Animal Physiology

A Series of Books in Biology Editor: Donald Kennedy

Roger Eckert

UNIVERSITY OF CALIFORNIA, LOS ANGELES

Physiology

with Chapters 13 and 14 by

David Randall

THE UNIVERSITY OF BRITISH COLUMBIA

◫ W. H. FREEMAN AND COMPANY   *San Francisco*

Library of Congress Cataloging in Publication Data

Eckert, Roger
    Animal physiology.

    (A Series of books in biology)
    Bibliography: p.
    Includes index.
    1.   Physiology.   I.   Randall, David, 1938–
joint author.   II.   Title.
QP31.2.E24   591.1   77–6648
ISBN 0–7167–0570–2

Printed in the United States of America

10   9   8   7   6   5   4   3   2

To our children and students

Contents

CHAPTER TWELVE

Osmoregulation and Excretion 392

CHAPTER THIRTEEN   *by David Randall*

Circulation of Blood 433

CHAPTER FOURTEEN   *by David Randall*

Exchange of Gases 469

Preface

The diversity and adaptations of the several million species that make up the Animal Kingdom provide endless fascination and delight to those that love nature. Not the least of this pleasure derives from a consideration of how the bodies of animals function. At first it might appear that with so many kinds of animals adapted to such a variety of life styles and environments, the task of even beginning to understand and appreciate the physiology of animals would be overwhelming. Fortunately (for scientist and student alike), the concepts and principles that provide a basis for understanding animal function are relatively few, for evolution has been conservative as well as inventive. The basic principles and mechanisms of animal physiology form the central theme of this book.

A beginning course in physiology is a challenge for both teacher and student because of the interdisciplinary nature of the subject. Not all students, even by their junior and senior years, have had exposure to all the chemical, physical, and biological subject matter required for an adequate background. On the other hand, most students are eager to come to grips with the subject and get on with the more exciting levels of modern scientific insight. For this reason, I decided several years ago to prepare a textbook in animal physiology that presents the essential background material in a way that allows the student to review it on his or her own. In that way it is hoped that the student is led gently but quickly to the ideas and principles of animal function and an understanding of their experimental elucidation.

Thus this book was written with the student's comprehension the major consideration.

This book attempts to develop the major ideas in a simple and direct manner, stressing principles and mechanisms over the compilation of information, and illustrating the functional strategies that have evolved within the bounds of chemical and physical possibility. This is done with examples selected from the broad spectrum of animal life, ranging from the protozoa at one end to our species and other vertebrates at the other end. It is the common principles that have been stressed, however, rather than the exceptions. Thus the more esoteric and peripheral phenomena have intentionally received only passing attention, if, indeed, any at all, so as not to distract from central ideas. Math is used where essential, but priority is given to the development of a qualitative and intuitive understanding rather than to quantitative derivations.

The ideas developed in the text are illuminated and augmented by liberal use of illustrations and parenthetical "boxes." Other pedagogical aids are a 1000-word glossary and various chapter end materials, including summaries, exercises, suggested readings, and lists of literature cited. References to the literature within the body of the text and in legends have been made unobtrusively, but hopefully with enough frequency so that the student becomes aware of the role of scientists and their literature in the development of the subject. The text often uses the device of a narrative describing actual, composite, or thought experiments to provide a feeling for methods of investigation while presenting information.

Originally I set out to write this book alone, but it became evident that this would take too long and spread my efforts too thin. I was fortunate, therefore, to have been able to enlist the collaboration of David Randall of The University of British Columbia to write the two chapters on respiratory and circulatory physiology.

The chapters of this book can be grouped into five sections. The first two chapters are intended primarily as introduction and for review of the essential physical and chemical background not covered in later chapters. Chapters 3 and 4 are devoted to a survey of cell energetics and regulation of the intracellular milieu. Chapters 5 through 8 deal with excitable membranes, nerve signals, sensory mechanisms, and the function of the nervous system. Chapters 9 and 10 consider the phenomena of contractility and motility, and Chapters 11 through 14 cover the systems (endocrine, osmoregulatory, respiratory, and circulatory) responsible for the homeostasis and supply of the internal environment. Certain special topics, such as temperature regulation, reproductive mechanisms, and adaptations to stressful environments, are considered along with those subjects to which they are most closely related, an approach that we feel is appropriate for an elementary book that stresses the general principles of animal function.

Finally, I would hope that our readers will not hesitate to help us with their suggestions for improvements and corrections for the next edition.

August 1977   ROGER ECKERT

Acknowledgments

Many individuals provided invaluable help during the writing and preparation of this book. Special thanks are due to Kathlyn Powell for her excellent help in researching Chapter 11; in compiling the chapter end materials, the Glossary, and the Index; and in being generally helpful in the final stages of editing and proofreading. Kathleen Dunlap, Susan Tamayo, and Jim Tipton also helped in various ways. Many colleagues have read and criticized chapters or made helpful suggestions of one kind or another. Among them are Saul Barber, Peter Bentley, Howard Bern, Charles Brokaw, James Case. Fred Crescitelli, Philip Dunham, Brenda Eisenberg, John Forte, Alan Gelperin, Terry Hamilton, William Jacobus, Bob Janssen, David Jones, Robert Josephson, Donald Kennedy, Leonard Kirschner, James Larimer, Hans Machemer, DeForest Mellon, Jr., Christine Milliken, Lee Peachey, Hermann Rahn, Dean Smith, Clara Szego, John West, and Ernest Wright. Thanks also are due to our colleagues and students at the University of California, Los Angeles, and at The University of British Columbia for their patience while we were occupied with this project and for their inspiration and valuable comments; our families, too, gave us their patience and understanding during the thousands of hours that have gone into this project. Finally, thanks are due Jill Leland for her excellent rendition of the figures, to Jack Nye for his design and page layout, and to Dick Johnson for his very able, careful, and conscientious work as manuscript editor.

Animal Physiology

CHAPTER ONE

The Meaning of Physiology

Animal physiology can be defined as the study of animal function. The ultimate goal of this subject is to understand, in physical and chemical terms, the mechanisms that operate in living organisms at all levels, ranging from the subcellular to the integrated whole animal. This goal is indeed an ambitious one, for each living organism, even a single cell, is incredibly complex. For this reason it has proved convenient to divide the subject of physiology into a number of subspecialties. These include general and cell physiology; organ, organismic, and environmental physiology; respiratory, circulatory, digestive, endocrine, developmental, neuro-, behavioral, and sensory physiology; and others. In spite of these somewhat contrived divisions, it has become apparent that common principles recur throughout, providing a thread of continuity. It has also become apparent that these principles arise from the properties of matter and energy.

In an elementary textbook, it is necessary to introduce the specialties somewhat arbitrarily as separate chapters so as to avoid overwhelming the student with complexity. It is helpful to remind the reader, however, that the various body functions require the coordinated activity of a number of tissues and organs. The brain, for example, cannot function without a constant supply of blood, carrying oxygen and glucose, provided by the pumping of the heart. The heart cannot survive more than minutes without oxygen supplied to the blood by the lungs. The lungs cannot function without neural commands to the respiratory muscles from the brain. Similar examples abound also at subcellular levels of function. Thus many chemical reactions in the cell require the integrity and metabolic activity of biological membranes, whereas the latter depend on some of these same reactions for production of energy-donor molecules required for the regulatory functions of the membrane.

Why Animal Physiology?

From a biological standpoint, the human species is part of the Animal Kingdom, sharing a common evolutionary history, a common planet, and the same laws of physics and chemistry. The same principles and mechanisms of Mendelian and molecular genetics hold for us that operate for the creatures of the field, sea, and sky. Moreover, the fundamental biological processes that, in sum total, are termed "life," are shared in common by all animal species. Thus the processes that give rise to the beating of the heart in the human body are fundamentally no different from those that underlie cardiac functions in a fish, frog, snake, bird, or ape. Likewise, the molecular and electrical events that produce a nerve impulse in the human brain are fundamentally no different from those that produce an impulse in the nerve of a squid, crab, or rat. In fact, most of what we have learned about the function of human cells, tissues, and organs has first been learned on various species of both vertebrates and invertebrates.

The first step in physiological research is to ask a question—for example, "Which inorganic ion carries the current that initiates the nerve impulse?" The next steps include the choice of tissue in which to investigate the problem. In studying nerve cells, it is extremely helpful to use one that is large, so as to facilitate certain procedures. For that reason, the major findings on nerve function have been made in work done on the giant axons of the cuttlefish and squid (see Chapter 5). Subsequent experiments, done with newer methods and with the benefit of the groundwork laid by the work on the squid, have confirmed that the nerves of humans and all other animals function in basically the same way. Our purpose, in this book, is to emphasize those processes that are basic to all animal groups and to see how they have been investigated. In addition, we will note special adaptations that serve to illuminate the ways in which environmental challenges have been met during the course of evolution by selection of functional specializations.

Physiology and Medicine

The time is past when students unquestioningly accept a program of study simply because someone has decided that it is "good" for them. For that reason we will briefly consider why an understanding of body functions is relevant to the daily existence of modern man. First and most obvious is that physiology, especially as it applies to the human body, is the corner-stone of scientific medical practice. Throughout the ages, as in today's primitive societies, the approach to disease and malfunction has been almost entirely empirical—that is, by trial and error. Because this process has been applied over such long periods of time, human societies have found that certain ailments improve in response to certain treatments, be they herbs, hot water baths, acupuncture, or even the psychological treatments of witch doctors. In fact, the medicinal effects of many modern drugs—aspirin, for example—have been discovered by purely empirical means, and the primary actions of some important medicines remain unknown. As our understanding grows of function and malfunction of living tissue, it is becoming increasingly more feasible to develop effective, scientifically sound treatments for human ills. A physician who understands body function is better equipped to make intelligent and insightful diagnoses and decisions for effective treatment. Those who do not are, in effect, modern versions of the medicine man, dispensing drugs with little more understanding than that obtained from the advertising brochures of pharmaceutical firms.

Physiology and the Human Experience

Besides satisfying a natural curiosity as to how our bodies live, move, metabolize food, and procreate—basic physical manifestations of life—the study of physiology is of great philosophical interest in helping us understand the nervous and sensory systems—those biological substrata of the human spirit in which resides all subjective experience: consciousness, awareness, thought, memory, learning, language, perception, and intellect—the sum of what is most specially human.

All animals, including humans, depend entirely on their sense organs and nervous system for information about the environment and the internal status of their bodies. Sensory input, together with the genetically inherited organization and properties of the nervous system, is responsible for all "knowledge," and determines how each animal behaves. (Some have claimed that there are channels of sensory input that bypass the physiological senses, but evidence in support of extrasensory perception has been equivocal and totally unconvincing to the scientific community at large.) Our ultimate dependence on our sense organs and the very personal nature of sensory perception becomes profoundly evident when we contemplate the problem of communicating subjective experience. For example, how would you explain to an individual who has been totally blind since birth the visual sensations we term "red" or "green," or even "light" and "dark"?

It is difficult to say to what extent physiological and biochemical studies will explain higher mental experiences and answer such questions as "How does the brain 'remember' past experiences?" or "How is a mental image of a visual scene generated from past or present input to the eyes?" Questions about the origin of subjective experience may or may not be entirely answerable, but they are of such fundamental importance to human self-knowledge that the quest for answers must certainly equal or exceed in philosophical importance any other intellectual endeavor. The elucidation of the molecular basis of heredity and the exploration of the moon were the great scientific and technological adventures of the past 20 years. The elucidation of the mechanisms that give rise to human behavior and higher brain functions will undoubtedly be the great scientific adventure of the coming decades.

it above 40°C is generally sufficient to render it inactive, since it no longer properly "fits" the substrate molecule.

GENETICS AND PHYSIOLOGY

It is generally agreed among scientists that the information content of a deoxyribonucleic acid (DNA) molecule is the result of many generations of natural selection. Those spontaneous alterations (mutations) in the base sequence of the germ-line DNA that enhance the survival of the organism to reproduce are thereby statistically retained, and increase in frequency of occurrence in the population of organisms. Conversely, those alterations in the base sequence of the DNA that render the organisms less well adapted to their environment will lessen the chances of reproduction and thus will be statistically suppressed and perhaps eliminated. Though it is common knowledge that Darwinian evolution has determined the basic structural details of all living species, it should be evident that function (which is closely tied to structure,

Central Themes in Physiology

As in all other fields, certain principles recur throughout the study of animal function. We will consider a few of these here. You will doubtless discover more as you go on to later chapters.

FUNCTION IS BASED ON STRUCTURE

The movement of an animal during locomotion depends on the structure of muscles and skeletal elements (e.g., bones). The movement produced by a contracting muscle depends on how it is attached to these elements and how they articulate with each other. In such a relatively familiar example, the relation between structure and function is obvious. The dependence of function on structure becomes more subtle, but no less real, as we direct our attention to the lower levels of organization—tissue, cell, organelle, etc. (Fig. 1-1). One of the most intensively studied examples of functional dependence on structure is the contractile machinery of skeletal muscle (Chapter 9). Our understanding of how a muscle contracts rests largely on an understanding of the ultrastructure of the contractile machinery as well as on its chemical properties.

The principle that structure is the basis of function applies to the biochemical events as well. The interaction of an enzyme with its substrates, for example, depends on the configurations and electron distributions of the interacting molecules. Changing the shape of an enzyme molecule (i.e., denaturing it) by heating

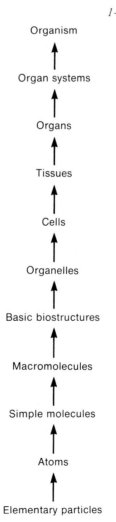

Organism

↑

Organ systems

↑

Organs

↑

Tissues

↑

Cells

↑

Organelles

↑

Basic biostructures

↑

Macromolecules

↑

Simple molecules

↑

Atoms

↑

Elementary particles

1-1. Structural hierarchy in a metazoan animal. In a protozoan, the cell is also the organism. "Basic biostructures" include membranes, microtubules, and filaments. At each level, function depends on the structural organization of that level and those below.

as noted above) has also evolved through Darwinian means. Nevertheless, since evolutionary pressure can work only within the confines of chemical and physical laws, the nature and function of living systems are ultimately limited by the fundamental chemical and physical properties of the constituent elements and molecules.

Toward the end of the nineteenth century, August Weismann elaborated a theory of heredity in which he postulated the *continuity of the germ plasm*—namely, that genetic material passed on from metazoan parents to their offspring is contained in a line of *germ cells* that, in each generation, is derived directly from parent germ cells, creating an uninterrupted lineage. This germ plasm is hereditarily independent of the somatic cells, which arise from the germ cells and die off at the end of each generation. DNA is the molecular equivalent of Weismann's germ plasm, and can be viewed as a continuous lineage of replicating strands that are passed from generation to generation within a species (Fig. 1-2).

The blind process of evolution is centered on the survival of the germ-line DNA, for it is the informational content of the DNA that encodes a species, and once the germ line is lost, that species becomes immediately and irreversibly extinct. Every somatic structure and function outside the continuous, generation-to-generation lineage of germ-line DNA is subservient to the survival of the germ line. Conversely, the soma owes its origin to the DNA.

There exists, then, a symbiotic relationship between the germ-line DNA and the rest of the organism. Neither can survive without the other. The soma owes its existence to the DNA, and the DNA cannot survive without the somatic functions concerned with the short-term survival of the organism. The philosophical loop is closed, so to speak, with the realization that the structure and function of a species, and even its be-

1–2. Concept of germ-line continuity. The germ-line is preserved by the physiological activities of each succeeding generation. Natural selection favors those physiological processes that enhance the probability of reproduction, and thus the transfer of the DNA to the next somatic generation.

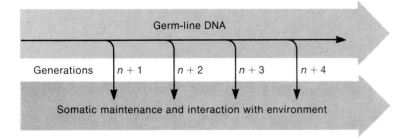

havior, have evolved through natural selection for one ultimate "purpose"—to enhance the probability of the survival of the germ-line DNA of the species. To this end, the somatic functions of an organism are all directly or indirectly concerned with the acquisition and conversion of energy and matter from the environment. All else is frosting on the biological cake.

THE PRINCIPLE OF HOMEOSTASIS

The nineteenth century French pioneer of modern physiology, Claude Bernard, was the first to enunciate the importance of *homeostasis* in animal function when he noted the ability of mammals to regulate the condition of their internal environments within rather narrow limits. This is familiar to all of us from routine clinical measurements on human blood and measurements of our body temperatures. "Constancy of the internal milieu," as Bernard phrased it, has been found to be a nearly universal phenomenon in living systems, allowing animals and plants to survive in stressful and varying environments (Fig. 1-3). The evolution of homeostasis is believed to have been the single most important factor that has allowed animals to venture from physiologically friendly environments and to invade environments more hostile to life processes.

Regulation of the internal milieu applies to unicellular organisms as well as to the most complex vertebrates. In the latter and in other metazoans the composition of the fluid surrounding the cells of all tissues is subjected to constant regulation so that its composition (and even temperature in birds and mammals) is kept within a narrow range. Single-celled animals, the protozoa, have been able to invade fresh water and other osmotically stressful environments because the concentrations of salts, sugars, amino acids, and other solutes in the cytoplasm are regulated by membrane permeability, active transport, and other mechanisms that maintain these concentrations within limits favorable to the metabolic requirements of the cell, and quite different from the extracellular environment. The same is true for the individual cells of the metazoan organism, which also regulate their cytoplasmic milieu.

The regulatory processes of cells and multicellular organisms are based primarily on the principle of *feedback* (see Box 1-1). A man-made system can, in principle, be made so accurate that it will produce a predicted result under ideal, defined conditions. Living systems, however, do not function under ideal conditions; they must be able to function under the variable conditions to which they are subjected by the vagaries of nature. Control in the face of the finite accuracy of genetic and metabolic mechanisms—to say nothing of external perturbations—requires con-

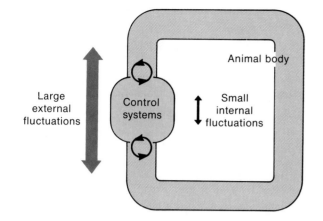

1-3. *Physiological regulatory systems maintain internal conditions within a relatively small range of fluctuation in the face of large variations in the external environment.*

tinuous regulation, which involves continuous sampling and correction. For example, suppose that an experienced driver is placed in a car on a straight, 10-mile long stretch of traffic-free highway, is allowed to position the car, is blindfolded, and is then required to drive the 10 miles without deviating from his lane. The slightest asymmetry in the neuromotor or sensory systems of the driver, or in the steering mechanism of the car—not to mention wind or unevenness of the road surface—makes this an impossible task. On the other hand, if the blindfold is removed, the driver will utilize feedback to stay in his lane. As he perceives a gradual drift to one side of the lane or the other, due to whatever internal or external perturbations, he will simply correct by a compensatory motor output applied to the steering wheel. This can be summarized in the terms used in Box 1-1. The visual system of the driver acts as the sensor in this case, while his neuromotor system, by causing a correctional movement in the direction opposite to the perceived error, acts as the inverting amplifier that corrects for deviations from the set point.

Another example of the regulation by negative feedback can be demonstrated with a thermostatic device that senses whether the temperature of a hot water bath is equal to or above or below the set point (Fig. 1-4). As long as the water temperature is below the set-point temperature, the sensor maintains the heater switch "on." As soon as the set-point temperature is achieved, the heater switch is opened, and further heating ceases until the temperature again drops below the set point. The "thermostat" that controls mammalian body temperature (situated in the brain) is set for about 37°C. Toxins produced by certain pathogens change the set point of this thermostat to a higher temperature, so that a fever develops.

Examples of physiological feedback systems occur in intermediary metabolism (Chapter 3), in neural control of muscle (Chapter 8), in circulatory control (Chapter 13), in respiration (Chapter 14), and in endocrine control (Chapter 11).

1-4. *Example of a regulated system. A bimetal spiral, fixed at its center, unwinds slightly as the temperature of the water bath drops. The circuit is completed as the contacts touch, allowing electric current to flow through the heating coil. As the water warms, the contacts separate. The desired temperature set point is adjusted by positioning the contact of the thermostat.*

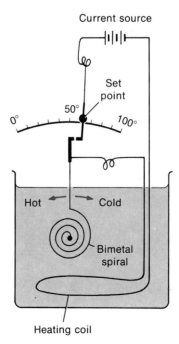

BOX 1-1 THE FEEDBACK PRINCIPLE

A servosystem uses *feedback* to maintain a given preselected state. Feedback is widely employed in biological systems, as well as in technology and engineering. Feedback can be either positive or negative, each producing profoundly different effects.

POSITIVE FEEDBACK

In the system shown in the upper diagram of the figure, an applied disturbance or perturbation acting on the *controlled system* is detected by a *sensor* and introduced at the *input* of an *amplifier*. Suppose the signal is amplified but that its sign (plus or minus) remains unchanged. In that case the *output* of the amplifier, when fed back to the controlled system, is reamplified and has the same effect as the original perturbation, reinforcing the perturbation of the controlled system. This configuration, which is called *positive feedback*, tends to be highly unstable, because the output becomes progressively stronger. A familiar example occurs in public address systems when the output of the loudspeaker is inadvertently picked up by the microphone and reamplified, generating a loud squeal. Although a tiny perturbation at the input can cause a much larger effect at the output, the output of the system is usually limited in some way. Thus, in the example of the public address system, the intensity of the output is limited by the power of the audio amplifier and speakers or by saturation of the microphone signal. In biological systems, the response may be limited by the amount of energy or substrate available. An important biological example of positive feedback occurs in the nerve impulse (Chapter 5). It should be noted that positive feedback is generally used to produce a regenerative, explosive, or autocatalytic effect.

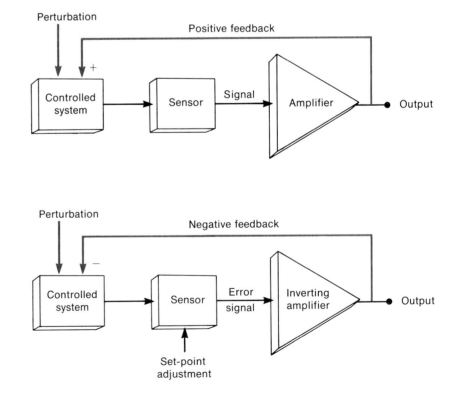

Basic elements of feedback systems. Top. Positive feedback occurs when a perturbation acting on a system is amplified and the amplifier output is "fed back" to the system without sign inversion. Bottom. Negative feedback occurs if somewhere in the feedback loop there is a "sign" inversion. In that case, the inverted signal stabilizes the controlled system at the set point. A change in sensitivity of the sensor is one way in which the set point can be adjusted.

Imagine an amplifier in which the "sign" of the output is opposite to that of the input. Such signal inversion provides the basis for *negative feedback* (see lower diagram), which can be used to regulate a certain parameter (e.g., length, temperature, voltage, concentration) in the controlled system.

When the sensor detects a change in state (e.g., change in length, temperature, voltage, concentration) of the controlled system, it produces an *error signal* proportional to the difference between the *set point* to which the system is to be held and the actual state of the system. The error signal is introduced into an amplifier that both amplifies and inverts (i.e., changes sign). The inverted output of the amplifier, fed back to the system, counteracts the perturbation. The inversion of sign (i.e., *negative* feedback) is the most fundamental feature of feedback control. The inverted output of the amplifier, by counteracting the perturbation, reduces the error signal, and the system tends to stabilize near the set point. Thus negative feedback is used to regulate and stabilize. Since the sensor or the amplifier can generally be biased, any selected set point can be automatically maintained.

A hypothetical negative-feedback loop with infinite amplification would hold the system in precisely its set point state, because the slightest error signal would result in a massive output from the amplifier to counteract the perturbation. Since no amplifier—either electronic or biological—produces infinite amplification, negative feedback only approximates the set point during perturbation. The less amplification the system has, the less accurate is its control.

Finally, it should be noted that the elements of the physical example of feedback described here occur in a number of variations. For example, sensor and amplifier functions are, in some instances, carried out by a single element, and in others the inversion of sign may take place at the sensor. Nonetheless, the principles remain unchanged.

Summary

Animal physiology is concerned with the physical and chemical processes that take place in tissues and organs and form the bases of organismic function. The field is subdivided into many areas that are often interdependent and are interrelated by common genetic, physical, and chemical principles. Medicine, the practical application of physiology, is constantly evolving from a trial-and-error, empirical approach toward practice founded on a rational understanding of cell and tissue function.

Besides practical application, physiology has philosophical value for us. This is apparent, for example, in a consideration of subjective human experience. All that we experience in life depends on the properties of our sensory and nervous systems. An understanding of how living organisms function helps us understand "what we are," and enhances our appreciation of our place in this world.

Three major ideas in physiology are (1) that function is based on structure at all levels, beginning with atoms, molecules, and cell organelles; (2) that regulation of the intra- or extracellular environment (or both) provides the required constancy of conditions necessary for reliable and coordinated chemical and physical processes; and (3) that cell and tissue functions have arisen through Darwinian evolution and are genetically determined.

EXERCISES

1. Give an example of a simple structure-function relationship in physiology, and describe its conditions of operation.

2. What evolutionary advantage does successful maintenance of internal homeostasis confer upon an animal species?

3. Why is negative rather than positive feedback required for maintenance of a constant state (i.e., homeostasis)?

4. Continuous regulation (i.e., homeostasis) of the internal environment is achieved through negative feedback. Describe an example and explain how the principle of negative feedback achieves regulation in the example.

5. Positive feedback is much more rare than negative feedback in biological systems. Give one example and explain the effect of positive feedback in that example.

6. Why can it be said that there exists a symbiotic relationship between the germ-line DNA and the somatic portions of the cell and organism?

SUGGESTED READING

Bayliss, L. E. 1966. *Living Control Systems.* W. H. Freeman and Company, San Francisco.

Bernard, C. 1872. *Physiologie General.* Hatchette et Cie., Paris.

Grodius, F. S. 1963. *Control Theory and Biological Systems.* Columbia Univ. Press, New York.

CHAPTER TWO

Physical and Chemical Concepts

The living organisms found on our planet form a vast and varied array, ranging from viruses, bacteria, and protozoa to flowering plants, invertebrates, and the "higher" animals. In spite of this immense diversity, all forms of life as we know it are similar in certain fundamentals. Thus all animals, plants, and micro-organisms on our planet consist of the same chemical elements and of similar types of organic molecules. Moreover, all life processes take place in a milieu of water, and depend on the physical-chemical properties of this ubiquitous and very special solvent. That all living organisms share a common biochemistry is one of the powerful evidences in support of their evolutionary kinship, the common thread that runs through all areas of biological study.

Biologists generally agree that life arose through processes of chance and natural selection under appropriate environmental conditions on the primitive Earth. Experiments first performed by Stanley Miller show that certain molecules essential for primitive life (e.g., amino acids, peptides, nucleic acids) are formed

by the action of lightning-like electric discharges upon an atmosphere of methane, ammonia, and water—a simple mixture believed to be similar in composition to that of the primitive atmosphere about four billion years ago. The early atmosphere is believed to have been modified during subsequent eons by photosynthetic plants, which added the immense quantities of oxygen now present and which are capable of taking up nitrogen compounds for incorporation into nitrogenous biological compounds. The experimental formation of simple organic molecules under conditions similar to those that may have prevailed in the primeval atmosphere suggests that such molecules may have accumulated in ancient shallow seas, forming an organic "soup" in which life may then have undergone its first evolutionary stages of organization.

To what degree did the origin of life depend on the "right" conditions? Would life of another sort have appeared on Earth if the chemical and physical environment had been quite different? Suppose there had been no carbon atom? As we shall see below, the occurrence of life as we know it and can imagine it depends heavily on the "fitness of the environment." That is to say, life would be either nonexistent or vastly different if some of the fundamental properties of matter had been different.

A controversy once raged between the vitalists, who believed life was based on special "vital" principles not found in the inanimate world, and the mechanists, who maintained that life can ultimately be explained in physical and chemical terms. Until the early part of the nineteenth century, students of the natural world supposed that the chemical composition of living matter differed fundamentally from that of inanimate minerals. The vitalist view held that "organic" substances can only be produced by living organisms, setting them apart in a mysterious way from the inorganic world. This concept met its end in 1828, when Wöhler synthesized the organic molecule urea (Fig. 2-1) from lead cyanate and ammonia. Wöhler's reagents were obtained from mineral sources. His successful organic synthesis set the stage for modern chemical and physical studies aimed at elucidating the mechanisms of life processes. It is now possible to duplicate in isolated cell-free systems nearly every synthetic and metabolic reaction normally performed by living cells.

The majority of biologists now agree that the biochemical and physiological processes of the living organism are based solely on the physical and chemical properties of the elements and compounds that constitute the living system. At first glance this may appear to be a gross oversimplification, for certainly the properties of living systems seem far too marvelous and complex to be explained by a mere mixture of elements and compounds. Therein, of course, lies part of the answer. Living systems are not simple chemical "soups," but are highly organized structures composed of complex macromolecules, such as nucleic acids, chromosomes, and ribosomes. Macromolecules of many kinds participate in the regulation and direction of chemical activities within living cells. Organelles, such as the cell membrane, lysosomes, and mitochondria, (Fig. 2-2) lend structural organization to the living system by separating it into compartments and subcompartments. They also hold molecules in functionally important spatial relations to one another. Cells are organized into tissues, tissues into organs, and those into interacting systems. Thus, the organism consists of an organizational hierarchy, with each higher level imparting further functional complexity to the whole. In this book we will begin with the most elementary, the chemical level, and progress to the more complex levels of organization.

2–1. *Urea.*

$$NH_2-\overset{\overset{\displaystyle O}{\|}}{C}-NH_2$$

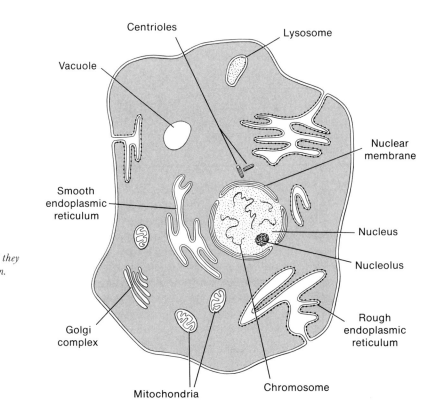

2–2. *Simplified diagram of an animal cell. The openings of the reticulum to the exterior, if they actually exist, are much smaller than shown.* [*After Keeton, 1972.*]

Centrioles

Lysosome

Vacuole

Nuclear membrane

Smooth endoplasmic reticulum

Nucleus

Nucleolus

Golgi complex

Rough endoplasmic reticulum

Mitochondria

Chromosome

Atoms, Bonds, and Molecules

Figure 2-3 shows the periodic table of the chemical elements, of which all matter is composed. Table 2-1 lists the major components of the earth's mineral crust, the human body, and sea water in their order of abundance in each. As the table shows, about 99% of the human body is made up of hydrogen, oxygen, nitrogen, and carbon. This holds true for all living organisms. Is the preponderance of these elements in living systems simply a matter of chance, or is there a mechanistic explanation for their uniform prevalence in the great diversity of organisms that have evolved over the past three billion years?

George Wald, who has contributed much to our understanding of the chemical basis of vision, has argued that the biological predominance of hydrogen, oxygen, nitrogen, and carbon is not at all a matter of chance, but is the inevitable result of certain fundamental atomic properties of these elements—properties that render them especially suited for the chemistry of life. We will review briefly the factors that influence the chemical behavior of atoms, and then return to Wald's thesis.

Atomic structure is far more complex and subtle than can be fully described here; for our purposes, we need consider only the very simplest features. Each atom consists of a dense nucleus of protons and neutrons surrounded by a "cloud" of electrons equal in number to the protons in the nucleus. Since the negatively charged electrons are equal in number to the positively charged protons, each atom in its elemental state carries no net electric charge. The electrons do not occupy fixed orbits, but their statistical

Table 2-1. Comparison of the chemical composition of the human body with that of seawater and the earth's crust. Values are percentages of total numbers of atoms.

Human body		Seawater		Earth's crust	
H	63	H	66	O	47
O	25.5	O	33	Si	28
C	9.5	Cl	0.33	Al	7.9
N	1.4	Na	0.28	Fe	4.5
Ca	0.31	Mg	0.033	Ca	3.5
P	0.22	S	0.017	Na	2.5
Cl	0.03	Ca	0.006	K	2.5
K	0.06	K	0.006	Mg	2.2
S	0.05	C	0.0014	Ti	0.46
Na	0.03	Br	0.0005	H	0.22
Mg	0.01			C	0.19
All others < 0.01		All others < 0.1		All others < 0.1	

Source: *Biology: An Appreciation of Life,* CRM Books, Del Mar, California, 1972.

*Because figures have been rounded off, totals do not amount to 100.

2-3. The periodic table. Note that each row corresponds to a different orbital shell.

First shell	1 H																	2 He
Second shell	3 Li	4 Be											5 B	6 C	7 N	8 O	9 F	10 Ne
Third shell	11 Na	12 Mg											13 Al	14 Si	15 P	16 S	17 Cl	18 Ar
Fourth shell	19 K	20 Ca	21 Sc	22 Ti	23 V	24 Cr	25 Mn	26 Fe	27 Co	28 Ni	29 Cu	30 Zn	31 Ga	32 Ge	33 As	34 Se	35 Br	36 Kr
Fifth shell	37 Rb	38 Sr	39 Y	40 Zr	41 Nb	42 Mo	43 Tc	44 Ru	45 Rh	46 Pd	47 Ag	48 Cd	49 In	50 Sn	51 Sb	52 Te	53 I	54 Xe
Sixth shell	55 Cs	56 Ba	57 La	72 Hf	73 Ta	74 W	75 Re	76 Os	77 Ir	78 Pt	79 Au	80 Hg	81 Tl	82 Pb	83 Bi	84 Po	85 At	86 Rn
Seventh shell	87 Fr	88 Ra	89 Ac	104	105	106												

58 Ce	59 Pr	60 Nd	61 Pm	62 Sm	63 Eu	64 Gd	65 Tb	66 Dy	67 Ho	68 Er	69 Tm	70 Yb	71 Lu	
90 Th	91 Pa	92 U	93 Np	94 Pu	95 Am	96 Cm	97 Bk	98 Cf	99 Es	100 Fm	101 Md	102 No	103 Lw	

2-4. *The first shell of He is filled (2 electrons), but that of H is not.*

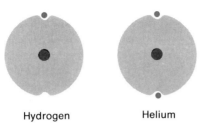

Hydrogen   Helium

2-5. *The first four orbital shells, showing the number of electrons necessary to fill each shell.*

18e⁻
8e⁻
8e⁻
2e⁻
1ˢᵗ shell
2ⁿᵈ shell
3ʳᵈ shell
4ᵗʰ shell

2-6. *Both hydrogen and oxygen have unfilled outer shells.*

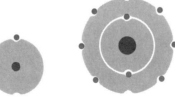

Hydrogen   Oxygen

2-7. *The outer shell of chlorine is more distant from its nucleus than is that of fluorine. Thus the outermost electrons of chlorine are less strongly attracted by the nucleus than those of fluorine.*

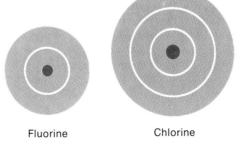

Fluorine   Chlorine

distribution is such that they occupy some positions with greater probabilities than others. This distribution is quite systematic, so that in an atom with one or two electrons, the orbital paths are virtually confined to a single "shell" around the nucleus, as in the hydrogen and helium atoms (Fig. 2-4). In atoms with three to ten electrons (Li, Be, B, C, N, O, F, Ne), this first shell is complete when occupied by two electrons; the remaining electrons occupy a second shell outside the first. The second shell can contain up to eight electrons. In atoms with more than ten protons and ten electrons, a third shell is formed, which can accommodate up to eight electrons, and so on (Fig. 2-5).

When the outermost shell of an atom contains the maximum number of electrons possible in that shell (two in the first shell, eight in both the second and the third, eighteen in the fourth, etc.)—that is to say, when it cannot accommodate additional electrons—the atom is highly stable and resists reactions with other atoms. This is true of all the noble gases, such as helium and neon, which appear at the far right of the periodic table. Most elements, however, have incomplete outer electron shells, and are therefore reactive with certain other atoms. Hydrogen, for example, has one rather than two electrons in its only shell, and oxygen has only six, instead of eight, electrons in its outer shell (Fig. 2-6). Thus the hydrogen atom and the oxygen atom both have a tendency to gain electrons—hydrogen one, and oxygen two—so as to fill their respective outer shells and bring them into the electron configuration of a noble gas.

While the number of electrons in the outer shell has an important influence upon the physical characteristics and reactivity of an atom, other physical features are also important in determining its chemical properties. One of these is the size (or weight) of the atom. The heavier an atom (i.e., the more protons and neutrons in its nucleus), the more electrons surround the nucleus. As the number of electrons exceeds ten and a third shell of electrons exists, the valence electrons—that is, those of the outermost shell—are correspondingly more distant from the compact nucleus, and hence less strongly attracted by it than the valence electrons of atoms with only two shells (Fig. 2-7). (Recall that electrostatic interactions between monopoles diminish with the square of distance.) Thus chlorine, with seven electrons in its third and outer shell, is less reactive than flourine, which has seven electrons in its second and outer shell. Both atoms have a tendency to gain one electron to complete the outermost shell, but this tendency is greater in fluorine, since its outermost shell feels a stronger electrostatic pull from its nucleus than the larger chlorine atom. As a result, with all other things being equal, a small atom forms stronger and hence more stable bonds with other atoms than does a large atom.

The Fitness of H, O, N, and C for Life

Now we can return to Wald's thesis that certain elements lend themselves especially well to the chemistry of living systems. Examination of the periodic table (Fig. 2-3) reveals that of the common elements of the Earth's crust, only H, O, N, and C have two or fewer electron shells. Helium and neon are virtually inert, rare gases, while boron and fluorine form relatively rare salts. The metals lithium and beryllium form easily dissociated ionic bonds. In contrast, H, O, N, and C will form strong covalent bonds by attracting one, two, three, and four electrons, respectively, to complete their outer electron shells.

Why are strong bonds important? Consider, for example, the biological chaos that would result if the chemical bonds in the hereditary macromolecule deoxyribonucleic acid (DNA) were easily dissociated. DNA, made up of H, O, N, C, and P, seldom undergoes alterations (i.e., mutations) during replication.* Although occasional mutations are essential for the process of evolution, it is important for the short-term integrity of each organism and each species that stable bonds reliably hold together the structures of DNA and other macromolecules.

Three of the four major biologically important elements (O, N, C) are among the very few to form double or triple bonds, which greatly increases the variety of molecular configurations that can be formed by reaction of these elements. Oxygen, for example, can oxidize carbon to form carbon dioxide.

$$O=C=O$$

Since the two double bonds satisfy the tendencies of the three atoms of this molecule to react, the CO_2 molecule is relatively inert and is therefore able to diffuse readily from its source of production to become available for recycling through the photosynthetic process of green plants.

The ability of the carbon atom to form four single or two double bonds endows it with great potential for varieties of atomic combinations with itself and other atoms. Thus carbon can form straight or branched chains and ring structures (Fig. 2-8), and together with the other atoms provides an almost infinite diversity of molecular structures and configurations.

Silicon, which is in the same column and just below carbon in the periodic table, has some properties similar to those of carbon. Unlike carbon, however, it is larger and does not form double bonds. Therefore it combines with two atoms of oxygen by two single bonds only:

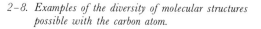

leaving incomplete outer shells in all three atoms of silicon dioxide. Since tendency to bond remains unfulfilled, the silicon dioxide molecule readily bonds with others of its kind, forming the huge polymeric molecules that make up silicate rocks and sand. Thus it is evident that silicon, even though it has some properties similar to those of carbon, is eminently more suited for the formation of stone than it is for large-scale participation in the organization of biological molecules.

Besides its important role in combining with hydrogen to form water, oxygen acts as the final electron acceptor in the sequence of oxidations through which chemical energy is released by cell metabolism (Chapter 3). This important ability to oxidize (accept electrons from) other atoms and molecules is due to the oxygen atom's incomplete outer electron shell and relatively low atomic weight.

In addition to the four major biological elements, other elements participate in cell chemistry, though in lesser numbers. These include phosphorus and sulfur; the ions of four metallic elements (Na^+, K^+, Mg^{2+}, and Ca^{2+}); and the chloride ion (Cl^-). We will return to those later.

2-8. Examples of the diversity of molecular structures possible with the carbon atom.

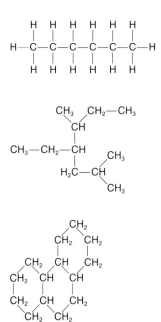

*On the average, less than once per gene in every 10,000 replications.

Water

Water is directly and intimately involved in all details of animal physiology, but because it is so common, water is often regarded with disinterest, as an inert space filler in living systems. The truth is, of course, that water is a highly reactive substance—quite different both physically and chemically from most other liquids. Water possesses a number of unusual and special properties of great importance for living systems. Indeed, life as we know it would be impossible if water did not have these properties. The first living systems presumably arose in the aqueous environment of shallow seas. It is therefore not surprising that the living organisms of the present are intimately adapted at the molecular level to the special properties of water. Today even terrestrial animals consist 75% or more of water, and much of their physiological effort is devoted to the conservation of body water and the regulation of the chemical composition of the internal aqueous environment.

The special properties of water so important to life stem directly from its molecular structure; therefore we should begin with a brief consideration of the water molecule.

THE WATER MOLECULE

Water molecules are held together by *polar covalent bonds* between one oxygen and two hydrogen atoms. The polarity (i.e., uneven charge distribution) of the covalent bonds results from the high electronegativity of the oxygen atom relative to hydrogen—an expression of the strong tendency of the oxygen atom to acquire electrons from other atoms, such as hydrogen. This high electronegativity causes the electrons of the two hydrogen atoms in the water molecule to occupy positions statistically closer to the oxygen atom than to the parent hydrogen atoms. The bond is therefore about 40% ionic in character, and the following partial charge distributions exist (δ represents the local partial charge of each hydrogen atom):

$$\underset{2\delta-}{\overset{\overset{\delta+}{H}\quad\overset{\delta+}{H}}{\underset{O}{\diagdown\diagup}}}$$

The water molecule can also be depicted in terms of molecular orbitals, as in Figure 2-9. The angle between the two oxygen–hydrogen bonds, rather than being 90°, as predicted for purely covalent bonding, is found to be 104.5°. The increased angle can be ascribed to the mutual repulsion of the two positively charged hydrogen nuclei, which tends to force them apart. In the hydride of sulfur, H_2S, the S—H bonds are purely covalent; there is no asymmetrical charge distribution as in H_2O. Thus the bond angle in H_2S is 90°. Because of the semipolar nature of H—O bonds, H_2O differs greatly, both chemically and physically, from H_2S and other related hydrides. Why is this?

The water molecule's uneven distribution of electrons, due to the semipolar nature of the H—O bond, causes the water molecule to act at a *dipole*. That is, it behaves somewhat like a bar magnet, but instead of having two opposite magnetic poles, it has two opposite electric poles (+ and −) (Fig. 2-9). As a result, it tends to align with an electrostatic field. The *dipole moment* is the turning force exerted on the molecule by an external field. The high dipole moment of water (4.8 debyes) is the most important physical feature of the molecule, and accounts for many of its rather special properties.

The most important chemical feature of water is its ability to form *hydrogen bonds* between the nearly electron-bare, positively charged protons (hydrogen atoms) of one water molecule and the negatively charged electron-rich oxygens of neighboring water molecules (Fig. 2-10). In each water molecule, four of the eight electrons in the outer shell of the oxygen atom are covalently bonded with the two hydrogens. This leaves two pairs of electrons free to interact electrostatically (i.e., to form hydrogen bonds) with the electron-poor hydrogen atoms of neighboring water molecules. Since the angle between the two covalent

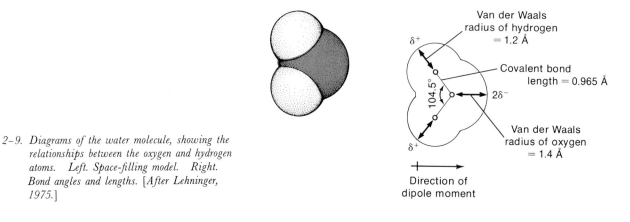

2-9. *Diagrams of the water molecule, showing the relationships between the oxygen and hydrogen atoms. Left. Space-filling model. Right. Bond angles and lengths. [After Lehninger, 1975.]*

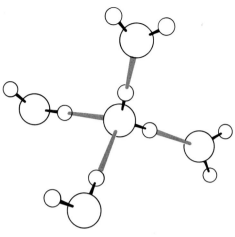

2-10. *The tetrahedral nature of hydrogen bonding between water molecules.*

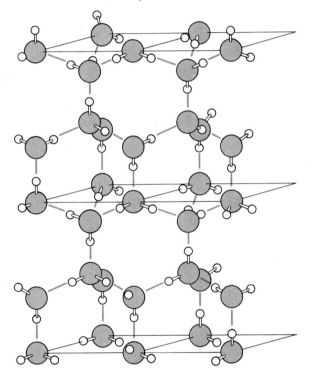

2-11. *The crystalline structure of ice. [After Loewy and Siekovitz, 1969.]*

PROPERTIES OF WATER

The hydrogen-bonded structure of water is highly labile and transient, for the lifetime of a hydrogen bond in liquid water is only about 10^{-10} to 10^{-11} s.

This is due to the relatively weak nature of the hydrogen bond. It takes only 4.5 kcal/mole to break the hydrogen bond, whereas the covalent O—H bond within the water molecule has an energy of 110 kcal/mole. As a result, no specific groups of H_2O molecules remain bonded for more than a brief instant, yet a statistically constant fraction of the population is joined together by hydrogen bonding at all times at a given temperature.

In spite of the modest strength of the hydrogen bond, it increases the total energy (i.e., heat) required to separate individual molecules from the rest of the population. For this reason, the *melting* and *boiling points* and the *heat of vaporization* of water are much higher than those of other common hydrides of elements related to oxygen (e.g., NH_3, HF, H_2S). Of the common hydrides, only water has a boiling point (100°C) far above temperatures common to the surface of the earth. The statistical loose bonding between water molecules also endows water with an unusually high *surface tension* and *cohesiveness*.

It is widely agreed that the oceans and lakes would have turned to solid ice except at the surface if ice were denser (heavier) than water and formed from the bottom up. Ice is less dense than water because it has an open crystalline lattice, whereas water, with its more random molecular organization, has a more closely packed, dense molecular population.

Water as a Solvent

The medieval alchemists, looking for the universal solvent, were never able to find a more effective and "universal" solvent than water. The solvent characteristics of water are due largely to its high dielectric constant,* a manifestation of its electrostatic polarity. This is illustrated especially well by the *ionic compounds*, or *electrolytes*, which include salts, acids, and bases, and which all share the property of dissociating into ions when dissolved in water. (Solutes that undergo no dissociation, and therefore do not increase the conductivity of a solution, are termed *nonelectrolytes*. Common examples of nonelectrolytes are the sugars, alcohols,

bonds of water is about 105°, groups of hydrogen-bonded water molecules form tetrahedral arrangements. This is the basis for the crystalline structure of the most common form of ice (Fig. 2-11).

---

*The dielectric constant is a measure of the effect that water or any dielectric substance has in diminishing the electrostatic force between two charges separated by water or another dielectric medium; that force is given by the relation

$$f = \frac{q_1 q_2}{\varepsilon d^2}$$

where f is the force (in dynes) between the two electrostatic charges q_1 and q_2 (in esu), d is the distance (in cm) between the charges, and ε is the dielectric constant.

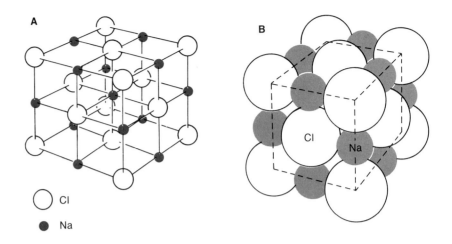

2-12. A. *Internal structure of the sodium chloride crystal lattice.* B. *Representation of relative ionic sizes of* Na^+ *and* Cl^-. [*After Mahan, 1966.*]

○ Cl

● Na

and oils.) Figure 2-12 illustrates the arrangement of the ions Na^+ and Cl^- in a sodium chloride crystal. The highly structured array is held together firmly by the electrostatic attraction between the positively charged sodium ions and the negatively charged chloride ions. A *nonpolar* liquid, such as hexane, cannot dissolve the crystal because no source of energy exists in the nonpolar solvent to break an ion away from the rest of the crystal. Water, however, can dissolve the NaCl crystal, just as it can dissolve most other ionic compounds (e.g., salts, acids, bases), because the dipolar water molecules can overcome the electrostatic interactions between the individual ions, as shown in Figure 2-13. The partial negative charge of the oxygen

causes weak electrostatic binding with the positively charged *cation* (Na^+ in this case), and the partial positive charge on the hydrogen causes weak electrostatic binding with the negatively charged *anion* (Cl^- in this case). The clustering of water molecules about individual ions and polar molecules is called *solvation* or *hydration*.

The water molecules surround the ions, orienting themselves so that their positive poles face anions and their negative poles face cations, thereby further reducing the electrostatic attraction between the dissolved cations and anions of an ionic compound. In a sense, the H_2O molecules act as insulators. The first shell of water molecules attracts a second shell of less tightly bound, oppositely oriented water molecules. The second shell may even attract more water in a third shell. Thus the ion may carry a considerable quantity of *water of hydration*. The effective diameter of the hydrated ion varies inversely with the diameter of the ion of a given charge. For example, the ionic radii of Na^+ and K^+ are 0.095 and 0.113 nm, respectively, whereas their effective hydrated radii are 0.24 and 0.17, respectively. The reason for this inverse relationship is that the electrostatic force between the nucleus of the ion and the dipolar water molecule decreases markedly distance between the water molecule and the nucleus of the ion (Fig. 2-14). Thus the smaller ion binds water more strongly, and thereby carries a large number of water molecules with it.

Water also dissolves certain organic substances (e.g., alcohols and sugars) that do not dissociate into ions in solution, but these small organic molecules do have polar properties. In contrast, water does not dissolve or dissolve in compounds that are completely nonpolar, such as fats and oils, for it cannot react with them by hydrogen bonding. It does, however, react partially with *amphipathic* compounds, which have a polar group and a nonpolar group. A good example is a soap molecule (Fig. 2-15), which has a *hydrophilic* (water-attracting) polar head and a *hydrophobic* (water-

2-13. *Hydration of a salt by water molecules. The oxygens of the water molecules are attracted to the cations, and the hydrogens of the water molecules are attracted to the anions.* [*After CRM Books Editorial Staff,* Biology Today, *CRM Books, Del Mar, California.*]

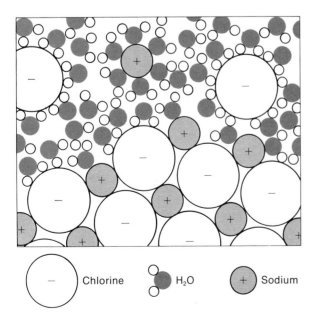

○— Chlorine   ○●○ H_2O ⊕ Sodium

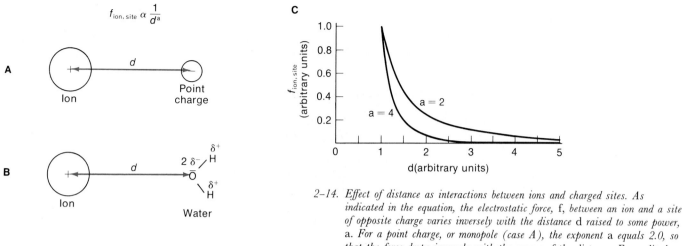

$$f_{\text{ion, site}} \, \alpha \, \frac{1}{d^a}$$

A — Ion —— d —— Point charge

B — Ion —— d —— $2\,\delta^- \overset{\delta^+}{\underset{\delta^+}{\overset{H}{\diagup}}} O \underset{H}{\diagdown}$ Water

C

2–14. Effect of distance as interactions between ions and charged sites. As indicated in the equation, the electrostatic force, f, between an ion and a site of opposite charge varies inversely with the distance d raised to some power, a. For a point charge, or monopole (case A), the exponent a equals 2.0, so that the force drops inversely with the square of the distance. For a dipole such as the water molecule, the value of a can be as high as 4.0. The drop in electrostatic force as a function of distance is illustrated in the graph in part C for these two values of a.

repelling) nonpolar tail. If a mixture of water and sodium oleate is shaken, the water will disperse the latter into minute droplets. The sodium oleate molecules in such a droplet, or *micelle*, are arranged in the configuration shown in Figure 2-16, with their hydrophobic, nonpolar tail groups huddled in the center and their hydrophilic, polar head groups arranged around the perimeter—facing outward, so as to interact with the water. The same behavior is exhibited by phospholipid molecules (p. 33), which also consist of hydrophobic and hydrophilic groups. This tendency of water to cause amphipathic molecules to form micelles is important in the formation of biological membranes in living cells (Chapter 4), and may have provided the basis for the first cell-like organization of a living system in the organic-rich shallow seas in which life is believed to have undergone its first evolutionary stages.

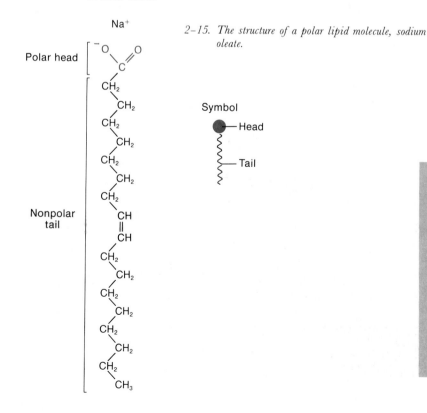

2–15. The structure of a polar lipid molecule, sodium oleate.

Sodium oleate

Na$^+$

Polar head

Nonpolar tail

Symbol
— Head
— Tail

2–16. Behavior of a polar lipid in a polar solvent, such as water. The hydrophobic ends of the molecule tend to avoid contact with the polar solvent by grouping at the center of the micelle. [After Lehninger, 1975.]

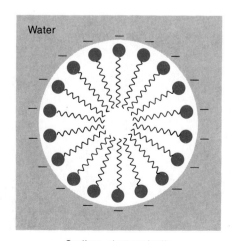

Sodium oleate micelle

2-17. *Dynamic nature of the hydrogen bond in water. Resonance can cause separation of charges, producing hydronium and hydroxyl ions. [After Dowben, 1969.]*

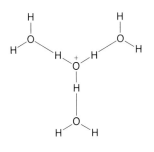

2-18. *The hydronium ion in solution, surrounded by three hydrogen-bonded water molecules. [After Lehninger, 1975.]*

2-19. *Proton migration between water molecules. Each molecule in turn exists briefly as a hydronium ion. [After Lehninger, 1975.]*

IONIZATION OF WATER

The dynamic nature of hydrogen bonding between molecules of water can be depicted as in Figure 2-17, which shows how the covalent and hydrogen bonds may exchange places from one instant to the next. Because of the ever-changing nature of the bonding relations between adjacent water molecules, there is a finite probability that three hydrogen atoms will associate with one oxygen to form a *hydronium* ion, H_3O^+, leaving another oxygen atom with only one hydrogen to form a *hydroxyl* ion, OH^-. This probability is actually quite small. At any given time, a liter of pure water at 25°C contains only 1.0×10^{-7} mole of H_3O^+ and an equal number of hydroxyl ions. The positively charged hydrogen atoms of the hydronium ion attract the electronegative (oxygen) ends surrounding nondissociated water molecules to form a stable hydrated hydronium ion (Fig. 2-18).

The dissociation of water is conveniently written as

$$H_2O \rightleftharpoons H^+ + OH^-$$

Nevertheless, the reader should bear in mind that the proton (H^+) is not, in fact, free in solution but becomes part of the hydronium ion. A proton can, however, migrate to a surrounding H_2O molecule, converting it to H_3O^+ or displacing one of its protons to another water molecule (Fig. 2-19). A sequence of such migrations and displacements can, in the fashion of falling dominoes, conduct over relatively long distances, with any one proton traveling but a short distance. There is some evidence that such proton conduction may play an important role in some biochemical processes, such as photosynthesis and respiratory chain phosphorylation.

ACIDS AND BASES

According to the Brønsted definition of acid and base, H_3O^+ is *acidic* and OH^- is *basic*. That is to say, the former can donate a proton, and the latter can accept a proton. Thus any substance that can form a hydrogen ion, H^+, is termed an acid, and any substance that combines with a hydrogen ion is termed a base. An acid-base reaction always involves such a *conjugate acid-base pair*—the proton donor and the proton acceptor, H_3O^+ and OH^- in the example of water. Water is said to be *amphoteric* because it acts either as acid or as base. Amino acids also have amphoteric properties (p. 19).

Examples of acids are:

hydrochloric acid	HCl	$\rightleftharpoons$	$H^+ + Cl^-$
carbonic acid	H_2CO_3	$\rightleftharpoons$	$H^+ + HCO_3^-$
ammonium	NH_4	$\rightleftharpoons$	$H^+ + NH_3^-$
water	H_2O	$\rightleftharpoons$	$H^+ + OH^-$

Examples of bases are:

ammonia	$NH_3 + H^+$	$\rightleftharpoons$	NH_4^+
sodium hydroxide	$NaOH + H^+$	$\rightleftharpoons$	$Na^+ + H_2O$
phosphate	$HPO_4^{2-} + H^+$	$\rightleftharpoons$	$H_2PO_4^-$
water	$H_2O + H^+$	$\rightleftharpoons$	H_3O^+

The dissociation of water into acid and base is an equilibrium process and can be described by the Law of Mass Action, which states that the rate of a chemical reation is proportional to the active masses of the reacting substances. For example, the equilibrium constant for the reaction

$$H_2O \rightleftharpoons H^+ + OH^-$$

is given by

$$K_{eq} = \frac{[H^+][OH^-]}{[H_2O]}. \tag{2-1}$$

The concentration of water remains virtually unaltered by its partial dissociation into H^+ and OH^-, since the concentration of each of the dissociated products is only 10^{-7} M (10^{-7} mole/liter), whereas the concentration of water in a liter of pure water ($= 1000$ g) is 1000 g/liter divided by the gram molecular weight of water, 18 g/mole, or 55.5 M (55.5 moles/liter). Equation 2-1 can thus be simplified to

$$55.5 \, K_{eq} = [H^+][OH^-].$$

Recall that a consequence of Law of the Mass Action is the reciprocal relation between the concentrations of two compounds in an equilibrium system. This is apparent in the constant K_{eq}, which may be lumped with the molarity of water (55.5) into a constant that will be termed the *ion product* of water, K_w. At 25°C this has a value of 1×10^{-14}:

$$K_w = [H^+][OH^-] = 10^{-14}.$$

This follows from the fact, noted above, that $[H^+]$ and $[OH^-]$ each equal 10^{-7} mole/liter. If $[H^+]$ for some reason increases, as when an acid substance is dissolved in water, $[OH^-]$ will decrease so as to keep $K_w = 10^{-14}$. This, of course, is the basis for the *pH scale*, the standard for acidity and basicity, measured as concentration of H^+ (actually H_3O^+). It will be noted in Table 2-2 that the pH scale is logarithmic and ranges from 1.0 M H^+ to 10^{-14} M H^+. The term

pH is a sort of logarithmic shorthand. It is defined as

$$pH = \log_{10} \frac{1}{[H^+]}$$

or

$$pH = -\log_{10}[H^+].$$

Thus a 10^{-3} M solution of a strong acid, such as HCl, which dissociates completely in water, has a pH of 3.0. A solution in which $[H^+] = [OH^-] = 10^{-7}$ M has a pH of 7.0, and so forth. A solution with a pH of 7 is said to be neutral—that is, neither acidic nor basic. The pH of a solution can be conveniently measured as the voltage produced by H^+ diffusing through the proton-selective glass envelope of an electrode immersed in the solution (Fig. 2-20).

THE BIOLOGICAL IMPORTANCE OF pH

The hydrogen ion and hydroxyl ion concentrations are important in biological systems because protons are free to move from the H_3O^+ to associate with and thereby neutralize negatively charged groups, and hydroxyl ions are available to neutralize positively charged groups. This is especially important in amino acids and proteins, which contain both carboxyl (i.e., $-COOH$) and amino (i.e., $-NH_2$) groups. In solution amino acids normally exist in a dipolar configuration termed a *zwitterion*:

undissociated   zwitterion

Table 2-2. The pH scale.

pH	$[H^+]$ (moles/liter)	$[OH^-]$ (moles/liter)
0	10^0	10^{-14}
1	10^{-1}	10^{-13}
2	10^{-2}	10^{-12}
3	10^{-3}	10^{-11}
4	10^{-4}	10^{-10}
5	10^{-5}	10^{-9}
6	10^{-6}	10^{-8}
7	10^{-7}	10^{-7}
8	10^{-8}	10^{-6}
9	10^{-9}	10^{-5}
10	10^{-10}	10^{-4}
11	10^{-11}	10^{-3}
12	10^{-12}	10^{-2}
13	10^{-13}	10^{-1}
14	10^{-14}	10^0

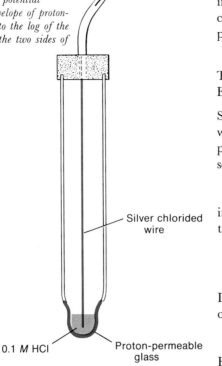

2-20. *When the pH electrode is immersed in a solution of different [H⁺], the potential difference set up across the envelope of proton-selective glass is proportional to the log of the ratio of H⁺ concentrations on the two sides of the H⁺-selective glass.*

pH meter

Silver chlorided wire

0.1 M HCl

Proton-permeable glass

Note that at a certain pH of the solution (the *isoelectric point*) the net charge of the amino acid in both undissociated and zwitterion forms is zero. In the event that the acidity of the solution is increased, the H^+ concentration of the solution will increase. As a result, the probability of a proton neutralizing a carboxyl group will be greater than the probability of a hydroxyl ion removing the extra proton from the amino group. A large proportion of the amino acid molecules will then bear a net positive charge:

$$\underset{\substack{| \\ H}}{\overset{\substack{NH_3^+ \\ |}}{R-C-COO^-}} + H^+ \rightleftharpoons \underset{\substack{| \\ H}}{\overset{\substack{NH_3^+ \\ |}}{R-C-COOH}}$$

Raising the pH will, of course, have the opposite effect. Each species of zwitterion has a characteristic isoelectric point—namely, a pH value at which it has a net charge (statistically) of zero. A number of amino acids have no amphoteric groups other than the alpha —COOH and alpha —NH₃ groups, which enter into peptide bonds (p. 37). Others, however, have additional carboxyl or amino side groups that can become acidic or basic. Dissociable side groups in a macromolecule will determine to a large extent the electrical properties of the molecule, and will render it sensitive to the pH of its environment. This is most dramatically evident in altered properties of the active site (p. 56) of an enzyme. Since the binding of a substrate to the active site of an enzyme generally includes electrostatic interactions, the formation of the enzyme-substrate complex is highly pH dependent, showing highest probability at an optimum pH.

THE HENDERSON-HASSELBALCH EQUATION

Some acids, such as HCl, dissociate completely, whereas others, such as acetic acid, dissociate only partially. For the generalized expression for the dissociation of an acid,

$$HA \rightleftharpoons H^+ + A^-$$

in which A^- is the anion of the acid HA, the dissociation constant is derived from the Mass Action Law:

$$K' = \frac{[H^+][A^-]}{[HA]}. \qquad (2\text{-}2)$$

It is convenient to use the logarithmic transformation of K', namely pK', which is analogous to pH. Thus

$$pK' = -\log_{10} K'.$$

Hence $pK' = 11$ means $K' = 10^{-11}$. A low pK' indicates a strong acid, a high pK' a weak acid.

Acid-base problems can be simplified by rearranging equation 2-2. Taking the log of both sides, we obtain

$$\log K' = \log [H^+] + \log \frac{[A^-]}{[HA]} \qquad (2\text{-}3)$$

Rearranging gives us

$$-\log [H^+] = -\log K' + \log \frac{[A^-]}{[HA]}. \qquad (2\text{-}4)$$

Substituting pH for $-\log [H^+]$ and pK' for $-\log K$:

$$pH = pK' + \log \frac{[A^-]}{[HA]}. \qquad (2\text{-}5)$$

Thus

$$pH = pK' + \log \frac{[\text{proton acceptor}]}{[\text{proton donor}]}.$$

This is the *Henderson-Hasselbalch equation*, which permits the calculation of the pH of a conjugate acid-base pair, given the pK' and the molar ratio of the pair. Conversely, it permits the calculation of the pK', given the pH of a solution of known molar ratio.

BUFFER SYSTEMS

Because of the effect of pH on the ionization of basic and acidic groups in proteins and other biological molecules, the pH of intra- and extracellular fluids must be held within the narrow limits in which the enzyme systems have evolved. Deviations of one pH unit or more generally disrupt the orderly functioning of a living system. This sensitivity to the acidity of the aqueous intracellular milieu exists in part because reaction rates of different enzyme systems (Chapter 3) become mismatched and uncoordinated. For example, the pH of human blood is maintained at 7.4 by means of natural pH *buffers*. A buffered system is one that undergoes little change in pH over a certain pH range upon addition of relatively large amounts of an acid or a base.

A buffer must contain an acid (HA) to neutralize added bases and a base (A^-) to neutralize added acids. (We have already seen that HA is an acid because it acts as an H^+ donor and that A^- is a base because it acts as an H^+ acceptor.) The greatest buffering capacity of such a conjugate acid-base pair therefore occurs when [HA] and [A^-] are both large and equal. Referring to the Henderson-Hasselbalch equation (Eq. 2-5), we see that this situation exists when pH = pK' (since $\log_{10} 1 = 0$). This is also apparent from that portion of a titration curve (Fig. 2-21) along which there is relatively little change in pH.

The most effective buffer systems are combinations of weak acids and their salts. The former dissociate only slightly, thus ensuring a large reservoir of HA, whereas the latter dissociate completely, providing a large reservoir of A^-. Added H^+ therefore combines with A^- to form HA, and added OH^- combines with H^+ to form HOH. As H^+ is thereby removed, it is replaced by dissociation of HA. Figure 2-22 shows a buffer system based on acetic acid (HAc) and one of its salts (NaAc). The most important inorganic buffer systems in the body fluids are the bicarbonates and phosphates. Amino acids, peptides, and proteins, because of their weak-acid side groups, form an important class of organic buffers in the cytoplasm and extracellular plasma.

2-21. The greatest buffering capacity of a conjugate acid-base system is obtained when pH = pK. On the graph, this point corresponds to the part of the curve with the shallowest slope (small pH changes with large amounts of OH^- added).

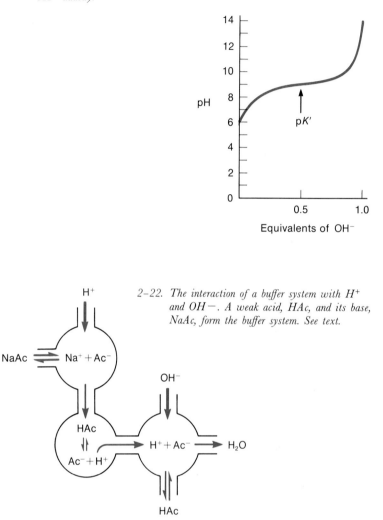

2-22. The interaction of a buffer system with H^+ and OH^-. A weak acid, HAc, and its base, NaAc, form the buffer system. See text.

Solutions and their Colligative Properties

It is a convention in chemistry to express the quantity of any pure substance in *moles*. This unit is arbitrarily defined as the number of atoms or molecules in X grams of the substance, where X is equal to the atomic weight or molecular weight of the substance. Thus 12.00 g of the pure nuclide ^{12}C is 1 mole of ^{12}C, or 6.022×10^{23} (Avogadro's number) carbon atoms. Conversely, there are 6.022×10^{23} molecules in 2.00 g (or 1 mole) of H_2, in 28 g (or 1 mole) of N_2, and in 32 g (or 1 mole) of O_2.

For some purposes, it is necessary to express the amount of solute in terms of molality—the number of moles of solute in 1000 g of solvent (*not* solution). If 1 mole of a soluble substance (e.g., 342.3 g of sucrose) is dissolved in 1000 g of water, the resulting solution is said to be a *one molal* solution. Although 1 liter of water equals 1000 g, the total volume of 1000 g of water plus 1 mole of the substance will be somewhat greater or lesser than one liter by some unpredictable amount. Molality, therefore, is generally an inconvenient way of stating concentration. A more useful measure of concentration in physiology is *molarity*. A *one molar* (1 M) solution is one in which 1 mole of solute is dissolved in a *total final volume* of 1 liter. This is written 1 mole/liter or 1 M. In the laboratory, a 1 M solution is made by simply adding enough water to

1 mole of the solute to bring the volume of the final solution up to 1 liter. A millimolar (mM) solution contains 1/1000 mole/liter, and a micromolar (μM) solution contains 10^{-6} mole/liter. If a solution contains *equimolar* concentrations of two solutes, then the number of molecules of one solute equals the number of molecules of the other solute per unit volume of solution.

Since the molarity of a solution describes the number of individual *particles* dispersed in a given volume of solution, the concept becomes somewhat more complex for electrolytes than for nonelectrolytes because of ionic dissociation. As an example, one mole of NaCl dissolved in H_2O produces nearly twice as many particles as a mole equivalent weight of glucose, since the salt dissociates into Na^+ and Cl^-. Because of electrostatic interaction between the cations and anions of the dissolved electrolyte there is a statistical probability that at any instant some Na^+ will be associated with Cl^-. The electrolyte therefore behaves as if it were not 100% dissociated. Because the electrostatic force between ions decreases with the square of the distance between them (see footnote, p. 29), the electrolyte will effectively become more dissociated if the solution is more dilute. Thus the *activity* (i.e., effective free concentration) of an ion depends on its tendency to dissociate in solution, as well as on its total concentration. Table 2-3 lists the *activity coefficients** of some common electrolytes. Those that dissociate to a large extent (i.e., have a large activity coefficient) are termed *strong electrolytes* (e.g., KCl, NaCl, HCl), and those that dissociate only slightly are termed *weak electrolytes.*

Solute particles, irrespective of their chemical nature impart to the solution a set of physical properties, including depression of the freezing point, elevation of the boiling point, and depression of the water vapor pressure. The solute particles also give the solution an osmotic pressure. These *colligative properties* are intimately related to each other, and are all quantitively related to the number of solute particles dissolved in a given volume of solvent—that is, the molality. Thus 1 mole of an ideal solute—that is, one in which the particles neither dissociate nor associate—dissolved in 1000 g of water at standard pressure (760 Torr) depresses the freezing point by 1.86°C and elevates the boiling point by 0.54°C. In an ideal apparatus for determining osmotic pressure, such a solution will exhibit an osmotic pressure of 22.4 atmospheres at standard temperature (0°C). Since colligative properties depend on the total number of solute particles in a given volume of solvent, the colligative properties of 10 mM NaCl (strongly dissociating electrolyte) solution will be nearly equivalent to those of a 20 mM sucrose solution—more precisely, equivalent to an 18 mM sucrose solution, since the dissociation constant of NaCl at a concentration of 10 mM is 0.9 (see Table 2-3).*

OSMOSIS

Osmotic pressure is the colligative property of greatest importance to living systems. It was first noted by Abbé Nollet, in 1748, that if pure water is placed on one side of an animal membrane (e.g., bladder wall) and an aqueous solution is placed on the other side, the water passes through the membrane into the solution. This was termed *osmosis* (from Greek for "push"). It was later found that this phenomenon produces a hydrostatic pressure gradient. As can be seen in Figure 2-23, the pressure difference causes a rise in the level of the solution as water diffuses through the *semipermeable membrane* into the solution. The rise in the level of the solution continues until the net rate of water movement (the net *flux*) across the membrane becomes zero. This occurs when the hydrostatic pressure of the solution (b) is sufficient to force water molecules back through the membrane (from b to a) at the same rate that osmosis causes water molecules to diffuse from a to b. The hydrostatic back pressure required to cancel the osmotic diffusion of water from side a to side b is termed the *osmotic pressure* of solution b.

Pfeffer, in 1877, made the first quantitative studies of osmotic pressure. By depositing a coating of ferrocyanide on the surface of porous clay cups, he produced membranes that would allow water molecules

Table 2-3. Activity coefficients of representative electrolytes at various molal concentrations.

Substance	Molalities				
	0.01	0.05	0.10	1.00	2.00
KCl	0.899	0.815	0.764	0.597	0.569
NaCl	0.903	0.821	0.778	0.656	0.670
HCl	0.904	0.829	0.796	0.810	1.019
$CaCl_2$	0.732	0.582	0.528	0.725	1.555
H_2SO_4	0.617	0.397	0.313	0.150	0.147
$MgSO_4$	0.150	0.068	0.049	—	—

Source: E. S. West, *Textbook of Biophysical Chemistry*, Macmillan, New York, 1964.

*The activity coefficient is defined by the relation $\gamma = a/m$, in which m is the molal concentration and a the activity, which is defined as the effective concentration of the substance as indicated by the properties in solution.

*The activity coefficients are given for various *molal* concentrations rather than *molar* concentrations. At low concentrations, however, molarity and molality are nearly identical.

to diffuse through it far more freely than sucrose molecules, and which was also strong enough, because of the clay substratum, to withstand relatively high pressures without rupturing. Using these membranes, he was able to make the first direct measurements of osmotic pressure. Some of his results are shown in Table 2-4. He found, first, that osmotic pressure, P, is proportional to the concentration, C, of the solute and, second, that it is proportional to the absolute temperature, T (degrees Kelvin, °K).

$$P = K_1 C \qquad (2\text{-}6)$$

and

$$P = K_2 T, \qquad (2\text{-}7)$$

in which K_1 and K_2 are constants of proportionality. Van't Hoff went on to relate these observations to the gas laws, and showed that solute molecules in solution behave thermodynamically like gas molecules. Thus

$$P = \frac{nRT}{V}, \qquad (2\text{-}8)$$

in which n = the number of moles of solute, R = the molar gas constant (0.082 liter-atm/°K-mole), and V = the volume in liters. Like the gas laws, however, this expression for osmotic pressure holds true only for dilute solutions; corrections must be made for concentrated solutions.

To demonstrate the role of a semipermeable membrane in osmosis, let us suppose that a 1.0 M aqueous solution of sucrose is carefully layered under an 0.01 M aqueous solution of sucrose. There would be net diffusion of water molecules from the solution of lower sucrose concentration (the 0.01 M solution) into the 1.0 M sucrose solution, and sucrose would show net diffusion in the opposite direction. If we were to place a membrane between these two solutions that would allow water molecules, but not sucrose molecules, to pass through it, the water molecules would still show a net diffusion from the solution in which H_2O is more concentrated (the 0.01 M sucrose solution) into the 1.0 M sucrose solution, in which the concentration of H_2O is lower. The sucrose, however, would be prevented from diffusing because of the membrane barrier. The result is a net diffusion of water (*osmotic flow*) through the membrane from the solution of lower solute concentration to the solution of higher solute concentration. As explained in Chapters 4 and 12, this provides the basis for net water movement across many biological membranes and epithelia.

OSMOTICITY AND TONICITY

Two solutions that exert the same osmotic pressure are said to be *isomotic* to each other. If one solution exerts less osmotic pressure than the other, it is *hypo-*

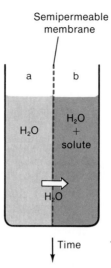

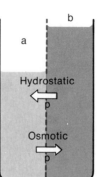

2-23. *Osmotic pressure forces water to enter compartment b from compartment a until the hydrostatic pressure difference equals the opposing osmotic pressure difference. When the pressures are equal, the flux is zero. Side* a *contains pure water; side* b, *water with impermeant solute.*

Table 2-4. *Results obtained by Pfeffer in experimental measurements of the osmotic pressure of sucrose solutions of various concentrations.*

Percent sucrose	Osmotic pressure (atm)	Ratio of osmotic pressure to percent sucrose
1	0.70	0.70
2	1.34	0.67
4	2.74	0.68
6	4.10	0.68

Source: Getman and F. Daniels, *Outlines of Theoretical Chemistry,* Wiley, New York.

osmotic with respect to the other solution; if it exerts more osmotic pressure, it is *hyperosmotic. Osmoticity* (or *osmolarity*) is defined on the basis of an ideal osmometer—one in which the osmotic membrane allows water to pass but completely prevents the solute from passing. Thus all solutions with the same number of dissolved particles per unit volume have the same osmoticity and are thus defined as isosmotic. In contrast, *tonicity* is defined in terms of the response of cells or tissues immersed in a solution. If cells ac-

Table 2-5. *Osmolarity of two electrolyte solutions and various human body fluids.*

Fluid	Osmolarity (milliosmols)
1 % KCl	135
1 % NaCl	172
Cerebrospinal fluid	154
Saliva	30–80
Seminal plasma	230–330
Blood serum	155
Tears	157
Urine	30–700

Source: A. V. Wolf, *Aqueous Solutions and Body Fluids,* Hoeber Medical Division, Harper & Row, New York, 1966.

2-24. *A. When KCl is added to compartment I of a container divided by a permeable membrane, K^+ and Cl^- diffuse across the membrane until the concentrations are equal on either side. B. If an impermeant anion is added to compartment I, then K^+ is forced to diffuse back into compartment I, whereas Cl^- diffuses into compartment II until electrochemical equilibrium is established.*

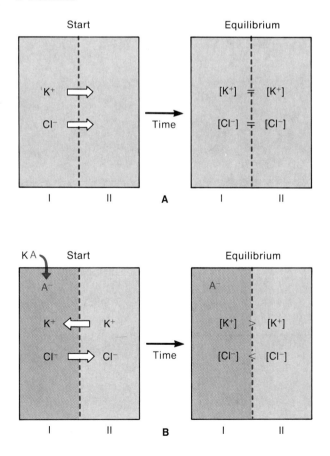

tually behaved as ideal osmometers, tonicity and osmoticity would be equivalent, but this is not generally true. For example, sea urchin eggs maintain a constant volume in a solution of NaCl that is isosmotic relative to sea water, but swell if immersed in a solution of $CaCl_2$ that is isosmotic relative to sea water. The NaCl solution is therefore isotonic relative to the sea urchin egg, whereas the $CaCl_2$ solution is hypotonic relative to the sea urchin egg. The tonicity of a solution depends on the permeability of the cell membranes and tissues in question, as well as on the concentration of the solution. The more readily the solute passes through the cell membrane, the lower the tonicity of a solution of given concentration or osmolarity. Thus the terms *isotonic, hypertonic,* and *hypotonic* are meaningful only in reference to actual experimental determinations on living cells or tissues.

The sum of the concentrations of solutes in a solution is sometimes obtained by measuring the colligative properties of the solution (e.g., by measuring the depression of freezing point). Concentrations measured in this way are often expressed in *osmoles* or *milliosmoles.* These units are, in theory, equivalent to the molarity of a solution of an ideal nondissociating solute exhibiting the same colligative properties. The osmolarities of some biological or biologically important fluids are listed in Table 2-5.

DONNAN EQUILIBRIUM

In 1911 the physical chemist Donnan examined the distribution of diffusible solutes separated by a membrane that is freely permeable to water and electrolytes but totally impermeable to one species of ion confined to one of two compartments. In this situation, the diffusible solutes become unequally distributed among the two compartments, as explained below.

To begin with, pure water is placed in both compartments, and some KCl is dissolved in the water in one of these compartments. The dissolved salt (K^+ and Cl^-) will diffuse through the membrane until the system is in equilibrium—that is, until the concentrations of K^+ and Cl^- become equal on both sides of the membrane (Fig. 2-24, A). Donnan found that if the K salt of a nondiffusible anion (a macromolecule, A^-, having multiple negative charges) is added to the solution in compartment I, the K^+ and Cl^- become redistributed until a new equilibrium is established by movement of some K^+ and some Cl^- from side I to II (Fig. 2-24, B). *Donnan equilibrium* is characterized by a reciprocal distribution of K^+ and Cl^+ such that

$$\frac{[K^+]_I}{[K^+]_{II}} = \frac{[Cl^-]_{II}}{[Cl^-]_I}.$$

The diffusible cation, K^+, becomes more concentrated in the compartment in which the nondiffusible anion,

Cl⁻, is confined than in the other, whereas the diffusible anion, Cl⁻, becomes less concentrated in that compartment than in the other.

This equilibrium situation arises from the following physical requirements:

1. There must be electroneutrality in both compartments. That is, within each compartment, the total number of positive charges must *virtually* equal the total number of negative charges. Thus, in this example, $[K^+] = [Cl^-]$ in compartment II.

2. The diffusible ions K^+ and Cl^- must, statistically, cross the membrane in pairs in order to maintain electrical neutrality. The probability that they will cross together is proportional to the product $[K^+][Cl^-]$.

3. At equilibrium the rate of diffusion of KCl in one direction through the membrane must equal the rate of KCl diffusion in the opposite direction. Thus, at equilibrium the product $[K^+][Cl^-]$ in one compartment must be equal to the same product in the other compartment. Letting x, y, and z represent the concentrations of the ions in compartments I and II, as shown in Figure 2-25, we can express the equilibrium condition (i.e., equality of the product $[K^+][Cl^-]$ in the two compartments) algebraically:

$$x^2 = y(y + z). \qquad (2\text{-}9)$$

This equation also holds, of course, if A^- is not present, for in that case K^+ and Cl^- are equally distributed and $z = 0$ and $x = y$.

By rearranging Equation 2-9, it becomes evident that, at equilibrium, the distributions of the diffusible ions in the two compartments are reciprocal:

$$\frac{x}{y} = \frac{y + z}{x}. \qquad (2\text{-}10)$$

Thus it is evident that as the concentration of the nondiffusible anion z is increased, the concentrations of the diffusible anion chloride (x in II and y in I) will become increasingly divergent.

This explanation of Donnan equilibrium uses an ideal set of conditions for the sake of simplicity. The living cell and its surface membrane are, of course, far more complex. The "nondiffusible anion" in this example represents various anionic side groups of proteins and other large molecules. The cell membrane is permeable to a large variety of ions and molecules to varying extents. Although the physical and mathematical principles recognized by Donnan play a role in regulating the distribution of some electrolytes in living cells, it has become increasingly evident that some *non*equilibrium mechanisms, such as active transport (Chapter 4), also play important roles in the distribution of many substances, including certain ions, across the cell membrane. Thus the cell cannot be con-

I	II
$Z = [A^-]_I$	
	$X = [K^+]_{II}$
$(Y + Z) = [K^+]_I$	
	$X = [Cl^-]_{II}$
$Y = [Cl^-]_I$	

2-25. *Algebraic description of the equilibrium condition established in Figure 2-24, B after the impermeable anion is added to compartment I.*

sidered a passive osmometer, and the distribution of substances across biological membranes cannot be predicted entirely by the Donnan principles.

Electric Current in Aqueous Solutions

Water conducts electric current far more readily than oils or other nonpolar liquids, and is therefore said to exhibit a higher *conductivity* than nonpolar liquids. Conductivity in aqueous solutions is defined as the amount of charge transferred by the migration of ions under a given potential. Thus the conductivity of water depends entirely on the presence of charged atoms or molecules (ions) in solution. Electrons, which carry electric current in metals and semiconductors, play no direct role in the flow of electric current in aqueous solutions. Pure water contains the ions H_3O^+ and OH^-. Since they are present in low concentrations (10^{-7}M at $25°C$), the electrical conductivity of pure water, though far higher than that of nonpolar liquids, is still relatively low. Conductivity is greatly enhanced by the addition of electrolytes, which, instead of dissolving as molecules, dissociate into cations and anions.

The role of ions in conducting electric current is illustrated in Figure 2-26, which shows two electrodes immersed in a solution of potassium chloride and

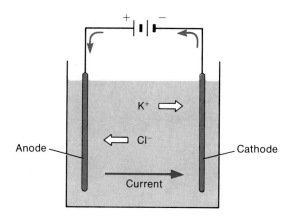

2-26. *Flow of current through an electrolyte solution. Solid arrows indicate direction of current flow. Open arrows indicate direction of ion flow.*

Table 2-6. *The electrical mobilities of some ions at 25°C extrapolated to infinite dilution.*

Ion	Mobility (10^{-4} cm²/volt-sec)
H+	36.3
Na+	5.2
K+	7.62
NH$_4$+	7.60
Mg²+	5.4
Li+	4.0

Source: A. L. Lehninger, *Biochemistry,* Worth Publishing, New York, 1970.

2-27. *Analogy between the flow of electrons in a wire and the flow of water in a pipe.*

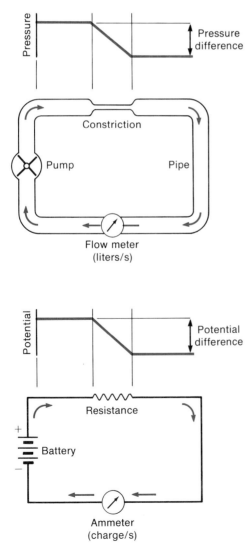

connected by wires to a source of electromotive force (i.e., potential difference), the two terminals marked + and −. The electromotive force causes a current (i.e., a unidirectional displacement of positive electric charge) to flow through the electrolyte solution from one electrode to the other.

What does the electric current consist of? In the wire, it consists of the displacement of electrons from the outer shell of one metal atom to another, then to another, and so on. In the KCl solution, electric charge is carried primarily by K+ and Cl− ions (and by displacement of OH−, H$_3$0+ and H+, but this contribution is so small that it will be ignored). When a potential difference (voltage) is applied to an electrolyte solution, the cations, K+, migrate toward the *cathode* (electrode with the negative potential) and the anions, Cl−, migrate toward the *anode* (electrode with positive potential). The rate at which each species of ion migrates in solution is termed its *mobility.* This is determined by the ions hydrated mass and the amount of charge (monovalent, divalent, or trivalent) that it bears. The mobilities of some common ions are given in Table 2-6. It is well to remember that ionic current is crudely analogous to a wave of falling dominoes, in which each domino (ion) is displaced just enough to cause a displacement of the next domino. Instead of interacting mechanically, like falling dominoes, ions influence each other through electrostatic interactions, with like charges repelling one another.

The current in a solution is said by convention to flow in the direction of cation migration. Anions flow in the opposite direction. The rate with which positive charges are displaced past a given point in the solution, plus the rate at which negative charges are displaced past a given point in the solution, plus the rate at which negative charges are displaced in the opposite direction, determines the intensity of the electric *current.* Current is a measure of the number of unit charges flowing past a point in one second, and is thus analogous to the volume of water that flows per second past a point in a pipe (Fig. 2-27, top).

An electric current always meets some resistance to its flow, just as water meets a mechanical resistance due to such factors as friction during its flow through a pipe. In order for the charges to flow through an electrical *resistance,* there must be an electrostatic force acting on the charges. This force (analogous to hydrostatic pressure in plumbing) is the difference in electric pressure, or *potential, E,* between the two ends of the resistive pathway (Fig. 2-27, bottom). This *potential,* or *voltage difference,* or electromotive force (emf) is related to the current, *I,* and resistance, *R,* as described by *Ohm's Law* (Box 2-1). To force a given current (number of charges moving past a point per unit time) through a pathway of twice the resistance requires twice the voltage (Fig. 2-28, A). Similarly, the current will be

BOX 2-1 ELECTRICAL TERMINOLOGY AND CONVENTIONS

Charge (*q*) is measured in units of *coulombs*. To convert one gram equivalent weight of a monovalent ion to its elemental form (or vice versa) requires a charge of 96,500 coulombs (one *faraday*). Thus, in loose terms, a coulomb is equivalent to 1/96,500 gram equivalent of electrons. The charge on one electron is -1.6×10^{-19} coulomb. If this is multiplied by Avogadro's number, the total charge is one faraday or $-96,487$ coulombs/mole.

Current (*I*) is the flow of charge. A current of one coulomb per second is called an *ampere* (A). By convention the direction of current flow is the direction that a positive charge moves (i.e., from the anode to the cathode).

Voltage (*E*) is the electromotive force, or electric potential expressed in volts. When the work required to move one coulomb of charge from one point to a point of higher potential is one joule (J), or 1/4.184 cal, the potential difference between these points is said to be one *volt* (V).

Resistance (*R*) is the property that hinders the flow of current. The unit is the *ohm* (Ω), defined as the resistance of a column of mercury 1 mm² in cross-sectional area and 106.3 cm long. $R = \rho \times$ length/cross-sectional area.

Resistivity (ρ) is the resistance of a conductor 1 cm in length and 1 cm² in cross-sectional area.

Conductance (*G*) is the reciprocal of resistance, $G = 1/R$. The unit is the *mho*.

Conductivity is the reciprocal of resistivity.

Ohm's Law states that current is proportional to voltage and inversely proportional to resistance:

$$I = \frac{E}{R} \text{ or } E = IR.$$

Thus a potential of one volt across a resistance of one ohm will result in a current of one ampere. Conversely, a current of one ampere flowing through a resistance of one ohm produces a potential difference across that resistance of one volt.

Capacitance (*C*). A capacitor (or condenser) consists of two conductors separated by an insulator. If a battery is connected in series to the two conductors, charges will move from one to the other until the potential difference across the plates is equal to the electromotive force (emf, in volts) of the battery, or until the insulation breaks down. No charges move "bodily" across the insulation between the plates in an ideal capacitor, but charges of one sign accumulating on one plate electrostatically repel similar charges on the opposite plate. The *capacity*, or charge-storing ability, of the capacitor is given in *farads* (F). If a potential of one volt is applied across a capacitor and one coulomb of positive charge is thereby accumulated by one plate and lost by the other plate, the capacitor is said to have a capacity of one farad:

$$C = \frac{q}{E} = \frac{1 \text{ coulomb}}{1 \text{ volt}} = 1 \text{ farad.}$$

Symbols

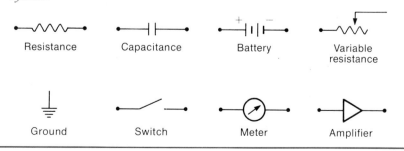

| Resistance | Capacitance | Battery | Variable resistance |
| Ground | Switch | Meter | Amplifier |

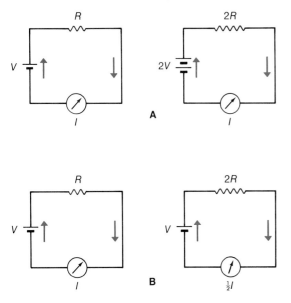

2-28. *Representation of electrical relationships described by Ohm's Law. A. Current remains unchanged if voltage and resistance are both doubled. B. Current drops by half if resistance alone is doubled.*

tance encountered by the current. This, again, is analogous to the effect of the cross-sectional area of a pipe carrying water. Third, the total resistance to current flow increases with the distance traversed in solution by the current. The resistance encountered by a current passing through a distance of 2 cm of electrolyte solution is twice the resistance encountered in traversing 1 cm of the same solution. The ions carrying current are distributed more or less evenly throughout a solution. Since the electromotive force (i.e., voltage) applied between the two electrodes sets up a widespread electric field, the current does not follow a straight path. Instead, it arches out in curved paths between the two electrodes (Fig. 2-29). It does so because more ions are brought into play than are present in a direct path between the two electrodes, thus providing a lower effective resistance to the flow of electric current.

The widespread importance of electrical phenomena in animal physiology will become apparent in later chapters. Familiarity with basic concepts of electricity is also of immense value in understanding laboratory instruments.

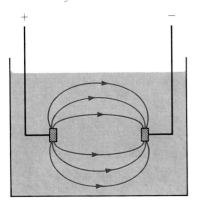

2-29. *Current flow through a volume of electrolyte solution spreads so as to decrease current density.*

Ion Selectivity

Ions free in solution inside or outside living cells will interact electrostatically with one another and with a variety of *ion-binding sites* on such biological substances as cell membranes and macromolecules. These sites carry electric charges. Their interactions with ions are based on the same principles that determine ion exchange at sites on such inorganic materials as soil particles, glass, and certain plastics. *Ion-site* interactions are highly important in certain physiological mechanisms, such as enzyme activation (p. 63) and membrane transport (p. 88), in which selective binding of ions plays a prominent role.

The energetic basis for interaction between an ion and an ion-binding site is the electrostatic attraction between the two, and is identical in principle to the interactions that occur between anions and cations in free solution. Thus a site with a negative charge or a partial negative charge (recall the partial charge on the oxygen of the water molecule, p. 14) attracts cations, and a site with a positive charge attracts anions. Two or more species of cations in solution will compete with each other to bind electrostatically to an anionic (i.e., electronegative) site. The negatively charged site will show an order of binding preference among cation species, ranging from those that bind most strongly to those that bind least strongly. This order to preference is termed the *affinity sequence,* or *selectivity sequence,* of the site.

reduced to half its value if the resistance it encounters is doubled while the voltage is kept constant (Fig. 2-28, B).

Three major factors determine the resistance to current flow in a solution. First, the availability of charge carriers in the solution (i.e., the ion concentration). The more dilute an electrolyte solution, the higher its resistance, and thus the lower its *conductivity* (Box 2-1). This makes sense, since fewer ions are available to carry current. Second, the smaller the cross-sectional area of the solution in a plane perpendicular to the direction of current flow, the higher the resis-

The most extensively studied selectivity sequences are those of the five alkali-earth metal ions (lithium, sodium, potassium, rubidium, cesium). Of the 120* possible sequences for these ions, only eleven have been observed in nature (Fig. 2-30). Sequence I (Cs^+, Rb^+, K^+, Na^+, Li^+) corresponds to the order of decreasing ionic radius (Fig. 2-31), hence increasing degree of hydration in water. Sequence XI, the reverse of sequence I, corresponds to the order of increasing ionic radius, and hence decreasing degree of hydration.

Cation-binding sites on organic molecules are generally oxygen atoms in such groups as silicates ($-SiO^-$), carbonyls ($R-C=O$), carboxylates ($R-COO^-$), and ethers (R_1-O-R_2). As was noted earlier (p. 13), the oxygen atom is strongly electron hungry, and draws electrons from surrounding atoms in the molecule. In such neutral groups as the carbonyls or ethers, these sites can be treated as having a partial negative charge due to the statistically higher number of electrons around the oxygen atoms. (Since the group itself is neutral, there must also, of course, be partial positive charges on the other atoms, as shown in Fig. 2-32.) The oxygens of silicates and carboxylates carry a full negative charge when ionized.

The energetics of electrostatic interaction of a site with an ion are expressed in terms of potential energy—namely, the energy U of bringing together two charges, q_+ and q_-, in a vacuum from a separation of infinity to the new distance of separation $d^†$:

$$U = \frac{(q_+ q_-)}{d^a}. \qquad (2\text{-}11)$$

The exponent a, in the case of two monopoles each carrying a full charge (i.e., a monovalent anion and a monovalent cation), is equal to one. For a dipolar molecule, such as water—that is, one in which there are centers of both negative and positive charge (but no net charge)—the energy of interaction falls off more rapidly with distance (i.e., a in Equation 2-11 is greater than unity).

Since the nucleus of a small atom can more closely approach another atom than can the nucleus of a large atom, it is evident that *small* monovalent cations can interact more strongly with an electronegative site than *large* monovalent cations. The consequence of this is that, *in a vacuum* (i.e., without interference from

*5! = 5 × 4 × 3 × 2 × 1 = 120 possible rankings of the five cations.

†The form of Equation 2-11 should not be confused with Coulomb's Law, in which the electrostatic force, f, of two monopoles varies inversely with the dielectric constant, ε, and the *square* of the distance, d, between them:

$$f = \frac{q_+ q_-}{\varepsilon d^2}.$$

2-30. *The eleven selectivity sequences exhibited by different anionic sites that bind the five alkali-earth metal ions.*

I	$Cs^+ > Rb^+ > K^+ > Na^+ > Li^+$
II	$Rb^+ > Cs^+ > K^+ > Na^+ > Li^+$
III	$Rb^+ > K^+ > Cs^+ > Na^+ > Li^+$
IV	$K^+ > Rb^+ > Cs^+ > Na^+ > Li^+$
V	$K^+ > Rb^+ > Na^+ > Cs^+ > Li^+$
VI	$K^+ > Na^+ > Rb^+ > Cs^+ > Li^+$
VII	$Na^+ > K^+ > Rb^+ > Cs^+ > Li^+$
VIII	$Na^+ > K^+ > Rb^+ > Li^+ > Cs^+$
IX	$Na^+ > K^+ > Li^+ > Rb^+ > Cs^+$
X	$Na^+ > Li^+ > K^+ > Rb^+ > Cs^+$
XI	$Li^+ > Na^+ > K^+ > Rb^+ > Cs^+$

2-31. *Scale drawings of the water molecule and unhydrated alkali-earth metal ions to show relative sizes.* [Hille, 1972.]

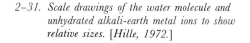

2-32. *Electron-cloud distributions of molecular side groups.*

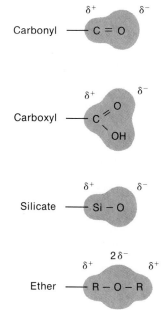

water molecules), the order of binding strength (from strongest to weakest) between an electronegative site and the alkali-metal cations should be $Li^+ > Na^+ > K^+ > RB^+ > Cs^+$, the order of increasing atomic size (sequence XI in Fig. 2-30). Thus, in a vacuum, lithium will bind more strongly to an anionic site than the cesium ion, because it carries the same unit charge but has a smaller *distance of closest approach.*

In an aqueous environment (i.e., in a solution as opposed to a vacuum) the coulombic relation (Eq. 2-11) between atomic radius and affinity for a given electronegative fixed site is modified by the electrostatic interaction of the cation with water. This interaction is due to the polar nature of the water molecule. The cation, attracted to both the electron-rich oxygen atom of the fixed monopolar site and the electron-rich oxygen atom of the dipolar water molecule, is caught in a tug-of-war, so to speak, between the free energy of electrostatic binding to water,

$$\Delta G_{\text{ion, water}},$$

and the free energy of electrostatic binding to the electronegative fixed site,

$$\Delta G_{\text{ion, site}}.$$

The energetic competition between water and site can be expressed as

$$\Delta G_{\text{ion, site}} - \Delta G_{\text{ion, water}}. \qquad (2\text{-}12)$$

It is evident that a site with a strong electrostatic field will compete most successfully with water for the cation, whereas a site with a relatively weak field strength will compete less successfully for the cation (Fig. 2-33).

How is it that different sites exhibit different selectivity sequences for the five alkali-metal cations (Fig. 2-30)? Because the selectivity of a given site for two cations, a and b, is a measure of the affinities of a and b for the site versus their affinities for water, it is necessary to compare the binding energies of the two ions first to the site and then to water. The difference in binding energies of the two ions to the site is given as

$$\Delta G_{a, \text{ site}} - \Delta G_{b, \text{ site}}, \qquad (2\text{-}13)$$

where $\Delta G_{a, \text{ site}}$ and $\Delta G_{b, \text{ site}}$ are the free energies of binding between the respective cations and the site. Similarly, the difference in their binding energies to water is

$$\Delta G_{a, \text{ water}} - \Delta G_{b, \text{ water}}, \qquad (2\text{-}14)$$

where $\Delta G_{a, \text{ water}}$ and $\Delta G_{b, \text{ water}}$ are the respective free energies of binding to water. The relative affinities of the two cations for the site in the presence of water will be governed by the difference between these expressions—that is, the *difference* between the relative binding energies of the two ions to the site on the one hand and their relative binding energies to water on the other hand:

$$(\Delta G_{a, \text{ site}} - \Delta G_{b, \text{ site}}) \\ - (\Delta G_{a, \text{ water}} - \Delta G_{b, \text{ water}}). \qquad (2\text{-}15)$$

Thus it is not the affinity of an ion for the site alone that determines how well it competes with another ion for the site, but also its affinity for water. *The selectivity of a site depends on the balance between the energies of hydration of various ions and their energies of binding with the site.*

Next we must recall that the fall off in potential energy with increasing distance depends on the elec-

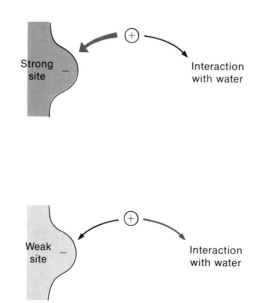

2–33. *Top. The force of attraction of a small monovalent cation to a* strong *anionic point site is greater than its attraction to water (and vice versa for a large monovalent cation). Bottom. The force of attraction of a small monovalent cation to a* weak *point site is less than its attraction to water (and vice versa for large monovalent cation).*

tron distribution of the site with which the cation interacts (p. 29). Thus the exponent a in Equation 2-11 is unity for a monopolar site, whereas for a dipolar site, such as a water molecule, the potential energy of interaction drops off as the square of distance (i.e., a in Eq. 2-11 equals 2). The effect this has on the relative affinities of large and small cations to monopolar sites and water is illustrated in Figure 2-34. Shown at the left is a monopolar, fixed, anionic site. Plotted above it is the change in energy of interaction as a function of distance between centers of charge for a weak and a strong site. At the right is a water molecule and a corresponding plot showing how the potential energy decreases with the square of distance. The difference between energies of interaction of two ions of different size is seen to be much larger for water than for the monopolar fixed site.

To illustrate the way in which this gives rise to a selectivity sequence, let us consider the electrostatic asymmetry between water and two monopolar anionic sites, A and B, which differ in their field strengths. The energies of electrostatic interaction of the five alkali cations with sites A and B and with water are plotted in Figure 2-35.

The upper and middle curves represent the free energies of binding of each of the alkali cations to sites A and B, assuming that the cations approach each site from an infinite distance in a vacuum. The curve labeled "water" represents the energies required to bring the alkali cations from a vacuum into water (i.e., the "ion-hydration energies"). The *differences* in the cation binding energies to sites A and B and to water determine the selectivity sequences of the two anionic sites. The energy differences are indicated by the vertical brackets, which are numbered in the order of their lengths. The selectivity sequences for the hypothetical sites A and B in Figure 2-35 are thus seen to be

Site A: $Na > Li > K > Rb > Cs$ Sequence X
Site B: $Na > K > Rb > Li > Cs$ Sequence VIII.

The eleven selectivity sequences found in nature (Fig. 2-30) arise from an orderly permutation of relative selectivities depending on these principles. Thus sequence I, characteristic of a weak site, corresponds to the order of decreasing ionic radius, and sequence XI, characteristic of a very strong site, corresponds to the order of increasing ionic radius. Each of the intervening sequences, II to X, differs from the previous sequence by the inversion of one pair of cations. Inspection of Figure 2-30, beginning with sequence I, shows that these inversions take place first among the largest cations (Cs^+, Rb^+, K^+) and last among the smallest cations (Na^+, Li^+). The reason for this is that, with increasing field strength of the monopolar site, the expression $\Delta G_{\text{ion, site}} - \Delta G_{\text{ion, water}}$ (Eq. 2-12) be-

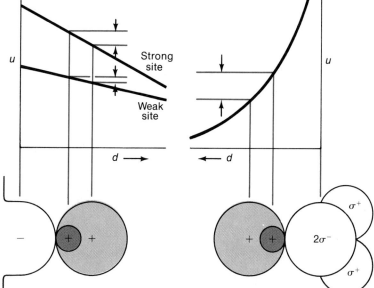

2-34. *Interaction of a large (lightly colored) and a small (darkly colored) cation with a monopolar, fixed, negatively charged site (left) and with a dipolar site, such as a water molecule (right). The upper graphs show the potential energy of interaction, U, as a function of distance, d, between centers of charge. Differences in curves are exaggerated.*

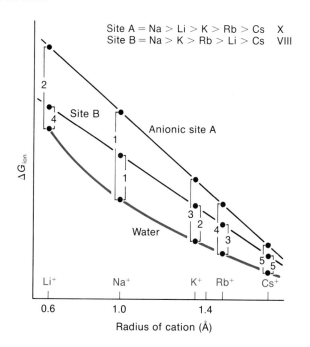

2-35. *Graph of the electrostatic interactions between water, five monovalent cations, and two monopolar anionic sites with differing field strengths. The nonlinearity of the water curve gives rise to the selectivity sequences indicated for each site by the order of numbered brackets. The brackets represent the difference for each ion between energies of interaction with each site and with water.*

Site A = Na > Li > K > Rb > Cs   X
Site B = Na > K > Rb > Li > Cs   VIII

comes negative first for the largest of the ions, which becomes attracted more strongly by water than by the site before the next largest, and so on. Thus the progression of inversions among pairs of cations, from largest to smallest.

Although we have limited our considerations to the monovalent alkali-metal cations, the same principles can be applied to explain selectivity sequences of the divalent alkali-earth cations (Mg^{2+} Ca^{2+}, Sr^{2+}, Ba^{2+}) and the monovalent halide anions (F^-, Cl^-, Br^-, I^-). Selectivity sequences exhibited by these ions are shown in Figure 2-36.

Finally, it should be pointed out that in addition to the principles of electrostatic interaction described above, there are steric constraints on the binding of ions with some sites. If, for example, a site is situated so that an interacting ion must squeeze into a narrow depression or hollow in or between molecules, the hydrated size of the ion will, of course, also have an effect upon the total energy required to reach and interact with the site.

2-36. *A. Selectivity sequences found in nature for divalent cations. B. Selectivity sequences for halide ions.*

A

I $Ba^{++} > Sr^{++} > Ca^{++} > Mg^{++}$

II $Ba^{++} > Ca^{++} > Sr^{++} > Mg^{++}$

III $Ca^{++} > Ba^{++} > Sr^{++} > Mg^{++}$

IV $Ca^{++} > Ba^{++} > Mg^{++} > Sr^{++}$

V $Ca^{++} > Mg^{++} > Ba^{++} > Sr^{++}$

VI $Ca^{++} > Mg^{++} > Sr^{++} > Ba^{++}$

VII $Mg^{++} > Ca^{++} > Sr^{++} > Ba^{++}$

B

I $I^- > Br^- > Cl^- > F^-$

II $Br^- > I^- > Cl^- > F^-$

III $Br^- > Cl^- > I^- > F^-$

IV $Cl^- > Br^- > I^- > F^-$

V $Cl^- > Br^- > F^- > I^-$

VI $Cl^- > F^- > Br^- > I^-$

VII $F^- > Cl^- > Br^- > I^-$

Biological Molecules

The precise molecular composition of an organism more complex than a virus has never been fully determined. This state of ignorance results largely from the incredible numbers and complexity of molecular species in an organism, even a unicellular one. This complexity is further compounded by the fact that no two animal species have the same molecular composition. In fact, the molecular composition of no individual of a species is identical to that of any other in the same species except in those reproduced by cellular fission (e.g., the two daughter cells of an amoeba or monozygotous mammalian twins). Such biochemical diversity is a major factor in evolution, for it provides an enormous number of variables in a population of organisms, and acts as the raw material, so to speak, on which natural selection operates. This diversity is in part made possible by the great potential for structural variability exhibited by the carbon atom, with its ability to form four highly stable bonds (p. 13). In fact, carbon is the "backbone" molecule for the four major classes of organic compounds found in living organisms—lipids, carbohydrates, proteins, and nucleic acids. We will review the chemical structures of these substances briefly as major classes, and consider some properties important to their roles in physiology. More specialized texts, such as Lehninger's and Stryer's biochemistry books, may be consulted for further details.

LIPIDS

Lipids are among the simplest of the biological molecules. The best known are the fats. Each fat molecule consists of a glycerol molecule connected through ester bonds with three fatty acid chains. They are therefore termed *triglycerides*. When they are *hydrolyzed* (i.e., digested) by the insertion of H^+ and OH^- into the ester bonds, the fats break down into glycerol and the individual *fatty acids*, each of which contains an even number of carbon atoms (Fig. 2-37). Some of the carbon atoms of the fatty acid chain may be linked by single bonds and some by double bonds, or the entire chain may be *saturated* with hydrogens, leaving no double bonds between the carbons. The degree of saturation and the length of the fatty acid chains (i.e., number of carbon atoms) determine the physical properties of the fat.

Fats with short chains and unsaturated fatty acids have low melting points (Table 2-7). These are oils or soft fats at room temperatures. Conversely, fats with long chains and saturated fatty acids are solids at room temperatures. That is why the process of hydrogenation (saturating the fatty acid chains with hydrogens, and thereby breaking the double bonds) converts oily peanut butter into smooth, greasy peanut butter, and vegetable oil into Crisco. It is generally agreed that saturated fatty acids are more readily converted by metabolic processes into the *steroid* cholesterol (Fig. 2-38), and thus are more likely to contribute to cardiovascular disease in humans.

Lipids act as energy stores, and are typically accumulated in the fat vacuoles of specialized adipose cells in vertebrates. Because of their low solubility in water, these energy-rich molecules can be stored in large concentrations in the body without requiring large quantities of water as a solvent. Triglyceride energy stores are also rendered highly compact by the relatively high proportions of hydrogen and carbon and low proportions of oxygen in the molecule. Thus one gram of triglyceride will yield about two times as much energy upon oxidation as one gram of carbohydrate (Table 2-8).

In *phospholipids* one of the outer fatty acid chains of the triglyceride is replaced with a phosphate-containing group. As is explained in Chapter 4, the *phospholipids* are important in the formation of biological membranes, because they exhibit *hydrophilic* (i.e., water-soluble) and *lipophilic* (i.e., lipid-soluble) properties at the head and tail ends, respectively, of their molecules. This allows a layer of oriented phospholipid molecules to form the transition between an aqueous phase and a lipid phase. Other groups of lipids are the waxes, glycolipids, sterols, and sphingolipids.

2–37. Hydrolysis of a triglyceride. R represents a fatty acid radical.

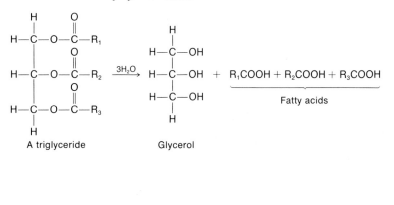

A triglyceride   Glycerol

2–38. The steroid cholesterol.

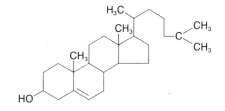

Table 2-7. *Melting points of various fatty acids. Unsaturated bonds lower the melting point of a molecule, as can be seen by a comparison of saturated and unsaturated molecules of equivalent chain length.*

Fatty acid	Structure	Melting point (K)
SATURATED		
Lauric acid	$CH_3(CH_2)_{10}COOH$	44
Palmitic acid	$CH_3(CH_2)_{14}COOH$	63
Arachidic acid	$CH_3(CH_2)_{18}COOH$	75
Lignoceric acid	$CH_3(CH_2)_{22}COOH$	84
UNSATURATED		
Oleic acid	$CH_3(CH_2)_7CH{=}^{CIS}CH(CH_2)_7COOH$	13
Linoleic acid	$CH_3(CH_2)_4(CH{=}CHCH_2)_2(CH_2)_6COOH$	−5
Arachidonic acid	$CH_3(CH_2)_4(CH{=}CHCH_2)_4(CH_2)_2COOH$	−50

Source: R. M. Dowben, *Cell Biology,* Harper & Row, New York, 1971.

Table 2-8. *The energy-producing capacity of the three foodstuffs.*

Substrate	Energy content (Kcal/g)
Carbohydrates	4.0
Proteins	4.5
Fats	9.5

2-39. *Structures of a monosaccharide, glucose (top), and a disaccharide, sucrose (bottom).*

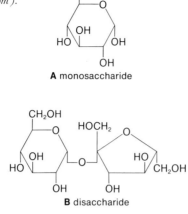

A monosaccharide

B disaccharide

2-40. *A portion of the polysaccharide glycogen. Branches occur every eight to ten glucose residues.*

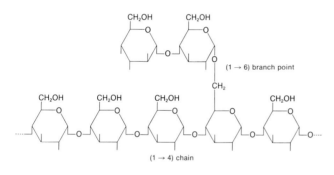

(1 → 6) branch point

(1 → 4) chain

2-41. *Chitin, a polymer of* n-*acetyl glucosamine.*

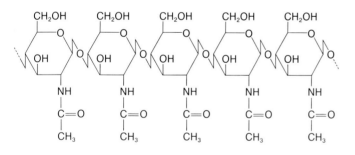

2-42. *The pentose sugar ribose.*

CARBOHYDRATES

Carbohydrate molecules have the ratio of one carbon to two hydrogens to one oxygen atom. In organic chemical terms they are polyhydroxyl aldehydes and ketones. They include the mono- and disaccharide *sugars* (Fig. 2-39) and the polymerized sugars known as *starches* (Fig. 2-40). Monosaccharides are typically ring structures containing five or six carbons, with one carbon outside the ring and an oxygen atom completing the ring. The hexose (6-carbon) sugar glucose is manufactured in green plants from H_2O and CO_2 by the process of photosynthesis (Fig. 2-39, A). All the energy trapped by photosynthesis and transmitted as chemical energy to the living world (i.e., all plant and animal tissues) is channeled through such 6-carbon sugars as glucose. As is noted in the next chapter, glucose is completely or partially degraded to water and CO_2 during cell respiration, with the release of the chemical energy that was stored in its molecular structure during photosynthesis. Cells also contain synthetic mechanisms by which glucose is modified and/or built up to form other monosaccharides or di- and polysaccharides, such as sucrose (Fig. 2-39, B) or starch.

Cells store carbohydrates as starches—substances that consist of polymerized D-glucose (Fig. 2-40). The form found in animal cells is a highly branched polymer termed *glycogen*, in which the glucose residues are joined in a carbon 1 to carbon 4 linkage. The branches are between carbons 1 and 6. Like fats, these high-molecular-weight carbohydrate polymers require a minimum of water as a solvent, and constitute a concentrated form of food reserve in the cell. In vertebrates, glycogen is found in the form of minute intracellular granules, primarily in liver and muscle cells (Fig. 9-21, A).

Carbohydrate polymers form structural substances. *Chitin*, which is a major constituent of the exoskeletons of insects and crustaceans, is a cellulose-like polymer of an amino-acid-containing hexose termed D-glucosamine (Fig. 2-41). Like the plant polymer cellulose, it is flexible and elastic and insoluble in water.

An important pentose (i.e., 5-carbon) sugar is *ribose* (Fig. 2-42), which occurs in the backbones of all nucleic acid molecules.

PROTEINS

Proteins are the most complex and the most abundant organic molecules in the living cell, making up more than half the mass of a cell as measured by dry weight. Proteins are made up of linear chains of *amino acids* (Table 2-9). All the hereditary information encoded in a cell's genetic material is transmitted initially to protein molecules: the *amino acid sequence* laid down

Table 2-9. Side groups or radicals (see Fig. 2-43) of the 20 common α-amino acids.

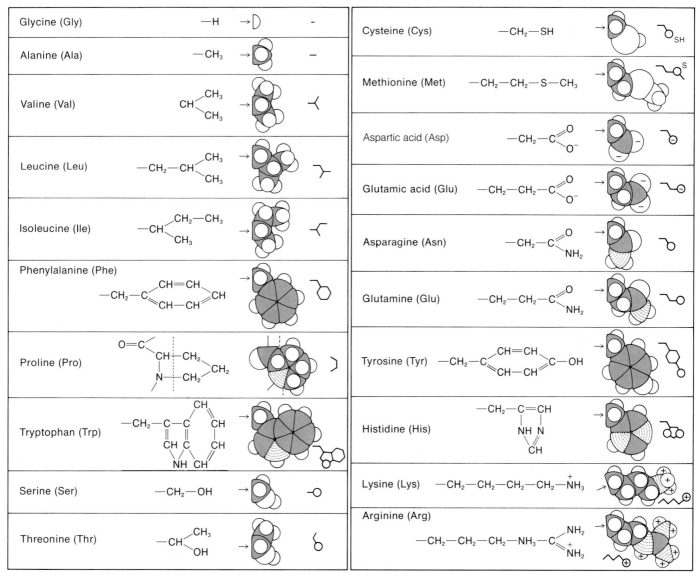

Source: G. H. Haggis et al., *Introduction to Molecular Biology,* Longman, London, 1964.

during protein synthesis is the expression of this information, and is the primary determinant of the properties of any protein molecule. Since there are about twenty different amino acid building blocks, an impressive variety of different amino acid sequences is possible. Suppose, for example, that one were to construct a polypeptide molecule consisting of one of each of those twenty building blocks. How many different linear arrangements could one make without ever repeating the same sequence of amino acids? This is determined by multiplying $20 \times 19 \times 18 \times 17 \times 16 \cdots \times 2 \times 1$ (i.e., 20!), or 10^{18}. Even this startling figure shrinks by comparison when one is reminded that a polypeptide containing only twenty amino acids is relatively small (mol. wt. about 2400).

For a more typical protein of molecular weight 35,000, containing only twelve kinds of amino acids, the number of possible sequences exceeds 10^{300}. Thus it is not at all surprising that the number of known enzymes (which are all proteins) exceeds 1000, with many unknown enzymes presumably still to be discovered.

While enzymes constitute the largest functional group of proteins, there are many nonenzymatic proteins, all coded and transcribed by the same genetic mechanisms. Table 2-10 gives a classification of proteins on the basis of biological function, with a few examples.

The amino acids that make up proteins are all of the *alpha* type, since the *amino group* in each one arises from the alpha carbon atom of the molecule. The

Biological Molecules 35

Table 2-10. Classification of proteins according to biological function.

Type and examples	Occurrence or function
ENZYMES	
Ribonuclease	Hydrolyzes RNA
Cytochrome *c*	Transfers electrons
Trypsin	Hydrolyzes some peptides
STORAGE PROTEINS	
Ovalbumin	Egg-white protein
Casein	Milk protein
Ferritin	Iron storage in spleen
TRANSPORT PROTEINS	
Hemoglobin	Transports O_2 in blood of vertebrates
Hemocyanin	Transports O_2 in blood of some invertebrates
Myoglobin	Transports O_2 in muscle
Serum albumin	Transports fatty acids in blood
CONTRACTILE PROTEINS	
Myosin	Stationary filaments in myofibril
Actin	Moving filaments in myofibril
Dynein	Cilia and flagella
PROTECTIVE PROTEINS IN VERTEBRATE BLOOD	
Antibodies	Form complexes with foreign proteins
Fibrinogen	Precursor of fibrin in blood clotting
Thrombin	Component of clotting mechanism
TOXINS	
Clostridium botulinum toxin	Causes bacterial food poisoning
Snake venoms	Enzymes that hydrolyze phosphoglycerides
HORMONES	
Insulin	Regulates glucose metabolism
Adrenocorticotrophic hormone	Regulates corticosteroid synthesis
Growth hormone	Stimulates growth of bones
STRUCTURAL PROTEINS	
Glycoproteins	Cell coats and walls
α-Keratin	Skin, feathers, nails, hoofs
Sclerotin	Exoskeletons of insects
Fibroin	Silk of cocoons, spider webs
Collagen	Fibrous connective tissue (tendons, bone, cartilage)
Elastin	Elastic connective tissue (ligaments)

Source: A. L. Lehninger, *Biochemistry,* Worth Publishing, New York, 1970.

twenty common amino acids differ from one another in the structure of the side groups (Fig. 2-43). The side groups are the letters in that protein alphabet, just as the four purine and pyrimidine bases are the molecular alphabet in DNA (p. 40). The specific linear sequence of amino acid residues of a polypeptide is termed its *primary structure*. The *amino acid residues* of a polypeptide chain are linked to their neighbors by covalent *peptide bonds* to form a planar *amide group*. The peptide bond is formed by a condensation in which one molecule of water is removed. A protein molecule may consist of one, two, or several polypeptide chains, either covalently linked or held together by weaker bonding.

The primary structure of a polypeptide chain determines the three-dimensional conformation it will assume in a given environment. This depends on the nature and position of the side groups that project from the peptide backbone (Fig. 2-44). In addition to

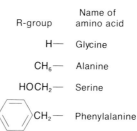

2-43. Generalized amino acid structure; R represents a side group (radical) of which four examples are shown. See also Table 2-9.

Common to all
amino acids

General structure of α-amino acids

R-group	Name of amino acid
H—	Glycine
CH_6—	Alanine
$HOCH_2$—	Serine
⬡CH_2—	Phenylalanine

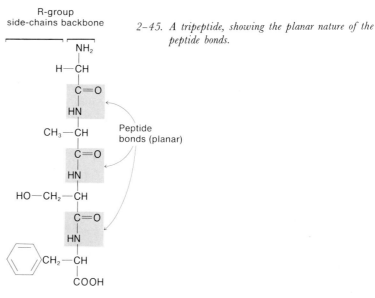

2-44. Ionic side-chains in protein molecules. [After Klotz, 1960.]

the primary structure—that is, the amino acid sequence—there are additional levels of conformation, designated *secondary, tertiary,* and *quaternary.* Secondary structure refers to the conformation of the polypeptide chain; tertiary structure refers to the foldings of the chain to produce globular or rod-like molecules; and quaternary structure refers to the joining of two or more protein molecules to form dimers, trimers, and occasionally even larger aggregates.

Because of its semi-double-bond nature, the C—N peptide bond is not free to rotate, hence the atoms of the amide group are confined to a single plane (Fig. 2-45). This leaves two out of three bonds of the peptide backbone free to rotate. Pauling and Corey, using precisely constructed atomic models, found that the simplest stable arrangement is a helix, as shown in

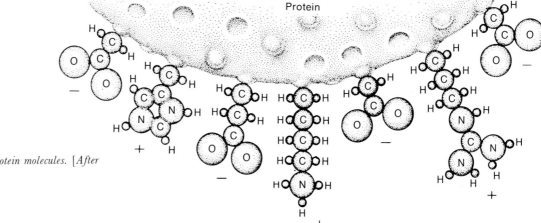

2-45. A tripeptide, showing the planar nature of the peptide bonds.

Glycylalanylserylphenylalanine

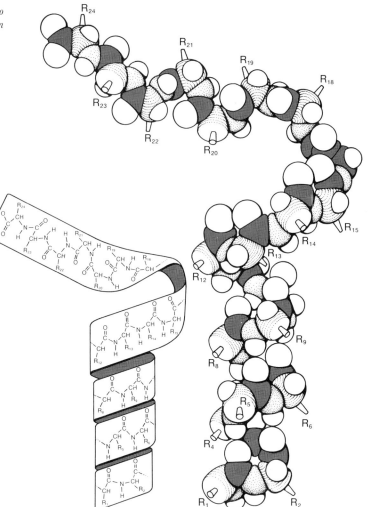

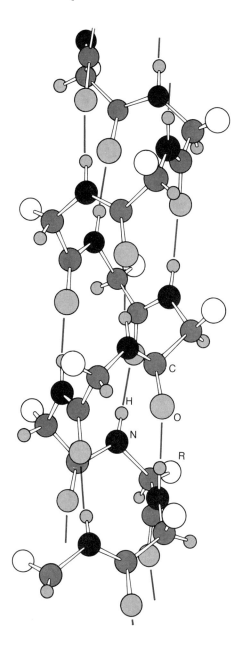

Figure 2-46. In this so-called *alpha-helix,* the plane of each amide group is parallel to the major axis of the helix, and there are 3.6 amino acid residues per turn. The side group of each amino acid residue extends outward from the helical backbone, free for interaction with other side groups or other molecules. The stability of the alpha-helix is enhanced substantially by hydrogen bonding (p. 14) between the oxygen of a carbonyl group and the hydrogen atom of the amide group four residues ahead (Fig. 2-47). Thus a peptide chain will assume the conformation of the alpha-helix spontaneously, provided that the side groups do not interfere. Long peptide chains with an uninterrupted alpha-helix conformation are characteristic of fibrous proteins, such as those that form hair, fingernails and claws, wool, horn, and feathers. Silk, which is produced by caterpillars, is an exception, having a secondary structure consisting of pleated sheets (*beta-keratin*) rather than the alpha-helix.

Intracellular proteins that are not purely structural in function have a more or less globular conformation.

These *globular proteins* also contain alpha-helices, but only in relatively short segments. In these proteins the polypeptide chain assumes a globular tertiary structure. The tertiary structure is in large part due to the properties of certain of the amino acid side groups. In the side group of the amino acid proline, for example (Fig. 2-48), the N—C bond cannot rotate, even though it is not a peptide bond, because the nitrogen atom is part of a rigid ring. Thus whenever proline (or hydroxyproline) occurs in a peptide chain, it interrupts the alpha helix, and the peptide backbone is bent at an angle, contributing to a globular conformation. Another factor that influences the tertiary structure of a protein is the electric charge on individual side groups and their resulting coulombic (electrostatic) interactions with other side groups. The side group of the amino acid cysteine is worthy of special note. The sulfhydryl group (i.e., —SH) plays an important role in covalently cross-linking the protein structure (i.e., connecting two separate peptide chains or holding a chain in a folded position), because two cysteine residues can be joined by a disulfide linkage (Fig. 2-49). Since the sulfhydryl group is highly reactive, it is not surprising that one or more cysteine residues frequently occupy the active sites (p. 56) of enzymes. The toxicity of mercury and other heavy metals is due in part to their reaction with the sulfur atom of cysteine, displacing the H atoms. This can poison (i.e., render catalytically inoperative) the active site of an enzyme.

In addition to covalent —S—S— bonding between cysteine residues, the tertiary structure of a protein depends directly on the conformation of certain residues, coulombic interactions, hydrogen bonding, and van der Waals forces. The last three interactions are relatively weak and are heat labile. This is why heating a protein tends to denature it—that is, cause it to unfold and alter its tertiary structure. In this way, high temperatures can render enzymes inactive and thus be fatal to living cells.

An important property of proteins is their ability to undergo *self-assembly*. That is to say, the amino acid sequence of the peptide chain—and hence the positions of the various different amino acid side groups—determines not only the secondary and tertiary structure of the molecule, but may also produce sites of specific attractive interaction with certain other protein molecules, allowing several subunit molecules to assemble, forming stable quaternary complexes (Fig. 2-50). These interactions can take place when the subunit molecules have complementary regions of interaction on their surfaces, so that (a) negatively charged groups of one subunit fit against positively charged groups of another subunit and (b) hydrophobic, nonpolar side groups on the subunits meet to the mutual exclusion of water molecules. Some enzymes and other proteins are not single protein molecules, but consist of molecu-

2-48. Diagram showing how a proline residue can alter the direction of a polypeptide chain, "kinking" the α-helix formation and thereby contributing to the conformation of the protein molecule.

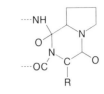

2-49. Formation of a disulfide bond, important in the determination of the tertiary structure of a protein by linking together portions of polypeptide chains.

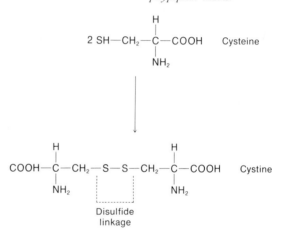

2-50. A representation of the quaternary structure of the protein collagen, which consists of three α-helixes, each twisted into a "superhelix." The superhelixes are held to each other by hydrogen bonding. [After Dowben, 1971.]

2-51. *The molecular structure of hemoglobin, which is composed of two α- and two β-chains. A. The α- and β-chains are held together by disulfide bonds. [After Dowben, 1971.] B. Crystallographic reconstruction of the molecule. Discs represent heme groups, which bind oxygen. [After Lehninger, 1970.]*

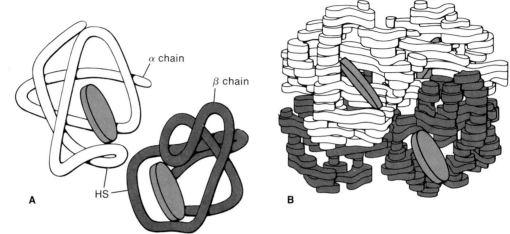

lar subunits bound together in this way without co-valent bonds. For example, the respiratory pigment hemoglobin consists of four subunits, two *alpha* and two *beta polypeptide molecules* (Fig. 2-51,A). These molecules will assemble themselves spontaneously if added separately to a solution and mixed. The manner in which they fit together is seen in Figure 2-51,B.

NUCLEIC ACIDS

Deoxyribonucleic acid (DNA) was first isolated from white blood cells and fish sperm in 1869 by Miescher. During the next decades the chemical composition of DNA was gradually worked out, and evidence slowly accumulated that implicated it in the mechanisms of heredity. It is now common knowledge that DNA, which is associated with the chromosomes, carries in its subunit sequence coded information that is passed from each cell to its daughter cells, and from one generation of organisms to the next. It is the substance of Mendel's genes.

A second group of nucleic acids, *ribonucleic acid (RNA)*, was subsequently discovered; it is now known to be instrumental in translating the coded message of the DNA into sequences of amino acids in the synthesis of protein molecules.

The nucleic acids are polymers of *nucleotide* monomers, each of which consists of a *pyrimidine* or *purine* base (Fig. 2-52), a *pentose* sugar, and a *phosphoric acid* residue (Fig. 2-53). There are five major nucleotides: *adenine, thymine, guanine,* and *cytosine* are found in DNA, and *uracil* is found in place of thymine in RNA. The backbone of the polynucleotide chain (Fig. 2-54) consists of the sugar portions of the nucleotides linked together by the phosphodiester bonds of phosphate groups interpolated between the 3′ carbon of one pentose ring to the 5′ carbon of the next pentose. The purine and pyrimidine bases extend outward from the backbone, and are not involved in the repetitive, non-varying backbone. It is the sequence of the bases along this chain that codes the genetic information. The DNA chain (or strand) is coiled in the form of a helical

2-52. *Structures of the common purine and pyrimidine bases.*

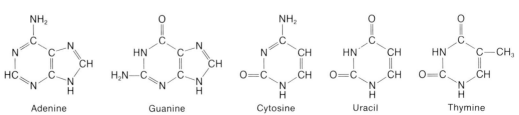

Adenine   Guanine   Cytosine   Uracil   Thymine

2-53. *Structure of a nucleic acid.*

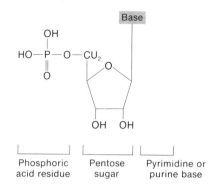

Phosphoric acid residue	Pentose sugar	Pyrimidine or purine base

2-55. *Helical conformation of a double strand of DNA. Note pairing of bases of the two complementary strands. [After Watson, 1965.]*

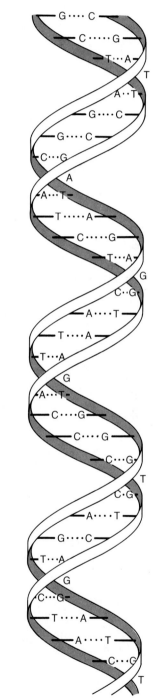

DNA

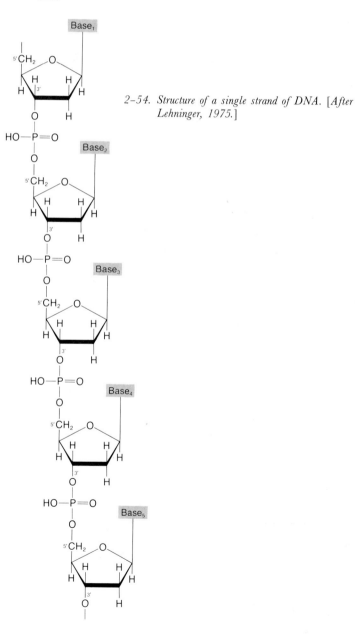

2-54. *Structure of a single strand of DNA. [After Lehninger, 1975.]*

staircase (Fig. 2-55) and is paired with a complimentary strand through hydrogen bonding (p. 14) between thymine-adenine pairs and between cytosine-guanine pairs, as shown in Figure 2-56. The conformations and molecular dimensions are such that other base-pair combinations will not form. This allows either DNA strand, upon separating from the other, to act as a template for the formation of its complimentary strand. The same principal allows a DNA strand to act as a template for *messenger RNA* (mRNA), as shown in Figure 2-56.

After formation in the nucleus of a complementary base sequence of mRNA from the DNA template, the mRNA strand, which now contains the information for the amino acid sequence of a polypeptide chain, leaves the nucleus and enters the cytoplasm to be "read out" by a *ribosome*. In this process of transcrip-

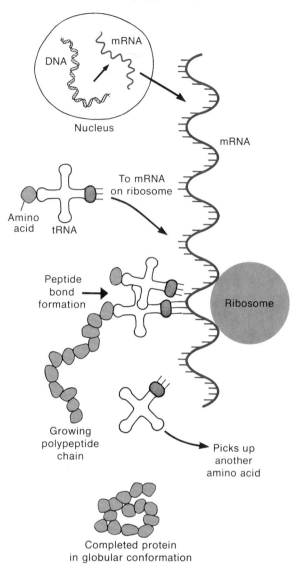

2–57. *Summary of protein synthesis.*

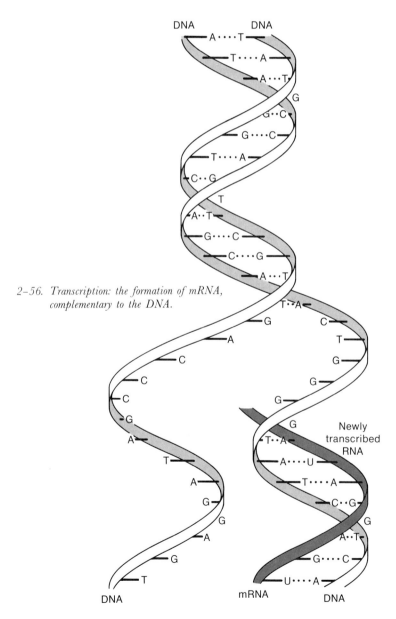

2–56. *Transcription: the formation of mRNA, complementary to the DNA.*

tion, certain sequences of three bases in the DNA code for certain amino acids. For example, GGU, GGC, CGA, and GGC all code for the amino acid glycine, and GCU, GCC, GCA, and GCT code for the amino acid alanine. Thus the genetic code consists of a four-letter alphabet (A, G, C, T) combined into three-letter words.

Once the primary structure (amino acid sequence) is formed, the new polypeptide chain curls and folds up by itself or together with other specific polypeptide chains to produce the characteristic secondary and tertiary structure of a protein molecule.

The major steps relating protein synthesis to nucleic acids are summarized for purposes of review in Figure 2-57. More detailed accounts may be found in the references listed under Suggested Reading at the end of the chapter.

Summary

Biologists generally accept the hypothesis that life on earth arose spontaneously in shallow seas under special conditions that no longer exist. It is believed that organic molecules, synthesized in the primitive atmosphere by reactions energized by lightning discharges or radiation, accumulated in the water over long periods, providing the raw material for primordial living cells.

Living matter is composed primarily of carbon, nitrogen, oxygen, and hydrogen in stable (convalently bonded) associations. Carbon, nitrogen, and oxygen are capable of double and triple bonding, which greatly increases the structural variety of biological molecules.

The polarity of the H_2O molecule is responsible for hydrogen bonding, which, besides linking H and O atoms of adjacent water molecules, confers upon water the many special properties that have profoundly shaped the evolution and survival of animal organisms. Water dissociates spontaneously into H^+ and OH^-. In one liter of pure water there is 10^{-7} mole of each ion. Many substances in solution contribute to an imbalance in H^+ and OH^- concentration, giving rise to acid-base behavior (i.e., donation and acceptance of protons). Their concentrations are measured by the pH system. The pH of biological fluids influences the charges carried by amino acid side groups, and hence the conformation and activity of proteins. Physiological buffering systems are necessary to maintain a narrow range of pH for the coordination of catalyzed reactions.

The colligative properties of solutions are proportional to the concentration of solute particles. Osmotic pressure is equal to the hydrostatic pressure necessary to balance osmotic flow (water movement across a semipermeable membrane) down a concentration gradient at equilibrium. The concept of tonicity describes the osmotic effects that a solution has on a given tissue, whereas osmoticity describes the number of dissolved particles per volume of solvent, as well as the behavior of a solution in an ideal osmometer.

The electrostatic force attracting an ion to a site of opposite charge is determined by the distance of closest approach of the ion to the site. The ion selectivity of a site for different ion species depends on the relative success of the site in competing with the dipolar water molecules to bind those different ion species.

There are four major groups of organic molecules of which animal cells are composed. The lipids, which include triglycerides (fats), fatty acids, waxes, sterols, and phospholipids, are important as energy stores and as constituents of biological membranes. The carbohydrates, which include sugars, starches, and structural polymers from such structural substances as chitin and cellulose. The sugars and starches are a major source of substrate for energy metabolism by cells. Proteins, made up of linearly arranged amino acid residues, form many structural materials, such as collagen, keratin, and subcellular fibrils and tubules. Enzymes are specialized proteins bearing catalytically active sites, and are important in nearly all biological reactions. The nucleic acids DNA and RNA encode and translate the genetic information necessary for the orderly synthesis of all the protein molecules in the cell.

EXERCISES

1. What evidence is there that the molecular building blocks of life might have arisen spontaneously on the primordial Earth?

2. What determines the reactivity of a given atom? Why?

3. What properties of C, H, O, and N make them especially well adapted for the construction of biological molecules?

4. Why is oxygen of such biological importance?

5. What important physical and chemical characteristics of H_2O can be directly related to the dipole nature of the water molecule?

6. What is the pH of a 1 mM solution of an acid that is 10% dissociated?

7. Why is a weak acid rather than a strong one required for a pH buffer system?

8. What is the difference between molality and molarity?

9. How many grams does a mole of CO_2 weigh?

10. Approximately how many particles are in a 1 mM solution of NaCl?

11. What is the approximate boiling point of a 1 molal solution of NaCl?

12. Explain the meanings of *isotonic* and *isosmotic*. How can a solution be isotonic but not isosmotic to another solution?

13. Why do some liquids conduct electricity while others do not?

14. How many ions flow past a point (equivalents/s) at a current of 1 mA?

15. What are the primary factors that govern the binding of two cations, *a* and *b*, to an electronegative binding site? Write the expression that integrates these factors into a meaningful quantity.

16. For which does the force of attraction for a univalent ion fall off most rapidly with distance: (a) a monopolar binding site or (b) a multipolar site? Give the expression relating force and distance for each site.

17. (a) What determines primary protein structure? (b) Secondary? (c) Tertiary? (d) Quaternary?

18. What special characteristic does cysteine have that makes it a likely participant in the active sites of enzyme molecules?

19. Why do proteins become denatured (structurally disorganized) at elevated temperatures?

SUGGESTED READING

Baker, J. J. W., and G. E. Allen. *Matter, Energy, and Life* (3rd ed.). Addison-Wesley, Reading, Mass.

Barry, J. M., and E. M. Barry. 1969. *An Introduction to the Structure of Biological Molecules.* Prentice-Hall, Englewood Cliffs, N. J.

Calvin, M., and M. J. Jorgenson (compilers). 1968. *Bio-organic Chemistry—Readings from Scientific American.* W. H. Freeman and Company, San Francisco.

Calvin, M., and W. A. Pryor (compilers). 1973. *Organic Chemistry of Life—Readings from Scientific American.* W. H. Freeman and Company, San Francisco.

Lehninger, A. L. 1975. *Biochemistry* (2nd ed.). Worth, New York.

Oparin, A. I. 1953. *The Origin of Life* (2nd ed.). Dover, New York.

Oparin, A. I. 1974. *The Origin of Life and Evolutionary Biochemistry.* Plenum Press, New York.

Stryer, L. 1975. *Biochemistry.* W. H. Freeman and Company, San Francisco.

Wald, G. 1954. *The Origin of Life.* Scientific American 191(2):44–53.

Watson, J. D. 1965. *Molecular Biology of the Gene.* Benjamin, New York.

REFERENCES CITED

Baker, J. J. W., and G. E. Allen. 1974. *Matter, Energy, and Life* (3rd ed.). Addison-Wesley, Reading, Mass.

CRM Books Editorial Staff, 1972. *Biology: An Appreciation of Life.* CRM Books, Del Mar, California.

CRM Books Editorial Staff. 1972. *Biology Today.* CRM Books, Del Mar, California.

Diamond, J. M., and E. M. Wright. 1969. Biological membranes: The physical basis of ion and nonelectrolyte selectivity. *Ann. Rev. Physiol.* 31:581–646.

Donnan, F. G. 1911. Theorie der Membrangleichgewichte und Membranpotentiale bei Vorhandensein von nicht dialysierenden Elektrolyten. Ein Beitrag zur physikalisch-chemischen Physiologie. *Z. Elektrochem.* 17:572–573.

Dowben, R. M. 1969. *General Physiology: A Molecular Approach.* Harper & Row, New York.

Dowben, R. M. 1971. *Cell Physiology.* Harper & Row, New York.

Getman, and F. Daniels. *Outlines of Theoretical Chemistry.* Wiley, New York.

Haggis, G. H., D. Michie, A. R. Muir, K. B. Roberts, and P. B. M. Walker. 1964. *Introduction to Molecular Biology.* Longman, London.

Hille, B. 1972. The permeability of the sodium channel to metal cations in myelinated nerve. *J. Gen. Physiol.* 59:637–658.

Keeton, W. T. 1972. *Biological Science* (2nd ed.). Norton, New York.

Klotz, I. M. 1960. *In* A. P. Fishman, M.D. (ed.), *Symposium on Salt and H$_2$O Metabolism.* New York Heart Association, Inc., American Heart Association.

Krasne, S., and G. Eisenman. 1972. Molecular basis of ion selectivity (Section V of Chapter 3) *In* G. Eisenman (ed.), *Membranes: A Series of Advances* (vol 2). Marcel Dekker. New York.

Lehninger, A. L. 1970. *Biochemistry.* Worth, New York. York.

Lehninger, A. L. 1975. *Biochemistry* (2nd ed.). Worth, New York.

Lemmon, R. M., and W. R. Erwin. 1975. High-energy reactions of carbon. *Scientific American* 232(1):72–79.

Loewy, A. G., and P. Siekevitz. 1969. *Cell Structure and Function.* Holt, Rinehart, & Winston, New York.

Mahan, B. H. 1966. *College Chemistry.* Addison-Wesley, New York.

Miescher, F. 1871. On the chemical composition of pus cells. *Hoppe-Seyler Med. Chem. Untersuch.* 4:441–460. [Translation in M. Gabriel and S. Fogel (eds.), 1955, *Great Experiments in Biology,* Prentice-Hall, Englewood Cliffs, New Jersey.]

Pauling, L., and R. B. Corey. 1953. Compound helical configurations of polypeptide chains: Structure of proteins of the L-keratin type. *Nature* (London) 171:59–61.

Watson, J. D. 1965. *Molecular Biology of the Gene.* Benjamin, New York.

West, E. S. 1964. *Textbook of Biophysical Chemistry.* Macmillan, New York.

Wolf, A. V. 1966. *Aqueous Solutions and Body Fluids.* Hoeber Medical Division, Harper & Row, New York.

CHAPTER THREE

Enzymes and Energetics

Animals can be viewed as chemical machines. As in all machines, every event, no matter how trivial, is accompanied by an energy transaction. For a machine to do work, energy must be transferred from one part of the system to another, usually with the conversion of at least part of the energy from one form to another. This is true even when the parts of the system are as minute as reacting molecules.

Animals are fueled by the intake of organic food molecules, which are subsequently degraded by digestive and metabolic processes in which chemical energy inherent in their molecular structures is made available for the energetic needs of the organism. Besides the energy required for such overt activity as muscle contraction, ciliary movement, and the active transport of molecules by membranes, chemical energy is required for the synthesis of complex biological molecules from simple chemical building blocks and for the subsequent organization of these molecules into organelles, cells, tissues, organ systems, and complete organisms. Because living organisms require continual maintenance, they must take in fuel and continuously expend energy to maintain function and structure. If energy intake drops below the amount required for maintenance, the organism will consume its own energy stores. When these are exhausted, it no longer has any source of energy; hence it cannot stave off the tendency to become disorganized nor can it continue to perform the necessary energy-requiring functions. The result is death.

All the material and energy transactions that take place in an organism are lumped under the term *metabolism*. At the intracellular level these transactions take place via intricate reaction sequences termed *metabolic pathways*, which in a single cell can involve thousands of different kinds of reactions. These reactions do not occur randomly, but in orderly sequences, regulated by a variety of genetic and chemical control mechanisms. Together with the organization of atoms and molecules into highly specific structures, it is *cell metabolism* that distinguishes living systems from the nonliving.

The processes of cell metabolism in animals are of two kinds: (1) the extraction of chemical energy from foodstuff molecules and the channelling of that energy into useful functions; (2) chemical alteration and rearrangement of nutrient molecules into small precursors of other kinds of biological molecules. An example of the first is the production of amino acids during the digestion of foodstuff proteins. The amino acids become available to the cell for the release of their chemical energy by oxidation to CO_2 and H_2O. An example of the second is the incorporation of amino acids in newly synthesized protein molecules in accord with the specifications of the genetic information of the cell. We are concerned here less with the biochemical details of cell metabolism as with the thermodynamic and chemical principles that underlie the transfer and utilization of chemical energy within the cell. Thus we will consider the mechanisms by which chemical energy is extracted from foodstuff molecules and the manner in which it is made available for the energy-requiring processes discussed in subsequent chapters.

Energy: Concepts and Definitions

Energy may be defined as the capacity to do work. Work, in turn, may be defined as the product of force times distance ($W = FD$); for example, when a force lifts a one kilogram weight a height of one meter, the force is 1 kg, and the mechanical work done is one m-kg (Table 3-1 shows the symbols and units used in measuring the several forms of work). The energy expended to do this work (i.e., the useful energy, not including that expended in overcoming friction or expended as heat) is also 1 m-kg. Once the kilogram mass is raised to the height of 1 m, it possesses, by virtue of its position, a potential energy of 1 m-kg, which can be converted to kinetic energy (energy of movement) if the mass is allowed to drop. Thus there are also different forms of energy. These include mechanical potential energy (e.g., a stretched spring or a lifted weight), chemical potential energy (e.g., gasoline, glucose), mechanical kinetic energy (e.g., a falling weight), thermal energy (actually kinetic energy at the

molecular level), electrical energy, and radiant energy. We will be concerned in this chapter primarily with the potential energy stored in the structure of molecules—namely, *chemical energy.*

Before continuing, it will be useful to recall the First and Second Laws of Thermodynamics.

The *First Law* states that energy is neither created nor lost in the Universe. Thus if one burns wood or coal to fuel a steam engine, this does not create new energy, but merely converts one form to another—in this example, chemical energy to thermal energy, thermal energy to mechanical energy, and mechanical energy to work.

The *Second Law* states that all the energy of the Universe will inevitably be degraded to heat and that the organization of matter will become totally randomized. In more formal terms, the Second Law states that the *entropy* of a closed system will progressively increase and that the amount of energy within the system capable of performing useful work will diminish. The term "entropy" refers to the degree of randomization of the system. A system that is ordered (nonrandom) contains energy in the form of its orderliness, because in becoming disordered (i.e., as a result of an increase in entropy) it can perform work. This is illustrated in Figure 3-1 (top), which shows gas molecules in thermal motion in a hypothetical system consisting of two compartments open to one another. Initially, the gas is confined almost entirely to compartment A, in which case the system possesses a certain degree of order. Clearly, this situation has a very small probability of occurring spontaneously if in the starting condition the gas molecules are evenly distributed between the two compartments. The gas molecules can all be forced into one compartment only by the expenditure of energy (e.g., a piston pushing the gas from one compartment to the other). As the gas is permitted to escape from compartment A into compartment B, the entropy of the system increases (i.e., the system becomes more random). The movement of molecules from compartment A to compartment B is a form of useful energy that can be made to do work on an appropriate apparatus placed near the opening between the two compartments.

Table 3-1. Various kinds of work, with symbols and units.

Type of work	Driving force	Displacement variable
Expansion work	$-P$ (pressure)	volume
Mechanical work	F (force)	length
Electrical work	E (electric potential)	electric charge
Surface work	Γ (surface tension)	surface area
Chemical work	μ (chemical potential)	mole numbers

Source: R. M. Dowben, *Cell Physiology,* Harper & Row, New York, 1971.

3-1. *A mechanical analogy of low and high entropy states. The situation shown at the top represents an organized, high-energy state in which nearly all the molecules are in compartment A. As they are allowed to diffuse, the molecules enter compartment B, thereby increasing the entropy and lowering the free energy of the system until equilibrium is reached (bottom). The change from a low- to a high-entropy state releases free energy, which in this model is harnessed by the paddle wheel. The ability to do work approaches zero as the system comes into equilibrium. [After Baker and Allen, 1965.]*

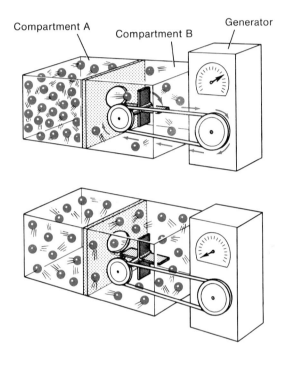

Compartment A   Compartment B   Generator

Once the system is fully randomized (i.e., entropy is maximal), no further work can be extracted from the system, even though the gas molecules remain in constant thermal motion (Fig. 3-1, bottom).

Orderliness increases as the organism develops from a fertilized egg to the adult. It has therefore been incorrectly said that living systems defy the Second Law. It should be recalled, however, that the Second Law refers to a closed system (e.g., the Universe), and animals are not closed systems. Living organisms maintain a relatively low entropy at the expense of energy obtained from their environment. Thus a rhinocerous eating, digesting, and metabolizing grass in quantities just sufficient to maintain constant weight ultimately increases the entropy of the matter it ingests (Fig. 3-2). Highly ordered food molecules in the grass are eventually converted to CO_2, H_2O, and low-molecular-weight nitrogen compounds, releasing energy trapped in the organization of the larger molecules. For example, the CO_2 and water represent a less highly ordered state of the atoms in the carbohydrate, and the metabolic breakdown of cellulose in the grass therefore represents an increase in entropy. At the same time, the cells of the rhinocerous utilize for their own energy requirements a portion of the chemical energy originally stored in the molecular organization of foodstuff molecules.

Living systems must function at relatively uniform temperatures and pressures, for there can be only minor temperature or pressure gradients between the various parts of an organism. For this reason, biological systems can utilize only that component of the total energy capable of doing work under isothermal conditions. This component is termed the *free energy*, symbolized by the letter G. Changes in free

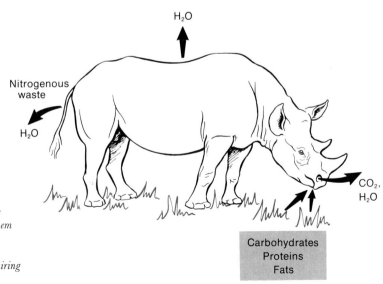

3-2. *Ingestion of food by an animal increases the entropy of the food molecules by breaking them down into smaller molecules of lower free energy content. The free energy liberated is utilized by animal cells to drive energy-requiring reactions.*

H_2O

Nitrogenous waste

H_2O

CO_2, H_2O

Carbohydrates
Proteins
Fats

energy are related to changes in heat and entropy by the equation

$$\Delta G = \Delta H - T\Delta S \qquad (3\text{-}1)$$

in which H is the heat produced or taken up by the reaction (also termed the *enthalpy*) T is absolute temperature, and S is entropy (in units of calories/mole-°K). From this equation, it is evident that in a reaction that produces no change in temperature ($\Delta H = 0$), there will be a decline in free energy (i.e., $^-\Delta G$) if there is a rise in entropy (i.e., $^+\Delta S$), and vice versa.

Since the direction of energy flow is toward increased entropy (Second Law), chemical reactions proceed spontaneously if they produce an increase in entropy (and thus a decrease in free energy). Stated otherwise, the reduction of free energy is the driving force in chemical reactions.

The inevitable trend toward increased entropy, with the inevitable degradation of useful chemical energy into useless thermal energy, requires that living systems must trap or capture new energy from time to time in order to maintain their structural and functional *status quo*. In fact, the ability to extract useful energy from their environment is one of the remarkable features that distinguish living systems from inanimate matter.

With the exception of chemotropic bacteria and algae, which obtain energy by the oxidation of inorganic compounds, all life on Earth depends on radiant energy from the Sun. This electromagnetic energy (including visible light) has its origin in the process of nuclear fusion—a conversion of the energy of atomic structure to radiant energy. In this process, four hydrogen nuclei are fused to form one helium nucleus, with the release of an enormous amount of radiant energy. A very small fraction of this radiant energy reaches the planet Earth, and a small portion of that is absorbed by chlorophyll molecules in green plants and algae. The photically activated chlorophyll molecule transfers this trapped energy, via activated electrons, to various electron acceptors. Eventually, these electrons become useful in the dark reactions of photosynthesis, in which the plant incorporates water and carbon dioxide to form glucose. The rearrangement of the atoms of water and carbon dioxide into carbohydrate molecules is brought about by the utilization of energy trapped by the chlorophyll. The chemical energy stored in the structure of glucose is available to the plant for controlled release during the processes of cell respiration (p. 64). All animals depend ultimately on the photosynthetic process for their energy requirements, utilizing such organic compounds as carbohydrates, fats, and proteins manufactured by green plants. Herbivores (e.g., grasshoppers, cattle)

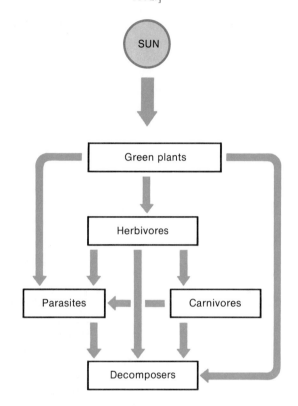

3–3. *The relation between trophic energy levels. Arrows indicate the direction of energy flow. Note the central position of green plants and herbivores. Bacterial decomposers are important in the recycling of organic matter.* [*After Keeton, 1972.*]

obtain these energy-rich compounds by feeding directly on plant materials, whereas predators (e.g., spiders, cats) and scavengers (e.g., lobsters, vultures) obtain them second, third, or fourth hand. The transfer of chemical energy between various *trophic levels* of the living world is diagrammed in Figure 3-3.

Later in this chapter we will consider the chemical pathways by which animal cells release energy through the oxidation of food molecules into H_2O and CO_2. First, however, it will be useful to examine some general principles of energy transfer in chemical reactions, and also some features of enzymes—the biological catalysts that allow biochemical reactions to proceed rapidly at biological temperatures.

Chemical Energy Transfer by Coupled Reactions

There are several categories of biochemical reactions, but the features of reaction rates and kinetics can be illustrated by a simple combination reaction in which two molecules react to form two new molecules:

$$A + B \rightleftharpoons C + D \qquad (3\text{-}2)$$

As the arrows indicate, this reaction is *reversible*. In theory, any chemical reaction is reversible—proceeding in either direction—provided that the products are not removed from the solution. In some reactions, however, the tendency for the reaction to go forward is so much greater than the tendency to go in reverse that for practical purposes they may be considered irreversible. A reaction tends to go forward if it liberates free energy (i.e., if the products contain less free energy than the reactants), and thus the reaction shows a negative free-energy change. In such a case, the reactants contain more potential energy than the products (Fig. 3-4,A), and the reaction is said to be *exergonic*, or *exothermic*. Such reactions typically liberate heat. An example is the oxidation of hydrogen:

$$2H_2 + O_2 \longrightarrow 2H_2O + \text{heat}.$$

This reaction is reversed by the energy of chlorophyll-trapped quanta in the process of photosynthesis:

$$2H_2O \xrightarrow{\text{light quantum}} 2H_2 + O_2.$$

This reaction, which requires the input of energy, is an example of an *endergonic*, or *endothermic*, "uphill" reaction (Fig. 3-4,B).

The amount of energy liberated or taken up by a reaction is related to the *equilibrium constant, K'_{eq}*, of the reaction. This is a constant of proportionality relating the concentrations of the products to the concentrations of the reactants when the reaction has reached equilibrium—that is, when the forward rate is equal to the reverse rate and the concentration of reactants and products has stabilized:

$$K'_{eq} = \frac{[C][D]}{[A][B]}. \qquad (3\text{-}3)$$

Here [A], [B], [C], [D] are the equilibrium molar concentrations of the reactants and products in Equation

3-2. It is evident that the greater the tendency for the reaction in Equation 3-2 to go to the right, the higher the value of its K'_{eq}. This tendency depends on the difference in free energy, ΔG, between the products C and D and the reactants A and B. The greater the drop in free energy, the more completely the reaction proceeds to the right and the higher its K'_{eq}. The equilibrium constant is related to the change in standard free energy, $\Delta G°$, of the system by the equation

$$\Delta G° = -RT \ln K'_{eq}. \qquad (3\text{-}4)$$

It is evident from inspection of Equation 3-4 that if K'_{eq} is greater than 1.0, $\Delta G°$ will be negative; and if less than 1.0, $\Delta G°$ will be positive. Exergonic reactions show a drop in free energy and hence have a negative $\Delta G°$. As a result they occur spontaneously without the need of external energy to "drive" them. Endergonic reactions have a positive $\Delta G°$; that is, they require the input of energy from a source other than the reactants.

Some biochemical processes in living cells are exergonic and others endergonic. Exergonic processes, since they proceed on their own under the appropriate conditions, present relatively little problem in energetics. Endergonic processes, however, must be "driven." This is generally done in the cell by means of *coupled reactions*, in which a *common intermediate* serves to transfer chemical energy from a molecule of relatively high energy content to a reactant of lower energy content. As a result the reactant is converted into a molecule of higher energy content, and can undergo the required reaction by releasing some of this energy. The principle is illustrated in Figure 3-5 with compounds A, X, Y, and Z. The asterisk on A represents a group having a high energy content. This group is transferred, with the loss of some free energy, to X, transforming the latter to a high-energy common intermediate. As indicated in the figure, this reaction, like reactions 2 and 3, is exergonic. In the second reaction, the high-energy group is transferred

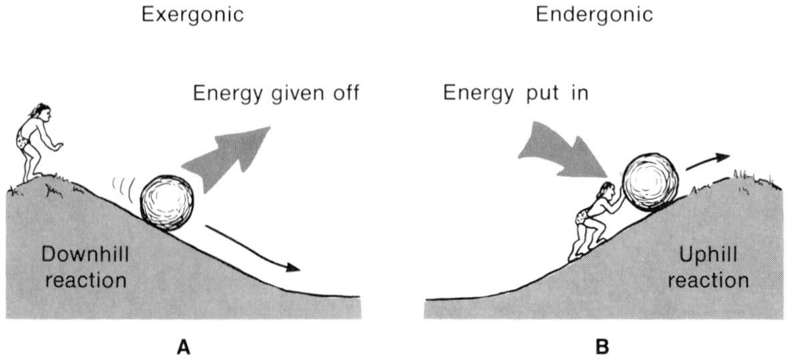

3–4. *A. An exergonic (downhill) reaction is one in which the products have less potential energy than the reactants. B. An endergonic (uphill) reaction requires energy input, as the products contain more potential energy than the reactants.* [*After Baker and Allen, 1965.*]

Exergonic

Energy given off

Downhill reaction

A

Endergonic

Energy put in

Uphill reaction

B

from A* to reactant Y, again with the loss of some free energy. With its newly acquired high-energy group, reactant Y (now Y*) can react spontaneously with Z to form the compound YZ, which has a higher free-energy content than Y + Z, but a lower energy content than Y* + Z. Thus the chemical energy inherent in the A* molecule is utilized with the help of the common intermediates X* and Y* for the synthesis of YZ from Y and Z.

A mechanical analogy of a coupled reaction is seen in Figure 3-6. The 10-kg weight on the left can lose its potential energy of 10 m-kg by dropping a distance of one meter, in which case it will lift the 3-kg weight on the right the same distance. Because the two weights are connected with a rope over a pulley, the fall of the 10-kg weight is coupled to the rise of the 3-kg weight, which initially had no potential energy of its own. It is evident that the falling weight can raise the other only if it weighs more. Likewise, an exergonic reaction can "drive" an endergonic reaction only if the former liberates more free energy than the latter requires. As a consequence, some energy is lost, and the efficiency is, of necessity, less than 100%.

3–5. *Coupled reactions. A high-energy molecule, A*, transfers energy to a common intermediate, X, forming X*. This compound in turn reacts exergonically with Y, producing Y*, which then reacts exergonically with Z. Without the chemical energy contributed by X*, the reaction Y + Z, being endergonic, would not proceed.*

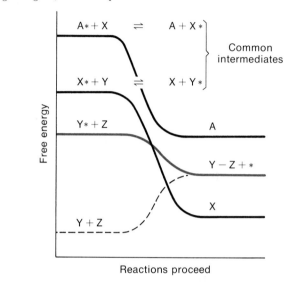

ATP and the High-energy Phosphate Group

The most ubiquitous energy-rich common intermediate is the nucleotide *adenosine triphosphate* (ATP), which can donate its terminal energy-rich phosphate group to any of a large number of organic acceptor molecules (e.g., sugars, amino acids, nucleotides). The *phosphorylation* raises the free-energy level of the acceptor molecule, allowing it to react exergonically in enzyme-catalyzed biochemical reactions.

The ATP molecule consists of an adenosine group, made up of the pyrimidine base adenine and the 5-carbon sugar residue ribose, and a triphosphate group (Fig. 3-7). Much of the free energy of the molecule resides in the mutual electrostatic repulsion of the three phosphate units, with their positively charged phosphorus atoms and negatively charged oxygen atoms. The mutual repulsion of these phosphate units is analogous to the repulsion of bar magnets (Fig. 3-8), with their north and south poles aligned, held together by a sticky wax. If the wax, which is analogous to the oxygen–phosphorus bonds in ATP, is softened by warming, the energy stored by virtue of the proximity of the mutually repelling magnets is released as the magnets spring apart. Likewise, the breaking of the bonds between the phosphate units of ATP results in the release of free energy. Once the terminal phosphate group is removed by hydrolysis (Fig. 3-9), the

3–6. *Mechanical analogy of a coupled reaction: the fall of the 10 kgm weight provides the energy required to lift the 3 kgm weight.*

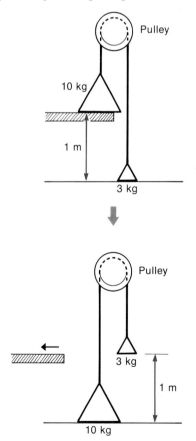

3-7. *Structural formula for ATP. The wavy bond symbols represent the structurally stored energy of the terminal and subterminal phosphate groups. [After Baker and Allen, 1965.]*

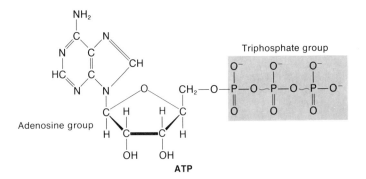

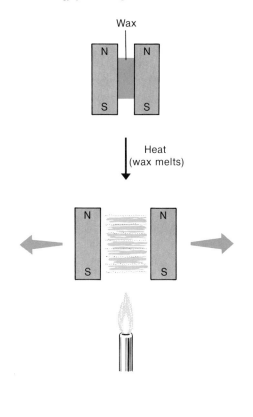

3-8. *Magnetic analogy of the phosphate high-energy bond. Energy is stored in pushing the magnets together against bonding wax. When the wax melts, the magnets fly apart, releasing the energy. In this analogy, the flame supplies the activation energy for melting the wax.*

mutual repulsion of the two products, *adenosine diphosphate* (ADP) and inorganic phosphate (P_i) is such that the probability of their recombining is very low. That is to say, their recombination is highly endergonic. As Table 3-2 shows, the standard free energy for the hydrolysis of ATP under standard conditions is -7.3 kcal.

The role of ATP in driving otherwise endergonic reactions by means of coupled reactions is illustrated by the condensation of the two compounds X and Y.

$$X + ATP \rightleftharpoons X\text{—phosphate} + ADP$$

$$\Delta G° = -3.0 \text{ kcal/mole}$$

$$X\text{—phosphate} + Y \rightleftharpoons XY + P_i$$

$$\Delta G° = -2.3 \text{ kcal/mole}$$

The total free energy liberated in these two reactions (-5.3 kcal) will be equal to the sum of free energy changes of the two parent reactions:

$$ATP + HOH \rightleftharpoons ADP + P_i$$

$$\Delta G° = -7.3 \text{ kcal/mole}$$

$$X + Y \rightleftharpoons XY \qquad \Delta G° = \underline{+2.0 \text{ kcal/mole}}$$

$$-5.3 \text{ kcal/mole}$$

Although ATP and other nucleoside triphosphates, such as GMP, are responsible for the transfer of energy in many coupled reactions, it should be stressed that the mechanism of a common intermediate is widely employed in biochemical reaction sequences. Thus portions of molecules—and even atoms, such as hydrogen—are transferred along with chemical energy from one molecule to another by common intermediates in consecutive reactions. The high-energy nucleotides are special only in that they act as *general energy currency* in a large number of energy-requiring reactions. In

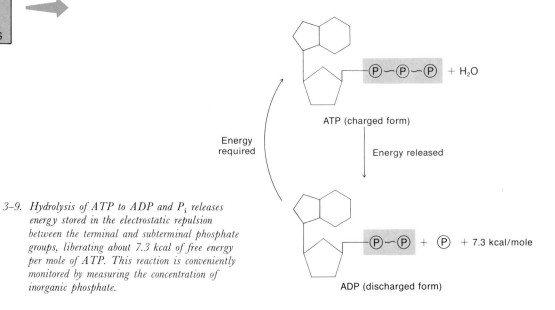

3-9. *Hydrolysis of ATP to ADP and P_i releases energy stored in the electrostatic repulsion between the terminal and subterminal phosphate groups, liberating about 7.3 kcal of free energy per mole of ATP. This reaction is conveniently monitored by measuring the concentration of inorganic phosphate.*

this role, ADP is the "discharged" form, and ATP is the "charged" form (Fig. 3-9). As we shall see later on, there are various mechanisms in the biochemical machinery of the cell for channeling chemical energy into the formation of ATP. The ADP-ATP system is used to channel chemical energy from those phosphate compounds having higher free energies of hydrolysis than ATP (Table 3-2). *Arginine phosphate* and *creatine phosphate* act as special reservoirs of chemical energy for the rapid phosphorylation of ADP to reconstitute ATP during vigorous muscle contraction. They are termed *phosphagens*. In vertebrate muscle and in some invertebrates, the transphosphorylation takes the form

Creatine phosphate + ADP $\underset{\text{enzyme}}{\overset{\text{transphosphorylase}}{\rightleftharpoons}}$

Creatine + ATP

$$\Delta G° = -3.0 \text{ kcal/mole}$$

Creatine phosphate alone is found in the vertebrates, whereas arginine phosphate is distributed widely in invertebrate muscles (Table 3-3).

Temperature and Reaction Rates

The rate at which a chemical reaction proceeds depends on the temperature. This is not surprising, since temperature is an expression of molecular motion. As temperature increases, so does the average molecular velocity. This increases the number of collisions per unit time and thereby increases the probability of successful interaction of the reactant molecules. Furthermore, as their velocities increase, the molecules possess higher kinetic energies, and thus are more likely to react upon collision. The kinetic energy required to cause two colliding molecules to react is termed the free energy of activation, or *activation energy*. It is measured as the number of calories required to bring all the molecules in a mole of reactant at a given temperature to a reactive (or *activated*) state.

The requirement for activation applies to exothermic as well as endothermic reactions. Although a reaction may have the potential for liberating free energy, it will not proceed unless the reactant molecules possess the necessary energy. This can be compared to a situation in which it is necessary to push a boulder over a low ridge before it is free to roll down a large hill (Fig. 3-10).

The relation between free energy and the progress of a reaction is shown in Figure 3-11. The reactants must first be raised to an energy state sufficient to activate them, allowing them to react. Since the reaction yields free energy, the energy state of the

Table 3-2. Standard free energy of hydrolysis of some phosphorylated compounds.

	$\Delta G°$ (kcal)	Phosphate group transfer potential*
Phosphoenolpyruvate	−14.8	14.8
1,3-Diphosphoglycerate	−11.8	11.8
Phosphocreatine	−10.3	10.3
Acetyl phosphate	−10.1	10.1
Phosphoarginine	−7.7	7.7
ATP	−7.3	7.3
Glucose 1-phosphate	−5.0	5.0
Fructose 6-phosphate	−3.8	3.8
Glucose 6-phosphate	−3.3	3.3
Glycerol 1-phosphate	−2.2	2.2

Source: A. L. Lehninger, *Biochemistry,* Worth, New York, 1970.

*Defined as $-\Delta G° \times 10^{-3}$, where $G°$ is the standard free energy at pH 7.0.

Table 3-3. Distribution of the two major phosphagens in the animal kingdom.

	Arginine phosphate	Creatine phosphate
Ciliata	+	−
Platyhelminthes	+	−
Annelida	−	+
Arthropoda	+	−
Mollusca		
Lamellibranchiata	+	−
Cephalopoda	+	−
Echinodermata		
Crinoidea	+	−
Asteroidea	+	−
Holothuroidea	+	−
Echinoidea	+	+
Ophiuroidea	−	+
Protochordata		
Tunicata	−	+
Enteropneusta	+	+
Cephalochorda	−	+
Vertebrata (all classes)	−	+

Source: E. Baldwin, *Comparative Biochemistry,* Cambridge Univ. Press, New York, 1964.

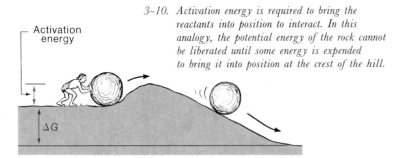

ΔG

3-10. *Activation energy is required to bring the reactants into position to interact. In this analogy, the potential energy of the rock cannot be liberated until some energy is expended to bring it into position at the crest of the hill.*

3-11. *The activation energy, ΔG*, of a reaction is lowered by the catalytic action of an enzyme. Note that the overall free energy change, ΔG°, is the same with or without the enzyme. E, enzyme; S, substrate; ES, activated enzyme-substrate complex.*

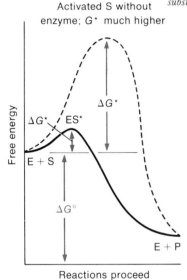

Activated S without enzyme; G* much higher

ΔG* ES*
ΔG*
E + S
ΔG*

Free energy

ΔG°

E + P

Reactions proceed

3-12. *The energy distribution in a population of substrate molecules is illustrated by the bell-shaped curves. A. Without enzyme, far fewer molecules (shaded area) have the required activation energy. B. By lowering the activation energy, an enzyme makes possible a large increase in the fraction of substrate molecules that have sufficient kinetic energy for the reaction to proceed. [After Lehninger, 1965.]*

products is lower than that of the reactants. Note that the overall free energy change of the reaction is independent of the activation energy required to produce the reaction.

In many industrial processes, both the reaction rate and the energy (i.e., the temperature) required to activate reactants are significantly reduced by the use of *catalysts*—substances that are neither consumed nor altered by a reaction, but which offer the advantage of facilitating the interaction of the reactant particles. Reactions in the living cell are similarly aided by biological catalysts called *enzymes*. Figure 3-11 shows the effect of an enzyme lowering the activation energy of a reaction. Note that the presence of the enzyme has no effect on the overall free-energy change (and hence the equilibrium constant) of the reaction; it merely increases the rate of reaction.

The increase in reaction rates produced by enzymes is extremely useful biologically because it allows reactions that would otherwise proceed at imperceptible rates to proceed at useful rates at biologically tolerable temperatures. Figure 3-12,A shows a normal distribution of particle velocities at a given temperature. Those molecules possessing the highest velocities (and hence, kinetic energies) have sufficient energy to react (shaded area). The effect of adding a catalyst is shown in Figure 3-12,B. The energy required for activation is reduced, so that a far larger number of molecules can react at the same temperature.

Another important advantage of catalyzed reactions is the possibility for regulating the rate of reaction by varying the concentration of catalyst. For example, when hydrogen and oxygen are burned noncatalytically they explode in an uncontrolled manner because the heat released by the rapid combustion of the H_2 produces a rapid ignition of the remaining unburned H_2. When hydrogen is oxidized slowly at a low temperature with small quantities of the catalytic agent platinum, the release of heat is

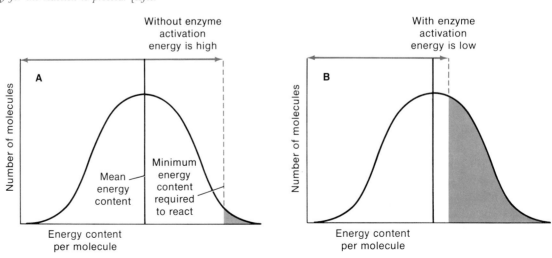

Without enzyme activation energy is high

A

Number of molecules

Mean energy content

Minimum energy content required to react

Energy content per molecule

With enzyme activation energy is low

B

Number of molecules

Energy content per molecule

slowed enough so that no explosion occurs. The quantity of platinum relative to the fuel (H_2) and oxidant (O_2) regulates the rate of combustion. Likewise, most biological reactions are regulated by the quantity or the *activity* (i.e., catalytic effectiveness) of certain enzymes.

Enzymes

Biological catalysts were first isolated from living cells in 1897 by the Buchner brothers by water extraction of yeast. These substances, which increase the rate of alcoholic fermentation, were found to be inactivated by heat, whereas the substrates were unaffected by heat. This was the first indication that enzymes are protein molecules. It was subsequently found that without exception each species of enzyme molecule is a protein of very specific amino acid composition and sequence. All of these proteins, or at least their enzymatically active portions, have a globular conformation (Fig. 3-13). Each cell contains literally thousands of species of enzyme molecules, which catalyze just as many reactions. The work of molecular geneticists indicates that enzymes are the primary gene products, regulating all the synthetic and metabolic activities of the cell. By specifying the structure of each enzyme molecule that is produced, the genetic apparatus is indirectly responsible for all enzymatic reactions in a cell.

ENZYME SPECIFICITY

Each enzyme is, to some degree, specific for a certain *substrate* (reactant molecule). Some enzymes act at certain types of bonds, and may therefore act on many different substrate molecules having such bonds. For example, trypsin, a *proteolytic enzyme** found in the digestive tract, catalyzes the hydrolysis of any peptide bond in which the carbonyl group is part of an arginine or lysine residue, regardless of the position of those bonds in the polypeptide chain of a protein (Fig. 3-14). Another intestinal proteolytic enzyme, carboxypeptidase, specifically catalyzes the hydrolysis of the peptide bond joining the terminal and subterminal amino acid residues in a polypeptide chain. Most enzymes are far more specific for their substrates. For example, the enzyme sucrase will only catalyze the hydrolysis of sucrose into glucose and fructose. Other disaccharides, such as lactose or maltose, are not attacked by that enzyme, but are hydrolyzed by enzymes specific for them (lactase and maltase). Many

*An enzyme that can hydrolize proteins and peptides.

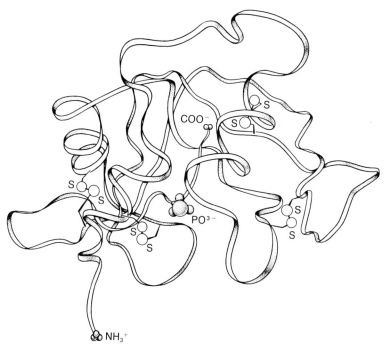

3-13. *The globular structure characteristic of enzymes is illustrated by this reconstruction of ribonuclease obtained from an ox. The phosphate ion is shown bound to the active site.* [*After Barry and Barry, 1969.*]

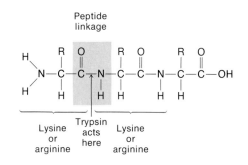

3-14. *Specificity of the enzyme trypsin, which selectively hydrolyzes the C-N bond of the peptide linkage between two lysines, two arginines, or between a lysine and an arginine residue.* [*After Baker and Allen, 1965.*]

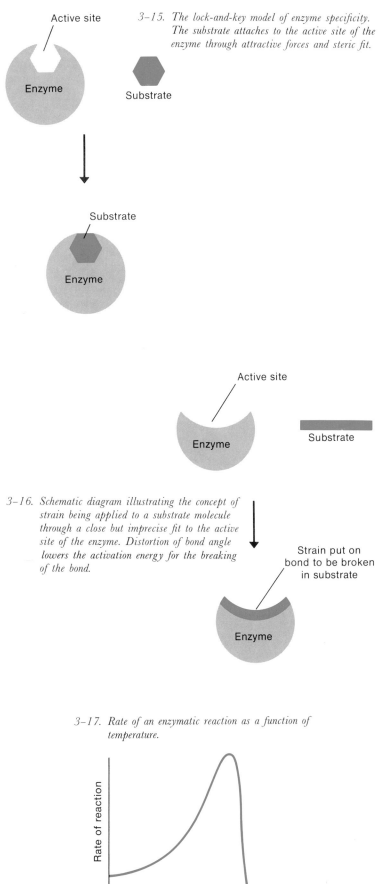

Active site

Enzyme

Substrate

3-15. *The lock-and-key model of enzyme specificity. The substrate attaches to the active site of the enzyme through attractive forces and steric fit.*

Substrate

Enzyme

Active site

Enzyme

Substrate

3-16. *Schematic diagram illustrating the concept of strain being applied to a substrate molecule through a close but imprecise fit to the active site of the enzyme. Distortion of bond angle lowers the activation energy for the breaking of the bond.*

Strain put on bond to be broken in substrate

Enzyme

3-17. *Rate of an enzymatic reaction as a function of temperature.*

Rate of reaction

Temperature

enzymes differentiate between optical isomers—molecules that are chemically and structurally identical except that one is the mirror image of the other. For example, the enzyme L-amino oxidase catalyzes the oxidation of the L-isomer of an α-keto acid, but is totally ineffective for the D-isomer of the molecule.

ACTIVE SITE

The steric specificity noted above is in agreement with the concept that the substrate molecule "fits" a special portion of the enzyme surface termed the *active site*. The enzyme molecule is made up of one or more peptide chains folded about so as to form the tertiary structure of a more-or-less globular protein of a specific conformation. The active site is thought to consist of the side groups of certain amino acid residues, which, in the tertiary structure, are brought into a conformation to which the substrate attaches through such attractive forces as electrostatic bonding, van der Waals forces, and hydrogen bonding, selectively fitting the active site (Fig. 3-15).

The steric specificity of the active site has been well established by testing the reactivity of chemical analogs of substrate molecules (i.e., molecules similar to but slightly different from the substrate molecule). The active site becomes increasingly less effective as the analog molecules depart further from the optimum in terms of interatomic distances, number and position of charged groups, and bond angles. According to one theory of enzyme action, the bond to be broken is selectively subjected to a strain by a slight mismatching of the substrate to the active site (Fig. 3-16). This strain on the bond purportedly increases the probability of its breaking, thereby facilitating the reaction. In any event, formation of such an *enzyme-substrate* complex (ES) changes the internal energy state of the substrate, increasing the probability of reactions. Upon completion of the reaction, the enzyme and products separate, and the enzyme molecule is free to form a complex with a new substrate molecule. Since the enzyme-substrate complex persists for a finite time, all the enzyme can become tied up as ES if the substrate concentration is high enough relative to the enzyme concentration.

Any factor that influences the conformation of the protein molecule, and hence the arrangement of amino acid side groups in the active site, will alter the activity of the enzyme. As was pointed out in Chapter 1, temperature is one such factor. An increase in temperature increases the probability of denaturation (disruption of the tertiary structure of peptide chains), thereby rendering increasing numbers of enzyme molecules inactive. For this reason, enzyme-catalyzed reactions give a characteristic curve of reaction rate versus temperature (Fig. 3-17). As temperature increases, the initial increase in reaction rate is due to the increased kinetic energy of substrate molecules. As temperature increases further, the rate of enzyme inactivation also increases due to unfolding of the protein as hydrogen bonds and other bonds are weakened. At a certain temperature (the *optimum temperature*), the rate of enzyme destruction by heat just offsets the increase in enzyme-substrate reactivity, and the two effects of elevated temperature cancel. At that temperature, the reaction rate is maximal. At higher temperatures, enzyme destruction becomes dominant, and the rate of reaction rapidly decreases. The temperature-sensitivity of enzymes and other protein molecules contributes to the lethal effects of excessive temperatures.

ALLOSTERIC MODULATION OF ENZYME ACTIVITY

Certain enzymes are subject to regulation of their activity by *modulator* or *regulator molecules,* which interact with a part of the enzyme molecule different from the active site. This part of the enzyme, termed the *allosteric site* when it combines with the modulator molecule, causes a change in the tertiary structure of the enzyme, changing the conformation of the active site (Fig. 3-18) and thereby decreasing (or in some cases increasing) affinity between the enzyme and its substrate. Allosteric enzymes operate at key points in metabolic pathways, and modulations of their activities play an important role in the regulation of these pathways.

pH SENSITIVITY

Electrostatic bonds often participate in the formation of an enzyme-substrate complex. Since H^+ and OH^- can act as counterions for electrostatic sites, a drop in pH leaves more positive sites available for interaction with negative groups on a substrate molecule; conversely, a rise in pH facilitates the binding of positive groups to negative sites on the enzyme. Thus it is not surprising that the activity of an enzyme will vary with the pH of the medium (Fig. 3-19) and that each enzyme has an optimum pH range.

COFACTORS

Some enzymes require the participation of small molecules called *cofactors* in order to perform their catalytic function. In that case the protein moiety is termed the *apoenzyme.* One class of cofactors consists of small organic molecules termed *coenzymes,* which *activate* their apoenzymes by accepting hydrogen atoms or protons from the enzyme-substrate complex. For example, the

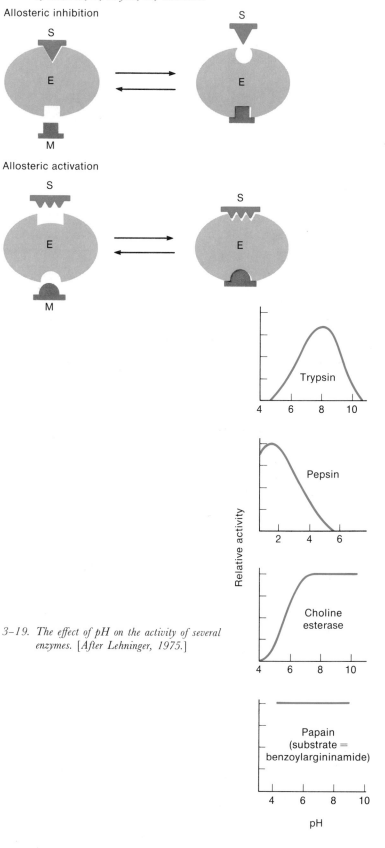

3-18. *Top. An allosteric modulator molecule can indirectly alter the configuration of the active site of an enzyme, thereby rendering the enzyme inactive. Noncompetitive inhibitors act by this mechanism.   Bottom. Conversely, an enzymatic site may be activated sterically by an allosteric modulator. S, substrate; E, enzyme; M, modulator.*

Allosteric inhibition

Allosteric activation

3-19. *The effect of pH on the activity of several enzymes. [After Lehninger, 1975.]*

Table 3-4. Some enzymes and enzyme modulators that require or contain metal ions as cofactors.

Zn^{2+}
 Alcohol dehydrogenase
 Carbonic anhydrase
 Carboxypeptidase
Mg^{2+}
 Phosphohydrolases
 Phosphotransferases
Mn^{2+}
 Arginase
 Phosphotransferases
Fe^{2+} or Fe^{3+}
 Cytochromes
 Peroxidase
 Catalase
 Ferredoxin
Cu^{2+} (Cu^{+})
 Tyrosinase
 Cytochrome oxidase
K^{+}
 Pyruvate phosphokinase
 (also requires Mg^{2+})
Na^{+}
 Plasma membrane ATPase
 (also requires K^{+} and Mg^{2+})
Ca^{2+}
 Protein kinase
 Troponin (muscle contraction modulator)

Source: A. L. Lehninger, *Biochemistry*, Worth, New York, 1970.

3-20. *Changes in concentration of substrate S and product P during the reaction* $S \longrightarrow P$.

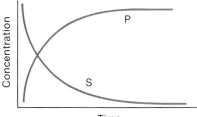

enzyme glutamate dehydrogenase requires the cofactor NAD (nicotinamide adenine dinucleotide) to accept hydrogen atoms from glutamate:

$$\text{Glutamate} + \text{NAD}_{ox} \Longleftrightarrow$$

$$\alpha\text{-Ketoglutarate} + \text{NAD}_{red} + \text{NH}_3$$

A number of coenzymes contain vitamins as part of the molecule. Since an apoenzyme cannot function without its coenzyme, it is not surprising that vitamin deficiencies can have profound pathological effects.

Other enzymes require monovalent or divalent metal ions as cofactors, generally in a highly selective manner (p. 28). Some ion-activated enzymes are listed in Table 3-4 along with their cofactor ions. Especially interesting is the calcium ion, which differs from most of the other common physiologically important ions in being present within cells at very low concentrations ($<10^{-6}$ M). Although other ions, such as Mg^{2+}, Na^+, K^+, and Cl^-, are generally present in nonlimiting concentrations, calcium is present in limiting concentrations for certain enzymes. The Ca^{2+} concentration of the cytoplasm is regulated by the surface membrane and by internal organelles, such as the mitochondria. In this way, the activity of calcium-activated enzymes can be regulated by the cell. Phenomena regulated by the concentration of calcium ions include muscle contraction, secretion of neurotransmitters and hormones, ciliary activity, assembly of microtubules, and ameboid movement.

ENZYME KINETICS

The rate at which a reaction proceeds depends on the concentrations of substrate, product, and active enzyme. For purposes of simplicity, let us imagine that the product is removed as fast as it is formed. The rate of reaction will be limited either by the concentration of enzyme or the concentration of substrate. Suppose further that the enzyme is present in excess, so that the concentration of the substrate A determines the rate at which A is converted to the product P:

$$A \xrightarrow{k} P.$$

The rate of conversion can be expressed as

$$\frac{-d[A]}{dt} = k[A], \tag{3-5}$$

in which [A] is the instantaneous concentration of the substrate, k is the *rate constant* of the reaction, and $-d[A]/dt$ is the rate at which A is converted to P. The disappearance of A and the appearance of P are plotted as functions of time in Figure 3-20. Note that as [A] decreases exponentially, [P] increases exponentially. An exponential time function is always generated when the rate of change of a quantity ($d[A]/dt$ in this example) is proportional to the instantaneous value of that quantity ([A] in this example). The kinetics of such a reaction is said to be *first order* (Fig. 3-21,B). The rate constant of a first-order reaction has the dimension of reciprocal time—that is, "per second," or s^{-1}. The rate constant can be inverted to yield the *time constant*, which has the dimension of time. Thus a first-order reaction with a rate constant of 10/s has a time constant of 1/10 s.

In a reaction with two substrates A and B, in the presence of enzyme,

$$A + B \xrightarrow{\;k\;} P,$$

the rate of disappearance of A will be proportional to the product [A][B]. Thus

$$\frac{d[A]}{dt} = k[A][B]. \qquad (3\text{-}6)$$

This reaction will proceed with *second-order kinetics.*

It is noteworthy that the order of the reaction is not determined by the number of substrate species participating as reactants, but instead by the number of species present in rate-limiting concentrations. Thus if B were present in great excess over A, the reaction $A + B \rightarrow P$ would become first-order, since its rate would be limited by only one substrate concentration.

The rate of reaction is independent of substrate concentrations when the enzyme is present in limiting concentrations and all the enzyme molecules are complexed with substrate (i.e., the enzyme is *saturated*). Such reactions proceed with *zero-order* kinetics (Fig. 3-21,A).

When the *initial* rate, v_0, of a reaction $S \rightarrow P$ is plotted as a function of substrate concentration, [S], at a constant enzyme concentration, we see that at low substrate concentrations the reaction is first-order (i.e., $v_0 \propto [S]$). At higher substrate concentrations, however, the reaction becomes zero-order, as all the enzyme is saturated with substrate, and the concentration of enzyme, not substrate, limits v_0 (Fig. 3-22). In the living cell, all orders of reaction, as well as mixed-order reactions, occur.

ENZYME-SUBSTRATE AFFINITY

The maximum rate of any reaction, V_{max}, occurs when all the enzyme catalyzing that reaction is tied up, or saturated, with substrate—that is, when S is present in excess and [E] is rate-limiting (Fig. 3-23). Each enzymatic reaction has a characteristic V_{max}. Although all enzymes can become saturated, they show great variation in the concentration of a given substrate that will produce saturation. The reason for this is that enzymes differ in affinity for their sub-

3-21. Zero- and first-order reaction kinetics plotted as straight lines. The symbol X represents the amount of substrate S reacting within time t, and a represents the initial amount of A at time zero. Note that the first-order plot is semilog, and therefore the straight line represents an exponential time course.

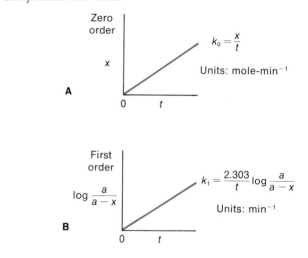

$$k_0 = \frac{x}{t}$$

Units: mole-min^{-1}

$$k_1 = \frac{2.303}{t} \log \frac{a}{a-x}$$

Units: min^{-1}

3-22. At a given enzyme concentration, the initial rate, v_0, of the reaction $S \longrightarrow P$ rises linearly with increasing substrate concentration until all of the enzyme becomes saturated, at which time [E] becomes rate-limiting.

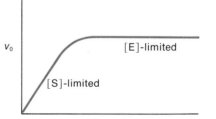

Substrate concentration

3-23. The Michaelis-Menton constant, K_M, is equal to the substrate concentration at which the reaction rate is one-half maximum. The black and colored plots are for different enzyme concentrations. Note that K_M is independent of [E].

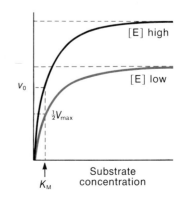

strates. The greater the tendency for the enzyme and substrate to form a complex, ES, the higher the percentage of total enzyme, E_t, tied up as ES at any given concentration of substrate. Conversely, the higher this affinity, the lower the substrate concentration required to saturate the enzyme.

An intimate relationship exists between the affinity of S to E and the kinetics of the reaction

$$S \xrightarrow{\text{E}} P.$$

The general theory of enzyme action and kinetics was proposed by L. Michaelis and M. L. Menten in 1913, and later extended by G. E. Briggs and J. B. S. Haldane. Their derivation of K_M can be found in most biochemistry texts. The *Michaelis-Menten equation* is the rate equation for a single enzyme-catalyzed substrate:

$$v_0 = \frac{V_{max}[S]}{K_M + [S]}, \tag{3-7}$$

where v_0 is the initial reaction rate at substrate concentration [S], V_{max} is the reaction rate with excess substrate, and K_M is the Michaelis-Menten constant. Let us take the special case in which $v_0 = \frac{1}{2}V_{max}$. Substituting for v_0 gives

$$\frac{V_{max}}{2} = \frac{V_{max}[S]}{K_M + [S]}. \tag{3-8}$$

Dividing by V_{max} gives

$$\frac{1}{2} = \frac{[S]}{K_M + [S]}. \tag{3-9}$$

Upon rearranging, we obtain

$$K_M + [S] = 2[S] \tag{3-10}$$

or

$$K_M = [S]. \tag{3-11}$$

Thus K_M equals the substrate concentration at which the initial reaction rate is half what it would be if the substrate were present to saturation.

Thus the Michaelis-Menten constant, K_M (in units of moles/liter) is a measure of the affinity of the enzyme for a substrate. For a given enzyme and substrate, it is equal to the substrate concentration at which the initial reaction is $\frac{1}{2}V_{max}$. By inference, then, K_M represents the concentration of substrate at which half the total enzyme present is combined with substrate in the enzyme-substrate complex; that is, $[E_t]/[ES] = 2$. The greater the affinity between an enzyme and its substrate, the lower the K_M of the enzyme-substrate interaction. As illustrated by the plots for two enzyme concentrations in Figure 3-23, K_M is independent of the enzyme concentration.

As Figure 3-23 shows, Equation 3-7 is a hyperbolic function, which cannot be accurately plotted without numerous data points. The equation can be algebraically transformed, however, into the Lineweaver-Burk form, which can be quickly and accurately plotted from few data points.

$$\frac{1}{v_0} = \frac{K_M}{V_{max}} \frac{1}{[S]} + \frac{1}{V_{max}}. \tag{3-12}$$

This gives a straight-line plot with a slope of K_M/V_{max} and with intercepts of $1/V_{max}$ on the $1/v_0$ axis and of $-1/K_M$ on the $1/[S]$ axis (Fig. 3-24). Thus one need know only V_{max} and one calculation for a given [S] in order to draw the curve. The intercept on the $1/[S]$ axis gives K_M.

ENZYME-INHIBITION

Certain molecules can inhibit the activity of an enzyme. Enzyme inhibition occurs in the living cell as a means of controlling enzymatic reactions. Through study of the molecular mechanisms of inhibition, enzymologists have discovered important features of the active site of an enzyme and of the mechanism of enzyme action.

Enzymes can be poisoned by agents that form highly stable covalent bonds with groups inside the active site, and thereby interfere with the formation of the enzyme-substrate complex. Such interference can produce *irreversible inhibition*. More relevant to normal cell function, however, are two kinds of *reversible inhibition*. The first, *competitive inhibition*, can be reversed by an increase in substrate concentration, whereas the

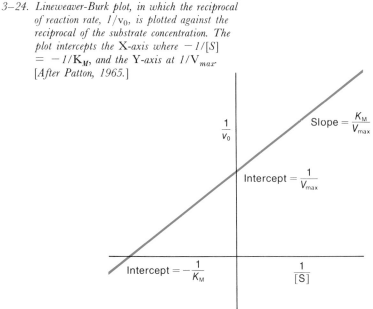

3–24. *Lineweaver-Burk plot, in which the reciprocal of reaction rate, $1/v_0$, is plotted against the reciprocal of the substrate concentration. The plot intercepts the X-axis where $-1/[S] = -1/K_M$, and the Y-axis at $1/V_{max}$. [After Patton, 1965.]*

second, *noncompetitive inhibition*, cannot be reversed. Competitive inhibitors appear to react directly with the active site of the enzyme, whereas noncompetitive inhibitors appear to react with a part of the enzyme other than the active site and exert their effects allosterically. Competitive inhibitors (Fig. 3-25) are generally analogs of the substrate molecule: noncompetitive inhibitors, however, can be completely different chemically from the substrate. A competitive inhibitor competes with substrate molecules for the active site. Thus increasing the concentration of one reduces the binding probability of the other. Since the noncompetitive inhibitor complexes with the allosteric site rather than the active site, it cannot be displaced from its binding site by the competition of substrate molecules, for the latter have no affinity for the allosteric site.

Competitive and noncompetitive inhibition are readily distinguishable in Lineweaver-Burk plots. The competitive inhibitor increases the slope of the plot, which corresponds to a decrease in reaction rate (Fig. 3-26,A). As the slope increases, however, the intercept on the $1/v_0$ axis remains the same; in other words, when extrapolated to infinite substrate concentration (i.e., $1/[S] = 0$), the rate of reaction in the presence of competitive inhibitor is the same as it is without the competitive inhibitor. The reason for this is that with increasing substrate concentration, the substrate competes successfully with the inhibitor for the active site, finally displacing the inhibitor completely in the hypothetical situation of infinite substrate concentration. The intercept with the $1/[S]$ axis indicates the K_M value. This is seen to shift toward a higher substrate concentration as the concentration of a competitive

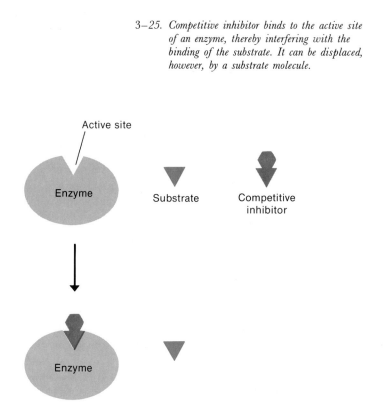

3–25. *Competitive inhibitor binds to the active site of an enzyme, thereby interfering with the binding of the substrate. It can be displaced, however, by a substrate molecule.*

3–26. *Lineweaver-Burk plots of competitive (left) and noncompetitive (right) inhibition. Note that K_M depends on the concentration of competitive inhibitor. The effect of the noncompetitive inhibitor is kinetically similar to a reduction in enzyme concentration, producing no change in K_M. I, inhibitor; S, substrate; K_I, dissociation constant of inhibitor-enzyme complex. [After Lehninger, 1975.]*

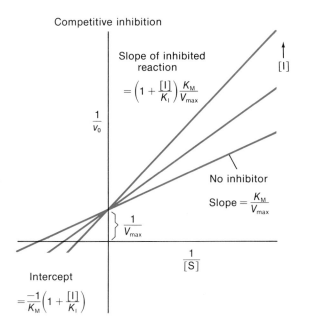

Competitive inhibition

Slope of inhibited reaction

$$= \left(1 + \frac{[I]}{K_I}\right) \frac{K_M}{V_{max}}$$

No inhibitor

$$\text{Slope} = \frac{K_M}{V_{max}}$$

$\frac{1}{V_{max}}$

Intercept

$$= \frac{-1}{K_M}\left(1 + \frac{[I]}{K_I}\right)$$

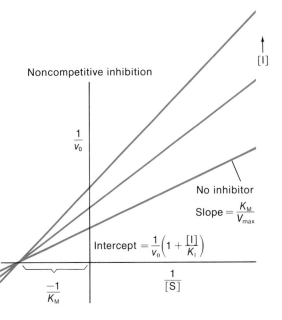

Noncompetitive inhibition

No inhibitor

$$\text{Slope} = \frac{K_M}{V_{max}}$$

$$\text{Intercept} = \frac{1}{v_0}\left(1 + \frac{[I]}{K_I}\right)$$

$\frac{-1}{K_M}$

inhibitor is raised. This merely means that it takes a higher concentration of substrate in the presence of competing molecules (i.e., competitive inhibitor) to keep half of the enzyme molecules at any instant complexed with the substrate.

Noncompetitive inhibitors also produce an increase in slope in the Lineweaver-Burk plot (Fig. 3-26,B), but this is accompanied by a drop in reaction rate at infinite substrate concentration. This drop is seen as an increase in the value at which the plot crosses the $1/v_0$ axis. These kinetic effects result from the failure of increased substrate concentration to remove a noncompetitive inhibitor from the allosteric site of the enzyme. This has the same effect as destruction of those enzyme molecules complexed with the inhibitor. Concomitantly, the curves intersect the $1/[S]$ axis at the same point with or without the noncompetitive inhibitor, indicating no change in K_M for the enzyme in the presence of the noncompetitive inhibitor. As noted earlier, the effect of the noncompetitive inhibitor is equivalent to lowering the enzyme concentration. It is not surprising, then, that the K_M of an enzyme is unaltered by addition of a noncompetitive inhibitor, for, as noted above, K_M is independent of [E].

Metabolic Regulatory Mechanisms

Without any regulation of reaction rates, cell metabolism would be uncoordinated and undirected. Growth, differentiation, and maintenance would be impossible, to say nothing of compensatory responses of the biological machine to externally imposed stresses. Most control is exerted through the quantity or activity of the various enzymes that catalyze nearly all biochemical reactions. The three major types of metabolic control are described below.

GENETIC CONTROL OF ENZYME SYNTHESIS

The number of molecules of an enzyme present in a cell is a function of the rate of synthesis and the rate of destruction of enzyme molecules. Enzyme molecules are denatured by temperature increases (p. 56), and they are broken down by the action of proteolytic enzymes. The rate of synthesis can be limited under special circumstances, such as inadequate diet, by the availability or unavailability of amino acid precursors, but the rate of synthesis of a particular enzyme is normally regulated by genetic mechanisms. *Structural genes* (i.e., sections of the DNA molecule coding the amino acid sequence of one or more peptide chains that make up the enzyme molecule) can be "turned

off" by the action of *repressor proteins*, which are coded by a *regulator gene*. The repressor molecule interferes with the transcription of the structural gene from DNA to RNA by binding to a third type of genetic locus called the *operator*. The latter controls the transcription into messenger RNA of one or more structural genes that constitute the *operon* subserved by that operator. The synthesis of enzymes coded by the operon is collectively controlled by the interaction of the regulator gene with the operator locus. This is illustrated in Figure 3-27. Certain small molecules combine with the repressor protein, rendering it incapable of combining with the operator locus. This halts repression of the structural genes and permits the synthesis of the enzymes that had previously been repressed. This scheme, proposed by Jacob and Monod in 1961, explains the phenomenon of *enzyme induction*, in which cells synthesize certain enzymes only after they are exposed to the substrates (or related molecules) for those enzymes (Fig. 3-28). This is an example of metabolic economy, for inducible enzymes are synthesized only as needed. When the substrate is present, it combines with the repressor, halting repression (i.e., allowing transcription) of the respective operon. Thus the segments of DNA that previously lay dormant become available for specifying the amino acid sequences of the induced enzymes.

The transcription of structural genes (and hence the synthesis of particular enzymes) is also regulated in some instances by the *end products* of a biosynthetic reaction sequence. But the repressor molecule synthesized by the regulator gene remains inactive until it combines with a small organic molecule—the *corepressor*, produced at the end of a biosynthetic reaction sequence (Fig. 3-29). The repressor and corepressor together combine with the operator to prevent transcription of the structural gene for an enzyme that acts early in the biosynthetic pathway. In this way the synthetic pathway and the rate of production of its end product are kept in check. If the end product begins to accumulate for any reason, such as a reduction of its incorporation into cell structures, the entire synthetic pathway is slowed by a drop in the rate of synthesis of the regulated enzyme.

Genetic regulatory mechanisms are of great importance in the development of an organism. Each somatic cell in an organism contains the same information coded in its DNA; cells in different tissues, however, contain widely divergent amounts of the different enzymes coded by the genetic material. It is evident that in any given tissue some genes are turned on while others are turned off. This may occur in part through mechanisms of enzyme induction and repression in response to differences in the local chemical environments of different cells and tissues in the developing organism.

3-27. The operon model of regulation of enzyme synthesis by the control of gene expression. [After Goldsby, 1967.]

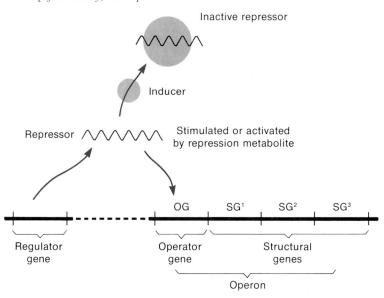

3-28. Time course of induction of enzyme synthesis by the addition of the substrate for the enzyme. [After Dowben, 1971.]

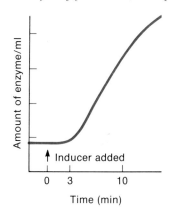

METABOLIC FEEDBACK INHIBITION

Some metabolic pathways have built-in mechanisms for direct (i.e., nongenetic) self-regulation (Fig. 3-30). In these reaction sequences it is usually the first enzyme of the sequence that acts as a *regulatory enzyme,* because its activity is subject to modulation by the concentration of the end product of the sequence. This usually takes the form of inhibition of the activity of that enzyme by some interaction with the end-product molecule. Such *end-product inhibition* limits the rate of accumulation of the end-product by slowing the entire sequence. The interaction of the end-product molecule with the enzyme molecule has been shown to occur at a site other than the catalytically active site. Thus the end product acts as a modulator molecule that reduces the activity of the enzyme molecule by an allosteric mechanism (p. 57). Most regulatory enzymes catalyze reactions that are virtually irreversible under cellular conditions, and therefore are not subject to mass-action kinetics, which would tend to slow the reaction as the concentration of product increases.

ENZYME ACTIVATION

The requirement for cofactors exhibited by some enzymes (p. 57) provides the cell with another means of regulating the rate of biochemical reactions. The intracellular free concentration of certain ions depends on diffusion and active transport across mem-

3-29. The repressive effect of an end-product synthesis of an enzyme. Top. The negative feedback loop in which synthesis of E_l is repressed by accumulation of a product several steps further along the pathway. The end product binds to the represser molecule to inactivate the gene for E_l. Bottom. The level of E_l drops as the level of end product rises.

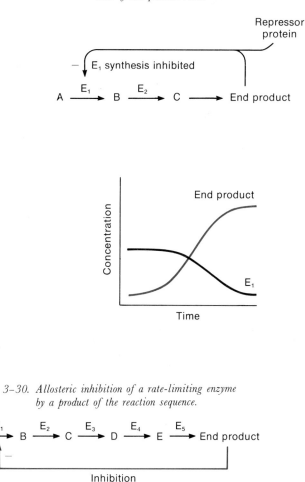

3-30. Allosteric inhibition of a rate-limiting enzyme by a product of the reaction sequence.

branes that separate the cytoplasmic compartment of the cell from the cell exterior and intracellular stores of certain ions (Chapter 4). By regulating the levels of cofactor ions, the cell can modulate the concentration of cofactor ions and the activity of certain enzymes. This appears to take place in the sequence of events that follow the fertilization of the sea urchin egg. Evidence obtained with ion-sensitive intracellular probes indicates a dramatic increase in the cytoplasmic concentration of certain ions subsequent to fertilization. It will be interesting to learn if this increase in concentration turns on some of the enzyme activity responsible for the early stages of cleavage and differentiation in the developing egg. There is also growing evidence that certain hormones act by altering the activity of specific enzymes of the target cells (Chapter 11).

Metabolic Production of ATP

For the sake of argument we can continue the analogy between an animal and a machine introduced at the beginning of this chapter. If we compare the energy utilization of an animal with that of an automobile, we note that both types of machine require the intermittent intake of chemical fuel to energize their activities. Their use of fuel differs, however, in at least one very important aspect. In the automobile engine, the organic fuel molecules in the gasoline are oxidized (ideally) to CO_2 and H_2O in one explosive step. The heat generated by the rapid oxidation produces a great increase in the pressure of gases in the cylinder. In this way, the chemical energy of the fuel is converted to mechanical movement (kinetic energy). This conversion depends on the high temperatures produced by the burning gasoline, for the chemical energy of the gasoline is converted directly into heat, and heat

can be used to do work only if there is a temperature and pressure difference between two parts of the machine.

Since living systems are capable of sustaining only small temperature and pressure gradients, the heat provided by the simple one-step combustion of fuel would be essentially useless for energizing the activities of a living system. For this reason cells have evolved metabolic mechanisms for the stepwise conversion of chemical energy in a series of discrete reactions. The energy of foodstuff molecules is recovered for useful work through the formation of intermediate compounds of progressively lower energy content. At each exergonic step some of the chemical energy is liberated as heat, while the rest is transferred as free energy to the reaction products. Chemical energy conserved and stored in the structure of intermediate compounds is then transferred to the general-purpose high-energy intermediate ATP and to other high-energy intermediates through which chemical energy is made available for a wide variety of cellular processes (Fig. 3-31).

Chemical energy is extracted primarily from three classes of food molecules: carbohydrates, lipids, and proteins. After digestion these generally enter the circulatory system as 5- or 6-carbon sugars, fatty acids, and amino acids, respectively (Fig. 3-32). These small molecules then enter into the tissues and cells of the animal, where they may (1) be immediately broken down into smaller molecules for the extraction of chemical energy or for rearrangement and recombination into other types of molecules *or* (2) be built up into larger molecules, such as polysaccharides (e.g., glycogen), fats, or proteins. With few exceptions these too will eventually be broken down and eliminated as CO_2, H_2O, and urea. Nearly all molecular constituents of a cell are in dynamic equilibrium, constantly being replaced by components newly synthesized from the simpler organic molecules.

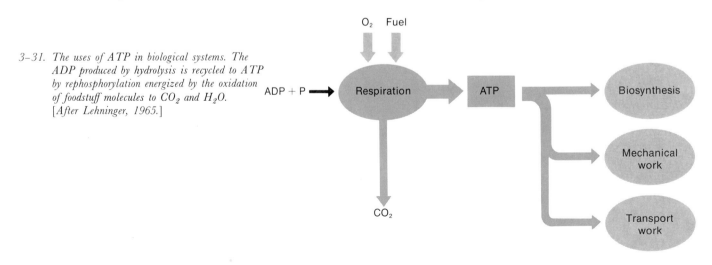

3–31. *The uses of ATP in biological systems. The ADP produced by hydrolysis is recycled to ATP by rephosphorylation energized by the oxidation of foodstuff molecules to CO_2 and H_2O.* [*After Lehninger, 1965.*]

Some simple organisms, including certain bacteria and yeasts, as well as a few invertebrate species, can live indefinitely under totally *anaerobic* (i.e., essentially oxygen-free) conditions. The anaerobes fall into two groups: *obligatory anaerobes,* those that cannot grow in the presence of oxygen (e.g., the botulism bacterium, *Clostridium botulinum*), and *facultative anaerobes,* those, like the yeasts, that survive and reproduce well either in the absence or in the presence of oxygen. All vertebrates and most invertebrates require molecular oxygen for cell respiration, and are therefore termed *aerobic.* Even these generally possess tissues that can metabolize anaerobically for periods of time, building up an *oxygen debt* that is repaid when sufficient oxygen becomes available.

As these observations suggest, there are two kinds of energy-yielding metabolic pathways in animal tissues: one termed *aerobic metabolism,* in which foodstuffs are finally oxidized completely to CO_2 and water by molecular oxygen; and another, termed *anaerobic metabolism,* in which foodstuff molecules are oxidized incompletely to lactic acid (Fig. 3-33). The energy yield per molecule of glucose in anaerobic metabolism is only a fraction of the energy yield for aerobic metabolism. For this reason, cells with high metabolic rates survive only briefly when their tissues are deprived of oxygen. The nerve cells of the mammalian brain are a familiar example. An oxygen deficiency lasting only a few minutes will lead to massive cell death and permanently impaired brain function.

In animal cells, aerobic metabolism is intimately associated with the *mitochondria.* These organelles, just visible in the light microscope, had to await the electron microscope for their detailed description (Fig. 3-34). They consist of an *outer membrane* and an *inner membrane,* which are not connected with each other. These two membranes carry out completely different functions. The inner membrane is thrown into folds termed *cristae,* which serve to increase the area of the inner membrane relative to the outer membrane. The space within the confines of the inner membrane is termed the *matrix compartment,* and the space between the two membranes is the *outer space.* As we shall see below, the inner membrane is very important in the production of ATP during aerobic metabolism. The matrix compartment contains DNA, which is involved in replication of the mitochondria, ribosomes, and dense granules, which consist primarily of salts of calcium.

Mitochondria are quite numerous in most cells, with estimates ranging from 800 to 2500 for a liver cell. They also tend to congregate most densely in those portions of a cell which are most active in utilizing ATP.

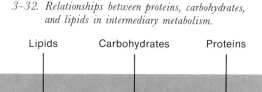
3–32. Relationships between proteins, carbohydrates, and lipids in intermediary metabolism.

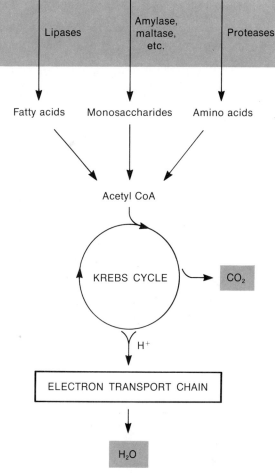

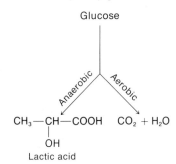
3–33. The two fates of glucose catabolism.

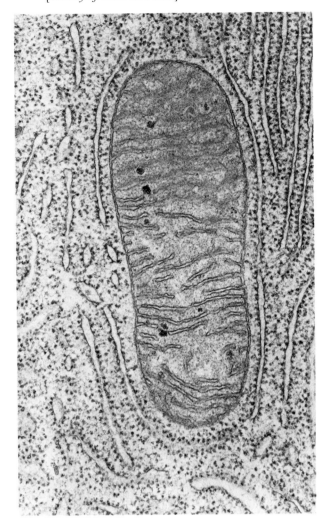

3-34. *An electron micrograph of a mitochondrion in a bat pancreas cell. Magnification 50,000×.* [*Courtesy of Keith R. Porter.*]

Oxidation, Phosphorylation, and Energy Transfer

Before continuing on to consider the biochemical pathways in cellular energy metabolism, we will see how chemical energy, liberated during metabolism, is conserved and channeled into high-energy intermediates. You will remember that when a complex organic molecule is taken apart, free energy is liberated, thus increasing the entropy (degree of randomness) of the constituent matter. This occurs when glucose is oxidized to carbon dioxide and water by combustion in the overall reaction

$$C_6H_{12}O_6 + 6O_2 \rightarrow 6CO_2 + 6H_2O$$

$$\Delta G° = -686 \text{ kcal/mole.}$$

The 686,000 calories liberated by the oxidation of one mole of glucose is the difference between the free energy incorporated into the structure of the glucose molecule during photosynthesis and the total free energy contained in the CO_2 and H_2O produced. If one mole of glucose is oxidized to carbon dioxide and water in a one-step combustion (i.e., if it is burned), the free energy change will appear simply as 686 kcal of heat. During cell respiration, however, a portion of this energy, instead of appearing as heat, is conserved as useful chemical energy and is channeled into ATP through the phosphorylation of ADP (p. 70). The overall reaction for the metabolic oxidation of glucose by the cell can be written as

$$C_6H_{12}O_6 + 38P_i + 38ADP + 6O_2$$

$$\rightarrow 6CO_2 + 6H_2O + 38ATP$$

$$\Delta G° = -420 \text{ kcal (as heat).}$$

Thus 266 kcal (686 minus 420) is incorporated into 38 moles of ATP (7 kcal/mole ATP).

How is the free energy of the glucose molecule transferred to ATP? In order to understand this, we must first recall that oxidation of a molecule is most broadly defined as the transfer of electrons from that molecule to another molecule. In an oxidation-reduction reaction, the *reductant* (electron donor) is oxidized by the *oxidant* (electron acceptor). Together they form a *redox pair*:

$$\text{Electron donor} \rightleftharpoons e^- + \text{electron acceptor}$$

or

$$\text{Reductant} \rightleftharpoons ne^- + \text{oxidant,}$$

where n is the number of electrons transferred. Whenever electrons are accepted from a reductant by an oxidant, energy is liberated, for the electrons move into a more stable (higher entropy) situation in transferring to the oxidant. This is akin to water dropping from one level to a lower level. It is the *difference* between the two levels that determines the energy liberated.

Thus, chemical energy is liberated when electrons are transferred from a compound of a given *electron pressure* (tendency to donate electrons) to one of lower electron pressure. If a molecule has a higher electron pressure than the molecule with which it undergoes a redox reaction, it is said to have a greater *reduction potential,* and will act as a reducing agent; if it has less electron pressure, it will act as an oxidant. The free energy change in each reaction is proportional to the difference between the electron pressures of the two molecules of the redox pair.

In aerobic cell metabolism, electrons move to progressively lower energy levels from compounds of high electron pressure to compounds of lower electron pressure. The *final electron acceptor* in aerobic metabolism is molecular oxygen. Oxygen presumably became the

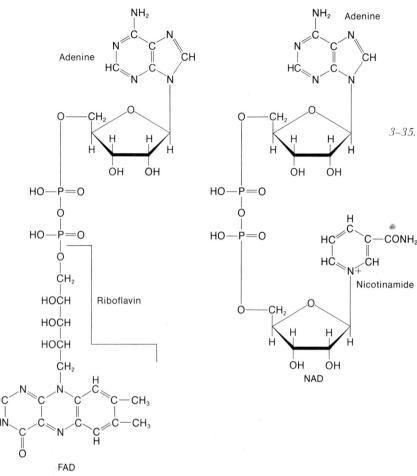

3-35. *Structure of flavin adenine dinucleotide (FAD) and nicotinamide adenine dinucleotide (NAD). [After Lehninger, 1975.]*

universal final oxidant because of its very low electron pressure (strongly oxidizing nature) and its abundance on the Earth's surface as a result of photosynthesis. Since oxygen acts merely as an electron acceptor, it is possible in theory to support aerobic metabolism without O_2, provided that a suitable electron acceptor is supplied in place of oxygen.

In being transferred from glucose to oxygen, electrons undergo an enormous drop in both reduction potential and free energy. One of the functions of cell metabolism is to transport electrons gently from glucose to oxygen in a series of small steps instead of one large drop. This is accomplished by means of two mechanisms found in all cells. First, as we have noted earlier, the conversion of foodstuff molecules such as glucose to the fully oxidized end products (e.g., CO_2 and H_2O) is accomplished in a series of many small intermediate stages of molecular change and oxidation. Second, electrons removed from substrate molecules are passed to oxygen via a series of electron acceptors and donors of progressively lower electron pressure. As we shall see below, this allows energy to be channeled into the synthesis of ATP in "packets" of appropriate size.

THE ELECTRON-TRANSFERRING COENZYMES

Electrons together with protons (i.e., hydrogen) are removed from substrate molecules during certain reactions along metabolic pathways by enzymes collectively termed *dehydrogenases*. These enzymes all function in conjunction with *pyridine* or *flavin* coenzymes. The most common are *nicotinamide adenine dinucleotide (NAD)* and *flavin adenine dinucleotide (FAD)*. Their structural formulas are shown in Figure 3-35. These coenzymes act as electron acceptors in their oxidized form and as electron donors in their reduced form:

Reduced substrate + NAD⁺ ⇌

NADH + H⁺ + oxidized substrate.

A very convenient feature for studies of these coenzymes is that their absorption spectra in the ultraviolet range differ for the reduced and oxidized forms (Fig. 3-36). They also undergo a change in ultraviolet-excited fluoresence upon oxidation and reduction. These two features have permitted physiologists and biochemists to use photometric methods to monitor

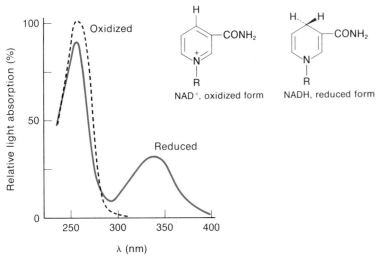

3-36. *Absorption spectra of NAD⁺ and NADH₂. Since the difference in absorption is greatest at 340 nm, that wavelength is used to monitor the reduction of NAD⁺ to NADH. [After Lehninger, 1975.]*

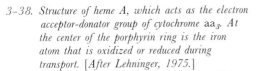

3-37. *The oxidation of NADH₂ leads to the release of free energy (−52 kcal).*

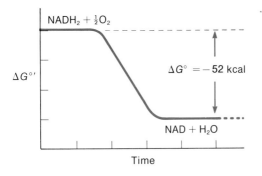

3-38. *Structure of heme A, which acts as the electron acceptor-donator group of cytochrome aa₃. At the center of the porphyrin ring is the iron atom that is oxidized or reduced during transport. [After Lehninger, 1975.]*

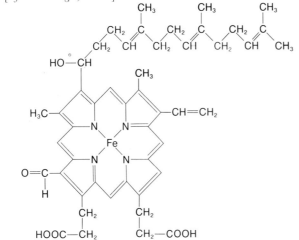

changes in the amount of reduced coenzyme under experimental conditions in living cells.

The energy level of the reduced coenzyme molecule, NADH or FADH, is very high relative to oxygen. As a result, the transfer of two electrons from NADH to O_2 produces a change in free energy of about −52 kcal/mole (Fig. 3-37). This energy represents a large proportion of the 686 kcal of free energy available from the oxidation of glucose, for one mole of glucose yields 10 moles of reduced NAD and 2 moles of reduced FAD. Multiplying 12×52 gives a total of 624 kcal. Thus 91 percent of the free energy of glucose is transferred to the electron-transferring coenzymes to be released in subsequent stages of electron transfer. As noted above, 226 kcal of this free energy is eventually retained by the synthesis of ATP.

The Electron Transport Chain

It is significant that in spite of the large difference in electron pressure between NADH and O_2 there is no enzymatic mechanism by which reduced NAD and FAD can be directly oxidized by oxygen. Instead, an elaborate *electron transport chain* or *respiratory chain* has evolved in which the electrons move through about seven discrete steps from the high reducing potential of NADH and FADH to the final electron acceptor, molecular oxygen. This sequence of electron transfers is the final common pathway for all electrons during aerobic metabolism. Its function, as we will see, is to utilize the energy of electron transfer efficiently for the phosphorylation of ADP to ATP.

The electron transport chain consists of a sequence of enzymes termed *cytochromes,* each of which contains a deeply colored *heme* group. The heme group consists, essentially, of a *porphyrin* ring with an *iron* atom at its center (Fig. 3-38), and is similar to the pigmented heme group in the hemoglobin molecule of vertebrate red blood cells. The functional order of the cytochrome sequence is diagrammed in Figure 3-39. From left to right each successive cytochrome molecule has a lower electron pressure than its predecessor. As a result, electrons are transferred from NAD down the cytochrome chain in a series of seven coupled reactions ending with the reduction of molecular oxygen. Only the last enzyme in the chain, *cytochrome a₃,* is able to transfer its electrons directly to oxygen.

The cytochromes show characteristic absorption spectra in their oxidized and reduced forms, absorbing more strongly in the red when reduced (Fig. 3-40). This behavior led to the first discoveries of their function by Keilin in 1925. Using a spectroscope, he discovered that the flight muscles of insects contain compounds that are oxidized and reduced during

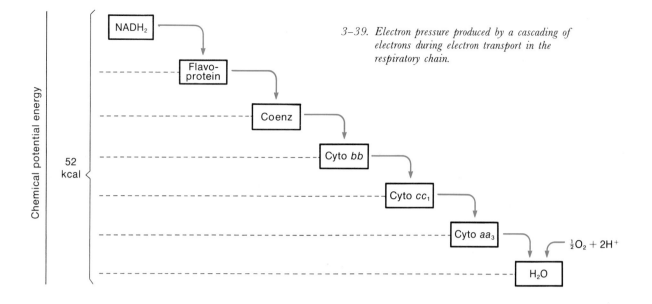

NADH₂

Flavo-protein

Coenz

Cyto *bb*

Cyto *cc₁*

Cyto *aa₃*

½O₂ + 2H⁺

H₂O

Chemical potential energy

52 kcal

3–39. *Electron pressure produced by a cascading of electrons during electron transport in the respiratory chain.*

respiration. He named these compounds cytochromes, and hypothesized that they transfer electrons from energy-rich substrates to oxygen. When the final step—electron transfer by cytochrome oxidase (composed of subunits of *a* and *a₃*) to O₂—is blocked by cyanide, the effect on electron transport is identical to the removal of molecular oxygen. Electrons pile up, so to speak, because transport is interrupted along the chain, reducing all the cytochrome molecules above the point of the block. Another poison, *antimycin*, blocks the flow of electrons from cytochrome b to c (Fig. 3-41), causing the cytochromes above the block to become fully reduced, and those below the block to become completely oxidized. Such selective poisoning at various points along the respiratory chain has en-

3–40. *The absorption spectra of reduced and oxidized cytochrome* c. [*After Lehninger, 1975.*]

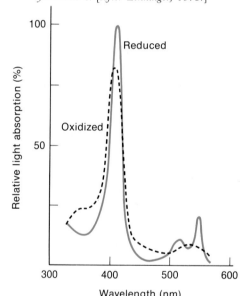

3–41. *Electron transport chain. Broken arrows indicate where the chain can be uncoupled by respiratory poisons. ADP is phosphorylated to ATP at three points during the transport of one pair of electrons along the respiratory chain. FP, flavoprotein; Q, coenzyme Q. Symbols b, c, c₁, a, a₃ refer to the respective cytochromes, shown working in pairs transporting pairs of electrons.*

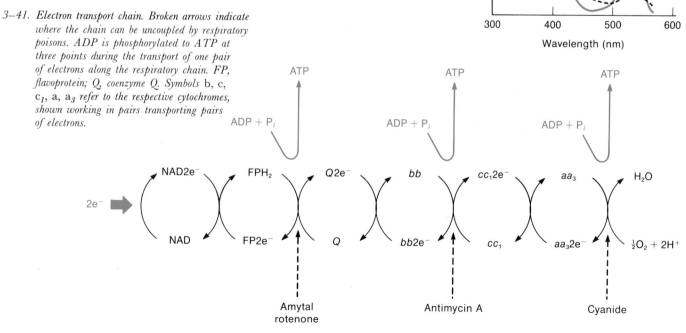

abled biochemists to work out the order of electron transfer, using spectrophotometric methods to follow the oxidation or reduction of the cytochromes.

A great energetic advantage is provided by the cascading of electrons through a series of small discrete steps rather than by allowing direct reduction of oxygen by NADH. The "logic" of the electron transport system becomes apparent when it is recalled that the standard currency in biological energy exchange is small compared with the total change in free energy produced by the transfer of electrons from NADH to oxygen. It requires a minimum of 7.3 kcal to synthesize ATP from ADP and inorganic phosphate (p. 52), whereas 52 kcal would be released in a one-step oxidation of NADH, permitting the formation of only one molecule of ATP. This would conserve only 14% (7.3 divided by 52) of the available free energy in the form of ATP, the rest being lost as heat. To avoid this loss, the large energy drop that would be experienced by the electrons in direct oxidation is subdivided into smaller steps of free energy change. Thus the electron transport system is a mechanism for releasing quantities of energy in doses just large enough for efficient synthesis of ATP. As noted below, there are three stages of electron transfer along the *respiratory chain,* each with a drop in free energy adequate to drive the phosphorylation of ADP to form ATP (Fig. 3-41).

The actual synthesis of ATP from ADP and inorganic phosphate during electron transport is termed *oxidative phosphorylation* or *respiratory chain phosphorylation.* The phosphorylation of ADP to ATP occurs when electrons are transferred from (1) flavoprotein to coenzyme Q, (2) from cytochrome b to cytochromes c and c_1 and (3) from cytochromes aa_3 (cytochrome oxidase) to molecular oxygen. Thus for each pair of electrons that pass along the entire chain, three molecules of ATP are generated from three molecules of ADP and three molecules of inorganic phosphate (P_i). Each pair of electrons finally reduces one half molecule of O_2 to form one molecule of water:

$$2e^- + 2H^+ + \tfrac{1}{2}O_2 \longrightarrow H_2O$$

By comparing the amount of oxygen consumed (i.e., converted to water) and the amount of inorganic phosphate consumed (i.e., incorporated into ATP), we can establish the *P/O ratio* (inorganic phosphate to atomic oxygen ratio). For example, if one oxidative phosphorylation occurs at each of the three steps noted above, three moles of inorganic phosphate will be incorporated into ATP for each mole of oxygen atoms ($1/2 O_2$) consumed in the formation of H_2O. Thus $P/O = 3$. Certain electron carriers, however, bypass the first stage of phosphorylation, reducing coenzyme Q directly, in which case electron transport allows only two ATP phosphorylations per pair of electrons and $P/O = 2$.

Three major theories have been developed to explain how the synthesis of ATP is *coupled* at the molecular level to the free energy liberated during electron transfer. All three, however, are currently subjects of dispute; for this reason, we will not digress to consider possible mechanisms of oxidative phosphorylation. Nonetheless, it is interesting to note that oxidative phosphorylation becomes *uncoupled* from electron transport whenever anything happens that makes the inner mitochondrial membrane "leaky." If the membrane is broken or if a chemical agent is used to increase its permeability to H^+ or other cations, the production of ATP drops or ceases while both electron transport and the reduction of O_2 to H_2O continue, all the released energy being given off as heat. Oxidative phosphorylation is also uncoupled from electron transport by certain drugs, such as dinitrophenol (DNP). Because this drug reduces the efficiency of energy metabolism, it was once prescribed by physicians to help patients lose weight. Its use as a weight-reducing drug was discontinued when it was found to produce pathological side effects.

Glycolysis

The term *glycolysis,* which means "breakdown of sugar," refers to the pathway of reactions leading from glucose to pyruvic acid (Figs. 3-42, 3-43). This sequence of reactions, the most fundamental in the energy metabolism of animal cells, is required for both anaerobic and aerobic release of energy from foodstuffs. The glycolytic pathway is also termed the *Embden-Meyerhof pathway* after the two German biochemists who worked out the details of glycolysis in the 1930's.

Glucose is first phosphorylated by ATP, either during the phosphorolysis of glycogen (Fig. 3-44) or in the reaction

Glucose + ATP $\longrightarrow$ glucose-6-phosphate + ADP.

After conversion of glucose (step 2 in Fig. 3-42) to *fructose-6-phosphate,* the *hexose* (6-carbon sugar) is again phosphorylated to *fructose 1,6-diphosphate* at the expense of a second mole of ATP (step 3). At first glance it would seem uneconomical for the cell to expend two moles of ATP to phosphorylate one mole of hexose, since the object of glycolysis is to produce ATP. On closer examination, however, the phosphorylation of glucose does make sense. As a result of phosphorylation, the hexose and *triose* (3-carbon sugar) phosphate molecules become ionized, and as explained in Chapter 2, polar molecules have very low membrane permeabilities. Thus, although the unphosphorylated glucose is free to enter (or leave) the cell by diffusion

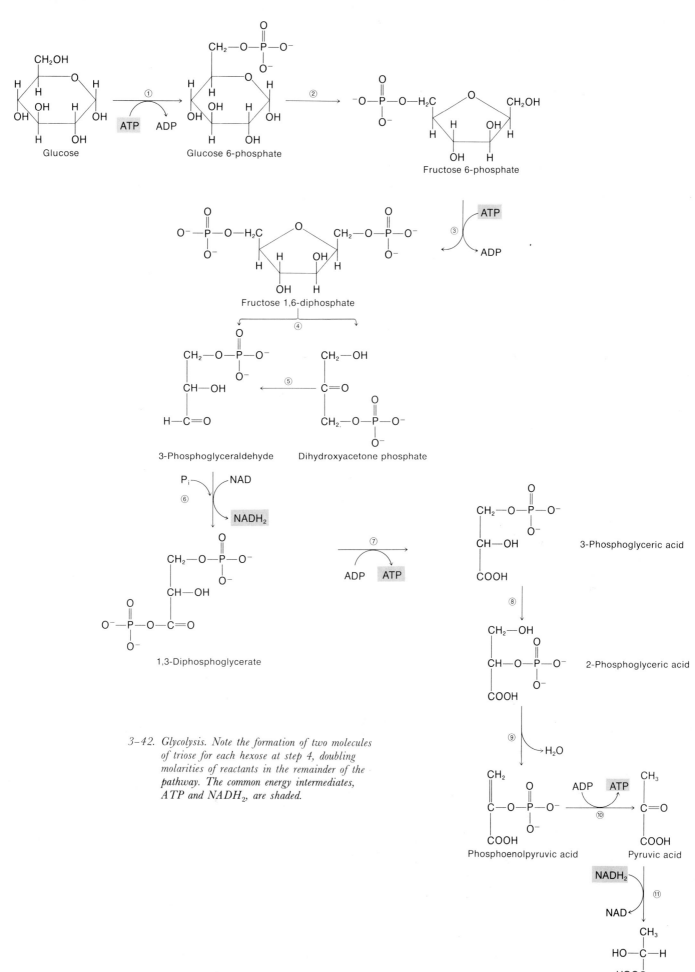

3-42. *Glycolysis. Note the formation of two molecules of triose for each hexose at step 4, doubling molarities of reactants in the remainder of the pathway. The common energy intermediates, ATP and NADH₂, are shaded.*

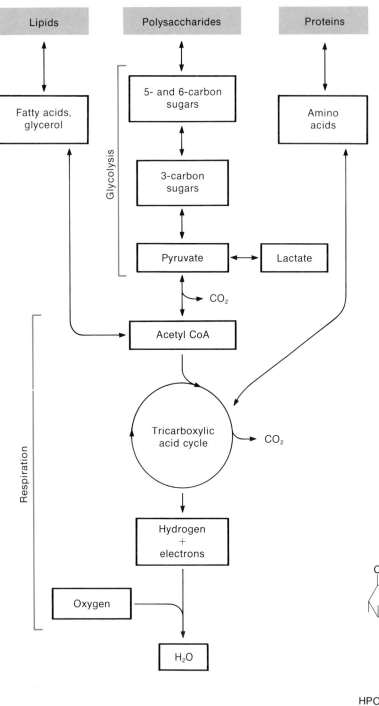

3-43. Metabolic interrelations between fats, carbohydrates, and proteins. Each class of foodstuff can fuel the tricarboxylic acid cycle.

through the surface membrane, the phosphorylated form is conveniently trapped along with its phosphorylated derivatives within the cell. The two moles of ATP expended in these so-called *priming phosphorylations* are, in fact, not really lost, for later in the glycolytic pathway these phosphate groups—and their intramolecular free energies—are transferred to ADP (step 10 in Fig. 3-42), thereby conserving the energy of the phosphate groups utilized in the priming phosphorylations.

Fructose 1,6-diphosphate is cleaved in step 4 into two triose sugars, *glyceraldehyde 3-phosphate* and *dihydroxyacetone phosphate.* The latter molecule is enzymatically rearranged into the former, so that each mole of glucose yields two moles of glyceraldehyde 3-phosphate, both of which follow the same pathway. This completes the *first stage of glycolysis,* which is concerned with the conversion of each mole of 6-carbon sugar into two moles of the 3-carbon sugar glyceraldehyde 3-phosphate (steps 1 to 5).

The *second stage of glycolysis* begins with the oxidation of glyceraldehyde 3-phosphate to *1,3-diphosphoglycerate* (step 6). This reaction is very important, because the addition of the second phosphate group to the triose molecule conserves the energy that would otherwise be released by oxidation of the aldehyde group. The elucidation of the mechanism of this reaction and of the following one (step 7), in which ADP is directly phosphorylated to ATP by the substrate, is considered among the most important contributions to modern biology; through these discoveries Otto Warburg and his colleagues provided, in the late 1930's, the first insight into a mechanism by which chemical energy of oxidation is conserved in the form of ATP. This is termed a *substrate-level phosphorylation* to distinguish it from respiratory chain phosphorylation.

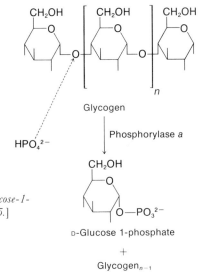

3-44. Phosphorylation of glycogen to glucose-1-phosphate. [After Lehninger, 1975.]

In steps 8 to 10, 3-phosphoglyceric acid is converted to *2-phosphoglyceric acid,* water is removed to form *phosphoenolpyruvate,* and in step 10 the latter yields its phosphate group to ADP, forming ATP and *pyruvic acid.* Thus the glycolytic pathway ends with two moles of pyruvic acid produced from each mole of glucose. The phosphorylation of each mole of hexose consumes two moles of ATP, and each mole of triose generates two moles of ATP (steps 7 and 10). Since each mole of glucose yields two moles of triose, the net gain per mole of glucose in anaerobic glycolysis is two moles of ATP (Fig. 3-45).

In the absence of oxygen—that is, during *anaerobic glycolysis* the reduction of pyruvic acid to *lactate* (step 11, Fig. 3-42) or ethanol (in certain microorganisms such as yeast) serves the very important function of oxidizing the $NADH_2$ formed in step 6 back to NAD. In this case the electrons of $NADH_2$ are accepted by pyruvate instead of oxygen. Without this *anaerobic oxidation* of the reduced coenzyme, there would be a depletion of the oxidized form of the coenzyme, and glycolysis would be blocked for lack of an electron acceptor at step 5 (the oxidation of 3-phosphoglyceraldehyde to 1,3-diphosphoglycerate) in the absence of molecular oxygen. The anaerobic $NAD \rightleftharpoons NADH_2$ cycle that operates between steps 6 and 11 is shown in Figure 3-46. During *aerobic glycolysis,* this mole of $NADH_2$ is oxidized with the concomitant production of three moles of ATP by molecular oxygen via the electron transport system discussed earlier.

Tricarboxylic Acid (Krebs) Cycle

Under aerobic conditions, pyruvic acid is decarboxylated; that is, one mole of CO_2 is removed, leaving a 2-carbon *acetate* residue (Fig. 3-47). The oxidized form of the coenzyme NAD accepts one hydrogen atom from pyruvic acid and one from *coenzyme A.* This allows the 2-carbon residue from the pyruvic acid to be condensed with the coenzyme to form *acetyl coenzyme A.* The coenzyme acts as a carrier for the acetate residue, transferring it to *oxaloacetatic acid* in the next reaction, in which free coenzyme A is released. Coenzyme A is not consumed, but repeatedly transfers acetate residues from pyruvic acid to oxaloacetate.

All the reactions of the glycolytic pathway up to the formation of pyruvic acid occur in free solution in the *cytosol* (unstructured fluid phase of the cytoplasm). The formation of acetyl coenzyme A and CO_2 from pyruvic acid is followed by the eight major reactions of the *tricarboxylic acid* (TCA) *cycle* (Fig. 3-48), in which each acetate residue is degraded to two additional molecules of CO_2 and two molecules of H_2O. These

3-45. The utilization and production of ATP during glycolysis. Note that net ATP production equals two moles of ATP per mole of glucose oxidized to pyruvic acid. [After Vander et al., 1975.]

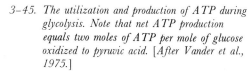
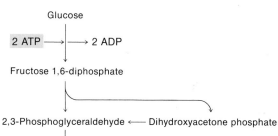
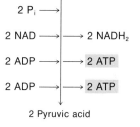
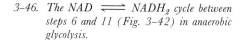

3-46. The NAD $\rightleftharpoons$ NADH$_2$ cycle between steps 6 and 11 (Fig. 3-42) in anaerobic glycolysis.

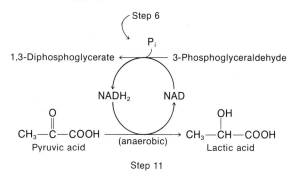
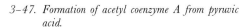

3-47. Formation of acetyl coenzyme A from pyruvic acid.

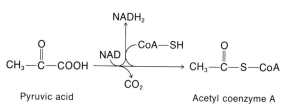

3-48. *The tricarboxylic acid (Krebs) cycle. With each circuit, one acetate group is fed in at step 2. The equivalent in C, O, and H atoms is removed in later steps as CO_2 and as $H^+ + e^-$ entering the electron-transport chain.*

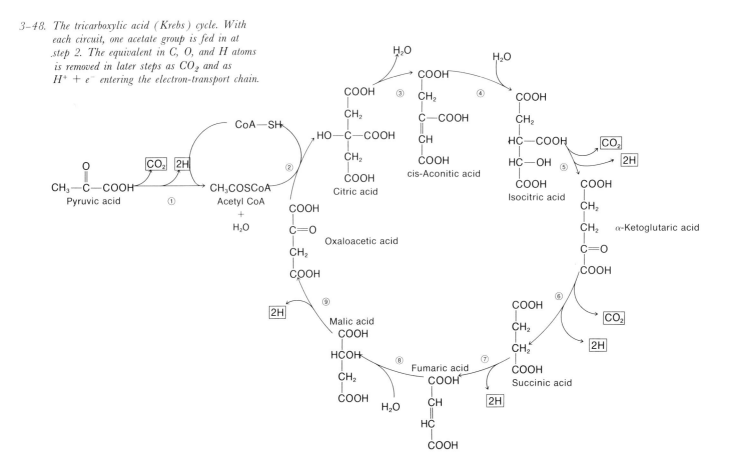

3-49. *The production of CO_2, $NADH_2$, and $FADH_2$ in the tricarboxylic acid cycle.* [After Vander et al., 1975.]

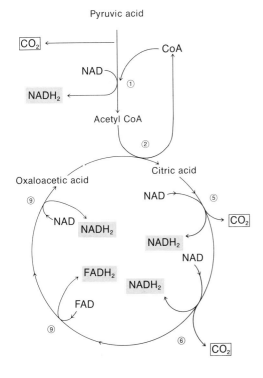

reactions are all catalyzed by enzymes confined to the matrix compartment of the mitochondrion. The overall reaction is

$$2CH_3-\overset{\overset{\displaystyle O}{\|}}{C}-COOH + 5O_2 \longrightarrow 6CO_2 + 4H_2O.$$

The tricarboxylic acid cycle is also known as the *Krebs cycle* in honor of Hans Krebs, who in the early 1940's elucidated the major features of the reaction sequence and its cyclic nature. The 2-carbon acetate residue of acetyl coenzyme A is first condensed with the 4-carbon oxaloacetic acid to form the 6-carbon *citric acid* (step 2, Fig. 3-48). In steps 5 and 6, two carboxyl groups of *isocitric acid* are removed to form the second and third molecules of CO_2. Moreover, four hydrogen atoms are transferred to NAD to form two moles of $NADH_2$. Step 7 takes place on the inner mitochondrial membrane, to which is bound *succinic dehydrogenase.* This enzyme, along with FAD, removes two hydrogen atoms from *succinic acid* to form *fumaric acid.* Another oxidation occurs at step 9 when *malic acid* is converted to *oxaloacetic acid* by the transfer to two hydrogen atoms to NAD. A new acetate residue is then condensed with the oxaloacetate to reconstitute the citric acid molecule, and thus the cycle repeats.

Each time one circuit of the TCA cycle is completed, two carbon atoms and four oxygen atoms are removed as two moles of CO_2 (Fig. 3-49), and with each circuit eight hydrogen atoms are removed, two at a time. These hydrogens (as electrons accompanied by protons) are oxidized to H_2O by molecular oxygen via NAD, FAD, and the cytochrome of the respiratory chain. The CO_2 leaves the mitochondrion and then the cell by simple diffusion, and is then eliminated as a gas via the circulatory and respiratory systems.

Efficiency of Energy Metabolism

The direct oxidation (burning) of glucose and its metabolic oxidation both liberate the same amount of free energy—namely, 686 kcal. If water is boiled by the heat of burning glucose to produce steam pressure for a steam engine, the mechanical output of the engine divided by the free energy drop of 686 kcal represents the efficiency of the conversion of chemical to mechanical energy. Modern steam engines have attained efficiencies of approximately 30 percent. Now let us see how efficiently the living cell transfers chemical energy from glucose to ATP.

Under standard conditions, it takes about 7 kcal to phosphorylate one mole of ADP to form ATP (p. 52). If the free energy of glucose were conserved with an efficiency of 100 percent, each mole of glucose could energize the synthesis of 98 (i.e., $686/7 = 98$) moles of ATP from ADP and inorganic phosphate. As we shall see below, only 38 moles of ATP is synthesized, giving an overall efficiency of about 42% or more.* The remaining free energy is liberated as metabolic heat, which accounts for a part of the heat that warms and thereby increases the metabolic rate of the tissue. Essentially all the energy incorporated into ATP and transferred to other molecules is eventually degraded to heat. The oxidation of fossil fuels represents a long-delayed return of stored energy to the original low-energy, high-entropy (p. 47) state of CO_2 and water.

It is interesting to compare the efficiencies of anaerobic versus aerobic glucose metabolism, keeping in

mind that since each mole of glucose yields two moles of the 3-carbon derivatives, it is necessary to double all the molarities beyond step 5 of glycolysis. In anaerobic glycolysis, there is a net production of two moles of ATP per mole of glucose (Fig. 3-45), since two of the four moles produced by substrate-level phosphorylation of ADP are consumed in the priming phosphorylations. The two moles of $NADH_2$ produced by the oxidation of 3-phosphoglyceraldehyde (step 6, Fig. 3-42) are oxidized again to NAD when the two pairs of hydrogen atoms are transferred to two moles of pyruvic acid to form two moles of lactic acid under anaerobic conditions (Fig. 3-46).

Under aerobic conditions, each of the two moles of $NADH_2$ produced in glycolysis by the oxidation of 3-phosphoglyceraldehyde yield 3 moles of ATP during respiratory phosphorylation (Fig. 3-41). Pyruvic acid goes on to fuel the TCA cycle, yielding a total of ten pairs of hydrogen atoms for every two moles of pyruvic acid (Fig. 3-48). Eight pairs are carried by NAD, yielding 24 moles of ATP, while two pairs are carried by the coenzyme FAD, yielding four moles of ATP. Finally, two moles of ATP are produced by substrate-level phosphorylation during the oxidation of α-ketoglutaric acid from succinic acid (step 6 in the TCA cycle). This adds up to 38 moles of ATP per mole of glucose during aerobic respiration. As noted above, only two moles is produced during anaerobic respiration. Thus, although aerobic respiration conserves about 42% of the free energy of the glucose molecule, anaerobic respiration conserves only about 2%. Stated differently, the energy conservation of glucose metabolism via aerobic glycolysis and the TCA cycle is about 20 times as efficient as that via anaerobic glycolysis. It is not surprising, then, that most animals carry on aerobic metabolism and require molecular oxygen for survival.

Oxygen Debt

When animal tissue, such as active muscle, receives less O_2 than is required to produce adequate amounts of ATP by respiratory chain phosphorylation, some of the pyruvic acid, instead of going on to fuel the TCA cycle, is reduced to lactic acid. For every two moles of pyruvic acid reduced, two moles of $NADH_2$ are oxidized (Fig. 3-46), costing six moles of ATP that might have been synthesized by respiratory chain phosphorylation. If the oxygen deficiency is maintained, lactic acid concentrations rise, and some may be lost into the extracellular space and circulatory system. When the muscle stops its strenuous activity, the accumulated lactic acid is oxidized by NAD and the enzyme lactate dehydrogenase back to pyruvic

*The 42% calculated here is for standard conditions. The efficiency of energy conservation may in fact be as high as 60%, for under intracellular conditions the free energy of hydrolysis of ATP has been estimated to be greater than that under standard conditions. The energetic efficiency of ATP production is therefore substantially better than that of a steam engine, or in fact better than any other method as yet devised by man for converting chemical energy to mechanical energy.

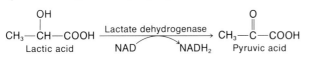

acid (Fig. 3-50). Respiratory chain oxidation of the $NADH_2$ produced in this reaction restores the ATP forfeited during the anaerobic formation of lactic acid. Moreover, the pyruvic acid regenerated from lactic acid goes on to fuel the TCA cycle. Thus the oxygen-poor state of the tissue results in a switch to anaerobic glycolysis, in which ATP is formed with low efficiency. But the unused chemical energy is stored in the tissue as lactic acid, and later becomes available for aerobic metabolism when sufficient oxygen is available. With cessation of heavy exercise, the respiratory and circulatory systems continue for some time to supply large amounts of oxygen in order to "repay" the oxygen debt that was built up as an accumulation of lactic acid.

Summary

A major characteristic of biological systems is that they maintain a low state of entropy—that is, they are highly and improbably organized. This requires steady expenditure of energy derived from foodstuff molecules by the processes of energy metabolism. In the living cell, metabolism occurs as orderly, regulated sequences of chemical reactions catalyzed by enzymes. Chemical reactions spontaneously tend to go down an energy gradient, decreasing free energy and increasing entropy. Living systems appear to defy entropy, but they do not; they merely exist at the expense of chemical energy obtained from their environment.

Energy-requiring biological reactions utilize ATP, a triply phosphorylated nucleotide that serves as a common intermediate capable of contributing chemical energy stored in the form of its terminal phosphate bond. This is accomplished by means of coupled reactions in which an endergonic (energy-requiring) reaction is driven by an exergonic reaction. ATP is reconstituted from ADP by the oxidation of foodstuff molecules, which have their origin in the radiant solar energy trapped during the process of photosynthesis in green plants. Thus all animals depend on energy ultimately derived from the Sun.

Catalysis by globular protein molecules called enzymes lowers the energy required to activate reactants sufficiently for reaction, therefore increasing the rate of reaction at a given temperature. This allows cell chemistry to proceed at reasonable body temperatures. The catalytic effectiveness of an enzyme is produced by virtue of sterically and electrostatically specific binding between the active site of the enzyme and the substrate molecule. This produces favorable spatial relations between the reacting molecules. Regulation of enzyme concentrations appropriate to the needs, function, and environment of the cell is performed genetically through enzyme induction and repression. The activity of some enzymes can also be controlled allosterically—that is, by conformational changes of the active site, which result from the binding of regulatory molecules or ions to the enzyme molecule at a site that is distinct from the active site of the enzyme.

The disassembly of carbohydrate molecules through oxidation is the major source of chemical energy within the animal cell. This occurs anaerobically in the cytosol via glycolysis (to lactic acid) and aerobically via the tricarboxylic acid cycle to CO_2 and H_2O. The liberation of free energy from chemical bond energy in metabolism occurs by transfer of electrons from an electron donor (reducer) to an oxidizer. During glycolysis and oxidative phosphorylation, the release of free energy is budgeted in small steps compatible with the amounts of free energy required to phosphorylate ADP to ATP. For example, during oxidative phosphorylation, electrons are transported in increments down a chain of electron acceptors and electron donors. Thus an electron pressure gradient exists from the reduced coenzymes NADH and FADH, through the electron-transport chain of cytochromes, to the ultimate electron-acceptor, molecular oxygen. It is the electron-hungry nature of the oxygen atom, and its abundance on the surface of the Earth, that makes it the ideal terminal electron acceptor in living systems.

During glycolysis, glucose is broken down into two 3-carbon molecules of lactate by anaerobic oxidation, with the formation of two ATP molecules, or to pyruvic acid in preparation for aerobic respiration. In the tricarboxylic acid cycle, pyruvic acid is oxidized completely to CO_2 and H_2O, accompanied by the formation of 36 more ATP molecules. Biological systems therefore attain efficiencies of at least 42%, considerably better than those of any man-made engine energized by the oxidation of organic fuels.

EXERCISES

1. Living systems would appear to defy the Second Law of Thermodynamics because of their high degree of maintained order. How do you reconcile the low entropy of an organism with this fundamental physical law?

2. At a particular temperature, will a reaction with $\Delta S > \Delta H$ be endergonic or exergonic?

3. Under what conditions will an endergonic reaction proceed?

4. What is ΔG for a system at equilibrium?

5. How does ATP "donate" stored chemical energy to an endergonic reaction?

6. Explain what is meant by a "coupled reaction."

7. How does increased temperature increase the rate of a chemical reaction?

8. What factors contribute to making the temperature optimal for an enzymatic reaction?

9. How does a catalyst increase the rate of a reaction?

10. Why is catalysis necessary in living organisms?

11. How do enzymes exhibit substrate or bond specificity?

12. How does pH affect the activity of an enzyme?

13. How was the conformational theory of active site specificity shown to be correct?

14. What factors can influence the rate of enzyme-catalyzed reactions?

15. The Michaelis-Menten constant, K_M, is equal to the substrate concentration at which a particular reaction proceeds at half its maximum velocity, V_{max}. Does a high K_M indicate a greater or a lesser enzyme-substrate affinity?

16. Why does a high substrate concentration reverse the effects of a competitive inhibitor and yet have no effect on a noncompetitive inhibitor?

17. How does each type of inhibition affect the Michaelis-Menten constant, K_M. Explain why.

18. Why does aerobic metabolism yield much more energy per food molecule than anaerobic?

19. What is the advantage of incremental drops in electron pressure over a single large drop in electron pressure in oxidative phosphorylation?

20. How is energy liberated in discrete amounts in the electron-transport chain?

21. How does the mechanism of energy release by the tricarboxylic acid cycle differ from that during glycolysis?

22. Suggest reasons why animal life evolved with O_2 as the final electron acceptor.

SUGGESTED READING

Boyer, P. D. 1970–1974. *The Enzymes.* Academic, New York.

Bender, M. L., and L. J. Brubacher. 1973. *Catalysis and Enzyme Action.* McGraw-Hill, New York.

Haynes, R. H., and P. C. Hanawalt (compilers). 1973. *The Chemical Basis of Life—Readings from Scientific American.* W. H. Freeman and Company, San Francisco.

Lehninger, A. L. 1971. *Bioenergetics* (2nd ed.). Benjamin, Menlo Park, California.

Lehninger, A. L. 1975. *Biochemistry.* Worth, New York.

Malcolm, A. D. 1971. *Enzymes: An Introduction to Biological Catalysis.* Methuen, London.

Watson, J. D. 1965. *The Molecular Biology of the Gene.* Benjamin, New York.

REFERENCES CITED

Baker, J. J. W., and G. E. Allen. 1965. *Matter, Energy, and Life.* Addison-Wesley, Reading, Mass.

Baldwin, E. 1964. *Comparative Biochemistry.* Cambridge Univ. Press, New York.

Barry, J. M., and E. M. Barry. 1969. *An Introduction to the Structure of Biological Molecules.* Prentice-Hall, Englewood Cliffs, New Jersey.

Buchner, E. 1897. Alcoholic fermentation without yeast cells. *Ber. Duet. Chem. Ges.* 30:117. [Translation in M. Gabriel and S. Fogel (eds.), 1955, *Great Experiments in Biology,* Prentice-Hall, Englewood Cliffs, New Jersey.]

Dowben, R. M. 1971. *Cell Biology.* Harper & Row, New York.

Goldsby, R. A. 1967. *Cells and Energy.* Macmillan, New York.

Guthe, K. F. 1968. *The Physiology of Cells.* Macmillan, New York.

Jacob, F., and J. Monod. 1961a. Genetic regulatory mechanisms in the synthesis of proteins. *J. Molec. Biol.* 3:318–356.

Jacob, F. and J. Monod. 1961b. On the regulation of gene activity. *Cold Spring Harbor Symp. Quant. Biol.* 26:193–209.

Keeton, W. T. 1972. *Biological Science* (2nd ed.). Norton, New York.

Krebs, H. A., and W. A. Johnson, 1937. The role of citric acid in intermediate metabolism in animal tissues. *Enzymologia* 4:148–156.

Lehninger, A. L. 1965. *Bioenergetics.* Benjamin, Menlo Park, California.

Lehninger, A.L. 1975. *Biochemistry.* Worth, New York.

Michaelis, L., and M. L. Menten. 1913. Der Kinetik der Invertinwirkung. *Biochem. Z.* 49:333–369.

Patton, A. R. 1965. *Biochemical Energetics and Kinetics.* Saunders, Philadelphia.

Rosenberg, E. 1971. *Cell and Molecular Biology.* Holt, Rinehart, & Winston, New York.

Vander, A. J., J. H. Sherman, and D. S. Luciano. 1975. *Human Physiology.* McGraw-Hill, New York.

Warburg, O. 1930. The enzyme problem and biological oxidations. *Bull. Johns Hopkins Hospital* 4:148–156.

CHAPTER FOUR

Permeability and Transport

The membranes found both at the surface of all living cells and within them perform functions of great importance to the integrity and activities of cells and tissues. So important and varied are these functions in nearly all areas of physiology that two chapters are required to provide an elementary understanding of biological membranes. We will begin here by considering membrane structure and transport functions. The electrical behavior of cell membranes follows in the next chapter.

The most obvious function of membranes is compartmentalization. The surface membrane of the cell (synonymous with *cell membrane, plasma membrane, plasmalemma*) separates the intracellular substance from the extracellular fluid. The surface membrane is first of all a formidable barrier to rapid diffusion, permitting the establishment of large differences between the concentrations of substances inside the cell and their concentrations in the extracellular fluid. The existence of such *concentration gradients* implies, moreover, that the membrane actively participates in the transport of substances into or out of the cell. Indeed,

the cell membrane regulates the cytoplasmic concentration of dissolved ions and molecules rather precisely, establishing an intracellular milieu conducive to the finely balanced metabolic and synthetic activities of the cell.

Membranes are not limited to the cell surface; they are present in great profusion throughout the cell interior, providing the basic structure of such organelles as the mitochondrion, the chloroplast, the Golgi apparatus, the nucleus, the various types of vesicles, and the endoplasmic reticulum. Membranes are the most ubiquitous of all intracellular structures. Experimental studies also demonstrated that containment and regulation of the cell contents is only one function of membranes. Other functions include the oxidation of succinic acid, as well as electron transport and respiratory chain phosphorylation, by enzyme systems intimately associated with the inner membrane of mitochondria (p. 65); enzymatic assembly of secretory products in Golgi apparatus membranes; transduction of environmental stimuli into electrical signals (Chapter 7); conduction of bioelectric impulses (Chap-

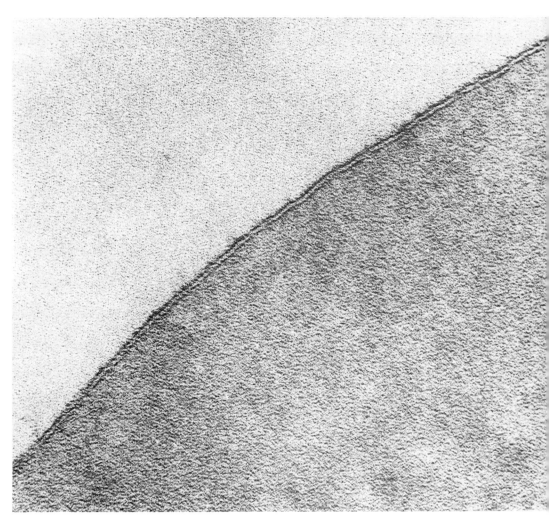

4–1. *Electron micrograph of plasma membrane seen in cross section. The cell interior (lower right,) is separated from the cell exterior by the surface membrane, which is seen as a dark-light-dark profile about 100 Å thick. The dark-light-dark sandwich-like appearance is due to the differential staining of the "unit membrane" by an electron-opaque substance during preparation of the tissue.* [Robertson, 1960.]

ter 6); release of synaptic transmitter substances (Chapter 6); and pinocytosis. Finally, it should not be overlooked that membranes perform the functions of compartmentalization and concentration of solutes within the various organelles, producing micro-environments that differ from the environment of the cytosol.

Evidence for the Existence of Membranes

As recently as the 1930's, the existence of a differentiated membrane structure at the surface of the cell was still a matter of uncertainty and debate. Since there was little or no direct anatomical evidence for biological membranes at that time, their existence could only be inferred from physiological studies. The first observations on the diffusion-limiting properties of the cell surface were made in the mid-nineteenth

century by Nägeli, who noticed that the cell surface acts as a barrier to free diffusion of dyes into the cell from the extracellular fluid. From this he deduced the presence of a "plasma membrane." He also discovered the osmotic behavior of cells, noting that cells swell when placed in dilute solutions and shrink in concentrated solutions. Several years later Pfeffer drew a parallel between the osmotic properties of artificial semipermeable membranes (which he made by precipitating copper ferrocyanide on the surface of a porous ceramic cup) and the osmotic properties of living cells. This added to the growing evidence that living tissue obeys the laws of physics and chemistry.

Using red blood cells as osmometers (indicators of osmotic pressure), Overton discovered late in the nineteenth century that there is a close relation between the lipid solubility of a substance and its ability to penetrate the cell membrane: the greater its lipid solubility, the less effective it is in producing osmotic shrinkage of the cell. He correctly interpreted this to indicate that high lipid solubilities allow a substance to penetrate the cell membrane more readily. This was the first evidence that membranes contain substantial quantities of lipids.

Morphological evidence for the existence of a discrete cell membrane came with the development of methods for ultrathin sectioning of tissues chemically fixed for electron microscopy. Seen at the surface of every cell type is a continuous layer (Fig. 4-1) that takes on electron-opaque stains more strongly than the free cytoplasm. The range of membrane thickness is 60 to 120 Å.

Because of the fundamental importance of membranes to nearly all aspects of animal physiology, we will summarize the evidence supporting their functional and anatomical reality.

1. Every method of fixation and every electron-microscopic technique consistently reveals a continuous structure at the surface of all cells. Methods of tissue preparation include such divergent techniques as osmium or gluteraldehyde fixation and rapid freezing without prior fixation.

2. The outermost surface of the cell imposes a far greater barrier to diffusion than an equivalent thickness of the external medium or the cytoplasm. This is manifested by the high electrical resistance (resistance to flow of ions) and electrical capacitance that are measured just at the very surface of the cell when ultrafine electrodes are passed through the surface membrane (Chapter 5). The electrical resistance of the cell membrane is in the range 10^3 to 10^4 Ω-cm^2, whereas the same thickness of Ringer solution has a resistance of about 10^{-5} ohm-cm^2. This means that the cell membrane retards the diffusion of inorganic ions by a factor of 10^8 to 10^9. Certain dyes injected into the cell through glass microcapillary pipettes diffuse freely within the cell but do not cross the surface barrier. Conversely, these same dyes do not cross the surface barrier if applied externally. If the surface is damaged by a microneedle, pigments and dyes rapidly leave or enter the cell through the region of surface damage.

3. Various mechanical and chemical means of destroying, extracting, or stretching the membrane eliminate or reduce the effectiveness of the cell's normal diffusion barrier. For example, when the cell membrane is removed by a chemical agent, substances that can only very slowly cross the normal diffusion barrier are free to enter the cell.

4. Some pharmacological agents that exert specific actions on the surface membrane can do so from only one side of the membrane or the other. For example, the pufferfish poison tetrodotoxin (p. 133) interferes with the sodium system of the nerve cell membrane only if applied to the outside of the cell. The same is true of ouabain, a drug that blocks the active transport of sodium ions across the membrane (p. 95). Conversely, tetraethylammonium (p. 137) must be injected into some cells in order to exert its action of blocking the permeability of the cell membrane to potassium ions.

5. It is possible to remove the cytoplasm from some cells and still keep the membrane intact; provided that ATP is supplied as a source of chemical energy, the membrane will continue to function as a diffusion barrier and will even exhibit such metabolic processes as active transport.

Molecular Components of Membranes

Membranes consist almost entirely of lipids and proteins. The relative amounts of lipid and protein vary greatly among the membranes of different organelles. The enzymatic properties of membranes are, of course, due to *membrane proteins,* such as the flavoproteins and cytochromes of mitochondrial inner membranes, the ATPase associated with active transport mechanisms, and the adenylate cyclase that catalyzes the conversion of ATP to cyclic AMP (p. 105). Proteins other than enzymes have also been isolated from some membranes, including those of mitochondria. In one such nonenzymatic protein, alteration of the molecular structure by the substitution of a single amino acid residue leads to the leakage of cytochrome *a* from the mitochondrion. Thus nonenzymatic proteins as well as enzymes appear to be functionally important in membranes.

Relatively little is known about membrane proteins, partly because enzymes tend to lose their activity when they are extracted from the membranes for study *in vitro.* Some of these proteins are intimately associated with lipid molecules because of lipophilic groups exposed on the surface of the protein molecule. The protein-lipid complex is termed a *lipoprotein.*

Membrane lipids, being smaller and simpler molecules than membrane proteins, are more completely known, and can be conveniently divided into three major classes. The *phosphoglycerides* (e.g., the phosphatidyl ethanolamine and phosphatidyl choline) are characterized by a glycerine backbone; the *sphingolipids* (e.g., the sphingomyelins), have backbones made of sphingosine bases. These two classes of molecules are *amphipathic;* that is, they have polar heads and nonpolar tails (Fig. 4-2). The polar head groups are hydrophilic (water soluble), and the nonpolar tail groups are hydrophobic (water insoluble).

The dual nature of these membrane lipids, with their hydrophilic heads and hydrophobic tails, is important to the organization of biological membranes,

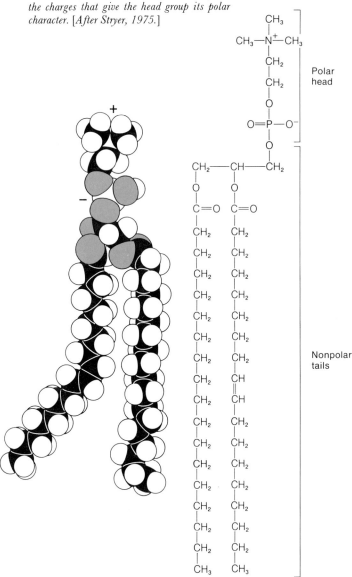

4-2. *Phosphatidyl choline, a phosphoglyceride. Note the charges that give the head group its polar character.* [*After Stryer, 1975.*]

4-3. *Orientation of phospholipid molecules at an air/water interface. The polar heads of the molecules seek the company of water, and the hydrophobic tails project into the air.*

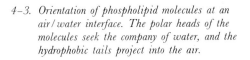

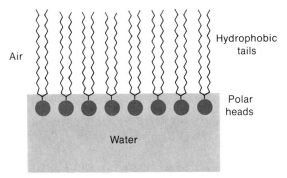

4-4. *Cholesterol, a sterol.* [*After Lehninger, 1975.*]

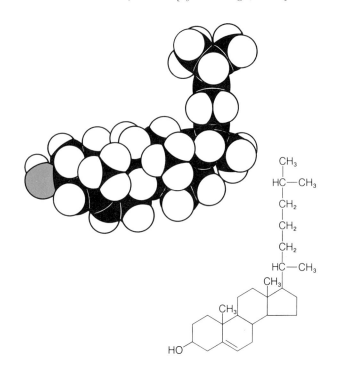

for the polar heads of these molecules seek the company of water (Fig. 4-3), and their nonpolar tails seek each other's company and are mutually attracted by van der Waals forces. Thus these molecules are ideally suited to form an interface between a nonaqueous lipid environment ("phase") within the membrane and the aqueous intra- and extracellular phases in contact with the two membrane surfaces. This concept forms the basis of the most widely accepted models of membrane structure, as discussed below.

The remaining major class of membrane lipids is the *sterols* (e.g., cholesterol) (Fig. 4-4). The sterols are largely nonpolar and only slightly soluble in water. In aqueous solution they form complexes with proteins. The complexes are far more water soluble than the sterols are alone. Once in the membrane, the sterol molecule fits snugly between the hydrocarbon tails of the phospholipids and sphingolipids (Fig. 4-5), and acts to increase the viscosity of the hydrocarbon core of the membrane.

The hydrophobicity of the hydrocarbon tails of the phospolipids is believed to be responsible for the low permeability of membranes to polar substances (e.g., the inorganic ions and such polar nonelectrolytes as sucrose and inulin).

Membrane lipids are important to the activity of some membrane-bound enzyme molecules. For example, the highly organized enzyme systems of mitochondrial membranes are inactivated when extracted and isolated from membrane lipids. Likewise, certain transport enzymes associated with the surface mem-

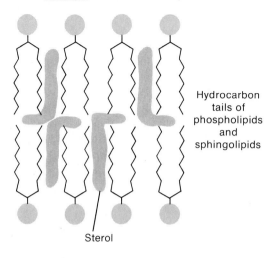

4–5. *The nonpolar sterols insert themselves between the hydrocarbon tails of the polar lipids in the membrane.*

Hydrocarbon tails of phospholipids and sphingolipids

Sterol

brane lose their enzymatic activity if deprived of specific lipids. The enzyme β-galactosidase, isolated from surface membranes, can be reactivated by the addition of phosphatidyl serine; other phospholipids, however, are ineffective. These examples illustrate the functional interrelations of the various molecules that make up a membrane.

Membrane Structure

The precise molecular mechanisms involved in various membrane functions are poorly understood. To study these mechanisms, it is helpful to know how the molecules of the membrane are assembled into functioning units. But the structural and functional integrity of the membrane is lost when its components are isolated and purified, and this places severe limitations on studies of membrane organization and substructure. To make matters still more difficult, it appears as if there is a broad spectrum of membrane types. It is now apparent that many of the controversies between proponents of different theories of membrane organization arose because of this diversity.

Information on structure and organization of membranes has come principally from three approaches: (1) chemical dissection, (2) inferences based on the physical properties of membranes, and (3) preparation of "artificial" membranes into which selected molecules are introduced in order to study their functions.

SIMPLE BILAYER MODELS

In 1925 Gorter and Grendel published the results of experiments that led to one of the major models of membrane organization. They dissolved the lipids from red blood cell ghosts* and allowed the extracted membrane lipids to spread out on the surface of water in a trough. Because of their asymmetry, lipid molecules become oriented so that their polar head groups form hydrogen bonds with the water and their hydrophobic hydrocarbon chains stick up into the air, as in Figure 4-3. The film of dispersed lipid molecules at the air-water interface was gently compressed laterally, and the force required to compress the film was measured. This force was low as long as the lipid molecules were dispersed on the surface. The formation of a uniformly compact monolayer was signaled by a sharp increase in the force required for further lateral compression (Fig. 4-6). The area of the monolayer of lipid was then measured, and was found to be about twice the calculated surface area of the cell membranes from which they were extracted. Gorter and Grendel concluded from this observation that the lipid of the cell membrane is arranged in a bilayer composed of

4–6. *Gorter and Grendel's experiment, which led to the lipid bilayer model of the membrane. Lateral compression of the lipid film produces an abrupt increase in the measured force, indicating the point at which the molecules are crowded into a dense single layer.*

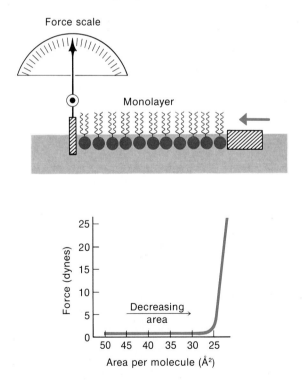

Force scale

Monolayer

Decreasing area

*A "ghost" is the empty membrane sac remaining after the red blood cell is hemolyzed by a hypotonic solution.

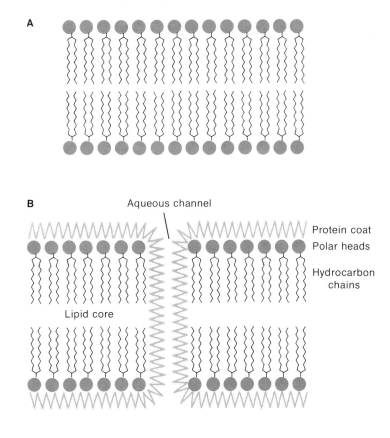

4-7. A. The Gorter-Grendel bimolecular leaflet. B. Danielli membrane model, showing both lipid and protein components of the membrane.

A

B

Aqueous channel

Protein coat
Polar heads

Hydrocarbon
chains

Lipid core

two monomolecular layers of molecules oriented so that the two are apposed to one another, with the hydrophobic hydrocarbon ends of the ordered molecules facing inward, or toward each other, and the polar groups facing outward, or toward the aqueous phases adjacent to the surfaces of the double layer (Fig. 4-7,A). This is the essence of the *bimolecular leaflet* or *lipid bilayer* model of membrane structure. Evidence for this concept is listed in Box 4-1.

A similar model developed subsequently by Danielli is based on the same double layer of phospholipid molecules, but in addition contains protein-lined pores and a layer of protein molecules on the surfaces of the lipid bilayer (Fig. 4-7,B). Danielli's original reason for adding surface proteins to the model was to account for the relatively low surface tension of cell membranes compared to that of an oil-water interface. The low surface tension is now understood to result from the hydrophilic properties of the phospholipid head groups of the bilayer molecules.

THE MOSAIC BILAYER MODEL

As we have already noted, chemical fractionation of membranes confirms that proteins are a component of membranes; moreover, the enzymatic properties of membranes exhibited in active transport and other metabolic functions require the participation of proteins. For some time it was speculated that these proteins have a globular conformation or some other conformation, since all other known enzymes are globular proteins or have active groups that are globular. Optical studies have recently confirmed the globular studies of membrane proteins. On the basis of this and other evidence, Singer and his coworkers have proposed that such proteins are integrated with the lipid bilayer, with some protein molecules penetrating the bilayer completely and others penetrating only partially (Fig. 4-8). These integral proteins are thought to be amphipathic, their nonpolar portions buried in the hydrocarbon core of the bilayer and their polar portions protruding from the core to form a hydrophilic surface with charged amino acid side groups in the aqueous phase. Uncharged hydrophobic side groups, on the other hand, are associated with the hydrocarbon bilayer (Fig. 4-9).

Morphological evidence for the mosaic arrangement of globular proteins in a lipid bilayer is seen in Figure 4-10, which shows three freeze-etch electron micrographs of the surface of a membrane. Globular units in the membrane are removed by progressive proteolytic digestion. The specificity of the protein-digesting enzyme used in this experiment indicates that these globular units are proteins.

The mosaic bilayer model appears to offer the most acceptable modern structural picture of the surface membrane and most of the intracellular membranes. It incorporates both large areas of uninterrupted phospholipid bilayer, for which there is very strong evidence, and the globular proteins responsible for the metabolic activities of membranes. It is also consistent with the evidence for intimate interaction between membrane proteins and lipids in the form of lipoproteins.

SUBUNIT MODELS

In some membranes, such as those of mitochondria and visual receptor cells, the mosaic bilayer model appears to be modified so that the lipid bilayer is largely obliterated by identical repeating macromolecular units. In visual receptor cells (p. 221), these units are molecules of visual pigment, consisting primarily of protein. In mitochondrial membranes, which have an unusually high proportion of protein, there is specialization for intense enzymatic activity, and the

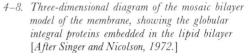

4-8. Three-dimensional diagram of the mosaic bilayer model of the membrane, showing the globular integral proteins embedded in the lipid bilayer [After Singer and Nicolson, 1972.]

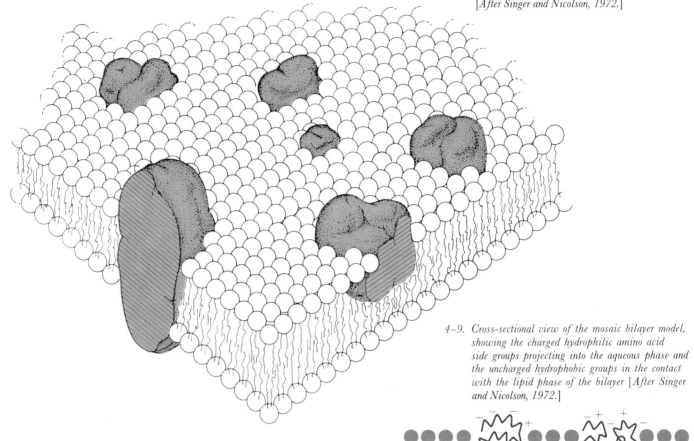

4-9. Cross-sectional view of the mosaic bilayer model, showing the charged hydrophilic amino acid side groups projecting into the aqueous phase and the uncharged hydrophobic groups in the contact with the lipid phase of the bilayer [After Singer and Nicolson, 1972.]

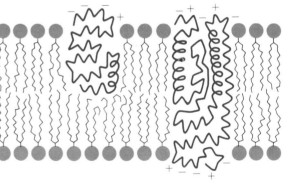

4-10. Freeze-etch electron micrographs showing morphological evidence for the mosaic membrane model. In each preparation, the membrane split along the middle of the bilayer, exposing membrane-embedded particles with diameters of 50–80 Å. Digestion with a proteolytic enzyme produced progressive loss of these particles, indicating that they are globular proteins inserted into the lipid phase of the membrane. A. control. B. 45% of the particles digested. C. 70% digested. Magnification 55,000×. [Courtesy of L. H. Engstrom and D. Branton.]

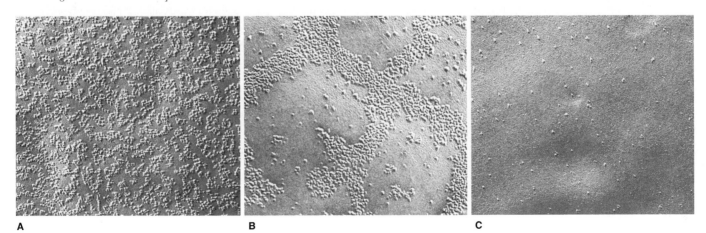

A

B

C

BOX 4-1 EVIDENCES FOR THE LIPID BILAYER MEMBRANE

1. The lipid content of membranes is consistent with a bilayer of oriented lipid molecules, as first shown by Gorter and Grendel.

2. The ease with which nonelectrolytes pass through the membrane corresponds to their partitioning between oil and water. (Fig. 4-16). That is to say, the greater the tendency for a molecule to leave an aqueous phase for a lipid phase, the more permeant the molecule. This suggests that substances crossing the membrane encounter a barrier layer of lipid. Moreover, certain lipid-insoluble substances must first be converted to a lipid-soluble form (by attachment of a lipid-soluble molecule) before they can cross the membrane.

3. The capacitance of biological membranes, typically 10^{-6} F/cm^2, is the same as that of a layer of lipid the thickness of two phospholipid molecules placed end-to-end (i.e., 60 to 75 Å).

4. When fixed with permanganate, membranes appear as triple-layered profiles, a lightly staining central zone sandwiched between two electron-dense outer layers (Fig. 4-1), with a total thickness of about 75 Å. In 1955 Robertson named this three-layered structure the *unit membrane*. The unit-membrane concept is consistent with a bimolecular layer of lipid between two layers of protein.

5. The thickness of a lipid bilayer calculated as twice the length of a single membrane lipid molecule agrees roughly with the dimensions of the inner zone (ca. 75 Å) of the unit membrane seen in electron micrographs.

6. The freeze-etch electron microscopy (see figure below) shows that membranes have a preferential plane of splitting down the middle, which is consistent with separation of a bilayer into two monolayers.

7. Reconstituted or "artificial" lipid bilayers (Box 4-2), similar in thickness and presumed structure to the bimolecular lipid core of the Danielli model, have permeabilities and electrical properties fundamentally similar to those of cell membranes.

Freeze-etch electron micrograph of a unit membrane. After rapid freezing, the tissue was cracked so as to reveal natural planes of cleavage. After brief evaporation of surface ice to bring out details of the structure, a metal film was deposited from one direction to produce a shadowed appearance in the electron microscope. In this micrograph, the membrane is seen as a sandwich structure. The dark section at the left is a step in the fracture surface where the membrane split for a short distance along the center of the bilayer. Magnification 120,000×. [Courtesy of D. Branton.]

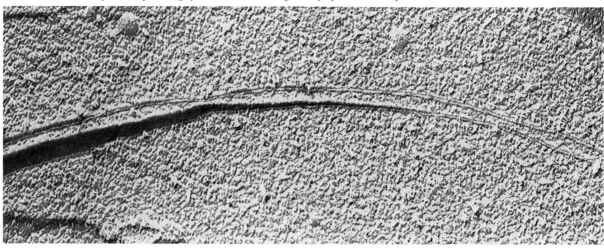

subunits appear to be complexes of enzyme molecules. Electron micrographs suggest repeating units having a globular shape (Fig. 4-11). Fractionation of mitochondrial membranes has yielded several components with specific enzymatic functions. When those components are allowed to reassemble, they regain the ability to perform the complete sequence of reactions characteristic of the intact membrane. On the other hand, mixtures containing all the dissociated components of the membrane are unable to perform the sequence of reactions. This suggests that an important function of certain membranes is to bestow a highly ordered structural arrangement on enzymatic subunits involved in tightly coupled sequential reactions.

It now appears that at one end of the spectrum of membrane organization, there is the metabolically inert myelin sheath (Fig. 4-12) of certain nerve cells, in which the lipid bilayer is largely uninterrupted. At the other end of the spectrum, there is the rapidly metabolizing mitochondrial membrane, composed almost entirely of repeating subunits of ordered enzymatic aggregates. In between these extremes is the surface membrane and most intracellular membranes, in which the mosaic bilayer is interrupted here and there by lipoprotein molecules or aggregates of molecules. Thus the basic structure of the bilayer appears to be modified as required for the functional specializations of different membranes.

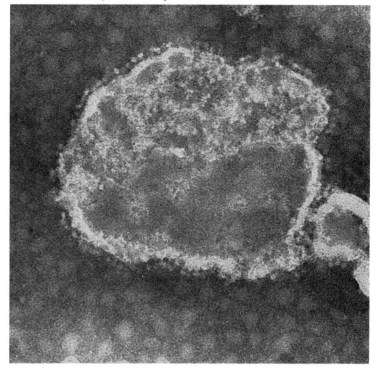

4-11. Electron micrograph of negatively strained fragment of the inner mitochondrial membrane prepared from mammalian heart muscle. Magnification 152,000×. Note the orderly arrangement of knob-like projections. [Courtesy of B. Tandler.]

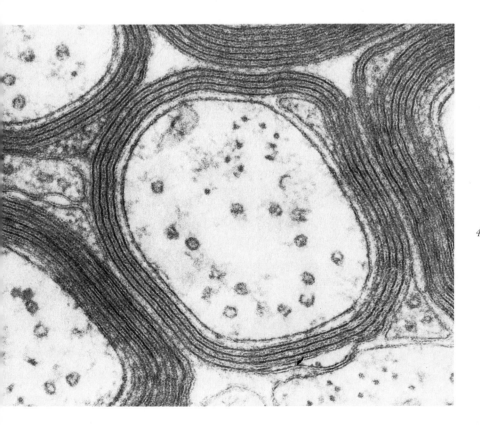

4-12. Electron micrograph of myelin sheath surrounding a nerve fiber cut in cross section. The sheath is formed during development by many layers of Schwann cell surface membrane wrapped spirally around the nerve fiber. Magnification 75,000×. [Peters and Vaughn, 1970.]

Membrane Transport

Membranes are never seen to terminate with free ends; they always form enclosed compartments. The largest of these is, of course, formed by the surface membrane. This compartment encloses the cytosol (free cytoplasm) and all cell organelles and inclusions, such as mitochondria, vesicles, nucleus, and reticulum. Many of these constitute still smaller subcompartments, separated from the cytosol by their own surface membranes. Membranes act as very significant barriers to free diffusion. Similarly, the membrane that forms each subcompartment limits the movement of substances into and out of it. The enormous retardation of free diffusion enables membranes, with the aid of metabolic mechanisms, to regulate the *net* movement, and hence the concentrations of substances in cellular or subcellular compartments. The active metabolic processes behind this will be discussed further on.

At this point it is useful to consider some definitions and physical relations pertinent to the diffusion of solutes across a membrane.

4-13. *Movement of a solute through a membrane. A. The arrows represent the actual unidirectional fluxes of a substance between compartments I and II. B. The single arrow indicates the resulting net flux.*

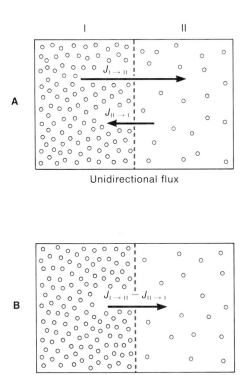

If a solute exists on both sides of a membrane through which it can diffuse, it will exhibit a *unidirectional flux* in each direction (Fig. 4-13,A). The flux can be expressed as the amount of the solute that penetrates a unit area of membrane every second in the direction under consideration, or

$$J = \frac{ds}{dt} \Big/ \text{ unit area} \qquad (4\text{-}1)$$

in which J is the unidirectional flux, s is the amount of solute in moles, t, the time in seconds, and ds/dt is the amount of solute traversing a unit area of membrane per second in the direction under consideration. The flux in one direction (say, from cell exterior to cell interior) will be considered independent of the flux in the opposite direction. Thus, if the *influx* and *efflux* are equal, the net flux is zero. If the unidirectional flux is greater in one direction, there is said to be a *net flux*, which is the difference in the two unidirectional fluxes (Fig. 4-13,B).

The *permeability* of the membrane to a substance refers to the rate at which that substance penetrates the membrane under a given set of conditions. A greater permeability will be accompanied by a greater flux if other factors remain equal. If it is assumed that the membrane is a homogeneous barrier and that a continuous concentration gradient exists for a non-electrolyte substance between the side of high concentration (I) and the side of low concentration (II), then

$$ds/dt = PA(C_{\mathrm{I}} - C_{\mathrm{II}}) \qquad (4\text{-}2)$$

in which ds/dt is the amount of the substance crossing a unit area of membrane per unit time (moles/cm^2/s), A is the area of membrane under consideration (cm^2) C_{I} and C_{II} are the respective concentrations (moles/cm^3) of the substance on the two sides of the membrane, and P is the *permeability constant* of the substance, with the dimension of velocity (cm/s).

The permeability constant incorporates all the factors inherent in the membrane and in the substance in question—factors that determine the probability with which a molecule of that substance will cross the membrane. This can be expressed formally as

$$P = WRT\frac{k}{a} \qquad (4\text{-}3)$$

in which W is the *mobility* of the substance within the membrane (the more viscous the membrane or the larger the molecule, the lower the mobility), R and T are the gas constant and absolute temperature, k is the partition coefficient (p. 91) of the substance, and a is the thickness of the membrane.

Permeability constants for different membranes and different substances vary greatly. The permeability of red blood cells to different solutes ranges from 10^{-8} to 10^{-3} cm/s. Furthermore, the permeability of many membranes to given substances can be altered greatly by hormones and other molecules that react with receptor sites on the membrane and thereby influence channel size or carrier mechanisms. Antidiuretic hormone (Chapter 12), for example, can increase the water permeability of the renal collecting duct in mammals by as much as ten times. Similarly, neural transmitter substances, acting on specialized portions of the surface membranes of nerve and muscle cells, produce large increases in permeability to such ions as Na^+, K^+, Ca^{2+}, or Cl^-.

Mechanisms of Permeation

There are three major routes by which substances are believed to cross membranes (Fig. 4-14). In the first, the molecule remains in the aqueous phase and diffuses through *aqueous channels* or "pores" in the membrane. In the second, the molecule leaves the aqueous phase on one side of the membrane, dissolves directly in the lipid layer of the membrane, diffuses across the thickness of the lipid or protein layer, and finally enters the aqueous phase on the opposite side of the membrane. In the third route, the molecule combines with a *carrier* molecule dissolved in the membrane. This carrier "mediates" or "facilitates" the transport of the solute molecule across the membrane, hence the term *carrier-mediated* (or *facilitated*) *transport* is used. Some carriers act passively, simply allowing the solute molecules to diffuse more readily across the membrane, down a concentration or electrochemical gradient. This is termed *carrier-mediated* (or *facilitated*) *diffusion*. Other carriers, by being coupled to a source of metabolic energy, are able to transport (or "pump") solutes against a concentration or electrochemical gradient. This form of carrier-mediated transport is called *active transport*.

DIFFUSION THROUGH MEMBRANE CHANNELS

Some evidence suggests that water and certain other polar substances can pass through channels or pores which penetrate the lipid bilayer. Since water has a very low solubility in long-chain hydrocarbons, it can be predicted that its diffusion through a lipid bilayer will be very slow. It is significant that the permeabilities of natural membranes and of artificial lipid bilayers to water are far higher than predicted for truly uninterrupted lipid films. Since there is no protein in the artificial lipid bilayer, the pores must be formed in the lipid without the aid of protein components.

The same may hold for natural membranes as well. The fatty acid chains in the lipid bilayer are in an essentially fluid state; thus the water-permeable channels appear to be transient structures that result from thermal fluctuations in the molecular order of the bilayer. Since proteins form a significant part of biological membranes, there is the possibility that fixed aqueous channels are formed by hydrophilic portions of protein molecules, as in Figure 4-7,B.

Studies of the permeabilities of cell membranes to other polar substances give an estimated 7 Å for the *equivalent pore size*—the pore size that would account for the rate of diffusion across the membrane. Thus, if membrane pores do exist, they presumably have diameters of less than 10 Å, close to the practical limits of resolution of contemporary electron-microscopes and fixation methods.

It is interesting to note that only a very small percentage of membrane area need be occupied by ionic and water channels in order to account for the observed rate of diffusion of polar substances through the membrane. For example, four rod-shaped molecules of the antibiotic nystatin line up to form a cylindrical channel through either natural or artificial (Box 4-2) membranes. The pores thus formed permit the passage

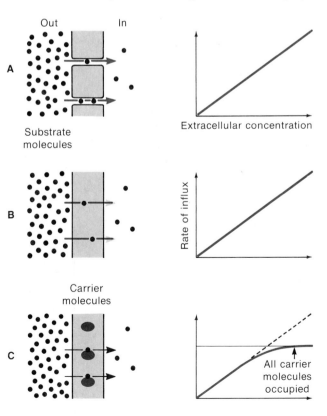

4-14. *Three major mechanisms by which substances cross membranes. A. Diffusion through labile or fixed aqueous channels. B. Dissolving in lipid phase. C. Carrier-mediated transport (either mediated diffusion or active transport).*

BOX 4-2   ARTIFICIAL MEMBRANES

Many of our present concepts of how molecules and ions pass across membranes have grown out of experiments and observations on artificial membranes that consist of reconstituted bilayers similar to the bimolecular leaflet which forms the basis of the Danielli and Singer models (Fig. 4-8, A). Artificial membranes are extremely useful in studies of permeation mechanisms because they can be made from chemically defined mixtures of lipids, or from less well-defined lipids extracted from biological membranes. Selected substances can also be added to test their effects on permeability.

The principle of bilayer formation is shown in the figure. The most stable configuration attained consists of two layers of lipid molecules whose hydrophobic, lipophilic hydrocarbon tails are loosely associated to form a liquid-lipid phase sandwiched between the hydrophilic, polar ends of the molecules, which are directed outward toward the aqueous medium. The thickness of the lipid film is easily determined from the interference color of light reflected from the two surfaces of the film. Membranes with thicknesses of approximately 70 Å (black interference color) are most commonly used. These membranes have electrical conductances (ion permeabilities) and capacitances consistent with their thickness and lipid composition. It is significant that their electric capacitance and permeability to water are both similar to those of cell membranes. Although their permeability to ions is much lower than that of actual cell membranes, the addition of certain ionophores (molecules that facilitate the diffusion of ions across membranes) increases it to values that are characteristic of cell membranes.

A bilayer of lipid formed in a 1 mm opening between two chambers.   A. A small amount of the lipid in a solvent such as hexane is placed in the opening. As it assumes the more stable bilayer configuration, the interference color changes from gray to black.   B. The chambers are filled with the test medium. The permeability to electrolytes can be measured electrically. [After Kotyk and Janáček, 1970.]

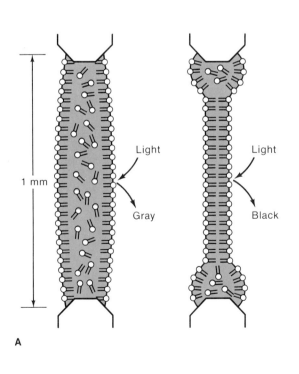

1 mm

Light

Gray

Light

Black

A

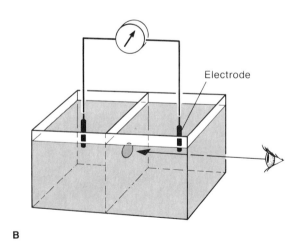

Electrode

B

of water, urea, and chloride, all of which are less than 4 Å in diameter. Larger molecules cannot penetrate the channel. Cations are excluded, presumably because the channel includes fixed positive sites along its walls (Fig. 4-15). Incorporation of nystatin into artificial membranes produces an insignificant increase in membrane area occupied by fixed pores (0.000% to 0.01%), but it produces a 100,000-fold increase in membrane permeability to chloride ions. In principle, then, very little membrane area need be devoted to pores to account for the ion permeabilities of natural membranes. This receives support from the fact that the electric capacitance of the cell membrane remains relatively unchanged during large changes in its permeability.

SIMPLE DIFFUSION THROUGH THE LIPID BILAYER

If a solute molecule comes into contact with the lipid layer of the membrane, it may enter into the lipid phase by virtue of its thermal energy and cross the lipid layer, finally emerging into the aqueous phase again on one side of the membrane or the other. In order to leave the aqueous phase and enter the lipid phase, a solute must first break all of its hydrogen bonds with water. This requires kinetic energy in amounts of about 5 kcal per hydrogen bond. Thus it is evident that those molecules with a minimum of hydrogen bonding with water will most readily enter the lipid bilayer, whereas polar molecules such as water and inorganic ions will dissolve in the bilayer with extremely low probability.

Factors such as molecular weight and molecular shape have a modifying effect on the mobility (Eq. 4-3) of nonelectrolytes within the membrane, but the primary factor that determines the diffusion of a nonelectrolyte across the lipid bilayer is its *partition coefficient*. As early as 1899 Overton suggested that nonelectrolyte permeability is correlated with the lipid-water partition coefficient of the test solute, which is described at equilibrium by the equation

$$k = \frac{\text{solute concentration in lipid}}{\text{solute concentration in water}}. \quad (4\text{-}4)$$

Collander systematically tested this idea in the giant algal cell *Chara* by plotting the permeability coefficient (Eq. 4-3) against the partition coefficient. His results are graphed in Figure 4-16, which shows a nearly linear relationship between lipid solubility and permeability of a substance. Note that in Equation 4-3 the quantities W and T can vary only slightly. However, nonelectrolytes exhibit a wide range of partition coefficients (k). For example, the value for urethan is 1000 times that for glycerol (Fig. 4-16). The reason

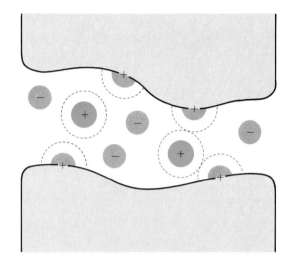

4-15. A hypothetical membrane channel lined with positive charges. These allow anions to pass but retard the diffusion of cations through the channel.

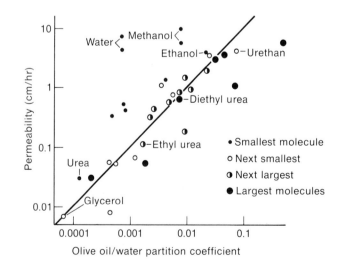

4-16. Membrane permeability of nonelectrolytes plotted against their respective oil/water partition coefficients. Note that the permeability of nonelectrolytes is independent of molecular size. [After Collander, 1937.]

4–17. Structures of two 6-carbon molecules—hexanol and mannitol. Note the difference in the number of hydroxyl groups. Hexanol is poorly soluble in water, whereas mannitol is highly soluble due to its H-bonding capacity.

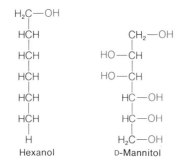

Hexanol   D-Mannitol

4–18. Graph showing the relationship between permeability coefficient and number of possible hydrogen bonds in a molecule. Hydrogen bonds greatly decrease the lipid solubility and hence the permeability. [After Stein, 1967.]

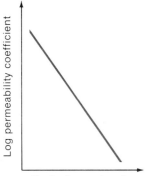

4–19. The effect of a competitive inhibitor on the transport kinetics of a particular substrate molecule (S) passing through a membrane. The inhibitor (the analog) reduces the rate of transport. A. Accumulation of S slowed by the analog. B. A Lineweaver-Burk plot shows that the inhibition is competitive.

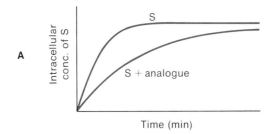

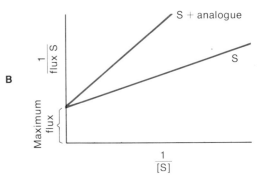

for these differences can be illustrated by considering the two molecules shown in Figure 4-17. The molecular structures are quite similar except that hexanol contains only one —OH group and mannitol contains six. The —OH groups facilitate hydrogen bonding to water and therefore decrease lipid solubility. In fact, each additional hydrogen bond results in a 40-fold decrease in the partition coefficient. This, in turn, is reflected in an increase in permeability (Fig. 4-18). Hexanol, therefore, diffuses across membranes much more readily than mannitol.

FACILITATED DIFFUSION

Simple diffusion through pores or through the lipid bilayer exhibits *nonsaturation kinetics* (Fig. 4-14,A,B). The rate of influx increases in proportion to the concentration of the solute in the extracellular fluid because the net rate of influx is determined by the difference in the number of ions impinging on the two sides of the cell membrane. This proportionality between external concentration and rate of influx (Fig. 4-14,A,B) holds true for most permeant substances at low concentrations. At higher concentrations, some solutes exhibit a saturation effect; that is, the rate of influx reaches a plateau beyond which a further increase in solute concentration produces no further increase in the rate of influx (Fig. 4-14,C). Such *saturation kinetics* are taken as evidence that lipid-soluble "carrier" molecules in the membrane facilitate passage of the solute molecules through the barrier. Since the number of carrier molecules and the rate at which they react with and traverse the membrane must be finite, the rate of diffusion of the solute will reach a maximum when all the carrier molecules are occupied.

The carrier hypothesis assumes the formation of a carrier-substrate complex similar in concept to an enzyme-substrate complex. This means simply that the carrier and the solute molecule temporarily form a complex based on bonding and/or steric specificity. This is consistent with the observation that carrier-mediated transport exhibits Michaelis-Menten kinetics (p. 60). Characteristic of such kinetics is that the number of interactions with a carrier or enzyme reaches a maximum when the carrier or enzyme molecules are all occupied by substrate molecules. Also characteristic is inhibition by certain chemical analogs of the substrate. Addition of these analogs reduces the rate of transport of the substrate across the membrane at a given substrate concentration (Fig. 4-19,A). The two curves in the Lineweaver-Burk plot (Fig. 4-19,B) intercept the ordinate at the same point for an infinite concentration of the substrate (i.e., when $1/[S] = 0$), indicating that the inhibition is a competitive one, rather than an irreversible poisoning of the transport system.

Our understanding of membrane carriers has recently been advanced by the discovery of naturally occurring antibiotic molecules from soil-dwelling fungi. Some of these *ionophores*, like valinomycin or monactin (Fig. 4-20), are donut-shaped; others, like gramocidin and nystatin, are rod-shaped. These molecules enter the membrane because they have hydrophobic surfaces. As the concentration of the ionophore in the membrane is increased, there is a proportional increase in permeability to ions (Fig. 4-21).

The donut-shaped ionophores act as membrane carriers by sequestering an ion in the "hole" of the cyclic molecule (Fig. 4-20). Monactin, for example, has no net charge, but has six inwardly directed electronegative oxygens with which such cations as K^+ form electrostatic bonds. Ionophore molecules have nonpolar groups on their exterior, hence they readily enter the lipid bilayer of the membrane. Thus a cation, sitting snugly within the polar core of the ionophore, can be safely carried through the unfriendly nonpolar interior of the lipid bilayer (Fig. 4-22). In nature, ionophores are produced by various fungi as antibiotics, which destroy bacterial cells by upsetting their ionic balance.

Three factors in particular determine the rate of ion permeation via a carrier system.

1. The affinity between the carrier molecule and the ion. For any given carrier molecule there is a sequence of ion preference consistent with Eisenman's concept of ion selectivity (Chapter 2). The greater the affinity, the more rapidly the carrier combines with an ion.

2. The concentration of the carrier in the lipid membrane.

3. The mobility of the carrier in the lipid phase. As the proportion of cholesterol (a naturally occurring phospholipid) in the lipid layer is increased, the rate of transport of the ion drops. This may be due to an increase in the viscosity of the lipid layer with in-

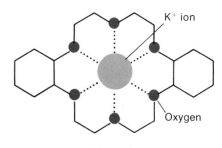

4-20. *Molecular structure of the donut-shaped ionophore monactin. The oxygen atoms are electron-rich, thus providing an energetic environment for cations similar to that produced by the oxygen atoms of water. The K^+ ion is not drawn to scale.*

4-21. *Relationship between ionophore concentration and membrane permeability to ions carried by the ionophore. The permeability is approximated by the electrical conductance λ. The ionophore enters the membrane from the solution in amounts proportional to its concentration in solution. [After Läuger, 1972.]*

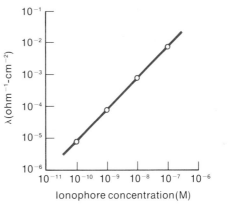

4-22. *The transport of an inorganic ion across the lipid phase of the membrane by a carrier ionophore; in this example, monactin.*

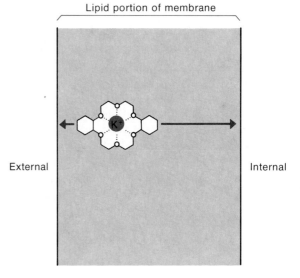

creased cholesterol concentration and a consequent drop in the mobility of the carrier molecule in the membrane.

ACTIVE TRANSPORT

Both simple diffusion and facilitated transport are passive processes in which no energy is released other than the potential energy that may exist in the form of differences in solute concentrations on opposite sides of the membrane. As diffusion proceeds, the solute concentrations in the two compartments approach equilibrium (Fig. 4-23). When the concentrations on the two sides of the membrane are in equilibrium, no further net diffusion occurs, although equal and opposite unidirectional fluxes continue.

Most solutes distributed across the surface membrane of a living cell are not, of course, in equilibrium. The concentration of an ion or molecule may be several times higher on one side of the cell membrane than on the other, even though it can diffuse through the membrane down its concentration gradient. Active processes of the membrane can maintain the transmembrane concentrations of such substances well out of equilibrium by the continual expenditure of chemical energy in the form of ATP. The mechanisms that actively transport substances against a gradient are loosely termed *membrane pumps*. When the source of energy for such pumps is cut off, active uphill transport ceases; passive diffusion then determines the distribution of substances to which the membrane is permeable, and the concentrations of these substances gradually redistribute toward equilibrium (Fig. 4-24).

Sodium ions, for example, are actively transported outward across the cell membrane at the same rate as they leak in. This is attributed to the *sodium pump*, a poorly understood ATP-requiring enzyme system that operates in the cell membrane. In the steady state, the number of sodium ions "pumped" or transported out of the cell is equal to the number of sodium ions that leak in. Thus, even though there is a continual turnover of Na^+ (and other ion species) across the membrane, the net Na flux over any period of time is zero. There are two factors that determine how large a sodium ion concentration gradient will be built up between the cell interior and cell exterior. These are (1) the rate of active transport of Na^+ and (2) the rate at which it can leak (i.e., diffuse passively) back into the cell. The rate at which the membrane allows sodium to leak back into the cell determines, of course, the rate at which the sodium pump has to work in order to maintain a given ratio of extracellular to intracellular Na^+. There is evidence that an increase in the intracellular concentration of sodium leads to an increase in the rate of Na extrusion by the pump (which may merely be due to the increased availability of intracellular Na^+ to the carrier molecules in the membrane).

No concrete picture of the mechanism of active transport exists at this time, but several basic features can be recognized.

1. *Transport can take place against substantial concentration gradients.* The most commonly studied membrane pump is the one that transports Na^+ from the cell interior to the external fluid. The cytoplasm typically has a free Na^+ concentration about 1/10th that of the extracellular fluid.

4-23. The equilibration in concentration by diffusion of a solute across a membrane with time. At time zero, the solute was confined to compartment I. At infinite time, the concentrations in I and II are equal.

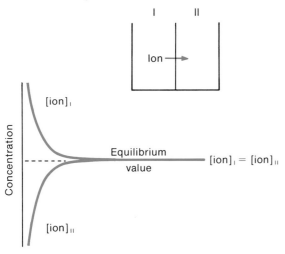

4-24. The active transport of ions requires a source of metabolic energy. If that energy supply is interrupted by the use of a metabolic inhibitor, active transport stops. In this hypothetical case, the cell was presented with a transportable substance at time zero.

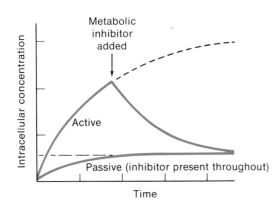

2. *ATP or other sources of chemical bond energy are required.* Metabolic poisons that stop the production of ATP bring active transport to a halt (Fig. 4-24).

3. *Certain membrane pumps exchange one kind of molecule or ion from one side of the membrane for another kind of molecule or ion from the other side.* In nerve cells, this is illustrated by the active outward transport of Na^+ concomitant with the inward transport of K^+. This usually involves the obligatory exchange of two potassium ions for three sodium ions. When external K^+ is removed, the sodium ions that normally would have been exchanged for potassium are no longer pumped out. The membranes of red blood cells and some nerve cells contain a transport ATPase that is activated by intracellular Na^+ and extracellular K^+ (Fig. 4-25,A).

4. *Some pumps can perform electrical work by producing a unidirectional flux of ions.* For example, some forms of the sodium pump are K-independent, and do not exchange K^+ for Na^+. These and others in which there is a net movement of positive charge across the membrane perform electrical work as well as osmotic work. Such a pump is said to be *electrogenic* because it produces a difference in electric charge across the membrane, which can be measured as a potential difference (p. 26).

5. *Active transport can be selectively inhibited by certain metabolic blocking agents.* When the cardiac glycoside *ouabain* is applied to the extracellular surface of the membrane, it blocks the K-dependent active extrusion of Na^+ from the cell. *Ethacrynic acid* inhibits the Na-activated ATPase responsible for the K-independent component of sodium pumping.

6. *Energy released by the hydrolysis of ATP is coupled to transport by enzymes (ATPases) present in the membrane.* Active transport exhibits enzyme kinetics, competitive inhibition by analog molecules, and sometimes a high degree of steric specificity. For example, D-glucose is actively transported into most cells, whereas its optical isomer L-glucose is not. Sodium- and potassium-activated ATPases have been isolated from red blood cell membranes. These enzymes catalyze the hydrolysis of ATP into ADP and inorganic phosphate only in the presence of Na^+ and K^+, and bind the specific Na pump inhibitor ouabain. Since ouabain binds to the membrane and blocks the Na-K pump, this evidence indicates that these ATPases are, in fact, involved in active transport of sodium and potassium.

Although the molecular mechanism for active transport remains a matter of speculation, several theories exist. According to one scheme (Fig. 4-26), a carrier molecule that has a specific site binds the transport substrate, S (e.g., Na^+). In its activated state, this site binds the substrate on one side of the membrane and releases it on the other side, producing a net flux

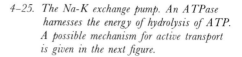

4-25. *The Na-K exchange pump. An ATPase harnesses the energy of hydrolysis of ATP. A possible mechanism for active transport is given in the next figure.*

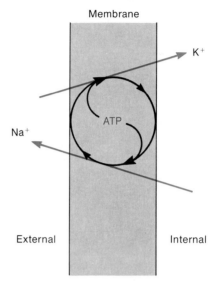

4-26. *A proposed mechanism for active transport of a substrate into the cell. The hydrolysis of ATP provides the energy for producing a change in the carrier molecule that enables it to pick up a substrate molecule on the exterior surface. A similar model can be constructed for transport in the opposite direction.*

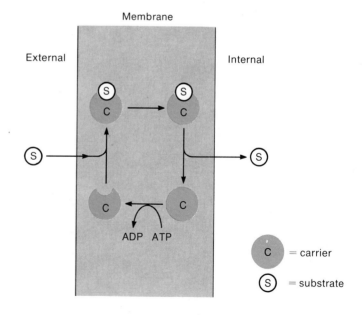

in one direction. Once the substrate is released, the site must be reactivated by a conformational change or phosphorylation of the carrier molecule by ATP. The ATPase, which hydrolyzes the ATP, may be part of the carrier molecule or may be separate from it. The carrier, once primed by the conformational change, accepts another molecule of substrate, and the cycle repeats. This scheme is intended only as a generalization, and is largely hypothetical.

As described, the actual process of metabolically energized transport takes place across the cell membrane, pumping molecules either into or out of the cell. However, the organization of cells into an epithelial sheet makes possible the active transport of substances from one side of the epithelial sheet to the other. Thus the epithelium of amphibian skin and bladder, fish gills, the vertebrate cornea, kidney tubules, the intestine, and many other tissues, are known to transport salts and other substances. Trans-epithelial transport will be discussed in Chapter 12.

4-27. *Effect of Na+ concentration on uptake of the amino acid alanine. A. Intracellular content as a function of time with and without extracellular Na+ present. B. Lineaweaver-Burk plots with and without extracellular Na+. The common intercept indicates that at infinite concentration of alanine, the rate of transport is independent of [Na+]ext. [After Schultz and Curran, 1969.]*

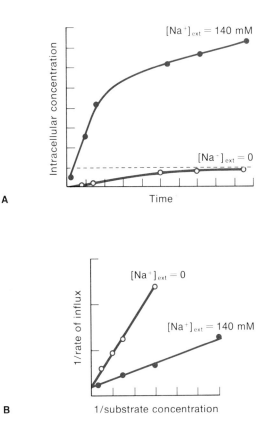

A

B

Transport Energized by the Concentration Gradient of Another Substance

The transport of some substances, such as Na^+, K^+, amino acids, and sugars, depends in some cases not only on the concentration of the substance in question, but also on the concentration of another substance. This has already been noted for the Na-K pump. Examples also exist that are not *directly* dependent on metabolic energy.

CODIFFUSION

Figure 4-27,A shows the time course of the accumulation (uptake by cell) of the amino acid alanine in the presence and absence of extracellular sodium. In the presence of Na^+, the amino acid is taken up by the cell until the internal concentration is 7 to 10 times that of the external concentration. In the absence of Na^+, the intracellular concentration of alanine merely approaches the extracellular concentration. As the Lineweaver-Burk plots show (Fig. 4-27,B), the maximum rate of alanine influx approaches the same maximum (intercept on ordinate) with or without extracellular Na^+. In both cases the rate of influx shows saturation kinetics, indicating a carrier mechanism. The different slopes of the two plots indicate that the effect of extracellular Na^+ is to enhance the activity of the alanine carrier. Increasing the intracellular Na^+ concentration by blocking the sodium pump with ouabain has the same effect as decreasing the extracellular Na^+ concentration. Thus it appears to be the sodium gradient that is important for inward alanine transport, and not merely the presence of sodium ions in the extracellular fluid.

The transport of amino acids and sugars appears to be *coupled* to inward Na^+ leakage by means of a *common carrier*. The carrier molecule apparently binds both Na^+ and the organic substrate molecule before it can transport either (Fig. 4-28). The tendency for Na^+ to diffuse down its concentration gradient is what drives this carrier system. Anything that reduces the concentration gradient of Na^+ (low extracellular Na^+ or increased intracellular Na^+) reduces the inwardly directed driving force and thereby reduces the coupled transport of amino acids and sugars into the cell. If the direction of the sodium gradient is experimentally reversed, the direction of transport of these molecules is also reversed. The transport of Na^+ in this case also depends on the presence of amino acids and sugars. In the absence of amino acids and sugars, the common carrier will not transport Na^+. As a result, the inward leakage of Na^+ is reduced.

The common carrier appears to shuttle between the two sides of the membrane passively, without *direct* utilization of metabolic energy. The coupled uphill transport of organic molecules derives its energy from the downhill diffusion of sodium ions, but the potential energy stored in the sodium gradient is, of course, derived from metabolic energy that drives the sodium pump (Fig. 4-29). The sodium concentration gradient is, in fact, another form of common energy currency used to drive several endergonic processes.

EXCHANGE DIFFUSION

The sodium concentration gradient also plays a role in the maintainance of a very low intracellular calcium concentration in certain cells. In most cells, if not all, the intracellular calcium concentration is several orders of magnitude below the extracellular concentrations ($< 10^{-6}$ M), and certain cell functions are regulated by changes in the intracellular calcium concentration. Efflux of Ca^{2+} from heart muscle and nerve cells is reduced when extracellular Na^+ is removed. This suggests that Ca^{2+} is extruded from the cell in exchange for Na^+ leaking in, with the opposing movements of these two ions coupled to one another by an *exchange carrier*. One view is that Ca^{2+} and Na^+ both compete for the carrier, but since Na^+ is less concentrated inside the cell than outside, it competes less effectively for the carrier on the inner surface of the membrane than it does on the outer surface, the converse being true for the cell exterior. As a result, there is a net efflux of Ca^{2+}. Again, the immediate source of energy is the Na^+ gradient, which ultimately depends on the ATP-energized active transport of Na^+. There is evidence that Ca^{2+} is also transported by an ATP-energized Ca pump.

Membrane Selectivity

Each kind of membrane transport displays selectivity, and the selectivity generally differs in a given membrane for different transport systems. For example, when the sodium in a physiological saline solution used to bathe a nerve cell is replaced with lithium ions, the Li^+ readily passes through the sodium channels, which open during electrical excitation of the nerve cell membrane. The other alkali-metal cations, K^+, Rb^+, and Cs^+, are essentially impermeant through these channels. On the other hand, the ATPase of the sodium pump in the same membrane is highly specific for intracellular Na^+, and is not activated by lithium ions. Lithium ions will therefore gradually accumulate in the cell. This is an example of electrolyte selectivity. We will now consider mechanisms of selectivity for both electrolytes and nonelectrolytes.

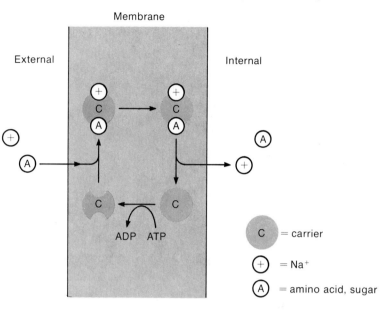

4-28. *Hypothetical mechanism of Na-mediated Codiffusion of amino acids (or sugars). The carrier must bind both the Na^+ and the amino acid before it will transport either.*

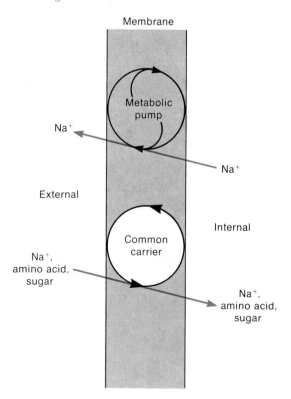

4-29. *The transport of amino acids and sugars depends ultimately on the chemical energy of ATP derived from cell metabolism. The Na^+ concentration gradient acts as an intermediate form of potential energy utilized to drive the organic molecules against their concentration gradients.*

MECHANISMS OF SELECTIVITY FOR ELECTROLYTES

The most commonly encountered example of selectivity is the ability of the resting membrane to distinguish K^+ from the other major monovalent cation, Na^+. The resting nerve cell is about 30 times more permeable to K^+ than to Na^+. At first glance, one might conclude that these ions are distinguished on the basis of their hydrated size, with K^+ passing freely through channels that are too small for Na^+. The sieving hypothesis is not adequate, however, to explain most other mechanisms of membrane selectivity. For example, during the excitation of nerve or muscle membrane (Chapter 5), the Na^+ permeability of the membrane increases about 300-fold to a value about 10 times greater than the K^+ permeability at rest. If, during excitation, the membrane were suddenly to develop channels that pass the Na^+ ion on the basis of size alone, the sieving hypothesis would predict a simultaneous increase in permeability to K^+ through the same channels. Since this does not happen, the membrane's selectivity must rest on mechanisms other than those based on size alone.

One factor that influences permeation of ions was illustrated in Figure 4-15, which shows fixed charges producing a net positivity on the walls of a hypothetical membrane channel. Such a channel would preferentially pass anions of appropriate size, but would hinder passage of cations by electrostatic repulsion.

Diamond and Wright reviewed the selectivity exhibited by various membranes and found that nearly all experimentally demonstrated selectivity sequences (Fig. 2-30) for the alkali cations (Ca^+, Rb^+, K^+, Na^+, Li^+) fall into one of the eleven predicted ion sequences. Some membranes show preferences that correspond to the order of decreasing ion diameter (Sequence I, Fig. 2-30), whereas others show a selectivity sequence that corresponds to increasing size (sequence XI, Fig. 2-30). Since these are only two of the 11 observed membrane selectivity sequences, correlations between ion diameters, hydrated or nonhydrated, appear to be secondary to more subtle interactions.

The thermodynamic basis for interactions between ions and electrostatic sites on enzymes and membranes is discussed on pages 28 to 32. The probability of binding between an ion and a polar site on the membrane is determined by the differences between the electrostatic attraction of the ion to water and to specific electrostatically charged sites on the membrane. The greater the electrostatic attraction of an ion to the site relative to its attraction to water, the more successfully it competes with other ions for the site. This theory does not specify the mechanism of permeation, but simply explains a major factor that determines the ion selectivity characteristics of membrane channels and carriers. Ion-selective sites reside on carrier molecules operating in mediated or active transport of ions, and they may be present at the entrance to or in the lumen of a transmembrane channel.

MECHANISMS OF SELECTIVITY FOR NONELECTROLYTES

As was shown in Figure 4-16, there is a somewhat linear relationship between permeability and partition coefficient for most nonelectrolytes. This is one of the major evidences that those substances cross the membrane by dissolving in (i.e., entering) the lipid bilayer and simply diffusing across it. In relation to Equation 4-3, this means that the permeability of those nonelectrolytes is limited primarily by the partition coefficient, k. Those few nonelectrolytes that deviate from the linear relation between partition coefficient and permeability (Fig. 4-16) all do so in the direction of greater than predicted permeability. One explanation for these deviations is that these substances cross the membrane by carrier-mediated transport, and hence show higher permeabilities than can be accounted for by simple diffusion through the lipid layer.

Osmotic Regulation by the Cell Membrane

As seen in Figure 4-30, the concentrations of solutes in the cytosol differ significantly from concentrations in

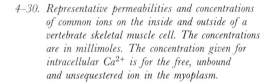

4–30. *Representative permeabilities and concentrations of common ions on the inside and outside of a vertebrate skeletal muscle cell. The concentrations are in millimoles. The concentration given for intracellular Ca^{2+} is for the free, unbound and unsequestered ion in the myoplasm.*

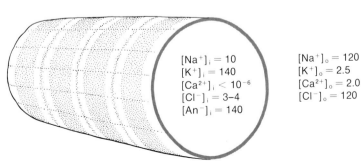

$[Na^+]_i = 10$
$[K^+]_i = 140$
$[Ca^{2+}]_i < 10^{-6}$
$[Cl^-]_i = 3-4$
$[An^-]_i = 140$

$[Na^+]_o = 120$
$[K^+]_o = 2.5$
$[Ca^{2+}]_o = 2.0$
$[Cl^-]_o = 120$

the extracellular fluid. This is due to (1) metabolic production or modification of impermeant substances inside the cell, (2) active transport of substances into or out of the cell or intracellular compartments, and (3) passive distribution according to the principles of Donnan equilibrium (p. 24). In this section we will make an overview of the various factors that regulate the steady state distributions of inorganic ions and cell volume.

CELL VOLUME

Plant and bacterial cells possess rigid walls secreted by the cell membrane. These walls place an upper limit on the size of the cell, allowing the osmotic buildup of turgor pressure in these cells. In contrast, animal cells have no rigid walls, and therefore cannot build up any significant intracellular pressure. As a result, they change size when placed in different concentrations of impermeable substances dissolved in water. This is due to osmotic movement of water (p. 22). As shown in Figure 4-31, a cell will swell in hypotonic solution and shrink in hypertonic solution.

A test solution containing a completely impermeant solute produces a maintained shrinkage of the cell. The shrinkage is merely transient, however, if the solute enters the cell slowly, in which case the cell will eventually swell beyond its original volume (Fig. 4-32).

The osmotically active intracellular solutes consist of colloidal molecules of proteins and peptides as well as smaller molecules and ions. Proteins with a net electric charge attract ions of the opposite charge (termed *counterions*), confining them to the cell interior as well, thereby adding to the osmotic pressure of the cell. This is treated in more detail in the section on Donnan equilibrium. The concentration of impermeant solutes is higher inside the cell than outside; thus the cell faces the problem of osmotic swelling by entry of water and permeant solutes. There are two ways in which the surface membrane might prevent osmotic swelling. One is to pump water out as fast as it leaks in; there is no evidence that this occurs, although a similar effect is achieved by the contractile vacuole of certain protozoans. The other, which appears to be the major mechanism for regulation of cell volume, is the active extrusion of solutes that leak into the cell (Fig. 4-32). Thus, at steady-state, Na^+, the major osmotic constituent outside the cell, is extruded from the cell by active transport as rapidly as it leaks in. In effect, there is no net entry. The situation is osmotically equivalent to complete sodium impermeability. Since Na^+ is not allowed to accumulate in the cell, there is no compensatory osmotic influx of water.

The high extracellular sodium concentration (relative to intracellular) is important in balancing the other osmotically active solutes in the cytoplasm. The

4–31. *Osmotic changes in the volume of a red blood cell. A. In an isotonic solution, the cell volume remains unchanged. B. In a more dilute solution, water (arrow) enters the cell because of the higher osmoticity of the cytoplasm with respect to the solution, producing swelling. C. Water leaves the cell in a more concentrated medium, causing shrinkage.*

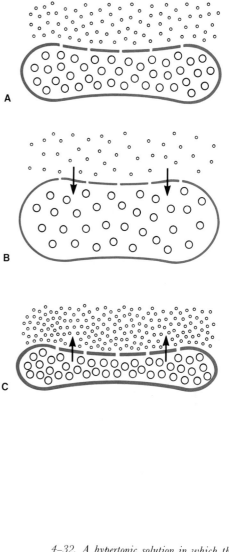

4–32. *A hypertonic solution in which the solute is completely impermeant causes maintained shrinkage of the cell. If the solute slowly enters the cell, it is followed by the osmotic flow of water and eventually produces swelling.*

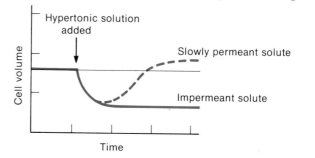

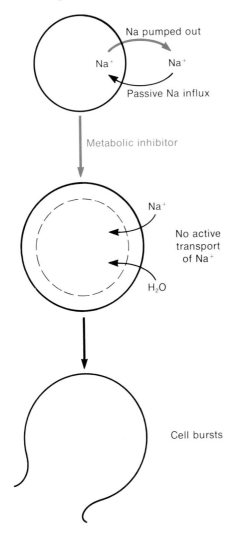

4-33. *Addition of a metabolic inhibitor results in an inability of the cell to pump out the Na⁺ that steadily leaks in. As a result, [Na⁺]ᵢ rises, water follows osmotically, and the cell bursts due to massive swelling.*

Na pumped out

Na^+ Na^+

Passive Na influx

Metabolic inhibitor

Na^+

No active transport of Na^+

H_2O

Cell bursts

importance of active transport in maintaining the sodium gradient, and thereby the osmolarity of the cell and the cell volume, is seen when the energy metabolism of the cell is interrupted by metabolic poisons (Fig. 4-33). Without ATP to energize uphill extrusion of Na^+, the sodium ion, together with its chloride counterion, leaks into the cell, and water follows osmotically, causing the cell to swell.

DISTRIBUTION OF PERMEANT IONS

Although the intracellular concentrations of solutes (Table 4-1) differ somewhat among different cell types and different organisms, certain generalizations can be made. The most concentrated inorganic ion in the cytosol is K^+, which is typically 10 to 30 times as concentrated in the cytosol as in the extracellular fluid. Conversely, the internal concentrations of free Na^+ and Cl^- are typically less (ca. 1/10th) than the external concentrations. Another important generalization is that the intracellular concentration of Ca^{2+} is maintained several orders of magnitude below the extracellular concentration. This is due in part to active transport of Ca^{2+} out across the cell membrane. and in part to the *sequestering* of this ion within such organelles as the mitochondria and reticulum. As a result, the activity of Ca^{2+} in the cytosol is generally well below 10^{-6} M.

Cell membranes are typically far more permeable (ca. 30 times) to K^+ than to Na^+. Membrane permeability to chloride varies. In some cells (Table 4-1) it is similar to potassium while in others it is much lower. From what we know about Donnan equilibrium (p. 24), it is evident that K^+ and Cl^- will distribute themselves so that the product of the concentrations of the two ions in the one compartment equals the product of the two in the other compartment. Since K^+ and Cl^- are by far the most concentrated permeant ions in the tissue, they distribute themselves in a way that approaches an ideal Donnan equilibrium; that is, the *KCl product* ($[K^+][Cl^+]$) of the cell interior is equal to the product of their concentrations in the

Table 4-1. *Internal and external concentrations of electrolytes in some nerve and muscle tissues.*

Tissue	Internal concentrations (mM)			External concentrations (mM)			Ratios, inside/outside		
	Na^+	K^+	Cl^-	Na^+	K^+	Cl^-	Na^+	K^+	Cl^-
Squid nerve	49	410	40	440	22	560	1/9	19/1	1/14
Crab leg nerve	52	410	26	510	12	540	1/10	34/1	1/21
Frog sartorius muscle	10	140	4	120	2.5	120	1/12	56/1	1/30

extracellular solution (Fig. 4-34). Since the cell interior contains impermeant anions in the form of proteins, with a preponderance of negative sites, such as carboxyl, the KCl distribution is such that K^+ is more concentrated inside and Cl^- less concentrated inside than in the extracellular solution.

As noted earlier (p. 95), one type of Na pump exchanges extracellular K^+ for intracellular Na^+. Because of the relatively high permeability of the membrane for K^+, this ion immediately redistributes itself passively, and the active uptake of K^+ has little direct effect on the intracellular potassium concentration.

Pinocytosis and Exocytosis

Membranes of some cells can transfer minute bulk quantities of material into or out of the cell. The membrane does this by first trapping the material on one side of itself in a vesicle formed from a tiny invagination or evagination. The vesicle then pinches off, isolating the material on the other side of the membrane (Fig. 4-35). Digestion or rupture of the vesicle liberates the contents. When the transfer is from cell exterior to interior, it is termed *pinocytosis;* when the transfer is from the interior to exterior, it is termed *exocytosis.* The ingestion of large particles of solid material in this manner by ameboid cells (i.e., amoebae, white blood cells, etc.) is termed *phagocytosis.* This can be stimulated to occur at a high rate in *Amoeba* by the addition of certain proteins, such as gamma globulins, to the medium.

A form of exocytosis plays an important role in the nervous system (Chapter 6). The presynaptic terminals of nerve cells (p. 168) contain many membrane-limited internal vesicles about 500 Å in diameter, which contain the neural transmitter substance. It now appears that these vesicles can coalesce with the surface membrane of the nerve terminal and release their contents to the cell exterior. This occurs with greatly enhanced probability when the terminal is invaded by a nerve impulse and serves to release the synaptic transmitter that interacts with the postsynaptic membrane.

Implicit in the theory of exocytosis is that the membrane of the vesicle is incorporated into the surface membrane, allowing all of the free contents—hormones and accessory molecules—to diffuse away into the interstitial space. This raises the question of what keeps the surface area of the plasma membrane from continually growing with the addition of new vesicle membranes. The answer appears to be that new *microvesicles* are formed by pinocytotic budding from the surface membrane, as suggested in Figure 11-6. Evidence favoring the formation of new secretory vesicles

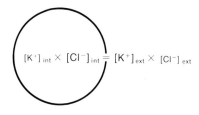

4–34. *The KCl product. The distribution of K^+ and Cl^- will be governed by Donnan equilibrium, provided the membrane is permeable to Cl^- and does not actively transport this ion.*

$$[K^+]_{int} \times [Cl^-]_{int} = [K^+]_{ext} \times [Cl^-]_{ext}$$

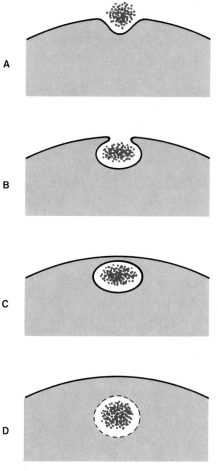

4–35. *Stages of vesicle formation during pinocytosis. A. Invagination begins. C. Vesicle pinches off. D. Vesicle membrane disintegrates, releasing engulfed material.*

4-36. *Possible role of microtubules in secretion, as hypothesized for pancreatic beta cells. The microtubules, often seen at secretory sites with vesicles attached in series, may propel the vesicles to the membrane in an energy-requiring process regulated by calcium ions. Different stages are shown from top to bottom. [After Lacy, 1971.]*

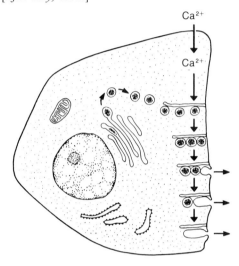

4-37. *Possible role of neurostennin in secretion of transmitter substance at nerve terminals. The protein stennin, which exhibits ATPase activity, is associated with the vesicles; the protein neurin is associated with the cell membrane. It is postulated that Ca-sensitive ATPase activity of the neurostennin complex liberates the energy from ATP required for exocytosis.*

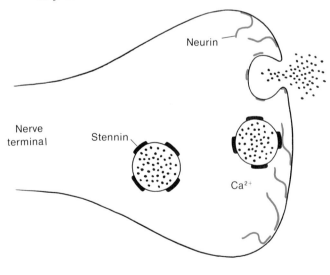

by this kind of pinocytotic process comes to us from experiments in which a large electron-opaque molecule, *horseradish peroxidase*, is introduced into the extracellular fluid and its progress followed with electron-microscopical methods. It subsequently appears inside the cell only within vesicles. Since the large size of the horseradish peroxidase molecule prevents its penetration by direct passage across biological membranes, it must be taken up in bulk by a process similar to pinocytosis during the formation of the microvesicles—that is, while they are budding off from the plasmalemma into the cytoplasm. It is not now known whether this occurs immediately after exocytosis and at the same site, so that the old vesicle membrane becomes incorporated into new vesicles, or at some other place on the surface membrane.

The vesicle membrane itself may participate actively in the initial steps leading to exocytosis. The secretory granules of the adrenal medulla (Chapter 11) have been found to be rich in an unusual phospholipid, *lysolecithin*, which facilitates the fusion of membranes and thus may help the vesicle membrane fuse with the surface membrane. Before fusion of the two membranes can take place, the secretory granule (or vesicle) must come into contact with the plasmalemma. Release of secretory products can be blocked by *colchicine*, an antimitotic agent that leads to the disassembly of microtubules, or by *cytochalasin*, an agent that disrupts microfilaments. This pharmacological evidence has led to the suggestion that microtubules or microfilaments participate in the movement of secretory granules toward sites of exocytotic release on the inner side of the surface membrane (Fig. 4-36). Although there is some doubt as to the specificity of these pharmacological agents, secretory vesicles are often seen associated with microtubules in the electron microscope.

An exciting lead in the search for the mechanism of exocytosis is the identification of two proteins in nerve endings isolated from mammalian brain by Berl et al. (1973). One, termed *stennin*, is associated with the synaptic vesicles, has properties similar to the muscle protein myosin, and exhibits ATPase activity. The other, termed *neurin*, is a filamentous protein similar to muscle actin, and appears to be attached to the inner surface of the plasmalemma. In the presence of Ca^{2+}, these two proteins interact as *neurostennin*, and it has been suggested that this interaction brings the secretory vesicle into contact with the inner surface of the plasmalemma as a key step in the secretory process. This idea is combined with the concept of exocytosis in Figure 4-37, as an alternative to the microtubule hypothesis shown in the previous figure.

Membrane Regulation of Metabolic Activity

CALCIUM AND METABOLIC REGULATION

By regulating the intracellular concentrations of inorganic ions, the cell membrane indirectly controls many intracellular reactions, ranging from energy metabolism to muscle contraction. This is possible because ions, especially certain of the divalent metal cations, act as cofactors in many enzymatic reactions. In recent years the calcium ion has been implicated as a rate-limiting agent in a number of cellular functions. The intracellular Ca^{2+} concentration is normally kept very low by outward transport and by calcium-sequestering mechanisms inside the cell (Box 4-3). For this reason, relatively small increments in the absolute calcium concentration in the cytosol can produce large increases in the relative concentration of this ion (Fig. 4-38). By permitting a transient increase in the influx of Ca^{2+} in response to certain stimuli, cell membranes can exert control over metabolic functions. For example, both the activation of the contractile mechanism in smooth muscle and the release of hormones from endocrine cells depend on the influx of Ca^{2+} through the excited surface membrane. In vertebrate skeletal muscle and in mammalian heart, the calcium that activates contraction is released from intracellular membrane-limited compartments. Other examples of Ca-regulated cell functions will be given in later chapters.

Membrane-regulated Ca^{2+} also plays a role in the control of energy metabolism. It does this at two known points and perhaps at others along the pathways leading from the breakdown of glycogen to the production of ATP (Fig. 3-42). Calcium ions are required as a cofactor for the enzyme phosphorylase *a*, which catalyses the breakdown of glycogen to glucose-6-phosphate, the raw material for glycolysis. Moreover, Ca^{2+} has been shown to increase the rate of respiratory chain phosphorylation in mitochondria. An increase in intracellular $[Ca^{2+}]$ is therefore able to accelerate the breakdown of glycogen stores and increase the rate of respiratory chain phosphorylation, thereby increasing the production of ATP.

The effect of Ca^{2+} on metabolism in living cells can be monitored indirectly by measuring the fluorescence (ultraviolet-stimulated visible light emission) of reduced pyridine nucleotide (NADH). Since the oxidized form (NAD) of the nucleotide does not fluoresce, the reduction of NAD to NADH (p. 67) can be followed photometrically. With this technique it has been shown that membrane excitation (production of action potentials) in nerves leads to increased energy metabolism as indicated by an increase in fluorescence

associated with increased levels of NADH. This effect is abolished when Ca^{2+} is removed from the external medium (Fig. 4-39). With each nerve impulse, there is a small calcium influx (10^{-14} moles/cm^2 of cell membrane).

MEMBRANE-BOUND ENZYMES

It was noted earlier in this chapter that membranes perform catalytic functions by means of enzymes associated with the lipid bilayer. A familiar example exists in the enzymes that govern the electron transport and respiratory chain phosphorylation associated

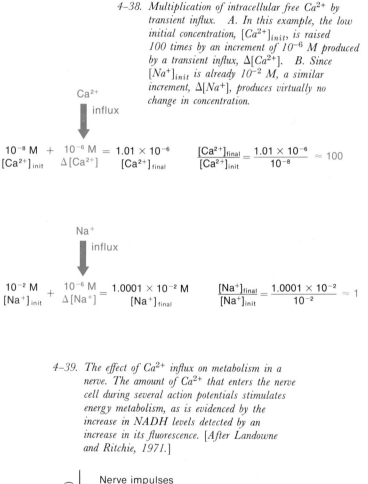

4-38. *Multiplication of intracellular free Ca^{2+} by transient influx. A. In this example, the low initial concentration, $[Ca^{2+}]_{init}$, is raised 100 times by an increment of 10^{-6} M produced by a transient influx, $\Delta[Ca^{2+}]$. B. Since $[Na^+]_{init}$ is already 10^{-2} M, a similar increment, $\Delta[Na^+]$, produces virtually no change in concentration.*

4-39. *The effect of Ca^{2+} influx on metabolism in a nerve. The amount of Ca^{2+} that enters the nerve cell during several action potentials stimulates energy metabolism, as is evidenced by the increase in NADH levels detected by an increase in its fluorescence. [After Landowne and Ritchie, 1971.]*

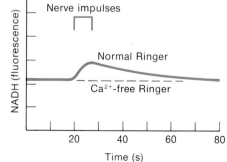

BOX 4-3   CALCIUM AS A MEMBRANE MESSENGER

Before his death in 1959, L. V. Heilbrunn was the pioneering advocate of Ca^{2+} as the agent responsible for regulating many intracellular functions. This idea was somewhat ahead of its time, because the techniques for manipulating Ca^{2+} in low concentrations had not yet been developed. We now know that he was essentially correct in major respects, although in his lifetime his proposals were considered somewhat extreme and controversial.

Although the *total* Ca^{2+} content of most cells is not particularly low, it has become an almost universal principle that the activity, or free ionized concentration of Ca^{2+}, $[Ca^{2+}]_i$, in the cytosol is maintained at extraordinarily low levels, usually well below 10^{-6} M. Extracellular $[Ca^{2+}]$ is typically 10^{-2} M. The discrepancy between total and free intracellular concentrations of Ca^{2+} arises in part from the sequestering of Ca^{2+} within such membrane-bound organelles as mitochondria and reticulum. Certain agents, if allowed to enter the cell, cause a release of Ca^{2+} from those stores and thereby cause a rise in $[Ca^{2+}]_i$. These agents include caffeine, theophylline, ruthenium red, lithium, abnormally high $[Na^+]_i$, and, depending on the cell type, increased or decreased cAMP. Anything that interferes with energy metabolism slows active transport of Ca^{2+}, and thereby also leads to a rise in $[Ca^{2+}]_i$. The low concentration of free Ca^{2+} is possible, of course, only because of uphill transport of Ca^{2+} against very large concentration differences.

The strategy behind maintaining a very low $[Ca^{2+}]_i$ is quite simple. Numerous intracellular functions are highly sensitive to changes in the concentration of Ca^{2+}. With $[Ca^{2+}]_i$ very low, small increments in the *amount* of free Ca^{2+} result in large *percentage* increments in free Ca^{2+}. This is illustrated by comparing the relative changes in $[Ca^{2+}]_i$ and $[Na^+]_i$ that result from the entrance of equal quantities of these two ion species into the cell in response to a transient increase in the permeability of the membrane to both ions (Fig. 4-38). In this example, $[CA^{2+}]_i$ undergoes a 100-fold increase. Thus a small influx of Ca^{2+} can produce a large effect on the free Ca^{2+} concentration.

Agents or stimuli (i.e., hormones, potential changes) that act on the membrane to increase its permeability to Ca^{2+} by this means produce an increase in $[Ca^{2+}]_i$ and stimulate the Ca-sensitive reactions in the cell. Calcium may therefore be thought of as a *coupling agent* or *messenger* between stimuli acting on the cell membrane and processes that take place deep inside the cell.

Two technical advances have been very helpful in recent studies of the physiological functions of Ca^{2+}. The first makes it possible to adjust $[Ca^{2+}]$ at concentrations below the levels of normal Ca contamination of distilled water (i.e., $<10^{-5}$ M Ca^{2+}). This is done by adding known amounts of both $CaCl_2$ and a calcium chelating agent, such as EGTA or EDTA,* to a solution. This produces a *pCa buffer system* analogous to that of a pH buffer. The $CaCl_2$ behaves like the strong acid, and the Ca-EGTA or Ca-EDTA (which dissociate extremely weakly) acts like the weak acid. By this means, free Ca^{2+} can be buffered at, for example, 10^{-8} M in the face of much larger quantities of total Ca^{2+}.

The other important methodological advance was the discovery in 1963 of a jellyfish protein named *aequorin*, which emits light when it complexes with Ca^{2+}. Since light can be measured with very sensitive instruments, injection of aequorin into cells has provided a means of detecting minute changes in the intracellular free Ca^{2+} levels.

*EGTA = ethyleneglycol-*bis*(β-aminoethylether)-N,N'-tetraacetic acid;   EDTA = ethylenediaminetetraacetic acid.

with the inner mitochondrial membrane. Other examples are the active transport ATPases of the surface membrane.

Intensive investigations have recently focused on adenylate cyclase, a ubiquitous enzyme that converts ATP into cyclic AMP (cAMP). The importance of cyclic AMP as the "second messenger" for certain hormones and its wide-ranging role in cell metabolism are considered in Chapter 11. In his initial studies on cyclic AMP, Sutherland noted that the activity of adenylate cyclase (and hence cyclic AMP production) in cell-free homogenates of liver is activated by hormones that stimulate the enzyme when applied to the exterior of intact cells. He then examined the various fractions of the cell-free homogenate of liver tissue and found that adenylate cyclase activity disappears if the cell membrane fragments of the homogenate are removed. In other words, the enzyme is intimately associated with the membrane. In this context, it is interesting to note that cyclic AMP does not penetrate the surface membrane if placed in the extracellular fluid (an analogue, dibutyryl cAMP) does enter as a result of enhanced lipid solubility). Furthermore, there is evidence that hormones that stimulate adenylate cyclase activity do so without entering the cell. Thus it appears that the hormone acts on the outer surface of the cell membrane and that the cyclic AMP derived from ATP is produced at the inner surface of the membrane. The scheme shown in Figure 11-37 assumes that the receptor-enzyme complex extends through the lipid bilayer, with its enzymatic active site exposed on the intracellular side of the membrane and its hormone-receptor site exposed on the outer surface of the membrane. A hormone molecule that binds to the extracellular receptor site appears to activate the intracellular enzymatic site by an allosteric mechanism.

Cell–Cell Membrane Junctions

In certain tissues, including epithelium, smooth muscle, cardiac muscle, central nervous tissues, and many embryonic tissues, cells are sometimes connected to their neighbors by specializations of apposed surface membranes. These specializations are of two major types, termed *gap junctions* and *tight junctions* (Figs. 4-40, 4-41).

GAP JUNCTIONS

The distance between two membranes of a gap junction is only 20 Å, whereas the membranes at a gap junction are connected by a hexagonal array of sub-units about 50 Å in diameter (Fig. 4-42) that resemble miniature donuts whose hollow centers form passageways between the interior of one cell and the interior of the neighboring cell. The gap junction permits the passage of ions and molecules between cells. The continuity of the cell–cell passageways through the gap junction has been demonstrated by the injection of a fluorescent dye, such as fluorescene (mol. wt. 332) and procion yellow (mol. wt. 500), into one cell and following its diffusion into the neighboring cells (Fig. 4-43). This has been corroborated for direct exchange of ions by the finding that electric current readily passes directly from one cell into another if gap junctions are present (p. 166). Since the intercellular channels in these junctions appear to pass molecules of at least molecular weight 500, it is possible that they may also pass long, thin informational molecules such as messenger RNA in cell–cell communication.

Gap junctions are labile, and are uncoupled by any treatment that increases the intracellular level of the divalent cations Ca^{2+} and Mg^{2+}. This has been demonstrated by direct injection of Ca^{2+} or Mg^{2+} into a coupled cell, by lowering temperature, or, by the use of poisons that inhibit energy metabolism. Uncoupling of cells from their neighbors is indicated in these experiments by the loss of electrical transmission between cells. Thus gap junctions are maintained intact only if the metabolic activity of the surface membrane maintains sufficiently low concentrations of intracellular free Ca^{2+} and Mg^{2+}.

TIGHT JUNCTIONS

In tight junctions, the outer surfaces of the two apposing cell membranes make nearly direct contact (Fig. 4-40,C), occluding the extracellular space between the adjacent cells at the points of contact. Tight junctions are found most commonly in epithelial tissues in the form of a *zonula occludens,* which completely encircles each cell, eliminating any direct extracellular passage between the two surfaces of an epithelial tissue. The zonula occludens is important in transport epithelia (Chapter 12), for it eliminates leakage past the cells situated between the two sides of an epithelium and requires that all substances pass through the membrane and cytoplasm of the epithelial cells. Unlike gap junctions, tight junctions appear to have no special channels for cell–cell communication.

Two other types of cell junction, shown in Figure 4-41, are the *zonula adherens* and the *macula adherens* (more commonly termed *desmosome*). These junctions serve primarily in the function of structural bonding of neighboring cells.

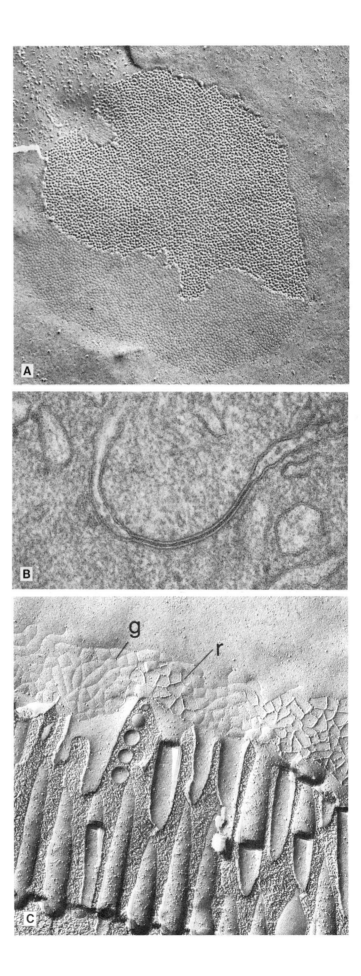

4-40. *Electron micrographs showing junctions between membranes of neighboring cells. A. Freeze-fracture preparation of a gap junction between pancreatic cells in guinea pig, showing characteristic densely packed particles. Note that a fragment of the uppermost membrane is fractured away, giving a view of the particles that connected it with the membrane of the adjacent cell below, which is now visible. Pits associated with the particles can be seen in the surrounding portions of the upper membrane. Magnification 78,500×. B. Transverse thin section showing gap junction between two mouse liver cells. Note close apposition of unit membranes and the connecting particles. 130,000×. C. Freeze-fracture preparation from rat small intestine showing lacework of tight junctions connecting two epithelial cells, one above and one below the plane of cleavage. The grooves (g) belong to the upper cell and the corresponding ridges (r) to the lower cell. The cylindrical projections at the bottom are the microvilli (mv) of the epithelial cells. Magnification 55,000×. [Courtesy of N. B. Gilula and D. S. Friend.]*

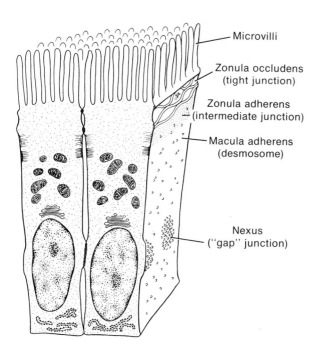

Microvilli

Zonula occludens
(tight junction)

Zonula adherens
(intermediate junction)

Macula adherens
(desmosome)

Nexus
("gap" junction)

4-41. *Artist's reconstruction of intercellular junctions found between adjacent epithelial cells like those that line the mammalian small intestine. The membranes and associated structures are drawn disproportionately large. [After Weinstein and McNutt, 1972.]*

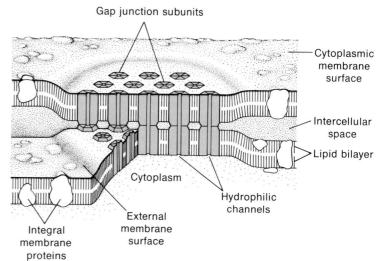

Gap junction subunits

Cytoplasmic membrane surface

Intercellular space

Lipid bilayer

Cytoplasm

Hydrophilic channels

Integral membrane proteins

External membrane surface

4-42. *Diagram of a gap junction. The two membranes each contain an array of hexagonal subunits, each of which connects with a matching subunit in the apposed membrane. A channel appears to penetrate both subunits, providing a path of communication between the connected cells. [After Staehelin, 1974.]*

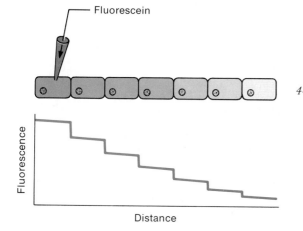

Fluorescein

A

B

Fluorescence

Distance

4-43. *Injection of fluorescent dye in one cell of a group of electrically coupled epithelial cells of insect salivary gland. Subsequent diffusion of the dye into neighboring cells without loss into extracellular space indicates that there are direct pathways from the cytoplasm of one cell to the cytoplasm of the adjacent cell. Gap junctions can invariably be found between such coupled cells.*

Summary

Membranes form one class of fundamental structures of the cell. They form not only the surface but serve as the structural bases of numerous cellular organelles. They are responsible for (1) cellular and subcellular compartmentalization, (2) maintenance of the intracellular milieu by virtue of selective permeability and transport mechanisms, (3) regulating cell metabolism by determining the concentrations of enzyme cofactors and substrates, (4) metabolic activities carried out by enzymes that are often present in ordered arrays in or on the membrane, (5) electric signals that conduct messages and/or regulate the transport of substances across the membrane, and (6) endo- and exocytosis of bulk material.

The foundation structure of membranes is a lipid bilayer in which the hydrophilic "heads" of the phospholipid molecules face outward and the lipophilic "tails" face inward, toward the center of the bilayer. The most widely accepted model of membrane structure has a "mosaic" of globular proteins, including enzymes, penetrating the bilayer.

Permeability is a measure of the ease with which a substance traverses a membrane. There are several ways in which substances cross the membrane. Water and some small polar molecules diffuse very slowly through transient aqueous channels created by thermal motion. Nonpolar molecules can diffuse more readily through the lipid phase of the membrane. There is evidence for the existence of fixed channels that are more-or-less specific for certain ions and molecules. Diffusion of some substances across the membrane can occur via carrier molecules that complex with the substance, facilitating its movement across the membrane while the carrier shuttles within the lipid phase of the membrane.

Active transport of a substance occurs by means of carriers, and requires metabolic energy, usually provided by ATP. It is responsible for the movement of a substance across a membrane against a concentration gradient. The most familiar active transport system is the sodium "pump," which maintains the intracellular Na^+ concentration below that of the cell exterior. The energy stored in the form of an extracellular/intracellular Na^+ concentration gradient is utilized to "drive" the uphill movement of a number of other substances, such as calcium ions, amino acids, and sugars by means of exchange diffusion and coupled transport. The Na^+ gradient is also important for the production of electric signals, such as nerve impulses.

Surface membranes and the intracellular membrane that enclose such organelles as mitochondria exert control on metabolic activities by regulating the concentrations of substances that affect enzyme activity. Most notable is the regulation of the intracellular calcium ion concentration at levels below 1 μmole/liter (typically between 10^{-8} and 10^{-6} mole/liter). Various cellular processes that are sensitive to small increments in the intracellular calcium ion concentration are controlled by changes in the permeability of the membrane to calcium ions, and hence changes in the net flux of Ca^{2+} between cell interior and exterior.

The surface membrane also contains protein complexes that have receptor components specific for blood-borne stimulus substances such as certain hormones or substrate molecules. It is believed that these substances interact with the receptor molecules in such a way that they allosterically influence enzymatic activities of active sites of enzymes in the protein complex—sites that project into the cytoplasmic side of the membrane. By such means, extracellular substances can influence metabolic events on the inner surface of the membrane.

EXERCISES

1. What are some of the physiological functions of membranes?

2. What is the evidence for the existence of membranes as real physical barriers?

3. What is the evidence for the lipid bilayer model of the membrane?

4. What is the evidence for a mosaic of globular proteins set into the lipid bilayer of the membrane?

5. What factors determine the permeability of the membrane to a given electrolyte? Nonelectrolyte?

6. Describe the probable mechanisms by which water and other small ($<10\mathring{A}$ diam.) polar molecules pass through the membrane.

7. Why do nonpolar substances diffuse more easily than polar substances through the membrane?

8. Active transport and facilitated diffusion both show saturation kinetics. What does this tell us about the mechanisms underlying these two kinds of transport?

9. How does facilitated diffusion differ from simple diffusion?

10. What factors influence the rate of facilitated diffusion of ions across a membrane?

11. How does active transport differ from facilitated diffusion?

12. Why can the sodium concentration gradient be considered a common cellular energy currency?

13. What are some parameters by which the membrane discriminates between ions of the same charge?

14. Explain the osmotic consequences of poisoning the metabolism of a cell.

15. How does the cell maintain a higher concentration of K^+ inside the cell than in the extracellular fluid?

16. What is the significance of the low intracellular concentration of free Ca^{2+} in the control of energy metabolism and other cell functions?

17. How do hormones cause metabolic changes within a cell without physically entering the cell?

18. What are the morphological and functional distinctions between gap and tight junctions?

19. A given cell is 40 times as permeable to K^+ and Cl^- as to any other ions present. If the inside/outside ratio of K^+ is 25, what would the approximate inside/outside ratio of Cl^- be?

SUGGESTED READING

Green, D. E., and J. F. Danielli (eds.) 1972. *Membrane Structure and its Biological Applications.* New York Acad. Sciences.

Cereijido, M., and C. A. Rotunno. 1970. *Introduction to the Study of Biological Membranes.* Gordon & Breach, Science Publishers, New York.

Jain, M. K. 1972. *The Bimolecular Lipid Membrane: A System.* Van Nostrand Reinhold, New York.

Levine, Y. K. 1972. Physical studies of membrane structure. *Progr. Biophys. Mol. Biol.* 24:1–74.

Lightfoot, E. N. 1974. *Transport Phenomena and Living Systems.* Wiley, New York.

Lockwood, A. P. M. 1971. *The Membranes of Animal Cells.* Edward Arnold, London.

Sleigh, M.A., and D. H. Jennings. 1974. *Transport at the Cellular Level.* (Symposia of the Society for Experimental Biology, No. 28.) Cambridge Univ. Press, New York.

Solomon, A. K. 1962. Pumps in the living cell. *Scientific American* 207(2):100–118. [Also available as Offprint 131.]

Vanderkooi, G., and D. E. Green. 1971. New insights into biological membrane structure. *BioScience* 21 (9):409–415.

Weissmann, G., and R. Clairborne. (eds.). 1975. *Cell Membranes.* Hospital Practice Publishing Co., New York.

REFERENCES CITED

Briggs, G. E. 1963. Rate of uptake of salts by plant cells in relation to an anion pump. *J. Exp. Botany* 14:1191.

Collander, R. 1937. The permeability of plant protoplasts to non-electrolytes. *Trans. Faraday Soc.* 33:985–990.

Davson, H. 1970. *A Textbook of General Physiology* (4th ed.). Churchill, London.

Davson, H., and J. F. Danielli. 1943. *The Permeability of Natural Membranes.* Cambridge Univ. Press, New York.

Diamond, J. M., and E. M. Wright. 1969. Biological membranes: The physical basis of ion and non-electrolyte selectivity. *Ann. Rev. Physiol.* 31:581–646.

Dunham, P. B., and J. F. Hoffman. 1970. Partial purification of the ouabain-binding component and of Na, K-ATPase from human red cell membranes. *Proc. Nat. Acad. Sci.* 66:936–943.

Gorter, E., and F. Grendel. 1925. On bimolecular layers of lipoids on the chromocytes of blood. *J. Exp. Med.* 41:439–443.

Kotyk, A., and K. Janácek. 1970. *Cell Membrane Transport.* Plenum Press. New York.

Landowne, D., and J. M. Ritchie. 1971. On the control of glycogenolysis in mammalian nervous tissue by calcium. *J. Physiol.* 212:503–517.

Länger, P. 1972. Carrier-mediated ion transport. *Science* 178:24.

Lehninger, A. L. 1970. *Biochemistry.* Worth, New York.

Nägeli, K. W. 1884. *Mechanish-Physiologische Theorie der Abstammungslehre.* Oldenbourg, München.

Overton, E. 1902. Beitrage zur allgmeinen Muskel und Nervenphysiologie. *Pflüger's Arch. Ges. Physiol.* 92:115–280.

Overton, E. 1899. Vierteljahresschr. Naturforsch. Ges. Zurich 44:88.

Peters, A., and J. E. Vaughn. 1970. Morphology and development of the myelin sheath. *In* D. N. Davison and A. Peters (eds.), *Myelination.* Charles C. Thomas, Springfield.

Pfeffer, W. F. P. 1899. *Osmotische Unterschungen.* Engleman, Leipzig, Germany.

Robertson, J. D. 1960. The molecular structure and contact relationships of cell membranes. *Progr. Biophys.* 10:343–418.

Schultz, S. G., and P. F. Curran. 1969. The role of sodium in non-electrolyte transport across animal cell membranes. *The Physiologist* 12:437–452.

Singer, S. J., and G. L. Nicolson. 1972. The fluid mosaic model of the structure of cell membranes. *Science* 175:720–731.

Sleigh, M. A., and D. H. Jennings. 1974. *Transport at the Cellular Level* (Society for Experimental Biologists Symposia Ser., No. 28). Cambridge Univ. Press, New York.

Solomon, A. K. 1960. Pores in the cell membrane. *Scientific American 203*(6):146–156. [Also available as Offprint 76.]

Staehelin, L. A. 1974. Structure and function of intercellular junctions. *Int. Rev. Cytol.* 39:191–283.

Stein, W. D. 1967. *The Movement of Molecules Across Cell Membranes.* Academic Press, New York.

Sutherland, E. W. 1970. On the biological role of cyclic AMP. *J. Am. Med. Assoc.* 714:1281–1288.

Sutherland, E. W., G. A. Robison, and R. W. Butcher. 1971. *Cyclic AMP.* Academic Press, New York.

Weinstein, R. S., and N. S. McNutt. 1972. Cell junctions. *New England Journal of Medicine* 286:521–524.

CHAPTER FIVE

Ions and Impulses

The origin of electrochemical theory and the discovery that living tissues produce electric currents can both be traced to observations made late in the eighteenth century by Luigi Galvani, a professor of anatomy at Bologna, Italy. Working with a nerve-muscle preparation from a frog leg, Galvani noted that muscles contract when dissimilar metals in contact with each other are brought into contact with the tissue, one metal touching the muscle and the other touching the nerve. Galvani and his nephew Giovanni Aldini ascribed this response to a discharge of "animal electricity" delivered by the nerves and stored in the muscle. They postulated that an "electric fluid" passed from the muscle through the metal and back into the nerve, and that the discharge of electricity from the muscle triggered the contraction. This interpretation, published in 1791, was largely incorrect in retrospect; nevertheless, this work provided the stimulus that led many inquisitive amateur and professional scientists of that revolutionary age to investigate two new and important areas of science, the physiology of excitation in nerve and muscle and the chemical origin of electricity.

Alessandro Volta, a physicist at Pavia, Italy, quickly took up Galvani's experiments and in 1792 proposed that the electric stimulus leading to contraction in Galvani's experiments came not from a discharge of current from the tissue, as claimed by Galvani and Aldini, but was in fact generated outside the tissue by the contact of dissimilar metals with the saline fluids of the tissue. It took several years for Volta to demonstrate unequivocally the electrolytic origin of electric currents from dissimilar metals, for there was no physical instrument available at that time sufficiently sensitive to detect weak currents. Indeed, the nerve-muscle preparation from the frog leg was probably the most sensitive indicator of electric current then available.

In his search for a means of producing stronger sources of electricity, Volta found that he could avoid having to use Galvani's nerve-muscle preparation by multiplying the current with a series of metal-saline cells. The fruit of his labor was the so-called Voltaic pile—a stack of alternating silver and zinc plates separated by saline-soaked papers. This first "wet-cell" battery produced proportionately higher voltages

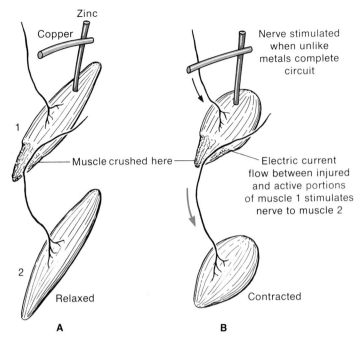

5–1. *Experiment performed by Matteucci in which the current produced in the upper muscle during a twitch stimulated the nerve to the lower muscle, causing the latter to twitch also. The upper muscle was activated in B by stimulating its motor nerve directly with current produced by electrolysis between dissimilar metals.*

5–2. *The oscilloscope. A beam of electrons "writes" on the phosphor screen while driven from left to right by a gradually changing sawtooth voltage. Signals applied to the oscilloscope input are amplified and fed to the vertical deflection plates. Vertical deflection of the beam allows the signal voltage to be plotted against time.*

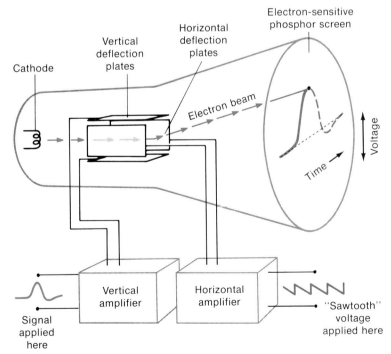

than can be produced by a single silver-zinc cell.

Galvani's original experiments did not really prove the existence of "animal electricity," but did demonstrate the sensitivity of excitable tissues to minute electric currents. In 1840, Carlo Matteucci used the action current of a contracting muscle to stimulate a second nerve-muscle preparation (Fig. 5-1). His experiment was the first recorded demonstration that excitable tissue produces electric current.

Since the nineteenth century, it has become evident that the production and processing of all signals in the nervous system and the contraction of muscle depend on the electrical properties of cell membranes.

Methods of Electrical Stimulation and Recording

Electrical phenomena* in the tissues of the nervous system and in muscle can be detected by placing two electrodes in the tissue to measure the flow of electric currents through the extracellular fluids. Since these currents originate across cell membranes, a more direct and quantitative approach is to measure electrical events across the membrane of a single cell. This is done by comparing the electric potential (voltage) of one side of the membrane with that of the other side. Subtracting one from the other gives the *potential difference*, which is commonly called the *membrane potential*. One sensing electrode is placed in electrical continuity with one side of the membrane, and another in electrical continuity with the other side of the membrane. In this way the potential difference can be detected and electronically amplified for display on a recording instrument, such as an oscilloscope (Fig. 5-2). This was impossible to do satisfactorily except in certain very large cells until Ling and Gerard (1949) perfected the glass capillary *microelectrode* (Fig. 5-3,A). Because of its minute tip diameter, this type of electrode can be passed through the surface membranes of many kinds of cells with negligible damage to the membrane.

Once the fine capillary tip has penetrated the membrane, the cytoplasm is in continuity with the wire leading into the amplifier via a fine column of electrolyte that fills the inside of the capillary electrode, usually a 3 M solution of KCl. Thus the intracellular potential can be compared to that of the extracellular fluid. The membrane potential, V_m, is always given as the intracellular potential minus the extracellular potential.

*A review of the electrical definitions and conventions on p. 27 may be useful before continuing.

5-3. *Glass capillary microelectrodes inserted through the membrane of a cell. The electrode at the left passes current into or out of the cell. Current flows in a circuit through the wires, bath, electrodes, and cell membrane. The high-ohm resistor has far greater resistance than the other resistances in the stimulating circuit, and therefore maintains the constancy of the stimulating current. The recording amplifier has a very high input resistance, preventing any appreciable current from leaving the cell through the recording electrode.*

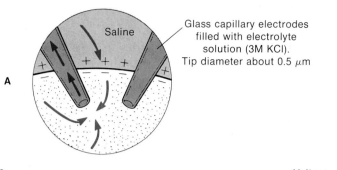

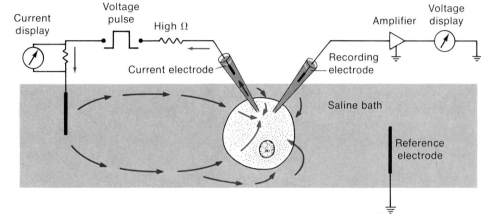

A simple stimulating and recording arrangement is shown in Figure 5-3,B. A cell is immersed in a physiological saline solution that is connected by means of a reference electrode to a point held at "ground" potential. Before the tip of the recording microelectrode enters the cell, the microelectrode and the reference electrode are at the same potential. The potential then recorded by the microelectrode is defined as zero (Fig. 5-4,A). As the tip of the microelectrode is advanced, a negative voltage, or potential, suddenly appears on the voltage display, indicating penetration of the surface membrane (Fig. 5-4,B; in electrophysiological recordings, negative potentials are conventionally shown as downward displacements on the oscilloscope screen). The steady negativity recorded by the electrode tip in the cytoplasm is the *resting potential* of the cell membrane, and is given in *millivolts* (mV, thousandths of a volt). Resting potentials of various cells range from as little as -10 mV to as much as about -100 mV.

The potential sensed by the intracellular electrode does not change as the tip is advanced further into the cell. Thus the entire potential difference between the cell interior and cell exterior exists across the surface membrane.

The electrical properties of the cell membrane can be examined by passing a pulse of current through the membrane to produce a perturbation in the membrane potential. A second microelectrode, the current electrode, delivers the stimulating current (Fig. 5-3,B, left). This current can be made to flow across

5-4. *A. Outside of the cell, the electrode records zero potential difference with respect to the reference level. B. Upon penetrating the membrane, the electrode records a negative potential difference. The negative resting potential is shown as a downward deflection on the oscilloscope screen.*

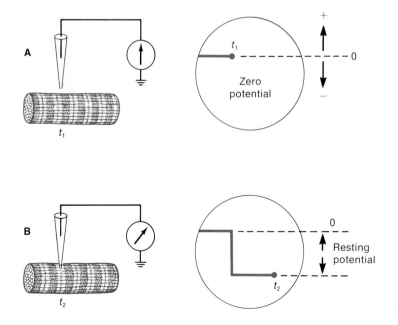

5-5. The cell membrane is able to separate charges
because it is very thin. The charges form a
diffuse layer on each side and interact electrostatically across the thin barrier.

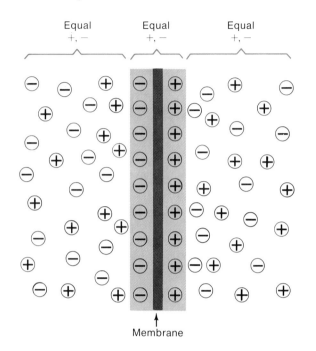

Membrane

the membrane in either the inward (bath to cytoplasm) or the outward (cytoplasm to bath) direction,*
depending on the polarity of the electric current applied to the electrode.

Passive Membrane Properties and Electrotonic Potentials

It was shown in the previous chapter that membranes
act as barriers to the free diffusion of various substances, including all ions. The rate at which ions
traverse a membrane is as much as 10^8 times lower
than the average rate at which they diffuse across an
equivalent distance (50–100 Å) of cytoplasm or extracellular fluid. Since electric current in an aqueous
solution is a flow of ions, the relatively low mobility
of ions through the lipid bilayer is equivalent to a
high electrical resistance. *Membrane resistance* is a measure of the ease with which ions move across the membrane under the influence of a potential difference,

*As was noted in Chapter 2, all the current carried in
solution and through the membrane is in the form of migrating ions. By convention, the flow of ionic current is from
a region of relative positivity to one of relative negativity,
and corresponds to the direction of cation migration.

and is one of the two physical properties that underlie
the passive electrical behavior of cell membranes.

MEMBRANE CAPACITANCE

Because they are very thin (<150 Å) and are virtually
impermeable to ions over most of their surface areas,
cell membranes are able to violate the principle of
electroneutrality at the microscopic level. In the bulk
phase of a solution, the number of positive charges
must equal the number of negative charges. Thus
one cannot make a pure solution of NaCl that contains appreciably more Na^+ than Cl^- or vice versa.
Nevertheless, because membranes are so thin, they
can separate charge on a submicroscopic scale. Negative charges accumulated at or near one surface of a
membrane will interact electrostatically over the short
distance of membrane thickness with positive charges
on the other side (Fig. 5-5). The ability of membranes
to accumulate and separate charge gives rise to the
second important electrical property, which is termed
membrane capacitance (Box 5-1).

Capacitance increases in proportion to the dielectric constant of the material separating the charges,
and decreases with increasing distance between
charges. Most membranes appear to contain a layer
of lipid about 50 Å thick. If we assume that the lipid
has a dielectric constant of 3, which is about that
of an 18-carbon fatty acid, the membrane capacitance can be calculated to be about 1 microfarad
($1 \mu F = 10^{-6}$ F) per cm^2. Measured values for membranes range from 1 to 3 $\mu F/cm^2$.

It is helpful to conceptualize the properties resistance and capacitance in the form of an *equivalent
circuit* (Fig. 5-6,A) in which a capacitor is wired in
parallel with a resistor. The resistor represents the
hydrophilic ion—permeable channels or carriers of the
membrane, and the capacitor represents the major
area of lipid bilayer, which is impermeable to ions.

The properties of membrane resistance and capacitance can be illustrated with the experimental setup
shown in Figure 5-3,B. Consider a current of constant
intensity, ΔI (amperes), passed across the membrane
from the reference electrode in the bath to the current
electrode in the cell. This current is applied as a square
pulse with an abrupt onset. All the current must pass
through the membrane to make a complete circuit.
While crossing the membrane, the current distributes
itself between the parallel resistance and capacitance
of the membrane (Fig. 5-6,A).

The response of the membrane to an applied pulse
of current, shown in Figure 5-6,B, is termed an *electrotonic potential*, which refers to the potential change
produced by the current flowing through the fundamental capacitance and resistance of the membrane.

MEMBRANE RESISTANCE
AND CONDUCTANCE

The membrane potential shifts in response to a step of constant current with an exponential time course toward a steady-state level as the current charges the membrane capacitance (Box 5-1). The displacement, ΔV_m (or ΔE_m) of the membrane potential from the resting value to the asymptotic value is a function of both the magnitude of the applied current (ΔI) and the resistance (R) that the current encounters as it passes across the membrane of a cell. The relationship between applied current, resistance, and recorded steady-state voltage is described by Ohm's Law (p. 27), which states that *the voltage across a conductor* (i.e., the membrane) *is proportional to both the current passed through the conductor and the resistance of the conductor.* Thus

$$\Delta E_m = \Delta IR, \qquad (5\text{-}1)$$

or

$$R = \frac{\Delta E_m}{\Delta I}.$$

Consider two spherical cells, one small, the other large, both with membranes having the same *specific resistance*, R_m, to electric current (i.e., the same resistance for a square centimeter of membrane). For a given increment of current, ΔI, the large cell will show a smaller increment of voltage, ΔE_m, because the same current will flow through a larger area of membrane; the current density will therefore be smaller across the membrane of the large cell than across the membrane of the smaller cell. This principle is illustrated by the fact that a current passing through two equal parallel resistors produces half the potential drop as the same current passing through only one of these resistors. Thus, if all else is equal, a large cell will have a lower input resistance than a small cell (Fig. 5-7). Because

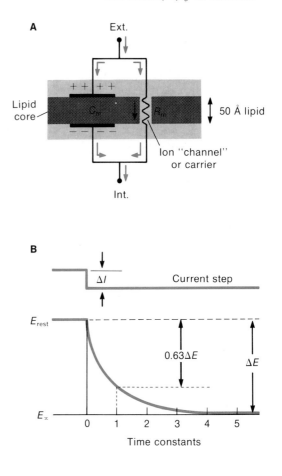

5–6. *A. Simplest equivalent circuit for a cell membrane, showing membrane capacitance,* C_m, *and resistance,* R_m. *Arrows indicate direction of current. B. Electrotonic response of a cell membrane to an applied pulse of inward-going current,* ΔI. *The time required for the voltage to reach 63% of its asymptotic value is proportional to both the resistance and the capacitance of the membrane. This is termed the time constant,* τ, *of the membrane.*

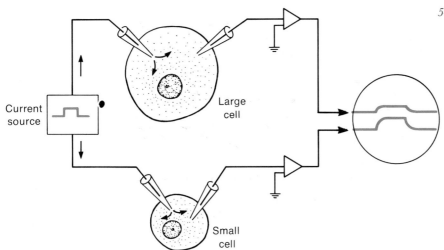

5–7. *Effect of cell size on voltage response to a given current. The input resistance of the larger cell is lower than that of the smaller cell. Thus passage of the same amount of current into both cells results in a larger potential change in the smaller cell as predicted by Ohm's Law.*

BOX 5-1   CAPACITANCE AND TIME CONSTANT

Consider a constant current, I, applied in an abrupt, step-like pulse to a capacitor in parallel with a resistor (Fig. 5-6). The potential, E_c (in volts), developed across the capacitor is proportional to the charge, q (in coulombs), accumulated by a capacitor. The proportionality constant, C (in farads), is an indication of the ability of the capacitor to accumulate and store charge. Thus

$$q = E_c C. \qquad (1)$$

The *capacitive current*, i_c, is defined as the charge accumulated per unit time:

$$i_c = \frac{dq}{dt}. \qquad (2)$$

Differentiation of Equation 1 shows that the rate of charge accumulation is proportional to the rate of change of potential across the capacitor, since C remains constant throughout:

$$\frac{dq}{dt} = C\frac{dE_c}{dt}. \qquad (3)$$

Finally, by substitution into Equation 2, we obtain

$$i_c = C\frac{dE_c}{dt}. \qquad (4)$$

That is, the current at any instant through a capacitor is proportional to the rate of change of the potential at that instant.

As current passes through a capacitor, the accumulated charge causes the potential across the capacitor to increase. The voltage produced across the capacitor repels new charges, and the rate of charging drops. Hence the capacitive current, i_c, varies inversely with E_c (see bottom part of figure), and diminishes with an exponential time course.

A. The equivalent circuit for a cell membrane across which an abrupt pulse of constant current is passed. The high resistance, high R, is used to supply an unvarying current.   B. Time courses of resistive current, i_r, capacitive current, i_c; membrane potential, V_m (i.e., the potential across both the membrane resistance and capacitance), and the total membrane current, I_m.

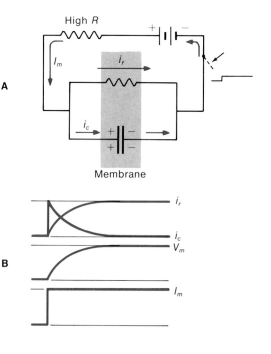

The relationship between potential and time during the charging of the capacitance is given by the equation

$$E_t = E_\infty(1 - e^{-t/RC}), \qquad (5)$$

where E_∞ is the potential across the capacitor at $t = \infty$ after a constant current is applied to the network, t is the time in seconds after the beginning of the current pulse, R is the resistance of the circuit in ohms, C is the capacitance of the circuit in farads, E_t is the potential across the capacitor at time t after the onset of the current pulse.

When t is equal to the product RC, then $E_t = E_\infty(1 - 1/e) = 0.63E_\infty$. The value of t (in seconds) that equals RC is termed the *time constant* (T) of the process. Note that it is independent of both E_∞ and current strength, and is the time required for the voltage across a charging capacitor to reach 63% of the asymptotic value E_∞ or the time required for the voltage across a discharging capacitor to drop by 63% (Fig. 5-6,B).

The current applied to the membrane flows initially through the capacitance of the membrane: As the capacitance charges (or discharges) exponentially, an increasing fraction of the total current passes through the resistive component of the membrane (see upper part of figure). After several time constants have elapsed, the potential closely approaches an asymptote, and all the applied current flows through the membrane resistance. When the applied current is terminated, the charge stored across the capacitor leaks back through the resistor, R_m, and the potential returns to the rest level with an exponential time course.

---

the *input resistance*, R, of a cell (i.e., the total resistance encountered by current flowing into or out of the cell) is a function of both membrane area, A, and specific resistance, R_m, of the membrane, it is useful when comparing membranes of different cells to correct for the effect of membrane area on the current density ($\Delta I/A$). Thus the specific resistance is calculated as

$$R_m = \frac{\text{input resistance (ohms)}}{\text{membrane area (cm}^2)},$$

or

$$R_m = \frac{\Delta E_m}{\Delta I/A} \qquad (5\text{-}2)$$

$$= \frac{\Delta E_m}{\Delta I} A.$$

Since $\Delta E_m/\Delta I$ has the units of ohms and area is in square centimeters, R_m is in units of ohm-cm^2. Specific resistances of membranes range from hundreds to tens of thousands of ohm-cm^2.

The reciprocal of the specific resistance of a membrane is the *membrane conductance*, g_m (in units of mhos/cm^2). Conductance is related to the ionic permeability of the membrane, but conductance and permeability are not synonymous. Conductance to a given species of ion is defined by Ohm's Law as the current carried by that species of ion divided by the electromotive force acting on that species. Thus membrane conductance for species X is defined as

$$g_X = \frac{I_X}{\text{emf}_X}, \qquad (5\text{-}3)$$

in which g_X is the membrane conductance for ion species X, I_X is the net current carried by that species, and emf$_X$ is the electromotive force (in volts) acting on that species. Although emf$_X$ varies with membrane potential, as noted below, it is not identical with membrane potential.

Even though a membrane may be permeable to ion X, the conductance, g_X, depends on the presence of this species in the solution; unless it is present, it cannot carry current. It is also evident that permeability of nonelectrolytes does not contribute any conductance, since a nonelectrolyte does not carry a charge, and hence cannot carry current.

The membrane conductance, g_m, is a constant that describes the ratio of the increment in current, ΔI, required to produce a small shift in membrane potential, ΔE_m. Figure 5-8,A shows the *current-voltage curve* of a membrane in which this ratio (i.e., the membrane conductance) remains constant over a moderate range of voltage differences across the membrane. This kind of behavior, which corresponds to the simple equivalent circuit shown in Figure 5-6,A is found in some electrically "silent" cells, such as connective tissue cells (neuroglia) in the nervous system. Figure 5-8,B shows

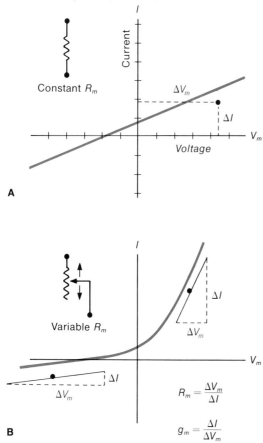

sults in a uniform electrotonic potential over the entire membrane of the spherical cell. But in a highly asymmetrical cell, such as a segment of an axon, the longitudinal flow of a current injected at one point undergoes a progressive decline with distance, as some of it leaks out at each point across the cell membrane.

Such long, cylindrical, membrane-limited processes have certain similarities to an insulated submarine cable. The cytoplasm is analogous to the conducting core of the cable, and the membrane is analogous to the insulation. Moreover, the extracellular fluid bathing the cell is analogous to the sea water that surrounds the submarine cable. The *cable properties* of nerve and muscle cells play an important role in the conduction of impulses along the cell membrane, as described in Chapter 6.

Current distributes itself along the axon according to the passive electrical properties described by the equivalent circuit shown in Figure 5-9. The components R_m and C_m are the same as in Figure 5-6,A, and represent the linearly distributed passive resistance and capacitance of the inactive membrane. They are depicted as discrete elements only for the sake of convenience. We will first ignore the membrane capacitance and assume that current flows only through the resistors.

According to Kirchoff's First Law, the sum of all the currents leaving a point must equal the sum of all the currents entering that point. Kirchoff's Law, together with Ohm's Law, requires that the current distribute itself in inverse proportion to the resistances of the various routes open to it at each branching point. Thus, when the switch in the equivalent circuit of Figure 5-9 is closed, the pulse (ΔI) of constant intensity current will distribute itself accordingly, and flow across the "membrane" at all points (0, 1, 2, 3, 4). It will be diminished by each longitudinal resistor, R_l, encountered, because longitudinal resistance is cumulative. At each branching point, 0, 1, 2, 3, 4, the current divides, with the same proportion passing through each R_m and the remainder through the R_l. The transmembrane current through the R_m's is therefore a decreasing exponential function of longitudinal distance from the point of current injection. Since all the R_m's in the circuit are of the same resistance, Ohm's Law requires that the potentials developed across the R_m's also decrease exponentially with distance. Thus the transmembrane steady-state electrotonic potential (ΔE) will diminish exponentially with distance along the axon (Fig. 5-9).

The exponential decay of a steady-state electrotonic potential with distance is described by the cable equation applied to axons by Hodgkin and Rushton (1946):

$$E_x = E_0 \, e^{-x/\lambda}. \qquad (5\text{-}4)$$

a nonlinear current-voltage curve that is characteristic of membranes in which conductance changes as a function of membrane potential. Such changes are the basis for membrane excitation, described further on.

Effect of Cell Geometry

Membrane resistance and capacitance are properties that influence the way in which membrane potentials and currents spread with distance along a cylindrical cell, such as a muscle fiber or a nerve cell. In a spherical cell, like that shown in Figure 5-3, there is little difference in the amplitude of an electrotonic potential from one point across the membrane to another because the resistance of the cell membrane is high compared to the resistance a current encounters on passing through the cytoplasm or the bath solution. The result is that a current injected into a spherical cell spreads out and passes through the membrane with relatively uniform density over the entire cell surface. This re-

Here E_x is the potential change measured at a distance x from the point ($x = 0$) at which the current is injected, and E_0 is the potential change at the point $x = 0$. The symbol λ is the *length* (or *space*) *constant*, which is related to the resistance of the axon by the expression

$$\lambda = \sqrt{\frac{r_m}{r_i + r_o}} = \sqrt{\frac{r_m}{r_l}}, \qquad (5\text{-}5)$$

in which r_m is the resistance of a unit length of axon membrane, and r_l is the summed longitudinal internal and external resistances over a unit length ($r_i + r_o$). Inspection of Equation 5-4 reveals that when $x = \lambda$,

$$E_x = E_0 \, e^{-1} = E_0 \frac{1}{e} = 0.37 E_0.$$

Therefore, λ is defined as the distance over which a steady state electrotonic potential shows a 63% drop in amplitude (Fig. 5-10).

Note in Equation 5-5 that the value of λ is directly proportional to the square roots of both r_m and $1/r_l$ This means that *electrotonic spread of current along the interior of an axon is enhanced by a high membrane resistance and/or low longitudinal resistance.* It will be explained in Chapter 6 that the velocity of conduction of an action potential is closely related to the effectiveness of electrotonic spread in the axon. Cable properties of nerve cells also are important in the information-processing of the nervous system, to be discussed in Chapter 8.

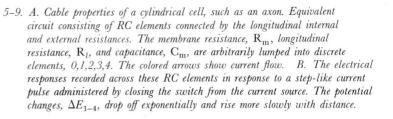

5–9. *A. Cable properties of a cylindrical cell, such as an axon. Equivalent circuit consisting of RC elements connected by the longitudinal internal and external resistances. The membrane resistance,* R_m, *longitudinal resistance,* R_l, *and capacitance,* C_m, *are arbitrarily lumped into discrete elements, 0,1,2,3,4. The colored arrows show current flow. B. The electrical responses recorded across these RC elements in response to a step-like current pulse administered by closing the switch from the current source. The potential changes,* ΔE_{1-4}, *drop off exponentially and rise more slowly with distance.*

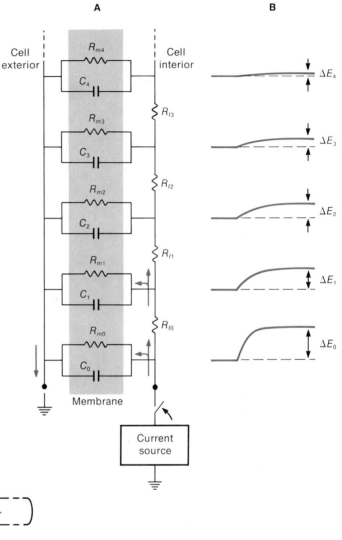

5–10. *The drop in potential with distance along a nerve or muscle fiber from the point of current injection. The length constant,* λ, *is defined as that distance over which the potential falls by* $1 - 1/e$ *(63%) from its value,* E_0, *at the point of injection.*

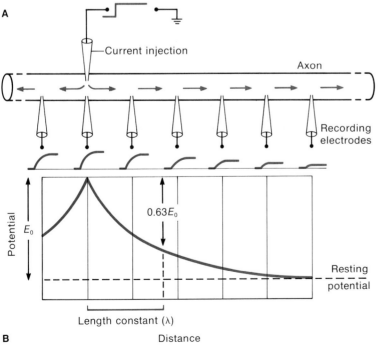

5-11. *Equilibrium. A hypothetical membrane permeable to only K^+ separates compartments I and II, containing the concentrations of KCl indicated. The net movement of K^+ across the membrane is zero when the electromotive force acting on K^+ balances the concentration gradient. See text for details.*

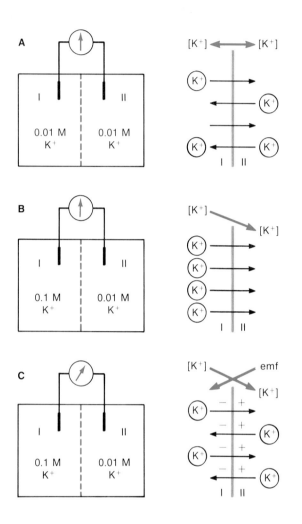

Equilibrium Potentials

Figure 5-11 shows a chamber divided into two compartments by a selectively permeable membrane, one that is permeable only to potassium ions. At the start of the experiment (not shown), each compartment contains pure distilled water. Electrodes inserted one each into the two compartments record no potential difference across the membrane. Potassium chloride is then added to bring the KCl concentration to 0.01 M in each compartment. Since the membrane is permeable to K^+ but *not* to Cl^-, K^+ can diffuse across the membrane without its counterion. On the average, for each K^+ ion that passes in one direction through

the membrane another will pass in the opposite direction under these conditions. As long as the two compartments contain the same concentration of KCl, the net K^+ flux is zero and the potential difference between the two sides of the membrane remains zero (Fig. 5-11,A). We then add KCl to compartment I to produce an instantaneous concentration of 0.1 M (10 times that of compartment II, Fig. 5-11,B). As K^+ now exhibits net diffusion from compartment I to II, a potential difference will quickly develop across the membrane and the voltmeter will indicate that compartment I is more negative than compartment II (Fig. 5-11,C). This potential difference is maintained indefinitely, provided there is no leakage of Cl^- into compartment II.

How do we explain the steadily maintained potential difference? For every K^+ ion that is statistically available for diffusion through the membrane from compartment II to I, ten potassium ions in I are available to pass through the membrane to compartment II. That is, the K^+ concentration gradient produces a *chemical potential difference,* causing an initial net diffusion through the membrane from I to II (Fig. 5-11,B). Each additional K^+ ion that diffuses from I to II adds its positive charge to that side, and Cl^- is left behind, since it cannot accompany K^+ across this hypothetical membrane. As K^+ ions accumulate in compartment II and Cl^- ions are left behind in compartment I, the potential difference across the membrane quickly rises, since the membrane then separates a *slight* excess of positive charges on one side from a *slight* excess of negative charges on the other, as in Fig. 5-5. Each K^+ now entering the membrane has two forces acting on it: a chemical potential difference favoring net K^+ flux from I to II, and an *electric potential difference* favoring net K^+ flux from II to I (Fig. 5-11,C). These two opposite forces come into equilibrium and remain balanced, the electrical potential difference precisely offsetting the tendency for K^+ to diffuse down its concentration gradient. The potassium ion is then said to be in *electrochemical equilibrium;* the potential difference that is established in this way is termed the *equilibrium potential* for the ion in question (in this case, the potassium equilibrium potential, E_K). When an ion is in electrochemical equilibrium it undergoes no net flux across the membrane (even if the membrane is freely permeable), regardless of the concentration gradient of that species. If for any reason the membrane potential, V_m, is not at the equilibrium potential, E_X, for ion X, the electromotive force acting on that ion (emf_X) is the difference between the two potentials:

$$emf_X = V_m - E_X. \qquad (5\text{-}6)$$

To illustrate the equilibrium state between ionic concentration gradient and the resulting electric potential gradient, a simple analogy is given in Figure

5-12. A mass hangs suspended from a spring. As gravity pulls the mass down, tension develops in the spring. This tension becomes equal to and opposite to the force of gravity acting on the mass; the system is therefore in equilibrium, with the mass suspended on the stretched spring. The weight is analogous to the chemical gradient, and the tension developed in the spring is analogous to the equilibrium potential developed across the membrane. The weight produces the tension in the spring by stretching it, and the tension in turn keeps the weight suspended. Likewise, movement of charge from compartment I to II produces the electrical "tension" (potential difference); the potential difference in turn prevents further movement of charge, and thereby balances the unequal ionic concentrations.

The equivalent electrical circuit for the development of the membrane potential in Figure 5-11,C is given in Figure 5-13. Positive charge (in the form of potassium ions), driven by the emf acting on potassium (i.e., $V_m - E_K$), leaks through the potassium conductance (i.e., R_K) of the membrane so as to accumulate on the other side of the membrane. That is, it "charges up" the membrane capacitance (C_m). When the voltage across the capacitance of the membrane equals the potassium equilibrium potential (i.e., when $V_m - E_K = 0$), net K$^+$ diffusion ceases and the system is at equilibrium, side II positive with respect to side I. Although the electrochemical gradient for the chloride ion is in the opposite direction, it has no effect because our hypothetical membrane is impermeable to chloride ions.

It will be explained on page 122 that the amount of K$^+$ crossing the membrane to produce the potential difference is so small that there is *virtually no change in concentration* of that ion in the two compartments.

THE NERNST RELATION

It seems right, intuitively, that the equilibrium potential of an ion should increase in value with an increase in its concentration gradient across the membrane, just as the tension developed in a spring (Fig. 5-12) increases with mass. In other words, a greater chemical potential difference across the membrane should develop a greater electric potential difference in order to offset the tendency for the ions to diffuse down their concentration gradient. The equilibrium potential, in fact, is proportional to the *logarithm* of the ratio of the concentrations in the two compartments. The relation between concentration ratios and membrane potential was derived in the latter part of the nineteenth century by Nernst from the gas laws. The derivation can be found in physical chemistry texts as well as in specialized texts, such as the one by Katz (1966). The

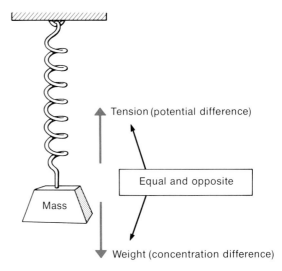

5–12. Physical analogy illustrating electrochemical equilibrium. The tension in the spring is analogous to the potential difference produced by diffusion of an ion across a semipermeable membrane. The weight of the mass is analogous to the concentration difference of the ion.

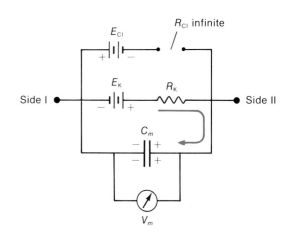

5–13. Equivalent electrical circuit for development of a potential across the membrane in Figure 5-11. E_K supplies the emf for K$^+$ to carry current through the membrane's K channels, R_K. This causes the buildup of positive charge on side II of the membrane capacitance, C_m.

equilibrium potential depends on the absolute temperature, the valence of the diffusible ion, and, of course, the ratio of concentrations on the two sides of the membrane:

$$E_X = \frac{RT}{Fz} \ln \frac{[X]_I}{[X]_{II}}. \qquad (5\text{-}7)$$

Here R is the gas constant, T is the absolute temperature (°Kelvin), F is the Faraday constant (96,500 coulombs/g-equivalent charge), z is the valence of ion X, $[X]_I$ and $[X]_{II}$ are the concentrations (more accurately, activities) of ion X on sides I and II of the membrane, and E_X is the equilibrium potential for ion X (potential of side II minus side I). At a temperature of 18°C and with a monovalent ion, and converting from ln to log, the Nernst equation can be reduced to

$$E_X = 0.058 \text{ Volt} \log \frac{[X]_I}{[X]_{II}}. \qquad (5\text{-}8)$$

Note that E_X will be positive if X is a cation and the ratio $[X]_I/[X]_{II}$ is greater than unity. The sign will become negative if the ratio is less than one. Likewise, the signs will be reversed if X is an anion rather than a cation, because z will be negative.

Suppose $[K^+]_I = 0.1$ M and $[K^+]_{II} = 0.01$ M, as in Figure 5-11. Using Equation 5-8, we obtain

$$E_K = 0.058 \log \frac{0.1}{0.01} = 0.058 \log 10 = 0.058\text{V}.$$

Thus side II will have a potential of $+58$ mV with respect to side I. Since log 100 is 2 and log 1000 is 3, the Nernst relation predicts a rise in potential difference of 58 mV every time the concentration difference of the permeant ion is increased by a factor of 10. When the potential is plotted as a function of log $[K^+]_I/[K^+]_{II}$, the relation has a slope of $+58$ mV per tenfold increase in the ratio (Fig. 5-14). It is apparent

from Equation 5-7 that if the ion is a divalent cation (i.e., $z = +2$), Equation 5-8 becomes $E_X = 0.029 \log ([X]_I/[X]_{II})$, and the slope of the relation becomes 29 mV per tenfold increase in the ratio.

Charge Separation by Membranes

How many ions actually diffuse across 1 cm² of the membrane in Figure 5-11 before the membrane potential equals E_K? This is easy to calculate for a system with a single diffusible ion. The number of excess potassium ions accumulated on side II (and excess chloride ions left behind on side I) depends on two factors: (1) the potassium equilibrium potential, and (2) the capacitance of the membrane. You will remember that the charge, q (in coulombs), accumulated across a capacitor is proportional to both the capacitance, C, of the capacitor and the voltage, E, developed across the capacitor (Eq. 1, Box 5-1). Biological membranes typically have capacitances of about 1 μF (10^{-6} F) per cm². We can calculate the coulombs of charge that diffuse across 1 cm² of membrane when the membrane separates a tenfold difference in the concentrations of a diffusible monovalent cation (i.e., a potential difference of 58 mV after equilibrium is achieved):

$$q = CE$$
$$= (10^{-6} \text{ F/cm}^2)(5.8 \times 10^{-2} \text{ V})$$
$$= 5.8 \times 10^{-8} \text{ coulombs/cm}^2.$$

There are 96,500 coulombs of charge (1 faraday) in 1 gram equivalent weight, or 1 mole, of a monovalent ion. Thus the amount of K^+ in moles required to transfer 5.8×10^{-8} coulombs across 1 cm² of membrane is calculated by dividing the number of coulombs in one faraday:

$$\frac{5.8 \times 10^{-8} \text{ coulombs/cm}^2}{9.65 \times 10^4 \text{ coulombs/mole } K^+}$$
$$= 6 \times 10^{-13} \text{ mole } K^+/\text{cm}^2.$$

The number of K^+ ions accumulated on side II of the membrane in Figure 5-11 is found by multiplying the number of moles by Avogadro's number (6×10^{23} molecules/mole):

$$(6 \times 10^{-13})(6 \times 10^{23}) = 3.6 \times 10^{11} \text{ K}^+ \text{ ions/cm}^2.$$

An equal number of Cl^- ions remain in excess on side I of the membrane. This number is more than 10,000,000 smaller than the number of potassium ions in a cubic centimeter of solution II (6×10^{18} K$^+$ ions). Thus the concentrations in compartments I and II are virtually unchanged as a result of the charge separa-

5-14. Relationship between the equilibrium potential of a monovalent ion, such as K$^+$, and the ratio of concentrations of that ion on the two sides of the membrane.

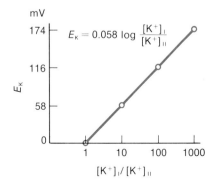

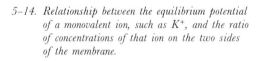

tion acros. the membrane. Even though there is a slight separation of anions from cations across the membrane, the segregation exists only on a microscopic scale, separated by about the thickness of the membrane (Fig. 5-5). The rule of electroneutrality—that positive charges must equal negative charges—remains essentially unviolated on the macroscopic scale.

The Resting Potential

PASSIVE CHARGE DISTRIBUTION

The principle of equilibrium potentials was illustrated above with a highly simplified, ideal system in which only one ionic species could diffuse across the membrane. This principle will now be applied to biological membranes, which are permeable in varying degrees to all of the inorganic ions present in tissues.

It is evident that the electrochemical gradient of an ionic species has no effect on the membrane potential if the membrane is impermeable to that species. After all, nonpermeant ions cannot carry charge from one side of the membrane to the other. It follows that a species to which the membrane is only slightly permeable will have a smaller effect on the membrane potential than another species that can diffuse across the membrane more freely. It is, in fact, the ease with which ions can cross the membrane that determines the charge distribution and, hence, the potential across the membrane. On this basis, Goldman (1943) derived an equation that is related to the Nernst relation and which takes into consideration the relative permeability of each species of ion:

$$V_m = \frac{RT}{F} \ln \frac{P_K[K^+]_o + P_{Na}[Na^+]_o + P_{Cl}[Cl^-]_i}{P_K[K^+]_i + P_{Na}[Na^+]_i + P_{Cl}[Cl^-]_o} \quad (5\text{-}9)$$

in which P_K, P_{Na}, and P_{Cl} are the respective permeability constants (p. 88) of the major ion species in the intra- and extracellular solutions.

Thus the probability that the ions of one species will cross the membrane is proportional to the product of their concentration (more accurately, their thermodynamic *activity*) on that side and the permeability of the membrane to that species. As a result, the contribution of an ion species to the membrane potential diminishes as its concentration is reduced. This point is illustrated in Figure 5-15, in which the membrane potential of a living cell is plotted as a function of the concentration of extracellular K^+, the ion most important in determining the resting potential. At the higher K^+ concentrations, the slope of the plot is +58 mV per 10-fold increase in potassium concen-

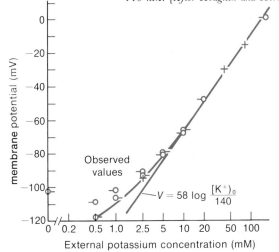

5-15. *The resting potential of a frog muscle cell plotted against the extracellular K^+ concentration. The theoretical -58-mV change for every 10-fold increase in the ratio of $[K^+]_o/[K^+]_i$, as predicted by the Nernst equation, is shown as a straight line. The measured values are shown by the plotted points. Curved line was calculated from Equation 5-9, using $P_{Na} = 0.01\ P_K$. $[K^+]_i$ was taken as 140 nM. [After Hodgkin and Horowitz, 1960.]*

tration. At lower K^+ concentrations, the curve deviates because Na^+ becomes a more important contributor, in spite of its low permeability, as the product $P_{Na}[Na^+]_o$ approaches $P_K[K^+]_o$. In the lower ranges of $[K^+]_o$, the membrane potential deviates from the potassium equilibrium potential, tending slightly upward (i.e., toward the sodium equilibrium potential). Keynes (1954) had already determined the permeability constants for the major ions in frog muscle with the use of radio-isotopes. The permeability of sodium was found to be about 0.01 times that of potassium. Chloride is in electrochemical equilibrium across the muscle membrane (i.e., $E_{Cl} = V_m$) and can therefore be ignored. Thus, for muscle cell membranes, the Goldman equation can be simplified to

$$V_m = \frac{RT}{F} \ln \frac{[K^+]_o + 0.01[Na^+]_o}{[K^+]_i + 0.01[Na^+]_i}$$

$$= 0.058 \log \frac{2.5 + (0.01)(120)}{140 + (0.01)(10)}$$

$$= -92 \text{ mV}.$$

Microelectrode measurements of the resting potential in muscle cells range from -90 to -100 mV.

Resting potentials of muscle, nerve, and other cells are far more sensitive to changes in the extracellular potassium level than to changes in the concentrations of other cations. This results, as we have seen, from the predominant permeability of most cell membranes to

K⁺. Large changes in [Na⁺] have almost no effect on the resting potential because of the low permeability of most cells to sodium ions when the membrane is at the resting potential. Resting potentials of different cell types range from a few millivolts to a hundred or more millivolts negative. The internal negativity of cells is due to their high internal potassium concentrations relative to extracellular potassium concentrations.

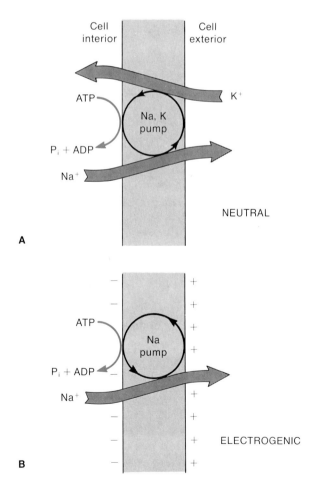

5-16. *A. Idealized neutral pump in which 1 K⁺ is exchanged for 1 Na⁺. In this case, the Na pump plays an indirect role in the resting potential by maintaining low internal Na⁺ and high internal K⁺ concentrations. B. The pump is electrogenic if it produces a net movement of charge across the membrane. The most common Na pump exchanges 3 Na⁺ for 2K⁺, and is therefore electrogenic.*

CHARGE DISTRIBUTION BY ACTIVE TRANSPORT

An idealized membrane (Figs. 5-11, 5-13) permeable to only one ion species will maintain a constant membrane potential indefinitely without expenditure of energy, because it is in a state of thermodynamic equilibrium. Real membranes, however, are leaky to varying degrees to all inorganic ions. Thus, although Na⁺ is far less permeant than K⁺, it slowly leaks into the cell. If it were not removed from the cell interior at the same rate at which it leaks in, Na⁺ would accumulate in the cell, replacing an equal amount of positive charge, largely in the form of internal K⁺. The high internal [K⁺] and low internal [Na⁺] result from the continual active transport of Na⁺ out of the cell (p. 94). In some Na pumps, the exchange of K⁺ for Na⁺ is coupled, and inward movement of K⁺ in exchange for Na⁺ is obligatory. Even without coupled K uptake, potassium ions, which are relatively permeant, move into the cell passively to replace the Na⁺ pumped out so as to maintain electroneutrality of the cytoplasm.

When metabolically energized transport is eliminated by general inhibitors of oxidative metabolism, such as cyanide or azide, or by specific inhibitors of Na transport, such as ouabain, Na⁺ exhibits a net influx, internal K⁺ is gradually displaced, and the resting potential shows a corresponding *slow* decay as the ratio [K⁺]ᵢ/[K⁺]ₒ gradually decreases. Over the long term, it is the metabolically energized extrusion of Na⁺ that keeps the Na⁺ and K⁺ concentration gradients from running downhill to equilibrium. By continual maintenance of the potassium concentration gradient, the sodium pump plays an important *indirect* role in determining the resting potential (Fig. 5-16,A), even though it may not directly affect the membrane potential by generating electric current.

Active transport has been shown to contribute *directly*, as well as indirectly, to the resting potential of some cells. This occurs when Na⁺ is transported from cell interior to exterior without one-to-one coupled exchange for K⁺ (Fig. 5-16,B). The pump is then said to be *electrogenic* rather than *neutral* because it is directly responsible for a steady transfer of positive charge (i.e., Na⁺) out of the cell. The pump is also electrogenic if the ratio of coupled Na⁺ to exchanged K⁺ is greater than one, as in the pump that exchanges three sodiums for two potassiums (p. 95). The potential contributed by an electrogenic pump depends on the rate at which sodium can leak back into the cell. The tendency to leak back increases, of course, as the resting potential is increased (made more negative) by the pump.

Permeability-controlled Changes
in Membrane Potential

It is again helpful to think of the membrane as a capacitance in parallel with a conductance (Fig. 5-17,A). This time, however, we must include a separate conductance in the equivalent circuit for each species of ion being considered, plus some batteries to represent the equilibrium potential of each species. It is because of this means of representation that the electrochemical potential of an ion is sometimes referred to as a "battery" (e.g., K-battery, Na-battery).

In the resting state, the membrane is predominantly permeable to K^+, hence the resting membrane potential approximates E_K. Potassium is nearly in electrochemical equilibrium across the resting membrane. Sodium, more concentrated outside the cell than inside, has an electrochemical gradient opposite that of K^+, and an equilibrium potential of opposite polarity to that of potassium. The Na potential, E_{Na}, is positive, whereas E_K is negative (Fig. 5-17,B). Because the sodium equilibrium potential is far from the resting potential, there is a large electrochemical potential $(V_m - E_{Na})$ acting on Na^+. This emf is a substantial source of potential energy, which is released in some cells by stimuli that increase the permeability of the membrane so as to permit a transient *inward sodium current* (i.e., net influx of Na^+) through the membrane.

The effect of a temporary increase in the Na conductance, g_{Na}, is illustrated in Figure 5-17,B. When the Na conductance in series with E_{Na} increases, Na^+ will flow through the increased Na^+ conductance into the cell, adding positive charge to the inside surface of the capacitor, C_m (Fig. 5-17,A), until a new steady-state potential is attained between E_K and E_{Na}, and K^+ (which is now out of equilibrium) carries charges out of the cell at the same rate as Na^+ carries them in. When g_{Na} is restored to its previous low level, the membrane potential returns to its original value near E_K. Thus the membrane will undergo a *depolarization* in response to an increase in its sodium conductance.

Changes in membrane permeabilities, and the concomitant changes in ionic currents, are important for producing changes in the membrane potential. Appropriate stimuli applied to some membranes cause an increase in permeability to a given species of ion. Energy stored as a concentration gradient of the species is thereby released, producing a change in membrane potential. This release of electrochemical energy through alterations in membrane conductance is termed *membrane excitation*. A membrane that changes its conductance in response to stimulation is said to be an *excitable membrane*.

Membranes display various types of excitability.

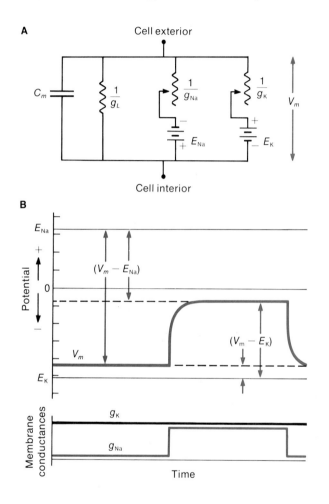

5-17. A. Equivalent circuit for a biological membrane, showing the electrically excited conductances for Na^+ and K^+. The remaining conductances are lumped as $1/g_L$. The concentration batteries E_{Na} and E_K are connected in series with the respective conductances. Note that these batteries have opposite polarities. B. Changes in membrane potential, V_m (top), produced by changes in sodium conductance, g_{Na} (bottom). Note the changes in the terms $(V_m - E_{Na})$ and $(V_m - E_K)$ produced by the change in V_m. Note also that E_K and E_{Na} remain constant throughout.

Some, like the membranes of liver cells and neuroglia, show essentially none. Other membranes, such as those of nerve, muscle, and receptor cells, are excited by certain stimuli, such as depolarizing current, light, chemicals, temperature changes, and mechanical strain. Highly developed sensitivity to a particular form of stimulus energy is characteristic of the membranes of sensory receptors (Chapter 7).

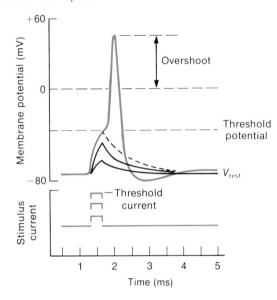

5-18. *An action potential produced by a nerve cell membrane in response to a depolarizing stimulus that brought the membrane to the threshold potential. Smaller polarizations failed to evoke the all-or-none response.*

Action Potentials

GENERAL FEATURES

Action potentials* are produced by the membranes of neurons and muscle cells, as well as by some receptor cells, secretory cells, and protozoa. They perform two major functions: (1) rapid transmission of information over long distances, in nerve and muscle fibers, and (2) control of effector responses, such as muscle contraction and the release of neurotransmitters and hormones.

The properties of electric excitation can be illustrated by simple experiments using the arrangement in Figure 5-3. When current pulses are passed so that positive charge is forced from the bath inward across the membrane and out of the cell via the current electrode, the potential difference across the membrane increases (*hyperpolarizes*) because additional positive charge is removed from the inner side of the membrane and added to the outer surface of the membrane. With hyperpolarizing stimulation, the membrane produces no response other than the potential change due to the simple capacitive-resistive properties described earlier in this chapter. If, on the other hand, direction

*The shape of the recorded action potential has led to the term "spike" in neurophysiological jargon. *Spike, impulse,* and *action potential* are generally used interchangeably.

of the current is reversed, so as to add positive charge to the inner surface of the cell membrane, the potential difference decreases and the cell is said to become *depolarized.* As the strength of the outward current pulse is progressively increased, the membrane is depolarized to progressively greater levels (Fig. 5-18). At a critical level, a small increase in current produces a strongly disproportionate increase in membrane response, and an action potential is generated. The intensity of stimulating current just sufficient to displace the membrane to the *threshold potential,* and thus to elicit the action potential is defined as the *threshold current.* No consistent values can be assigned to either the threshold current intensity or the threshold potential, because these depend on several factors, such as the condition of the membrane and the conditions of its environment, the duration of the current pulse, and the resistance of the membrane. The generation by a membrane of an active electrical response is termed *membrane excitation.*

Once the threshold potential is attained, the upstroke becomes *regenerative* (i.e., self-stimulating; autocatalytic). The cell interior continues to increase in positive potential until the membrane potential overshoots zero (i.e., reverses polarity) and reaches a peak of +30 to +50 mV (Fig. 5-18). The portion of the action potential on the positive side of zero is called the *overshoot.* It is the regenerative property of the action potential that permits it to propagate itself along a nerve cell axon or a muscle fiber for long distances without any decline in amplitude. Propagation of the action potential is discussed in Chapter 6.

Because there are no responses (under a given set of conditions) that are intermediate in size between a full response and a minute, abortive response, the action potential is said to be *all-or-none.* Although the amount of overshoot can change if the condition of the membrane or the compositions of the intra- or extracellular solutions change, this does not contradict the all-or-none principle, which is simply that the amplitude of the response (action potential) is independent of the intensity of the stimulus. An analogy can be drawn with the flushing of a toilet. Once initiated, the flush generally continues until the tank is emptied, independent of the pressure applied to the lever to initiate the operation.

Another feature that is characteristic of an action potential is the rapid repolarization from the peak of the overshoot to the resting level (Fig. 5-18). Action potentials range in duration from less than a millisecond in some nerve fibers (axons) to nearly a second in heart muscle cells.

When the interval between two action potentials is reduced, the second one becomes progressively smaller, and suddenly fails completely if initiated soon after the end of the first action potential (Fig. 5-19,A). The interval at which the second spike fails depends on the stimulus strength. No stimulus, however, is sufficient to evoke a second action potential during the *absolute refractory period*, which exists during and persists for a short period after an action potential. Spikes of diminished amplitude occur during the *relative refractory period*, when the threshold is higher than normal. The threshold potential progressively decreases (i.e., excitability increases) with time during this period to the level characteristic of the resting membrane before stimulation (Fig. 5-19,B). Diminished excitability (*refractoriness*) during and immediately after the action potential prevents fusion of impulses and permits the propagation of discrete impulses.

The membrane undergoes a time-dependent decrease in excitability (i.e., threshold increase) during subthreshold depolarizations. This can be demonstrated by depolarizing the membrane gradually with a current of steadily increasing intensity rather than with an abrupt step-like stimulus current. Greater depolarizations are required to elicit an action potential with such a slowly increasing current (Fig. 5-20). This characteristic of excitable membranes—a result of time-dependent changes in the sensitivity of membrane channels to depolarization—is termed *accommodation*.

Accommodation of excitable membranes also occurs during the passage of a constant-intensity current. Some nerve cell membranes accomodate rapidly and generate only one or two spikes at the beginning of a prolonged constant-current stimulus; others accommodate more slowly, and therefore fire repetitively with gradually decreasing frequency in response to a maintained current of constant intensity (Fig. 5-21). It will be seen in Chapter 7 that accommodation is important in sensory physiology, for it is one of several factors that determine whether a maintained stimulus will elicit a transient or maintained discharge in a sensory neuron.

5-19. *Top. Refractoriness following an action potential. Five pair of stimuli (A_1, B_1 to A_5, B_5) were delivered with progressively shorter intervals between the first stimulus (A) and the second (B) in each pair. During the relatively refractory period, spike B became smaller. During the absolutely refractory period, no second spike can be elicited. Bottom. Time course of change in excitability.*

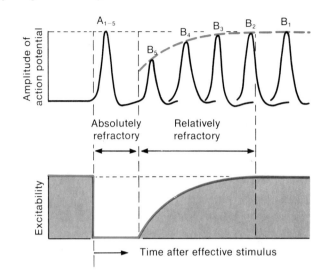

5-20. *Accommodation. The threshold current changes with time during subthreshold stimulation. Thus slowly increasing currents (b to d) are less effective in reaching thresholds than an abruptly increasing current (a). [After Davson, 1964.]*

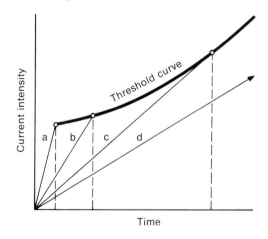

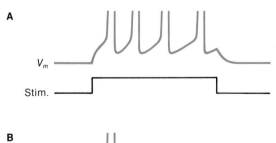

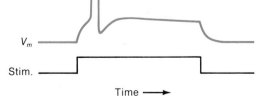

5-21. *Accommodation of impulse discharge during a constant-stimulus current. A. Some membranes show little accommodation except for a progressive lengthening of the interspike interval. B. Other membranes produce only one or two impulses in response to a similar stimulus. Tops of action potentials are cut off.*

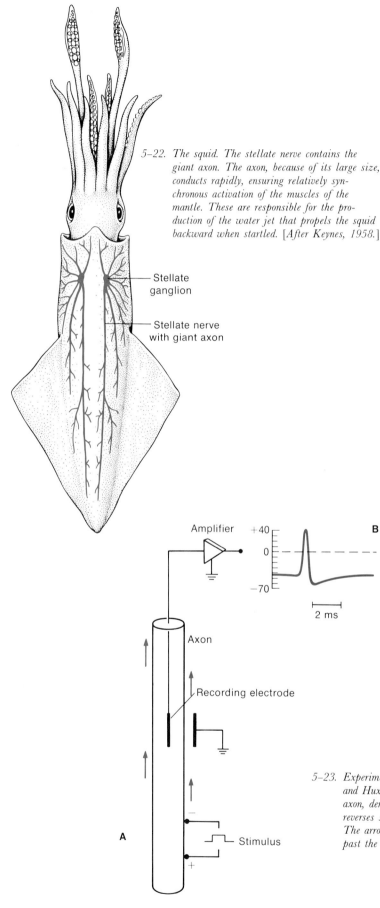

5-22. *The squid. The stellate nerve contains the giant axon. The axon, because of its large size, conducts rapidly, ensuring relatively synchronous activation of the muscles of the mantle. These are responsible for the production of the water jet that propels the squid backward when startled.* [*After Keynes, 1958.*]

Stellate
ganglion

Stellate nerve
with giant axon

Amplifier

B

2 ms

Axon

Recording electrode

A

Stimulus

Ionic Basis of Action Potentials

Much of what we know about electrically excitable membranes began with a report in 1936 by the British zoologist J. Z. Young that certain longitudinal structures in squids and cuttlefish (Fig. 5-22) previously thought to be blood vessels were really extraordinarily large axons. He quickly recognized the potential usefulness of these *giant axons* for the study of membrane physiology, for their unusually large diameters (up to 1 mm) allow electrode wires to be inserted longitudinally for stimulation and recording (Fig. 5-23,A).

The first major discoveries made with the squid axon were published separately in 1939 by K. S. Cole and H. J. Curtis, working at Woods Hole, Mass., and by A. L. Hodgkin and A. F. Huxley, working in Plymouth, England. Cole and Curtis demonstrated an increase in membrane conductance (without any significant change in capacitance) concomitant with the passage of the action potential (Fig. 5-24). This was consistent with the proposal made in 1917 by J. Bernstein, a student of Nernst, that the action potential is a simple collapse of membrane polarization due to a transient *non*selective increase in membrane permeability to inorganic ions. Hodgkin and Huxley simultaneously found that the membrane potential does not simply go to zero during the action potential, but instead reverses sign during the impulse (Fig. 5-23,B). This important detail was at odds with Bernstein's assumption that the permeability increase during excitation was nonspecific and resulted in a simple collapse of membrane polarization.

Hodgkin and Katz (1949) subsequently found that the action potential fails to develop if the extracellular Na^+ is removed. When extracellular Na^+ is present in reduced concentration, the rate of depolarization decreases, and the amplitude of the action potential diminishes (Fig. 5-25). This led them to propose the *sodium hypothesis*—namely, that the upstroke and overshoot of the action potential results from an influx of Na^+ through a transiently increased membrane permeability to sodium.

5-23. *Experimental set-up (A) with which Hodgkin and Huxley (1939), using the squid giant axon, demonstrated that the membrane potential reverses sign during the action potential (B). The arrows show propagation of the impulse past the recording electrodes.*

The sodium hypothesis receives support from the following considerations and observations.

1. The extracellular concentration of Na$^+$ exceeds the intracellular concentration by a factor of about 10, so that E_{Na} is about +50 to +60 mV. Thus both the electrical and the chemical potentials tend to drive Na$^+$ through the membrane into the cell. The emf acting on Na$^+$ is $V_m - E_{Na}$.

2. Since it carries a positive charge, Na$^+$ will produce an increased intracellular positive potential as it enters the cell.

3. The overshoot of the action potential approaches the calculated Na$^+$ equilibrium potential:

$$E_{Na} = \frac{RT}{Fz} \ln \frac{[Na^+]_o}{[Na^+]_i} = 0.058 \log 10$$

$$= +58 \text{ mV}.$$

4. The overshoot varies, as noted above, with the extracellular Na$^+$ concentration as predicted for a change in E_{Na}.

EXPERIMENTAL CONFIRMATION OF THE SODIUM HYPOTHESIS

After World War II, which interrupted their work on the squid axon, Hodgkin and Huxley (1952a,b) obtained further evidence in support of the sodium hypothesis with a powerful new electronic technique termed *voltage clamping* (Box 5-2). In a nutshell, this method, first applied to the squid giant axon, employs a feedback system that abruptly changes and maintains ("clamps") the membrane voltage constant at any preselected value while the ionic current that flows across the membrane is monitored. This approach includes fewer uncontrolled variables than does the simpler approach in which the membrane is permitted to produce an action potential in response to a pulse of depolarizing current (Figs. 5-3, 5-18).

Fig. 5-26 shows that a *hyper*polarizing voltage step (trace a) results in a very small and constant inward membrane current (trace a') during maintained hyperpolarization. A *de*polarizing potential step of the same magnitude (trace b) is accompanied by a stronger and more complex sequence of membrane currents (trace b'). The initial transient downward deflection of trace b' indicates an early surge of inward current. This subsides in 1 or 2 ms and is followed by a more slowly developing, *delayed outward current* (upward deflection of the trace). The *early inward current* is especially interesting, since it represents an influx of positive charge into the cell and could therefore be related to the upstroke of the action potential believed to be due to an influx of Na$^+$.

5-24. *Change in membrane conductance during the action potential in squid axon. This classical display from Cole and Curtis (1939) includes the action potential and an envelope of high-frequency oscillation, which indicates by its increase in width the increased membrane conductance during and briefly following the action potential. By repeating this with different frequencies of oscillation, Cole and Curtis found the membrane capacitance to remain constant. Time markers are 1 ms apart.*

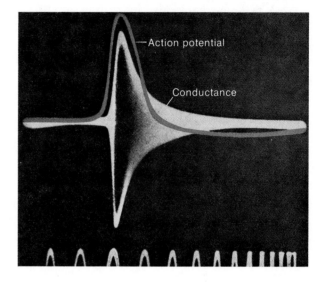

5-25. *Dependence on Na$^+$ of the overshoot of the action potential in the squid giant axon. Trace 1 shows the control action potential in the normal solution (i.e., sea water). Traces 2 to 5 show the progressive change with time after the replacement with artificial seawater containing choline chloride in place of NaCl. Trace 6 was made after replacement of normal seawater at the end of the experiment. [After Hodgkin and Katz, 1949.]*

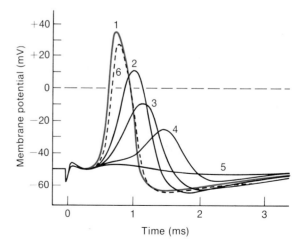

BOX 5-2   THE VOLTAGE-CLAMP METHOD

With this technique, the membrane potential is held constant in time, and is held uniform over a selected length of axon by electronic feedback while variations in current through that area of membrane are measured. The potential difference across the membrane is stepped abruptly from a steady holding potential to a selected stimulus potential. There are two strategic reasons for clamping the membrane potential in an abrupt step from a steady holding potential to a new stimulus potential:

1. Total membrane current (I_m) is made up of resistive current, i_r, and capacitive current, i_c. Capacitive current is proportional to both the rate of change of membrane potential and the membrane capacitance, C_m:

$$i_c = \frac{dV_m}{dt}C_m. \tag{1}$$

Since

$$I_m = i_r + i_c, \tag{2}$$

by substitution,

$$I_m = i_r + \frac{dV_m}{dt}C_m. \tag{3}$$

With the membrane potential clamped at a constant value, dV_m/dt equals zero, and

$$I_m = i_r. \tag{4}$$

Thus all the membrane current after the abrupt step in voltage passes through the

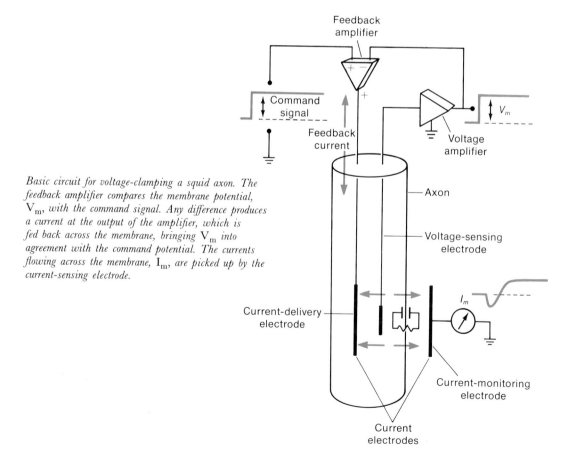

Basic circuit for voltage-clamping a squid axon. The feedback amplifier compares the membrane potential, V_m, with the command signal. Any difference produces a current at the output of the amplifier, which is fed back across the membrane, bringing V_m into agreement with the command potential. The currents flowing across the membrane, I_m, are picked up by the current-sensing electrode.

membrane conductances. The current delivered to charge up the membrane capacitance to this level is over in a fraction of a millisecond, and can therefore be ignored.

2. In the unclamped membrane, conductance and potential interact with one another (Fig. 5-34). By clamping the potential at a fixed value, one major variable V_m, is held constant, and the complexity of the analysis is greatly reduced.

In voltage-clamping, the potential recorded from inside the axon is compared by a differential amplifier with an electronically generated "command" potential (see figure). The voltage difference between the membrane potential and the command signal is amplified, and the output of the amplifier supplies a feedback current that passes across the membrane in the direction that brings the membrane potential into agreement with the command signal (the amplifier inverts the polarity—plus to minus and vice versa—of the potential recorded from inside the axon). If the inside of the axon is slightly more negative than the command signal, a positive current flows from the amplifier output to the current electrode inside the axon and across the membrane to produce an increase in intracellular positivity until the potential inside the axon agrees precisely with the command signal. This automatic adjustment by the amplifier is complete within a fraction of a millisecond after a step-like command potential is presented to the control amplifier. If the membrane becomes permeable to an ion (e.g., Na^+) that carries a current across the membrane into the axon, the entering charge is immediately removed by the feadback system so as to keep the membrane voltage constant. The current supplied or removed by the amplifier to maintain the selected membrane potential is identical to the current crossing the membrane, I_m.

By replacing the Na^+ in the extracellular medium with choline ion, an organic molecule to which the membrane is essentially impermeable, Hodgkin and Huxley tested the hypothesis that sodium carries the early inward membrane current. The result, seen in Figure 5-27, was the disappearance of the early inward current, with a small transient outward current appearing in its place. The delayed outward current was unaffected. Returning the axon to the normal Na-containing bathing solution restored the early inward current. This indicated that the early inward current is produced by a transient influx of Na^+ across the membrane into the cell. According to this interpretation, a sudden depolarization produces a transient rise in the sodium conductance of the membrane, Na^+ moves through this conductance (e.g., Na channels) according to Equation 5-3:

$$I_{Na} = g_{Na}(V_m - E_{Na}). \qquad (5-10)$$

In the normal extracellular environment, the electrochemical gradient ($V_m - E_{Na}$) drives Na^+ into the cell when g_{Na} rises. When extracellular Na^+ is replaced by choline, the electrochemical gradient of Na^+ becomes reversed, and hence the direction of the Na current is outward, as shown in Figure 5-27.

These investigators then proceeded to separate the time course of the early inward current from the delayed outward current. They lowered the external

sodium concentration, so that Na^+ would be in approximate equilibrium when the membrane potential was depolarized by 56 mV. The membrane was then stimulated by such a potential step (Fig. 5-28,A). Since Na^+ was in equilibrium at the stimulus voltage (i.e., $V_m - E_{Na} = 0$), no Na current flowed in response to the depolarizing potential step (Fig. 5-28,B). What remained was the delayed outward current, which was later shown to be carried by K^+ (p. 136). The delayed-current curve was then subtracted from the complex curve obtained with normal Na-containing solution. The difference between these two curves (shaded area, Fig. 5-28,B) represents the time course of the current carried inward through the membrane by Na^+, and is plotted in Figure 5-28,C.

What does the time course of sodium current tell us about the behavior of the membrane? It is necessary, first, to note in Equation 5-10 that the sodium current, I_{Na}, is determined according to Ohm's Law by two factors: (1) the conductance, g_{Na}, of the membrane to Na^+ and (2) the electrochemical driving force, or emf, acting on Na^+ (i.e., $V_m - E_{Na}$). This means that when the membrane is suddenly shifted to a steady depolarized level, the time course of the sodium current must be proportional to the time course of the underlying change in the sodium conductance produced by the depolarization. The time course of increased I_{Na} in Figure 5-28,C can therefore

5-26. *Results of a voltage-clamp experiment. A hyperpolarization (trace a) results in a small, constant membrane current (a'). A depolarization produces an initial inward current (downward deflection in trace b') followed by a slowly developing, delayed outward current (upward in trace b'). [After Hodgkin, Huxley, and Katz, 1952.]*

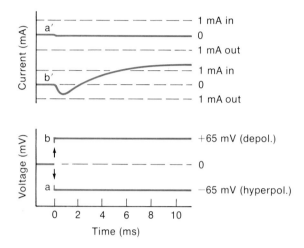

5-28. *Separation of the time course of the early inward Na current from that of the delayed outward current. A. Voltage change. B. Trace a, current recorded in normal sea water; trace b, current carried by K^+ alone in low-Na^+ seawater. C. Trace b subtracted from trace A gives time course of Na current, trace c. [After Hodgkin, 1952a.]*

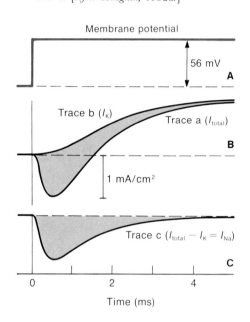

5-27. *A sodium substitution experiment on squid axon. In Na-free solution, the early inward current is abolished (center column). Note the small early outward currents under Na-free conditions. Return to normal Na-containing sea water restored the inward current (right-hand column). Choline was used as a substitute for Na^+. The numbers at left indicate the amplitude of the positive-going stimulus voltage. The calibration scales indicate current, all divisions being equivalent. [After Hodgkin and Huxley, 1952a.]*

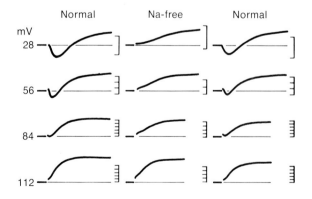

be equated with the time course of the increased sodium conductance. Note that although V_m is held constant at the depolarized potential, the Na conductance, after reaching a maximum within 1 ms, rapidly subsides to its low prestimulus level (Fig. 5-28,C). Thus there are two separate processes. The increase in Na conductance evoked by a depolarization is termed *sodium activation*, and its subsequent time-dependent return to the base level is due to *inactivation* of the sodium channels. When the proteolytic enzyme pronase is perfused through the squid axon, it eliminates Na-inactivation, so that the inward Na current persists during prolonged depolarizations. This suggests that a protein molecule participates in the process of Na-inactivation.

The Sodium Channel

A number of observations suggest that the sodium current passes through a finite number of channels in the excited membrane (Fig. 5-29). These channels have a high selectivity for Li$^+$ and Na$^+$ relative to other ions (Fig. 5-30). *Tetrodotoxin* (TTX), a compound extracted from the viscera of the Japanese pufferfish, blocks sodium activation by inserting itself into the sodium channels (Fig. 5-31). Experiments on several types of nerves have shown that less than 100 molecules of TTX bind to the sodium-selective sites in 1 μm^2 of axon membrane, completely blocking the increase in sodium conductance that normally accompanies depolarization. The kinetics of the blocking indicate that each TTX molecule blocks a single Na channel. Thus the number of channels per square micrometer must be less than 100. If all of these channels are simultaneously open, the total cross-sectional area occupied by all the Na channels (assuming a channel diameter of 5 Å, Fig. 5-31,B) will be less than 1/50,000th of the membrane surface area. That this minute fraction of the surface is occupied by channels is consistent with the Danielli and Singer membrane models (p. 84), in which large areas of uninterrupted lipid bilayer account for the low permeability of the membrane to polar molecules. The invariant capacitance of the membrane during large conductance changes is also consistent with the infinitesimal fraction of membrane area occupied by ion-conducting channels.

The way in which the sodium channel is *gated* (i.e., turned "on" and "off") by membrane depolarization is not understood. One possibility, of course, is that there is a mechanical barrier to sodium ions at rest and that the barrier transiently opens and then closes when the membrane is depolarized (Fig. 5-29,A). The major evidence favoring a physical reordering or conformational change is the recent discovery of minute *gating currents* associated with the opening and closing of the Na channels. These are interpreted as arising from movements of charged groups associated with the gating mechanism of the Na channel.

The Regenerative Nature of Electrical Excitation

By subjecting the membrane to sudden changes in potential of different values, Hodgkin and Huxley demonstrated that the peak intensity of the early inward current depends on the value of the stimulating potential, V_m. As Figure 5-32 shows, the peak current increases with moderate positive-going steps, but then

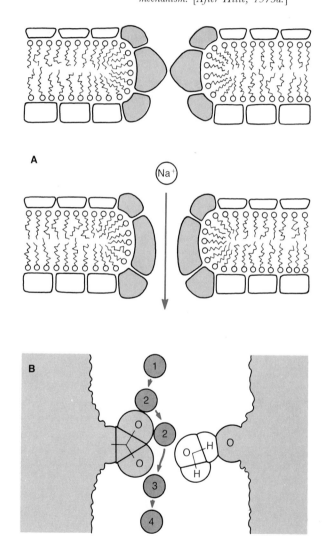

5-29. Models of the Na channel of excited membranes. A. General model. The "gate" in the channel is shown closed at the top and open at the bottom. The elements comprising the channel and gate are believed to be proteins. [Davison, 1967.] B. Recent, more specific model of the Na channel, showing four stages (1, 2, 3, 4) in the passage of a Na$^+$ ion (shaded circle) through the channel. A water molecule is hydrogen-bonded to a strongly electronegative oxygen at the right. The two oxygens at the left are part of a carboxyl group. The sodium ion interacts electrostatically with the oxygen atoms in passing through the channel. This model does not include a gating mechanism. [After Hille, 1975a.]

5-30. The relative selectivity of the sodium channel is indicated by the ratios of permeability coefficients of ions that pass through the early Na channel of the squid axon. [After Taylor, 1967.]

Li	Na	K	Rb	Cs	Choline
1.1	1	1/12	1/40	1/60	1/73

5-31. *The pufferfish poison, tetrodotoxin. A. Molecular structure of TTX.
B. Space-filling model of the toxin as it is believed to fit into the Na
channel (Hille, 1975b). C. Effect of TTX on the early inward current.
Traces are recorded at 15-s intervals after the application of 1.5×10^{-7}
M TTX to squid axon. Note reduction in size of early current, whereas late
current remains unchanged.* [After Moore and Narahashi, 1967.]

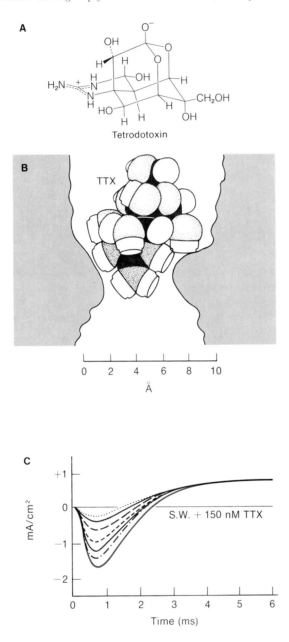

5-32. *Current-voltage relations of the early inward current.
A. Voltage and current recordings on which plot B is
based. B. Early current amplitude plotted against V_m.
Curve straightens out in the presence of tetrodotoxin
(broken line), revealing the nonspecific conductance of the
unexcited membrane. C. Changes in Na conductance,
Δg_{Na}, plotted on the same voltage scale. Note that the
maximum inward current in plot B coincides with
saturation of the Na conductance. With g_{Na} turned fully
on the inward current drops linearly toward E_{Na} in
curve B.*

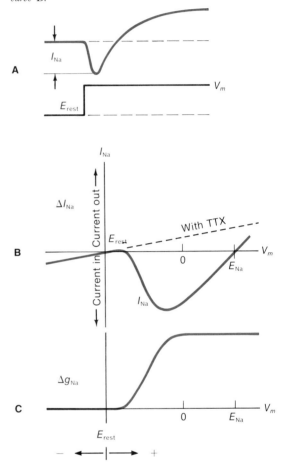

decreases with greater positive potential. To understand the decrease, it is necessary to refer to Equation
5-10, in which the sodium current, I_{Na}, is a function of
the term $(V_m - E_{Na})$ as well as the sodium conductance. Thus, as V_m approaches the potential, E_{Na},
at which sodium is in electrochemical equilibrium
(about $+55$ mV), I_{Na} must approach zero even though
g_{Na} is very high. Figure 5-33,A shows plots of sodium

conductances at various stimulus potentials. The plots
were calculated with Equation 5-10 from data similar
to those in Figure 5-32. In Figure 5-33,B it can be seen
that the g_{Na} transient increases sigmoidally with depolarization, reaching a plateau when the membrane
is depolarized by more than 100 mV.

The increase in sodium conductance produced by
depolarization is the basis of the regenerative behavior
necessary for the production of an all-or-none action
potential. When the membrane is allowed to respond
freely to a stimulus without voltage-clamp control,
as in Figure 5-18, an increase in g_{Na} produced by a
depolarizing stimulus allows Na^+ to flow inward across
the membrane, carrying its positive charge into the
cell and thus producing further depolarization. The

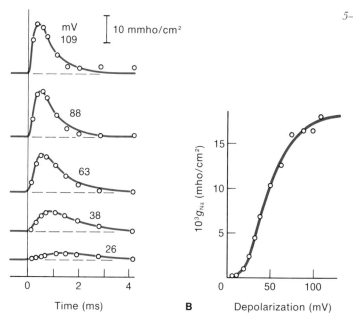

A   Time (ms)   B   Depolarization (mV)

5–33. A. Plots of g_{Na} against time at different amplitudes of depolarization given in mV. [Hodgkin, 1957.]   B. Maximum values of g_{Na} at each potential plotted against amplitude of depolarization. This is similar to the idealized curve in Figure 5–32,C, but is based on actual measurements. [After Hodgkin and Huxley, 1952.]

5–34. The Hodgkin Cycle. The broken line indicates where the voltage clamp interrupts the positive-feedback loop. With the loop closed, the system is regenerative, and accounts for the upstroke of the action potential.

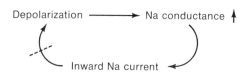

additional depolarization due to Na influx produces a further increase in the sodium conductance (Fig. 5-34), and this permits a further increase in the rate of Na influx. The circular relation between membrane potential and Na conductance is known as the *Hodgkin Cycle*. This is an example of positive feedback, which is inherently unstable and explosive, so to speak. The rapidity of the upstroke of the action potential is due in part to the regenerative, explosive nature of the Hodgkin Cycle. The upstroke is limited in extent, however, by E_{Na}, for the potential produced by the Na current is self-limiting by its dependence on the driving force, $V_m - E_{Na}$, and therefore cannot exceed the Na equilibrium potential. For a further description of the relations between membrane voltage and membrane current, see Box 5-3.

BOX 5-3   CURRENT-VOLTAGE RELATIONS

When the peak intensity of the early Na current is plotted against stimulus voltage, a current-voltage curve results that is characteristic of electrically excitable membranes (Fig. 5-32,B). A series of voltage-clamp steps are applied, beginning at a *holding potential*, similar to the normal resting potential, shown by the origin of the voltage axis. The membrane is depolarized in a series of test pulses, each beginning at the holding potential and stepping abruptly to a selected potential along the voltage axis. The early current (Fig. 5-32,A) recorded in response to each potential step is then plotted as a function of the test potential, V_m.

As the voltage steps reach more positive values (i.e., from left to right on the voltage axis), the current-voltage plot (Fig. 5-32,B) first shows a region of positive slope in which an increase in positive potential is accompanied by an increase in outward current, essentially as predicted for a resistor behaving according to Ohm's law. At potentials somewhat more positive, there begins a region of negative (descending) slope along which each increment in positive potential produces an increment in inward current.

The region of negative slope in the sodium current curve (Fig. 5-32,B) results from the progressive increase in g_{Na}, which occurs with increased depolarization along that segment of the voltage axis (Fig. 5-32,C). At the potential at which g_{Na} reaches a maximum (Fig. 5-32,C), the transient inward Na current is at a maximum (bottom of curve in Figure 5-32,B). At yet more positive potentials, the emf acting on Na^+ (i.e., $V_m - E_{Na}$) drops linearly with further increase in positivity. Thus the current-voltage plot crosses the voltage axis (i.e., zero current) at $V_m = E_{Na}$.

It is interesting to note that the current that flows into the cell through the increased sodium conductance of the membrane crosses the membrane in the direction opposite to that in which the stimulating current delivered by an electrode must pass to depolarize the membrane. How can both outward stimulating current and inward Na current cause depolarization? The apparent contradiction is resolved if one simply thinks of the channels of increased sodium conductance as current sources that inject current (positive charge in the form of Na^+) into the cell, just as a microelectrode inserted through the membrane can inject positive charge. In both cases, the current entering the cell adds positive charge to the cell interior, depolarizing the membrane.

Delayed Outward Potassium Current

The regenerative increase in sodium conductance is responsible, as we have seen, for the upstroke of the action potential. How, then, is the membrane potential subsequently returned to the resting level? Hodgkin and Huxley suspected that the delayed outward current in Figure 5-28 corresponds to the efflux of positive charge that shifts the membrane potential from the peak of the overshoot to the resting potential. The intensity of the delayed current during maintained potential steps is plotted in Figure 5-35 against

membrane potential. The slope of the curve (conductance) increases as the membrane potential is made more positive. Another way of stating this is that in the steady state, several milliseconds after a potential change, the membrane current passes more readily (i.e., rectifies) in the outward direction than in the inward direction. This behavior is known as delayed rectification.

It was logical to suppose that the delayed outward current evoked by a depolarization is carried by potassium ions, because the electrochemical potential acting on K^+ (Eq. 5-6) increases as the interior is made progressively more positive than E_K. Thus the tendency for K^+ to leak out and carry positive charge out of the cell increases as the cell interior is made more positive. At the peak of the action potential, the emf tending to drive K^+ out of the cell and restore the resting potential is at a maximum. It should not be overlooked, however, that the experiments clearly indicate (Fig. 5-28) that there is a time-dependent turning on of a conductance that allows this current to flow.

Hodgkin and Huxley (1953) used radioactive potassium to measure the movement of K^+ across the membrane during the passage of steadily applied current. The results showed that potassium efflux was small during inward current and large during outward current. Moreover, the K efflux agreed quantitatively with the amount of charge carried by the outward current (Fig. 5-36). This provided convincing

5–35. *Current-voltage relations of the delayed outward current. The method used to obtain this plot is the same as that for Figure 5–32,B except that the current was measured about 5 ms after E_m was applied, as shown in the inset. Note that after this delay, the membrane passes current more easily in the outward than in the inward direction.*

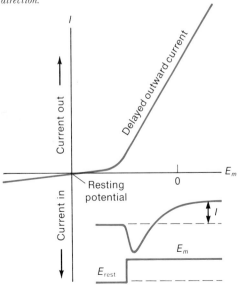

5–36. *Efflux of radioactively labeled K^+ plotted against membrane current during steady electrical depolarization of squid axon. The proportionality provides strong evidence that K^+ carries the late outward current. [After Hodgkin, 1957.]*

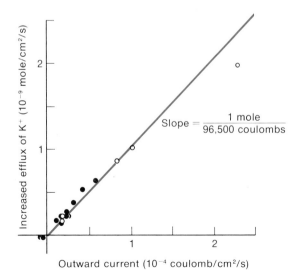

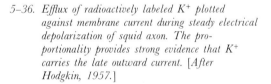

evidence that the delayed outward current is carried by K[+]. The delayed increase in membrane conductance to K[+] upon depolarization is termed *potassium activation*.

The delayed increase in potassium permeability can be suppressed by some agents. Procaine and xylocaine, both local anesthetics, diminish potassium activation as well as sodium activation, and thereby block impulse conduction in nerves. Tetraethylammonium ions (TEA), when injected into an axon, interfere only with potassium activation. As a result, repolarization is delayed and the action potential is prolonged.

The Action Potential Summarized in Terms of Ionic Mechanisms

The sequence of events that produce the action potential can be outlined with reference to the equivalent circuit in Figure 5-37 and the graphs in Figure 5-38.

1. Stimulating current of threshold intensity is passed from an electrode inside the cell across the membrane to the exterior. This applies positive charge to the intracellular side of the membrane, partially discharging the membrane capacitance, C_m (Fig. 5-37) and causing the depolarization from points *a* to *b* in Figure 5-38.

2. As the membrane potential approaches threshold, the sodium conductance of the membrane increases slightly. Below threshold, K efflux is sufficient to cancel the charge carried by Na influx. The potential at which Na influx begins strongly to exceed K efflux is the threshold (*b*).

3. The net inward current causes the membrane to depolarize further. The depolarization becomes regenerative, since each increment of positive potential increases g_{Na}, and this further hastens the inflow of Na[+], producing another increment in positive potential (Hodgkin cycle). This produces the upstroke.

4. As the membrane potential approaches E_{Na} the electromotive force ($V_m - E_{Na}$) acting on Na[+] becomes progressively smaller. This causes the rate of potential change to slow progressively from point *c* until the overshoot reaches a maximum somewhat short of E_{Na} (point *d*). The peak of the overshoot is about $+120$ mV from the resting potential. Thus the initial passive depolarization to threshold (ca. $+20$ mV) produced by the stimulating current is *amplified* five or six times by the regenerative depolarization of the membrane.

5. The sodium conductance declines due to an inherent relaxation of the open Na channels—that is, Na inactivation.

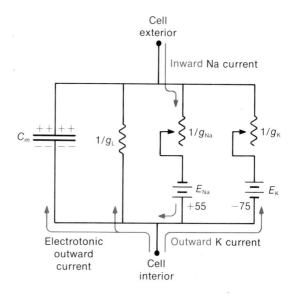

5-37. An equivalent circuit describing the electrical behavior of the axon membrane during an action potential. C_m, membrane capacitance; g_L, lumped nonspecific conductances of the membrane; g_{Na}, g_K, sodium and potassium variable conductances sensitive to membrane potential. Arrows indicate ionic currents.

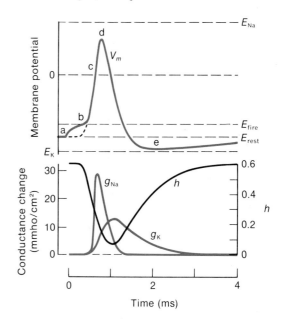

5-38. An action potential (top), with underlying changes in Na[+] and K[+] conductances plotted below. The value h (right-hand scale) represents the ability of the sodium channels to become activated (i.e., opened) by a depolarization. Note that the decrease in h far outlasts the increase in g_{Na}. [After Hodgkin, 1957.]

6. The delayed potassium conductance starts to increase. This allows K^+ to diffuse rapidly outward, removing positive charge from the cell and thereby repolarizing the membrane to the resting level (*d* to *e*).

Upon completion of the repolarization, the number of potassium ions having left the cell equals the number of sodium ions that initially entered the axon. Na^+-inactiviation and high potassium conductance persist for several milliseconds after the action potential. This produces the depressed excitability characteristic of the absolute and relative refractory periods. Sodium inactivation and potassium activation also contribute to the increase in threshold that accompanies a subthreshold depolarization (accommodation, Fig. 5-20). The different degrees of accommodation observed in different membranes result from quantitative differences in time- and voltage-dependencies of Na inactivation and K activation.

Changes in Ion Concentration During Excitation

It is important to note that the ionic movements responsible for the potential changes of a single action potential are extremely small and *do not appreciably change the intracellular ionic concentrations* in any but the smallest cells or axons.

It can be calculated from the principles discussed on page 122 that about 10^{-12} moles of Na^+ crossing 1 cm^2 of membrane is sufficient to produce an action potential of 100 mV amplitude. This is only 160 sodium ions per square micrometer. Because of the partial canceling effect of simultaneous K outflow, the actual number is closer to 500 sodium ions per μm^2 per impulse. Extending the calculation, it becomes evident that a single action potential changes the internal Na^+ concentration of a squid axon 1 mm in diameter by only 1 part in more than 100,000. For this reason, a squid axon can generate thousands of impulses with the sodium pump incapacitated by a metabolic poison. Eventually, of course, the concentrations, and hence the equilibrium potentials, of Na^+ and K^+ will show significant shifts toward equilibration.

In axons of smaller diameter, the increased surface-to-volume ratio results in more significant change in axoplasmic concentration with a single action potential. For example, in mammalian "C" fibers (axons), which have diameters of only 10^{-3} mm, the flux from a single impulse changes the internal Na^+ and K^+ concentrations by about 1%. This results in a drop in resting potential of about 0.3 mV, and, for ten action potentials in close succession, a depolarization of 2 mV. Thus in axons of small diameter, it is important that the intracellular resting concentrations of Na^+ and K^+ be restored rapidly by active transport before cumulative ion fluxes produce significant changes in ion gradients.

Note that *metabolic "pumping" of ions across the cell membrane does not enter directly into the production or recovery of an action potential,* but serves to maintain the ionic concentration gradients required for the production of membrane currents.

Internal Perfusion Experiments

An additional advantage presented by the squid giant axon is the possibility of removing its axoplasm and replacing it with artificial test solutions to control or alter at will the internal concentrations of ions and metabolites. As shown in Figure 5-39,A, the axoplasm can be gently expelled in a manner not unlike the squeezing of toothpaste from a tube. The axon can then be perfused with an artificial solution (Fig. 5-39B). It was found that the resting potential varies approximately as predicted by Equation 5-9 when K^+ is altered. The ability of the membrane to produce action potentials remains unimpaired by the removal of axoplasm (Fig. 5-40,A). Increases in the intracellular sodium ion concentration cause a smaller overshoot by the action potential (Fig. 5-40,B), as predicted by Equation 5-7. The ionic hypothesis of resting and action potentials, derived originally from the effects of changing the extracellular concentrations of various ions, is confirmed by the effects of altered internal ion concentrations. This provided the final evidence that it is the *gradient* of ion concentrations across the membrane, and not the absolute concentrations, that contributes to the electrical behavior of the membrane.

Action Potentials Generated by Ions other than Sodium

The ionic hypothesis was initially tested and confirmed by experiments on the Na action potential of the giant axon of squid. Subsequent work on other tissues has shown the hypothesis to be universally correct in its major features. Sodium, however, is not unique as the carrier of the regenerative depolarizing current. If lithium is provided in place of Na^+, it will substitute for Na^+ in carrying the inward current through the Na channels in nerve and muscle and will

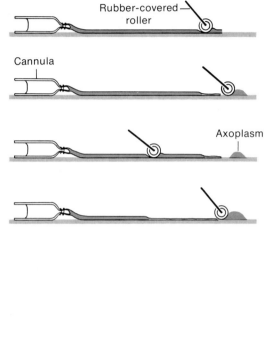

5–39. *Technique used for perfusing the squid giant axon. A. Axoplasm is gently rolled out little by little. B. Axon suspended between two cannulae, with test solution perfused axially through axon. The internal electrode records potentials. [After Baker, Hodgkin, and Shaw, 1961.]*

Rubber-covered roller

Cannula

Axoplasm

A

produce normal action potentials. But cells exposed to lithium gradually depolarize because the Li$^+$ that enters the cell is not extruded by the sodium pump, and therefore accumulates in the cell, permanently displacing an equivalent amount of K$^+$. The reduction in the potassium concentration gradient results in a lower resting potential. The steady depolarization inactivates the sodium mechanism and finally renders the axon inexcitable. The therapeutic action of small doses of LiCl$_2$ administered to manic-depressive patients may be caused by small modifications in nerve cell excitability.

There are, in addition to the Na channel, membrane channels selective for other ions capable of carrying inward current in response to depolarizing stimuli. A particularly odd case occurs in certain excitable algae such as *Nitella* and *Chara*. These elon-

5–40. *A. Comparison of action potential in an extruded axon perfused with isotonic potassium sulfate (top) and an intact axon (bottom). B. Effect of $[Na^+]_i$ on overshoot in perfused axon. Record a, K_2SO_4; record b, one quarter of the K$^+$ replaced with Na$^+$; record c, one-half the K$^+$ replaced with Na$^+$. External Na$^+$ normal throughout. [After Baker, Hodgkin, and Shaw, 1961.]*

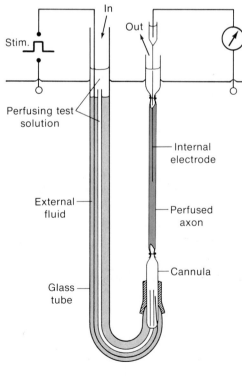

Stim.

In
Out

Perfusing test solution

Internal electrode

External fluid

Perfused axon

Cannula

Glass tube

B

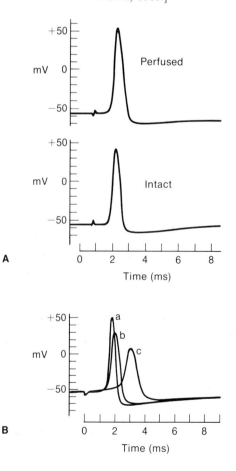

A

B

gated cells generate action potentials in which the upstroke is produced by a Cl efflux. The loss of negative charge by anion efflux is, of course, electrically equivalent to a cation influx.

CALCIUM CHANNELS

In recent years, evidence has accumulated for the widespread occurrence of electrically excitable Ca channels. Calcium ions carry all or part of the regenerative depolarizing current through such channels in crustacean muscle fibers, in smooth muscle cells, in the cell bodies and terminals of many nerve cells, in embryonic cells, and in the ciliate *Paramecium*. In such membranes, Ca^{2+} may carry the inward current together with Na^+ or by itself. In the latter case, the Ca current usually is not strong enough to produce an all-or-none action potential, and instead produces a *calcium response,* the size of which depends on the stimulus depolarization. This is seen at the upper left in Figure 5-41.

The electrically excited Ca channels are rendered defective or are eliminated by certain mutations in *Paramecium.* This can be seen in Figure 5-41 at the right. Failure of the channels to open in response to a depolarizing stimulus renders the membrane inexcitable, and the response is the simple exponential

change in voltage similar to that produced when a pulse of current is passed across a capacitance in parallel with a resistance. The effect of this mutation is similar to the Na-blocking effect that tetrodotoxin produces by rendering the Na channels of the squid axon inoperable.

The calcium channels of metazoan excitable cells are blocked to greater or lesser extents by certain divalent and trivalent cations, most notably Co^{2+}, Mn^{2+}, Ni^{2+}, and La^{3+}. These ions compete with Ca^{2+} at anionic sites associated with the channel, but do not pass through the channel as readily as Ca^{2+}. The ions Sr^{2+} and Ba^{2+}, on the other hand, compete with Ca^{2+} but are equally as capable, or more so, of carrying current through the Ca channels to produce action potentials. This is illustrated by the large all-or-none action potentials produced by *Paramecium* in a barium solution compared to the small graded responses obtained in a Ca solution (Fig. 5-41, left).

Calcium and Membrane Excitability

Calcium plays several important roles in the electrical behavior of excitable membranes and in modifying the electrical properties of membranes. It had been known for some time that the concentration of extracellular Ca^{2+} influences the threshold of firing in nerve and muscle membranes. Frankenhaeuser and Hodgkin (1957) had shown that the current-voltage curve of the early Na current (Fig. 5-32,B) is displaced along the voltage axis toward more positive potentials in high $[Ca^{2+}]_o$ and toward more negative potentials in low $[Ca^{2+}]_o$—in either case, about 12 mV per fivefold change in $[Ca^{2+}]_o$. This is ascribed to a nonspecific *screening effect* of the divalent cation; that is to say, the Ca^{2+} associates as a counterion with nega-

5-41. *Electrical excitability of a wild-type* Paramecium *(left) compared with the inexcitability of the membrane mutant "pawn," which has defective Ca channels (right). A. Bath solution consisted of 1 mM CaCl$_2$, 4 mM KCl and 1 mM tris-HCl (pH 7.2). The wild type shows graded calcium responses to depolarizing current, while the "pawn" mutant shows pure electrotonic responses. B. Bath solution consisted of 1 mM CaCl$_2$, 4 mM BaCl$_2$, 1 mM Tris-HCl. The wild type exhibits strong all-or-none barium action potentials, produced by Ba^{2+} carrying current through Ca channels, and the "pawn" again shows only electrotonic responses. The lower set of traces in each record indicates the stimulus current. [After Kung and Eckert, 1972.]*

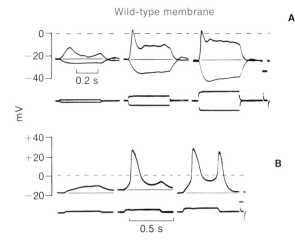
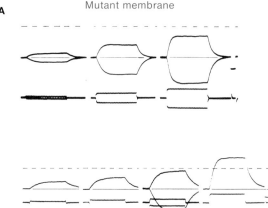

tive sites on the membrane and thereby changes the voltage profile across the membrane and solution close to the membrane, causing the membrane to experience a different voltage gradient in different Ca^{2+} concentrations, even though the voltages measured between the bulk intra- and extracellular phases remain unchanged. Other divalent cations, such as Mg^{2+}, also produce the nonspecific screening effect.

More recently, evidence has accumulated that *intra*cellular Ca^{2+}, as well, strongly influences the electrical behavior of various excitable membranes, but in a more specific manner. This occurs through an action on the potassium conductance. An increase in $[Ca^{2+}]_i$ produces an increase in the resting (i.e. non-electrically stimulated) potassium permeability in nerve cell bodies, some sensory receptor cells, red blood cells. This has been shown by direct injection of Ca^{2+} through a micropipette or by loading the cells in other ways.

Still more recent evidence shows that during or immediately after the inward flow of Ca^{2+} through membrane Ca channels in response to depolarization, the Ca^{2+} strongly activates an outward K current. This K current adds to the K current that turns on directly in response to the depolarization itself. The K-activating effect of Ca influx helps repolarize the membrane in those cells in which the inward depolarizing current is carried by Ca^{2+}. Very little Ca current is seen in the squid axon; in keeping with this observation, the K conductance in this membrane is independent of $[Ca^{2+}]_i$.

Barium ions can substitute for Ca^{2+} in carrying current through membrane channels that normally carry Ca^{2+}. But Ba^{2+} does not show the same effect as Ca^{2+} in turning on the K^+ permeability. As a result, membranes that have a Ca system (e.g., crustacean muscle, nerve cell bodies, and axon terminals, *Paramecium*) produce prolonged action potentials in barium (Fig. 5-42) that resemble myocardial potentials. The repolarizing K current normally turned on by Ca influx fails to turn on, or turns on weakly, in response to a barium influx. Since repolarization depends largely on the activation of the K system, the action potential in which the upstroke is produced by an influx of Ba^{2+} exhibits a prolonged duration. A similar prolongation has been produced without the use of barium by injecting into the cell a compound (EGTA) that binds free Ca^{2+} and prevents the accumulation of intracellular free Ca^{2+} during an action potential.

PERSISTENT Ca CURRENTS

As explained earlier, an important characteristic of the Na channel is that it becomes spontaneously in-

activated even when the membrane is artificially maintained in a depolarized condition. In squid axon, the channel opens and automatically shuts, all in a matter of about a millisecond. Recent experiments on membranes of nerve cell bodies in gastropods have shown that the calcium channel in those membranes exhibits extremely slow inactivation during maintained depolarization (Fig. 5-43). This is interesting in part because it allows time for significant amounts of Ca^{2+} to move through the membrane into the cell during depolarization. As discussed in Box 4-3, modulation of intracellular $[Ca^{2+}]$ by membrane permeability changes is an important regulatory mechanism for a variety of cell functions.

MYOCARDIAL POTENTIALS

Except in certain minor details, the action potentials of vertebrate skeletal muscle resemble those of neurons, and need no further comment here. Action po-

5-42. *Calcium-barium competition and duration of the action potential in* Paramecium. *Top. Overshoot of action potential plotted against extracellular barium concentration. Bottom. Duration of action potential plotted against Ba^{2+} concentration. A. Calcium concentration held constant at 1 mM. B. $[Ca^{2+}]_o$ varied with $[Ba^{2+}]_o$ to maintain constant ratio. The overshoot increases with increased $[Ba^{2+}]_o$ in both cases, but the duration of the action potential increases as the concentration ratio Ba^{2+}/Ca^{2+} increases. [After Naitoh and Eckert, 1968.]*

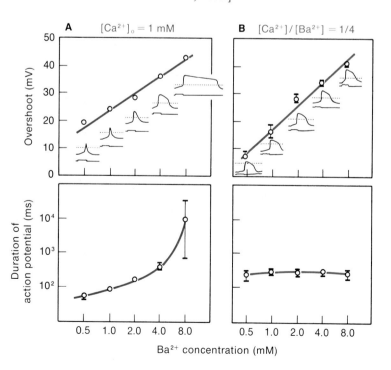

5-43. *Persistent calcium system in a snail neuron.* A. *Inward current (downward deflection of trace) during prolonged (1/2 s) depolarizations of three amplitudes (shown at left). The depolarization began and ended as shown by arrows. The recording was interrupted at the gap for 250 ms.* B. *Plot of the late current (colored curve) recorded 200 ms after onset of the voltage pulse against membrane potential during the pulse. Note the small inward current carried by Ca²⁺ between −45 and −28 mV. This small inward current is obscured at less negative potentials by the strong outward K current [After Eckert and Lux, 1976.]*

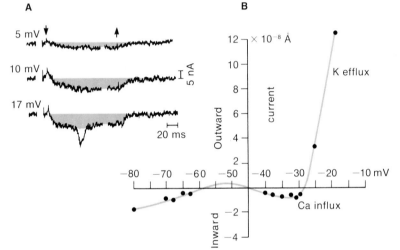

5-44. *Cardiac action potentials.* A *and* B *are from different cells in the sinus venosus of the frog. Note the slowly depolarizing pacemaker potentials between the action potentials.* C *was recorded from the atrial muscle. [After Hutter and Trautwein, 1956.]* D. *Action potential recorded from a cell in the ventricle of the frog. [After Orkand, 1968.] Note the abrupt origin of the action potential in nonpacemaker tissue.*

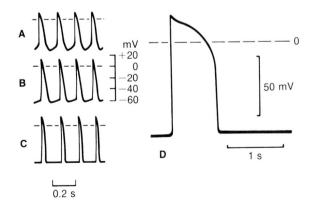

tentials of cardiac muscle, however, differ in certain respects from those of nerve and skeletal muscle. The most striking feature of the action potential in the ventricle of the heart is its long duration, up to 1 s in amphibians (Fig. 5-44,D). The long duration allows time for full contraction of the *myocardium* (heart muscle). Following a rapid upstroke, there is a protracted, slowly descending *plateau* terminated by a rapid repolarization. The upstroke is due primarily to inward current carried by Na⁺, as in squid axon. The evidence indicates that the prolonged plateau results largely from a high Ca conductance. The rapid repolarization following the plateau appears to be due to a drop in Ca conductance together with an increase in K conductance.

PACEMAKER POTENTIALS

Rhythmic "firing" of action potentials occurs in a number of excitable tissues. In some receptor and nerve cells a steady stimulus produces a steady *train* of impulses (Fig. 5-21,A). Certain *pacemaker* cells are spontaneously active, firing at a steady rate without input from any extrinsic source. There are several possible mechanisms based on the ionic hypothesis which might produce *autorhythmicity*. A familiar example of autorhythmicity is known from the pacemaker tissues of vertebrate hearts (Fig. 5-44). The membranes of cells in the pacemaker region (sinoauricular node) have no fixed resting potential, but undergo a steady depolarization termed a *pacemaker potential* preceding each action potential (Fig. 5-44,A,B). The interval between cardiac action potentials depends in part on the rate of depolarization during the pacemaker activity. A slower depolarization brings the membrane to the firing level later, and thus decreases the frequency of spontaneous discharge. The action potential initiated in the pacemaker cells is conducted and transmitted electrically through the myocardium to excite the remaining cells of the heart. A pacemaker cell can be recognized by the pacemaker depolarization, which is absent in the other cells, whose upstrokes arise abruptly out of their resting potentials (Fig. 5-44,C,D).

Pacemaker activity has its origin in time-dependent changes in membrane conductance. In the atrial cells of the frog heart, the pacemaker depolarization begins immediately after the previous action potential, when the potassium conductance of the membrane is very high. The potassium conductance then gradually drops, and the membrane shows a corresponding depolarization due to a moderately high steady conductance for sodium. The pacemaker depolarization continues until the electrically excited sodium conductance (not to be confused with the resting Na conductance) is activated, and the rapid regenerative upstroke of the cardiac action potential takes over.

Acetylcholine, which slows the heart when released by activity of the vagus nerve (p. 158), does so by increasing potassium conductance of the pacemaker cells. This keeps the membrane potential near E_K for a longer time, thereby slowing the pacemaker depolarization, and thus delaying the onset of the next upstroke (Fig. 5-45).

Figure 5-46 summarizes a recent proposal for the rhythmic generation of pacemaker waves which underlie the "bursting" of spontaneously oscillating neurons in snails and other molluscs. These neurons exhibit a persistent Ca current (Fig. 5-43) which is turned on by a depolarization due to a decrease in potassium conductance (I) which occurs following the previous wave. This weak Ca current adds to the depolarization and is weakly regenerative (II), and results in a rise in $[Ca^{2+}]_i$ with time (III). The rise in $[Ca^{2+}]_i$ turns on g_K (IV), and the membrane begins to repolarize as K^+ carries charge out of the cell. The repolarization turns off g_{Ca} (V), which increases the rate of repolarization. The cycle resumes after a pause as $[Ca^{2+}]_i$ is lowered by the Ca pump, allowing g_K to drop again (I'), leading to a new pacemaker depolarization (Eckert and Lux, 1976).

Summary

The electrical properties of the cell membrane can be conceptualized with the help of an equivalent electric circuit. The lipid bilayer has the property of capacitance; that is, it does not readily allow charge carriers (i.e., ions) to pass through, but because it is very thin (ca. 50 Å) it can store electric charge by means of electrostatic interaction between cations and anions on opposite sides of the membrane. Channels penetrating the lipid bilayer have the property of conductance, since they permit physical passage of ions across the membrane. These two properties, conductance (reciprocal of resistance) and capacitance, determine the time course of voltage changes produced across electrically active cell membranes.

An asymmetrical distribution of ions in solution on the two sides of a membrane can produce an electric potential across the membrane, depending on the relative permeabilities of the membrane to the ions present. If it is permeable to one ion species only, the membrane will develop a potential difference proportional to the log of the ratio of concentrations of the ion on opposite sides of the membrane, the difference in potential resulting from the electrostatic charge carried across the membrane by the diffusible ion. The

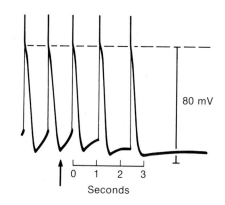

5-45. *The effect of acetylcholine on pacemaker activity in the mammalian heart. Acetylcholine was applied topically at the time indicated by the arrow, resulting in a depression of the pacemaker potential. [After Hecht, 1965.]*

80 mV

0 1 2 3

Seconds

5-46. *Proposed events (I to VI) responsible for pacemaker waves in spontaneously "bursting" neurons. During the slow depolarization, the Ca conductance, g_{Ca}, is turned on, allowing an influx of Ca^{2+}. As the $[Ca^{2+}]_i$ rises, it gradually activates the potassium conductance, g_K. Thereupon the membrane repolarizes toward E_K, causing the calcium conductance, g_{Ca}, to turn off. As a result, $[Ca^{2+}]_i$ drops, g_K drops, and the membrane potential slowly shifts away from E_K (i.e., depolarizes), turning on g_{Ca} and initiating a new cycle. The slow depolarizing pacemaker waves give rise to trains of action potentials as the wave reaches and exceeds the firing level. The wave at the left is shown without action potentials for the sake of simplicity.*

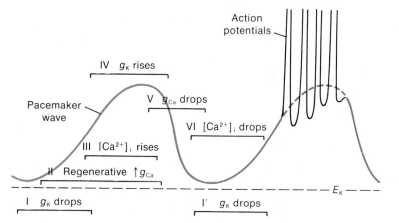

diffusional and electrostatic forces acting on that ion species will be equal and opposite at the so-called equilibrium potential, determined by the ratio of concentrations of that ion across the membrane. If the membrane shows significant permeability to more than one ion species, as is common in biological systems, the membrane potential reflects the contributed diffusion potentials of those ions. Since resting cell membranes are most permeable to K^+ and Cl^-, the resting potential is close to the equilibrium potentials of these two ions, which usually have similar but always oppositely directed concentration gradients. Since the free K^+ concentration of the cell interior is usually 10 to 60 times that of the cell exterior, the resting potential (inside voltage with respect to outside voltage) is -60 to -100 mV (i.e., -0.6 to -1×10^{-1} V). Since the sodium and calcium ions are more concentrated outside the cell than they are within the cytoplasm, they have a strong tendency to leak into the cell, and must be continually pumped out. Stimuli that increase the normally low permeability to either Na^+ or Ca^{2+} lead to a strong influx of one or the other, which tends to decrease the negative potential of (i.e., depolarize) the cell interior. A transient increase in Na^+ permeability, in fact, is responsible for the upstroke (depolarization) of the nerve impulse. Since this increase in sodium permeability is evoked by membrane depolarization, the upstroke of the nerve impulse is regenerative and causes the membrane potential to approach briefly the sodium equilibrium potential of $+50$ to $+60$ mV at the peak of the nerve impulse. A delayed rise in K permeability brought on by the voltage change across the membrane, together with rapid inactivation of the sodium permeability, brings the membrane back to the resting potential.

In some excitable membranes calcium ions carry all or part of the inward depolarizing current. In some of those membranes, the Ca^{2+} that enters turns on potassium channels, which hastens the repolarization process. The subsequent removal of intracellular Ca^{2+}, restoring $[Ca^{2+}]_i$ to the original low level, restores the resting K permeability.

EXERCISES

1. Galvani and Volta each considered the other's view of "animal electricity" (i.e., electrophysiology) incorrect. Explain why they were, in fact, both correct in certain respects.

2. What are the chief carriers of current in biological solutions and across membranes?

3. The cell membrane separates charge and therefore has a potential difference across it. Does this violate the rule of electroneutrality? Explain.

4. What is the structural basis for membrane capacitance? For conductance?

5. How is the time course of potential changes across the cell membrane related to the resistance and capacitance of the membrane?

6. A given intensity of injected current will produce a larger potential change in a small cell than in a large cell having similar membrane characteristics. Why?

7. A subthreshold current injected into an axon produces a potential change that decreases exponentially with distance from the point of injection. Why does the amplitude of the potential decrease with distance?

8. Explain why the side of the membrane having the higher concentration of the permeable cation is electrically negative.

9. In an artificial system in which the membrane is totally impermeable to all ion species but one, why would one expect a permanently unequal distribution of that ion to be maintained across the membrane?

10. In a living cell that is permeable to ions other than K^+, what prevents the K^+ from gradually being displaced from the cell interior by other cations?

11. For a cell that is 100 times more permeable to K^+ than to any other ion, use the Nernst Equation to determine the potential change produced by a doubling of the extracellular K^+ concentration.

12. What are the equilibrium potentials for each of the following ions of the given concentrations?
    (a) $[K^+]_o$ = 3 mM, $[K^+]_i$ = 150 mM.
    (b) $[Na^+]_o$ = 100 mM, $[Na^+]_i$ = 10 mM.
    (c) $[Ca^{2+}]_o$ = 10 mM, $[Ca^{2+}]_i$ = 10^{-6} mM.

13. In 1939, Cole and Curtis reported that membrane conductance increases but capacitance remains essentially unchanged during an action potential. Relate these findings to membrane structure and to changes in structure thought to occur during excitation.

14. Give two lines of evidence that Na^+ carries the inward current responsible for the upstroke of the action potential.

15. How did Hodgkin and Huxley show that the repolarization (return to resting potential) of the action potential is due in part to an increase in K permeability?

16. Does the Na pump play a *direct* role in any part of the action potential?

17. How is the Na pump *indirectly* important in the production of an action potential?

18. Explain the following classical phenomena in terms of the modern ionic hypothesis: (a) threshold potential, (b) all-or-none overshoot, (c) refractoriness, and (d) accommodation.

19. Calculate the approximate number of sodium ions entering through each square centimeter of axon surface during an action potential having an amplitude of 100 mV. (Recall that 1 coulomb is equivalent to 96,500 mole equivalents of charge; that membranes have a typical capacitance of 10^{-6} F/cm^2; and that Avogadro's number is 6.022×10^{23} atoms/mole.)

20. Why can it be said that an axon of large diameter undergoes essentially no change in ionic concentration during several action potentials, whereas the very thinnest axons undergo significant changes in concentration during several impulses?

21. The Hodgkin Cycle, which is responsible for the upstroke of the action potential, is an example of positive feedback in a biological system. Since positive feedback is inherently unstable, how does one account for the limited amplitude of the upstroke?

SUGGESTED READING

Adelman, W. J. 1971. *Biophysics and Physiology of Excitable Membranes.* Van Nostrand Reinhold, New York.

Aidley, D. J. 1971. *The Physiology of Excitable Cells.* Cambridge Univ. Press, New York.

Davies, M. 1973. *Functions of Biological Membranes.* Chapman and Hall, London.

Davson, H. 1970. *A Textbook of General Physiology* (4th ed.). Churchill, London.

Duncan, C. J. (ed.). 1976. *Calcium in Biological Systems.* Cambridge Univ. Press, New York.

Hille, B. 1970. Ionic channels in nerve membranes. *Prog. In Biophys. and Molec. Biol.* 21:1–32.

Hodgkin, A. L. 1964. *The Conduction of the Nervous Impulse.* Charles C. Thomas, Springfield.

Junge, D. 1976. *Nerve and Muscle Excitation.* Sinauer, Sunderland, Mass.

Katz, B. 1966. *Nerve, Muscle and Synapse.* McGraw-Hill, New York.

Thomas, R. C. 1972. Electrogenic sodium pump in nerve and muscle cells. *Physiol. Rev.* 52: 563–94.

REFERENCES CITED

Baker, P. F., M. P. Blaustcin, R. D. Keynes, J. Manil, T. I. Shaw, and R. A. Steinhardt. 1969. The ouabain-sensitive fluxes of sodium and potassium in squid giant axons. *J. Physiol.* 200:459–496.

Baker, P. F., A. L. Hodgkin, and T. I. Shaw. 1961. Replacement of the protoplasm of a giant nerve fibre with artificial solutions. *Nature* (London) 190:885–887.

Bernstein, J. 1917. *Electrobiologie.* Brunswick.

Cole, K. S., and H. J. Curtis. 1939. Electric impedence of the squid giant axon during activity. *J. General Physiol.* 22:649–670.

Cross, S. B., R. D. Keynes, and R. Rybová. 1965. The coupling of sodium efflux and potassium influx in frog muscle. *J. Physiol.* 181:865–880.

Davison, P. F. 1967. Protein of nervous tissue: Specificity, turnover, and functions. *In* F. O. Schmitt (ed.), *The Neurosciences: A Study Program*, Rockefeller Univ. Press, New York.

Davson, H. 1964. *Textbook of General Physiology* (3rd ed.). Little, Brown & Co., New York.

Eckert, R., and H. D. Lux. 1976. A voltage-sensitive persistent calcium conductance in neuronal somata of *Helix. J. Physiol.* 254:129–151.

Frankenhaeuser, B., and A. F. Huxley. 1957. The action of calcium on the electrical properties of squid axons. *J. Physiol.* 137:218–244.

Goldman, D. E. 1943. Potential, impedence, and rectification in membranes. *J. Gen. Physiol.* 27:37–60.

Grundfest, H. 1966. Comparative electrobiology of excitable membranes. *Adv. Comp. Physiol. Biochem.* 2:1–116.

Hecht, H. H. 1965. Comparative physiological and morphological aspects of pacemaker tissues. *Ann. New York Acad. Science* 127:49–83.

Hille, B. 1975a. Ionic selectivity, saturation and block in sodium channels. A four barrier model. *J. Gen. Physiol.* 66:535–560.

Hille, B. 1975b. The receptor for tetrodotoxin and saxitoxin. *Biophysical Journal* 15:615–619.

Hodgkin, A. L. 1951. The ionic bases of electrical activity in nerve and muscle. *Biol. Rev.* 26:339–409.

Hodgkin, A. L. 1958. Ionic movements and electrical activity in giant nerve fibres. *Proc. Roy. Soc.* (London) Ser. B. 148:1–37.

Hodgkin, A. L., and P. Horowicz. 1959. The influence of potassium and chloride ions on the membrane potential of single muscle fibres. *J. Physiol.* 148:127–60.

Hodgkin, A. L., and A. F. Huxley. 1939. Action potentials recorded from inside a nerve fibre. *Nature* (London) 144:710–711.

Hodgkin, A. L., and A. F. Huxley. 1952a. Currents carried by sodium and potassium ions through the membrane of the giant axon of *Loligo. J. Physiol.* 116:449–472.

Hodgkin, A. L., and A. F. Huxley. 1952b. A quantitative description of membrane current and its application to conduction and excitation in nerve. *J. Physiol.* 117:500–544.

Hodgkin, A. L., and A. F. Huxley. 1953. The mobility and diffusion coefficient of potassium in giant axons from *Sepia. J. Physiol.* 119:513–528.

Hodgkin, A. L., A. F. Huxley, and B. Katz. 1952. Measurement of current voltage relations in the membrane of the giant axon of *Loligo. J. Physiol.* 116:424–448.

Hodgkin, A. L., and B. Katz. 1949. The effect of sodium ions on the electrical activity of the giant axon of the squid. *J. Physiol.* 108:37–77.

Hodgkin, A. L., and R. D. Keynes. 1957. Movements of labelled calcium in squid giant axons. *J. Physiol.* 138:253–281.

Hodgkin, A. L., and W. A. H. Rushton. 1946. The electrical constants of a crustacean nerve fibre. *Proc. Roy. Soc.* (London) Ser. B. 133:444–479.

Hutter, O. F., and W. Trautwein. 1956. Vagal and sympathetic effects on the pacemaker fibers in the sinus venosus of the heart. *J. Gen. Physiol.* 39:715–733.

Katz, B. 1961. The transmission of impulses from nerve to muscle, and the subcellular unit of synaptic action. (Croonian Lecture). *Proc. Roy. Soc.* (London) Ser. B. 115:455–477.

Keynes, R. D. 1954. The ionic fluxes in frog muscle. *Proc. Roy. Soc.* (London) Ser. B 142:359–382.

Keynes, R. D. 1958. The nerve impulse and the squid. *Scientific American* 199(6):83–90. [Also available as Offprint 58.]

Kung, C., and R. Eckert. 1972. Genetic modification of electric properties in an excitable membrane. *Proc. Nat. Acad. Sci.* 69:93–97.

Ling, G., and R. W. Gerard. 1949. The normal membrane potential of frog sartorius fibres. *J. Cell. Comp. Physiol.* 34:383–396.

Moore, J. W., and T. Narahashi. 1967. Tetrodotoxin's highly selective blockage of an ionic channel. *Fed. Proc.* 26:1655–1663.

Naitoh, Y., and R. Eckert. 1968. Electrical properties of *Paramecium caudatum*. All-or-none electrogenesis. *Z. vergl. Physiol.* 61:453–472.

Orkand, R. K. 1968. Facilitation of heart muscle contraction and its dependence on external Ca^{++} and Na^+. *J. Physiol.* 196:311–325.

Taylor, R. E. 1967. The role of inorganic ions in the nerve impulse. *In* F. O. Schmitt (ed.), *The Neurosciences: A Study Program.* Rockefeller Univ. Press, New York.

Young, J. Z. 1936. The giant nerve fibers and epistellar body of cephalopods. *Quart. J. Microscopical* Sci. 78:367–386.

CHAPTER SIX

Nerve Cells and Signals

Neurobiology, the study of the nervous system, has grown with great momentum in recent years. Now that biological scientists have elucidated many of the major outlines of somatic cell and tissue function, and the way in which macromolecules store and transfer information, they are turning with increasing interest to the nervous system, which also stores and analyzes information. The task of analyzing the functioning of the nervous system, however, is even more problematic than that of revealing the secrets of the gene, for unlike a strand of DNA, which is organized in essentially a one-dimensional order, the physical organization of the nervous system is three-dimensional, and extremely intricate at that, even in the most simple invertebrate species.

The question of how the nervous system gives rise to perception and behavior is undoubtedly one of the greatest of all challenges to science, for to unravel the functioning of the nervous system, the brain is called upon to analyze and understand itself. Whether such subjective phenomena as perception and consciousness will ever be understood in physical and chemical terms

can only be conjectured. For the present, we must be content to approach some of the simpler aspects of neural function—namely, such phenomena as sensory reception (Chapter 7), nervous integration, and motor control (Chapter 8). In this chapter, we will begin by considering the properties of the cells that make up the nervous system and the means they use to communicate with each other.

Neural Organization

Nervous systems are undoubtedly the most intricately organized structures to have evolved on Earth. The human nervous system contains 10^{10} to 10^{11} *neurons* (nerve cells) plus as many or more inexcitable supportive cells termed *glial cells*. Even the commonly studied "simple" nervous systems of invertebrates consist of tens or hundreds of thousands of neurons. It should therefore come as a relief to learn that, regardless of their number, all neurons operate by means of two basic types of electrical signals, as described below. Thus the complexity of the nervous system lies not in its variety of signals, but in the number and intricacy of the interconnections made between its many cells.

Nerves are the functional units of the nervous system; they are analogous, in a way, to the electrical components of a telephone system or a computer, but much more complex. They occur in a variety of shapes and sizes (Fig. 6-1). A vertebrate *motoneuron* (motor neuron), which originates in the spinal cord and innervates skeletal muscle fibers, is shown diagrammatically in Figure 6-2. In these neurons, the surface membrane of the *dendrites* and the *soma* (cell body) is innervated by the terminals of other nerve cells. The *axon* (nerve fiber) carries action potentials from the *spike-initiating zone* in the *axon hillock* to the *axon terminals,* which innervate muscle cells. The dendrites and the axon are processes that grow out from the soma during development, and into which there is a slow but steady flow of proteins and other constituents synthesized in the soma. Once disconnected from the cell body, these processes gradually deteriorate and die within a few days or weeks. Regeneration (regrowth) of axons is essentially absent in mammals; in the lower inver-

6–1. Three morphological types of neurons. There are wide variations within each type. Arrows indicate the direction of propagation of action potentials. [After Montagna, 1959.]

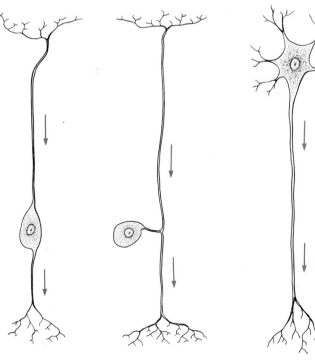

Bipolar   Unipolar   Multipolar

6–2. A vertebrate spinal motoneuron, with the functions of different parts indicated. The flow of information is indicated by colored arrows. Axon and surrounding myelin sheaths shown in longitudinal section.

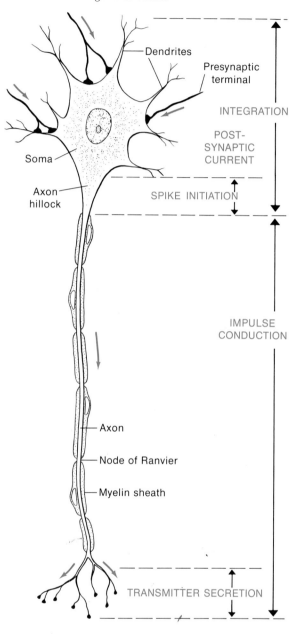

Dendrites
Presynaptic terminal
INTEGRATION
POST-SYNAPTIC CURRENT
Soma
SPIKE INITIATION
Axon hillock
IMPULSE CONDUCTION
Axon
Node of Ranvier
Myelin sheath
TRANSMITTER SECRETION

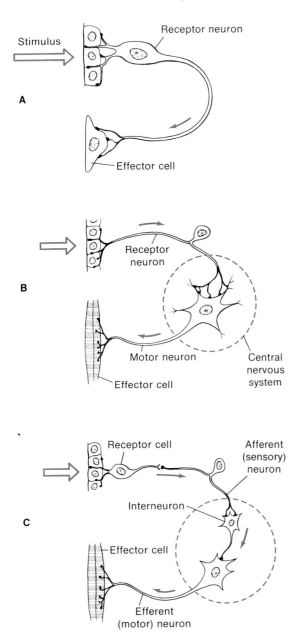

6-3. *Examples of simple reflex arcs.   A. Hypothetical primitive receptor cell directly innervating an effector cell.   B. Monosynaptic reflex arc.   C. Arc including several synaptic relays. Broken circles enclose portions that are within the central nervous system.*

tebrates, regeneration and reinnervation of muscles occur quite readily.

The physiological behavior of a neuron depends largely on the electrical properties of its surface membrane. These are not uniformly distributed over the neuron surface, but are specialized in different regions for different functions. Thus the electrically excitable axon membrane is specialized for the conduction of impulses. The membrane of the axon terminals is specialized to secrete a *transmitter substance* into the extracellular space for the purpose of activating the cells with which it makes special junctions termed *synapses* (p. 166). The membrane of the dendrites and the soma has regions of special sensitivity to transmitter substances released by the terminals of other nerve cells. *Postsynaptic currents* produced in the dendrites and the soma in response to those transmitters are *integrated* (i.e., "put together"; summed algebraically) to produce *postsynaptic potentials* in the dendrites, soma, and axon hillock. The anatomical form of a neuron and the distribution of the various membrane properties over its surface determine the way in which these currents are integrated, and thus the way in which the neuron behaves as a functioning unit in a neural network (i.e., a group of interacting neurons).

The simplest neural network is a *reflex arc.* The primordial reflex arc may have consisted of a *receptor cell* directly innervating an *effector cell* (Fig. 6-3,A). As neural circuitry became more complex through the process of evolution, centralized nervous systems developed to permit compactness and economy as well as complexity of interconnections. Long sensory and motor axons became useful to connect the receptors and effectors at the periphery to the central nervous system. This gave rise to the *monosynaptic reflex arc* (Fig. 6-3,B), in which a sensory neuron makes synaptic connection in the *central nervous system* with a motoneuron that innervates a muscle. The result is a reflex excitation of the effector organ whenever a stimulus sets up sufficiently intense activity (impulses) in the sensory neuron. Polysynaptic pathways with *interneurons* connecting the sensory and motor neurons are actually more common (Fig. 3,C). Interneurons have become progressively more numerous through evolution, vastly increasing the behavioral potential of animals and gradually improving their ability to learn from experience and to associate combinations of stimuli. It is noteworthy that the most elementary components of the reflex arc—namely, the sensory input pathways and the *final common pathways* of motor output—remain essentially unchanged from the most primitive invertebrates to the most complex vertebrates. The vast increase in neural capability that evolution has produced is a manifestation of the complex interneuronal circuitry that lies between the sensory neurons and the motor neurons, and it is the function of this circuitry about which we know the least.

THE TWO MAJOR TYPES OF SIGNALS EMPLOYED BY NEURONS

The nervous system detects, transmits, and processes information largely by means of electrical and chemical signals. The electrical signals can be detected with the help of electrodes, amplifiers, and oscilloscopes as changes in potential difference across the surface membranes of neurons and other excitable cells. The major types of electrical signals in a reflex arc are illustrated in Figure 6-4. Stimulus energy impinging on specialized receptor endings of neurons produce *receptor potentials* that are *graded* (i.e., amplitude-modulated) according to the stimulus energy intercepted and which generally continue for as long as the stimulus persists (see Chapter 7). Since the time course and intensity of the receptor potential more or less mimics the stimulus, it can be said to be an electrical analogue of the stimulus. The receptor potential spreads electrotonically (p. 118) in the sensory endings of the nerve cell, and therefore decays progressively with distance from its site of origin. These amplitude-modulated analogue signals from the receptor region are therefore incapable of transmitting information over appreciable distances. If the information is to be transmitted to the central nervous system, it must be converted into action potentials (frequency-modulated impulses), which are conducted without decrement (i.e., without loss of signal strength) by the axon of the sensory neuron.

The impulses arriving at the central terminals of a sensory neuron cause the release of a transmitter substance. The action of the transmitter (discussed at length later in this chapter) produces in the *postsynaptic* neuron a potential change that is graded in amplitude as a function of the impulse frequency in the *presynaptic* neuron (Fig. 6-4). Within limits, the higher the presynaptic frequency, the greater the postsynaptic depolarization. The *postsynaptic potentials* are also analogues (although nonlinear and quite distorted) of the original stimulus. The postsynaptic depolarization, if large enough, then initiates a train of impulses in the postsynaptic neuron. Thus, in this simplified overview, we see graded, local, analogue-type membrane potential changes alternating along the pathway with all-or-none, far-traveling conducted impulses. These appear to be the two major types of electrical signals used by nervous system. The graded potentials occur at sensory and postsynaptic membranes, and the impulses are confined largely to the conducting structures, such as axons, that lie in between.

6–4. *The alternation of graded and all-or-none electrical signals in a neural pathway. The receptor potential produced in the sensory endings of the afferent (sensory) nerve cell is an analogue copy of the stimulus. This spreads through the soma and sets up all-or-none propagated action potentials in the axon. On arriving at the terminals, the action potentials cause the release of a transmitter that sets up a graded synaptic potential in the next neuron. If this reaches the spike threshold, it will initiate a new train of action potentials. As described in Chapter 8, much of the information-processing in the nervous system occurs between the arrival of impulses at the terminals of one neuron and the initiation of impulses in the next neuron.*

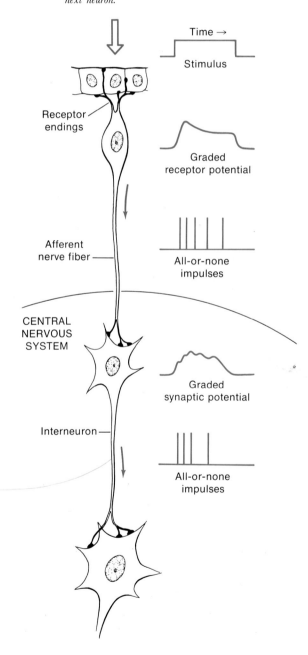

6-5. *Nerve net in subumbrellar surface of the jellyfish* Aurelia, *viewed in oblique light. The axons running in all directions innervate muscles that cause contraction of the umbrella.* [*Horridge, 1954.*]

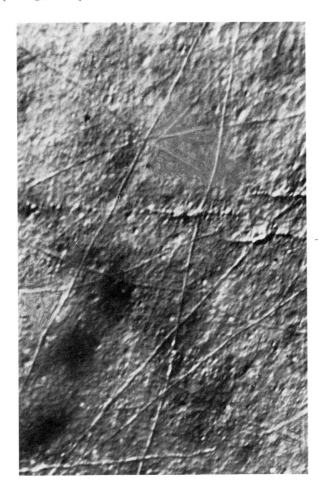

Evolution of Nervous Systems

Those nervous systems that are anatomically the most simply organized consist of very fine nerve fibers (axons) criss-crossing as a diffuse network (Fig. 6-5) and making synaptic contacts at points of intersection. Such *nerve nets*, found most extensively in the coelenterates, show little or no preference in the direction of conduction. A stimulus applied to one part of the organism produces a response that spreads to some degree from the point of stimulation. If the stimulus is repeated at brief intervals, the system "facilitates," spreading the response further. Very little is known about the synaptic mechanisms in diffuse nerve nets, because the nerve fibers are extremely fine, and do not lend themselves to intracellular recording techniques. Coelenterates and ctenophores show the beginnings of an organization of neurons into reflex arcs.

A major advance in the evolution of nervous systems was the organization of neurons into ganglia. This is first seen in the coelenterates. A *ganglion* is an organized cluster of many neuron cell bodies (Fig. 6-6). This mode of organization permits extensive interconnections among those neurons with an economy of collateral processes. The collaterals (side branches arising from the axons) form arborizations and make contacts in the *neuropil*. Although the neuropil gives the appearance of a confused tangle of fine processes, recent studies done with injected fluorescent dyes (Fig. 6-7) indicate that these aborized collaterals are relatively uniform from one specimen to another. More significant is the physiological evidence that connections in the neuropil are so orderly that similar synaptic connections can be observed between homologous neurons in different individuals of the same species.

In segmented invertebrates, each body segment is equipped with a ganglion. A segmental ganglion usually serves the reflex functions of the segment it occupies, plus one or more adjacent body segments. The ganglia of successive body segments are joined by nerve fiber trunks called *connectives*. The result is a series of ganglia and connectives constituting the *ventral nerve cord* characteristic of annelids and arthropods (Fig. 6-8), in which segmental organization is most clearly seen. The segmental ganglia of these animals provide convenient material for neurophysiological investigation because of the relatively small numbers of neurons in each segment and the redundancy cf structure and function from one segment in the nerve cord to the next. Thus an analysis of the interactions of the neurons of one segment provides the basic picture for all other segments of the nerve cord, which goes a long way toward an integrated understanding of the nervous system of such an animal.

An important development in the evolution of complex behavior was the trend toward fusion of several of the more anterior ganglia into superganglia or "brains." These are more complex than the segmental ganglia, and exert varying degrees of control over the other ganglia. The prominence of the brain over the more posterior portions of the central nervous system results, in part, from the relatively large amount of sensory input entering the brain from the large number of receptors at the anterior of an animal, and in part from the development of regulatory centers in the brain.

In contrast to worms and arthropods, which are segmentally structured and have bilateral symmetry, echinoderms typically have a nerve ring around an axis of secondary radial symmetry. Perhaps as a result of the radial symmetry, there is no brain-like ganglion in the echinoderms. The molluscs have nonsegmental

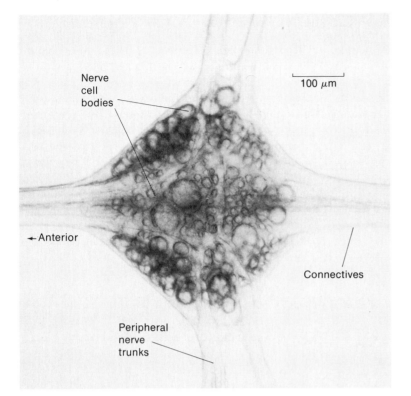

Nerve
cell
bodies

100 μm

←Anterior

Connectives

Peripheral
nerve
trunks

6–6. *Photomicrograph of a living segmental ganglion of the leech* Hirudo, *showing the nerve cell bodies. The paired connectives at the left and right contain axons, and connect the ganglion to similar ganglia in adjacent body segments. The peripheral nerve trunks emerging laterally carry motor and sensory axons to the viscera and muscle.* [Van Essen, 1973.]

6–7. *Sensory neuron in leech ganglion, injected with the fluorescent dye procion yellow before fixation. The dye remains within the cell, diffusing into all branches. Note the numerous small branches for synaptic contact with dendrites of other cells. The two large axons enter the peripheral nerve trunks at the left.* [Van Essen, 1973.]

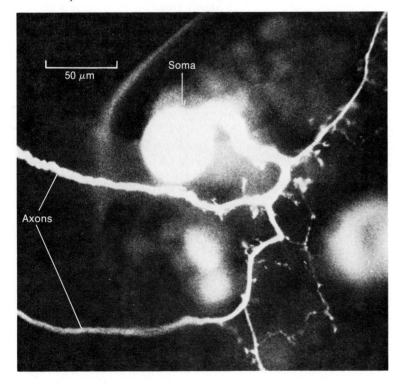

50 μm

Soma

Axons

6–8. *The ventral nerve cord of the lobster* Homarus *illustrates the segmented arrangement of the nervous system in many invertebrates. The roots emerging from the ganglia carry sensory and motor axons.* [After Berndt, 1903.]

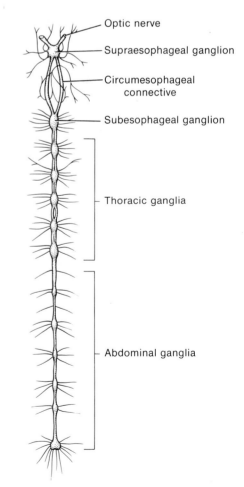

Optic nerve

Supraesophageal ganglion

Circumesophageal
connective

Subesophageal ganglion

Thoracic ganglia

Abdominal ganglia

Evolution of Nervous Systems   153

nervous systems with several dissimilar ganglia connected by long nerve trunks. Opisthobranch molluscs, like the sea hare *Aplysia*, have a number of neurons with extraordinarily large cell bodies, some as large as 1 or 2 mm in diameter. These have become a favorite material for the study of cellular neurophysiology, for they can be recognized visually from preparation to preparation as individual neurons, and lend themselves well to long-term electrical recording.

The octopus has the most complex nervous system of all invertebrates. The brain alone is estimated to contain about 10^8 neurons. These are arranged in a series of highly specialized lobes and tracts that evolved from the more dispersed ganglia of the lower molluscs.

The Vertebrate Nervous System

The organization of anterior ganglia into a multifunctional brain shows the highest development in the vertebrates, although a rudimentary segmentation remains in the form of the cranial and spinal nerve roots (Fig. 6-9). In spite of its awesome structural complexity, the vertebrate nervous system offers certain advantages for experimental neurophysiology. One of these, expressed as the so-called *Bell-Magendie rule*, is that the *afferent* (sensory) nerve fibers enter the central nervous system (CNS) via the dorsal roots of the cranial and spinal nerves whereas the *efferent* (motor) nerve fibers leave the CNS via the ventral roots (Figs. 6-10, 6-11). The motor axons arise from cells in the

6–9. *The brain and spinal cord of a frog (left) and human (right) in ventral aspect. Rudimentary segmentation remains in the form of cranial and spinal neurons. [After Wiedersheim, 1907; Neal and Rand, 1936.]*

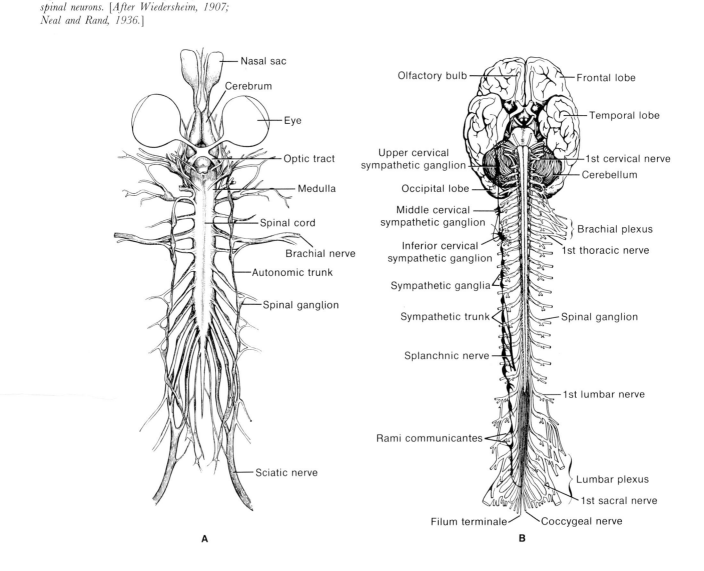

A

B

ventral horn of the spinal cord. The afferent fibers arise from monopolar cell bodies in the *dorsal root* or *spinal ganglia* (Fig. 6-11). The segregation of sensory and motor axons into dorsal and ventral roots makes it possible selectively to stimulate, or to eliminate by transection, the sensory input to or motor output from the central nervous system.

Another convenience to neurophysiologists is the high degree of redundancy of neurons of any given type in the vertebrate central nervous system. In the arthropod nervous system, a single motoneuron may innervate essentially all the muscle fibers of one muscle, and in some cases more than one muscle of a limb. In vertebrates, each skeletal muscle typically is innervated by a large *pool* of several hundred motoneurons, each of which controls a *motor unit* consisting of up to 100 muscle fibers. Since the motoneurons of each pool are qualitatively similar in physiological properties, data obtained from one motoneuron are largely representative of the whole pool. If this redundancy were not the case, and if all neurons were substantially different in their functional properties from all others, attempts by neurophysiologists to analyze the functions of the vertebrate nervous system would be utterly hopeless.

MAJOR PARTS OF THE CENTRAL NERVOUS SYSTEM

The *spinal cord,* enclosed in the vertebral column (Fig. 6-12), is the site of the cervical, thoracic, lumbar, and sacral segmental reflex connections. Ascending (sensory) and descending (motor) interneurons form well-defined tracts of *white matter* located in the periphery of the spinal cord, which gets its color from the myelin sheathing of the axons. The more centrally located *gray matter* of the spinal cord contains the cell bodies, dendrites, and presynaptic terminals, which are all nonmyelinated. A central canal is a fluid-filled lumen that is continuous with the *ventricles* of the brain. The enlarged portion of the upper spinal cord forms the *medulla oblongata* (Figs. 6-9, 6-13). This contains centers for the control of respiration and cardiovascular reflexes (Chapters 13 and 14). The spinal cord contains the reflex connections for locomotion and other limb movements and for such visceral functions as bladder control and erection of penis or clitoris. Spinal reflexes, however, are under descending control from various portions of the brain.

The *cerebellum,* which overlies the medulla, consists of a pair of hemispheres that are convoluted in the higher vertebrates. It integrates input from the semicircular canals and other proprioceptors (position and movement sensors) and from the visual and auditory

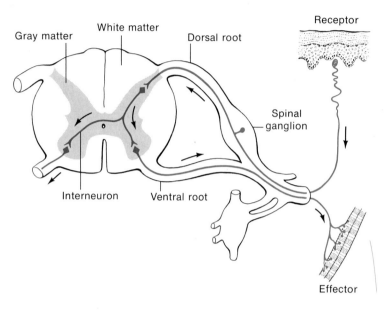

6-10. *Organization of the vertebrate spinal cord and its segmental roots, shown in cross section. Shown in color are the neurons that form a polysynaptic reflex arc between skin receptor endings and skeletal muscle innervation. Note that the cell body of the afferent neuron resides in the spinal ganglion. [After Montagna, 1959.]*

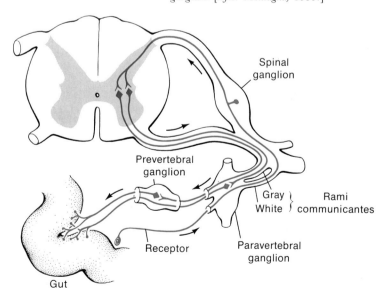

6-11. *Autonomic reflex arc. Sensory input passes directly through the paravertebral ganglion of the autonomic chain. Motor output synapses in either the paravertebral or the prevertebral ganglion. [After Montagna, 1959.]*

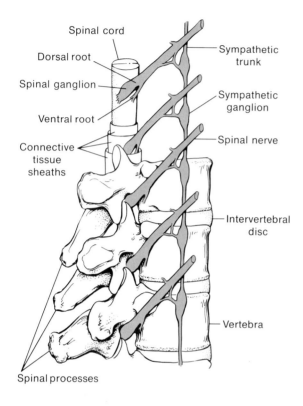

6–12. *Vertebral column and spinal cord. The spinal cord runs through openings in the vertebrae, the spinal nerves emerging through between the vertebrae. Nervous tissue is shown in color.*

Spinal cord

Dorsal root

Spinal ganglion

Ventral root

Connective tissue sheaths

Spinal processes

Sympathetic trunk

Sympathetic ganglion

Spinal nerve

Intervertebral disc

Vertebra

systems. These inputs are compared in the cerebellum, and the resulting output helps coordinate the motor signals responsible for maintaining posture, for orientation of the animal in space, and for accurate limb movements.

The *hypothalamus* contains a number of centers that control visceral functions and concomitant emotional reactions having to do with feeding, drinking, sexual appetite, pleasure, rage, and temperature control. Hormone-secreting neurons in the hypothalamus control water and electrolyte balance and the secretory activity of the pituitary gland. Further discussion of the endocrine functions of the hypothalamus is found in Chapter 11.

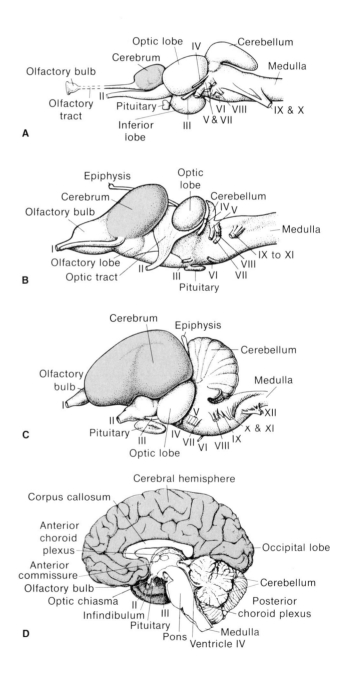

6–13. *Representative vertebrate brains. A. Fish. B. Frog. C. Bird. D. Human. Note the gradual increase in the size of the cerebrum with evolutionary development. The cerebellum, which has an important function in the coordination of movement, is highly developed in birds and mammals. [After Romer, 1955.]*

The *cerebral hemisphere* shows the most dramatic changes in the course of vertebrate evolution (Fig. 6-13). In the higher mammals, the *cortex* (surface layer of gray matter) is thrown into prominent folds that greatly increase the cortical area. Some areas of the cerebral cortex are purely sensory, and others are purely motor. During neurosurgery, local electric stimulation of the *somatosensory cortex* evokes sensations in waking patients, who are able to tell the surgeon to which part of the periphery the sensation is projected (felt). This is one evidence that *all sensation* takes place in the central nervous system—primarily in the sensory portions of the cerebral cortex. Peripheral stimulation produces the converse result; local points in the somatosensory cortex produce electrical signals in response to sensory input when specific areas of skin are stimulated. Both approaches have permitted the point-by-point construction of a somatosensory map (Fig. 6-14, left). The *auditory cortex* of the temporal lobe and the *visual cortex* of the occipital lobe are both purely sensory, and direct electrical stimulation of these areas during neurosurgery evokes rudimentary auditory and visual sensations.

Anterior to the central sulcus (groove) is the *motor cortex,* which also exhibits topographical representation of the periphery (Fig. 6-14, right). Large *pyramidal cells,* with their somata in the motor cortex, send axons down the spinal cord and make synaptic connections on the motoneurons that innervate the skeletal muscles. These cells maintain a steady background of low-level synaptic input to the motoneurons. An increase in the activity of the pyramidal cells results in synaptic activation of the motoneurons and forceful movements of the limb. This occurs naturally when a subject consciously generates a strong contraction of a muscle; it also occurs experimentally when the pyramidal cells of the motor cortex are directly stimulated with electrodes.

6–14. *Sensory and motor homunculi in the human cortex. Left. Map of a transverse section of the somatosensory cortex depicts the point localization of areas corresponding to their peripheral projections—that is, the places in the periphery where the stimuli are subjectively "felt." Note that the region representing the genitalia is tucked discreetly out of sight into the intercerebral cleft. Right. Transverse section through the motor cortex, showing the projection of cortical regions to the skeletal musculature. [After Penfield and Rasmussen, 1950.]*

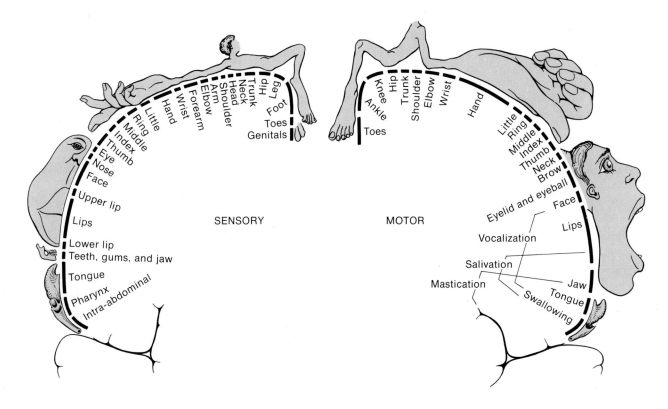

SENSORY

MOTOR

6–15. *The autonomic nervous system.   Left. Sympathetic or thoracocolumbar division.   Right. Parasympathetic or craniosacral division. Postganglionic neurons represented by broken lines. The major differences in organization are shown at the bottom. The preganglionic endings liberate acetylcholine (ACh) in both divisions. The postganglionic endings of the parasympathetic division also liberate ACh, but the postganglionic endings of the sympathetic system liberate norepinephrine (NE). [After Noback and Demarest, 1972.]*

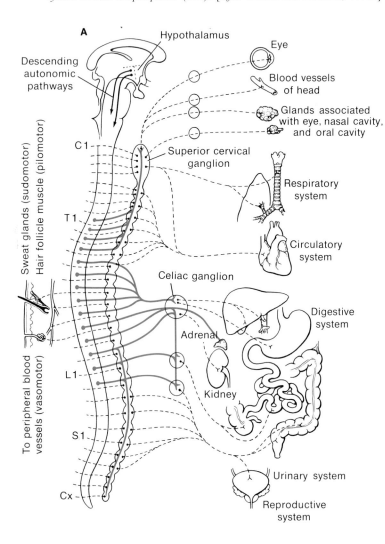

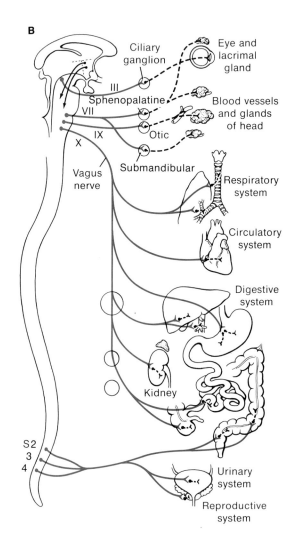

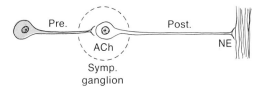

Sympathetic

Parasympathetic

In primitive mammals, essentially the entire cortex consists of sensory or motor areas, and the cortex is without the strong convolutions that increase its area in higher mammals. In humans especially, and in other higher mammals, large portions of the cortex are "unassigned" to either sensory or motor functions. Unassigned areas are involved in intersensory associations, memory, and (in humans) speech.

Visceral functions, largely without conscious control, are regulated in large part by the two divisions of the *autonomic nervous system* (Fig. 6-15). The autonomic reflex arc is shown in Figure 6-11. The afferent (sensory) side of the arc is largely indistinguishable from the somatic reflex arc (Fig. 6-10); in fact, the same sensory fiber may activate both somatic and autonomic reflexes. The two arcs differ primarily in the location of the motoneuron. In the autonomic system, it lies completely outside the central nervous system. The somatic motoneurons lie within the gray matter of the spinal cord.

In the *sympathetic division* of the autonomic system, the preganglionic neurons arise from thoracic and lumbar divisions of the spinal cord (Fig. 6-15,A), and synapse with the *postganglionic* (motor) neurons in the *paravertebral chain* of autonomic ganglia. The *parasympathetic division* arises from cranial and sacral divisions of the central nervous system (Fig. 6-15,B). Parasympathetic interneurons characteristically synapse with postganglionic neurons in or near the visceral end organs rather than in separate ganglia.

The parasympathetic and sympathetic systems innervate the same end organs, but, in general, liberate different neural transmitter substances and have generally opposing actions on visceral functions. Pacemaker activity of the heart, for example, is inhibited by the liberation of the transmitter *acetylcholine* (ACh) from parasympathetic neurons, but is accelerated by *noradrenaline* liberated from the sympathetic innervation to the heart. These actions of the parasympathetic and sympathetic systems are reversed in the digestive tract, where parasympathetic *cholinergic* (ACh-liberating) innervation stimulates and sympathetic *adrenergic* (noradrenaline-liberating) innervation inhibits intestinal motility and digestive secretion. The sympathetic system generally mobilizes the organism for strenuous or stressful activity, diverting resources from the viscera to the somatic musculature.

Propagation of Nerve Impulses

Communication between different parts of the nervous system depends on the propagation of nerve impulses (action potentials) along the axons of neurons. Simi-

lar propagation also occurs in certain muscle cells. As noted in the previous chapter, the action potential entails a potential change across the surface membrane that is about 5 times as large as the threshold depolarization. With this *safety factor*, the excited portion of an axon is able to excite the portions ahead of it and thereby cause the action potential to propagate along the axon.

To understand the way in which impulses propagate, it is necessary to recall from Chapter 5 that the electrically excited membrane becomes permeable to Na^+, so that this ion carries a momentary current into the excited region of an axon. This current spreads longitudinally along the inside of the axon and leaks transversely outward across the membrane. This electrotonic spread of *local circuit current* is due to the cable properties of the axon (Fig. 5-9). Thus the influx of sodium, producing the upstroke of the action potential

6–16. *The action potential in a nerve (A) is accompanied by local circuit current flowing across the membrane, as shown in part B. The "foot" is produced by outward current depolarizing the membrane ahead of the active (Na entering) region. Outward current in the inactive regions is carried across the membrane primarily by K^+.*

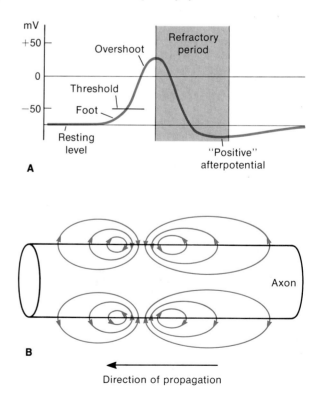

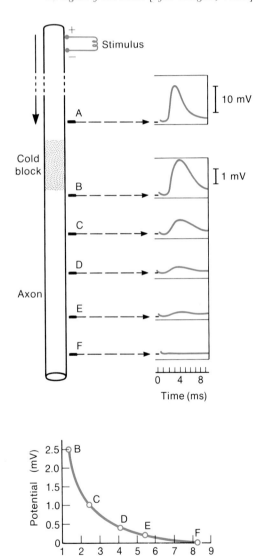

6–17. *Experiment in which Hodgkin demonstrated that the action potential generates current that produces an electrotonic depolarization of the membrane ahead of the active portion.   Top. Section (stippled area) was blocked by cooling, and potentials recorded at points B to F. Bottom. The electrotonic potential was found to decrease exponentially with distance from the region of the block. [After Hodgkin, 1937.]*

(Fig. 6-16,A) results in a current that spreads longitudinally, both forward and backward within the axon (Fig. 6-16,B).

Consider only that part of the current that flows forward longitudinally within the axon—that is, in the direction of impulse propagation (to the left in Fig. 6-16,B). In order to complete its circuit, this current must flow out across unexcited portions of the membrane ahead of the region of inward Na flux and then back to the active region. Current flowing outward across the unexcited membrane reduces the potential difference across that part of the membrane, partially discharging the membrane capacitance to produce the *foot* of the propagated impulse (compare Figs. 5-18 and 6-16,A). Such electrotonic depolarization of the inactive membrane ahead of the active region was first clearly demonstrated with the experiment shown in Figure 6-17, done by Hodgkin as a college student in 1937.

As the membrane ahead of the impulse is depolarized to the firing level by local circuit current, the sodium conductance of that region increases, initiating the regenerative sequence that produces the all-or-none action potential. The newly excited region then generates the local circuit current that depolarizes and thereby excites portions of the axon ahead of it. Thus local circuit current from each excited region depolarizes and excites in turn the next region ahead of it. The signal is continuously boosted and maintained at full strength in this manner as it travels along the axon.

Some of the current that enters an axon at the excited portion spreads backward longitudinally— that is, in the direction from which the impulse originated. This current does not stimulate, since the membrane just behind the advancing action potential is in a refractory state.

Propagation of an impulse depends on (a) the electrical excitability of the axon membrane, which results in a 5-fold regenerative amplification of the electrotonic potential that reaches threshold, and (b) the cable properties of the axon, which permit the electrotonic spread of local circuit current from the region of sodium influx to nearby regions of inactive membrane.

One might ask why extracellular action currents from one conducting axon do not excite other nearby axons, creating "cross talk" between the axons. The answer, in short, is that the resistances of the inactive membranes are so much greater than the resistance of the extracellular current path that only a minute fraction of the total current produced by an active membrane flows into a neighboring inactive axon. Because of this extracellular shunting action, the currents developed by an active axon are normally too small to excite neighboring inactive neurons.

VELOCITY OF PROPAGATION

Johannes Müller declared in the 1830's that the velocity of the action potential would never be measured. He reasoned that the action potential, being an electrical impulse, must travel with a speed approaching that of light (3×10^{10} cm/s), and was therefore too fast to resolve over biological distances, even with the best instruments available at that time.

Within ten years, one of his own students, Hermann von Helmholtz, had measured the velocity of impulse propagation in frog nerves by an elegantly simple method (Fig. 6-18), which can easily be duplicated in a student laboratory course. The nerve is stimulated at each of two locations 3 cm apart, and the latency to the peak of the muscle twitch is determined. Suppose the latency decreases by 1 ms when the stimulating electrode is moved to the more distal (closer to the muscle) position. The velocity of propagation, V_p, is calculated as

$$V_p = \frac{\Delta d}{\Delta t} = \frac{3 \text{ cm}}{1 \text{ ms}} = 3 \times 10^3 \text{ cm/s}.$$

This is seven orders of magnitude slower than the velocity of electric current flow in a copper wire or in an electrolyte solution. From this kind of experiment, Helmholtz correctly concluded that the nerve impulse is more complex than a simple longitudinal flow of current within the nerve fiber.

The velocity of impulse propagation in various axons ranges from 120 m/s in some large axons down to several centimeters/sec in very thin axons. Differences in conduction velocity are illustrated in Table 6-1 and Fig. 6-19.

The velocity of conduction depends in large part on the rate at which the membrane at any given distance ahead of the active region is depolarized to threshold by the local circuit currents. The greater the length constant (p. 119), the farther the local circuit current flow, the more rapid the depolarization of the membrane in advance of the excited region, and hence the greater the velocity of propagation. The effect on conduction velocity of decreasing the

6-19. *Conduction velocities of different axons in a frog nerve. A. Experimental setup for stimulating and recording from the nerve bundle B. The externally recorded compound action potentials (the summed signals from all active fibers in the bundle). The α-fibers have the largest diameter and highest conduction velocity. The γ-fibers have the smallest and slowest of those shown here (Table 6-1).*

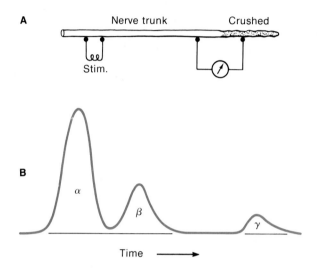

Table 6-1. Classification of frog nerve fibers on the basis of diameter and conduction velocity.

Fiber class		Fiber diameter (μm)	Velocity (m/s)
A	α	18.5	42
	β	14.0	25
	γ	11.0	17
B		—	4.2
C		2.5	0.4–0.5

Source: J. Erlanger and H. S. Gasser (1937). *Electrical Signs of Nervous Activity*, Univ. Pennsylvania Press, Philadelphia.

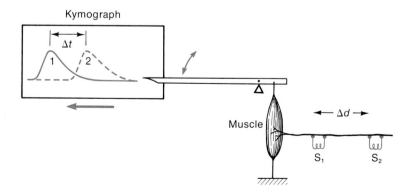

6-18. *Experimental apparatus similar to that used by Helmholtz to measure the velocity of propagation of nerve impulses in a frog nerve. Stimulus electrodes were used first at position S_1 and then at position S_2. The kymograph moved a smoked paper while the lever scratched a tracing in the layer of soot.*

BOX 6-1   EXTRACELLULAR SIGNS OF IMPULSE CONDUCTION

Nerve impulses can be recorded with a pair of extracellular recording leads (see figure below). The electronics are designed so that a negative potential in lead *A* will cause the oscilloscope beam to go up while a similar potential recorded by lead *B* will make the beam go down; positive potentials do the opposite. An action potential passing along an axon is seen as a wave of negative potential, because the cell exterior becomes more negative than its surroundings when sodium flows into the cell to produce the overshoot. As a result, the action potential passing two electrodes makes a biphasic wave shape on the oscilloscope (part A of figure).

The recording is simplified by preventing invasion of the part of the axon that is in contact with electrode *B*. This is done by anaesthetizing, cooling, or crushing that part of the axon (part B of figure). A similar effect can be obtained by placing electrode *B* in the bath, at some distance from the axon (part C of figure).

Extracellular recordings of action potentials in a nerve bundle.   A. Biphasic recording.   B. Recording with one electrode on a crushed part of the nerve.   C. Recording with reference to the bath. Times t_1 *to* t_5 *show the progression of the impulse (shaded areas) and corresponding times on oscilloscope recordings. The oscilloscope signal is produced by electronic subtraction of electrode B's signal from electrode A's signal.*

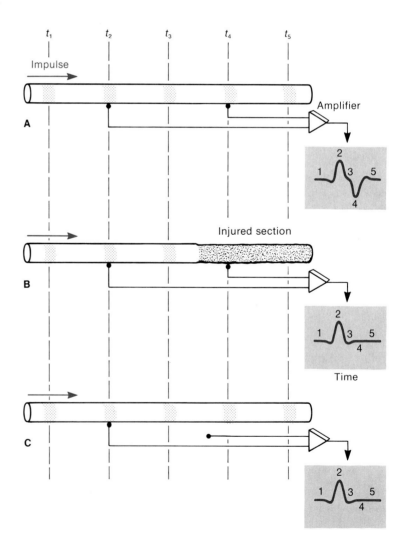

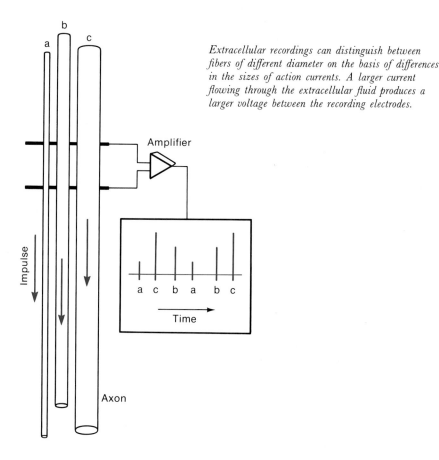

Extracellular recordings can distinguish between fibers of different diameter on the basis of differences in the sizes of action currents. A larger current flowing through the extracellular fluid produces a larger voltage between the recording electrodes.

Extracellular recordings are frequently made from nerve bundles or tracts made up of many axons. The summed activity of many axons gives a compound recording whose characteristics depend on the numbers of axons conducting and their relative timing and current strength. Larger axons generate larger extracellular currents because membrane current increases in proportion to membrane area. The size of the action potential recorded with extracellular electrodes is proportional to the amount of current flowing through the extracellular fluid. Thus action potentials from axons of large diameter appear bigger when recorded extracellularly, even though the potential changes across their membranes are no larger than those of smaller nerve fibers. Because of these amplitude differences in extracellularly recorded action potentials, the signals originating in individual axons can often be distinguished by their size in such recordings (see figure above).

---

length constant can be demonstrated by placing an axon in oil or in air. This leaves only a thin film of saline on the surface of the axon, and the length constant is decreased because the external longitudinal resistance (r_o in Eq. 5-5) is thereby raised. Under these conditions, the rate of conduction is slower than if the axon is immersed in saline.

Evolution has exploited two means for increasing the length constants of axons, and thereby the velocity of impulse propagation. One, typified by the giant axons of squid, arthropods, annelids, and teleosts, is an *increase in axonal diameter* and thereby a

reduction in internal longitudinal resistance (r_i in Eq. 5-5). This is explained further in Box 6-2. Giant axons have evolved in some species for rapid and synchronous activation of locomotor reflexes, as in the mantle of squid and the escape or withdrawal reflexes of certain arthropods (e.g., crayfish, cockroach) and annelids (e.g., earthworm).

The other evolutionary means of increasing conduction velocity, developed only in the vertebrates, is the *insulation of segments of the axon with myelin*. This greatly increases the length constant of these segments, thus enhancing efficient longitudinal current spread.

BOX 6-2 AXON DIAMETER AND CONDUCTION VELOCITY

The transverse resistance, r_m, of a unit length, l, of axon membrane is *inversely proportional to the radius*, ρ, of the axon. The reason is that the area, A_s, of a cylindrical surface of unit length is equal to $2\pi\rho l$. The longitudinal resistance, r_i, of a unit length of axoplasm is inversely proportional to the cross-sectional area, A_x, of the axon. Since $A_x = \pi\rho^2$, the resistance r_i is *inversely proportional to the square of the radius*. It follows that, with any given increase in radius, the drop in r_i will be greater than the drop in r_m. Since $\lambda = \sqrt{r_m / r_i + r_o}$ (Eq. 5-5), the disproportionate drop in longitudinal resistance, r_i, which accompanies an increase in axon diameter, results in an increased length constant.

Because propagation velocity depends on the *rate* of depolarization at a given distance, x, ahead of the action potential, membrane capacitance cannot be ignored. Note that the time constant $(r_m \times c_m)$ of a unit length of axon membrane remains constant with changes in axon diameter, because capacitance, c_m, *increases* in direct proportion, whereas the resistance, r_m, *decreases* in direct proportion to an increase in membrane area. The increase in length constant that accompanies increased axon diameter therefore occurs without an increase in the time constant of the membrane; increase in diameter results in a greater membrane current at distance x without an increase in membrane time constant. The increased rate of depolarization brings the membrane to threshold sooner and results in an increase in velocity of conduction.

SALTATORY CONDUCTION

Myelin is laid down during development by a kind of glial cell termed a *Schwann cell*, which grows around the axon, leaving behind a tightly wrapped, multilayered sheath of Schwann cell membrane (Fig. 6-20). Cross sections of the sheath show a periodic 120 Å spacing, which represents the repeated layering of Schwann cell membrane. Each unit membrane contributes to the high transverse resistance of the sheath. Because of its many layers of membrane, the myelin sheath has far less capacitance than a single unit membrane. The multilayered sheath is interrupted at regular intervals (*nodes of Ranvier*), directly exposing short sections of electrically excitable axon membrane to the extracellular fluid. Between nodes, the sheath is closely applied to the axon membrane, nearly obliterating the extracellular space of the axon membrane. Moreover, the internodal axon membrane appears to lack the mechanism for sodium activation.

The insulating properties of the myelin greatly increase the length constant of the axon, since its effect is the same as increasing r_m in Equation 5-5. Because of the high insulating resistance along the internode, the local circuit current in advance of the action potential leaves the axon almost exclusively at the nodes of Ranvier. Moreover, very little current is expended in discharging membrane capacitance along the internodes because of the low capacitance of the thick myelin sheath. The action potential at one node electrotonically depolarizes the membrane at the next node, and thus the action potential does not propagate with continuity along the axon membrane as it does in nonmyelinated nerve fibers, such as the squid axon. Instead, it is produced only at the small areas of membrane exposed at the nodes of Ranvier. The result is *saltatory conduction*, a series of discontinuous action potentials, one at each node, as illustrated in Figure 6-21. The velocity of signal transmission is greatly enhanced, for the electrotonic spread of local circuit current occurs more rapidly over internodal distances than would continuous impulse propagation over the same distance.

Cable theory describes the spread of electrotonic currents in an axon in terms analogous to the passive spread of current in a submarine cable (p. 118). By the same analogy, the saltatory propagation of an action potential in a myelinated axon can be compared to the transmission of a signal in a submarine cable equipped with amplifier stations spaced along the cable to boost the signal and compensate for cable losses. In this analogy, the excitable membrane of the nodes of Ranvier performs the function of boosting the signal along the myelinated segments of axon, which are analogous to the segments of cable linking the amplifier stations. Saltatory conduction was first demonstrated by Tasaki in 1939, and was later confirmed by Huxley and Stämpfli with the experiment illustrated in Figure 6-22.

6-20. *Node of Ranvier. A short segment of axon is exposed between two myelin-wrapped internodes. This is the part that becomes excited during saltatory conduction. Figure 4-12 shows an electron micrograph of the multiple layers of Schwann cell membrane that constitute the myelin sheath. [After Bunge et al., 1961.]*

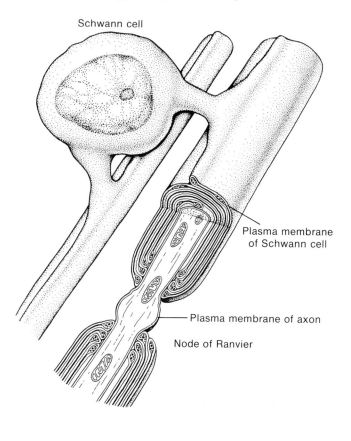

Schwann cell

Plasma membrane of Schwann cell

Plasma membrane of axon

Node of Ranvier

6-22. *The demonstration of saltatory conduction in a myelinated neuron. A. Axon threaded through fine opening in insulating wall. B. As the axon is gradually pulled through, there are discrete discontinuities in time of recording of the action potential, indicating that the active current is produced only at the nodes, numbered R_1 to R_5. [After Huxley and Stämpfli, 1949.]*

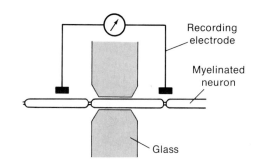

Recording electrode

Myelinated neuron

Glass

A

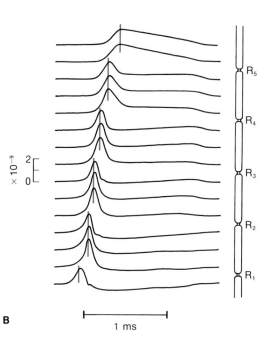

$\times 10^{-9}$ $\genfrac{}{}{0pt}{}{2}{0}$

R_5

R_4

R_3

R_2

R_1

B |—— 1 ms ——|

6-21. *Saltatory conduction in a myelinated axon. Top. The action potentials (inward Na^+, outward K^+) occur only at the nodes of Ranvier, and current spreads longitudinally between nodes. The action potential jumps from node to node. Bottom. The circles indicate the intracellular potentials present at each corresponding node at the instant shown in the upper part of the diagram.*

Direction of propagation

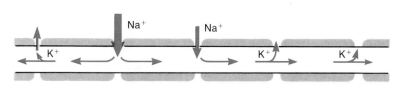

Na^+ Na^+

K^+ K^+ K^+

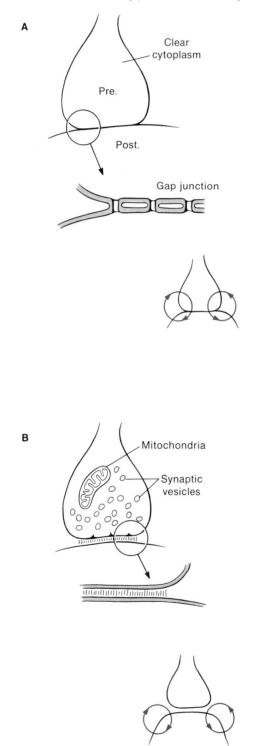

6–23. *Two kinds of synaptic transmission. A. Electrical synapse. Gap junctions between pre- and postsynaptic membranes permit current to flow through fine intercellular channels (inset). The action current from the presynaptic cell simply flows into the postynaptic cell, depolarizing it. B. Chemical synapse. No intercellular continuity. Synaptic current flows only across the postsynaptic membrane in response to transmitter-activated opening of membrane channels. [After Whittaker, 1968.]*

Concept of the Synapse

In 1897, long before the morphological basis for neuron–neuron interactions became known, the functional junction between two neurons was given the name *synapse* by Sir Charles Sherrington, who is regarded as the founder of modern neurophysiology. It was his conclusion that "The neurone itself is visibly a continuum from end to end, but continuity fails to be demonstrable where neurone meets neurone—at the synapse. There a different kind of transmission may occur." Although Sherrington had no direct information about the microstructure or microphysiology of these specialized regions of interaction between excitable cells, he displayed extraordinary insight, gained from his cleverly designed experiments on the spinal reflexes of cats and dogs. He deduced that some synapses are *excitatory*, leading to the initiation of action potentials, and that others are *inhibitory*, counteracting the initiation of action potentials.

It is now known that there are two categories of synapses, *chemically transmitting* and *electrically transmitting*. Electrical synapses will be considered first, since they behave more simply.

Transmission at Electrical Synapses

At an electrical synapse, the pre- and postsynaptic membranes are in close apposition (Fig. 6-23,A), forming gap junctions (p. 105), through which electric current flows preferentially from one cell into the other. The injection of a subthreshold current pulse into cell *A* (Fig. 6-24) elicits a change in the membrane potential of that cell. If a significant fraction of the current injected into cell *A* spreads directly through gap junctions into cell *B*, it will cause a detectable change in the membrane potential of cell *B* as well. Since only part of the total current injected into cell *A* crosses into cell *B*, the electrotonic potential change recorded across the membrane of cell *B* will always be less than that recorded in cell *A*. The ratio of the potential change in cell *B* to the potential change in cell *A* gives the *attenuation factor* of the electrical synapse. The gap junctions through which the current flows from one cell to the other are generally (but not always) symmetrical in resistance—that is current meets the same resistance in either direction. Differences in the input resistances alone of the cells *A* and *B* can lead to different attenuation factors, depending on which cell the current is injected into.

An electrical junction between two neurons will allow local circuit current from an action potential in one to spread into the other and depolarize it. Transmission of an action potential through an electrical synapse is basically no different from propagation within one cell, since both phenomena depend on the electrotonic spread of local circuit current ahead of the action potential to depolarize and excite new regions of membrane. Since the safety factor of an action potential is about 5 (p. 159), the attenuation in amplitude from one cell to the next must generally be no greater than 5-fold in order for the electrotonic depolarization of the postsynaptic cell to reach threshold and initiate an impulse. It would therefore be very difficult for a single action potential in a fine axon to supply enough local circuit current across an electrical synapse to elicit an action potential in a comparatively large cell, such as a muscle fiber, because of the enormous membrane area (and hence low input resistance) of the muscle fiber compared to the motor axon. This is undoubtedly one evolutionary reason why electrical synapses are not as widespread as chemical synapses.

Electrical transmission between excitable cells was first demonstrated by Furshpan and Potter in 1959, in the crayfish. The synapse between the crayfish lateral giant nerve fiber and a large motor axon has the unusual property of passing current preferentially in one direction (Fig. 6-25). Electrical transmission occurs between cells in the central nervous system, smooth muscle, cardiac muscle, receptor cells, and sensory axons. Electrical synapses function with shorter *synaptic delay* than chemical synapses, and are therefore well suited for the synchronization of electrical activity in a group of nerve cells.

6-24. A. In electrically coupled cells, injection of current into one cell elicits potential changes in both cells. B. This coupling is generally symmetrical, current passing equally well in either direction.

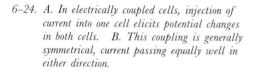

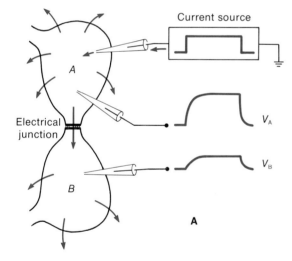

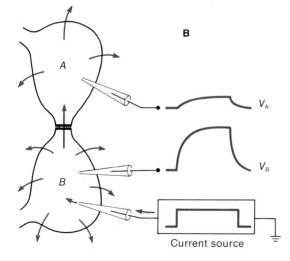

6-25. The giant electrical synapse in the crayfish. Top. The arrangement used for recording from and stimulating the pre- and postsynaptic axons. Bottom left. An action potential produced in the presynaptic (lateral giant) axon electrically excites an action potential in the postsynaptic (giant motor) axon. Bottom right. An action potential in the postsynaptic axon does not produce a significant potential change in the presynaptic axon. Injection of current pulses shows that there is preferential flow of current from pre- to postsynaptic cells. This is unusual for an electrical synapse. [After Furshpan and Potter, 1959.]

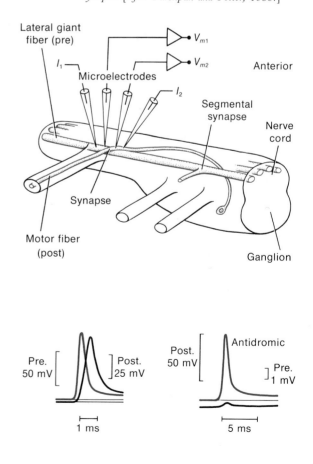

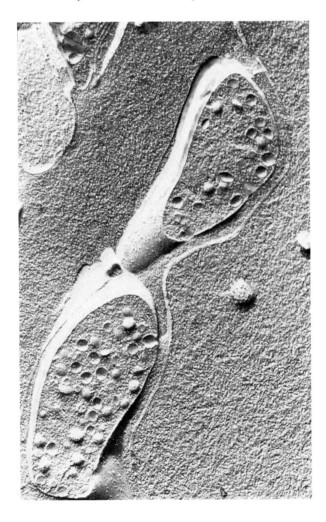

6–26. *Synaptic terminal as seen in transverse section in a freeze-etched specimen of an electric organ of the ray* Torpedo. *Synaptic vesicles can be seen in the terminal, with two vesicles frozen in place as they were opening into the synaptic cleft. Magnification 40,000×.* [Nickel and Potter, 1970.]

Transmission at Chemical Synapses

Most synaptic transmission occurs through the secretion of a transmitter substance by the terminals of the presynaptic neuron. The transmitter diffuses to the closely apposed surface of the postsynaptic cell, where it interacts with membrane receptor molecules to produce changes in the ionic conductance of the *postsynaptic membrane*. A *synaptic current* flows that produces a *postsynaptic potential*. Generally speaking, chemical transmission is more flexible than electrical transmission, and allows a greater range of interactions between cells with fewer anatomic restrictions. Chemical transmitters also allow amplification of small presynaptic currents into large postsynaptic currents, as described below.

The great histologist Ramon y Cajal, using Golgi's silver impregnation technique, had shown early in this century that neurons appear histologically to be discrete units. In spite of this, some anatomists held the belief that neural tissue is made up of a continuous reticulum rather than morphologically separate neurons. Unequivocal evidence for cellular discontinuity between neurons came with the development of electron microscopy in the 1940's.

The verity of chemical transmission and the existence of transmitter substances was also debated for decades. The first direct evidence for chemical transmitter substances was obtained by Otto Loewi, who found that inhibition of one frog heart by stimulation of the vagus nerve produced a substance that could cause a second frog heart to beat more slowly. Loewi's finding led to the subsequent identification of *acetylcholine (ACh)* as the transmitter substance released by the postganglionic neurons in response to stimulation of the vagus nerve (Fig. 6-15,B), and by motoneurons innervating skeletal muscle in vertebrates.

MORPHOLOGY OF CHEMICAL SYNAPSES

Chemical transmission occurs across an extracellular *synaptic cleft,* a space of about 200 Å that separates the membranes of the pre- and postsynaptic cells (Fig. 6-23,B). The presynaptic terminal contains hundreds or thousands of membrane-bound *synaptic vesicles* (Fig. 6-26), about 400 Å in diameter, each containing 1×10^4 to 5×10^4 molecules of the transmitter substance. During synaptic transmission, the transmitter substance is released into the synaptic cleft, and reaches the postsynaptic membrane by diffusion. The cleft is filled with a mucopolysaccharide that "glues" together the pre- and postsynaptic membranes, which usually show some degree of thickening at the synapse.

The most extensive studies of synaptic transmission have been done with the *motor endplate* (i.e., neuromuscular synapse) of vertebrate skeletal muscle (Fig. 6-27),

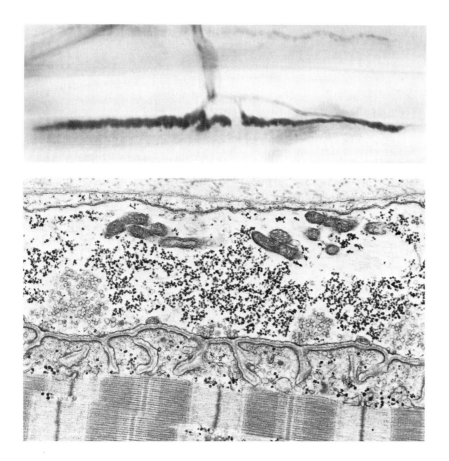

6-27. *Frog motor endplate (neuromuscular synapse). Top. Light micrograph of a whole mount preparation showing motor nerve approaching from above and branching to left and right along the surface of a muscle fiber (note striations). A histochemical reaction has stained the acetycholinesterase in the postsynaptic (muscle) membrane black. Bottom. Electron micrograph of the endplate region. The muscle cell appears at the bottom, showing striated myofibrils. The muscle membrane shows extensive infoldings, termed "junctional folds." The axon terminal is seen in longitudinal section above, and contains pale synaptic vesicles grouped in bunches over regions of presynaptic membrane thickenings, forming the active zones. Above them are seen denser granules and mitochondria. The synaptic cleft is filled with an amorphous mucopolysaccharide.* [McMahan et al., 1972.]

especially with the endplates of the frog sartorius muscle. Except for the identities of various transmitter substances and certain quantitative differences, synaptic transmission between neurons in the central nervous system is similar to transmission at nerve-muscle synapses, such as the motor endplate. It will serve as the model system in much of what follows on chemical transmission.

An examination of Figure 6-27 in the light of the three-dimensional reconstruction of the frog motor endplate* in Figure 6-28 shows that it consists of specializations of the postsynaptic membrane, the motor nerve terminal, and Schwann cells. The axon terminal bifurcates, and each approximately 1-µm-thick branch lies in a longitudinal depression along the surface of the muscle fiber. The muscle membrane lining the depression is thrown into transverse *junctional folds* at intervals of 1 to 2 µm. Directly above these folds within the nerve terminal are the *active zones,* transverse regions of slight thickening of the presynaptic membrane, above which are clustered the synaptic vesicles. There is evidence that the vesicles are released along

*The term "endplate" does not accurately describe the organization of the neuromuscular (N-M) junction of amphibians, having been first applied to the N-M junction of mammals, which is more plate-like and less strung out than the amphibian endplate.

the active zones by the process of *exocytosis* (p. 101). Examples of exocytosis can be seen in Figure 6-26. Transmitter release from the presynaptic terminal is triggered by the arrival of an action potential in the presynaptic terminal.

Once released, the transmitter—acetylcholine in vertebrate neuromuscular synapses—is subject to hydrolysis by the enzyme *acetylcholinesterase.* The presence of this enzyme can be detected by histochemical means (Fig. 6-27) and is found to be located in the synaptic folds of the frog endplate. Before it is completely hydrolyzed the acetylcholine interacts with receptor molecules located in the postsynaptic membrane of the endplate, causing closely associated ion channels to open briefly.

SYNAPTIC POTENTIALS

In 1942, Kuffler reported experiments on single fibers of frog muscle in which extracellular recordings showed depolarizations intimately associated with the motor endplate. These occurred in response to motor nerve impulses, and preceded the action potential generated across the membrane of the muscle cell. Since these potential changes were recorded with greatest amplitude at the endplate, and gradually disappeared with distance as recordings were made further away from

6-28. *Three-dimensional reconstruction of the frog endplate based on electron-microscopical data. The nerve terminal lies in a longitudinal depression in the surface of the muscle fiber. The depression contains transverse* junctional *folds (jf). Overlying the junctional folds are* active zones *(az) in the nerve terminal, rich in synaptic vesicles (sv). A Schwann cell (S) overlies the terminal, sending slender fingers underneath the terminal. Compare with Figure 6-26. [After Peper et al., 1974.]*

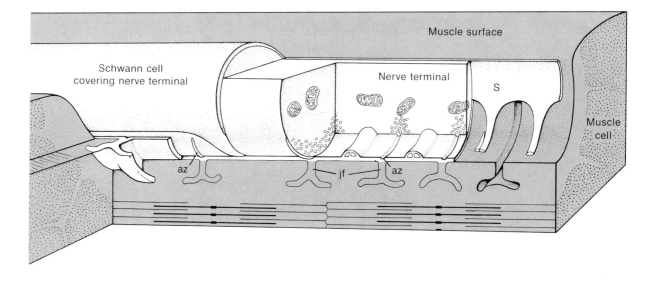

the endplate region, they were termed *endplate potentials.* It was concluded that the propagated action potential in the muscle cell arises from a local depolarization of the postsynaptic membrane associated with the arrival of an action potential in the presynaptic terminal.

The development of the glass capillary microelectrode (p. 112) in the late 1940's made it possible to go far beyond these early exploratory experiments. Described below is a composite of intracellular studies—based especially on those reported from the laboratory of Sir Bernard Katz—of synaptic transmission at the frog neuromuscular synapse (i.e., frog endplate).

A microelectrode inserted into a muscle fiber at a distance of several millimeters from the region of the endplate will record the resting potential. If the motor axon innervating the muscle is given a single shock (Fig. 6-29,A), the electrode will record an all-or-none *muscle* action potential after a delay of several milliseconds. Every time the motor axon is stimulated, a muscle action potential will be recorded, and the muscle fiber will respond with a twitch. If increasing concentrations of the South American arrow poison *curare* (d-tubocurarine) are applied, a concentration will be found at which there is a sudden (all-or-none) failure of the muscle action potential and a concomitant failure of the muscle fiber to contract. The action

potentials of the motor axon, however, will remain unaffected, and so will the ability of the muscle fiber to give an action potential and contract in response to an electrical stimulus applied directly to it. Since the presynaptic and postsynaptic action potentials remain unaffected by the poison, we can conclude that curare somehow interferes with synaptic transmission.

If the same experiment is repeated with the microelectrode inserted in the muscle fiber close to (within <0.1 mm) the endplate region (Fig. 6-29,B), the following observations are noted. (1) As the concentration of curare is gradually raised, the action potential arises not abruptly from the resting potential, but instead from a depolarization that is distinctly slower in time course and lower in amplitude than the action potential. This slow potential wave is the *endplate potential,* or *excitatory postsynaptic potential* (e.p.s.p.). (2) The blocking agent, curare, reduces the amplitude of the endplate potentials. (3) The endplate potential must reach a minimum level (the threshold or *firing level*) to trigger the muscle action potential, hence the abrupt failure of the action potential as the amplitude of the endplate potential is reduced below the spike threshold by increased concentrations of curare.

At a concentration of curare sufficient to reduce the size of the endplate potential to just below the firing level, the action potential is eliminated, and the end-plate potential is revealed without the superimposed action potential (Fig. 6-29,C).

Intracellular recordings of the endplate potential at different points along the muscle fiber show that its amplitude drops exponentially with distance from the endplate (Fig. 6-30). In contrast to the action potential, which propagates in an unattenuated manner because of its regenerative nature, the synaptic potential spreads electrotonically.

POSTSYNAPTIC EXCITATION

In Chapter 5, it was shown that changes in membrane conductance to one or more species of ion shift the membrane potential toward a new level, in accord with Equation 5-9. The flow of ions that produces such a potential shift constitutes an electric current that transfers charge from one side of the membrane to the other. Chemical transmission depends on the ability of the transmitter substance to produce a specific change in the conductance of the postsynaptic membrane, for this determines the direction and extent of ionic current flow across the postsynaptic membrane. In vertebrate muscle, the conductance of the postsynaptic membrane increases in response to the transmitter acetylcholine.

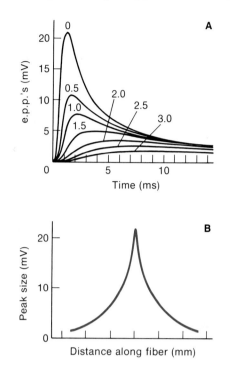

6–30. A. Recordings of endplate potentials at various distances from the endplate region. B. The peak potential decreases more or less exponentially with increased distance from the endplate. [After Fatt and Katz, 1951.]

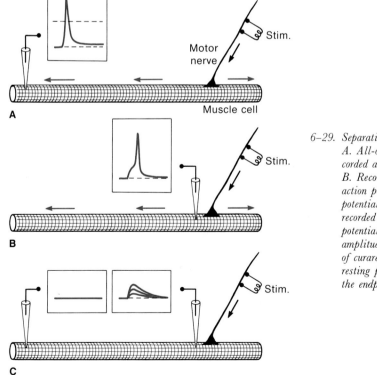

6–29. Separation of endplate and action potentials. A. All-or-none muscle action potential is recorded at a distance from the endplate region. B. Recording close to the endplate shows the action potential arising out of the endplate potential. C. Endplate potentials can be recorded without the superimposed action potential if the e.p.p. is reduced to an amplitude below the firing level by application of curare. In that case, only the undisturbed resting potential is recorded at a distance from the endplate region.

The ionic currents responsible for the endplate potential can be recorded independently of any membrane potential change by holding the postsynaptic potential constant by voltage clamping (Box 5-2) the membrane in the region of the endplate (Fig. 6-31,A). When the motor nerve is stimulated while the membrane potential is held constant by electronic feedback, the release of transmitter by the motor nerve ending is followed by a characteristic *endplate current*, or *synaptic current* (Fig. 6-31,B). This current represents the flow of ions down their electrochemical gradients through channels opened by the action of the transmitter on receptor molecules in the postsynaptic membrane of the muscle fiber.

The ions carrying the endplate current were identified by changing the extracellular concentrations of ions and noting the effects on the current. In this way, it was found that the inward synaptic current at the endplate is carried by an influx of Na^+, and that this is partially cancelled by a simultaneous efflux of K^+. Thus the transmitter, ACh, increases the conductance of the muscle postsynaptic membrane to both K^+ and Na^+. As a result, the *reversal potential* (Box 6-3) for the postsynaptic potential in this tissue lies somewhere between E_{Na} and E_K; at about -15 mV.

6–31. Comparison of synaptic current with synaptic potential in frog motor endplates.   A. Voltage-clamping the muscle membrane holds the postsynaptic potential constant while the endplate current is recorded. B. Stimulation of motor axon produces synaptic current (lower trace). When membrane is unclamped, an endplate potential is produced (upper trace), which decays much more slowly than the underlying endplate current. This is explained in the text.

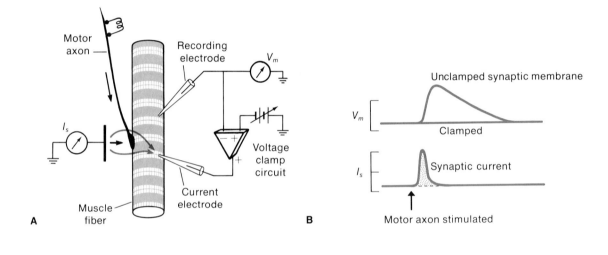

BOX 6-3   REVERSAL POTENTIALS

When a membrane responding to a chemical transmitter or other stimulus undergoes a transient increase in conductance to one or more ions, such as Na^+ and K^+, the membrane potential shifts *toward* a new level somewhere between the equilibrium potentials (p. 120) of the permeant ions. This can be demonstrated by testing the effect of the steady background potential on the amplitude and polarity of the endplate potential (see figure on p. 173). The presynaptic axon is stimulated while the postsynaptic potential is recorded intracellularly. A polarizing microelectrode is used to pass a current across the postsynaptic membrane so as to set the prevailing membrane potential of the endplate region at various selected levels. The amplitude of the synaptic potential progressively diminishes as the membrane is depolarized by applied current. Somewhere between -15 and -30 mV, the synaptic potential disappears. This defines the *reversal potential*. Setting the membrane potential at progressively more positive levels causes the synaptic potential to reappear, but with its polarity reversed. At the reversal potential, the two ionic species (Na^+ and K^+), to which the membrane has become more permeable because of the action of the transmitter, flow in opposite

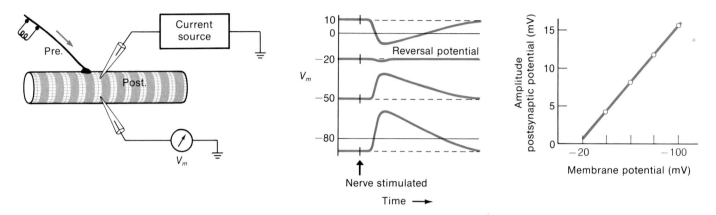

Left. Experimental method for determining the reversal level of a synaptic potential. Polarizing current injected with one electrode is used to displace the membrane potential to different levels during synaptic stimulation via the motor nerve. The responses are recorded with the other electrode. Middle. The synaptic potential reverses sign at potentials more positive than the reversal potential. At the reversal potential, the transmitter produces no potential change. Right. The amplitude of the e.p.p. is plotted against membrane potential.

directions (K^+ out of the cell, Na^+ into the cell) at equal rates. When the membrane is initially at the resting potential, close to E_K, the difference ($V_m - E_K$) is small and $V_m - E_{Na}$ is large, hence the synaptic current begins primarily as an influx of Na^+.

The value of the reversal potential depends on the relative conductances of the permeant ions. Assuming that only Na^+ and K^+ are permeant, the reversal level can be related to conductances by using Equation 5-3.

$$I_K = g_K (E_m - E_K), \tag{1}$$

$$I_{Na} = g_{Na} (E_m - E_{Na}). \tag{2}$$

At the reversal potential, I_K and I_{Na} must be equal and opposite regardless of the relative conductances. Thus, when E_m is at the reversal potential, E_{rev},

$$-I_K = I_{Na}. \tag{3}$$

Therefore, from Equations 1 and 2,

$$g_K (E_m - E_K) = g_{Na}(E_m - E_{Na}). \tag{4}$$

It is obvious that if g_K is greater than g_{Na}, then E_m must be closer to E_K than to E_{Na}, and vice versa.

Solving for E_m ($= E_{rev}$) gives

$$E_m = \left(\frac{g_K}{g_{Na}+g_K}\right)E_K + \left(\frac{g_{Na}}{g_K+g_{Na}}\right)E_{Na}. \tag{5}$$

From this it is apparent that E_{rev} will not simply be the algebraic sum of E_{Na} and E_K, but will lie somewhere between the two, depending on the ratio g_{Na}/g_K. Thus, if g_{Na} and g_K become equal to each other (e.g., as in frog muscle), the membrane potential will shift toward the reversal potential, which in this case lies exactly halfway between E_{Na} and E_K:

$$E_{rev} = 1/2E_K + 1/2E_{Na} = 1/2(E_K + E_{Na}).$$

For frog muscle, E_K is about -90 mV and E_{Na} about $+50$, hence during synaptic activation, $E_{rev} = 1/2(-90 + 50) = -20$ mV.

To summarize, the reversal potentials of different membrane currents differ according to the species of ions that participate, the equilibrium potentials of those ions, and the relative conductances to each of the kinds of ions.

It is evident from Figure 6-31,B that the postsynaptic potential has a much longer duration than the postsynaptic current. The reason for the protracted decay of the potential becomes apparent when one recalls that the postsynaptic current is essentially no different in its effect than an artificially injected current. The decay rate of the synaptic potential is dependent on the time constant (Box 5-1) of the postsynaptic cell. After the postsynaptic current has depolarized the membrane, the transmitter-activated channels close again, and the charge that has accumulated in the postsynaptic cell slowly leaks out through the resting conductance of the cell membrane, restoring the membrane to the resting potential.

The amplitude of the endplate potential in vertebrate skeletal twitch muscle generally exceeds the firing level by a considerable margin. Because of this, the neuromuscular synapse of skeletal muscle has no integrative (information-processing) role, but merely relays all-or-none excitation from the motor nerve to the muscle. By using a postsynaptic blocking agent, such as curare, the amplitude of the endplate potential can be reduced to less than the firing level (Fig. 6-29,C). It then behaves in a manner more typical of arthropod neuromuscular synapses and of most synapses between neurons in which individual synaptic potentials are very small (several millivolts at most), and integrative processes such as summation (Chapter 8) are required to elicit an action potential.

POSTSYNAPTIC INHIBITION

A synaptic event that increases the probability of initiation of an action potential in the postsynaptic cell is termed excitatory; conversely, an event that reduces that probability is termed inhibitory. Thus any postsynaptic potential whose reversal potential is more positive than the firing level has an excitatory effect (Fig. 6-32,A), and *any postsynaptic potential whose reversal potential is on the negative side of the firing level is inhibitory in effect, regardless of whether it produces a hyperpolarization or a small depolarization* (Fig. 6-32,B). The effect of an inhibitory transmitter acting on a given cell simultaneously with an excitatory transmitter is to reduce the size of the excitatory potential and keep it from reaching the threshold potential (Fig. 6-32,C).

The inhibitory postsynaptic potential of some neurons is due to an increased Cl^- conductance; in others, it is due to the increased conductance of both K^+ and Cl^-. Both of these ions typically have equilibrium potentials in the general vicinity of the resting potential, well below the firing level.

Inhibition does not require hyperpolarization from the resting potential. Thus, if the reversal potential for a transmitter action happens to be equal to the resting

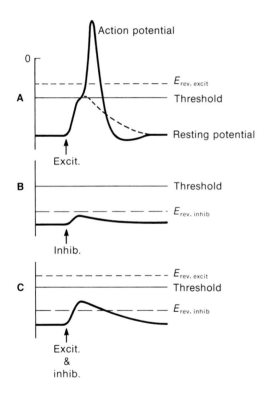

6–32. *Inhibitory-excitatory interaction.   A. An action potential arises out of an excitatory postsynaptic potential if the latter exceeds threshold.   B. An inhibitory postsynaptic potential may depolarize, but its reversal potential is below threshold.   C. An inhibitory transmitter acting simultaneously with an excitatory transmitter can keep the membrane potential below threshold.*

potential, no synaptic current and no potential change will result from the increase in postsynaptic conductance caused by the action of the inhibitory transmitter (Box 6-3). Even though the conductance to Cl⁻ and/or K⁺ increases, the membrane potential will remain constant at the rest level. The transmitter will have an inhibitory action, since it will tend to hold V_m below the firing level, which has a more positive potential. If the reversal potential is several millivolts more negative than the resting potential, the action of the transmitter will hyperpolarize the cell toward that level (Fig. 6-33). If the reversal potential for the transmitter action is more positive than the resting potential, the transmitter will produce a small postsynaptic depolarization (Fig. 6-32,B). A transmitter is defined as inhibitory if the increased membrane conductance resulting from its action keeps the postsynaptic membrane from reaching the firing level (Fig. 6-32,C).

Whether the action of a transmitter depolarizes or hyperpolarizes depends on (1) the conductance changes produced by its interaction with receptor sites on the postsynaptic membrane and (2) the equilibrium potentials of the ions to which the membrane becomes more permeable (Fig. 6-33).

It follows that a normally inhibitory transmitter can be made to have an excitatory action by an experimental redistribution of the appropriate ionic gradients across the postsynaptic membrane. This has, in fact, been done in neurons of the mammalian spinal cord and in the snail. In certain snail neurons, the effect of the natural transmitter (acetylcholine) is to increase the chloride conductance of the postsynaptic membrane. In one such group of cells (H cells), the intracellular Cl⁻ concentration is relatively low, so that E_{Cl} is more negative than the resting potential. The neural transmitter acetylcholine produces a hyperpolarization when applied to the H cells by opening Cl channels, allowing Cl⁻ to flow into the cell, shifting the membrane potential toward E_{Cl} (Fig. 6-34,A). When the extracellular chloride is replaced with sulfate, which cannot pass through the chloride channels, application of acetylcholine leads to an efflux of Cl⁻, which now has an outwardly directed electrochemical gradient. This efflux of negative charge produces both a depolarization and an increase in the frequency of action potentials (Fig. 6-34,B). Thus acetylcholine, the transmitter that is normally inhibitory in these cells, will produce excitation if the electrochemical gradient of the chloride ion is reversed.*

*It is interesting that other cells in the snail (D cells) maintain a high intracellular Cl⁻ concentration by active Cl pumping. In these cells, ACh produces a similar increase in Cl permeability. Since the Cl gradient is outward in D cells, they depolarize in response to the normal transmitter, ACh.

6–33. *Top. Comparison of depolarizing and hyperpolarizing conductance changes. Transmitter D evokes a depolarizing postsynaptic potential because the conductance increase that it produces leads to a net inward current (carried primarily by Na⁺) that adds positive charge to cell interior. Its reversal potential is relatively positive. Transmitter H produces a hyperpolarizing synaptic potential because the conductance increase that it produces is primarily to ions (e.g., K⁺ and/or Cl⁻) that will carry net current out of the cell (i.e., add negative charge to cell interior). Bottom. The direction of current flow through the postsynaptic membrane is the opposite for currents D and H.*

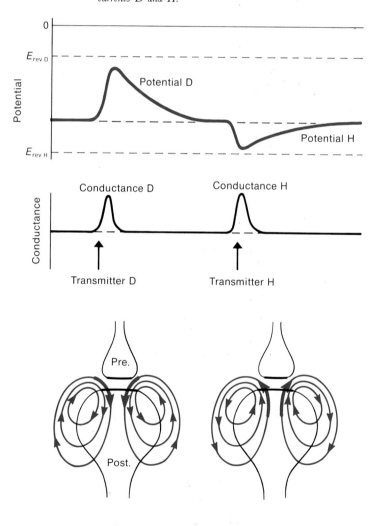

6-34. *The importance of ionic gradients in determining the direction of potential changes produced in response to a transmitter substance. A. ACh applied to H cells in the snail brain produces a hyperpolarization because Cl⁻ flows into the cell down its concentration gradient. B. By exchanging the extracellular Cl⁻ with SO₄²⁻ the direction of potential change is reversed. Opening of the chloride channels by the transmitter now causes a depolarization because the new concentration gradient causes Cl⁻ to flow out of the cell. The effect on impulse discharge is shown at the right. [After Kurkut and Thomas, 1963.]*

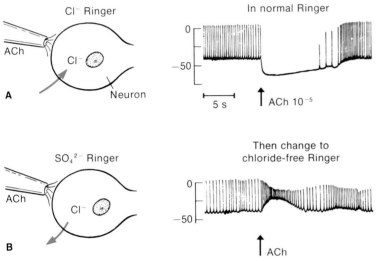

6-35. *Anatomical basis for presynaptic inhibition in a crustacean muscle. An inhibitory neuron synapses with the presynaptic terminals of an excitatory axon. Release of inhibitory transmitter increases the K and Cl conductance of the excitatory terminal, reducing the size of the action potential in the terminal and hence the amount of transmitter released from the terminal. Postsynaptic inhibition occurs where the inhibitor terminates on the muscle fiber directly. [After Lang and Atwood, 1973.]*

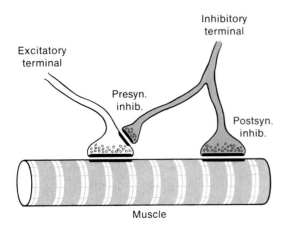

There is, of course, nothing inherently "excitatory" or "inhibitory" about a transmitter substance. For example, acetylcholine is the excitatory transmitter at the motor endplate and at synapses of sympathetic ganglia, producing a predominant increase in Na and K conductance in the postsynaptic membrane. In contrast, it is an inhibitory transmitter at parasympathetic endings in the heart and viscera, producing an increase in K and/or Cl conductance. The molecular properties of the receptor sites on the postsynaptic membrane determine the ion specificity of the permeability increase that is set up across the postsynaptic membrane when these sites react with the transmitter molecules. The relative ionic permeabilities and the electrochemical gradients of the permeant ions determine the reversal level of the synaptic potential, and thus whether the postsynaptic effect is excitatory or inhibitory.

Although vertebrate skeletal muscle receives only excitatory innervation, various invertebrate muscle fibers and neurons of the central nervous systems of vertebrates and invertebrates receive inhibitory as well as excitatory motor axons. It will become evident in Chapter 8 that inhibition is equally as important as excitation in the functioning of nervous systems.

PRESYNAPTIC INHIBITION

Neural inhibition can also result from the action of an inhibitory terminal ending on the presynaptic terminal of an excitatory axon (Fig. 6-35), causing a reduction in the amount of transmitter *released* from the excitatory terminal. The inhibitory transmitter apparently increases the membrane permeability of the presynaptic terminals of the excitatory axon to K⁺ and Cl⁻. This increase in conductance reduces the size of the action potential invading the excitatory terminal, thereby reducing the amount of excitatory transmitter released. The end effect of *presynaptic inhibition* is that the postsynaptic cell receives less excitatory transmitter and thus produces a smaller excitatory postsynaptic potential.

Postsynaptic Receptors and Channels

The transmitter, as we have seen, interacts with the postsynaptic membrane to produce conductance changes to certain ions. This interaction must entail two major events:

1. The transmitter combines with the receptor site on the postsynaptic membrane. The receptor site can be blocked by substances like curare (in the case of muscle ACh receptors), which compete with the transmitter for the site.

2. Interaction of a receptor site with the transmitter molecule must cause a previously closed ion channel to open transiently. This requires that the receptor site be intimately associated with the channel. The receptor may be either a molecule separate from those that make up the channel, or it may be simply a part of the channel.

During the opening of the channel a minute current (single-channel current) must flow through the opened channel. A large number of such single-channel currents must sum to produce the synaptic current in response to the tens or hundreds of thousands of transmitter molecules released from the presynaptic terminal in response to a presynaptic action potential.

THE ACETYLCHOLINE RECEPTOR

The problem of isolating, identifying, and characterizing the molecule that binds the transmitter and transduces this binding into the opening of a channel is not a simple one, since the number of channel molecules relative to the total number of protein molecules in the membrane is rather small. In such studies, advantage is taken of two biological aids. One is the occurrence of an acetylcholine receptor in high densities on one surface of the *electroplax* (flattened cells originating embryonically from muscle tissue) found in the powerful electric organs of certain elasmobranch and teleost fish. The high receptor content of these tissues provides useful yields during the chemical isolation of the receptor. The second aid is the use of α-bungarotoxin (*BuTX*), a synaptic blocking agent isolated from the venom of the krait, a member of the cobra family. Since BuTX binds irreversibly to the ACh receptor, it can be isotopically labeled and then used as a tagging molecule for the identification and isolation of the receptor.

The ACh receptor is a protein of as yet uncertain molecular weight. One suggestion is that the receptor is made up of subunits (monomers) of molecular weight 42,000 that polymerize predominantly to a hexamer of molecular weight 252,000. This size agrees with that of particles seen by freeze-etch electron microscopy in electroplax membranes.

The ACh receptor is located on the exterior side of the cell membrane, as deduced from the fact that ACh injected into a muscle cell near the endplate produces no electrical effect. Whether the molecule or molecules that constitute the ACh receptor is also a part of the ACh-activated channel is not yet known.

ACh-ACTIVATED CHANNELS

As we have seen, the postsynaptic channels of the motor endplate of frog skeletal muscle become perme-able to both K^+ and Na^+ when activated by ACh. This results in an inward current with a reversal potential of about -15 mV. Normally these channels and the associated ACh receptors are confined to the postsynaptic membrane in the endplate region. The density of ACh-activated channels at the frog endplate has been estimated at about $6500/\mu m^2$.

When a muscle is *denervated* by section of the motor nerve, ACh sensitivity gradually spreads from the endplate region over most or all of each muscle cell, indicating that receptors and channels, normally confined to the endplate region and suppressed elsewhere in the membrane, appear at extrajunctional sites. The normal suppression of *extrajunctional receptors* (and channels) is mediated in part by a poorly understood *trophic action* of the motoneuron that innervates the muscle cell, and in part by contractile activity of the innervated muscle cell. If the motor axon is allowed to reinnervate the muscle, the extrajunctional receptors disappear, and sensitivity to ACh again becomes confined to the junctional (i.e., endplate) region.

The sparse distribution of extrajunctional channels that develop in denervated muscle has been exploited in a recent study of the *gating* of the ACh-activated Na-K channel in frog muscle by Neher and Sackmann (1976). The muscle membrane was voltage-clamped at a hyperpolarized potential in order to increase the driving force for inward synaptic current. A micropipette with a tip opening of 10 μm^2 was filled with Ringer's solution containing a low concentration of ACh or one of its agonists (compound having a similar action). The surface of a denervated muscle fiber was explored with the tip of the pipette, which was connected to a highly sensitive current-recording amplifier (Fig. 6-36,A). At certain spots on the surface, the pipette detected minute ($<5 \times 10^{-12}$ A) but distinct inward current pulses (Fig. 6-36,B) produced by the transient opening of the ACh-activated (or agonist-activated) channels. It is notable that those pulses are more or less rectangular in shape (i.e., turn abruptly "on" and "off") and are essentially all-or-none. This is, of course, to be expected if the channels exhibit two states, completely shut or completely open. The current pulses are absent unless the pipette contains ACh or an agonist, and occur with a frequency related to the concentration of the transmitter or agonist in the pipette. The conductance of a single open channel can be calculated from the current to be about $2 \times 10)^{-11}$ mhos (i.e., a resistance of about 5×10^{10} ohms).

It is significant that the average duration of the current pulses differs with the substance used to activate the channel. Thus the pulses produced by suberylcholine are longer than those produced by ACh, which are longer than those produced by carbachol. This is consistent with the idea that the affinities of the

6–36. Currents recorded from a single ACh-sensitive channel in denervated frog muscle. A. The muscle membrane is held at a high potential (−120 mV) by a voltage-clamp circuit while its surface is explored with a pipette containing a 2 × 10⁻⁷ M solution of the ACh agonist suberylcholine in Ringer's solution. B. With the opening of the pipette placed snugly over an ACh-sensitive channel, pulses of inward-going current are recorded by the pipette. These represent transient opening of the channel as the agonist interacts with the receptor site associated with the channel. [After Neher and Sakmann, 1976.]

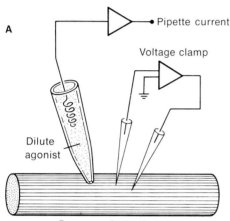

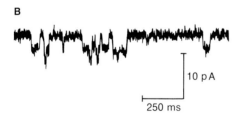

6–37. Molecular structure of acetylcholine.

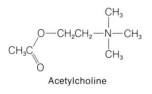

ACh receptor to these agents is in the order suberylcholine > ACh > carbachol.

The extrajunctional receptors studied in these experiments are not accompanied by the enzyme acetylcholinesterase, which rapidly hydrolyzes the ACh in the synaptic cleft. This may explain the long durations of channel opening seen in Figure 6-36. During transmission at the endplate, the synaptic current normally lasts only a few milliseconds because the ACh is rapidly hydrolyzed by the acetylcholinesterase.

Transmitter Substances

One of the more difficult problems in neurophysiology is the unequivocal chemical identification of transmitters acting at various synapses. A limited number of transmitters have been identified with certainty (Table 6-2). The most familiar transmitter substance is acetylcholine (Fig. 6-37), which is released by the terminals of vertebrate motor axons, by preganglionic terminals of the vertebrate autonomic system (Fig. 6-15), by postganglionic terminals of the parasympathetic division of the autonomic system, and by the presynaptic terminals of certain neurons of the vertebrate central nervous system. It also appears to act as the transmitter in a number of invertebrate neurons, including some cells of the molluscan central nervous system and sensory neurons of arthropods.

The ACh released from the terminals of *cholinergic* axons is hydrolyzed to choline and acetate by the enzyme acetylcholinesterase, which is present on the surface of the postsynaptic membrane (Fig. 6-38). The enzymatic destruction of ACh terminates its effect on the postsynaptic membrane. The choline is actively reabsorbed by the presynaptic endings, in which it is recycled by combination with acetyl coenzyme A (p. 73) to form a new molecule of acetylcholine.

The acetylcholinesterase molecule has two distinct sites (Fig. 6-39), an anionic site that binds the quaternary nitrogen of ACh, and an esteratic site that can donate electrons to the acetate portion of the ACh molecule, cleaving it from the choline moiety. This allows the hydrolysis of ACh and terminates the postsynaptic action of the transmitter. The esterase is inactivated by certain nerve gases and insecticides. With the esterase blocked, ACh lingers and builds up in the synaptic regions. This either prevents repolarization of the postsynaptic membrane or, in many types of synapses, causes inactivation of the ACh receptors. In either case, the normal functioning of the nervous and neuromuscular systems is disrupted, and death ensues very rapidly. The anticholinesterase *eserine* (=physostigmine) is used in the laboratory when it is necessary to retard the hydrolysis of acetylcholine.

Table 6-2. Some common neurotransmitters and their sites of action.

Substance	Site of action	Type of innervation	Status
Acetylcholine	Skeletal muscle; neuromuscular junction	Excitatory	Est.
	Autonomic nervous system:		
	preganglionic sympathetic	Excitatory	Est.
	pre- and postganglionic parasympathetic	Excitatory or inhibitory	Est.
	Renshaw cell in CNS	Excitatory	Est.
	Other CNS	—	Poss.
Norepinephrine	Most postganglionic sympathetic	Excitatory or inhibitory	Est.
	CNS	—	Poss.
Glutamic acid	CNS	Excitatory	Poss.
	Crustacea, CNS and PNS	Excitatory	Poss.
γ-aminobutyric acid (GABA)	CNS	Inhibitory	Poss.
	Crustacea, CNS and PNS	Inhibitory	Est.
Serotonin (5-hydroxy-tryptamine)	CNS	—	Poss.
Dopamine (3,4-dihydroxy-phenylethylamine)	CNS	—	Poss.

*Est. = established transmitter; poss. = possible transmitter.

6-38. Transmitter chemistry at a cholinergic synapse. Acetylcholine released from the terminal is hydrolyzed by acetylcholinesterase (AChE) on the surface of the postsynaptic membrane. Choline is taken up by the presynaptic terminal and re-acetylated to ACh. [After Mountcastle and Baldessarini, 1968.]

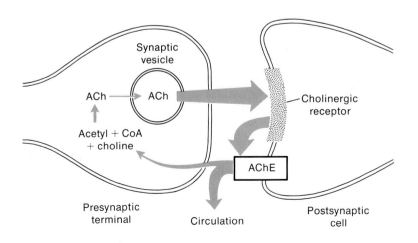

6-39. The steric relations between the active site on the acetylcholinesterase molecule and its substrate ACh.

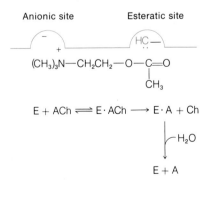

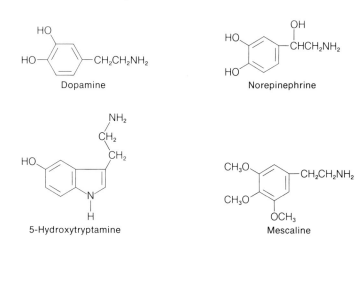

6-40. The monamines dopamine, norepinephrine, epinephrine (not shown), and 5-HT are a closely related group of transmitter substances found in vertebrate and invertebrate nervous systems. Mescaline, a psychoactive drug extracted from the peyote cactus, is believed to induce hallucinations by interfering with its analogue norepinephrine at synapses in the central nervous system.

Dopamine

Norepinephrine

5-Hydroxytryptamine

Mescaline

The monoamines *norepinephrine, dopamine, and 5-hydroxytryptamine* (5-HT) (Fig. 6-40) are closely related compounds found in certain groups of vertebrate and invertebrate neurons. They are most concentrated in nerve terminals, and have also been isolated in the synaptic vesicles of some nervous tissues. These substances can be detected in individual neurons, because they fluoresce in ultraviolet light after fixation with formaldehyde. They are found in the central and autonomic nervous systems, and are suspected of being transmitters. The evidence for the central role of dopamine is especially convincing. Norepinephrine (= noradrenalin) is known to be the excitatory transmitter at postganglionic cells of the sympathetic system (Fig. 6-15), such as the *chromaffin cells* of the adrenal medulla and the sympathetic neurons innervating the vertebrate heart. The chromaffin cells are derived embryologically from postganglionic neurons and secrete epinephrine as well as norepinephrine. These two *catecholamines* have similar pharmacological actions. The chemistry of norepinephrine at an *adrenergic* synapse is outlined briefly in Figure 6-41. The pathway for synthesis of norepinephrine from the amino acid phenylalanine (Fig. 6-42) shows the close relationship between dopamine and norepinephrine. It is interesting to note the structural similarities between these amines and certain extremely potent psychoactive drugs, such as mescaline (Fig. 6-40) and lysergic acid diethylamide (LSD).

There is growing evidence that certain amino acids, such as *glutamic* acid (Fig. 6-43) are released at excitatory synapses of the vertebrate central nervous system and at excitatory neuromuscular synapses (motor nerve terminals) in insects and crustaceans. *Gamma aminobutyric acid (GABA)* (Fig. 6-43) is the transmitter at the inhibitory motor synapse in crustacean muscle, and there is evidence that it may be one of the inhibitory transmitters in the vertebrate central nervous system.

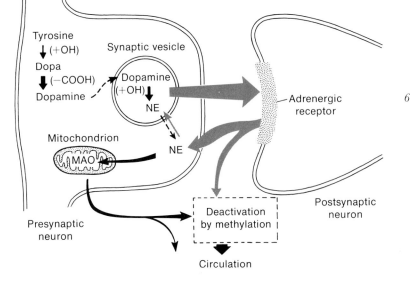

6-41. Transmitter chemistry at an adrenergic synapse. Norepinephrine (NE) is synthesized from the amino acid phenylalanine via tyrosine and stored in synaptic vesicles. After release, some NE is taken back up into the presynaptic terminal and some is deactivated by methylation and carried away in the blood. Cytoplasmic NE is either taken up into a synaptic vesicle or degraded by monamine oxidase (MAO). [After Mountcastle and Baldesarrini, 1968.]

6-42. *Biosynthetic pathway leading to epinephrine and norepinephrine.* [*After Eidusen, 1967.*]

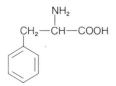

Phenylalanine

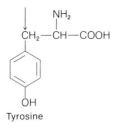

Tyrosine

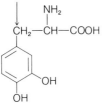

3,4-Dihydroxyphenylalanine (dopa)

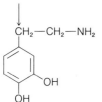

3,4-Dihydroxyphenylethylamine (dopamine)

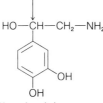

Norepinephrine

Epinephrine

6-43. *The structures of glutamate and γ-amino butyric acid (GABA). Glutamate, the neutral form of glutamic acid, has been identified as an excitatory transmitter in some central nervous systems and in the excitatory innervation of crustacean muscle. GABA is the inhibitory transmitter in arthropod muscle and at some synapses in central nervous systems.*

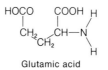

Glutamic acid

$$NH_2-CH_2-CH_2-CH_2-COOH$$
γ-Aminobutyric acid

Release of Transmitter

QUANTAL NATURE OF RELEASE

Fatt and Katz (1952a) reported miniature (<1 mV) spontaneous depolarizations recorded from the vicinity of the postsynaptic membrane of the motor endplate of frog muscle (Fig. 6-44). As the recording electrode was inserted at greater distances from the endplate, they found that these miniature depolarizations stopped being recorded. Since these potentials have the same shape, time course, and drug-sensitivity as the endplate potential, they were termed *miniature endplate potentials (m.e.p.p.'s)*.

A progressive increase in Mg^{2+} and/or decrease in Ca^{2+} causes the normal endplate potential to become smaller until, at the appropriate concentrations of these cations, it attains an amplitude similar to that of a spontaneously occurring m.e.p.p. By measuring postsynaptic responses to presynaptic motor nerve impulses under high Mg^{2+} and low Ca^{2+}, Fatt and Katz (1952b) found that (1) some motor impulses produce no response at all, (2) some produce m.e.p.p.'s having approximately the same amplitudes as spontaneous m.e.p.p.'s, and (3) some produce potentials whose amplitudes are integral multiples (e.g., 2x, 3x, 4x, etc.) of the mean amplitude of single spontaneous m.e.p.p.'s

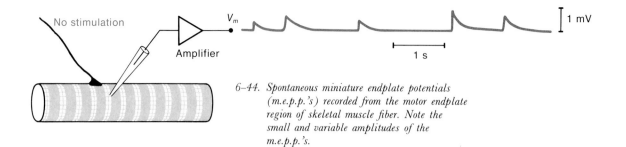

6–44. *Spontaneous miniature endplate potentials (m.e.p.p.'s) recorded from the motor endplate region of skeletal muscle fiber. Note the small and variable amplitudes of the m.e.p.p.'s.*

6–45. *Quantal release at the motor endplate.* *Top. A motor nerve is stimulated in a solution having a low [Ca²⁺] and a high [Mg²⁺], which reduces the amount of transmitter released in response to stimulation. Evoked endplate potentials have variable miniature amplitudes. Bottom. Histograms record the number of m.e.p.p.'s of various amplitudes (vertical bars). The upper histogram records spontaneously occurring m.e.p.p.'s evoked by motor-nerve stimulation. Note that there were large numbers of failures. The largest number of evoked m.e.p.p.'s had a size distribution similar to those of spontaneous m.e.p.p.'s. The continuous curves give the theoretical distributions obtained on the assumption that the evoked m.e.p.p.'s are made up of units corresponding to those that occur spontaneously.* [*Histograms from Del Castillo and Katz, 1954.*]

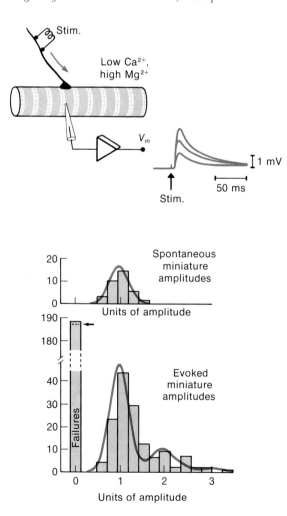

(Fig. 6-45). This suggested that the normal endplate potential results from the summation of many (100–250) units of transmitter released in unison.

Cooling the nerve-muscle preparation slows the release of transmitter from the nerve terminal and therefore results in an asynchronous release of these transmitter units. The jagged, step-wise rise of the endplate potential under these conditions, each peak presumably due to a separate unit of release, is further evidence that the endplate potential is made up of smaller units that, when normally released in unison, sum as a single, large depolarization.

The miniature endplate potential is now widely agreed to represent the postsynaptic response to a unit presynaptic release of the transmitter substance. The unit, termed a *quantum,* or packet, of transmitter, consists of 1×10^4 to 4×10^4 molecules of acetylcholine released into the subsynaptic cleft to activate in the frog about 2000 postsynaptic channels. The source of a single packet of transmitter was long believed to be a single presynaptic vesicle releasing its contents by exocytosis (Figs. 6-26, 6-46). With recently refined methods, however, it is seen that each m.e.p.p. itself consists of several (up to about 15) *subminiature potentials.* For this reason it now appears that the m.e.p.p. is produced by the simultaneous release of several vesicles, each of which contributes a subminiature potential. Further evidence suggests that this occurs by a synchronous release of a group of vesicles lined up along the inner surface of the terminal membrane at an active zone (Figs. 6-27, 6-28). According to this view, a spontaneous miniature endplate potential arises from the spontaneous "discharge" of a single active zone, and a normal endplate potential arises from the simultaneous discharge by an invading action potential of many (100–250) active zones (Kriebel et al., 1976; Wernig, 1976).

Miniature synaptic potentials and *quantal release,* first demonstrated in neuromuscular synapses, were subsequently demonstrated in neuron-to-neuron synapses of the central nervous system. These, too, have structures resembling the active zones of the motor nerve terminal.

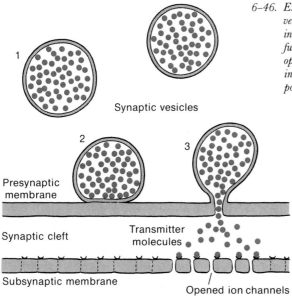

6–46. *Exocytosis of transmitter-containing synaptic vesicles. The vesicles release their contents into the synaptic cleft when their membranes fuse with the plasma membrane and an opening forms. The transmitter diffuses and interacts with receptor molecules on the postsynaptic membrane.* [*After Eccles, 1965.*]

Synaptic vesicles

Presynaptic membrane

Synaptic cleft

Transmitter molecules

Subsynaptic membrane

Opened ion channels

DEPOLARIZATION-RELEASE COUPLING

When the presynaptic membrane potential is at its resting level, the probability of quantal release is low, and the occasional release of the contents of synaptic vesicles is recorded postsynaptically as a spontaneous miniature endplate potential. The occurrence of a m.e.p.p. is random and independent of other m.e.p.p.'s, but when the presynaptic membrane is depolarized, the probability of quantal release increases (Fig. 6-47). This led to the conclusion that the depolarization of the terminal by an action potential (or local circuit currents from the action potential) that invades the presynaptic terminals is what causes the simultaneous release of many quantal units of transmitter.

The relation between presynaptic membrane potential and transmitter release was examined in the synapse of the squid giant axon by Katz and Miledi. Electrical excitability (Na activation) was eliminated by applying tetrodotoxin (p. 133), and potassium activation was blocked by injecting TEA (p. 137). This made it possible to depolarize the presynaptic membrane in a graded fashion by passing a current into the terminal through an intracellular electrode (Fig. 6-48,A). The postsynaptic potential, recorded with a third electrode, provided a highly sensitive microchemical assay of the transmitter released by the presynaptic membrane. The results (Fig. 6-48,B,C) show (1) that depolarization of the presynaptic membrane results in transmitter release (detected as postsynaptic depolarization) even though the normal mechanism of the action potential was eliminated, and (2) that the amplitude of the postsynaptic potential (and therefore transmitter release) increases with increased depolari-

6–47. *Electrically induced increase in the rate of m.e.p.p. occurrence. Electrotonic depolarization by application of current (below) to the presynaptic terminal increases the probability of transmitter release as evidenced by the increase in frequency of miniature endplate potentials seen in the upper trace.* [*After Katz and Miledi, 1967b.*]

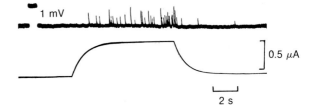

1 mV

0.5 μA

2 s

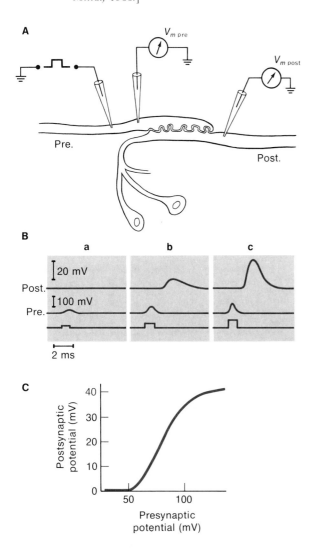

6-48. Relation between presynaptic depolarization and transmitter release at the squid giant synapse. A. The presynaptic membrane is depolarized with current from an intracellular electrode. B. Pre- and postsynaptic potentials are recorded with two additional microelectrodes. C. Increased presynaptic membrane depolarization results in increased transmitter release and hence increased amplitude of the postsynaptic potential. [After Katz and Miledi, 1966.]

zation of the *pre*synaptic membrane. The relationship between *post*synaptic potential and *pre*synaptic depolarization is not linear: a plot of the relationship rises sigmoidally to a plateau. The plateau is expected, of course, since the postsynaptic potential cannot exceed its reversal potential (Box 6-3), regardless of the quantity of transmitter released.

Evidence has accumulated that Ca^{2+} is an important limiting factor in the process of transmitter release. This can be seen in the reduction of transmitter release (and thus a reduced postsynaptic current) in response to a given presynaptic depolarization when the extracellular Ca^{2+} concentration is reduced (Fig. 6-49). If the sodium current of the action potential is blocked with TTX and TEA, the presynaptic terminal of the squid axon is seen to produce a local response when depolarized by a brief pulse of stimulating current (Fig. 6-50). This TTX-resistant, all-or-none response is produced only by the presynaptic membrane. Since its size varies with the Ca^{2+} concentration, and since it is eliminated by the addition of lanthanum ions (which block Ca influx), the prolonged all-or-none response in the terminal is termed a *calcium response*. Calcium influx has also been demonstrated in the nerve terminal of the squid axon by light emission from an injected Ca-sensitive protein, aequorin (p. 104). Thus we have several lines of evidence that calcium enters the terminals during impulse invasion of the axon terminal.

That calcium is required for transmitter release during impulse propagation into the presynaptic terminal was demonstrated very elegantly at the endplate of frog muscle bathed in a Ringer solution in which the calcium was replaced by magnesium. One capillary microelectrode, filled with a $CaCl_2$ solution and connected to an electrical apparatus to control the diffusion of Ca^{2+} from its tip, was positioned extracellularly at the endplate. A second electrode recorded both the arrival of the presynaptic action potential in the nerve terminal and the subsequent postsynaptic current (Fig. 6-51,A). When Ca^{2+} was prevented from diffusing out of the calcium pipette into the endplate region, only the presynaptic action current was recorded (Fig. 6-51,B). When Ca^{2+} was allowed to diffuse out of the pipette onto the synaptic region, an endplate current appeared (Fig. 6-51,C). The occurrence of the externally recorded endplate current required that the local concentration of Ca^{2+} be raised in time for the arrival of the presynaptic action potential in the terminals of the motor axon. If the pulse of Ca^{2+} was administered slightly after the arrival of the action potential, there was no postsynaptic response, indicating that no transmitter was released. Moreover, conditions that interfere with the entry of Ca^{2+} into the axon (e.g., low extracellular Ca^{2+}; competing ions, such as Mg^{2+} and La^{3+}) also prevent release of the

6–49. *Input-output relations of the squid synapse in different concentrations of extracellular Ca^{2+}. The method used is the same as that shown in Figure 6-48. The amplitude of the postsynaptic potential is plotted against the presynaptic amplitude. At lower calcium concentrations, the size of the postsynaptic potential evoked by any given presynaptic depolarization was reduced. [After Katz and Miledi, 1970.]*

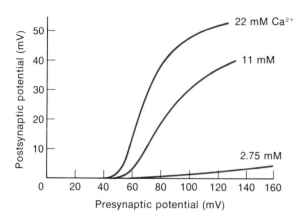

6–51. *The synaptic requirement for calcium. A. Motor fiber stimulated in a Ca-free saline, which prevents transmitter release. Ca^{2+} is delivered from the $CaCl_2$ pipette electrophoretically in precisely timed pulses relative to the arrival of the motor action potential at the endplate. B to E. The endplate current is recorded with an extracellular pipette electrode positioned on the endplate region. An inward postsynaptic current (C and D) is recorded only if the release of calcium from the pipette coincides with or occurs immediately prior to the arrival at the endplate of the presynaptic action potential. [After Katz, 1969.]*

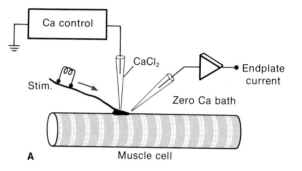

6–50. *The calcium response of the presynaptic terminal of the squid axon. Tetrodotoxin was employed to eliminate the Na current, so that the depolarization was not due to a Na current. TEA was used to limit K current that would otherwise cancel the Ca current. Two traces are shown, one showing a simple electrotonic depolarization during the period of current injection; the other, with a prolonged regenerative response due to excitation of the Ca system. [After Katz and Miledi, 1969.]*

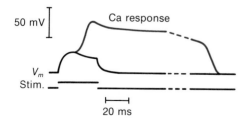

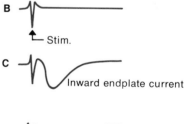

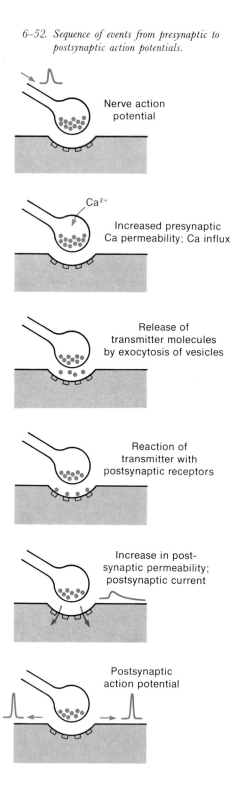

6–52. *Sequence of events from presynaptic to postsynaptic action potentials.*

Nerve action potential

Ca²⁺

Increased presynaptic Ca permeability; Ca influx

Release of transmitter molecules by exocytosis of vesicles

Reaction of transmitter with postsynaptic receptors

Increase in post-synaptic permeability; postsynaptic current

Postsynaptic action potential

neural transmitter in response to a presynaptic action potential. Thus the evidence indicates that Ca^{2+}, which enters during the time of arrival of the action potential, is responsible for triggering the release of transmitter. The intracellular role of Ca^{2+} in the release of transmitter is not fully understood. Perhaps Ca^{2+} is required for the fusion of synaptic vesicles with the inner surface of the cell membrane of the nerve terminal. The sequence of known events from presynaptic action potential to postsynaptic action potential is outlined in Figure 6-52. The calcium that enters the terminal is eventually pumped out again, but is initially removed from the cytosol by active uptake into mitochondria and other sequestering sites.

Modification of Synaptic Function by Past Activity

One of the most interesting properties of nervous systems is their *plasticity*—that is, their ability to modify behavior as a result of experience. This is evidenced in our lives by learning and by the development of reflexes, motor skills, and habits. This is an area about which very little concrete knowledge of physiological mechanisms exists, but it is widely suspected that modification of neural function by experience involves a change in *synaptic efficacy* (i.e., the effectiveness of a presynaptic impulse in producing a postsynaptic potential change). A change in synaptic efficacy is not the only way in which neural function might be modified, but at present it is the only one for which there is any experimental support. The evidence indicates that past activity produces some modification in the amount of transmitter released from presynaptic terminals.

FACILITATION

A change in synaptic efficacy can be illustrated by recording from the endplate region in a skeletal muscle fiber while applying two stimuli to the motor axon, the second stimulus following the first after varying intervals (Fig. 6-53). If the second synaptic potential begins before the first has subsided, they will sum, but the second will reach an amplitude greater than can be accounted for by summation alone. If the second synaptic potential begins soon after the first has completely subsided, it reaches a higher amplitude than the first one. This effect, which is termed synaptic *facilitation*, subsides in 100 to 200 ms at the motor endplate.

The best evidence indicates that facilitation is due to an increase in the intracellular free calcium ion concentration of the presynaptic terminal. Katz and Miledi used a carefully positioned micropipette to supply pulses of Ca^{2+} to the vicinity of the motor terminals of the endplate of a frog muscle immersed in a Ca^{2+}-free Ringer solution (Fig. 6-54,A). Figures 6-54,B,C show that the size of the endplate potential depends on the presence of Ca^{2+}. Moreover, facilitation of the postsynaptic potential evoked by the second stimulus is greatest when a pulse of Ca^{2+} coincides in time with the arrival of the first action potential at the motor endplate (Fig. 6-54,E). The first pulse of Ca^{2+} does not significantly enhance facilitation if it is given after the first action potential arrives at the motor nerve terminals (Fig. 6-54,D). Thus, to be effective in facilitation, calcium must be available to enter the presynaptic terminal during the invasion of the terminal by an action potential. It is presumed that some of this Ca^{2+} persists within the ending so as to sum with calcium entering in response to a second presynaptic action potential arriving after a short interval, and that the additional Ca^{2+} results in the release of a larger amount of transmitter, and hence a larger postsynaptic response.

There are several possible mechanisms by which calcium entry during the first presynaptic impulse may lead to a facilitation of the release of transmitter in response to the second presynaptic action potential:

1. The second presynaptic action potential may be accompanied by a greater influx of Ca^{2+} than the first. This might result from (a) more extensive invasion of the terminals by the second impulse, producing a larger depolarization, (b) an increased sensitivity to depolarization of the Ca channels due to the prior Ca influx, or (c) increased duration of the second action potential due to an effect on membrane conductances of the internal Ca^{2+} from the first impulse. The longer period of depolarization could allow a more protracted influx of Ca^{2+}.

2. A higher concentration of *free* Ca^{2+} could result during the second presynaptic impulse if the Ca^{2+} entering during the first impulse loads a large proportion of the nonspecific Ca-binding sites within the terminal. The increment of Ca^{2+} entering during the second impulse would then produce a large increment of ionized calcium available for activating the transmitter-release mechanism.

Each of these possibilities is compatible with present data. It will require more study to determine which of these mechanisms actually are responsible for synaptic facilitation.

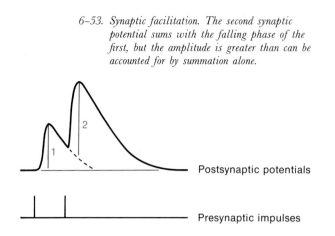

6-53. *Synaptic facilitation. The second synaptic potential sums with the falling phase of the first, but the amplitude is greater than can be accounted for by summation alone.*

6-54. *Dependence of facilitation of a second synaptic potential on availability of extracellular calcium during the first presynaptic action potential. A. The method of applying Ca pulses to the endplate region is the same as shown in Figure 6–51. B to E. Black bars show timing of Ca pulses. Facilitation occurs only if calcium is available when the first presynaptic action potential reaches the endplate. [After Katz and Miledi, 1968.]*

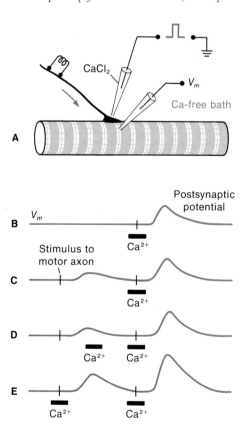

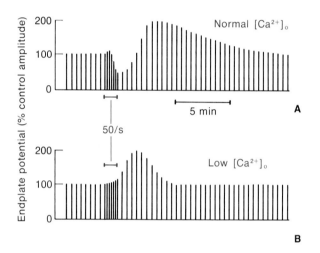

6-55. *Post-tetanic depression and post-tetanic potentiation of frog endplate potentials. A. When $[Ca^{2+}]_o$ is normal, a period of high-frequency motor stimulation is followed first by a depression of e.p.p.'s and delayed potentiation. B. When $[Ca^{2+}]_o$ is low, only an early phase of potentiation is seen. See text for explanation. [After Rosenthal, 1969.]*

POST-TETANIC POTENTIATION

When a presynaptic neuron is stimulated *tetanically* (i.e., at a high frequency), synaptic transmission is initially *depressed* following the tetanic stimulus. Test pulses applied at various times are then *potentiated* (i.e., increased in amplitude) over a period of up to many minutes. How does past activity affect the behavior of the synapse? A tentative answer is obtained in the experiment on curarized frog muscle shown in Figure 6-55. Endplate potentials are evoked first by

stimulation at a low control rate (e.g., 1 stimulus every 30 s). The rate is then increased to 50/s for a period of 20 s, after which a series of test stimuli are administered at the rate of 1 every 30 s. The results are plotted for a normal extracellular calcium concentration (1.8 mM) and for a low Ca^{2+} concentration ($1/8 \times$ normal). In the normal calcium concentration, a *post-tetanic depression* of the endplate potential occurs initially after the tetanic stimulation. After the depression, there follows a rapid increase in amplitude, termed *post-tetanic potentiation* (*PTP*), up to nearly twice the control amplitude. The amplitude of the endplate potential then returns to the control level in about 10 min. In Ringer solutions containing low calcium (Fig. 6-55,B), there is no depression, and the PTP subsides more rapidly.

These results have been interpreted as follows: During high-frequency stimulation in the normal extracellular calcium concentration (Fig. 6-55,A), the available transmitter units (i.e., vesicles containing ACh) in the presynaptic terminals are released faster than they can be replaced. Thus the amount of transmitter available for release is depressed immediately after a period of high-frequency discharge. The units are then replenished during the post-tetanic period, and the depression subsides. During tetanic stimulation, Ca^{2+} entering the terminals as a consequence of excitation accumulates and lingers on within the terminals as it is gradually pumped out of the terminals by active transport. It is believed that PTP and its slow decay reflect an increase and subsequent reduction in intracellular free calcium concentration. The increased $[Ca^{2+}]_i$ increases the probability of quantal release, and as the number of quanta available for release is replenished following the period of tetanic stimulation, the number released in response to a presynaptic impulse exceeds the control number (i.e., potentiation). In Ringer solutions containing low calcium (Fig. 6-55,B), the limited availability of Ca^{2+} lowers the number of synaptic vesicles released, and hence is accompanied by less depletion of available transmitter units. As a result, post-tetanic depression is absent, and PTP is just as pronounced but decays more rapidly, perhaps because the axon terminal is able to pump the accumulated calcium out more rapidly in the face of a lower extracellular calcium concentration.

A similar Ca-dependence for PTP has recently been demonstrated with preparations in which the Na system was poisoned with tetrodotoxin to eliminate the presynaptic action potential. The nerve terminals were depolarized directly with an extracellular electrode positioned on the endplate region. The occurrence of PTP in the absence of action potentials, and with artificial presynaptic depolarization, indicates that PTP is not due to an increase in the size of the action potentials invading the motor terminals.

Summary

The common unit of structure in the nervous system is the neuron, which communicates with other neurons or effector cells by electrical or chemical transmission across synapses. The neuron typically consists of (1) a soma, which contains the nucleus; (2) a variable number of dendrites, which, along with the soma (in some neurons), are supplied with synaptic inputs from the terminals of other neurons; and (3) an axon, which carries impulses to its presynaptic terminals. Arrival of impulses in the terminals leads to a release of a neurotransmitter substance.

The nervous system functions with two types of signals: graded, nonpropagating potential changes, and all-or-none, propagated action potentials. These generally alternate in a pathway, the graded potentials occurring at sensory and postsynaptic membranes, and the action potentials being confined largely to axons and associated structures. Intensity is coded by amplitude in the graded potentials and by frequency in the firing of action potentials.

During the course of evolution, primitive, distributed, structurally diffuse "nerve nets" characteristic of coelenterates became condensed into nerve cords and ganglia—first apparent in some jellyfish. During these changes, the anterior end, initially specialized as the sensory center, became differentiated as a superganglion or brain.

Information travels between different parts of the nervous system via action potentials, which are propagated without decrement along the axons. The velocity of propagation depends on axon diameter and on the presence (in some vertebrate axons) of myelin sheaths between bare sections termed nodes of Ranvier. In myelinated axons, saltatory conduction occurs from node to node, skipping the intimately sheathed portions in between, and thereby increasing the velocity.

Synapses are of two major types—electrical and chemical. The principle of electrical synaptic transmission is essentially that of impulse propagation; the current flows from one cell into another through low-resistance gap junctions and depolarizes the second cell. In chemical transmission, the presynaptic ending liberates a transmitter substance that interacts with receptor molecules on the postsynaptic membrane. This interaction opens ion-specific channels in the postsynaptic membrane, resulting in an ionic current that produces a synaptic potential across the postsynaptic membrane. The action of transmitter can be blocked by inhibitor substances that bind with the receptor molecule, as in the case of curare, a drug that blocks neuromuscular transmission in vertebrates.

A synapse can be either excitatory or inhibitory. In excitatory synapses, the action of the transmitter is to change the membrane conductance so as to shift the potential to or beyond the firing potential for the action potential. The action of the transmitter substance at an inhibitory synapse is to change the conductance so as to counteract depolarization to the firing level. The properties of excitation and inhibition are not inherent in the transmitter substances, but depend on the ion selectivity of the postsynaptic channels activated by the transmitters.

Both excitatory and inhibitory substances are stored in and released from vesicles found in the nerve terminal. The arrival of an action potential depolarizes the presynaptic membrane, allowing Ca^{2+} to enter the terminal. The calcium, in a manner as yet not understood, increases the probability that the vesicles will coalesce with the terminal membrane and release their contents by exocytosis into the synaptic cleft.

EXERCISES

1. Contrast the characteristics of the two basic types of electrical signals used in the nervous system.

2. Compare the encoding of intensity in graded signals, such as receptor potentials and synaptic potentials, with the encoding of intensity with all-or-none impulses.

3. What is the evidence that sensation arises in specific locations in the cerebral cortex?

4. Discuss the anatomical and functional differences between the sympathetic and parasympathetic divisions of the autonomic system.

5. Action potentials consist of electric currents. Explain why they do not propagate along axons with the velocity of an electric current in a wire.

6. If the action potential is not a simple linear flow of current, why can one draw an analogy between the behavior of a myelinated axon and a submarine cable?

7. How does an action potential propagate over long distances without loss of amplitude?

8. Explain why, if all else is equal, an axon of large diameter will conduct impulses at higher velocity than an axon of small diameter.

9. Explain why interrupted myelination increases the velocity of impulse conduction.

10. How can one determine experimentally if a junction between two nerve cells is an electrical or a chemical synapse?

11. Compare the properties of electrical and chemical synapses. Outline the presynaptic events leading to the release of transmitter substance.

12. What determines if a postsynaptic conductance change will be excitatory or inhibitory?

13. What factors determine whether a transmitter depolarizes or hyperpolarizes the postsynaptic membrane?

14. Explain how a synapse can produce a depolarizing postsynaptic potential and still be inhibitory.

15. What prevents the acetylcholine released from the presynaptic terminal from persisting and interfering with subsequent synaptic transmission?

16. Of what possible significance are the structural similarities between the monoamine neurotransmitters and such psychotropic agents as LSD and mescaline in explaining the effects of these agents?

17. What is the evidence that an endplate potential is composed of smaller units termed miniature endplate potentials?

18. How might previous synaptic activity affect the amplitude of postsynaptic potentials?

19. Explain why the amplitude of a postsynaptic potential is limited in spite of simultaneous release of many transmitter quanta.

SUGGESTED READING

Bullock, T. H., R. Orkand, and A. D. Grinnell. 1977. *Introduction To Nervous Systems.* W. H. Freeman and Company, San Francisco.

Cooper, J. R., F. E. Bloom, and R. Roth. 1974. *The Biochemical Basis of Neuropharmacology.* Oxford Univ. Press. New York.

Eccles, J. C. 1965. The synapse. *Scientific American* 212 (1):56-66. [Also available as Offprint 1001.]

Hall, Z., J. Hildebrand, and E. Kravitz. 1974. *The Chemistry of Synaptic Transmission.* Chiron Press, Newton, Mass.

Hodgkin, A. L. 1964. *The Conduction of the Nervous Impulse.* Charles C Thomas, Springfield, Ill.

Katz, B. 1966. *Nerve, Muscle and Synapse.* McGraw-Hill, New York.

Katz, B. 1969. *The Release of Neural Transmitter Substances.* Charles C Thomas, Springfield, Ill.

Kuffler, S., and Nicholls, J. 1976. *From Neuron to Brain.* Sinauer, New York.

Schmitt, F. O., and F. G. Worden. 1974. *The Neurosciences: Third Study Program.* The M.I.T. Press. Cambridge, Mass.

REFERENCES CITED

Aidley, D. J. 1971. *The Physiology of Excitable Cells.* Cambridge Univ. Press, New York.

Bennett, M. V. L. (ed.). 1974. *Synaptic Transmission and Neuronal Interaction.* Raven Press, New York.

Bullock, T. H., and G. A. Horridge. 1965. *Structure and Function in the Nervous System of Invertebrates.* W. H. Freeman and Company, San Francisco.

Bunge, M. B., R. P. Bunge, and H. Ris. 1961. Ultrastructural study of remyelination in an experimental lesion in adult cat spinal cord. *J. Biophys. Biochem. Cytol.* 10:67–94.

Cajal, S. R. 1911. *Histologie du Systeme Nerveux de l'Homme et des Vertebres.* Consejo Superior de Investigaciones Cientificas, Instituto Ramón y Cajal, Madrid.

Cajal, S. R. 1954. *Neuron Theory or Reticular Theory.* (English trans.) Consejo Superior de Investigaciones Cientificas, Madrid.

Del Castillo, J., and B. Katz. 1954. Quantal components of the end-plate potential. *J. Physiol.* 124:560–573.

Eccles, J. C. 1965. The synapse. *Scientific American* 212 (1):56–66. [Also available as Offprint 1001.]

Eiduson, S. 1967. The biochemistry of behavior. *Science Journal,* 3:113–117.

Erlanger, J., and H. S. Gasser. 1937. *Electrical Signs of Nervous Activity.* Univ. Pennsylvania Press, Philadelphia.

Fatt, P., and B. Katz. 1951. An analysis of the endplate potential recorded with an intracellular electrode. *J. Physiol.* 115:320–370.

Fatt, P., and B. Katz. 1952. Spontaneous subthreshold activity at motor nerve endings. *J. Physiol.* 117:109–128.

Furshpan, E. J., and D. D. Potter. 1959. Transmission at the giant motor synapses of the crayfish. *J. Physiol.* 145:289–325.

Helmholtz, H. 1866. *Handbuch der Physiologischen Optik.* Leipzig.

Hodgkin, A. L. 1937. Evidence for electrical transmission in nerve. *J. Physiol.* (London) 90:183–232.

Horridge, A. 1968. *Interneurons.* W. H. Freeman and Company, San Francisco.

Huxley, A. F., and R. Stämpfli. 1949. Evidence for saltatory conduction in peripheral myelinated nerve fibres. *J. Physiol.* 108:315–339.

Kandel, E., and H. Wachtel. 1968. The functional organization of neural aggregates in *Aplysia. In* F. D. Carlson (ed.), *Physiological and Biochemical Aspects of Nervous Integration.* Prentice-Hall. Englewood Cliffs, New Jersey.

Katz, B. 1969. *The Release of Neural Transmitter Substances.* Charles C Thomas. Springfield, Ill.

Katz, B., and R. Miledi. 1965. The effect of calcium on acetylcholine release from motor nerve terminals. *Proc. Roy. Soc.* Ser. B. 161:496–503.

Katz, B., and R. Miledi. 1966. Input-output relation of a single synapse. *Nature* (London) 212:1242–1245.

Katz, B., and R. Miledi. 1967a. Modification of transmitter release by electrical interference with motor nerve endings. *Proc. Roy. Soc.* Ser. B. 167:1–7.

Katz, B., and R. Miledi. 1967b. Tetrodotoxin and neuromuscular transmission *Proc. Roy. Soc.* Ser. B. 167:8–22.

Katz, B., and R. Miledi. 1968. The role of calcium in neuromuscular faciliation. *J. Physiol.* 195:481–492.

Katz, B., and R. Miledi. 1969. Tetrodotoxin-resistant electric activity in presynaptic terminals. *J. Physiol.* 203:459–487.

Katz, B., and R. Miledi. 1970. Further study of the role of calcium in synaptic transmission. *J. Physiol.* 207:789–801.

Kerkut, G. A., and R. C. Thomas. 1963. Acetylcholine and the spontaneous inhibitory post-synaptic potentials in the snail neurone. *Comp. Biochem. Physiol.* 8:39–45.

Kravitz, E. A. 1967. ACh, GABA, and GA: Physiological and chemical studies related to their roles as transmitter agents. *In* F. O. Schmitt (ed.), *The Neurosciences: A Study Program.* Rockefeller Univ. Press, New York.

Kriebel, M. E., F. Llados, and D. R. Matteson. 1976. Spontaneous subminiature endplate potentials in mouse diaphragm muscle: Evidence for synchronous release. *J. Physiol.* 262:553–581.

Kuffer, W. W. 1942. Further study on transmission in an isolated nerve-muscle fibre preparation. *J. Neurophysiol.* 6:99–110.

Lang, F., and H. Atwood. 1973. Crustacean neuromuscular mechanisms, functional morphology of nerve terminals and the mechanism of facilitation. *American Zool.* 13:337–338.

Loewi, O. 1921. Über humorale Übertragbarkeit der Herznervenwirkung *Pflügers Arch. ges. Physiol.* 189:239–242.

McMahan, M., N. C. Spitzer, and K. Peper. 1972. Visual identification of nerve terminals in living isolated skeletal muscle. *Proc. Roy. Soc.* 181:421–430.

Miledi, R. 1973. Transmitter release induced by injection of calcium ions into nerve terminals. *Proc. Roy. Soc.* Ser. B. 183:421–425.

Montagna, W. 1959. *Comparative Anatomy.* Wiley, New York.

Mountcastle, V. B., and R. J. Baldessarini. 1968. Synaptic transmission. *In* V. B. Mountcastle (ed.), *Medical Physiology.* Mosby, St. Louis, Missouri.

Neal, H. V., and H. W. Rand. 1936. *Comparative Anatomy.* Blakiston, Philadelphia, Penn.

Neher, E., and B. Sakmann. 1976. Single channel currents recorded from membrane of denervated frog muscle fibres. *Nature* (London) 260:799–802.

Nickel, E., and L. Potter. 1970. Synaptic vesicles in freeze-etched electric tissue of *Torpedo. Brain Res.* 23:95–100.

Noback, C. R., and R. J. Demarest. 1972. *The Nervous System: Introduction and Reviews.* McGraw-Hill, New York.

Penfield, W., and T. Rasmussen. 1950. *The Cerebral Cortex of Man.* Macmillan, New York.

Peper, K., F. Dreyer, C. Sandri, K. Ackert, and H. Moor. 1974. Structure and ultrastructure of the frog endplate. *Cell Tiss. Res.* 149:437–455.

Romer, A. S. 1955. *The Vertebrate Body.* Saunders, Philadelphia, Penn.

Rosenthal, J. 1969. Post-tetanic potentiation at the neuromuscular junction of the frog. *J. Physiol.* 203:121–133.

Sherrington, C. S. 1906. *The Integrated Action of the Nervous System.* Yale Univ. Press, New Haven, Conn.

Tasaki, I. 1939. The electro-saltatory transmission of the nerve impulse and the effect of narcosis upon the nerve fiber. *Am. J. Physiol.* 127:211–227.

Van Essen, D. 1973. The contribution of membrane hyperpolarization to adaptation and conduction block in sensory neurones of the leech. *J. Physiol.* 230:509–534.

Werchert, C. K. 1970. *Anatomy of the Chordates.* McGraw-Hill, New York.

Wernig, A. 1976. Localization of active sites in the neuromuscular function of the frog. *Brain Research* 118:63–72.

Whittaker, Victor. 1968. Synaptic transmission. *Proc. Nat. Acad. Sci.* 60:1081–91.

Wiedersheim, R. E. 1907. *Comparative Anatomy of Vertebrates.* MacMillan, London.

CHAPTER SEVEN

Receptors and Responses

Sense organs provide the only channels of communication into the nervous system from the external world. Thus sensory input—interacting with the organization and properties of the nervous system, inherited through genetic mechanisms and organized during the ontogeny of the animal—provides the animal with its entire store of "knowledge." This concept was recognized by Aristotle when he said, "Nothing is in the mind that does not pass through the senses." An understanding of how environmental information is converted into neural signals and how these signals are then processed would seem to have considerable philosophical as well as scientific interest.

The processes of *sensory reception* begin in sense organs—more specifically, in the *primary sensory receptor cells.* These receptor cells are tuned, so to speak, to specific *modalities* of stimuli. In the higher animals (extrapolating from human experience), a consequence of most sensory input is a subjective sensation identified with the stimulus. Thus light of wavelength 650 to 700 nm falling on the eye is perceived as "red"; sugar on the tongue is perceived as "sweet." Sensations are subjective phenomena generated by unknown physical and chemical means within the nervous system, and they are in no way inherent in the source of stimulation itself.

The traditional categorization of senses—sight, hearing, touch, taste, and smell—is both subjective and incomplete, for it fails to include certain types of *interoceptive* (internal) senses of which we are largely unconscious, such as positional receptors in muscles and joints, and certain sensory receptors that monitor the chemical and thermal conditions within the organism. A more physiological classification of receptors is based simply on the form of energy to which each is specially sensitive. We will classify receptors as *chemoreceptors, mechanoreceptors, photoreceptors, thermoreceptors,* and *electroreceptors.*

The first part of this chapter considers some of the general principles of sensory function, and the remainder deals in turn with the major senses and examines the physiology of selected sense organs. An understanding of the principles covered in Chapters 5 and 6 is assumed throughout.

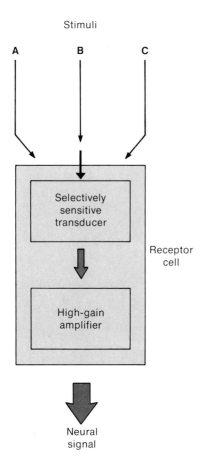

Stimuli

A   B   C

Selectively
sensitive
transducer

Receptor
cell

High-gain
amplifier

Neural
signal

7–1. *The major functions performed by sensory receptor cells in the processing of stimuli. Although many forms of stimulus energy may impinge upon a receptor, only one form is intercepted at weak to moderate levels of stimulus energy. This form is transduced and amplified into a neural signal.*

General Principles of Sensory Processing

RECEPTOR CELLS AS SELECTIVE TRANSDUCERS

As just noted, sensory processing begins in the *receptor cells*—more specifically, in specialized membranes of these cells.

Receptor cells perform two main functions in processing stimulus signals (Fig. 7-1). First, they are sensitive to specific forms of stimulus energy, ignoring other forms. That is to say, they exhibit differential sensitivity. Second, they act as *signal transducers* by releasing

bioelectric energy in response to stimulus energy. With the exception of electroreceptors, in which the stimulus is already an electrical signal, each receptor cell transduces the stimulus into a change in membrane potential. A receptor cell thus may perform a role analogous to that of a microphone, which converts the mechanical energy of sound to modulated electrical signals, or a role analogous to that of a photocell, which converts changing light intensities into corresponding electrical signals.

For example, the visual cells of the eye are far more sensitive to light than to any other form of energy. A single quantum in the wavelength range of 320 to 700 nanometers (1 nm = 10^{-9} meter) can excite a visual receptor cell. This excitation is admittedly very small, and by itself does not lead to the sensation of light, but its effect can sum with the effects of several other visual receptor cells simultaneously excited by single photons to produce in an observer the sensation of light. Although extremely sensitive to light, these receptor cells are quite insensitive to other stimuli, such as mechanical energy. Conversely, the hair cells found in the vertebrate ear are extremely sensitive to mechanical energy and quite insensitive to light. Thus each receptor cell type normally responds only to an *adequate stimulus.*

Photoreceptor cells contain a visual pigment that consists of molecules that capture quanta of light. As the light energy is trapped, the molecular structure undergoes a transient alteration. The pigment is part of the cell membrane, so the change in molecular conformation produces a change in membrane conductance, exciting the receptor cell. Excitation of the receptor cell gives rise to a neural signal. In contrast, a mechanoreceptor cell is equipped with a membrane that responds to a slight distortion or stretch. Thus the adequate stimulus of a receptor cell is determined largely by the molecular mechanisms built into its membrane (i.e., by its filtering characteristics).

RECEPTOR CELLS AS AMPLIFIERS

During transduction of the stimulus energy into a neural signal, many receptor cells exhibit varying degrees of *power amplification*. Among the most impressive are the receptors of the vertebrate eye and ear and the olfactory receptors of certain insects. In humans, as few as ten *rods* (a type of visual receptor cell), when stimulated simultaneously by one photon each, can lead to the sensation of a faint flash. Let us assume that this sensation is due to one extra action potential generated in the visual system. A single action potential releases about 10^{-11} watt-s/s of electric energy. Ten photons, on the other hand, contain a total of only 10^{-17} to 10^{-16} watt-s/s of radiant energy. In this crude comparison, we see a power amplification of at least 100,000 times between the sensory input and the neural output in the visual system. The amplifying ability of sensory systems is adaptively important, as it permits an animal to perceive weak signals from distant sources—for example, light and sound from an approaching predator.

STEPS BETWEEN STIMULUS INPUT AND SENSORY OUTPUT

A receptor cell that senses muscle length in the abdomen of crayfish and lobsters is diagrammed in Figure 7-2. Because it is relatively large, this *stretch receptor* has been useful for studies in which intracellular recording methods must be used. If the receptor is stimulated by a weak stretch applied to the muscle to which the dendrites attach, a steady sequence of impulses can be recorded from the axon. The frequency of firing depends on the amount of stretch applied. With a microelectrode inserted into the cell body, it is seen that a small stretch applied to the relaxed muscle leads to a small depolarization, the *receptor potential* (Fig. 7-3,A). A stronger stretch produces a larger receptor potential. Sufficiently large receptor potentials are accompanied by one or more action potentials.

What is the relation between stimulus, receptor potential, and action potential? The action potential (Fig. 7-3,B) can be eliminated by blocking the electrically excited sodium system with tetrodotoxin (p. 133). When this is done, the receptor potential remains (Fig. 7-3,C), indicating that it is produced by a different mechanism from the one that generates the all-or-none upstroke of the action potential. It is also seen that the receptor potential is graded with stimulus strength (Fig. 7-3,C) rather than all-or-none like the action potential (Fig. 7-3,A). In these respects, the receptor potential resembles the excitatory synaptic potential (p. 171) of muscle and nerve cells.

The stimulus and the receptor potential can be bypassed by injecting a depolarizing current into the receptor cell with a second electrode. When this is done, a steady train of impulses is evoked by the depolarization. The frequency of impulses is seen to be related more-or-less linearly to the amount of depolarization, showing a small drop in frequency with time.

Local stimulation of the receptor cell was used to test the ability of various parts of the cell membrane to produce sustained trains (sequences) of impulses. As shown in Figure 7-4, a sustained stimulus current produces a sustained steady frequency of discharge only when the current depolarizes the low-threshold axon hillock region, where the impulses are normally initiated. Other portions of the cell membrane show much more rapid accommodation (p. 127). Finally, measurements of membrane conductance have shown

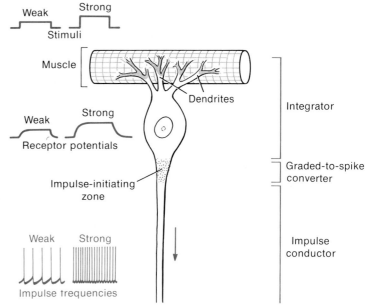

7–2. *Stretch receptor in the abdomen of a crayfish, consisting of a sensory neuron with its stretch-sensitive dendrites embedded in a special muscle bundle. When the tail of the crayfish bends, the muscle is stretched and the receptor is activated. Recordings show its electrical responses to both weak and strong stimuli. The parts of the neuron are functionally differentiated as labeled at the right. Graded receptor currents from the stretch-sensitive membrane of the dendrites are converted to all-or-none impulses at the impulse-initiating zone.*

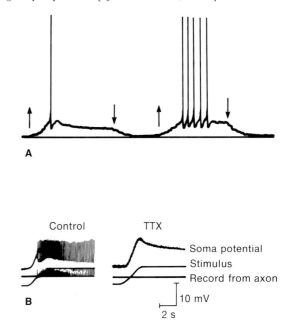

7–3. *Intracellular records from the stretch receptors of a crayfish. A. Response of quickly adapting receptor to a weak (left) and a strong (right) stimulus. Arrows indicate "on" and "off" of applied stretch. [Eyzaguire and Kuffler, 1955.] B. Slowly adapting receptor in normal saline (at left). With addition of tetrodotoxin (right), the action potentials are blocked, showing the underlying receptor potential. [After Loewenstein, 1971.]*

7-4. *Capacity of the axon hillock region of the slowly adapting crayfish stretch receptor to respond with a sustained discharge of impulses during sustained stimulation. Other areas of the cell show rapid adaptation to the steady stimulation.* [*After Nakajima and Onodera, 1969.*]

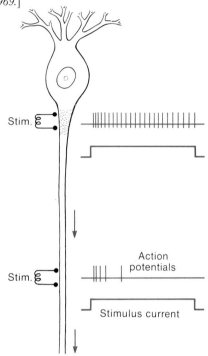

Stim.

Stim.

Action potentials

Stimulus current

that the effect of stimulating the stretch receptor is an increase in conductance to Na⁺ and K⁺.

We can now put together a general sequence of steps leading from a stimulus to a train of impulses in a sensory neuron (Fig. 7-5). The initial sensory transduction produces a change in membrane conductance in response to the stimulus. How this occurs is not entirely clear. In any case, a change in membrane conductance, such as an increase in sodium conductance, will cause a shift in the membrane potential in accord with the principles discussed earlier (p. 125). If the stimulus produces an increase in membrane conductance to sodium, the membrane potential will shift toward the equilibrium potential for Na⁺, and the cell interior will become more positive—that is, it will exhibit some degree of depolarization in accordance with Equation 5, Box 6-3. If the stimulus decreases the sodium conductance, the membrane potential will shift away from the sodium equilibrium potential, becoming more negative. Ions other than sodium (i.e., Ca^{2+} and K^+) are also involved in several receptors that have been studied. The *receptor current* is produced by the movement of ions that takes place in response to stimulus-evoked conductance changes.

As the intensity of a stimulus increases, greater numbers of channels in the membrane of the receptor cell respond (i.e., open or close). The result is an in-

7-5. *Sequence of events in a receptor cell from stimulus to sensory axon impulses. In some systems, the impulses are initiated in the receptor cell itself and travel to the central nervous system in the axon of that cell (left branch). In other systems, the receptor cell synaptically modulates impulse discharge in a second-order neuron (right branch).*

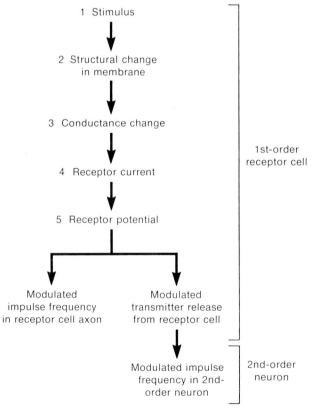

1 Stimulus

2 Structural change in membrane

3 Conductance change

4 Receptor current

5 Receptor potential

Modulated impulse frequency in receptor cell axon

Modulated transmitter release from receptor cell

1st-order receptor cell

Modulated impulse frequency in 2nd-order neuron

2nd-order neuron

creased (or decreased) conductance to certain ions, a resulting increase in the receptor current, and a larger receptor potential.

The signals produced in all steps leading up to and including the receptor potential are graded in amplitude. Unlike the sodium current of an action potential (p. 137), the receptor current is *not* regenerative and can therefore spread only by passive electrotonic means. In order for sensory information to be propagated over long distances into the central nervous system, the information contained in the receptor potential must, of course, be converted into action potentials. This is done in one of two ways (Fig. 7-6).

1. In some receptors, a depolarizing receptor potential spreads electrotonically from its site of origin in the *sensory zone* to a spike-initiating zone in the axon membrane, which then generates action potentials. The receptor zone may be part of the afferent neuron (Fig. 7-6,A and B), or part of a special receptor cell that is electrically coupled to the afferent neuron (not shown in figure). When the receptor potential spreads directly to the electrically excitable membrane and directly modulates the generation of action potentials, it has traditionally been termed a *generator potential.*

2. In others, a depolarizing or hyperpolarizing receptor potential spreads electrotonically to the presynaptic portion of the primary receptor cell, modulating the release of a transmitter substance (Fig. 7-6,C). The postsynaptic action of the transmitter then modulates the frequency of impulses generated in the axon of a secondary afferent fiber. In this case it is not necessary for the receptor cell itself to produce an action potential, because the role of long-distance conduction is performed by the secondary afferent fiber.

We see, then, that the receptor potential is the message with which the sensory portion of a receptor cell signals the secretory or impulse-generating regions.

SENSORY CODING

Individual action potentials carrying information from the different sense organs are essentially indistinguishable from one another. That is to say, the modality of the stimulus is *not* coded by any characteristics inherent in the individual action potentials. Rather, the modality perceived by the organism depends on the anatomical specificity with which the sensory neurons connect with the "higher" cognitive centers in the brain.

The only way in which the information carried in a single nerve fiber can be coded other than by anatomical specificity is by the temporal distribution of the impulses. Thus a high frequency of impulses represents

7–6. Conversion of the receptor potential into propagated impulses. Compare with previous figure. In A and B, the receptor current arising in the sensory zone spreads electrotonically to depolarize the spike-initiating zone directly. In both A and B, the receptor cell also provides the afferent sensory fiber, the only difference being the peripheral (A) and central (B) portions of the cell body. In C, a synapse intervenes between the sensory zone in the primary receptor cell and a secondary afferent fiber.

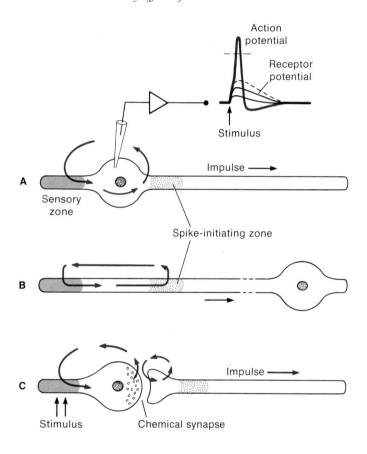

a strong stimulus, and a cessation of spontaneously occurring impulses means a reduction in the strength of the stimulus. There is no simple rule for sensory coding, because the relations between stimulus and sensory response differ in different kinds of receptors. Nevertheless, some generalizations can be made at the level of the receptor cell. As the intensity of a stimulus is increased, the receptor current is increased and a greater depolarization is produced. In many receptors, the impulse-initiating zone (Fig. 7-2) shows little accommodation in the face of a steady depolarization, and thus produces a steady train of impulses.

7–7. *Input-output relations of sense organs. A. In many receptors, the amplitude of the receptor potential is linearly related to the logarithm of stimulus intensity over a large range. B. The frequency of sensory impulses is linearly related (i.e., proportional) to the amplitude of the receptor potential. C. As a result of A and B, the impulse frequency in many sensory fibers varies linearly with the log of the stimulus intensity. The broken parts of the curves in B and C indicate the failure of impulses to follow due to refractoriness and axon membrane.*

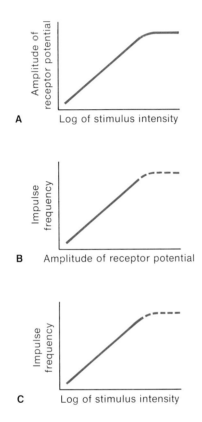

The amplitude of the receptor potential in most receptor cells is approximately proportional to the logarithm of the stimulus intensity (Fig. 7-7,A). The frequency of sensory impulses is related more-or-less linearly to the amplitude of the receptor potential (Fig. 7-7,B) up to the point at which the refractory state of the axon membrane after each impulse limits the rate of firing. As a consequence of those two relations, the impulse frequency in a slowly adapting receptor (discussed on p. 199) is generally a function of the logarithm of the stimulus intensity (Fig. 7-7,C). The impulses, upon reaching the central terminals of the sensory neurons, set up synaptic potentials that sum and facilitate as a function of the frequency of impulses. Thus the postsynaptic potential produced at this point is graded as a function of the stimulus intensity, and it can be regarded as a very crude analogue of the stimulus (Fig. 6-4).

The logarithmic relation between stimulus energy and sensory impulse frequency is interesting in view of the enormous range of stimulus intensities encountered by sense organs. For example, the difference in intensity between moonlight and sunlight is about 10^9 times. The human auditory system can perceive sounds that differ in energy by as much as 10^{12} times without significant distortion. The ability of sense organs to function over such enormous energy ranges is quite remarkable, and it depends to a large degree on the properties of the initial transduction process.

At low stimulus intensities, the receptor potential represents a very large amplification of energy. The amplification is progressively reduced as the stimulus energy increases. This logarithmic relation between stimulus intensity and amplitude of the receptor potential is predicted by the Goldman equation (p. 123), which states that the membrane potential varies with the log of the ion permeabilities multiplied by the concentrations of the ions distributed across the membrane. Thus changes in the permeability of Na^+, for example, should produce changes in membrane potential that are proportional to the log of stimulus-induced changes in Na permeability. Stimulus intensities normally encountered in the environment are generally within the logarithmic portion of the input-output curve. Some receptors depart from the logarithmic relationship, exhibiting some other kind of power function (e.g., Fig. 7-8,B).

Two factors limit the maximum sensory response to intense stimuli. Regardless of stimulus intensity, the receptor current will saturate as the membrane approaches a certain value (the reversal potential of the receptor current), which it cannot exceed. This is analogous to the reversal potential of a synaptic current (p. 172). In addition, impulse frequencies in sensory axons are limited by refractoriness following each impulse; thus most nerve fibers are limited to maximum impulse frequencies of several hundred or fewer per second.

The roughly logarithmic relationship between stimulus strength and receptor potential in many sense organs is interesting from an evolutionary point of view, because it makes far better adaptive sense than a simple proportional (i.e., linear) relationship. Consider, for example, the following argument. The maximum amplitude a receptor potential can achieve in a living cell is about 0.1 V. On the other hand, the smallest potential change that might be expected to modulate the impulse frequency of a train of action potentials in an afferent nerve fiber is about 0.00001 V. Thus a linear stimulus–potential relationship would have a usable range of intensity discrimination of only 10^4-fold—more than a hundred or a thousand times less than the range of sensitivity of some receptor cells. The logarithmic stimulus–response relationship (illustrated in Fig. 7-7,C) "compresses" the high-intensity end of the scale, thereby greatly extending the range of discrimination at the expense of absolute sensitivity.

Another consequence of the logarithmic relationship between receptor-potential amplitude and stimulus intensity is that a given *percentage* of change in stimulus intensity evokes the same *increment* of change (i.e., same number of millivolts) in the receptor potential over a large range of intensities. That is to say, a doubling of the stimulus intensity at the low end of the intensity range will evoke the same increase in receptor-potential amplitude as will a doubling of intensity at the high end of the range. In other words,

$$\frac{\Delta I}{I} = K,$$

where I is stimulus intensity and K is a constant. This relation is similar to that governing subjectively perceived changes in stimulus intensity, known in psychology as the *Weber–Fechner Law*.

Information about the *relative* intensities of stimuli and changes in stimulus intensity are more significant to an animal than are absolute values. For example, the detection of differences and changes in luminosity, such as those produced by an object moving in the visual field, is far more important for survival than are absolute measurements of luminosity. Moreover, the luminosities of different objects in a given light (e.g., at high noon) differ far less than do the changing levels of illumination (e.g., high noon versus dusk).

SENSORY ADAPTATION

How reliably is sensory information conveyed to the central nervous system? How do sense organs compare in fidelity with such physical sensors as thermometers, light meters, strain gauges, etc.? From our own experiences, we know that biological sensory systems are not trustworthy as indicators of absolute energy levels. Moreover, many sensations change with time. For example, when one dives into an unheated pool for a swim, the water initially feels colder than it does a minute or two later. A pleasantly sunny day may seem painfully bright for a few minutes after one emerges from a dimly lit interior. Phenomena of this type are lumped under the general term *sensory adaption*. Where does the adaption take place? There is no simple answer. Some adaptation occurs in the receptor cell, some occurs as a result of time-dependent changes in accessory tissues, and some occurs in the central nervous system.

Receptors exhibit various degrees of adaptation. So far we have considered only *tonic* (i.e., steady, slowly adapting) *receptors*—that is, those that continue to fire steadily in response to a constant stimulus. This is illus-

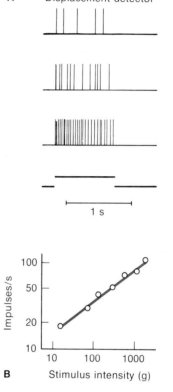

7–8. *Behavior of a displacement detector. This tonic (i.e., slowly adapting) mechanoreceptor responds to a steady displacement with a relatively steady frequency of impulses. A. Discharge at three stimulus intensities. B. A plot of steady-state discharge frequency against grams of tension applied.* [*After Schmidt, 1971.*]

trated by a mechanical displacement detector (Fig. 7-8). This tonic mechanoreceptor fires at an almost constant rate with constant stimulus. As the stimulus intensity is increased, the firing frequency rises as a power function of stimulus intensity (Fig. 7-8,B). Many receptors are of the *phasic* (i.e., quickly adapting) type, in which the firing subsides soon after the onset of a steady stimulus. In one class of phasic receptors, firing occurs only during changes in stimulus energy. For example, some mechanoreceptors fire only during the mechanical change, with the firing frequency a function of the velocity of displacement (Fig. 7-9).

Adaptation of a receptor organ can occur in at least three ways. First, the receptor membrane itself may fatigue in the face of a constant stimulus. Thus the receptor molecules in the membrane may require metabolic regeneration, as in visual receptors (p. 227).

7–9. *Behavior of a velocity detector. This rapidly adapting mechanoreceptor responds to the rate of change of position (i.e., velocity of displacement). A. The higher the rate of change, the higher the frequency of the impulse discharge. B. The number of impulses during a 0.5 s stretch varies with the log of the displacement velocity. [After Schmidt, 1971.]*

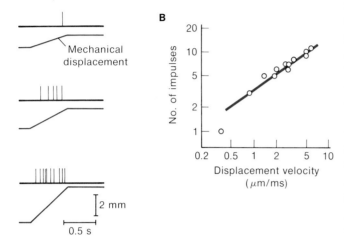

A   Velocity detector

7–10. *The phasic (A) and tonic (B) stretch receptors of the crayfish. The phasic receptor adapts quickly to a constant stretch, producing only a short train of impulses. The tonic receptor fires steadily during maintained stretch. [After Horridge, 1968.]*

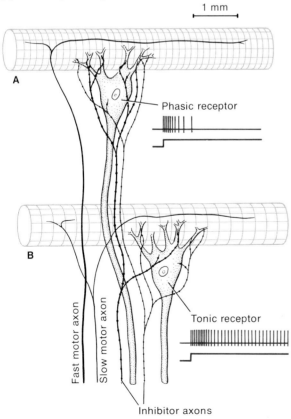

Second, the electrical properties of the receptor cell may change during sustained stimulation. In some receptors, sensitivity diminishes with accumulation of Ca^{2+} within the cell during the flow of receptor current carried in part by calcium ions. Third, accessory structures may show time-dependent changes, as with the pupil of the eye or the connective tissue associated with mechanoreceptors. The second and third of these mechanisms of adaptation are well illustrated by the stretch receptors of crayfish and lobsters. These occur in pairs; one receptor of each pair is a phasic receptor and the other a tonic receptor. A step increase in receptor muscle-fiber length produces a transient response in the former (Fig. 7-10,A) and a sustained discharge in the latter (Fig. 7-10,B). When the receptor current is bypassed by direct injection of depolarizing current with a microelectrode, the two receptor cells retain some of their differences. That is, the phasic receptor responds to a sustained current with a more rapid drop in firing frequency than does the tonic receptor under similar conditions of stimulation. But in both the phasic and the tonic stretch receptors, firing slows down to some extent as a result of a slackening of tension of the receptor muscle fibers after a sudden increase in length. The slackening is due to viscous properties of the tissue, which is not perfectly elastic.

The filtering effects of accessory structures are also important in the rapid adaptation of the *Pacinian corpuscle,* a pressure receptor found in the skin, muscles, mesentery, tendons, and joints of mammals (Fig. 7-11). It consists of a mechanically sensitive axon terminal, surrounded by concentric lamellae of connective tissue resembling the layers of an onion. When a corpuscle is deformed by something pressing on it, the disturbance is transmitted mechanically through these layers to the sensitive membrane of the axon terminal. The axon terminal normally responds with a brief, transient depolarization at both the "on" and the "off" of the deformation (Fig. 7-11,B). When the layers of the corpuscle are peeled away, permitting a mechanical stimulus to be applied directly to the naked axon, the receptor potential obtained is a far better analogue of the stimulus than that obtained in the undissected Pacinian corpuscle. Although the receptor potential still shows some degree of adaptation (the sag in Fig. 7-11,C), it gives only an "on" response. The rapid adaptation of the undissected Pacinian corpuscle to maintained deformation can be ascribed in part to the properties of the corpuscle, which preferentially passes rapid changes in pressure. This explains, in part, why we quickly lose awareness of moderate, steady pressure stimuli. The reader can demonstrate this by pinching the skin over the knuckles of one hand with two fingers of the other hand, noting that the sensation of pressure quickly subsides.

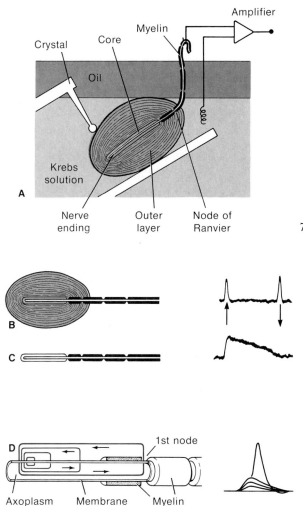

7–11. *Adaptation in the Pacinian corpuscle. A. Experimental arrangement for tapping the receptor with a crystal-driven stylus. The electrical recording was made between the hook electrode and the oil-water interface. B. Electrical response of the intact corpuscle. The "on" and "off" of the stimulus (arrows) both produce transient depolarizations. C. Electrical response was sustained during displacement after the lamellae were removed. D. Receptor current flow in response to deformation of the sensory zone of the axon. The impulse arises out of the receptor potential (right) at the first node of Ranvier. [After Loewenstein, 1960.]*

EFFERENT CONTROL OF RECEPTOR SENSITIVITY

The responsiveness of some sense organs is influenced by the central nervous system, which sends impulses through efferent (centrifugally conducting) axons that innervate the sense organ. For example, the stretch-receptor neurons in the abdominal musculature of crayfish and lobsters are innervated by efferent neurons that make inhibitory synapses on the dendrites and soma of the stretch-receptor cells (Fig. 7-10). The size of the receptor potential is diminished by a transmitter substance released by the inhibitory terminals, causing either a cessation of the sensory impulses produced by the stretch-receptor cells or a reduction in their frequency. The inhibitory fibers are activated reflexly by sensory discharge from the same receptor cells and in similar stretch receptors in neighboring body segments (Fig. 7-12). This indicates that the axon of the receptor cell must make synaptic connections in the CNS, either directly or via interneurons, with these inhibitory neurons. The central output—in this case, reflex— reduces the sensitivity of the receptor at the periphery to a given mechanical stimulus. One purpose of this may be to enhance differences in sensory output of adjacent segments. The subject of contrast enhancement by lateral inhibition is taken up in Chapter 8.

MECHANISMS THAT ENHANCE SENSITIVITY

Certain receptor cells exhibit spontaneous firing without any apparent sensory input. This has two important consequences. First, if the sensory fiber is in the process of firing spontaneously, any small increase in stimulus energy will produce an increase in its rate of

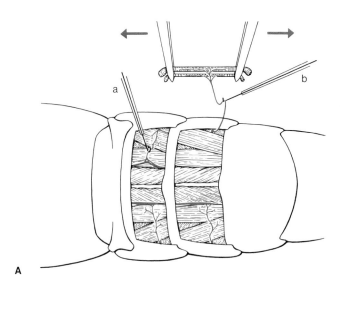

7-12. A. Reflex inhibition of muscle stretch receptors (see Fig. 7–10) in the tail of the crayfish. The muscle stretch receptors of one segment are removed with innervation intact, and recordings are made as shown with electrodes a and b. *B*. Electrode a records a steady train of action potentials from the tonic receptor in response to a steady stretch. When the isolated tonic receptor is stretched, electrode b records a train of sensory impulses and electrode a records a drop in frequency of firing in the undisturbed intact receptor. The activity recorded by electrode b results in the activation of an inhibitory axon, which inhibits the steady stretch-receptor output by electrode a. [After Eckert, 1961.]

A

B
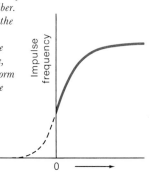
a
b

7-13. Impulse interval in a spontaneously firing receptor cell can be decreased by extremely small stimuli. This results from a slight increase in the slope of the pacemaker potential. (In reference to second-order sensory fibers, read "synaptic potential" instead of "pacemaker potential.")

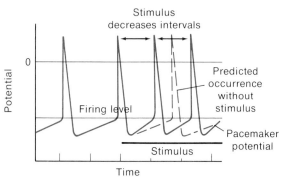

7-14. Typical input-output relations of a spontaneously active receptor cell or second-order sensory fiber. In the absence of any input above or below the norm ("0" on the abscissa), the cell fires spontaneously. Because this norm lies on the steep portion of the stimulus-frequency curve, any deviation in stimulus energy from the norm will produce either a decrease or an increase in the rate of firing.

firing. Small receptor currents in response to weak stimuli can modulate the impulse frequency by shortening the intervals between impulses (Fig. 7-13). Such modulation of impulse frequency lends far greater sensitivity than would be possible if the receptor current had to depolarize a completely inactive spike-initiating zone to the firing level. The input–output relations of such a sensory fiber are described by the sigmoid curve in Figure 7-14. In the unstimulated condition, the firing frequency is on the steep portion of the curve, and even a small input will produce a significant increase in firing frequency. Second, in some spontaneously active sensory neurons, modulation of impulse frequency can take the form of either an *increase* or a *decrease,* which permits the receptor to respond differentially to different stimulus polarities or directions. An example is seen in the discharge of the electroreceptor nerve of some fish (Fig. 7-37). The fibers in the nerve fire spontaneously in the absence of any electric field in the surrounding water. An electric field that causes current to flow into the receptor pit depolarizes the receptor and increases the firing frequency of the sensory nerve. A field that causes an outflow of current hyperpolarizes the receptor and decreases the afferent impulse frequency. The influence of electric field on the activity of electroreceptors is discussed further on page 216.

Another way in which the nervous system enhances its ability to differentiate between a "signal" (i.e., a change in stimulus energy) and the "noise" (i.e., background activity in the sensory afferents) is to average the input from a number of receptor cells simultaneously. Random signals in individual input channels are ignored, and only simultaneous input in several channels is interpreted as a stimulus. Thus a human observer cannot reliably perceive a single photon absorbed by a single receptor cell; but if each of several receptors simultaneously absorbs a photon, the observer experiences the sensation of light.

ORGANIZATION OF RECEPTORS INTO SENSE ORGANS

During the course of evolution, sensory systems developed from single, independent receptor units into complex sense organs, such as the vertebrate eye, in which receptor cells are organized into a tissue associated with elaborate accessory structures. The architecture of the accessory structures and the organization of the receptor cells permit far more intricate and accurate sampling of the environment than is possible by independent, isolated receptor cells.

The difference in capability between a simple receptor and a highly organized association of receptor and accessory structures in the form of a sense organ can be illustrated by comparing the barnacle "eye" with the vertebrate eye. The barnacle eye consists of three simple photoreceptor cells, which are not equipped with a lens and thus cannot process an image. The barnacle eye evidently evolved to carry out photoreception, but not vision. The photoreceptors of a barnacle merely signal changes in light intensity, which allows the nervous system to respond with appropriate protective reflexes when the shadow of a predator falls on the barnacle. The vertebrate eye, on the other hand, can form an optical image, certain parameters of which are encoded in the neural activity of the optic nerve. From this information, the central nervous system abstracts a complex neural counterpart of the image, which in turn gives rise to the subjective experience of "vision."

Chemoreception

The sensitivity of cells to specific molecules is widespread; this includes metabolic responses of tissues to chemical messengers as well as the ability of lower organisms such as bacteria to detect certain substances in the environment. We will restrict ourselves to special *chemoreceptor* cells that include both *gustatory* (taste) receptors, which detect dissolved ions and molecules, and *olfactory* (smell) receptors, which detect airborne molecules. Because airborne molecules enter an aqueous layer covering the membrane of an olfactory receptor, any fundamental distinction between olfactory and gustatory reception disappears. Figure 7-15 illustrates vertebrate taste and olfactory receptors and an insect olfactory receptor.

Chemosensory systems can be extraordinarily sensitive. A case in point is the sensitivity of antennal chemoreceptors of the male silkworm moth (*Bombyx mori*) to *bombycol*, the female's sex-attractant pheromone

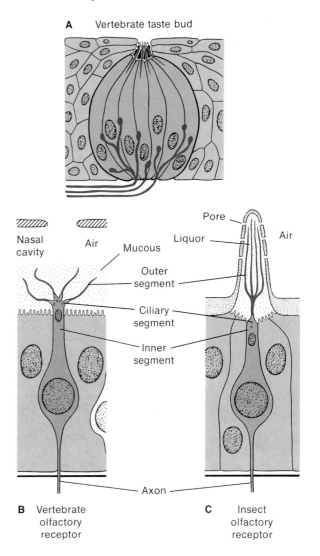

7-15. *Three types of chemoreceptor organs. A. Vertebrate taste bud with secondary sensory axons innervating the primary receptor cells. [After Murray and Murray, 1970.] Vertebrate (B) and insect (C) olfactory receptors send primary afferents to the central nervous system. Analogous structures are drawn similarly in B and C. In all three types, fine processes extend from the receptor cell into the mucous layer. In the insect, these are true dendrites. [Parts B and C after Steinbrecht, 1969.]*

A Vertebrate taste bud

Nasal cavity Air Mucous

Pore Liquor Air

Outer segment

Ciliary segment

Inner segment

Axon

B Vertebrate olfactory receptor

C Insect olfactory receptor

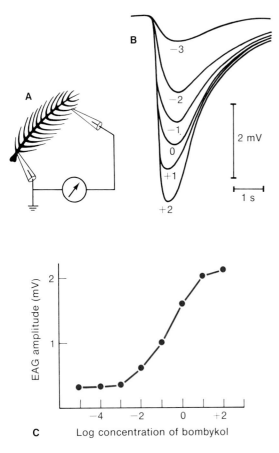

7-16. *Electrical responses of olfactory receptors in moth antennae stimulated with the pheromone bombykol. A. Method of recording. B. Electroantennograms (EAG) in response to various stimulus intensities. Numbers give relative concentration of bombycol in log units. C. Relationship between response amplitude and bombykol concentration, given in same units as in B. [After Boeckh et al., 1965.]*

(p. 336). The male responds behaviorally to concentrations as low as one molecule per 10^{17} molecules of air. The moth's receptors are highly specific, responding only to bombycol and a few of its chemical analogues. The zoological significance of this highly evolved stimulant–receptor system is obvious—it allows the male of the species to locate a single female at night from distances of up to several miles downwind.

Recordings of summed electrical responses of the antennal olfactory receptors of the moth have been used to investigate their sensitivity to bombycol (Fig. 7-16). This technique and single-unit recording have shown that only about 90 bombycol molecules impinging on a single receptor cell per second are required to produce a significant increase in the rate of firing of the cell. However, the male moth reacts behaviorally (i.e., flaps his wings excitedly) when only about 40 receptor cells (out of a total number of 20,000 per antenna) each intercept one molecule per second. Because the change in discharge rate of a single cell in response to a single odorant molecule is not readily apparent in electrophysiological recordings, it is inferred that the moth's central nervous system is capable of sensing very slight but simultaneous changes in impulse frequency in numerous sensory channels.

The *contact chemoreceptors* (taste hairs) of insects have proven very useful in electrophysiological studies of single chemoreceptor cells. These receptor cells send fine dendrites to the tips of hollow hairlike projections of the cuticle, called *sensilla*. Each sensillum has a minute pore that provides access for stimulant molecules to the sensory cells (Fig. 7-17). The sensillum contains several cells, each of which is sensitive to a different

7-17. *Electrical recording from a contact chemoreceptor sensillum of a fly. The dendrite of each neuron is sensitive to a different class (sugars, cations, anions, water) of substances. Electrical responses (right) are recorded through a crack made in the side of the sensillum.*

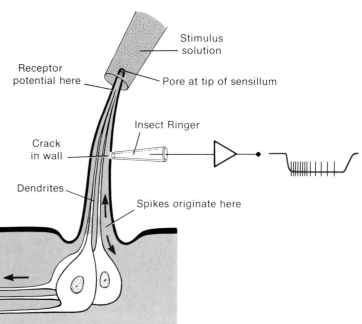

chemical stimulus (e.g., water, cations, anions, carbo-hydrates). In this case, a behavioral response can be evoked by appropriate stimulation of a single sensil-lum. A small drop of sugar solution applied to a sen-sillum on the foot causes the fly to respond by lowering its proboscis to feed. The effectiveness of various com-pounds in evoking this stereotyped behavior has been tested with this reflex. All compounds that release the feeding reflex also evoke electrical activity in the *sugar receptor,* one of the receptor cells in the sensillum. This receptor cell responds only to certain carbohydrates. Carbohydrates, such as D-ribose, that do not release feeding behavior also fail to stimulate the sugar recep-tor. It is interesting that the sugar receptor of the fly shows the same sequence of sensitivity (fructose > sucrose > glucose) as do the sweetness receptors of the human tongue.

The electrical activity of the contact chemoreceptors of the fly can be recorded either through the stimulus solution applied to the tip or through a crack made in the side wall of the sensillum (Fig. 7-17). Using the latter technique, it is possible to observe two compo-nents of the extracellularly recorded electrical response: a receptor potential (slow downward deflection of trace), and impulses. The receptor potential is pro-duced at the ends of the dendrites that extend to the tip of the sensillum, whereas the action potentials originate near the cell body. The long distance between the tip of the sensillum, where the stimulus acts on the *receptor membrane,* and the site of impulse initiation requires electrotonic spread of the receptor potential along the length of the dendrite to the site of impulse initiation.

Olfactory coding has been examined electrically in the olfactory epithelium of the frog by recording the activity of single receptor axons (electrode 2, Fig. 7-18,B) along with the summed potential (*electro-olfac-togram,* or *EOG*) of large numbers of olfactory receptors in the epithelium (electrode 1). Impulses from individ-ual receptors were superimposed electronically on the EOG before display on the oscilloscope. This technique permitted comparison of the activity of single units with the total response of many receptors to selected odor stimuli, or odorants. The results indicate that stimulus coding in the vertebrate nose is far more complex than that in the contact chemoreceptors of insects. Different receptors respond differently to the same odorant. In some sensory axons, a particular odorant increases the impulse frequency (Fig. 7-19, cell *a*); in other axons, the same odorant depresses impulse frequency (Fig. 7-19, cell *b*). Perhaps most interesting is the finding that odorants smelling alike to humans also have similar effects on some frog olfac-tory cells, but have differing effects on other cells (Fig. 7-20). It has not been possible to establish a one-to-one relation between certain smells and certain types of

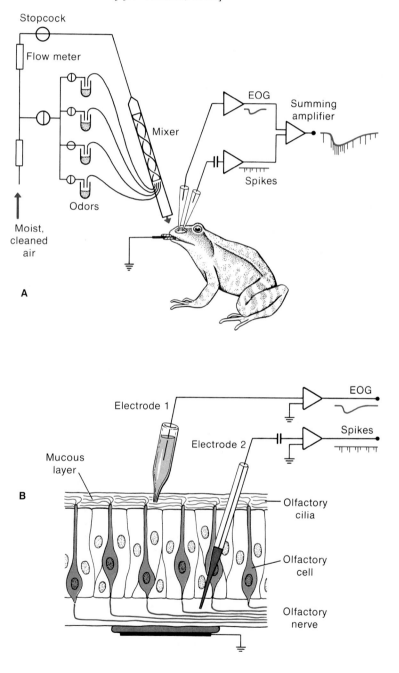

7-18. *Method for studying sensory coding in the olfactory epithelium of the frog. A. Various odors can be applied to the nasal epithelium while the electro-olfactogram (EOG) and spikes are recorded and summed to give a com-posite recording (right). B. Detail of tissue and electrodes. Electrode 1 records the overall EOG potential by virtue of its position. [After Gesteland, 1966.]*

7-19. *Responses of two different cells to the same odor (tetraethyl tin). Cell* a *is excited (i.e., spike frequency increases) while cell* b *is inhibited.* [After Gesteland, 1966.]

Cell a   Cell b

7-20. *Two substances that have similar effects on cell* a *have very different effects on cell* b. *Thus cell* b *can differentiate some odors that* a *cannot.* [After Gesteland, 1966.]

Resting discharge

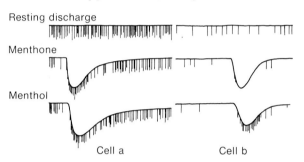

Menthone

Menthol

Cell a   Cell b

olfactory cells in the frog. Instead, each olfactory receptor cell may have a mosaic of odorant-receptor molecules with differing specificities. Depending on the proportions of receptor molecules having different olfactory specificities, a given olfactory cell may show various combinations of excitation or depression in response to a given odorant. The ability of mammals to distinguish among a wide variety of odorants may therefore reside in the ability of the olfactory centers of the brain to "recognize" a large number of different combinations of enhanced and depressed impulse frequencies arriving from various olfactory cells in the nasal epithelium.

How does a taste or olfactory receptor cell transduce a chemical stimulus? In the context of this question, we can recall the behavior of the postsynaptic membrane of a chemical synapse (p. 171), which can be regarded as the chemosensory membrane of the postsynaptic nerve or muscle cell. The postsynaptic receptor molecules of the vertebrate motor endplate, upon binding with ACh, undergo a conformational change that produces an increase in the conductance of the membrane to Na^+ and K^+, with the result that a synaptic current (in the present context, read also

7-21. *The seven basic odors, as postulated by Amoore and his co-workers. The odors of substances appear to be correlated with steric conformation of the odorant molecules. Models of representative molecules are shown for each category. In addition, "pungent" and "putrid" odorants have positive and negative charges, respectively. An odorant molecule appears to fit into a receptor site, which produces excitation of the olfactory cell. At the lower right is a cross section of a "pepperminty" site occupied by a molecule of 1-methone.* [After "The Stereochemical Theory of Odor" by J. E. Amoore and J. W. Johnston, Jr. Copyright © 1964 by Scientific American, Inc. All rights reserved.]

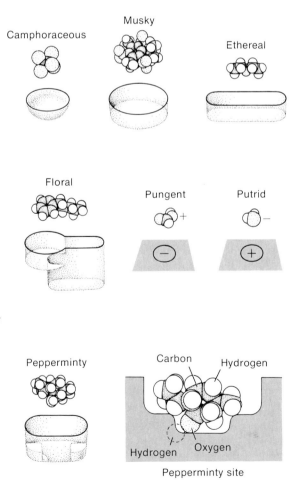

"receptor current") flows into the cell, depolarizes it, and generates action potentials.

The acetylcholine receptor molecule is known to be a protein (or group of protein molecules), because reagents that alter protein structure alter the properties of the receptor molecule. It is not surprising that the ACh receptor molecule is a protein, for protein molecules are known to undergo changes in shape in response to interactions with other molecules; a change in shape is one way in which a receptor molecule in a membrane might cause the opening of channels for the passage of an ionic receptor current through the membrane. Although no receptor molecules of chemosensory cells have yet been isolated, it is probable that they are proteins.

There appear to be several basic classes of receptor molecules in the nasal epithelium of mammals. Humans can distinguish several hundred different compounds on the basis of their odors, but it is not reasonable to suppose that corresponding to each odorant there is a different receptor molecule or receptor cell responsive only to that odorant. More likely, as we proposed in the case of the frog, there is a distribution of receptor molecules in different olfactory cells that permits the coding of combinations of basic odor types. According to a modern classification, there are seven primary odors: *camphoraceous, musky, floral, pepperminty, ethereal, pungent,* and *putrid.* Amoore based these categories on his observations of a correlation between steric conformation of odorant molecules and olfactory sensation in humans. Odorants that have different chemical formulae, but that share certain common features of molecular shape and dimensions, were found to have similar smells. The *stereochemical theory* of odor is that the odorant excites the olfactory receptor cell through a quasispecific steric fit between a receptor site on the olfactory cell and the odorant molecule (Fig. 7-21). Some molecules, because they have intermediate shapes and sizes, according to this theory, stimulate two or more kinds of receptor sites, producing intermediate odor sensations. Odorants that smell pungent and putrid appear to do so by virtue of their cationic and anionic properties, respectively.

Mechanoreception

The simplest mechanoreceptors are morphologically undifferentiated nerve endings found in the connective tissue of skin (Fig. 7-22). In many mechanoreceptors, there have evolved accessory structures whose function is the efficient transfer of mechanical energy to the receptor cells. These accessory structures are generally differentiated to filter the mechanical energy in some way. Examples are Pacinian corpuscles, in which the

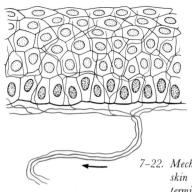

7-22. *Mechanoreceptors in the connective tissue of skin are morphologically undifferentiated axon terminals. [After "Biological Transducers" by W. R. Loewenstein. Copyright © 1960 by Scientific American, Inc. All rights reserved.]*

7-23. *A hair-like mechanoreceptor sensillum in the exoskeletons of insects. A. Location of joint-position receptors. Each hair plate contains a number of sensilla that sense the position of the joint. B. Anatomical detail of a sensillum at rest. C. Bending the sensillum stretches and deforms the dendrite of the receptor cell. [After Thurm, 1965.]*

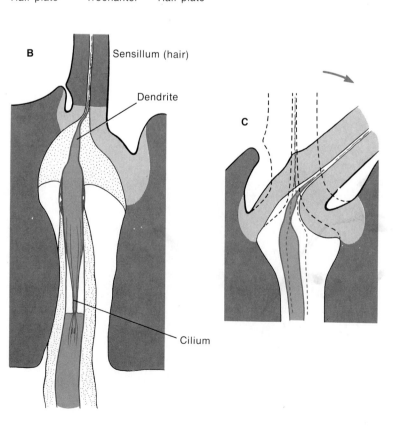

7-24. A simple hypothesis for explaining the increase in permeability to Na⁺ produced by
stretching a mechanoreceptor membrane. A. If
the diameter of the pores in the unstretched
receptor is just below the diameter of the Na⁺
ion, a small stretch (B) will increase the
diameter enough to allow sodium to flow into
the cell. It is not known if this is, in fact,
the way a mechanoreceptor functions.

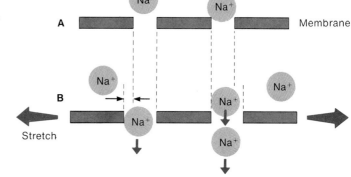

7-25. A. Electron micrograph of a cross section
through the cilia of a hair cell. The large
cilium with the 9 + 2 structure is the
kinocilium; the others are stereocilia. [Flock,
1967.]   B. A diagram showing anatomical
relations of the hair cell, stimulus direction,
and secondary afferent fibers.   C. Depending
on the direction in which the cilia are bent, the
hair cell can either increase or decrease its rate
of firing (compare with Fig. 7–14). [Harris
and Flock, 1967.]

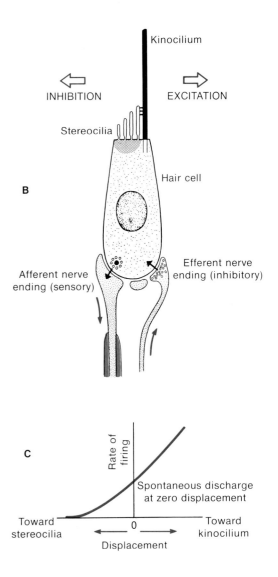

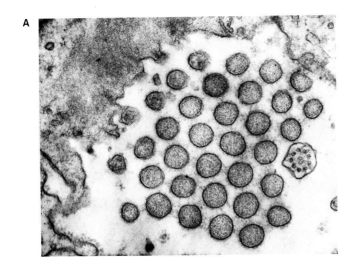

sensitive ending is covered by a capsule (Fig. 7-11); muscle stretch receptors, in which the mechanical sensitive neuronal endings are associated with specialized muscle fibers (Figs. 7-10 and 8-31); and the hair-like sensilla in the exoskeletons of arthropods (Fig. 7-23). The most elaborate accessory structures, used to detect and analyze sound waves, are found in the vertebrate middle and inner ear (Figs. 7-31 and 7-32).

The immediate stimulus thought to act on mechanoreceptors is a stretch or distortion of the surface membrane. Stretching the membrane of one of the large axons of the lobster has been shown to increase its permeability to sodium. One hypothesis for mechanoreceptor transduction is that stretching of the receptor membrane slightly enlarges ion-selective channels in the membrane. Such an enlargement of channels that would otherwise be just below the critical size for a specific ion might cause a large increase in permeability to that ion (Fig. 7-24). The very small amount of mechanical energy required to stretch the membrane just enough to produce an increased conductance to the ion would release a much larger amount of electrical energy stored as the concentration gradient of that ion.

HAIR CELLS

The hair cells of vertebrates (Fig. 7-25,A,B) are the primary mechanoreceptors in the lateral-line systems of fish and amphibians (Fig. 7-26), in the cochlear nerve of vertebrate organs of hearing (Figs. 7-31 and 7-32), and in the organs of equilibrium (semicircular canals) of vertebrates (Fig. 7-31). The name "hair cell" derives from the cilia that project from one end of each receptor—a single *kinocilium* and about two dozen *stereocilia*. The kinocilium has the 9 + 2 arrangement of microtubules similar to that of motile cilia (Chapter 10); however, the sensory cilia do not exhibit motility. The stereocilia contain many fine longitudinal filaments, and they are structurally and developmentally unrelated to the kinocilium. Although the kinocilium is present in the lateral line and vestibular hair cells, it is absent from the hair cells of the mammalian cochlea. The stereocilia are arranged in an order of increasing length from one side of the cell to the other; the kinocilium stands tallest of all (Fig. 7-25,B).

The hair cells are sensitive to the direction of the mechanical stimulus. Bending of the stereocilia toward the kinocilium leads to depolarization and excitation of the sensory fibers, whereas bending in the opposite direction leads to hyperpolarization and inhibition of the sensory fiber discharge (Fig. 7-25,B). Thus the receptor potential of the hair cell modulates the spontaneous activity of the sensory axon with which the hair cell makes a chemical synapse. Depending on the

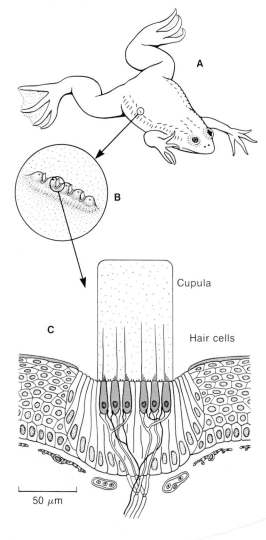

7–26. *Hair cells in the lateral-line system of an amphibian. Water motion causes displacement of the cupula, which stimulates the hair cells.*

Cupula

Hair cells

50 μm

direction in which the cilia are bent, the discharge rate is modulated above or below a spontaneous frequency corresponding to zero displacement (Fig. 7-25,C).

The receptor potential of hair cells in the lateral line of *Necturus* was correlated with mechanical stimuli and nerve-fiber discharges by simultaneous recording of the intracellular receptor-cell potential and the impulses of the sensory axons (Fig. 7-27). It was found that depolarization of the receptor (upward deflection in trace *a*) increases discharge frequency, and that hyperpolarization (downward deflection of trace *a*) reduces discharge frequency. The astounding feature of the recording is the very small potential changes produced in the hair cell (<0.1 mV) in response to relatively large mechanical displacements of the gelatinous *cupula* in which the cilia are imbedded. The ability to modulate sensory discharge with very small

7-27. Simultaneous recordings of the receptor potentials and action potentials in hair cells of the lateral line in a salamander. Electrode placement is shown at left. The receptor potential is seen to modulate the frequency of action potentials in the secondary afferents; depolarization increases the frequency, and hyperpolarization decreases it. [After Harris et al., 1970.]

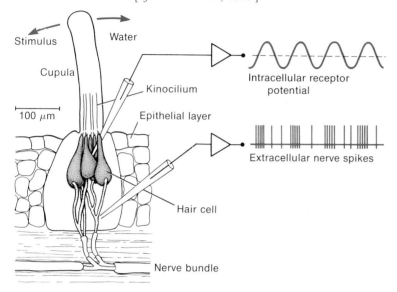

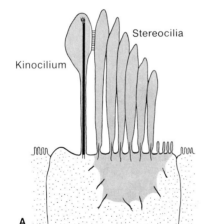

changes in receptor-cell potential is characteristic of the hair cells and of the electroreceptor cells (p. 216) derived from them. There appears to be a steady release of synaptic transmitter by the hair cell. Changes in membrane potential modulate the rate of release, thereby modulating the frequency of firing of the sensory axon.

The anatomy of the hair cell suggests a possible mechanism of directional sensitivity. The kinocilium is attached with minute filaments to the adjacent stereocilium (Fig. 7-28,A), so that displacement toward the kinocilium depresses the membrane at the base of the kinocilium (Fig. 7-28,B), while displacement away from the kinocilium lifts the membrane matrix, which appears to be inflexible. The depression of the kinocilium stretches the sensitive membrane at its base, while a lifting of the kinocilium, may relieve a resting stress. The changes in stress on the stretch-sensitive membrane may produce corresponding changes in ionic permeability, which would account for the depolarization and hyperpolarization produced when the cilia are displaced toward and away from the kinocilium, respectively.

ORGANS OF EQUILIBRIUM

The simplest organs that have evolved to detect position with respect to gravity and to detect acceleration are invertebrate *statocysts*. Forms of this organ are found in a number of animal groups, ranging from jellyfish to vertebrates. The organ consists of a hollow cavity lined with mechanoreceptor cells that are generally ciliated and that make contact with a *statolith* (sand grains, calcareous concretions, etc.). The statolith is either taken up from the animal's surroundings or secreted by the epithelium of the statocyst. In either case, the statolith has a higher specific gravity than the surrounding fluid. If a lobster, for example, is tilted to one side, the statolith stimulates the receptor cells

7-28. Mechanics of transduction in the hair cell, hypothesized on the basis of studies of the ultrastructure. A. Unstimulated state. The kinocilium (left) is attached near its tip to the tallest stereocilium. The stereocilia are anchored at their bases in a dense matrix. B. Movement to the left causes the kinocilium to act as a plunger, depressing and stretching the sensory membrane at its base. C. Movement to the right has the opposite effect, relieving resting tension on the membrane. [After Hillman, 1969.]

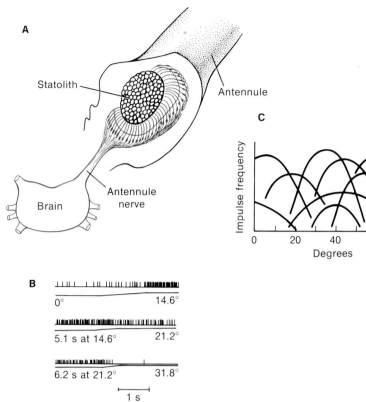

A

Statolith

Antennule

Brain

Antennule nerve

C

Impulse frequency

0   20   40   60
Degrees

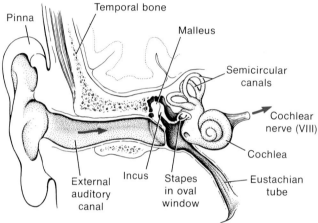

7–29. *Statocyst of the lobster. A. A statolith rests on the sensory processes of an array of neurons. B. Electrophysiological records from the nerve fibers in response to the tilting of the lobster. The trace below the recording indicates tilting. C. A plot of impulse frequency versus position of the animal shows that each cell responds with maximum discharge at an optimum position. [After* Interneurons *by G. A. Horridge. W. H. Freeman and Company. Copyright © 1968.]*

B

0°   14.6°

5.1 s at 14.6°   21.2°

6.2 s at 21.2°   31.8°

1 s

7–30. *The major parts of the human ear. [After Beck, 1971.]*

Temporal bone

Pinna

Malleus

Semicircular canals

Cochlear nerve (VIII)

Cochlea

Eustachian tube

External auditory canal

Incus

Stapes in oval window

7–31. *Semicircular canals and cochlea. The stapes is removed in order to show the oval window. The pathway of sound in the cochlea is shown by arrows. [After Beck, 1971.]*

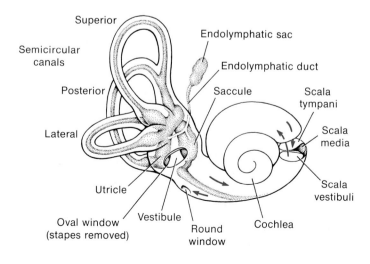

Superior

Endolymphatic sac

Semicircular canals

Endolymphatic duct

Posterior

Saccule

Scala tympani

Lateral

Scala media

Scala vestibuli

Utricle

Oval window (stapes removed)

Vestibule

Round window

Cochlea

on that side of the statocyst, causing a tonic (steady) discharge in the sensory fibers of the stimulated receptor cells (Fig. 7-29). Each cell has an optimum angle at which its discharge is maximal. The sensory discharge produced by tilting the lobster sets up reflex movements of the appendages, which right the animal.

The vertebrate organs of equilibrium reside in the three *semicircular canals* of the inner ear, which lie in three mutually perpendicular planes (Figs. 7-30, 7-31). They detect changes in the rate of rotation or translation of the head. As the head is accelerated in one of these planes, the inertia of the endolymph fluid in the corresponding canal results in relative motion of the endolymph past a gelatinous projection, the cupula. Movement of the cupula stimulates the hair cells. The hair cells are all oriented with the kinocilium on the same side. Thus they are all excited by acceleration of the head in one direction and inhibited by acceleration in the other direction. The sensory signals from the semicircular canals provide information about movements of the head, and that information is integrated with other sensory input in the cerebellum (p. 155) to control postural reflexes.

The Mammalian Ear

STRUCTURE AND FUNCTION OF THE COCHLEA

The hair cells of the mammalian ear are located in the *organ of Corti* in the *cochlea* (Fig. 7-32). They resemble the hair cells of the lateral line system of lower vertebrates except that the kinocilium is absent, leaving only the stereocilia. Most of the structures of the ear aid in the transformation of sound waves (airborne vibrations) into movements of the organ of Corti, which stimulate the hair cells; the hair cells, in turn, excite the sensory axons of the auditory nerve. We

7-32. Details of mammalian cochlear anatomy. A. Cross section through cochlear canal, showing the two outer chambers and the organ of Corti in the central canal attached to the basilar membrane. B. The arrangement of the hair cells in the organ of Corti. Note the cilia in contact with the tectorial membrane. [After Wersäll et al., 1965.]

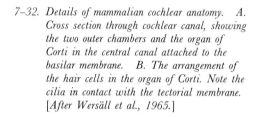

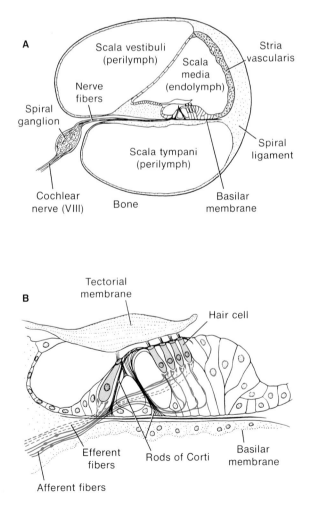

shall now consider the way in which frequency and intensity of sound are encoded by the cochlea and the nerves that innervate it.

The cochlea, a tapered tube encased in the mastoid bone, is coiled in mammals—somewhat like the shell of a snail. It is divided internally into three longitudinal compartments (Figs. 7-32,A). Continuity exists between the two outer compartments (*scala tympani* and *scala vestibuli*) via the *helicotrema*, an opening located near the apical end of the cochlea. This space is filled with an aqueous *perilymph*. Between these compartments, and bounded by the *basilar membrane* and Reissner's membrane, is another compartment, the *scala media*, filled with a fluid *endolymph*. The organ of Corti, which bears the hair cells, lies within the scala media and is attached to the basilar membrane. The cilia of the hair cells project from the surface of the basilar membrane to make contact with the overlying tectorial membrane (Fig. 7-32). Airborne vibrations impinging on the *eardrum* are transmitted through the auditory ossicles and through the *oval window* to the perilymph (Fig. 7-31). The ossicles amplify the pressure of vibrations set up in the eardrum by airborne vibrations. Because the area of the oval window is only about 1/25th the area of the eardrum, the sound energy is concentrated in a smaller area, and the force per unit area (pressure) is increased. This is important, as the inertia of the fluid is greater than that of air.

Vibrations applied to the oval window pass through the cochlear fluids and the membranes (Reissner's and basement) separating the cochlear compartments before dissipating their energy through the membrane-covered *round window*. The distribution of perturbations within the cochlea depends on the frequencies of vibrations entering the oval window. To visualize this, imagine a displacement of the eardrum transferred through the ossicles of the middle ear to the oval window. Very low frequencies displace the incompressible perilymph along the scala tympani, through the helicotrema, and back through the scala vestibuli toward the round window. In contrast, rapid displacements due to high sound frequencies show a greater tendency to take a shortcut from the scala tympani to the scala vestibuli by displacing the intervening membranes and endolymph. This finding is based on observations by Von Békésy made on exposed cochleae. His studies showed (1) that the perturbations of the basilar membrane in response to a pure (sine wave) tone have the same frequency as the tone, (2) that these perturbations, regardless of frequency, move as a traveling wave over the *whole length* of the basilar membrane, and (3) that the location along the basilar membrane of the maximum amplitude of the wave is a function of the frequency of the tone. Thus each point along the basilar membrane is displaced most effectively by some unique frequency.

EXCITATION OF THE COCHLEAR HAIR CELLS

Electrical recordings from several places in the cochlea show fluctuations in electric potential that are similar in frequency, phase, and amplitude to the sound waves that produce them. These *cochlear microphonics,* as they are called, result from the summation of receptor currents from the numerous hair cells stimulated by movements of the basilar membrane. The receptor currents of the hair cells faithfully signal movements of the basilar membrane over the whole audible sound-frequency spectrum (~ 20 to 20,000 Hz in young humans). The hair cells make synaptic contact with sensory axons of the *eighth cranial nerve,* axons that terminate in the cochlear nucleus. Synaptic output of the hair cells modulates the firing frequency in the auditory nerve fibers. At *low* frequencies, these afferent nerve fibers discharge impulses in synchrony with the receptor potentials produced in the hair cells. But at frequencies approaching 1,000 Hz and beyond, the frequency of discharge is limited by refractoriness of the axons. (The coding of tonal frequency is discussed in the following subsection.)

Serious gaps remain in our understanding of the way that movements of the basilar membrane produce receptor potentials in the hair cells. The initial transductional step appears to be a lateral shearing (i.e., relative sliding) component of motion between the organ of Corti and the tectorial membrane, to which the stereocilia of the hair cells are attached. The shearing component of the movement is a consequence of the arrangement of the pivot points of the basilar and tectorial membranes (Fig. 7-33). Because of this, a perturbation of the basilar membrane applies a lateral displacement to the tips of the stereocilia. This displacement presumably increases or decreases the tension on the mechanoreceptor membrane near the attachments of the cilia at the apical end of the hair cell (Fig. 7-28). According to this theory, an upward displacement of the basilar membrane produces a shearing movement that bends the stereocilia in the direction of the missing kinocilium, causing an increase in conductance of the receptor membrane and a flow of current from the scala media through the receptor membrane into the hair cell (Fig. 7-34). This current slightly depolarizes the membrane at the basal end of the hair cell and increases the release of synaptic transmitter there, producing an increase in rate of discharge of the associated sensory axon. Conversely, a downward displacement of the basilar membrane will cause the stereocilia to be bent away from the side of the missing kinocilium, relieving some of the tension on the receptor membrane and reducing the steady depolarizing receptor current.

The emf responsible for the receptor current origi-

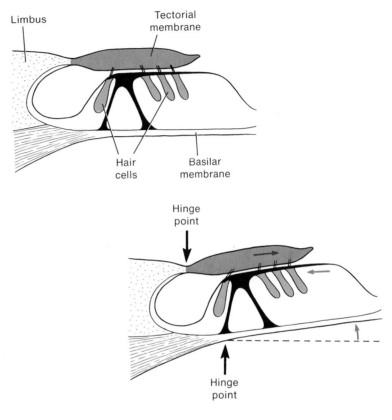

7–33. *Diagram of the presumed shearing force applied to the cilia as a result of an upward movement of the basilar membrane. The tectorial membrane slides over the organ of Corti because the tectorial membrane and the basilar membrane have laterally displaced points of pivoting. The movements are greatly exaggerated.* [*After Davis, 1968.*]

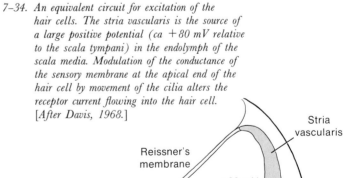
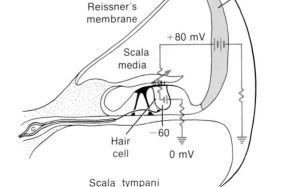

7–34. *An equivalent circuit for excitation of the hair cells. The stria vascularis is the source of a large positive potential (ca +80 mV relative to the scala tympani) in the endolymph of the scala media. Modulation of the conductance of the sensory membrane at the apical end of the hair cell by movement of the cilia alters the receptor current flowing into the hair cell.* [*After Davis, 1968.*]

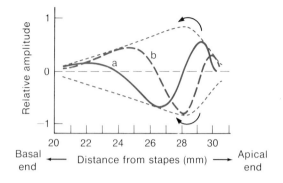

7-35. *Profile of a traveling wave moving along the basilar membrane, stopped at two times,* a *and* b. *The light broken line shows the envelope generated by the movements. Amplitudes are greatly exaggerated. [After von Békésy, 1960.]*

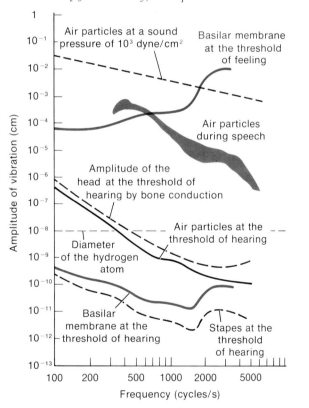

7-36. *The amplitudes of vibration of air particles and basilar membrane at different sound frequencies and intensities. Note the dimensions relative to the size of the hydrogen atom. [After von Békésy, 1962.]*

nates in part from an electrogenic pumping (p. 95) of K^+ from the blood into the endolymph by the *stria vascularis* (Fig. 7-34), a capillary bed specialized for active transport. The stria thereby acts as a battery, generating a large positive potential of about $+80$ mV in the scala media relative to the scala tympani. This potential is in series with the resting potential of the hair cell, about -60 mV, giving a total emf at the receptor membrane of about 140 mV. It is conjectured that stimulation of the hair cell changes the resistance of the receptor membrane at its apical end (variable resistance in Fig. 7-34), and that this modulates the flow of current from the endolymphatic space through the hair cell to the perilymphatic space, producing receptor potentials in the hair cell. The receptor potentials modulate the release of synaptic transmitter, thereby influencing the discharge of the afferent fibers in the auditory nerve.

FREQUENCY ANALYSIS BY THE COCHLEA

Helmholtz noted in 1868 that the basilar membrane consists of many transverse bands increasing in length from the proximal end (round window) to the apical end of the basilar membrane. This reminded him of the strings of a piano and led to his *resonance theory,* which proposed that various parts along the length of the basilar membrane vibrate to the exclusion of other parts of the basilar membrane in resonance with a specific tonal frequency (just as the appropriate string of a piano will resonate in response to a tone from a tuning fork). This theory was later challenged by von Békésy (1960), who found (as noted above) that the movements of the basilar membrane are *not* standing waves like those of a piano (as Helmholtz suggested), but consist instead of *traveling waves* that move from the narrow end of the basilar membrane toward the broader apical end (Fig. 7-32). These waves have the same frequency as the sound entering the ear, but their velocity is much less than that of sound in air. A familiar example of a traveling wave is seen when a rope, secured at one end, is given a shake at the free end. The basilar membrane differs from the rope in that its mechanical properties change along its length. The progressive increase in mechanical compliance (i.e., looseness) of the basilar membrane—from its narrow end toward its broad end—results in changes in the amplitude of traveling waves as they move along the membrane (Fig. 7-35). The position at which the displacement of the basilar membrane has its maximum amplitude (and hence maximum stimulation of hair cells and sensory axons) depends on the frequency of the traveling waves, and hence on the frequency of the stimulating sound. At high sound frequencies, the traveling waves produce maximum displacements near the basal end of the cochlea. At low sound frequencies, the region of maximum displacement of the basilar membrane shifts toward the apical end of the cochlea. The extent of displacement at any point along the basilar membrane determines how strongly the hair cells are stimulated, and thus the rate of discharge of sensory fibers arising from different parts of the basilar membrane. It is in this way that the basilar membrane and its receptor cells analyze the sound-frequency spectrum. As explained in Box 7-1,

BOX 7-1   VON BÉKÉSY'S MODEL OF THE COCHLEA

How can a pure tone of one frequency be discriminated from other tones if traveling waves pass along the entire basilar membrane? Von Békésy provided important clues by experimenting with a mechanical model of the cochlea and basilar membrane (see part A of figure). The model "basilar membrane," which is tapered along its length like its biological counterpart, consists of a thin metal membrane with a rib along its length. Traveling waves of selected frequencies are set up along the "basilar membrane" by sine wave perturbations produced by a mechanical driver at one end. The driver is analogous to the stapes on the oval window. A subject's forearm is placed on the rib, so that the tactile receptors in the skin of the arm can feel the movements of the "basilar membrane." The tactile receptors in this model are analogous to the cochlear hair cells along the length of the real basilar membrane.

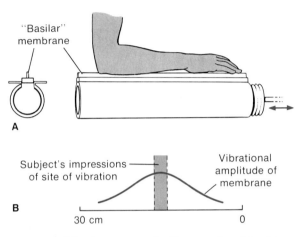

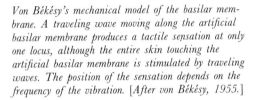

Von Békésy's mechanical model of the basilar membrane. A traveling wave moving along the artificial basilar membrane produces a tactile sensation at only one locus, although the entire skin touching the artificial basilar membrane is stimulated by traveling waves. The position of the sensation depends on the frequency of the vibration. [After von Békésy, 1955.]

The important finding made with this model is that vibrational waves traveling along the skin of the forearm are felt in only one narrow transverse band (see part B of figure). The band of sensation moves along the arm as the frequency of stimulation is altered, and corresponds to the region at which the traveling wave in the artificial basilar membrane reaches its maximum amplitude. Presumably the subject "feels" the vibration only in the region of maximum displacement because the strong sensory signals arriving in the brain from the region of maximum displacement inhibit weaker signals arriving from surrounding regions (a form of *lateral inhibition*, p. 248). It is believed that lateral inhibition accounts for the auditory system's ability to distinguish tones even though traveling waves stimulate receptors along the entire length of the basilar membrane. Efferent axons from the central auditory centers make inhibitory synaptic connections with the hair cells (Fig. 7-32,B). These inhibitory efferents to the hair cells may be activated centrally by sensory activity arising from hair cells of relatively higher and lower frequency loci of the basilar membrane. Thus the activity of weakly stimulated hair cells at one point along the basilar membrane may be suppressed by inhibitory efferents reflexly activated by receptors at a point along the basilar membrane more strongly stimulated by the tone. This effect would suppress all receptors except those receiving maximum mechanical stimulation.

frequency discrimination is enhanced by neural mechanisms.

It should be stressed that the diagrams of traveling waves in Figure 7-35 exaggerate greatly the actual amplitudes of displacement of the basilar membrane. The loudest sounds produce displacements of the basilar membrane of only about 1 μm. It has been calculated that for sound levels that are just perceptible to the mammalian auditory system, the amplitude of vibration of the basilar membrane may be as small as 10^{-11} cm (Fig. 7-36). It seems incredible that such miniscule movements (more than 1000 times smaller than the diameter of a hydrogen atom) should have any effect on the receptor cells. At this time, we can only assume that such movements produce small changes in the firing rates of a large number of sensory fibers, and that these changes are detected statistically in the auditory centers of the brain.

Electroreceptors

Hair cells located in the skin of certain fish have lost their cilia and have become modified for the detection of electrical currents in the water. The sources of these currents are the electric organs found in *weak electric fish* (such as the Mormyrids) or external currents that originate in the active tissues of other animals in the vicinity. The electroreceptors are distributed over the body in the lateral-line system (Fig. 7-37,A).

In weak electric fish (as opposed to *strong electric fish*, such as the electric eel), electrical pulses produced by modified muscle or nerve tissue at one end of the body re-enter the fish over much of its surface, through pores in the epithelium. At the base of each pore, the current encounters an *electroreceptor cell* (Fig. 7-37,B), which makes synaptic contact with eighth-nerve axons that innervate the receptors of the lateral line system. The receptor-cell membrane that faces the exterior has a lower electrical resistance than the membrane at the base of the cell. The result is that the membrane at the base limits the current flow through this cell and responds to a current flowing from outside

the fish into the pore with a positive-going shift in membrane potential (depolarization). The depolarization of the membrane at the base of the receptor cell causes the release of synaptic transmitter to exceed the spontaneous rate of release, and hence increases the frequency of firing in the sensory nerve fiber that innervates the receptor. Conversely, a current flowing out of the body of the fish hyperpolarizes the membrane at the base of the receptor cell and reduces the release of transmitter to less than the spontaneous rate. Thus the firing frequency goes up or down depending on the direction of current flowing through the electroreceptor cell (Fig. 7-37,B,C). The sensitivity of these receptors and their innervation, like that of the hair cells of the vertebrate ear, is truly remarkable. As seen in Figure 7-37,C, changes in sensory nerve discharge occur in response to changes in receptor-cell membrane potential of as little as several microvolts (millionths of a volt).

Electroreceptors capable of detecting minute fields are used extensively for orientation, communication, and detection of objects by weak electric fish and by certain nonelectric fish, such as catfish and elasmo-

7–37. A. The positions of the electric organ and the lateral-line nerve trunk and the distribution of electroreceptor pores in the weak electric fish Gnathonemus petersii. *B. At the base of each pore is an electroreceptor cell whose apical membrane has a low electrical resistance compared to the basal membrane. C. The spontaneously active receptor (a) is extremely sensitive to inward (b) and outward (c) current through the receptor pore. [After Bennett, 1968.]*

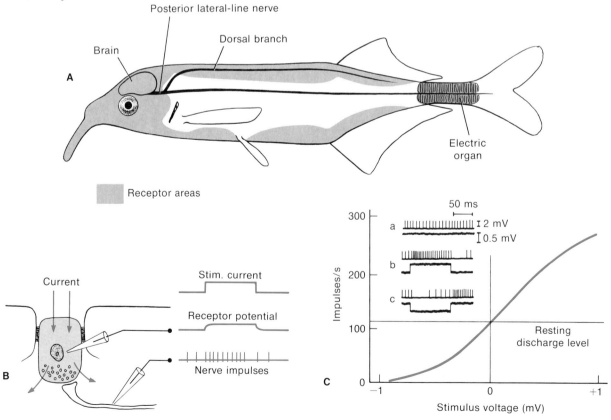

branchs. The latter can detect prey by the electric currents produced by the tissues of the prey. In contrast to the eels, torpedos, and other fish that produce powerful currents to stun prey, the weak electric fish produce a series of synchronous depolarizations in the cells of their electric organs. The currents of these cells sum to produce a train of current pulses that flow through the water from the posterior to the anterior end of the fish (Fig. 7-38). Any object whose conductivity differs from that of the water will distort the lines of current flow. The lateral line electroreceptors detect the distribution of current flowing back into the fish through the lateral line pores on the head and anterior end of the body, and this sensory information is then processed in the greatly enlarged cerebellum of the fish, enabling it to detect and locate objects in its immediate environment.

Thermoreceptors

Certain receptor cells are specialized for detecting and signaling temperature. Some of these are in the skin, and thus detect the temperature of the external environment. Others, especially important in the homeotherms (mammals and birds), monitor the temperature of the internal organs and provide feedback to the temperature-regulating mechanisms of the body.

Relatively little is known about thermoreception other than some relations between stimulus and response. Some temperature receptors have remarkable sensitivity. The infrared detectors in the facial pits of rattlesnakes (Fig. 7-39,A) increase their firing rate transiently in response to temperature increases as small as 0.002° C. This sensitivity is also seen in behavioral tests. A rattlesnake can detect the radiant heat (infrared wavelengths) from a mouse 40 cm away if the mouse is 10° C above the ambient temperature. Because these receptors are located on a connective tissue membrane deep within the facial pits, the snake is able to detect the direction of the infrared source (Fig. 7-39,B). The infrared-receptor organ consists of the branching endings of sensory nerve fibers, and shows no structural specializations.

The mechanisms by which temperature changes alter receptor output are not known. Both the skin and the upper surface of the tongue in mammals have two kinds of temperature receptors, those that increase firing when warmed ("warm" receptors) and those that increase firing when cooled ("cold" receptors). These categories are distinguished on the basis of responses to temperature changes near normal body temperature (about 37° C), because both kinds of receptors show peaks beyond which the response to temperature changes is reversed (Fig. 7-40).

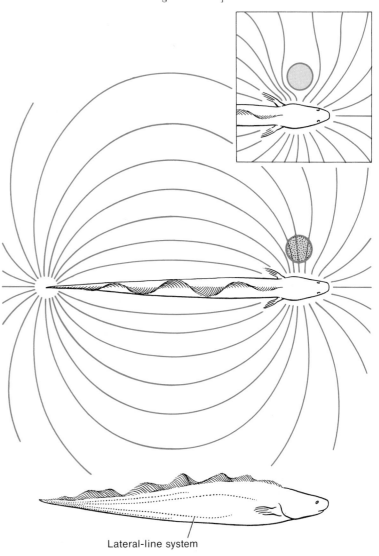

7–38. Current flowing between the electric organ (in the tail) and receptor pores in the head. An object having a conductivity greater than the water deflects current toward axis of flow. An object whose conductivity is lower than that of the water (inset) diverts the current away from the axis of flow. [After "Electrical Location by Fishes" by H. W. Lissman. Copyright © 1963 by Scientific American, Inc. All rights reserved.]

Lateral-line system

7–39. A. Structure of the facial pit of the rattlesnake Crotalus viridis. B. The positions of the facial pits lend directional sensitivity to the thermoreceptors within the pits. [After Bullock and Diecke, 1956.]

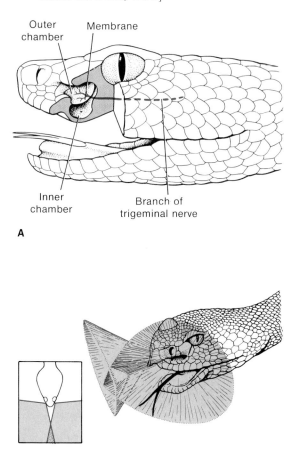

A

B

7–40. A. Responses of "cold" and "warm" receptors of the mammalian tongue. B. Frequency changes of a "cold" fiber upon cooling, then rewarming, at temperatures above the point of maximum resting frequency. C. Same as in B, except at temperatures below the point of maximum resting frequency. [After Zotterman, 1953.]

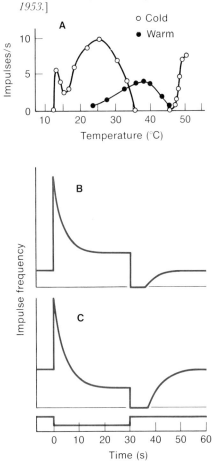

Photoreceptors

All photoreceptors have in common the presence of photoexcitable pigments associated with the receptor membrane. These photopigment molecules, which are the primary sites of photoreception, are altered by the absorption of light in such a way as to change the conductance of the membranes in which they reside. The vertebrates and the invertebrates have evolved different mechanisms by which the primary transduction process influences the conductance of the photoreceptor membrane and alters the membrane potential of the receptor cell. Let us first consider the simpler of the two mechanisms.

INVERTEBRATE PHOTORECEPTOR CELLS

The most intensively studied invertebrate photoreceptors are in the *lateral eye* of the horseshoe crab*, *Limulus polyphemus*. Most of the early electrical recording from single visual receptor cells was done with this *compound eye,* because the receptor cells and the nerve cells with which they connect lend themselves well to simple recording techniques. Although invertebrate photoreceptors and their organization into eyes show great variety, they appear to employ principles common to all.

*This "living fossil" is an arachnid, closely related to the spiders; it is not a crustacean.

The receptor cells at the base of a single *ommatidium* in the lateral eye of the horseshoe crab are shown in Figure 7-41. Ommatidia are the redundant functional units of the compound eye. Each ommatidium lies beneath an hexagonal facet of the cornea. A central dendrite arising from the *eccentric cell* is surrounded by about twelve *retinular cells*, the primary photoreceptors. Each retinular cell has a *rhabdomere*, consisting of the surface membrane thrown into a dense profusion of tubular evaginations termed *microvilli* (Fig. 7-42). Thus the surface area of the cell membrane is greatly expanded in the rhabdomere. Light enters through the lens and is absorbed by molecules of the photopigment located on or in the receptor membrane forming the rhabdomere. Small (3 to 8 mV) transient depolarizations of the membrane potential occur in the retinular cells of *Limulus* when the eye is exposed to very dim

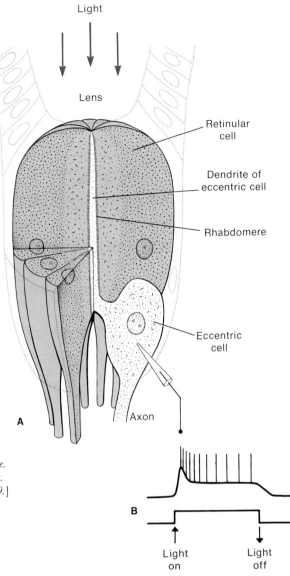

7–41. An ommatidium in the compound eye of the horseshoe crab Limulus polyphemus. *A. Light enters via the lens at the top and is intercepted by visual pigment in the retinular cells, which are arranged like the segments of an orange around the dendrite of the eccentric cell. B. Intracellularly recorded signal in response to a light stimulus. Receptor potential arising in the retinular cells spreads through gap junctions to the eccentric cell, which produces action potentials.* [*Part A After "How Cells Receive Stimuli" by W. H. Miller, F. Ratliff, and H. K. Hartline. Copyright © 1961 by Scientific American, Inc. All rights reserved. Part B after Fuortes, 1959.*]

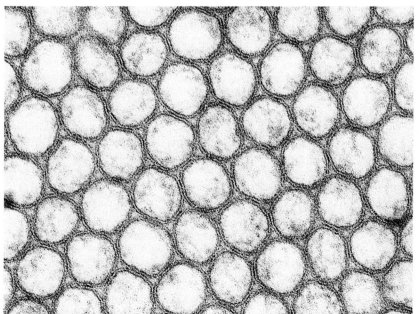

7–42. Electron-microscopic view of a rhabdomere in Limulus. *Note the profusion of microvilli (shown in cross section), the site of visual pigment concentration. Magnification 170,000 ×. [Courtesy of A. Lasansky.]*

7-43. *For light flashes of duration less than 1 s, the frequency of impulses in the eccentric cell axon is proportional to the logarithm of the number of photons impinging on the ommatidium. Therefore, for these short flashes, a short and bright flash can produce the same impulse discharge as a longer and dimmer flash. [After Hartline, 1934.]*

Duration

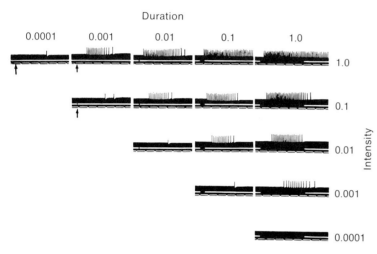

illumination. These "quantum bumps" on the recording increase in frequency when photons are allowed to impinge on the receptor with greater frequency. The small transient depolarizations are evidently the electrical signals generated by the absorption of individual quanta of light by single photopigment molecules. Simple calculations demonstrate that the power amplification of this process is between 10^5 and 10^6 times. How does a single photon captured by a molecule of photopigment lead to the rapid release of so many times its own energy? One obvious possibility is that the pigment molecule undergoes a conformational change when it absorbs a photon, and thereby opens up a channel in the membrane for the diffusion of ions down an electrochemical gradient. This appears to be what happens in most invertebrate photoreceptors. In these receptors, light produces an increase in membrane conductance, primarily to Na^+ and Ca^{2+}. This is seen as a depolarizing receptor potential. When the light goes off, these conductances diminish again, and the membrane repolarizes.

Although the primary photoreceptors of *Limulus* (the retinular cells) have axons, they apparently do not support action potentials. Instead, the receptor current spreads electrotonically through low-resistance junctions from the retinular cells into the dendrite of the eccentric cell. The depolarizing current spreads into the cell body and axon of the eccentric cell, and there the electrotonic depolarization leads to the generation of action potentials (Fig. 7-41,B), which are conducted in the optic nerve by the axon of the eccentric cell to the central nervous system. Thus the one axon of the eccentric cell carries all the information for the ommatidium. This is just as well, for the retinular cells are all electrically coupled, and act with the eccentric cell as one unit. In the next chapter (p. 248), we will see how the neighboring ommatidia interact in the initial stages of processing visual information.

Studies on the *Limulus* eye were begun by Hartline in the mid-1930's. By recording impulses in the axons of the optic nerve, he was able to correlate primary receptor activity with stimulus parameters. One of the most significant generalizations that came from his work is that a number of the simpler psychophysical (i.e., quantified subjective) features of human vision parallel the electrical behavior of single visual cells. This suggests that some of the very simple features of visual perception originate in the behavior of the photoreceptor cells, and are relatively unmodified by the nervous system. Examples follow.

Impulse frequencies recorded from the axons of single ommatidia are proportional to the logarithm of the stimulating light intensity (Fig. 7-43, right-hand column). This logarithmic relation is also true of a human subject's judgment of intensity in comparing different light intensities.

7-44. *Flicker fusion at the level of the receptor cell. The on-off pattern of the light stimulus is shown by the trace below the electrical recording. A. At a frequency of 10 flashes/s, the frequency of receptor potentials is also 10/s. At 12 flashes/s, the receptor potentials begin to lag behind the light flashes, and the grouping of impulses begins to break down. B. At high frequencies (here about 17 flashes/s), the receptor potentials fuse into an essentially constant depolarization, and the impulses no longer correspond in time to light flashes. [After "How Cells Receive Stimuli" by W. H. Miller, F. Ratliff, and H. K. Hartline. Copyright © 1961 by Scientific American, Inc. All rights reserved.]*

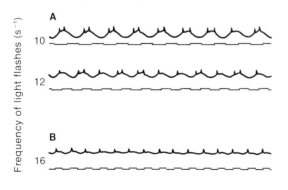

The receptor's response to light flashes less than 1 s in duration is proportional to the total number of photons in the flash, irrespective of flash duration (Fig. 7-43). That is, the number of impulses generated remains constant, provided that the product of the intensity and duration of the flash are kept constant. This is reasonable, because the response should be determined (within limits) by the number of photopigment molecules altered by the photons impinging on the receptor. For flashes of short duration, a human observer cannot tell the difference between reciprocal changes in intensity and duration of the flash.

The frequency of impulses in the eccentric cell is directly proportional to the amplitude of the receptor potential. If the receptor is stimulated with a flickering light, the membrane will follow it by fluctuating with the same frequency up to a rate of nearly 10 flashes/s (Fig. 7-44). Beyond this frequency, the receptor potential can no longer follow the flashes, hence the ripples in the membrane potential fuse into a steady level of depolarization. The impulses then no longer group with the flashes, but show a steady rate of discharge. When grouping of impulses fails, the central nervous system no longer receives information about the rate of flicker, and the light might as well be constant. This appears to be the reason why a human subject cannot tell the difference between a steady light and one (such as a lamp powered by a current of 60 cycles/s) that flickers at a rate above the *critical fusion frequency*.

VISUAL RECEPTOR CELLS OF VERTEBRATES

In mammals, birds, and many other vertebrates, the receptor cells (*rods* or *cones*) are most closely packed in the *fovea*, or *area centralis*, which is the small (1 mm^2) central part of the retina specialized for highest *visual acuity* (angular discrimination). In humans, and other mammals with color vision, the fovea contains only cones, whereas the remainder of the retina contains rods as well as cones. In mammals, the cones are responsible for color vision, and the more sensitive rods are restricted to achromatic vision. This distinction between rods and cones does not pertain to all vertebrates. In fact, some retinas contain only rods but may nonetheless be capable of color vision (discussed in the following section).

The two types of vertebrate photoreceptor cells are structurally and functionally more uniform than the great variety of photoreceptors found in the invertebrates. Each receptor cell contains a rudimentary *cilium* that connects the *outer segment,* which contains the receptor membranes, to the inner segment, which contains the nucleus, mitochondria, synaptic contacts, etc. (Figs. 7-45, 7-46). The receptor membranes of vertebrate visual cells consist of flattened lamellae derived from the surface membrane near the origin of

7–45. *Electron micrograph of a portion of a visual rod. Inner (below) and outer (above) segments are attached by a modified cilium. The outer segment contains numerous flattened lamellar sacs, or "disks." The inner segment contains nucleus, mitochondria, and other common organelles. Magnification 28,000 ×. [Courtesy of T. Kuwabara.]*

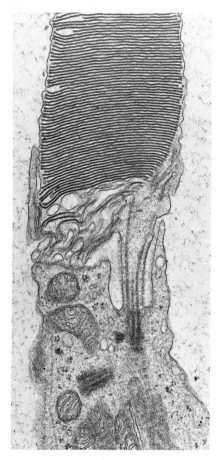

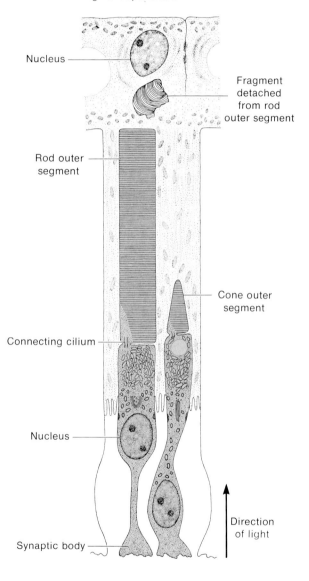

7–46. *Rod and cone of the frog. Note that the outer segments are pointed away from the source of light, toward the pigment epithelium at the back of the eye. As the visual cells grow, fragments detach from the apical ends and a new membrane reseals the outer segment. [After "Visual Cells" by R. W. Young. Copyright © by Scientific American, Inc. All rights reserved.]*

Pigment epithelium

Nucleus

Fragment detached from rod outer segment

Rod outer segment

Cone outer segment

Connecting cilium

Nucleus

Synaptic body

Direction of light

the outer segment. In the cones (Fig. 7-47,B) of mammals and some other vertebrates, the lumen of each lamella is open to the cell exterior. In rods, the lamellae pinch off completely during the continual growth of the outer segment so as to form flattened sacs, or *disks* (Fig. 7-47,A), which are stacked like hollow pancakes or pita bread on top of one another within the outer segment. The stack of disks is completely contained within the surface membrane of the visual cell. The *inside* surface of the membrane composing each sac corresponds to the *outside* surface of the cell membrane, because the disk is formed as an invagination of the outer membrane. The photopigment molecules have been shown to be intimately associated with these membranes. Because the disks of the rod outer segment are the sites of light absorption, they must be responsible for the primary steps in photochemical transduction.

In vertebrate rods and cones, light produces a *hyperpolarizing* receptor potential (Fig. 7-48) instead of a depolarization as seen in the photoreceptor of *Limulus*. Membrane-conductance measurements before and during illumination have shown that the effect of light in these cells is to *decrease* the sodium conductance of the receptor membrane. In the dark, the surface membrane of the vertebrate photoreceptor is nearly equally permeable to both Na^+ and K^+. The result is a resting potential about halfway between E_K and E_{Na}. Sodium ions leak into the outer segment and are continually pumped out at the same rate across the membrane of the inner segment (Fig. 7-49,A). When light is absorbed by the photopigment, the sodium conductance of the outer segment decreases, the *dark current* decreases (Fig. 7-49,B), and the membrane potential hyperpolarizes toward E_K (Fig. 7-48,B) according to Equation 5 in Box 6-3. When the light ceases, the sodium conductance of the membrane increases to its high resting value and the membrane potential settles back to the resting level between E_{Na} and E_K.

How does illumination produce a *decrease* in Na conductance? The implications of this question become evident when it is recalled that the absorption of a single quantum of light by a single photopigment molecule produces a change in electrical activity. Because the resting membrane has a high sodium permeability, it is highly unlikely that the conductance could be altered significantly if the photochemical reaction of one photopigment molecule closes only one Na channel. The effect of one photon must be amplified in some way so as to close many Na channels and thereby produce a decrease in the dark current during illumination. It has been proposed by Hagins and Yoshikami (1974) that the photochemical alteration of a photopigment molecule in the membrane of a disk opens a calcium channel in that membrane (Fig. 7-50,B). Calcium ions stored at a high concen-

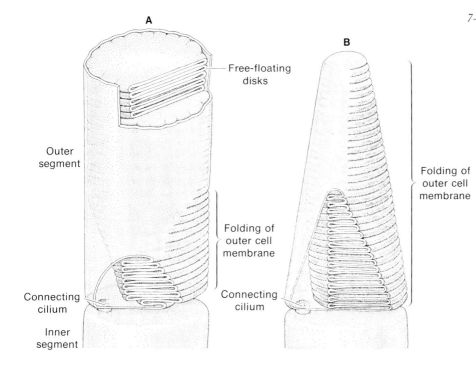

A

Free-floating disks

Outer segment

Folding of outer cell membrane

Connecting cilium

Inner segment

B

Folding of outer cell membrane

Connecting cilium

7–47. *Formation of the receptor membranes in a rod (A) and cone (B) of the frog retina. The rod lamellar sacs become detached after folding in from the surface membrane at the base of the outer segment. The surface membrane of a cone remains intact after folding in.* [*After "Visual Cells" by R. W. Young. Copyright* © *1970 by Scientific American, Inc. All rights reserved.*]

INVERTEBRATE   VERTEBRATE

E_{Na}

Membrane potential

0

Rest

Rest

E_K

Time

Increased g_{Na} Decreased g_{Na}

Light on   Light on

7–48. *Electrical responses to light by invertebrate and vertebrate visual cells. Most invertebrate photoreceptors undergo an* increase *in Na (and perhaps Ca) conductance in response to light. The membrane potential shifts toward* E_{Na}, *producing a depolarization. Vertebrate photoreceptors respond with a* decrease *in Na conductance. This causes a shift away from* E_{Na} *toward* E_K, *producing a hyperpolarization.* [*After Toyoda et al., 1969.*]

tration inside the disk then leak out into the cytoplasm of the rod outer segment and diffuse to the surface membrane of the rod, blocking the sodium channels through which the Na current flows in the dark. Because many calcium ions can flow through a single photon-activated calcium channel, and each calcium ion can block the inflow through a Na channel of many sodium ions, this mechanism could account for the large power amplification exhibited by the photoreceptor cell. This hypothesis is supported by experi-ments showing that the local application of Ca^{2+} or of certain drugs (theophylline, caffeine) that release internal stores of Ca^{2+} mimics the effect of light in hyperpolarizing the photoreceptor cell.

If this hypothesis is correct, the function of the membrane-limited flattened sacs (disks) of the outer segment is similar to that of the Ca-sequestering sarcoplasmic reticulum, which releases Ca^{2+} into the myoplasm of the striated muscle cell to activate the contractile mechanism. In some vertebrate cones, the

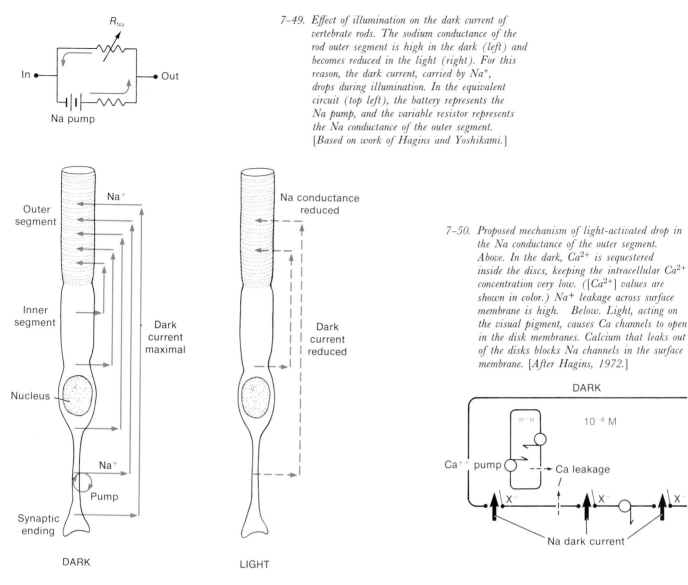

7–49. *Effect of illumination on the dark current of vertebrate rods. The sodium conductance of the rod outer segment is high in the dark (left) and becomes reduced in the light (right). For this reason, the dark current, carried by Na+, drops during illumination. In the equivalent circuit (top left), the battery represents the Na pump, and the variable resistor represents the Na conductance of the outer segment. [Based on work of Hagins and Yoshikami.]*

7–50. *Proposed mechanism of light-activated drop in the Na conductance of the outer segment. Above. In the dark, Ca²⁺ is sequestered inside the discs, keeping the intracellular Ca²⁺ concentration very low. ([Ca²⁺] values are shown in color.) Na⁺ leakage across surface membrane is high. Below. Light, acting on the visual pigment, causes Ca channels to open in the disk membranes. Calcium that leaks out of the disks blocks Na channels in the surface membrane. [After Hagins, 1972.]*

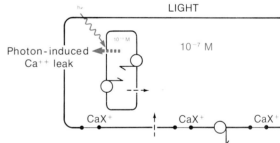

photosensitive membranes remain continuous with the surface membranes, so that the interior of each disk is continuous with the extracellular space (Fig. 7-47). Calcium ion enters the cytoplasm of such cones through the invaginated membranes from the cell exterior, where the calcium concentration is high relative to the cell interior. Calcium is continually pumped out of the cytoplasm into the disks of rods and into the extracellular spaces of cones. This maintains a low cytoplasmic calcium concentration, so that in the dark

the sodium channels are open and Na⁺ carries a strong dark current (Fig. 7-50,A). In the next chapter, we see that illumination of a vertebrate visual-receptor cell produces a hyperpolarization of the bipolar cell that it innervates. This appears to be caused by a reduction, during the hyperpolarization of the visual-receptor cell, of the rate at which excitatory transmitter is released; the transmitter is constantly emitted from the receptor cell in the dark.

Visual Pigments

The spectrum of electromagnetic radiation extends from gamma rays, with wavelengths as short as 10^{-12} cm, to radio waves, with wavelengths greater than 10^6 cm (Fig. 7-51). The portion of the electromagnetic spectrum between 10^{-8} cm and 10^{-2} cm is termed *light*. Only a small portion of this segment of the spectrum is visible to us, ranging from about 400 to about 740 nm. Below this range is the ultraviolet (UV) portion of the spectrum and above it the infrared, neither of which is visible to humans. There is nothing qualitatively special about those portions of the spectrum that renders them invisible to us. What we see depends on which wavelengths, upon reaching the visual cells, are absorbed by *visual pigments*. For example, persons who have had their lenses (which absorb UV) removed because of cataracts can see into the ultraviolet range, which is invisible to the normal eye. The compound eyes of insects can see into the ultraviolet, and thus some flowers with patterns of UV-reflecting pigments will not look the same to insects as they do to mammals.

The energy in a quantum of radiation is equal to Planck's constant divided by the wavelength (in cm):

$$E = \frac{2.854}{\lambda} \text{ g-cal/mole.}$$

Thus the energy in a quantum increases as the wavelength of radiation decreases. Quanta with wavelengths below 1 nm have so much energy that they break bonds and atomic nuclei. Quanta with wavelengths greater than 1000 nm lack sufficient energy to affect molecular structure. The pigments evolved by living organisms for capturing the sun's radiant energy were selected for their maximal absorption between these limits. When a quantum of radiation is absorbed by a photopigment molecule, it raises the energy state of the molecule by increasing the orbital diameter of the electrons associated with a conjugated double bond. This is the basis of the photosynthetic conversion of radiant energy into chemical energy in plants; it is also the basis of visual excitation in animals. It is interesting that all known organic pigments owe their photochemical properties to the presence of a carbon chain or ring having alternating single and double bonds.

PHOTOCHEMISTRY OF VISUAL PIGMENTS

The concept that a pigment is essential for the process of photoreception originated with Draper, who concluded in 1872 that, in order to be detected, light must be absorbed by molecules in the receptor system. Boll found in 1877 that the characteristic reddish-purple color of the frog's retina fades (*bleaches*) with exposure to light. The light-sensitive substance *rhodopsin*, respon-

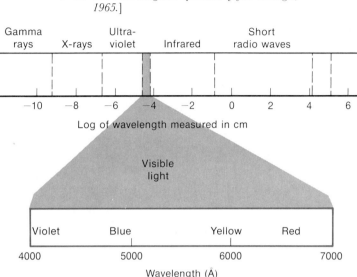

7-51. The electromagnetic spectrum. [After Lehniger, 1965.]

sible for the color, was extracted in 1878 by Kühne, who also found that once the pigment is bleached by light, its reddish-purple color can be restored by keeping the retina in the dark, provided that the receptor cells remain in contact with the pigment epithelium at the back of the eye.

Rhodopsin has since been shown to absorb light maximally at wavelengths of about 500 nm. It is found in the outer segments of rods in many vertebrate species and in the photoreceptors of many invertebrates. Rhodopsin molecules are present in the receptor membranes in high density—5×10^{12} molecules per cm^2, which is equivalent to an intermolecular spacing in the membrane of about 50 Å.

All visual pigments that have been studied consist of two major components: one, a lipoprotein moiety called an *opsin;* the other, a prosthetic group consisting in all instances of either *retinal* (Fig. 7-52; retinal is the aldehyde of the carotenoid vitamin A_1, which is the alcohol retinol) or *3-dehydroretinal* (the aldehyde of vitamin A_2, the alcohol 3-dehydroretinol). To be more specific, a visual pigment molecule is made up of (1) the prosthetic group, (2) a protein moiety to which is attached (3) a six-sugar polysaccharide chain and (4) a variable number (30 or more) of phospholipid molecules. The lipoprotein opsin (which includes 2 through 4 in the preceding list) appears to be part of the mosaic structure of the visual receptor membrane; the carotenoid prosthetic group exchanges between the visual receptor membrane and the pigment epithelium at the back of the retina during bleaching and regeneration of the visual pigment. The pigment in the

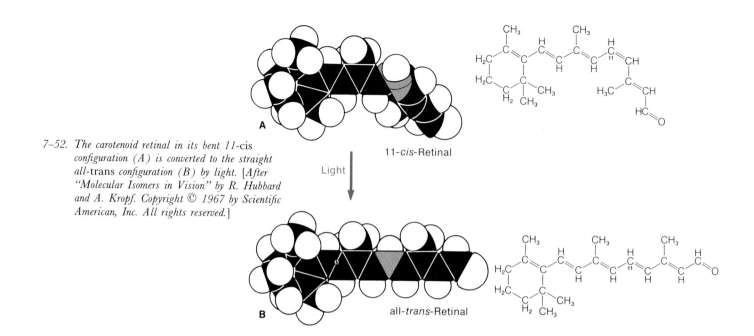

7–52. The carotenoid retinal in its bent 11-cis configuration (A) is converted to the straight all-trans configuration (B) by light. [After "Molecular Isomers in Vision" by R. Hubbard and A. Kropf. Copyright © 1967 by Scientific American, Inc. All rights reserved.]

7–53. Hypothetical mechanism by which isomerization of retinal might alter the conformation of the opsin. A. In this scheme, the 11-cis isomer fits snugly into the protein molecule before photochemical isomerization. B. Upon reacting with light, the retinal is converted to the all-trans form and, in straightening out, permits a relaxation of a part of the opsin.

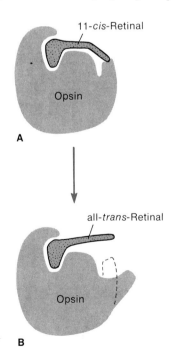

epithelium is photochemically inactive and unrelated to the visual pigment. It keeps light from scattering and reflecting diffusely back toward the retina.

The effect of light on rhodopsin, representative of the effect of light on all the visual pigments, can be summarized as

$$rhodopsin \underset{dark}{\overset{light}{\rightleftharpoons}} retinal + opsin.$$
$$\searrow$$
$$retinol$$

In the absence of light, the opsin and the retinal are closely associated, with the retinal in the 11-cis configuration (Fig. 7-52,A). It is believed that the retinal fits snugly into a special site on the opsin (Fig. 7-53). The absorption of a quantum of light isomerizes the 11-cis retinal into the all-trans configuration, forming lumirhodopsin (Fig. 7-54). The cis–trans isomerization is the only action of light on the visual pigment, and this initial step (the conversion of 11-cis retinal to all-trans retinal) is the only reaction in the sequence that does not proceed spontaneously. All the subsequent steps are energy-yielding reactions, and all proceed spontaneously at physiological (body) temperatures. The conversion from 11-cis to all-trans straightens out the conjugated chain of the retinal. As a result, the opsin undergoes a change in molecular conformation, because the all-trans retinal no longer fits into the special site on the opsin (Fig. 7-52,B). It is the conformational change in the opsin that presumably results in the opening in the membrane of a conductance channel, of which the opsin is believed to be a part. In this context, it is interesting that vertebrate visual pigment behaves in gel-filtration analysis as if it has undergone a 36% increase in volume upon becoming bleached by

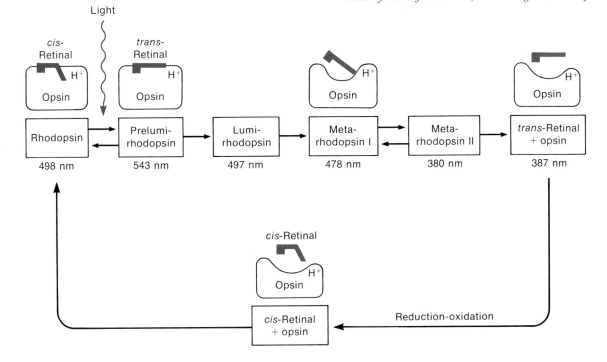

7-54. *The visual pigment cycle. A sequence of reactions beginning with photochemical isomerization of retinal leads to the dissociation of rhodopsin into retinol and the opsin. See text for details. [After "How Light Interacts with Living Matter" by S. B. Hendricks. Copyright © 1968 by Scientific American, Inc. All rights reserved.]*

exposure to light. It has therefore been suggested that the retinal group "locks" the opsin into a compact conformation (Fig. 7-53,A), which is altered to a less compact form when the retinal undergoes isomerization from the *cis* to the *trans* conformation by the action of light (Fig. 7-53,B).

Subsequent chemical permutations of the retinal (Fig. 7-54) are irrelevant to the excitation of the visual receptor cell, but are necessary for the regeneration of rhodopsin. *Metarhodopsin* is hydrolyzed spontaneously to retinal and opsin. The all-*trans* retinal is then re-isomerized to the 11-*cis* retinal. This requires the action of an enzyme and consumes chemical energy. The newly reformed 11-*cis* retinal then combines spontaneously with the opsin to form rhodopsin. Retinal and the opsin are both reused in repeated cycles of bleaching and reconstitution. Any retinal that is lost or chemically degraded is replenished from vitamin A_1 (retinol) stored in the cells of the pigment epithelium, which actively take up the vitamin from the blood. A nutritional deficiency of vitamin A_1 is reflected in a decrease in the amount of retinal that is synthesized, and hence a decrease in the amount of rhodopsin. The result is a decrease in photosensitivity of the eye, commonly known as "night blindness."

Any opsin can combine either with 11-*cis* retinal or with 11-*cis* 3-dehydroretinal to form a visual pig-

ment molecule. For a given pigment, the *absorption spectrum* depends on the electronic substructure of the *chromophore*, the photon-absorbing portion of the pigment molecule, consisting of the carotenoid prosthetic group and closely associated portions of the opsin.

Retinal acts as the prosthetic group for three cone pigments in humans, in addition to the rod pigment, rhodopsin. Each of the cone pigments has a different absorption spectrum and is important in color vision, as described in the following subsection. The other carotenoid found in visual cells, 3-dehydroretinal—which differs from retinal by a single double bond in its ring structure—occurs in the *porphyropsins*, a class of pigments found in rods, and in other visual pigments present in cones.

The distribution of the rhodopsins, as compared with the porphyropsins, shows an interesting ecological trend. In land vertebrates, the visual receptor cells are supplied by the pigment epithelium with retinol only, and thus the visual pigments of land vertebrates are all rhodopsins. Rhodopsins are also found in invertebrates such as *Limulus*, insects, and crustaceans. Porphyropsins are most common in freshwater and euryhaline fishes and in some amphibians. An interesting case is that of the grass frog, in which the tadpole at first has only porphyropsins, while the adult has only rhodopsins. During the course of metamorphosis, dehydroretinol supplied in the bloodstream is gradually replaced by retinol. Fishes that migrate from fresh water to salt water similarly change from porphyropsin to rhodopsin in anticipation of the marine environment. There is a correlation between the presence of visual pigments with higher red-sensitivity (e.g., porphyropsins) and longer-wavelength light in the environment. Thus it is suspected that the adaptive significance of the changeover from porphyropsin to rhodopsin during seaward migration of euryhaline fishes lies in the greater absorbance of rhodopsin for shorter wavelength (blue) light, which is prevalent at ocean depths.

COLOR VISION

In 1666, Newton demonstrated that white light can be separated into a number of colors by passing it through a prism. Each *spectral color* is monochromatic—that is, it cannot be separated into other colors. It was already known, however, that a painter could match any spectral color (e.g., orange) by mixing two pure pigments (e.g., red and yellow), each reflecting a wavelength different from that of the spectral color. Thus there seemed to be a paradox between Newton's demonstration that there are an infinite number of colors and the growing awareness of Renaissance painters that all colors can be produced by combinations of three primary pigments—red, yellow, and blue. This paradox was resolved by the suggestion of Thomas Young in 1801 that the receptors in the eye are selective for the three *primary colors*: red, yellow, and blue. Young was able in this way to reconcile the infinite variety of spectral colors that can be duplicated with the limited

number of painter's pigments by proposing that each class of color receptor is excited to a greater or lesser degree by any wavelength of light, so that the "red" and "yellow" receptors would be stimulated, respectively, by separate monochromatic "red" and "yellow" wavelengths or that both would be stimulated to a lesser degree by monochromatic orange light. In other words, the sensation for "orange" is the result of the simultaneous excitation of "red" receptors and "yellow" receptors.

Young's *trichromacy theory* was supported by the extensive psychophysical investigations of Maxwell and Helmholtz in the nineteenth century, and those of Rushton in more recent years, but the direct evidence for three classes of color receptors had to wait until 1964, when Marks made the first spectrophotometric (color-absorption) measurements on single cones of the goldfish retina (Fig. 7-55). He found three classes of cones, each with a different maximum absorption wavelength corresponding to one of three visual pigments. Similar measurements on human and monkey retinas produced the same findings. It is a principle of photochemistry that light made up of different wavelengths energizes photochemical reactions in accord with the proportions of each wavelength absorbed. A photon that is not absorbed has no effect on the pigment molecule. Once absorbed, the photon transfers part of its energy to the molecule. This suggests that a photoreceptor cell will be excited by different wavelengths (as recorded by the *action spectrum*) in proportion to the efficiency with which its pigments absorb those wavelengths (as recorded by the *absorption spectrum*).

The existence of three pigment classes of cones was corroborated by the demonstration that there are three electrophysiological classes with action spectra corresponding to the absorption spectra (Fig. 7-56). Thus we can now state Young's trichromacy theory in terms of cone pigments. There are three classes of cones, each of which contains a visual pigment that is maximally sensitive to either red, blue, or green light. The electrical output of each class depends on the number of quanta that excite the photopigment. The sensation of color apparently arises from the proportions of neural output from the three classes of cones. According to this concept, excitation of the blue-absorbing cones alone will give the sensation of "blue," but in combination with red-absorbing cones they will give the sensation of "purple."

What about the rods? In humans, and probably in other primates, color vision is mediated entirely by the cones. In the human retina, the rods are found entirely outside the fovea and are important primarily for vision at low light levels because they show greater convergence (Fig. 8-11) in their neural connections and thus produce greater summation of weak stimuli than do the cones. For this reason, we see only shades of

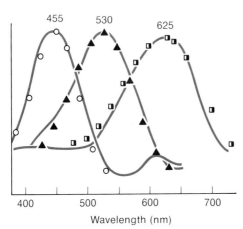

7–55. Microspectrophotometric measurements on the cones reveals three classes of absorption spectra, each representing a different pigment with a different absorption maximum. [After Marks, 1965.]

BOX 7-2 THE ELECTRORETINOGRAM

It is sometimes useful to record the summed electrical activity of the eye, for this is much easier than recording from single cells with microelectrodes. The recording electrode (generally a saline wick) is placed on the cornea, and the indifferent electrode is attached to another part of the body. When a light is flashed on the eye, a complex waveform is recorded (see part A of figure). This *electroretinogram (ERG)* results from the summed activity of the visual cells and the neurons in the retina (Fig. 8-20). After years of debate about the structural correlates of the various components of the ERG, it is now evident that the *a* wave is due to the receptor current produced by the visual receptor cells. This is followed by the *b* wave, which is produced by electrical activity of the retinal neurons that innervate the receptor cells. The *c* wave is found only in vertebrates, and appears to be produced by the nonretinal pigmented epithelial cells against which the outer segments of the visual cells abut. In tadpoles, only the *a* wave is produced before synaptic contacts are established; the *a* wave is produced alone also in adult frog retinas after synaptic transmission is eliminated by means of a blocking agent.

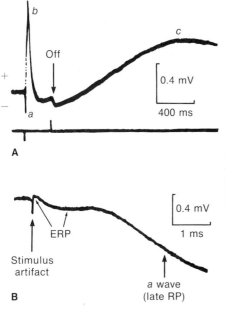

A

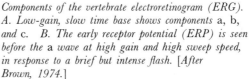

B

Components of the vertebrate electroretinogram (ERG). A. Low-gain, slow time base shows components a, b, and c.   B. The early receptor potential (ERP) is seen before the a wave at high gain and high sweep speed, in response to a brief but intense flash. [After Brown, 1974.]

When the stimulus is a very intense brief flash, another component can be recorded with minimum latency after the onset of the flash, before the ERG develops (see part B of figure). This *early receptor potential (ERP)*, discovered in recent years, differs from the classical ERG in several fundamental respects. It increases linearly in amplitude with flash intensity (rather than logarithmically like the ERG) and saturates when the flash is intense enough to bleach all the visual pigment molecules. Fixation of the retina in gluteraldehyde abolishes the ERG, but leaves the early receptor potential intact. These, plus other lines of evidence, suggest that the early receptor potential represents a charge displacement that accompanies a change in the conformation of the pigment molecules of the receptor membrane. The visual pigment molecules are all aligned similarly so that, upon absorption of light quanta, their minute individual shifts in charge add up to generate the early receptor potential. The ERP is not the electrical event that leads to excitation of the receptor; instead, it occurs concomitantly with the structural change in the visual pigment, which is believed to be an early step in the transduction of light energy into a change in receptor-membrane conductance.

7-56. *The action spectra of three classes of cones in the carp. A to C. Electrical responses of single cones to flashes of different wavelength, as shown by the scale at the top. D. When the responses were plotted, three classes of cones were found, each with an action spectrum approximating one of the absorption spectra in Figure 7-55. [After Tomita et al., 1967.]*

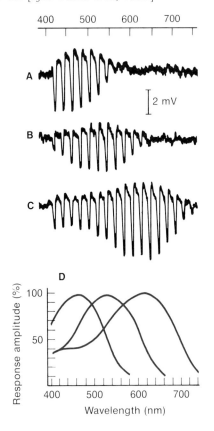

black and grey in very dim light, and we are most sensitive to dim light that falls outside the cone-populated fovea. For example, a dim star appears brighter if its image falls just outside the fovea onto a population of rods than it does if it falls on the fovea.

Color vision has been demonstrated in some fishes, amphibians, reptiles, and birds, all of which have cones. Most mammals are incapable of distinguishing colors, primates being the most notable exceptions. Few generalities can be made about the contribution of rods and cones to color vision in other animal groups. In general, retinas with cones are associated with color vision, but some examples of color classes among rods have been found. For example, frogs have two kinds of rods, red (containing rhodopsin, which absorbs in the blue-green) and green (containing a pigment that absorbs in the blue), in addition to cones. Among the invertebrates, the insects have a well-developed ability to distinguish color.

Optic Mechanisms

Primitive animals possess means of detecting the direction of light sources and changes in intensity; more highly evolved visual systems form images with optic mechanisms. In protozoa and flatworms, the direction of a light source is detected with the help of a screening pigment that casts a shadow on the photoreceptor. Some flagellates, for example, have a light-sensitive organelle near the base of the flagellum, shielded on one side by a pigmented "eye spot." This provides a crude indication of directionality. As the flagellate swims along, it rotates about its longitudinal axis roughly once per second. If it enters a beam of light shining from one side perpendicular to its path of locomotion, the eyespot is shaded each time the shielding pigment passes between the source of the light and the photosensitive part of the base of the flagellum. Each time this happens, the flagellum moves just enough to turn the flagellate slightly toward the side bearing the shielding pigment. Because this is in the same direction as the source of light, the flagellate turns by increments in the direction of the light source. This is an example of *positive phototaxis*. One group of dinoflagellate protozoans even has a subcellular lens-like organelle positioned to concentrate light on a "pigment cup." Although this organelle is capable of forming crude images, it seems unlikely that an image is utilized for visual discrimination by unicellular organisms. Vision also requires that the spatial details of an image formed by a lens be represented in neural activity that is processed by the central nervous system so as to abstract certain features of the optic image (Chapter 8).

The formation of an image requires a lens; but this is not enough. There must be a spatial sampling by the receptor cells of the optical image formed by the lens. In most image-forming eyes, this is done by a myriad of receptor cells arrayed on a retina, so that each individual receptor samples one portion of the image formed by the lens and conveys the temporal pattern of stimulation to the central nervous system. A very interesting and unusual mechanism of spatial sampling occurs in the eye of the copepod crustacean *Copilia*, which has only three receptor cells. A set of muscles moves these photoreceptors back and forth in the image plane to "scan" the image. The great disadvantage of this mechanism of optic sampling is the inability of a scanning system to form an instantaneous neural "image" of the optical image. The neural image produced by the scanning system of *Copilia* must of necessity be extremely coarse.

COMPOUND EYES

The compound eyes of arthropods solve the problem of image formation by having many optic units (the ommatidia) aimed at different parts of the visual field (Fig. 7-57). Each ommatidium samples an angular cone (about 2 to 3°) of the visual field. The visual acuity of such a compound eye is therefore less than that of the vertebrate eye, in which each receptor samples only 0.02° of the visual field. The *mosaic image* projected on the visual cells of an insect compound eye is therefore coarse compared to that of a vertebrate eye (Fig. 7-58).

The detailed structure and optics of compound eyes of different arthropods are varied and complex, and will therefore not be considered in detail here. The ommatidium of *Limulus* (Fig. 7-42) is one of the least complex, and represents one of two variants of the compound eye. In *Limulus* and in some insects, such as bees, the rhabdomeres of the retinular cells are grouped at the center of the ommatidium, and all "see" the same part of the optic field (Fig. 7-59,A).

The other variant of the compound eye is represented in the flies, whose retinular cells are arranged in an open circle, often with one or two retinular cells in the center. In this arrangement, each retinular cell of an ommatidium "sees" a different part of the field, but the retinular cells of neighboring ommatidia channel into the neural network in such a way that the axons of all seven (or so) of those retinular cells, which "see" the same part of the field, converge on the same postsynaptic neurons (Fig. 7-59,B). The convergent wiring of retinular cells receiving the same optic signal serves to maintain spatial coherence in the neural translation of the visual field.

Some insects and crustaceans can orient with respect to the sun even when the sun is blocked from their view. Sunlight is polarized differently over parts of the sky in relation to the position of the sun. It has been found that many arthropods can detect differences in the plane of the electric vector of polarized light entering the eye (Fig. 7-60,A). Measurements of birefringence (the ability of a substance to absorb light polarized in various planes) on retinular cells in the crayfish compound eye show that the absorption of polarized light is maximum when the plane of the electric vector of the light is parallel to the longitudinal axis of microvilli that form the rhabdomere of the retinular cell (Fig. 7-60). The rhabdomeres of the seven retinular cells of each ommatidium interdigitate as shown in Figure 7-60,A, and form two groups. The microvilli of each group are oriented at 90° to those of the other group. Polarized light, with its electric vector parallel to the microvilli of one group of receptor cells, is absorbed about twice as efficiently by that group of retinular cells than by the other group. If we assume that the photopigment molecules are oriented

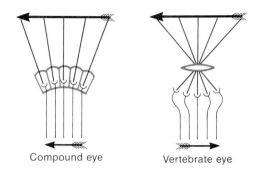

7–57. *Compound and simple eyes. Left. In a compound eye, each ommatidium samples a different point in the field through a separate lens. Right. In the simple eye, each receptor cell samples part of the field through a common lens.* [After Kirschfeld, 1971.]

Compound eye   Vertebrate eye

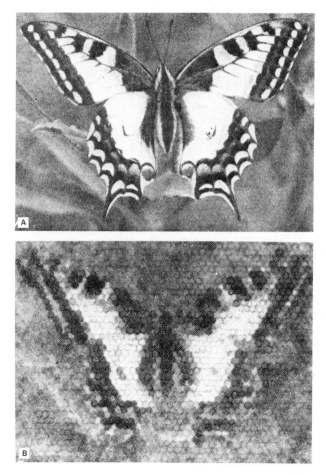

7–58. *Visual acuity of a compound eye. At the top is a photograph of the butterfly* Papilio machaon. *At the bottom is the mosaic image of that picture approximately as it would be perceived by a dragonfly at a distance of 10 cm.* [Mazokhin-Porshnyakov, 1969.]

7-59. A. In one type of compound eye (e.g., that of Limulus), all of the retinular cells of one ommatidium "look at" about the same point in space. B. In another type, one retinular cell in each of seven or eight ommatidia looks at the same point in the visual field. The outputs of these cells, each in a different ommatidium, converge on the same secondary cell. [Part B after Kirschfeld, 1971.]

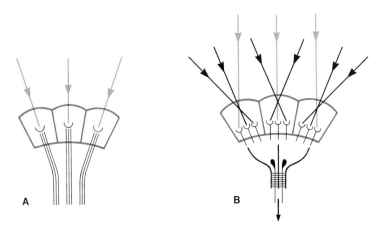

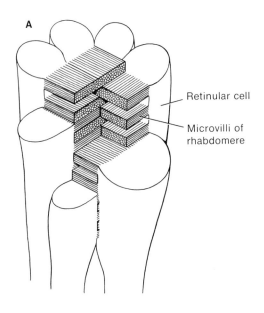

7-60. The polarized-light detector of the crustacean eye. A. The interdigitating rhabdomeres of separate retinular cells give rise to two sets of mutually perpendicular microvilli. [After Horridge, 1968.] B. Electron micrograph of a section of the rhabdome formed by two sets of microvilli, the upper set sectioned parallel to the axes of the microvilli, the lower set sectioned perpendicular to the axis of orientation. Magnification 24,400 ×. [Waterman et al., 1969.]

Retinular cell

Microvilli of rhabdomere

systematically in the microvilli, preferentially absorbing light with its electric vector parallel to the microvilli, this arrangement provides the anatomical basis for the detection of planes of polarized light by arthropods. Electrical recordings from single retinular cells (Fig. 7-61) have shown that the electrical response to a given intensity of light depends on the plane of polarization of the stimulating light, consistent with the preferential absorption of light polarized parallel to the microvilli. Unlike the situation in the ommatidium of the horseshoe crab, Limulus (Fig. 7-42), each retinular cell in the ommatidia of crustaceans and insects independently sends sensory information along its own axon. Thus the relative degree of excitation of the retinular cells whose microvilli are orientated in different directions can be utilized at higher centers in the visual system to analyze the relation between planes of polarized light incident upon the compound eye, and this information can in turn be used by the animal for orientation or navigation.

THE VERTEBRATE EYE

Vertebrate eyes have certain structural features similar to those of a camera (Figs. 7-57 and 7-62). The lens focuses light that enters through the pupil and forms an inverted image on the retina. In a camera, the image is focused on the film by moving the lens along the optic axis. For close objects, the lens must be moved away from the film to keep the image focused. The eyes of certain bony fish also focus by this method. The eyes of higher vertebrates are not equipped to move the lens along the optic axis; instead, the image is focused by changing the shape of the lens, and there-

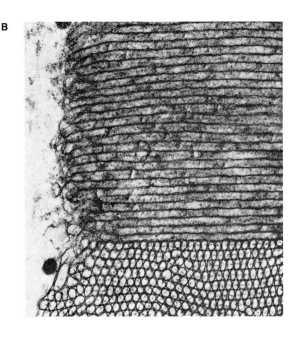

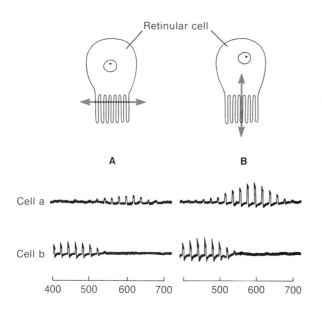

A   B

Cell a

Cell b

400   500   600   700   500   600   700

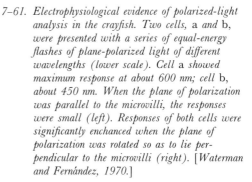

7–61. *Electrophysiological evidence of polarized-light analysis in the crayfish. Two cells,* a *and* b, *were presented with a series of equal-energy flashes of plane-polarized light of different wavelengths (lower scale). Cell* a *showed maximum response at about 600 nm; cell* b, *about 450 nm. When the plane of polarization was parallel to the microvilli, the responses were small (left). Responses of both cells were significantly enchanced when the plane of polarization was rotated so as to lie perpendicular to the microvilli (right).* [*Waterman and Fernández, 1970.*]

by its *focal length.* The lens is suspended from radially oriented fibers of the *zonula.* These connective tissue fibers, which originate in the outer margin of the ciliary body, exert radial tension on the outer rim (equator) of the lens. When the radially oriented muscles of the ciliary body are relaxed, the lens is somewhat flattened by the elastic tension exerted on the equator of the lens by the fibers of the zonula. *Accommodation* to closer objects is accomplished by contraction of the radially oriented smooth muscle fibers of the *ciliary body.* When these contract, the origins of the zonula fibers near the outer edge of the ciliary body are moved toward the lens. This relieves the tension exerted on the equator of the lens by the zonula fibers and allows the lens to bulge more and thereby to shorten its focal length, bringing closer objects into focus. Most of the refraction occurs as light passes from air into the corneal surface, for this is where the light encounters the greatest change in refractive index. However, modifications of the focal length of the lens by contraction of the ciliary body are superimposed on the basic lens effect of the corneal surface to accommodate to objects at different distances. The ability to accommodate decreases with age in humans, hence the need for bifocal eyeglasses.

The most remarkable thing about accommodation is not the mechanism for altering the shape of the lens, but the neural mechanism by which the correct focus of a "selected" image on the retina is reflexly adjusted by nerve impulses to the ciliary muscle. This is related in principle, if not in detail, to the neural mechanisms responsible for *binocular convergence,* in which the left and right eyes are positioned so that the images

formed fall on analogous portions of the two retinas, regardless of the distance and hence the angle formed by the object and the two eyes.

In a camera, the intensity of light admitted to the film is controlled by adjusting the aperture of a mechanical diaphragm through which light is admitted when the shutter opens. The eye has an opaque *iris diaphragm* analogous to the mechanical diaphragm of a camera. In the center of the iris, there is an aperture, the *pupil,* through which light enters the eye. When circular, smooth muscle fibers in the iris contract, the pupillary diameter decreases, and the proportion of light entering the eye is reduced. Contraction of radially oriented muscle fibers causes the pupil to enlarge. The contraction of these muscles, and hence the diameter of the pupil, is controlled by a neural reflex originating in the retina. The *pupillary reflex* can be seen in a dimly lit room in response to sudden illumination of another person's eye with a flashlight.

Changes in pupillary diameter are transient. The pupil gradually returns to its average size after several minutes. Moreover, the area of the pupil can change only about fivefold, which makes it no match for the changes in intensity of illumination normally encountered by the eye; these changes amount to many orders of magnitude. The pupillary reflex can account for only a small component of visual adaptation to differing ambient light levels; it is useful primarily for making rapid adjustments to moderate changes in light intensity. Bleaching and regeneration of visual pigment and neural adaptation are the more effective means by which the eye adapts to extremes of illumination. One consequence of pupillary constriction is

7-62. *The mammalian eye. An inverted image is focused on the retina at the back of the eye. The refraction of light is diagrammatically simplified, for refraction of light at the air-cornea interface has not been shown. The ciliary body is anchored near the limbal zone; when it contracts, tension on the zonula fibers is reduced, allowing the lens to bulge elastically. The visual axis differs from the optic axis because the fovea does not lie precisely in the path of the optic axis.*

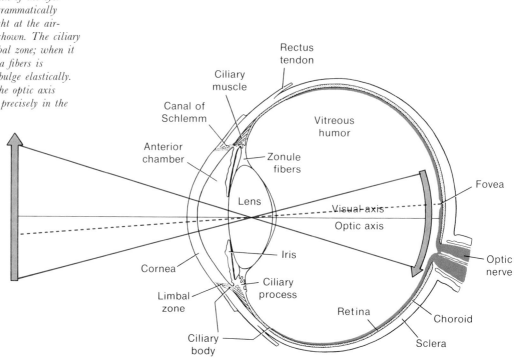

an improved image on the retina, because the edges of the lens, which are optically imperfect and introduce much aberration, are screened off as the pupil becomes smaller. Furthermore, depth of focus increases with decreased pupillary diameter, just as it does in a camera when the aperture is reduced.

The structure and function of the vertebrate retina are included in the discussion of visual information processing in the following chapter.

Summary

Receptor cells are specialized to detect specific modalities (i.e., qualities) of stimulus energy while largely ignoring other modalities. They are also specialized for transduction of the stimulus into an electrical signal, usually (but not always) a depolarization. The transduction process generally exhibits greatest sensitivity in the lower ranges of stimulus strength, producing receptor signals several orders of magnitude stronger than the stimulus energy. In most receptor cells, the primary sites of reception and transduction are in the cell membrane or intracellular membranes, which undergo changes in ionic permeability in response to the stimulus. The receptor potential, in turn, initiates action potentials by electrotonic spread to the impulse-initiating zone of the sensory neuron. Stimulus intensity is typically encoded in the frequency of impulses, which is roughly proportional to the log of the intensity up to a limiting frequency. The log relationship between stimulus and response magnitudes permits reception over a large dynamic range while retaining high sensitivity at low stimulus intensities. The time-dependent loss of sensitivity to a maintained stimulus is termed sensory adaptation. Some receptor cells adapt rapidly, others slowly.

Some receptor cells occur individually, but others are organized into sensory tissues and organs, such as the nasal epithelium or the retina of the eye. The anatomical organization can play an important role in the functioning of the sensory organ. For example, the image formed by the visual system depends on the presence of a lens and a mosaic of many visual receptor cells in the retina.

Chemoreception (taste, smell) is poorly understood. One theory is that it depends on steric specificity—the ability of stimulus molecules to "fit" into protein receptor sites on the receptor-cell membrane. Mechanoreception occurs as a result of distortion or stretching of receptor membrane, producing changes in ion conductances. The deflection of hair cells provides directional information that is utilized by organs of equilibrium and hearing and by the lateral-line system in fish.

The vertebrate cochlea analyzes sound frequencies according to their effectiveness in displacing different portions of the basilar membrane, which bears hair cells. Traveling waves of the basilar membrane, set up by sound-stimulated movements of the eardrum and auditory ossicles, stimulate the hair cells, which in turn modulate their synaptic action on axons of the auditory nerve.

Electroreceptors of fish are modified hair cells that have lost their cilia, but retain a similar high degree of sensitivity. Instead of producing a receptor current with its apical membrane, the electroreceptor responds to exogenous currents channelled across the low-resistance apical membrane.

Visual receptors employ photoexcitable membrane-bound pigment molecules that undergo a conformational change upon absorption of a photon. This produces a change in the conductance of the receptor membrane. All visual pigments consist of one protein molecule (opsin) combined with one carotenoid chromophore moiety, either retinal or dehydroretinal. Differences in the opsin moiety determine the absorption spectrum of the visual pigment. It is the *cis-trans* isomerization of the carotenoid that initiates all visual responses.

Some vertebrates have three types of cones in the fovea, each with a visual pigment maximally sensitive to a different part of the spectrum. The integration of input from each of these cones produces the sensation of color vision. Rods, which are present in greater densities in the periphery of the retina outside the fovea, are more sensitive than cones, and also show much greater synaptic convergence. They contain only one pigment type. As a result, they exhibit low acuity, high sensitivity to shades of grey and white, but no color discrimination.

EXERCISES

1. Visual receptor cells can be stimulated by pressure, heat, and electricity, as well as by light. How is this reconciled with the concept of receptor specificity?

2. Outline the steps from energy absorption in a receptor cell to the initiation of impulses in a sensory neuron innervating the receptor cell.

3. Why must receptor potentials be converted into action potentials?

4. All sensory information enters the central nervous system in the form of action potentials having similar properties. How, then, does the CNS differentiate among various stimulus modalities?

5. How are stimulus intensities that differ by up to ten orders of magnitude all handled by the same receptor cells?

6. What is the typical relationship between stimulus intensity and impulse frequency? What advantage does this offer?

7. Discuss three mechanisms that contribute to sensory adaptation.

8. Discuss an example of central nervous modulation of receptor sensitivity.

9. Chemoreception probably requires the presence of protein receptor molecules on or in receptor membranes. What properties of proteins are probably most important in chemoreception?

10. Von Békésy noted that sound waves produce traveling waves that propagate along the entire length of the basilar membrane. Explain how his theory accounts for frequency discrimination in the cochlea.

11. How does von Békésy's traveling-wave hypothesis of frequency discrimination differ from Helmholtz's resonance hypothesis?

12. How are movements of the basilar membrane converted into auditory nerve impulses?

13. How does spontaneous firing enhance the sensitivity of certain receptor systems—for example, lateral line electroreceptors?

14. How is the presence of an object perceived by electroreceptors of the weak electric fish?

15. What features of receptor-cell behavior help determine the flicker-fusion frequency of the visual system?

16. How does the calcium ion appear to be involved in the visual process of vertebrate visual receptor cells? How is it involved in retinular cell adaptation in *Limulus?*

17. Outline the photochemical steps in the transduction of light energy in visual receptors.

18. What modern evidence substantiates Young's trichromacy theory of color vision?

19. How is polarized light perceived in arthropods?

20. Compare the ways in which mammalian and teleost (bony fishes) lenses are focused.

21. Visible light is restricted to a narrow band between about 350 and 700 nm. Why should vision have evolved to use these wavelengths?

SUGGESTED READING

Burkhardt, D., W. Schleidt, and H. Altner. 1967. *Signals in the Animal World.* McGraw-Hill, New York.

Burtt, E. T. 1974. *The Senses of Animals.* Springer-Verlag, New York.

Cold Spring Harbor Laboratory of Quantitative Biology. 1965. *Sensory Receptors.* [*Symposia on Quantitative Biology,* vol. 30.], New York.

Geldard, F. A. 1972. *The Human Senses.* Wiley, New York.

Kennedy, D. (compiler). 1967. *From Cell to Organism. Readings from Scientific American.* W. H. Freeman and Company, San Francisco. [See Part IV in particular.]

Loewenstein, W. R. 1971. *Handbook of Sensory Physiology: Principles of Receptor Physiology.* Springer-Verlag, New York.

McGough, J. L., N. M. Weinberger, and R. E. Whalen (compilers). 1967. *Psychobiology: The Biological Bases of Behavior. Readings from Scientific American.* W. H. Freeman and Company, San Francisco.

Mellon, D. 1968. *The Physiology of Sense Organs.* W. H. Freeman and Company, San Francisco.

Rushton, W. A. H. 1972. Pigments and signals in colour vision. *J. Physiol.* 220:1–31P.

von Békésy, G. 1960. *Experiments in Hearing.* McGraw-Hill, New York.

REFERENCES CITED

Ammore, J. E., J. W. Johnston, and M. Rubin. 1964. The stereochemical theory of odor. *Scientific American* 210 (2):42–49.

Baylor, D. A., and P. M. O'Bryan. 1971. Electrical signaling in vertebrate photoreceptors. *Fed. Proc.* 30:79–83.

Beck, W. S. 1971. *Human Design.* Harcourt Brace Jovanovich, New York.

Bennett, M. V. L. 1968. Similarities between chemical and electrical mediated transmission. *In* F. D. Carlson (ed.), *Physiological and Biochemical Aspects of Nervous Integration.* Prentice-Hall, Englewood Cliffs, New Jersey.

Bennett, M. V. L., and A. B. Steinbach. 1969. *Neuro-Biology of Cerebellar Evolution and Development.* American Medical Association—Educational and Research Foundation, Chicago.

Boeckh, J., K. E. Kaissling, and D. Schneider. 1965. Insect olfactory receptors. *Cold Spring Harbor Symp. Quant. Biol.* 30:263–280.

Boll, R. 1877. Zur Anatomie und Physiologie der Retina. *Arch. Anat. Physiol.* 4–35.

Brown, K. T. 1968. The electroretinogram: Its components and their origins. *Vision. Res.* 8:633–677.

Brown, K. T. 1974. Physiology of the retina. *In* V. B. Mountcastle (ed.), *Medical Physiology* (13th ed.). C. V. Mosby, St. Louis, Mo.

Brown, K. T., and M. Murakami. 1964a. A new receptor potential of the monkey retina with no detectable latency. *Nature* (London) 201:626–628.

Brown, K. T., and M. Murakami. 1964b. Receptive field organization of S-potentials and receptor potentials in light and dark adapted states. *Fed. Proc.* 23:517.

Bullock, T. H., and F. P. J. Diecke. 1956. Properties of an infrared receptor. *J. Physiol.* 134:47–87.

Davis, H. 1968. Mechanisms of the inner ear. *Ann. Otol. Rhinol. Larynol.* 77:644–655.

Draper, J. W. 1872. On the distribution of chemical force in the spectrum. *Phil. Mag.* 44(ser. 4):422–443.

Eckert, R. O. 1961. Reflex relationships of the abdominal stretch receptors of the crayfish. *J. Cell. Comp. Physiol.* 57:149–162.

Eyzaguirre, C., and S. W. Kuffler. 1955. Processes of excitation in the dendrites and in the soma of single isolated sensory nerve cells of the lobster and crayfish. *J. Gen. Physiol.* 39:87–119.

Flock, A. 1967. Ultrastructure and function in the lateral line organs. *In* P. H. Cahn (ed.), *Lateral Line Detectors*. Indiana Univ. Press, Bloomington.

Frishkopf, L. S. 1969. Distribution and anatomy of lateral line in the tail of the mudpuppy. *J. Acoust. Soc. Amer.* 45:300–301.

Fuortes, M. C. F. 1959. Initiation of impulses in visual cells of *Limulus*. *J. Physiol.* 148:14–28.

Gesteland, R. C. 1966. The mechanics of smell. *Discovery* 27(2). Proprietors, Professional and Industrial Pub. Co., London.

Gordon, M. S. 1972. *Animal Physiology: Principles and Adaptations*. Macmillan, New York.

Hagins, W. A. 1972. The visual process: Excitatory mechanisms in the primary receptor cells. *Ann. Rev. Biophys. Bioeng.* 1:131–158.

Hagins, W. A., and S. Yoshikami. 1974. Proceedings: A role for Ca^{2+} in excitation of retinal rods and cones. *Exp. Eye Res.* 18:299–305.

Harris, G. G., and A. Flock. 1967. Spontaneous and evoked activity from *Xenopus laevis* lateral line. *In* P. H. Cahn (ed.), *Lateral Line Detectors*. Indiana Univ. Press, Bloomington.

Harris, G. G., L. S. Frishkopf, and A. Flock. 1970. Receptor potentials from hair cells of the lateral line. *Science* 167:76–79.

Hartline, H. K. 1934. Intensity and duration in the excitation of single photoreceptor units. *J. Cell. Comp. Physiol.* 5:229–274.

Hendricks, S. B. 1968. How light interacts with living matter. *Scientific American* 219(3):175–186.

Hillman, D. E. 1969. New ultrastructural findings regarding a vestibular ciliary apparatus and its possible functional significance. *Brain Res.* 13:407–412.

Horridge, G. A. 1968. *Interneurons*. W. H. Freeman and Company, San Francisco.

Hubbard, R., and A. Kropf. 1967. Molecular isomers in vision. *Scientific American* 216(6):64–76. [Also available as offprint 1075.]

Kirschfeld, K. 1971. *Verhandlungen der Gesellschaft Deutscher Naturforscher und Ärtze*. Springer-Verlag, Berlin.

Kühne, W. 1878. *On the Photochemistry of the Retina and on Visual Purple*. Ed. with notes by M. Foster. Macmillan, London.

Lehninger, A. L. 1965. *Bioenergetics*. Benjamin, New York.

Lissman, H. W. 1963. Electric location by fishes. *Scientific American* 208(3):50–59. [Also available as offprint 152.]

Loewenstein, W. R. 1960. Biological transducers. *Scientific American* 203(2):98–108.

Loewenstein, W. R. 1971. *Handbook of Sensory Physiology: Principles of Receptor Physiology*. Springer-Verlag, New York.

Marks, W. B. 1965. Visual pigments of single goldfish cones. *J. Physiol.* 178:14–32.

Mazokhin-Porshnyakov, G. A. 1969. *Insect Vision*. Plenum Press, New York.

Miller, W., F. Ratliff, and H. K. Hartline. 1961. How cells receive stimuli. *Scientific American* 205(3):223–238. [Also available as offprint 99.]

Mountcastle, V. B. 1974. Physiology of sensory receptors: Introduction to sensory processes. *In* V. B. Mountcastle (ed.), *Medical Physiology* (Vol. 2), pp. 1345–1371. Mosby, St. Louis, Mo.

Murray, R., and A. Murray. 1970. *Taste and Smell in Vertebrates*. Churchill, London.

Murray, R. W. 1962. Temperature receptors in animals. *Symp. Soc. Exp. Biol.* (16):245:266.

Nakajima, S., and K. Onodera. 1969. Membrane properties of the stretch receptor neurones of crayfish with particular reference to mechanisms of sensory adaptations. *J. Physiol.* 200:161–185.

Schmidt, R. F. 1971. Möglichkeiten und Grenzen der Hautsinne. *Klinische Wochenschrift* 49:530–540.

Steinbrecht, R. A. 1969. Comparative morphology of olfactory receptors. *In* C. Pfaffman, *Olfaction and Taste* (Vol. 3). Rockefeller Univ. Press, New York.

Thurm, U. 1965. An insect mechanoreceptor. *Cold Spring Harbor Symp. Quant. Biol.* 30:75–82.

Tomita, T., A. Kaneko, M. Murakami, and E. L. Pautler. 1967. Spectral response curves of single cones in the carp. *Vision Res.* 7:519–531.

Toyoda, J., H. Nosaki, and T. Tomita. 1969. Light induced resistance changes in single photoreceptors of *Necturus* and *Gekko*. *Vision Res.* 9:453–463.

von Békésy, G. 1955. Human skin perception of traveling waves similar to those of the cochlea. *J. Acoust. Soc. Amer.* 27:830–841.

von Békésy, G. 1960. *Experiments in Hearing*. McGraw-Hill, New York.

von Békésy, G. 1962. The gap between the hearing of external and internal sounds. *Symp. Soc. Exp. Biol.* 16:267–288.

von Békésy, G. 1970. Traveling waves as frequency analyzers in the cochlea. *Nature* 225:1207–1209.

Waterman, T., H. Fernández, and T. Goldsmith. 1969. Dichroism of photosensitive pigment in rhabdoms of the crayfish *Orconectes*. *J. Gen. Physiol.* 54:415–432.

Waterman, T. H., and H. R. Fernández. 1970. E-vector and wavelength discrimination by retinular cells of the crayfish *Procambarus. Z. Vergl. Physiol.* 68:157–174.

Wendler, G. 1964. Laufen und Stehen der Stabheuschrecke *Carausius morosus:* Sinnesborstenfelder in den Beingelenken als Glieder von Regelkreisen. *Z. Vergl. Physiol.* 48:198–250.

Wersäll, J., A. Flock, and P. G. Lundquist. 1965. Structural basis for directional sensitivity in cochlear and vestibular sensory receptors. *Cold Spring Harbor Symp. Quant. Biol.* 30:115–132.

Young, R. W. 1970. Visual cells, *Scientific American* 223(4):89–91. [Also available as offprint 1201.]

Young, T. 1802. On the theory of light and colors. *Phil. Trans. Roy. Soc.* 92:12–48.

CHAPTER EIGHT

Integration and Behavior

There are few features of the natural world that have captured the human imagination more than the behavior of animals. The behavior of the human species is the basis of nearly all literature and all religions, and for the past century it has been the subject of intensive study by behavioral scientists. In spite of this effort, human behavior remains one of the least thoroughly understood areas of biology. Some scientists are of the opinion that an understanding of the nervous system is essential to a solid understanding of human and other animal behavior.

At the most complex levels of behavior, the nervous system must still be viewed as a "black box" that will produce a more or less predictable output, depending on past and present sensory input. To start, however, it is best to examine certain simple components of animal behavior that can be understood in mechanistic terms. It should be noted first that all behavioral acts are ultimately generated by the motor output of the nervous system, which controls the contraction of muscles. The motor output, in turn, is strongly influenced by sensory input. The movements (behavior) of an organism are constantly modified by stimuli

from the environment. Some of these input–output relations are simple and predictable reflexes independent of cerebral control. Other kinds of behavior are highly dependent on information stored from past experience, and therefore are less predictable to an observer. The neurophysiological mechanisms of such complex behavior, involving learning and memory, are very poorly understood, but it is agreed that the physical substratum for complex behavior is the vast array of neural circuitry that lies between the relatively simple afferent sensory pathways and efferent motor pathways. Symbolized by the central box in Figure 8.1, this enormously complex interface between the sensory and motor sides of the nervous system is understood only in the most fragmentary sense.

Some Generalizations

Several generalizations can be made about the organization and function of the nervous system. First, the anatomical substratum consists of highly and specifi-

8–1. *Major functional divisions of the central nervous system. Genetic determination and past experience both contribute to the organization of the central nervous system, which can be crudely divided, as shown, into parts that process sensory input, associative circuits that integrate various inputs and make decisions influenced by past sensory input, and networks that in turn generate appropriate neuromotor output.*

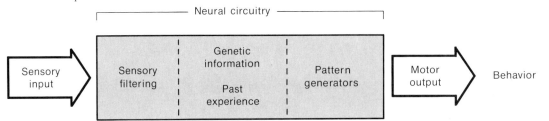

8–2. *Effect of rerouting sensory information. A. The normal reflex of a frog to a noxious stimulus applied to the leg is withdrawal of that leg. B. If the dorsal roots are cut and are allowed to regrow as shown, the frog will exhibit withdrawal of the contralateral leg. The reason for this is that sensory input from the right leg has been channeled to the motor network of the left leg. [After "The Growth of Nerve Circuits" by R. W. Sperry. Copyright © 1959 by Scientific American, Inc. All rights reserved.]*

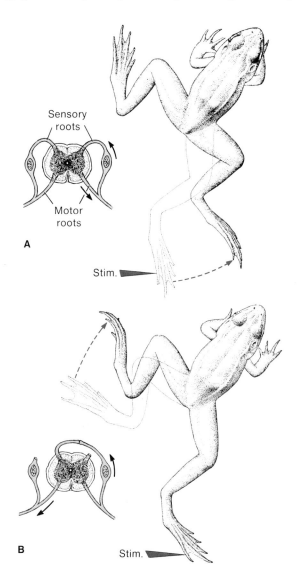

cally organized connections between neurons of the nervous system. These circuits are established during the development of the nervous system; they are subsequently maintained and modified by use during the entire lifetime of the organism. The consequences of experimentally altering neural connections has been demonstrated in the frog by surgically disconnecting and incorrectly reconnecting the sensory fibers entering the spinal cord from one side to the dorsal root of the opposite side. A noxious stimulus to the leg of an unoperated frog causes reflex withdrawal of the leg (Fig. 8-2,A). In the case where the connections were surgically redirected (Fig. 8-2,B), the stimulus evoked an inappropriate movement of the other leg.

The importance of specificity of neural connections was recognized formally a century ago by Johannes Müller when he stated that the modality of a sensation is determined ultimately by the central connections of the nerve fibers activated by a stimulus, rather than by the nature of the stimulus applied to the sense organ. We now use the term *labeled lines* to indicate that the modality of sensory activity in a "line" (i.e., afferent neuron or sequence of neurons) is "labeled" by its central connections. There is widespread agreement that this is the major—perhaps the only—way in which sensory modality is conveyed to the central nervous system. Suggestions that stimulus modality is coded in impulse patterns have received little experimental support.

The various senses are represented centrally by "assigned" regions of the brain (Fig. 6-14). Direct electrical stimulation of any one of those regions evokes the same sensation in the subject's consciousness as would be produced by stimulation of the corresponding sense organ.

The second generalization is that the synaptic and electrical properties of individual neurons determine the way each neuron responds to the sum total of the synaptic signals impinging on it. Each active neuron, by virtue of the connections it makes, influences in turn the activity of other neurons.

The third and most sweeping generalization we can make about the nervous system is that *its complexity and variety of functions are manifestations of the complexity and variety of neural circuits, and not of a large variety of different kinds of signals.* The two basic kinds of signals, (1) propagated, all-or-none (action potentials) and (2) non-propagated, graded (synaptic and receptor potentials), are illustrated in Figure 6-4.

These circuits, or *networks* of neurons, can be grouped into several major categories (Fig. 8-1). One includes the *sensory filter networks,* which pass on only certain features of a complex sensory input while ignoring other features. Their function is to serve as selective filters for certain kinds of information—a function that should not be confused with the energy-filtering properties of receptor cells and their accessory structures.

Another category includes the *pattern generators,* networks whose function is the production of stereotyped movements, such as locomotion and respiration. Such patterning networks pass on more information than they receive. They are able to do so because some of the information they pass on is obtained from the genetic material and is built into the network during its development, and some is obtained ("stored") from past experience. The output of some pattern generators is cyclic—for example, those governing locomotion and respiration. That of others is noncyclic, such as those governing tongue ejection of frogs and toads when catching insects.

Superimposed on these are a more general kind of network, the reflex arc noted earlier (p. 150), in which moment-to-moment changes in sensory input evoke immediate stereotyped motor output. Some reflexes involve the participation of a filter network on the input side and a programmed pattern generator on the output side (Fig. 8-1). An example is the feeding reflex of the frog (p. 248). The simplest reflexes (e.g., the knee jerk) involve neither kind of network.

There was a long-standing question about the generation of locomotor output: To what extent is it dependent on moment-to-moment sensory input, and to what extent does it arise from autonomous motor output of pattern-generating networks independent of sensory input? It will become evident that both play important roles in locomotion.

The way in which groups of neurons are organized (interconnected) determines how networks function. A cyberneticist (student of information theory) would say that these characteristics of the neural network constitute biochemical and structural information (network information) that the network uses to process sensory information in order to produce a motor output. The basic information for the organization of neural networks is carried in the genetic material of the species. In the more advanced groups of animals, however, networks can be modified by experience—that is, by processes of learning (the mechanics of which are still very poorly understood).

Integrative Properties of Single Nerve Cells

Nervous systems continuously process sensory information—discard it, store it as a memory, or use it to generate behavioral reactions. The processing of neural signals is given the general term *integration,* defined as "combining into an integral whole." At the level of a single neuron, this means to react to incoming information from various synaptic inputs so as to produce or fail to produce propagated impulses. Thus each neuron integrates the various excitatory and inhibitory synaptic signals impinging on it as a function of amplitude and sign, point of origin on the neuron, and timing of these signals with respect to one another.

Much of our knowledge about neuronal integration has been obtained from the large α-*motoneurons* (Fig. 8-3), which have their cell bodies in the ventral horn

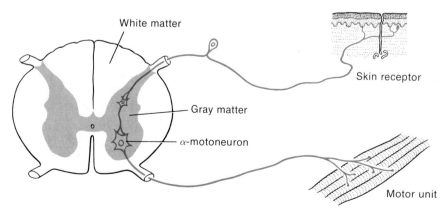

8-3. An α-motoneuron located in the ventral horn of gray matter. It is shown as part of a bisynaptic reflex arc in which a noxious stimulus applied to the skin results in excitation of the motoneuron via the interneuron. Activation of the motoneuron leads to contraction of its motor unit, the group of muscle fibers that it innervates.

White matter

Gray matter

α-motoneuron

Skin receptor

Motor unit

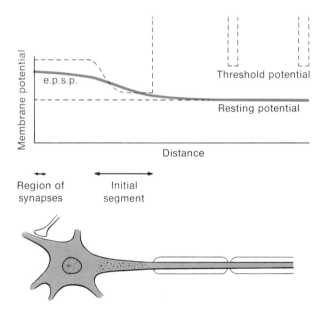

of the vertebrate spinal cord and which innervate groups of skeletal muscle fibers. Each motoneuron receives thousands of inhibitory and excitatory synaptic terminals on its dendrites and cell body. The frequency of firing (impulses per second) of a motoneuron in response to its synaptic input determines the strength of contraction of the muscle fibers it innervates.

SPATIAL SUMMATION

The action potentials generated in a motoneuron arise in the *initial segment* of the axon, which includes the axon hillock. This region has a lower firing level than do the soma and dendrites (Fig. 8-4), and therefore is the site of impulse initiation. Excitatory synaptic current must flow outward across the membrane of the *impulse-initiating zone* in order to depolarize the membrane toward the firing level. All the integrative activity of the motoneuron is centered on the production of action potentials (i.e., excitation) or the suppression of excitation (i.e., inhibition). Because only action potentials can carry information over distances exceeding a few millimeters, only those signals that lead to the production of action potentials can effect the contraction of muscle cells innervated by the motoneuron. Excitatory input that fails to reach threshold, either

by itself or by summation with other inputs, is effectively discarded.

Synaptic currents spread electrotonically from the synapses on dendrites and soma toward the impulse-initiating zone in accord with the cable properties of the neuron (p. 118). As shown in Figure 8-5, postsynaptic potentials become smaller as they spread away from their sites of origin and toward the impulse-initiating zone. A synaptic current set up at the end of a long slender dendrite will experience especially high decrement, and hence will exert a far smaller effect on the impulse-initiating zone than will synaptic current originating on the cell body close to the axon hillock. It is apparent, then, that the cable properties of the cell play a major role in the summation of synaptic currents originating in different parts of the neuron. Inhibitory synapses generally occur with highest density near the axon hillock, where they are most effective in preventing excitatory synaptic current from depolarizing the impulse-initiating zone to the firing level.

The integrative properties of motoneurons can be studied by first exposing several segments of the spinal cord of an anesthetized cat, so that a microelectrode can be lowered into the ventral horn of the gray matter and inserted into a single motoneuron soma. Stimulating electrodes are placed on bundles of afferent axons dissected from the dorsal root so that excitatory or inhibitory axons* can be made to fire as required for the experiment.

In the absence of presynaptic stimulation, the recording electrode inserted into the soma of the motoneuron records randomly occurring synaptic activity. Some of this is due to activity in presynaptic neurons not under the control of the investigator. But some of it results from spontaneous release of transmitter from inactive endings. This effect produces spontaneous *miniature postsynaptic potentials* with amplitudes of about 1 mV analogous to the m.e.p.p.'s recorded at the muscle endplate (Fig. 6-44). Stimulation of a single presynaptic excitatory fiber shows that a single presynaptic ending releases only one to several units of transmitter in response to a presynaptic action potential. In this respect, the excitatory synapses ending on a motoneuron differ from the endplate potential in vertebrate skeletal muscle, in which the motoneuron terminals release about 200–300 units of transmitter and produce an endplate potential of 60 mV or more. The transmitter released from a single synaptic ending on the motoneuron depolarizes the neuron by only about

---

*Whether these axons are excitatory or inhibitory depends on the transmitter substances they release and on the consequent conductance changes in the postsynaptic membrane. The criteria for excitatory and inhibitory synapses are discussed on p. 174.

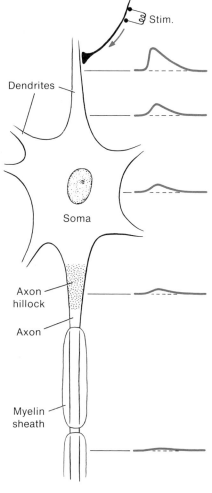

8–5. *Spatial decay of synaptic current in a neuron. The closer a synapse is to the impulse-initiating zone, the more effective the synaptic current will be in influencing the firing of the neuron.*

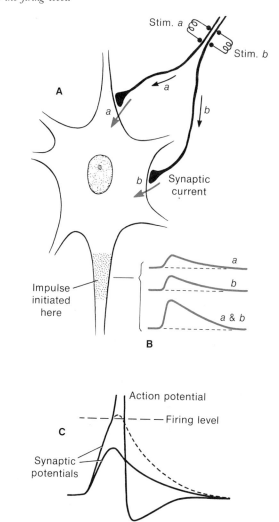

8–6. *Spatial summation in a motoneuron.   A. Two excitatory synaptic potentials, a and b, arising at widely separated synapses give rise to separate synaptic currents.   B. Synaptic potentials due to stimulation of either or both pathways a and b as they might be recorded at the impulse-initiating zone.   C. The summation of currents from many synapses is required to exceed the firing level.*

1 mV—far less than the amount required to shift the membrane potential to the firing level. The small effect of a single ending is very important in the integrative behavior of the neuron, for it means that *many* presynaptic terminals must be activated more or less simultaneously to reach the firing level and initiate a postsynaptic action potential.

As the strength of the stimulus current applied to the presynaptic axons is increased, an increasing number of excitatory axons is recruited. As these fire in unison, the total amount of transmitter released rises accordingly to produce a larger postsynaptic potential (Fig. 8-6,A). The increase in depolarization

occurs because of the additive effect of synaptic currents, and it is termed *spatial summation*. The transmitter released at the excitatory synapse causes a current to flow into the postsynaptic cell through the transmitter-activated channels, depolarizing the cell membrane. When a large enough number of presynaptic excitatory axons fires in unison, the summed e.p.s.p. exceeds the firing level, and a propagated action potential is initiated in the initial segment of the axon near the soma (Fig. 8-6,C). An action potential is suppressed when inhibitory transmitter is released simultaneously with excitatory transmitter (Fig. 8-7). The inhibitory transmitter opens channels

8–7. *Summation of excitatory and inhibitory synaptic*
currents. A. Stimulation of separate presynaptic
pathways gives rise to excitatory, a, *and*
inhibitory, b, *synaptic currents. B. Potentials*
produced by currents as they might be recorded
from the impulse-initiating zone.

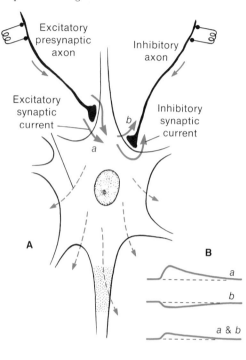

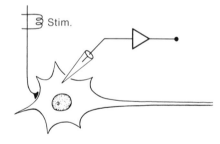

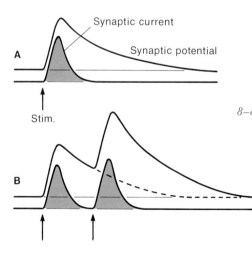

for K^+ and/or Cl^-, in the membrane, through which the inflowing excitatory postsynaptic current can escape out of the cell with minimal depolarization of the impulse-initiating zone.

TEMPORAL SUMMATION

Summation also occurs as a function of time. When a second postsynaptic potential is elicited within a short time after the first, it will "ride upon," or sum with, the first (Fig. 8-8). This effect is called *temporal summation*. The shorter the interval between two successive synaptic potentials, the higher the second rides on the first. Further summation can be achieved by additional stimuli, the third synaptic potential riding on the second, and so on. Under natural conditions, spatial and temporal summation generally occur together. For example, if different excitatory synapses on one motoneuron are active at slightly different times, their effects will sum both spatially and temporally.

Spatial and temporal summation both depend on the passive cable properties of cell membranes. Spatial summation occurs because of electrotonic spread (Fig. 5-10) in the cell. In Figure 8-8,B, it is evident that temporal summation does not require the summation of synaptic currents (i.e., the current that flows through the postsynaptic membrane channels opened in response to the neurotransmitter). The first synaptic current partially discharges the resting potential of the cell membrane. Because of the time constant of the membrane (p. 116), the potential returns to the resting level gradually after the synaptic current has ceased. The duration of the synaptic potential is therefore much longer than the duration of the synaptic current. If a second synaptic current flows before the resting potential is attained, it will cause a second depolarization to add to the falling phase of the first, even though the two synaptic currents do not overlap in time. Thus the time constant of the membrane makes possible the interaction of brief synaptic currents separated in time. The longer the time constant, the more effective the summation of asynchronous synaptic inputs. The time constant is about 10 ms in spinal motoneurons and up to 100 ms in other neurons.

8–8. *Temporal summation. A. A single stimulus*
evokes synaptic current (shaded signal) and more
slowly decaying synaptic potential. B.
Summation of synaptic currents is not required
for summation of synaptic potentials, because the
time course of the potential change exceeds the
time course of the synaptic current. Arrows
indicate time of stimulus to presynaptic axon.

Under normal conditions, the motoneuron is almost never electrically silent, but always exhibits *synaptic noise* (irregular fluctuations in membrane potential) due to a "background" level of activity in the presynaptic neurons. The result is a constantly changing, irregular membrane potential. Sufficient excitatory inputs will sum to trigger an action potential. The result is a constant background of low-level tonus (maintained tension) in a muscle as first one and then another motoneuron fires and causes the contraction of the muscle fibers it innervates. The membrane in the impulse-initiating zone fails to accommodate (p. 127) completely to maintained depolarization. Therefore, a maintained, intense synaptic input to the motoneuron causes it to fire a train of action potentials. The frequency of impulses in such a train rises with increased depolarization. The postsynaptic spike frequency thus reflects the intensity of excitatory synaptic input (Fig. 8-9).

To summarize, the generation of impulses by a neuron requires that depolarization of the low-threshold initial segment reaches the firing level. Beyond that level, the frequency of firing rises as the depolarization increases. The amount of depolarization depends on (1) the number of inhibitory and excitatory presynaptic endings active at any one time to produce spatial summation, (2) the frequency of presynaptic firing to produce temporal summation, and (3) the electrotonic spread of synaptic currents to the impulse-initiating zone from their places of origin in the dendrites and soma of the neuron.

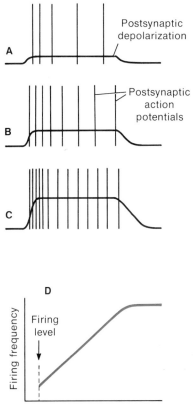

8–9. *At the spike-initiating zone of a motoneuron, the frequency of impulses generated is approximately proportional to the amplitude of a maintained depolarization. A to C. Depolarizing current is injected into the soma with one electrode, and potentials are recorded with another. Increasing depolarization causes an increased rate of firing. D. Steady-state firing frequency plotted against depolarization.*

Basic Neural Circuits

The number of possible combinations with which neurons can form different circuits is enormous. As noted above, a single neuron may receive thousands of presynaptic terminals from other neurons, some of which are excitatory, and others inhibitory. In addition, the neuron may itself branch many times and innervate many other neurons.

Divergence—the repeated branching of a neuron—gives it a widespread influence on many postsynaptic neurons (Fig. 8-10,A). *Convergence* of inputs upon a single neuron (Fig. 8-10,B) allows that unit to integrate signals from numerous presynaptic neurons. Most neurons, such as the spinal motoneuron discussed above, are not depolarized to the firing level without considerable spatial summation of excitatory synaptic input. As a result, those neurons fire only in response to more-or-less simultaneous activity in a number of presynaptic neurons.

Excitation of a neuron will be suppressed if sufficient numbers of its inhibitory synapses are active at the same time as the excitatory synapses. The inhibitory synapses on a neuron can be thought of as a variable gain (amplification) control that modulates the ease with which excitatory inputs can excite a neuron (Fig. 8-11,A). Thus the greater the number of active inhibitory synapses on a neuron, the greater the number of excitatory synapses that must be activated to depolarize the integrating neuron to the firing level. It is interesting, however, that with the appropriate circuitry, the end effect of activity in an inhibitory neuron can be an increase in the discharge frequency of another neuron (Fig. 8-11,B). This simply requires that the inhibitory neuron inhibit another inhibitory neuron, releasing tonic inhibition exerted by the latter on a third neuron.

Feedback is employed extensively in neural circuits. An example of positive feedback is shown in Figure 8-12,A, for a hypothetical reverberating circuit in which some branches of a neuron excite interneurons that feed back upon that neuron to re-excite it

8–10. *A. Divergence is the branching of one neuron so as to innervate several others. B. Convergence refers to the innervation by many cells of a single cell.*

A Divergence

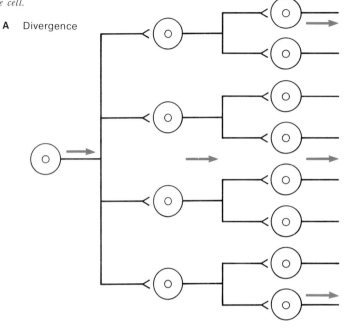

B Convergence

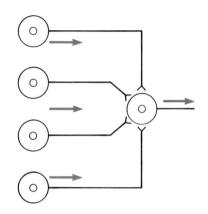

8–11. *Two consequences of activity in an inhibitory interneuron. A. With a single inhibitor in a sequence, the end effect is a reduced probability of firing in the terminal cell. B. If there are two inhibitors in the sequence of interneurons, and if the second one is tonically excited or spontaneously active, excitation of the first inhibitor will, in effect, increase the probability of firing in the terminal cell.*

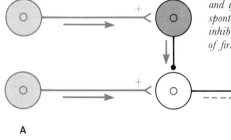

A

8–12. *Two simple circuits in which a branch of a neuron excites an interneuron that feeds back on it. A. If the interneuron is excitatory, the feedback is positive. B. An inhibitory interneuron produces negative feedback.*

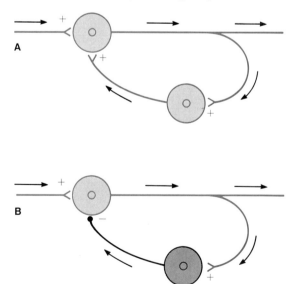

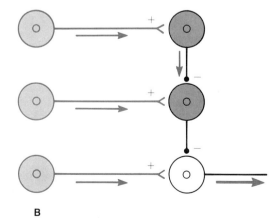

B

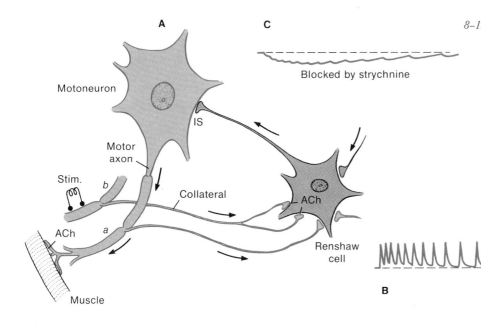

A

Motoneuron

IS

Motor
axon

Stim.

b

Collateral

ACh

a

ACh

Renshaw
cell

Muscle

C

Blocked by strychnine

B

8-13. *Inhibition of α-motoneurons by the Renshaw cells. A. Simplified diagram of motoneuron axons with their collateral axons innervating a group of Renshaw cells (only one is shown). The Renshaw cells make inhibitory endings on the motoneurons. B. Discharge of Renshaw cell in response to antidromically excited discharge in motoneuron b. C. Inhibitory postsynaptic potentials in motoneuron a in response to the Renshaw-cell discharge. These inhibitory potentials are blocked by strychnine. It is not known if the Renshaw cell feeds back on the same motoneurons that innervate it or only on others of the same pool of motoneurons. [After Eccles, 1969.]*

and keep it firing for extended periods. In theory, the neuron could continue to fire indefinitely once excited by synaptic input. If the interneuron in such a circuit is inhibitory instead of excitatory (Fig. 8-12,B), the result is negative feedback, which reduces any tendency for the neuron to fire repetitively. A well-known instance of inhibitory (negative) feedback occurs in the motoneuron pool of the vertebrate spinal cord. Here each α-motoneuron (the neurons that activate the skeletal muscle fibers) has small branches that innervate short inhibitory interneurons, the *Renshaw cells*. These feed back upon the motoneurons, so that the Renshaw cell is excited each time the motoneuron fires. The Renshaw cell responds with a high-frequency train of impulses (Fig. 8-13,B) that sets up inhibitory postsynaptic potentials in the motoneurons. Although the reason for the existence of this circuit is not entirely clear, we do know that it serves to keep the motor discharge in check. Strychnine interferes with the inhibitory synapses made by the Renshaw cells, and presumably with other inhibitory synapses. This is why the poison produces convulsions, spastic paralysis, and death due to loss of coordination of the respiratory muscles. These gruesome consequences of an inhibitory blocking agent demonstrate the pervading importance of synaptic inhibition in neural function.

Sensory Filter Networks

In the preceding chapter, we examined the processes of stimulus reception by sensory cells; the electrical signals produced by these cells are the first step in the events that give rise to sensory perception. We now consider subsequent steps in sensory processing, using the visual system as a model.

It has become evident that the processing of visual information by the nervous system is based to a large extent on two levels of organization. First, there is the specificity and orderliness of connections in the neural pathway, progressing from receptor cells through several orders of neurons into that portion of the cerebral cortex—the *visual cortex*—assigned to processing visual information. Developmental and electrophysiological studies indicate that individual cells—or at least very small groups of cells—are connected to each other with unambiguous specificity. Second, there is the behavior of the individual neurons arising from their synaptic and integrative mechanisms as described above.

The existence of *sensory filtering* is well documented in the visual system. Unlike a television system, in which there is a point-to-point transfer of light-dark-color information from the photocathode of the TV camera to the phosphor screen of the TV receiver, the visual system selects from the total stimulus input to

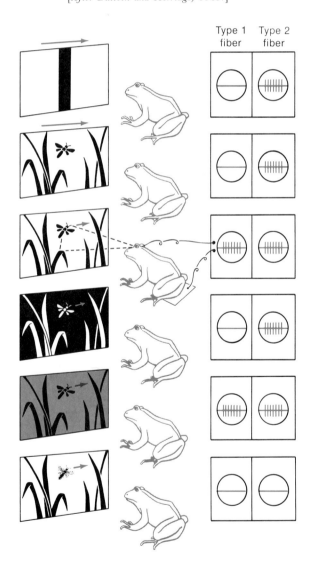

8–14. *Sensory filtering in the retina of the frog. The frog will respond to a small, moving object in the field but not to the movement of a background against the stationary small object or to other nonspecific visual stimuli. His response is seen behaviorally as the ejection of his sticky tongue. Certain fibers (type 1 in the figure) in the optic nerve become active only in response to the sight of a small, dark, sharply outlined object moving across a lighter background. Other fibers (type 2) are activated by a wide variety of movement in the field.* [*After Bullock and Horridge, 1965.*]

Type 1 fiber   Type 2 fiber

the eye certain features while largely ignoring the rest. Thus an individual cell in the visual cortex does not respond to the mere presence or absence of light impinging on a corresponding visual receptor cell, but reacts specifically to certain parameters of the visual input to numerous receptor cells. Each cell abstracts certain features of the image falling on the retina, such as straight borders or lines, their orientation, or their direction of movement.

A classic example of sensory filtering is shown in Figure 8-14. Recordings from the optic nerve of a frog show that nerve cells respond to certain features of the visual field. Some are more specific in this regard than others. One kind of fiber fires in response to a small object, such as a fly, moving against a light background containing stationary objects. It does not respond if the entire scene moves, or if the light is turned on or off. Because frogs catch flying insects, this class of visual neurons presumably tells the frog's brain that supper is on the wing, a bit of information undoubtedly more significant to the frog than most of the other details in the visual scene. Anyone who tries to maintain frogs in captivity soon learns that a frog does not recognize a dead insect as food. Apparently, to the frog, a dead fly does not appear at all similar to a moving fly. We next consider some neural mechanisms responsible for such sensory filtering.

LATERAL INHIBITION

Perhaps the simplest kinds of filtering that occur in sensory systems are those that enhance contrast. Differences in stimulus energy or quality, either in time or in space, are generally more significant as visual cues than the absolute energies or qualities of light from an image. The spatial enhancement of visual contrast can be seen in the abruptly stepped bands of Figure 8-15. These give the appearance of increasing luminosity (brightness) toward that side of each band bordering a darker band. Conversely, each band looks darker on the side bordering its lighter neighbor. This effect is an illusion, for the actual luminosity is uniform across the width of each band. (Use a pair of identical sheets of paper to mask out neighboring bands to convince yourself that this is so.)

How does the visual system enhance edge contrast so as to produce such an illusion? Our first understanding came from the compound eye of *Limulus* (p. 218). Although the organization of receptors is much simpler in the *Limulus* eye than in the retina of the vertebrate eye, relatively complex interactions do occur among the ommatidia. This was first noted in the laboratory of H. K. Hartline at Rockefeller University in the mid-1950's. A room light was turned on while the activity of a single ommatidium was being recorded in response to a bright stimulus light focused on that

8–15. Enhanced visual contrast. Each band is actually uniform, but appears to be lighter near its dark neighbor and darker near its light neighbor. The edge-to-edge uniformity of the luminosity can be demonstrated by covering the neighbors to either side of a band.

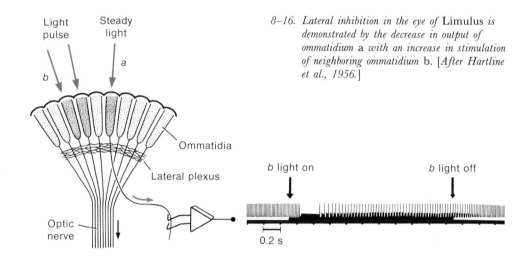

8–16. Lateral inhibition in the eye of Limulus is demonstrated by the decrease in output of ommatidium a with an increase in stimulation of neighboring ommatidium b. [After Hartline et al., 1956.]

ommatidium alone. The additional stimulus from the room light, rather than producing an increase in the frequency of discharge, caused the frequency in that unit to drop. It was subsequently demonstrated that excitation of the surrounding units by the diffuse light is what caused an inhibition (reduced frequency of firing) in the test ommatidium. This phenomenon, which was termed *lateral inhibition*, has since been observed in other visual systems as well as in some other sensory systems.

Evidence of the interaction of receptors in the eye of *Limulus* is illustrated in Figure 8-16; the steady discharge of ommatidium *A* is inhibited during the illumination of ommatidium group *B*. The inhibitory effects are, of course, reciprocal between interacting units, and they fall off with the distance between interacting ommatidia. Lateral inhibition in the *Limulus* eye is mediated through the so-called *lateral plexus,* which consists of collaterals from the eccentric cell axons, which form inhibitory synapses on one another. Lateral inhibition is illustrated in greatly simplified form in Figure 8-17. Because the inhibition exerted by a unit

8–17. Connections in the retina of Limulus responsible for lateral inhibition. Each eccentric cell axon gives off branches that make inhibitory synapses on the neighboring axons. These connections become fewer with distance away from each axon, hence the interaction becomes weaker between more distant neighbors.

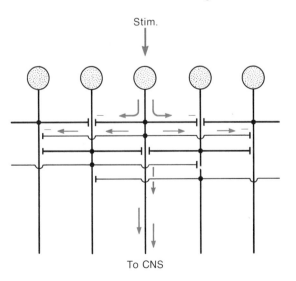

8-18. Accentuation of contrast at a border between dark and light. A light-dark border is moved across the compound eye (B) while the output of a single ommatidium is recorded (A). If all other ommatidia are masked, the output of the ommatidium will change in an abrupt, step-like manner (upper plot in A). If the light-dark border is allowed to pass over all the ommatidia, the output of the single ommatidium plotted against position of the border will generate a curve similar to the lower plot in A. This results from lateral inhibition, as explained in the text. [After "How Cells Receive Stimuli" by W. H. Miller, F. Ratliff, and H. K. Hartline.]

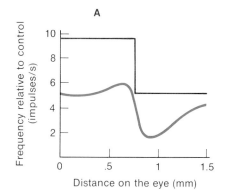

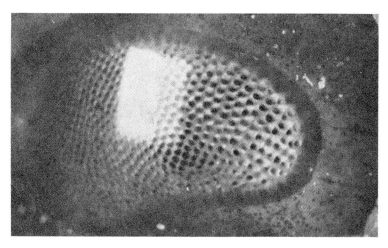

on its neighbors increases as its activity increases, the more strongly a unit is stimulated, the more strongly it will inhibit neighboring less-strongly-stimulated units. The more strongly stimulated unit receives weak inhibition from units stimulated less strongly. This enhances the contrast (increases the difference in response) between units subjected to different intensities of photostimulation (Fig. 8-18). This contrast is greatest for units immediately opposite each other across a bright-dim border. As a shadow slowly passes over a brightly lit compound eye, the impulse frequency recorded from one receptor unit increases as the edge of the shadow approaches that ommatidium. This occurs because the inhibition from nearly half the units neighboring that ommatidium is reduced as they become nearly quiescent in the shadow. Then, as the shadow passes over that ommatidium, its discharge frequency drops abruptly to a low level. At that moment, the unit is subjected not only to a weaker stimulus, but to strong inhibitory influence from nearly half of its neighbors still exposed to the bright light. As the edge progresses further beyond the selected unit, shading the rest of the neighboring ommatidia, inhibitory input to that unit from its neighbors is reduced, and that ommatidium assumes a new, somewhat higher frequency of firing.

Although the impulse-frequency profile in Figure 8-18,A was produced as a function of *time* by moving the edge of a shadow over the field of receptor units, it is obvious that a similar impulse-frequency profile would result as a function of *space.* If it were possible to record and to plot the discharge frequencies of all of the receptors along a straight line perpendicular to the edge of a stationary shadow, the result would be a frequency profile similar to that in Figure 8-18. Thus lateral inhibition serves to sharpen visual edges by increasing contrast at borders between areas of different luminosities, and this is what is experienced by an observer viewing the bands in Figure 8-15.

VISUAL PROCESSING IN THE VERTEBRATE RETINA

The vertebrate retina consists of the visual receptor cells (p. 221) and a network of neurons. These neurons belong to the central nervous system, even though the network is located at the periphery. It is not surprising, therefore, that the rather complex process of visual abstraction begins in the retina before the partially processed visual information is sent along the axons of the optic nerve (which is in fact a tract of the central nervous system) to higher centers of integration, the lateral geniculate bodies and the visual cortex (in birds and mammals) or optic tectum (in lower vertebrates) (Fig. 8-19). The signals in the optic nerve are carried by the axons of the *ganglion cells* located in the retina.

The visual receptor cells make indirect contact with the ganglion cells via the *bipolar cells* (Fig. 8-20). We will consider the receptors as the first-order cells, the bipolars as second-order, and the ganglion cells as third-order in the afferent pathway. This is admittedly oversimplified, because two other types of retinal neurons—the *horizontal cells* and the *amacrine cells*—participate in these connections and are particularly important for lateral interactions in the retina. The horizontals interconnect receptor cells and bipolars, and the amacrines interconnect bipolars and ganglion cells. Recent studies combining intracellular recording techniques with the injection of fluorescent marker dyes have succeeded in correlating electrical activity with each retinal cell type.

As noted in Chapter 7, the visual receptor cells of vertebrates produce hyperpolarizing potential shifts when illuminated, and never produce action potentials. Likewise, the horizontal cells show only graded, nonspiking potential changes, which in some species are always hyperpolarizing (Fig. 8-21). The bipolar cells also fail to produce spike potentials, but produce graded potential changes of both polarities, depending on the location of the stimulus. Thus the name "bipolar" can apply as well to the physiology of this type of cell as it does to the morphological feature that suggested it. The membrane potential of the ganglion cell changes inversely with that of the corresponding bipolar cells. It becomes depolarized and fires action potentials when bipolar cells synapsing on it are hyperpolarized, and it becomes hyperpolarized when its bipolar connections are depolarized. It has been conjectured that the bipolar steadily secretes a hyperpolarizing transmitter, and that its secretion is increased when the bipolar cell is depolarized and reduced when it is hyperpolarized. The amacrine cells show transient "on" and "off" effects in response to input from bipolar cells.

The bipolars generally connect more than one receptor to each ganglion cell, and they may also connect each receptor cell to several ganglion cells. Thus convergence and divergence already occur between first- and third-order cells of the visual system; both are minimal in the *area centralis,* where acuity is greatest and where there is a tendency for 1:1:1 connections between cones, bipolar cells, and ganglion cells. Outside the area centralis, ganglion cells receive input from many receptor cells, primarily rods, conveying on those ganglion cells a greater sensitivity to dim illumination.

Each ganglion cell is active spontaneously in the dark and responds to a spot of light directed at any point inside a more-or-less circular area of the retina (Fig. 8-24). Depending on which receptor cells are

8–19. *Visual pathways in mammal and amphibian. A. In the mammal, each side of the visual field is projected to the opposite side of the visual cortex. B. In the amphibian, the left and right optic tectums each receive projections of the entire field of view of the contralateral eye. [Part A after Noback and Demarest, 1972; part B after "Retinal Processing of Visual Images" by C. R. Michael. Copyright © 1969 by Scientific American, Inc. All rights reserved.]*

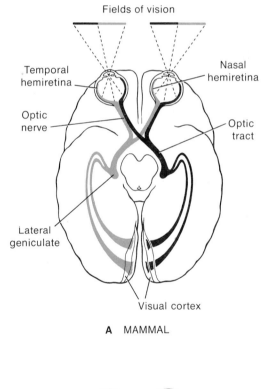

A MAMMAL

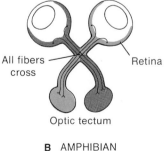

B AMPHIBIAN

8–20. *Cellular organization in the vertebrate retina. The bipolar cells carry signals from the visual receptor cells toward the ganglion cells, which give rise to the axons of the optic nerve. The horizontal and amacrine cells carry signals laterally. [After "Visual Cells" by R. W. Young. Copyright © 1970 by Scientific American, Inc. All rights reserved.]*

8–21. *Electrical responses of the retinal cells to a spot of light (left) and to an annulus (doughnut) of light (right). In this example, the ganglion cell has an "on"-center receptive field. The duration of the light stimulus is indicated in the lower trace on each record. Note that the bipolar and ganglion cells produce responses of opposite polarities to spot and annulus. This is believed to be due to lateral inhibition similar to that in Limulus. [After Werblin and Dowling, 1969.]*

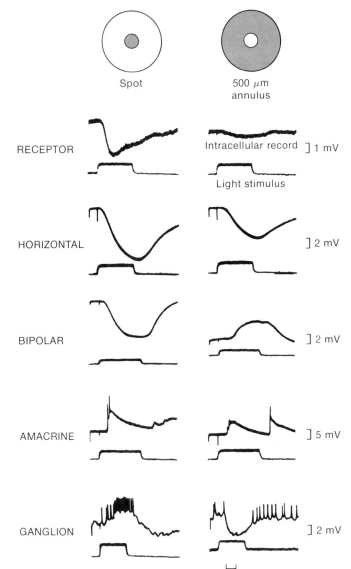

8–22. *The electrical behavior of "on"-center and "off"-center ganglion cells in the mammalian retina. A. An "on"-center cell fires in response to light in the center of its receptive field (upper trace). If the stimulus spot is outside the center, the firing is suppressed (lower trace). B. An "off"-center cell is inhibited by a spot of light in the center of its receptive field (upper trace) and excited by a spot of light falling on the surround (lower trace). [After "The Visual Cortex of the Brain" by D. H. Hubel. Copyright © 1963 by Scientific American, Inc. All rights reserved.]*

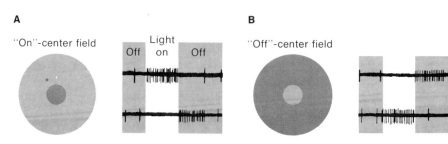

illuminated by a small spot of light, a ganglion cell may give an "on" response (increased rate of firing when stimulus light is turned on) or an "off" response (decreased rate of firing when stimulus light is turned on, and increased rate when stimulus light is turned off). The region of the retina in which illumination causes a response (either increased or decreased rate of firing) in a nerve cell is termed the *receptive field* of that cell. The receptive field of a ganglion cell is approximately centered on the ganglion cell and varies in extent from a few receptors in the center of the area centralis to several thousand receptor cells near the periphery of the retina. Thus the receptive field of a ganglion cell can be up to 2 mm in diameter.

Two *main* types of ganglion cells can be recognized. One type, the *"on"-center* cell, responds to illumination of a small region at the center of its receptive field with an "on" response (Fig. 8-22). Illumination of the receptive field in a concentric band (annulus) peripheral to the "on" region of such a cell causes an "off" response in the cell. This band is termed the *inhibitory surround* of the receptive field. Illumination of the entire receptive field results in a weak response or no response in that ganglion cell. The other type, the *"off"-center* cell, exhibits the converse behavior, ceasing its firing when the center of its receptive field is illuminated and increasing its firing when the surround is illuminated.

Because of the *antagonistic surround* of each receptive field, a small spot of light is more effective than diffuse illumination in affecting activity in the optic nerve. A small spot of light moved about on the retina will cause an increase in frequency of firing of an optic nerve fiber (axon of a ganglion cell) when the spot is in the "on" portion of that cell's receptive field. At the same time, the spot will be in the "off" portions of the receptive fields of other fibers. As the spot is moved about, it will turn fibers "on" or "off" according to its position in their individual receptive fields. Thus whether a spot of light will excite or inhibit a given ganglion cell depends on its position in the receptive field of that cell.

The center-surround organization of receptive fields is, of course, an example of lateral inhibition similar to that which we have already encountered above in the compound eye of *Limulus*. An interesting feature of the organization of the vertebrate retina is the presence of the two kinds of receptive fields characteristic of the "on"-center and "off"-center ganglion cells. How do these receptive fields arise? First, it should be noted that much of the lateral interaction in the retina takes place via the horizontal cells. These cells, which form the *outer plexiform layer* of the retina, have extensive lateral processes and are electrotonically interconnected. Since they make synaptic contact between the receptor cells and distant bipolar cells, they have laterally far-reaching effects on the bipolar cells. A spot of light stimulates

most effectively the local, *direct-line* pathway of receptor $\longrightarrow$ bipolar cell $\longrightarrow$ ganglion cell, and it activates less strongly the lateral, *indirect-line* pathway—namely, receptor $\longrightarrow$ horizontal cells $\longrightarrow$ bipolar cells $\longrightarrow$ ganglion cells. Since the horizontal cells form an extensive network through low-resistance electrical junctions, input from any receptor into a horizontal cell decays with distance in all directions from that receptor. Thus every bipolar cell gets input from surrounding receptor cells via the lateral network of horizontal cells, and this input falls off with lateral distance between stimulated receptors and bipolar cells.

Another key factor in the origin of "on"- and "off"-center receptive fields is the existence of two kinds of bipolar cells, *type A* and *type B* (Fig. 8-23) that exhibit mutually inverse responses to synaptic input from receptors and horizontal cells. Stimulated receptor cells directly hyperpolarize type A and directly depolarize type B bipolar cells. As noted above, all bipolar cells produce opposite-going potential changes in the ganglion cells that they innervate. Thus the ganglion cells innervated by type A bipolars are depolarized by direct-line activation and have "on"-center fields. Those innervated by type B bipolars have "off"-center receptive fields. Activity (i.e., hyperpolarization from receptor input) in the horizontal cells affects the two types of bipolar cells in opposite ways from input originating in the overlying receptor cells (Fig. 26). Thus an "on"-center ganglion cell will be excited by direct receptor input to type A bipolar cells, and be inhibited by receptor input to horizontal cells in response to illumination of the surround. The converse applies to the ganglion cells innervated by type B bipolars. The two opposing sets of responses of type A and type B bipolar cells result from differences in their postsynaptic responses to two different neurotransmitters, one released by the receptor cells and the other released by the horizontal cells.

In summary, then, ganglion cells having "on"-center and "off"-center receptive fields receive input from type A and type B bipolar cells, respectively. In both cases, the visual receptors in the antagonistic surround exert their effects on bipolar cells through the network of electrotonically interconnected horizontal cells. The direct input to the bipolar cells from overlying receptors and the indirect input via the horizontal cell network oppose each other, and thereby produce the contrasting center-surround effects.

The retina teaches us several lessons about neural organization that may well be of widespread importance in the rest of the central nervous system. First, we note that cells can signal each other without all-or-none activity if they are small and do not require impulses for long-distance propagation. This has the advantage of continuously graded analogue-to-analogue transformations more sensitive than those possible with intervening all-or-none activity. Second, excitation does

8–23. *Retinal organization responsible for "on"-and "off"-center receptive fields. Two kinds of bipolar cells,* B_A *and* B_B, *exhibit reciprocal responses to direct input from the receptors,* R, *and indirect visual input carried laterally by the horizontal cells,* H. *Activity leading to ganglion cell* (G) *discharge is indicated by colored shading. Activity that inhibits ganglion cell discharge is shown in gray. Type A bipolars become strongly hyperpolarized during activation of their overlying receptor cells and weakly depolarized in response to lateral input from horizontal cells. Type B bipolars show the converse behavior, becoming strongly depolarized by their receptors and weakly hyperpolarized by horizontal cell activity. The amacrine cells have been omitted for simplicity.* [*Based on Dowling, 1970.*]

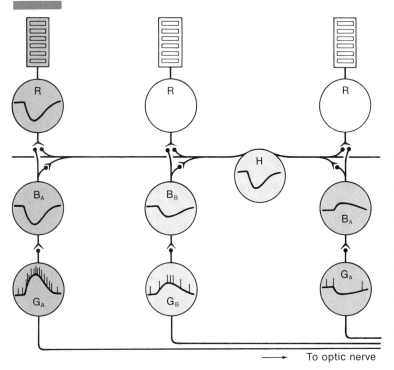

To optic nerve

not necessarily mean depolarization; in some nerve cells (e.g., visual receptors, horizontal and bipolar cells), hyperpolarization is the normal response that leads to synaptic transmission. Third, the postsynaptic response of a neuron cannot be predicted *a priori* from the sign of the presynaptic potential change. Thus, a cell can be depolarized in response to hyperpolarization of its presynaptic cell or vice versa. The postsynaptic response, it will be recalled, depends on the ionic currents produced in the postsynaptic cell in response to the modulated release of transmitter by the presynaptic neuron.

INFORMATION PROCESSING IN THE VISUAL CORTEX

In mammals and birds, the axons of the ganglion cells distribute themselves at the optic chiasm between ipsilateral (same) and contralateral (opposite) sides of the brain, as shown in Figure 8-19,A, whereas in vertebrates more primitive than birds, all optic fibers cross at the chiasm (Fig. 8-19,B). In the *geniculate body* of the thalamus, they synapse with fourth-order cells that go on to innervate fifth-order cortical neurons (simple cells) in Area 17 of the *visual cortex*, located at the rear of the cerebral hemispheres (Fig. 6-13). The receptive fields of the fourth-order cells in the geniculate body somewhat resemble those of the ganglion cells, except that contrast between brightly and dimly lit regions of the retina receives greater emphasis.

Among the most fruitful studies in sensory processing have been those of D. Hubel and T. Wiesel of Harvard University on the visual centers of the brain. While electrodes recorded the activity of individual neurons, a simple illuminated silhouette was projected onto a screen in the visual field of an anesthetized cat, and the responses of the neurons were correlated with the position, shape, and movement of the silhouette on the screen (Fig. 8-24,A).

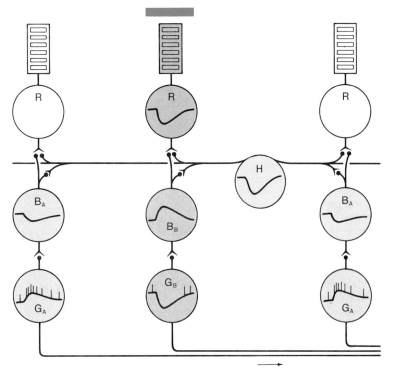

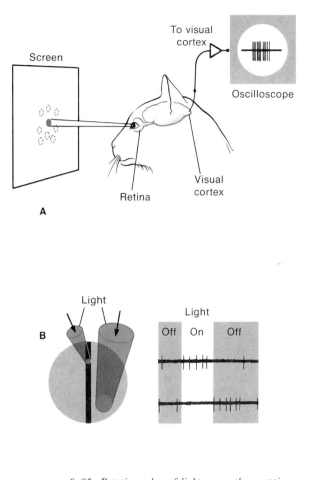

The *simple cells,* along with other neurons of the cortex, are arranged in an orderly array of vertical columns in the cortical tissue. They are believed to be the first way station in the visual cortex, and they have receptive fields very different from those of the retinal ganglion cells and the geniculate cells. Although the receptive fields of these neurons are of several types, they all have one thing in common. The "on" region of the field always makes a straight border with the "off" region, rather than a circular border as in the ganglion and the geniculate cells. In some simple cells, the receptive field has a bar-shaped "on" region surrounded by an "off" region (Fig. 8-24,B). Others have a receptive field consisting of an "off" bar surrounded by an "on" region. Still others have a receptive field consisting of a straight border with an "off" region on one side and an "on" region on the other side. As in ganglion and geniculate cells, the receptive field for a simple cell is in a fixed position on the retina.

The orientation and the location of the "on"–"off" boundary differs from one simple cell to another, so that a bar of light moved horizontally or vertically on the retina activates one simple cell after another as it enters one receptive field after another. Figure 8-25 shows the effect of rotating a bar of light about the center of the "on" area for a given simple cell. The bar has either no effect or an inhibitory effect on spontaneous activity in the simple cell when at right angles to the field, but elicits a maximum discharge when in register with the "on" region of the receptive field (this effect, of course, defines the receptive field). If the bar of light is then displaced so that it falls completely outside the "on" region onto the "off" region, the cell is inhibited.

How do the simple cells come to be specifically sensitive to straight bars or borders of precise orientation and location projected onto the retina? Hubel and Wiesel suggest that each simple cell with a "bar"-type receptive field receives excitatory connections from lateral geniculate cells whose "on" centers are

8–25. *Rotating a bar of light across the receptive field of a cortical simple cell produces a maximum discharge when the bar coincides with the "on" region of the receptive field, and partial excitation depending on the degree of overlap between the bar of light and the "on" region at other orientations.* [After "The Visual Cortex of the Brain" by D. H. Hubel. Copyright © 1963 by Scientific American, Inc. All rights reserved.]

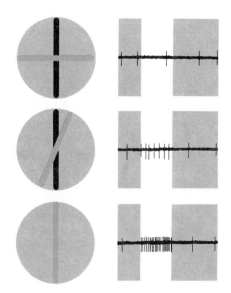

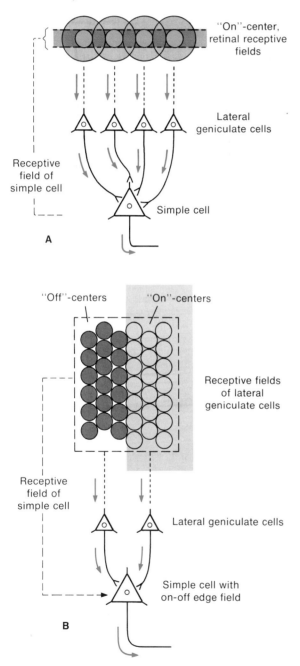

8-26. *Mechanisms responsible for cortical simple-cell receptive fields. A. The bar-shaped receptive field of a simple cell is believed to arise as the result of convergence of outputs from ganglion and lateral geniculate cells whose circular "on"-center receptive fields are linearly aligned, as shown. B. In a similar manner, an "on"-"off" edge receptive field may result from the convergence of "off"-center and "on"-center geniculate cells onto the simple cell, as shown.*

"On"-center, retinal receptive fields

Lateral geniculate cells

Receptive field of simple cell

Simple cell

A

"Off"-centers

"On"-centers

Receptive fields of lateral geniculate cells

Receptive field of simple cell

Lateral geniculate cells

Simple cell with on-off edge field

B

arranged linearly on the retina (Fig. 8-26,A). Simple cells with "border"-type receptive fields are presumed to receive inputs as shown in Figure 8-26,B. Thus the simple cell responds most strongly when all the receptors included in the "on"-center fields of the ganglion and the geniculate cells innervating that simple cell are illuminated while the receptors included in the "off" fields of these cells receive minimum illumination.

The next order of complexity is seen in another group of cortical neurons, the so-called *complex cells*. These are believed to be innervated by the simple cells, which would make them the sixth order in the visual hierarchy. Complex cells respond best to straight borders of specific angular orientation on the retina. Unlike the simple cells, however, complex cells do not have fixed receptive fields. Appropriate stimuli presented within relatively large portions of the retina are equally effective, whereas general illumination over the whole receptive area proves ineffective. Some complex cells respond to bars of light of specific orientation (Fig. 8-27,A), and others give an "on" response to a straight border with the light on one side, and an "off" response when the light is on the other side. Certain complex cells respond to a moving border progressing in one direction only (Fig. 8-27,B). Movement in the other direction evokes either no response at all or a weak one. This effect has been explained as follows. A complex cell appears to receive its input largely from the simple cells of one cortical column. The simple cells of one column all have their receptive fields in the same angular orientation, but systematically displaced with respect to one another. As a light–dark border moves through the corresponding receptive fields of these simple cells, they excite the complex cell in sequence as the light–dark edge passes in turn through each of the "on"–"off" borders in the receptive fields of the simple cells. Directional sensitivity in the complex cell results from the inhibitory effect of illuminating the "off" region of each simple cell's receptive field before illuminating the adjacent "on" region (Fig. 8-27,B). Remember that illumination of the entire receptive field is relatively ineffective in stimulating a cortical cell. If the border moves so as to illuminate each "on" region before the adjacent "off" region of the simple-cell receptive field, the complex cell will receive a sequence of excitation as one simple cell after another is excited.

The complex cells go on to innervate the so-called *hypercomplex cells* (seventh-order), which respond specifically to such silhouettes as corners and moving "tongues." The organization of the receptive fields of the hypercomplex cells is based on the same principles of visual processing that hold for the lower order cells.

BOX 8-1   SPECIFICITY OF NEURONAL CONNECTIONS AND INTERACTIONS

Note in Figure 8-19,A that the portions of the image falling on the temporal (ear-side) portion of one retina fall on the nasal portion of the other retina, and vice versa. The ganglion cells on the right side of each retina send their axons to the right side of the brain, and those on the left side send their axons to the left side of the brain. Thus it is evident that the right side of the brain "sees" the left half of the field of view, and that the left side of the brain "sees" the right half.

Hubel and Wiesel found that some individual cells of the right and left visual cortices have receptive fields in each of the two retinas, and that these fields are positioned so as to be optically in register. That is, cortical cells receive from both retinas input that arises from *corresponding parts of the image.* This means that these cortical cells receive extremely accurate neural projections from ganglion cells "seeing" the same part of the field but located in each of the two retinas. These findings confirm the suggestion of Johannes Müller over a century ago that information originating from analogous receptors (i.e., those "seeing" the same part of the visual field) on both right and left retinas converges on specific neurons in the brain. Such a high degree of morphological specificity is in direct contrast to the idea that the activity of the nervous system is diffusely organized, and that it is the patterning of electrical activity rather than the precise circuitry of neurons that is significant in coding neural messages. It is clear from recordings of single-unit activity in the visual cortex that each cell responds optimally to certain parameters of a stimulus. Furthermore, the behavior of that cell depends in large part on the behavior of cells from which it receives its input. A single impulse in a neuron is thus significant by virtue of the connections that neuron makes with other neurons.

The neurons of the visual cortex are arranged in a remarkably orderly manner. When a recording electrode is gradually advanced into the cortex perpendicular to its surface and past successive simple cells, it is seen that all of the cells of that vertical column have retinal receptive fields of the same orientation, but progressively displaced along the surface of the retina. Those cells forming the adjacent vertical column have receptive fields whose angles of orientation differ slightly from those of the first column and so on. This is an example of the orderliness of the vast number of connections present in the central nervous system. One of the major problems of modern neurobiology is to discover how connections are made during the development of the nervous system with such specificity and precision.

In summary, the visual system is organized primarily on the principle of convergence. Each cell receives inputs from numerous cells of lesser complexity of receptive field. The result is a hierarchy in which each complex cell receives input from a number of simple cells below it in the neuronal hierarchy and abstracts information from this input on the basis of their connections and synaptic mechanisms. The hypercomplex cell in turn receives input from numerous complex cells and makes a further abstraction. Although convergence is most evident in this scheme, a great deal of divergence also exists, for each receptor cell connects to many ganglion cells and ultimately to thousands of cortical cells. Thus the visual cortex does not receive a simple one-to-one projection from the retina. Instead, the activity of each neuron represents an abstraction of some relatively simple feature of the optic image.

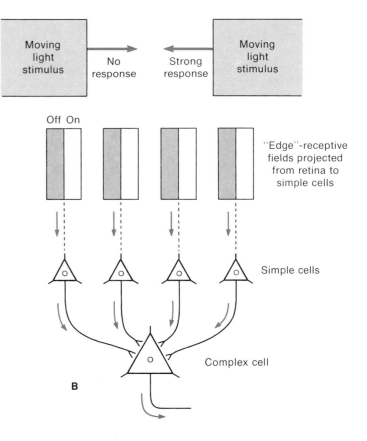

8-27. The origin of complex-cell responses. A. Some complex cells respond to bars of light of specific orientation anywhere within a large receptive field. This may occur by convergence of many simple cells having similarly oriented bar-shaped receptive fields. B. Some complex cells respond to edges of light moving in one direction only. This could result from convergence of a population of simple cells sensitive to light-dark edges of the same orientation. Excitation of the complex cell occurs if the edge moves so as to illuminate the "on" side of the simple-cell receptive fields before illumination of the "off" side. Movement in the opposite direction causes only inhibition.

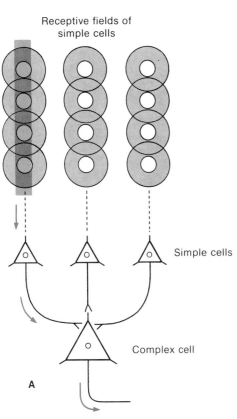

Neuromotor Networks

Although we now understand some of the elementary principles of sensory processing, a great deal remains obscure. As yet, we do not understand the neural mechanisms by which the nervous system gives rise in the mind's eye to the mental image from the optic image projected on the retina, nor for that matter how it gives rise to sensory perception of any kind. Likewise, the circuits that exist between sensory input and motor output constitute a highly complex and poorly understood no-man's land. These circuits, lumped together as a black box in Figure 8-28, receive filtered sensory input from past and present. They are also influenced by hormones acting on the genetically and developmentally determined neural networks. The end result of the central integration of past and present inputs is the coordinated motor output that we term the animal's behavior. We next consider some of the simpler examples of neuromotor control.

THE STRETCH REFLEX

The most elementary neuromotor mechanisms are simple reflexes. In its rudimentary form, the *myotatic* (or *stretch*) *reflex* of vertebrates depends on only two kinds of neurons: the *1a afferent sensory fiber* and the α-motoneuron (Fig. 8-29). The 1a afferent fibers have sensory endings in the muscle that are sensitive to stretch, and they terminate synaptically in the spinal cord on the α-motoneurons to form a monosynaptic reflex arc. The sensory terminals of the 1a afferents spiral around the central noncontractile region of special *infrafusal* muscle fibers, which are distinct from the mass of *extrafusal* muscle fibers that constitutes the bulk of the muscle. The extrafusal muscle fibers are innervated by the α-motoneurons, and these fibers are the ones that cause the muscle to develop tension and shorten. The contraction of intrafusal muscle fibers

8–28. Block diagram of the circuitry between sensory input and motor output. See text for discussion.

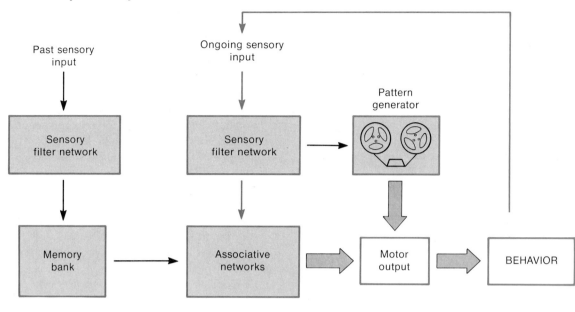

8–29. The myotatic reflex. A. Steady state with a light weight held up by contracting extrafusal fibers. B. Large weight puts greater load on the muscle, stretching it. This causes reflex contraction via 1a afferent excitation. The original length of the muscle is not completely restored because the gain of the feedback system is not infinite. Cutting the sensory input opens the feedback loop and allows the weight to stretch the muscle (broken outline) without compensatory contraction of the extrafusal fibers.

differs from that of the extrafusal fibers in two important ways: (1) it does not contribute significantly to muscle tension, because the intrafusal fibers are relatively few in number; and (2) the intrafusal fibers contract only near their ends and not in the central sensory region, and they contract in response to impulses in the γ-*efferent* motoneurons that innervate them.

Together with their motor and sensory innervation, the intrafusal muscle fibers are termed *muscle spindles,* or *stretch receptors.* It is important to note that they are attached in *parallel* with the extrafusal muscle fibers. Thus the muscle spindles are stretched when the muscle is stretched by an external force such as gravity or by contraction of an antagonist muscle. The stretch causes an increase in 1a afferent discharge, a reflex excitation of the α-motoneurons, and hence a compensatory shortening of the extrafusal muscle fibers (Fig. 8-29). On the other hand, contraction of the extrafusal fibers will reduce tension in the stretch receptors and so tend to reduce their sensory discharge.

Consider the reflex arc as a *feedback loop* (Box 1-1). If the system is perturbed by a force that stretches the muscle, the increased 1a afferent discharge synaptically evokes an increased motor discharge (Fig. 8-30). This results in an increased contraction of the extrafusal muscle fibers innervated by those motoneurons. This

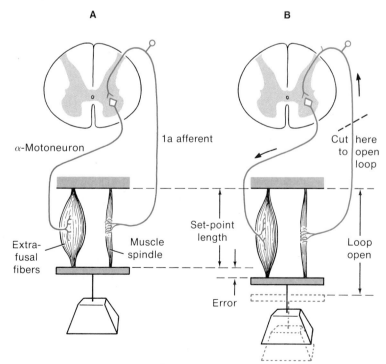

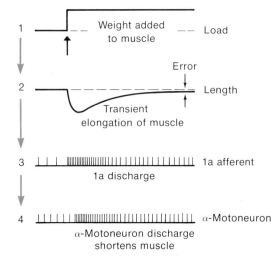

8-30. *Cause-effect sequence of the components of the myotatic reflex initiated by the sudden addition of a weight that stretches the muscle. The subsequent time-dependent shortening of the muscle is due to reflex activation of the α-motoneurons.*

1 — Weight added to muscle — Load

2 — Error — Length — Transient elongation of muscle

3 — 1a afferent — 1a discharge

4 — α-Motoneuron — α-Motoneuron discharge shortens muscle

reflex contraction counteracts the force that originally stretched the muscle, causing the muscle to return toward its initial length. Because the muscle spindles are connected in parallel with the extrafusal muscle fibers, the contraction of the extrafusal fibers lowers the sensory discharge in stretch receptors of that muscle. Shortening only approximates the original length, however, because the *gain* (i.e., amplification) of the feedback system is not infinite. The difference between the original length and the new length is termed the *error* (Figs. 8-29, 8-30).

From this simplified account, it is evident that the myotatic reflex constitutes a *load-compensating* feedback system that operates to keep the muscle close to a preset length, independent of the load (i.e., tension) acting on the muscle. This mechanism, which operates without conscious control, is important in maintaining posture. Postural muscles must keep the skeleton erect in the face of gravitational pull. Extensors, especially, are subject to stretch by the force of gravity. Flexion of a limb by gravity applies a stretch to the spindle receptor organs in the extensors. In response to this stretch, the 1a fibers discharge and synaptically excite the α-motoneurons innervating the extrafusal muscle fibers of the extensors. The ensuing contraction opposes the force that tends to flex the limb.

A familiar example of the stretch reflex is the knee-jerk reflex evoked by a tap applied to the tendons of the knee extensor muscles where they pass over the

knee joint. The tap results in a sudden stretch of the muscle and its spindle organs. The reflex discharge of the α-motoneurons produces the brief extension of the lower leg.

The myotatic reflex loop can be "opened" for analysis by interrupting the 1a sensory feedback. This is done by sectioning the dorsal root through which the 1a afferents enter the spinal cord (Fig. 8-29,B). This operation causes the corresponding muscles to lose their tone, and they no longer contract reflexly when stretched. This observation led to Sherrington's discovery of the myotatic reflex in his pioneering neurophysiological studies on dogs and cats in the early part of this century. It was interesting that the muscles should go limp even though the motor innervation remained intact and connected to the spinal cord. This indicated to Sherrington that the 1a afferents provide continual synaptic input to the α-motoneurons and are responsible in part for muscle tone, the state of partial contraction present in the otherwise inactive muscle.

CENTRAL CONTROL OF MUSCLE LENGTH

The account of the stretch reflex just given is simplified by omitting the mechanism that determines the *set point* of the sensory portion of the feedback system. The set point is that length of the muscle spindle at which the 1a discharge produces just enough reflex α-motoneuron discharge (and hence extrafusal muscle contraction) to balance the forces tending to stretch the muscle. It is analogous to the thermostat setting in a cooling system. As the temperature drops to the set point, the compressor is turned off by a temperature-sensitive switch. When the temperature subsequently rises above the set point, the thermostat produces a signal (closing of temperature-sensitive switch) that turns the compressor on until the temperature is again lowered to the set point.

What determines the set-point spindle length in the myotatic reflex? Before answering this, it must be recalled that the contractile portions at the ends of the intrafusal muscle fibers are arranged *in series* with the noncontractile sensory regions midway along these fibers (Fig. 8-31). The contractile portions of the fibers are innervated by the γ-motoneurons, which have their cell bodies located in the gray matter of ventral horn of the spinal cord (Fig. 8-32). These motoneurons are smaller than the α-motoneurons that innervate the extrafusal fibers, and their axons (γ-efferents) innervate only the intrafusal muscle fibers of the spindle organs. The γ-motoneurons and the intrafusal muscle fibers are collectively termed the *fusimotor system.* Activation of the fusimotor system by neural commands from the motor centers of the brain or from reflex connections in the spinal cord causes shortening of the contractile portions of the intrafusal fibers, which *stretches the noncontractile sensory portion* of the intrafusal fibers.* This causes an increase in 1a sensory activity and reflex shortening of the extrafusal muscle fibers until the spindle organs reach their new set-point length (Fig. 8-33). A stretch applied to the muscle will now set up additional 1a sensory discharge, which will cause additional firing of α-motoneurons and maintenance of the new set-point length. Likewise, a reduction in the steady excitation of the fusimotor system by signals from the brain resets the system to maintain a greater length. The γ-system is also activated reflexly along with the α-motor system in response to painful stimuli to the skin (Fig. 8-32). This serves to keep the muscle spindle from going slack during the reflex contraction of the extrafusal muscle fibers. This dynamically changing set point assures a steady 1a input to the α-motoneurons essential for maintained tone and maintains responsiveness of the spindle organs to externally imposed stretch.

Relatively slow movements and postural attitudes may be controlled through adjustments of the set point by the γ-system and reflex activation of the α-system that maintains the muscle at any given set-point length. Rapid and forceful movements are mediated by direct activation of the α-motoneurons by nerve fibers descending from the cerebral cortex (Fig. 8-33,C) and via polysynaptic reflexes initiated from pain receptors.

GOLGI TENDON REFLEX

A second kind of receptor in muscle is the *Golgi tendon organ*, formed by sensory arborizations of the so-called *1b afferent neurons* terminating in the tendons of skeletal muscle (Fig. 8-34,A). These endings in the tendon are sensitive to tension developed in the muscle during contraction. Because they are in series with the muscle fibers (rather than in parallel like the spindle organs), the Golgi tendon organs sense muscle tension rather than length. They indirectly innervate the α-motoneurons of the corresponding muscle through inhibitory interneurons (Fig. 8-34,B), and thus act to dampen the α-motor output. The role of the 1b reflex is not entirely clear, but it is conjectured that the tension-sensing feedback to the α-motoneurons helps correct for imperfections in the length-control mechanism of the myotatic reflex. Thus as the α-motoneurons fatigue during a maintained 1a input, the 1b afferents will signal the drop in tension by slowing their firing rate. This reduces the 1b inhibition on the α-motoneurons and leads to compensatory increases in motor output.

*It is important to note that separate activation of the α-motoneurons and γ-motoneurons has contrary effects on the stretch-sensitive tissue of the spindle organ.

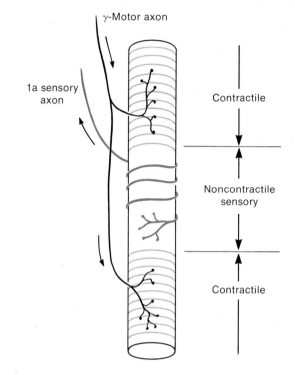

8–31. *Simplified structure of an intrafusal muscle, the 1a sensory axon, and γ-motoneuron innervation. The striated part of the muscle is contractile. The central region is noncontractile, and is stretched either by γ-motoneuron activity or by elongation of the muscle within which it resides.*

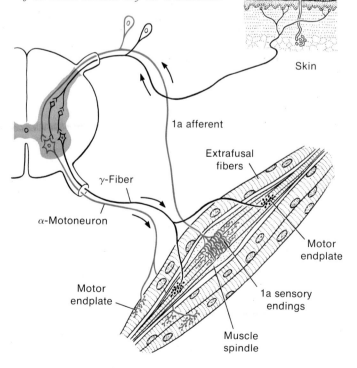

8–32. *The γ and α systems shown together. Painful stimuli to the skin activate both systems simultaneously, shortening the muscle. Stretching of the muscle activates only the α-motoneuron.*

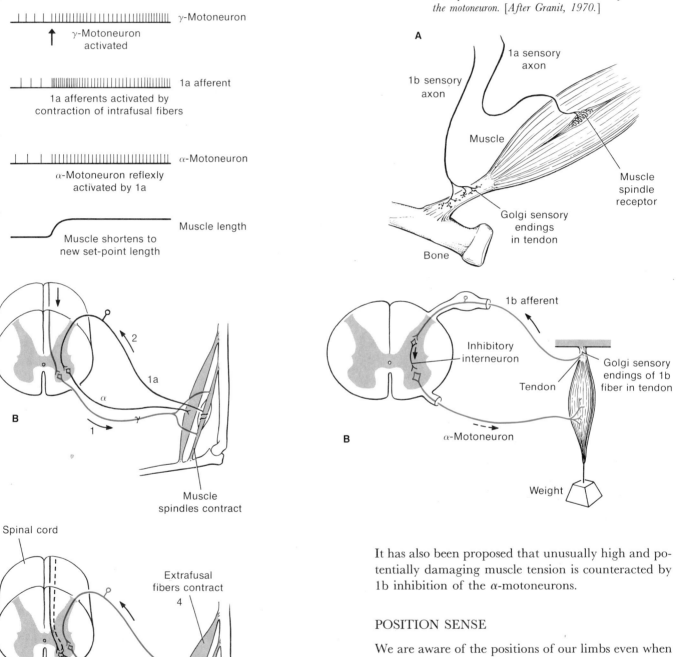

8–33. *Reflex control of muscle length.* A. *Gamma control. Cause-effect sequence (1–4) in the establishment of a new set-point by the fusimotor system. Activation of the γ-motoneurons causes the intrafusal fibers to contract, stretching the sensory portion of the spindle. This stimulates the 1a sensory axons to fire and activate the α-motoneurons. The muscle contracts until tension on the sensory portion of the spindle is reduced. B. Diagram of steps 1 and 2 from part A. C. Steps 3 and 4.* [After "How We Control the Actions of Our Muscles" by P. A. Merton. Copyright © 1972 by Scientific American, Inc. All rights reserved.]

A

1 |||||||||||||||||||||||||||||||||||||| γ-Motoneuron

       γ-Motoneuron activated

2 | | |||||||||||||||||||||||||||||| | | | 1a afferent

       1a afferents activated by contraction of intrafusal fibers

3 | | ||||||||||||||||||||||||||||| α-Motoneuron

       α-Motoneuron reflexly activated by 1a

4   Muscle length

       Muscle shortens to new set-point length

B   Muscle spindles contract

C   Spinal cord   Extrafusal fibers contract

8–34. A. *The Golgi tendon organ.* B. *The connections it makes in the spinal cord. The inhibitory interneuron is responsible for limiting tension development in the motor unit innervated by the motoneuron.* [After Granit, 1970.]

A   1b sensory axon   1a sensory axon   Muscle   Muscle spindle receptor   Golgi sensory endings in tendon   Bone

B   1b afferent   Inhibitory interneuron   Golgi sensory endings of 1b fiber in tendon   Tendon   α-Motoneuron   Weight

It has also been proposed that unusually high and potentially damaging muscle tension is counteracted by 1b inhibition of the α-motoneurons.

POSITION SENSE

We are aware of the positions of our limbs even when blindfolded. It is possible to touch one's nose on the first try with both eyes shut. Neither the spindle organs nor the Golgi tendon organs give any conscious sensation of limb or joint position, but injection of a local anesthetic into a joint eliminates conscious sensation of the position of the limb. This demonstrates that mechanoreceptors in the articulating surfaces of each joint monitor its position. The information thus obtained enters the consciousness as a sense of limb position.

RECIPROCAL INNERVATION

Limb movement about a given joint requires the cooperation of the various muscles that act on that joint. Contraction in one set of muscles is coordinated by relaxation of its *antagonists* (i.e., those that have the opposite action), so that mutually antagonistic sets of muscles do not counteract each other.

Consider two muscles, *A* and *B*, that produce opposite movements about a joint (Fig. 8-35). When muscle *A* is stretched, its 1a afferents activate reflexly the α-motoneurons that cause contraction. At the same time, branches of the 1a afferents of muscle *A* activate inhibitory interneurons ending on the α-motoneurons of muscle *B*. Thus, although a stretch applied to muscle *A* produces contraction in that muscle, it simultaneously produces relaxation in the antagonistic muscle. Conversely, a stretch applied to muscle *B* sets up a myotatic reflex in that muscle and reciprocally inhibits the α-motoneurons to muscle *A*. Without this *reciprocal inhibition*, the contraction of one muscle would evoke reflex contraction of its antagonists in response to stretch.

Inhibitory circuitry is also important in the muscular coordination of movements of different limbs in vertebrates. This is most clearly demonstrated in *decerebrate* animals. Decerebration—cutting through the brainstem above the respiratory centers in the medulla to disconnect the pathways between the forebrain and the spinal cord—results in exaggerated spinal reflexes, because cerebral modification of spinal reflexes is prevented. A noxious stimulus to the skin of limb *A* will cause a reflex withdrawal (flexion) of that limb. This is accompanied by a reflexive extension of the contralateral limb. This extension happens because, simultaneous with the activation of flexor motoneurons in limb *A,* there is inhibition of flexor motoneurons and excitation of extensor motoneurons of limb *B*.

CENTRALLY GENERATED MOTOR OUTPUT

Locomotory and respiratory movements typically consist of rhythmic movements controlled by repetitive patterns of neuromotor discharge. Each phase of such a neuromotor cycle is both preceded and followed by characteristic motoneuron discharges that are consistently related to each other in time. This raises a fundamental question. To what degree are cyclic patterns of movement due (1) to reflex sequences in which movement stimulates mechanoreceptors whereby it reflexly evokes the next movement, and so on, or (2)

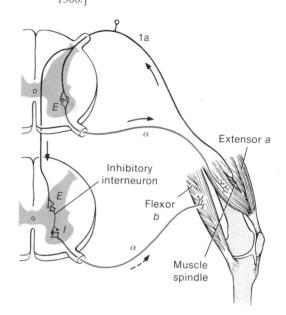

8–35. *Reflex connections of two antagonistic muscles. When muscle* a *is reflexly activated by stretch, the motoneurons to its antagonist,* b, *receive input from inhibitory interneurons reflexly activated by the 1a afferents of muscle* a. *Excitatory and inhibitory synapses are labeled* E *and* I, *respectively.* [*After Eccles, 1960.*]

to centrally generated sequences of motor output (which constitute a *motor score*) that arise independently of sensory input? This question has been examined in a number of animals. As might be expected, both mechanisms have been found to function in some instances, and one or the other has been found to predominate strongly in others.

Central motor patterns have been most clearly demonstrated in some of the simpler, more stereotyped nervous systems of invertebrates, such as the neuromotor system that controls wingbeat in grasshoppers. The various muscles that cause alternate up-and-down movements of the two pairs of wings are controlled by an appropriate sequence of nerve impulses carried by several motor axons (Fig. 8-36). The output patterns of the motoneurons continue to occur in proper phase relation to one another even after all sensory input from the muscles or joints of the wings is eliminated. This suggests that the motor output pattern is generated by a "central flight motor" consisting of a network of neurons—a network that perhaps has some features in common with the hypothetical circuit shown in Figure 8-37. In this scheme, motoneurons *B* and *C* receive excitatory input from a third neuron, *A*. Neurons *B* and *C* inhibit each other, so that when one is active the other is silent. It is also necessary that *B* and *C* accommodate, or fatigue, as they generate their respective trains of impulses. As *B* becomes active,

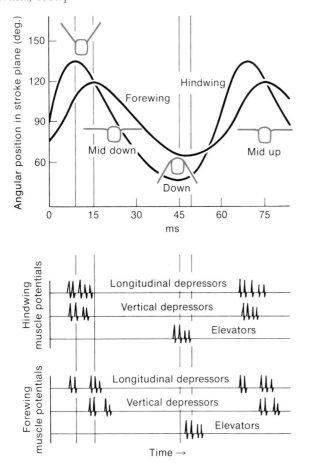

8-36. *The centrally generated motor-output rhythms (below) in flight muscles of grasshoppers are correlated with wing position (above) during one and one-half cycles of wingbeat. Each deflection of the baseline represents time of firing of several motor units. The phase relations of firing of different muscles is determined in the central nervous system and is independent of sensory input. [After Wilson, 1964.]*

8-37. *Hypothetical circuits capable of generating rhythms of alternating discharge in paired motoneurons.   Above. Input from interneuron A drives both B and C motoneurons. Because of fatigue and mutual inhibition, B and C fire alternating trains.   Below. Same as above, except that B and C are interneurons that drive rapidly adapting motoneurons D and E, which produce short trains. [After Wilson, 1966.]*

it inhibits *C* until *B* accommodates. Then *C* becomes active and inhibits *B* until *C* accommodates. Thus *B* and *C* continue indefinitely to give alternating trains of impulses. Although the output pattern depends on excitatory input from *A,* it is largely independent of the pattern in neuron *A.* The addition of rapidly accommodating neurons in series with *B* and *C* results in shorter trains at the same frequency of alternation (Fig. 8-37,B). These model systems work when they are simulated by computers, but such networks have only been inferred indirectly in the locust and other animals. There is direct experimental evidence, on the other hand, that some nerve cells generate repetitive trains of impulses independent of any synaptic input (p. 142). Such spontaneously oscillating neurons may also participate in the generation of centrally patterned motor output.

What role, if any, does sensory input play in the control of centrally programmed motor output? Sensory feedback from stretch receptors at the bases of the locust's wings, stimulated by the movement of the wings, increases the frequency of the motor rhythm. In the absence of feedback from the wing joints (i.e., when the receptors are destroyed), the neuromotor output slows down to about half its normal frequency, but the phase relations of impulses in the different motoneurons are retained. The original frequency can be restored by electrical stimulation of the nerve roots containing the sensory axons of the wing-joint receptors (Fig. 8-38,B). It is interesting that although the motor output rhythm increases in frequency when provided with sensory input, the timing of the motor output is independent of the timing of impulses in the sensory nerves. Randomly ordered stimulation of the sensory nerves is just as effective in speeding up the motor output as a regular train of stimuli. Thus proprioceptive feedback is not required for the correct sequence of motor impulses to the various muscles producing the alternating up-and-down wing movements. Nevertheless, once the central flight motor is turned on, sensory feedback from the wing-joint receptors provides positive feedback that increases the central excitatory state (Fig. 8-38,C).

What turns the flight motor "on" and "off"? When the grasshopper jumps off to fly, hair receptors on the head are stimulated by the passing air. This specific sensory input initiates the output of the flight motor. When the insect alights, the motor is turned off by signals originating in tarsal (i.e., foot) mechanoreceptors. These signals stop, of course, the next time the insect jumps off to fly.

Endogenous pattern-generating networks have been shown to exist in a number of other invertebrate nervous systems. The cyclic motor output to the abdominal swimmerets of the crayfish persists in the isolated nerve cord and even in single ganglia. This intrinsic rhythm is initiated and maintained by activity of command interneurons that descend from the supraesophageal ganglion. Although the intrinsic bursting pattern requires maintained activity from one and perhaps several of the interneurons, there is no simple one-to-one relationship between the firing pattern of the interneuron and the pattern of the motor output to the swimmerets.

Varying degrees of central neural automaticity also occur in the vertebrates. Respiratory movements persist in mammals when sensory input from the thoracic muscles is eliminated by cutting the appropriate sensory roots. Toads in which all sensory roots except those of the cranial nerves have been cut still show some rudimentary coordinated walking movements, although these are hard to demonstrate due to the loss of neuromotor tone that results from interruption of the myotatic reflex arc (p. 260). Motor output to the swimming muscles of sharks continues to fire in the normal alternating way when segmental sensory input is eliminated. But the intersegmental sequencing (anterior-to-posterior waves) of motor output disappears in the absence of sensory input, and all the segments fire together, left and right motor outputs firing alternately with each other. This results in violent, alternating lateral flexions of the shark's entire body instead of the sinuous traveling waves that normally propel it through the water. Thus sensory input appears to be required in the shark to coordinate the motor output in a spatial sequence that progresses in waves from anterior to posterior segments.

8–38. *The role of proprioceptive feedback in grasshopper flight. A. The experimental arrangement. An eviscerated grasshopper or locust is mounted so that it can flap its wings when stimulated by air blowing on facial receptor hairs. Electrodes for recording motor output and for stimulating receptor nerves are fixed in place. B. The result of sensory input is to speed up the frequency of the endogenous rhythm of motor output. C. Cyclic organization of behavior. External sensory input (puff of air on hair receptors) stimulates behavior (flying). The wing movements stimulate proprioceptors that provide further input that stimulates the flight motor. [After Wilson, 1964, 1970.]*

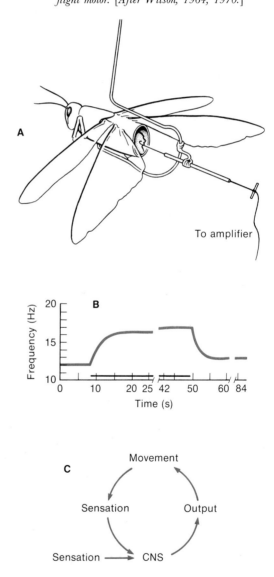

Programmed Behavior

"RELEASE" OF STEREOTYPED MOTOR OUTPUT

The stimulation of appropriate neurons in the central nervous system can elicit coordinated movements of varying degrees of complexity. Electrical stimulation of one such *command interneuron* in the nerve cord of the crayfish causes the animal to assume the defense posture, with open claws held high and body arched upward on extended forelegs. The appropriate sensory input excites this interneuron, and it (via its widespread processes) effects the excitation of some motoneurons and the inhibition of others, thereby eliciting the fixed defensive posture. It is characteristic of command interneurons of arthropods that they activate many muscles in a coordinated manner, and produce reciprocal actions in a given body segment. That is, antagonists are inhibited while protagonists are excited. Those command interneurons that are most effective in eliciting a coordinated pattern of motor response are generally the least easily activated by simple sensory input. A number of command interneurons have been described in the nervous systems of arthropods, including some (noted in the next section) that act as "on" or "off" switches for internally generated, repetitive patterns of motor output.

Command interneurons must not be confused with motoneurons. As stated by Sherrington early in the century, motoneurons are the *final common pathways* of animal behavior. Each motoneuron activates its motor unit of muscle cells, and thus produces only one component of movement in the complex sequence of movements that, together, constitute a behavioral act. This was illustrated very nicely by A. O. D. Willows in the nudibranch (i.e., sea slug) *Tritonia* (Fig. 8-39). Stimulation of specific neurons in the brain of this mollusc produces specific movements in the semirestrained experimental animal. Activity in one neuron causes contraction of a set of muscles on one side while activity in its counterpart on the opposite side causes contraction of homologous muscles on the other side. This is not surprising. What is more noteworthy is the ability of a command interneuron to control the orchestrated activation of motoneurons so as to produce a well-defined temporal pattern of swimming movements (Fig. 8-40). This command interneuron is activated synaptically by sensory input when the *Tritonia* is touched by its natural predator, a starfish. The escape-swimming program thus *released* by the appropriate sensory input consists of an intrinsic motor program, for it is played out even in the isolated nervous system deprived of reflex feedback from receptor organs.

8–39. Stimulation of identified nerve cells in the brain of the marine nudibranch Tritonia *results in stereotyped postures or behavior patterns. Stimulation of the small cells indicated in the pleural ganglion elicits the alternating movements of swimming. [After "Giant Brain Cells in Mollusks" by A. O. D. Willows. Copyright © 1971 by Scientific American, Inc. All rights reserved.]*

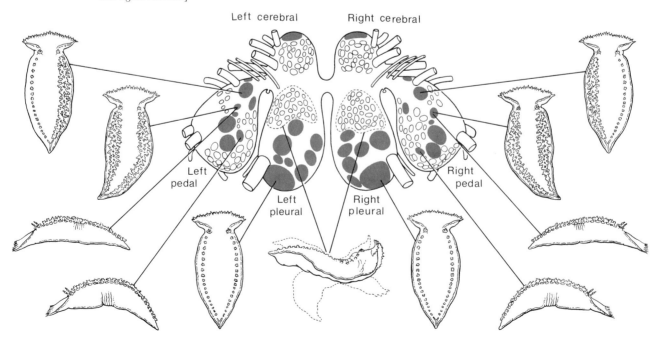

Left cerebral   Right cerebral

Left pedal   Left pleural   Right pleural   Right pedal

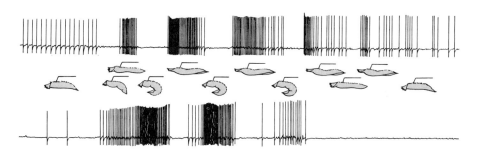

Animal Orientation

TAXES AND CORRECTIVE RESPONSES

It is common knowledge among tenement dwellers that cockroaches abandon their tasty morsels and scurry back to their crevices when a kitchen light is turned on at night. This behavior is an example of *negative phototaxis*. Another simple form of *taxis* is shown by the flatworm (Fig. 8-41). An animal that is programmed to turn toward the light exhibits *positive phototaxis*. Loeb suggested early in the twentieth century that simple taxes like these result from asymmetrical motor activation by asymmetrical sensory input. According to this view, negative phototaxis occurs when the light impinging on one eye leads to a stronger ipsilateral motor output (i.e., on the same side as that eye), causing the animal to veer away from the source of the light. Positive phototaxis occurs if the light stimulus to an eye stimulates contralateral locomotor output, causing the animal to turn toward the source of light. The concept of a *sensorimotor servosystem* (Fig. 8-42) as the basis for locomotor orientation is supported by the simple observation that positively phototaxic animals blinded in one eye will orient so that the intact eye points away from the light. It appears to apply in a number of cases of orientation toward or away from stimuli such as light, heat, odor, sound, and gravity.

Sensory information is used to correct structural or functional asymmetries of central pattern generators or of the structures (wings, legs, fins, etc.) that influence locomotion. A locust continues to fly in a straight line after one of its four wings is partially or entirely removed. Even an intact tethered locust (Fig. 8-43,A) will roll about its longitudinal axis if induced to fly in the dark. The roll is due to the slight asymmetry of the wings and of the centrally generated motor output (Fig. 8-43,B). The locust ceases to roll when it is provided with a visual cue in the form of an artificial horizon (Fig. 8-43,A). This stabilization is the direct

8-41. *Negative phototaxis in the flatworm* Dugesia. *Top. Upon entering the beam of light, the worm turns away from the source until illumination to the two primitive eyes (bottom) is equalized. Pigmented cup of epithelial cells conveys some directional sensitivity to the eye. [After Wells, 1968.]*

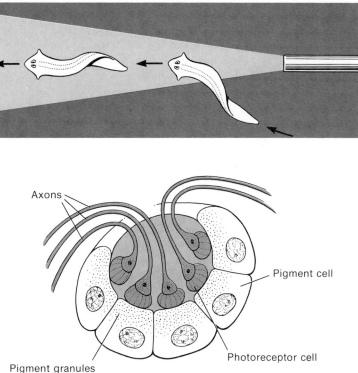

Axons

Pigment cell

Photoreceptor cell

Pigment granules lining the eye cup

8-42. *Jacque Loeb's hypothesis of negative (left) and positive (right) taxis. At the left, stronger illumination of one eye leads to stronger locomotor movements of the appendages on the homolateral side. At the right, stronger illumination of one eye causes stronger locomotor movements of the contralateral appendages. [After "Flight Orientation in Locusts" by J. M. Cahmi. Copyright © 1971 by Scientific American, Inc. All rights reserved.]*

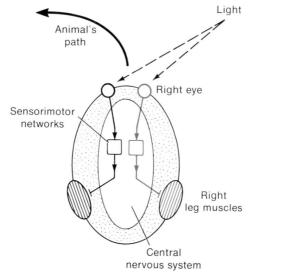
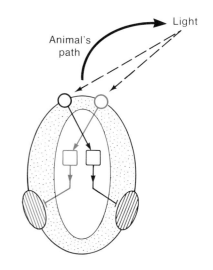

8-43. *Visual correction of endogenous neuromotor asymmetry. A. Experimental arrangement. The locust is tethered so as to be free to roll while flying in a wind tunnel. An artificial horizon is provided when the lamp is on. When the lamp is turned off, the flying locust has no visual clues as to flight orientation; consequently, it rolls slowly about its longitudinal axis as a result of asymmetrical output to muscles of the two wings. B. Electrical recordings of left and right flight muscles during flight of a locust that has had one hindwing removed. In this recording of flight with the lamp off, the output to both left and right wing muscles was equal, as in the normal animal. Because of the missing hindwing, this motor output produced severe rolling during flight. C. When the light was turned on, output to the intact wing was reduced in order to compensate and prevent rolling. After the light was turned off, removing the visual reference, the output again became symmetrical and rolling resumed. [After Wilson, 1968.]*

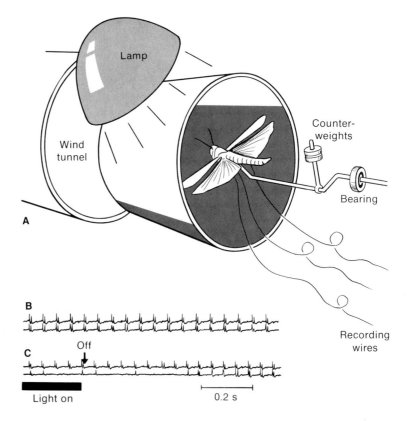

result of a correction in the motor output to the wings (Fig. 8-43,C). Visual input provides information to the central flight motor, regulating the relative outputs to the left and right sets of wing muscles so as to maintain a level horizon.

The importance of sensory feedback correction of orientation and locomotion in humans is confirmed in our daily experience. The driver of a car, for example, continually makes minor steering adjustments: his eyes are the sensors in a feedback system in which the driver's neuromuscular system coupled to the car's steering mechanism corrects any deviations from the set point (i.e., center of the lane). Even if the road were perfectly straight, the driver could not close his eyes without eventually deviating from the course because of asymmetries in the driver's neuromotor system, to say nothing of side winds or imperfections in the road and vehicle. Related to this is the finding that blindfolded human subjects, either walking or driving in an open flat field, will take a more-or-less circular course, the size and direction (right or left) of the average radius differing from one subject to another. Similar turning biases are seen in animals at all phylogenetic levels. But visual and other exteroceptive feedback can compensate for inherent locomotor biases due to congenital asymmetries in the neuromotor apparatus.

NAVIGATION

The ability of certain animals to navigate over long distances is truly impressive. Birds use star patterns, the sun, landmarks, and perhaps even the Earth's magnetic field. Bats become familiar with the sonar "image" of the landscape, and can find their way back to their roosts as readily as if they were using visual images. Bees use the sun's position and the pattern of polarized light in the sky to keep track of the direction of the hive or a source of food. Birds and bees both possess internal *clock-compasses* that they use to correct for time-dependent changes in the position of celestial indicators (sun, stars). A bird can maintain a correct bearing through the course of a day (or night) even though the celestial indicator progresses across the sky with the rotation of the Earth. If a bee or bird is put on a day–night schedule with "dawn" and "dusk" shifted by several hours, it will enter the incorrect time into its internal clock-compass and will orient with a compass deviation equivalent to the artificial phase shift in the day–night cycle.

The navigational abilities of certain animals have become surrounded by an aura of mystery because of our lack of understanding of the cues they use to sense direction. The long-distance migration of the American eel (*Anguilla rostrata*) is a case in point. These fish migrate from their spawning grounds in the Sargasso Sea to the Atlantic coast of North America, a distance of about 1,000 km. Suggestions that they might employ the Earth's magnetic field have been scoffed at because of the field's low density. Nevertheless, the movement of the sea water in ocean currents acts as an enormous generator, for the water functions as a conductor moving through the Earth's magnetic field. The geoelectric fields set up in the sea by ocean currents, such as the Gulf Stream, reach intensities of about 0.5 μV/cm. This is equivalent to a 1.0 volt drop over 20 km. Classical (Pavlovian) conditioning has been used to train eels to slow their heart rates in response to electric fields. Once trained, the eels showed reduced heart rates in response to dc fields as low as 0.002 μV/cm. Because the fields generated in the ocean are one or two orders of magnitude greater, it is entirely possible that the eel uses the orientation of a geoelectric field for navigational purposes.

Behavior in Animals Without Nervous Systems

Early claims that subcellular "neuromotor" systems exist in certain protozoa have not survived modern scrutiny, hence it can safely be concluded that the unicellular organisms have nothing analogous to the circuitry of a metazoan nervous system. Nonetheless, protozoans are capable of detecting stimuli and responding adaptively. Some even exhibit a very rudimentary kind of memory. How is this possible without a nervous system?

When a ciliate, such as *Paramecium*, bumps into an obstacle, it reverses the beat of its cilia, swims backward a short distance, pivots about its posterior end, and resumes forward locomotion, usually at some angle to its previous path (Fig. 8-44,A). This is termed the *avoiding reaction*. In contrast, a mechanical stimulus to the posterior end causes the paramecium to swim forward more rapidly, the *escape reaction*. Although these responses have the superficial appearance of being purposive, electrophysiological studies show them to be purely mechanistic.

As explained in Chapter 10, the frequency and the direction of ciliary beat in protozoans is controlled directly or indirectly by the membrane potential. Depolarization causes the cilia to reverse their beat, so that the ciliate swims backward, whereas hyperpolarization evokes an increased rate of beat in the forward-swimming direction. Electrical recordings were made from paramecia with intracellular microelectrodes while applying mechanical stimuli to selected parts of the cell surface (Fig. 8-45). Mechanical stimulation at the anterior end elicited a depolar-

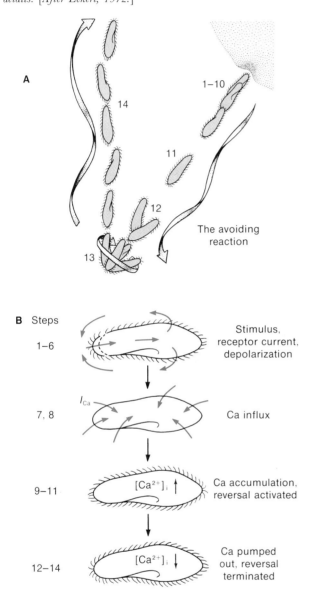

8-44. *The avoiding reaction in* Paramecium. *A. After colliding with an object, the ciliate backs up, rotates, and heads off in a new direction.* [After Grell, 1973.] *B. Ionic events that give rise to this behavior; the numbers refer to steps shown in part A. See text for details.* [After Eckert, 1972.]

A

1–10

14

11

12

13

The avoiding reaction

B Steps

1–6

Stimulus, receptor current, depolarization

I_{Ca}

7, 8

Ca influx

9–11

$[Ca^{2+}]_i$ ↑

Ca accumulation, reversal activated

12–14

$[Ca^{2+}]_i$ ↓

Ca pumped out, reversal terminated

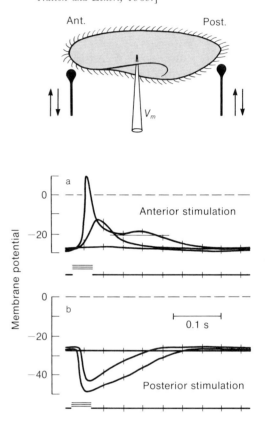

8-45. *Receptor potentials in* Paramecium. *The anterior or posterior ends of the ciliate were stimulated mechanically with a crystal-driven microprobe while an intracellular electrode recorded responses. Stimulation of the anterior produced a depolarizing receptor potential, a, and stimulation of the posterior produced a hyperpolarizing receptor potential, b. The lower trace in each set shows relative intensity and the duration of each stimulus. Note gradation of response amplitudes.* [After Naitoh and Eckert, 1969.]

Ant.   Post.

V_m

Membrane potential

a

0

−20

Anterior stimulation

0

b

0.1 s

−20

−40

Posterior stimulation

ization graded in intensity with the stimulus (curve *a*); stimulation of the posterior end elicited a graded hyperpolarization (curve *b*).

Why do the opposite ends of the paramecium give different electrical responses to the same kind of stimulation? Experiments using different concentrations of the external cations K^+ and Ca^{2+} revealed that mechanical stimulation of the anterior end causes an increase in calcium permeability. Because calcium is about 10,000 times more concentrated outside the

cell than inside (p. 104), the local increase in calcium permeability produced by the mechanical stimulus results in a transient influx of Ca^{2+}. This constitutes a depolarizing receptor current. The depolarization spreads electrotonically throughout the entire cell. A similar mechanical stimulus to the posterior surface leads to a local increase in potassium-ion permeability, and the consequent efflux of K^+ constitutes a hyperpolarizing receptor current that spreads throughout the cell. Thus the very different electrical consequences of mechanical stimulation at anterior and posterior ends are due to differences in the ion-selective channels activated in the cell membrane by stimuli at the opposite ends of the ciliate.

The depolarizing receptor potential acts as an electrical stimulus for the entire cell membrane, causing it to become more permeable to calcium ions and hence produces a *calcium response* (Fig. 8-46). This is a graded (as opposed to all-or-none) regenerative response of the membrane, similar to those that occur in crustacean muscle (Fig. 9-37). The resulting influx of calcium ions through the surface membrane into the cilia leads to a reversal in the beat direction of the cilia, and hence to a retreat of the swimming paramecium from obstacles that it bumps into.

The calcium response of the paramecium membrane is not all-or-none like that of a true action potential, but is instead graded with stimulus intensity. An all-or-none response is unnecessary in this system because the cell is short enough so that electrotonic spread communicates the signal to the entire cell. Because the calcium response is graded with stimulus intensity, a more violent stimulus results in a more vigorous avoiding reaction by the ciliate, and a weak stimulus evokes a weak reaction. It is not clear why the hyperpolarization produced by mechanical stimulation of the hind end causes the cilia to beat faster.

The trumpet-shaped ciliate *Stentor* spends most of the time attached to the substratum at its narrow base (Fig. 8-47,A). When a mechanical disturbance of sufficient strength is applied to the surface of the cell, it contracts longitudinally with the aid of an internal system of microfilaments. It is interesting that the probability of occurrence of this all-or-none contraction diminishes with repeated stimuli. The response to a carefully controlled mechanical stimulus decreases exponentially with number of trials (Fig. 8-47,B). This resembles a simple type of learning in metazoans termed *habituation,* in which the nervous system eventually ignores a stimulus after it is presented several times. Recordings made from *Stentor* with intracellular

8-46. *The control of swimming by membrane potential in* Paramecium. *The depolarizing receptor potential in response to stimulation of the anterior gives rise to a second potential, the spike-like Ca^{2+} response. This is graded with the stimulus strength and evokes reversed beating of the cilia and hence backward swimming. The hyperpolarizing potential elicited by mechanical stimulation of the posterior causes the cilia to beat more rapidly in the forward-swimming direction. [After Eckert, 1972.]*

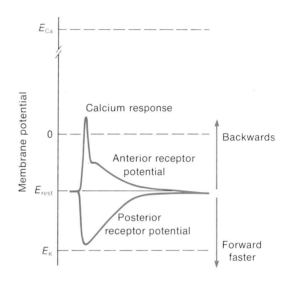

8-47. *Habituation in* Stentor. *A. Behavior in response to adverse stimuli: (1) undisturbed posture; (2) bending away from stimulus; (3) cilia reverse; (4) cell contracts; (5, 5') cell swims away. With repeated stimulation, the responses decrease, with the responses toward the left becoming more probable than those toward the right. [After Jennings, 1906.] B. Decay of probability of contraction as a function of number of trials in which* Stentor *is mechanically stimulated. [After Wood, 1970–1971.]*

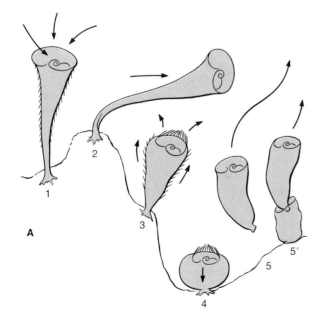

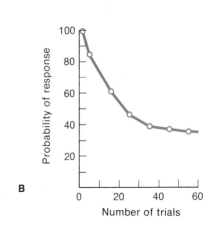

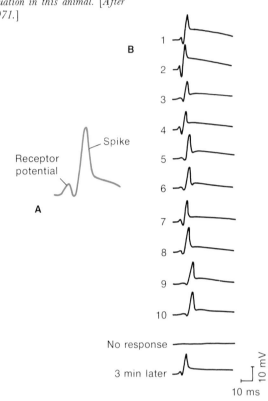

8-48. *Receptor potentials and action potentials recorded from* Stentor. *A. Control recording. B. Series of potentials elicited at 1-min intervals by mechanical stimulation. Note decrease in amplitude of receptor potentials with time. Eventually, the receptor potential fails to reach threshold for the action potential. The reduced probability of eliciting the action potential with repeated stimulation results in behavioral habituation in this animal. [After Wood, 1970–1971.]*

Spike

Receptor potential

A

B

1
2
3
4
5
6
7
8
9
10

No response

3 min later

10 mV

10 ms

trophysiological properties of the Protozoa. The similarity between the electrical properties of nerve cells and protozoa suggests that these properties are very general and very ancient. This lends support to the view that the evolution of nervous systems has taken place, primarily, by the development of increasingly sophisticated neural circuits rather than through changes in fundamental properties of nerve cells.

Genetics and Instinctive Behavior

It was noted in the early chapters of this book that the function of biological tissues ultimately depends on molecular structure and on the organization of molecules into organelles and tissues, which in turn is regulated by the information stored in the genetic material. The evidence for genetic influences on the physiology of animal behavior comes from several lines. First, there are long-standing observations that animals at all phyletic levels are born with locomotory and behavioral patterns that are expressed *de novo* without the opportunity for practice and learning. These kinds of behavior are termed *instinctive*. This suggests that some complex neural functions are programmed in the genetic material in the form of anatomical and physiological organization of the nervous system. Examples of such genetically fixed behaviors are shown in Figure 8-49. These can often be modified through experience, but only to a limited extent.

A well-documented example of genetically programmed motor output is seen in the wing movements responsible for the "chirps" and "trills" in the courting song of the male cricket. The patterns of cricket songs are species-specific and are largely independent of environmental factors other than temperature. Moreover, the sound pattern is directly related to the pattern of motor impulses to the sound-producing muscles. F_1 hybrids of two species, one with a short trill (2 sound pulses) and the other with a long trill (about 10 sound pulses) produce trills with an intermediate number (about 4) of pulses. Backcrosses to produce various genetic combinations demonstrated that the neural network producing the song pattern is under rigid genetic control, sufficiently precise to specify differences as small as the exact number of impulses in the motor output to the chirp-producing muscles.

A similar finding, using hybridization, has been used to confirm the genetic fixity of more complex vertebrate behavior. Closely related species of fowl with different behavior patterns were mated. The hybrid offspring exhibited hybrid behavior patterns with some components from one parent species and other components from the other parent species. Of course, care was taken to isolate the hybrids from either parent

electrodes show that a mechanical stimulus elicits a receptor potential that in turn evokes an all-or-none action potential (Fig. 8-48,A). Contraction follows the action potential. As the mechanical stimulus is applied repeatedly to the cell at 1-min intervals, the receptor potential becomes progressively smaller until finally it is no longer large enough to evoke the all-or-none action potential (Fig. 8-48,B). Thus the probability of a behavioral response to mechanical stimulation decreases as the size of the receptor potential decreases. It is not known why repeated stimulation produces a progressive reduction in the receptor potential.

It is evident from these two examples that the surface membrane of a unicellular organism can perform the functions of sensory reception, simple integration of receptor signals, and control of the motor response—and that a rather simple modification of membrane function can give rise to an elementary form of memory. Thus the rudiments of the sensory-neuromotor systems of metazoans are present already in the elec-

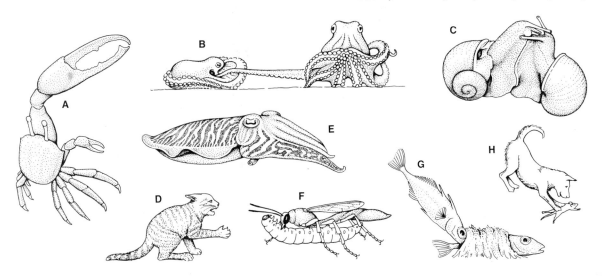

species to rule out any possibility of learning by exposure to adults.

At birth, the calves of some ungulates walk about immediately and react to stimuli in much the same way as do adults of the species. Nevertheless, advocates of the idea that all behavior is learned (the "nurture" camp of the "nature-versus-nurture" controversy) have contended that the rudiments of feeding and loco-motor behavior is learned gradually by the fetus through movements in the mammalian womb or the avian egg. This argument is difficult to disprove directly, because it is not practical to control behavior *in utero*. But tadpoles can be raised from eggs in the presence of an anesthetic; these tadpoles show normal movement patterns when the anesthetic is removed.

Observations on certain migratory birds also indicate that complex behavioral information is transmitted through the genetic material. It was common knowledge that certain birds navigate over vast stretches of ocean devoid of landmarks. Some species of nocturnally migrating birds such as garden warblers, when exposed to the night sky in a planetarium, orient with respect to certain patterns of stars (Fig. 8-50). As night progresses, and the projected constellation is moved across the dome to mimic the Earth's rotation, the birds orient themselves in the "correct" direction with respect to the projected sky, continually compensating for the time-dependent shift in position of the constellation about the Earth's axis. Arbitrary changes in the position of the projected sky produce corresponding changes in the orientation of the birds.

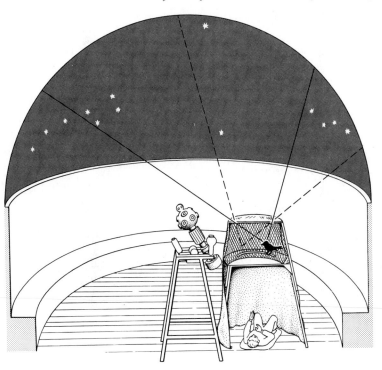

BOX 8-2   GENETIC APPROACHES TO NEURAL MECHANISMS AND BEHAVIOR

Neurobiologists have recently started to use the approach originally used by molecular biologists, that of examining the effects of single mutations on the functioning of a complex system. This approach was initially applied to neurobiology by S. Benzer at Cal Tech. Hundreds of behavioral mutants of the fruitfly *Drosophila* have been isolated that exhibit abnormal locomotor responses to visual stimuli. Wild-type (i.e., normal) fruitflies will walk toward a light, exhibiting positive phototaxis. If only one eye is blind, the fly walks with the defective eye toward the light, as predicted by Loeb's hypothesis (Fig. 8-42). Mutants that are blind fail to show this behavior, of course, and are of interest primarily to students to the visual process. One line of mutants shows a normal electroretinogram and a normal optokinetic response to moving patterns of alternating black and white stripes, which indicates that it can see, but it shows no phototaxis. The locomotor mutants include "Runner," which walks very quickly; "Hyperkinetic," which jumps when a shadow passes over; and "Easily Shocked," which goes into convulsions upon mechanical stimulation. In all cases, modification of the genetic material (i.e., mutation) must have produced a structural or chemical modification in one or more loci of the nervous system. The major interest in such behavioral mutants arises from the possibilities they present to identify structural or chemical mechanisms involved in the altered behavior. This approach, termed *genetic dissection*, attempts to identify and analyze individual steps or components in a complex physiological process by genetically eliminating or altering them.

8–51. Models used to study the aggressive behavior of male sticklebacks. Responses to these models indicate that the stimulus that releases the aggressive behavior is the horizontal red underside of the intruding male. Vertically oriented males elicit no response. The shape of the model fish is of little importance. [After Tinbergen, 1951.]

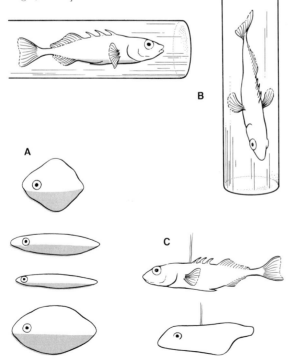

With no sun or stars visible, some birds have the ability to orient with respect to geomagnetic cues.

The ability to orient with respect to stellar patterns, complete with time compensation to account for the Earth's rotation, is fully present in birds that have been artificially hatched indoors and shielded from prior exposure to the sky. This is significant because there is no way under those conditions for the birds to have learned from practice to orient properly in relation to the sky. We must therefore conclude that information necessary for celestial navigation resides in the genetic material, and that the developing nervous system of the bird is programmed to generate the appropriate behavior when it is presented with the appropriate visual input from the night sky.

A classic example of instinct is the release of aggressive behavior in the courting male of the three-spined stickleback by the appearance of another male. With models of various shapes and coloration, it was determined that the *sign stimulus* that releases this behavior is the red underside characteristic of the males (Fig. 8-51,A). The shape of the model male is relatively unimportant, but the red underside loses its effectiveness as a sign stimulus if the fish is in any orientation other than horizontal (Fig. 8-51,B). Thus it is not simply the color red, but the proper combination of visual inputs, that acts to release the aggressive behavior.

The genetic origin of the innate releasing mechanism for the aggressive behavior of the male stickleback is evident in another stickleback species discovered in a mountain lake. The sign stimulus in this species is a *black* underbelly. Having evolved from a population of the red-bellied stock when the lake was formed tens of thousands of years ago by glacial action, this isolated group, in which the males have black bellies, now is genetically programmed to react to underbellies that are black instead of red.

It is reasonable to say that behavior in higher animals has both genetic and learned components, the contributions of heredity and experience showing wide variations among the different behavioral acts and among the different species. Genetically programmed behavior is most dominant in animals with simple nervous systems. Examples of learned behavior are too familiar to enumerate here, and the problems of learning and memory too poorly understood to consider in depth in a textbook that stresses known mechanisms. It will suffice here to note that the larger (in numbers of neurons) and hence the more complex a nervous system, the greater its potential to learn from experience. This potential enables it to depart from a limited repertoire of inherited, fixed patterns of behavior. For example, the octopus, which has the most elaborate nervous system of all invertebrates, shows the greatest ability to modify its behavior adaptively as the result of experience. There is no biological evidence that the human brain differs qualitatively from brains of some of the more intelligent mammals, such as chimpanzees or porpoises. But certain refinements having to do with language and cognitive ability have opened the way to qualitative advances in the processing of information. The senses are no more acute in humans than in other mammals, but the human nervous system can make more sophisticated abstractions by virtue of its more highly developed associative powers. Moreover, with the aid of language, the human species has been able to accumulate, record, and transmit information and experiences to succeeding generations, allowing the species to break out of the confines of time and the limitations imposed by having to relearn anew with each generation.

Summary

Lying between the sensory inputs and motor outputs of the central nervous system are highly complex neural networks responsible for all reflex and higher functions of the nervous system. The connections of this central network appear to be preprogrammed genetically to a large extent, but during development and thereafter they are sustained or modified by use. In spite of its complexity of organization and function, the nervous system operates with only two fundamental kinds of signals: all-or-none and graded potentials.

The integration of sensory input and subsequent activity depends on two major sets of factors: (1) the organization of circuits formed by interacting neurons and (2) the integrative properties of the individual neurons. The latter depend on the anatomical layout of the neuron and its connections and on the properties of the cell membrane and synapses. Simultaneous synaptic activity impinging on a neuron sums spatially because of the cable properties of the neuron. Synaptic activity also undergoes temporal summation as permitted by the time constant of the membrane. At the same time, there is interaction of excitatory and inhibitory input, the former tending to exceed the firing level and the latter counteracting depolarization to the firing level.

The simplest neural networks are monosynaptic reflex arcs. The most familiar example is the stretch reflex of vertebrates. The elongation of a muscle stimulates stretch receptors, which include the sensory endings of 1a afferent axons. These fibers enter the spinal cord and make direct synaptic connection with the α-motoneurons that activate contraction of the muscle. This reflex contraction counteracts the force that caused the initial elongation of the muscle. Simultaneously, collateral branches of the 1a afferent synaptically activate interneurons that make inhibitory synapses on the α-motoneurons to the antoganist muscles. This reflex inhibition of contraction of the antagonist muscles eliminates their opposition to the reflex contraction of the protagonist muscle.

Locomotor movements of animals are based in part on central "motor scores," which program the sequence of muscle contractions to produce the coordinated locomotor movements. Feedback from proprioceptors exerts varying degrees of influence in different animal groups on the strength and frequency of the movements.

The central nervous system "filters" sensory input—namely, it enhances certain features of the incoming stimuli. A classic example of neural filtering is lateral inhibition, which produces enhanced contrast in apparent luminosity at visual edges, in intensity of sound between adjacent frequencies in the audio spectrum, and in apparent vibration perceived between adjacent somatosensory loci. Electrical recording from cells in the visual cortex suggests that there is a hierarchical arrangement of neurons and that the specificity of sensory features evoking activity in the neurons increases with each level, until only very specific features of the visual stimulus evoke responses at the higher levels. Moreover, there appears to be a close anatomical arrangement into columns of cortical cells responding to stimuli that are similar but systematically displaced in the visual field. This is one example of how the processing of visual information, and perhaps other sensory information, is not a diffuse process, but is highly ordered both anatomically and physiologically.

Because of the complexity of nervous systems, animal behavior cannot yet be explained completely in neurophysiological terms. Although it is clear that some behavior patterns are genetically programmed, the roles of learning and experience have become increasingly important in behavior as evolution has progressed.

Sensory-motor behavior, as well as a rudimentary form of learning termed habituation, occurs in single-celled organisms. These phenomena have been traced to the electrophysiological properties of the cell membrane, similar to the properties of nerve cells. This lends support to the view that the properties of single nerve cells are ancient, and that the intricacies and variations that occur in the nervous systems of higher organisms are the result, primarily, of the evolution of neural networks.

Finally, evidence is presented that some forms of behavior are programmed into the nervous system by the genetic dictation of neural organization. Only this can explain instances where animals exhibit certain complex behaviors without prior opportunity to learn.

EXERCISES

1. Since all action potentials are fundamentally alike, how is the modality of input from the various sense organs recognized by the central nervous system?

2. Why is it that impulses originate in the axon hillock of a vertebrate motoneuron rather than at the postsynaptic membranes of the dendrites and soma?

3. Since postsynaptic potentials decay as they spread, where on a neuron would you expect a synapse to exert the strongest influence?

4. How can increased rate of firing of an inhibitory interneuron result in an increased rate of firing of other neurons?

5. What is meant by spatial summation? temporal summation? What are the membrane properties responsible for each?

6. What is responsible for the continuous low-level synaptic input and slow tonic firing in motoneurons?

7. Explain the two means with which the nervous system controls the intensity of contraction of a muscle.

8. Each eye of a primate sees about the same field, but the right hemisphere of the brain "sees" the left half of the visual field while the left hemisphere "sees" the right half of the field. How does this occur?

9. Why does the evening sky appear to have a lighter band outlining the silhouette of a mountain range?

10. What is meant by the "receptive field" of a neuron?

11. Explain the circuitry that results in the sensitivity to a bar of light of a specific orientation in a "simple cell" in the visual cortex.

12. What would happen to a subject if all of his muscle spindles ceased to function?

13. How is the set-point length of a muscle regulated by the nervous system?

14. What basic difference in arrangement is there between the muscle spindle and the Golgi tendon organ?

15. Relate the answer for Exercise 14 to the differences in reflex function between the 1a and 1b afferent fibers.

16. How does a mammal sense the relative position of its limbs?

17. The ciliate *Paramecium* has no nervous system, yet responds to collision with an object by reversing beat, backing off, and resuming forward locomotion in a new direction. How is this accomplished?

18. The nervous system is sometimes compared to a telephone system. Explain why this analogy is a particularly poor one.

19. Discuss some of the evidence that some complex behavior patterns are inherited and cannot be ascribed entirely to learning.

20. Cite observations that suggest that the major factor responsible for differences in the functioning of different nervous systems is neural circuitry and not the properties of single nerve cells.

SUGGESTED READING

Bullock, T. H., R. Orkand, and A. D. Grinnell. 1977. *Integrative Neurobiology.* W. H. Freeman and Company, San Francisco.

Chalmers, N., R. Crawley, and S. P. R. Rose (eds.). 1971. *The Biological Bases of Behavior.* Open Univ. Press (Harper & Row), New York.

Dethier, V. G., and E. Stellar. 1970. *Animal Behavior.* Prentice Hall, Englewood Cliffs, N.J.

Eccles, J. C. 1973. *The Understanding of the Brain.* McGraw-Hill, New York.

Fentress, J. C. 1976. *Simpler Networks and Behavior.* Sinauer, New York.

Kandel, E. R. 1976. *Cellular Basis of Behavior.* W. H. Freeman and Company, San Francisco.

Kuffler, S. W., and J. Nicholls. 1976. *From Neuron to Brain.* Sinauer, New York.

Kutscher, C. L. 1971. *Readings in Comparative Studies of Animal Behavior.* Xerox College Pub. Co., Waltham, Mass.

Manning, A. 1972. *An Introduction to Animal Behavior.* Addison-Wesley, Menlo Park, Calif.

Sherrington, C. S. 1906. *The Integrative Action of the Nervous System* (2nd ed., 1947). Yale Univ. Press, New Haven.

REFERENCES CITED

Buddenbrock, W. von. 1956. *The Love of Animals.* Muller, London.

Bullock, T. H., and G. A. Horridge. 1965. *Structure and Function in the Nervous Systems of Invertebrates.* W. H. Freeman and Company, San Francisco.

Camhi, J. M. 1971. Flight orientation in locusts. *Scientific American* 225(2):74–81. [Also available as Offprint 1231.]

Dowling, J. E. 1970. Organization of vertebrate retinas. *Investig. Ophthal.* 9:655–680.

Eccles, J. 1960. The nature of central inhibition. *Proc. Roy. Soc. Ser. B* 153:445–476.

Eccles, J. C. 1969. Historical introduction to central cholinergic transmission and its behavioral aspects. *Fed. Proc.* 28(1):90–94.

Eckert, R. 1972. Bioelectric control of ciliary activity. *Science* 176:473–481.

Granit, R. 1970. *The Basis of Motor Control.* Academic Press, New York.

Grell, K. G. 1973. *Protozoology.* Springer-Verlag, New York.

Hartline, H. K., and F. Ratliff. 1957. Inhibitory interaction of receptor units in the eye of *Limulus. J. Gen. Physiol.* 40:357–376.

Hartline, H. K., H. G. Wanger, and F. Ratliff. 1956. Inhibition in the eye of *Limulus. J. Gen. Physiol.* 39:651–673.

Hotta, Y., and S. Benzer. 1970. Genetic dissection of the *Drosophila* nervous system by means of mosaics. *Proc. Nat. Acad. Sci.* 67:1156–1163.

Hubel, D. H. 1963. The visual cortex of the brain. *Scientific American* 209(5):54–62. [Also available as Offprint 168.]

Hubel, D. H., and T. N. Wiesel. 1960. Receptive fields of optic nerve fibers in the spider monkey. *J. Physiol.* (London) 154:572–580.

Jennings, H. S. 1906. *Behavior of the Lower Animals.* Columbia Univ. Press, New York.

Lindemann, W. 1955. Über die Jugendentwicklung beim Luchs (*Lyns* 1. *lynx* Kerr.) und bei der Wildkatze (*Feliss. sylvestris* Schreb.). *Behavior* 8:1–45.

Loeb, J. 1918. *Force Movements, Tropisms, and Animal Conduct.* Lippincott, Philadelphia.

Lorenz, K. Z. *Man Meets Dog* (translated from the German by M. K. Wilson). Methuen, London.

Merton, P. A. 1972. How we control the contractions of our muscles. *Scientific American* 226(5):30–37. [Also available as Offprint 1249.]

Michael, C. R. 1969. Retinal processing of visual images. *Scientific American* 220(5):104–114. [Also available as Offprint 1143.]

Miller, W. H., F. Ratliff, and H. K. Hartline. 1961. How cells receive stimuli. *Scientific American* 205(3):222–238. [Also available as Offprint 99.]

Naitoh, Y., and R. Eckert. 1969. Ionic mechanisms controlling behavioral responses of *Paramecium* to mechanical stimulation. *Science* 164:963–965.

Noback, C. R., and R. J. Demarest. 1972. *The Nervous System: Introduction and Review.* McGraw-Hill, New York.

Sauer, E. G. F. 1958. Celestial navigation by birds. *Scientific American* 199(2):42–47. [Also available as Offprint 133.]

Sherrington, C. S. 1906. *The Integrative Action of the Nervous System* (2nd ed., 1947). Yale Univ. Press, New Haven.

Sperry, R. W. 1959. The growth of nerve circuits. *Scientific American* 201(5):68–75.

Stent, G. S. 1972. Cellular communication. *Scientific American* 227(3):42–51. [Also available as Offprint 1257.]

Tartar, V. 1961. *The Biology of Stentor.* Pergamon Press, London.

Tinbergen, N. 1951. *The Study of Instinct.* Clarendon Press, Oxford.

Vander, A. J., D. S. Luciano, and J. H. Sherman. 1970. *Human Physiology.* McGraw-Hill, New York.

Wells, M. 1968. *Lower Animals.* McGraw-Hill, New York.

Werblin, F. S., and J. E. Dowling. 1969. Organization of the retina of the mudpuppy, *Necturus maculosus:* II, Intracellular recording. *J. Neurophys.* 32:339–355.

Willows, A. O. D. 1967. Behavioral acts elicited by stimulation of single identifiable brain cells. *Science* 157:570–574.

Willows, A. O. D. 1971. Giant brain cells in mollusks. *Scientific American* 224(2):68–75.

Wilson, D. M. 1964. *Neural Theory and Modeling.* Stanford Univ. Press.

Wilson, D. M. 1966. Central nervous system mechanisms for the generation of rhythmic behavior in anthropods. *Symp. Soc. Exp. Biol.* 20:199–228.

Wilson, D. M. 1968. Inherent asymmetry and reflex modulation of the locust flight motor pattern. *J. Exp. Biol.* 48:631–641.

Wilson, D. M. 1970. Neural operations in arthropod ganglia. *In* F. O. Schmitt (ed.), *The Neurosciences: A Second Study Program.* Rockefeller Univ. Press, New York.

Wilson, D. M., and E. Gettrup. 1963. A stretch reflex controlling wingbeat frequency in grasshopper. *J. Exp. Biol.* 40:171–185.

Wood, D. C. 1970–1971. Electrophysiological correlates of the response decrement produced by mechanical stimuli in the protozoan, *Stentor coeruleus. J. Neurobiol.* 2:1–11.

Young, R. W. 1970. Visual cells. *Scientific American* 223(4):80–91. [Also available as Offprint 1201.]

CHAPTER NINE

Muscle and Movement

The most overt examples of animal movements—such as locomotion, eating, copulation, and communication—are expressions of neural commands translated into coordinated muscle activity. The contractions of muscles are the most apparent and dramatic macroscopic signs of animal life, and have therefore excited the imagination since the times of the ancients. In the second century, Galen postulated that "animal spirits" flow from nerves into muscle, inflating the muscle so as to increase its diameter at the expense of its length. As recently as the 1950s, it was postulated that muscles shorten as the result of a shortening of linear molecules of "contractile proteins." It was suggested that such molecules possess helical configurations and that changes in the pitch of the helix produce changes in length. This hypothesis, however, was short-lived, and the development of new techniques subsequently led to a dramatic improvement in our knowledge of muscle function. As a result, our understanding of how muscles function is more complete and intellectually satisfying than most other areas of physiological knowledge. Through evidence from electron microscopy, biochemistry, and biophysics, we have learned how the contractile mechanism of muscle is organized and how it produces shortening. It is also becoming clear how the process of contraction is initiated and controlled by the electrical activity of the muscle-cell membrane.

Muscles are classified on both morphological and functional grounds into two major types, *smooth* and *striated*. Because the most is known about the structure and function of vertebrate striated muscle, we use it as the model system throughout much of this chapter. Striated muscle can be subdivided into skeletal and cardiac muscle. This division, however, is not a basic one, since the organization and function of the contractile mechanism are nearly identical in both. Differences in function between these two types arise primarily from quantitative differences in the electrical properties of their surface membranes.

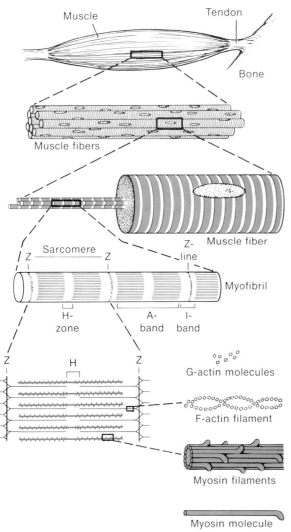

Muscle
Tendon
Bone
Muscle fibers
Muscle fiber
Z-line
Sarcomere
Z Z
Myofibril
H-zone
A-band
I-band
Z H Z
G-actin molecules
F-actin filament
Myosin filaments
Myosin molecule

Structural Basis of Contraction

The hierarchy of organization of skeletal muscle tissue is shown in Figure 9-1. The cells (or *fibers*) of striated muscle typically extend from the tendon or other connective tissue attached to one bone to a tendon attached to another bone, and they thus function in parallel. Striated muscle fibers range from 5 to 100 μm in diameter, and may be as much as several centimeters or more in length. Their extraordinary size is possible because of their syncytial origin; that is, they arise from single cells, the *myoblasts*, which fuse into *myotubes*. These in turn differentiate into the multinucleate membrane-limited *muscle fiber*. Each fiber is made up of numerous parallel subunits termed *myofibrils*, which consist of longitudinally repeated units termed *sarcomeres*, which are bounded by *Z-lines*. The sarcomere of a myofibril is the functional unit of striated muscle. The myofibrils of one muscle fiber are lined up with sarcomeres in register, giving the fiber a banded or *striated* appearance in the light microscope.

The fine structure of striated muscle is an elegant example of structure as the basis of function. The electron micrograph in Figure 9-2 shows a longitudinal section of several myofibrils. Extending in both directions from the Z-line of a myofibril are numerous *thin filaments* consisting largely of the protein *actin*. These interdigitate with *thick filaments* made up of the protein *myosin*. The myosin filaments make up the largest portion of the sarcomere, the *A-band* (the "A" stands for "anisotropic," as this band strongly polarizes visible light). The light region in the center of the A-band is called the *H-zone* (the "H" stands for *hell*, German for "bright"). The portion of the sarcomere between two A-bands is called the *I-band* (the "I" stands for "isotropic," as these bands are relatively nonpolarizing). A cross section through the I-band reveals profiles of only the actin filaments (Fig. 9-3) and a cross section

9-2. *Electron micrograph of frog muscle in a longitudinal thin section that includes two whole and two half sarcomeres of three myofibrils. I-, H-, and A-bands and Z-line are labeled. Dark granules between fibrils are glycogen. Magnification 20,000×. [Courtesy of L. D. Peachey.]*

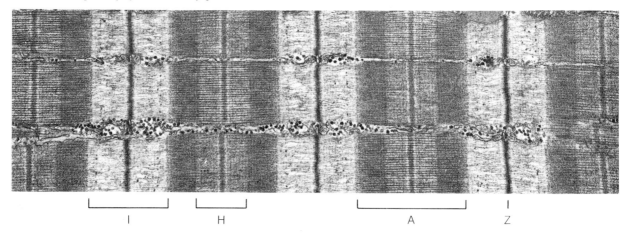

I   H   A   Z

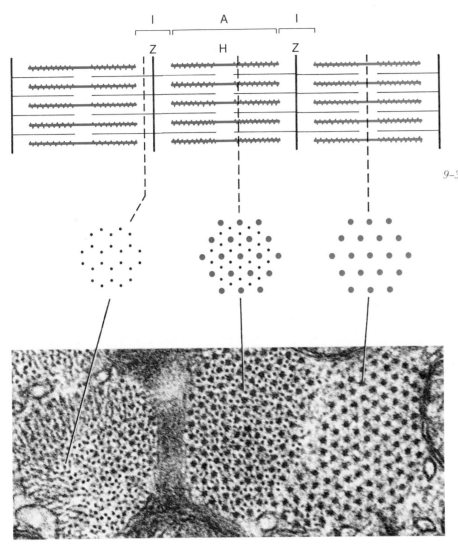

9–3. *Organization of the myofibril. Top. Diagram of three sarcomeres, showing thick and thin myofilaments forming I-, A-, and H-bands and Z-lines. Middle. Imaginary sections through the sarcomere at different levels show profiles of thin (left) and thick (right) filaments, and both types (center). Bottom. Electron micrograph of a cross section in which the sarcomeres of adjacent myofibrils are out of register, and can thus be matched with the corresponding profiles shown above. Spider monkey extraocular muscle. Magnification 100,000×. [Courtesy of L. D. Peachey.]*

9–4. *The myosin cross bridges. A. Electron micrograph in which they can be seen as faint projections extending from the myosin toward the actin filaments. [Huxley, 1963.] B. The double helical arrangement of cross bridges on the thick filaments, shown enlarged relative to part A. [After Huxley, 1969.]*

through the H-zone reveals profiles of only the myosin filaments. In the region of overlap, each myosin filament is surrounded by six actin (thin) filaments; it shares these with surrounding myosin (thick) filaments. Each actin filament is surrounded by three myosin filaments.

Close inspection with the electron microscope shows small projections, termed *cross bridges,* that extend outward from the myosin filaments (Fig. 9-4,A). These projections make contact with the actin filaments during contraction. The cross bridges are arranged in a double-helix pattern along the myosin filament (Fig. 9-4,B). The cross bridges are spaced about 143 Å apart along the axis of one helix. The angular displacement around the filament between successive cross bridges is 60°.

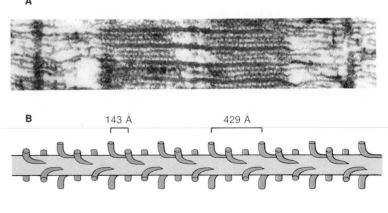

A

B   143 Å   429 Å

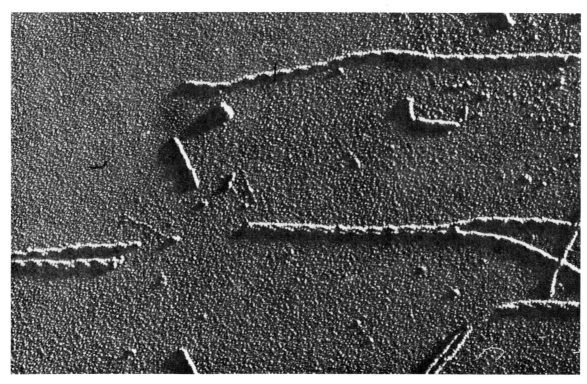

A

9–5. *Actin filaments. A. Electron micrograph of F-actin filaments. Note the double-helical arrangement of globular monomers. The specimen was prepared for microscopy by shadowing with a thin film of metal. Magnification 150,000×. [Courtesy of R. V. Rice.] B. Diagram showing the double helix of F-actin, made up of G-actin monomers. This structure has been deduced from electron micrographs (as in A) and from X-ray diffraction studies. [After Huxley, 1969.]*

B

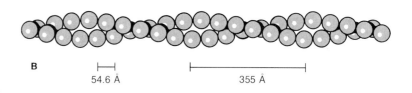

54.6 Å   355 Å

SUBSTRUCTURE OF THE MYOFILAMENTS

It has been known since the work of Kühne in the mid-nineteenth century that different protein fractions can be extracted from muscle by soaking minced muscle in water containing various concentrations of salts. Nonstructural soluble proteins, such as myoglobin, are extracted by distilled water. The actin and myosin filaments are solubilized by highly concentrated salt solutions, which break the bonds that hold together their respective monomers. Along with actin and myosin, certain other proteins are extracted in this way. Our present knowledge of muscle contraction rests in part on the isolation of actin and myosin filaments and on subsequent analyses of their structures and compositions.

Isolated fragments of myofibrils several sarcomeres in length can be prepared by homogenizing fresh muscle in a laboratory blender. Gentle homogeniza-

tion in a *relaxing solution* of Mg^{2+}, ATP, and a calcium *chelating agent* such as EGTA prevents the formation of bonds between the myosin cross bridges and the actin filaments. As a result, the myofibril falls apart into its constituent actin and myosin filaments.

The *actin filament* resembles two strings of beads twisted into a double helix (Fig. 9-5). Each "bead" is a molecule of G-actin, so called because of its globular shape. The molecules of G-actin (diameter 55 Å) are polymerized to form the long double helix of F-actin, so called because of its fiber-like appearance. This polymerization can be produced *in vitro* with purified preparations of G-actin. The F-actin double helix has a pitch of about 710 Å, so that its two strands cross over each other once every 355 Å. It should not be confused with the far smaller α-helix of peptide chains (p. 38). Actin filaments are about 1 μm long and 80 Å thick, and they are joined at one end to the material that constitutes the Z-line. Positioned in the grooves of the actin helix are the filamentous molecules of the protein *tropomyosin.* Attached to each tropomyosin is a complex of globular protein molecules collectively called *troponin.* The troponin complexes are spaced out along the actin filament at intervals of about 400 Å. As described further on, troponin and tropomyosin together play an important role in the control of muscle contraction.

The individual monomers that polymerize to form the *myosin filament* are long and thin, with an average length of 1500 Å and a width of about 20 Å (Fig. 9-6). One end of the myosin molecule forms the globular double "head region," which is about 40 Å thick and 200 Å long. The long slender portion of the molecule constitutes its "neck" and "tail."

When the myosin molecule is treated with the proteolytic enzyme trypsin, it separates into two parts—the so-called *light meromyosin (LMM)* and *heavy meromyosin (HMM).* The LMM constitutes the major part of the tail region, and the HMM makes up the globular head and a thin segment of "neck." The head region is of special interest, for it contains all the enzymatic and actin-binding activity of the parent molecule. The myosin molecule consists of two peptide chains twisted about each other the full length of the straight portion. The head is actually a composite of the globular ends of the two peptide chains.

Myosin molecules, like the molecules of G-actin, will aggregate and polymerize *in vitro* so as to reconstitute myosin (A-band) filaments. This occurs spontaneously *in vitro* when the ionic strength of a solution of myosin molecules is lowered. The first step in the formation of myosin filaments occurs when several myosin molecules aggregate with tails overlapping and heads pointing outward from the region of overlap in opposite directions (Fig. 9-7). The result is a short filament with a central region bare of heads. The filament grows as molecules of myosin add onto each end, with their tails pointing toward the center of the filament and overlapping with the tails of previously added molecules. With the addition of each myosin molecule, a new "head" projects laterally from the filament. Because the myosin molecules add on symmetrically to the growing ends, the heads on each half of the filament are oriented opposite those of the other half. Aggregation continues until the myosin filament is about 1.5 μm long and 120 Å thick. Why filaments stop growing at that length is not clear. This behavior holds special interest because the length at which *in vitro* polymerization ceases is identical with the length of the myosin filament *in vivo.* Natural and reconstituted myosin filaments exhibit other similarities. The heavy meromyosin components (head and neck) of the individual myosin molecules project from the reconstituted filaments, and these projections correspond to the cross bridges of natural myosin filaments.

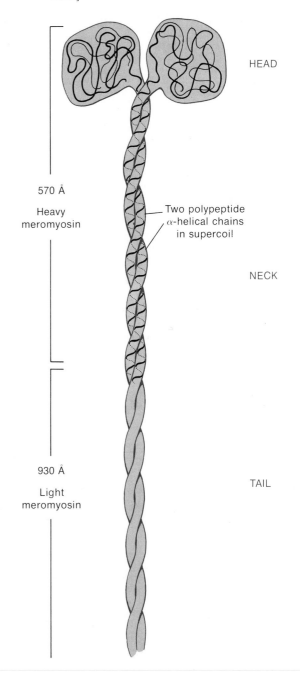

9-6. *Schematic illustration of the myosin molecule, with globular head and long thin tail. Light and heavy meromyosin are differentiated on the basis of trypsin digestion, which breaks the myosin molecule into those two parts.* [After Lehninger, 1975.]

HEAD

570 Å
Heavy meromyosin

Two polypeptide α-helical chains in supercoil

NECK

930 Å
Light meromyosin

TAIL

9-7. *A. The spontaneous* in vitro *formation of thick filaments from myosin molecules. B. Electron micrographs of myosin molecules assembled into thick filaments of various lengths. Note double-ended organization. [Huxley, 1969.]*

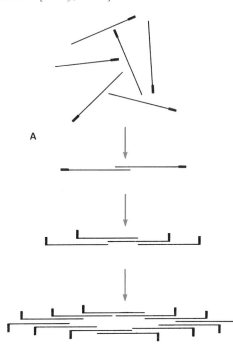

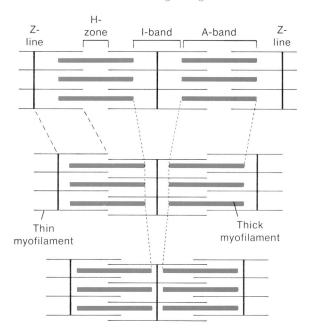

9-8. *Relations of the myofilaments during shortening of two sarcomeres. Note that the A-band retains a constant width during sliding.*

Sliding-Filament Theory of Muscle Contraction

The bands that define the sarcomeres were first observed by light microscopy well over a century ago. It was also observed that the sarcomeres undergo changes in length during stretch or contraction of the muscle, and that these changes correspond to the change in muscle length. Using a specially built interference light microscope, which permitted more accurate measurement of the sarcomeres, A. F. Huxley and R. Niedergerke in 1954 confirmed earlier reports that the A-bands maintain a constant width during shortening of the muscle, whereas the I-bands and the H-zone become narrower. When the muscle is stretched, the A-band again maintains constant width, but the I-bands and H-zone broaden. That same year, J. Hanson and H. E. Huxley reported that the myosin (A-band) and actin (I-band) filaments seen in electron micrographs do not change their lengths when the sarcomere shortens or is stretched (Fig. 9-8). Instead, the *extent of overlap* between actin and myosin filaments changes as the sarcomere changes length. Largely on the basis of these two points of evidence, H. E. Huxley and A. F. Huxley independently proposed in 1954 the *sliding-filament theory of muscle contraction.* This theory states that shortening of the sarcomere (and hence the muscle fiber) during contraction occurs as a consequence of active sliding of the thin (actin) filaments between the thick (myosin) filaments. Shortening results when the actin filaments are drawn further in toward the center of the A-band. When the muscle relaxes or is stretched, the overlap between thin and thick filaments is reduced.

The sliding-filament theory differed radically from earlier hypotheses of muscle contraction. Some workers had suggested that contraction might be due to a shortening of the protein molecules themselves, either as a result of increased folding of plaited molecules or as a result of changes in the helical pitch or diameter of helical molecules. In contrast, the sliding-filament theory holds that filaments of constant length slide past each other as a result of forces developed between the actin and myosin filaments. Evidence that cross bridges produce the sliding force is presented below.

It was noted that the myosin monomers that make up one half of the thick filament are assembled with their heads all pointing toward one Z-line, whereas those that make up the other half are oriented with their heads toward the other Z-line. This arrangement is crucial to the sliding-filament mechanism, because it allows actin filaments to slide symmetrically from both sides of a sarcomere toward the center of the A-band, accounting for the shortening of the sarcomere.

LENGTH-TENSION CURVE

One of the strongest evidences for the sliding-filament theory is the relation between amount of overlap between actin and myosin filaments and the tension produced by the active sarcomere at various amounts of filament overlap. It was reasoned by A. F. Huxley and R. Niedergerke that if each myosin cross bridge that interacts with the actin filament provides an increment of tension, the total tension produced by the sarcomere should be proportional to the number of cross bridges that can interact with actin filaments. Because the number of myosin cross bridges that can interact with the actin filaments increases linearly with the distance of filament overlap, tension should be proportional to the amount of overlap. The sliding-filament theory also predicts that no *active* tension (i.e., beyond that due to the elasticity of the muscle fiber) will be developed if the sarcomere is stretched so far that there is no longer any overlap between actin and myosin filaments.

To test these predicted relations between filament overlap and tension, single amphibian muscle fibers were stimulated to contract at different fixed sarcomere lengths, which, of course, are linearly related to the amount of overlap between the actin and myosin filaments (Fig. 9-9). This was done with the aid of an electromechanical system that controlled muscle-fiber tension so as to hold the sarcomeres at any desired constant length. The tension required to do so was measured and plotted as a function of sarcomere length. Tension was found to increase linearly with decreasing sarcomere length between 3.65 μm and 2.25 μm. When the sarcomere was allowed to shorten until the actin filaments overlapped completely with

9–9. *Relations between filament overlap and contractile force. A. The length-tension curve for muscle. The state of the sarcomere is shown at critical points on the curve. B. The critical stages in overlap between actin and myosin during sliding (as represented in A) are shown at the bottom. The upper diagram in this part of the figure establishes the dimensional nomenclature used in the other parts. [After Gordon et al., 1966.]*

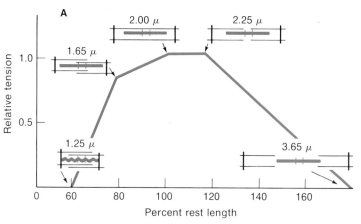

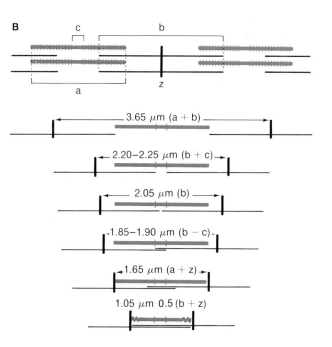

the segment of the myosin filament that bears the cross bridges, the tension was maximal. When the fiber was stretched until there was no overlap at all, stimulation produced no tension beyond the passive elastic tension of the resting state. At the other extreme, when the fiber was allowed to shorten until the actin filaments from the two halves of the sarcomere collided, tension decreased with further shortening. Tension decreased still more steeply when shortening was allowed to proceed beyond the point at which the myosin filaments crumpled up against the Z-line.

It is crucial in these experiments that the length measurements be made on small groups of sarcomeres of uniform behavior near the center of the muscle fiber. Measurements made earlier with less precise techniques yielded rounded curves, because the various sarcomeres of a whole muscle—and, indeed, of a single fiber—were in different stages of overlap at any instant. From the length–tension relation, it was predicted that muscles with longer actin and myosin filaments (long sarcomeres) should develop greater tensions. This prediction has since been confirmed.

Cross-Bridge Function and the Production of Force

The most fundamental questions in muscle research are concerned with the precise functioning of the cross bridges. According to recent versions of the sliding-filament theory, the energy for muscle contraction comes from the sequential binding of several sites on the myosin head to sites on the actin filament. ATP is then hydrolyzed to provide the energy to release the head of the cross bridge from the actin filament, freeing it for another cycle of sequential binding further along the actin filament. The following subsections explain this model in detail.

CHEMISTRY OF CROSS-BRIDGE ACTIVITY

Clues to the chemistry of cross bridge interaction with the actin filaments have their origin in studies begun several decades ago on crude and purified extracts of muscle. Semipurified solutions of actin and myosin—extracted from freshly minced rabbit muscle with concentrated salt solutions and subsequently precipitated by ammonium chloride—exhibited several interesting physical properties. Among them are (1) the formation of an actin–myosin, or *actomyosin,* complex that has a distinctly higher viscosity than a disassociated mixture of actin and myosin, and (2) the formation of a precipitate of the actomyosin gel, which contracts upon addition of Mg^{2+}-ATP in the presence

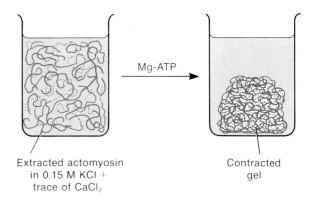

9–10. Syneresis of an actomyosin extract upon the addition of Mg-ATP.

Extracted actomyosin in 0.15 M KCl + trace of $CaCl_2$

Mg-ATP

Contracted gel

of small amounts of calcium (initially the calcium was present as a contaminant and was therefore overlooked). The contraction of the gel squeezes water out from between its molecular lattice (Fig. 9-10). This process, termed *syneresis* by polymer chemists, proved useful in muscle chemistry as a test-tube analogue of muscle contraction.

When mixed together, the actin and myosin solutions form the actomyosin complex spontaneously without ATP. This explains the high viscosity that results when an actin solution is added to a myosin solution. But the actomyosin complex require Mg^{2+}-ATP to undergo syneresis. The ATPase activity (i.e., ensymatic hydrolysis of the terminal phosphate bond of ATP) of the myosin catalyses the following reaction:

$$Mg\text{-}ATP + \text{actomyosin} \rightarrow \text{actomyosin-}Mg^{2+}\text{-ATP}$$
$$\rightarrow \text{actomyosin-}Mg^{2+}\text{-ADP} + P_i$$

Binding of myosin to actin takes place either in the absence of ATP or when the ATPase site is poisoned. This suggests that binding of actin to myosin occurs at a site different from the ATPase site of the myosin. Even though different parts of the myosin appear to be involved, there is an interaction between the actin-binding site of the myosin and the enzymatic site for splitting of ATP, for the ATPase activity of myosin is greatly enhanced by the formation of the actomyosin complex. This is evident from the observation that the ATPase activity of myosin by itself is much lower than that of actomyosin. The formation of the actomyosin complex may activate the ATPase site by an allosteric mechanism. The head portion alone shows all the ATPase and actin-binding activity of the myosin. This is also the only part of the myosin molecule that comes in contact with the actin filament in the living muscle.

CROSS-BRIDGE ATTACHMENT AND MUSCLE CONTRACTION

The technique of X-ray diffraction has made it possible to correlate tension with cross-bridge position in contracting muscle. The X-ray diffraction pattern of insect fibrillar flight muscle* (p. 308) was projected onto a lead screen (Fig. 9-11,A). The screen had a hole in the position corresponding to the spot produced by the inherent periodicity of the actin (Fig. 9-4). Without going into the theory of X-ray diffraction, we can simply state that the intensity of the X-rays of such a spot on the diffraction pattern is a function of the number of units in the specimen that produce the X-ray spot. Thus, as the cross bridges swing out from the myosin filament and attach to the actin, they scatter X-rays away from the spot corresponding to the actin periodicity, and that spot then receives less intense bombardment of X-rays. The intensity of X-radiation producing that spot was monitored by means of a Geiger counter placed behind the opening in the lead screen. When the muscle was made to undergo oscillatory contractions and relaxations, the fluctuating intensity of the actin spot was correlated with fluctuating muscle tension; the relationship is plotted in Figure 9-11,B. Increased muscle tension was correlated with decreased signal due to cross-bridge attachment to the actin filaments (Fig. 9-12,A,B), thus supporting the idea that the sliding movement between the myosin and actin filaments results from forces produced by the cross bridges acting on the actin filaments.

*This muscle was used because it can be made to oscillate spontaneously between relaxation and contraction without nervous control after the ions and soluble molecules are extracted by low-temperature storage in a water-glycerol solution.

9–11. The use of an X-ray diffraction technique to correlate muscle tension with cross-bridge movement. A. Experimental arrangement for X-ray diffraction studies. A Geiger counter behind a hole in the lead screen monitors the fluctuations in intensity of the X-ray spot produced by reflections from the actin. The intensity of the spot declines as cross bridges attach to the actin and obscure its intrinsic periodicity. B. Tension in water beetle flight muscle undergoing cyclic contraction is plotted in broken curve. The intensity of the X-ray spot declines (i.e., number of cross-bridge attachments increases; solid line) as the tension in the muscle rises. Note the high X-ray intensity for relaxed muscle. [After Miller and Traeger, 1971.]

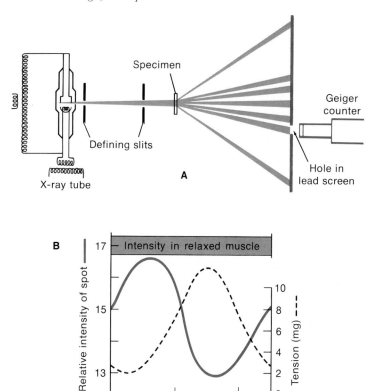

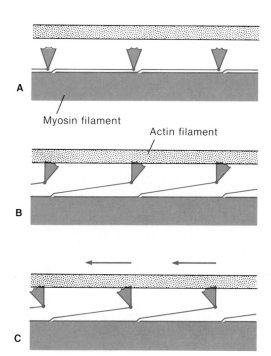

9–12. Sequence of events in the attachment of cross bridges to actin filaments. A. Relaxed state. B. Myosin heads attach to actin. C. Rotation of heads pulls on actin filament, causing it to slide past myosin filament. Although the cross bridges are shown acting in unison, they actually act out of synchrony. [After Huxley, 1969; Huxley and Simmons, 1971.]

9-13. *Mechanism proposed for cross-bridge function. This model shows four sites on the myosin head. These sites, M_1 to M_4, interact in sequence (left to right) with sites on the actin. The rocking motion produced in this manner causes the myosin head to pull on the elastic cross-bridge link, stretching it. This tension pulls the actin filament toward the left, causing it to slide past the myosin filament. [After Huxley and Simmons, 1971.]*

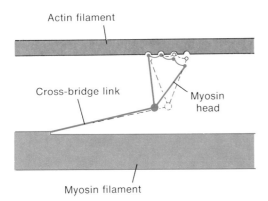

Actin filament

Cross-bridge link

Myosin head

Myosin filament

The cross bridges must alternately attach to the actin filament, exert force, detach, and reattach at another locus. For maintained active contraction, the activity of the cross bridges must be asynchronous, so that at any instant some of them are attached while others are detached from the actin. It is presumed that, after detaching, the cross bridge reattaches to the actin filament further toward the Z-line, because there is continued sliding in that direction during shortening.

One of the major problems in cross-bridge function is to understand how chemical energy is transduced into mechanical energy. How do the cross bridges produce a sliding force between thick and thin filaments? There have been a number of suggestions. The most widely accepted view is that a *rotation* of the myosin head (Fig. 9-12,B,C) produces force, and that this force is transmitted to the thick filament through the neck of the myosin molecule, the neck forming the *cross-bridge link* between the head of the myosin molecule and the thick filament. In this hypothesis, the *link* acts as a connection between the myosin head and the thick filament, transmitting the force produced by rotation of the head on the actin filament.

Recent studies of the mechanical properties of contracting muscle by A. F. Huxley and R. M. Simmons have provided support for this view of cross-bridge function. They obtained evidence that much of the elasticity that exists *in series* with the contractile component (see Series Elastic Components, p. 301) of the muscle resides in the cross bridges themselves. They

have postulated that the cross-bridge link is the site of the elasticity, and that the elastic stretching of the link serves the important function of storing mechanical energy as the head makes a rotational movement against the actin filament (Fig. 9-13). According to their hypothesis, several sites on the head interact with sites on the actin filament. These sites are arranged in an order of increasing myosin-actin affinities (left to right in Fig. 9-13). Thus, after site M_1 attaches, the tendency is for the head to rotate so that site M_2 attaches, then M_3, and so forth. This causes point B to move toward the right in Figure 9-13.

The elasticity of the link (segment A to B in Fig. 9-13) would allow the rotational movement to occur without abrupt changes in tension. Once stretched, the link would transmit its tension smoothly to the thick filament, contributing force to promote filament sliding. One of the major evidences in favor of this scheme is the finding by Huxley and Simmons that the series elasticity of a muscle fiber is proportional to the amount of thick- and thin-filament overlap, and hence is proportional to the number of attached cross bridges. They also found that sudden small decreases in length are accompanied by very rapid recovery of tension, which they explain as being due merely to the rotation of the cross-bridge heads into their more stable positions of interaction with actin sites (i.e., from the M_1 to the M_4 position of interaction).

The sequence of events in cross-bridge function most widely accepted at this time can be summarized as follows.

1. The head of the cross bridge attaches to the actin filament at the first of a sequence of stable sites. It then goes to the second, third, and successive sites, each of which exhibits a greater myosin-actin affinity than the previous one (i.e., a lower energy state).

2. This produces a rocking, or rotation, of the myosin head (Fig. 9-12), causing it to pull on the cross-bridge link connecting the myosin head to the thick filament. The elasticity of the link allows the step-like rocking of the head to progress without sudden, large transients in tension in the link.

3. Tension in the link is transmitted to the myosin filament, and sliding occurs, allowing the tension built up in the stretching of the link to subside.

4. When the rotation of the head is complete, Mg^{2+}-ATP (attached to the ATPase site of the head region before Step 1) is hydrolyzed by the ATPase, and the free energy released is utilized to detach the myosin head from the actin filament. The cross bridge is then free to repeat the cycle a little further along the actin filament. In this way, sliding is produced in small incremental steps of cross-bridge attachment, rotation, and detachment.

Two things are especially noteworthy in this sequence. First, ATP is not utilized directly to produce cross-bridge force, but to detach the cross bridge and "recharge" the myosin head so that it can repeat the cycle. This may take place by means of a conformational change in the head region. Second, cross-bridge attachment requires the presence of free intracellular Ca^{2+} concentrations above 10^{-6} M. The role of calcium in controlling cross-bridge function is discussed in the following subsections.

Role of Calcium in Contraction

CROSS-BRIDGE ACTIVATION

Evidence gradually accumulated that calcium ions play an important role in contractile activity of muscle. This was realized only gradually, because calcium is active in such low (10^{-6} M or below) sarcoplasmic concentrations, and before the discovery of calcium-chelating agents such as EDTA and EGTA, it was not feasible to keep the Ca^{2+} concentration of experimental solutions to such low levels. The earliest evidence for a physiological role of Ca^{2+} came from the work of S. Ringer in the late nineteenth century. Ringer found that the isolated frog heart stops contracting if calcium is omitted from the bathing saline. Later, when electrophysiological methods were available, it was found that contraction ceases in low Ca^{2+}, even though cardiac action potentials continue.

The possibility that Ca^{2+} participates in the regulation of muscle contraction was tested by the introduction of various cations into the interior of muscle fibers by T. Kamada and H. Kinosita in 1943, and later by L. V. Heilbrunn and F. J. Wierczinski. Of all the ions tested, only calcium was found to produce contraction at concentrations commensurate with those normally found in living tissue. It was subsequently found that skeletal muscle fails to contract in response to depolarization after its internal calcium stores are depleted, and that extracted models of skeletal muscle fibers (Box 9-1) fail to contract in response to added ATP if Ca^{2+} is absent.

The quantitative relation between sarcoplasmic free Ca^{2+} concentration and muscle contraction has been determined more recently by peeling off the surface membrane and exposing the naked myofibrils to solutions of different calcium concentrations. As seen in Figure 9-14,A, the tension rises sigmoidally from zero at a calcium concentration of about 10^{-8} M to a maximum at about 5×10^{-6} M. This is closely paralleled by the calcium dependence of ATP hydrolysis (ATPase activity) of homogenized myofibrils (Fig. 9-14,B). These lines of evidence suggest that Ca^{2+} might act as cofactor for the ATPase activity of myosin, but this turned out *not* to be so.

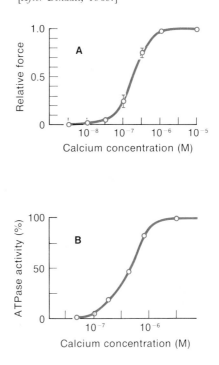

9-14. A. *Relationship between the Ca concentration and the force produced in a glycerinated muscle.* [*After Hellam and Podolsky, 1967.*] B. *ATPase activity in a suspension of isolated myofibrils as a function of Ca concentration.* [*After Bendall, 1969.*]

In *semi*-purified extracts of actomyosin, the hydrolysis of ATP and syneresis require the presence of minute ($\geq 10^{-7}$ M) amounts of Ca^{2+}. The low-level requirement for calcium was initially overlooked because calcium is normally present as a contaminant of even the most pure off-the-shelf salts. As noted earlier, it was only after the introduction of calcium-chelating agents that this problem was recognized and overcome.

The calcium dependence of ATPase activity and syneresis disappeared when the actomyosin extracts were purified sufficiently to remove from the actin filaments the closely associated proteins troponin and tropomyosin. It then became evident that Ca^{2+} is not directly required for the contractile activity of actin and myosin. Magnesium is, in fact, the only ion necessary for the ATPase activity of myosin. It became clear, then, that the calcium requirement for activation of the ATPase, and hence for contraction, is closely tied to the presence of troponin and tropomyosin.

How, then, does Ca^{2+} induce contraction? As noted earlier, the ATPase activity of a pure myosin solution is low, but shows a great increase when purified actin is added. This indicates that *the ATPase site of the myosin is activated when myosin binds to actin*. In the intact muscle, the ATPase site of the cross bridge is activated when the cross bridge attaches to the actin filament. Experi-

BOX 9-1   EXTRACTED CELL MODELS

One of the key advances in cell physiology was made in the late 1940's when Albert Szent-Györgyi developed the glycerine-extracted muscle "model," which he and his followers used to elucidate certain facets of muscle activity. After a muscle fiber has been soaked in a solution made up of equal parts of glycerine and water at subzero temperatures for several days or weeks, the cell membrane is disrupted and all soluble substances are leached out, leaving the contractile mechanism intact. The glycerine acts as an antifreeze, and also solubilizes membranes. The subfreezing storage temperature serves to keep the enzymes active while slowing catabolic processes that would cause the cells to digest themselves. The *glycerinated fibers* can be made to contract and relax under the appropriate conditions. The significance of using *extracted, reactivated* cells is that they allow the investigator to control the composition of the intracellular milieu without interference from the regulatory mechanisms of the cell membrane and other metabolic processes.

More recently, this method of producing extracted models of cells has been improved upon by the use of nonionic detergents, such as the Triton X series. These agents, used at about zero degrees, rapidly solubilize the lipid components of the cell membrane, allowing dissolved metabolites to diffuse out of the cell and substances in the extracellular medium to diffuse rapidly into the cell. Because this all takes place within minutes instead of days, much time is saved and enzymatic activity remains higher. Many of the structurally fixed enzymes remain active, permitting the reactivation of motile cells such as amoebae, fibroblasts, and ciliates by external application of ATP and essential ions.

---

ments done in S. Ebashi's laboratory indicate that troponin and tropomyosin, which have been found to lie in the grooves of the actin helix (Fig. 9-15), inhibit the attachment of cross bridges to actin. Troponin is the only protein in the actin and myosin filaments with a high binding affinity for Ca^{2+}, each troponin complex binding four calcium ions. The troponin complex occurs every 400 Å along the actin filament, attached to both the actin filament and the tropomyosin molecule. In the resting state, the tropomyosin lies in a position that interferes sterically with the binding of the myosin heads to the actin filament. Upon binding Ca^{2+}, the troponin undergoes a change in conformation that moves the tropomyosin out of the way, permitting the myosin cross bridges to attach to actin sites (Fig. 9-15,B). Thus, binding of Ca^{2+} to troponin removes a constant inhibition of the cross bridge, sliding-filament mechanism. It is inferred from experiments like those shown in Figures 9-14 and 9-16 that release of cross-bridge inhibition occurs at free calcium concentrations above 10^{-7} M.

CROSS-BRIDGE INACTIVATION AND MUSCLE RELAXATION

In the resting state, an internal system of membrane-limited sacs, the *sarcoplasmic reticulum* (p. 294), actively takes up Ca^{2+}. This process keeps the levels of free Ca^{2+} below 10^{-7} M. At those concentrations, very little calcium binds to the troponin, and the cross bridges remain inactive. Thus removal of Ca^{2+} from the sarcoplasm by the reticulum causes the muscle to relax after a contraction.

Because ATP supplies the energy for contraction, one might conclude that relaxation can also be produced by removal of ATP. This, it turns out, does not happen.

A muscle becomes rigid and inextensible when all of its ATP and phosphagen stores are depleted. This state, known as *rigor mortis,* is due to the failure of the cross bridges to detach from the actin filaments. That Mg^{2+}-ATP is required for relaxation has been known since the early experiments with glycerine-extracted models of muscle (Box 9-1). In the presence of Ca^{2+}, the extracted muscle contracts when Mg^{2+}-ATP is added (Fig. 9-16,A), and subsequently relaxes if Ca^{2+} is removed. Relaxation, like contraction, occurs only if Mg^{2+}-ATP is present (Fig. 9-16,B). Why should ATP be required for relaxation as well as for contraction? In the living muscle, the cross-bridge bond with actin is broken only by the hydrolysis of ATP. If there is no available ATP, the cross bridges remain attached, and the muscle goes into rigor. Normally there is an adequate supply of ATP, and the cross bridges readily detach. The muscle then relaxes if the sarcoplasmic

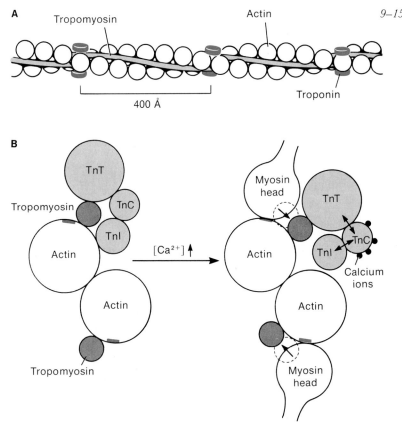

A

Tropomyosin   Actin

400 Å

Troponin

B

TnT

Tropomyosin

TnC

TnI

Actin

$[Ca^{2+}]\uparrow$

Actin

Tropomyosin

Myosin head

TnT

TnC

TnI

Actin

Calcium ions

Actin

Myosin head

9–15. *Muscle regulatory proteins. A. The arrangement of troponin and tropomyosin on the actin filament, as first postulated by Ebashi (1969). B. A more recent model, shown in cross section, of their manner of action. At left, under resting conditions of low $[Ca^{2+}]_i$, the troponin complex, consisting of units C (TnC), T (TnT), and I (TnI), bonds in such a way with the actin and tropomyosin as to cause the latter to interfere sterically with the attachment of the cross-bridge heads to the myosin-binding sites of the actin. At right, an increase in sarcoplasmic $[Ca^{2+}]$ allows TnC to bind Ca^{2+}, causing a change in subunit affinities and a consequent shift of the tropomyosin molecule away from the myosin-binding site. The cross-bridge activity can then proceed until the Ca^{2+} is removed from the TnC.*

free calcium concentration is below the level required to allow cross-bridge attachment to the actin filaments.

Thus muscle relaxation depends on the presence of Mg^{2+}-ATP to break the myosin-actin complex and on a calcium concentration sufficiently low to prevent reattachment of the cross bridges to the actin filaments.

Electromechanical Coupling

The arrival of an action potential at the terminals of the motor axon that innervates a vertebrate skeletal muscle fiber causes the release of the neurotransmitter acetylcholine. This leads to a postsynaptic potential at the muscle endplate (Chapter 6), which in turn triggers an all-or-none action potential in the surface membrane of the muscle fiber. This action potential propagates away from the endplate in both directions, so as to excite the entire muscle-fiber membrane. The contractile mechanism responds with a latency of several milliseconds from the peak of the action potential. Whenever the action potential occurs, the muscle fiber responds with an all-or-none twitch (Fig. 9-17). Somehow the action potential sets in motion the sequence of events leading to contraction. We will now consider the *coupling* of contraction to the electrical events that accompany the action potential.

9–16. *Dependence of tension in glycerine-extracted muscle on Mg-ATP and Ca^{2+}. A. Contraction requires Ca^{2+}. B. Mg-ATP is required for both contraction and relaxation.*

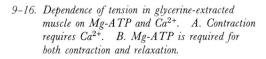
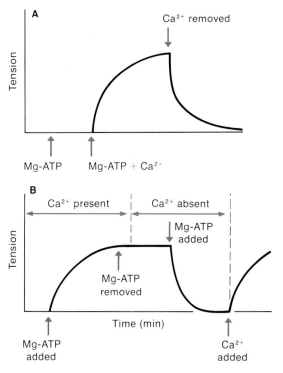

A

Tension

Ca^{2+} removed

Mg-ATP   Mg-ATP + Ca^{2+}

B

Ca^{2+} present Ca^{2+} absent

Tension

Mg-ATP added

Mg-ATP removed

Time (min)

Mg-ATP added Ca^{2+} added

BOX 9-2   CONTRACTILE PROTEINS IN NONMUSCLE CELLS

Active movements of various kinds occur in all cells. These movements include cell cleavage, in which the cleavage furrow constricts to divide the cell, and chromosome movements by the spindle fibers during mitosis and meiosis. Many cells exhibit locomotory movements. The most familiar of these are ciliary (Chapter 10) and amoeboid movement. The amoebae propel themselves by flowing into *pseudopodia*. Other amoeboid cells are the phagocytes and fibroblasts of vertebrates.

Most active cell movements appear to arise from the interactions of filaments. In recent years, molecules closely resembling myosin and actin have been identified in many cells, ranging from sea urchin eggs to brain cells.

It has been found that actin and myosin isolated from muscle and from various nonmuscle cells such as the slime mold will cross-react with one another. That is, muscle myosin will decorate actin filaments isolated from other cell types, and vice versa. This observation, together with biochemical characterization, indicates that the myosins and actins found in a variety of cells are basically similar. There is one interesting variable that has become apparent in studies of various actin-myosin systems. The interaction of actin and myosin in skeletal muscle is regulated by an interaction of Ca^{2+} with the regulatory proteins (i.e., troponin and tropomyosin) associated with the actin, a process termed *actin-regulated* contraction. In vertebrate smooth muscle and many invertebrate muscles, as well as in several amoeboid cells, the actin-myosin interaction is regulated by an action of Ca^{2+} on the myosin. These systems are termed *myosin-regulated*. The regulatory action of Ca^{2+} in these systems also depends on the presence of a protein other than actin or myosin. This protein, like troponin in the actin-regulated systems, appears to interact with calcium to permit the myosin heads to attach to the actin filaments.

The manner in which actin and myosin interact to produce movement in nonmuscle cells is not yet understood, but it is under study in several laboratories.

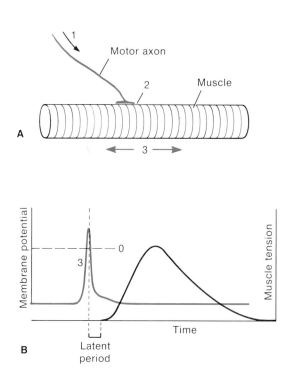

9-17. *Excitation of muscle fiber. A. Action potential in motor nerve (1) leads to postsynaptic potential (2), and this gives rise to a propagated muscle action potential (3). B. The action potential in the muscle fiber is followed after a latent period by an all-or-none contraction.*

MEMBRANE POTENTIAL AND CONTRACTION

Replacing some of the Na$^+$ with K$^+$ in the extracellular fluid depolarizes the cell membrane (Chapter 5). This provides a convenient way of depolarizing the muscle membrane to different levels, for the degree of depolarization depends on the K$^+$ concentration. Muscle fibers show a transient contraction (termed *contracture*, to differentiate from a normal contraction) in response to sudden, maintained depolarizations. Single frog muscle fibers were exposed to various concentrations of K$^+$ while membrane potential and muscle tension were monitored (Fig. 9-18,A). With depolarization, tension begins to develop at about -60 mV (the mechanical threshold) (Fig. 9-18,B); with a further depolarization, tension increases sigmoidally, reaching a maximum at about -25 mV. This demonstrates that the contractile system is capable of *graded contraction* in response to varying degrees of reduced membrane potential.

During the action potential, the membrane swings from a resting value of about -90 mV to an overshoot of about $+50$ mV, an excursion of 140 mV. The peak is as much as 75 mV more positive than the potential required to give a maximum contracture (Fig. 9-19). Thus the muscle twitch is all-or-none because the action potential is all-or-none, and the potential greatly exceeds the plateau (Fig. 9-18,B) at which mechanical activation during steady depolarization is saturated.

The direct physical influence of a potential difference across the surface membrane can extend only several micrometers at most from both surfaces of the membrane. Thus a potential change across the surface membrane cannot exert a direct effect on the great bulk of myofibrils in a muscle fiber 50 to 100 μm in diameter. It therefore became necessary to look for a substance or a process that couples changes in surface membrane potentials to the myofibrils deep within the muscle fiber. The local circuit currents produced by a propagated action potential were ruled out because currents of physiological magnitude passed between two microelectrodes inserted in a muscle fiber produced no contraction.

During the 1930's and 1940's, L. V. Heilbrunn emphasized the importance of calcium in cellular processes, and showed that Ca^{2+} injected into a muscle fiber initiates contraction. He proposed that the physiological contraction of muscle is also controlled by intracellular changes in calcium concentration. We now know that this hypothesis is essentially correct. It was widely rejected at first, however, because (1) before the discovery of the sarcoplasmic reticulum it was assumed that, to initiate contraction, calcium would have to enter the cell entirely through the surface membrane, and (2) A. V. Hill pointed out in 1948 that

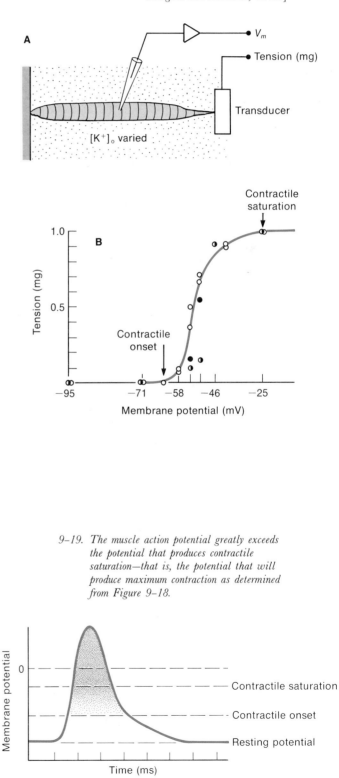

9–18. *Relation between membrane potential and contractile tension. A. Experimental setup for measuring tension and potential changes in an isolated muscle fiber in response to various external concentrations of KCl. B. Membrane depolarized to varying degrees by adjusting the KCl concentration. The tension was found to rise sigmoidally with depolarization.* [*After Hodgkin and Horowicz, 1960.*]

9–19. *The muscle action potential greatly exceeds the potential that produces contractile saturation—that is, the potential that will produce maximum contraction as determined from Figure 9–18.*

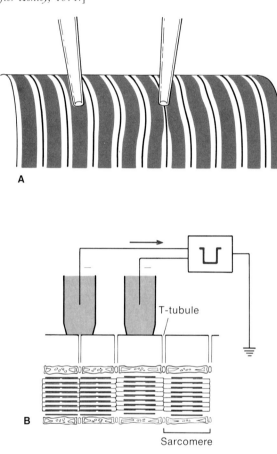

A

B

Sarcomere

the rate of diffusion of an ion or molecule from the surface membrane to the center of a muscle fiber 25 to 50 μm in radius is several times too slow to account for the short latent period (about 2 ms) between the action potential at the surface membrane and activation of the entire cross-section of the muscle fiber. Hill correctly concluded that a *process* rather than a substance must communicate the surface signal to myofibrils deep within the muscle fiber in order to initiate contraction. As we shall see below, the surface signal is conducted into the cell interior, where it causes the release of intracellular Ca^{2+} from internal storage depots. The Ca^{2+} released in this way permits the cross bridges to enter into action and produce active sliding.

THE SARCOTUBULAR SYSTEM

Anatomical and physiological evidence for a process of intracellular communication linking the surface membrane to the internal myofibrils came to light about 10 years after Hill's calculation. In 1958, A. F. Huxley and R. E. Taylor stimulated the surface of single muscle fibers of the frog with glass-capillary stimulating electrodes (Fig. 9-20). Externally applied pulses of current too small to initiate an action potential, but sufficient to produce depolarization of the membrane under the opening of the microelectrode, were observed to produce local contractions near the surface of the fiber. Listed here are Huxley and Taylor's most significant findings.

1. Local contractions occur only if the tip of the capillary is positioned on the fiber surface with its opening over a Z-line.

2. This happens only at certain loci spaced around the perimeter of the fiber along each Z-line.

3. Contractions spread further inward as the intensity of stimulating current is raised.

4. Contractions are limited to both half-sarcomeres immediately on either side of the Z-line over which the electrode is positioned; thus there is inward spread, but no longitudinal spread, of the graded contraction.

Electron micrographs of amphibian skeletal muscle have provided the anatomical correlate of these findings. Running around the perimeter of each myofibril at the level of the Z-line is a membrane-limited *transverse tubule* (*T-tubule*) less than 0.1 μm in diameter, which branches so that it is continuous with similar tubules surrounding neighboring myofibrils at the same level (Fig. 9-21). The anastomosing system of tubules eventually reaches and connects with the surface membrane. For some time it was uncertain whether continuity exists between the lumen of the T-tubule system and the cell exterior. Continuity was finally confirmed by the demonstration that ferritin and horseradish peroxidase (large electron-opaque protein molecules) placed in the bath find their way into the T-tubules before the tissue is fixed for electron microscopy. Because these molecules do not cross cell membranes, the T-tubules must be open to the extracellular space, arising as invaginations of the surface membrane.

The T-tubule system provides the anatomical link between the surface membrane and the myofibrils deep inside the muscle fiber. With Huxley's stimulating pipette placed over the entrance to a T-tubule at the surface membrane (Fig. 9-20), stimulating current spreads down the tubule to initiate contraction deep within the muscle fiber. This conclusion is supported by comparative studies that correlate the location of the T-tubule system with surface sensitivity to current. In muscles where the T-tubules are located at the ends of the A-band instead of at the Z-line (e.g., crab,

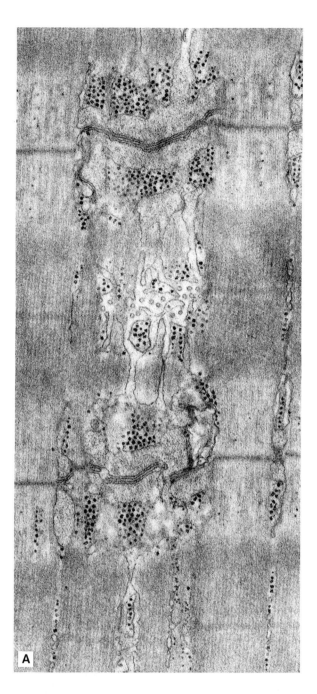

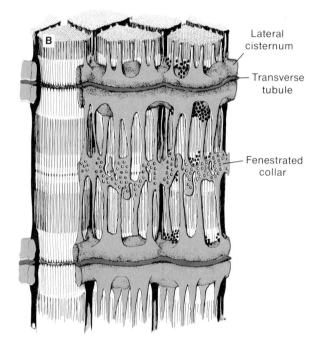

9–21. *Electron micrograph (A) and diagram (B) showing the sarcoplasmic reticulum (light color) and transverse tubules (dark color) of striated skeletal muscle of the frog. Dark spots are glycogen granules.* [*Peachey, 1965.*]

Lateral cisternum

Transverse tubule

Fenestrated collar

Fig. 9-22, and lizard), the current-sensitive spots on the surface membrane are found at the edges of the A-band.

The role of the T-tubules in the process that couples activation of the sarcomeres to depolarization of the surface membrane was demonstrated by breaking the connections of the T-tubules to the surface membrane through osmotic shock with a 50% glycerol solution. When the tubules are disconnected from the surface membrane in this way, membrane depolarization no longer evokes a contraction. Thus physical uncoupling of the T-tubule system results in functional uncoupling of the contractile system from the surface membrane.

The inward spread of electrical signals down the T-tubules was at first thought to be simply electrotonic. Recent work has demonstrated that the spread of contraction to the center of a twitch fiber in response to membrane depolarization is reduced by adding tetrodotoxin (p. 133) or by lowering the Na^+ concentration. Either treatment will reduce or eliminate sodium action potentials. It appears, then, that the action potential characteristic of the surface membrane of a vertebrate twitch fiber is carried deep into the muscle fiber along the membranes of the transverse tubules. In muscle fibers that do not produce action potentials (e.g., many arthropod muscles), the T-tubules carry pas-

9-22. Crab muscle. A. Structure of crab muscle fiber resembles that of vertebrate fibers, except for larger diameter, deep clefts, and location of T-tubules. B. The current-sensitive spots are located at the edges of the A-bands, which suggested that the T-tubules open to the surface near the edges of the A-bands, rather than at the Z-lines as in vertebrate muscle. This hypothesis was subsequently confirmed with the electron microscope. [After Ashley, 1971.]

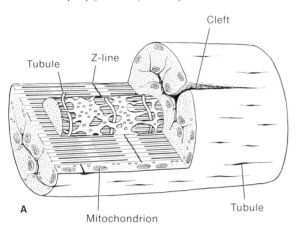

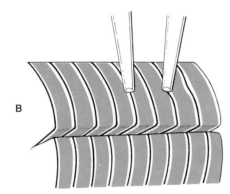

sive electrotonic signals in keeping with the graded depolarizations of the surface membrane.

SARCOPLASMIC RETICULUM

In addition to the system of transverse tubules, there is the *sarcoplasmic reticulum* (*SR*), which is wrapped separately as a hollow collar around each myofibril from one Z-line to another (Fig. 9-21). The SR surrounding each sarcomere consists of a membrane-enclosed compartment separate from the sarcoplasm. The *terminal cisternae* of the SRs of two adjacent sarcomeres make intimate contact with the T-tubule, which is sand-

wiched between them. The manner in which the depolarization of the T-tubules conveys a signal to the terminal cisternae of the SR remains unknown. There is speculation, but no direct evidence, that the region of contact between the T-tubule and terminal cisternae of the SR may be specialized as a low-resistance pathway for the spread of electric current between the interior of the T-tubule and the lumen of the SR.

When isolated by fractionation techniques, membranes of the sarcoplasmic reticulum form microscopic vesicles about 1 μm in diameter. These can take up calcium ions from the surrounding medium. If oxalate is present, a calcium oxalate precipitate is seen to form within the vesicles as the calcium concentration within the vesicles increases because of active calcium transport by the membrane of the reticulum. In unfractionated tissue, the calcium oxalate can be visualized in the terminal cisternae with the electron microscope. The calcium-sequestering activity of the SR is sufficiently powerful to keep the concentration of free Ca^{2+} in the sarcoplasm of the resting muscle below 10^{-7} M, which is sufficient to remove the calcium bound to the troponin and prevent contraction.

CALCIUM RELEASE BY THE SARCOPLASMIC RETICULUM

Once it became known that calcium ions are accumulated by the SR, it seemed likely that muscle contraction is initiated by release of Ca^{2+} from the interior of the SR cisternae into the sarcoplasm. Direct evidence that free sarcoplasmic Ca^{2+} increases in response to stimulation has come from a photometric method that utilizes the calcium-sensitive protein *aequorin* (extracted from the jellyfish *Aequorea*). When a molecule of aequorin combines with two Ca^{2+} ions, it emits a photon of visible light. After aequorin is injected into the large muscle fiber of the giant barnacle, a photomultiplier can be used to monitor changes in light emission (Fig. 9-23) as calcium undergoes transient concentration changes. Depolarization of the muscle membrane is followed by light emission, which begins before an increase in tension is recorded from the muscle fiber (Fig. 9-24). Increased intensity or duration of depolarization produces greater light emission (indicating a greater calcium concentration) along with greater tension (Fig. 9-25). In this way, tension developed in response to membrane depolarization has been directly correlated with transients in the concentration of free Ca^{2+} in the sarcoplasm.

Contraction is normally controlled electrically by membrane depolarization. A muscle fiber will nevertheless contract without any change in membrane potential if placed in a solution containing a small amount of caffeine or theophylline, methyl xanthenes that produce contracture by causing the release of calcium

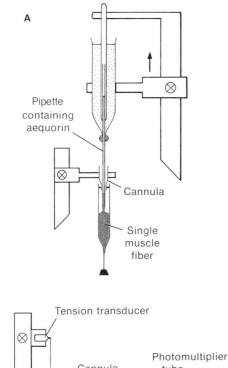

9-23. *Method for injecting aequorin and monitoring calcium transients in muscle fibers. A. Setup for injection. B. A photomultiplier tube monitors the light emission brought about by Ca²⁺ reacting with aequorin. The tension produced by muscle contraction is measured with a force transducer. [After Ashley, 1971.]*

A

Pipette containing aequorin

Cannula

Single muscle fiber

B

Tension transducer

Cannula

Photomultiplier tube

To oscilloscope

Cannulated single muscle fiber

Photocathode window

Tension lever

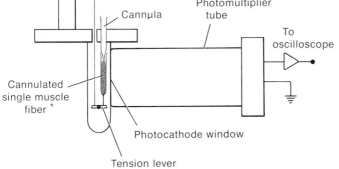

9-24. *Relation of calcium transient to excitation and contraction in an aequorin-injected crustacean muscle. A pulse of outward-going current (1) caused a graded depolarization of the surface membrane (2). This elicited a signal from the calcium-sensitive aequorin (3) and development of tension (4). The aequorin signal (colored trace) is related to the square of the sarcoplasmic free Ca concentration. [After Ashley and Ridgway, 1970.]*

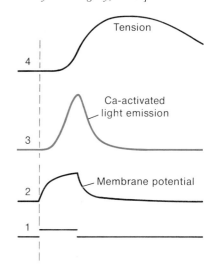

Tension

Ca-activated light emission

Membrane potential

9-25. *The tension developed in response to a depolarizing current in a crustacean muscle fiber is closely related to the total amount of light from the injected aequorin in the kind of experiment shown in Figures 9-23 and 9-24. [After Ashley and Ridgway, 1970.]*

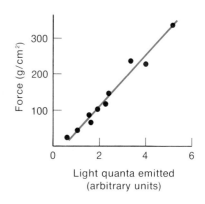

sequestered in the SR. The increase in sarcoplasmic free Ca²⁺ in response to caffeine has been demonstrated with a colorimetric method similar in principle to the photometric method depicted in Figure 9-23. After removal of caffeine, the calcium is taken up again by the SR, and the muscle relaxes.

There is an interesting correlation between structure of the sarcotubular system and muscle function. Mus-cles that contract and relax very rapidly have a highly developed sarcoplasmic reticulum and extensive systems of transverse tubules. Those that contract and relax slowly have either a rudimentary or a less well-developed SR. This, of course, correlates with the efficiency of the SR in regulating the changes in calcium concentrations that turn the contractile system on and off.

9-26. *Steps in the sequence of excitation-contraction coupling. (1) Action potential propagates along surface membrane of muscle fiber and conducts down T-tubule (2). The signal is communicated to the lateral cisternae of the SR (3), which thereupon release sequestered Ca²⁺ (4). The calcium then relieves the inhibition of actin-myosin interaction by binding to troponin (5). The myosin cross bridges attach to the actin filaments, and produce sliding of the filaments (6).*

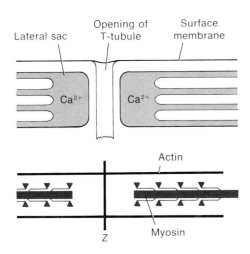

A RELAXED

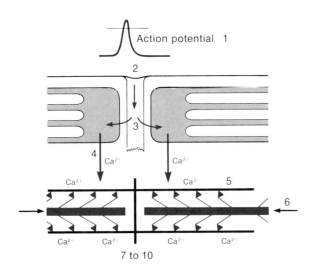

B CONTRACTING

CONTRACTION AND RELAXATION SUMMARIZED

The events controlling contraction of skeletal muscle are summarized in Figure 9-26 as follows.

1. The surface membrane of the muscle fiber is depolarized by an action potential, or in some muscles by synaptic potentials.

2. The signal is conducted deep into the muscle fiber along the T-tubules.

3. The electrical signal spreads from the T-tubules to the sarcoplasmic reticulum.

4. This signal brings about the release of calcium ions sequestered in the reticulum.

5. The free Ca^{2+} concentration of the sarcoplasm increases from a resting value below about 10^{-7} M to an active level of about 10^{-6} M or higher. Calcium binds to the troponin, and a conformational change takes place.

6. This causes a change in the position of the tropomyosin molecule, eliminating steric inhibition of cross-bridge binding to the actin filaments.

7. Cross bridges attach to the actin filaments and undergo a sequential interaction of sites that causes the myosin head to rock against the actin filament, pulling on the cross-bridge link.

8. This produces active sliding of the actin filaments into the A-band. The sarcomere shortens a small distance.

9. Prior to the next cycle of cross-bridge movement, ATP (bound to the ATPase site on the myosin head) is hydrolyzed, and the energy of hydrolysis is employed to detach the myosin head from the actin filament. The head is then free to attach to the next site along the actin filament and repeat the cycle described in item 7. During a single contraction, each cross bridge attaches, pulls, and detaches many times as it progresses along the actin filament toward the Z-line.

10. Finally, the free Ca^{2+} level of the sarcoplasm is again lowered through active calcium uptake by the SR; the tropomyosin again inhibits cross-bridge attachment, and the muscle relaxes until the next depolarization.

Mechanical Properties of Contracting Muscle

Now that we have reviewed the sliding-filament and cross-bridge mechanisms, we can examine the mechanical and contractile properties of a whole muscle. Many of the mechanical properties of contracting

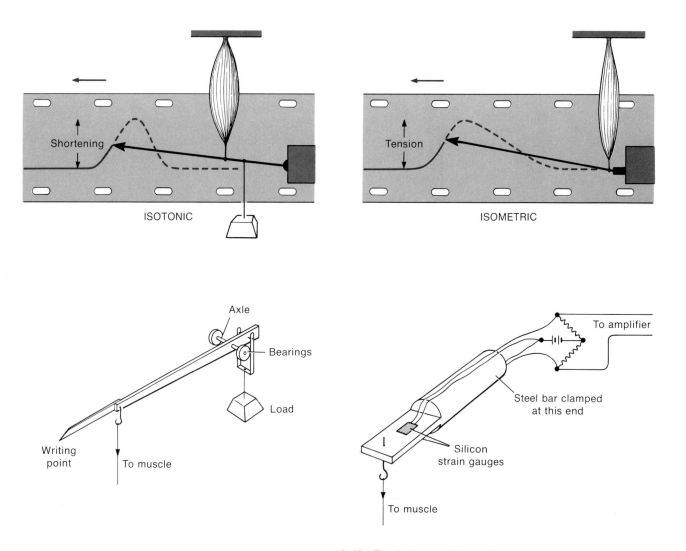

9–27. *Two basic ways of measuring contraction of a muscle. The principles are illustrated at the top, and the instruments are shown at the bottom. Left. In isotonic contractions, change in the length of a muscle is recorded while it contracts with constant tension. Right. In isometric contractions, tension change is recorded while the length of the muscle is held constant. [After Wilkie, 1968.]*

muscle were elucidated during the first half of this century, before the mechanism of contraction was understood. It is interesting to re-examine these classical findings in the light of the sliding-filament theory.

Contraction is expressed in two different ways, in terms of shortening or in terms of tension. Two corresponding means are used to measure activity of the contractile system. In one, changes in muscle length are measured during contraction while the muscle shortens against a load (Fig. 9-27,A). This is called *isotonic contraction,* because the tension remains constant. In the other method, the muscle is held at an essentially constant length while tension produced during contraction is measured with a strain gauge (Fig. 9-27,B). This is called *isometric contraction.* Although

there is no appreciable external shortening during isometric contraction, there is a small amount of *internal* shortening (sliding of actin filaments into A-band) due to stretching of intracellular components and extracellular connective tissue in series with the muscle fibers. The time course of isometric contraction differs greatly among muscles of different animals and among different muscles of the same animal (Fig. 9-28).

One simple physical concept is essential to an understanding of the following paragraphs: the tension in one element of a linear series (e.g., one link in a chain) is equal to the tension in each of the other elements in the series. This holds true for tension generated by contraction or produced by an external weight pulling on the muscle.

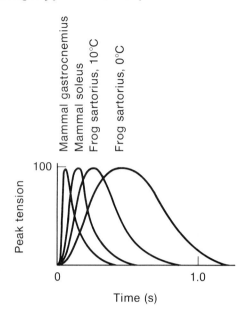

9-28. Time courses of isometric twitches in various muscles. The peak tensions are normalized to the same height. [After Wilkie, 1968.]

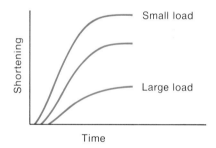

9-29. The effect on rate and extent of isotonic shortening of increasing the load on a muscle. In each case, tetanic stimulation was begun at time zero. [After Wilkie, 1968.]

9-30. Force-velocity relations in isotonic contractions. As the load to be lifted increases, the maximum shortening decreases. The broken line represents mechanical power (force × velocity) produced by the muscle under various loads. [After Wilkie, 1968.]

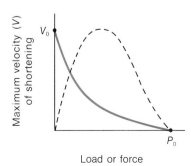

VELOCITY OF SHORTENING

The velocity with which two points along a muscle fiber approach each other (i.e., the fiber shortens) under a given load is a linear function of the number of sarcomeres present *in series* between these two points. Assuming that all the sarcomeres of one muscle fiber shorten by the same increment per unit time, the overall reduction in length in that time will be directly proportional to the number of sarcomeres in series. What this means, in brief, is that the opposite ends of a long muscle approach each other with higher velocity than do those of a short muscle. This is undoubtedly an important factor in the evolution of skeletal morphology.

In contrast to velocity of shortening, maximum tension is independent of the number of sarcomeres in series (length of muscle). Just as a chain is no stronger than its weakest link, the tension developed by a myofibril cannot exceed the tension developed by its weakest sarcomere. The contractile tension produced by a muscle fiber is proportional to the number of myofibrils (or more precisely, actin and myosin filaments) working in parallel. Thus a thick muscle can lift more than an equivalent thin muscle, regardless of length. Physical exercise increases the number of myofibrils and mitochondria per muscle fiber. This is seen as both an increase in size and an increase in strength of the muscle.

LATENT PERIOD

The effect on the kinetics of the isotonic twitch of increasing the load on the muscle is seen in Figure 9-29. As the load is increased, the muscle takes more time to lift the weight clear of its support. The reason for this is that the muscle needs time to develop tension (see below); the greater the weight, the longer the time required to build up the necessary tension. The muscle also shortens less with greater loads. Even with the lightest load, there is a latent period—the sum of all the delays between membrane excitation, propagation via the T-tubules into the fiber, time for Ca release and diffusion, and activation of the cross bridges by attachment to the actin filaments. The time from peak of the action potential to the first sign of tension in frog muscle is about 2 ms.

FORCE-VELOCITY CURVE

It also is apparent in Figure 9-29 that the initial velocity of shortening decreases as the load increases. Maximum velocity is attained when the load is zero—in which case, of course, the force (tension) developed by the muscle is also zero.

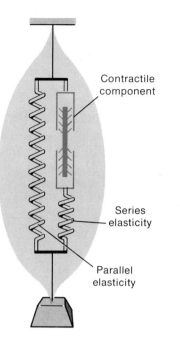

Contractile component

Series elasticity

Parallel elasticity

The relation between load and maximum velocity of shortening is plotted in Figure 9-30. The velocity drops as the force necessary to lift the load (i.e., weight of load) increases. If the load is made sufficiently heavy, there is no *external* shortening, and the contraction (by definition) is isometric. The dependence of velocity of shortening on load is easily understood in the light of the sliding-filament theory. The tendency for the actin filaments to slip backward against the production of force by cross-bridge activity should increase as the load increases.

A. V. Hill measured the velocity of shortening under various loads in different muscles and found that for each muscle the force-velocity relation could be consistently described by the hyperbolic equation

$$V = \frac{b(P_0 - P)}{P + a},$$

where V is initial velocity of shortening; P, the force (or load); P_0, maximum isometric tension of that muscle; b, a constant with dimensions of velocity; and a, a constant with dimensions of force. Unfortunately, although Hill's equation describes the force-velocity relation, it provides no real insight into the mechanism of muscle contraction. Aubert devised an exponential equation—entirely different from Hill's—that fits the force–velocity data equally well. An empirical equation is but a model of the physical process, and models often have no true relation to the real system other than that they describe its behavior. Our present knowledge of muscle physiology has grown out of many concrete morphological, chemical, and biophysical data.

9–31. *Mechanics of contraction. Left. A muscle represented as a contractile component in series and in parallel with elastic components. Below. The beginning of contraction (A): the weight rests on the substratum; sliding of filament begins to exert stretch on series elasticity. Tension building up with progressive stretching of series elasticity (B): contraction is isometric to this point. Once tension equals the weight of the load (C), the load is lifted and the contraction becomes isotonic. Note progressive increase in overlap of filaments and in number of active cross bridges throughout the contraction. [After Vander et al., 1975.]*

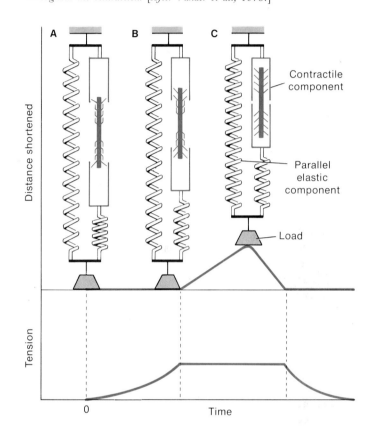

SERIES ELASTIC COMPONENTS

The muscle can be represented (Fig. 9-31) as a contractile component in *parallel* with an elastic* component (sarcolemma, connective tissue, etc.) and *in series* with a second elastic component, the so-called *series elastic components (SEC)*. Lumped into the category of series elastic components are tendons, connective tissues linking muscle fibers to the tendons, and perhaps the Z-line material. An important component contributing to series elasticity appears to be the elasticity of the cross-bridge links. Thus Figure 9-31 is greatly simplified.

As the contractile component shortens, it must stretch the SEC while tension is developed and transmitted to the external load (Fig. 9-31,A,B). When the tension developed in the SEC equals the weight of the

*Elasticity is defined by Hooke's Law, which states that the length of an object with ideal elasticity increases in proportion to the force applied.

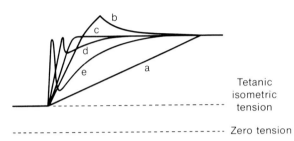

9–32. *Changes in tension in muscle stretched at different velocities during maximum tetanus. Curves* a *through* d *show increasing velocities of stretch applied to muscle.* [*After Gasser and Hill, 1924.*]

Tetanic
isometric
tension

Zero tension

9–33. *Overall length remains constant during stretching of the series elasticity by the contractile elements during an isometric twitch (B) and tetanus (C).* [*After Vander et al., 1975.*]

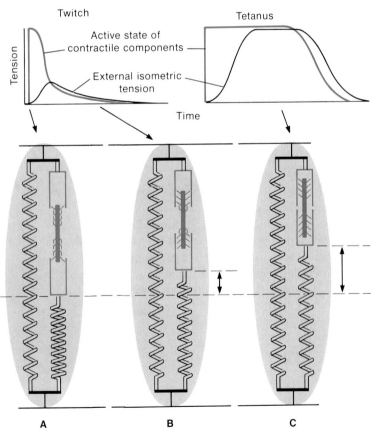

load, the muscle begins to shorten externally and lift the load (Fig. 9-31,C). In Figure 9-31,B the contraction is isometric, whereas in Figure 9-31,C it becomes isotonic with a load. At maximum tension during an isometric contraction, the series elastic components stretch by an amount equivalent to about 2% of the muscle length. This means that the contractile component must shorten by an equivalent amount even though the external length of the muscle, under those conditions, does not change.

It takes time for the filaments to slide past each other by cross-bridge activity as the series elastic components become stretched and tension builds up. Thus the development of tension in a muscle progresses with time as a function of internal shortening. The effect of the series elasticity is to slow development of tension in the muscle and to smooth out abrupt changes in cross-bridge activity.

ACTIVE STATE

Shortening or tension reaches a maximum within 10 to 100 ms, depending on the kind of muscle and the load. At first glance, this might suggest that the contractile mechanism is activated with a similar slowly rising time course. It is important, however, not to confuse the time course of tension developed by the muscle with the time course of cross-bridge activity. It will be recalled that, upon excitation and release of Ca^{2+} from the SR, the cross-bridges first attach to the actin filaments before active sliding begins. Moreover, sliding must first take up the slack in the SEC before full tension is developed (Fig. 9-31).

The state of cross-bridge activity that prevails before the muscle has had a chance to develop full tension can be determined by application of *quick stretches* with a special apparatus at various times after stimulation before and during the twitch (Fig. 9-32). The object of applying a quick stretch to the muscle is to stretch the series elastic components and thereby eliminate the time normally required for the contractile mechanism to take up the slack in the SEC. In this way, the state of cross-bridge activity can be measured with improved time resolution. The tension recorded by the sensing device during the quick stretch represents the tensile strength of the contractile mechanism at the instant of the quick stretch. This depends on the holding strength of the cross bridges at the instant of stretch, because the cross bridges will slip and the filaments will simply slide past each other, preventing the development of any higher tension. Thus the tension just necessary to make the thick and thin filaments slide apart approximates the load-carrying capacity of the muscle at the time of stretch. This tension should be proportional to the average number of active cross bridges per sarcomere.

In the relaxed state, muscle has very little resistance to stretch other than the compliance of connective tissue, sarcolemmae, etc. The quick-stretch technique revealed that, after stimulation, the resistance to stretch rises steeply and reaches a maximum within 100 ms. This is about the time when external shortening or tension in the unstretched muscle is just getting under way (Fig. 9-33). After a brief plateau, the load-carrying ability decreases to the low level characteristic of the relaxed muscle.

The increase in load-carrying ability of the muscle, as determined by quick-stretch experiments, is termed the *active state,* and corresponds to the formation of actomyosin complexes by the attachment of myosin cross bridges to actin filaments and by subsequent shortening activity of the cross bridges. Because cross-bridge activity is controlled by the concentration of free Ca^{2+} in the sarcoplasm, the time course of the active state is believed to approximate the time course of increased calcium concentration in the sarcoplasm.

TWITCH AND TETANUS TENSIONS

Two obvious questions are raised by a comparison of active state and twitch tension in Figure 9-33. First, why does the tension recorded during the simple twitch reach its maximum while the active state is decaying? Second, why is the maximum tension produced by the muscle during a twitch so much lower than the maximum tension of which the contractile mechanism is actually capable?

During a single twitch, the active state is rapidly terminated by the Ca-sequestering activity of the SR, which removes the Ca^{2+} soon after it is released. Thus the active state begins to decay before the filaments have had time to slide far enough to stretch the SEC to a fully developed tension (Fig. 9-33). For this reason, the tension of which the contractile system is capable cannot be realized in a single twitch. Before the peak of twitch tension, the contractile elements store potential energy in the SEC by progressive stretching. If a second action potential follows the first before the SR can remove the previously released Ca^{2+}, the calcium level remains high in the sarcoplasm, and the active state is prolonged. With the active state prolonged, isometric tension continues to increase with time until the tension produced by internal shortening of the contractile components and stretching of series elastic components is just sufficient to cause cross bridges to slip and prevent further shortening of the contractile components. The muscle has then reached full *tetanus tension.* (The prolongation of the active state by repeated action potentials is called *tetanus.*) Depending on the repetition rate of muscle action potentials, varying degrees of twitch fusion and tetanus tension are produced (Fig. 9-34).

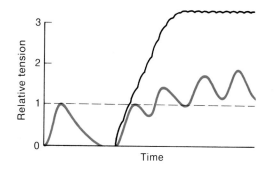

9-34. *Varying degrees of tetanus are produced, depending on the frequency of muscle action potentials. A single twitch is seen at left. The higher stimulus frequency produces a higher and smoother tension curve.*

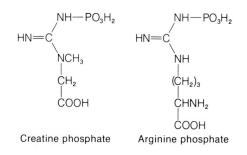

9-35. *Two phosphagens responsible for the rephosphorylation of ADP produced from ATP during muscle contraction.*

Creatine phosphate   Arginine phosphate

ENERGY, HEAT, AND WORK

The immediate source of energy for the contractile process is ATP:

$$ATP \rightleftharpoons ADP + P_i + \text{Free energy}$$

The concentration of ATP in muscle, however, is only 2 to 4 mM, hence ATP is quickly used up in sustained contraction. The ATP is rapidly regenerated by rephosphorylation of ADP by an energy-rich phosphagen compound (p. 53). In the vertebrates and several invertebrates, the phosphagen is creatine phosphate; in the muscles of most invertebrates, it is arginine phosphate (Fig. 9-35). The enzyme creatine phosphokinase catalyzes the transphosphorylation:

$$PC + ADP \rightleftharpoons C + ATP$$

This reaction proceeds freely to supply ATP during exercise. The level of ATP in active muscle shows no substantial decline as long as the phosphagen has not been depleted.

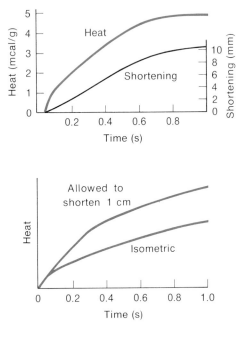

9-36. *Heat production during muscle contraction.*
A. The heat produced is composed of two components—the activation heat (a relatively constant amount presumed to be associated with the processes of excitation, release and reuptake of calcium, and activation) and a variable heat of shortening (related to the distance through which the muscle shortens).
B. If allowed to shorten, the muscle produces more heat than if contracting isometrically.
[After Hill, 1938.]

During and after contraction, the heat production of the muscle rises above the basal (resting) level. There is a relatively fixed production of heat associated with the process of excitation and activation; this is termed the *activation heat*. Added to this, there is the *heat of shortening*, which is proportional to the distance through which the muscle is allowed to shorten during the contraction. It should be noted that when a muscle shortens as it lifts a load, the energy released in the muscle is the sum of the work done (weight × distance) and the heat produced. The energy liberated as heat is about five times as great as the energy converted into work. This level of efficiency is typical of biological processes. What is unusual about the energy utilization of muscle is its high degree of control. One example of this is seen in Figure 9-36. With increased shortening, there is a proportional increase in heat liberated. This is now understandable in terms of the sliding-filament mechanism. With increased overlap of actin and myosin filaments, the number of activated cross-bridge ATPase sites increases linearly with the degree of overlap. Those cross bridges that are out of reach of the actin filaments cannot attach, and therefore cannot enzymatically hydrolyze ATP to do work and liberate heat.

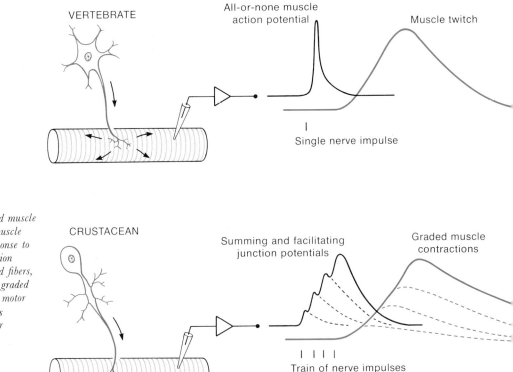

9-37. *Comparison of vertebrate and arthropod muscle excitation. Top. Vertebrate twitch muscle produces an all-or-none twitch in response to each all-or-none, conducted muscle action potential. Bottom. In many arthropod fibers, contractions are graded in response to graded electrotonic potentials produced at the motor synapses. In those muscles, nerve fibers carry the impulses to distributed motor synapses.*

Neural Control of Muscle Contraction

Effective animal movements require that contractions of muscles be correctly timed with respect to each other. Their timing is of course regulated by the timing of motor impulses generated by the central nervous system. In addition, it is necessary that the degree or strength of contraction of each muscle be regulated by the nervous system. A motor system limited to all-or-none contractions of entire skeletal muscles would produce spastic behavior with a very limited repertoire of movement. Fine control of muscle contraction has been achieved in different organisms by various means during the course of evolution. Vertebrate and arthropod neuromuscular mechanisms lend themselves especially well to comparison because of the great divergence of "designs" that have evolved for the neural control of contraction in these two groups.

VERTEBRATE NEUROMOTOR ORGANIZATION

Vertebrate skeletal muscle is innervated by motoneurons (p. 241) whose cell bodies are located in the ventral horn of the gray matter of the spinal cord. The motor axon leaves the spinal cord by a ventral root, continues to the muscle via a peripheral nerve trunk, and finally branches repeatedly to innervate about 100 skeletal muscle fibers.

The motoneuron and the muscle fibers that it innervates form a *motor unit* (Fig. 8-3). An action potential originating as a consequence of synaptic input to the motoneuron travels from its site of origin in the axon hillock along the axon toward the periphery, spreading into all the terminal branches of the axon to the endplates that innervate the muscle fibers of that motor unit. A postsynaptic potential is produced in each muscle fiber by the action of the neuromuscular transmitter substance acetylcholine. In twitch muscle, such as the sartorius muscle of the frog, this depolarization always exceeds the firing level for the muscle action potential (Fig. 9-37,A); therefore, each time the motoneuron fires (generates an action potential), all the muscle fibers of the motor unit are fully activated by the release of transmitter from all the motor terminals of that neuron. Whether the contractions consist of single twitches or of sustained tetanic contractions depends on the frequency of motor impulses generated by the synaptic input to the motoneuron.

The degree with which tension can be modulated in such an all-or-none motor unit is very small, because there is no gradation between inactivity and a twitch. With repeated motor impulses, the response is rather uneven except at firing rates high enough to elicit a full tetanic contraction (Fig. 9-33). In the vertebrates, the problem of increasing overall muscle tension in a graded fashion is solved by increasing the number of motor units active at any moment, termed *recruitment* of motor units, and by varying the average frequency with which the motoneurons fire. If, for example, a small number of the motor units of a given muscle are maximally active, the muscle will contract with a small fraction of maximum tension. On the other hand, if all the motoneurons of the muscle are recruited to fire at a high rate, all the motor units that constitute the muscle are brought into a state of full tetanus, producing a maximal contraction of the muscle.

The advantages of the neuromotor organization of vertebrate twitch muscle are that it is able to produce rapid, powerful contractions as well as finely graded tensions. The cost of this flexibility is a large number of motoneurons serving each muscle.

Slow motor systems in certain postural muscles (e.g., *rectus abdominus*) of frog, the extraocular muscles of mammals, and the intrafusal fibers of muscle spindles (p. 261) contain a type of striated muscle fiber that does not produce all-or-none action potentials. These *slow muscle fibers* receive a multiterminal innervation—that is, the motor nerve makes many synapses along the length of each fiber. They also exhibit strongly facilitating synaptic potentials, and it is the synaptic potentials that produce the graded depolarizations responsible for their slow, graded contractions. In these respects, these muscles are similar to those of crustaceans, described in the following subsection. Slow muscle fibers generally are found where slow, sustained contractions are required.

Except for the extraocular muscles and intrafusal spindle fibers, mammals and birds do not have multiterminal, nonspiking muscle fibers. But the skeletal muscles of these two classes of vertebrates contain several types of twitch muscle. Muscles occupied primarily with postural functions tend to contain a high percentage of muscle fibers that produce all-or-none twitches of slower time course and low fusion frequency (Box 9-3). Muscles concerned with rapid movements contain a high percentage of fast twitch fibers that exhibit high tetanus fusion frequencies. Between the extreme fast and slow twitch fibers, there exist muscle fibers of intermediate properties.

ARTHROPOD NEUROMUSCULAR ORGANIZATION

Arthropod nervous systems consist of a relatively small number of neurons, hence large numbers of motor units are not available to produce fine gradations of movement by varying the recruitment of motor units. Moreover, many types of arthropod muscles do not

BOX 9-3 TROPHIC EFFECTS OF NERVES ON MUSCLES

Slow fibers predominate in postural muscles. They are redder in color (hence the dark meat of fowl) than fast fibers (light meat) because of their higher myoglobin content (Chapter 14). Other quantitative differences in the enzyme content of fast and slow twitch fibers are related to their contractile properties. The myosin ATPase activity of fast fibers is higher than that of slow fibers. On the other hand, slow muscle fibers are chemically specialized for greater endurance and maintained tensions.

Crossed-innervation experiment.   Top. Two muscles, a and b, have fast and slow contractile properties, as illustrated by the recordings of twitch and tetanus tensions at the right.   Bottom. Cutting the nerves and crossing them, to allow reciprocal regeneration of the "incorrect" nerve to each of the two muscles, causes each muscle to assume the properties of the other. This experiment suggests that the contractile properties are determined to a large extent by the nerve innervating the muscle. The contractile changes have been shown to parallel biochemical change in the cross-innervated muscles. [After Close, 1971.]

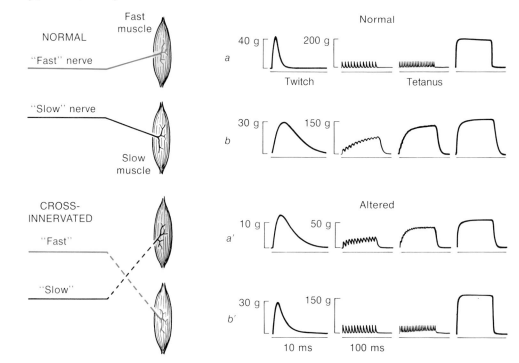

Cross-reinnervation experiments indicate that biochemical and physiological differences between fast and slow muscle fibers are determined by the nerve fibers that innervate them. For example, when motor nerves that normally innervate slow muscle fibers are transplanted into denervated fast fibers, they will, upon innervation, induce properties characteristic of slow fibers (see figure). One hypothesis is that different *trophic substances* released from the axon terminals influence the transcription of genetic information in the muscle fibers. Trophic substances elaborated by nerves to regulate the molecular biology of target cells have not yet been demonstrated.

It was recently reported that the amount of contractile activity, dependent, of course, on the average frequency of impulses in the motor nerve, plays an important role in determining whether a muscle exhibits "slow" or "fast" biochemical and physiological properties, irrespective of the identity of the nerve innervating the muscle. Thus the differences between slow and fast muscle may be due, at least in part, to differences in steady impulse activity of the motor nerves that innervate them. Some of the differences in biochemical and contractile properties may, indeed, arise within each muscle fiber as a consequence of the amount of contractile activity it experiences.

produce action potentials or do so only in response to synaptic input from certain motor endings. In these muscles, contraction is controlled by *graded* depolarization of the muscle-fiber membrane. As seen in Figure 9-18, the tension developed in a single muscle fiber is a function of membrane depolarization, the two being related by the release of Ca^{2+} from the SR (Fig. 9-26). This appears to be true for all muscle fibers. Muscle fibers that do not produce all-or-none action potentials respond with graded release of calcium—and, hence, graded tension—in response to graded changes in synaptic depolarization. The latter is determined in part by the frequency of impulses in the motor axon.

The vertebrate twitch muscle fiber is innervated at only one or two restricted regions—the endplates, where the motor axon forms minute presynaptic arborizations. The postsynaptic action potential originates at or near an endplate and spreads nondecrementally along the muscle fiber (Fig. 9-37,A). In contrast, the motor axons innervating crustacean skeletal muscle fiber make numerous synapses along the entire length of the muscle fiber (Fig. 9-37,B). This is called *multi-terminal innervation.* Because the motor axon carries the message along the entire length of the muscle fiber, there is no need for a propagated action potential in the muscle fiber. Many crustacean muscle fibers do not, in fact, generate all-or-none action potentials, but produce graded responses (Fig. 9-37,B). The postsynaptic potentials exhibit a large degree of facilitation and temporal summation (pp. 186, 244) at the distributed neuromuscular synapses. The shorter the interval between excitatory synaptic potentials, the greater the depolarization of the muscle membrane. Because the coupling between membrane potential and tension is graded (Fig. 9-18), each muscle fiber can produce a wide range of contractions, instead of being limited, like vertebrate twitch muscle, to all-or-none twitches or tetanus. For this reason, arthropod muscles can function quite well over a large range of tensions with very few motor units. In some arthropod muscles, a single motoneuron innervates all or most of the fibers of the muscle.

The flexibility of peripheral control of contraction is further enhanced in the crustaceans and other arthropods by *multineuronal innervation*—that is, each muscle fiber receives branches from several motor axons, including one or two inhibitory axons (Fig. 9-38). Firing of the inhibitor counteracts the depolarization induced by the excitatory motor nerves. There is usually one excitor axon that produces larger excitatory synaptic potentials in the muscle fiber. This *fast excitor axon* can generate a strong contraction with less facilitation and summation than can a *slow excitor axon,* which must fire repeatedly at high frequency to produce similar levels of depolarizations, and hence contraction, in the muscle fiber.

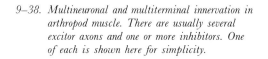

9–38. *Multineuronal and multiterminal innervation in arthropod muscle. There are usually several excitor axons and one or more inhibitors. One of each is shown here for simplicity.*

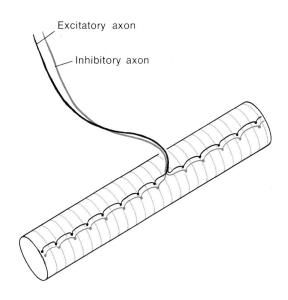

Excitatory axon

Inhibitory axon

The variety and complexity of peripheral motor organization is increased still further by the presence in most arthropod muscles of several types of muscle fibers exhibiting different electrical, contractile, and morphological properties. On the one end of the spectrum, there are fibers with rapid all-or-none contractions, which resemble vertebrate twitch fibers (Fig. 9-39,A). A series of intracellular current pulses evokes a series of electrotonic depolarizations until the firing level is exceeded and the membrane responds with an all-or-none action potential. This elicits an all-or-none fast twitch. At the opposite end of the spectrum of crustacean muscle-fiber types are the fibers (Fig. 9-39,C) in which the electrical responses show little sign of regenerative depolarization and the contractions are fully graded with the amount of depolarization. Between these two extremes is a continuum of intermediate muscle-fiber types (Fig. 9-39,B). The differences in contractile behavior of these fiber types are correlated with morphological differences. The slowly contracting fibers have relatively fewer transverse tubules and less sarcoplasmic reticulum than the rapidly contracting fibers.

9-39. *Summary of the variations in crustacean muscle-fiber properties. Membrane potentials shown at top, stimulating current in the middle, and tension at the bottom of each set of records. A. All-or-none twitch fibers; these produce action potentials and fast twitches. B. Intermediate graded fibers; these produce non-propagating graded potentials and graded contractions. C. Slow-muscle fibers; these produce only electrotonic potentials, and contract very slowly. [After Hoyle, 1967.]*

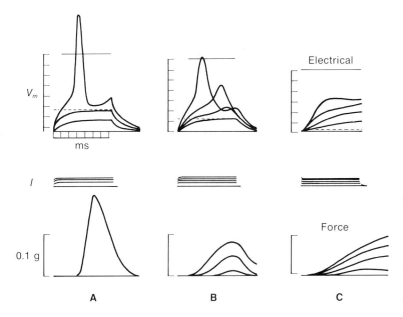

ASYNCHRONOUS FLIGHT MUSCLES

One type of striated skeletal muscle is a notable exception to the rule that each contraction is evoked by a depolarization of the surface membrane. The flight muscles of most species of four orders of insects (bees and wasps, flies, beetles, and bugs) show no relation between the timing of the individual contractions of the muscles and the timing of the arrival of motor impulses. These muscles are termed *asynchronous* to distinguish them from muscles that contract in synchrony with each motor impulse. They are known also as *fibrillar muscles*. Although the timing of contraction has no relation to the timing of neural input to these muscles, a constant train of motor impulses and muscle depolarizations maintains the muscle in an active condition.

In species of small insects, the wingbeat frequency (and the frequency of wing-muscle contractions) far exceeds the maximum maintained discharge rates of which axons are capable. Wingbeat frequency increases with decrease in wing size. A tiny midge, for example, will have a wingbeat frequency of more than 1000 cycles/s.

How do the contractions of fibrillar muscle occur with a timing that is independent of membrane potentials? As in other muscles, the active state (cross-bridge activity) of fibrillar muscle requires that there be a sufficient Ca^{2+} concentration in the sarcoplasm. The sarcoplasmic calcium concentration is maintained at a steady activating level as long as there is steady neural input to the muscle. But the active state is not initiated until the muscle is given a sudden stretch. Conversely, the active state is terminated if tension is released. The role that changes in length play in producing repetitive contractions was examined in glycerine-extracted (Box 9-1) fibrillar muscles lacking functional cell membranes. In the presence of constant levels of Ca^{2+} above 10^{-7} M, the extracted muscle will contract (actively develop tension) in response to an applied stretch and oscillate between contractions and relaxations if provided with a resonant mechanical system (Fig. 9-40). When the calcium levels are reduced to 10^{-9} M, the muscle fails to contract.

Insects having asynchronous muscles have musculoskeletal configurations with two stable states. Contractions of the antagonist flight muscles produce changes in the shape of the thorax, which favor only two wing positions—up or down (Fig. 9-41,B). As the *elevators* (muscles that elevate the wings by pulling down roof of thorax) contract, they cause the roof of the thorax to snap down past the "click" point (much as in a clicker toy). This does three things: (1) elevates the wings; (2) stretches, and thereby activates, the *depressors* (muscles that lower the wings); and (3) slackens the elevator muscles suddenly, thereby inactivating them. The cycle is completed in reverse as the stretch-activated depressors produce an upward deformation of the room of the thorax until it "clicks" back to the raised (wing-depressing) position (Fig. 9-41,B, bottom).

When nervous input to these muscles ceases, the muscle membrane repolarizes and the sarcoplasmic calcium levels drop, with the result that the cross bridges are unable to attach to the actin filaments. Externally applied stretch then no longer produces an active state, and the flight movements stop. Thus motor input to fibrillar muscle acts largely as an on–off switch. The frequency of contraction depends on the mechanical properties of the muscle and the mechanical resonance of the flight apparatus (thorax, muscles, wings). Thus, if the wings are clipped short, the wingbeat frequency will increase, even though the nerve impulses occur with unchanged frequency.

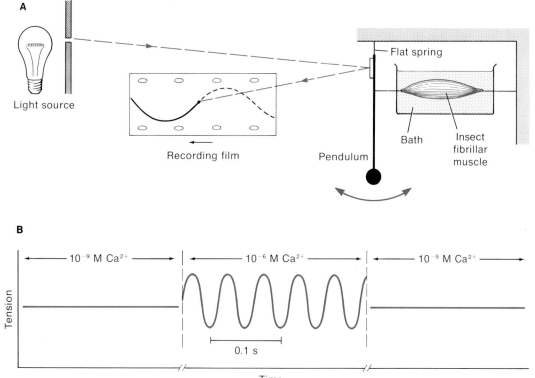

9–40. *Calcium dependence of oscillatory contractions in glycerinated asynchronous flight muscle of a water beetle.   A. Experimental method. The pendulum provides the mechanical resonance in place of the thoracic exoskeleton and wings of beetle. Contraction of muscle causes movement of the pendulum to the right. As the pendulum continues its movement due to momentum, tension in the muscle drops, inactivating it. Muscle is reactivated when the pendulum swings back to left and stretches the muscle. Movements are recorded on film as shown.   B. Ability of extracted flight muscle to produce oscillations is dependent on calcium concentration of reactivation solution. [After Jewell and Rüegg, 1966.]*

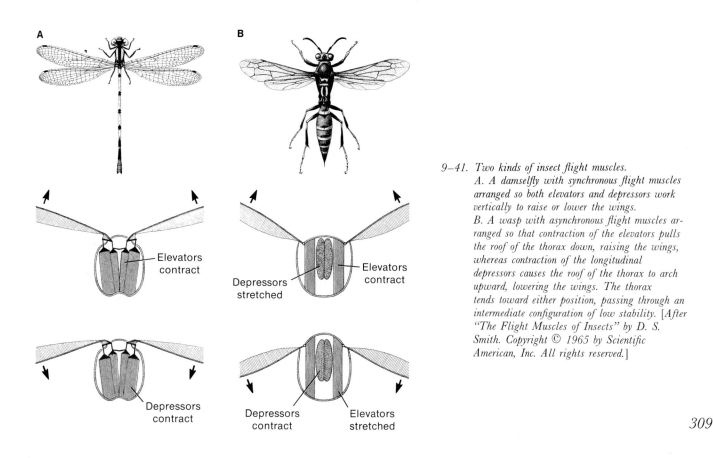

9–41. *Two kinds of insect flight muscles.*
A. A damselfly with synchronous flight muscles arranged so both elevators and depressors work vertically to raise or lower the wings.
B. A wasp with asynchronous flight muscles arranged so that contraction of the elevators pulls the roof of the thorax down, raising the wings, whereas contraction of the longitudinal depressors causes the roof of the thorax to arch upward, lowering the wings. The thorax tends toward either position, passing through an intermediate configuration of low stability. [After "The Flight Muscles of Insects" by D. S. Smith. Copyright © 1965 by Scientific American, Inc. All rights reserved.]

309

9-42. *Gross morphology of three major classes of vertebrate muscle. A. Striated muscle fibers are cylindrical and multinucleate. B. Cardiac muscle cells are joined end-to-end by electrical junctions, and therefore are electrically continuous. C. Smooth-muscle fibers are small and spindle-shaped, each with a single nucleus. They are joined laterally into electrically coupled groups. The innervation is diffuse, the transmitter arising from varicosities along the motor nerve.*

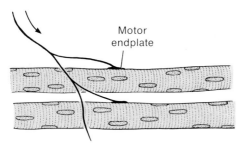

Motor endplate

A STRIATED

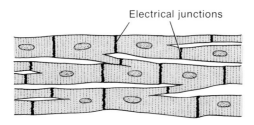

Electrical junctions

B CARDIAC

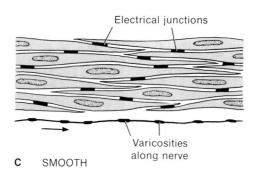

Electrical junctions

Varicosities along nerve

C SMOOTH

Cardiac Muscle

The contractile mechanism of vertebrate ventricular muscle (Fig. 9-42,B) fundamentally resembles that of skeletal twitch muscle. The major specializations are in the action potential (p. 126), which differs from that of nerve and skeletal muscle in the following ways.

1. It has a plateau hundreds of milliseconds long following the upstroke (Fig. 9-43,B). The long duration of the action potential relative to the velocity of conduction insures that all the cells of the ventricle are excited approximately in unison, causing the ventricular muscle to contract as a unit. This is essential for the efficient pumping action of the heart (p. 438).

2. Each cardiac action potential is followed by a refractory period of several hundred milliseconds. This long period of refractoriness prevents tetanic contraction, requiring the muscle to relax and permitting the ventricle to fill with blood between action potentials. As a result of regularly paced, prolonged action potentials, the heart contracts and relaxes at a rate suitable for its function as a pump.

The cells of mammalian cardiac muscle possess an elaborate sarcoplasmic reticulum and system of transverse tubules (Fig. 9-44). Like skeletal twitch muscle, cardiac muscle is activated by the release of Ca^{2+} from the sarcoplasmic reticulum. The cardiac muscle of amphibians is more simply organized than that of higher vertebrates, and has therefore proved useful in elementary studies of how contraction is regulated by the electrical activity of the cell membrane. Cardiac muscle of the frog has only a rudimentary reticulum and tubular system. Like those of smooth muscle, the cell of the frog heart are much smaller than skeletal muscle fibers. The relatively large surface-to-volume ratios of these small cells reduces the "need" for an elaborate intracellular reticulum for the storage, release, and uptake of Ca^{2+}. Instead, much of the calcium supplied for contraction in smooth muscle and amphibian heart enters these cells through the surface membrane as a result of the membrane's increased calcium permeability during depolarization (see discussion of calcium action potentials, pp. 140–141).

The relation between membrane potential and tension in small strips of frog ventricle is shown in Figure 9-45,B. As the cell is depolarized (Fig. 9-45,A), Ca^{2+} diffuses into the cell because of the increased calcium conductance of the surface membrane. Because the influx of Ca^{2+} is voltage dependent, tension develops as a function of depolarization, with greater depolarization producing greater tension. Reduction of the extracellular Ca^{2+} concentration results in a weaker contraction for a given depolarization (Fig. 9-45,B), presumably because less Ca^{2+} enters the cell when the concentration difference between cell interior and exterior is reduced.

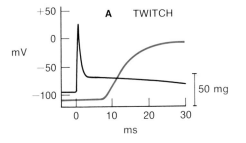

9-43. *Relationships between electrical (black traces) and mechanical (colored traces) activity in three major classes of vertebrate muscle. A. Striated muscle. [After Hodgkin and Horowicz, 1957.] B. Cardiac muscle. [After Brooks et al., 1955.] C. Smooth muscle. [After Marshall, 1962.]*

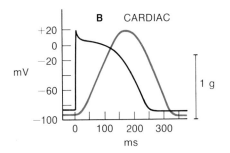

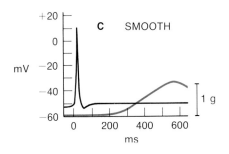

9-44. *Structure of mammalian ventricular cardiac muscle. The intercalated disk consists of the two membranes of two cells joined end-to-end by numerous gap junctions. [After Threadgold, 1967.]*

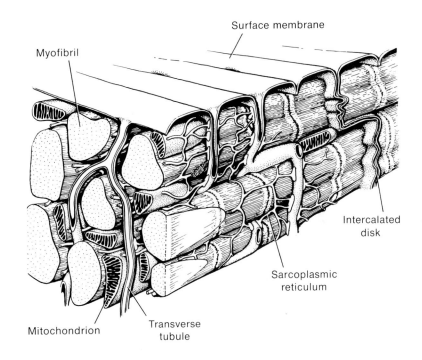

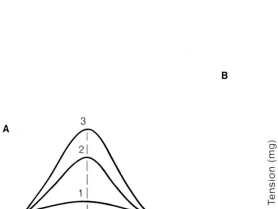

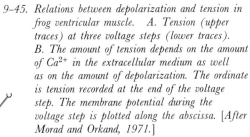
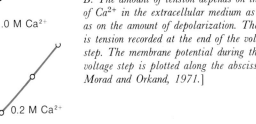

9-45. *Relations between depolarization and tension in frog ventricular muscle. A. Tension (upper traces) at three voltage steps (lower traces). B. The amount of tension depends on the amount of Ca^{2+} in the extracellular medium as well as on the amount of depolarization. The ordinate is tension recorded at the end of the voltage step. The membrane potential during the voltage step is plotted along the abscissa. [After Morad and Orkand, 1971.]*

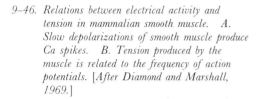

9-46. *Relations between electrical activity and tension in mammalian smooth muscle. A. Slow depolarizations of smooth muscle produce Ca spikes. B. Tension produced by the muscle is related to the frequency of action potentials. [After Diamond and Marshall, 1969.]*

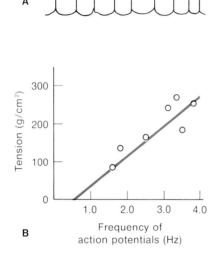

smooth-muscle cells can perform calcium-regulating functions similar to those ascribed to the membranes of the SR of striated muscle. Calcium is constantly pumped outward across the surface membrane so as to keep internal levels of that ion very low. Whenever the membrane becomes depolarized, it becomes more permeable to calcium ions. This permits an influx of Ca^{2+}, which activates contraction. Relaxation, according to this hypothesis, occurs when the calcium permeability returns to the low resting level while the membrane pumps out calcium. Large depolarizations lead to action potentials in which calcium carries the inward current (Fig. 9-46,A). Action potentials produce the greatest Ca influx, and thus evoke the largest contractions. Tension is graded with fluctuations in membrane potential (Fig. 9-46,B).*

An interesting feature of smooth muscle is the sensitivity of the membrane to mechanical stimuli. Stretching the muscle produces some depolarization, and this produces some contraction. As a result, muscle tension is maintained over a large range of muscle length. Because there is no sarcomere structure with which to gauge the overlap of actin and myosin filaments, it is difficult to interpret the length–tension relations of smooth muscle. Smooth muscle contracts and relaxes far more slowly than striated muscle, and is generally capable of more sustained contractions.

Smooth Muscle

Muscles are termed "smooth" if they lack the characteristic striations produced by the organized groups of actin and myosin filaments that form sarcomeres. The filaments of smooth muscle are distributed somewhat randomly within the myoplasm. There are several types of smooth muscle, distinguished on the basis of cell morphology. For example, the byssus retractor muscle and the adductor muscles of bivalve mollusks have long cylindrical cells, and the smooth muscle that forms the walls of vertebrate visceral organs (e.g., alimentary canal, urinary bladder, ureters, arteries, and arterioles) consists of small, mononucleate, spindle-shaped cells 2–20 μm in diameter and 10 to 100 times as long as they are wide (Fig. 9-42,C). Groups of these cells are connected to each other by gap junctions (p. 105) that permit the electrotonic spread of current from cell to cell. Such cells are thus electrically coupled in bundles about 100 μm across and several mm long. Such coupled groups of cells form functional units.

In the cells of smooth muscle, the sarcoplasmic reticulum characteristic of striated muscle is either absent or rudimentary in form. This is possible because the cells of smooth muscle are small and therefore have large surface-to-volume ratios. No point in the cytoplasm is more than a few micrometers distance from the surface membrane. Thus the surface membrane of

Musculo-skeletal Systems

To do work, a muscle must be able to transfer the energy of its contraction to a load. This can be done with a mechanical system such as the vertebrate skeleton, with its levers, joints, pulleys, and muscle attachments (Fig. 9-47). A number of factors determine the speed with which contracting muscles can move a distal part of the body (e.g., the foot) relative to a proximal part (e.g., the knee). These factors include the relative distances between joints and muscle attachments, limb length, and muscle length and strength. It will be recalled that, all else being equal, a long muscle will shorten faster than a short muscle (p. 300). The simple principles of lever mechanics will be recalled from elementary physics. The variations in skeletal architecture among various animals are the result of adaptations for different modes of locomotion (Fig. 9-48).

The arthropod exoskeleton also consists of rigid elements connected by joints, but is arranged as a

---

*For an account of metabolic mechanisms augmenting the electrical regulation of smooth-muscle activity, see p. 382.

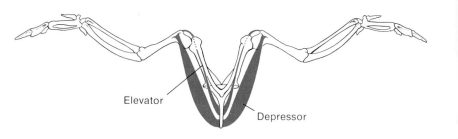

9-47. *Lever mechanics of musculo-skeletal system, illustrated by the flight apparatus of a bird. A tendon passes over the joint attaching to the humerus so as to produce a pulley-like effect to lift the wing. [After Darling et al., 1962.]*

Elevator

Depressor

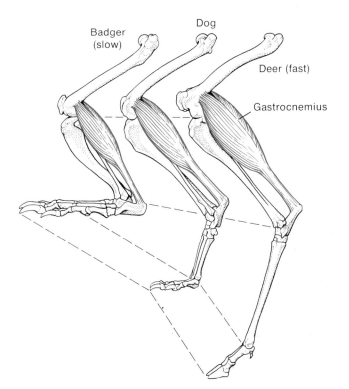

Badger (slow)

Dog

Deer (fast)

Gastrocnemius

9-48. *Adaptations for strength and speed in skeleton and musculature of three mammals. Each is scaled so that the femurs are all of the same length. The lengthened metatarsals of the deer and dog result in a longer foot and altered ankle posture, which afford these two species a much higher running speed than the badger. The legs of the badger have evolved an efficient structure for the strength required to dig burrows. Note the differences in the ratio of the length of the foot to the length of the heel bone. The greater this ratio, the higher the speed of movement of the toes in response to a given contraction of the gastrocnemius.*

9-49. *A hydrostatic skeleton. The sea anemone has no rigid skeleton, but antagonistic muscles can act against each other through the incompressibility of the fluids contained within the animal.*

protective armor enclosing the muscles and other tissues. It functions on the same mechanical principles as an endoskeleton. Many invertebrates have no rigid skeletons, but even these animals are generally able to move, change shape, and propel themselves by muscle contractions. Some animals, such as coelenterate polyps and annelid worms, utilize a hydrostatic "skeleton" (Fig. 9-49) in which opposing circularly and longitudinally arranged layers of muscle contract against an incompressible aqueous fluid contained within a lumen. Contraction of longitudinal muscles shortens the organism; contraction of circular muscles elongates it. Movements along the vertebrate digestive tract arise in a similar manner.

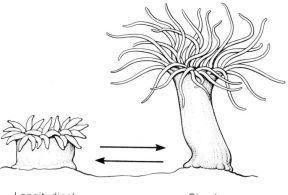

Longitudinal muscles contract

Circular muscles contract

Summary

Muscles are classified into two types—striated and smooth. Because striated muscle has been so intensively studied, its structure is perhaps better understood than that of any other tissue. Its striated appearance is the result of the regular arrangement of parallel myofilaments, which produce the banded sarcomeres. The sarcomere consists of myosin and actin filaments. Myosin filaments, which make up the A-band, interdigitate and slide between the thinner actin filaments, which make up the I-bands. During muscle activity, active sliding is produced by interactions between the actin filaments and the cross bridges that project from the myosin filaments. The head of the myosin cross bridge exhibits ATPase activity only when bound to an actin site. Hydrolysis of ATP, which requires Mg^{2+}, produces a conformational change that leads to the detachment of the cross bridge from the actin filament. The myosin head then reattaches further along the actin filament, with the first of several sites. As successive sites attach and detach, the head undergoes a rotation against the actin filament, pulling on the cross-bridge link. This in turn pulls on the thick filament from which it arises, causing the myosin filament to slide past the thin filament toward the end of the sarcomere. Because this happens symmetrically at both ends of the thick filaments, the sarcomere shortens. A number of classical muscle properties can now be understood in the light of this sliding-filament model of muscle contraction.

At rest, attachment of the myosin heads is prevented by steric hindrance of the actin sites by tropomyosin, a long protein molecule associated with the actin filament. When the muscle cell is depolarized, as by an action potential, calcium ions are released from within the sarcoplasmic reticulum. Calcium ions entering the sarcoplasm then bind to troponin, a group of three globular protein molecules attached to both the actin and the tropomyosin. The Ca^{2+} effects a conformational change in the troponin, and this in turn moves the tropomyosin molecule so that it no longer offers hindrance to the binding of the myosin cross-bridge heads to the actin filament. In that way calcium regulates muscle contraction. As the surface membrane repolarizes, the sarcoplasmic reticulum begins pumping up the Ca^{2+} again, removing it from the troponin, terminating the active state of the muscle and causing it to relax.

The electrical activity of the surface membrane is carried into the cell interior by thin invaginating projections of the surface membrane termed transverse tubules. These come into close apposition with the lateral cisternae of the collars of sarcoplasmic reticulum that wrap around each sarcomere of each myofibril. Although the nature of the signal transmitted from transverse tubules to lateral cisternae is not known, it is evident that depolarization of the transverse tubules leads to the release of Ca^{2+} from the sarcoplasmic reticulum. The rise in free Ca^{2+} in the sarcoplasm is the final signal that couples activation of the contractile mechanism to depolarization of the surface membrane.

The control of muscle tension by the nervous system has evolved in several ways in different animal groups. Vertebrate striated muscle responds to single motoneuron impulses with all-or-none twitches, because it contracts in response to all-or-none action potentials. Many arthropod striated muscle fibers give graded contractions in response to graded, nonconducted depolarizations at synapses distributed along each muscle fiber. Most arthropod muscle fibers have an inhibitory innervation in addition to being innervated by several kinds of excitatory motor axons.

Smooth-muscle cells are usually spindle-shaped, and they are electrically coupled to one another in groups. They show both slow-wave electrical activity and action potentials in response to diffuse transmitter release by innervating nerves. Actin and myosin fibers are present, but not in the organized manner characteristic of striated muscle. The calcium that activates contraction enters primarily from the cell exterior during depolarization; this is feasible in smooth muscle because the contractions are slow and because the small cells have a large surface-to-volume ratio.

Vertebrate cardiac muscle is organized very much like skeletal striated muscle except that (1) the fibers are electrically coupled for rapid through-conduction of the action potential, and (2) the ionic mechanisms of the muscle are specialized for pacemaker activity in the atrial wall and for prolonged action potentials in the ventricular wall.

EXERCISES

1. Distinguish each of the following levels of muscle organization: myofilaments, myofibrils, muscle fibers, and muscle.

2. What kinds of evidence led to the sliding-filament hypothesis?

3. Draw and label from memory the various components of the sarcomere.

4. Discuss the functions of myosin, actin, troponin, and tropomyosin.

5. Why do muscles become stiff several hours after an animal dies?

6. How is the force responsible for sliding produced by the cross bridges?

7. Explain how calcium regulates muscle contraction.

8. List the steps involved in muscle contraction and relaxation.

9. Outline the evidence for the coupling function of the sarcotubular system.

10. How is depolarization of the surface membrane of a muscle fiber communicated to the calcium-sequestering reticulum?

11. A muscle attached to a 50-g weight requires more time before it lifts the weight off a table than it requires to lift a 5-g weight. Explain why.

12. Discuss the factors that determine the production of heat during contraction.

13. What limits the tension attainable by a myofibril? by a muscle?

14. Why does velocity of shortening decrease as heavier loads are placed on a muscle?

15. Explain the effect of the series elastic components on tension developed in muscle.

16. Define the active state of muscle.

17. How is a vertebrate twitch muscle, the fibers of which are activated all-or-none by single motor impulses, controlled so as to give graded contractions?

18. How do arthropods achieve graded muscular contraction with only a very limited number of motoneurons?

19. What factors determine wingbeat frequency in insect fibrillar muscle?

20. Discuss the major functional differences between skeletal, smooth, and cardiac muscle.

SUGGESTED READING

Bendall, J. R. 1969. *Muscles, Molecules, and Movement.* American Elsevier, New York.

Carlson, F. D., and D. R. Wilkie. 1974. *Muscle Physiology.* Prentice-Hall, Englewood Cliffs, N.J.

Cold Spring Harbor Laboratory of Quantitative Biology. 1973. *The Mechanism of Muscle Contraction.* [*C.S.H. Symp. Quant. Biol.,* vol. 37.]

Duncan, C. J. (ed.). 1976. *Calcium in Biological Systems* [*Symp. Soc. Exp. Biol.,* vol. 30]. Cambridge Univ. Press, New York.

Huddart, H. 1975. *The Comparative Structure and Function of Muscle.* Pergamon Press, New York.

Huxley, H. E. 1969. The mechanism of muscular contraction. *Science* 164:1356–1365.

Podolsky, R. (ed.). 1971. *Contractility of Muscle and Related Processes.* Prentice-Hall, Englewood Cliffs, N.J.

Tonomura, Y. 1973. *Muscle, Proteins, Muscle Contraction, and Cation Transport.* University Park Press, Baltimore.

Weber, A., and J. M. Murray. 1973. Molecular control mechanisms in muscle contraction. *Physiol. Rev.* 53:612–673.

Wessells, N. K. 1968. *Vertebrate Adaptations. Readings from Scientific American.* W. H. Freeman and Company, San Francisco.

Ashley, C. C. 1971. Calcium and the activation of skeletal muscle. *Endeavor* 30(109):18–25.

Ashley, C. C., and E. B. Ridgway. 1970. On the relationships between membrane potential, calcium transient, and tension in single barnacle muscle fibres. *J. Physiol.* 209:105–130.

Aubert, X. 1956. La relation entre la force et la vitesse d'allongement et de raccourcissement du muscle strié. *Arch. S. Int. Physiol. Biochem.* 64:121.

Bendall, J. R. 1969. *Muscles, Molecules, and Movement.* American Elsevier, New York.

Bennett, M. R. 1972. *Autonomic Neuromuscular Transmission.* Cambridge Univ. Press, New York.

Bloom, W., and D. W. Fawcett. 1968. *A Textbook of Histology* (9th ed.). Saunders, Philadelphia.

Brooks, C. M. C., B. F. Hoffman, E. E. Suckling, and O. Orias. 1955. *Excitability of the Heart.* Grune and Stratton, New York.

Close, R. 1971. Neural influences on physiological properties of fast and slow limb muscles. *In* R. J. Podolsky (ed.), *Contractility of Muscle Cells and Related Processes.* Prentice-Hall, Englewood Cliffs, N.J.

Cohen, C. 1975. The protein switch of muscle contraction. *Scientific American* 233(5):36–45.

Davson, H. 1964. *A Textbook of General Physiology.* Little, Brown & Co., Boston.

Diamond, J., and J. M. Marshall. 1969. A comparison of the effects of various muscle relaxants on the electrical and mechanical activity of rat uterus. *J. Pharmac. Exp. Ther.* 168:21–30.

Ebashi, S., and M. Endo. 1968. Calcium ion and muscle contraction. *Progr. Biophys.* 161:125–183.

Ebashi, S., M. Endo, and I. Ohtsuki. 1969. Control of muscle contraction. *Quart. Rev. Biophys.* 2:351–384.

Gasser, H. S., and A. V. Hill. 1924. Dynamics of muscular contraction. *Proc. Roy. Soc.* (London) Ser B 96:398.

Gordon, A. M., A. F. Huxley, and F. J. Julian. 1966. The variation in isometric tension with sarcomere length in vertebrate muscle fibers. *J. Physiol.* 184:170–192.

Hanson, J., and H. E. Huxley. 1955. The structural basis of contraction in striated muscle. *Symp. Soc. Exper. Biol.* 9:228–264.

Heilbrunn, L. V. 1940. The action of calcium on muscle protoplasm. *Physiol. Zool.* 13:88–94.

Heilbrunn, L. V., and F. J. Wierczinski. 1947. The action of various cations on muscle protoplasm. *J. Cell. Comp. Physiol.* 29:15–32.

Hellam, D. C., and R. J. Podolsky. 1967. Force measurements in skinned muscle fibres. *J. Physiol.* 200:807–819.

Hildebrand, M. 1960. How animals run. *Scientific American* 202(5):148–157.

Hill, A. V. 1938. The heat of shortening and the dynamic constants of muscle. *Proc. Roy. Soc.* (London) Ser. B 126:136–195.

Hill, A. V. 1948. On the time required for diffusion and its relation to processes in muscle. *Proc. Roy. Soc.* (London) Ser. B 135:446–453.

Hodgkin, A. L., and P. Horowicz. 1957. The differential action of hypertonic solutions on the twitch and action potential of a muscle fibre. *J. Physiol.* 136:17–18.

Hodgkin, A. L., and P. Horowicz. 1960. Potassium contractures in single muscle fibres. *J. Physiol.* 153:386–403.

Hoyle, G. 1967. Specificity of muscle. *In* Wiersma, C. A. G. (ed.), *Invertebrate Nervous Systems.* Univ. Chicago Press.

Huxley, A. F., and R. Niedergerke. 1954. Structural changes in muscle during contraction: Interference microscopy of living muscle fibres. *Nature* (London) 173:971–973.

Huxley, A. F., and R. M. Simmons. 1971. Proposed mechanism of force generation in striated muscle. *Nature* 233:533–538.

Huxley, A. F., and R. E. Taylor. 1958. Local activation of striated muscle fibres. *J. Phsiol.* 144:426–441.

Huxley, H. E. 1963. Electron microscope studies on the structure of material and synthetic protein filaments from striated muscle. *J. Molec. Biol.* 7:281–308.

Huxley, H. E. 1969. The mechanism of muscular contraction. *Science* 164:1356–1365.

Huxley, H. E., and J. Hanson. 1954. Changes in the cross-striations of muscle during contraction and stretch and their structural interpretation. *Nature* (London) 173:973–976.

Jewell, R. R., and J. C. Rüegg. 1966. Oscillatory contraction of insect fibrillar muscle after glycerol extraction. *Proc. Roy. Soc.* (London) Ser. B 164:428–459.

Kamada, T., and H. Kinosita. 1943. Disturbances initiated from naked surface of muscle protoplasm. *Jap. J. Physiol.* 10:469–493.

Lehninger, A. L. 1970. *Biochemistry.* Worth, New York.

Marshall, J. M. 1962. Regulation of activity in uterine smooth muscle. *Physiol. Rev.* 42:213–227.

Miller, A., and R. T. Tregear. 1971. X-ray studies on the structure and function of vertebrate and invertebrate muscle. *In* R. J. Podolsky (ed.), *Contractility of Muscle Cells and Related Processes.* Prentice-Hall, Englewood Cliffs, N.J.

Morad, M., and R. Orkand. 1971. Excitation-contraction coupling in frog ventricle: Evidence from voltage clamp studies. *J. Physiol.* 219:167–189.

Peachey, L. D. 1965. Transverse tubules in excitation-contraction coupling. *Fed. Proc.* 24:1124–1134.

Ringer, S., and D. W. Buxton. 1887. Upon the similarity and dissimilarity of the behavior of cardiac and skeletal muscle when brought into relation with solutions containing sodium, calcium, and potassium salts. *J. Physiol.* 8:288–295.

Smith, D. S. 1965. The flight muscles of insects. *Scientific American* 212(6):76–88.

Szent-Györgyi, A. 1945. Studies on muscle. *Acta Physiol. Scand.* 9(Suppt. 25).

Szent-Syörgyi, A. 1947. *Chemistry of Muscular Contraction.* Academic Press, New York.

Szent-Györgyi, A. 1949. Free energy relations and contraction of actomyosin. *Biol. Bull.* 96:140–167.

Threadgold, L. J. 1967. *Ultra-structure of the Animal Cell.* Pergamon Press, New York.

Vander, A. J., J. H. Sherman, and D. S. Luciano. 1975. *Human Physiology.* McGraw-Hill, New York.

Wilkie, D. R. 1968. *Muscle.* Edward Arnold, London.

CHAPTER TEN

Cilia and Flagella

The cilia and flagella of eucaryotic cells arise from cellular organelles homologous with centrioles. They are developmentally and structurally unrelated to bacterial flagella and the nonmotile "stereocilia" found in eighth-nerve mechanoreceptors of vertebrates (p. 209). The organelles we will consider have a characteristic organization of "9 + 2" (or occasionally 9 + 1 or 9 + 3) tubular substructures. These organelles are generally termed *flagella* (singular, *flagellum*) if relatively long, or *cilia* (singular, *cilium*) if short. There appears to be no fundamental difference in structure or mechanism between a cilium and a flagellum; cilia generally occur in large numbers on a cell, whereas flagella generally occur singly or in pairs.

Flagella are familiar as the motile organelles that propel spermatozoa and flagellates by means of traveling waves (Fig. 10-1). Several examples of flagella are also found in epithelia, such as the flame cells of flatworms and the collar cells of sponges. Flagella are about 0.2 μm in diameter and attain lengths up to 100 or 200 μm. Cilia have the same diameter but are generally less than 15 μm in length. Cilia on the sur-

face of certain groups of protozoa and invertebrate larvae provide the propulsive energy for locomotion (Fig. 10-2), and those on certain epithelial cells of metazoans move mucus-trapped particles over the surface or serve to circulate water to facilitate either feeding or respiration. The cilia of the mammalian trachea and bronchioles serve to move mucus-trapped particles up and out of the respiratory system. Tobacco smoke paralyzes the cilia, preventing this function when most needed. The cilia of the mammalian fallopian tubes are important in transporting the ovum.

Function, Form, and Composition

TYPES OF MOVEMENTS

There are several types of beating patterns, all of which can generally be ascribed to bending or propagated bending. The most easily described are those in which all the bending takes place in two dimensions rather

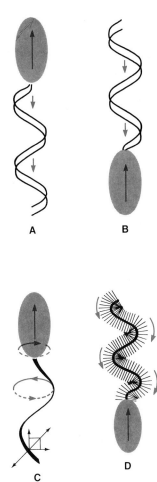

10–1. *Examples of flagellar motion in different proto-*
zoans.   A, B. Planar waves. Organism moves
in direction opposite to direction of wave
propagation. In some species, the flagellum leads
(as in B).   C. Helical waves produce more
complex force vectors, adding a counterturning
spin to the body.   D. Mastigonemes, hair-like
filaments projecting normal to the surface of
the flagellum of Mastigamoeba setosa,
reverse the direction of thrust, causing the
cell to be propelled in the same direction as
flagellar wave propagation. This happens
because the mastigonemes projecting on the
outside of the curvature of a traveling wave
swing in the direction opposite to the move-
ment of the wave (curved arrows).   E.
Peranema trichophorum *exhibits beating*
movements restricted to the terminal portion of
its flagellum. The power stroke is shown at
the right, propelling the cell forward. The
recovery stroke, which exerts less force on the
medium, is shown at left. [Part A after Jahn
et al., 1964; Parts B and C after Grell, 1968;
Part D after Jahn and Votta, 1972; Part E
after Jahn and Bovee, 1967.]

10–2. *Photomicrograph of a swimming* Paramecium
multimicronucleatum *in interference con-*
trast, showing metachronal waves of ciliary
activity. Arrows indicate cilia performing
power stroke toward rear (bottom of page),
thereby propelling specimen forward. [Machemer,
1972.]

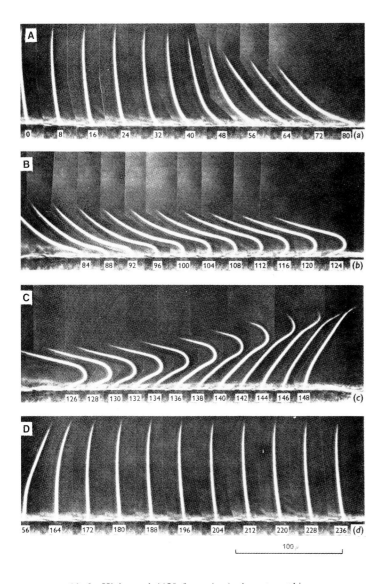

than in three. This kind of movement has been analyzed in cilia with the aid of high-speed photography (Fig. 10-3). The beating cycle can be divided into two parts, a *power* (or *effective*) *stroke* and a *recovery stroke.* During the power stroke, the cilium is relatively straight, and bends mostly near its base. Following the power stroke, the recovery stroke begins with a reverse bend near the base, which travels up the shaft of the cilium as the basal portion swings in the recovery direction. The result is that the cilium applies a minimum of force to the extracellular medium on its return to the starting position for the next power stroke, which is executed at a higher velocity than the recovery stroke. These movements result in a vector of net force applied to the extracellular medium.

Planar, or two-dimensional, movement is characteristic of epithelial cilia in the metazoa, especially those in which many long, closely grouped cilia function together to form a *cirrus* (found in clam gills) or *comb-plate* (in ctenophores). The cilia of protozoans and some epithelia beat in a more complex three-dimensional pattern. The power stroke is nearly planar, but during the recovery stroke the cilium departs from that plane of movement, leaning far over toward one side, close to the cell surface (Fig. 10-4).

Flagella show several forms of movement (Fig. 10-1), some with planar waves and some with helical movements. At first glance, one might suppose that the undulatory movements of flagella are due to passive traveling waves set up by active movements of the basal end of the flagellum—analogous to the motion of a whip. Several lines of evidence indicate that this is not the case. Instead, bending forces are generated along the entire length of the organelle or along whatever part undergoes movement. (1) If passive waves were set up by active movement near the base, they would show progressively diminishing amplitude as they move toward the free end. The traveling waves seen in flagella of sea urchin sperm show no such decrease in their amplitude (Fig. 10-5). (2) Isolated flagella can move independently of their normal attachments. (3) In some flagella, the waves begin at the free end and travel toward the base (Fig. 10-1,B). (4) The movement of some flagella is restricted to a small portion of the free end; the proximal region remains immobile and straight (Fig. 10-1,E).

FINE STRUCTURE

The major structures in a cilium or flagellum are microtubules, which extend continuously from end to end of the organelle. The hierarchy of microtubular organization is shown in Figure 10-6. In the shaft of the cilium or flagellum, nine microtubular doublets form a ring around a central pair of microtubules, which originate above the basal plate. Some flagella have

10–3. *High-speed (450 frames/sec) cinematographic analysis of the movement of the giant compound cilium found on mussel gills. Frames are numbered below. Frames were cut out and arranged in this montage. Every eighth frame is shown in parts A and D, every fourth in B, and every second in C. The power stroke extends from frame 40 to about frame 84; the recovery stroke extends from about frame 84 to frame 148. Following the recovery stroke, the cilium stands upright until the next power stroke. The movement of this specialized compound giant cilium is largely two-dimensional, and thus simpler than the three-dimensional movements characteristic of protozoan cilia.* [Baba and Hiramoto, 1970.]

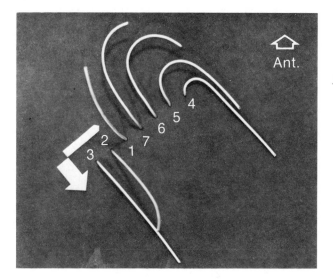

10-4. *Reconstructed stages in the ciliary cycle of* Paramecium. *Seven cilia along a line perpendicular to the metachronal wave are numbered in the sequence exhibited by a single cilium. The power stroke (steps 1–3) is planar in form; the recovery stroke (steps 4–7) takes place close to the cell surface, with the cilium leaning to one side. The small arrow shows direction of metachronal wave. The anterior of the ciliate is indicated by the arrow marked "ant." Based on photomicrographs of beating cilia. [Machemer, 1972.]*

10-5. *The beating form of sea-urchin sperm tails. Left. The traveling waves in the flagellum remain constant in amplitude throughout the length of the flagellum, as seen in multiple stroboscopic exposures. Right. Straight sections alternate with regions of circular arcs. [After Brokaw, 1965.]*

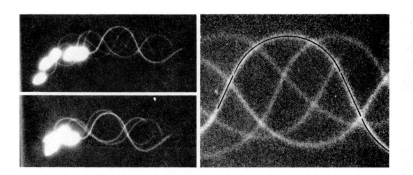

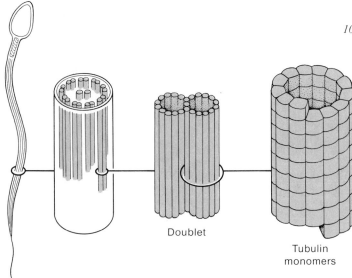

Doublet

Tubulin
monomers

10-6. *Hierarchy of axonemal substructure. The building blocks of the microtubules are tubulin monomers arranged as shown at the right. The axoneme, surrounded by the surface membrane, makes up the major portion of the sperm tail. [After "How Living Cells Change Shape" by N. Wessells. Copyright © 1971 by Scientific American, Inc. All rights reserved.]*

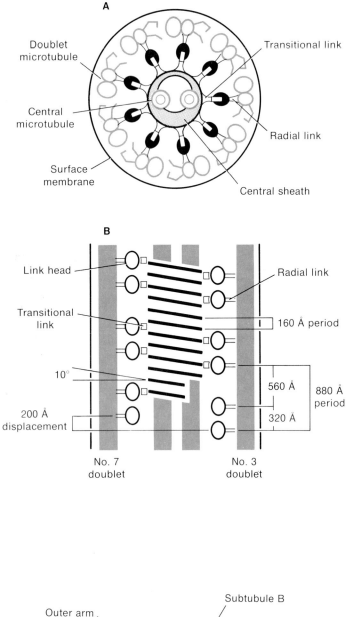

10-7. *Structural components of a flagellum, shown in cross section (A) and transverse section (B). Drawings based on electron micrographs of blowfly sperm tails. [After Warner, 1970.]*

A

Doublet microtubule

Central microtubule

Surface membrane

Transitional link

Radial link

Central sheath

B

Link head

Transitional link

10°

200 Å displacement

No. 7 doublet

Radial link

160 Å period

560 Å

880 Å period

320 Å

No. 3 doublet

only one central microtubule and others have three, but the 9 + 2 pattern is typical of the vast majority of cilia and flagella. The nine doublets and two central microtubules, together with their associated structures, form the *axoneme,* which is fully enclosed in an evaginated extension of the cell membrane (Fig. 10-7).

The microtubules of the axoneme have a substructure of globular protein molecules (diameter 40 Å) called *tubulin.* In the central pair, these molecules are organized into about thirteen longitudinal protofilaments per tubule. The outer nine doublets have a similar substructure of globular protein particles organized into protofilaments. The protofilaments of the doublets are assembled into one complete tubule, *tubule A,* and an attached incomplete *tubule B* (Fig. 10-8).

Tubule A of each doublet bears two *arms* that point toward tubule B of the next doublet clockwise around the ring (as viewed from base toward tip of the shaft). The arms, which repeat at intervals along tubule A, consist of a protein, *dynein,* which exhibits Mg-activated ATPase activity. Thus far, dynein is the only component of the axoneme that has been shown to have ATPase activity, but other ATPases in the axoneme have not been ruled out.

Each peripheral doublet also bears a series of *radial links.* These have been seen in some flagella to occur in pairs along the entire length of each doublet, as shown in Figure 10-7,B. Each radial link bears a swelling, or head, which can be seen in some sections to make contact with a corresponding protuberance on the *central sheath.* The arrangement of radial links along the length of each microtubular doublet is regularly displaced from one doublet to the next. The result is a helical progression of links (Fig. 10-7,B) reminiscent of the arrangement of cross bridges emerging from the myosin filaments in striated muscle.

At the base of each cilium or flagellum is a *basal body* (also called *kinetosome*) homologous with the centrioles, organelles that give rise to the microfilaments and tubules (e.g., the spindle fibers of dividing cells). The basal body is a short squat cylinder with an outer wall of nine triplet tubules.

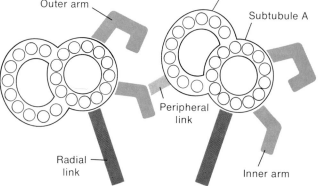

Outer arm

Subtubule B

Subtubule A

Peripheral link

Radial link

Inner arm

10-8. *Organization of the doublet microtubules and associated structures. The dynein arms extend from subtubule A toward subtubule B of the neighboring doublet. The compositions of the peripheral and radial links are not yet known. This highly schematic interpretation is based on electron-microscopical studies of the cilia of the clam* Elliptio. *[After Warner and Satir, 1973.]*

MOVEMENT AS RELATED TO STRUCTURE

Electron-microscopical studies on clam-gill cilia, which beat in a single plane, and on cilia of the parasitic protozoan *Opalina*, which beat with a complex three-dimensional movement, both indicate that bending of the shaft consistently occurs in a plane passing between the two central tubules and perpendicular to a line passing through both the central tubules. This is especially interesting in the cilia of *Opalina*, because they bend in a three-dimensional pattern, which is shifted when the effective stroke changes its direction in response to membrane depolarization (described below). The perpendicular relation between the central pair and the plane of bending holds true near the base as well as near the tip of the cilium. It has not yet been possible to determine if the central pair rotates independently during changes in the direction of bending or if the entire axoneme rotates as a unit. Furthermore, it remains uncertain whether the central pair determines the direction of bending of the shaft or simply complies passively and rotates so as to give the least resistance to bending.

An additional structural correlation with the plane of bending—one that is characteristic of epithelial cilia—is the presence of a bridge (Fig. 10-8) between two of the nine outer doublets. The bridge appears to be a modification of the arms. A radius drawn from the bridge to the center of the axoneme lies in the plane of bending.

CHEMISTRY OF CILIA AND FLAGELLA

Intact cilia can be isolated from ciliated protozoa by a procedure utilizing a calcium-binding agent and ethanol, and flagella can easily be broken away from sperm heads by mechanical treatment. Initial studies of whole cilia revealed several protein fractions, one of which showed ATPase activity. The localization of the different protein components and ATPase in the axoneme was made possible by the technique of chemical dissection, applied to the cilia of *Tetrahymena* by Gibbons in 1965. The first step after isolation of the cilia is extraction with a detergent that removes the cell membrane and the amorphous matrix of the ciliary shaft. The remaining axoneme is then dialyzed against a solution of low ionic strength containing EDTA, an agent that chelates both Ca^{2+} and Mg^{2+}. This extraction procedure removes the two central tubules and the arms from the outer nine doublets. The ring of nine outer doublets otherwise remains intact. Ultracentrifugation of the dialysate (extract obtained by dialysis) produces two principal protein fractions. One, which sediments slowly, contains the protein of the two central fibrils; the other fraction consists of the ATPase *dynein*, which occurs as a monomer and as more rapidly sedimenting polymers of various lengths. Gibbons showed that the enzymatic activity of *dynein* requires a divalent ion, such as Mg^{2+}, and liberates inorganic phosphate from ATP (Fig. 10-9). The dynein monomer is a globular protein about 140 Å long and 80 Å in diameter. It polymerizes to form a unit about 400 to 5,000 Å long (Fig. 10-10).

When the purified dynein fraction is mixed with the extracted axonemes, the dynein polymer reattaches to the A-tubules of the outer nine doublets to reconstitute the extracted arms. The periodicity of the arms along the length of the A-tubule is of approximately the same order of magnitude as the length of the dynein

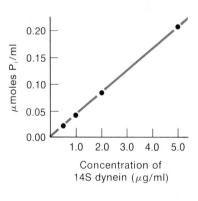

10-9. *ATPase activity of the 14S dynein molecule. The release of inorganic phosphate during an incubation period of 20 min is plotted as a function of dynein concentration.* [*After Gibbons, 1966.*]

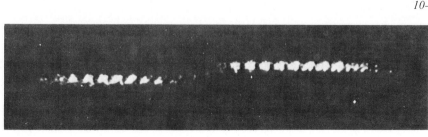

10-10. *Electron micrograph of the isolated dynein polymer, which is composed of monomer subunits 140 Å long and 80 Å in diameter.* [*Courtesy of I. Gibbons.*]

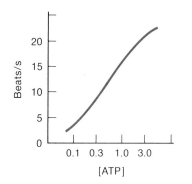

10-11. *The frequency of beating of glycerol-extracted cilia as a function of the ATP concentration.* [*After Brokaw, 1967.*]

10-12. *Two hypothetical mechanisms to explain the active bending of cilia. A. If the peripheral doublets on one side contract, the axoneme should bend toward the side undergoing contraction. This would work on the same principle as the bending of a bimetal strip, which changes shape as temperature changes cause differential contraction of the metals. B. If the doublets are fixed at the base and the doublets on one side of the axoneme slide actively in relation to the others, the axoneme should bend toward the doublets that tend to slide away from the base.* [*After Brokaw, 1968.*]

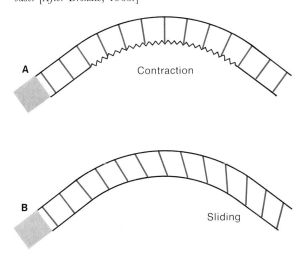

monomer. This suggests that the individual arms consist of dynein monomers linked in longitudinal polymeric filaments bound to the A-tubules of the outer doublets. Because of their location and their ATPase activity, it has been proposed that the dynein arms serve a function analogous to that of the cross bridges of striated muscle, utilizing the energy released by hydrolysis of ATP for mechanical work.

The outer nine doublets are composed of at least two species of globular protein subunits, collectively termed *tubulin.* In amino acid composition, dimensions, and electrophoretic behavior, tubulin approximates

actin from muscle. Although it does not polymerize into a double helix, as actin does, and shows some other minor differences, the general resemblance to actin is interesting in view of analogous functions suggested for tubulin.

ENERGETICS OF CILIARY MOVEMENT

Studies with models of cilia and flagella prepared by using detergents or 50% glycerol to remove the flagellar membrane and soluble constituents (Box 9-1) have shown that Mg^{2+}-ATP supplies the chemical energy for their movement. Beating stops in the absence of ATP, and beating frequency is a function of ATP concentration (Fig. 10-11).

Protozoan cilia contain the enzyme arginine kinase, which catalyzes the reaction

$$ADP + phosphoarginine + H^+ \rightleftharpoons ATP + arginine$$

This enzyme performs the same function in the muscles of certain invertebrates. The phosphoarginine acts as a reservoir for the high-energy phosphate bond, providing a rapidly available source of chemical energy for recharging the purine nucleotide. Gibbons (1965) found that each molecule of dynein hydrolyzes 11 to 35 molecules of ATP per second. Because flagella beat about that many times per second, this suggests that on the average each dynein molecule hydrolyzes one ATP molecule per cycle of movement.

Mechanisms of Bending

Whereas the contraction of a muscle fiber is simply a shortening in one dimension, the active movements of cilia and flagella are two- or three-dimensional, which makes the mechanism of ciliary movement much more difficult to study than that of muscle. In addition, these organelles are very small and cannot be attached to a mechanical transducer for simple tension measurements. As a result, we do not yet have a thoroughly tested theory for the mechanism of ciliary and flagellar movement. Nevertheless, recent findings, described below, suggest a sliding-tubule mechanism as the basis for ciliary and flagellar motility.

SLIDING-TUBULE HYPOTHESIS

There are two ways in which the ring of nine doublets might behave during bending of the axoneme: (1) the doublets on the inside curvature of the axoneme might *contract,* as illustrated in Figure 10-12,A (or the tubules on the outside curvature might expand), or (2) the doublets on the inside curvature of the bending axoneme might *slide* relative to the others while all the doublets maintain a constant length (Fig. 10-12,B). It now appears that the second of these two possibilities is the basis for ciliary and flagellar motility. The evidence for this conclusion follows.

Satir (1972) has shown in recent years that the microtubules of the axoneme slide past each other during bending of the ciliary shaft. This was demonstrated by careful electron-microscopical examination of the terminations of the outer nine doublets in cilia fixed instantaneously with osmium while in various phases of the beating cycle. The microtubules on the inside curvature of the cilium always project beyond those that happen to be located on the outer arc of the curved cilium, regardless of the part of the ciliary cycle in which the cilium is stopped by the fixative (Fig. 10-13). This is precisely what would be expected if the microtubules maintain a constant length while sliding past one another. But this evidence does not in itself distinguish between (1) active sliding between microtubules, which would *cause* bending of the shaft, and (2) passive sliding, which might occur as the *result* of bending produced by another process.

Active sliding would require a physical means for the development of force between apposed or adjacent doublets or between doublets and the central sheath. In muscle this force is developed with cross bridges from the myosin acting upon the actin filaments. The axoneme contains at least two structures that might behave in a manner analogous to that of the cross bridges of muscle. These structures are the dynein arms that project from the A-tubules of the outer nine doublets toward the B-tubules and the radial links that project inward from the A-tubules toward the central sheath (Fig. 10-7). No ATPase activity has as yet been traced to the radial links; therefore, unless such an ATPase can be demonstrated, it is unlikely that the radial links perform a function analogous to the role of myosin cross bridges in muscle contraction. On the other hand, the ATPase activity of the dynein arms suggests that they are somehow involved in the process of mechano-chemical transduction.

Summers and Gibbons have recently demonstrated active sliding of the outer doublets energized by ATP. Flagella of sea urchin sperm were extracted with the detergent Triton X-100 to remove the surface membrane and the soluble components in the shaft (Box 9-1). The extracted axonemes were then briefly exposed to the enzyme trypsin, which attacks certain peptide bonds. The trypsin treatment modifies the axonemes so that subsequent exposure to ATP and Mg^{2+} causes them initially to elongate and then to dissociate into individual tubules and groups of tubules. Examination with dark-field microscopy revealed that the elongation results from a longi-

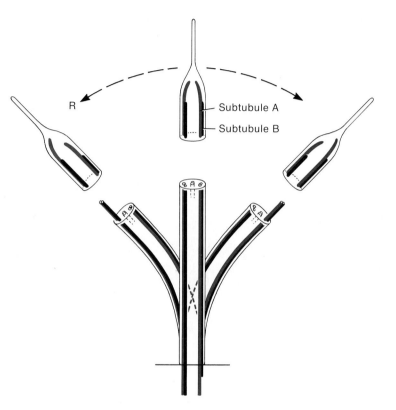

10-13. *Electron-microscopical evidence for the sliding-filament hypothesis of ciliary-flagellar movement. Cilia fixed instantaneously with osmium while beating were examined electron-microscopically at their tips. The outer doublets were found to extend further toward the ciliary apex on the inside of the bend, regardless of the part of the beating cycle in which the cilium was stopped.* [*After Satir, 1972.*]

Subtubule A
Subtubule B

tudinal sliding of the nine outer doublets with respect to one another (Fig. 10-14), so that the total length of overlapping tubules increases to as much as five times the length of individual tubules. These results may be interpreted as follows. In the living cilium, ATP energizes a sliding action between the dynein arms and the B-tubule of the next doublet. This active movement is opposed by an elastic restraint, perhaps the attachment of the nine outer doublets to the central sheath via the radial links. The limited sliding motion produced in this way is responsible for the bending of the flagellum (or cilium). When the trypsin has digested certain structures, unrestrained sliding takes place upon addition of Mg^{2+}-ATP, producing a progressive elongation of the total structure as one doublet slides along upon another, which in turn slides along upon still another, and so forth (Fig.

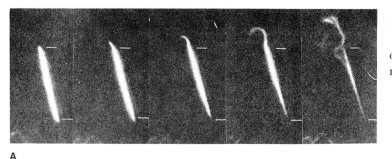

10–14. Direct evidence for ATP-energized sliding of doublets. The addition of Mg-ATP to Triton-extracted, trypsin-treated sea-urchin flagella causes tubules to slide past each other. A. Dark-field light micrographs of such a preparation taken at 10- to 30-s intervals. The two white lines indicate the initial position of each end of the fragment. [Summers and Gibbons, 1971.] B, C. Schematic interpretation of these findings.

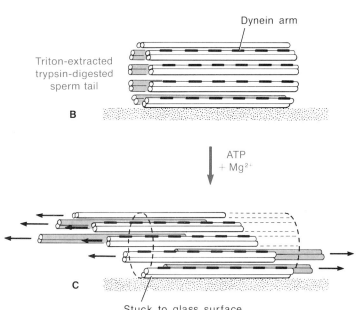

10-14,B). This sliding has the same energetic and ionic requirements as reactivated beating in extracted models.

Thus the observations of Satir (Fig. 10-13) and the experiments by Summers and Gibbons (Fig. 10-14) leave little doubt that ciliary and flagellar movements are produced by a sliding-tubule mechanism somewhat similar in principle to the sliding-filament mechanism of muscle. A major question that remains at this time is how the radially arrayed set of nine doublets is regulated to undergo sliding movements that produce the various kinds of asymmetrical movements characteristic of beating cilia and flagella.

PROPAGATION OF BENDING ALONG THE AXONEME

It has been suggested that the cell membrane, which is continuous over the surface of the ciliary shaft, conducts an electric impulse that travels along the shaft and triggers active bending along the way. Although this might explain how the traveling wave of mechanical activity is propagated along the axoneme in cilia and flagella, the regulation of bend propagation by membrane impulses has been ruled out by experiments with glycerinated or detergent-extracted preparations in which the membrane is either physically or functionally eliminated. In such models, bend propagation and other movements of individual cilia are fully retained. A plausible hypothesis that accounts for the propagation of the bend along the shaft of a cilium or flagellum has emerged from the sliding-tubule hypothesis. Brokaw (1965) has suggested that the propagation of bending along the axoneme of a flagellum can be attributed to a sliding mechanism. If it is assumed that in the inactive segments of the axoneme there is some resistance to relative sliding of the tubules, it will be apparent that active sliding within one section of the axoneme will produce passive bending in opposite directions of the inactive sections on either side of the actively sliding section (Fig. 10-15,B).

Longitudinal propagation of activity along the axoneme can be explained if it is assumed that the bending of an inactive region stimulates it to become active (Fig. 10-15). Sliding forces produced by chemomechanical transduction in the active region will be transferred longitudinally to adjacent inactive regions, causing these to bend passively. The passive bending initiated by nearby active sliding initiates active sliding that bends the next section, and so on, along the length of the axoneme. A mathematical model based on this hypothesis has been used for computer simulation of movement patterns that closely resemble real flagellar movements (Fig. 10-16). Sensitivity to mechanical strain is seen in the "giant cilium" found on the gill filament of clams. This cilium (actually a closely packed bundle of very long individual cilia) remains poised indefinitely at the end of its effective stroke under certain ionic conditions (Fig. 10-17,A). If then given a small passive displacement with a microneedle, the cirrus initiates a complete cycle of active bending (Fig. 10-17,D to G). Intracellular electrical recordings show no potential changes across the cell membrane associated with the mechanical stimulus or the active mechanical response. Apparently the mechanical stimulus acts directly on the mechanism responsible for active sliding.

Evidence that ATPase activity is stimulated by mechanical forces associated with flagellar movements was obtained by slowing the frequency of movements of glycerinated sperm tails by increasing the viscosity of the medium in which they were suspended. This produced a reduction in ATP hydrolysis. Thus it is clear that the rate of ATP hydrolysis depends on the frequency with which inactive regions are stimulated by regions undergoing active bending. A relation between passive tension on cross bridges and ATP hydrolysis is observed in insect fibrillar muscle (p. 308), in which ATPase activity and tension production of the cross bridges are stimulated by externally applied tension.

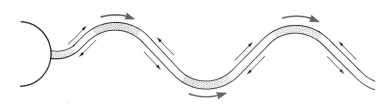

10-16. *Propagation of alternating linear and bent regions of axoneme along sperm-tail flagellum. Small arrows show proposed active counter-sliding of axoneural tubules in active straight segments. This is believed to produce passive bending of the inactive neighboring segment.*

10-15. *Diagram illustrating the idea that active sliding in a straight section of the axoneme of a flagellum produces passive bending in opposite directions in adjacent inactive regions. If passive bending activates the sliding mechanism (B), the sequence of alternating straight and curved regions will propagate along the axoneme (C). See text and Figure 10–16.*

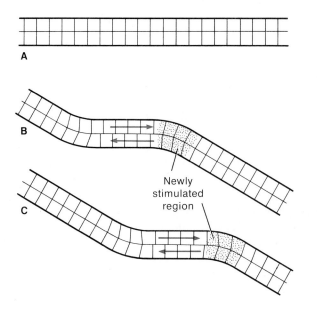

10-17. *Mechanical activation of the giant cilium of the clam. A crystal-driven microstylus is used to give the stationary cilium an abrupt displacement (B). This initiates an entire beat cycle (B–G). [After Thurm, 1968.]*

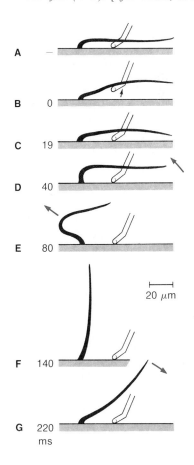

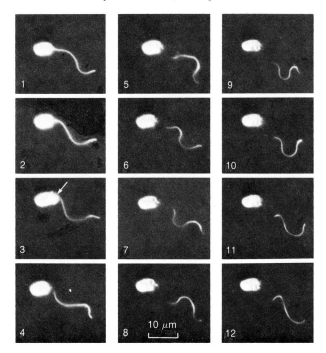

beat when it is severed near the base and separated from the basal body (Fig. 10-18). It must be concluded that, in at least some species, the beat can originate in the shaft itself.

The cilia of certain vertebrate epithelia (e.g., frog palate) increase their frequency of beating in response to acetylcholine (ACh) and slow down in response to epinephrine. They also increase beating frequency when nerves that release ACh in the tissue are stimulated. Brief electrical stimulation of the nerve innervating the ciliated gills of the mussel *Mytilus* results in a transient cessation of ciliary activity (Fig. 10-19). This is presumed to result from the action of a transmitter substance released by the nerve terminals. The neurotransmitter 5-hydroxytryptamine (5-HT) accelerates the cilia of clam and mussel gills, mimicking the excitatory effect of stimulating the branchial nerve.

How does a neurotransmitter influence the frequency of ciliary beating? One hypothesis suggests that certain transmitter substances produce changes in the permeability of the cell membrane to ions that influence the rate of energy metabolism in the cell. In this way, a neurotransmitter substance might change the cytoplasmic levels of a rate-limiting factor such as ATP. Some ciliated cells are activated to a high frequency of beating when mechanically stimulated. In experiments with the epithelial cells of the amphibian oviduct, it has been observed that the cilio-activating effect of mechanical stimulation disappears when Ca^{2+} is prevented from entering the cell through the stimulated membrane. Direct injection of Ca^{2+} restores beating in decalcified cells, and injection of ATP into normally beating cells increases the frequency of beating.

Coordination of Ciliary Movement

Questions of control and coordination of movement exist at three principal levels. First, there is the question of how the beat is initiated and how the beating frequency is regulated. Second, there is the question of what causes the individual cilia of a population to beat with a timing that produces *metachronal waves* that sweep steadily and repeatedly over the ciliary field (Fig. 10-2). Third, there is the question of how the cilia of protozoa and certain metazoan epithelia are controlled so as to undergo changes in the spatial organization of the beat, most evident as a change in the direction of the power stroke and in the direction of the metachronal waves.

SPONTANEITY AND BEATING FREQUENCY

Cilia and flagella exhibit endogenous rhythmicity. The organelles can beat spontaneously after isolation from a cell, and will beat after extraction of the cell membrane and cytoplasmic metabolites by glycerination or treatment with detergents (Box 9-1) if provided with an external supply of ATP and essential ions. In certain species, the flagellum continues to

CILIARY REVERSAL

Most epithelial cilia beat in a fixed direction, but the cilia of protozoa and of the epithelium of tunicate larvae can alter the direction of the power stroke.

The most extensive investigations of ciliary reversal have been made on ciliated protozoa. There is an intimate relation between change in the direction of ciliary beat and changes in the direction of metachronal waves. A shift in the direction of the effective stroke is accompanied by a similar shift in the direction of metachronism. This relation was used to correlate direction of ciliary beating with the membrane potential in *Opalina*. The membrane potential was altered by changes in the KCl concentration of the external medium, and the orientation of the metachronal waves was plotted against membrane potential (Fig. 10-20). As the membrane is depolarized, the direction of the power stroke shifts in a clockwise direction until the beat is directed toward the anterior. In the free-swimming cell, this produces backward

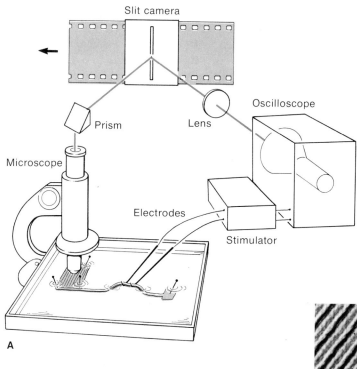

A

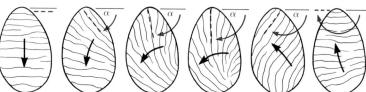

B

10-19. *Method of studying the neural control of ciliary beating. Electrical stimulation of the nerve that innervates the gills of the mussel* Mytilus *stops the ciliary beat. A. The experimental apparatus. A steadily moving strip of film travels past a slit while the image of the metachronal waves of the beating cilia move along the longitudinal axis of the slit. B. This movement produces a diagonal pattern on the film. Alterations in the activity of the cilia interrupt this pattern. C. Records showing the stoppage of the beat of cilia in response to nerve stimulation.* [Takahashi and Murakami, 1968.]

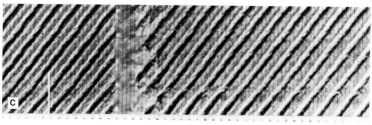

C

10-20. *Orientation of the metachronal waves as a function of membrane potential. The ciliate* Opalina *was immersed in various concentrations of KCl to set the membrane to different potentials. The potentials were recorded with a microelectrode and the orientation of metachronal waves (angle α) plotted against the membrane potential (top). The more depolarized the membrane, the more anteriorly directed are the waves. The different symbols in the graph refer to different specimens. Direction of wave propagation on the surface of* Opalina *is shown below, with depolarization progressing from left to right.* [After Kinosita, 1954.]

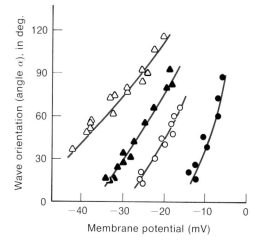

Wave orientation (angle α), in deg.

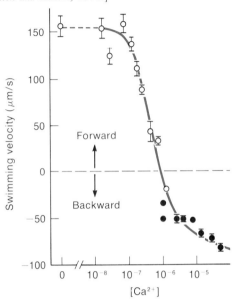

10-21. *Relation between* Ca^{2+} *concentration and direction of ciliary beat in Triton-extracted models of* Paramecium. *Extracted cells swim if reactivated with Mg-ATP. Swimming is forward if* Ca^{2+} *is below* 10^{-6} *M and backward if above that concentration.* [*After Naitoh and Kaneko, 1972.*]

10-22. *The calcium response of* Paramecium. *Injection of brief current pulses of three different intensities (bottom trace) produces responses of increasing intensity (A to C). The colored areas indicate approximately the depolarization contributed by the influx of* Ca^{2+} *into the cell. The cilia respond to the graded influx of* Ca^{2+} *with reversed beating of graded strength and duration.* [*After Eckert, 1972.*]

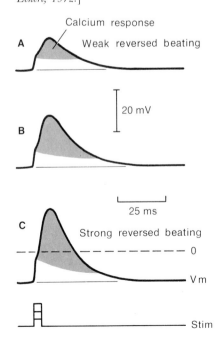

locomotion. This shift in the direction of the power stroke is termed *ciliary reversal*. The orientation of the beat is graded with membrane depolarization in somewhat the same way that muscle contraction is graded when the membrane is artificially depolarized.

The mechanism that produces reversal of the direction of effective stroke, like the mechanism for muscle contraction, requires a certain concentration of Ca^{2+}. If Ca^{2+} is absent from the extracellular fluid, the cilia do not reverse their direction of beating in response to depolarization. The high calcium sensitivity of the ciliary apparatus was recently demonstrated by Y. Naitoh and H. Kaneko (1972) in detergent-extracted specimens of *Paramecium*. After membrane is destroyed as a diffusion barrier with Triton X-100 (a nonionic detergent), the cells can be reactivated to swim in a solution of ATP and Mg^{2+}. If the concentration of Ca^{2+} in the reactivation solution is held at less than 10^{-6} mole/liter, the ciliated cells swim forward; if it is higher, the cilia beat in reverse, causing the ciliated cells to swim backward (Fig. 10-21). Because the ciliary apparatus of the extracted *Paramecium* is exposed directly to the reactivation medium ($ATP + MgCl_2 + CaCl_2$), these results indicate that the direction of the ciliary power stroke is normally controlled by the internal concentration of Ca^{2+}. ATP is required for the Ca-activated reversal. If Mg^{2+} is omitted from the reactivation medium, the cilia fail to beat, but they will shift toward the anterior-pointing orientation as the concentration of Ca^{2+} is increased, provided that ATP is present.

In the living ciliate, the concentration of free Ca^{2+} in the cytoplasm is determined by a balance between efflux of Ca^{2+} produced by a metabolically-energized calcium pump and the influx of calcium through calcium channels or carriers in the surface membrane. If the permeability of the membrane to Ca^{2+} increases in response to a stimulus, the balance shifts and the intracellular concentration of Ca^{2+} rises. Electrophysiological experiments have shown that depolarization of the cell membrane in *Paramecium* increases the permeability of the membrane to Ca^{2+} (much as depolarization increases sodium conductance in squid axon; see Chapter 5). The influx of Ca^{2+} that occurs in response to depolarization is seen in electrical recordings as an impulse-like Ca^{2+} response (Fig. 10-22) that is graded with stimulus intensity rather than being all-or-none like a nerve impulse. The influx of Ca^{2+} through channels in the membrane covering the cilia leads to a rise in the Ca^{2+} concentration within the cilia. The intraciliary Ca^{2+} alters the activity of the sliding tubules so as to produce a reversal in the orientation of the ciliary movements. Thus it is the influx of Ca^{2+} due to increased calcium conductance that couples a membrane depolarization produced by a sensory stimulus (p. 270) to the reversal of ciliary

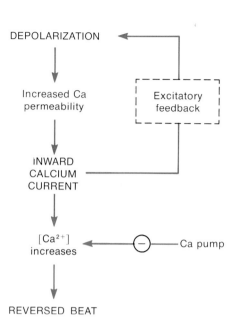

DEPOLARIZATION

Increased Ca
permeability

Excitatory
feedback

INWARD
CALCIUM
CURRENT

$[Ca^{2+}]$
increases ← ⊖ — Ca pump

REVERSED BEAT

10–23. *Coupling of ciliary reversal to membrane depolarization. Depolarization produced by stimulation of the membrane causes calcium channels to open. The large electrochemical gradient of Ca^{2+} causes it to flow through these channels into the cell, primarily into the cilia, as most channels are located in the portions of membrane covering the cilia. This inward Ca^{2+} flux is seen as a calcium response, a weakly regenerative, spike-like depolarization. The increase in ciliary free Ca^{2+} causes the beat to undergo a change in direction of power stroke. Removal of the Ca^{2+} by membrane-transport mechanisms or by diffusion into the rest of the cell is followed by restoration of normal beating. [Eckert, 1972.]*

10–24. *Metachronal waves in* Opalina. *Specimen was fixed instantaneously with osmium and then shadowed with gold for examination by scanning electron microscope. Part B is an enlargement from part A, and measures 17 μm across the lower edge. [Tamm, 1970.]*

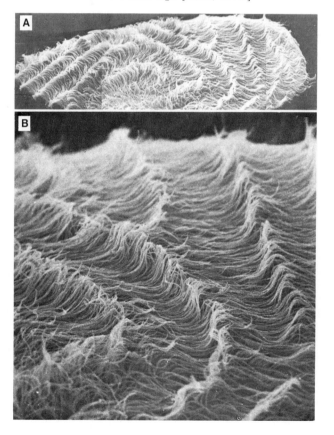

beating in ciliates such as *Paramecium* (Fig. 10-23). A similar depolarization-induced calcium influx occurs at the presynaptic nerve terminal, where it leads to the release of the synaptic transmitter (Chapter 6); another occurs in smooth muscle and amphibian cardiac muscle, where it activates contraction. Although it is apparent that Ca^{2+} participates in the orientation of ciliary beating, almost nothing is known as yet about the Ca-activated mechanism within the axoneme that shifts the direction of the effective stroke.

METACHRONISM

The term "metachronism" refers to the waves of in-phase activity that spread over a population of cilia much like the ripples in a windblown field of wheat. In general, the direction of the waves is at right angles to the planes of the effective stroke. Figure 10-24 shows an instantaneously fixed specimen of the ciliate *Opalina*. As can be seen, all cilia are in phase along one axis—the axis of the wave front. At right angles to this, there is a phase shift from one cilium to the next, producing the sequence of waves. As the cilia produce their cyclic movements, the waves move smoothly at right angles to the axis of the wavefront.

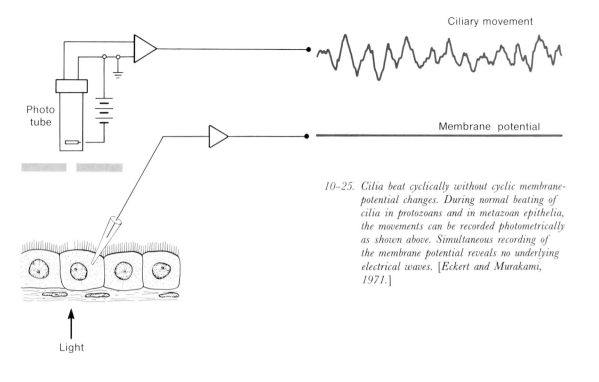

Ciliary movement

Membrane potential

Photo
tube

Light

10-25. *Cilia beat cyclically without cyclic membrane-
potential changes. During normal beating of
cilia in protozoans and in metazoan epithelia,
the movements can be recorded photometrically
as shown above. Simultaneous recording of
the membrane potential reveals no underlying
electrical waves.* [*Eckert and Murakami,
1971.*]

Two hypotheses have been devised to explain the coordination of cilia in metachronal waves. The *neuroid hypothesis* proposes that repetitive signals carried by a cellular epithelium or cell membrane arise at a pacemaker region in one part of the epithelium or cell membrane and sweep over the surface, triggering or entraining each cilium as the signals pass. There are various versions of the neuroid hypothesis, some involving the surface membrane and others the intracellular fibrils connecting the basal bodies. The idea common to all versions is that the progression of the metachronal wave results directly from propagated coordinating signals of some kind. The *coupled-oscillator* hypothesis holds that metachronal waves arise as a consequence of viscous coupling between neighboring cilia through their fluid medium, and perhaps as a consequence of the sensitivity of the cilium to passive bending, already described.

There is no convincing evidence in support of the neuroid hypothesis. For example, no electrical signals recorded across the cell membrane can be correlated with ciliary beating, either in protozoa or in vertebrate epithelium (Fig. 10-25). The evidence to the contrary is most convincing. In extracted models of *Paramecium* lacking a functional cell membrane, well-coordinated metachronism has been demonstrated following Mg^{2+}–ATP reactivation (Fig. 10-21). It has been proposed for many years that intracellular fibrils associated with the basal bodies act as pathways for conduction, as though they were components of a miniature intracellular nervous system. The concept of an internal network of signal-conducting fibrils is difficult to reconcile with the infinite variability in the

direction of wave progression correlated with graded changes in membrane potential (Fig. 10-20). Nevertheless, this view was reinforced by a report in 1920 that the cilia at the posterior end of the ciliate *Euplotes* fail to reverse their direction of beating in coordination with the cilia of the anterior end once the intracellular "neuromotor" fibrils between the groups are cut. This observation was never confirmed. More recent work has demonstrated that the fibrils are not involved; instead, the coordinated reversal of beating depends on a depolarization of the membrane, which occurs uniformly over the cell by electrotonic spread.

There is considerable evidence that the metachronal waves arise as a consequence of viscous coupling between the organelles resulting from the viscosity of the extracellular medium. The role of viscous coupling was first suggested in 1922 by Gray, who studied a population of independently undulating spirochetes (type of bacteria) and found that, as they were crowded more closely together, they fell into a common rhythm, each beating in harmony with its neighbors, apparently as a result of mutual interference. Mechanical interaction does not require that cilia be in direct contact, because they are loosely coupled to their neighbors through the viscous drag of the extracellular fluid. Although each cilium has an inherent spontaneous beating frequency, it becomes entrained to beat nearly in phase with its closest neighbors along the axis of greatest physical interaction, because that requires less energy than does beating out of phase against its neighbors. This axis is determined by the form and orientation of the beat of individual cilia and by their spacing along the cell surface.

Summary

The cilia and flagella of eucaryotic cells arise from basal bodies homologous with centrioles, and have a basic "9 + 2" organization of tubules. The two central tubules are surrounded by a ring of nine doublet tubules. Like other cellular microtubules, these tubules form by polymerization of tubulin, a protein monomer. The nine doublet tubules of cilia and flagella have arms positioned at intervals along the length of tubule A and project toward tubule B of the next doublet. These arms are composed of monomers of a protein termed dynein, which exhibits ATPase activity. It is believed that the dynein arms are involved in producing a sliding movement between adjacent doublets.

Spokes radiate from the sheath that surrounds the central pair of tubules to the nine doublet tubules. Although the function of these spokes is not clear, they appear to become displaced longitudinally along their respective doublets as the shaft of the cilium or flagellum is bent. When extracted and trypsinized flagella are supplied with ATP, the doublets slide past one another, suggesting that the movements of cilia and flagella depend on a sliding-tubule mechanism similar in principle to the sliding-filament mechanism of muscle. When cilia bend, the doublets on the inside of the bend are seen to project out beyond the other doublets near the tip of the cilium. This also suggests that bending is produced not by selective contraction of the doublets, but by relative sliding between doublets.

Analysis of undulating movements of flagella show that straight regions alternate with bending regions. The bends propagate along the shaft without diminishing in amplitude, indicating that—unlike the traveling wave of a whip, which is produced by active movement at one end only—force is generated along the entire length of the flagellum. It has been proposed that the bends propagate by a regenerative mechanical process, with the strain produced by an actively sliding region being transferred to the inactive portion ahead to activate the force-generating mechanism that causes the tubules in the previously inactive region to initiate active sliding.

In vertebrate epithelial cilia, frequency appears to be determined by cytoplasmic concentrations of ATP and Ca^{2+}, which are controlled by membrane permeability regulated by neurotransmitters. In protozoa, Ca^{2+} influx due to cell-membrane depolarization induces a reversal of the direction of the power stroke.

Although individual cilia exhibit endogenous rhythmicity, populations of cilia exhibit a coordinated wave of motion called metachronism. No electrical signals corresponding to phases of the beating cycle occur over the cell membrane. Instead, the entrainment of neighboring cilia is a hydrodynamic phenomenon; the viscous drag of the medium between cilia brings about coherent bending of all the cilia along the paths of greatest force production.

EXERCISES

1. Discuss evidence that flagellar movements are not generated solely at the base and simply propagated in whip-like fashion toward the tip.

2. Describe the properties and functions of the two main protein fractions found in the ciliary axoneme.

3. What is the evidence that ATP supplies the energy for ciliary and flagellar bending?

4. Discuss the evidence in favor of the sliding-tubule hypothesis.

5. Describe an experiment that suggests that the cilia can respond to passive bending by generating active bending.

6. How do nerves regulate the activity of epithelial cilia?

7. How is reversal of ciliary beat regulated by membrane depolarization in the protozoa?

8. Discuss evidence for the viscous-coupling hypothesis of metachronism.

9. What evidence indicates that the cycle of ciliary beating is independent of cyclic regulation by the cell membrane?

SUGGESTED READING

Eckert, R. 1972. Bioelectric control of ciliary activity. *Science* 176:473–481.

Holwill, M. E. J. 1966. Physical aspects of flagellar movement. *Physiol. Rev.* 46(4):696–785.

Inoué, S., and R. E. Stephens (eds.). 1975. *Molecules and Cell Movement* (Symposium Soc. Gen. Physiology). Vol. 30. Raven Press, New York.

Satir, P. 1974. How cilia move. *Scientific American* 231(4):44–52. [Also available as offprint 1304.]

Sleigh, M. A. 1962. *The Biology of Cilia and Flagella.* Pergamon Press, New York.

Sleigh, M. A. 1971. Cilia. *Endeavor* 30(109):11–17.

Sleigh, M. A. (ed.). 1974. *Cilia and Flagella.* Academic Press, New York.

REFERENCES CITED

Baba, S. A., and Y. Hiramoto. 1970. A quantitative analysis of ciliary movement by means of high speed microcinematography. *J. Exp. Biol.* 52:645–690.

Brokaw, C. J. 1965. Non-sinusoidal bending waves of sperm flagella. *J. Exp. Biol.* 43:155–169.

Brokaw, C. J. 1967. ATP usage by flagella. *Science* 156:76–78.

Brokaw, C. J. 1968. Mechanisms of sperm movement. *Symp. Soc. Exper. Biol.* 22:101–117.

Brokaw, C. J. 1971. Bend propagation by a sliding filament model for flagella. *J. Exper. Biol.* 55:289–304.

Eckert, R. 1972. Bioelectric control of ciliary activity. *Science* 176:473–481.

Eckert, R., and A. Murakami. 1971. Control of ciliary activity. *In* R. Podolsky (ed.), *Contractility of Muscle Cells and Related Processes.* Prentice-Hall, Englewood Cliffs, N.J.

Gibbons, I. R. 1965. Chemical dissection of cilia. *Arch. Biol.* 76:317–352.

Gibbons, I. R. 1966. Studies on the adenosine triphosphate activity of 14s and 30s dynein from cilia of *Tetrahymena. J. Biol. Chem.* 241:5590–5596.

Goldstein, S. F., M. E. J. Holwill, and N. R. Silvester. 1970. High speed recording of laser damage. *Visual* 8:245–248.

Gray, J. 1922. The mechanism of ciliary movement. *Roy. Soc. Proc.* Ser. B 93:104–121.

Grell, K. G. 1973. *Protozoology.* Springer-Verlag, New York.

Jahn, T. L., and E. C. Bovee. 1967. Motile behavior of protozoa. *In* T. T. Chen (ed.), *Research in Protozoology* (vol. 1). Pergamon Press, New York.

Jahn, T. L., M. D. Landman, and J. R. Fonseca. 1964. The mechanism of locomotion of flagellates, II: Function of mastigonemes of *Ochromonas. J. Protozool.* 11:291–296.

Jahn, T. L., and J. J. Votta. 1972. Locomotion of protozoa. *Ann. Rev. Fluid Mech.* 4:93–116.

Jarosch, R. 1972. The participation of rotating fibrils in biological movements. *Acta Protozool.* 11:23–38.

Kinosita, H. 1954. Electric potentials and ciliary response in *Opalina. J. Fac. Sci. Tokyo U. Sec. 4* 7:1–14.

Machemer, H. 1972. *J. Mechanochem. Cell Motil.* 1:57–66.

Naitoh, Y., and H. Kaneko. 1972. Reactivated Triton-extracted models of *Paramecium:* Modification of ciliary movement by calcium ions. *Science* 176:523–524.

Satir, P. 1973. Structural basis of ciliary activity. *In* A. Perez-Miravette (ed.), *Behavior of Microorganisms.* Plenum Press, New York.

Summers, K., and I. R. Gibbons. 1971. Adenosine triphosphate-induced sliding of tubules in trypsin-treated flagella of sea-urchin sperm. *Proc. Nat. Acad. Sci.* 68:3092–3096.

Takahashi, K., and A. Murakami. 1968. Nervous inhibition of ciliary motion in the gill of the mussel *Mytilus edulis. J. Fac. Sci.* (Tokyo Univ., Sec. IV) 2:359–372.

Tamm, S. L., and G. A. Horridge. 1970. The relation between the orientation of the central fibrils and the direction of beat in cilia of *Opalina. Proc Roy. Soc.* (London) Ser. B 175:219–233.

Thurm, U. 1968. Steps in transducer process of mechanoreceptors. *Symp. Zool. Soc. London* 23:199–216.

Warner, F. D. 1970. New observations on flagellar fine structure. *J. Cell Biol.* 47(1):159–182.

Warner, F. D., and P. Satir. 1973. The substructure of ciliary microtubules. *J. Cell Sci.* 12:313–326.

Wessels, N. 1971. How living cells change shape. *Scientific American* 225(4):76–82. [Also available as offprint 1233.]

CHAPTER ELEVEN

Chemical Messengers

Without regulation and coordination, the chemistry of living cells would be chaotic, and life in its present form would be impossible. This chapter is about special agents employed to control the activities of the cells, tissues, and organs in the animal body. Chemical regulation of cellular processes makes its appearance in some of the most primitive plant and animal species. For example, individual amebae of the cellular slime molds exhibit aggregating behavior in response to a substance originally termed "acrasin" but now known to be the ubiquitous regulatory molecule *cyclic adenosine 3', 5'-monophosphate* (cAMP). An example of a still more primitive kind of chemical regulation is seen in the freshwater coelenterate *Hydra*. The water from a crowded culture of *Hydra* induces the differentiation of reproductive tissues in that animal. This effect is now ascribed to the high CO_2 concentration built up by a dense culture. These two examples of primitive regulation include a nonspecific substance, CO_2, and the substance cAMP, which is now known to be widely employed by cells as a special regulatory agent—one that we will return to later in this chapter.

We have already seen in Chapter 3 that most of the thousands of reactions that occur within the cell depend on the catalytic action of specific enzyme molecules. Biochemical reaction rates depend on the number of enzyme molecules present in the cell and on the catalytic activity of those enzymes. From this it follows that regulation of both the amount and activity of enzymes is ultimately essential for the regulation and coordination of all biochemical and physiological processes.

Chemical Regulation

The concentration of an enzyme within a cell depends on its rate of synthesis and its rate of degradation. Synthesis is controlled by the genetic machinery (Fig. 2-57). The rate of synthesis drops if the section of DNA that codes the amino acid sequence of an enzyme is shielded by a histone protein or if the synthesis of messenger RNA for that enzyme is otherwise slowed or prevented. Similarly, enzyme synthesis will be slowed by anything that interferes with translation of the mRNA sequence to the amino acid sequence of a polypeptide that goes into the enzyme molecule. Conversely, factors that facilitate these steps will increase the rate of synthesis of the enzyme, and hence its amount, assuming that the rate of degradation remains unaffected.

The catalytic effectiveness (i.e., activity) of an enzyme is measured in *turnover number,* which is the number of molecules of substrate per second with which one mole of the enzyme reacts to produce the product molecule(s). Many enzymes require a cofactor—an ion or small molecule that combines with the protein molecule to form the active enzyme complex. If the cofactor is present in limiting concentrations within the cell, the activity of the enzyme can be regulated by alterations in the concentration of the cofactor. In contrast, some enzymes do not become catalytically effective until an inhibitor molecule is removed from them.

An important and common regulatory cofactor is the calcium ion, which is present within cells in low concentrations compared with such common inorganic ions as Mg^{2+}, Na^+, K^+, and Cl^-. Changes in intracellular Ca^{2+} concentration play an essential role in many physiological and biochemical functions (p. 103). The special role of calcium as a widespread intracellular messenger and regulatory agent is related to its very low concentration ($<10^{-6}$ M) in the cytosol. Minute changes in the net flux of Ca^{2+} across the cell membrane or the membranes of cytoplasmic organelles can thereby produce substantial *percentage* changes in the intracellular free Ca^{2+} concentration (Box 4-3).

How do Ca^{2+} and other intracellular regulatory agents exert their effects on intracellular events? There is no single answer, because there appear to be several ways in which biochemical regulation occurs. A number of enzymes exhibit allosteric regulation (p. 57). For example, an ion such as Ca^{2+}, a metabolic end product, or a specific regulatory molecule, may combine with a site on the enzyme molecule in such a way as to alter the tertiary conformation of the enzyme and thereby modify the catalytic efficiency of the active site on another part of the enzyme molecule. The control of precursor availability and concentration is another effective means of regulating a reaction rate. For example, if the supply of glucose available to the glycolytic pathway should be reduced, the initial reaction

$$\text{glucose} + \text{ATP} \rightarrow \text{glucose-6-phosphate} + \text{ADP}$$

would be slowed, and so would the rate of glycolysis. The level of glucose in a cell may be regulated by the glucose permeability of the cell membrane, by the level of glucose in the blood, or by the rate at which glycogen stored within the cell is broken down enzymatically to glucose-6-phosphate.

Thus there is a variety of "bottlenecks" in even the simplest biochemical pathways. These have been exploited by the process of natural selection for the evolution of biochemical control mechanisms.

Hormones as Messengers

Chemical regulatory agents may be divided into two groups: those that are simple, widespread, and relatively nonspecific (e.g., CO_2, H^+, O_2, Ca^{2+}) and those, like cAMP, that are generally more complex and produced specifically as regulators or *messengers.* Some species utilize chemical messengers as means of communication between individuals of that species. A familiar example of such a *pheromone* is bombykol, the powerful female sex attractant of the commercial silkworm moth (p. 203).

Pheromones occur in a wide variety of animal groups, but are most familiar in the insects, in which they function not only as sex attractants, but also as a means of identifying the members of a colony or caste. In certain marine invertebrates, such as clams and starfish, spawning of eggs and sperm is triggered by pheromones liberated along with the gametes. Thus the spawning of one individual triggers spawning in others of both sexes. The adaptive value of such *epidemic spawning* is that it enhances the probability that sperm and egg will meet and that fertilization will occur. The hormone *crustecdysone,* a steroid that induces molting in crabs, also serves as the female sex attractant, producing behavioral responses in males at concentrations in the seawater as low as 10^{-13} M.

Both invertebrates and vertebrates have specialized tissues that secrete regulatory molecules into the interstitial fluid and blood and act upon distant *target cells* within the same organism. These tissues constitute the various *endocrine glands.* The messenger molecules they secrete are termed *hormones.* This term was introduced by E. H. Starling in 1905 in first describing secretin (p. 362), and comes from the Greek for "I arouse." In the course of their circuit through the blood and interstitial fluid, the hormone molecules encounter *receptor molecules,* which are specific for the hormone and which reside at the surface of the target cells or within them. By an interaction of hormone molecule with receptor molecule, there is initiated in the target cells a series of steps that influence one or more aspects of the physiology or metabolism of those cells. Although hormone molecules come into contact

Table 11-1. Classification of chemical messengers.

Messenger type	Origin	Mode of action	Examples
Neurotransmitters	Nerve cells	Synaptic transmission; distances transported are short, duration of activity brief	Acetylcholine 5-Hydroxytryptamine Norepinephrine
Neurohormones	Nerve cells	Endocrine function; transported by circulation	Vertebrate neurohypophysial hormones Arthropod brain hormone
Glandular hormones	Nonneural endocrine tissues	Endocrine function; transported throughout body to distant target organs	Epinephrine Ecdysone Juvenile hormone Insulin
Pheromones	Glands opening to the outside	Intraspecific communication between individuals	Bombykol
Cyclic nucleotides	Most cells	Intracellular messenger action within same cell; "second messenger" for many hormones	cAMP cGMP
Inorganic ions	Extracellular or intracellular stores	Activation of enzymes; coupling agent between membrane and enzymes	Ca^{2+}

with all the tissues in the body, only cells that contain receptors specific for the hormone are affected by the hormone.

Because the amount of hormone produced by an endocrine gland is generally very small, its concentration in the blood remains very low. The target cells, however, are extraordinarily sensitive to the hormone. Thus some target cells respond to plasma concentrations of hormone as low as 10^{-12} M. If the human taste buds were that sensitive to sugar, we would be able to detect a pinch of sugar dissolved in a large swimming pool full of coffee.

Because the secretion and circulation of hormones both take place relatively slowly, endocrine systems are best suited for long-term regulatory functions, such as maintenance of blood osmolarity, blood sugar and metabolic levels (antidiuretic hormone, insulin, growth hormone, thyroxine), for control of sexual activity and the reproductive cycles (sex hormones), and for the modification of behavior (various hormones). It seems apparent, then, that the slow, steady actions of the endocrines complement the more rapid performance of the nervous system in coordinating bodily functions.

Hormonal properties can be summarized as follows:

1. Hormones are produced and secreted by endocrine cells in trace amounts.

2. They circulate in the blood and reach all tissues.

3. They react with specific receptor molecules present in certain target cells.

4. Hormones act in catalytic quantities, frequently by activating specific enzymes.

5. A single hormone may have multiple effects on a single target tissue or on several different target tissues.

As has been noted, hormones constitute but one of several classes of chemical messengers. Some of the other classes are included in Table 11-1.

Table 11-2. Some forms of the neurohypophysial hormones in different animal groups.

Name	Positions of amino acid residues									Animal group
	1	2	3	4	5	6	7	8	9	
Parent molecule	Cys—Tyr—··· ····—Asn—Cys—Pro— ····—Gly—(NH₂)									
Oxytocin	Cys—Tyr— Ile —Gln—Asn—Cys—Pro—Leu—Gly—(NH₂)									Mammals
Arginine vasopressin	Cys—Tyr—Phe—Gln—Asn—Cys—Pro—Arg—Gly—(NH₂)									Mammals
Lysine vasopressin	Cys—Tyr—Phe—Gln—Asn—Cys—Pro—Lys—Gly—(NH₂)									Pigs and relatives
Arginine vasotocin	Cys—Tyr— Ile —Gln—Asn—Cys—Pro—Arg—Gly—(NH₂)									Birds, reptiles, amphibians, and fishes
Isotocin	Cys—Tyr— Ile —Ser—Asn—Cys—Pro— Ile —Gly—(NH₂)									Some teleost fishes
Mesotocin	Cys—Tyr— Ile —Gln—Asn—Cys—Pro— Ile —Gly—(NH₂)									Reptiles, amphibia, and lungfish
Glumitocin	Cys—Tyr— Ile —Ser—Asn—Cys—Pro—Gln—Gly—(NH₂)									Some Cartilaginous fishes

Frieden, E., and H. Lipner, *Biochemical Endocrinology of the Vertebrates*, Prentice-Hall, Englewood Cliffs, N.J., 1971.

Classification of Hormones

STRUCTURAL CLASSIFICATION OF HORMONES

It must be assumed that some hormones remain undiscovered. Thus no classification is certain to be complete. Nevertheless, we can place most of the known hormones into three molecular groups: (1) amines, (2) steroids, and (3) polypeptides and proteins (Fig. 11-1). The simplest are the amines. They are among the first to have been discovered, epinephrine having been described, and its function recognized, at the beginning of this century. The largest and most complex are the polypeptides, which include some small proteins. The peptide hormones are particularly interesting as models of molecular evolution. The sequence of amino acid residues in a given polypeptide hormone (e.g., vasopressin, Table 11-2) is, of course, genetically determined; within different animal groups, substitutions of individual amino acid residues produce different analogues of the polypeptide. From inspection of Table 11-2, it is evident that some residues never undergo substitution, and are presumably necessary for function; those that do (positions 3, 4, and 8) seem to be functionally neutral, and probably serve only to place the essential residues in the positions appropriate for the activity of the polypeptide.

FUNCTIONAL CLASSIFICATION

The actions of hormones on their target tissues are diverse, and not easily subject to generalization. It is possible, however, to recognize three major classes of endocrine-mediated effects (Table 11-3). *Kinetic effects* include pigment migration, muscle contraction, and glandular secretion. *Metabolic effects* consist mainly of changes in the rate and balance of reactions and concentrations of tissue constituents. *Morphogenetic effects* have to do with growth and differentiation. Hormones often have multiple effects, and some in fact cut across at least two of the classes mentioned above. For example, the thyroid hormones have metabolic effects on cells as well as morphogenetic effects on certain tissues. This suggests that the hormones do not produce their end effects directly, but instead activate intermediate processes, which may differ in different tissues or cell types. This is, in fact, borne out by recent studies of how hormones act at the cellular level.

The mechanisms of hormone action are considered in the last section of this chapter. In the meantime, we will keep in mind that there are two major loci for hormone action. Some hormones readily penetrate the surface membranes of their target cells, and react or combine with internal cell constituents. This is characteristic of the steroids, whose lipid solubility allows them to pass readily across membranes. Most other hormone molecules, either because of their large

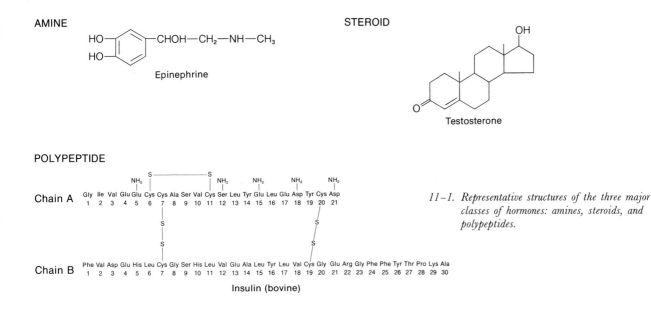

AMINE

Epinephrine

STEROID

Testosterone

POLYPEPTIDE

Chain A
Gly Ile Val Glu Glu Cys Cys Ala Ser Val Cys Ser Leu Tyr Glu Leu Glu Asp Tyr Cys Asp
1   2   3   4   5   6   7   8   9   10 11 12 13 14 15 16 17 18 19 20 21

Chain B
Phe Val Asp Glu His Leu Cys Gly Ser His Leu Val Glu Ala Leu Tyr Leu Val Cys Gly Glu Arg Gly Phe Phe Tyr Thr Pro Lys Ala
1   2   3   4   5   6   7   8   9   10 11 12 13 14 15 16 17 18 19 20 21 22 23 24 25 26 27 28 29 30

Insulin (bovine)

11–1. Representative structures of the three major classes of hormones: amines, steroids, and polypeptides.

Table 11-3. The main types of effects of vertebrate hormones.

Class of effect	Effect on target tissues	Hormones
Kinetic	Contraction of muscle	Epinephrine, oxytocin
	Concentration and dispersion of pigment	Melatonin
	Secretion of exocrine glands	Secretin
	Secretion of endocrine glands	ACTH, TSH, FSH, releasing hormones
Metabolic	Control of respiration rate	Thyroxin
	Carbohydrate and protein balance	Insulin, growth hormone
	Electrolyte and water balance	ADH, aldosterone
	Ca and P balance	Parathormone, calcitonin
Morphogenetic	General growth	Growth hormone
	Moulting	Thyroxin
	Metamorphosis	Thyroxin
	Regeneration	GH
	Gonad maturation	FSH
	Gamete release	LH
	Differentiation of genital ducts	
	Development of secondary sexual characteristics	Estrogens and androgens

Source: After P. M. Jenkins, *Animal Hormones* (Vol. I, Kinetic and Metabolic Hormones), Pergamon Press, New York, 1962.

size or their polar properties, cannot readily enter the cell, and are known to interact with receptors located in the surface membrane. These receptor molecules are, in turn, associated with enzymes whose activity is modulated by the hormone-receptor interaction.

Thus it is easy to see how one hormone can produce multiple effects. By activating different membrane enzymes associated with similar receptor molecules, a given hormone can produce entirely different effects in different cells or, for that matter, in the same cell. Conversely, hormone-receptor specificities and receptor-enzyme specificities account for different *channels of action* of different hormones (Fig. 11-2).

IDENTIFICATION OF ENDOCRINE GLANDS AND HORMONES

The various endocrine tissues are structurally and chemically diverse. Some contain more than one kind of secretory cell, each elaborating a different hormone. Unlike *exocrine glands* (e.g., salivary glands, enzyme-secreting cells of the pancreas, prostate, mammary glands, etc.), which empty their secretions into ducts, endocrine tissues liberate their secretions (i.e., hormones) directly into the extracellular space, from which the hormone diffuses into the blood. Since there is no common morphological plan for endocrine glands, nor any distinctive gross morphological feature (other than a rich vascularization), such as a secretory duct, it has proved difficult in some cases to establish unequivocally whether tissues suspected of having an endocrine function actually have such a function. No single characteristic can be used for this purpose, so the following set of criteria has been used to establish whether a tissue has an endocrine function:

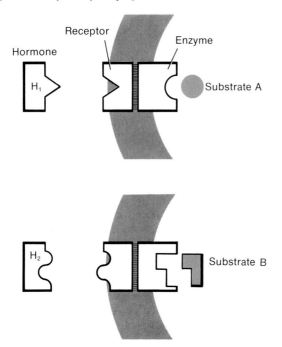

11–2. *Hormone-response specificity. Hormones H_1 and H_2 can produce different responses in the same or different target cells by virtue of hormone-receptor and receptor-enzyme specificities.*

1. Ablation of the suspected tissue should produce deficiency symptoms in the subject.

2. Replacement (i.e., reimplantation) of the ablated tissue elsewhere in the body should prevent or reverse these deficiency symptoms. If the effects produced by removal of the tissue are due to the absence of a blood-borne substance produced by that tissue, replacement of the ablated tissue should restore the missing hormone. Misleading results may be expected, however, when ablation-and-reimplantation experiments are done with tissues closely associated with the nervous system (p. 344) because of the interruption of neural connections.

3. Deficiency symptoms should be relieved by replacing the suspected hormone by injection. This is the most important criterion for identification of a suspected endocrine tissue and its hormone. It is also the basis of *replacement therapy,* which is so important for patients who for medical reasons have lost the function of an endocrine gland. For example, the effects of surgical removal of the thyroid gland because of a malignancy can be compensated by daily administration of thyroxine. Likewise, replacement therapy successfully maintains normal function when it is necessary to remove the gonads or when the insulin-secreting cells of the pancreas fail.

These three classical criteria for the identification of endocrine glands and hormones are now supplemented by a variety of modern approaches. For example, electron-microscopical investigation of the tissue may be employed to locate the membrane-limited *secretory granules* (secretory vesicles),* 1000–4000 Å in diameter, that contain the hormone. Once a hormone has been isolated in purified form, its molecular composition can be determined. Such efforts have opened the way for artificial synthesis of hormones important for replacement therapy.

Regulation of Hormone Secretion

FEEDBACK CONTROL

The secretory activities of endocrine tissues are, with very few exceptions (e.g., the cells that produce growth hormone), modulated by negative feedback (Box 1-1). That is, the concentration of the hormone itself, or a response to the hormone by a target tissue, will have an inhibitory effect on the synthetic or secretory processes responsible for the elaboration of the hormone in question. There is both *short-loop* and *long-loop* feedback (Fig. 11-3).

In *short-loop* feedback, either a product of the target tissue or an effect produced by it acts directly back on the endocrine tissue that elaborates the hormone. This keeps hormone secretion in check. Negative feedback, as the name implies, requires a sign inversion somewhere in the loop, usually some inhibitory effect that the product of the target tissue has on the endocrine tissue. As the concentration of the hormone rises, it indirectly inhibits any further increase in its own plasma concentration.

A long loop operates on the same principle, but it includes more elements (Fig. 11-3). Regardless of the number of elements in the loop, there must be an odd number of sign inversions to produce the regulatory effect. For example, two sign inversions (i.e., inhibitions) in the same loop will not do, for two negatives would cancel each other, producing an overall positive feedback.

Negative-feedback control is illustrated by the secretion of ADH in response to increased osmolarity of the blood plasma. Upon reaching the kidney, the ADH increases water reabsorption in the collecting

---

*These are similar in many respects to synaptic vesicles (p. 168), which are about 400 Å in diameter. We will use the terms "secretory granule" and "secretory vesicle" interchangeably, depending on whether the emphasis is on its contents (granule) or its limiting membrane (vesicle).

duct from the pre-urine (p. 407), counteracting the loss of fluid. As a consequence, plasma osmolarity is stabilized, and, in turn, so is the secretory activity of the ADH-producing tissue.

The negative-feedback signal acting to slow the output of an endocrine tissue may be a physiological response to the hormone secreted by that tissue (e.g., reduced osmolarity in the ADH loop; reduced blood glucose levels in the insulin loop, p. 359) or it may be the rise in concentration of a second hormone, the secretion of which is stimulated by the first hormone (e.g., high *estrogen* levels inhibit production of the gonadotropic hormone that stimulates estrogen production, p. 365). Thus the negative-feedback signal may be simply the reduction of a stimulus to the endocrine cells or it may be an active inhibition of secretion of the hormone.

Although negative feedback is common in physiological processes, positive feedback is rare, since it is of no use in maintaining a steady state. Nevertheless, there is an interesting example of positive feedback in the generation of the *menstrual cycle*. Low levels of estrogens stimulate the secretion of *follicle-stimulating hormone (FSH)*, which, in turn, stimulates the secretion of estrogen—a positive feedback relationship that increases the levels of both estrogen and FSH in the blood. As the hormone levels rise sufficiently, positive feedback is terminated as negative feedback takes over. This happens because *high* concentrations of the estrogen *inhibit* FSH production, causing a change in feedback sign. Secretion of both FSH and estrogen is thereby largely curtailed until another cycle of positive feedback begins to build up the concentrations of these hormones. The familiar cyclic changes that characterize the menstrual cycle depend in part on the alternation between positive and negative feedback as well as on the lags inherent in the time required for the rise and fall of plasma hormone levels (Fig. 11-39).

INTRACELLULAR PACKAGING AND STORAGE OF HORMONES

Endocrine cells, like other secretory cells, generally show a morphological polarity, with the synthesis and packaging of the hormone taking place at one part of the cell and its secretion taking place at another part. This is illustrated in Figure 11-4. The nature of synthesis and storage varies from one class of hormones to another. For example, the steroid hormones, all derived from cholesterol, appear to be secreted in molecular (i.e., unpackaged) form. Most other hormones are packaged in membrane-bound vesicles within the secretory cell, later to be liberated into the extracellular space.

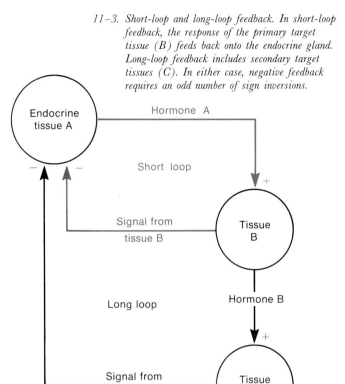

11-3. Short-loop and long-loop feedback. In short-loop feedback, the response of the primary target tissue (B) feeds back onto the endocrine gland. Long-loop feedback includes secondary target tissues (C). In either case, negative feedback requires an odd number of sign inversions.

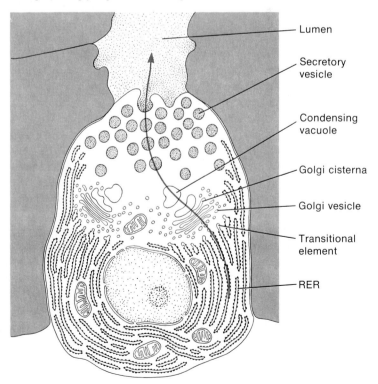

11-4. Representative epithelial endocrine cell. The colored arrow represents the general pathway of hormone production and secretion, beginning with the rough endoplasmic reticulum (RER) and ending with the exocytosis of secretory granules. [After Jamieson, 1975.]

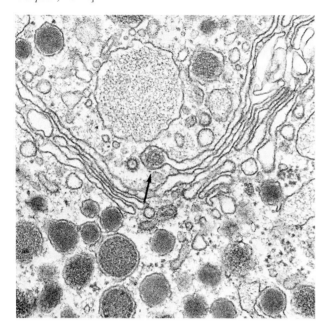

11-5. *Electron micrograph showing a Golgi apparatus in an anterior pituitary gonadotroph cell. Notice the relatively dense free secretory granules and the one budding off from the Golgi cisterna (arrow). Magnification 20,000×. [From Farquhar, 1971.]*

The protein and peptide hormones are synthesized on messenger RNA templates of the polyribosomes (polysomes) of the *rough endoplasmic reticulum (RER)* and accumulate within the reticulum. Pulse-chase radiography—a tracer technique in which radioactively labeled amino acid is incorporated for a brief period into newly synthesized proteins—permits observation of the intracellular travels of secretory proteins. From the RER, the polypeptides pass into the smooth, polysome-free portions of the endoplasmic reticulum, termed *transitional elements* (Fig. 11-4), where the membrane of the reticulum buds off, encapsulating the secretory products. These vesicles then migrate to the Golgi complex, which consists of a stacked set of slightly concave, nearly flat membrane saccules with closely associated free vesicles and vacuoles (Fig. 11-5). In an as yet unknown way, the protein is delivered to the Golgi saccules. Microscopic studies suggest that the membranes of the vesicle and saccule become fused. Within the Golgi complex, which contains enzymes bound to the luminal membrane surfaces, some proteins are altered by the addition of sugar residues and others (e.g., insulin) by the excision of fragments joining two polypeptide chains. It is believed that in a process that begins in the *Golgi cisternae,* but which takes place mainly in the *condensing vacuoles* (Fig. 11-4), water is drawn out of the future secretary vesicle osmotically, with the result that the protein becomes

concentrated 20–25 times. The mature secretory vesicle eventually reaches the plasma membrane to await the appropriate signal to release its inclusions to the cell exterior.

Retention of the hormone within the secretory vesicle is accomplished by a variety of means. Hormones of large molecular weight, such as proteins, are retained simply because of their size, which renders them incapable of crossing the membrane of the vesicle. Some small hormone molecules are bound to larger accessory molecules, usually proteins. There is evidence that the catecholamines noradrenaline and adrenaline (p. 357) are kept in their secretory vesicles at least in part by continual active uptake into the vesicles from the cytosol. The tranquilizing drug *reserpine* interferes with this uptake, thereby causing the catecholamines to leak out of their secretory vesicles and out of the secretory cells.

The duration of storage of a hormone within a secretory tissue varies widely. The steroid hormones appear to diffuse out of the cell across the surface membrane in a matter of minutes after synthesis, as they are not packaged in vesicles and, being lipid soluble, readily cross membranes. Secretory residues of most endocrine cells are held until their release is stimulated by mechanisms discussed below. The thyroid hormones are secreted into the extracellular storage spaces of spherical clusters of cells termed *follicles,* and are stored there for up to several months. Once secreted into the circulation, a hormone can still be considered stored in the bloodstream, the length of this phase of storage depending on the rate of degradation or uptake by cells. Many hormones are, in fact, carried in the circulation by *binding proteins,* and remain inactive until they dissociate from the protein.

SECRETORY MECHANISMS

There are several conceivable mechanisms by which hormones stored within the cell in secretory vesicles might find their way to the cell exterior. For most hormones (except the steroids, which appear not to be stored in vesicles), the most widely accepted theory is that the entire contents of a vesicle is delivered to the cell exterior by the process of exocytosis (p. 101). A current view of the formation, transport, release, and reconstitution of secretory vesicles is summarized in Figure 11-6.

Secretion occurs in response to appropriate stimulation of the endocrine cell. The stimulus may be the arrival of another hormone or neurotransmitter at the membrane of the secreting cell (e.g., the release of acetylcholine in the chromaffin tissue of the adrenal medulla) or may result from a nonhumoral stimulus (e.g., stimulation of the ADH-secreting neurons by an increase in plasma osmoticity). In neurosecretory nerve cells (next section), the stimulus sets up action potentials that travel to the axon terminals and there elicit the release of hormone from the endings. It is clear that depolarization in the form of the impulse leads to secretion in these cells. This has been demonstrated by stimulating such cells electrically at a distance from their endings, so as to set up impulses, while monitoring the release of hormone from the endings. The rate of hormone secretion increases with increased frequency of impulses (Fig. 11-7). Depolarization *without* the production of action potentials—for example, by experimental increase of the extracellular K^+ concentration—is also accompanied by a rise in the rate of hormone secretion. Secretion rises to a maximum with increasing $[K^+]_o$, and hence with increasing depolarization (Fig. 11-8). At still higher concentrations, secretion decreases. The stimulation of secretion by depolarization suggests that the action potential also evokes secretion by virtue of its depolarization. In either case, there must be a means by which the depolarization of the surface membrane stimulates the process of secretion. Because of the well-known role of Ca^{2+} in regulating neurotransmitter release, it came as no surprise that calcium has also been implicated in the coupling of hormone secretion to membrane stimulation.

The evidence that Ca^{2+} is the *secretogogue* that couples secretion to membrane stimulation comes from experiments on several kinds of endocrine tissues. The findings discussed below were obtained by Douglas (1974) and his associates using the release of ADH from the neurohypophysis as an experimental system.

1. Stimuli that lead to increased hormone secretion (e.g., high K^+ concentration) also lead to increased uptake of radioactively labeled Ca^{2+}. This uptake increases as $[Ca^{2+}]_o$ is raised, and decreases as $[Ca^{2+}]_o$ is lowered.

2. The rate of potassium-stimulated release of hormone is a function of $[Ca^{2+}]_o$. Over a wide range of concentrations, the output of hormone from endocrine tissues increases as $[Ca^{2+}]_o$ increases (Fig. 11-9). Below the optimum calcium concentration (2 to 4 mM, the normal plasma concentration), secretion drops off to about $\frac{1}{6}$ as much at 0.1 mM Ca^{2+}. This is consistent with the idea that calcium channels opened by depolarization allow Ca^{2+} to flow down its concentration gradient and through the cell membranes. As the extracellular concentration is altered, so is the rate of Ca influx during depolarization. The consequent rise in $[Ca^{2+}]_i$, in turn, determines the rate of hormone secretion. Thus secretion drops at low $[Ca^{2+}]$. For reasons that are not understood, it also drops at extracellular concentrations higher than 4 or 5 mM Ca^{2+}.

11-6. Formation and fate of secretory vesicles. After their formation by the Golgi apparatus (top), secretory vesicles are transported to the site of release. In a secretory neuron, as shown here, this entails transport of the vesicles down the axon to the terminals (bottom), where release occurs by exocytosis. Vesicles may be reformed by a pinocytotic process, possibly using the same membrane that made up the original vesicle. The microvesicles thus formed then aggregate and eventually become incorporated into new secretory vesicles. [After Douglas, 1974.]

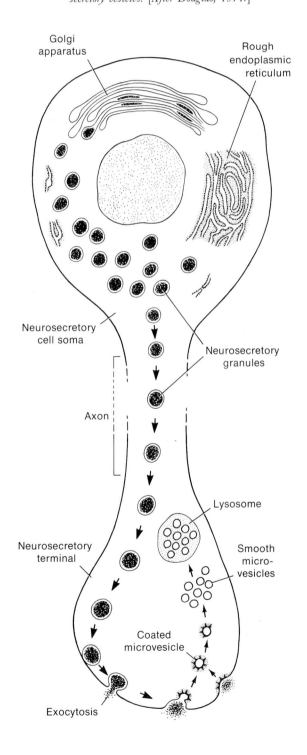

Golgi apparatus

Rough endoplasmic reticulum

Neurosecretory cell soma

Neurosecretory granules

Axon

Lysosome

Neurosecretory terminal

Smooth microvesicles

Coated microvesicle

Exocytosis

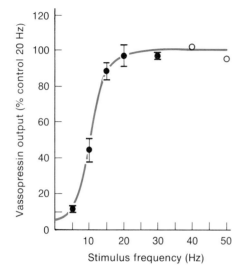

11-7. Relation between electrical stimulation and the release of vasopressin from the rat neurohypophysis. The stimulus pulses at each frequency were continued for 5 min. [After Mikiten, 1967.]

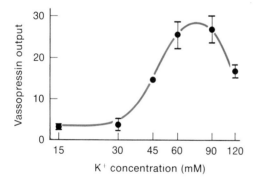

11-8. Vasopressin release (arbitrary units) as a function of potassium depolarization. Freshly dissected neurohypophyses were placed in incubation media of different K^+ content for 10 min, after which the released vasopressin was assayed. [After Douglas, 1974.]

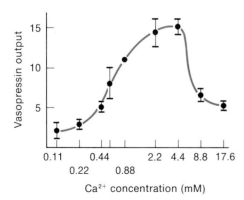

11-9. The calcium dependence of vasopressin secretion by the neurohypophysis in response to depolarization by 60 mmole of potassium. [After Douglas, 1974].

3. Treatments that produce a rise in intracellular $[Ca^{2+}]$ by nonphysiological means also produce an increase in hormone secretion. For example, the addition of calcium ionophores (i.e., molecules that facilitate the diffusion of Ca^{2+} across membranes) to the extracellular fluid in the presence of Ca^{2+} stimulates strong hormone secretion. Moreover, either a lowering of extracellular Na^+ or a lowering of temperature will produce a gradual increase in basal (i.e., unstimulated) hormone secretion. Both these treatments are known to favor a rise in the concentration of intracellular free Ca^{2+}.

4. If agents that block Ca^{2+} influx through cell membranes (e.g., Co^{2+}, Mn^{2+}, La^{3+}, the organic drug D600) are present in the extracellular fluid, they interfere with the secretory response to stimuli that normally evoke hormone release.

Thus calcium appears to be the agent that mediates *excitation-secretion coupling* in nonneural and neural endocrine cells as well as in ordinary nerve cells (p. 184). Barium or strontium ions (but not Mg^{2+} or any other ions) can replace Ca^{2+} in this role. The relations between stimuli, membrane potential, calcium concentration, and secretion are summarized for three types of secretory cells in Figure 11-10.

Any stimulus that leads to an influx of Ca^{2+} in the output portion of the cell (colored in Fig. 11-10) is followed by an increase in secretory activity. The stimulus is sensed by the receptors in the input region of the cell (shaded gray). In neurosecretory cells (see next section) and in ordinary nerve cells, the input and output regions are separated by a conducting region. Incoming stimuli (synaptic input, physical or chemical changes in the plasma) produce a depolarizing permeability change that, in turn, leads to an increased frequency of impulse firing in the axon. By invading and depolarizing the terminal membranes, impulses (action potentials) cause calcium-permeable channels to open. The influx of Ca^{2+} then triggers exocytosis.

Neuroendocrine Relations

The endocrine system is closely associated with the nervous system. This is most obvious in those endocrine tissues that are made up of nerve cells or have a neural embryological origin. For example, the *chromaffin cells* of the *adrenal medulla*, which secrete the catecholamines epinephrine and norepinephrine are embryologically as well as functionally distinct from the steroid-secreting tissue of the *adrenal cortex*. The chromaffin cells are derived from the embryonic tissue that also gives rise to postganglionic sympathetic neurons of the autonomic ganglia (Fig. 6-15). They are, in fact, the postganglionic cells of the preganglionic sympathetic neurons that arise in the thoracolumbar segments of the autonomic ganglia. Their secretory activity is stimulated by acetylcholine released from the pre-ganglionic sympathetic fibers that terminate in the chromaffin tissue.

Another important example of neuroendocrine affinity is seen in the secretory neurons of the vertebrate hypothalamus, which will be discussed below.

NEUROSECRETION

Nerve cells that produce hormones and secrete them into the bloodstream belong to a special class of neurons termed *neurosecretory cells*. These are at the same time nerve cells and endocrine cells. *Neurosecretion* occurs in nearly all metazoans, but has been most extensively studied in the insects, crustaceans, annelids, mollusks, and vertebrates.

In principle, there is little difference between an ordinary nerve cell and most neurosecretory cells. The release of a hormone from the terminals of a neurosecretory cell is similar to the release of a transmitter substance from a simple nerve cell. The major distinctions are morphological. Ordinary nerve cells form synapses with other cells at their terminations, whereas neurosecretory axons terminate close to capillaries and release their secretions into the interstitial space (Figs. 11-11, 11-12), whence they diffuse into the bloodstream and are carried away to target tissues elsewhere in the organism. The neurosecretory hormone is packaged within the neuron soma into vesicles that are 1000–4000 Å in diameter (Fig. 11-12), as compared to the 300–600 Å vesicles that contain the neurotransmitter substances of ordinary nerve cells. Neurosecretory hormones, generally peptides, are produced in the soma and transported along the axon to the axon terminals (Fig. 11-6).

Electrophysiological studies in the lower vertebrates and in invertebrates have shown that the impulses recorded from neurosecretory nerve terminals are several times the duration of terminal impulses in ordinary nerve cells (Fig. 11-10). It has been postulated that the prolonged depolarization permits correspondingly large amounts of Ca^{2+} to enter the terminal during each action potential. This could, in turn, effect the release of neurosecretory hormone into the general circulation in quantities larger than the minute amounts of neurotransmitter that are released from ordinary nerve cell terminals to diffuse a short distance across the synaptic cleft.

The term *neurohumor* has been used to describe both synaptic neurotransmitters and neurosecretory hormones (Table 11-1). Many of the hormones discussed in this chapter are produced by neurosecretory cells, most notably the hormones of the hypothalamus and insect brain.

11-10. Functional organization of three secretory cell types. A. Ordinary neuron. B. Neurosecretory neuron. C. Simple endocrine cell. Input regions shaded gray; output regions shaded in color. The influx of Ca^{2+} in the output region triggers exocytosis. Depolarization is initiated in the input region and spreads to the output region either electrotonically (in the simple endocrine cell) or by action potentials (in neurons). Note the prolonged action potential characteristic of neurosecretory terminals. Some simple endocrine cells are activated to secrete without depolarization as an intermediate step between chemical stimulus and Ca^{2+} influx.

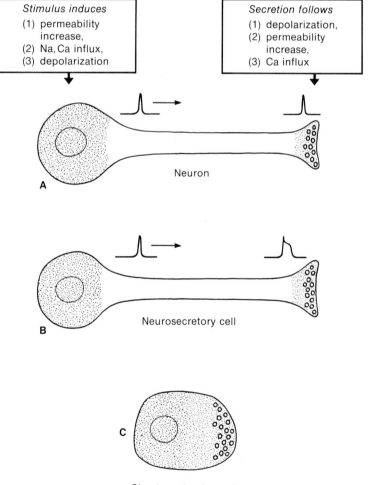

Stimulus induces
(1) permeability increase,
(2) Na, Ca influx,
(3) depolarization

Secretion follows
(1) depolarization,
(2) permeability increase,
(3) Ca influx

Neuron

Neurosecretory cell

Simple endocrine cell

11–11. *Organization of a neurosecretory system.*

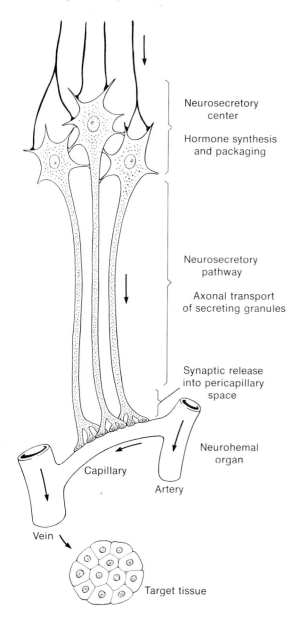

Neurosecretory
center

Hormone synthesis
and packaging

Neurosecretory
pathway

Axonal transport
of secreting granules

Synaptic release
into pericapillary
space

Neurohemal
organ

Capillary

Artery

Vein

Target tissue

11–12. *Terminals of neurosecretory axons in the
neurohypophysis of the hamster, as seen with
the electron microscope. The large dark bodies
are the secretory vesicles (or granules).
The terminals end upon an endothelial basement membrane that separates the terminals
from a fenestrated capillary wall. The large
dark object at the bottom is a red blood cell
in the capillary. Magnification 27,000×.
[After Douglas et al., 1971.]*

The *axonal transport* of secretory products can be demonstrated in the axons of neurosecretory cells by ligating the bundle of axons with a fine silk strand and then examining the proximal (toward the cell body) and distal sides of the ligature at different times. When the neurosecretory material is stained with a specific dye, it can be seen to dam up on the proximal side of the ligature. The distal side of the ligature shows a depletion of the material. The neurosecretory material is produced in the cell body and is then transported distally within the axon toward the terminal, where it is eventually released. Since the discovery of axonal transport in the 1930's, it has been found that there are both slow and fast transport systems in a given axon. Neurosecretory granules have been reported to be transported by the fast system at rates up to 2800 mm/day.

The Vertebrate Endocrine System

To discuss in any detail all the vertebrate endocrine glands, their hormones, and their interrelations would require one or more separate volumes. We will limit this section to a brief consideration of several of the more familiar endocrine tissues. The major vertebrate hormones—their origin, structure, target tissues, actions, and regulation—are summarized in Tables 11-4 to 11-11. More detailed information can be found in the Selected Reading section at the end of this chapter.

Much of this section will be devoted to the hormones of the *hypophysis,* or *pituitary gland,* a small but complex appendage at the base of the hypothalamus. This organ secretes at least nine hormones, many of

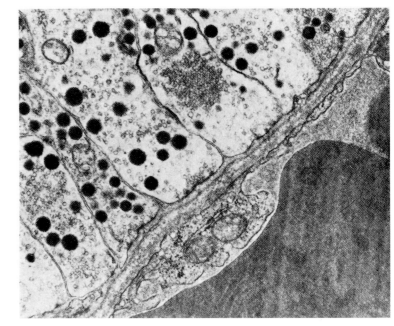

which regulate the functions of other endocrine tissues. For this reason, the hypophysis has been termed the "master gland." Recently, however, it has been discovered that the pituitary tissue is, in fact, itself under the control of neurosecretory cells located in the hypothalamus.

Hypothalamus and Pituitary

THE NEUROHYPOPHYSIAL HORMONES

The *posterior lobe* of the pituitary gland (Fig. 11-13) consists of the *pars intermedia* and the *pars nervosa*, more commonly termed the *neurohypophysis*. The neurohypophysis consists of neurosecretory axons and their terminals (Fig. 11-12). The cell bodies of these axons reside in the *supraoptic* and *paraventricular* nuclei of the hypothalamus. The secretory products, synthesized and packaged in the cell bodies, are transported to the axon terminals in the posterior lobe, within which they are released into a capillary bed. The *hypothalamo-hypophysial* system was the first example of neurosecretion discovered in the vertebrates. Below we consider more recently discovered, but equally important, neurosecretory connections between the hypothalamus and other portions of the pituitary gland.

The neurohypophysial secretory endings release two octapeptides: *vasopressin*, also termed antidiuretic hormone (ADH) and *oxytocin* (Table 11-4). Both are mildly effective in fostering contractions of the smooth-muscle tissue in arterioles and the uterus. In mammals, oxytocin is best known for its function of stimulating the uterine contractions during parturition and for stimulating the release of milk from the mammary gland; in birds, it stimulates motility of the oviduct. The foremost function of ADH is the stimulation of water retention in the kidney (p. 417). These functions are summarized in Figure 11-14.

These neurosecretory hormones occur in several molecular forms, differing from one vertebrate species to another in the identity of the amino acid residues at three loci in the peptide chain (Table 11-2). There is no clear structural distinction between the oxytocins and the vasopressins. The names are assigned on the basis of their physiological actions (Table 11-4).

Within their respective neurosecretory cells, these two neurophypophysial peptides are associated with cysteine-rich protein molecules termed *neurophysins*. Within the secretory granules, the hormone molecules appear to be noncovalently complexed in the ratio of 1:1 with the neurophysin molecules, of which there are two major fractions, neurophysin I and neurophysin II. Oxytocin is associated with I and vasopressin with II. The role of these proteins is not clear, since they have no hormone activity, even though they are secreted along with the two hormones. It is conjectured that a

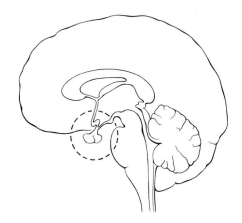

11–13. The mammalian hypophysis, or pituitary gland, situated at the base of the hypothalamus. The major components are the anterior lobe (adenohypophysis) and the posterior lobe (neurohypophysis and pars intermedia). The neurohypophysis is an extension of the brain. The adenohypophysis consists of nonneural glandular tissue.

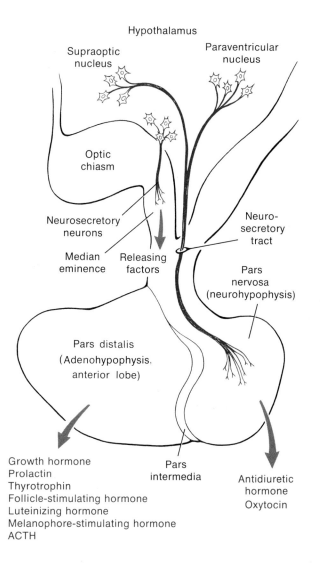

Table 11-4. Hormones of the neurohypophysis.

Hormone	Structure	Target tissue	Primary action	Regulation
Vasopressin, or antidiuretic hormone (ADH)	Peptide	Kidney	Increased water resorption	Decreases in plasma osmotic pressure, blood volume, and blood pressure cause increased release of hormone
		Arterial smooth muscle	Smooth muscle contraction	
Oxytocin	Peptide	Uterus	Smooth muscle contraction	In mammals, decreases in progesterone level, suckling stimulus, and cervical distention cause release of hormone in a positive feedback loop; increased progesterone inhibits release
		Mammary glands	Milk ejection	

11–14. The neurohypophysis and its target organs. Osmoreceptors in the hypothalamus, baroreceptors in the aorta, and exteroceptive sensory input all influence the neurosecretion of ADH. High plasma solute concentration and low blood pressure resulting from low plasma volume stimulate ADH output. Oxytocin is released during labor and nursing.

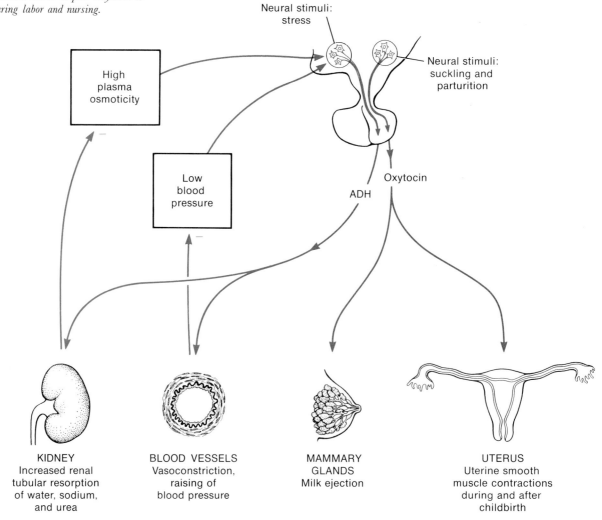

Neural stimuli: stress

Neural stimuli: suckling and parturition

High plasma osmoticity

Low blood pressure

ADH

Oxytocin

KIDNEY
Increased renal tubular resorption of water, sodium, and urea

BLOOD VESSELS
Vasoconstriction, raising of blood pressure

MAMMARY GLANDS
Milk ejection

UTERUS
Uterine smooth muscle contractions during and after childbirth

parent protein molecule is enzymatically cleaved, producing the 8-residue peptide and the neurophysin moiety, both of which are secreted during exocytosis. One possible role of the neurophysin is that of a *storage protein*, which serves to retain the hormone in the secretory granules until release. A storage protein is also found associated with epinephrine and norepinephrine in the chromaffin granules of the adrenal medulla.

ADENOHYPOPHYSIAL HORMONES

The *anterior lobe* of the pituitary, also termed the *adenohypophysis* (Fig. 11-13), secretes at least seven peptide hormones (Table 11-5). In contrast to the hormones of the neurohypophysis, the hormones of the adenohypophysis do not originate in neurosecretory cells, but instead from simple secretory cells that reside entirely within the anterior lobe. These cells occur in three histochemically distinct types, but are otherwise difficult to distinguish. It appears that the acidophils (cells that take up acidic stains) secrete *growth hormone* (*GH;* also termed *somatotropin*) and *prolactin,* and that the basophils secrete *thyroid-stimulating hormone (TSH)* and the gonadotropins *luteinizing hormone (LH)* and *follicle-stimulating hormone (FSH)*. The sources of *adenocorticotropic hormone (ACTH)* and *melanocyte-stimulating hormone (MSH)* are uncertain.

HYPOTHALAMIC CONTROL OF THE ADENOHYPOPHYSIS

In recent years, evidence has been accumulating that indicates that the secretory activity of the adenohypophysial endocrine cells is regulated by at least seven short-range *hypothalamic hormones* of neurosecretory origin. Four of these are *releasing hormones* (or *factors*), and three are *release-inhibiting hormones.* They are produced by neurosecretory cells that are located in the hypothalamus and have endings in the *median eminence* at the floor of the hypothalamus. These hormones are nearly all polypeptides, and are named according to their actions on adenohypophysial secretion (Table 11-6). Only in recent years has the elaborate neuroendocrine organization of the hypothalamus and pituitary become known and much more undoubtedly will be learned. As early as the 1930's, studies revealed that capillaries in the median eminence converge to form a series of *portal vessels* that carry blood from the neurosecretory tissue to the secretory tissue of the anterior pituitary. There they break up again into a capillary bed before finally converging into the venous system (Fig. 11-15). The portal system enhances chemical communication from the hypothalamus to the adenohypophysis by carrying the hypothalamic hormones directly to the interstitium of the adenohypophysis. In the adenohypophysis, the hypothalamic hormones come into contact with the endocrine cells that secrete the seven anterior pituitary hormones,

either stimulating or inhibiting their secretory activity. The discovery of the hypothalamic releasing hormones has proved to be one of the more important recent developments in vertebrate endocrinology, opening an entire new area of investigation into the orchestration of vertebrate endocrine function.

The first physiological evidence for the neurohumoral control of the anterior pituitary gland came in the late 1950's with the discovery of a substance that stimulates the release of adrenocorticotropic hormone (ACTH) from the anterior pituitary. This substance, obtained by the extraction of thousands of pig brains, was given the name *corticotropic releasing hormone (CRH)*. Minute amounts of CRH are liberated from neurosecretory cells in the hypothalamus when they are activated by neural input in response to a variety of stressful stimuli to the organism (e.g., cold, fright, sustained pain). The axons of these cells terminate close to capillaries in the median eminence, from which their secretions are carried directly via the portal vessels to the capillary bed of the anterior pituitary (Fig. 11-15). Because there is a direct portal connection from the hypothalamus to the anterior pituitary, the amount of releasing hormone (in this case CRH) required to produce effective concentrations in the anterior pituitary tissue need not be large. Once the releasing hormones enter the total circulation, they are diluted to ineffective concentrations, and are enzymatically degraded within several minutes.

The three release-inhibiting hormones of the hypothalamo-hypophysial relay system suppress the release from the adenohypophysis of melanocyte-stimulating hormone (MSH), prolactin, and growth hormone (GH). Of these, growth hormone is also under the control of a releasing hormone (Table 11-6). It is interesting that the target tissues of these three hormones do not produce any agents or effects that act by negative feedback on the hypothalamus or adenohypophysis. From a teleological point of view, it would seem that the hypothalamic release-inhibiting hormones provide a means of inhibitory control of secretion in the absence of negative feedback from target tissues. These relations are summarized in Figure 11-16, which shows the closed, short and long feedback loops of the hypothalamo-hypophysial relay system, controlled by ACTH, TSH, FSH, LH, and the open-loop control of nonendocrine tissues by GH, prolactin, and MSH.

Metabolic and Developmental Hormones

GLUCOCORTICOIDS

Cells of the adrenal cortex are stimulated by ACTH to synthesize and secrete a family of steroids termed

Table 11-5. Hormones of the adenohypophysis.

Hormone	Structure	Target tissue	Primary action	Regulation
Adrenocorti-cotrophin (ACTH)	Peptide	Adrenal cortex	Increases steroidogene-sis and secretion in adrenal cortex	CRH secretion stimu-lates release; ACTH inhibits release
Thyroid-stimulating hormone (TSH)	Peptide (glyco-protein)	Thyroid gland	Increases thyroid hormone synthesis and secretion	TRH induces secretion; thyroid hormones block release
Growth hormone (GH)	Peptide	All tissues	Tissue growth; increases RNA synthesis, protein synthesis, transport of glucose and amino acids, lipolysis, and antibody formation	GRH secretion stimu-lates release
Follicle-stimulating hormone (FSH)	Peptide	Seminiferous tubules (male); ovarian follicles (female)	In male, increases sperm production; in female, stimulates follicle maturation	FSH/LH-RH stimulates release
Luteinizing hormone (LH)	Peptide	Ovarian inter-stitial cells (female); testicular interstitial cells (male)	Induces final maturation of follicle, estrogen secretion, ovulation, corpus luteum forma-tion, and progesterone secretion; in males, increases synthesis and secretion of androgens	FSH/LH-RH stimulates release
Prolactin	Peptide	Mammary glands (alveolar cells)	Increases synthesis of milk proteins and growth of mammary glands	Secretion is continuously blocked by PIH secre-tion; increased estro-gen and a decrease in PIH secretion permits release
Melanocyte-stimulating hormone (MSH)	Peptide	Melanophores (ectotherm pigment cells); melanocytes (endotherm pigment cells)	Increases melanin syn-thesis in melanophores and melanocytes; increases dispersal in melanophores (skin darkening)	MIH secretion inhibits release

glucocorticoids (Table 11-7) derived from cholesterol. These include *cortisone, cortisol, corticosterone,* and *11-deoxycorticosterone* (Fig. 11-17). The basal level of a secretion is maintained by a feedback action of gluco-corticoids on the CRH-secreting neurons of the hypo-thalamus (Fig. 11-18). This basal level of glucocorti-coid secretion undergoes a diurnal rhythm resulting from cyclically varying CRH-secretion, which appears to be influenced by the rest-activity cycle of the animal. Basal glucocorticoid levels in humans are maximal during the early hours of the morning prior to waking. This is adaptively useful because of the energy-mobilizing consequences of these hormones.

The glucocorticoids act on the liver, increasing the synthesis of enzymes that promote *gluconeogenesis* (synthesis of glucose from substances other than carbohydrates). The glucose is released into the circulation, causing a rise in blood glucose levels. Some of the glucose is stored as glycogen in the liver. While glucose is mobilized by the liver, the uptake of amino acids by muscle tissues is decreased, and amino acids are released from muscle cells into the circulation. This increases the quantity of amino acids available for deamination and conversion into glucose in the liver under glucocorticoid stimulation. Another consequence is mobilization of fatty acids from stores of fat in adipose tissue. Again, this has the effect of increasing the available substrates for gluconeogenesis in the liver. All of these actions tend to produce *hyperglycemia* (i.e., increased blood glucose levels). The mobilization of glucose produced from noncarbohydrate sources increases the availability of quick energy to muscle and nervous tissue.

THYROID HORMONES

Thyroid-stimulating hormone (TSH), released from the adenohypophysis, maintains the volume, weight, and secretory activity of the thyroid gland. As its name implies, it stimulates the release of thyroid hormones. The two major thyroid hormones, *thyroxine* and *3,5,3-triiodothyronine*, are synthesized in the follicles of the thyroid tissue from two iodinated tyrosine molecules (Fig. 11-19). Iodine is actively accumulated by the thyroid tissue from the blood.

Table 11-6. Hypothalamic releasing hormones.

Hormone	Structure	Target tissue	Primary action	Regulation
Corticotropic releasing hormone (CRH)	Polypeptide	Adenohypophysis	Stimulates ACTH release	Stressful neural input increases secretion; ACTH inhibits secretion
TSH-releasing hormone (TRH)	Polypeptide	Adenohypophysis	Stimulates TSH release	Large meals and low body temperatures induce secretion
GH-releasing hormone (GRH)	Polypeptide	Adenohypophysis	Stimulates GH release	Insulin stimulates secretion
FSH- and LH-releasing hormone (FSH/LH-RH)	Polypeptide	Adenohypophysis	Stimulates release of FSH and LH	In the male, low blood testosterone levels stimulate secretion; in the female, neural input and decreased estrogen levels stimulate secretion; high blood FSH or LH inhibits secretion
GH-inhibiting hormone (GIH) (or somatostatin)	Polypeptide	Adenohypophysis	Inhibits GH release; interferes with TSH release	Hypoglycemia and exercise induce secretion; hormone is rapidly inactivated in body tissues
Prolactin-release-inhibiting hormone (PIH)	?	Adenohypophysis	Inhibits prolactin release	High levels of prolactin increase secretion; estrogen, testosterone, and neural stimuli (suckling) inhibit secretion
MSH-release-inhibiting hormone (MIH)	Polypeptide	Adenohypophysis	Inhibits MSH release	Melatonin stimulates secretion

11-15. The hypophysial portal relay system.
Left. Releasing or release-inhibiting hormones secreted by neurosecretory endings in the median eminence are carried via the portal vessels to the adenohypophysis, where they stimulate (or inhibit) secretory activity.
Right. Input from various neural sources to the hypothalamus elicits the secretion of release and release-inhibiting hormones in the median eminence. Compare with Figure 11-16.

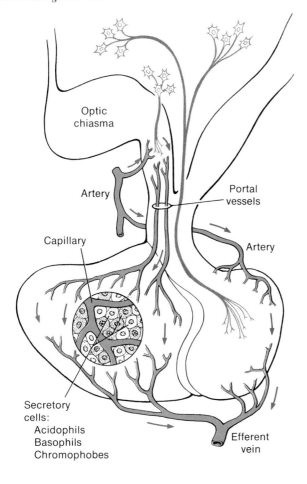

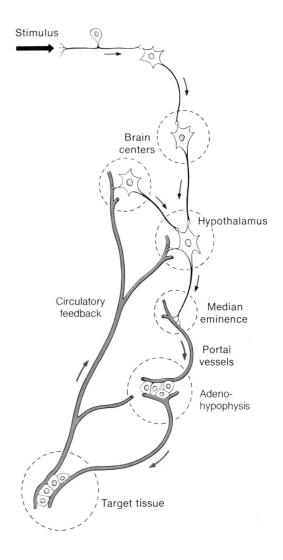

The release of thyroid-stimulating hormone is regulated by the secretion of TSH-releasing hormone (TRH) from the median eminence. Both the hypothalamic neurosecretory cells, which produce TRH, and the TSH-secreting cells of the adenohypophysis are inhibited by a rise in the circulating levels of thyroid hormones (Fig. 11-20). Superimposed upon this chemical regulation, however, is neural stimulation of the hypothalamus; either a low skin temperature or a large meal will reflexly stimulate the release of hypothalamic TRH.

The thyroid hormones act on liver, kidney, heart, and skeletal muscle in much the same way that epinephrine does (p. 357) in breaking down liver glycogen to glucose, producing a rise in plasma glucose levels. The thyroid hormones also stimulate cellular respiration, producing an increase in oxygen consumption and metabolic rate. These effects differ from those produced by epinephrine. Instead of occurring rapidly, they have a large latency; after a rise in thyroid hormone concentration, up to 48 hours may pass before these effects are seen.

The acceleration of metabolism stimulated by thyroid hormones leads to a rise in heat production. This is of major importance in the *thermoregulation* of homeotherms (birds and mammals). The catecholamines (p. 357) also participate in thermoregulatory responses.

The thyroid hormones have only limited thermo-

Table 11-7. Hormones that regulate energy metabolism.

Hormone	Tissue of origin	Structure	Target tissue	Primary action	Regulation
Insulin	Pancreas β-cells	Peptide	All tissues	Increases glucose and amino acid uptake by cells; increases GRH secretion	High plasma glucose, presence of glucagon, pancreozymin, secretin, gastrin, and GH increase secretion
Glucagon	Pancreas α-cells	Peptide	Liver	Stimulates glycogenolysis and releases glucose from liver	Low serum glucose, presence of pancreozymin, insulin, and GH increase secretion
Thyroxin	Thyroid	Amino acid derivative	Most cells, but especially those of muscle, heart, liver, and kidney	Increases metabolic rate, growth and development; promotes amphibian metamorphosis, thermogenesis	TSH secretion induces release
Norepinephrine and epinephrine	Adrenal medulla, chromaffin cells	Amino acid derivative (catecholamine)	Most cells	Increases cardiac activity; induces vasoconstriction; increases glycolysis, hyperglycemia, and lipolysis; influences secretion of hypothalamic releasing hormones	Sympathetic stimulation via splanchnic nerves increases secretion
Growth hormone (GH)	Adenohypophysis	Peptide	All tissues	Stimulates RNA synthesis, protein synthesis, and tissue growth; increases transport of glucose and amino acids into cells; increases lipolysis and antibody formation	GRH secretion stimulates release; GIH secretion inhibits release
Glucocorticoids	Adrenal cortex	Steroid	Most cells	Balances metabolism of carbohydrates, proteins, and fats; exhibits antiinflammatory action	Increased ACTH level stimulates secretion

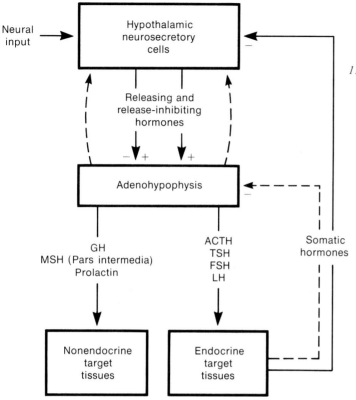

Neural input →

Hypothalamic neurosecretory cells

Releasing and release-inhibiting hormones

− + +

Adenohypophysis −

GH
MSH (Pars intermedia)
Prolactin

ACTH
TSH
FSH
LH

Somatic hormones

Nonendocrine target tissues

Endocrine target tissues

11–16. Regulatory pathways for the adenohypophysial hormones. Production of GH, MSH, and prolactin is regulated by release hormones and release-inhibiting hormones carried by the portal vessels from the median eminence. In contrast, ACTH, TSH, FSH, and LH all stimulate the release of hormones from somatic (i.e., nonpituitary) target tissues, and those hormones exert negative feedback on the hypothalamic neurosecretory cells and perhaps also on the corresponding adenohypophysial cells themselves.

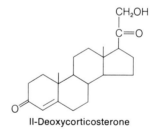

Il-Deoxycorticosterone

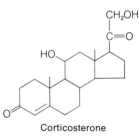

Corticosterone

11–17. Structures of some adrenal steroids.

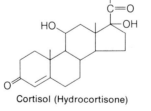

Cortisol (Hydrocortisone)

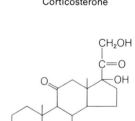

Cortisone

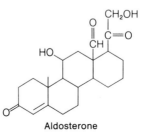

Aldosterone

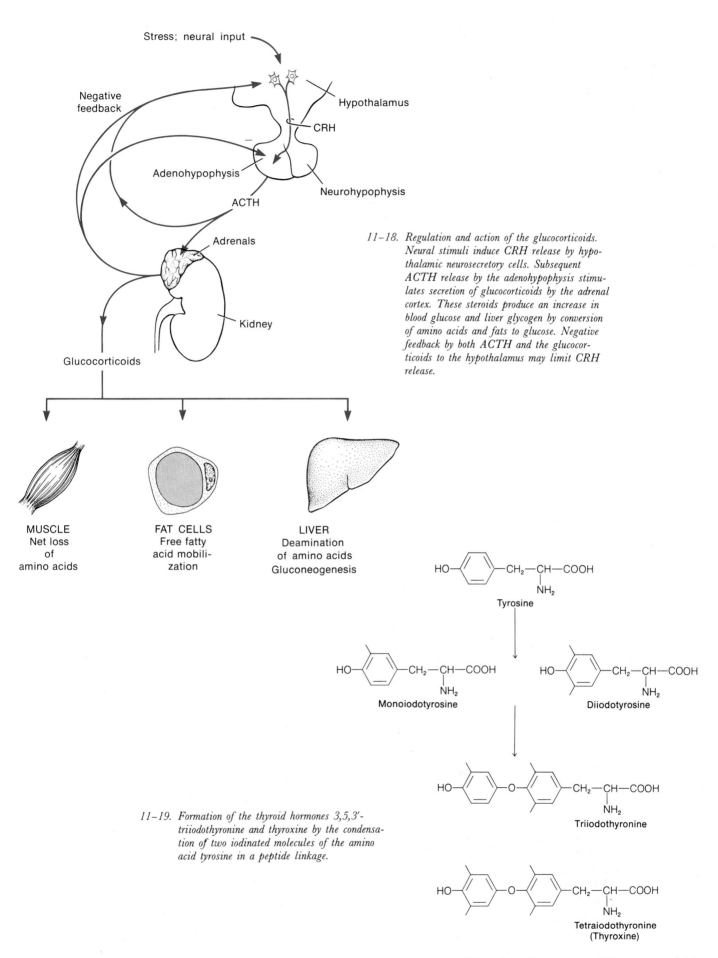

11-18. *Regulation and action of the glucocorticoids. Neural stimuli induce CRH release by hypothalamic neurosecretory cells. Subsequent ACTH release by the adenohypophysis stimulates secretion of glucocorticoids by the adrenal cortex. These steroids produce an increase in blood glucose and liver glycogen by conversion of amino acids and fats to glucose. Negative feedback by both ACTH and the glucocorticoids to the hypothalamus may limit CRH release.*

MUSCLE
Net loss
of
amino acids

FAT CELLS
Free fatty
acid mobili-
zation

LIVER
Deamination
of amino acids
Gluconeogenesis

Tyrosine

Monoiodotyrosine

Diiodotyrosine

Triiodothyronine

Tetraiodothyronine
(Thyroxine)

11-19. *Formation of the thyroid hormones 3,5,3'-triiodothyronine and thyroxine by the condensation of two iodinated molecules of the amino acid tyrosine in a peptide linkage.*

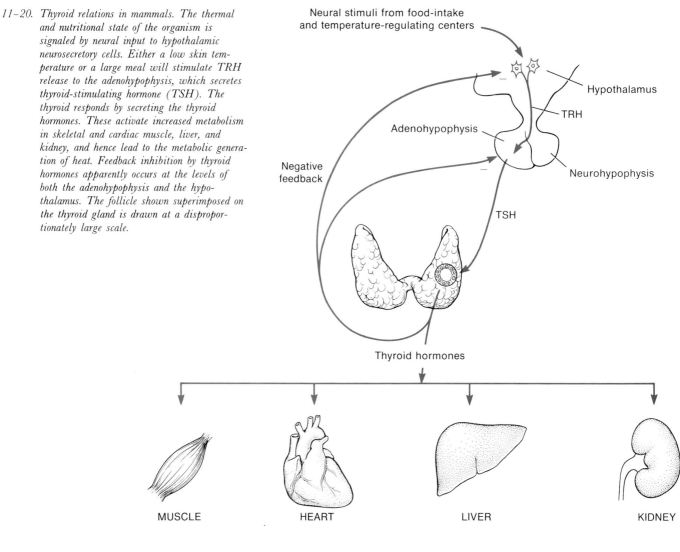

11–20. *Thyroid relations in mammals. The thermal and nutritional state of the organism is signaled by neural input to hypothalamic neurosecretory cells. Either a low skin temperature or a large meal will stimulate TRH release to the adenohypophysis, which secretes thyroid-stimulating hormone (TSH). The thyroid responds by secreting the thyroid hormones. These activate increased metabolism in skeletal and cardiac muscle, liver, and kidney, and hence lead to the metabolic generation of heat. Feedback inhibition by thyroid hormones apparently occurs at the levels of both the adenohypophysis and the hypothalamus. The follicle shown superimposed on the thyroid gland is drawn at a disproportionately large scale.*

Neural stimuli from food-intake and temperature-regulating centers

Hypothalamus

TRH

Adenohypophysis

Neurohypophysis

Negative feedback

TSH

Thyroid hormones

MUSCLE   HEART   LIVER   KIDNEY

Increased oxygen consumption and heat production

genic effect in poikilotherms, although these hormones do have important metabolic and developmental effects. In teleost fish, thyroid hormones seem to stimulate the increased energy metabolism required for osmoregulation in the face of osmotic stress. Thyroxine has been reported to play a role in physiological adaptation to changes in environmental salinity associated with the migrations of euryhaline teleosts (such as salmon) from seawater into fresh water. In some teleosts, increased thyroid secretion induces a behavioral preference for salt water; in others, a preference for freshwater.

The thyroid hormones play important and varied roles in the development and maturation of various vertebrate groups. The developmental effects of thyroid hormones occur only in the presence of growth hormone and vice versa. Both GH and the thyroid hormones acting together promote protein synthesis during development. *Hypothyroidism* during early stages of development in fish, birds, and mammals results in *cretinism*, a deficiency disease in which somatic, neural, and sexual development are severely retarded, the metabolic rate is reduced to as little as about half the normal rate, and resistance to infection is reduced. In young humans, the lack of dietary iodine causes cretinism, and in adults it causes goiter, a malady characterized by an enlargement of the throat due to hypertrophy of the thyroid tissue. Hypertrophy is caused by excessive TSH production. This excessive production results from the absence of negative feedback to the hypothalamus in the form of thyroid hormones. Both cretinism and goiter have been reduced in areas where table salt is routinely "iodized" and the populace is no longer dependent on natural trace amounts of iodine in food.

The role of thyroid hormones in development is

especially dramatic in the metamorphosis of amphibians. In the absence of thyroxine or triiodothyronine, tadpoles fail to metamorphose into frogs. The role of thyroid hormones in amphibian metamorphosis is outlined in Figure 11-21. The development of tadpole into frog occurs in three stages. (1) During *premetamorphosis* (lasting about 20 days), the immature thyroid binds iodine and synthesizes the hormones. (2) The first part of metamorphosis, *prometamorphosis,* is characterized by slow morphological changes, growth of the thyroid gland, iodine concentration and binding, increased secretory activity of the thyroid tissue, and differentiation of the median eminence and hypothalamus. (3) In the final stage, the *metamorphic climax,* in which the adult form emerges, the median eminence undergoes its final differentiation and becomes highly vascularized. It has been suggested that this enhances metamorphosis in two ways. First, secretion of prolactin, which tends to inhibit or slow metamorphosis, is itself inhibited by increasing secretion of the hypothalamic release-inhibiting hormone, PIH (Table 11-6) with development of the median eminence. Second, the differentiation of the median eminence, which occurs in response to rising levels of thyroid hormone, results in greater TRH (Table 11-6) release and hence increased TSH and thyroid hormone production. This, of course, is a case of positive feedback, which is inherently unstable. The elaboration of TSH and thyroid hormones is kept from getting out of hand, so to speak, by negative feedback in the form of inhibition of TRH release by thyroid hormone (Fig. 11-21). Sensitivity of metamorphosing tissues to thyroid hormones increases with development, but postmetamorphic growth in the frog occurs under the direction of growth hormone.

THE CATECHOLAMINES

The chromaffin tissue of the adrenal medulla secretes catecholamines in response to activation of the preganglionic neurons of the sympathetic nervous system (Fig. 6-15). Whereas postganglionic sympathetic nerve cells secrete norepinephrine almost exclusively, the chromaffin cells secrete mostly epinephrine (Fig. 6-42), norepinephrine amounting to about one-fourth the total secretion. Cells that contain catecholamines can be conveniently identified in appropriately fixed preparations by a characteristic yellow fluorescence when viewed in ultraviolet light, the fluorescence arising from the catecholamine molecules stored in the secretory granules of these cells. Fluorescence and electron microscopy both indicate that epinephrine and norepinephrine are produced in two different sets of cells intermingled in the chromaffin tissue of the adrenal medulla.

11–21. The role of thyroid hormones in the control of metamorphosis in the frog. During the first 20 days (premetamorphosis), the median eminence is undifferentiated, and TRH and TSH secretion is low. The thyroid gland is also poorly developed and inactive except for iodine binding and hormone synthesis. The next 20 days (prometamorphosis) are characterized by increasing differentiation of the median eminence, with enhanced TRH and hence TSH output. This provides the stimulation for maturation of the thyroid gland, with increasing iodine uptake and secretory activity. Tissue sensitivity to the thyroid hormones (TH) is age-dependent, and thus determines in part the time table of morphological transformations during amphibian metamorphosis. [After Spratt, 1971.]

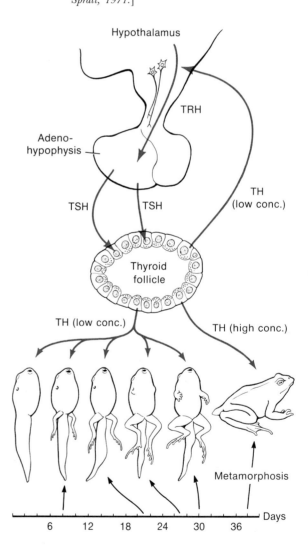

Table 11-8. Physiological responses to epinephrine and norepinephrine.

	Epinephrine	Norepinephrine
Heart rate	Increase	Decrease*
Cardiac output	Increase	Variable
Total peripheral resistance	Decrease	Increase
Blood pressure	Rise	Greater rise
Respiration	Stimulation	Stimulation
Skin vessels	Constriction	Constriction
Muscle vessels	Dilatation	Constriction
Bronchus	Dilatation	Less dilatation
Metabolism	Increase	Slight increase
Oxygen consumption	Increase	No effect
Blood sugar	Increase	Slight increase
Uterus *in vivo* in late pregnancy	Inhibition	Stimulation
Kidney	Vasoconstriction	Vasoconstriction

Source: G. H. Bell, J. N. Davidson, and H. Scarborough, *Textbook of Physiology and Biochemistry,* Churchill Livingstone, Edinburgh, 1972.
*Increases rate of isolated heart.

The two adrenal catecholamines have a large number of actions, most of which contribute to the sympathetic "fight or flight" response to emergencies. They stimulate glycogenolysis in the liver, but to a lesser extent than glucagon (p. 359), and in addition have a strong glycogenolytic effect in skeletal and cardiac muscle (p. 377). The effect is to mobilize glucose. In addition, these hormones stimulate the strength and rate of heart beat and the contraction of vascular smooth muscle, thereby raising the blood pressure.

Epinephrine and norepinephrine are not equivalent in their actions (Table 11-8), although in some tissues they exert similar effects. Differences in their actions are due to differences in the membrane receptor molecules with which they interact. Epinephrine binds most effectively to β-*adrenergic* receptors*, and norepinephrine binds to α-*adrenergic receptors*. The receptors can be distinguished by the use of drugs that activate

*The term "adrenergic" comes from *Adrenaline,* the patented British trade name for epinephrine.

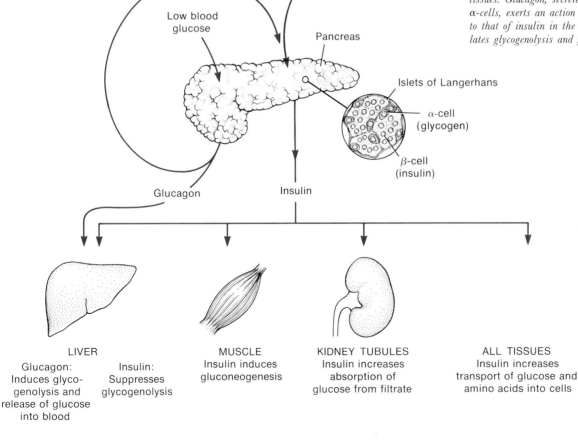

11–22. Relationships of insulin and glucagon in the regulation of glucose metabolism. High levels of blood glucose and glucagon and/or gastrointestinal hormones signalling food ingestion stimulate the pancreatic β-cells to secrete insulin, which stimulates glucose uptake in all tissues. Glucagon, secreted by pancreatic α-cells, exerts an action that is antagonistic to that of insulin in the liver, where it stimulates glycogenolysis and glucose release.

High blood glucose; gastrointestinal hormone secretion

Low blood glucose

Pancreas

Islets of Langerhans

α-cell (glycogen)

β-cell (insulin)

Glucagon

Insulin

LIVER
Glucagon: Induces glycogenolysis and release of glucose into blood

Insulin: Suppresses glycogenolysis

MUSCLE
Insulin induces gluconeogenesis

KIDNEY TUBULES
Insulin increases absorption of glucose from filtrate

ALL TISSUES
Insulin increases transport of glucose and amino acids into cells

one or the other receptor type, eliciting responses characteristic of one or the other catecholamine.

INSULIN AND GLUCAGON

The level of glucose in the blood is enhanced by uptake from the gut and release into the circulation from storage within cells. The level drops as a result of uptake into various tissues for metabolism or storage. The uptake of glucose into cells is stimulated by *insulin,* which is secreted by the β-cells of the *pancreatic islets,* small patches of endocrine tissue scattered throughout the exocrine tissue of the *pancreas.* Insulin facilitates the movement of glucose from its higher concentration in the plasma to its lower concentration in the cells of tissues and organs. It does this by increasing the permeability of cell membranes to glucose. Once glucose has entered a cell, it is immediately phosphorylated to prevent its uncontrolled escape. In muscle, glucose is either metabolized or converted into glycogen for storage. In the cells of the liver, insulin increases energy storage by stimulating glycogenesis (polymerization of glucose into glycogen) and lipogenesis. Adipose cells also respond to insulin by increasing glucose uptake and lipogenesis. Insulin and GH share the property of promoting the uptake and incorporation of amino acids into protein; insulin also inhibits the conversion of amino acids into glucose by gluconeogenesis, an action counter to that of the glucocorticoids.

High blood glucose acts as the major secretory stimulus to the β-cells of the pancreas, which respond by discharging insulin (Fig. 11-22). The release of insulin is also stimulated by glucagon (see below) and GH.

Diabetes mellitus in humans is a disorder of the pancreatic β-cells, in which insulin production is either lost or impaired. The symptoms can be reversed by administration of insulin or an agent with similar pharmacological properties. Insulin deficiency causes severe hyperglycemia, *glycosuria* (spillover of excess glucose into the urine), reduced ability to metabolize carbohydrates or convert them into fat, and loss of protein, which is broken down for energy in place of glucose. In addition, mobilized fat particles that cannot be rapidly metabolized accumulate in the blood as ketone bodies. These are excreted in the urine but can also interfere with liver function.

Glucagon is secreted by the α_2-cells of the pancreatic islets in response to *hypoglycemia* (low levels of blood glucose). This hormone stimulates glycogenolysis, gluconeogenesis, and glucose release by the liver as other defenses against glucose starvation of tissues. The molecular basis of the action of glucagon on cell metabolism is understood perhaps better than that of

any other hormone, and we will return to that subject below (p. 377).

GROWTH HORMONE

Closely related in function to the thyroid hormones is growth hormone (GH, or somatotropin), which is dependent upon the thyroid hormones for its synthesis in the adenohypophysis. The growth-enhancing effects of GH and the thyroid hormones are difficult to separate because the action of each relies on the presence of the other hormone. The action ascribed to GH is tissue growth—in particular, the development of bone from cartilage. GH-stimulated tissue growth occurs by an increase in cell number. The importance of GH in the regulation of growth is seen in humans in the extreme cases of *gigantism,* caused by infantile GH hypersecretion; *acromegaly* (enlargement of bones of the head and of the extremities), caused by late onset of GH hypersecretion; and *dwarfism,* caused by hyposecretion of GH.

The metabolic effects of GH are diverse (Fig. 11-23). It depresses glycogenolysis and initiates the mobilization of stored fat. GH strongly promotes protein synthesis and the utilization of fatty acids for energy. The fatty acids released from adipose tissue into the bloodstream in response to GH are converted in the liver to glucose and released into the circulation. GH-stimulated fatty acid uptake in muscle promotes the synthesis of glucose within muscle cells, and thereby helps conserve glycogen stores.

The release of GH is stimulated by a rise in plasma insulin levels as well as by a drop in glucose levels. Insulin levels rise after food ingestion. Glucose and amino acids absorbed from the intestine are taken up into the cells and immediately catabolized or stored as glycogen or proteins. Fatty acids and glucose are taken up into the liver, where lipogenesis and glycogenesis proceed. At the same time, the increase in blood glucose stimulates the release of insulin from the pancreas, and the insulin stimulates the release of GRH from the hypothalamus and thus promotes the release of growth hormone. GH reaches its peak plasma level several hours after the meal, when immediate energy supplies (e.g., blood glucose, amino acids, and fatty acids) are less abundant. GH acts to liberate fatty acids from adipose tissue; the liberated fatty acids are taken up by muscle as an energy source and by the liver for gluconeogenesis. In most tissues other than the central nervous system, GH suppresses glycolysis, thereby conserving glucose for use by the CNS.

Growth hormone stimulates insulin secretion in two ways. First, it acts directly on the β-cells; second, its hyperglycemic action leads to a stimulation of insulin

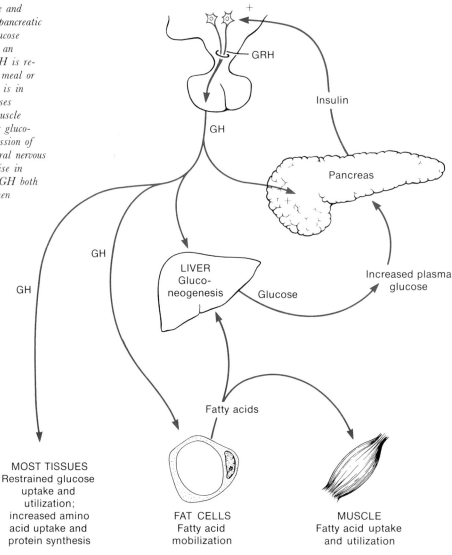

11–23. Synergistic action of growth hormone and insulin. Output of insulin from the pancreatic β-cells in response to high blood glucose initiates GRH discharge to promote an increased secretion of GH. When GH is released, usually several hours after a meal or after prolonged exercise, free glucose is in shorter supply. Growth hormone causes lipolysis and fatty acid uptake by muscle tissue for energy and by the liver for gluconeogenesis. There is a general depression of glucose oxidation, except in the central nervous system, where it is essential. The rise in plasma glucose and the presence of GH both stimulate insulin secretion, which then stimulates glucose uptake into cells.

secretion by elevated plasma glucose levels. The insulin released "corrects" the GH-induced hyperglycemia by promoting the cellular uptake of glucose. Thus there is a certain cooperativity. In brief, these two hormones have the following major actions:

1. GH promotes glucose synthesis and hyperglycemia at the expense of stored fat, without depleting glycogen or proteins.

2. Insulin promotes increased uptake and utilization of plasma glucose by the cells, stoking the fires of glycolysis.

Hormonal Regulation of Electrolyte Balance

The hormones that regulate electrolyte and water balance (Chapter 12) are:

1. Antidiuretic hormone (vasopressin), which increases the water permeability of the collecting ducts of the kidney, the end effect of which is a resorption and conservation of urinary water.

2. The *mineralocorticoids,* in particular *aldosterone,* which enhance retention of sodium (and, indirectly, chloride) by the kidney.

3. *Calcitonin* and *parathyroid hormone,* two hormones important in the metabolism of calcium in bone, plasma, kidney, and other tissues (Table 11-9).

Antidiuretic hormone is discussed in the sections on renal function (p. 417) and the neurohypophysis (p. 347). We will first turn our attention to the mineralocorticoids, secreted by the adrenal cortex and derived, like the other steroid hormones, from cholesterol. The major representative of this group is *aldosterone.* This very potent steroid acts on the distal tubule of the nephron (Fig. 12-26), increasing the rate of Na resorp-

Table 11-9. Other vertebrate hormones.

Hormone	Tissue of origin	Structure	Target tissue	Primary action	Regulation
Melatonin	Pineal gland	Amino acid derivative	Melanophores (ectotherms)	Induces aggregation of melanin (skin blanching)	Darkness (or blinding) increases synthesis and secretion; light reduces synthesis and secretion
			Melanocytes (endotherms)	May regulate secretion of the gonadotrophin-releasing hormones	
Calcitonin (CT)	Thyroid	Peptide	Bones, kidney	Decreases bone calcium release; decreases blood calcium levels; increases calcium and phosphorus excretion	Elevation of plasma $[Ca^{2+}]$ increases secretion
Parathyroid hormone (PTH)	Parathyroid	Peptide	Bones, kidney, intestine	Increases blood calcium and phosphorus levels; increases mobilization of bone calcium; decreases calcium excretion from kidney; increases intestinal calcium absorption	Decline in plasma $[Ca^{2+}]$ increases secretion
Erythropoietin	Kidney	Peptide	Bone marrow	Causes hyperplasia of the bone marrow; increases production and release of erythrocytes	Low atmospheric O_2 and anemia increase secretion
Relaxin	Ovary	Peptide	Pelvic ligaments	Induces relaxation of pelvic ligaments and cervix	Increased progesterone and estrogen levels late in pregnancy increase secretion
Renin	Kidney	Peptide	Adrenal cortex	Increases synthesis and secretion of angiotensin	Increased renal sympathetic activity, decreased plasma $[Na^+]$, decreased renal arteriole distension and decreased blood volume or pressure increase secretion

tion. It does this by stimulating the active exchange of plasma K^+ and H^+ for Na^+ in the glomerular filtrate. Rather than direct stimulation of a Na pump, it appears that increased Na transport arises from an aldosterone-induced increase in *sodium permeability* of the renal cell in the membrane on the *mucosal side* (i.e., facing the lumen) of the tubular epithelium. As a consequence of this increase in Na permeability of the luminal membrane, there is an increased influx of Na^+ from the tubular lumen into the epithelial cells (followed by Cl^-). The rise in intracellular $[Na^+]$ provides the pump on the *serosal side* of the cells (i.e., facing the blood) with a higher Na^+ concentration and thus increases the rate of Na transport from the kidney tubule across the epithelial cell layer into the interstitial fluid and blood. Aldosterone works the same way in certain other *transport epithelia,* such as the bladder wall and integument of amphibians. In mammals, this hormone promotes Na^+ resorption in the salivary glands, sweat glands, and colon.

The secretion of aldosterone in mammals is stimulated by *angiotensin.* This agent is activated in the blood by the enzyme *renin,* which is produced in the kidney (p. 411) in response to a decline in blood volume, blood pressure, or Na^+ concentration. This feedback loop (Fig. 12-23) thus tends to stabilize the plasma Na^+ concentration.

Millimolar changes in the concentration of calcium ion in the plasma and other extracellular tissue fluids are more critical than changes in the concentration of most other common metal ions because of its role as a regulatory agent in many cellular processes. This ion is actively absorbed through the intestinal wall into the plasma and is deposited in bone, the major depot for storage of calcium. Elimination of Ca^{2+} from the body occurs through the kidney. Calcitonin, parathyroid hormone (*PTH* or *parathormone*), and *vitamin D* all participate in the regulation of Ca^{2+} and PO_4^{3-} exchange between the skeleton and the blood.

Vitamin D is a steroid-like compound that is synthesized in the skin in response to sunlight, and is ingested along with some dietary oils. It is converted in the liver and kidneys into *1,25-dihydroxycholecalciferol,* which stimulates intestinal Ca absorption.

Parathyroid hormone is secreted from the paired parathyroid glands (Fig. 11-24). Release occurs in response to a drop in plasma Ca levels. In its short span of activity (a half-life of about 20 min.), it promotes Ca mobilization from bone, increases renal Ca uptake from kidney tubules, increases renal phosphate excretion, and, with the help of vitamin D, enhances intestinal Ca absorption (Fig. 11-24).

Calcitonin is secreted from the *parafollicular* (or *C*) *cells* in the thyroid gland in response to high calcium levels in the plasma. It rapidly suppresses Ca loss from bone. Calcitonin acts more rapidly on bone than parathyroid hormone, and produces the dominating effect.

Although the two hormones act opposingly, there is no feedback interaction between them. The dominance of calcitonin prevents hypercalcaemia and extensive dissolution of the skeleton. Essentially, then, bone acts as a large reservoir and buffer for Ca^{2+} and PO_4^{3-}. Plasma Ca^{2+} and PO_4^{3-} are held within narrow limits by parathyroid hormone and calcitonin, which have opposite actions, regulating the flux of these minerals between plasma and bone.

Gastrointestinal Hormones

A flow of digestive juices into the gastrointestinal lumen normally begins with feeding. There are two avenues for the control of gastrointestinal secretion: the autonomic nervous system and the endocrine cells of the stomach and intestine. Stimulation of gastric secretion by the vagus nerve occurs as a conditioned reflex in response to sensory or psychological input, as was first discovered in dogs by Pavlov. More relevant here is the secretion of the gastrointestinal hormones (Table 11-10). The arrival of food proteins in the stomach stimulates the secretion into the blood of *gastrin* by cells in the pyloric mucosa of the stomach (Fig. 11-25). This hormone acts back on the stomach tissues, stimulating the flow of HCl- and pepsin-rich *gastric juices* from cells of the gastric mucosa. Counteracting this flow and gastric motility is *enterogastrone,* released from the small intestine in response to the entry of fats and acid into the duodenum.

Elevated levels of hydrogen ion, resulting from the gastric flow of hydrochloric acid, also stimulate the secretion of *enterogastrone* (= *secretin**) from the mucosa of the small intestine. This acts on the exocrine portion of the pancreas, causing it to discharge a watery bicarbonate solution, which neutralizes the acid arriving from the stomach. Secretin also stimulates the liver to secrete bile and depresses the motility of the stomach.

Cholecystokinin (= *pancreozymin*) also secreted in response to intestinal fatty acids, stimulates pancreatic secretion and contraction of the smooth muscular wall of the gall bladder, forcing bile into the duodenum. Bile (a weakly basic mixture of cholesterol, lecithin, and inorganic salts), bile salts (organic salts), and bile pigments (the hemoglobin metabolites *biliverdin* and *bilirubin*) are produced in the liver and transported via the hepatic duct to the gall bladder for storage. This mixture disperses fats into fine droplets, facilitating the breakdown of the fats by lipases, and hence the absorption of lipids by the intestine.

*The discovery of secretin by Bayliss and Starling, between 1902 and 1905, marked the first unequivocal demonstration of a hormone.

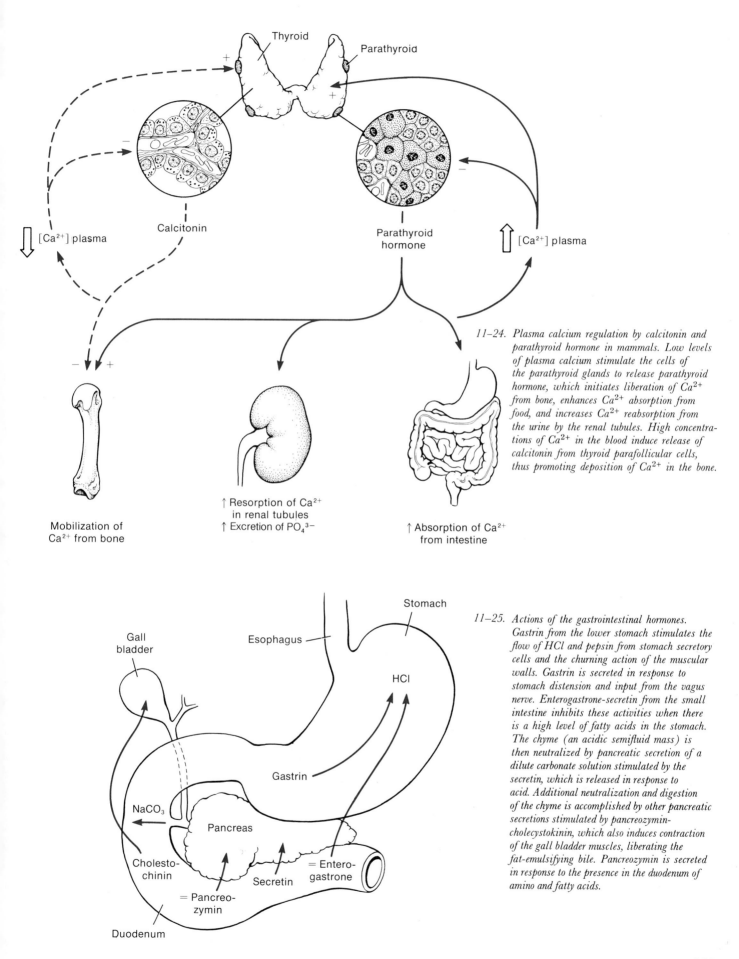

11–24. *Plasma calcium regulation by calcitonin and parathyroid hormone in mammals. Low levels of plasma calcium stimulate the cells of the parathyroid glands to release parathyroid hormone, which initiates liberation of Ca^{2+} from bone, enhances Ca^{2+} absorption from food, and increases Ca^{2+} reabsorption from the urine by the renal tubules. High concentrations of Ca^{2+} in the blood induce release of calcitonin from thyroid parafollicular cells, thus promoting deposition of Ca^{2+} in the bone.*

Thyroid
Parathyroid
$[Ca^{2+}]$ plasma
Calcitonin
Parathyroid hormone
$[Ca^{2+}]$ plasma

Mobilization of Ca^{2+} from bone

↑ Resorption of Ca^{2+} in renal tubules
↑ Excretion of PO_4^{3-}

↑ Absorption of Ca^{2+} from intestine

11–25. *Actions of the gastrointestinal hormones. Gastrin from the lower stomach stimulates the flow of HCl and pepsin from stomach secretory cells and the churning action of the muscular walls. Gastrin is secreted in response to stomach distension and input from the vagus nerve. Enterogastrone-secretin from the small intestine inhibits these activities when there is a high level of fatty acids in the stomach. The chyme (an acidic semifluid mass) is then neutralized by pancreatic secretion of a dilute carbonate solution stimulated by the secretin, which is released in response to acid. Additional neutralization and digestion of the chyme is accomplished by other pancreatic secretions stimulated by pancreozymin-cholecystokinin, which also induces contraction of the gall bladder muscles, liberating the fat-emulsifying bile. Pancreozymin is secreted in response to the presence in the duodenum of amino and fatty acids.*

Gall bladder
Esophagus
Stomach
HCl
Gastrin
$NaCO_3$
Pancreas
Cholesto-chinin
= Pancreo-zymin
Secretin
= Entero-gastrone
Duodenum

11-26. *Synthesis of sex hormones from cholesterol.*

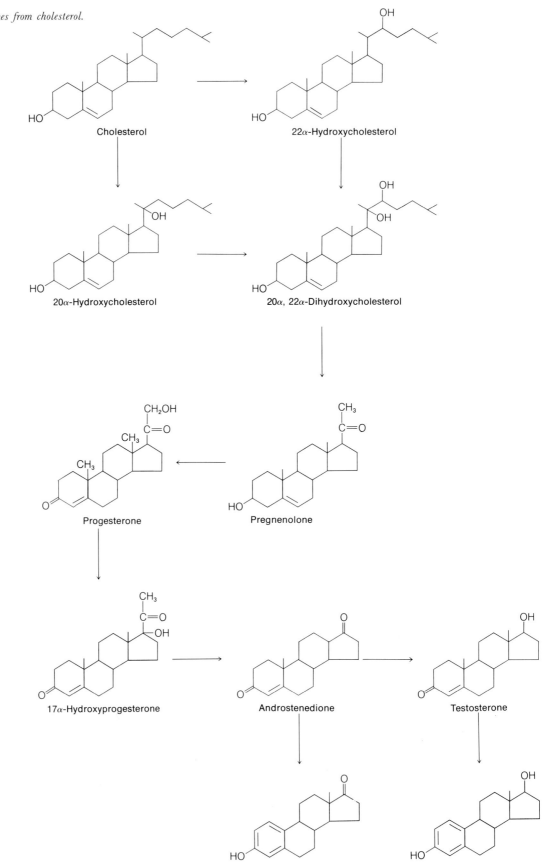

The Sex Hormones

The sex hormones of vertebrates—steroids derived from cholesterol (Fig. 11-26) in the gonads and adrenal cortex of both sexes—include the *estrogens*, the *androgens*, and *progesterone*. Apparently the only function of progesterone in males is as a biosynthetic intermediate. The estrogens and androgens are important in various aspects of growth, development, and morphological differentiation, as well as in the development and regulation of sexual and reproductive behavior and cycles. Estrogens predominate in the female, and androgens predominate in the male. The production and secretion of these steroids is under the control of *follicle-stimulating hormone (FSH)* and *luteinizing hormone (LH)* (Table 11-5). Both of these *gonadotropins* are present in both sexes.

The mammalian testes consist primarily of tubules lined with germ cells, the *seminiferous tubules* (Fig. 11-27).

11-27. Regulation and actions of testosterone. A decrease in blood testosterone stimulates the secretion of the releasing hormone FSH/LH-RH, which promotes the release of FSH and LH. FSH promotes spermatogenesis in the seminiferous tubules, as well as estrogen secretion from the interstitial cells. Some of the actions of testosterone are indicated at the bottom of the figure. Excessive levels are inhibitory to the FSH/LH-RH-secreting neurons of the hypothalamus.

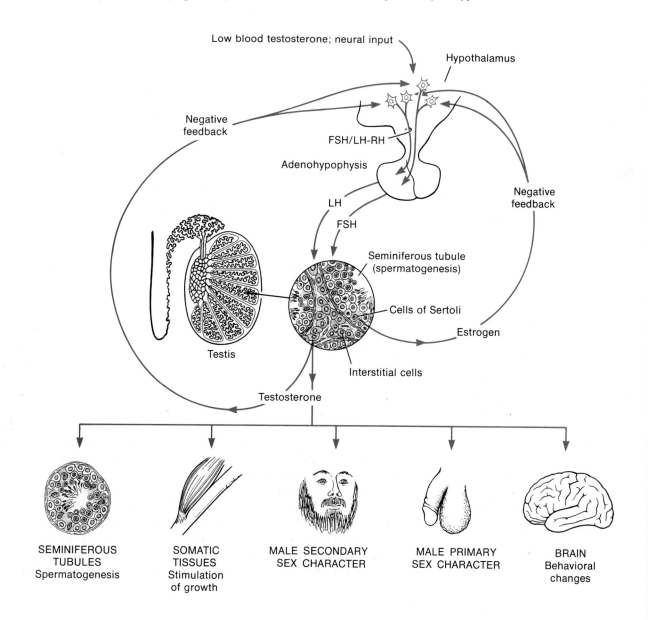

Low blood testosterone; neural input

Hypothalamus

Negative feedback

FSH/LH-RH

Adenohypophysis

LH

FSH

Negative feedback

Seminiferous tubule (spermatogenesis)

Cells of Sertoli

Estrogen

Testis

Interstitial cells

Testosterone

SEMINIFEROUS TUBULES
Spermatogenesis

SOMATIC TISSUES
Stimulation of growth

MALE SECONDARY SEX CHARACTER

MALE PRIMARY SEX CHARACTER

BRAIN
Behavioral changes

Table 11-10. Gastrointestinal hormones.

Hormone	Tissue of origin	Structure	Target tissue	Primary action	Regulation
Gastrin	Stomach and duodenum	Peptide	Secretory cells and muscles of stomach	Stimulates HCl production and secretion and pepsin secretion; stimulates gastric motility	Vagus nerve stimulation and presence of food in stomach and duodenum (distension, chemical stimulus) stimulate secretion
Cholecystokinin (= pancreozymin)	Stomach and Duodenum	Peptide	Gall bladder	Causes contraction of gall bladder	Presence of fatty acids and amino acids in duodenum stimulates secretion
			Pancreas	Stimulates digestive enzyme secretion and duodenal acid neutralization; maintains structural and functional integrity of pancreas	
Secretin (= enterogastrone)	Duodenum	Peptide	Pancreas; secretory cells and muscles of stomach	Water and salt secretion, acid neutralization in small intestine. Inhibits gastric motility and HCl secretion	Food and presence of strong acids in stomach, duodenum, and proximal gut stimulate secretion

Under stimulation by FSH, spermatogenesis occurs in these tubules after sexual maturity, either continuously or seasonally, depending on the species. The *cells of Sertoli,* which also line the tubules, are responsible for the synthesis and secretion of androgen in small amounts, promoting differentiation of the spermatogonia, which give rise to the mature sperm. The *interstitial cells,* or *Leydig cells,* which lie between the seminiferous tubules, are the main site of steroid synthesis in the testes, also promoted by LH. The testicular androgens, of which *testosterone* (Table 11-11) and *androstenedione* are the most important, trigger development of the penis, vas deferens, seminal vesicles, prostate gland, epididymis, and such secondary sex characteristics as the lion's mane, the rooster's comb and plumage, and facial hair in male humans. The androgens also contribute to general growth and protein synthesis—in particular, the synthesis of myofibrillar proteins, as evidenced by the enhanced muscularity of the males relative to the females of many vertebrate species.

The estrogens are a family of steroids produced in the vertebrate ovary, testis, and adrenal cortex. Cholesterol is converted to progesterone, which is then transformed to the androgens, androstenedione, and testosterone. The estrogens, of which *estradiol-17β* is the most potent, are made from these androgens. The estrogens are responsible for the development of the female sexual apparatus, secondary sex characteristics (Fig. 11-28), and the regulation of reproductive cycles, but their function in the male is not yet understood.

Prenatal sexual differentiation of the genital tract is dependent upon the secretion or absence of androgens during a critical period in development. Without them, the female configuration develops with the Müllerian ducts retained and the Wolffian ducts eliminated. In the presence of androgens, the male tract develops (Wolffian ducts retained; Müllerian ducts eliminated). In normal male development, maternal estrogen is bound to a protein that serves to keep the circulating levels of estrogens within the male fetus low.

Table 11-11. Steroid hormones.

Hormone	Tissue of origin	Target tissue	Primary action	Regulation
Testosterone (Androgen)	Testes	Most tissues	Promotes development and maintenance of masculine characteristics and behavior	Increased LH level stimulates secretion
Estradiol-17β (Estrogen)	Ovary	Most tissues	Promotes development and maintenance of female characteristics and behavior	Increased FSH and LH levels stimulate secretion
Progesterone (Progestin)	Corpus luteum	Uterus, mammary glands	Maintains uterine endometrium and stimulates mammary duct formation	Increased LH and Prolactin levels stimulate secretion
Cortisol (glucocorticoid)	Adrenal cortex	Liver, adipose tissue and muscle	Stimulates the transfer of amino acids from muscle and fatty acids from adipose cells to liver; gluconeogenesis; anti-inflammatory action	Increased ACTH level stimulates secretion
Aldosterone (mineralo-corticoid)	Adrenal cortex	Distal kidney tubules	Promotes resorption of Na^+ from urinary filtrate	Angiotensin II stimulates secretion

REPRODUCTIVE CYCLES

Simultaneous reproduction within an entire population can be of obvious survival value to a species. The gathering of large numbers of individuals of both sexes for mating, bearing young, and tending to the needs of the young during their period of high vulnerability can be timed to coincide with favorable weather and an adequate food supply. Moreover, the sudden appearance of large numbers of defenseless individuals of a species can have an overwhelming effect on even the most voracious of predators, permitting the survival of enough individuals of the new generation to assure survival of the species. In general, reproductive cycles arise from within the animal, but in many species the inner cycles are entrained by environmental signals, such as the changes in day length that accompany the change of seasons.

In vertebrates, the neuroendocrine mechanisms of the hypothalamus and adenohypophysis play important roles in the sexual and reproductive cycles. The pituitary gonadotropins (LH and FSH) maintain the activity of the testes and ovaries. Steroid-secreting cells in the gonads and the adrenal cortex are responsible for secretion of sex hormones. Secretion of pituitary gonadotropin is modulated by the feedback of sex steroids to the hypothalamic neurons, which secrete the corresponding releasing hormones (Table 11-6), and possibly by direct action of these steroids on the corresponding endocrine cells of the adenohypophysis. The interactions between the gonadotropins and steroids provide the endocrine basis for the cyclicity most apparent in the mammalian female.

The female bird or mammal is born with her full complement of *oocytes* (each of which gives rise to one *ovum*), and each oocyte becomes embedded in a *follicle* within the ovary. Most of the follicles and their oocytes degenerate early, but even before puberty some develop just short of yolk formation or maturation. In humans, about 400 ova are released between *menarche* (onset of *menstruation*) and *menopause*. Oogenesis in lower vertebrates occurs throughout life.

In mammalian females, a chemical fugue begins with the first trickle of *follicle-stimulating hormone* (Table 11-5) during puberty. FSH stimulates development of the follicles to the ripe form, each a fluid-filled cavity enclosed by a membranous sac of several cell layers in which the ovum is embedded. One of these layers, the *theca interna*, is the ovarian site of estrogen biosynthesis and secretion. The adult ovarian cortex contains follicles in all stages of growth from *primary* to *Graafian*

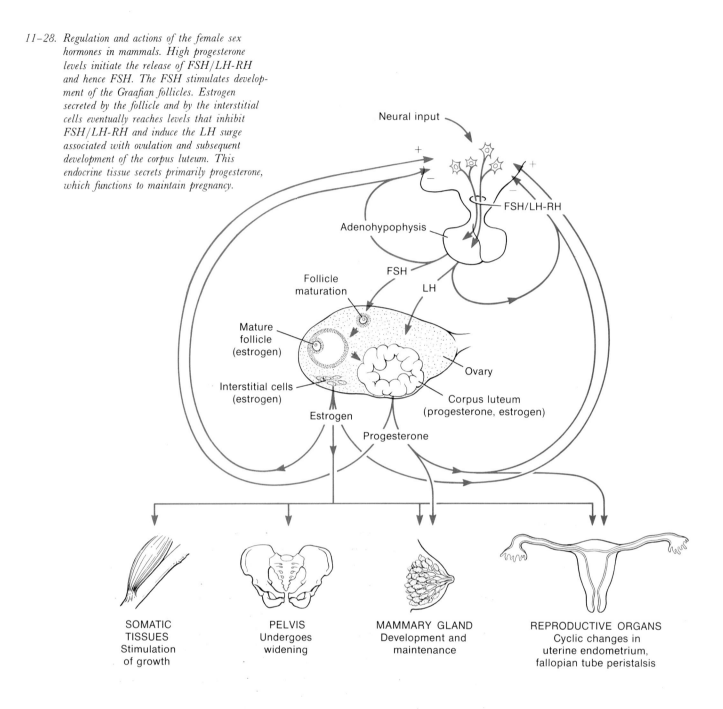

11–28. *Regulation and actions of the female sex hormones in mammals. High progesterone levels initiate the release of FSH/LH-RH and hence FSH. The FSH stimulates development of the Graafian follicles. Estrogen secreted by the follicle and by the interstitial cells eventually reaches levels that inhibit FSH/LH-RH and induce the LH surge associated with ovulation and subsequent development of the corpus luteum. This endocrine tissue secrets primarily progesterone, which functions to maintain pregnancy.*

Neural input

Adenohypophysis

FSH/LH-RH

FSH

LH

Follicle maturation

Mature follicle (estrogen)

Interstitial cells (estrogen)

Estrogen

Progesterone

Ovary

Corpus luteum (progesterone, estrogen)

SOMATIC TISSUES
Stimulation of growth

PELVIS
Undergoes widening

MAMMARY GLAND
Development and maintenance

REPRODUCTIVE ORGANS
Cyclic changes in uterine endometrium, fallopian tube peristalsis

follicles. The FSH-induced ripening of the follicle leads to the production and release of estrogen into the blood (Fig. 11-29). At low concentrations, estrogen feeds back onto hypothalamic FSH/LH-RH secreting cells, *stimulating* increased release of FSH and thereby accelerating follicle maturation. At high levels, however, estrogen, possibly by lowering the sensitivities of the adenohypophysial secretory cells, *inhibits* the release of FSH and initiates, via FSH/LH-releasing hormone (Table 11-6), a surge of *luteinizing hormone* (Table 11-5). This peak of *LH* output precipitates ovulation. The ovum bursts forth from the follicle and begins its journey down the ciliated fallopian tube. At that time, estrogen secretion declines, and under the influence of LH the follicle becomes transformed into a temporary endocrine tissue, the *corpus luteum*. During the *luteal phase*, the corpus luteum secretes estrogen and progesterone, which is responsible for proliferation of the *endometrial tissue* lining the uterus. A low concentration of progesterone permits adenohypophysial release of LH, resulting in further development of the corpus luteum and the secretion of more progesterone. When high levels of progesterone are reached, negative feedback is exerted by an inhibitory action of high progesterone levels on the hypothalamic cells that secrete FSH/LH-releasing hormone, thereby terminating LH release. In the absence of fertilization and implantation of an ovum, the subsequent degeneration of the corpus luteum brings steroid secretion to a halt. In humans and some other primates, this precipitates the *mensus*, or shedding of the uterine lining. With the reduction in estrogen concentration, FSH/LH-RH secretion resumes, and a new cycle is thereby initiated.

In the event that an ovum is fertilized and becomes implanted in the endometrium of a placental mammal, an as yet poorly understood endocrine signal—possibly involving the prostaglandins (Table 11-12)—prevents lysis of the active corpus luteum, and progesterone secretion continues. FSH and LH are not secreted until after parturition (birth of the fetus). In many mammals, including humans, the corpus luteum continues to grow and to secrete progesterone and some estrogen until the placenta is able to take over, at which time the corpus luteum degenerates. In other mammals, such as the rat, the secretions of the corpus luteum, which are stimulated by prolactin, are essential to the maintenance of pregnancy throughout its

11–29. The primate menstrual cycle. Before ovulation, FSH promotes maturation of the follicle, which secretes estrogen. At low levels of this steroid, a positive-feedback loop exists, estrogen in turn stimulating FSH release. At high estrogen levels, FSH release is inhibited while a surge of LH is initiated. The LH induces the corpus luteum to secrete progesterone and some estrogen, which remain at high levels if implantation and pregnancy occur. In the absence of implantation, the progesterone and estrogen levels reach a peak and then fall, initiating menstruation. In either case, high progesterone levels act as a negative feedback on the release of LH, which decreases after ovulation. If no implantation occurs, the high progesterone level that prevails just before menstruation initiates the secretion of FSH, renewing the cycle. This rhythmicity is the result of the alternating dominances of the two steroids and the two gonadotropic hormones. [After McNaught and Callander, 1975.]

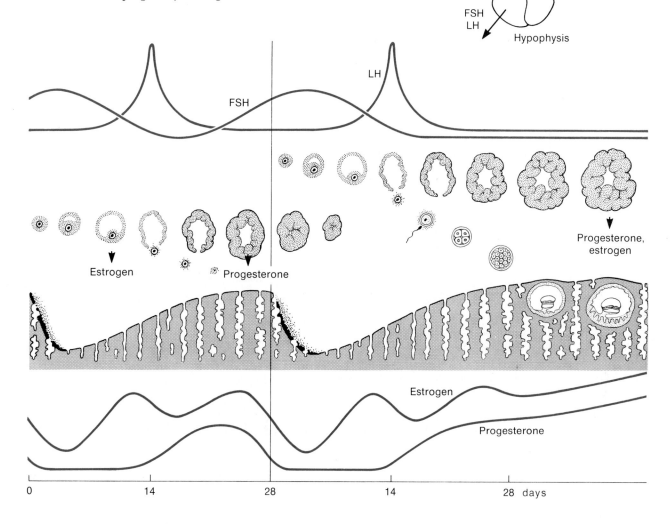

Table 11-12. Prostaglandins.

Hormone	Tissue of origin	Structure	Target tissues	Primary action	Regulation
Prostaglandins	Seminal vesicles	Cyclical unsaturated fatty acids	Uterus, ovaries, fallopian tubes	Potentiates smooth muscle contraction and possibly luteolysis; may mediate LH stimulation of estrogen; and progesterone synthesis	Introduced during coitus with semen
	Kidney		Blood vessels (especially renal)	Regulates vasodilation or constriction	Increased angiotensin II and increased epinephrine stimulate secretion; inactivated in lungs and liver.
	Neural tissue		Adrenergic terminals	Blocks norepinephrine sensitive adenylate cyclase	Neural activity increases level
	Most cells		Most cells	Alters cAMP levels	

term. Progesterone prevents ovulation during gestation and, with estrogen, initiates growth of the mammary gland ducts in preparation for lactation.

Birth control pills contain small amounts of progesterone-like and estrogen-like synthetic steroids. Taken daily, these steroids mimic the stage of pregnancy, preventing ovulation and also acting on the endometrium, thereby providing a highly effective (ca. 99%) means of avoiding conception.

Ovulation and the secretion of LH are cyclically spontaneous in some groups of mammals, including primates, as described above, but in others ovulation depends to a large degree on stimuli associated with coitus. The durations of the follicular and luteal phases of the reproductive cycle vary among different mammalian groups. They are about equal in the primate *menstrual cycle,* but in the *estrus cycle* of many other mammals (Fig. 11-30) the luteal phase is much shorter. The number of cycles per year also varies

among species. The human menstrual cycle of approximately 28 days normally occurs thirteen times a year. Among the other mammals, some have only one estrus cycle per year (usually in the Spring) and others are polyestrous throughout the year.

In mammals, *prolactin* (Table 11-5) aids in the preparation of the mammary glands for lactation. After parturition, a decrease in progesterone levels apparently interferes with the hypothalamic secretion of *prolactin-inhibiting hormone* (Table 11-6), permitting the release of prolactin. Milk production is mediated by prolactin along with the glucocorticoids, and the release of the milk is induced by oxytocin (Table 11-4). In both males and females of some species of birds (e.g., pigeons), prolactin stimulates secretion of "crop milk," a nutritive substance fed to chicks by regurgitation. In many birds, prolactin stimulates the development of brood patches—highly vascularized bald regions on the undersides for incubating eggs.

BOX 11-1   HORMONES AND BEHAVIOR

There are numerous examples of behavior whose development or expression is under hormonal control. The most familiar examples are seen in the sexual behavior of animals. In temperate-zone birds, the progressive increase in day length with approaching springtime induces growth of the gonads, testicular weight in some species increasing up to 500 times; this is accompanied by a large rise in the levels of sex hormones, which in turn promotes the development of various aspects of sexual behavior, such as selection of territory and singing in the male and nest-building in the female. Although hormones play a direct role in such behavior, they also play indirect roles by promoting the differentiation of sex-related morphological features, such as plumage, color, and voice. The behavior of one sex also releases (p. 274) behavioral responses in the other sex. An interesting example is the stimulation of nest-building behavior in female canaries by the singing of courting males. The poorer the repertoire of the male, the less intense the nest-building. Conversely, the more elaborate the serenade, the more intense the efforts of the female. Although the nest-building behavior itself is promoted by increased progesterone levels in the female, it is nevertheless dependent on the appropriate sensory input. Similarly, the singing of the male, though promoted by testosterone, depends for development of quantity and quality on exposure to the songs of the older, more experienced males.

Some behavioral differences between male and female mammals are due to differences in levels of sex hormones. Increased levels of androgens circulating in the blood lead to greater sexual receptivity in females and to greater sexual aggressiveness in males—in short, increased sexual arousability in both sexes. The more general behavioral consequences of castration in male domestic animals and humans have been known for centuries. Thus an aggressive bull is readily converted into a placid ox. More recently, it has been shown that aggressive behavior can be restored in castrated mice by administering either estradiol or testosterone. In contrast, simultaneous progesterone administration interferes with the induction of aggressiveness.

The modification of behavior by hormones implies that certain hormones can modify the properties of certain nerve cells. Direct evidence for endocrine influences on single nerve cells has been obtained in several studies. Recordings from single units in the lateral areas of the hypothalamus of rats at different times during the estrus cycle show that the percentage of neurons synaptically inhibited by such stimuli as pain, cold, or mechanical stimulation of the cervix is higher during estrus (period of female receptivity) than at other times. They found a similar augmentation of synaptic inhibition in that part of the hypothalamus when the estrogen was administered to the rat. The neurons in another part of the hypothalamus, the septum, were found to respond differently to estrogen. These cells exhibit a decrease in reflex inhibition in response to cervical stimulation, pain, and cold during estrus or when estrogen is administered. Thus an increase in the plasma level of estrogen, whether due to ovarian secretion during estrus or to experimental administration of the hormone, increases the inhibitory effects of sensory input in some neurons while decreasing it in others. Specific changes in neural excitability in various parts of the hypothalamus are also seen in response to progesterone and to prolactin.

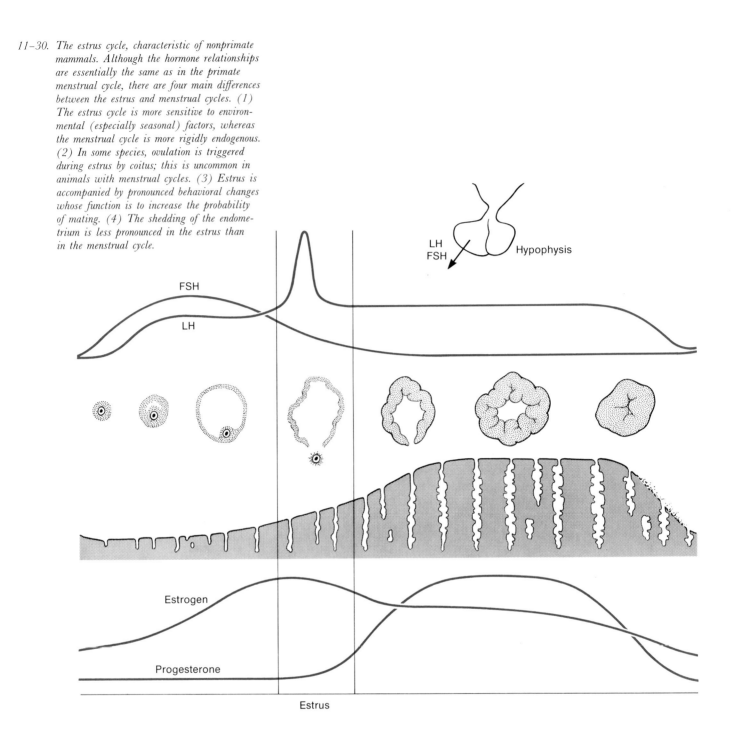

11–30. *The estrus cycle, characteristic of nonprimate mammals. Although the hormone relationships are essentially the same as in the primate menstrual cycle, there are four main differences between the estrus and menstrual cycles. (1) The estrus cycle is more sensitive to environmental (especially seasonal) factors, whereas the menstrual cycle is more rigidly endogenous. (2) In some species, ovulation is triggered during estrus by coitus; this is uncommon in animals with menstrual cycles. (3) Estrus is accompanied by pronounced behavioral changes whose function is to increase the probability of mating. (4) The shedding of the endometrium is less pronounced in the estrus than in the menstrual cycle.*

FSH

LH

LH
FSH

Hypophysis

Estrogen

Progesterone

Estrus

Invertebrate Endocrine Systems

Endocrine cells—in particular, neurosecretory cells—have been identified in most invertebrate groups, including the primitive hydroid coelenterates. In *Hydra*, for example, neurons secrete what is believed to be a growth-promoting hormone during budding, regeneration, and growth. In most of the invertebrate groups investigated so far, the presence of hormones has been mainly inferred from morphological observations rather than demonstrated biochemically. This is of course understandable because of the great diversity of groups among the invertebrates. The endocrinology of development and metamorphosis in insects has been widely studied, however, and is appropriate for a brief overview here.

ENDOCRINE REGULATION OF DEVELOPMENT IN INSECTS

The life cycle of *hemimetabolous* insects, such as the Hemiptera (bugs) and Orthoptera (locusts, roaches), begins with the development of the egg into an immature *nymphal* stage. The nymph eats and grows and undergoes several molts, replacing its old exoskeleton with a soft new one that expands to a larger size before hardening. The stages between molts are termed *instars*. The final nymphal instar gives rise to the *adult* stage. The development of *holometabolous* classes, such as the Diptera (flies), Lepidoptera (butterflies, moths), and Coleoptera (beetles), is more complex. The egg develops into a *larva* (e.g., maggot, "worm," or caterpillar), which grows through several instars. The last larval instar undergoes an especially pronounced tanning and stiffening of its cuticle, becoming outwardly dormant during the *pupal* stage. The pupa undergoes extensive internal reorganization and finally gives rise to the adult form, which shows little if any morphological resemblance to the previous stages. The larval stage of a holometabolous insect is specialized for eating, and is therefore the one that causes the major damage to many agricultural crops. The adult is the reproductive stage, and in some species is not even equipped to feed.

The first experiments to demonstrate a probable endocrine control of insect development were done between 1917 and 1922 by Kopeč, who ligatured the last larval instars of a moth at various positions along their length. He found that when the ligature was tied before a certain critical period, the larva would pupate anteriorly to the ligature but remain larval posteriorly. Cutting the nerve cord had no effect, hence he concluded that a circulating, pupa-inducing substance had its origin in a tissue located in the anterior portion of the larva. By testing various tissues, Kopeč found that removal of the brain prevents pupation and that reimplantation of the brain allows it to proceed again. It was subsequently found that a hormone secreted by cells in the brain stimulates the activity of the *prothoracic (thoracic) glands,* the tissue that elaborates the hormone that induces molting. Thus ligaturing posteriorly to the prothoracic glands after their activation by the *brain hormone* prevents pupation of the abdomen, whereas ligaturing anteriorly allows pupation to proceed. In the former case, pupation can be initiated by implanting activated prothoracic glands into the isolated abdomen.

The hardiness of insects makes them ideal subjects for the kind of experiments that were to demonstrate the humoral control of molting and metamorphosis. It is possible to carry out extended parabiosis experiments (Fig. 11-31) in which two insects or two parts of one insect are joined so that they share a common circulation, exchanging body fluid. Windows made of glass cover-slip material make it possible to observe developmental changes.

The endocrine control of development and molting in insects depends on four major hormones (Table 11-13). The insect endocrine system responsible for

development and metabolic regulation, is characterized by the following cells and functions:

1. Neurosecretory cells, which have their cell bodies in the *pars intercerebralis* of the brain (Fig. 11-32), manufacture the *brain hormone* (also termed *thoracotropic hormone*). The chemical structure of this hormone is not known, but it appears to be a small protein.

2. The so-called brain hormone is shipped via axoplasmic transport to storage organs termed the *corpora cardiaca* (Fig. 11-32). Each corpus cardiacum consists largely of the endings of the neurosecretory cells arising in the pars. It appears to act as a *neurohemal organ,* a depot for storage and release of the neurosecretory hormone* into blood spaces.

---

*The transport via neurosecretory axons of hormone from cells in the brain to an appendage of neural tissue where it is stored and released into the circulation is reminiscent of the vertebrate hypothalamo-hypophysial system. Since most vertebrate and invertebrate neuroendocrine systems are not phylogenetically homologous, they offer remarkable examples of convergent evolution in widely divergent animal groups.

11–31. Parabiosis as a method in insect endocrinology. Insect tissues readily survive in the face of such radical surgery as transection and decapitation. In this experiment by Williams (1947), the abdomen of one pupa is joined to another pupa through a glass tube. Cover-glass windows at either end permit visual inspection of the developing tissues.

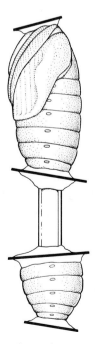

Table 11-13. Insect hormones.

Hormone	Tissue of origin	Structure	Target tissue	Primary action	R...
Brain hormone (thoracotropin)	Neuro-secretory cells in brain	Polypeptide	Prothoracic gland	Stimulates ecdysone release	Transr... o brai... ous impulses (from stretching of alimentary canal during large feed-ing in larva) stimulates secre-tion; increased secretion of juvenile hormone inhibits release
Ecdysone (molting hormone)	Thoracic glands	Steroid	Epidermis	Increases synthesis of RNA, protein, mitochondria, endoplasmic retic-ulum; stimulates secretion of new cuticle	Secretion stimulated by brain hormone
Juvenile hormone (JH)	Corpora allata	Terpene derivative	Epidermis ovarian follicles, sex accessory glands	Promotes synthesis of larval struc-tures; inhibits metamorphosis; activates ovarian follicles and sex accessory glands	Endogenous "clock"
Bursicon	Neuro-secretory cells of the cere-bral gan-glion and the thoracic ganglion	Polypeptide	Epidermis	Promotes cuticle development; in-duces tanning of cuticle of newly molted adults	Stimuli associated with emergence stimu-late secretion
Diapause hormone (moth ♀)	Neuro-secretory cells in subeso-phageal ganglion	Polypeptide	Ovaries, eggs	Induces diapause; lengthens larval and pupal instars	Release is con-trolled by the central nervous system and ap-pears to be antagonized by JH
Eclosion hormone				Induces emergence of adult from puparium	Endogenous "clock"

3. Brain hormone, released from the corpora cardi-aca, activates the thoracic gland to secrete the molt-inducing hormone *ecdysone* (Fig. 11-33), a steroid that closely resembles cholesterol and the verebrate steroid hormones, differing from these primarily in its larger number of hydroxyl groups, which greatly increase the water solubility of the steroid. Insects synthesize the ecdysone from cholesterol in their diets.

4. Other neurosecretory cells in the brain and nerve cord produce *bursicon*, a hormone that influences certain aspects of cuticle development, including the process of tanning, which is completed several hours after each molt. This hormone is a small protein with a molecular weight of about 40,000.

5. The *corpora allata* (Fig. 11-32), located at the posterior ends of the corpora cardiaca, are nonneural secretory organs responsible for secretion of *juvenile hormone (JH)* (Fig. 11-34), a modified hydrocarbon chain. This substance, acting in association with ecdysone, promotes the retention of the immature or "juvenile" characteristics of the larva, thereby post-poning metamorphosis until the adult stage.

11-32. *The general anatomy of the insect neuroendo-*
crine system. Neurosecretory cells arising in the
pars intercerebralis send their axons to the
neurohaemal organs of the corpora cardiaca,
the organs from which the brain hormone is
released. The corpora allata are nonneural
endocrine glands that secrete juvenile hormone.
The thoracic glands, located further caudally,
are not shown. [After Scharrer, 1952.]

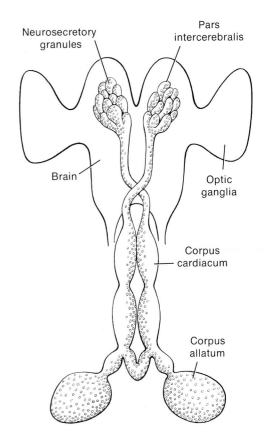

The presence of juvenile hormone in the early nymphal instar was demonstrated in experiments in which parabiotic coupling (Fig. 11-31) of the early instar to a final instar prevented the latter from pupating. The circulating concentration of JH is at its highest early in larval life, dropping to a minimum at the end of the pupal period (Fig. 11-35). Metamorphosis to the adult stage occurs when juvenile hormone is virtually absent in the circulation. The concentration then rises again in the adult. This final rise in the concentration of juvenile hormone occurs in response to feeding by the adult. In the male, JH promotes development of the accessory sexual organs; in the females of most insects it promotes maturation of the eggs.

The interaction of the insect developmental hormones is illustrated with the life cycle of a moth (Fig. 11-36). Prolonged exposure to cold stimulates the synthesis of brain hormone, which in turn stimulates the thoracic gland to secrete ecdysone. Growth continues through a series of instars, which remain larval as long as the concentration of juvenile hormone remains above a minimum. This process of growth and molting is usually completed in four or five instars, during which there is a progressive decline in juvenile hormone (Fig. 11-35) until a low concentration of JH induces pupation. As this stage of quiet reorganization progresses, the level of JH is gradually reduced until metamorphosis to the adult form finally occurs.

Thus the normal development of an insect depends on precisely adjusted concentrations of juvenile hormone at each stage. This is somewhat analogous to the role of thyroid hormones in the regulation of amphibian development. In both cases, disturbance of the relations between hormone concentration and developmental stage leads to abnormal development. Because of its potency in preventing maturation in insects, juvenile hormone or synthetic analogues have been proposed as potential nontoxic, ecologically sound means of combating insect pests.

11-33. *Ecdysone. This steroid moulting hormone is*
synthesized in and liberated by the thoracic
glands of insects. Subsequent to release,
α-ecdysone, shown here, is converted in the
blood into the physiologically active β form by
relocation of the upper hydroxyl group.

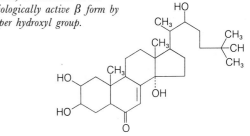

11-34. *A juvenile hormone extracted from the cecropia*
moth Hyalophora cecropia. This is one
of several analogues that occur naturally
in insects and their food plants and which
are active in the retention of juvenile
characteristics.

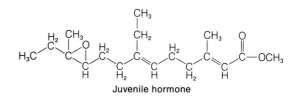

Juvenile hormone

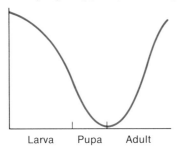

11–35. *Changes in the level of juvenile hormone during the insect life cycle. Metamorphosis to the adult form can occur only if its concentration is very low. After the adult insect has fed, secretion of JH recurs, regulating ovarian activity and stimulating development of male accessory organs.* [After Spratt, 1971.]

11–36. *Hormone interactions in insect metamorphosis, illustrated by the developmental sequence of the cecropia moth.* [After Spratt, 1971.]

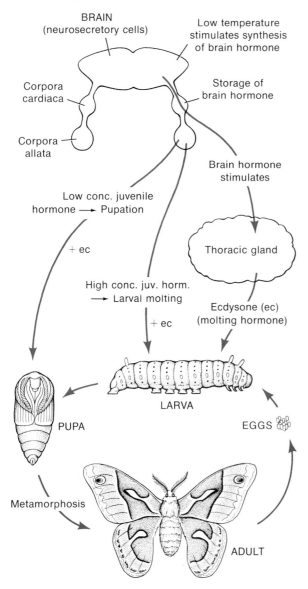

Mechanisms of Hormone Action

cAMP AS SECOND MESSENGER

The advance of science depends on two forms of progress. There is the everyday growth of scientific knowledge by the slow but steady accumulation of data in thousands of laboratories. This represents by far the major effort expounded by the entire community of scientists. These small-scale but essential increments of progress generally build upon another kind of advance—the major leap forward, generally unanticipated, and providing the revolutionary new insight or point of departure. Such "breakthroughs" open new paths of inquiry, which are then explored by the step-by-step everyday mode of progress until the next major breakthrough provides new insight and again alters the course of daily investigation.

The discovery of *cyclic adenosine 3′, 5′-monophosphate (cAMP)*—and the investigations, started in the mid-1950's by the late E. W. Sutherland and associates, of its role as a cellular regulatory agent—is an example of a fundamental advance in biological science. The discovery of the regulatory role of cAMP ranks equal in importance to the discovery of the role of its parent molecule ATP as the major energy currency of the cell. Sutherland's discovery has led to a vast accumulation of data from many types of cells, confirming the importance and ubiquitousness of this and the related nucleotide *cyclic guanosine 3′, 5′-monophosphate (cGMP)* as cellular regulatory agents.

The related discovery of the membrane-bound enzyme *adenylate cyclase* (adenyl cyclase) provided the first evidence for a link between extracellular hormones and intracellular messenger molecules, and led to the hypothesis of the *second messenger*, outlined in Figure 11-37. This hypothesis states that a receptor molecule projecting at the outer surface of the target-cell membrane interacts with a hormone molecule for which the receptor is specific. This interaction causes a conformational change in the receptor, which leads to an allosteric activation of adenylate cyclase. The latter, according to this scheme, is closely associated with the receptor molecule, but faces the cytoplasm. The activated cyclase catalyzes the hydrolysis of adenosine triphosphate to cAMP. The cyclic nucleotide then stimulates or inhibits enzymes or processes that are specific for the type of target cell. The conversion of ATP to cAMP (Fig. 11-38) requires Mg^{2+} and a trace of Ca^{2+}.

The intracellular level of cAMP depends not only on the rate at which it is synthesized, but also on the rate at which it is inactivated by conversion to ordinary adenosine 5′-monophosphate, AMP, a reaction

11–37. *The first and second messengers. The "first messenger" is the circulating hormone. The hormone-receptor interaction activates the adenylate cyclase, which catalyzes the synthesis of cAMP from ATP. cAMP acts as an intracellular "second messenger," leading to the stimulation of certain cellular reactions. It does this by removing inhibition from protein kinases. Degradation of cAMP to AMP can be inhibited by addition of methyl xanthines, such as caffeine and theophylline, and in many cells by an elevation in intracellular Ca^{2+} concentration.*

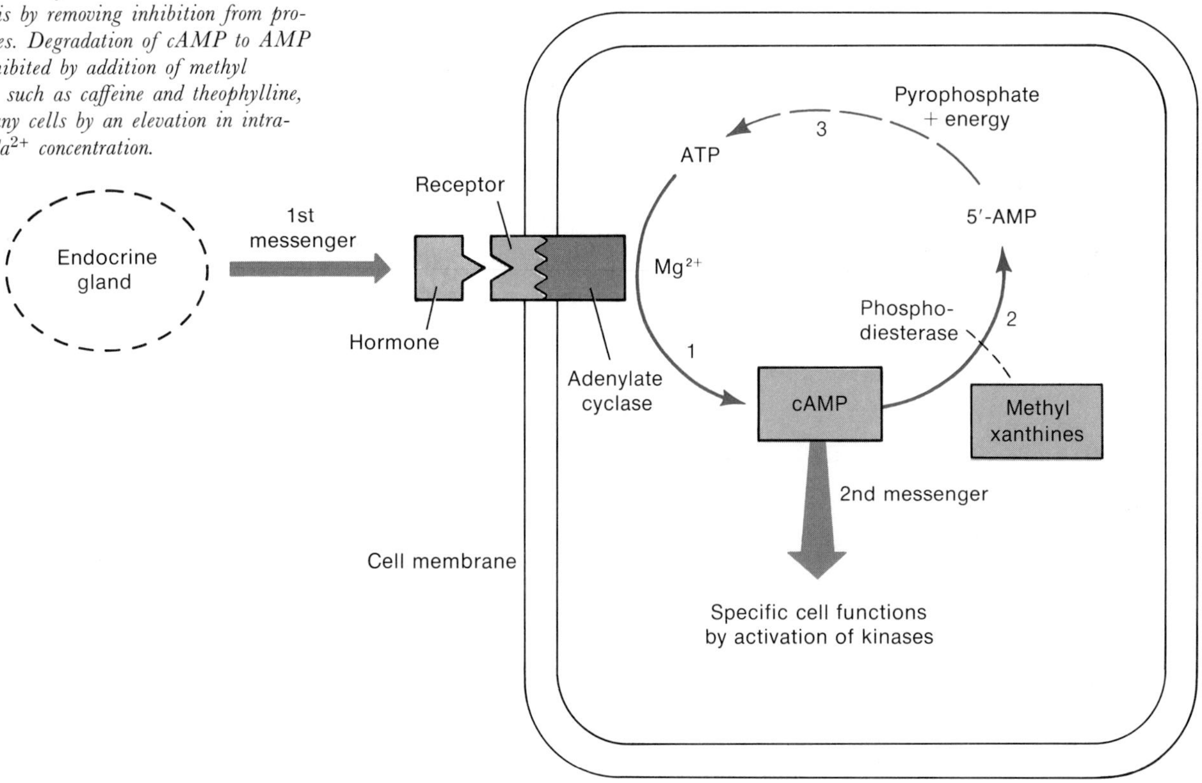

catalyzed by a *phosphodiesterase* (Fig. 11-38). Thus there exists a cycle of

$$ATP \xrightarrow{\;1\;} cAMP \xrightarrow{\;2\;} AMP$$
$$\underset{3}{\underline{\hspace{3cm}}}$$

The last of these steps, regeneration of ATP from ADP, is energized by intermediate metabolism (Chapter 3). The level of cAMP is determined by the balance between steps 1 and 2, with step 1 in many endocrine target tissues under the control of hormones that modulate the activity of adenylate cyclase. Step 2, dependent on phosphodiesterase activity, can be slowed by the addition of the methyl xanthines caffeine or theophylline,* which inhibit phosphodiesterase activity, and can thereby increase the intracellular concentration of cAMP. The basal concentration of cAMP within the cells can be as low as 10^{-12}M.

*Theophylline is the stimulant found in tea, analogous to caffeine in coffee.

cAMP AND HORMONE-INDUCED MOBILIZATION OF GLUCOSE

It will be useful at this point to review the sequence in which the role of cAMP as second messenger has been most completely worked out—namely, the endocrine-stimulated mobilization of glucose from glycogen (Fig. 11-39,A).

It had been known for some time that the hormone glucagon causes glycogenolysis in the liver and that epinephrine does the same in skeletal and cardiac muscle. Sutherland and his associates, working with liver tissue, found that an increase in cAMP levels due to activation of adenylate cyclase occurs in the presence of the hormone glucagon. The cAMP was found to promote breakdown of glycogen into glucose, inhibit the synthesis of glycogen from glucose, and stimulate the formation of glucose from lactate and amino acids. The end effect is a rise in blood glucose.

The interaction of the hormone (glucagon in liver and epinephrine in skeletal and cardiac muscle) with

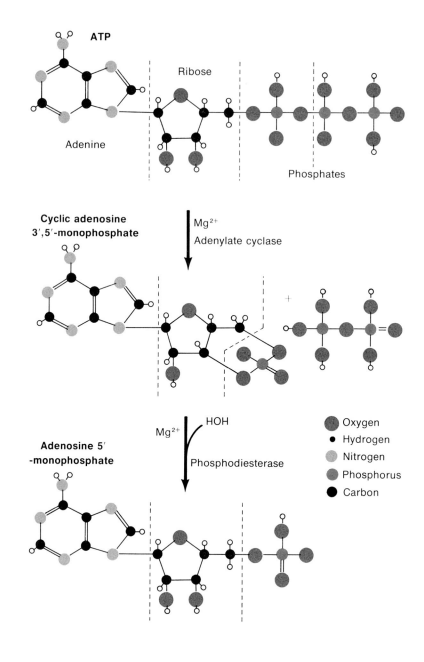

11–38. *Synthesis and degradation of cAMP. Membrane-bound adenylate cyclase catalyzes the conversion of intracellular ATP to cAMP in response to hormone-receptor interaction at the outer cell surface. Removal of cAMP from the system occurs via the phosphodiesterase-catalyzed hydrolysis of the ribose-phosphate bond, converting the cAMP to adenosine 5′-monophosphate (AMP), which is recycled by metabolic phosphorylation to ATP.*

the membrane-bound receptor activates the adenylate cyclase. The activation may take place through an intermediate molecule within the membrane, termed the *transducer* (not shown in the figures). In any event, the result is an increased rate of cAMP synthesis from ATP (Fig. 11-39, steps 1 and 2). The immediate action of cAMP—one that appears to be the common step in most if not all cAMP-regulated systems—is the activation of a *protein kinase* (step 3). The cAMP molecule does this by complexing with an *inhibitory subunit* associated with the protein kinase (Fig. 11-40). Once activated, the protein kinase is free to catalyze the

phosphorylation (from ATP) of another enzyme, *phosphorylase kinase* to *phosphorylase kinase-PO_4*, which in turn catalyzes the phosphorylation of *phosphorylase b* to *phosphorylase a-PO_4* (steps 4 and 5). It is the latter enzyme that then phosphorylates glycogen residues to glucose-1-PO_4 (step 6), making the glucose available for use within the cell in the glycolytic pathway or for release from the cell as unphosphorylated glucose (Fig. 3-44).

It is interesting that the pathway leading to the *activation* of phosphorylase *a*, the enzyme that breaks down glycogen into glucose, concomitantly produces an *inhibition* of *glycogen synthetase,* the enzyme that cat-

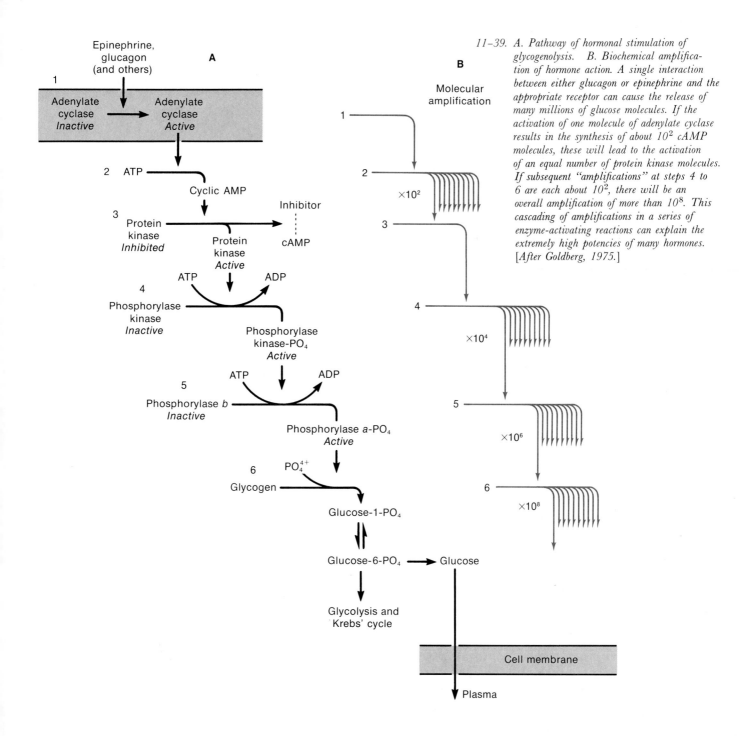

Epinephrine, glucagon (and others)

A

1

Adenylate cyclase *Inactive* → Adenylate cyclase *Active*

2 ATP

Cyclic AMP

Inhibitor

3 Protein kinase *Inhibited*

Protein kinase *Active*

cAMP

ATP → ADP

4 Phosphorylase kinase *Inactive*

Phosphorylase kinase-PO_4 *Active*

ATP → ADP

5 Phosphorylase *b* *Inactive*

Phosphorylase *a*-PO_4 *Active*

6 PO_4^{4+}

Glycogen

Glucose-1-PO_4

Glucose-6-PO_4 → Glucose

Glycolysis and Krebs' cycle

B

Molecular amplification

1

2 $\times 10^2$

3

4 $\times 10^4$

5 $\times 10^6$

6 $\times 10^8$

Cell membrane

Plasma

11–39. A. Pathway of hormonal stimulation of glycogenolysis. B. Biochemical amplification of hormone action. A single interaction between either glucagon or epinephrine and the appropriate receptor can cause the release of many millions of glucose molecules. If the activation of one molecule of adenylate cyclase results in the synthesis of about 10^2 cAMP molecules, these will lead to the activation of an equal number of protein kinase molecules. If subsequent "amplifications" at steps 4 to 6 are each about 10^2, there will be an overall amplification of more than 10^8. This cascading of amplifications in a series of enzyme-activating reactions can explain the extremely high potencies of many hormones. [After Goldberg, 1975.]

alyzes the polymerization of glucose into glycogen. The inhibition results from a phosphorylation of the glycogen synthetase by a protein kinase. Thus the hormone-stimulated rise in cAMP stimulates (by phosphorylation) the enzyme that breaks down glycogen and inhibits (also by phosphorylation) the enzyme that resynthesizes it from glucose. This synergistic effect is important, for it keeps the rise in glucose from driving by mass action a resynthesis of glycogen from glucose. It is also an example of the multiplicity of cAMP-mediated effects which take place simultaneously within a single cell.

MULTIPLE ACTIONS OF cAMP

Since the initial discovery of cAMP in the role of a messenger linking glucose mobilization to hormone action in liver and muscle, the production of cAMP has been found to be stimulated in a large number of target tissues by the appropriate hormones. Furthermore, when cAMP (or a more permeant and less metabolizable analogue, such as dibutyryl cAMP) is applied to those tissues, it has been found to mimic the effects normally induced by the hormones. These effects can often also be produced by blocking the

11–40. Mediation of various hormone actions by cAMP. Hormone association with the membrane receptor leads to the synthesis of cAMP from ATP. cAMP then removes the inhibition of a protein kinase by removing an inhibitory subunit from the kinase. The active protein kinase can then phosphorylate another intracellular enzyme, thereby either activating or repressing it, depending upon the enzyme. Since there are various forms of kinase with different substrates that they phosphorylate, the hormone-induced increase in cAMP concentration can lead to any of a variety of effects, depending on the macromolecular specializations of the target cell. [After Goldberg, 1975.]

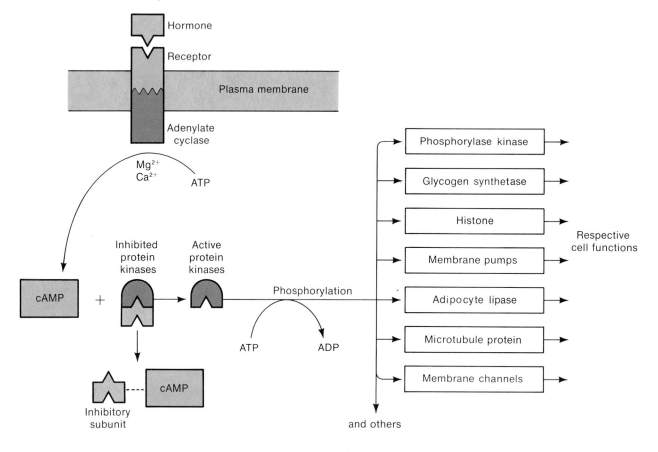

phosphodiesterase with methyl xanthines (Fig. 11-37). These lines of evidence are all taken to indicate that cAMP acts as the intracellular messenger in a large variety of target tissues. Examples of cAMP-mediated hormone actions on target cells are:

1. Enhanced synthesis and release of hormone in various endocrine tissues, including the release of insulin from pancreatic β-cells, the secretory response of anterior pituitary to hypothalamic releasing hormone, responses of endocrine tissues to various trophic hormones, such as ACTH, FSH, TSH.

2. ADH-stimulated increases in water permeability of the kidney collecting duct.

3. Stimulation of lipid mobilization and inhibition of fat storage in adipose (fat) tissue by epinephrine, glucagon, and TSH.

4. Epinephrine-evoked increased rate and force of beating in cardiac muscle.

5. Postsynaptic changes in membrane permeability in response to the neural transmitter dopamine.

How, one might ask, can the same messenger molecule be responsible for mediating such a diversity of biochemical and physiological responses? In all mammalian systems that have been studied so far, the step that follows hormone-stimulated cAMP production is the activation of a protein kinase by removal of an inhibitory subunit by the cAMP (Fig. 11-40). The key to the diversity of effects that cAMP exerts lies in the different forms of protein kinase, each one effective in phosphorylating a different substrate protein. There is generally more than one protein kinase in a given type of cell. This, of course, is the reason why a hormone

BOX 11-2 AMPLIFICATION OF HORMONE ACTION

The sequence of steps between the binding of glucagon or epinephrine and the breakdown of glycogen is rather complex (Fig. 11-39,A). It would be simpler, of course, for cAMP to activate the final enzyme in the sequence directly and thereby save several steps. On the other hand, the large number of steps makes sense if one considers the need for amplification—that is, for producing a large effect from a few hormone molecules. The concept of *biochemical amplification* is illustrated in Figure 11-39,B. Each enzymatic step, beginning with number 1 and ending with number 6 (with the exception of step 2), is an *activating reaction* that converts a catalytically inactive (or weakly active) molecule into an active enzyme. The result is a cascading of amplification through four steps. If it is assumed, conservatively, that each activated enzyme molecule catalyzes the activation of 100 inactive molecules in the next step, then four steps would produce an overall amplification of 10^8. Thus the interaction of one molecule of glucagon or epinephrine with the membrane receptor of liver or muscle can result in the mobilization of about 100,000,000 or more molecules of glucose. Since the basal intracellular concentration of cAMP is very low (10^{-12} to 10^{-8} M), a small increase in the number of cAMP molecules can be equivalent to a large percentage change in cAMP concentration, and a few hormone molecules can produce large relative changes in cAMP levels.

can exert multiple effects in one or more cell types, using cAMP as second messenger in evoking each response. The action of cAMP in any given cell is determined by the particular protein kinases that it encounters and activates as it is produced in response to the hormone.

It is apparent, then, that the relations between hormones and the responses of their target tissues are determined by genetic and developmental mechanisms. First, there are hormone-receptor specificities that determine which cells will recognize a given hormone. Second, there is molecular specificity between cAMP-activated protein kinase and the protein (often an enzyme) that is phosphorylated and thereby activated by the kinase.

INTERACTIONS BETWEEN CYCLIC AMP AND CALCIUM

Not much time had passed after the discovery of cAMP before various laboratories noted that effects ascribed to cAMP were often mimicked by Ca^{2+}, were Ca^{2+}-dependent or were reinforced by Ca^{2+}. Such observations have been compiled by Rasmussen (Table 11-14), who has proposed that Ca^{2+} also acts in the role of a messenger, often regulating and/or being regulated by cAMP. It has become evident that the relations between Ca^{2+} and cAMP are complex and therefore not always identical in different tissues. Pre-

sented here are some examples of how Ca^{2+} and cAMP can participate in regulating cell processes.

Two pathways leading to glycogenolysis in skeletal muscle are shown in Figure 11-41. Skeletal muscle responds to epinephrine with the sequence of enzyme activations—already familiar from Figure 11-39—that leads to the breakdown of glycogen to glucose-6-phosphate. In that sequence, phosphorylase kinase is sensitized to *resting* calcium levels (i.e., $<10^{-7}$ M) by cAMP-induced phosphorylation. This is shown in the *right-hand branch*. The *left-hand branch* shows the Ca^{2+}-stimulated pathway, which is activated during muscle contraction by the increase in the concentration of intracellular free Ca^{2+} that results from release of Ca^{2+} by the sarcoplasmic reticulum. The increased $[Ca^{2+}]_i$ enhances phosphorylase kinase activity independent of a hormone-stimulated rise in cAMP.

The two pathways leading to glycogenolysis in muscle owe their characteristics to the differences in the relative activities of phosphorylase kinase and phosphorylase kinase-PO_4 at different Ca^{2+} concentrations. The phosphorylase kinase requires an intracellular Ca^{2+} concentration of 10^{-6} to 10^{-5} M, characteristic of the contracting muscle, before it will catalyse the conversion of phosphorylase *b* to phosphorylase *a* (Fig. 11-42). In contrast, phosphorylase kinase-PO_4 (produced in response to epinephrine) catalyzes this reaction at intracellular calcium concentrations below 10^{-6} M, which is the calcium concentration characteristic of the relaxed muscle. Thus glucose is mobilized

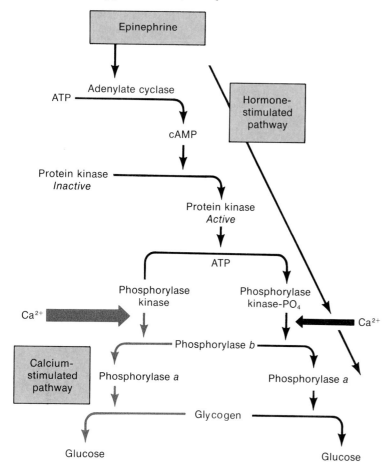

11-41. *Supplementary activation of glycogenolysis in skeletal muscle by* Ca^{2+}. *At the right is the same epinephrine-stimulated pathway shown in Figure 11-39,A. The branch at the left, also leading to the same end product, is independent of hormone stimulation, but is instead stimulated by a rise in* $[Ca^{2+}]_i$, *as explained in the text. [After Rasmussen, 1975.]*

11-42. *Calcium sensitivity of the phosphorylated ("activated") and unphosphorylated forms of phosphorylase kinase (see Fig. 11-41). The phosphorylated form shows greater activity at lower calcium concentrations. [After Rasmussen, 1975.]*

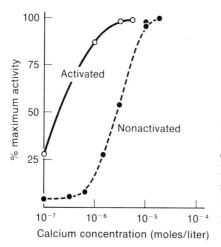

via phosphorylase kinase as needed in response to increases in $[Ca^{2+}]_i$ during contraction. The epinephrine-stimulated mobilization of glucose via phosphorylase kinase-PO_4, however, is useful for anticipating energy needs or augmenting the calcium-activated mobilization in the "fight or flight" syndrome characteristic of the sympathetic division of the autonomic nervous system (Fig. 6-15,A), which stimulates the secretion of the catecholamines, epinephrine, and norepinephrine.

Another example of Ca^{2+}-cAMP interaction is seen in the smooth muscle of the mammalian intestine. Acetylcholine released from parasympathetic postganglionic neurons (Fig. 6-15,B) causes a depolarization and concomitant influx of Ca^{2+} in the spindle-shaped cells of smooth muscle (Fig. 11-43,A). As the $[Ca^{2+}]_i$ rises, the cells contract. At the same time, the elevated $[Ca^{2+}]_i$ stimulates the activity of both the phosphodiesterase and the adenylate cyclase, the effect on the latter outweighing that of the former, thereby producing an elevation in cAMP concentration (Fig. 11-43,B). The rise in cAMP stimulates the calcium pump, which transports Ca^{2+} out of the cell and into the Ca^{2+}-sequestering reticulum (not shown). The result of this negative-feedback regulation of the intracellular Ca^{2+} concentrations is to re-establish the resting $[Ca^{2+}]_i$ and the resting muscle tension when stimulation by ACh ceases.

cAMP also mediates the relaxation of smooth muscle in response to the secretion of epinephrine by the adrenal medulla and the liberation of norepinephrine from sympathetic postganglionic neurons. The catecholamines stimulate cAMP production in smooth muscle by activation of adenylate cyclase (Fig. 11-44,A). The rise in cAMP concentration stimulates the pumping of Ca^{2+} from the cytosol, as we have already noted, fostering relaxation of the contractile mechanism. Concomitantly, the drop in $[Ca^{2+}]_i$ leads to a reduction in adenylate cyclase activity and hence a reduction in cAMP synthesis (Fig. 11-44,B). A steady state of Ca^{2+} and cAMP levels is thereby restored, ensuring relaxation of the contractile mechanism.

The dynamic nature of cAMP metabolism is illustrated by the discovery that in cardiac muscle the concentration of cAMP undergoes fluctuations correlated with the cycle of beating. Thus the concentration of cAMP is highest in samples of heart tissue rapidly frozen just before or just at the beginning of contraction. The cAMP concentrations at that time are about 50% higher than during the relaxed phase. It may be that the increase in $[Ca^{2+}]_i$ during contraction raises cAMP levels by stimulating adenylate cyclase activity. By analogy with smooth muscle, a rise in cAMP may stimulate the calcium pump of the sarcoplasmic reticulum, helping restore the low $[Ca^{2+}]_i$ required for relaxation of the contractile apparatus.

The relations between Ca^{2+} and cAMP are still

Table 11-14. Partial list of Ca²⁺ and cAMP-dependent responses of tissues to electrical and chemical stimuli.

Tissue	Stimulus	Response	Ca²⁺ required	cAMP produced
Synapses	Depolarization	Transmitter release	+	+
Anterior pituitary	GHR	Growth hormone release	+	+
Anterior pituitary	FSH/LH-RH	LH release	+	+
Anterior pituitary	TRH	TSH release	+	+
Posterior pituitary	Depolarization	Vasopressin release	+	?
β-cell, pancreas	Glucose	Insulin release	+	+
Adrenal cortex	ACTH	Steroid release	+	+
Adrenal medulla	Depolarization	Epinephrine release	+	−
Liver	Glucagon	Glucose synthesis and release	?	+
Thyroid	TSH	Thyroxine release	+	+
Corpus luteum	LH	Progesterone release	+	+
Heart	Epinephrine	Glycogenolysis	+	+
Melanocyte	MSH	Melanin dispersion	+	+
Adipose cell	Epinephrine	Lipolysis	+	+

Source: H. Rasmussen, Cell communication, calcium ions, and cyclic adenosine monophosphate, Science, 170(1970):404–412.

A ACh induces contraction

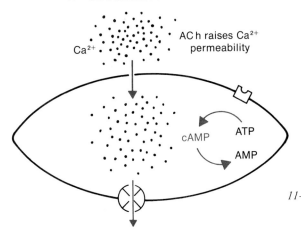

B Feedback limits duration of contraction

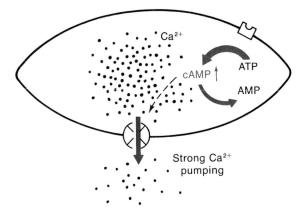

11–43. Ca-mediated and cAMP-mediated smooth muscle responses to acetylcholine. A. Contraction is produced by an influx of Ca²⁺ in response to depolarization in response to ACh. B. The increased [Ca²⁺]ᵢ interferes with phosphodiesterase activity, leading to an increase in the cAMP level. The cAMP stimulates the Ca pump, lowering [Ca²⁺]ᵢ and thus causing smooth muscle to relax. [After Rasmussen, 1975.]

11–44. *cAMP-mediated relaxation of smooth muscle in response to epinephrine. A. Epinephrine activates adenylate cyclase. cAMP then rises and stimulates the Ca^{2+} pump, causing $[Ca^{2+}]_i$ to fall. B. The drop in $[Ca^{2+}]_i$ removes Ca^{2+}-inhibition of phosphodiesterase activity, and the cAMP levels tend toward their steady-state resting levels. [After Rasmussen, 1975.]*

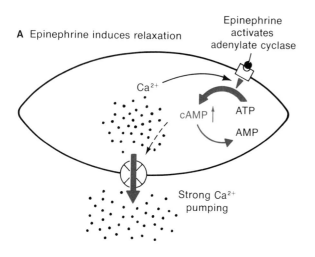

A Epinephrine induces relaxation

Epinephrine activates adenylate cyclase

Ca²⁺

cAMP ↑   ATP

AMP

Strong Ca²⁺ pumping

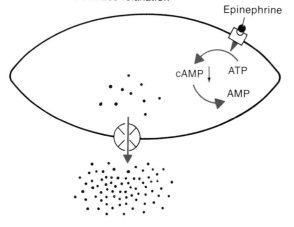

B Feedback stabilizes relaxation

Epinephrine

cAMP ↓   ATP

AMP

under intensive study. They are difficult to sort out because of the following complexities:

1. Calcium ion affects adenylate cyclase activity differently at different concentrations. At low concentrations, Ca^{2+} enhances the activity of that enzyme; at high concentrations, Ca^{2+} inhibits the activity of the cyclase and tends to suppress cAMP levels. The optimal concentrations probably differ in different cell types, and are not yet well understood.

2. Calcium in some cells has been shown to modulate the activity of the phosphodiesterase, in that way influencing the rate of cAMP breakdown.

3. In some cells, Ca^{2+} has been found to stimulate the production of cGMP (see below), whose actions often oppose those of cAMP.

4. cAMP stimulates uptake of Ca^{2+} into reticula on the one hand, but facilitates release of Ca^{2+} from mitochondria. The latter effect may account for the ability of caffeine or other methyl xanthines (p. 377) to induce muscle contraction in the absence of membrane depolarization, and the ability of methyl xanthines or cAMP to release hormones from some tissues in the absence of extracellular Ca^{2+}. The net effect of a rise in cAMP on $[Ca^{2+}]_i$ will depend, then, on which effect is greater—the release of Ca^{2+} from mitochondria or the enhanced uptake of Ca^{2+} into reticula.

Because of these multiple effects of Ca^{2+} on cAMP metabolism on the one hand and of cAMP on intracellular calcium metabolism on the other hand, it is not yet possible to predict in any given tissue what effect a change in the concentration of one of these agents will have on the concentration of the other.

CYCLIC GMP

The study of cAMP metabolism is further complicated by the existence of the other regulatory nucleotide, cyclic guanosine 3′,5′-monophosphate (cGMP) (Fig. 11-45). This nucleotide, present in cells at concentrations even lower than those of cAMP, is produced

11–45. *Cyclic guanosine 3′,5′-monophosphate (cGMP). This cyclic nucleotide differs from cAMP only in one portion (shown shaded) of its purine group. Compare with Figure 11-38. cGMP is synthesized from GTP by guanylate cyclase, is active in extremely low concentrations, and appears to act in an opposite sense to cAMP in many tissues.*

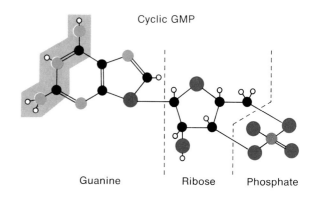

Cyclic GMP

Guanine   Ribose   Phosphate

Table 11–15. Opposing cyclic nucleotide-mediated cellular responses.

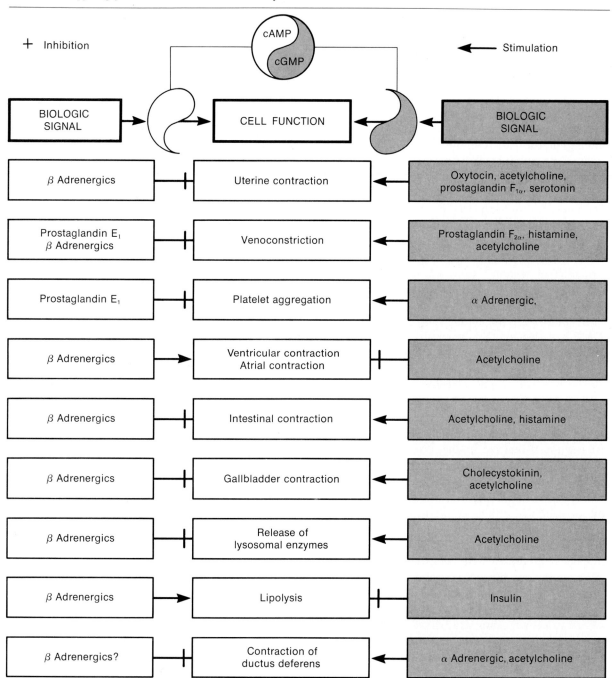

Source: N. D. Goldberg, Cyclic nucleotides and cell function, in G. Weissmann and R. Claiborne (eds.), *Cell Membranes: Biochemistry, Cell Biology and Pathology,* Hospital Practice Publishing Co., Inc., New York, 1975.

from GTP (guanosine triphosphate) by the enzyme *guanylate cyclase,* which occurs in the cytoplasm as well as in cell membranes. cGMP generally promotes responses opposite to those promoted by cAMP (Table 11-15). For example, in heart muscle, as we noted above, epinephrine stimulates the production of cAMP. Acetylcholine, on the other hand, stimulates the production of cGMP. ACh and the catecholamines have opposing effects on the rate and strength of heartbeat, the former decreasing them and the latter increasing them. This suggests that cAMP (whose production is stimulated by β-adrenergic receptor binding of the catecholamines) and cGMP (whose production is stimulated by acetylcholine) have opposing intracellular actions. Activation of the β-adrenergic receptors of cardiac muscle, brain, smooth muscle, and lymphocytes simultaneously produces a rise in the level of cAMP and a drop in the level of cGMP. Conversely, ACh causes a drop in the level of cAMP while producing a rise in the level of cGMP. Table 11-15 lists a number of responses in which cAMP and cGMP mediate the actions of different hormones that produce opposing effects on the target cells. The see-saw relations and counter-regulatory effects of cAMP and cGMP have led to a Yin-Yang analogy for the function of these two important agents (Goldberg, 1975).

Cyclic GMP production is particularly sensitive to $[Ca^{2+}]$. In every system in which GMP is the intermediary for a hormone-elicited effect, the hormone is ineffective if Ca^{2+} is absent from the extracellular fluid. Studies on isolated guanylate cyclase indicate that the enzyme is inactive in the absence of Ca^{2+}, and becomes progressively more active with increases in $[Ca^{2+}]$. In contrast, isolated preparations of adenylate cyclase are stimulated by Ca^{2+} at low concentrations, but are inhibited at high concentrations as well as at zero $[Ca^{2+}]$. Thus the optimum $[Ca^{2+}]$ for this enzyme is lower than for guanylate cyclase. In view of the differences in the calcium sensitivities of these two enzymes, the relative concentrations of cAMP and cGMP can in principle be influenced by intracellular free Ca^{2+}. In addition, the greater calcium responsiveness of cGMP synthesis suggests that in some systems Ca^{2+} may act as a second messenger to stimulate the production of cGMP, which would then act as a "third" messenger.

Hormone Action on Genetic Mechanisms

Steroid hormones appear to penetrate the surface membrane and act on internal receptor sites. Some, it appears, exert their cellular actions by modulating the expression of the genetic program. Presumptive

evidence for this comes from several sources. Injection of the insect growth and molting hormone ecdysone (p. 374) into larvae of the fly *Chironomus* is followed after a short delay (15–30 min) by the appearance of *puffs* at specific loci on the chromosomes of the salivary gland (Fig. 11-46). The larval salivary gland is used because the chromosomes are polytene (composed of many chromatin strands), and are therefore "giant" sized, with easily observed bands. The puffing consists of a swelling of one or more of the bands, and indicates the elaboration of a specific messenger RNA. Other tissues in the larval fly respond to ecdysone by puffing of other bands, suggesting that the programmed response to ecdysone is tissue specific and results in different synthetic activity in different tissues. It is still not clear how ecdysone influences the transcription of DNA to RNA.

The steroid hormones of vertebrates also exert powerful effects on the genetic machinery. This is evidenced by the stimulation of synthesis of certain proteins in restricted tissues in response to steroid hormones in the general circulation. For example, the androgens stimulate the synthesis of myofibrillar proteins, but only in striated muscle cells, not in other tissues.

Because of their low molecular weight (ca. 300; similar to sucrose) and their lipid solubility, steroid hormones can readily enter and leave cells by diffusing across membranes. It was therefore interesting to find by autoradiography that steroid hormones accumulate in the nuclei of their target cells, but not in the nuclei of other cells. This specific accumulation occurs very rapidly and persists for some time after the labeled steroid is removed from the circulation. These findings, made in the 1960's, suggested that these must be steroid-hormone-specific binding molecules within target cells. Such receptor molecules were found by fractionating target tissue incubated with labeled hormone and separating components of different molecular weight by sucrose-density-gradient centrifugation. Toft and Gorski did this using estradiol as the hormone and rat uterus as the target tissue. The receptor-hormone complex was identified by the radioactivity of the tritiated estradiol; the receptor turned out to be a protein molecule with a molecular weight of about 200,000. This protein, which binds estradiol very strongly, was present in uterine tissues but not in other tissues. Most significant was the observation that substances that mimic the hormonal action of estradiol in the uterus were all bound by this protein. It therefore appears that the formation of the hormone-protein complex is an intermediate in the chain of events that leads to the end effect of estradiol action in the uterus. Similar receptor proteins have since been identified in the target tissues of the other steroid hormones. Conversely, the receptor molecules were found only in the target tissues of the respective hormones.

The steroid hormone is initially bound by the recep-

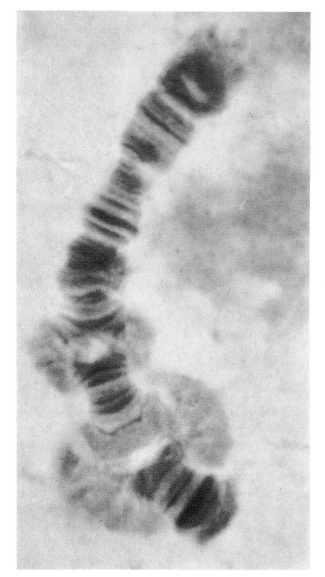

11-46. *Puffing induced by ecdysone in a giant chromosome of the fly* Chironomus. *Two puffs are seen in the bottom portion of the chromosome.* [*From "Chromosome Puffs" by W. Beerman and U. Clever. Copyright © 1964 by Scientific American, Inc. All rights reserved.*]

11-47. *Postulated mechanism of steroid hormone action. A. Steroids diffuse randomly into and out of nontarget cells without interaction or binding. B. Target cells, however, preferentially retain specific steroid hormone molecules, which complex in the cytoplasm with receptor protein molecules consisting of two subunits. C. These complexes then accumulate in the nucleus, where they bind to a specific fraction of the group of heterogeneous nonhistine proteins associated with the DNA in the chromatin. It has been proposed that this association makes a segment of the DNA available for gene transcription. D. The resulting messenger RNA is then translated into a protein by the ribosomes.*

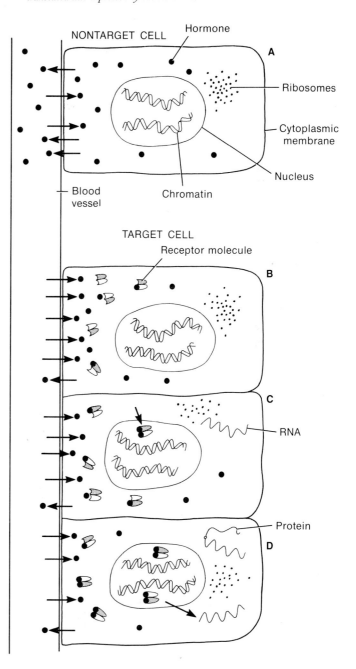

tor protein in the cytoplasm before the complex enters the nucleus (Fig. 11-47), as seen in labeling and fractionation experiments. Initially, nearly all the label appears in the cytoplasm, and, with time, increasing amounts appear in the nucleus. In the absence of the hormone, the receptor protein is distributed more or less uniformly between nucleus and cytoplasm. With the addition of hormone, the hormone-receptor complex accumulates in the nucleus, suggesting that the complex binds selectively to some component of the nucleus. This component is the *chromatin*, the substance of chromosomes, which consists of DNA, the fairly uniform basic protein *histone,* and a group of heterogeneous acid proteins collectively termed the *nonhistone chromosomal proteins* (*NCP*). As it turns out, the hormone-and-receptor complex binds to a fraction of the NCPs, which, unlike the histones, are specific for each tissue.

Summary

Physiological and biochemical processes are controlled and coordinated in the animal body in large part by special blood-borne messenger molecules termed hormones, which are liberated by the cells of endocrine secretory tissues. In vertebrates, these messenger molecules belong to three categories: amines, steroids, and peptides. After liberation from the endocrine tissues in which they originate, the molecules of a hormone are distributed by the circulation in low concentrations throughout the body, where they come in contact with target cells that exhibit a specific and high sensitivity to the hormone molecules.

The peptide and amine hormones bind to receptors on the surface membranes of the target cells. This interaction produces a signal (perhaps a conformational change in the receptor molecule) that is transmitted to the active site of an associated membrane-bound enzyme facing the cytoplasm. The membrane-bound enzyme adenylate cyclase participates in the initial response to many of these hormones, mediating many and diverse cell responses. This enzyme catalyzes the conversion of ATP to cyclic adenosine $3',5'$-monophosphate (cAMP), which acts as a "second messenger," conveying the influence of the extracellular "first messenger," the hormone, to the cell interior. The cAMP does this by activating a protein kinase by removal of an inhibitory subunit from the enzyme. In the cAMP-mediated action, the target cell's ultimate chemical or metabolic responses to the hormone depends on the nature of the protein kinases present in the cell and is therefore subject to activation by the cAMP. A given kinase will phosphorylate a certain protein, generally an enzyme, activating it and thereby determining which cell reactions or functions are stimulated.

The steroid hormones, being lipid-soluble, enter cells freely, and appear at least in some cases to influence the transcription of certain genes. The steroid hormone molecules bind to free receptor protein molecules present in the cytoplasm and nucleus. The hormone-receptor complex binds to chromatin in the nucleus in such a way that transcription of one or more codons into RNA is stimulated.

Secretion of most hormones occurs by exocytotic expulsion of hormone molecules contained within minute secretory vesicles, a process requiring the intervention of Ca^{2+}, which enters the secretory cell through the surface membrane. The secretory activities of many endocrine tissues are modulated by the action of hormones that arise in other tissues. The hypothalamus, for example, is the site of neurosecretory cells that secrete polypeptide hormones that are carried into the anterior pituitary gland by a system of portal vessels. There they stimulate (or inhibit) the secretion of other polypeptide hormones. The hormones of the anterior pituitary in turn stimulate secretion of hormones in various other endocrine tissues throughout the body. Feedback from the responses of target glands and other target tissues plays a major role in preventing runaway activity by endocrine tissues. Thus the secretion of a hormone becomes reduced when the secreting cells sense a signal associated with the increased activity of the target tissue.

The nervous system is intimately involved in the endocrine physiology of both vertebrates and invertebrates. This is especially evident in neurosecretory systems, made up of neurons that secrete hormones into the circulation. Both neural and nonneural endocrine secretions are important in the regulation of diverse kinetic, metabolic, and morphogenetic events.

EXERCISES

1. Give three examples of chemical regulation that do not involve hormones.

2. What criteria must be met before a tissue can be unequivocally identified as having an endocrine function?

3. Give one example each of negative and positive feedback control of hormone secretion.

4. Discuss the evidence that calcium plays an important role in hormone secretion.

5. Give two examples that illustrate the intimate functional association of the nervous and endocrine systems.

6. How do the glucocorticoids (also growth hormone and glucagon) combat hypoglycemia?

7. What role do the thyroid hormones play in mammalian thermoregulation?

8. How does insulin produce its hypoglycemic effects?

9. What factors influence secretion of growth hormone?

10. Compare the mechanisms and sites of action of aldosterone and ADH in the mammalian kidney.

11. Discuss the endocrine regulation of plasma calcium levels.

12. What biochemical reason would explain why the average man has larger muscles than the average woman?

13. Discuss the endocrine control of the menstrual cycle.

14. How is conception prevented by the use of birth control pills?

15. Give some examples of endocrine influence on animal behavior.

16. Discuss the role of juvenile hormone in the development and metamorphosis of an insect.

17. Explain how it can be that the actions of epinephrine and glucagon are similar but are specific to different tissues.

18. How does cAMP activate a protein kinase?

19. If cAMP is the "second messenger" in many different target tissues, how do you explain the multitude of specific and distinct responses?

20. Explain how a small number of hormone molecules can elicit responses involving millions of times as many molecules.

21. How can a working muscle mobilize glycogen stores without stimulation of glycogenolysis by epinephrine?

22. Discuss the interrelations between Ca^{2+} and cAMP levels within some cells.

SUGGESTED READING

Barrington, E. J. W. 1975. *An Introduction to General and Comparative Endocrinology* (2nd ed.). Clarendon Press, Oxford.

Catt, K. J. 1971. *An ABC of Endocrinology*. Little, Brown & Co., Boston.

Frieden, E. H. 1976. *Chemical Endocrinology*. Academic Press, New York.

Frieden, E., and H. Lipner 1971. *Biochemical Endocrinology of the Vertebrates*. Prentice-Hall, Englewood Cliffs, N.J.

O'Malley, B. W., and W. T. Schrader. 1976. The receptors of steroid hormones. *Scientific American* 234:32–43. W. H. Freeman and Company, San Francisco.

Sawin, C. T. 1969. *The Hormones*. Little, Brown & Co., Boston.

Tepperman, J. 1973. *Metabolic and Endocrine Physiology*. (3rd ed.). Year Book Medical Publishers, Inc., Chicago, Ill.

Turner, C. D., and J. T. Bagnara. 1976. *General Endocrinology*. Saunders, Philadelphia.

Weissman, G., and R. Claiborne (eds.) 1975. *Cell Membranes: Biochemistry, Cell Biology and Pathology*. Chapters 18, 19, 20. Hospital Practice Publishing Co., Inc., New York.

REFERENCES CITED

Anderson, L. L., J. D. Bast, and R. M. Melampy. 1973. Relaxin in ovarian tissue during different reproductive stages in the rat. *J. Endocrinology* 59:371–372.

Anderson, R. G. G. 1972. Cyclic AMP and calcium ions in mechanical and metabolic responses of smooth muscles. *Acta Physiol. Scand.* (Suppl.) 382.

Barrington, E. J. W. 1967. *Invertebrate Structure and Function*. Houghton Mifflin, Boston.

Beck, W. S. 1971. *Human Design*. Harcourt Brace Javonovich, New York.

Becker, H. D., D. D. Reeder, and J. C. Thompson. 1975. Vagal control of gastrin release. *In* J. C. Thompson (ed.), *Gastrointestinal Hormones: A Symposium.* Univ. Texas Press, Austin and London.

Beerman, W., and U. Clever. 1964. *Chromosome Puffs. Scientific American* 210(4):50–58.

Bell, G. H., J. N. Davidson, and H. Scarborough. 1972. *Textbook of Physiology and Biochemistry* (8th ed.). Churchill Livingstone, Edinburgh.

Berl, S., S. Puszkin, and W. J. Nicklas. 1973. Actomyosin-like protein in brain. *Science* 179:441–446.

Cooper, J. R., F. E. Bloom, and R. H. Roth. 1974. *The Biochemical Basis of Neuropharmacology.* Oxford Univ. Press, New York.

Douglas, W. W., J. Nagasawa, and R. Schulz. 1971. Electron microscopic studies on the mechanism of secretion of posterior pituitary hormones and significance of microvesicles ("synaptic vesicles"): Evidence of secretion by exocytosis and formation of microvesicles as a by-product of this process. *In* H. Heller and K. Lederis (eds.), *Mem. Soc. Endocrin. No. 19, Subcellular organization and function in endocrine tissues.* The Syndics of the Cambridge Univ. Press, New York.

Douglas, W. W. 1974. Mechanism of release of neurohypophysial hormones: Stimulus-secretion coupling. *In* R. O. Greep (ed.), *Handbook of Physiology.* Section 7. Endocrinology (Vol. IV, Part I, Pituitary Gland). American Physiological Society, Washington, D.C.

Farquhar, M. G. 1971. Processing of secretory products by cells of the anterior pituitary gland. *Mem. Soc. Endocrin.* 19:79–124.

Frieden, E. and H. Lipner. 1971. *Biochemical Endocrinology of the Vertebrates.* Prentice-Hall, Englewood Cliffs, N.J.

Frohman, L. A. 1975. Neurotransmitters as regulators of endocrine function. *Hospital Practice* 10:54–67.

Goldberg, N. D. 1975. Cyclic nucleotides and cell function. *In* G. Weissman and R. Claiborne (eds.), *Cell Membranes: Biochemistry, Cell Biology and Pathology.* Chapter 19. Hospital Practice Publishing Co., Inc., New York.

Iversen, L. L. 1974. Biochemical aspects of synaptic modulation. *In* F. O. Schmitt and F. G. Worden (eds.), *The Neurosciences: Third Study Program.* The Rockefeller Univ. Press, New York.

Jamieson, J. D. 1975. Membranes and Secretion. *In* G. Weissman and R. Claiborne (eds.), *Cell Membranes, Biochemistry, Cell Biology and Pathology.* Chapter 15. Hospital Practice Publishing Co., Inc. New York.

Jenkins, P. M. 1962. *Animal Hormones. I. Kinetic and Metabolic Hormones.* Pergamon Press, New York.

Kopeč, S. 1917. Experiments on metamorphosis in insects. *Bull. Acad. Sci. Cracovie.* 57–60.

Kopeč, S. 1922. Studies on the necessity of the brain for the inception of insect metamorphosis. *Biol. Bull.* 42:323–342.

Lacy, P. E. 1971. Microtubule-microfilament system in beta cell secretion. *In* S. Taylor (ed.), *Proceedings of the 3rd International Symposium on Endocrinology* (London).

McGiff, J. C. 1975. Prostaglandins as regulators of blood pressure. *Hospital Practice* 10:101-112.

McNaught, A. B., and R. Callander. 1975. *Illustrated Physiology.* Churchill Livingstone, New York.

Meyer, H. H. 1975. Release of secretin and cholecystokinin. *In* J. C. Thompson (ed.), *Gastrointestinal Hormones: A Symposium.* Univ. Texas Press, Austin and London.

Mikiten, T. M. 1967. Electrically stimulated release of vasopressin from rat neurohypophyses *in vitro* (Ph.D. thesis). Yeshiva University, New York.

Novak, V. J. A. 1975. *Insect Hormones.* Wiley, New York.

O'Malley, B. W., and W. T. Schrader. 1976. The receptors of steroid hormones. *Scientific American* 234(2):32–43.

Pharriss, B. B., S. A. Tillson, and R. R. Erickson. 1975. Prostaglandins in luteal function. *Rec. Prog. Horm. Res.* 28:51–89.

Prosser, C. L. (ed.). 1973. *Comparative Animal Physiology* (3rd ed.). Saunders, Philadelphia.

Rasmussen, H. 1970. Cell communication, calcium ions, and cyclic adenosine monophosphate. *Science* 170:404–412.

Rasmussen, H. 1975. Ions as "second messengers". *In* G. Weissman and R. Claiborne (eds.), *Cell Membranes, Biochemistry, Cell Biology, and Pathology.* Chapter 20. Hospital Practice Publishing Co., Inc., New York.

Rayford, P. L., H. R. Fender, N. I. Ramus, D. D. Reeder, and J. C. Thompson. 1975. Release and half-life of CCK in man. *In* J. C. Thompson (ed.), *Gastrointestinal Hormones: A Symposium.* Univ. Texas Press. Austin and London.

Robison, G. A., R. W. Butcher, and E. W. Sutherland (eds.). 1971. *Cyclic AMP.* Academic Press, New York.

Samuelsson, B. 1971. The synthetic and biological role of prostaglandins. *Biochem. Soc. Symp.* 35:101–102.

Sanger, F. 1960. The chemistry of insulin. *Brit. Medical Bull.* 16:183–188.

Scharrer, B. 1952. Neurosecretion. XI. The Effects of nerve section on the intercerebralis-cardiacum-allatum system of the insect *Leucophaea maderae. Biol. Bull.* 102:261–272.

Shaw, J. E., and S. A. Tillson. 1974. Interactions between the prostaglandins and steroid hormones. *In* M. H. Briggs and G. A. Christie (eds.), *Advances in Steroid Biochemistry and Pharmacology* (vol. 4). Academic Press, New York.

Sláma, K., M. Romaňuk, and F. Sorm. 1974. *Insect Hormones and BioAnalogues.* Springer-Verlag, New York.

Spratt, N. T., Jr. 1971. *Developmental Biology.* Wadsworth, Belmont, Calif.

Thompson, J. C., P. L. Rayford, N. I. Ramus, H. R. Fender, and H. V. Villar. 1975. Patterns of release and uptake of heterogeneous forms of gastrin. *In* J. C. Thompson (ed.), *Gastrointestinal Hormones: A Symposium.* Univ. Texas Press, Austin and London.

Tombes, A. S. 1970. *An Introduction to Invertebrate Endocrinology.* Academic Press, New York.

Villar, H. V., H. R. Fender, P. L. Rayford, N. I. Ramus, and J. C. Thompson. 1975. Inhibition of gastrin release and gastric secretion by GIP and VID. *In* J. C. Thompson (ed.), *Gastrointestinal Hormones: A Symposium.* Univ. Texas Press, Austin and London.

Villee, D. B. 1975. *Human Endocrinology: A Developmental Approach.* Saunders, Philadelphia.

Wigglesworth, V. B. 1970. *Insect Hormones.* W. H. Freeman and Company, San Francisco.

Wigglesworth, V. B. 1972. *The Principles of Insect Physiology.* Chapman & Hall, London.

Whitcomb, W. H. 1971. Erythropoietic inhibition in polycythemic plasma following transfusion or hypoxia. *In* J. W. Fisher (ed.), *Kidney Hormones.* Academic Press, New York.

Williams, C. M. 1947. Physiology of insect diapause. II. Interaction between the pupal brain and prothoracic glands in the metamorphosis of the giant silkworm *Platysamia cecropia. Biol. Bull.* 93:89–98.

CHAPTER TWELVE

Osmoregulation and Excretion

The unique physical and chemical properties of water have played a major role in the origin of living organisms, and water thus is indispensable for all biochemical and physiological processes. These properties of water, described in Chapter 2, made it possible for life as we know it to arise several billion years ago in a shallow, somewhat salty sea. Living cells to this day carry this aqueous heritage in their intracellular milieu, and, moreover, are generally dependent on the immediate presence of extracellular water, even if merely a very thin layer. The macromolecular machinery of living cells also requires certain inorganic molecules and ions, which play a variety of important roles in both the intra- and extracellular fluids (Table 12-1).

The ability to survive in an osmotically unfavorable environment was achieved in the more advanced animal groups by the evolution of a *stable internal environment,* which acts to buffer the internal tissues against the vagaries and extremes of the external environment (Fig. 12-1). One of the requirements in the regulation of the internal environment is that adequate quantities of water be retained. Another major requirement for cell survival is the presence, in appropriate concentrations, of various solutes, such as salts and nutrient molecules. Some cells require an ionic environment that is more or less an approximation of sea water—namely, fluid high in sodium and chloride and relatively low in the other major ions, such as potassium and the divalent cations (Tables 12-2, 12-3). For the simpler forms of marine invertebrates, this is easily accomplished, as the seawater itself acts as the extracellular medium; for some of the more complex forms, the internal fluids are in near ionic equilibrium with the sea water. In most multicellular animals, there are mechanisms for regulating (between broad or narrow limits) the concentration of extracellular solutes (Fig. 12-1). Finally, the cellular environment must be freed of toxic wastes that accumulate as byproducts of metabolism. In the simplest and smallest marine and aquatic organisms, this happens simply by diffusion into the surrounding water. In animals that have evolved circulatory systems, the blood typically passes through excretory organs, generally

Table 12-1. Major inorganic ions of tissues

Ion	Distribution	Some Functions
Na⁺	Main extracellular cation	Contributes major osmotic pressure of extracellular fluid
		Concentration gradient set up by Na pump provides potential energy for transport of substances across cell membrane
		Carries inward current for membrane excitation
K⁺	Main cytoplasmic cation	Contributes to osmotic pressure of cytoplasm
		Establishes the resting potential
		Activates some enzymes
		Carries outward current for membrane repolarization
Ca²⁺	Low concentration in cells	Stabilizes membranes
		Regulates muscle contraction
		Involved in "cementing" cells together
		Carries inward current in some excitable membranes (e.g., smooth and cardiac muscle)
		Regulates activity of many enzymes
		Regulates exocytosis
Mg²⁺	Intra- and extracellular	Stabilizes membranes
		Antagonist of Ca action in many functions
		Acts as cofactor for many enzymes (e.g., myosin ATPase)
PO_4^{3-} HCO_3^-	Intra- and extracellular	Buffers H⁺ concentration
Cl⁻	Main anion of tissues	Counterion for cations and positively charged groups of proteins

Table 12-2. Electrolyte composition of the human body fluids.

Electrolytes	Serum (meq/liter)	Interstitial fluid (meq/liter)	Intracellular fluid (muscle) (meq/kg H_2O)
CATIONS			
Na⁺	142	145	±10
K⁺	4	4	156
Ca²⁺	5		3.3
Mg²⁺	2		26
Totals	153	149	195
ANIONS			
Cl⁻	104	114	±2
HCO_3^-	27	31	±8
HPO_4^{2-}	2		95
SO_4^{2-}	1		20
Organic acids	6		
Protein	13		55
Totals	153	145	180+

Note: Some of the ions contained within cells are not all freely dissolved in the cytoplasm, but may also be sequestered within cytoplasmic organelles. Thus the true free calcium concentration in the cytoplasm is typically below 10^{-6} meq/kg H_2O rather than the overall value given in the table.

12-1. *Regulatory systems act as buffers between the external and internal environments of the more advanced groups of animals. The cells and tissues of these animals are protected from large fluctuations in the external environment, such as osmotic extremes, since the composition of the internal extracellular fluids is maintained within narrow limits.*

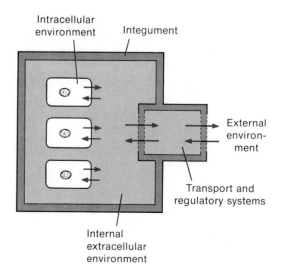

Table 12-3. Composition of extracellular fluids of nonmammalian vertebrates (concentrations in mM).

	Habitat*	Milliosmoles	[Na$^+$]	[K$^+$]	[Ca^{2+}]	[Mg^{2+}]	[Cl$^-$]	[SO$_4^{2-}$]	[HPO$_4^{2-}$]	Urea
SEAWATER		1000	459	9.8	10.1	52.5	538	26.6		
CYCLOSTOMATA										
Epatretus (hagfish)	SW	1002	554	6.8	8.8	23.4	532	1.7	2.1	3
Lampetra (lamprey)	FW	248	120	3.2	1.9	2.1	96	2.7	—	0.4
CHONDRICHTHYES										
Dogfish shark	SW	1075	269	4.3	3.2	1.1	258	1	1.1	376
Carchahrhinus (freshwater shark)	FW	—	200	8	3	2	180	0.5	4.0	132
TELEOSTEI										
Paralichthys (flounder)	SW	337	180	4	3	1	160	0.2	—	—
Carassius (goldfish)	FW	293	142	2	6	3	107	—	—	
AMPHIBIA										
Rana esculenta (frog)	FW	210	92	3	2.3	1.6	70	—	—	2
Scaphiopus (toad)	Ter.	456	184	4	—	—	122	—	—	148
	FW	305	159	5	—	—	102	—	—	39
Rana cancrivora (frog)	FW	290	125	9	—	—	98	—	—	40
	80% SW	830	252	14	—	—	227	—	—	350
REPTILIA										
Pelamis (sea snake)	SW	—	264	11			198	—	—	—
Alligator	FW	278	140	3.6	5.1	3.0	111	—	—	—
AVES										
Anas (duck)	SW	313	147	3.0	2.5		112	—	1.7	—
	FW	294	138	3.1	2.4		103	—	1.6	—
	Dehyd.	411	190	—	—		142	—	—	—
Zenaidura macroura (mourning dove)	FW	372	176	—	—		136	—	—	—

Source: B. M. Schmidt-Nielsen and W. C. Mackay, 1972, "Comparative physiology of electrolyte and water regulation, with emphasis on sodium, potassium, chloride, urea and osmotic pressure," in M. H. Maxwell and C. R. Kleeman (eds.), Clinical Disorders of Fluid and Electrolyte Metabolism, McGraw-Hill, New York.

*SW = seawater; FW = fresh water; Ter. = terrestrial.

termed kidneys, in which the removal of organic wastes is closely coordinated with the basic osmoregulatory functions of the organ.

The ability to maintain a suitable internal environment in the face of osmotic stress has played a most important role in animal evolution. There are two main reasons. First, animals are restricted in their geographic distribution by environmental factors, one of the most important being the osmotic nature of the environment. Second, geographic dispersal followed by genetic isolation is an important mechanism for the divergence of species in the process of evolution. If, for example, the arthropods and the vertebrates had not evolved means of regulating their extracellular compartments, they would have been far less successful in their invasion of the osmotically hostile freshwater and terrestrial environments. As a consequence, the number and diversity of arthropod and vertebrate species would now be limited largely to those found in the oceans and fresh waters of the world, which support far less than half the living species of animals. In the absence of terrestrial arthropods and vertebrates, other groups would have evolved with greater diversity to fill the vacant terrestrial niches.

Thus the animal groups that have been most successful in colonizing extreme osmotic environments have evolved means of regulating their water content and the concentration of solutes dissolved in their body water. There is always a difference between the optimal intracellular and extracellular concentrations of ions. A number of mechanisms are employed to handle those problems and reconcile the differences (a) between intracellular and extracellular compartments and (b) between the extracellular compartment and the external environment. These are collectively termed *osmoregulatory mechanisms,* a word coined in 1902 by Höber to refer to the regulation of osmotic pressure and ionic concentrations in the extracellular compartment of the animal body.

The evolution of efficient osmoregulatory mechanisms had extraordinarily far-reaching effects on other aspects of animal speciation and diversification. The various adaptations and physiological mechanisms evolved by animals to cope with the rigors of the osmotic environment form especially fascinating examples of the resourcefulness of evolutionary adaptation. This was the theme of an excellent book by the late Homer Smith entitled *From Fish to Philosopher.*

In this chapter, we will first consider the osmotic environment and the types of responses that various animals use to cope with environmental osmotic extremes. We will then go on to the mechanisms of osmoregulation, beginning first with the movement of water and solutes across multicellular epithelial layers and then go on to special organs of osmoregulation. Finally, we will consider the related problem of eliminating toxic nitrogenous wastes produced during the metabolism of proteins.

General Considerations

Although there may be hourly and daily variations in osmotic balance, an animal is generally in long term osmotic steady state. That is to say, on the average, the input-output balance sheet over an extended period sums up to zero (Fig. 12-2). Water enters with food and drink, and in a freshwater environment may enter through the integument. Water leaves the body in the urine, in the feces, and by evaporation through the integument and lungs.

The problem of osmotic regulation does not end with the intake and output of water. If that were so, osmoregulation would be a relatively simple matter: a frog sitting in fresh water far more dilute than its body fluids would merely have to eliminate the same amount of water as leaks in through its skin, and a camel would just stop urinating between oases. Osmoregulation also includes the requirement of maintaining favorable solute concentrations in the extracellular compartment. Thus the frog immersed in hypotonic (p. 24) pond water is also faced with the problem of retaining salts, which tend to be washed out as water is taken in and then lost or eliminated. The camel must compromise between conserving water and eliminat-

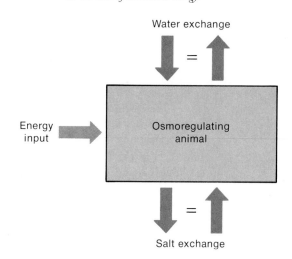

12-2. *In a strictly osmoregulating animal, the amounts of internal salt and water are held relatively constant in the face of environmental changes. This requires that intake and outflow of water and salts be equal over an extended period of time. Such osmotic homeostasis is maintained at the cost of metabolic energy.*

12-3. *Two major classes of osmotic exchange between an animal and its environment. Obligatory exchanges are those that occur in response to physical factors over which the animal has little short-term physiological control. Controlled exchanges are those that the animal can vary physiologically to maintain internal homeostasis. Substances entering the animal by either path can leave by the other path.*

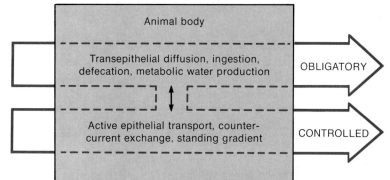

ing toxic end-products of metabolism, such as urea; it must regulate the salt concentrations of its extracellular fluids as it loses water through evaporation and through the production of urine.

The osmotic exchanges that take place between an animal and its environment can be divided into two classes (Fig. 12-3). First, there are *obligatory exchanges*—namely, those that occur mainly in response to physical factors over which the animal has little or no physiological control. Second, there are *regulated exchanges,* which, as the name indicates, are physiologically controlled and serve to aid in maintaining internal homeostasis. Regulation of osmotic exchange forms the major theme of this chapter. The various factors that contribute to the obligatory exchange have been reviewed by Bentley (1971); these are outlined below.

FACTORS INFLUENCING OBLIGATORY EXCHANGE

1. *Gradients between the extracellular compartment and the environment.* The greater the difference between the concentration of a substance in the external medium and in the body fluids, the greater the tendency for net diffusion in the direction of low concentration. Thus, although a frog immersed in a pond tends to take up water from its hypotonic environment, a bony fish in seawater is faced with the problem of losing water into the hypertonic sea water.

2. *Surface/volume ratio.* The volume of an animal varies with the cube of its linear dimensions, whereas its surface area varies with the square of its linear dimensions. That is, the surface/volume ratio is greater for small animals than for large animals. It follows that the surface area of the integument, through which water or a solute can exchange with the environment, is greater relative to the water content of a small animal than for a large animal. This means that for a given net rate of exchange across the integument ($mol/s/cm^2$), a small animal will desiccate (or hydrate) more rapidly than a larger animal of the same shape.

3. *Permeability of the integument.* The integument acts as a barrier between the extracellular compartment and the environment. The permeability of the integument to water and solutes varies with animal groups. Amphibians have moist, highly permeable skins, through which they exchange O_2 and CO_2 and through which water and ions move by passive diffusion. Amphibian skin compensates for loss of electrolytes by active transport of salts from the aquatic environment into the animal. Fish gills are necessarily permeable, since they engage in the exchange of O_2 and CO_2 between the blood and the aqueous environment. These also engage in active transport of salts.

4. *Feeding.* Water and solutes are taken in during feeding. The diet may include excess water or excess salts. A gull feeding on seashore invertebrates ingests a relatively high quantity of salt relative to water and must therefore have special means of excreting the excess salt. A freshwater fish or amphibian, on the other hand, ingests large quantities of water relative to salts, and requires special means of conserving salts.

5. *Temperature, exercise, and respiration.* Because of its high heat of vaporization (p. 15), water is ideally suited for the elimination of body heat by evaporation from epithelial surfaces. During evaporation, those water molecules with the highest energy content enter the gaseous phase and thus take with them their thermal energy. As a result, the water left behind becomes cooler. The importance of water in temperature regulation leads to conflicts and compromises between physiological adaptation to environmental temperatures and osmotic stresses in terrestrial animals. Desert animals, faced with both high temperatures and a meager water supply, are especially hard-pressed, since they must avoid becoming overheated and yet avoid losing large quantities of body water. Conversely, strenuous exercise generates high body temperatures due to muscle metabolism, and must be compensated by a high rate of heat dissipation. This can be accomplished best by evaporative cooling over respiratory surfaces, such as the lungs, air passages, and tongue, or by evaporative water loss through the skin. Even during basal conditions (no exercise beyond breathing), the nature of the respiratory mechanism of many terrestrial animals leads to the loss of water through the respiratory surfaces.

6. *Metabolic factors.* Those end products of metabolism that cannot be used by the organism must be eliminated. Carbon dioxide diffuses into the environment from the respiratory surfaces. Water, the other major end product of cellular respiration, is produced in small enough quantities so that its elimination is no problem. In fact, this so-called *metabolic water* must be conserved in some animals: it is the major source of water for many desert-dwellers. The kangaroo rat, for example, minimizes water loss by being nocturnal, and can therefore exist exclusively on dry seeds. Osmotic problems are posed by the production of nitrogenous end products of metabolism, such as ammonia, urea, and uric acid. Ammonia, which is rather toxic, is highly soluble, and therefore poses no problem for aquatic or marine invertebrates, from which it merely diffuses into the aqueous environment. Uric acid requires little water for its elimination, since it is relatively insoluble in water, and is therefore the preferred form of nitrogenous waste in certain terrestrial groups, such as lizards and birds.

OSMOREGULATORS AND OSMOCONFORMERS

Animals that maintain an internal osmolarity different from the medium in which they are immersed have been termed *osmoregulators.* This category includes all groups of vertebrates (Fig. 12-4) and some inverte-

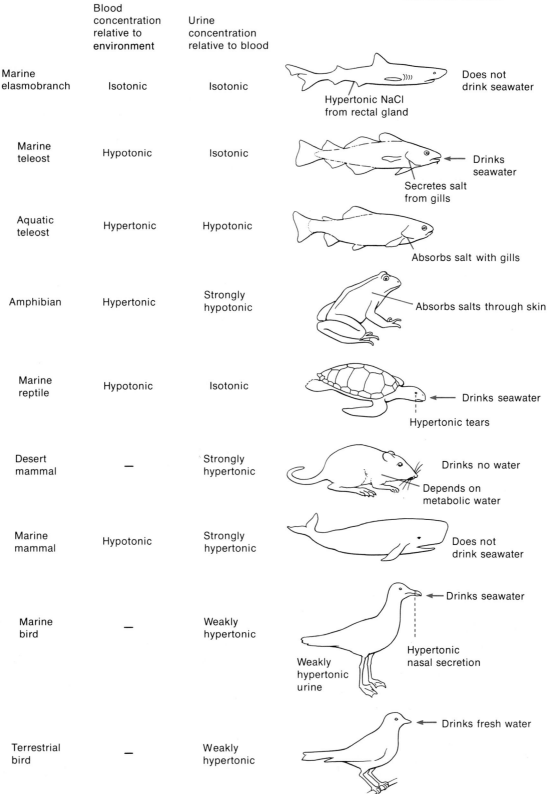

12-4. Exchange of water and salt in some vertebrates. Only active exchange is indicated; passive loss of water through skin, lungs, and alimentary tract are not indicated.

	Blood concentration relative to environment	Urine concentration relative to blood		
Marine elasmobranch	Isotonic	Isotonic		Does not drink seawater, Hypertonic NaCl from rectal gland
Marine teleost	Hypotonic	Isotonic		Drinks seawater, Secretes salt from gills
Aquatic teleost	Hypertonic	Hypotonic		Absorbs salt with gills
Amphibian	Hypertonic	Strongly hypotonic		Absorbs salts through skin
Marine reptile	Hypotonic	Isotonic		Drinks seawater, Hypertonic tears
Desert mammal	—	Strongly hypertonic		Drinks no water, Depends on metabolic water
Marine mammal	Hypotonic	Strongly hypertonic		Does not drink seawater
Marine bird	—	Weakly hypertonic		Drinks seawater, Hypertonic nasal secretion, Weakly hypertonic urine
Terrestrial bird	—	Weakly hypertonic		Drinks fresh water

12–5. Relation between the osmolarity of body fluids and that of the environment for three classes of brackish-water animals.

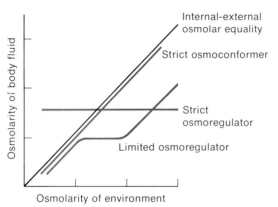

12–6. Two pathways, extracellular and transcellular, for passage of substances across on epithelial layer. Active transport takes place only across cell membranes, hence all actively transported molecules follow the transcellular pathway.

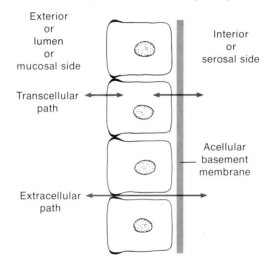

brates. An animal that does not actively control the osmotic condition of its body fluids and instead conforms to the osmolarity of the ambient medium is termed an *osmoconformer*. These categories represent two extremes of adaptation. Most vertebrates are strict osmoregulators, the composition of the body fluid being maintained within a small range of variation. Many terrestrial invertebrates, as well, osmoregulate to a large degree. Aquatic, brackish-water, and marine invertebrates are exposed to various concentrations of inorganic salts dissolved in the aqueous environment. Thus some are *strict osmoregulators,* some *limited osmoregulators,* and some strict *osmoconformers.* This is illustrated in Figure 12-5, in which the osmolarity (p. 23) of the extracellular compartment is plotted against the osmolarity of the aqueous environment.

As the osmolarity of the environment changes, the osmolarity of a strict osmoconformer changes by an equal amount, paralleling the line that shows internal-external osmolar equality. In contrast, a strict osmoregulator maintains a constant internal osmolarity, so as to produce a horizontal plot parallel with the abcissa. Limited osmoregulators are able to regulate over one range of osmolarities and conform over another range.

It is evident that there are two ways in which a species can handle large differences in environmental osmolarity. First, it may act as an osmoconformer and display a high degree of *cellular tolerance* to osmotic change. Second, it may act as an osmoregulator, and maintain strict extracellular osmotic homeostasis in the face of large external differences in salt concentration. In osmoregulating animals, the internal tissues are generally not able to cope with more than minor changes in extracellular osmolarity, and depend entirely on the osmotic regulation of the extracellular fluid. We do not understand why the cells of some animals can tolerate large osmotic variations while those of other animals have a more limited osmotic tolerance.

Epithelial Transport

The osmoregulatory activities of animals are carried out by a variety of specialized tissues and organs, some of which we will consider later in this chapter. Common to all of them is the transport of water and solutes across epithelia. These tissues have several features in common. First, they occur at surfaces that separate the internal space of the organism from the environment. This is not always evident, because the external space may extend in a tortuous way deep into the body, as in the lumen of the intestine. Second, the cells forming the outermost living layer of the epithelium are generally sealed together by tight junctions (p. 105), which to varying degrees in different epithelia obliterate extracellular passages between the *serosal* (inner) and *mucosal* (external) sides of the epithelium (Fig. 12-6). In some epithelia, such as the endothelium of capillary walls, the junctions are leaky. As a consequence, water and solute molecules can cross these epithelia by diffusing within the passages that exist between the epithelial cells. Since diffusion of material through extracellular passages is not coupled to any metabolically energized transport mechanism, such passages allow only passive diffusional movements of water and ions. Substances that are actively transported across an epithelium must follow *transcellular pathways* in which the cell membrane participates. Such substances must cross the cell membrane first on one side of the cell and then on the other side of the cell. As discussed below, the functional properties of the surface membrane of an epithelial cell are dissimilar in some respects on the serosal and mucosal surfaces of the cell. This asymmetry is important to epithelial active transport.

ACTIVE SALT TRANSPORT ACROSS EPITHELIA

Metabolically energized transport of ions from one side of an epithelium to the other side has been demonstrated in a number of epithelial tissues, including amphibian skin and urinary bladder, fish gills, insect and vertebrate intestine, vertebrate kidney tubule, and gall bladder. Much of the initial work on epithelial active transport was done on the skin of the frog. In amphibians, the skin acts as a major osmoregulatory organ. Salt is actively transported from the mucosal side (i.e., facing the pond water) to the serosal side of the skin to compensate for the osmotic flux of water from the hypotonic pond water into the frog. This water is subsequently eliminated in the form of a copious urine that is hypotonic relative to the extracellular fluid.

Frog skin was developed as a preparation for use in studying epithelial transport in the 1930's and 1940's by the German physiologist Ernst Huf and the Danish physiologist Hans Ussing. A piece of abdominal skin several square centimeters in area is removed from an anesthetized and decapitated frog and placed between two halves of an *Ussing chamber* (Fig. 12-7). The dissection is very simple, since the skin of the frog lies largely unattached over an extensive lymph space. Once it is gently clamped between two compartments of a chamber, a test solution—for example, frog Ringer (Table 12-4)—is introduced, with the frog skin acting as a partition between the two compartments. The compartment facing the mucosal side of the skin can be designated as the outside, and the one facing the serosal side can be designated as the inside compartment. Air is bubbled through the two solutions to keep them well oxygenated.

In 1947, Ussing reported the first experiments in which two isotopes of the same ion were used to measure bidirectional fluxes. The Ringer solution in the outside compartment was prepared with the isotope ^{22}Na$^+$ and the Ringer in the inside compartment was prepared with ^{24}Na$^+$ The appearance of each of the two isotopes on the opposite side of the skin was followed as a function of time. The two isotopes were switched around in other experiments of the same type to rule out any effects due to possible (but unlikely) differences in transport rates inherent in the isotopes themselves. In all experiments, it was found that Na$^+$ shows a net movement across the skin from the outside

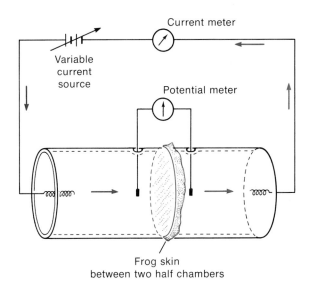

12-7. Ussing chamber. The frog skin separates the two half-chambers, each filled with Ringer's or other test solution. The current source is adjusted until the potential difference across the skin is zero. Under those conditions, the current flowing through the circuit (and thus through the skin) is equivalent to the rate of charge transferred by the active movement of sodium ions across the skin.

Current meter

Variable current source

Potential meter

Frog skin between two half chambers

to the inside compartments. That is to say, more ions move in that direction than in the opposite direction. The net movement of sodium ions is apparently the result of active transport, for it (1) occurs without any concentration gradient, even *against* an electrochemical gradient; (2) is inhibited by general metabolic inhibitors, such as cyanide and iodoacetic acid, and by specific transport inhibitors, such as ouabain; (3) displays a strong temperature dependence; (4) exhibits saturation kinetics; and (5) shows chemical specificity. For a review of active transport, the reader is referred back to Chapter 4.

The initial experiments of Ussing led to several important questions. For example, is the inward active transport of Na$^+$ independent of the transport of counterions? If so, can one demonstrate an electric current that corresponds to the net movement of charge carried by Na$^+$? How is transport carried out across a layer of cells? We will come back to these basic questions later.

The electrical correlates of active sodium transport were reported by Ussing and Zerahn in 1951. They reasoned that if Na$^+$ alone is actively transported across the epithelium, there should be quantitative agreement between the number of sodium ions transported across a unit area of skin per second and the strength of the resulting current (i.e. charges crossing the membrane per second). Under ordinary conditions,

Table 12-4. *Physiological salines (concentrations in mmoles/liter).*

	NaCl	KCl	CaCl$_2$	MgCl$_2$	NaHCO$_3$	Other Constituents
MARINE						
Artificial seawater	470	10.0	10.0	25.0	2.0	Buffer
Lobster	455	13.5	16.5	4.0	4.0	H$_3$BO$_3$ + NaOH buffer
Squid	475	10.3	10.6	53.1	25.7	Phosphate to pH 7.6
Dogfish	224	1.35	1.8	1.1	2.38	Glucose 15 Urea 333
FRESHWATER						
Artificial pond water	0.5	0.05	0.4		0.2	
Leech	115	4	1.8			Glucose 10 Tris buffer 10
Crayfish	207	5.4	13.6	2.64	2.4	
Freshwater Fish	101.8	3.38	1.36		2.5	MgSO$_4$ 1.19
Frog	112	1.9	1.1		2.4	Glucose 11.1 NaH$_2$PO$_4$ 0.7
TERRESTRIAL						
Cockroach	210	3.1	1.8			Phosphate buffer to pH 7.2
Lizard	116	3.2	1.2		2.0	NaH$_2$PO$_4$ 0.3 Glucose 1.7 MgSO$_4$ 1.4
Bird	117	2.33	5.8		28	MgSO$_4$ 2.12
Mammal Tyrode	138	2.7	1.84	1.06	11.9	NaH$_2$PO$_4$ 0.5
Mammal Krebs	119	5.0	2.5	1.0	2.5	NaH$_2$PO$_4$ 0.5 Glucose 11.0

Source: C. L. Prosser, 1973, *Comparative Animal Physiology* (vol. I), W. B. Saunders, Philadelphia.

12–8. *Active transport of Na$^+$ from the mucosal to the serosal side of the skin leaves the mucosal side with an excess of Cl$^-$, and hence a net negative charge, whereas the serosal side has a net positive charge. The result is that Cl$^-$ is drawn across the skin by the potential difference. In this way, both Na$^+$ and Cl$^-$ are transported across the skin even though the isolated skin actively transports only Na$^+$. Recent evidence indicates that in the intact frog, some of the chloride is also transported actively.*

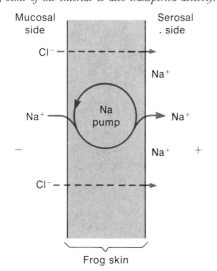

Frog skin

this comparison is hard to make, since the measured current would be reduced by the movement of Cl$^-$, which would tend to accompany Na$^+$. Such a passive movement of Cl$^-$ is expected if the active transport of Na$^+$ builds up a potential difference (i.e., voltage) across the skin. As soon as the inside chamber gains a few excess cations, that side would become more positive, and Cl$^-$ would be electrostatically drawn across the skin (Fig. 12-8). To avoid any electrochemical gradients, Ussing and Zerahn neutralized the charge difference, and hence the potential difference, by drawing off positive charges with an external electrical network at the same rate as they appeared across the skin (Fig. 12-7). The adjustment to zero potential difference accomplished two important things. First, Na$^+$ would not be hindered in its movement by the buildup of a potential that would counteract its net movement by active transport. Second, the current flowing through the external circuit (identical, of course, to the current flowing through the skin) could be compared to the net amount of sodium ions transported through the skin. If the current were in quantitative agreement with the net sodium transport measured by isotopic means, it could be concluded that only Na^+ is actively transported, for a simultaneous transport of Cl^- in the same direction would reduce the electric current proportionately. Obviously, if one chloride ion were transported for each Na^+ ion, the net electric current would be zero.

In these experiments, Ussing and Zerahn found a close agreement between the skin current and the isotopically measured sodium flux (Fig. 12-9). Both the current and the net transport of Na^+ are reduced or abolished by ouabain, the Na-pump inhibitor, by metabolic inhibitors, and by Na-free solutions in the external compartment. This provides further evidence that in the isolated frog skin, active sodium transport seems to predominate over that of any other active ion.

When the external short-circuiting current is removed, the frog skin quickly develops a potential difference due to the active transport of Na^+ to the serosal side. The potential difference between the two sides leads, in turn, to a passive inward movement of chloride down its electrochemical gradient (Fig. 12-8). Thus the active transport of Na^+ alone is sufficient to produce a net influx of NaCl. There is now evidence, however, that under more natural conditions (e.g., in the intact frog, with the external surface of the skin bathed in a dilute solution more closely approximating pond water), the skin also actively transports Cl^- in the same direction as Na^+.

The ability of the frog skin to generate an electric current by active sodium transport is illustrated by the fanciful prospect shown in Figure 12-10. In reality, the electrical work performed by the frog's skin probably serves no function other than to produce a passive uptake of Cl^- as described above, and to provide physiologists with a convenient means of monitoring Na transport in the isolated skin.

We can now turn to the problem of how a net movement of ions is produced across an epithelium. It will be recalled (Fig. 12-6) that adjacent cells of a transport epithelium are intimately tied together with tight junctions. Let us assume for the sake of simplicity that this eliminates all extracellular passageways for the diffusion of ions between the two sides of the epithelium (in reality, there are minute residual extracellular passages). This would force all substances that cross the epithelium to traverse the epithelial cell membrane twice, first traversing the membrane on one side of the cell and then leaving through the membrane on the other side. Active transport by this route rquires that the cell membrane of each epithelial cell be differentiated, so that the portion of the cell membrane facing the serosal side of the epithelium differs in functional properties from that portion of the membrane facing the mucosal side. Experiments on frog skin have provided several lines of evidence to support this hypothesis. For example:

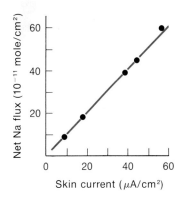

12–9. *Agreement between frog skin current and the net Na flux across a unit area of skin. Relating the current (Coulombs/s) to the flux (eq/s) through Faraday's constant (96,500 Coulombs/geq) shows a close agreement between the net transport of sodium and the skin current. The latter is therefore considered to be primarily a sodium current in the isolated frog skin.* [After Ussing, 1954.]

12–10. *A fanciful application of the electrical work done by the frog skin during the active transport of Na^+.* [After Lindley, 1970.]

1. Ouabain, which blocks the Na pump, inhibits transepithelial Na transport only when applied to the serosal side of the epithelium. It is ineffective on the mucosal side.

2. Potassium must be present in the solution on the serosal side for active sodium transport to take place, but is not required on the mucosal side.

12-11. *Profile of electric potential of the frog skin (or toad bladder) as recorded by a microelectrode passed slowly from the medium on the mucosal side through the epithelial layer (A) to the serosal medium (B). The solutions on the two sides of the skin are electrically isolated except through the skin. The cell interior is positive with respect to the mucosal medium and negative with respect to the serosal fluid. The composition of the two solutions is identical. [After Hoshiko, 1961.]*

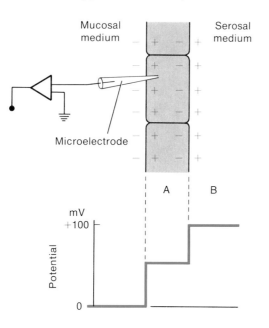

12-12. *Model devised by Koefoed-Johnsen and Ussing for transepithelial sodium transport in frog skin. Sodium diffuses passively down its concentration gradient into the cell from the mucosal solution. K⁺ diffuses out of the cell into the serosal space as it is displaced by Na influx. In the face of these leaks, a Na-K exchange pump in the serosal membrane of the cell maintains the high internal K⁺ and low internal Na⁺ concentrations. [Koefoed-Johnsen and Ussing, 1958.]*

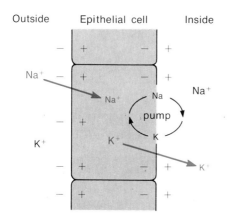

3. Measurements with microelectrodes show that the potential generated across the skin by sodium transport is the sum of two positive increases in potential recorded as an electrode is passed through the epithelial cell layer (Fig. 12-11). The first increase occurs upon penetration of the mucosal membrane, and the second occurs when the electrode tip has passed through the cell and emerges on the serosal side. This is consistent with an active transport of Na^+ out of the cell across the serosal surface membrane and with a passive leakage of Na^+ into the cell from the mucosal side to replenish the Na^+ pumped out into the extracellular fluid of the serosal side.

Such evidence led to the model of epithelial transport shown in Figure 12-12. According to this model, a Na–K exchange pump is located in the membrane of the serosal side of the epithelial cell. This membrane behaves in the manner typical of many cell membranes, pumping Na^+ out in exchange for K^+, thus maintaining a high intracellular potassium concentration and a low intracellular sodium concentration. The outward diffusion of potassium ions across the membrane on this side of the cell produces an inside negative resting potential (p. 123). The situation on the mucosal side is different. The cell membrane on this side of the cell is relatively impermeable to potassium. Moreover, sodium ions are not pumped out; instead, a net *inward* diffusion of sodium across this membrane (apparently facilitated by carriers in the membrane; p. 92) replaces the Na^+ pumped out of the cell on the serosal side. This model explains why Na-pump inhibitors exert an effect only from the serosal side of the epithelium, and why only changes in the concentration of K^+ on that side influence the rate of Na transport. Moreover, the net diffusion of sodium into the epithelial cell from the mucosal side explains why the cell interior is electrically positive relative to the extracellular medium on the mucosal side.

Thus there is a net flow of Na^+ across the frog skin from the mucosal side to the serosal side as a result of the functional asymmetries of the membranes on the two sides. The driving force is none other than the active transport of Na^+ that is common to the cells of all tissues.

The frog skin has served as a model system for the general problem of epithelial salt transport. Although details may differ from one type of epithelial tissue to another, the major features, listed below, are probably common to all transport epithelia.

1. To varying degrees, tight junctions obliterate extracellular passages. As a result, transport through epithelial cells assumes major importance in transepithelial fluxes of water and solutes.

2. Mucosal and serosal portions of the cell membranes exhibit functional differences, being asymmetrical in both pumping activity and membrane permeabilities.

3. The active transport of cations across the skin is accompanied by the passive diffusion of anions or by exchange for another cation, minimizing the buildup of electric potentials. The converse applies to actively transported anions.

4. Epithelia may actively transport more than one ion species. Thus the skins of certain species of frog actively transport Cl^- as well as Na^+. Active transport of chloride ion in these preparations appears to be more susceptible to the disturbance caused by isolating the frog skin than to the effect of sodium transport. This may explain the predominance of Na transport in isolated frog-skin preparations.

TRANSPORT OF WATER

A number of epithelia absorb or secrete fluids; for example, the stomach secretes gastric juice, the choroid plexus secretes cerebrospinal fluid, the gall bladder secretes bile fluid, and the kidney tubules of birds and mammals absorb water from the glomerular filtrate. In some of these tissues, water is transported across an epithelium in the absence of or against a gradient of water concentration. A number of possible explanations for uphill water transport have been given, but all these hypotheses can be placed in one of two major categories: (1) water is transported by a specific water-carrier mechanism driven by metabolic energy; (2) water is transported secondarily as the consequence of solute transport. The latter includes classical osmosis, in which water undergoes a net diffusion in one direction due to concentration gradients built up by solute transport, and electroosmosis, in which water moves through a membrane containing fixed charges when a potential difference exists across the membrane.

So far, there has been no convincing evidence to indicate that water is actively transported by a primary water-carrier pump, except, perhaps, in the rectum of certain insects (p. 426). The case for electroosmosis is equally unconvincing. For some time it also appeared as though classical osmosis could be ruled out, for it was found that some epithelia (e.g., intestinal lumen, gall bladder) can transport water from the side of low water concentration to the side of high water concentration.

The osmotic hypothesis of water transport received a boost when Peter Curran pointed out in 1965 that an osmotic gradient produced by active salt transport from one subcompartment of the epithelium into the other could, in theory, result in a net flow of water across the epithelium (Fig. 12-13). Biological correlates of Curran's model were subsequently found in the epithelium of mammalian gall bladder by Diamond and Tormey in 1966, which led to the *standing-gradient hypothesis* of *solute-coupled water transport* of Diamond and Bossert. A simplified schematic version is shown in Figure 12-14. Two anatomical features are of major importance: (1) the tight junctions near the luminal (mucosal) surface, which obliterate extracellular passages through the epithelium, and (2) the lateral intercellular spaces, or intercellular *clefts,* between adjacent cells. These clefts are closed at the luminal ends by the tight junctions and open at the basal ends.

The basis for the standing-gradient hypothesis is the active transport of salt across the portions of the epithelial cell membranes facing the intercellular clefts. It is suggested that as salt is transported out of the cell into these long, narrow clefts, a gradient will be set up such that the salt concentration will be highest near the luminal ends of the clefts, diminishing toward the open ends of the clefts, where it comes into equilibrium with the bulk phase bathing the serosal surface (Fig. 12-15,A). As a consequence of the high extracellular osmolarity in the clefts, water is osmotically drawn from within the cell across the cell membrane into the intercellular space. The water leaving the cell is replaced by water drawn osmotically into the cell at the mucosal surface. The water that enters the clefts gradually moves, together with solute, out into the bulk phase on the serosal side. In this way, the steady, active extrusion of salt by one surface membrane of the cell produces a standing concentration gradient in the narrow intercellular spaces. This results in a steady osmotic flow of water from the

12–13. Curran's model for solute-linked water transport. Solute (e.g., Na^+) is pumped by barrier A *from compartment 1 to compartment 2. Semibarrier* B *slows diffusion of solute into compartment 3 and thereby keeps the osmolarity high in 2. The rise in osmolarity in compartment 2 causes water to be drawn from 1 into 2. In the steady state, both water and solutes diffuse into compartment 3 at the same rate at which they appear in 2. [After Curran, 1965.]*

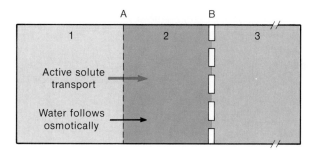

12–14. *The biological counterpart of Curran's 3-compartment model for solute-coupled water transport. The compartments corresponding to those in Figure 12-13 are numbered 1, 2, and 3. Salt transported actively into the intercellular clefts produces a high osmolarity within the clefts. Water flows osmotically into the clefts across the cell, and the bulk solution flows through the freely permeable basement membrane and into the bulk fluid of the interstitium. A and B label the barriers analogous to A and B in Figure 12-13. [After Diamond and Tormey, 1966a.]*

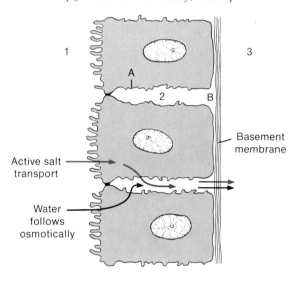

1   3

A

2   B

Basement membrane

Active salt transport

Water follows osmotically

mucosal to the serosal side. This solute-coupled water transport can take the opposite direction if there is active salt transport in the opposite direction (Fig. 12-15,B).

The general applicability of the standing-gradient mechanism of solute-coupled water transport is supported by ultrastructural studies showing that the necessary cellular geometry—namely, narrow intercellular spaces closed off at the luminal end by tight junctions—is present in all the water-transporting epithelia that have been examined. In epithelia fixed during conditions that produce water transport, these spaces are dilated; in epithelia fixed in the absence of water transport, the intercellular clefts are largely obliterated. Solute-linked water transport has been implicated as the mode of uphill water transport in several epithelia (Fig. 12-16).

12–16. *Solute-linked water transport under three conditions. A. No osmotic gradient. B. Gradient in the direction of increasing osmolarity. C. Gradient in the direction of higher water concentration (i.e., decreasing osmolarity). The numbers indicate osmolarity. [After Schmidt-Nielsen, 1971.]*

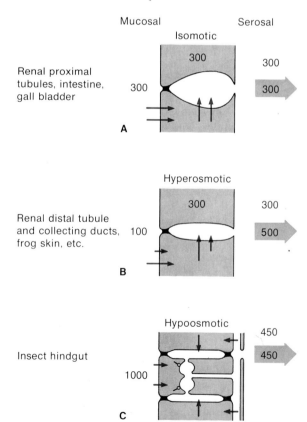

Mucosal   Serosal

Isomotic

Renal proximal tubules, intestine, gall bladder

300

300   300

A

Hyperosmotic

Renal distal tubule and collecting ducts, frog skin, etc.

300   300

100   500

B

Hypoosmotic

Insect hindgut

450

1000   450

C

12–15. *The standing-gradient flow system operating in "forward" and "backward" directions. The direction of water flow depends on the direction of salt pumping. The density of the dots shows the relative osmolarity. [After Diamond, 1971.]*

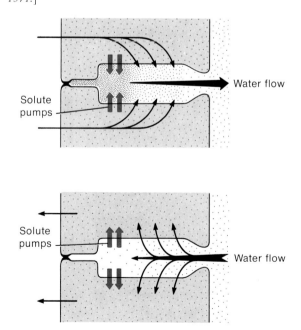

Solute pumps

Water flow

Solute pumps

Water flow

Osmoregulatory Organs

Transport epithelia, such as frog skin and mammalian gall bladder (discussed above), incorporate the basic cellular mechanisms of all excretory or osmoregulatory organs. The capabilities of transport epithelia are greatly enhanced in many osmoregulatory organs by anatomical specialization and differentiation. This is exquisitely evident in the kidneys of higher vertebrates. Here, in addition to a high degree of cellular differentiation for transepithelial transport, there is the added dimension of "plumbing"; that is, the epithelium is organized into tubules that are anatomically arranged so as to enhance the transport capabilities of the tubular epithelium. This combination of cell function and tissue organization has produced a marvelously efficient osmoregulatory and excretory organ. We will now examine the mammalian kidney in some detail before going on to consider briefly the osmoregulatory organs of some other animals.

The Vertebrate Kidney

To speak of the vertebrate kidney would be misleading unless we note that it is organized somewhat differently in different groups of vertebrates. This can best be done after we first consider the mammalian kidney. The mammalian kidney performs certain functions that in lower vertebrates are shared by such organs as the skin and bladder of amphibians, the gills of fishes, and the salt glands of reptiles and birds. It is also the osmoregulatory organ of which we have the most complete understanding, thanks to intensive research over the past four decades.

ANATOMY

The gross anatomy of the mammalian kidney is shown in Figure 12-17. The organs are in pairs, one located on each side against the dorsal inner surface of the lower back, outside the peritoneum. In view of their small size (about 1% of total body weight in humans), they receive a remarkably large amount of blood, carrying about 20-25 percent of the total cardiac output. Surrounding the hollow *pelvis* is the *medulla,* which sends *papillae* projecting into the pelvis. The outer functional layer, termed the *cortex,* is covered by a tough *capsule* of connective tissue. The pelvis gives rise to the *ureters,* tubes that empty into the *urinary bladder.* The urine leaves the bladder during *micturition* (urination) via the *urethra,* which leads to the end of the penis in males and into the vulva in females. The formation of *urine* is completed as it reaches the pelvic cavity of the kidney. The urine is then carried to the

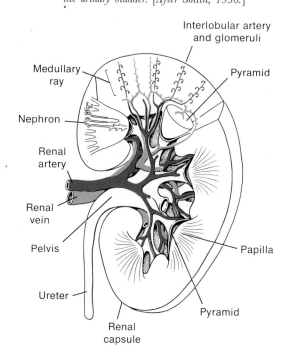

12-17. *Anatomy of the mammalian kidney. The nephrons (see next figure) are arranged in parallel, with their collecting ducts opening through the papillae into a central cavity termed the renal pelvis. The urine passes from the pelvis into the ureter, which takes it to the urinary bladder. [After Smith, 1956.]*

bladder and expelled without further modification. For this reason, the portions of the urinary tract below the kidney might be considered mere plumbing. Fortunately, this plumbing is equipped to allow occasional release of stored urine rather than a continual dribble. This is accomplished by the neural control of a skeletal muscle sphincter around the opening of the bladder, which leads into the urethra. As the bladder wall is stretched by gradual filling of the bladder, stretch receptors in the wall of the bladder generate nerve impulses that are carried by sensing neurons to the spinal cord and brain, producing the associated sensation. The sphincter can then be relaxed by cessation of motor impulses, allowing the smooth muscle of the bladder wall to contract under autonomic control and empty the contents.

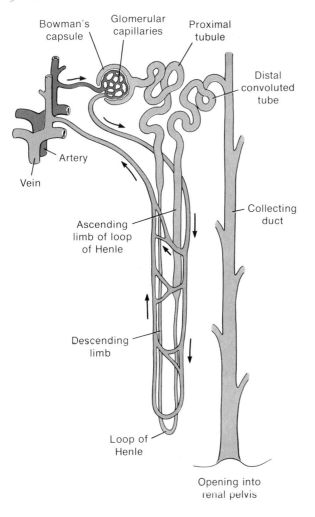

12–18. *The unit of kidney function, the nephron, with its blood supply. The renal tubule and collecting duct are shown in gray, the vascular elements in color. The blood first passes through the capillaries of the glomerulus and then flows through the hairpin loops of the vasa recta, which plunges deep into the medulla of the kidney along with the loop of Henle.*

Bowman's capsule
Glomerular capillaries
Proximal tubule
Distal convoluted tube
Artery
Vein
Collecting duct
Ascending limb of loop of Henle
Descending limb
Loop of Henle
Opening into renal pelvis

The functional unit of the mammalian kidney is the *nephron* (Fig. 12-18), an intricate epithelial tube that is closed at one end and that opens into the renal pelvis through collecting ducts at the other end. At the closed end, the nephron is expanded—somewhat like a balloon that has been pushed in from one end toward its neck—to form the cup-shaped *Bowman's capsule*. The lumen of the capsule is continuous with the narrow lumen that extends through the *renal tubule*. Associated with the capsule is the tuft of capillaries that forms the *glomerulus* inside Bowman's capsule. This remarkable structure is responsible for the first step in urine formation. A *filtrate* of the blood passes through the single-cell layer of the capillary walls, through a basement membrane, and finally through another single-cell layer of epithelium that forms the wall of Bowman's capsule. The filtrate accumulates in the lumen of the capsule to begin its trip through the various segments of the renal tubule, finally descending the *collecting duct* into the renal pelvis. The wall of the renal tubule is one cell layer thick; this epithelium separates the lumen, which contains the urinary filtrate, from the interstitial fluid. In some portions of the nephron, these epithelial cells are morphologically specialized for transport, bearing a dense pile of *microvilli* on their luminal surfaces (Fig. 12-19). The epithelial cells are tied together by tight junctions, which restrict extracellular diffusion between the lumen and interstitial space surrounding the renal tubule.

Several regions of the nephron can be distinguished on morphological or functional grounds. One is Bowman's capsule, already noted above. Others are the *proximal convoluted tubule,* which merges with a long narrow portion that forms the hairpin-like *loop of Henle.* This, in turn, consists of a *descending limb* and an *ascending limb.* The latter merges into the *distal convoluted tubule,* which finally joins a collecting duct serving several tubules. The number of nephrons per kidney

12–19. *Diagram of a proximal tubular cell. The surface membrane facing the lumen of the proximal tubule of the nephron is thrown into finger-like projections termed microvilli, greatly increasing its surface area. Mitochondria are concentrated near the serosal surface.* [*After Rhodin, 1954.*]

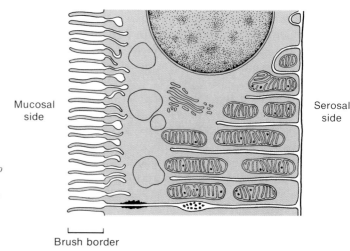

Mucosal side

Serosal side

Brush border

varies from several hundred in lower vertebrates to many thousands in small mammals, and a million or more in humans and other large species.

Before continuing, we might make several observations about the loop of Henle. This feature is known only in birds and mammals and is believed to be of central importance in concentrating the urine. Vertebrates that lack the loop of Henle are incapable of producing a urine that is hyperosmotic relative to the blood. In mammals, the nephron is so oriented that the loop of Henle and the collecting duct lie parallel to each other and in a radial orientation in the kidney. The glomeruli are found in the renal cortex, and the loops of Henle reach down into the papillae of the medulla.

The anatomy of the renal circulatory system also appears to be important in the function of the nephron. The vascular plumbing leading to the capillaries of the glomerulus is designed for maximum pressure difference between inflowing and outflowing blood. As we will see below, this aids in the filtration of plasma into the lumen of Bowman's capsule. The pressure in an artery drops linearly with distance, assuming constant diameter. It is significant that the glomerulus and the artery that supplies it are connected by a very short length of arteriole, minimizing the pressure drop (Fig. 12-18). The capillary tuft then recombines to form a second segment of arteriole. This is unusual, for in most other tissues the capillaries empty into venules, which in turn merge into veins. The blood, upon leaving the glomerulus, located in the renal cortex, enters the second arteriole and is carried into the medulla in a descending and subsequently ascending loop of anastomosing (interconnecting) capillaries before leaving the kidney via a vein. We will return later to the functional significance of this circulatory loop, which lies in parallel with the loop of Henle.

AN OVERVIEW OF URINE FORMATION

The initial stage of urine formation is the filtration of plasma* and the accumulation of the ultrafiltrate in the lumen of Bowman's capsule. The glomerular filtrate contains essentially all the constituents of the blood except for the blood cells and proteins. Filtration in the glomerulus is so extensive that 15–25% of the water and solutes are removed from the plasma that flows through it. The glomerular filtrate is produced at the rate of 125 ml/min, or about 200 liters/day, in human kidneys. When this number is compared to the normal intake of water, it is evident that unless most

of the glomerular filtrate is subsequently resorbed into the bloodstream, the body would be quickly dehydrated. *Resorption* is one of the important functions of the nephron. As we will see later, 99% of the water, and nearly as large a proportion of the salts, is resorbed before formation of the urine is completed. Some substances, however, appear in the urine in concentrations higher than can be accounted for by the rate of plasma filtration, which means that those substances are *secreted* into the lumen of the nephron during formation of the urine.

It is apparent, then, that there are three processes that contribute to the ultimate composition of the urine (Fig. 12-20):

1. *Glomerular filtration* of water and nonprotein solutes (crystalloids, such as Na$^+$, K$^+$, Cl$^-$, glucose, and urea) in approximately the proportions in which they occur in the plasma. This has been determined by direct sampling of the glomerular filtrate by micropuncture and removal (Fig. 12-21). With the exception

12-20. *The three processes involved in urine formation in the glomerular nephron. Filtration, the initial step, takes place in Bowman's capsule. Absorption and secretion take place along the renal tubule. The final product of these three processes is the urine.*

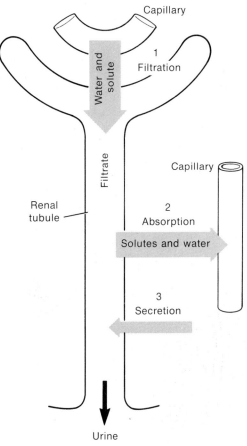

---

*Plasma is the fluid portion of the blood that remains when the various blood cells are removed.

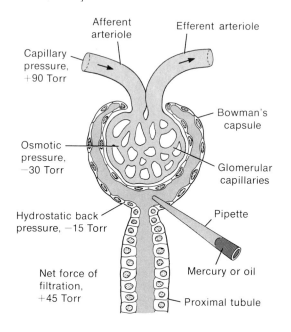

that blood cells and large proteins are excluded, the process of glomerular filtration is completely nonselective and based entirely on molecular size (Table 12-5).

2. *Tubular resorption* of approximately 99 percent of the water and most of the salts. The resorption is somewhat selective, resulting in the concentration (relative to water and salt) of waste products such as urea.

3. *Tubular secretion* of a number of substances. This is relatively selective and is responsible for the regulation of blood concentrations of H^+ and the pH buffer bicarbonate as well as the elimination of foreign substances, such as drugs.

Thus the kidney may be considered a "black box" in which the final concentration of any substance in the urine is a function of one, two, or all three of these processes. This is best illustrated by some simple quantitative comparisons of the amounts of various substances appearing in the urine and the amounts of those substances appearing in the glomerular filtrate in Bowman's capsule.

Renal clearance is defined as the volume of plasma that contains a quantity of filtered substance equal to the amount that appears in a unit of time in the glomerular filtrate. The total renal clearance is the quantity of ultrafiltrate in milliliters produced by the kidney in one minute. A substance that is freely filtered along with water into the nephron, but which

Table 12-5. *Relation between molecular size and the ratio of the concentration of the substance in the filtrate appearing in Bowman's capsule to its concentration in the plasma, [filtrate]/[filtrand].*

Substance	Mol. wt. (g)	Dimensions in Angstrom units		[filtrate] / [filtrand]
		Radius from Diffusion Coefficient	Dimensions from X-Ray Diffraction	
Water	18	1.0		1.0
Urea	60	1.6		1.0
Glucose	180	3.6		1.0
Sucrose	342	4.4		1.0
Insulin	5,500	14.8		0.98
Myoglobin	17,000	19.5	⊢54⊣ ⥮8	0.75
Egg albumin	43,500	28.5	⊢88⊣ ⥮22	0.22
Hemoglobin	68,000	32.5	⊢54⊣ ⥮32	0.03
Serum albumin	69,000	35.5	⊢150⊣ ⥮36	<0.01

Source: R. F. Pitts, *Physiology of the Kidney and Body Fluids,* Year Book Medical Publ., Chicago, 1968.

BOX 12-1   RENAL CLEARANCE

A substance that passes freely from the blood into Bowman's capsule during formation of the glomerular filtrate, and subsequently is neither secreted nor resorbed by the renal tubule, can be very useful in renal physiology because it exhibits a renal clearance equal to the glomerular filtration rate. Thus inulin, a substance that has been found to meet these criteria, has been used routinely to determine the glomerular filtration rate of intact kidneys. In such studies, the substance is first injected into the subject's circulation and allowed to mix to uniform concentration in the blood stream. A sample of blood is removed, and the plasma inulin concentration, P, is determined from the sample. The rate of appearance of inulin in the urine is determined by multiplying the concentration, U, of inulin in the urine by the volume of urine, V, produced per minute. The amount of inulin appearing in the urine per minute (VU) must equal the rate of plasma filtration (GFR) multiplied by the plasma concentration of inulin, P:

$$\frac{VU}{(\text{GFR})P} = \frac{\text{amt. inulin appearing in urine/min}}{\text{amt. inulin removed from blood/min}} = 1.$$

In this special case, the substance in question, inulin, is freely filtered and unchanged by tubular absorption or secretion. Therefore, the GFR and the clearance, C, of the substance are equal. Substituting C for GFR gives, for inulin,

$$\frac{VU}{CP} = 1.$$

Therefore,

$$\frac{VU}{P} = C = \text{plasma clearance (ml/min).}$$

If the amount of substance x appearing in the urine per minute deviates from the amount of x present in the volume of plasma that is filtered per minute, this will be reflected in a value of C_x that differs from that of the inulin plasma clearance C. For example, if the inulin clearance of a subject, and hence the GFR, is 125 ml/min and substance x exhibits a clearance of 62.5 ml/min,

$$\frac{VU_x}{P_x} = C_x = 62.5 \text{ ml/min}$$
$$= 0.5(\text{GFR}).$$

In this case, a volume of plasma *equivalent* to half that filtered each minute is cleared of substance x. Stated differently, only half the amount of substance x present in a volume of blood plasma equal to the volume filtered each minute actually appears in the urine per minute. There are two possible reasons why the plasma clearance for a substance would be less than the glomerular filtration rate. First, it may not be freely filterable: it may be hindered in the filtration process by binding to serum proteins, by its large molecular size, which would interfere with filtration, or some other factor. Second, it may be freely filtered, but the amount of x that appears in the urine might be reduced by tubular resorption. As a matter of fact, most molecules below a molecular weight of about 100 are freely filtered (Table 12-5). Many of these are either partially resorbed or partially secreted, and the extent of resorption or secretion can be gauged by the plasma clearance of a substance. Resorption reduces the plasma clearance to below the glomerular filtration rate. Tubular secretion, however, will cause more of a substance to appear in the urine than is carried into the tubule by glomerular filtration.

is neither resorbed nor secreted, permits the calculation of total renal clearance merely by dividing the amount of the nontransported substance appearing in the urine by the concentration of that substance in the plasma. One such molecule is inulin (*not* insulin), a small starchlike carbohydrate (mol. wt. 500). Since the inulin molecule is neither resorbed nor secreted by the renal tubule, the *inulin clearance* is identical with the rate at which the glomerular filtrate is produced, the *glomerular filtration rate* (GFR), generally given in milliliters per minute. Having determined the GFR, and knowing the concentration of a substance in the plasma (thus also its concentration in the ultrafiltrate), it is easy to calculate whether it undergoes a net resorption or net secretion during the passage of the ultrafiltrate along the renal tubule (Box 12-1). Thus, if less of a substance appears in the urine than was filtered in the glomerulus, it must have undergone some resorption in the tubule. This is true for water, NaCl, glucose, and many other essential constituents of the blood. If, however, the quantity of a substance appearing in the urine over a period of time is greater than the amount that passed into the nephron because of glomerular filtration, it can be concluded that this substance is actively secreted into the lumen of the tubule. The *clearance technique* is of limited usefulness in studies of renal function, since it indicates only the *net* output of the kidney relative to input, and fails to provide insight into the physiological details. Nevertheless, it is useful clinically, and it indicates that some substances are resorbed while others are secreted. It does not indicate if a substance is both resorbed and secreted by different portions of the nephron, as is true for potassium ions.

Glucose clearance offers a simple example of a clinical application. A healthy mammal exhibits a plasma glucose clearance of zero ml/min. That is to say, even though the glucose molecule is small and is freely filtered by the glomerulus, it is completely resorbed (up to certain concentrations) by the epithelium of the renal tubule. The appearance of glucose in the urine is usually due to its presence in excessive concentration in the blood plasma. In diabetes mellitus, appearance of glucose in the urine is due to saturation of carriers responsible for glucose transport in the epithelial cells of the tubular epithelium. Examination of Figure 12-22 reveals that there is a maximum rate (mg/min) at which glucose can be removed from the tubular urine by resorption. This *transfer maximum*, or TM, is about 375 mg/min in humans. Below plasma glucose levels of 200 mg % all the glucose appearing in the glomerular filtrate is resorbed. At about 400 mg %, the carrier mechanism is fully saturated, so that any additional amount of glucose appearing in the filtrate will be passed out in the urine. The arterial plasma glucose concentration in humans

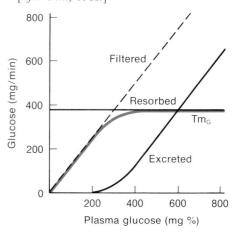

12-22. *Relation of urine glucose to blood glucose levels. The concentration of glucose in the glomerular filtrate (broken line) is proportional to the plasma glucose concentration. The renal tubules are capable of resorbing the glucose by active transport at rates up to 375 mg/min (Tm_G). Glucose entering the filtrate in excess of this rate is necessarily excreted in the urine.* [*After Pitts, 1968.*]

is normally held at about 100 mg % by an endocrine feedback loop involving insulin. Since this is well below the TM for glucose, normal urine contains essentially no glucose.

GLOMERULAR FILTRATION

The process of ultrafiltration in the glomerulus (Fig. 12-21) depends on two factors: (1) a pressure gradient from the lumen of the capillary to the lumen of Bowman's capsule, and (2) the sieve-like properties of the three-layered tissue separating these two compartments. The pressure gradient results from the sum of the hydrostatic pressure difference between the two compartments and the osmotic pressure difference. The latter arises because of the separation of proteins during the filtration process. In humans, the proteins remaining in the capillary plasma produce an osmotic pressure difference of about −30 Torr (mm Hg), and the hydrostatic pressure difference (capillary blood pressure minus intracapsular back pressure in the renal tubule) is about +75 Torr (Table 12-6). The result is a net filtration pressure of about +45 Torr. It is this pressure acting on the high water and crystalloid permeability of the glomerular ultrasieve (about 100 times higher than the permeability of systemic capillaries) that produces the phenomenal rate of filtrate formation by the millions of glomeruli in each human kidney of 125 ml/min, or 200 liters/ day. It is important to note that the filtration process in the kidney is entirely passive, deriving its energy from the hydrostatic pressure of the blood, which is maintained by the contractions of the heart.

The kidneys are perfused by 500–600 ml of plasma per minute, or 20–25% of the cardiac output, yet constitute less than 1% of the body weight. This preferential perfusion takes place in a relatively low-resistance vascular bed within the kidney. A high renal blood pressure is the result of the relatively direct arterial supply; since arteries and arterioles are large in diameter and short in length, the loss of pressure due to friction is minimized. The efferent arterioles (those taking the blood away from the glomeruli) are of smaller diameter, providing greater resistance and hence maintaining a higher pressure within the glomeruli.

The control of the glomerular filtration rate is not entirely clear. Since the amount of salt and water passing into Bowman's capsule is more than 100 times greater than the amount appearing in the urine, large changes in GFR could result in the disruption of salt and water balance, or would at least require heroic corrective action by mechanisms of resorption and secretion. In the human kidney, the renal blood flow remains quite constant in spite of large changes in systemic blood pressure. This, of course, aids in maintaining a constant glomerular filtration rate. The GFR, moreover, can also remain quite constant in the face of altered renal blood flow.

The kidneys receive a nerve supply from the sympathetic system (p. 159), which innervates the *juxtaglomerular apparatus* (*JGA*), shown in Figure 12-23. The JGA consists of specialized cells in closely apposed segments of the *afferent arteriole* and the distal segment of the renal tubule. Activation of these nerves is thought to induce the release of a proteolytic enzyme, *renin*, from certain cells of the JGA located primarily in the wall of the afferent arteriole which carries blood into the glomerular capillaries in Bowman's capsule. Renin is also liberated from those cells in response to local stimuli such as distension of the arteriolar walls due to increased blood pressure, and a rise in the sodium concentration of the pre-urine inside the distal tubule of the nephron. The salt concentration is believed to be sensed by cells in the tubular wall which are in close communication with the renin secreting cells of the arteriole. As indicated in Figure 12-23, renin released into the arteriole acts on a glycoprotein molecule that is manufactured in the liver and is present in the plasma, *α-2-globulin*. Renin cleaves a leucine-leucine bond in the globulin molecule, releasing a 10-residue peptide, *angiotensin I*. A *converting enzyme* then removes two additional amino acids to form the 8-residue peptide *angiotensin II*. This hormone has several actions, among them to stimulate the secretion of the steroid hormone *aldosterone* (p. 360) from the adrenal cortex, and to cause general and probably also local specific vasoconstriction (constriction of arterioles). The manner in which the renin-

Table 12-6. Balance sheet of pressures (in torr) involved in glomerular ultrafiltration as illustrated in Figure 12-21.

	Salamander	Man
Glomerular capillary pressure	17.7	90
Intracapsular pressure	−1.5	−15
Net hydrostatic pressure	16.2	75
Osmotic pressure	−10.4	−30
Net filtration pressure	5.8	45

Source: R. F. Pitts, *Physiology of the Kidney and Body Fluids,* Year Book Medical Publ., Chicago, 1968.

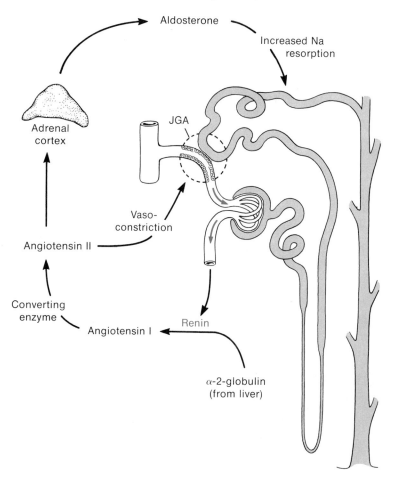

12-23. The renin-angiotensin feedback loops. The juxtaglomerular apparatus consists of renin-secreting cells located primarily in the smooth muscle layer of the wall of the afferent arteriole and of osmotically sensitive cells in the closely apposed wall of the distal segment of the renal tubule. Renin, liberated by such stimuli as arteriolar constriction due to decreased pressure in the vessel and to low salt concentration in the tubule, leads to an increase in the titre of angiotensin II and aldosterone. Angiotensin II causes general and local constriction of arterioles. Aldosterone stimulates salt transport out of the renal tubule.

12-24. The stopped-flow microperfusion technique.
A. A micropipette is inserted into Bowman's
capsule (left), and oil is injected until it
enters the proximal tubule.   B. Perfusion fluid
is injected through a second pipette into the
middle of the column of oil, forcing a droplet
ahead of it.   C. The tubule is full when the
droplet reaches the far end of the tubule.
D. After about 20 min, the fluid is collected
for microanalysis by the injection of a second
liquid behind the oil remaining near the
glomerulus. [After "Pumps in the Living
Cell" by Arthur K. Solomon. Copyright
© 1962 by Scientific American, Inc. All
rights reserved.]

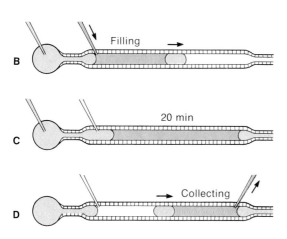

12-25. Perfusion of a cannulated segment of renal
tubule. The perfusate is subjected to chemical
and radiotracer analysis to determine the fluxes
of ions across the tubular wall.

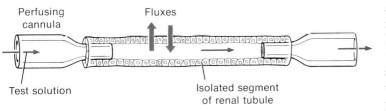

angiotensin system regulates local blood pressure within the kidney remains uncertain.

Aldosterone has a powerful stimulating effect on the active transport of NaCl from the lumen to the interstitial space across the wall of the renal tubule. Thus one ultimate effect of renin secretion into the afferent arteriole is an increased recovery of NaCl from the glomerular filtrate. This has the obvious regulatory effect of compensating for increased loss of NaCl into the glomerular filtrate when increased

pressure in the afferent arteriole produces an increased rate of glomerular filtration (recall that renin is released in response to distention of the arteriolar wall).

The stimulation of renin secretion in response to increased intratubular NaCl concentration also has a regulatory effect. If for some reason the tubular salt concentration becomes abnormally high, the stimulated secretion of renin will increase NaCl recovery via the angiotensin-aldosterone pathway.

TUBULAR RESORPTION

Glomerular filtration is only the first step in urine formation; as the filtrate makes its way through the nephron, its original composition is quickly modified. The human kidneys produce about 200 liters of filtrate per day, but the final volume of urine is only about $1\frac{1}{2}$ liters. Of the 1800 g of NaCl in the original filtrate only 10g appears in the urine. Essentially all of the glucose filtered is resorbed (Fig. 12-22), but varying amounts of other filtered solutes are resorbed from the tubular lumen or secreted into the lumen.

The details of tubular function vary from species to species. Our knowledge of the changes in urinary composition along different portions of the nephron is based to a large extent on the technique of micropuncture, first developed by Alfred Richards and his co-workers in the 1930's. A glass capillary micropipette is used to remove a minute sample of the tubular fluid from the lumen of the nephron. The osmolarity of the sample is then determined by measuring its freezing point. The lower the freezing point, the higher its osmolarity (p. 22). Subsequent modifications of this technique include the injection of oil into the tubule to isolate a portion of the lumen and analyze the action of that section of the tubule on injected samples of defined solution (Fig. 12-24). Microchemical methods are now used to determine the concentrations of individual ion species in the sample. Techniques have recently been developed by which a given segment of renal tubule can be steadily perfused and the perfusate analyzed (Fig. 12-25). The major findings on tubular transport, summarized in Figure 12-26, are listed below.

1. The *proximal convoluted tubule* initiates the process of concentrating the glomerular filtrate. In this segment, about 75 percent of the Na^+ is removed from the lumen by active transport, and a nearly proportional amount of water and certain other solutes, such as Cl^-, follow passively. The result is a tubular fluid of reduced volume that is isosmotic with respect to the plasma and interstitial fluids.

Using the stopped-flow perfusion technique (Fig. 12-24), Solomon and his co-workers found that when the NaCl concentration inside the tubule is decreased, the movement of water also decreases. This is just the opposite of the result that should be expected if the water moves by simple osmotic diffusion, and it indicates that water transport is coupled to active sodium transport. The coupling is presumably due to a standing-gradient mechanism (p. 403). The actual "pumping" of sodium ions takes place at the serosal surface of the epithelial cells of the proximal tubule, the same as in frog skin and gall bladder epithelia. In amphibians, this active transport leaves the tubular lumen about 20 mV negative relative to the fluid surrounding the nephron. This potential difference accounts for the passive net diffusion of Cl$^-$ out of the proximal tubule as the counterion for sodium. At the most distal portion of the proximal tubule (where it joins the thin descending limb of the loop of Henle, the glomerular filtrate is already reduced to one-fourth its original volume. As a result of the reduction in the volume of tubular fluid, substances that are not transported across the tubule or that do not passively diffuse across it become four times as concentrated toward the end of the proximal tubule as in the original filtrate. In spite of this great reduction in the volume of tubular fluid, the fluid at this point is isosmotic relative to the fluid outside the nephron, having an osmolarity of about 300 milliosmoles (Fig. 12-26). It is interesting to note that the active transport of Na$^+$ and Cl$^-$ alone can account for the major changes in volume of the fluid along the proximal tubule and for the increased concentration of urea and many other filtered substances.

The proximal tubule is ideally structured for the massive resorption of salt and water. Numerous microvilli at the luminal border of the tubular epithelial cells form the so-called *brush border* (Fig. 12-19). This greatly increases the area of membrane and thereby reduces the barrier to diffusion of salt and water from the tubular lumen into the epithelial cell. The serosal border has a smaller surface area, and hence offers a greater resistance to the back leakage of Na$^+$ pumped out of the cell across that membrane.

2. The *descending limb of the loop of Henle* has proved too small for micropuncture studies, but success has recently been obtained in perfusing segments of the renal tubule and determining the alterations produced in the perfusate during its passage through the tubule (Fig. 12-25). Using this approach, Maurice Burg and his co-workers at the National Institutes of Health have demonstrated that there is no active salt transport in the descending loop. Moreover, this segment exhibits very low permeability to NaCl and urea, but is highly permeable to water. As will be described below, the descending loop plays an entirely passive but important, role in the urine-concentrating system of the nephron.

3. The *thin segment* of the ascending limb was also shown by perfusion experiments to be inactive in salt transport. Nevertheless, it is highly permeable to Na$^+$ and Cl$^-$. Its permeability to urea is low to moderate.

4. The *medullary thick ascending limb* differs from the rest of the loop of Henle in that it exhibits active transport of Cl$^-$ outward from the lumen to the interstitial space. This portion of the nephron has a very low permeability to water. As a result of chloride resorption (and accompanying passive transport of Na$^+$), the fluid reaching the junction of the ascending limb and the distal convoluted tubule is somewhat

12-26. Overview of ion and water fluxes along the renal tubule of a mammal. Numbers indicate milliosmoles/liter. The shaded portion of the collecting duct is ADH-sensitive. The osmotic gradient in the extracellular fluid is indicated by the gray wedge. [After Pitts, 1959.]

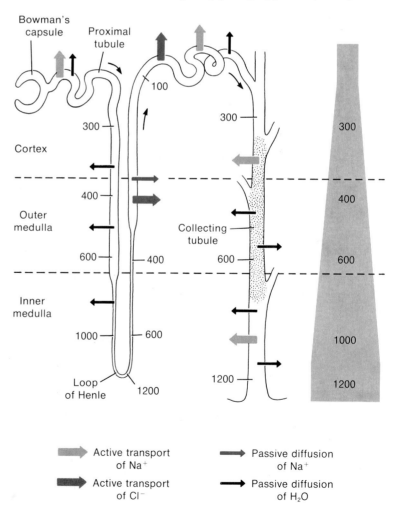

hypoosmotic relative to the interstitial fluid. The importance of salt resorption by the ascending tubule will be discussed at greater length in the section on the countercurrent mechanism.

5. The movement of salt and water across the *distal convoluted tubule* is complex; the distal tubule is made up of several morphologically and functionally different segments in series. In some species, sodium resorption appears to occur, whereas in others it does not. The distal tubule is important in the transport of K^+, H^+, and NH_3 into the nephron and Na^+, Cl^-, and HCO_3^- out of the nephron.

6. The *collecting ducts* remove water from the hypotonic fluid entering the distal tubule, and thereby produce a hyperosmotic urine. The duct also resorbs NaCl by active transport of Na^+; it is impermeable to salts and exhibits a variable permeability to water. The rate at which water is resorbed in the collecting duct is under delicate feedback control via *antidiuretic hormone* (ADH) secreted by the neurosecretory cells of the hypothalamus (p. 347). ADH renders the duct permeable to water. As the tubular fluid passes down the collecting duct deep into the renal medulla, it encounters an increasingly hyperosmotic interstitial fluid (Fig. 12-26). The result in the presence of ADH

is a progressive increase in the concentration of the tubular fluid as water is osmotically drawn across the epithelium of the collecting duct into the hypertonic interstitial fluid of the renal medulla.

THE CONCENTRATING MECHANISM OF THE NEPHRON

There is a clear-cut correlation between the architecture of the vertebrate nephron and its ability to manufacture a urine that is hypertonic relative to the body fluids. Nephrons capable of producing a hypertonic urine (i.e., those of mammals and birds) all have a loop of Henle. In general, the longer the loop, the greater the concentrating power of the nephron. Thus desert mammals have both the longest loops of Henle and the most hypertonic urine. This, together with the progressive increase in tonicity of intra- and extra-tubular fluids toward the deeper regions of the renal medulla, led Hargitay and Kuhn to propose in 1951 that the loop of Henle acts as a *countercurrent multiplier* (Box 12-2). Though a very attractive and plausible hypothesis, it has proven rather difficult to test because of the difficulty of sampling the intratubular fluid in the thin portion of the nephron. Studies of the freezing point depression of the fluid in slices of frozen kidney

---

BOX 12-2 COUNTERCURRENT SYSTEMS

In 1944, Craig published a method of concentrating chemical compounds based on the countercurrent principle. This has proved useful in many industrial and laboratory applications. As in many other instances, man's ingenuity turns out to be a latter-day reflection of Nature's inventiveness; countercurrent mechanisms have since been found to operate in a variety of biological systems, including the vertebrate kidney, the gas secreting organ of swim bladders and gills of fish, and in the limbs of various birds and mammals that live in cold climates.

The principle can be illustrated with a hypothetical countercurrent multiplier that employs an active-transport mechanism much like the one that operates in the mammalian kidney. The model system shown in part A of the figure consists of a tube bent into a loop with a common dividing wall between the two limbs. A sodium chloride solution flows in one limb of the tube and then out the other. Let us assume that within the common wall separating the two limbs of the tube, there is a mechanism that actively transports NaCl from the outflow limb to the inflow limb of the tube, without any accompanying movement of water. As bulk flow carries the fluid along the inflow limb, the effect of NaCl transport is cumulative, and the salt concentration becomes progressively higher. As the fluid rounds the bend and begins flowing through the other limb, its salt concentration progressively falls as a result of the cumulative effect of outward NaCl transport along the length of the outflow limb. By the time it reaches the end of that limb, its osmolarity is slightly lower than that of the fresh fluid beginning its inward flow in the other limb.

This example resembles the loop of Henle in principle but not in detail. The loop of Henle has no common wall dividing the two limbs; nevertheless, the limbs are coupled functionally through the interstitial fluid, so that the NaCl pumped out of the ascending limb can diffuse the short distance toward the descending limb and cause osmotic resorption of water from that limb.

Of special interest are the following general points about the countercurrent principle:

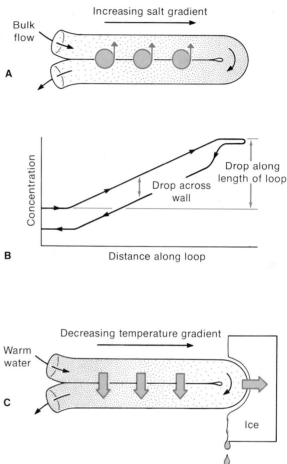

Active and passive models illustrating the counter-current principle. A. Active system. A salt solution flows through a U-shaped tube with a common dividing wall that pumps salt from the outflow to the inflow limb. B. A plot of salt concentration along the two limbs, illustrating the principle that the concentration difference across the wall at any point is small relative to the total concentration difference along the length of the loop. The length of the loop as well as the efficiency of transport across the wall will determine the overall difference along the entire length of the loop. C. Passive system. Warm water flows down the input limb and gives up part of its heat to cooler water flowing in the opposite direction in the outflow limb. Some heat is lost to the heat sink represented by the ice, but much of the heat is conserved by passive transfer from the inflow to the outflow limbs.

1. The standing concentration gradient set up in both limbs is due to both the continual movement of fluid through the system and the cumulative effect of transfer from the outflow limb to the inflow limb. The gradient would disappear if fluid movement were to cease or if transport across the partition were to cease.

2. The difference in concentration from left to right and right to left of the two limbs of the countercurrent multiplier is far greater than the difference across the partition at any one point (part B of the figure). As a consequence, the countercurrent multiplier can produce greater concentration changes than would be attained by a simple transport epithelium without the configuration of a countercurrent system. The longer the multiplier, the greater the concentration differences that can be attained.

3. The multiplier system can work only if it contains an asymmetry. In this case, there is an active net transport of salt in one direction across the partition. Counter-current systems are also used to conserve heat (part C of the figure). In the extremities of birds and mammals that inhabit cold climates, there is a temperature differential between the arterial and venous flow of blood, because the blood is cooled as it descends into the leg. The arterial blood gives up some of its heat to the venous blood leaving the leg, thereby reducing the amount lost to the environment.

reveal that the osmolarity of both the intratubular and extratubular fluid shows a gradient from the upper to the lower ends of the loop of Henle. This gradient is represented by the gray wedge in Figure 12-26. The fluid that enters the descending limb from the proximal tubule is approximately isosmotic with respect to the extracellular fluid at that point (in the outer portion of the renal medulla), having a concentration of about 300 milliosmoles. The concentration of the fluid gradually increases as it makes its way down the descending limb toward the hairpin turn in the loop, where its concentration reaches 1000–3000 milliosmoles. At this point, too, it is nearly isosmotic relative to the surrounding extracellular fluid in the deep portion of the renal medulla.

The tubular fluid flowing down the descending limb comes into osmotic equilibrium with the interstitial fluid because the walls of the descending limb are relatively permeable to water and impermeable to salt. Thus the concentration of the tubular fluid, initially about 300 milliosmoles, approaches the 1000-3000 milliosmole concentration of the interstitial fluid around the hairpin turn of the loop (Fig. 23-26). As the fluid flows up into the thick segment of the ascending limb, it undergoes a progressive loss of NaCl (but not water) as the result of an active extrusion of Cl⁻, with sodium ions following passively. The thin and thick segments of the ascending limb are relatively impermeable to water, as noted earlier.

The osmotic asymmetry between the descending and ascending limbs of the loop of Henle, together with the countercurrent hypothesis, can account for the *cortico-medullary concentration gradient*. The osmotic loss of water from the descending limb allows the lumen of that limb to approach osmotic equilibrium with the interstitial fluid. Since the fluid is moving along within the lumen, the progressive removal of water from the lumen leads to a progressively higher concentration of solute as the fluid approaches the bend in the loop of Henle (Fig. 12-27). The result is a standing gradient in which the salt concentration becomes progressively higher with distance into the depths of the renal medulla. This gradient is responsible for the final osmotic removal of water from the collecting ducts, producing a hyperosmotic urine.

A countercurrent feature in the organization of the circulation around the nephron aids in maintaining the standing concentration gradient in the interstitium. Blood descends from the cortex into the deeper portions of the medulla in capillaries that form loop-like networks around each nephron (Fig. 12-18). It then ascends toward the cortex. In this circuit, the blood takes up salt and gives up water osmotically, and the surrounding interstitial fluid becomes increasingly hyperosmotic during the descent of the blood into the medullary depths. The reverse occurs as the blood returns back up toward the cortex and encounters an interstitium of progressively lower osmolarity.

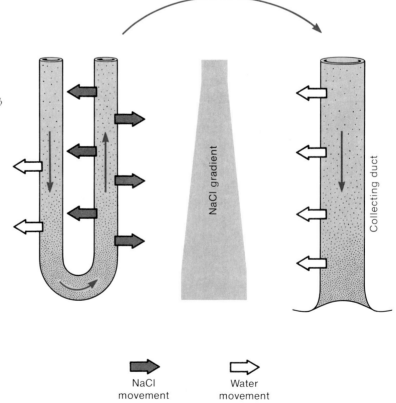

12–27. *Countercurrent model of the loop of Henle. The gray arrows indicate the active Cl⁻ transport and passive codiffusion of Na⁺. The diffusion of NaCl into the descending limb is purely passive, and occurs because of the concentration buildup in the interstitial fluid. The gradient of extracellular salt concentration is indicated by the gray wedge. The osmotic movement of water into the interstitial fluid is shown by open arrows.*

NaCl gradient

Collecting duct

NaCl movement

Water movement

To summarize, the formation of urine begins with the concentration of the glomerular filtrate into a hyperosmotic fluid in the proximal tubule, where 75% of the salt and water are removed in osmotically equivalent amounts, leaving urea and certain other substances behind. In its course through the loop of Henle and the distal tubule, there is little net change in osmolarity, but the countercurrent mechanism sets up a concentration gradient parallel to the loop. This gradient provides the basis for the osmotic removal of water from the fluid descending the collecting duct within the medulla. It is interesting also to note that this process takes place without active transport of water.

REGULATION OF WATER RETENTION

An animal can experience osmotic stress due to changes in temperature or salinity and to the ingestion of food and drink. Perturbations in the osmotic state of the body fluids are minimized through feedback mechanisms by which the osmoregulatory organs adjust their activity so as to maintain the internal status quo. These feedback control mechanisms may be neural, endocrine, or a combination of the two.

The control of water retention by the mammalian kidney is a well-known example of such regulation. The tubular fluid is concentrated by the osmotic removal of water as it passes down the collecting duct into the hyperosmotic depths of the renal medulla (Fig. 12-27). This provides a means of regulating the amount of water passed in the urine. The rate at which water is osmotically drawn out across the wall of the collecting duct from the urine into the interstitial fluid depends on the water permeability of the epithelium that forms the wall of the collecting duct. The antidiuretic hormone, released from the neurohypophysis, regulates the water permeability of the collecting duct, and thereby controls the amount of water leaving the animal in the urine. The higher the level of ADH in the blood, the more permeable the epithelial wall of the collecting duct, and hence the more water is drawn out of the urine as it passes down the duct toward the renal pelvis (Fig. 12-28). The level of ADH in the blood is a function of the osmotic pressure of the plasma. Osmotically sensitive neurons with cell bodies located in the hypothalamus respond to increased plasma osmolarity by an increased rate of firing. These are neurosecretory cells that send their axons to the neurohypophysis, the posterior lobe of the pituitary gland. The increased neural activity of these cells increases the rate at which ADH is released into the blood stream from their axon terminals, and thus increases the blood level of ADH. The negative-feedback effect of this neuroendocrine mechanism is illustrated in Figure 12-29. If, for example, the osmo-

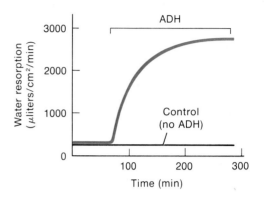

12–28. *Effect of ADH on osmotic resorption of water from the collecting duct into the interstitial fluid. The osmolarity of the fluid perfused through the duct was 125 milliosmoles/liter; that of the external bath, 290 milliosmoles/liter. The hormone was applied during the period indicated. [After Grantham, 1971.]*

12–29. *Feedback regulation of blood osmolarity by the action of antidiuretic hormone on the collecting duct. ADH increases the water permeability of the stippled region, enhancing the rate of osmotic removal of water from the urine. The increased recovery of water counteracts the conditions that stimulate ADH secretion.*

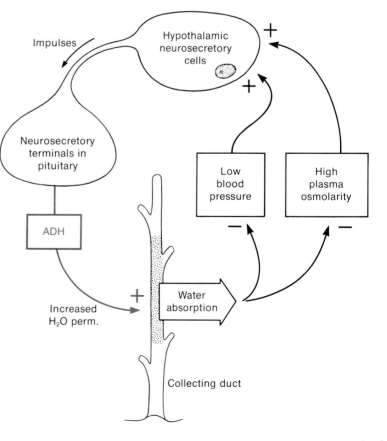

larity of the blood is increased as a result of desiccation, the activity of the neurosecretory neurons is increased, more ADH is released, the collecting ducts become more permeable, and water is osmotically drawn from the urine at a higher rate. This results in the excretion of a more concentrated urine. As the osmolarity of the blood gradually decreases toward the set-point level, ADH secretion is reduced. The hypothalamic cells that produce and release ADH also receive inhibitory input from receptors that respond to increases in blood pressure. These are located in various parts of the circulatory system, but the major ones are located in the left atrium of the heart. Any factor that raises the arterial blood pressure (e.g., an increase in blood volume due to dilution by ingested water) will inhibit the ADH-releasing hypothalamic cells and thereby result in an increased loss of body water through the urine. Conversely, any factor that reduces the blood pressure will reflexly lead to the retention of body water by stimulating the release of ADH.

In humans, the ingestion of ethyl alcohol inhibits the release of ADH and as a result leads to copious urination and an increase of plasma osmolarity beyond the normal set-point level. Some degree of dehydration results, and this contributes to the uncomfortable feeling of a "hangover."

The action of mammalian ADH and related peptides of nonmammalian species is not limited to the kidney. These antidiuretic hormones, applied to frog skin and toad bladder, also increase the water permeability of those epithelia.

ADAPTATIONS OF THE VERTEBRATE KIDNEY

The evolution of the vertebrate nephron is summarized in Fig. 12-30. A primitive forerunner is found in some prochordates, in which the proximal end of the nephron opens into the coelom. The simplest vertebrate nephron occurs in certain marine teleosts that have neither glomerulus nor Bowman's capsule. In

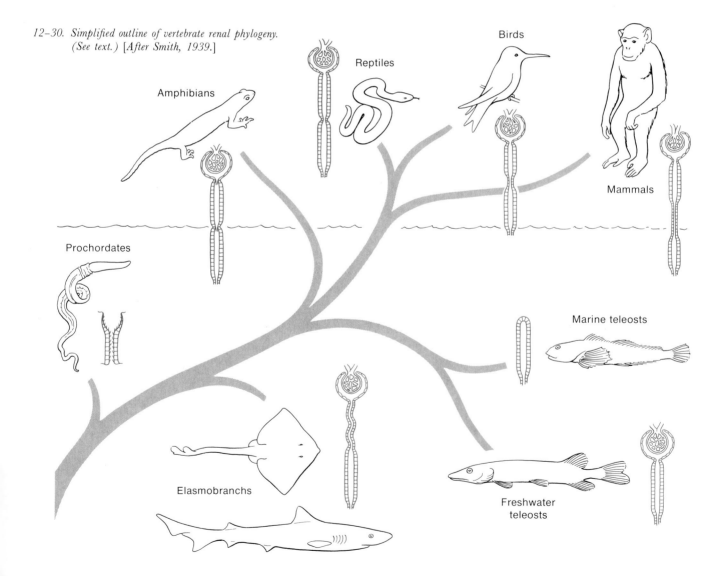

12-30. Simplified outline of vertebrate renal phylogeny. (See text.) [After Smith, 1939.]

such *aglomerular* kidneys, the urine is formed entir[e] by secretion and perhaps resorption, since there is [no] specialized mechanism for the production of a filtra[te]. The opposite extreme, again, is seen in the mari[ne] hagfishes (class Cyclostomata); the glomeruli are present in these animals, but the tubules are absent and the Bowman's capsules empty directly into the collecting duct. Although we have little information on the physiology of these primitive nephrons, morphology suggests that the kidneys of these vertebrates carry out little or no osmoregulation, serving primarily to turn over a certain fraction of blood, water, and crystalloids per unit time as a means of preventing the toxic build up of nitrogenous wastes. Water and salts lost in the urine are, of course, replaced from the external environment.

Thus the extracellular fluids of the most primitive living vertebrate, the hagfish, are similar to seawater in concentration of major salts (Table 12-3), and their plasma is essentially isotonic relative to seawater. The plasma of sharks and rays (class Chondrichthyes) is lower in the concentrations of the major ions (Table 12-3) but nonetheless hyperosmotic relative to seawater. This results from the retention of large concentrations of urea in the plasma. The teleosts (modern bony fishes) represent the next level of osmoregulation, for they maintain a plasma that is hypoosmotic relative to seawater and hyperosmotic relative to fresh water. They do this without recourse to the retention of an organic osmotic agent such as urea. An interesting exception to this is seen in the coelocanth *Latameria,* which has recently been found to have a high plasma urea concentration much like that of the sharks and rays. This is the only living species of the subclass of bony fishes (Sarcopterygii) that gave rise to the terrestrial vertebrates.

As a general rule, freshwater teleosts (subclass Actinopterygii) have larger glomeruli and more of them than do their marine relatives. This is also true for all the higher vertebrates. In lower vertebrates up to the reptiles, the kidney is incapable of producing a hypertonic urine (i.e., of higher osmolarity than the plasma). This is closely correlated with the organization of the nephron, for without a countercurrent system the kidney cannot produce a urine of significantly greater osmolarity than the plasma. Only birds and mammals have a loop of Henle, and thus only these animals have renal plumbing that is so organized as to allow countercurrent multiplication. The avian kidney resembles that of mammals, except that some of the nephrons are without loops of Henle and the loop of Henle in some birds is oriented perpendicular to the collecting duct, producing a less efficient concentrating mechanism. In mammals, there is a nice correlation between the length of the loop and the ability to concentrate the urine. The loop of Henle is longest in desert dwellers,

[s]h as the kangaroo rat; these long loops produce [lar]ger overall gradients in osmolarity from renal cortex [to] medulla, thus permitting strong osmotic extraction [of] water from the collecting duct.

Vertebrate Osmoregulatory Organs other than the Kidney

Although the kidney is the most highly developed organ of osmoregulation among the vertebrates, it should be noted that several other vertebrate organs are also important in the maintenance of osmotic homeostasis.

OSMOREGULATORY FUNCTIONS OF FISH GILLS

The epithelial surface area of a gill must be large if it is to function efficiently as an organ for respiratory gas exchange (Chapter 14). This feature also makes these organs well suited for osmotic and excretory exchange with the environment. Thus the gills of teleost fishes are active in such diverse functions as gas exchange, ion transport, excretion of nitrogenous wastes, and maintaining acid-base balance. Recent evidence indicates that such multifunctional activity also takes place in the gills of some invertebrates and vertebrates that have been less intensively investigated.

Marine and freshwater teleosts maintain plasma osmolarities that differ significantly from those of their aqueous environments. Some species—for example, the salmon of the Pacific Northwest—are able to maintain a more-or-less constant plasma osmolarity even though they migrate between marine and freshwater environments. The osmotic homeostasis of the teleost fishes depends to a large degree on the active transport of salts across the epithelium of the gills. In fresh water, the osmotic gradient for water dictates that water diffuses passively across the gills into the fish. The kidney prevents hydration of the fish by a copious production of urine that is hypoosmotic relative to the plasma. It has been suggested that the gut plays only a minor osmoregulatory role in freshwater fishes, for they appear to drink very little, and can live without a net loss of salts during experimental starvation, even though there is a steady excretion of salts via the kidneys. The loss of sodium and chloride ions through the kidneys is countered by the active uptake of NaCl through the gills from the freshwater environment (Fig. 12-31,A). In seawater, the osmotic gradient is reversed, and water diffuses out through the extensive area of the gill surfaces, tending to dehydrate the fish. To replace this water, the fish swallows seawater, which

12–31. *Salt and water exchange in freshwater and marine teleosts. Solid arrows indicate active transport; broken arrows, passive transport. Note the active role of the gills in salt transport in both groups.* [After Prosser, 1973.]

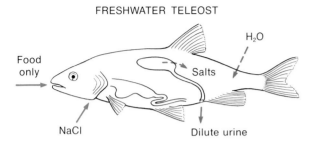

FRESHWATER TELEOST

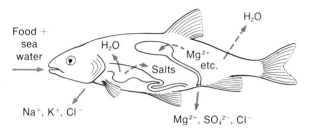

MARINE TELEOST

enters the blood stream by absorption from the digestive tract. In marine fish, the salts that enter along with the ingested water are removed by the active outward transport of monovalent ions (Na^+, Cl^-, K^+) across the epithelium of the gills and by the excretion of divalent ions (Mg^{2+}, Ca^{2+}) by the kidney (Fig. 12-31,B). The kidneys contribute to the conservation of plasma water by producing limited quantities of urine which is isotonic relative to the plasma. Thus the teleost gill plays a central role in coping with osmotic stress.

The structure of a teleost gill is seen in Figure 12-32,A. The blood transfusing the gill flows along two major pathways, the central compartment inside the filament and the lumen inside the lamellae. The epithelium separating the blood from the external water consists of two distinct cell types. The epithelium of the lamellae consists entirely of flat cells no more than 3–5 μm thick, containing few mitochondria.

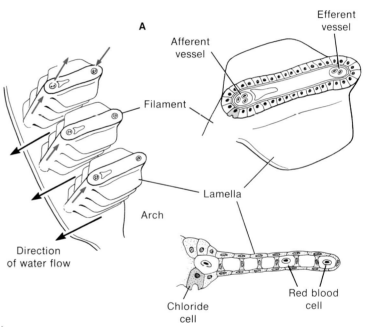

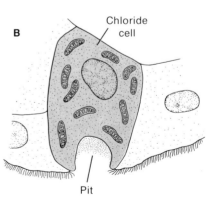

12–32. *The teleost gill as an osmoregulatory organ. A. Gill filaments extending up from the gill arch. Blood flows in capillaries, as shown by colored arrows. Flattened lamellae (right) extend out from the filaments. The lamellae contain extensive spaces through which blood circulates. B. Chloride cell bordered by flat respiratory epithelial cells.* [After Maetz, 1971.]

These are clearly best suited for respiratory exchange, acting as minimal barriers for diffusion of gases. The epithelium covering the gill filaments consists of these cells plus a second type that is more columnar in shape and several times thicker from base to apex than the flat cells (Fig. 12-32,B). These so-called *chloride cells* are heavily laden with mitochondria and with enzymes related to NaCl transport, such as Na,K-activated ATPases, and carbonic anhydrase. Glutamic dehydrogenase and other enzymes associated with nitrogen metabolism and excretion are also present in high concentrations. These cells were first described in 1932 by Keys and Willmer, who ascribed to them the transport of chloride because they exhibit histochemical similarities to cells that secrete hydrochloric acid in the amphibian stomach, and because it had already been shown that the teleost gill is the site of extrarenal excretion of chloride (and sodium). More recent microscopical studies have confirmed the presence of high levels of chloride in these cells, especially in the pit that develops on the mucosal (external) border of these cells in fish that have become adapted to high salinities.

It is especially interesting that the direction of salt transport across the gill epithelium changes so as to adapt to changes in environmental salinity in species that migrate between seawater and fresh water. Salts are actively taken up in fresh water and actively excreted in salt water. In experiments done to study the effects of transferring such fishes from low to high salinities, it was found that the physiological adaptation of the gills (i.e., change from inward pumping to outward pumping of NaCl) is a gradual process, involving the synthesis and/or destruction of molecular components of the epithelial transport systems and the appearance of specialized cells. When the external salinity is experimentally reduced, characteristic changes occur in the chloride cells, including the disappearance of the pits on the chloride cells. Conversely, exposure to high salinities results in the appearance of the pits, an increase in the number of chloride cells, and a corresponding increase in the activity of Na,K-activated ATPases, and carbonic anhydrase in the gill. When *euryhaline* fishes (i.e., those able to tolerate a wide range of salinities) are transferred from fresh water to salt water, new ion-pump activity ensues after a delay of about a day. It is not known how external salinity induces those osmoregulatory changes, but two alternatives have been suggested; high external salinity may exert a direct action on the epithelial cells of the gills, or the initial rise in internal osmolarity may act via endocrine mechanisms to influence epithelial differentiation and metabolism. Another question is whether adaptation to high salinity results from a change in the function of existing chloride cells or if new cells with a salt-extrusion mechanism replace the chloride cells that have a salt-uptake mechanism.

Since the chloride cells were first characterized and associated with the transport of chloride ions, they have been found to be responsible for the exchange of other ions as well, including H^+, Na^+, K^+, NH_4^+, and HCO_3^-. Although it is difficult to demonstrate rigorously that the chloride cells alone take part in the transport and exchange of those ions, a variety of evidence, including the changes that the chloride cells undergo during adaptation to high salinities, indicates that they are the major site of active exchange in the gills of teleost fishes.

AVIAN AND REPTILIAN SALT GLANDS

In 1957, Knut Schmidt-Nielsen and his co-workers, investigating the means by which marine birds maintain their osmotic balance without access to fresh water, discovered that the *nasal salt glands* secrete a hypertonic solution of NaCl. It was found in those early studies that if cormorants or gulls are administered seawater by intravenous injection or by stomach tube, the increase in the plasma salt concentration leads to a prolonged nasal secretion of fluid with an osmolarity of two to three times that of the plasma. Salt glands have subsequently been described in many species of birds and reptiles, especially those subjected to the osmotic stress of a marine or desert environment. These species include nearly all marine birds, ostriches, the marine iguana, sea snakes, and marine turtles as well as many terrestrial reptiles.

The salt glands of birds occupy shallow depressions in the skull above the eyes (Fig. 12-33). The gland consists of many lobes about 1 mm in diameter, each of which drains via branching secretory tubules and a central canal (Fig. 12-34) into a duct that, in turn, runs through the beak and empties into the nostrils. Active secretion takes place across the epithelium of the secretory tubules, and consists of characteristic secretory cells that have a profusion of deep infoldings at their basal ends and are heavily laden with mitochondria. As in other transport epithelia, adjacent cells are tied together by tight junctions, which preclude the massive leakage of water or solutes past the cells, from one side of the epithelium to the other.

The formation of nasal gland fluid does not include filtration, as does the formation of urine by the glomerular kidney. The absence of filtration can be deduced from the failure of small filterable molecules, such as inulin (p. 409) or sucrose, to appear in the nasal gland fluid after they have been injected into the blood stream. Although our knowledge of cellular mechanisms in the salt gland is limited, there is good evidence that active transport takes place at the surface of the cell facing the lumen of the gland. A Na,K-activated ATPase has been localized at the basal membrane, and the application of ouabain (p. 95) to the basal

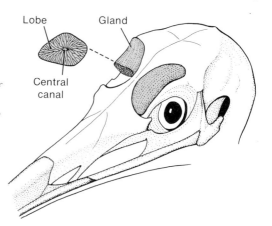

12–33. *Avian salt glands are located above the orbit and drain via ducts into the nasal region. The gland consists of a longitudinal arrangement of many lobes. Each lobe consists of tubules and capillaries (see Fig. 12-34) arranged radially around a central canal. The secretion collects in a duct that empties into the nasal region.*

12–34. *Microscopic structure of a salt gland. Lobes (not shown) contain thousands of branching tubules radiating from a central duct. Single tubules are surrounded by capillaries in which blood flows counter to the flow of secretory fluid in the tubule. This countercurrent flow facilitates the transfer of salt from the blood to the tubule, since the uphill gradient of salt concentration between capillary and tubule lumen is thereby minimized at each point along the length of the tubule (see Box 12-2). [After "Salt Glands" by K. Schmidt-Nielsen. Copyright © 1959 by Scientific American, Inc. All rights reserved.]*

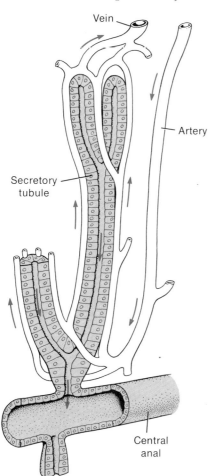

surface of the epithelium blocks salt transport. Since this inhibitor does not pass across epithelia, and can block the pump only by direct contact with the transport mechanism, the sodium transport mechanism appears to operate in the basal membrane of the epithelial cell.

The avian salt gland appears to be organized as a countercurrent system that might aid in concentrating salts in the secreted fluid. The capillaries are so arranged that the flow of blood is parallel to the secretory tubules, and occurs in the direction opposite to the flow of secretory fluid (Fig. 12-34). This maintains a minimal concentration gradient from blood to tubular lumen along the entire length of a tubule, and thereby minimizes the concentration gradient for uphill transport from the plasma to the secretory fluid.

The secretory activity of the salt gland is controlled by the nervous system. Sensory endings in the heart respond to an increase in plasma tonicity by a sensory discharge. This activity results in the activation of parasympathetic cholinergic neurons that innervate the salt gland. Acetylcholine liberated from the terminals of those neurons stimulates the secretion of the salt gland. There is no direct evidence that the functioning of the salt gland is controlled through endocrine mechanisms.

The salt glands convey an important survival advantage to marine birds and reptiles, for they enable the animal to secrete salt ingested with seawater without the loss of much water. Whereas terrestrial mammals secrete all their salts in a urine that is more dilute than sea water, the gull, for example, retains some water after all the NaCl ingested with seawater is secreted via the salt glands (Fig. 12-35). This water can then be passed or lost without stress through the kidneys, lungs, skin, and intestine.

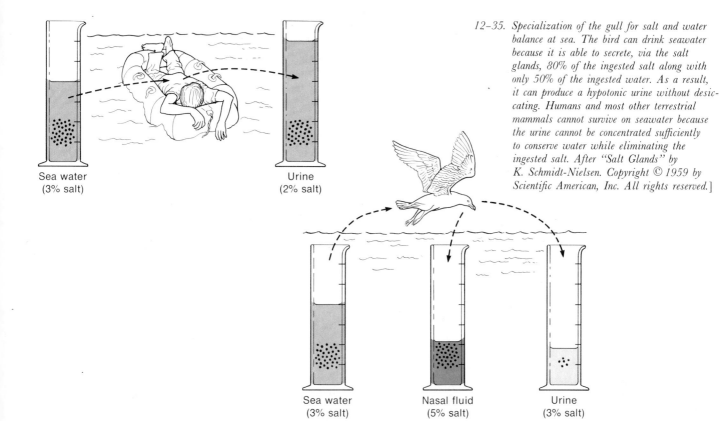

Sea water
(3% salt)

Urine
(2% salt)

Sea water
(3% salt)

Nasal fluid
(5% salt)

Urine
(3% salt)

Invertebrate Osmoregulatory Organs

The invertebrates exhibit far greater evolutionary diversity than the vertebrates, and have evolved a variety of osmoregulatory organs unrelated to the vertebrate kidney. In general, invertebrate osmoregulatory organs employ mechanisms of filtration, resorption, and secretion similar in principle to those of the vertebrate kidney to produce a urine that is significantly different in osmolarity and composition from the body fluids. That there has been convergent evolution of physiological mechanisms in nonhomologous organs underscores the utility of these mechanisms. In addition, there is some evidence, still controversial, that urine and feces are dehydrated by active transport of water across the epithelium in the hindgut of some insects. Should this evidence be verified in future studies, it will represent a mechanism of osmoregulation for which there is as yet no evidence among the vertebrates.

FILTRATION-REABSORPTION ORGANS

Filtration of plasma, similar in principle to that which occurs in Bowman's capsule of vertebrates, appears to underlie the formation of the primary urine in both mollusks and crustaceans. This conclusion is derived from several observations:

1. When polymers such as inulin are injected into the blood stream or coelomic fluid, they appear in high concentrations in the urine. Since it is unlikely that they are actively secreted, they must enter the urine during a filtration process in which all those molecules below a certain size pass through a sieve-like membrane of tissue. During the resorption of water and essential solutes, these polymers remain behind in the urine.

2. The normal urine of some animals is found to contain little or no glucose, even though substantial levels occur in the blood. In several mollusks, for example, when the blood glucose is elevated by artificial means, such as by injection, glucose appears in the urine. In each species, glucose appears in the urine at a characteristic threshold concentration of blood glucose. As in the vertebrate kidney (Fig. 12-22), the urine glucose concentration rises linearly with blood glucose concentration beyond that point. By analogy with the vertebrate kidney, this behavior is believed to result from a saturation of the transport system by which the glucose that entered the tubular fluid via filtration is resorbed from the filtrate into the blood. Once the

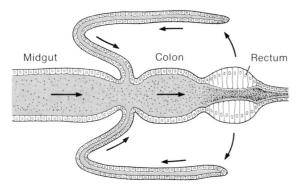

12–36. *The insect excretory system. The proto-urine is produced by secretion into the lumen of the malpighian tubules and flows into the rectum, where it is concentrated by the extraction of water. The decrease in volume of the urine in the rectum is evidence for the resorption of water rather than secretion of solutes. [After Wigglesworth, 1932.]*

Midgut   Colon   Rectum

transport system is saturated, the "spillover" of glucose in the urine is proportional to its concentration in the blood. More conclusive evidence is obtained with the drug *phlorizin,* which is known to block active glucose transport. When phlorizin is administered to mollusks and crustaceans, glucose appears in the urine even at normal blood glucose levels. The most reasonable explanation for this effect is that glucose enters the urine as part of a filtrate and remains in the urine when the resorption mechanism is blocked by phlorizin.

3. Analysis of tubular fluids near suspected sites of filtration indicate a crystalloid composition similar to that of the plasma.

4. The rate of urine formation has been found in some animals to depend on the blood pressure. This relationship is consistent with a filtration mechanism, but the change in blood pressure may also produce a change in the circulation to the osmoregulatory organ.

The site of primary urine formation by filtration is known in only a few invertebrates. In a number of marine and freshwater mollusks, filtration takes place across the wall of the heart into the pericardial cavity, and the filtrate is conducted to the "kidney" through a special canal. Glucose, amino acids, and essential electrolytes are resorbed in the kidney. In the crayfish, the major organ of osmoregulation is the so-called *antennal gland.* Part of that organ, the *coelomosac,* contains tubules whose ultrastructure resembles the structure of the vertebrate glomerulus. The organ also exhibits structures that are morphologically analogous to the proximal and distal tubules of the vertebrate kidney. These observations have led to speculation

that the excretory fluid that collects in the coelomosac is produced by ultrafiltration.

Since the final urine in mollusks and crustaceans differs in composition from the initial filtrate, there must be either secretion of substances into the filtrate or resorption of substances from the filtrate. The resorption of electrolytes is well established in freshwater species, for the final urine has a lower salt concentration than both the plasma and the filtrate. Glucose must also be resorbed, since it is present in the plasma and in the filtrate, but is either absent or very low in concentration in the final urine.

It is interesting that the filtration-resorption type of osmoregulatory system has appeared in at least three and perhaps more phyla (Mollusca, Arthropoda, Chordata). This kind of system has the important advantage that all the low-molecular-weight constituents of the plasma are filtered into the ultrafiltrate in proportion to their concentration in the plasma. Physiologically important molecules, such as glucose, and, in freshwater animals, such ions as Na^+, K^+, Cl^-, and Ca^{2+}, are subsequently removed from the filtrate by tubular resorption, leaving toxic substances or unimportant molecules behind to be excreted in the urine. This avoids the need for active transport into the urine of toxic metabolites, or for that matter unnatural, man-made substances of a neutral or toxic nature encountered in the environment. A disadvantage of the filtration-resorption osmoregulatory system is its high energetic cost for the organism: the filtering of large quantities of plasma requires the active uptake of large quantities of salts, either in the excretory organ itself or in other organs, such as gills or skin. In frog skin, for example, it has been shown that one mole of oxygen must be reduced in the synthesis of ATP for every 16–18 moles of sodium ions transported. In freshwater clams, the cost of maintaining sodium balance amounts to about 20% of the total energy metabolism. In marine invertebrates, the filtration-resorption system proves metabolically less expensive, since salt conservation is much less of a problem.

SECRETORY-TYPE
OSMOREGULATORY ORGANS

In insects, the *Malpighian tubules* together with the *hindgut* form the major excretory-osmoregulatory system. In broad outline, this system (Fig. 12-36) consists of the long, thin Malpighian tubules, which empty into the alimentary canal at the junction of the midgut and hindgut and whose closed ends lie in the hemocoel (body cavity containing blood). The secretion formed in the tubules passes into the hindgut, where it is dehydrated and passed into the rectum and voided as a concentrated urine through the anus. With the evolution of tracheolar respiration in insects (Chapter 14), the importance of an efficient circulatory system was diminished. As a consequence, the Malpighian tubules do not receive a direct, pressurized arterial blood supply, as the mammalian nephron does. Instead, they are surrounded with blood, which is at a pressure essentially no greater than the pressure within the tubules. Since there is no significant pressure differential across the walls of the Malpighian tubules, filtration cannot play a role in urine formation. Instead, the urine must be formed entirely by secretion, with perhaps the subsequent resorption of some constituents of the secreted fluid. This is analogous to the formation of urine by secretion in the aglomerular kidneys of marine teleosts. The serosal surface of the Malpighian tubule exhibits a profusion of microvilli and mitochondria (Fig. 12-37), a specialization often associated with a highly active secretory epithelium.

The details of urine formation by tubular secretion differ among different insects, but some major features seem to be common throughout. Potassium and, to a lesser extent, sodium are secreted actively into the tubular lumen along with such waste products of nitrogen metabolism as uric acid or allantoin. It appears that the transport of K^+ is the major driving force for the formation of the tubular urine, with most of the other substances following passively. This has been concluded from the observations that (1) the tubular urine is more or less isotonic relative to the hemolymph; (2) the tubular urine has a high K^+ concentration in all insects; (3) the rate of tubular urine formation is a function of K^+ concentration in the fluid surrounding the tubule, higher potassium concentrations producing more rapid tubular urine accumulation; and (4) the formation of tubular urine is largely independent of the sodium concentration of the surrounding fluid. Although potassium is osmotically the most important substance actively transported, there is evidence that active transport plays an important role in the secretion of uric acid and other nitrogenous wastes.

The urine formed in the Malpighian tubules passes into the hindgut, where several important changes in its composition occur. The fluid formed in the Malpighian tubules is relatively uniform in composition from one species to another, and in each species it remains isotonic relative to the hemolymph under different osmoregulatory demands. In the hindgut, water and ions are removed in such amounts as to maintain the proper composition of the hemolymph. Thus it is in the hindgut that the composition of the final urine is determined. The most complete study of the osmoregulatory behavior of the hindgut has been done with the desert locust, *Schistocerca*. When a solution similar to hemolymph is injected into the hindgut of this insect, water, potassium, sodium, and chloride are

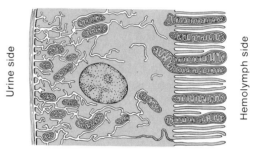

12–37. *Secretory cell in the wall of a Malpighian tubule of a cockroach. The surface facing the hemolymph is expanded into a dense pile of microvilli, some of which are distended by mitochondria. The side facing the lumen contains a profusion of branched invaginations.* [*After Oschman and Berridge, 1971.*]

Urine side

Hemolymph side

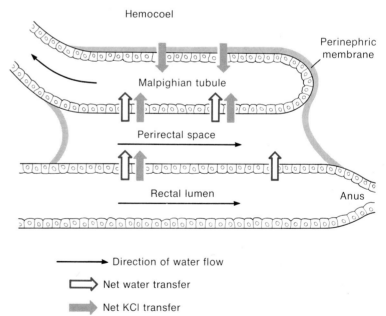

12–38. *Water-extraction apparatus of the rectum of the mealworm beetle* Tenebrio. *(See text.)* [*After Philips, 1970.*]

Hemocoel

Perinephric membrane

Malpighian tubule

Perirectal space

Rectal lumen

Anus

→ Direction of water flow

⇨ Net water transfer

⇨ Net KCl transfer

absorbed into the surrounding hemolymph. Evidence from electrical measurements suggests that the ions are transported actively.

The locust hindgut is capable of removing a large amount of water, producing a hypertonic urine, with urine/blood osmolarity ratios as high as 4. It has been argued that the uptake of water is active (i.e., directly coupled to the hydrolysis of an energy-donor molecule, such as ATP), since it takes place even against an osmotic gradient in which the osmolarity of the rectal contents is five times that of the hemolymph. In the mealworm *Tenebrio*, the urine/blood osmolarity ratio can be as high as 10, which is comparable to the concentrating ability of the most efficient mammalian kidneys. Alternatively, a purely physical mechanism may produce the net uphill movement of water without direct coupling of water transport to the release of chemical energy. It has been suggested, for example, that uphill transport of water in some species, such as *Tenebrio*, results from a countercurrent-like arrangement of the Malpighian tubules, the perinephric space, and the rectum, as illustrated in Figure 12-38. According to Philips (1970), water is drawn osmotically from the rectum into the Malpighian tubules because of the KCl gradient produced by active transport. The direction of bulk flow in these compartments is such that the osmotic gradient along the length of the complex is maximized, with the absolute osmolarities highest toward the anal end of the rectum. This may allow the concentrations near the anal end to exceed those of the hemolymph by several times. A standing-gradient system may also be responsible for solute-coupled uphill water transport in the hindgut of insects (Fig. 12-16,C). The question of active versus osmotic transport of water in the insect hindgut requires more study before it is resolved.

Very little is known about the feedback regulation of osmolarity among the invertebrates, but there is evidence for such regulation in insects. The bug *Rhodnius* becomes bloated after sucking blood from a mammalian host. Within 2–3 minutes, the Malpighian tubules increase their secretion of fluid by more than a thousand times, producing a copious urine. Artificially bloating the insect with a saline solution does not produce such diuresis in an unfed *Rhodnius*. It has also been found that isolated Malpighian tubules immersed in the hemolymph of unfed individuals remain quiescent, but if immersed in the hemolymph of a recently fed *Rhodnius* they produce a copious secretion. A factor that stimulates the secretion of these tubules can be extracted from neural tissue containing the cell bodies or axons of neurosecretory cells, primarily those of the metathoracic ganglion. Thus it appears that these cells release a diuretic hormone in response to a factor present in the ingested blood. The only identified neurohumor that simulates the diuretic action of the neuro-

secretory cells is 5-hydroxytryptamine. Similar findings on other insect species suggest that diuretic and antidiuretic hormones produced in the nervous system regulate the secretory activity of the Malpighian tubules or the resorptive activity of the rectum. In earthworms, the removal of the anterior ganglion results in the retention of water and a concomitant decrease in plasma osmolarity. Injection of homogenized brain tissue reverses these effects, suggesting a humoral mechanism.

Excretion of Nitrogenous Wastes

When amino acids are catabolized, the amino group is released. Unlike the atoms of the carbon skeleton of an amino acid, which can be oxidized to CO_2 and water, the amino group must either be salvaged for the resynthesis of amino acids or be excreted to avoid a toxic rise in the concentration of nitrogenous wastes.

The unused amino groups are excreted in one of three forms: *ammonia, urea,* or *uric acid* (Fig. 12-39). These three nitrogenous compounds differ in their properties, so that in the course of evolution some animal groups have found it more opportune to produce one or the other of these forms for excretory purposes during all or part of their life cycles. Most teleosts produce little or no urea. Instead, teleosts excrete their nitrogenous wastes primarily as ammonia. This approach is not feasible for land vertebrates, however, since ammonia is both highly toxic and highly soluble. For example, a blood concentration of 3×10^{-5} mole/liter of ammonia is fatal in rabbits. Large quantities of water would be required, therefore, to dissolve and carry off the ammonia, 300–500 ml for one gram of nitrogen in the form of ammonia. This is not feasible for land animals; they convert nitrogenous wastes either to uric acid or to urea instead. The former is only slightly soluble and hence is voided primarily as a pasty precipitate, only about 10 ml of water being required per gram of nitrogen. Although urea is quite soluble, it is far less toxic than ammonia; only about 50 ml of water is required to excrete one gram of urea. Uric acid is the choice of the birds and reptiles, which produce a *guano* containing white crystals of uric acid. Avian embryos produce ammonia for the first day or so, and then switch to uric acid, which is deposited within the egg as an insoluble solid and thus has no effect on the osmolarity of the precious little fluid contained in the egg. Lizards and snakes have various developmental schedules for switching from the production of ammonia and urea to the production of mainly uric acid. In species that lay their eggs in moist sand, the switch to uric acid production occurs late in development, but before hatching. The switch to uric acid production is a kind of biochemical metamorphosis that prepares the organism for a dry, terrestrial habitat.

The phylogenetic relations of nitrogen excretion among the vertebrates is illustrated in Figure 12-40. It is evident that there are overlaps of different excretory products in several groups. Thus the adults of a given species may excrete part of their nitrogen as ammonia, urea, or uric acid, and lesser quantities in the form of such compounds as creatinine, creatine, or trimethylamine oxide. This is generally related to habitat; terrestrial birds excrete about 90% of their nitrogenous wastes as uric acid and 3–4% as ammonia, but semiaquatic birds, such as ducks, excrete only 50%

12–39. *Molecular structures of the three common nitrogenous excretory products. Ammonia is both highly soluble and highly toxic. Uric acid is poorly soluble and nontoxic.*

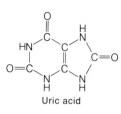

Ammonia   Urea   Uric acid

12–40. *Phylogenetic relations and nitrogen excretion among the vertebrates. The trunk of the tree includes extinct ancestral forms. Note the overlaps between ammonotelic, ureotelic, and uricotelic excretion in some of the groups. [After Schmidt-Nielsen and Mackay, 1972.]*

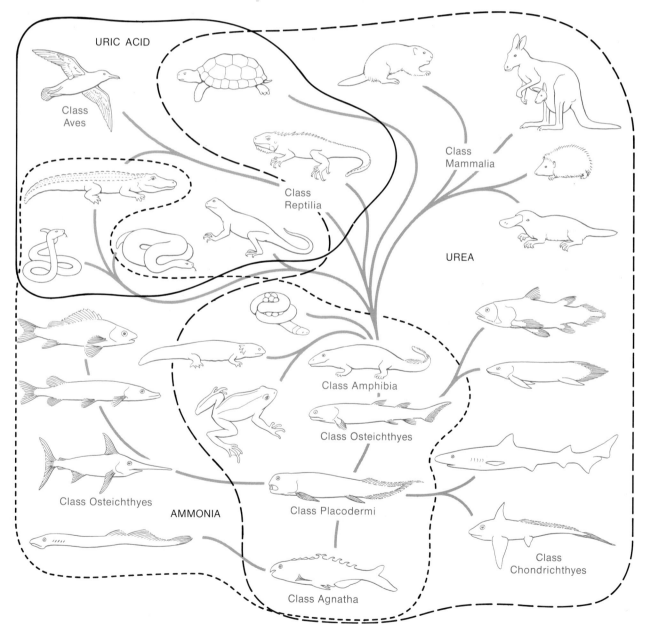

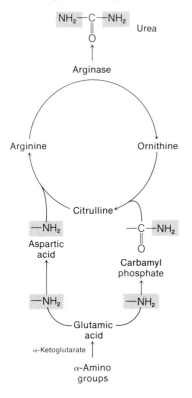

12–41. *The urea cycle. Alpha-amino groups derived by deamination of amino acids enter the cycle along with CO₂. Ureotelic animals contain large amounts of the enzyme arginase, which catalyzes the hydrolysis of arginine to ornithine and urea.* [*After Lehninger, 1970.*]

of their nitrogenous wastes as uric acid and 30% as ammonia. Mammals excrete most of their waste as urea.

In *ureotelic* (urea-excreting) animals, the synthesis of urea takes place primarily in the liver through the *urea cycle* (Fig. 12-41). Two amino groups and a molecule of CO_2 are added to ornithine to form arginine. The urea molecule is removed with the aid of the enzyme arginase, which is present in relatively large quantities in ureotelic animals.

In *ammonotelic* (ammonia-secreting) animals, the amino groups of various amino acids are transferred to glutamate, which is converted to *glutamine* (Fig. 12-42). Finally, the glutamine is deaminated in the kidney tubules, and ammonia is liberated into the tubular fluid. The ammonia can take up a proton to form the ammonium ion, NH_4^+, but because the ion is very poorly diffusible across cell membranes, the nitrogen leaves the tubular cells as NH_3. Since ammonia in both its free or ionized forms is highly toxic, it makes good sense that glutamine, which is nontoxic, should act as the amino-group carrier through blood and tissues until its deamination in the ammonotelic kidney.

Concentration of nitrogenous wastes in the urine of vertebrates takes place in two ways: (1) by glomerular filtration with subsequent removal of water and salts, leaving the waste molecules behind to be eliminated; and (2) by active tubular secretion of those molecules across the tubular epithelium into the urine. In the aglomerular kidneys of marine teleosts, secretion alone accounts for the passage of nitrogenous wastes into the urine. In the mammalian kidney, urea is passed into the urine by both filtration and secretion.

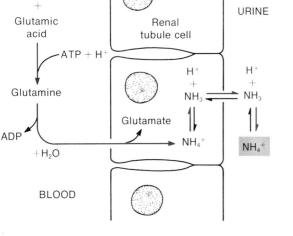

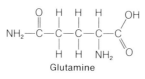

12–42. *Formation of ammonia. Glutamic acid is transaminated to form glutamine, which serves as the amino-group carrier in the blood. Within the cells of the kidney tubule, the amino group is removed as NH_4^+. The uncharged lipid-soluble form, NH_3, crosses the cell membrane into the urine.*

Summary

The extracellular environment in many marine and nonmarine animals broadly resembles dilute sea water. This similarity may have had its origin in the shallow, dilute primeval seas that are believed to have been the setting for the early evolution of animal life. The ability of many animals to regulate the composition of their internal environment is closely correlated with their ability to occupy ecological environments that are osmotically at odds with the osmotic requirements of their tissues. Osmoregulation requires the exchange of salts and water between the extracellular environment and the external environment to compensate for obligatory, or uncontrolled, losses and gains. The obligatory exchange of water depends on (1) the osmotic gradient that exists between the internal and external environments, (2) the surface/volume ratio of the animal, (3) the permeability of the integument, (4) the intake of food and water, (5) the evaporative losses required for thermoregulation, and (6) the disposal of digestive and metabolic waste through urine and feces.

The transport of solutes and water across epithelial layers is fundamental to all osmoregulatory activity. Such transport depends on an asymmetry in the permeability and pumping activities of the mucosal and serosal portions of epithelial cell membranes. On the serosal side of the cell, ions are actively transported across the membrane against an electrochemical gradient; on the mucosal side, ions cross the membrane by diffusion or facilitated diffusion. Diffusion of ions back through the epithelial layer is slow, because the spaces between cells are sealed by tight junctions. Water is transported across some epithelia by being drawn osmotically down a standing salt-concentration gradient built up by active salt transport between the epithelial cell interior and the intercellular clefts. There is no evidence for true active transport of water, with the possible exception of the insect hindgut.

Mammalian and avian kidneys utilize filtration, resorption, and secretion to produce a hypertonic urine. The filtration of the plasma in the glomerulus is dependent upon arterial pressure. Crystalloids and small organic molecules are filtered, leaving blood cells and large molecules behind. Salts and organic molecules such as sugars are partially resorbed in the renal tubules from the glomerular filtrate, and certain substances are secreted into the tubules. A countercurrent multiplier system in the loop of Henle sets up a steep extracellular salt concentration gradient that extends deep into the medulla of the kidney, so that water is drawn out of the collecting duct as it passes toward the renal pelvis. Endocrine feedback control of the water permeability of the collecting duct determines the volume of water resorbed and retained in the circulation. The final urine, then, is the product of filtration, resorption, and secretion. This allows the urinary composition to depart strongly from the proportions of substances occurring in the blood.

The formation of urine follows the same major outline in all or most vertebrates and invertebrates. A primary urine is formed that contains essentially all the small molecules and ions found in the blood. In most vertebrates and in the crustaceans and mollusks, this is accomplished by ultrafiltration; in insects, by the secretion through the epithelium of the Malpighian tubules of K^+, Na^+, and phosphate, with water and other small molecules, such as amino acids and sugars, following passively by osmosis and diffusion down their concentration gradients. The primary urine is modified by the selective resorption of ions and water and, in some animals, by secretion of substances by the tubular epithelium.

The gills of teleost fish perform osmoregulation by active transport of salts, the direction of transport being inward in freshwater fish and outward in marine fish. Marine birds and reptiles both utilize the nasal salt gland for the active secretion and expulsion of concentrated salts via epithelial tubules. Secretory activity by the salt gland is stimulated by neurons with osmosensory endings in the heart.

The nitrogen produced in the catabolism of amino acids and proteins is concentrated into one of three forms of nitrogenous waste, depending on the osmotic environment of different animal groups. Ammonia, highly toxic and soluble, requires large volumes of water to dilute; it is produced by teleosts. Uric acid is less toxic and poorly soluble; it is excreted as a semisolid suspension by birds and reptiles. Urea is the least toxic and requires a moderately small amount of water. Mammals convert their nitrogen into urea, and excrete it via the urine; elsmobranchs use urea as an osmotic agent in their blood.

EXERCISES

1. How has the development of osmoregulatory mechanisms affected animal evolution?

2. What factors influence obligatory osmotic exchange with the environment?

3. Given that cell membranes can transport substances only into or out of a cell, explain how substances are transported *through* cells.

4. Describe the experiments that first demonstrated active transport of Na^+ across an epithelium.

5. What is some of the evidence that active transport of Na^+ and K^+ occurs only across the serosal membranes of epithelial cells?

6. There is no convincing evidence for direct active transport of water. Explain one way in which water is moved by epithelia against a concentration gradient—that is, from a concentrated salt solution to a more dilute salt solution.

7. What factors determine the rate of ultrafiltration in the glomerulus?

8. If the intratubular fluid in the loop of Henle remains nearly isosmotic relative to the extracellular fluid along its path, and is even slightly hypotonic upon leaving the loop, in what way is the final urine made hypertonic?

9. Explain why the consumption of 1 liter of beer has a greater diuretic effect than the consumption of an equal volume of water?

10. What role does the kidney play in the regulation of blood pressure?

11. How do marine and freshwater fish maintain osmotic homeostasis?

12. Compare the function of aglomerular and glomerular vertebrate kidneys.

13. What evidence supports the existence of filtration-absorption organs of osmoregulation in mollusks and crustaceans?

14. Why is it more adaptive for animals to resorb essential physiological molecules or ions from urine than to secrete wastes actively into the urine?

15. How do insects produce concentrated, hypertonic urine and excrement?

16. In the course of evolution, terrestrial organisms have come to excrete mainly uric acid and urea rather than ammonia. What are the adaptive reasons for such a change?

17. Explain why gulls can drink seawater and survive but humans cannot.

18. After the injection of inulin into a small mammal, the plasma inulin concentration was found to be 1 mg/ml, the concentration in the urine 10 mg/ml, and the urine flow rate through the ureter 10 ml/hr. What was the rate of plasma filtration and the clearance in ml/min? How much water was resorbed in the tubules per hour?

19. What evidence is there that the mammalian nephron employs tubular secretion as one means of eliminating substances into the urine?

20. Countercurrent systems have evolved for gas-exchange in the gills and swim bladder of fish, for heat conservation in the vascular systems of the extremities of some homeotherms, and for establishing osmotic gradients in the kidneys of birds and mammals. Explain why the countercurrent system is more efficient in physical transport and transfer than a system in which fluids in opposed vessels flow in the same direction.

SUGGESTED READING

Bentley, P. J. 1971. *Endocrines and Osmoregulation.* Springer-Verlag, New York.

Bentley, P. J. 1972. Comparative endocrinology and osmoregulation. *Fed. Proc.* 31:1583–1624.

Brenner, B. M. 1974. Renal handling of sodium. *Fed. Proc.* 33:13–36.

Harvey, R. J. 1974. *The Kidneys and the Internal Environment.* Wiley, New York.

Moffat, D. B. 1971. *The Control of Water Balance by the Kidney.* Oxford Univ. Press, New York.

Pitts, R. F. 1968. *Physiology of the Kidney and Body Fluids* (2nd ed.). Year Book Medical Publishers, Chicago.

Smith, H. W. 1953. *From Fish to Philosopher.* Little, Brown & Co., Boston.

Wessels, N. K. 1968. *Vertebrate Adaptations: Readings from Scientific American.* Part IV. Water Balance and its Control. pp. 185–204. W. H. Freeman and Company, San Francisco.

REFERENCES CITED

Burg, M., J. Grantham, M. Abramow, and J. Orloff. 1966. Preparation and study of fragments of single rabbit nephrons. *Amer. J. Physiol.* 210:1293–1298.

Curran, P. F. 1960. Na, Cl, and water transport by rat ileum *in vitro. J. Gen. Physiol.* 43:1137–1148.

Curran, P. F. 1965. Ion transport in intestine and its coupling to other transport processes. *Fed. Proc.* 24:993–999.

Curran, P. F., and M. Cereijido. 1965. K fluxes in frog skin. *J. Gen. Physiol.* 48:1011–1033.

Diamond, J. M. 1971. Standing-gradient model of fluid transport in epithelia. *Fed. Proc.* 30:6–13.

Diamond, J. M., and W. H. Bossert. 1967. Standing-gradient osmotic flow, a mechanism for coupling of water and solute transport in epithelia. *J. Gen. Physiol.* 50:2061–2083.

Diamond, J. M., and J. McD. Tormey. 1966a. Studies on the structural basis of water transport across epithelial membranes. *Fed. Proc.* 25:1458–1463.

Diamond, J. M., and J. McD. Tormey. 1966b. Role of long extracellular channels in fluid transport across epithelia. *Nature* 210:817–820.

Grantham, J. J. 1971. Mode of water transport in mammalian renal collecting tubules. *Fed. Proc.* 30:14–21.

Hargitay, B., and W. Kuhn. 1951. Das Multiplikationsprinzipals Grundlage der Harnkonzentrierung in der Niere. *Z. Electrochem.* 55:539–558.

Hoshiko, T. 1961. Electrogenesis in frog skin. *In* H. M. Shanes (ed.), *Bio-Physics in Physiological and Pharmacological Actions.* American Association Advancement of Science, Washington, D.C.

Huf, E. G. 1935. Versuche über den Zusammenhang zwischen Stoffwechsel, Potentialbildung und Funktion der Froschhaut. *Pflügers Arch.* 235:655–673.

Koefoed-Johnsen, V., and H. H. Ussing. 1958. The nature of frog skin. *Acta. Physiol. Scand.* 42:298–308.

Lehninger, A. L. 1970. *Biochemistry.* Worth, New York.

Lindley, B. D. 1970. Fluxes across epithelia. *Amer. Zool.* 10:355–364.

Maetz, J. 1971. Fish gills: Mechanisms of salt transfer in fresh water and sea water. *Phil. Trans. Roy. Soc.* (London) Ser. B, 262:209–249.

Merck, Sharp, and Dohme. 1947. Cited by Hoar, W. S. in *General and Comparative Physiology.* Prentice-Hall, Englewood Cliffs, N.J.

Oschman, J. C. and M. J. Berridge. 1971. The structural basis of fluid secretion. *Fed. Proc.* 30:49–56.

Philips, J. E. 1970. Apparent transport of water in insect excretory system. *Amer. Zool.* 10:413–436.

Pitts, R. F. 1968. *Physiology of the Kidney and Body Fluids* (2nd ed.). Year Book Medical Publishers, Chicago.

Pitts, R. F. 1959. *The Physiological Basis of Diuretic Therapy.* Charles C Thomas, Springfield, Illinois.

Prosser, C. L. 1973. *Comparative Animal Physiology* (Vol. I). Saunders, Philadelphia.

Rhodin, J. 1954. Correlation of ultrastructural organization and function in normal and experimentally changed proximal convoluted tubule cells of the mouse kidney. Thesis, Karolinska Institute, Stockholm. *In* R. F. Pitts, *Physiology of the Kidney and Body Fluids.* Year Book Medical Publishers, Chicago, 1968.

Richards, A. N. 1935. Urine formation in the amphibian kidney. *Harvey Lect.* 93–118.

Schmidt-Nielsen, B. M. 1971. Introduction to comparative aspects of transport of hypertonic, isotonic, and hypotonic solutions by epithelial membranes. *Fed. Proc.* 30:3–5.

Schmidt-Nielsen, B. M., and W. C. Mackey. 1972. Comparative physiology of electrolyte and water regulation, with emphasis on sodium, potassium, chloride, urea, and osmotic pressure. *In* M. H. Maxwell, and C. R. Kleeman (eds.), *Clinical Disorders of Fluid and Electrolyte Metabolism.* McGraw-Hill, New York.

Schmidt-Nielsen, K. 1959. Salt glands. *Scientific American* 200(1):109–116.

Smith, H. W. 1939. *Physiology of the Kidney.* Univ. Kansas Press, Lawrence.

Smith, H. W. 1956. *Principles of Renal Physiology.* Oxford Univ. Press, New York.

Solomon, A. K. 1960. *In* A. Kleinzeller and A. Kotyk (eds.), *Symposium on Membrane Transport and Metabolism.* Academic Press, New York.

Solomon, A. K. 1962. Pumps in the living cell. *Scientific American.* 207(2):100–108.

Ussing, H. H. 1949. The active ion transport through the isolated frog skin in the light of tracer studies. *Acta. Physiol. Scand.* 17:11–37.

Ussing, H. H. 1954. Ion transport across biological membranes. *In* H. T. Clarke and D. Nachmansohn (eds.), *Ion Transport Across Membranes,* Academic Press, New York.

Ussing, H. H., and K. Zerahn. 1951. Active transport of sodium as the source of electric current in the short-circuit isolated frog skin. *Acta. Physiol. Scand.* 23:110–127.

Wigglesworth, V. B. 1932. On the function of the so-called rectal-glands of insects. *Q. Jour. Micro. Sci.* 75:131–150.

CHAPTER THIRTEEN

Circulation of Blood

Blood and the vessels in which it moves have evolved for the transport of materials between the various tissues of the body. These materials include respiratory gases, nutrients, waste products, hormones, antibodies, salts, and cells of various types. Blood acts as the vehicle for most homeostatic processes and, in several respects, has the properties of a complex tissue because of the variety of special cell types that it contains. Its movement through the animal body results from the forces imparted by rhythmic contractions of the heart, by the squeezing of blood vessels during body movements, and/or by the peristaltic contractions of smooth muscle surrounding blood vessels. (Fig. 13-1). The relative importance of each of these mechanisms in generating flow varies. In vertebrates, the heart plays the major role in blood circulation; in arthropods, movements of the limbs and contractions of the dorsal heart are equally important in generating blood flow; in the giant earthworm *Glossoscolex giganteus,* peristaltic contractions of the dorsal vessel are responsible for moving blood in an anterior direction and filling the five pairs of lateral hearts (Fig. 13-2). In all animals, valves and/or septa determine the direction of flow (Fig. 13-3), and sphincters surrounding blood vessels regulate the amount of blood that flows through a particular pathway, and thus control the distribution of blood within the body.

Many invertebrates have an *open circulation*—that is, a system in which blood pumped by the heart empties via an artery into an open fluid space to bathe cells (Fig. 13-4). In crustaceans and mollusks, blood is collected in the gills before returning via a sinus to the heart. Open-circulation systems have low pressures, seldom exceeding 5–10 mm Hg. Higher pressures have been recorded in portions of the open circulation of the terrestrial snail *Helix,* but these are exceptional. In snails, these high pressures are generated by contractions of the heart, whereas in some bivalve mollusks high pressures in the foot are generated by contractions of surrounding muscles rather than by the heart.

13-1. *Changes in blood flow caused by contractions of the heart (A), contractions of skeletal muscle (B), and peristalsis (C). Peristalsis has been observed in the venous system of the bat and in arteries of giant earthworms. [Part B after Barcroft and Swan, 1953.]*

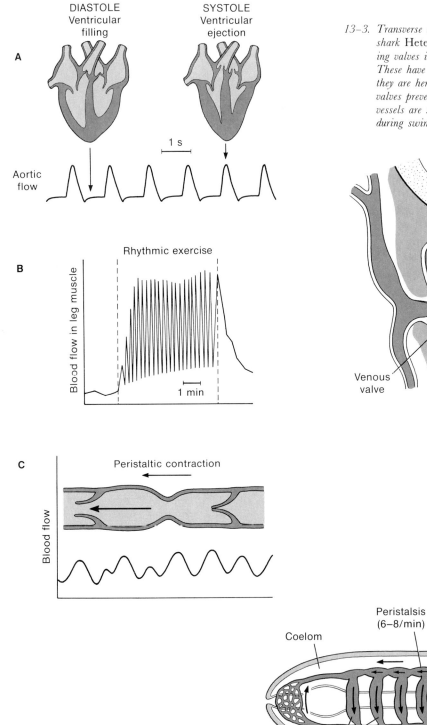

13-3. *Transverse section of the haemel canal of the shark* Heterodontus portus jacksoni, *showing valves in intercostal arteries and veins. These have their origins half a segment apart; they are here shown at the same level. These valves prevent the backflow of blood when vessels are squeezed by contracting muscles during swimming. [After Satchell, 1971.]*

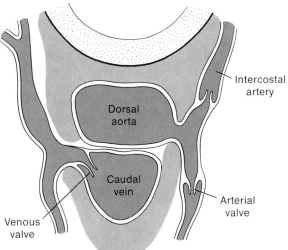

13-2. *Circulation in the giant earthworm* Glossoscolex giganteus. *[Data from Johansen and Martin, 1965.]*

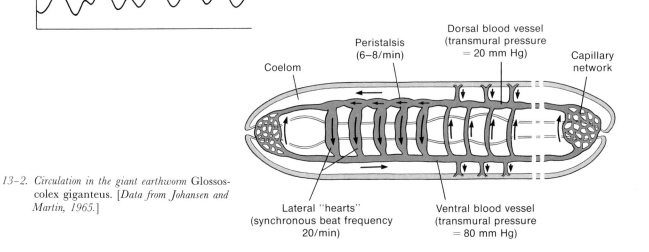

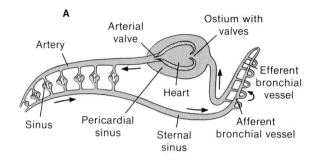

13–4. *Invertebrate circulations. A. Simplified diagram of the circulation in the crayfish. B. Simplified diagram of the circulation in a bivalve mollusk. C. Hearts and main blood vessels of a cephalopod. The broken arrows indicate the direction of water flow; other arrows, direction of blood flow.*

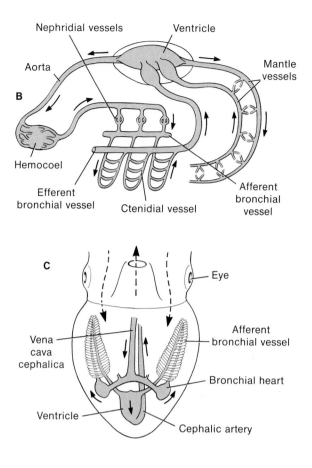

13–5. *The mammalian circulation. The percentages indicate the relative proportion of blood in different parts of the circulation.*

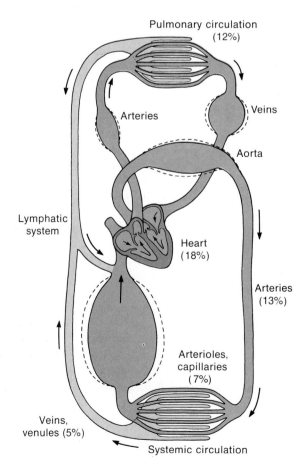

The functional significance of these high pressures in open circulations is that they appear to help the animal maintain posture.

Vertebrates, and some invertebrates, have a *closed circulation,* with blood flowing from the arterial to the venous circulation through *capillaries,* which constitute an extensive network of small tubes (Fig. 13-5). In most tissues, each cell is no more than two or three cells away from a capillary. The presence of this extensive network allows fine control of blood distribution but increases the impedance to flow and, therefore, the cost of circulating the blood. High arterial pressures are required to maintain an adequate rate of flow through these small capillaries. The pumping action of the heart fills the arterial system and maintains arterial pressure. Only a few capillaries are open at any one time, the rest being closed off by sphincters at the entrance to the capillary bed. Relaxation of these sphincters can produce sudden increases in flow, because the high pressure of the arterial system acts as a reservoir for maintaining capillary flow. The capillary walls are thin, thus allowing high rates of transfer of material between blood and tissues, but because the walls are permeable and pressures high, fluid can slowly filter across the capillary walls and into the spaces between cells. This fluid is returned to the circulation via a *lymphatic system,* a low-pressure tissue-drainage system connected to the cardiovascular system at points of low transmural pressure. Closed systems, therefore, are typified by high pressures, extensive capillary networks, and an associated lymphatic system for recycling fluid that has leaked into the tissue spaces.

Most blood pressures reported are in fact *transmural blood pressures*—that is, differences between pressures inside and outside of a blood vessel. In vertebrates, arterial transmural pressures typically range from 30 to 130 mm Hg. Similar pressures have been recorded in the arterial system of invertebrates with closed circulations. For instance, synchronous contractions of the five pairs of lateral hearts generate pressures of about 80 mm Hg in the ventral distributing vessel of the giant earthworm *Glossoscolex giganteus* (Fig. 13-2). These values, however, give no indication of flow:

blood flow is proportional *not to the transmural pressure,* but to the pressure difference *along* a vessel.

High blood pressures enable vertebrates to form an ultrafiltrate in the kidney, and this is correlated with the presence of a closed circulation. Animals with a low-pressure open circulation generally cannot produce an excretory fluid by ultrafiltration. In insects, for example, the primary excretory fluid is formed in the Malpighian tubules by secretion (p. 424).

Animals with an open circulation generally have a limited ability to alter the velocity and distribution of blood flow. As a result, in bivalve mollusks and other animals that have open circulations and use blood for gas transport, changes in oxygen uptake are usually slow and maximum rates of oxygen transfer low per unit weight. Insects have avoided this problem by evolving a tracheal system in which direct gas transport to tissues occurs through air-filled tubes that bypass the blood. Consequently, although insects have an open circulation, they have a large capacity for aerobic metabolism.

The Mammalian Heart

The mammalian heart consists of four chambers (Fig. 13-6). Blood returning from the lungs enters the *left atrium,* passes into the *left ventricle,* and is then ejected into the body circulation. Blood from the body collects in the right atrium, passes into the right ventricle and is pumped to the lungs. Valves prevent backflow of blood from the aorta to the ventricle, the atrium, and the veins. These valves are passive and are opened and closed by pressure differences between heart chambers. The atrio-ventricular valves (bicuspid and tricuspid valves; Fig. 13-6) are connected to the ventricular wall by fibrous strands. These strands prevent the valves from being everted into the atria when the ventricles contract and intraventricular pressures are much higher than those in the atria.

The heart muscle consists of three types of muscle fiber. Muscle cells found in the sinus node and the atrio-ventricular node are smaller than other myocardial cells, are only weakly contractile, are autorhythmic, and exhibit very slow conduction between cells. The largest myocardial cells are found in the ventricular endocardium and are also weakly contractile, but are specialized for fast conduction. The intermediate-sized myocardial cells are strongly contractile and constitute the bulk of the heart.

The walls of the ventricle, especially the left chamber, are thick and muscular; the inner portion of the wall, or *endocardium,* is generally more spongy than the outer region, or *epicardium.* The mammalian heart is contained within a fibrous but flexible bag, the *pericardium.*

13-6. *Cutaway view of the human heart, showing the rear portion, depicts the pacemaker and the path of its impulses. The pacemaker is the structure near the top of the heart; it is variously called the sinus node and the sinoatrial node. Impulses from the pacemaker spread along the paths indicated by the colored lines to the atrio-ventricular node, from which they are transmitted to the ventricles. Pacemaker cells differ from both nerve cells and muscle cells; they are usually described as modified muscle cells.* [After "The Heart's Pacemaker" by E. F. Adolph. Copyright © 1967 by Scientific American, Inc. All rights reserved.]

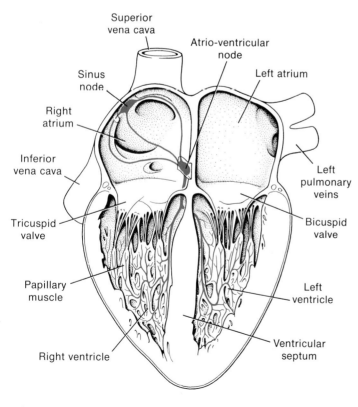

Superior vena cava

Atrio-ventricular node

Left atrium

Sinus node

Right atrium

Inferior vena cava

Left pulmonary veins

Tricuspid valve

Bicuspid valve

Papillary muscle

Left ventricle

Right ventricle

Ventricular septum

Electrical Activity of the Heart

Hearts are muscular pumps. Vertebrate cardiac and skeletal muscle fibers are similar except that the T-system (p. 294) is less extensive in myocardial (cardiac) cells and cardiac muscle cells are electrically coupled. Except for differences in the uptake and release of Ca^{2+}, the mechanisms of contraction of skeletal and cardiac muscle are generally considered to be alike.

A heartbeat consists of a rhythmic contraction and relaxation of the whole muscle mass. Contraction of each cell is associated with an action potential in that cell. The electrical activity is initiated in a pacemaker region of the heart, and electrical activity spreads over the heart from one cell to another because the cells are electrically coupled via membrane junctions. The nature and extent of coupling determines the pattern by which the electrical wave of excitation spreads over the heart and also influences the rate of conduction.

THE PACEMAKER REGION

The pacemaker region consists of cells that are capable of spontaneous activity (p. 142). Hearts may have many cells capable of pacemaker activity, but because all cardiac cells are electrically coupled, the cell (or group of cells) with the fastest intrinsic rate is the one that stimulates the whole heart to contract and which determines the heart rate. These pacemaker cells will normally overshadow those with slower pacemaker activity, but if the normal pacemaker were to stop, the other pacemaker cells would determine a new, lower heart rate. Thus cells with the capacity for spontaneous activity may be categorized as pacemakers and latent pacemakers. In the event that a latent pacemaker becomes uncoupled electrically from the pacemaker, it may beat and control a portion of cardiac muscle at a rate different from that of the normal pacemaker. Such a pacemaker is referred to as an *ectopic pacemaker.*

Pacemaker cells may be either neurons (as in many invertebrate hearts) or modified muscle cells (as in vertebrate and some invertebrate hearts). If the heartbeat is initiated in a neuron, the pacemaker is called a *neurogenic pacemaker;* if the beat is initiated in a modified muscle cell, the term *myogenic pacemaker* is used. Hearts are often categorized by the type of pacemaker, and hence are called either neurogenic or myogenic hearts.

Neurogenic Pacemakers. In many invertebrates, it is not clear whether the pacemaker is neurogenic or myogenic. Decapod crustacea, however, do have neurogenic hearts. The cardiac ganglion, situated on the heart and consisting of 9 or more neurons (depending on the species) acts as a pacemaker. If the cardiac ganglion is removed, the heart stops beating but the ganglion continues to be active and shows intrinsic rhythmicity. The cardiac ganglion consists of small and large cells. The small cells act as pacemakers and are connected to the large follower cells, which are all electrically coupled. Activity from the small pacemaker cells is fed into and integrated by the large follower cells and then distributed to the heart muscle. Some of the large follower cells have been shown to have the capacity to act as pacemakers. The cardiac ganglion is innervated by excitatory and inhibitory nerves that can alter the rate of firing of the ganglion and, therefore, the heart rate.

Myogenic Pacemakers. Vertebrate, molluscan, and many other invertebrate hearts are driven by myogenic pacemakers. These modified muscle cells have been studied extensively in a variety of vertebrate species. Pacemaker cells are usually only weakly contractile, are smaller than other heart cells, and are characterized by an unstable resting potential. The resting potential slowly depolarizes to a threshold level, at which time an action potential is produced. This slow depolarization is termed the pacemaker potential (Fig. 13-7). The ionic bases of pacemaker and action potentials are discussed in Chapter 5.

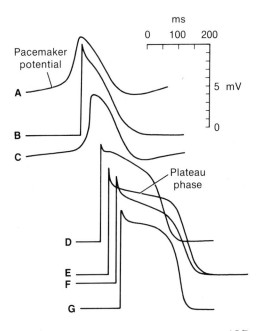

13-7. *Drawings of transmembrane action potentials recorded from the following sites: sinoatrial node (A), atrium (B), atrioventricular node (C), bundle of His (D), Purkinje fiber in a false tendon (E), terminal Purkinje fiber, (F), and ventricular muscle fiber (G). Note the sequence of activation at the various sites, as well as the differences in the amplitude, configuration, and duration of the action potentials. [After Hoffman and Cranefield, 1960.]*

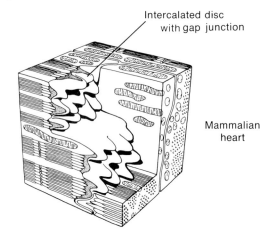

13–8. *Mammalian myocardial cells.* [*After Sjöstrand et al., 1958.*]

Intercalated disc with gap junction

Mammalian heart

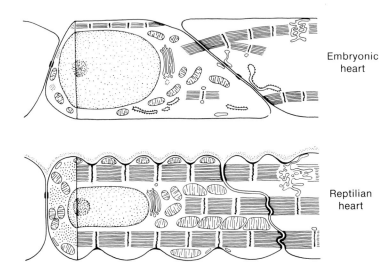

13–9. *Myocardial cells from a mammalian embryonic heart and a reptilian heart.* [*After Hirakow, 1970.*]

Embryonic heart

Reptilian heart

CARDIAC MUSCLE CELLS

Action potentials precede contraction in all cardiac muscle cells. The exact form of the action potential varies in different cells. All cardiac cells, except pacemaker cells, have a stable resting potential. Action potentials in cardiac muscle are of long duration compared with action potentials in skeletal muscle (Fig. 9-43). The action potential in skeletal muscle is complete and the membrane in a nonrefractory stage before the onset of contraction, hence repetitive stimulation and summation of contraction are possible. The long duration of the action potential in cardiac muscle ensures that the signal has time to travel over the entire atrial or ventricular muscle and produce a complete contraction of the entire chamber before any portion of the muscle can repolarize and relax. Because the refractory period is very long relative to the time course of relaxation, summation of contractions is avoided in cardiac muscle.

Cardiac muscle action potentials have a rapid depolarization phase associated with an increase in sodium conductance. Repolarization of the cell membrane is delayed and the cell remains depolarized for many milliseconds (Fig. 13-7). The duration of the plateau phase and the rates of depolarization and repolarization vary in different cells of the same heart. Atrial cells generally have an action potential of shorter duration than ventricular cells. The duration of the action potential in atrial or ventricular fibers from hearts of different species also varies. The duration of the action potential is one factor that determines the maximum frequency of the heartbeat; heart rates are normally higher in smaller mammals and the duration of the ventricular action potential shorter.

There is great diversity among the hearts of different invertebrate phyla, hence little generalization can be made about the ionic mechanisms of invertebrate hearts other than that participation of Ca^{2+} is widespread. For instance, bivalve mollusk hearts have a calcium action potential.

TRANSMISSION OF EXCITATION OVER THE HEART

Activity initiated in the pacemaker is conducted over the entire heart, depolarization in one cell resulting in the depolarization of neighboring cells by virtue of electrical coupling. Junctions between cells are formed by the close apposition of large areas of neighboring cells. Area of contact is increased by folding and interdigitation of membranes. Gap junctions (p. 105) represent regions of low resistance between cells and allow the transfer of electrical activity from one cell to the next across the *intercalated disks* (Fig. 13-8). The extent of infolding and interdigitation increases during development of the heart and is also variable among species (Fig. 13-9).

Although the junctions between cells can conduct in both directions, transmission is usually unidirectional because it is initiated in and spreads only from the pacemaker region. There are usually several pathways for excitation of any single cardiac muscle fiber, as intercellular connections are numerous. If a portion of the heart becomes nonfunctional, the wave of excitation can easily flow around that portion, so that the remainder of the heart can still be excited. The prolonged nature of cardiac action potentials ensures that multiple connections do not result in multiple stimulation and a reverberation of activity in cardiac muscle. An action potential initiated in the pacemaker region results in a single action potential in all other cardiac cells, and another pacemaker action potential is required for the next wave of excitation.

In the mammalian heart, the pacemaker is situated in the sinus node. The wave of excitation spreads over both atria in a concentric fashion at a velocity of about 0.3 m/s. The atria are connected electrically to the ventricles only through the atrio-ventricular node; other regions are joined by connective tissue that does not conduct the wave of excitation from atria to ventricles. Excitation spreads to the ventricle through small *junctional fibers,* in which the velocity of the wave of excitation is slowed to about 0.05 m/s. The junctional fibers are connected to nodal fibers, which in turn are connected via transitional fibers to the *bundle of His,* which consists of right and left bundles and covers the endocardium of the two ventricles. Conduction is slow through the nodal fibers (about 0.1 m/s), but rapid through the bundle of His, (1.5–2.5 m/s). The bundle of His delivers the wave of excitation to all regions of the endocardium almost simultaneously so that all the muscle fibers of the endocardium contract synchronously; the wave of excitation is followed almost immediately by contractions of ventricular epicardial cells as the wave of excitation passes at a velocity of 0.5 m/s from the endocardium to the epicardium. The functional significance of the arrangement of the cardiac muscle cells is its ability to deliver separate, synchronous contractions of the atria and the ventricles. Slow conduction through the atrio-ventricular node allows atrial contractions to precede ventricular contractions and allows time for blood to move from the atria into the ventricles.

Because of the large number of cells involved, the currents that flow during the synchronous activity of cardiac cells can be detected as small changes in potential from points all over the body. These potential changes—recorded as the electrocardiogram—are a reflection of electrical activity in the heart, and can be easily monitored and then anlayzed. A P-wave is associated with depolarization of the atrium, a QRS complex with depolarization of the ventricle, and a

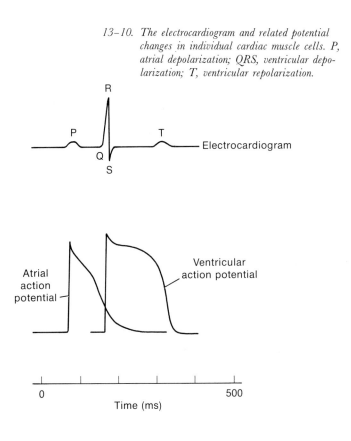

13–10. *The electrocardiogram and related potential changes in individual cardiac muscle cells. P, atrial depolarization; QRS, ventricular depolarization; T, ventricular repolarization.*

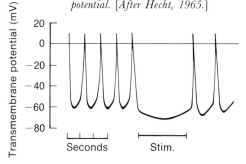

13–11. *The effect of vagus nerve stimulation on the pacemaker action potential. Several action potentials are shown. Stimulation of the vagus nerve produces a rise in diastolic transmembrane potential, a decrease in the rate of depolarization of the pacemaker potential, and a decrease in the duration of the action potential. [After Hecht, 1965.]*

T-wave with repolarization of the ventricle (Fig. 13-10). The exact form of the electrocardiogram is affected by the nature and position of recording electrodes as well as the physiological state of the heart.

Various compounds alter the properties of cardiac muscle cells. Acetylcholine, released from cholinergic nerve fibers, causes an increase in potassium conductance, and therefore hyperpolarizes the membrane and reduces the rate of depolarization of the pacemaker potential (p. 143). This increases the interval between action potentials and thus slows the heart rate (Fig. 13-11). Parasympathetic cholinergic fibers in the vagus

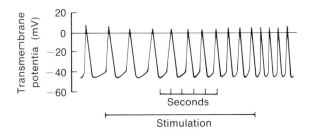

13–12. *The effect of sympathetic nerve stimulation on the pacemaker cell action potential. Several action potentials are shown. When the sympathetic nerves are stimulated, there is an increase in the rate of depolarization, which results in an increase in the frequency of firing of the pacemaker cell. [After Hutter and Trautwein, 1956.]*

nerve innervate the sinus node and atrio-ventricular node of the vertebrate heart. Acetylcholine reduces the velocity of conduction from atria to ventricles through the atrio-ventricular node. High levels of acetylcholine block transmission through the atrioventricular node, so that only every second or third wave of excitation is transmitted to the ventricle. Under these conditions, the atrial rate will be two or three times that in the ventricle. Alternatively, high levels of acetylcholine may block *conduction* through the atrio-ventricular node, giving rise to an ectopic pacemaker in the ventricle, with the result that the atria and ventricles are controlled by different pacemakers and contract at quite different rates, the two beats being uncoordinated.

Epinephrine and norepinephrine increase both the rate and force of contraction of the heart. The effect of these catecholamines on rate of contraction is mediated via the pacemaker, whereas the increased strength of contraction is a general effect on all myocardial cells. The increase in rate is due to changes in conductance in the pacemaker cell. Norepinephrine probably increases sodium conductance, increasing the rate of depolarization of the pacemaker potential and shortening the interval between successive action potentials (Fig. 13-12), thereby increasing heart rate. Norepinephrine also increases conduction velocity through the atrio-ventricular node. It is released from adrenergic nerve fibers that innervate the sinus node, atria, atrio-ventricular node, and the ventricle, so that sympathetic adrenergic stimulation has a direct effect on all portions of the heart. Metabolic actions of the catecholamines on cardiac cells are discussed in Chapters 5 and 11.

Mechanical Properties of the Heart

The heart consists of a number of muscular chambers connected in series and guarded by valves or, in a few cases, sphincters (e.g., in some molluscan hearts), which allow blood to flow in only one direction. Contractions of the heart result in the ejection of blood into the circulatory system. A series of chambers permits step increases in pressure as blood passes from the venous to the arterial side of the circulation.

CHANGES IN PRESSURE AND FLOW DURING A SINGLE HEART BEAT

Contractions of the heart cause fluctuations in pressure and flow. Figure 13-13 shows the general plan of a mammalian heart. During diastole, closed aortic valves maintain large pressure differences between the relaxed ventricles and the systemic and pulmonary aortae. The atrio-ventricular valves are open, and blood flows directly from the venous system into the ventricle. When the atria contract, pressures rise in the atria, and blood is ejected from the atria into the ventricles. Then the ventricles begin to contract. Pressures rise in the ventricles and exceed those in the atria. The atrio-ventricular valves close and prevent the backflow of blood into the atria. Ventricular contraction proceeds; during this phase, both the atrioventricular and the aortic valves are closed, so that the ventricle is a sealed chamber and there is no volume change. That is, the ventricular contraction is "isometric." Pressure within the ventricle increases rapidly and eventually exceeds that in the aorta. The aortic valves open, and the volume of the ventricle decreases as blood is ejected into the aorta. The ventricle then begins to relax, intraventricular pressures fall below the pressure in the aorta, the aortic valves close, and there is an isometric relaxation of the ventricle. The atrio-ventricular valves open when ventricular pressure falls below that in the atria. Ventricular filling starts once more, and the cycle is repeated. In the mammalian heart, the volume of blood forced into the ventricle by atrial contraction is much less than the volume of blood ejected into the aorta by ventricular contraction. In mammals, ventricular filling is determined to a large extent by venous filling pressure; blood flows from the veins, directly through the atria, into the ventricles. Atrial contraction simply tops off the nearly full ventricles with blood.

Contraction of cardiac muscle is complex, and can be divided into two phases. The first is an isometric contraction during which tension in the muscle and pressure in the ventricle increase rapidly. The second phase is essentially isotonic; tension does not change

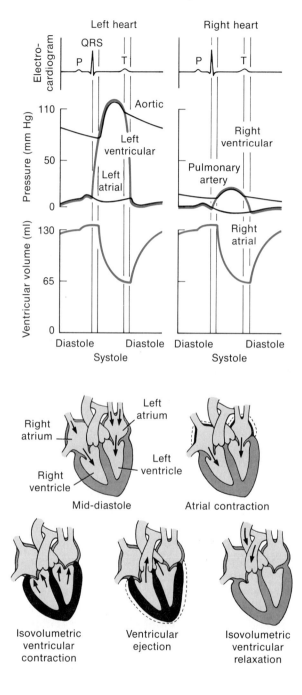

13–13. *Changes in pressure and volume in the ventricles and aorta (left) and pulmonary artery (right) during a single cardiac cycle.* [*After Vander et al., 1975.*]

very much, for as soon as the aortic valves open, blood is ejected rapidly from the ventricles into the arterial system with little increase in ventricular pressure. Thus tension is generated with almost no change in length, and then length changes with little change in tension; that is, during each contraction, cardiac muscle switches from an isometric to an isotonic contraction. Interestingly, it has been shown that in the isolated papillary muscle from a cat heart, the length-tension curves obtained from isotonic contractions of the heart are similar to length-force curves from isometric contractions. Thus cardiac muscle is adapted for generating both pressure and flow.

WORK DONE BY THE HEART

External work done is the product of mass times distance moved. In our present context, it is calculated as *pressure* times *flow*. Flow is directly related to the change in volume of the ventricle. Thus a plot of pressure times volume for a single contraction of a ventricle yields a *pressure-volume loop* whose area is proportional to the external work done by that ventricle. In Figure 13-14, pressure-volume loops have been plotted for the right and left ventricles of a mammalian heart. The two ventricles eject equal volumes of blood, but the pressures generated in the pulmonary circuit are much lower; consequently, the external work done by the right ventricle is much less than that done by the left ventricle. Blood is ejected from the ventricle only when intraventricular pressures exceed the arterial pressure. If the arterial pressure is elevated,

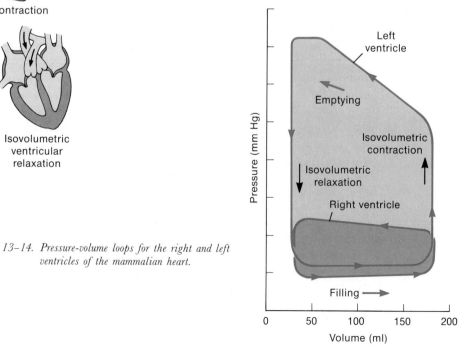

13–14. *Pressure-volume loops for the right and left ventricles of the mammalian heart.*

then more external work must be done by the heart to raise the intraventricular pressure enough to maintain stroke volume at the original level.

Not all energy expended by the heart will appear as changes in pressure and flow; some energy is expended to overcome frictional forces within the myocardium, and more will be dissipated as heat. The external work done by the heart, expressed as a fraction of the total energy expended, is termed the *efficiency of contraction.* The external work done can be determined from measurements of pressure and flow and converted into milliliters of O_2 consumed. This, in turn, can be expressed as a fraction of the total O_2 uptake by the heart in order to measure the efficiency of contraction. In fact, not more than 10–15% of the total energy expended by the heart appears as mechanical work.

Energy is expended to increase wall tension and raise *blood pressure* within the heart. According to the *Law of Laplace,* the relationship between wall tension and pressure in a hollow structure is related to the radius of curvature of the wall. If the structure is a sphere, then

$$P = 2y/R,$$

where P is the transmural pressure (the pressure difference across the wall of the sphere), y = the wall tension, and R = the radius of the sphere. According to this relation, a large heart must generate twice the wall tension of a heart half its size in order to develop a similar pressure. Thus more energy must be expended by larger hearts in developing pressure, and one might expect a larger ratio of muscle mass to total heart volume in these hearts. Hearts are not, of course, perfect spheres, but have a complex gross and microscopical morphology; nevertheless, the Law of Laplace applies in general. The energy expended in ejecting a given quantity of blood from the heart will depend on the efficiency of contraction, the pressures developed, and the size and shape of the heart. The cost of pumping blood in mammals is about 5–10% of the total energy expended by the animal.

STROKE VOLUME, HEART RATE, AND CARDIAC OUTPUT

Cardiac output is the volume of blood ejected per unit time from a ventricle. In mammals, it is the volume ejected from the right or left ventricle, not the combined volume from both ventricles. The volume of blood ejected by each beat of the heart is termed the *stroke volume,* and mean values can be determined by dividing cardiac output by heart rate.

Stroke volume is the difference between the volume of the ventricle just before contraction (end-diastolic volume) and the volume of the ventricle at the end of a contraction (end-systolic volume). The end-diastolic volume will be determined by

1. Venous filling pressure.
2. Pressures generated during atrial contraction.
3. Distensibility of the ventricular wall.
4. The time available for filling the ventricle.

The end systolic volume will be determined by

1. The ventricular pressures generated during systole.
2. The pressure in the outflow channel from the heart (aortic pressure).

Changes in stroke volume may result from changes in either end-diastolic or end-systolic volume.

In 1914, Starling observed that raising venous filling pressure causes an increase in end-diastolic volume and results in an increased stroke volume from an *in vitro* mammalian heart. End-systolic volume also increased, but not as much as end-diastolic volume. Thus cardiac muscle behaves in a way similar to that of skeletal muscle in so far as stretch of the relaxed muscle results in the development of increased tension during a contraction. Starling also observed that increases in arterial pressure result in a rise in both end-diastolic and end-systolic volume with little change in stroke volume. In this instance, the increased mechanical work required to maintain stroke volume at an elevated arterial pressure resulted from the increased stretch of cardiac muscle during diastole.

Otto Frank had previously derived a length-tension relationship for frog myocardium, and had demonstrated that contractile tension increases with stretch up to a maximum, and then decreases with further stretch. The increase in mechanical work from the ventricle caused by an increase in end-diastolic volume (or venous filling pressure) is therefore termed the *Frank-Starling mechanism.* The curves derived from measuring work output from the ventricle at different venous filling pressures are described as *Starling curves* (Fig. 13-15).

No single Starling curve, however, describes the relationship between venous filling pressure and work output from the ventricle. The mechanical, as well as electrical, properties of the heart are affected by a number of factors, including the level of activity in nerves innervating the heart and the composition of blood perfusing the myocardium. For instance, the relationship between ventricular work output and venous filling pressure is markedly affected by stimulation of sympathetic and parasympathetic nerves innervating the heart (Fig. 6-15).

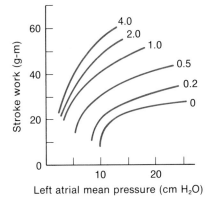

13-15. *Starling curves indicating the relationship between stroke work and venous filling pressure (left atrial mean pressure) at different levels of sympathetic nerve stimulation. The numbers indicate the stimulating frequency in Hz. [After Sarnoff and Mitchell, 1962.]*

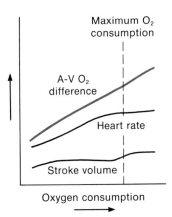

13-16. *Changes in heart rate, stroke volume, and arterial-venous oxygen difference during exertion in normal human subjects. Increases in cardiac output are associated with increases in heart rate rather than stroke volume except at very high levels of oxygen consumption, when heart rate levels off and stroke volume increases. [After Rushmer, 1965.]*

Catecholamines released from sympathetic nerves increase the distensibility and the force of contraction of the ventricle, hence both the rate and extent of ventricular filling and ventricular emptying are increased by catecholamines. The effects of cholinergic nerve activity on the rate and force of ventricular power output during each beat are much less marked than the effects of adrenergic stimulation, and are related to the reduced cholinergic innervation compared with the extensive adrenergic innervation of the ventricles.

The effects of sympathetic stimulation represent a series of integrated actions. Heart rate is increased by action on the membranes of pacemaker fibers. Conduction velocity over the heart is increased to produce a more nearly synchronous beat of the ventricle. There are increases in both the rate of production of ATP and in the rate of conversion of chemical energy to mechanical energy, leading to an increase in ventricular work. The rate of blood ejection increases during systole, so that the same or a slightly larger stroke volume is ejected in a much shorter time. Thus when adrenergic nerve stimulation increases the heart rate, the same or a larger stroke volume is ejected from the heart in a shorter time. Diastolic filling is augmented by the increased ventricular distensibility resulting from sympathetic stimulation. Thus, in mammals, both filling and emptying of the ventricles occurs more rapidly as heart rate increases. Stroke volume does not change very much, although there are small changes in both end-diastolic and end-systolic ventricular volumes in mammals.

It is possible to increase heart rate, and therefore cardiac output, merely by reducing the venous filling period. Nevertheless, the nature of the *coronary circulation* imposes limitations on the reduction in diastole. Coronary capillary flow is occluded during systole, but flow rises dramatically during diastole. A decrease in the diastolic period tends to reduce the period of coronary blood flow, and therefore the nutrition of the heart.

Increases in cardiac output with exercise are associated with changes in heart rate rather than stroke volume in mammals (Fig. 13-16). Following sympathetic denervation of the heart, exercise results in similar increases in cardiac output, but in this instance there are large changes in stroke volume rather than heart rate. The sympathetic nerves therefore play an important role in determining the relationship between heart rate and stroke volume but other additional factors are involved in mediating the increase in cardiac output with exercise.

The Pericardium

The heart is contained in a pericardial cavity and is surrounded by a pericardial membrane. The magnitude of the intrapericardial pressure change depends on the rigidity of the pericardium and the magnitude and rate of change of the heart volume. The membrane may be thin and flexible, as in mammals, in which case pressure changes that occur in the pericardial cavity during each heartbeat are negligible.

In elasmobranch fish, lungfish, and bivalve mollusks, contractions of the heart within a noncompliant

13-17. *The heart of the bivalve mollusk* Anodonta, *showing blood flow and pressure changes in the heart and pericardial cavity during ventricular diastole (left) and ventricular systole (right). Large black arrows indicate the movements of the walls of contracting chambers; small arrows indicate movements of walls of relaxing chambers. The colored arrows indicate the direction of blood flow. A, atrium; AAV, anterior aortic valve; AVV, atrio-ventricular valve; PC, pericardial cavity; PAV, posterior aortic valve; V, ventricle. [After Brand, 1972.]*

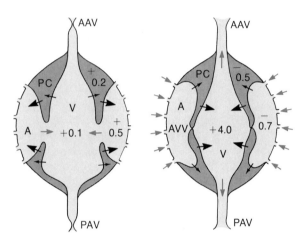

pericardium cause oscillations of pressure within the pericardial cavity. In the heart of bivalve mollusks (Fig. 13-17), contractions of the ventricle reduce pressure in the pericardial cavity and enhance flow into the atria from the venous system. Tension generated in the ventricular wall is utilized both to eject blood into the arterial system and to draw blood into the atria from the venous system. The elasmobranch heart consists of three chambers, atrium, ventricle, and conus, all contained within a pericardium (Fig. 13-18). The reduction in intrapericardial pressure during ventricular systole in elasmobranchs produces aspiratory forces that increase venous return to the heart. If the pericardial cavity is opened, cardiac output is reduced, hence the increased venous return to the atrium caused by reduced pericardial pressure is important in augmenting cardiac output. Contractions of the ventricle affect the conus as well as the atrium. The exit from the ventricle to the conus is guarded by a pair of flap valves, and there are from two to seven pairs of valves along the length of the conus. Just before ventricular systole, all valves except the set most distal to the ventricle are open. The conus and the ventricle are interconnected, but a closed valve at the exit of the conus maintains a pressure difference between the conus and the ventral aorta. During arterial systole, both the ventricle and the conus are filled with blood. Ventricular systole in elasmobranchs does not have an isovolumetric phase, because at the onset of contraction blood is moved from the ventricle into the conus. Pressure rises simultaneously in the ventricle and conus and eventually exceeds that in the ventral aorta. The distal valves open, and blood is ejected into the aorta. Conal systole begins after the onset of ventricular systole. During conal systole, the proximal valves close, preventing reflux of blood into the ventricle as

13-18. *The elasmobranch heart is contained in a noncompliant pericardium. Contractions of the ventricle create subatmospheric pressures in the pericardial cavity and assist atrial filling.*

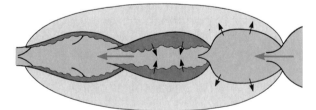

B Ventricular contraction

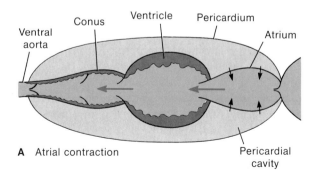

A Atrial contraction

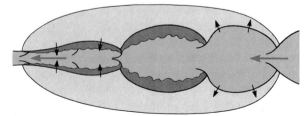

C Conal contraction

it relaxes. Conal systole proceeds relatively slowly away from the heart toward the aorta; each set of valves closes, in turn, to prevent backflow of blood. Conus length is variable among species; in general, more valves are found in those species with a longer conus.

Functional Morphology of the Vertebrate Heart

The mammalian heart is the focus of attention for studies of cardiac structure and function, and most of the foregoing discussion of electrical and mechanical properties refers to the adult mammalian heart. The structure of the heart varies in different vertebrates, and a comparative analysis of vertebrate circulatory systems produces insights into the relationships between heart structure and function. In fish, the heart consists of four chambers in series (Fig. 13-19). All chambers except the elastic bulbus are contractile. A unidirectional flow of blood through the heart is maintained by valves at the sino-atrial and atrio-ventricular junctions and at the exit of the ventricle. Blood pumped by the heart passes first through the gill (respiratory) circulation and then into a dorsal aorta that supplies the rest of the body (systemic circulation). In fish, the input pressures for the respiratory circulation are higher than those for the systemic circulation.

The pulmonary (respiratory) circulation of birds and mammals is maintained by much lower pressures than the systemic circulation because they have two series of heart chambers in parallel. The left side of the heart ejects blood into the systemic circuit, and the right side ejects blood into the pulmonary circulation (Fig. 13-6). The advantage of a high blood pressure is that rapid transit times and sudden changes in flow can be readily achieved for blood passing through small-diameter capillaries. High transmural pressures, however, result in filtration of fluid across the capillary wall, and therefore require an extensive lymphatic drainage of the tissues. In the mammalian lung, capillary flow can be maintained by relatively low input pressures, reducing the requirements for lymphatic drainage and avoiding the formation of large extracellular spaces that could increase diffusion distances between blood and air and impair the gas-transfer capacity of the lung. The advantage of a divided heart, like that of mammals, is that blood flow to the body and the lungs can be maintained by different input pressures. The disadvantage of a completely divided heart is that in order to avoid shifts in blood volume from the systemic to the pulmonary circuit, or vice versa, cardiac output must be the same in both sides

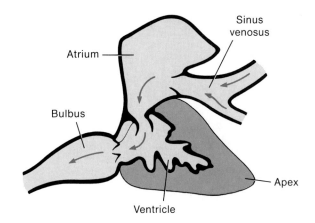

13–19. The trout heart. [After Randall, 1968.]

of the heart, independent of the requirements in the two circuits. Lungfish, amphibia, reptiles, bird embryos, and fetal mammals have either a divided ventricle or some other mechanism that allows the shunting of blood from one circulation to the other. These shunts usually result in the movement of blood from the right (respiratory, pulmonary) to the left (systemic) side of the heart during periods of reduced gas transfer in the lung. Blood returning from the body, instead of being pumped to the lung, is shunted from the right to the left side of the heart and once again ejected into the systemic circuit, bypassing the lungs. A single undivided ventricle permits variations in the ratio of flows to the pulmonary and systemic circuits, but the same pressures must be developed on both sides of the heart.

AMPHIBIA

The atria are completely subdivided in amphibia, but there is a single ventricle (Fig. 13-20) whereas in reptiles there is either partial or complete separation of the ventricle into two chambers (Figs. 13-21, 13-22).

In the frog, there is a separation of blood within the heart even though the ventricle is undivided. Blood from the lungs and skin is preferentially directed towards the body, whereas deoxygenated blood from the body is directed toward the pulmocutaneous arch. This separation of oxygenated and deoxygenated blood is aided by a spiral fold within the truncus arteriosus of the heart (Fig. 13-20). Deoxygenated blood leaves the ventricle first during systole and enters the low-impedance circuit of the lungs. Pressures rise in the pulmocutaneous arch and become similar to those in the systemic arch. Blood flows into both arches, the spiral fold partially dividing the systemic and pulmocutaneous flows within the truncus arteriosus.

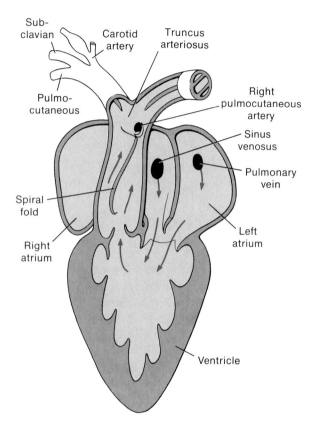

13-20. *Ventral view of the internal structure of the frog heart.* [After Goodrich, 1958.]

13-21. *Sections through the squamate heart. A. Frontal section dorsad of the cavum pulmonale. The probable reciprocal action of the atrioventricular valves is indicated by the double-headed arrows. B. Cross sections from near the apex (i) toward the base of the heart (iv). AVV, atrio-ventricular valve; CA, cavum arteriosum; CV, cavum venosum; IVC, interventricular canal; LA, left atrium; LAA, left aortic arch; LAVJ, left atrioventricular junction; PA, pulmonary arch; RA, right atrium; RAA, right aortic arch; RAVJ, right atrioventricular junction.* [After White, 1968.]

The volume flow to the lungs or body is inversely related to the impedance of the two circuits to blood flow. Immediately following a breath, the impedance to blood flow through the lung is low and blood flow is high; between breaths, impedance gradually increases and is associated with a fall in blood flow. These oscillations in lung blood flow are possible because of the partial division of the heart, which, while directing deoxygenated blood towards the pulmocutaneous arch, allows shunting in order to adjust the ratio of lung to systemic blood flow.

REPTILES

Noncrocodilian reptiles have a partially divided ventricle, whereas crocodilian reptiles have separate right and left ventricles. All reptiles have both right and left systemic arches.

In turtles, lizards, and snakes, the ventricle is partially subdivided by an incomplete muscular septum referred to as the horizontal septum, Muskelleiste, or muscular ridge. This horizontal septum separates the cavum pulmonare from the cavum venosum and cavum arteriosum, which in turn are partially separated by the verticle septum (Fig. 13-21). The right atrium contracts slightly before the left atrium and ejects deoxygenated blood into the cavum pulmonare across the free edge of the horizontal septum. Blood from the left atrium fills the cavum venosum and cavum arteriosum (Fig. 13-21). Blood in the cavum pulmonare is ejected into the pulmonary artery, but the cavum venosum and cavum arteriosum empty into the systemic arches. This process is aided by the fact that in some of the animals the contraction of the cavum pulmonare occurs slightly before that of the rest of the ventricle.

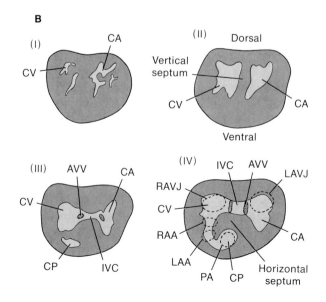

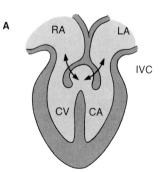

Blood pressure in the pulmonary circuit is usually less than that in the systemic circuit, and increased flow occurs earlier in the pulmonary artery than the systemic arches during each cardiac cycle. Measurements support the above view that oxygenated blood from the left atrium passes into the systemic circuit whereas deoxygenated blood from the right atrium is ejected into the pulmonary artery. In turtles, there may be some recirculation of arterial blood in the lung circuit; that is, there is probably a left to right shunt within the heart. During a dive, pulmonary vascular resistance increases in turtles, but systemic vascular resistance decreases, resulting in a right-to-left shunt and a decrease in pulmonary blood flow as compared with systemic blood flow. As in many other animals, there is a reduction in cardiac output associated with a marked slowing of the heart during a dive.

Crocodilian reptiles have two completely divided ventricles. There are also two systemic arches, the left arising from the right ventricle, the right systemic from the left ventricle. The systemic arches are connected via the foramen of Panizzae. When the reptile is breathing normally, the impedance to blood flow through the lungs is low, and pressures generated by the right ventricle are lower than those generated by the left ventricle. Blood ejected by the left ventricle flows into the right systemic arch and into the left systemic arch via the foramen of Panizzae (Fig. 13-22). Pressures in the left systemic arch remain higher than the pressure in the right ventricle; consequently, the valves at the base of the left systemic arch remain closed throughout the entire cardiac cycle. All blood ejected from the right ventricle passes into the pulmonary artery and flows to the lungs. Thus the crocodilian reptile is functionally the same as the mammal in that there is complete separation of systemic and pulmonary blood flow. The reptile, however, has the added capacity to shunt blood between the two circuits when the crocodile stops breathing and dives under water (Fig. 13-22). During this period, there is an increase in the impedance to flow in the pulmonary circuit, which results in a rise in right ventricular pressure. The increase in pulmonary impedance is probably due to a constriction of the pulmonary artery. Peak right ventricular pressure becomes equal to left ventricular pressure and exceeds left systemic pressure. As a result, the valves at the base of the left systemic arch open, and blood from the right ventricle is ejected into both the pulmonary and systemic circulations (Fig. 13-22). Thus a portion of the deoxygenated blood returning to the heart from the body is recirculated in the systemic circuit during apnea (periods of no breathing).

13-22. Diagrammatic view of the crocodilian heart. A. Crocodile breathing air. Left systemic arch is closed off from right ventricle, which ejects blood into the pulmonary artery. B. Crocodile submerged. Right ventricle ejects blood into both pulmonary artery and left systemic arch. There is an increase in resistance to flow in the pulmonary circuit and a rise in pulmonary and right ventricular pressure.

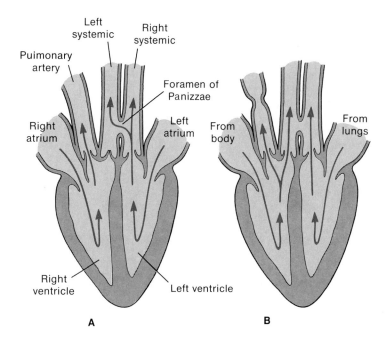

MAMMALIAN FETUS

At birth, mammals shift from a placental to a lung circulation, a process that involves several central cardiovascular readjustments. The lungs of the mammalian fetus are collapsed, presenting a high impedance to blood flow. Most of the blood ejected by the right ventricle is returned to the systemic circuit via the ductus arteriosus (Fig. 13-23), blood flow through the lungs is reduced, and there is a marked right-to-left shunt; that is, blood flows from the pulmonary to the systemic circuit. At birth, the lungs are inflated, reducing the impedance to flow in the pulmonary circuit. Blood ejected from the right ventricle passes into the lungs, resulting in an increased venous return to the left side of the heart. At the same time, the placental circulation disappears, and the impedance to flow increases markedly in the systemic circuit. Pressures in the systemic circuit rise above those in the pulmonary circulation and, if the ductus arteriosus remains open, result in a left-to-right shunt; that is, blood flows from the systemic to the pulmonary circuit. Generally, the ductus arteriosus becomes occluded, and blood flow through the ductus does not

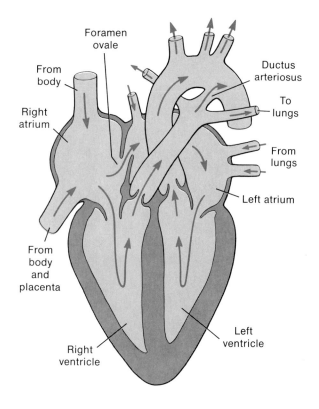

13–23. *Blood flow in the mammalian fetal heart. Blood returning from the placenta is shunted from the right to the left atrium through the foramen ovale.*

Foramen ovale

From body

Right atrium

From body and placenta

Right ventricle

Ductus arteriosus

To lungs

From lungs

Left atrium

Left ventricle

foramen ovale into the left atrium, is pumped into the left ventricle, is ejected into the aorta, and flows to the head and upper limbs. Deoxygenated blood in the right ventricle is preferentially directed toward the right ventricle, whence it flows into the systemic circuit via the ductus arteriosus. At birth, pressures in the left atrium exceed the pressure in the right atrium; as a result, the foramen ovale closes, eventually adhering to the interatrial wall to form a permanent closure.

BIRD EMBRYO

Oxygenated blood from the chorioallantois (which takes up oxygen that penetrates the egg shell) and deoxygenated blood from the head and body enter the right atrium of the bird embryo heart. The interatrial septum of the bird heart is fenestrated with several large and numerous small holes. Oxygenated blood from the chorioallantoic circulation passes from the right into the left atrium through holes in the interatrial septum. The oxygenated blood is pumped into the left ventricle and then ejected into the aorta, whence it flows to the head and body. In the adult bird, the pulmonary and systemic circulations are completely separated, as in mammals.

Hemodynamics

In vertebrates and other animals with a closed circulation, the blood flows in a continuous circuit. The velocity of flow at any point is related not to the proximity of the heart but to the cross-sectional area of the circulation. The highest velocities occur where the total cross-sectional area is least, and vice versa. The highest velocities occur in the pulmonary artery and the aorta in mammals; the velocity falls as blood passes through the capillaries and then rises as blood passes into the veins.

Since fluids are incompressible, blood pumped by the heart must cause flow of an equivalent volume in each other part of the circulation. Furthermore, unless there is some change in total blood volume, a reduction in volume in one part must lead to an increase in volume in the rest of the circulation.

LAMINAR AND TURBULENT FLOW

In nearly all portions of the circulation, blood flow is streamlined, or laminar. Laminar flow is characterized by a parabolic velocity profile across the vessel (Fig. 13-24). Flow is zero at the wall and maximum along the axis of the vessel. The blood adjacent to the vessel wall does not move, but the next layer of molecules

persist. If the ductus remains open after birth, however, blood flow to the lungs exceeds systemic flow because a portion of the left-ventricular output passes via the ductus arteriosus into the pulmonary artery and to the lung. Under these circumstances, systemic flow is often normal, but blood flow to the lungs may be twice systemic flow, and cardiac output from the left ventricle may exceed that from the right ventricle by a factor of two. The result is a marked hypertrophy of the left ventricle. The work done by the left ventricle during exercise is also much greater than normal, the capacity to increase output is limited, and, as a result, the maximum level of aerobic exercise is much reduced if the ductus arteriosus remains open after birth. Furthermore, blood pressure in the lungs is increased, leading to a greater fluid loss across lung capillary walls and may cause pulmonary congestion.

Fetal blood is oxygenated in the placenta. This oxygenated blood returns to the right atrium along with deoxygenated blood from the rest of the systemic circulation. There is a hole in the interatrial septum of the fetal heart, the foramen ovale, which permits flow from the right to the left atrium, but not in the reverse direction (Fig. 13-23). Oxygenated blood from the placenta enters the right atrium, flows through the

BOX 13-1 POTENTIAL ENERGY, PRESSURE, AND KINETIC ENERGY

Contractions of the heart raise the potential energy of the blood in the ventricle. The rise in potential energy can be measured as an increase in blood pressure. Differences in pressure between two points in a flow path establish a pressure gradient, and therefore the direction of flow—from high to low pressure. (An exception is a fluid at rest under gravity, where pressure increases uniformly with depth but flow does not occur.) Flowing blood has inertia, and energy is expended in setting the blood into motion, hence fluids in motion possess kinetic energy. In static fluids, potential energy is measured in terms of pressure; in fluids in motion, however, potential energy is measured in terms of both pressure and kinetic energy. How does kinetic energy compare with pressure? The answer is that kinetic energy is usually negligible. The kinetic energy per milliliter of fluid is given by $1/2(QV^2)$, where Q is the density of the fluid and V the velocity of flow. If the velocity is measured in cm/s and density in g/ml, then kinetic energy has the units of dynes/cm^2, the same as pressure. The maximum velocity of blood flow occurs at the base of the aorta in mammals, and is about 50 cm/s at the peak of ventricular ejection. The density of blood is about 1.055 g/ml. The kinetic energy of the blood in the aorta during peak ejection is $1/2 \times 1.055 \times 50^2$, or 1320 dynes/cm^2. Since a pressure of 1 mm Hg is equal to 1330 dynes/cm^2, the kinetic energy of the blood is close to 1 mm Hg. This is small compared with peak systolic transmural pressures of around 120 mm Hg. Blood velocity is low in the ventricle, but accelerates as blood is ejected into the aorta; that is, blood gains kinetic energy as it leaves the ventricle. Pressure is converted into kinetic energy as blood is ejected from the heart, and may account for most of the small drop in pressure that occurs between the ventricle and the aorta. Velocity, and therefore kinetic energy, is highest in the aorta. In the capillaries, the velocity is about 1 mm/s, and kinetic energy is virtually zero.

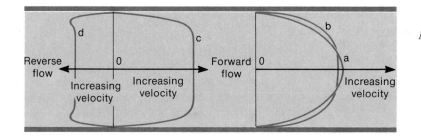

13–24. Velocity profiles for fluids flowing in tubes. Curve a: Continuous laminar flow, plasma. Curve b: Continuous laminar flow, blood. Curve c: Pulsatile laminar flow, blood at peak of forward motion. Curve d: Pulsatile laminar flow, blood at peak of flow reversal.

slides over this layer, and so on, each successive layer moving at an increasingly higher velocity, with the maximum at the center of the vessel. A pressure difference supplies the force required to slide adjacent layers past each other, and viscosity is a measure of the resistance to sliding between adjacent layers of fluid. An increase in viscosity will require a larger pressure difference to maintain the same rate of flow.

Turbulent flow occurs at certain points in the circulation. In turbulent flow, fluid moves in all directions at once, and much more energy is expended in moving fluid through a vessel under these conditions.

Laminar flow is silent and turbulent flow noisy; in the bloodstream, turbulence causes vibrations that produce the sounds of the circulation, and these sounds can be localized to indicate points of turbulence. Sounds can be heard when blood velocity in vessels exceeds a certain critical value, and in heart valves when they open and close. The Reynolds number, N_R, is an empirically derived value that indicates whether flow will be laminar or turbulent under a particular set of conditions. In smooth vessels of the circulation, flow will be turbulent if the Reynolds number is greater than about 1000. Small back eddies may

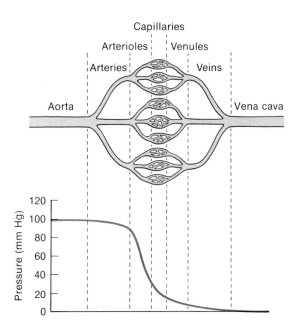

Capillaries
Arterioles | Venules
Arteries | Veins
Aorta | Vena cava

PRESSURE AND FLOW: POISEUILLE'S EQUATION

Pressures generated by the heart are dissipated by the flow of blood, and fall as the blood passes from the arterial to the venous side of the circulation (Fig. 13-25).

The relationship between pressure and steady laminar flow of fluid in a rigid tube is described by Poiseuille's Law, which states that the flow rate of a fluid, $\dot{Q}$, is directly proportional to the pressure difference, $P_1 - P_2$, and the fourth power of the radius of the tube, r, and inversely proportional to the tube length, L, and fluid viscosity, η:

$$\dot{Q} = \frac{(P_1 - P_2)\pi r^4}{8L\eta}.$$

As $\dot{Q}$ is proportional to r^4, very small changes in r will have a profound effect on $\dot{Q}$. A doubling of vessel diameter will lead to a sixteenfold increase in flow.

Poiseuille's equation applies to steady flows in straight rigid tubes. Blood pressure and flow are pulsatile, and blood is a complex fluid consisting of plasma and red blood cells. The blood vessel walls are not rigid, and as a result the oscillations in pressure and flow are not in phase; consequently, the relationship between the two is no longer accurately described by Poiseuille's equation. The extent of the deviation of the relationship between pressure and flow from that predicted by Poiseuille's equation is indicated by the value of a nondimensional constant α:

$$\alpha = r\frac{\sqrt{2\pi n f \rho}}{\eta},$$

where ρ and η are the density and viscosity of the fluid, respectively, f the frequency of oscillation, n the order of the harmonic component, and r the radius of the vessel. If α is 0.5 or less, then the relationship between pressure and flow is described by Poiseuille's equation. Values of α for the arterial systems of mammals and birds range from 1.3 to 16.7, depending on the species and the physiological state of the animal. Since most values of α for the arterial system are around 6, Poiseuille's equation is not applicable. The value for α in the small terminal arteries and veins is about 0.5, hence Poiseuille's equation can be used to analyze the relationship between pressure and flow in this portion of the circulation. Flow in the terminal arteries will therefore will be proportional to the pressure difference along the vessel and the fourth power of the radius and inversely proportional to the length of the vessel and the viscosity of blood.

RESISTANCE TO FLOW

Since it is often difficult or impossible to measure the radii of all vessels in a vascular bed, we designate

form at arterial branches and, like the back eddies in rivers, can become detached from the main flow regime and be carried downstream as small, discrete regions of turbulence. These eddies can form in the circulation at Reynolds numbers as low as 200. The Reynolds number is directly proportional to the flow rate, $\dot{Q}$ (ml/s), and inversely proportional to the inside radius of the vessel, r (cm), and the kinematic viscosity, K, of the blood:

$$N_R = \frac{2\dot{Q}}{\pi r K}$$

The kinematic viscosity is the ratio of viscosity to density. The larger the kinematic viscosity, the less the likelihood that turbulence will occur. The relative viscosity, and therefore the kinematic viscosity, increases with hematocrit (volume of red blood cells per unit volume of blood), so that the presence of red blood cells decreases the occurrence of turbulence in the blood stream. In general, blood velocity is seldom high enough to create turbulence. The highest flow rates in the mammalian circulation are in the proximal portions of the aorta and pulmonary artery, and turbulence may occur distal to the aortic and pulmonary valves at the peak of ventricular ejection or during backflow of blood as these valves close.

$8L\eta/\pi r^4$, the inverse of the term in Poiseuille's equation, as the resistance to flow, R, which is equal to the pressure difference $(P_1 - P_2)$ across a vascular bed divided by the flow rate, $\dot{Q}$:

$$R = \frac{P_1 - P_2}{\dot{Q}} = \frac{8L\eta}{\pi r^4}.$$

The resistance to flow in the peripheral circulation is sometimes expressed in resistance units or PRU's (Peripheral Resistance Units), 1 PRU being equal to the resistance in a vascular bed when a pressure difference of 1 mm Hg results in a flow of 1 ml/s; that is, 1 PRU = 1 mm Hg/cm^3/s, and since 1 mm Hg equals 1330 dynes/cm^2, then 1 PRU = 1330 dyne-s-cm^{-5}.

Blood flow is related not only to the pressure difference along a vessel but also to the resistance to flow, which is inversely proportional to the fourth power of the radius of the vessel. As pressure increases in an elastic vessel, so does the radius; as a result, flow increases as well. Let us consider a blood vessel with a constant pressure differential along its length but operating at different pressure levels—for example, input pressure 100 mm Hg, outflow pressure 90 mm Hg, and input pressure 20 mm Hg, outflow pressure 10 mm Hg. The flow rate in this vessel will be much greater at the higher pressure, if the vessel is distensible, simply because the radius will be increased and the resistance to flow reduced.

VISCOSITY OF BLOOD

Changes in viscosity have a marked effect on the flow of blood. The presence of red blood cells alters the viscous properties of blood. Plasma has a viscosity relative to water of about 1.8; the addition of red blood cells increases the relative viscosity, so that mammalian and bird blood at 37°C has a relative viscosity between 3 and 4. Thus blood behaves as though it were three or four times more viscous than water; this characteristic is due largely to the presence of red blood cells. In terms of blood flow, this means that larger pressure gradients are required to maintain the flow of blood through a vascular bed than would be needed if the vascular bed were perfused by plasma alone. Blood flowing through small tubes behaves as if the relative viscosity were much reduced. In fact, in tubes less than 1 mm in diameter (i.e., capillaries), the relative viscosity of blood decreases with diameter and approaches the viscosity of plasma.

The velocity profile across a vessel with steady laminar fluid flow is a parabola (Fig. 13-24). Maximum velocity is twice the mean velocity, which can be determined by dividing the flow rate by the cross-sectional area of the tube. The rate of change in velocity is maximal near the walls, and decreases toward the center of the vessel. In flowing blood, red cells tend to accumulate in the center of the vessel, where velocity is highest but the rate of change in velocity between adjacent layers smallest. This leaves the walls relatively free of cells, so that fluid flowing from this area into small side vessels will have a low level of red blood cells and consist almost entirely of plasma. Such a process is referred to as plasma skimming.

The accumulation of red blood cells in the center of a bloodstream means that blood viscosity is highest in the center and decreases toward the walls, because viscosity of blood increases with hematocrit (volume percentage of red blood cells per unit volume of blood). Flow is inversely related to viscosity, and a change in viscosity between the center and the walls of the bloodstream will alter the velocity profile. In blood whose viscosity is lowest at the walls, the effect will be to increase flow slightly at the walls and reduce flow slightly in the center—that is, slightly flatten the parabolic shape of the velocity profile (Fig. 13-24).

The velocity profile is a parabola if flow is laminar and steady. If flow is turbulent, there is little change in velocity across the vessel. If flow is laminar but pulsatile, as in arteries, the velocity profile is also flattened, so that blood velocity is similar across the core of the blood stream (Fig. 13-24).

COMPLIANCE IN THE CIRCULATORY SYSTEM

A further complication in analyzing the relationship between pressure and flow in the circulation is that blood vessels are not straight, rigid tubes, but contain elastic fibers that enable them to distend. As pressure increases, the walls are stretched and the volume of the vessel is enlarged. The ratio of change in volume to change in pressure is termed the compliance, or capacitance, of the system. The compliance of a system is related to its size and the elasticity of its walls. The larger the initial volume and the elasticity of the walls, the greater will be the compliance of the system.

The venous system is very compliant; small changes in pressure can produce large changes in volume. The venous system can therefore act as a *blood reservoir*, because large changes in volume have little effect on either venous pressure (and therefore the filling of the heart during diastole) or capillary blood flow. The arterial system is less compliant, because it has to act as a *pressure reservoir* in order to maintain capillary blood flow. An increase in compliance would reduce the sensitivity of the control system; nevertheless, the proximal portions of the arterial system *are* elastic in order to dampen the pressure pulse generated by contractions of the heart and to maintain flow in distal arteries during diastole.

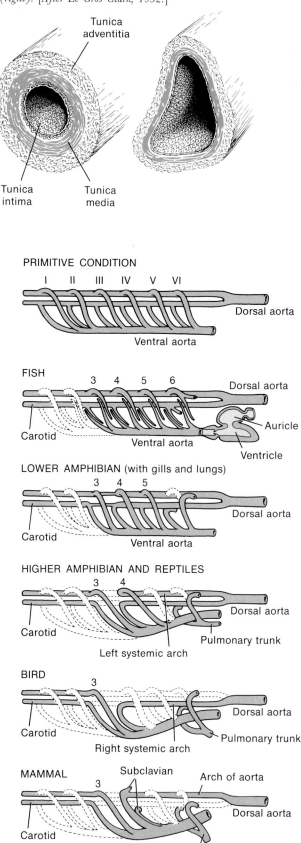

13–26. A diagram constructed to emphasize schematically the contrast between the cross-sectional appearance of an artery (left) and its corresponding vein (right). [After Le Gros Clark, 1952.]

Tunica adventitia

Tunica intima

Tunica media

PRIMITIVE CONDITION

I   II   III   IV   V   VI

Dorsal aorta

Ventral aorta

FISH

3   4   5   6

Dorsal aorta

Carotid

Ventral aorta

Auricle

Ventricle

LOWER AMPHIBIAN (with gills and lungs)

3   4   5

Dorsal aorta

Carotid

Ventral aorta

HIGHER AMPHIBIAN AND REPTILES

3   4

Dorsal aorta

Carotid

Pulmonary trunk

Left systemic arch

BIRD

3

Dorsal aorta

Carotid

Pulmonary trunk

Right systemic arch

MAMMAL

Subclavian

Arch of aorta

3

Dorsal aorta

Carotid

Pulmonary trunk

The Arterial System

All blood vessels are lined by endothelial cells. Capillaries consist of only an endothelial layer; the larger vessels have a surrounding layer of elastic and collagenous fibers. Circular and longitudinal smooth muscle fibers may intermingle with or surround the elastic and collagenous fibers. Blood vessels are covered by a limiting fibrous outer coat, termed the *tunica adventitia* (Fig. 13-26). The endothelial layer and the elastic fibers form the *tunica intima*, and the circular and longitudinal smooth muscle form the *tunica media*. The boundary between the *tunica intima* and the *tunica media* is not well defined; the tissues blend into one another. The thick walls of blood vessels require their own capillary circulation, termed the *vasa vasorum*. Large arteries often have more elastic tissue than small arteries. In general, arteries have thicker walls and much more smooth muscle than veins of similar outside diameter. The relatively thin walls of veins are responsible for their larger inside diameter. In some veins, muscular tissue is absent.

Elastic tubes are unstable and tend to balloon. In blood vessels, this is prevented by a collagen sheath that limits the expansion of the vessel. Ballooning of blood vessels (aneurisms) can occur if the collagen sheath breaks down.

The gross anatomy of the arterial system varies from one group to another, and it also undergoes changes during an individual's development. In vertebrates, major modifications of the structure of the arterial system are associated with the evolution of completely terrestrial forms. These modifications are correlated with changes in the structure of the heart (Fig. 13-27).

The arteries serve four main functions (see Fig. 13-28). The arteries are filled with blood by contractions of the heart, and they empty via arterioles into capillaries. Only a small number of capillaries (approximately 5–10%) are open at any one time; most are closed off by contractions of smooth-muscle sphincters at the entrance to capillary beds. The pressure in the arterial system is determined by the volume of blood it contains and the properties of its walls. If either is altered, the pressure will change. The volume of blood in the arteries is the resultant of filling by the heart and emptying via the capillaries. If cardiac output increases, then arterial blood pressure will rise, but if capillary flow is increased, blood pres-

13–27. Diagram showing the outcome of the primitive or embryonic aortic arches in a series of vertebrates from fishes to mammals. [After Guyer, 1948.]

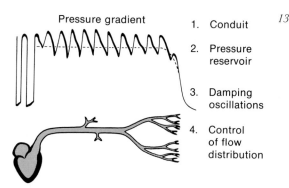

Pressure gradient

1. Conduit

2. Pressure reservoir

3. Damping oscillations

4. Control of flow distribution

13–28. Four functions of the systemic arterial system are represented schematically. The conduit function refers to the vascular channels along which blood flows toward the periphery with minimal frictional loss of pressure. The combination of distensible walls and high outflow resistance accounts for the pressure-reservoir function, which also allows damping of oscillations in pressure and flow. The sites of controlled hydraulic resistance in the peripheral vascular beds control the distribution of blood flow to the various tissues and organs. [After Rushmer, 1965.]

sure will fall. Normally, however, arterial blood pressure varies little, because the rates of filling and emptying are evenly matched by virtue of the increase in cardiac output that accompanies a rise in capillary flow. Capillary blood flow is proportional to the pressure difference between the arterial and venous systems. Thus arterial pressure exerts primary control over the rate of capillary blood flow, and is responsible for maintaining adequate perfusion of the tissues. Arterial pressure varies among species, generally ranging from 50 to 150 mm Hg. Pressure differences are small along large arteries (less than 1 mm Hg), but there may be considerable pressure differences along the small arteries and arterioles.

The elasticity of arterial walls serves to dampen the oscillations in pressure and flow generated by contractions of the heart. As blood is ejected into the arterial system, pressure rises and the vessels expand. As the heart relaxes, blood flow to the periphery is maintained by the elastic recoil of the vessel walls and by a reduction in arterial volume. If the arteries were rigid tubes, flow in the periphery would exhibit the same large oscillations that are observed at the exit of the ventricle.

The extent of elastic tissue in arteries varies depending on the particular function of each vessel. In fish, for example, blood pumped by the heart is forced into an elastic bulbus and a ventral aorta (Fig. 13-29). The blood then flows through the gills and passes into a dorsal aorta, the main conduit for the distribution of blood to the rest of the body. A smooth, continuous flow of blood is required in the gill capillaries for efficient gas transfer. The bulbus, the ventral aorta, and the arteries leading to the gills are very compliant, and act to smooth and maintain flow in the gills in the face of large oscillations produced by contractions of the heart (Fig. 13-30). The dorsal aorta is much less elastic than the ventral aorta; if it were as elastic as the ventral aorta, there would be a rapid rush of blood through the gills during each heartbeat, when the dorsal aorta is filled with blood. This would increase rather than decrease the oscillations in flow through the gills. The major compliance must take place *before, not after,* blood reaches the gills in order to dampen

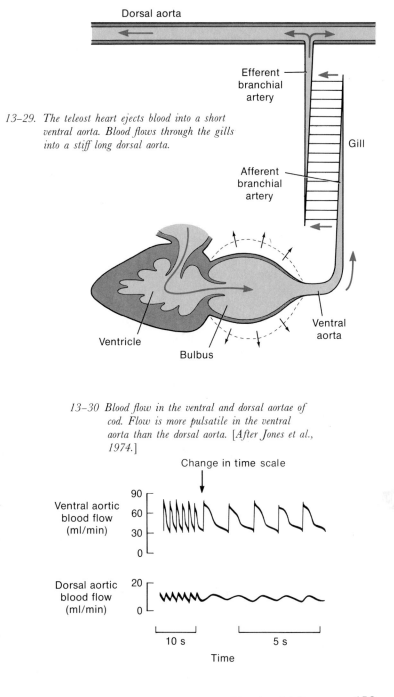

13–29. The teleost heart ejects blood into a short ventral aorta. Blood flows through the gills into a stiff long dorsal aorta.

13–30 Blood flow in the ventral and dorsal aortae of cod. Flow is more pulsatile in the ventral aorta than the dorsal aorta. [After Jones et al., 1974.]

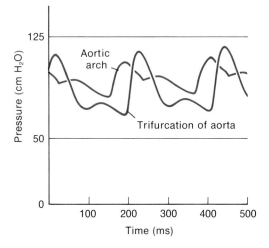

the oscillations in flow through the gills. The ventral aorta must be elastic and the large-volume dorsal aorta stiff in order to achieve a smoothing of flow through the gills.

Blood Pressure. The oscillations in pressure produced by the contractions and relaxations of the ventricle are reduced at the entrance to capillary beds and nonexistent in the venous system. Heart contractions cause small oscillations in pressure within capillaries. The pressure pulse travels at a velocity of 3 to 5 m/s. The velocity of the pressure pulse increases with decrease in artery diameter and increasing stiffness of the arterial wall. In the mammalian aorta, the pressure pulse travels at 3–5 m/s, and reaches 15–35 m/s in small arteries.

Peak blood pressure and the size of the pressure pulse within the mammalian and avian aorta both increase with distance from the heart (Fig. 13-31). There are three possible explanations for this rather odd phenomenon. First, pressure waves are reflected from peripheral branches of the arterial tree; the initial and reflected waves summate; and, where peaks coincide, the pressure pulse and peak pressure is greater than where they are out of phase. If the initial and reflected waves are 180° out of phase, then the oscillations in pressure will be reduced. It has been suggested that the heart is situated at a point where initial and reflected waves are out of phase, thus reducing peak arterial pressure in the aorta close to the ventricle.

As distance from the heart increases, the initial and reflected pressure waves move into phase, and a peaking of pressures is observed in the periphery. Second, the properties of the arterial walls change with distance from the heart; they become less elastic and the vessels taper, being of smaller diameter in the periphery. It is possible that these properties cause an increase in the magnitude of the pressure pulse with distance from the heart. Third, the pressure pulse is a complex wave form, consisting of several harmonics. Higher frequencies travel at higher velocities, and it has been suggested that the changing wave form of the pressure pulse is due to summation of different harmonics. This may be unimportant, as the distances are too small to allow summation of harmonics. The argument is concentrated on the relative importance of reflected waves and the changing geometry of the aorta and its wall elasticity in causing peaking of the pressure pulse.

GRAVITY AND BODY POSITION

When a person is lying down, the heart is at the same level as the feet and head, and pressures will be similar in arteries in the head, chest, and limbs. Once a person moves to a sitting or standing position, the relationship between the head, heart, and limbs changes with respect to gravity. Blood has a density of 1.055 compared with water, and this fluid must be lifted from the heart to the head when a person is standing. In addition, the heart is now a meter above the lower limbs. The result is an increase in arterial pressure in the lower limbs and a decrease in arterial pressure in the head. Vasoconstriction in the limbs is required to prevent the pooling of blood as position changes with respect to gravity. This problem is more acute in some species than in others. When the giraffe is standing with its head raised, its brain is placed about 6 m above the ground and 1.6 m above the heart. If the arterial pressure of blood perfusing the brain is to be maintained at around 100 mm Hg, aortic blood pressure must be between 200 and 300 mm Hg in order to lift blood to the raised head and force it through the brain capillaries at an adequate flow rate. Aortic blood pressures greater than 200 mm Hg have been recorded from an anesthetized giraffe with its head raised. As the giraffe lowers its head to the ground, arterial blood pressure must be reduced considerably if brain blood flow is to remain constant. The probable means of control is extensive dilation and constriction in capillary beds other than those in the head. As the giraffe raises its head, there is probably an extensive vasoconstriction of peripheral vessels. Flow to these capillary beds, however, cannot be varied without consequences. For example, there must be a fairly large, variable resistance to flow between the heart and the kidney in order to maintain blood pressure at the level of the nephron. If the kidney tubule were subjected to the enormous changes in blood pressure associated with the raising and lowering of the giraffe's head, the rate of formation of an ultrafiltrate would be very high, and would require that fluid be resorbed at an equally high rate each time arterial blood pressure is raised as the giraffe lifts its head. Thus the giraffe must have fairly complex mechanisms for adjusting peripheral resistance to flow in various capillary beds in order to maintain the flow of blood to its brain as it swings its head from ground level to a height of 6 m to eat the leaves near the top of an acacia. Similar problems must be faced by a number of other animals—for example, the camel, but to a lesser degree.

BLOOD FLOW

Oscillations in flow vary with distance from the heart (Fig. 13-32). They are largest at the exit to the ventricle, and decrease with distance from the heart. At the base of the aorta, flow is turbulent, and reverses during diastole due to closure of the aortic valves. In most other parts of the circulation, flow is laminar, and oscillations are damped by the compliance of the aorta and proximal arteries.

The velocity of flow in a closed circulation is proportional to the cross-sectional area of the circulation at that point. Blood velocity is maximal in the arteries, falls rapidly in the capillaries, but increases once more in the veins (Fig. 13-33). Mean velocity in the aorta—the point of maximum blood velocity—is about 33 cm/s in humans. The cross-sectional area of the aorta (about 2.5 cm^2) and cardiac output (about 5 liters/min) were used to estimate this mean velocity. If we assume that maximum velocity in the vessel is twice mean velocity (valid only if the velocity profile is a parabola), then maximum velocity of blood flow will be 66 cm/s. If cardiac output is increased by a factor of 6 during heavy exercise, maximum velocity is raised to 3.96 m/s. These maximum values for blood flow velocity can be compared with pressure-pulse velocities of 3–35 m/s; that is, the pressure pulse travels faster than the flow pulse.

The Venous System

The venous system acts as a conduit for the return of blood from the capillaries to the heart. It is a large-volume, low-pressure system with vessels of large inside diameter. In mammals, 50% of the total blood volume is contained in veins, and pressures seldom exceed 10 mm Hg. The walls of veins are much thinner than those of arteries and less elastic. The venous compli-

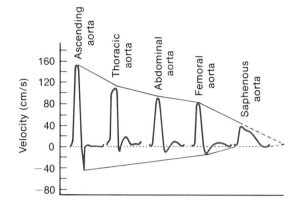

13-32 Changes in form in the pulsatile flow recorded in arteries of the dog ranging from the heart toward the periphery. There is a progressive decrease in amplitude until oscillatory flow is damped out in the capillaries (see Fig. 13-35). A backflow phase is observed in the large arteries; in the ascending aorta, it is probably related to a brief reflux of blood through the aortic valves. [After McDonald, 1960.]

13-33. Blood velocity is inversely proportional to the cross-sectional area of the circulation at any given point. Blood velocity is highest in arteries and veins and lowest in the capillaries; the converse is true for cross-sectional area. [After Feigl, 1974.]

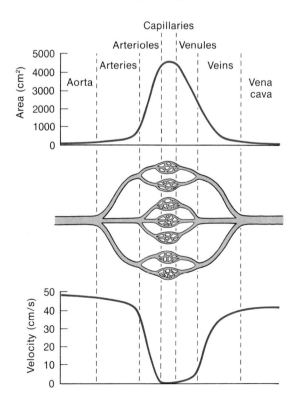

ance, unlike the arterial compliance, is related to its large volume rather than to the elasticity of its walls. The venous system acts as a storage reservoir for blood. In the event of blood loss, venous and not arterial volume decreases in order to maintain arterial pressure and capillary blood flow.

Blood flow in veins is affected by a number of factors other than contractions of the heart. Activity of limb muscles and pressure exerted by the diaphragm on the gut both result in the squeezing of veins in those parts of the body, fostering the return of blood to the heart. In the absence of skeletal muscle contraction, there may be considerable pooling of blood in the venous system of the limbs.

Breathing in mammals also contributes to the return of venous blood to the heart. The heart and large veins are contained within the thoracic cage. Expansion of the thoracic cage reduces pressure within the chest, with the result that blood is sucked from the veins of the head and abdominal cavity.

Peristaltic activity has been observed in the venules of the bat wing, and peristaltic contractions of smooth muscle may be important in some instances in causing venous blood flow.

When bleeding depletes the venous blood reservoir, the loss is compensated for by a reduction in venous volume. The walls of many veins are covered by smooth muscle innervated by sympathetic adrenergic fibers. Stimulation of these nerves causes vasoconstriction and a reduction in the size of the venous reservoir. This reflex allows some bleeding to take place without a drop in venous pressure. Blood donors actually lose part of their venous reservoir; the loss is temporary, however, and the venous system gradually expands as blood is replaced.

Venous smooth muscle also aids in regulating the distribution of blood in the venous system. Inactivity causes blood to become pooled in the limbs. When a person shifts from a sitting position to a standing position, the change in the relative positions of heart and brain with respect to gravity activates sympathetic adrenergic fibers that innervate limb veins, causing contraction of venous smooth muscle and thereby promoting the redistribution of pooled blood. Such venoconstriction is inadequate, however, to maintain good circulation if the standing position is held for long periods in the absence of limb movements, as when soldiers stand immobile during a review. Under such circumstances, venous return to the heart, cardiac output, arterial pressure, and flow of blood to the brain are all reduced, resulting in fainting. Similar problems affect bedridden patients who attempt to stand after several days of inactivity and space pilots returning to Earth after a long voyage. In the absence of body changes that shift the relative positions of the heart and brain with respect to gravity, the system of

corrections falls into disrepair, and the result is the pooling of blood. The reflex control of venous volume is normally re-established with use.

RETE MIRABILE

Many animals have a countercurrent arrangement (p. 414) of small arterioles and venules that form a *rete mirabile*. Before entering a tissue, the artery divides into a large number of small capillaries that parallel a series of venous capillaries leaving the tissue. The arterial capillaries are surrounded by venous capillaries and vice versa, forming an extensive exchange surface between inflowing and outflowing blood. Retial capillaries serve to transfer heat or gases between arterial blood entering a tissue and venous blood leaving it. For instance, tuna fish red muscle is warmer by several degrees than the rest of the body and the sea water. The red muscle has an extensive rete system (Fig. 13-34) in which heat is transferred from warm venous blood to the cool arterial blood entering the muscle. The rete serves to reduce the rate of heat loss from the muscle when ambient temperature changes—for instance, when the fish dives through the thermocline from the warm surface waters to the cooler, deeper waters in the ocean. Retial structures that lead to the limbs of many aquatic mammals help reduce the rate of heat loss when the animals are submerged. Venous blood returning to these structures from the limbs is warmed by arterial blood entering the flipper or limb, so conserving heat. Many teleost fish have a choroid rete that maintains high oxygen levels in the retina. The rete leading to the fish swim bladder reduces the loss of oxygen from that organ (see Chapter 4, p. 494), and the countercurrent arrangement of blood flow to the loop of Henle in the mammalian kidney permits the development of high Na levels in the kidney medulla.

CAPILLARIES

Most tissues have an extensive network of capillaries such that any single cell is not more than 3 or 4 cells away from a capillary. The capillary walls consist of a single layer of endothelial cells, which, although thin-walled, do not stretch or break easily when blood pressure is increased because they also have a small diameter (see p. 442). The capillaries are usually about 1 mm long and 10 to 25 μm in diameter, just large enough for red blood cells to squeeze through. Large leucocytes, however, may become lodged in capillaries, stopping blood flow. The leucocytes are either dislodged by a rise in blood pressure or migrate slowly along the vessel wall until they reach a larger vessel and are swept into the bloodstream.

The small arteries subdivide into *arterioles,* which subdivide to form capillaries. The arterioles lose the longitudinal smooth-muscle fibers present in arteries, and the number of circular smooth-muscle fibers decreases toward the capillary. The smooth-muscle fibers are arranged spirally around the arteriole and form a precapillary sphincter.

The capillaries empty into venules, which join to form veins. The veins and venules are valved, and a muscle sheath appears after the first postcapillary valve.

All capillaries combined have a volume of about 140% of the total blood volume of the animal; that is, there is insufficient blood to fill all capillaries at once. In fact, only 3–5% of all capillaries are open at any one time and only 5–7% of the total blood volume is contained in the capillaries. No capillary remains closed for long, however, as the precapillary sphincters open and close continuously, always shifting the pathway of blood flow through the capillary bed. The arrangement of arterioles and venules is such that all capillaries are only a short distance from an arteriole, and, as a result, a fairly uniform distribution of pressure and flow is possible within the capillary bed. Precapillary sphincters appear to be under local control, and are independent of nervous activity. The overall flow to the capillary bed is determined by smooth-muscle sphincters at the junction of the artery and arterioles; these sphincters are heavily innervated and under nervous control.

Capillary walls are permeable, and materials are transferred between blood and tissues. Lipid-soluble materials diffuse through the endothelial cells; other materials pass through the gaps between cells. Most proteins are not transferred across the capillary walls, but are retained in the blood. As a result, an osmotic gradient is established between plasma and the interstitial fluid, the plasma having a higher osmotic pressure than the interstitial fluid.

Transmural pressures of about 10 mm Hg have been recorded in capillaries by Weiderhielm and others (Figs. 13-35, 13-36). High pressures inside the capillary result in the filtration of fluid from the plasma into the interstitial space. This filtration pressure is opposed by the plasma colloid osmotic pressure. In the kidney, capillary pressure is high and filtration pressures exceed colloid osmotic pressures, hence an ultrafiltrate is formed in the kidney tubule. In most other tissues, filtration pressure is balanced by osmotic pressure, so that there is little *net* movement of fluid across capillary walls. Pressures are higher, however, at the arterial end than at the venous end of the capillary. At the arterial end of the capillary, where filtration pressure exceeds colloid osmotic pressure, there is a net loss of fluid; at the venous end of the capillary, where osmotic pressure exceeds filtration pressure

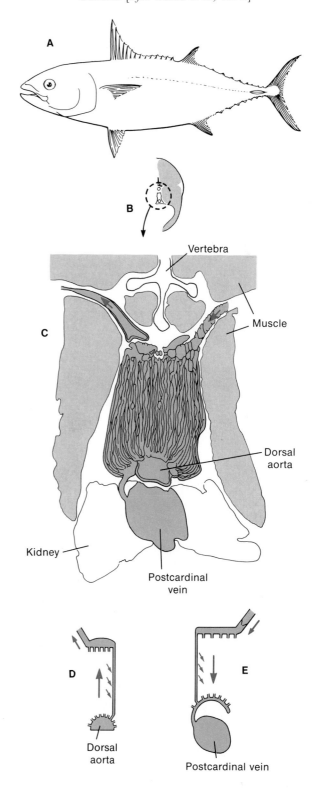

13–34. *Vascular heat-exchanger of skipjack tuna. A. Skipjack tuna. B. Cross section through body. C. Heat-exchanger, showing details of rete mirabile. D. Pattern of arterial blood flow. E. Pattern of venous blood flow. Small arrows indicate heat transfer from venules to arterioles. [After Stevens et al., 1974.]*

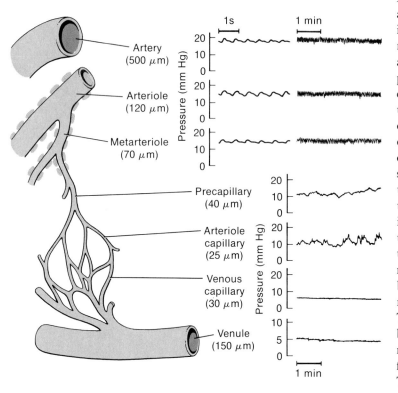

13-35. *Capillary bed of the frog mesentery. Blood pressure is smoothed, and falls from about 20 mm Hg to 5 mm Hg as it flows from the artery to the venule through the capillaries of the frog mesentery. [After Wiederhielm et al., 1964.]*

Artery (500 μm)

Arteriole (120 μm)

Metarteriole (70 μm)

Precapillary (40 μm)

Arteriole capillary (25 μm)

Venous capillary (30 μm)

Venule (150 μm)

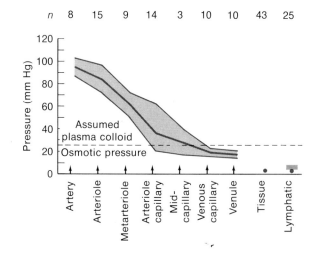

13-36 *Pressure in the blood circulation, lymphatics, and tissues in the subcutaneous layers of the bat wing. The shaded area represents $\bar{x} \pm 1\ SE$. [After Weiderhielm and Weston, 1973.]*

| n | 8 | 15 | 9 | 14 | 3 | 10 | 10 | 43 | 25 |

Assumed plasma colloid
Osmotic pressure

Artery — Arteriole — Metarteriole — Arteriole capillary — Mid-capillary — Venous capillary — Venule — Tissue — Lymphatic

(Fig. 13-36), there is a net uptake of fluid. Thus there is a circulation of fluid from the arterial end of the capillary into the interstitial space and back to the venous end of the capillary. If the loss and uptake processes are balanced, there will be no net loss of fluid. If however, there is a rise in capillary pressure, due to a rise in either arterial or venous pressure, it will result in increased filtration into the interstitial space and a net loss of fluid from the blood. In general, though, arterial pressure remains fairly constant in order to prevent large oscillations in tissue volume. A drop in colloid osmotic pressure, resulting from a loss of protein from the plasma either by excretion or by increased capillary wall permeability and the movement of proteins into the interstitial space, will reduce the osmotic pressure difference between plasma and interstitial fluid. If filtration pressure remains constant, this will also result in an increase in net fluid loss to the tissue spaces. Thus the volume and composition of interstitial fluid is closely correlated with the conditions for capillary blood flow. This varies in different tissues; in general, liver capillaries are fairly permeable, brain capillaries much less permeable. Brain blood flow changes little, but blood flow in skeletal muscle changes enormously between rest and exercise. Thus one might expect the interstititial fluid of the brain to vary less than that of the liver and skeletal muscle. In general, there are small net movements of fluid from the circulation into the interstitial spaces. This fluid does not collect in tissues, but is drained away via a low-pressure lymphatic system.

Lymphatic System

Lymphatic vessels are blind-ending capillaries that drain the interstitial spaces. The lymphatic capillaries join to form a tree-like structure with branches reaching to all tissues. The larger lymphatic vessels resemble veins, are surrounded by smooth muscle, and have been observed to contract rhythmically and spontaneously. The lymphatic vessels empty via a duct into the blood circulation at a point of low pressure. In mammals and many other vertebrates, the lymph vessels drain via a thoracic duct into the anterior cardinal vein.

The walls of lymphatic capillaries consist of a single layer of endothelial cells. The basement membrane is absent or discontinuous, and there are large pores between adjoining cells. This has been demonstrated by observing the passage of such substances as horse radish peroxidase or china ink particles through lymphatic capillary walls.

Lymphatic pressures are often as much as 1 mm Hg less than the surrounding tissue pressures. Interstitial fluid passes easily into the lymphatic channels. The vessels are valved and only permit flow away from the lymphatic capillaries. The larger lymphatic vessels are surrounded by smooth muscle and, in some instances, contract rhythmically, creating pressures of up to 10 mm Hg and driving fluid away from the tissues (Fig. 13-37). The vessels are also squeezed by contractions of the gut and skeletal muscle and by movements of the body generally, causing lymph flow. Lymph vessels are innervated by nerves but it is not clear what type of innervation exists, or the function of these nerves.

Many cyclostomes, fish, and amphibians have lymph hearts, which aid in the movement of fluid. A lymph heart located in the tail of the hagfish and many teleosts (Fig. 13-38) aids in propelling fluid toward the heart. Lymph hearts are present in reptiles but absent in mammals. Bird embryos have a pair of lymph hearts located in the region of the pelvis; these hearts persist in the adult bird of a few species. Frogs have very large-volume lymph spaces, the function of which is not clear. They could act as a reservoir for water or ions and/or as a fluid buffer between the skin and underlying tissues.

Lymph flow is variable, ranging from 4 to 900 ml/kg/hr in the human thoracic duct, 11 ml/hr being an average value for resting individuals. This is 1/3000 of the cardiac output during the same time period. Nevertheless, although it is small, lymphatic flow is important in draining tissues of excess interstitial fluid. Obstruction of lymphatic channels results in retention of fluid in tissue spaces, a condition termed "edema," which can be severe. In the tropical disease filariasis, larval nematodes, transmitted by mosquitoes to humans, invade the lymphatic system and cause the blockage of lymph channels and, in some cases, totally block lymphatic drainage from certain parts of the body. The consequent edema can cause parts of the body to become so severely swollen that the condition has come to be called *elephantiasis* because of the resemblance of the swollen, hardened tissues to the hide of an elephant.

The lymphatic vessels are not easily seen, as lymph is colorless; as a result, even though the lymphatic system was first described about 400 years ago, the lymphatic system has not been nearly as extensively studied as the cardiovascular system.

Regulation of Capillary Blood Flow

Capillary blood flow adjusts to meet the demands of the tissues. If the requirements change suddenly, as in skeletal muscle during exercise, then capillary flow also changes. If requirements for nutrients vary little

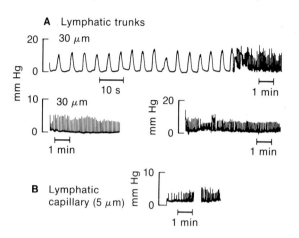

13–37. Pressures in lymphatic trunks and capillaries. [After Wiederhielm and Weston, 1973.]

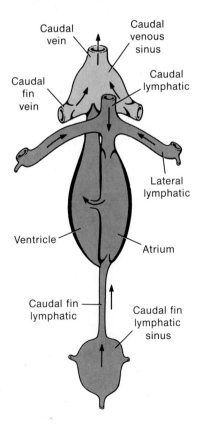

13–38. Schematic of the lymph heart located in the eel tail. The walls of the lymph heart contain skeletal muscle and beat rhythmically. Lymph is pumped into the caudal vein. [After Kampmeier, 1969.]

with time, as in the brain, then capillary flow also varies little.

The regulation of capillary flow can be divided into two main types, local and nervous control. *Local control* ensures that the most active tissue has the most dilated vessels and, therefore, the most blood flow. The degree of dilation is dependent on local conditions in the tissue, and, in general, it is those conditions associated with high levels of activity that cause vasodilation. *Nervous control* serves to maintain arterial pressure, and ensures that total flow in all capillaries is the same as cardiac output. The vertebrate brain and heart must be perfused with blood at all times. A failure in the perfusion of the human brain for only seconds will result in damage. Arterial pressure is maintained to ensure adequate perfusion of these structures. Nervous control of arterioles ensures that only a limited number of capillaries will be open at any moment, for if all capillaries were open, there would be a rapid drop in arterial pressure and blood flow to the brain would be reduced. The nervous control of capillary flow operates under a priority system. If arterial pressure falls, then blood flow to the gut, liver, and muscles is reduced in order to maintain flow to the brain and heart.

NERVOUS CONTROL OF CAPILLARY BLOOD FLOW

Arterioles are normally innervated by sympathetic nerves, some by parasympathetic nerves. Sympathetic nerves usually contain norepinephrine, which reacts with adrenergic receptors in vascular smooth muscle and usually causes a vasoconstriction of the arterioles.

Thus a generalized effect of sympathetic stimulation is to cause peripheral vasoconstriction and a rise in arterial blood pressure. This overall response is related to the release of norepinephrine from nerve endings; norepinephrine reacts with α-receptors (p. 358) in smooth muscle and results in an increase in smooth-muscle tension. Stimulation of a β-receptor often results in vasodilation, but this is only a generalized response reported for mammals. The response in any vascular bed depends on the type of catecholamine and the nature of the receptors involved and on the relationship between the catecholamine/receptor interaction and the change in muscle tone. Although stimulation of α-receptors is usually associated with a vasoconstriction and that of β-receptors with vasodilation, this is not invariably the case. An additional complicating factor is that *not all* sympathetic fibers are adrenergic. Some are cholinergic, releasing acetylcholine from their nerve endings. The effect of sympathetic cholinergic nerve activity is to cause vasodilation in skeletal muscle vasculature.

Some arterioles are innervated by parasympathetic nerves—for example, in the circulation to the brain and the lungs. Parasympathetic nerves contain cholinergic fibers that release acetylcholine from their nerve endings when stimulated (Fig. 6-38). In mammals, parasympathetic nerve stimulation causes vasodilation in arterioles.

Some parasympathetic nerves may release ATP and other purines from nerve endings; that is, the fibers may be purinergic rather than cholinergic. ATP causes vasodilation, and it is possible (though not demonstrated) that some purinergic nerves participate in the control of capillary blood flow.

LOCAL CONTROL OF CAPILLARY BLOOD FLOW

The term *hyperemia* means increased blood flow to an organ; *ischemia* means the cessation of such flow. *Active hyperemia* refers to the increase in blood flow that follows increased activity in an organ, particularly skeletal muscle. Active tissues, metabolizing aerobically, utilize O_2 and produce CO_2, H^+, and various other metabolites. There are also other ionic changes, for example, a rise in extracellular $[K^+]$ following exercise in skeletal muscle. Increases in CO_2, H^+, K^+ (in muscle), and various other metabolites, or a decrease in O_2 in the tissues, have all been shown to cause vasodilation and a local increase in capillary blood flow. That is, the most active tissue has the most dilated vessels and therefore the highest blood flow. The lung capillary bed is an exception: low O_2 causes local vasoconstriction rather than vasodilation. The reason for the difference is that in the lung, O_2 is being taken up by the blood, and the blood must therefore flow to the regions of high O_2; in tissues, however, O_2 is being delivered in the blood flowing to them, and the highest blood flow should be to the area of greatest need, which is indicated by regions of low O_2.

If blood flow to an organ is stopped by clamping the artery or by a powerful vasoconstriction, then there will be a much higher blood flow to that organ when the occlusion is removed than there was before the occlusion. This phenomenon is termed *reactive hyperemia*. Presumably during the ischemic period (period of no blood flow), O_2 levels are reduced and CO_2, H^+, and other metabolites build up and cause a local vasodilation. The result is that when the occlusion is removed, blood flow is much higher than normal.

Local injury in mammals and perhaps other vertebrates is accompanied by a marked vasodilation of vessels in the region of the injury. Histamine is released when cells are damaged and may mediate the vasodilation associated with local inflammation. Antihistamines ameliorate, but do not completely remove, this inflammation response. It is possible that another group of potent vasodilators, plasma kinins, may also be activated in damaged tissues. Kinins are formed by the action of many factors, including hypoxia, and by the action of proteolytic enzymes on kininogen, an α_2-globulin. Tissue damage results in the release of proteolytic enzymes that split kinins from kininogen, and the kinins then cause local vasodilation.

Serotonin (5-hydroxytryptamine), found in high concentration in the gut and blood platelets, acts as a vasoconstrictor or vasodilator, depending on the vascular bed and on the dose level.

Angiotensin II, like norepinephrine, has a vasoconstrictor effect on arterioles. It is formed by the action of renin on angiotensinogen, which circulates in the blood (p. 411).

Histamine, bradykinin, and serotonin cause an increase in capillary permeability, and large proteins and other macromolecules tend to distribute themselves more evenly between plasma and interstitial spaces. As a result, the colloid osmotic pressure difference across the capillary wall is reduced, filtration is increased, and tissue edema occurs. On the other hand, norepinephrine, angiotensin II, and vasopressin tend to promote absorption of fluid from the interstitial fluid into the blood. This could be achieved by reducing filtration pressure and/or the permeability of the capillaries.

Cardiovascular Control by the Central Nervous System

Central control of the cardiovascular system hinges on the regulation of arterial blood pressure, which is adjusted to maintain an adequate level of capillary blood flow. The central priorities appear to be (1) to maintain arterial pressure in order to deliver an adequate supply of blood to the brain and heart and, (2) once these requirements are satisfied, to supply blood to other organs of the body. Arterial pressure is also maintained within narrow limits to control capillary pressure and, therefore, tissue volume and the composition of the interstitial fluid.

Receptors monitor blood pressure at various sites in the cardiovascular system. Information from baroreceptors (pressure receptors), along with that from chemoreceptors monitoring O_2, CO_2, and pH in the blood, is transmitted to the brain. The integration of these inputs occurs in the mammalian brain at the level of the medulla oblongata and pons. This center of integration consists of a collection of neurons, and is referred to as the medullary cardiovascular center. It is influenced by inputs from other regions of the brain, including the hypothalamus, the amygdala nucleus, and the cortex. The output from the medullary cardiovascular center is fed into autonomic motor neurons that innervate the heart and smooth muscle of arterioles and veins.

BARORECEPTORS

There is a wide distribution of baroreceptors in the arterial system. The mammalian carotid sinus baroreceptors have been much more extensively studied than those of the aortic arch, subclavian, common carotid, or pulmonary arteries. In mammals, there appear to be only minor quantitative differences between the baroreceptors of the carotid sinus and the aortic arch. Birds have aortic-arch baroreceptors that are sensitive to intravascular pressure changes, but their physiological importance has yet to be determined.

The carotid sinus is a dilation of the internal carotid at its origin, where the walls are somewhat thinner than in other portions of the artery. The baroreceptors are finely branched nerve endings buried in the walls of the carotid sinus. Under normal physiological conditions, there is a resting discharge from the baroreceptors, and they increase their rate when the vessel wall is stretched (Fig. 13-39). An increase in blood pressure stretches the wall of the carotid sinus and causes an increase in discharge frequency from the baroreceptors. The relationship between blood pres-

13–39. *The relationship between the pressure pulse (top) and the impulse firing frequency (bottom) in a single carotid baroreceptor unit. [After Korner, 1971.]*

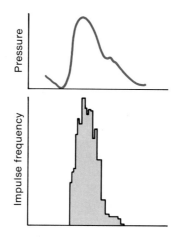

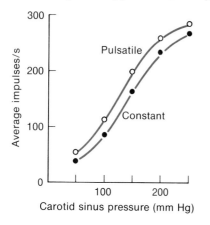

13–40. *Average impulse frequency, recorded from a multifiber preparation of the carotid sinus nerve in relation to mean carotid sinus pressure while the pressure in the sinus is either constant or pulsatile. [After Korner, 1971.]*

Table 13-1. *Open-loop reflex effects observed during changes in carotid sinus pressure.*

	Carotid Sinus Pressure	
Autonomic Effector	*Increased*	*Decreased*
Cardiac vagus	+ + + +	−
Cardiac sympathetic	−	+ + +
Splanchnic bed		
Resistance vessels	− −	+ +
Capacitance vessels	− −	+ +
Renal bed	~0	+
Muscle bed		
Resistance vessels	− − −	+ + + +
Capacitance vessels	−	+
Skin		
Resistance vessels	−	+ +
Capacitance vessels	?0	0
Adrenal catecholamines	~0	+ +
Antidiuretic hormone	?	+ +

Source: P. I. Korner, "Integrative Neural Cardiovascular Control," *Physiol. Revs.* 51(2):312–367.
Note: + = increased autonomic effect; − = decreased autonomic effect; 0 = no autonomic effect.

sure and baroreceptor impulse frequency is sigmoidal, the system being most sensitive over the physiological range of blood pressures. Arterial pressure oscillates in phase with contractions of the heart, the baroreceptor impulse frequency is higher when pressure is pulsatile than when it is constant (Fig. 13-40), and the carotid-sinus baroreceptors are most sensitive to frequencies of pressure oscillation between 1 and 10 cycles/s—that is, within the normal physiological range. Afferent fibers from the carotid sinus consist of about 15% myelinated fibers and 85% unmyelinated fibers. Most recordings of nervous activity are from the larger myelinated fibers. Stimulation of both fiber types results in a drop in blood pressure and a drop in heart rate, but the latter is more marked following stimulation of the unmyelinated fibers. The differential role, if any, of these two types of fibers in reflex cardiovascular control is not clear. Sympathetic efferent fibers terminate in the arterial wall near the baroreceptors; stimulation of these sympathetic fibers increases carotid sinus baroreceptor discharge, and under normal physiological conditions may alter the sensitivity of the receptors.

Information from baroreceptors is relayed through the medullary cardiovascular center in the medulla oblongata. An increase in blood pressure results in an increase in discharge frequency from the carotid sinus baroreceptors, which in turn causes a reflex reduction in both cardiac output and peripheral vascular resistance, which tends to reduce arterial blood pressure (Table 13-1). The reduction in cardiac output results from both a drop in the heart rate and the force of cardiac contraction. A reduction in arterial pressure reduces baroreceptor impulse frequency and causes a reflex increase in both cardiac output and peripheral resistance, which tends to increase arterial pressure. The carotid sinus baroreceptor reflex is therefore a negative feedback loop that tends to stabilize arterial blood pressure at a particular set-point. The set-point may be altered by interaction with other receptor inputs or be reset centrally within the medullary cardiovascular center by inputs from other regions of the brain (Fig. 13-41).

Mechanoreceptors in the wall of the atrium monitor both the rate of atrial filling and the force of atrial contraction. Type B atrial mechanoreceptors respond to an increase in atrial volume, and type A fibers respond to changes in tension in the atrial wall. The physiological significance of type A atrial fibers, which apparently monitor atrial systole, is not clear. Type B atrial receptors presumably monitor increased venous return to the heart. Increased discharge frequency from these type B atrial receptors causes an increase in heart rate if the initial rate is high. There is a reflex drop in arterial blood pressure and a rise in urine flow when the type B receptors are stimulated.

13-41. Circulatory control system in mammals. Changes in circulatory state are monitored by baroreceptors through changes in arterial pressure. Other mechanoreceptors and chemo-receptors provide collateral information about the physiological state of the body. The arterial set-point is altered by inputs from other areas of the brain, which are in turn influenced by a variety of peripheral inputs. [After Korner, 1971.]

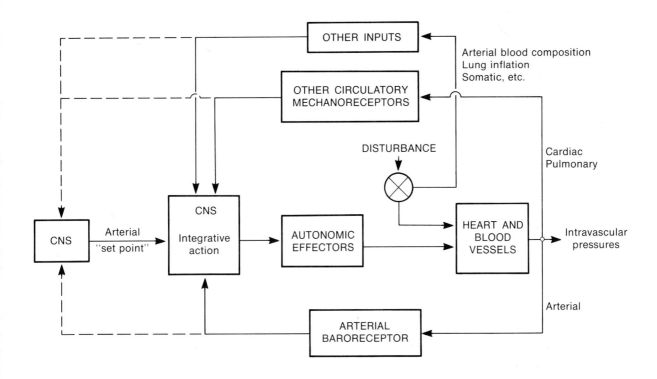

Mechanoreceptors embedded in the ventricular wall are stimulated by stretch of the ventricle when end-diastolic volume is large, and may also be activated by ventricular contractions, which produce very small end-systolic volumes—that is, a high heart rate and a very low end-diastolic volume, a situation that may follow extensive blood loss. Stimulation of these receptors tends to inhibit the sympathetic system and activate the parasympathetic system, resulting in an increase in renal blood flow (which will tend to reduce blood volume) and a decrease in heart rate.

ARTERIAL CHEMORECEPTORS

These receptors not only have important reflex effects on ventilation, but also have some effect on the cardiovascular system. They respond with an increase in discharge frequency to an increase in CO_2 or to decreases in oxygen and pH of blood perfusing the carotid and aortic bodies, where the chemoreceptors are situated. An increase in discharge frequency results in periph-

eral vasoconstriction and a slowing of the heart rate. This can cause a rise in arterial pressure, which then evokes reflex slowing of the heart by stimulation of the systemic baroreceptors. Nevertheless, chemoreceptor stimulation produces a bradycardia even when arterial pressure is regulated at a constant level. Chemoreceptor stimulation, therefore, has a direct effect on heart rate, as well as an indirect action via changes in arterial pressure, resulting from peripheral vasoconstriction. These reflex effects are only seen, however, if the animal is not breathing. Not surprisingly, there are many interactions between the control systems associated with ventilation and the cardiovascular system. The discharge pattern from stretch receptors in the lungs has a marked effect on the nature of the cardiovascular changes caused by chemoreceptor stimulation. That is, if the animal is breathing normally, changes in blood gas levels will cause one set of reflex changes; if, however, the animal is not breathing, then chemoreceptor stimulation results in quite a different series of cardiovascular changes (see below).

13–42. *Approximate distribution of cardiac output at rest and at different levels of exercise up to the maximal oxygen consumption (Max V_{O_2}) in a normal young man. Section labeled "viscera" reveals a progressive reduction in absolute blood flow and percentage of cardiac output distributed to splanchnic region and kidneys to augment muscle blood flow. Even skin is constricted during brief periods of exercise at high oxygen consumption. [After Rowell, 1974.]*

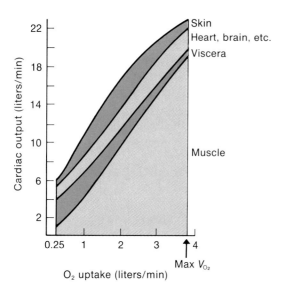

Cardiovascular Responses to Exercise and Diving

During exercise, the blood flow to skeletal muscle tissue in mammals is increased by a factor of 150 to 300% (Fig. 13-42). Cardiac output increases by a factor of 4 to 8 due to large increases in rate and small changes in stroke volume. There is increased sympathetic tone and decreased parasympathetic tone to the heart. Much of the increase in cardiac output can be accounted for by a decrease in peripheral resistance of about 50% the resting value and an increase in venous return due to pumping action of skeletal muscles on veins. The role of the cardiac nerves is to adjust heart rate to maintain stroke volume at a constant level rather than to cause the increase in cardiac output *per se*. The increase in heart rate is proportional to the decrease in peripheral resistance, for it has been shown in the dog that if peripheral resistance is held constant during exercise there is little change in heart rate. An increase in muscle blood flow may precede exercise, indicating that sympathetic cholinergic fibers may be causing skeletal muscle vasodilation, but active hyperemia is sufficient to maintain vasodilation during exercise. There are only small changes in arterial blood pressure, pH, and gas tensions. The oscillations in P_{CO_2} and P_{O_2} with breathing are somewhat larger, as is the arterial pulse pressure. The increased oscillations in pulse pressure are dampened to some extent because of increased elasticity of the arterial walls due to a rise in circulating catecholamines. It is probable that arterial chemoreceptors and baroreceptors play only a minor role in the cardiovascular changes associated with exercise. Motoneurons that innervate skeletal muscle are activated at the onset of exercise; it is possible that this activation system also initiates changes in lung ventilation and blood flow. Proprioceptive feedback from muscles may also play a role in increasing lung ventilation and cardiac output. Thus exercise is responsible for a complex series of integrated changes that maintain blood flow to the exercising muscle. Active hyperemia is primarily responsible for increasing blood flow to skeletal muscle; and increases in cardiac output are a direct result of the decrease in peripheral resistance. The exact role of a variety of other control systems is not clear.

Many air-breathing vertebrates can remain submerged for prolonged periods. During submersion, there are marked respiratory and cardiovascular changes. Breathing stops, and the cardiovascular system is adjusted to meter out the limited oxygen store to those organs that can least withstand anoxia (brain, heart, and some endocrine structures). Breathing stops during a dive because "water" receptors are stimulated and reflexly cause apnea (Fig. 13-43). The continued

A variety of inputs converge on the medullary cardiovascular center and cause reflex changes in circulation (Fig. 13-42). The output from the medullary cardiovascular center is fed into sympathetic and parasympathetic autonomic motoneurons that innervate the heart and blood vessels. Stimulation of sympathetic nerves increases the rate and force of contraction of the heart and causes arterial and venous vasoconstriction; the result is a marked increase in arterial blood pressure and cardiac output. In general, the reverse effects occur upon parasympathetic nerve stimulation, the end result being a drop in arterial blood pressure and cardiac output. Areas have been located within the medulla that, when stimulated, result in activation of either the sympathetic or the parasympathetic system. The pressor area results in sympathetic activation and a rise in blood pressure, whereas stimulation of the depressor area results in activation of the parasympathetic system and a drop in blood pressure. In general terms, various inputs affect the balance between pressor and depressor activity; some activate the pressor center and inhibit the depressor center, and other inputs have the reverse effect. Thus various inputs converge on the medullary cardiovascular center, are modified and integrated, resulting in an output that activates pressor or depressor areas and produces cardiovascular changes in response to changing requirements of the body or disturbances to the cardiovascular system.

utilization of oxygen by the brain and heart in the absence of breathing results in the gradual fall in blood oxygen and rise in blood carbon dioxide levels, stimulating the arterial chemoreceptors and causing peripheral vasoconstriction and a reduction in cardiac output associated with a profound bradycardia. The increase in peripheral resistance results from a marked rise in sympathetic tone, and involves constriction of fairly large arteries. Blood flow to skeletal muscle is reduced almost to zero in some diving mammals, and there is enlargement of the venous reservoir. Most of the blood pumped by the heart into the systemic circuit flows through the capillaries of the brain and heart. In some instances, there is a rise in arterial pressure, which results in arterial baroreceptor stimulation, and the bradycardia is maintained by a rise in both chemoreceptor and baroreceptor discharge frequency. The bradycardia is caused by an increase in parasympathetic and possibly a decrease in sympathetic activity in fibers innervating the heart.

Since the cardiovascular responses to diving can be elicited in decerebrate ducks, the medulla is presumed to be the site of integration of peripheral inputs. It has been shown in the seal, however, that the generation of the diving bradycardia can also involve some form of associative learning. In some trained seals, bradycardia occurs before the onset of the dive, and therefore before the stimulation of any peripheral receptors.

In birds, the "water" receptors are not directly involved in the cardiovascular changes associated with submersion. A decrease in heart rate is not observed either in submerged ducks breathing air through a tracheal cannula or in submerged ducks following carotid body denervation (Fig. 13-44). Thus the "water" receptors cause apnea, and the subsequent drop in blood P_{O_2} and pH and the rise in P_{CO_2} result in stimulation of the chemoreceptors, which then reflexly cause the cardiovascular changes.

Stimulation of lung stretch receptors modifies the reflex response initiated by chemoreceptor stimulation. In the absence of breathing, and hence stimulation of lung stretch receptors, different reflex responses are elicited by chemoreceptor stimulation than when the animal is breathing. Lung inflation tends to suppress reflex cardio-inhibition and peripheral vasoconstriction caused by stimulation of arterial chemoreceptors. The cardiovascular responses to hypoxia and hypercapnia (increased CO_2 levels) are therefore different when the animal is breathing than during a dive. Animals breathing air of low oxygen content show only minimal cardiovascular changes, including slight peripheral vasodilation and a small increase in heart rate. Reflex cardiovascular changes due to chemoreceptor stimulation are inhibited by lung inflation. Low oxygen levels in the blood cause peripheral vasodilation, which is partially offset by reduced blood

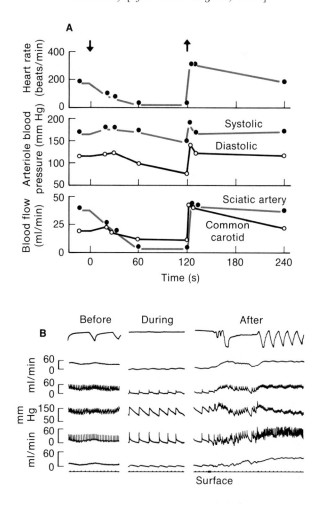

13–43. *Effect of submersion on normal ducks* (Anas Platyrhynchos). *A. Mean results from thirty-six dives on thirteen ducks (for carotid artery blood flow, mean values are from twenty-four dives on eight ducks). Downward pointing arrow indicates submersion, upward pointing arrow indicates emersion. B. Traces showing arterial blood pressure (and blood flow in the carotid and sciatic arteries) before, during, and after a normal dive of 2 min duration. In each series, the traces, from top to bottom, are (1) pneumogram (down on trace, inspiration), (2) mean blood flow through sciatic artery, (3) pulsatile blood flow through sciatic artery, (4) arterial blood pressure, (5) pulsatile blood flow through common carotid artery, (6) mean blood flow through common carotid artery. (Time markers in seconds.)* [After Butler and Jones, 1971.]

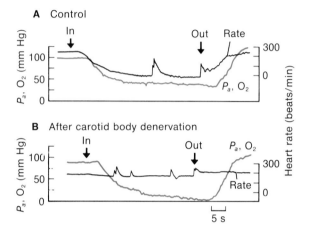

13-44. *Changes in heart rate and in brachiocephalic artery oxygen tension (mm Hg) during a period of submergences of the head in water indicated by the in-out arrows. Six-week-old Khaki Campbell unanesthetized duck. A. Control with all nerves intact. B. The same duck 3 weeks after denervation of the carotid bodies. [After Jones and Purves, 1970.]*

CO_2 levels (resulting from hyperventilation). The small decrease in peripheral resistance causes a drop in arterial pressure and a reflex increase in heart rate due to a reduction in baroreceptor discharge.

Thus, during a dive, stimulation of the "water" receptors inhibits breathing and the subsequent chemoreceptor respiratory drive, but not the chemoreceptor-induced cardiovascular changes. The absence of breathing results in reflex cardiovascular changes elicited by chemoreceptor stimulation. When the animal is breathing, however, any reflex cardiovascular changes associated with chemoreceptor stimulation are inhibited by activation of lung stretch receptors.

Summary

Circulatory systems can be divided into two broad categories—those with open and those with closed circulations. In open circulatory systems, transmural pressures are low, and blood pumped by the heart empties into a space in which blood bathes the cells directly. In closed circulations, blood passes via capillaries from the arterial to the venous circulation. Transmural pressures are high, and a slow leakage of fluid across capillary walls into the extracellular spaces is subsequently returned to the circulation via a lymphatic system.

The heart is a muscular pump that ejects blood into the arterial system. Excitation of the heart is initiated in a pacemaker, and the pattern of excitation of the rest of the muscle mass is determined by the nature of the contact between cells. The junctions between muscle fibers in the heart are of low resistance and allow the transfer of electrical activity from one cell to the next.

The initial phase of each heart contraction is isometric, followed by an isotonic phase in which blood is ejected into the arterial system. Cardiac output is dependent on venous inflow and, in mammals changes in cardiac output are mediated by changes in heart rate rather than stroke volume.

The arterial system acts as a pressure reservoir and a conduit for blood between heart and capillaries. The elastic arteries dampen oscillations in pressure and flow caused by contractions of the heart, and the muscular arterioles control the distribution of blood to the capillaries.

Blood flow is generally streamlined, but because the relationship between pressure and flow is complex, Poiseuille's equation applies only to flow in smaller arteries and capillaries.

Capillaries are the site of transfer of material between the blood and tissues. Only 3–5% of all capillaries are open to blood flow at any particular time, but no capillary remains closed for long, because they all open and close continuously. Capillary blood flow is controlled by nerves that innervate smooth muscle around arterioles. Changes in the composition of blood and extracellular fluid in the region of the capillary causes the vessels to either constrict or dilate so altering blood flow.

The venous system acts both as a conduit for blood between capillaries and the heart and as a blood reservoir. In mammals, 50% of the total blood volume is contained in veins.

Capillary blood flow is adjusted to meet the requirements of the tissues, and arterial pressure is adjusted to maintain capillary blood flow. Arterial baroreceptors monitor blood pressure and reflexly alter cardiac output and peripheral resistance to maintain arterial pressure. Atrial and ventricular mechanoreceptors monitor venous pressure and derivatives of the heart contraction to ensure that activity of the heart is correlated to blood inflow from the venous system and blood outflow into the arterial system. Arterial chemoreceptors and other sensory receptors feed information into the medullary cardiovascular center, where the inputs are integrated to ensure an appropriate response of the circulatory system to changing requirements of the animal, such as during exercise.

EXERCISES

1. Describe the properties of myogenic pacemakers.

2. Describe the transmission of excitation over the mammalian heart.

3. Describe the changes in pressure and flow during a single beat of the mammalian heart.

4. Discuss the factors that influence stroke volume of the heart.

5. What is the nature and function of the nervous innervation of the mammalian heart?

6. What is the effect on cardiac function of a rigid versus a compliant pericardium?

7. What is the functional significance of a partially divided ventricle in some reptiles?

8. Discuss the changes in circulation that occur at birth in the mammalian fetus.

9. Discuss the applicability of Poiseuille's equation to the relationship between pressure and flow in the circulation.

10. What are the functions served by the arterial system?

11. Describe the factors that determine capillary blood flow.

12. Describe the location and role in cardiovascular control of various baroreceptors and/or mechano-receptors in the mammalian circulatory system.

13. Compare and contrast the cardiovascular responses to breathing air low in oxygen with those associated with diving in mammals.

14. Describe the cardiovascular changes associated with exercise in mammals.

SUGGESTED READING

Farner, D. S., and J. R. King (eds). 1972. *Avian Biology* (Vol. II). Academic Press, New York.

Hoar, W. S., and D. J. Randall (eds.). 1970. *Fish Physiology* Vol. IV). Academic Press, New York.

Hoffman, B. F., and P. F. Cranfield. 1960. *Electrophysiology of the Heart.* McGraw-Hill, New York.

Korner, P. I. 1971. Integrative neural cardiovascular control. *Physiol. Revs.* 51:312–367.

McDonald, D. A. 1960. *Blood in Arteries.* Williams and Wilkins, Baltimore.

Paintal, A. S. 1973. Vagal sensory receptors and their reflex effects. *Physiol. Revs.* 53:159–227.

Robb, J. S. 1965. *Comparative Basic Cardiology.* Grune and Stratton, New York.

Ruch, T. C., and H. D. Patton. (eds.). 1974. *Physiology and Biophysics* (Vol. II, 20th ed.). Saunders, Philadelphia.

Satchell, G. H. 1971. *Circulation in Fishes.* Cambridge Univ. Press, New York.

Schmidt-Nielsen, K. 1972. *How Animals Work.* Cambridge Univ. Press, New York.

REFERENCES CITED

Adolph, E. F. 1967. The heart's pacemaker. *Scientific American* 216(3):32–37.

Barcroft, H., and H. J. C. Swan. 1953. *Sympathetic Control of Human Blood Vessels* (Monograms of the Physiological Society, No. 1). E. Arnold, London.

Brand, A. R. 1972. The mechanisms of blood circulation in *Anodonta anatina* (L.) Bivalvia Unionidae). *J. Expt. Biol.* 56:361–379.

Burnstock, G. 1972. Purinergic nerves. *Pharmacol. Revs.* 24:509–581.

Butler, P. J., and D. R. Jones. 1971. The effect of variations in heart rate and regional distribution of blood flow on the normal pressor response to diving in ducks. *J. Physiol.* 214:457–479.

Feigl, E. O. 1974. Physics of the cardiovascular system. T. C. Ruch and H. D. Patton (eds.), *Physiology and Biophysics* (Vol. II, 20th Ed.) Saunders, Philadelphia.

Goodrich, E. S. 1958. *Studies on the Structure and Development of Vertebrates* (Vol. II). Dover, New York.

Guyer, M. F. 1948. *Animal Biology* (4th Ed.). Harper and Bros., New York.

Hecht, H. H. 1965. Comparative physiological and morphological aspects of pacemaker tissues. *Ann. N.Y. Acad. Sci.* 127:49–83.

Hirakow, R. 1970. Ultrastructural characteristics of the mammalian and sauropsidan heart. *Amer. J. Cardiology.* 25:195–203.

Hoffman, B. F., and P. F. Cranefield. 1960. *Electrophysiology of the Heart.* McGraw-Hill, New York.

Hutter, O. F. and W. Trautwein. 1956. Vagal and sympathetic effects on the pacemaker fibers in the sinus venosus of the heart. *J. Gen. Physiol.* 39: 715–733.

Johansen, K., and A.W. Martin. 1965. Circulation in a giant earthworm, *Glossoscolex giganteus.* I. Contractile processes and pressure gradients in the large blood vessels. *J. Expt. Biol.* 43:333–347.

Jones, D. R., B. L. Langille, D. J. Randall, and G. Shelton. 1974. Blood flow in dorsal and ventral aortas of the cod, *Gadus morhua. Amer. J. Physiol.* 226:90–95.

Jones, D. R., and M. J. Purves. 1970. The effect of carotid body denervation upon the respiratory response to hypoxia and hypercapnia in the duck. *J. Physiol.* 211:295–309.

Kampmeier, O. F. 1969. *Evolution and Comparative Morphology of the Lymphatic System.* Charles C Thomas, Springfield, Illinois.

Korner, P. I. 1971. Integrative neural cardiovascular control. *Physiol. Revs.* 51(2):312–367.

Langille, B. J. 1975. A comparative study of central cardiovascular dynamics in vertebrates. PhD. Dissertation. Univ. British Columbia, Vancouver, Canada.

Le Gros Clark, W. E. 1952. *The Tissues of the Body* (3rd ed.). Clarendon Press, Oxford.

McDonald, D. A. 1960. *Blood Flow in Arteries* (Monographs of the Physiological Society, No. 7). E. Arnold, London.

Randall, D. J. 1968. Functional morphology of the heart in fishes. *Amer. Zool.* 8(2):179–189.

Rowell, L. B. 1974. Circulation to skeletal muscle. *In* T. C. Ruch and H. D. Patton (eds.), *Physiology and Biophysics* (Vol. II, 20th ed.). Saunders, Philadelphia.

Ruch, T. C., and H. D. Patton. 1974. *Physiology and Biophysics* (Vol. II, 20th ed.). Saunders, Philadelphia.

Rushmer, R. F. 1965a. Control of cardiac output. *In* T. C. Ruch and H. D. Patton (eds.), *Physiology and Biophysics* (19th ed.). Saunders, Philadelphia.

Rushmer, R. F. 1965b. General characteristics of the cardiovascular system. *In* T. C. Ruch and H. D. Patton (eds.), *Physiology and Biophysics* (19th ed.). Saunders, Philadelphia.

Rushmer, R. F. 1965c. The arterial system: Arteries and arterioles. *In* T. C. Ruch and H. D. Patton (eds.), *Physiology and Biophysics* (19th ed.). Saunders, Philadelphia.

Sarnoff, S. J., and J. H. Mitchell. 1962. The control of the function of the heart. In H. W. Magoun (ed.), *Handbook of Physiology* (Section 1, Neurophysiology, Vol. I). Williams & Wilkins, Baltimore.

Satchell, G. H. 1971. *Circulation in Fishes* (Cambridge Monographs in Experimental Biology Series, Vol. 18), Cambridge Univ. Press. London.

Scher, A. M., and W. G. L. Kerrick. 1974. Electrical characteristics of the cardiac cell. *In* T. C. Ruch and H. D. Patton (eds.), *Physiology and Biophysics* (Vol. II, 20th ed.). Saunders, Philadelphia.

Sjöstrand, F. S., E. Anderson-Cedergreen, and M. M. Dewey. 1958. The ultrastructure of the intercalated discs of frog, mouse, and guinea-pig cardiac muscle. *J. Ultrastr. Res.* 1:271-287.

Stevens, E. D., H. M. Lam, and J. Kendall. 1974. Vascular anatomy of the countercurrent heat exchanger of skipjack tuna. *J. Expt. Biol.* 61:145–153.

Vander, A. J., J. H. Sherman, and D. S. Luciano. 1975. *Human Physiology: The Mechanisms of Body Function* (2nd ed.). McGraw-Hill, New York.

White, F. N. 1968. Functional anatomy of the heart of reptiles. *Amer. Zool.* 8:211-219.

Wiederhielm, C. A., and B. U. Weston. 1973. Microvascular lymphatic and tissue pressures in the unanesthetized mammal. *Amer. J. Physiol.* 225: 992–996.

Wiederheilm, C. A., J. W. Woodbury, S. Kirk, and R. F. Rushmer. 1964. Pulsatile pressures in the microcirculation of frog's mesentery. *Amer. J. Physiol.* 207:173–176.

CHAPTER FOURTEEN

Exchange of Gases

Animals utilize oxygen and produce carbon dioxide during the course of cellular respiration, a process whose reactions take place at the level of the mitochondria, as described in Chapter 3. Oxygen is obtained from the environment, and carbon dioxide liberated into the environment. In order for cellular respiration to proceed, there must be a steady supply of O_2, and the waste product CO_2 must be continually removed. In this chapter, we will consider the means by which these gases are transferred between the environment and the mitochondria.

Oxygen and carbon dioxide are transferred passively across the body surface (i.e., skin or special respiratory epithelium) by diffusion. The mass of gas transferred across an epithelium, M, is determined by the area available for diffusion, A, the diffusion distance, x, the diffusion coefficient, D, and the concentration difference across the respiratory surface, $(a_1 - a_2)$:

$$M = \frac{DA(a_1 - a_2)}{x}.$$

Therefore, in order to facilitate the rate of gas transfer for a given concentration difference, the surface area of the respiratory epithelium should be as large as possible and diffusion distances as small as possible.

The oxygen requirements and CO_2 production of an animal increase in proportion to its mass, whereas the rate of gas transfer across the body surface is related to a large extent to surface area. It will be recalled that the area of a sphere increases as the square of its diameter, whereas the volume increases as the cube of its diameter. In very small animals, the distances for diffusion are small and the ratio of surface area to volume large. For this reason, diffusion alone is sufficient for the transfer of gases in small animals, such as rotifers and protozoa, which are less than 0.5 mm in diameter. Increases in size result in increases in diffusion distances and reductions in the ratio of surface area to volume. A circulatory system has evolved in larger animals to facilitate the transfer of gases between the body surface and the tissues. The circulatory system reduces diffusion distances, transferring gases by flow of blood between body surface

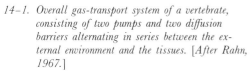

14-1. *Overall gas-transport system of a vertebrate, consisting of two pumps and two diffusion barriers alternating in series between the external environment and the tissues. [After Rahn, 1967.]*

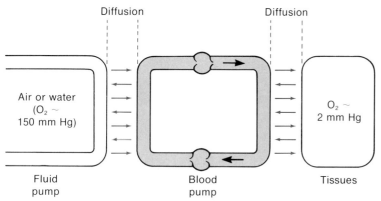

3. Bulk transport of gases by the blood.

4. Diffusion of oxygen and carbon dioxide across capillary walls between blood and mitochondria in tissue cells.

The rate of diffusion of a substance along a given gradient is inversely proportional to the square root of its molecular weight (or density) (Graham's Law). Oxygen and carbon dioxide molecules are of similar size and therefore will diffuse at similar rates, and they are also utilized (O_2) and produced (CO_2) at approximately the same rates. It can therefore be expected that a transfer system that meets the oxygen requirements of an animal will also ensure adequate rates of carbon dioxide removal.

The ratio of carbon dioxide produced to oxygen utilized during the same time period is termed the *respiratory quotient* (RQ):

$$RQ = \frac{ml\ CO_2\ produced/unit\ time}{ml\ O_2\ utilized/unit\ time}.$$

The RQ varies depending on the nature of the substrate being metabolized. The oxidation of fats, proteins, and carbohydrates results in RQ's of 0.7, 0.8, and 1.0, respectively. Different tissues exhibit different RQ's. For example, the mammalian brain has an RQ of 1.0, whereas resting mammalian muscle usually has an RQ of about 0.7. The RQ of the whole animal will depend upon the relative activity of different organs, the nature of the substrates being metabolized, and whether O_2 and CO_2 stores within the body are constant or changing. In general, however, the number of oxygen molecules utilized is approximately the same as the number of carbon dioxide molecules produced.

and tissues. Large surface-area/volume ratios are maintained in larger animals by the elaboration of special areas for the exchange of gases. In some animals, the whole body surface participates in gas transfer, but in large, active animals there is a specialized respiratory surface. This surface is covered by a thin layer of cells, the respiratory epithelium, which is between 0.5 and 5 μm thick and represents the major portion of the total body surface. In humans, for instance, the alveolar surface area of the lung is between 50 and 100 m^2, varying with age and lung inflation, whereas the area of the rest of the body surface area is less than 2 m^2.

Stagnation of the medium close to the surface of the respiratory epithelium is avoided in most animals by the exchange of air or water through breathing movements. Blood flows through an extensive capillary network and is spread in a thin film just beneath the respiratory surface, thereby reducing diffusion distances required to distribute the contained gases. The gases are transported between the respiratory surface and the tissues by bulk flow of blood. Gases diffuse between blood and tissues across the capillary wall. Once again, the area for diffusion is large and the diffusion distance between any cell and the nearest capillary small in order to facilitate gas transfer. Thus the transfer of gases in many animals takes place in several stages (Fig. 14-1):

1. Breathing movements, which assure a continual supply of air or water to the respiratory surface (e.g., lungs or gills).

2. Diffusion of oxygen and carbon dioxide across the respiratory epithelium.

Oxygen and Carbon Dioxide in Blood

RESPIRATORY PIGMENTS

Henry's Law (Box 14-1) applies only to gases that do not react chemically with the solvent. The oxygen content of the blood of most animals is greatly increased because oxygen combines with a *respiratory pigment*, of which hemoglobin is the best-known example (Fig. 14-2). In the absence of a respiratory pigment, the oxygen content of blood would be small. The Bunsen solubility coefficient of oxygen in blood at 37°C is 2.4 ml O_2/100 ml blood/atmosphere of oxygen pressure. Therefore, the concentration of O_2 in physical solution (i.e., not bound to a respiratory pigment) in human blood at a P_{O_2} of 95 mm Hg will be 2.4 × 95/760 = 0.3 ml O_2/100 ml blood, or

BOX 14-1 THE GAS LAWS

Over three hundred years ago, Boyle realized that at a given temperature the product of pressure and volume is constant for a given number of molecules of gas. Gay-Lussac's Law states that either the pressure or the volume of a gas is directly proportional to absolute temperature if the other is held constant. Combined, these laws are expressed in the equation of state for a gas:

$$PV = nR°K,$$

where P = pressure, V = volume, n = number of molecules of a gas, R = universal gas constant ($=0.08205$ liter-atm/°K-mole, or 8.314×10^7 ergs/°K-mole, or 1.987 cal/°K-mole), °K = absolute temperature. For accurate use, the equation should be modified using Van der Waals' constants.

The equation of state for a gas indicates that equal volumes of different gases at the same temperature and pressure contain equal numbers of molecules (Avogadro's Law). One mole of gas occupies approximately 22.414 liters at 0°C and 760 mm Hg. Because the number of molecules per unit volume is dependent on pressure and temperature, the conditions should always be stated along with the volume of gas. Gas volumes in physiology are usually reported as being at body temperature, atmospheric pressure, and saturated with water vapor (BTPS); or at ambient temperature and pressure, saturated with water vapor (ATPS); or at standard temperature and pressure (0°C, 760 mm Hg) and dry (zero water vapor pressure) (STPD).

Gas volumes measured at BTPS can be converted to ATPS or STPD volumes using the equation of state for a gas. For example, the volume of air expired from a mammalian lung at body temperature (37°C or $273 + 37 = 310$°K) is often measured at room temperature (e.g., 20°C or $273 + 20 = 293$°K). The drop in temperature will reduce the expired gas volume. A gas in contact with water will be saturated with water vapor. The water vapor pressure at 100% saturation varies with temperature. Expired air is saturated with water, but as temperature decreases, water will condense, and this will also reduce the expired gas volume. If the measured expired volume at 20°C is 500 ml, then, if the barometric pressure is 760 mm Hg and the water vapor pressure at 37°C and 20°C is 47.1 mm Hg and 17.5 mm Hg, respectively, the BTPS expired volume can be calculated as follows:

$$500 \times \frac{(760 - 17.5)}{(760 - 47.1)} \times \frac{(273 + 37)}{(273 + 20)} = 551 \text{ ml.}$$

Thus, under the conditions stated above, a gas volume of 551 ml within the lung is reduced to 500 ml following exhalation because of the drop in gas temperature and the condensation of water.

Dalton's Law of partial pressure states that the partial pressure of each gas in a mixture is independent of other gases present, so that the total pressure equals the sum of the partial pressures of all gases present. The partial pressure of a gas in a mixture will depend on the number of molecules present in a given volume at a given temperature. Usually oxygen accounts for 20.94% of all gas molecules present in dry air; thus, if the total pressure is 760 mm Hg, the partial pressure of oxygen, P_{O_2} will be $760 \times 0.2094 = 159$ mm Hg. But air usually contains water vapor, which contributes to the total pressure. If the air is 50% saturated with water vapor at 22°C, then the water vapor pressure is 10 mm Hg. If the total pressure is 760 mm Hg, the partial pressure of oxygen will be $(760 - 10)0.2094 = 157$ mm Hg. If the partial pressure of CO_2 in a gas mixture is 7.6 mm Hg and the total pressure is 760 mm Hg, then 1% of the molecules in air are CO_2.

Gases are soluble in liquids. The quantity of gas that dissolves at a given temperature is proportional to the partial pressure of that gas in the gas phase (*Henry's Law*). The quantity of gas, V, in solution equals αP, where P is the partial pressure of the gas and α is the *Bunsen solubility coefficient*, which is independent of P but varies with temperature. Thus the amount of any gas in solution may be expressed either as a partial pressure or as a gas content per unit volume, the gas content being expressed in grams, moles or milliliters per unit volume.

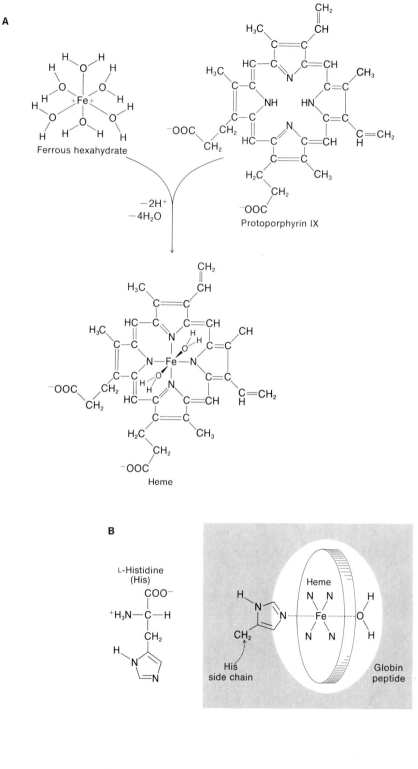

A

Ferrous hexahydrate

Protoporphyrin IX

$-2H^+$
$-4H_2O$

Heme

B

L-Histidine
(His)

His
side chain

Heme

Globin
peptide

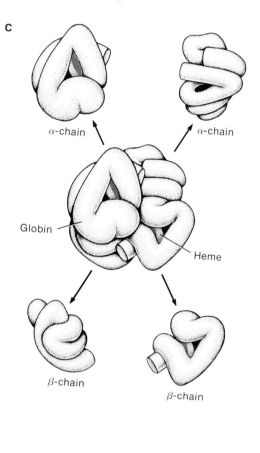

14–2. *A. The combination of ferrous ion and protoporphyrin IX to form heme. B. Schematic diagram of heme in a pocket formed by the globin molecule. A histidyl side chain from the globin acts as an additional ligand for the iron atom in heme. C. An "idealized," exploded diagram of the hemoglobin molecule. Two of the four heme units are visible in pockets formed by folds of the peptide chains.* [*After McGilverery, 1970.*]

C

α-chain

α-chain

Globin

Heme

β-chain

β-chain

0.3 vol % O_2. The total O_2 content of human arterial blood at a similar P_{O_2} is, in fact, 20 vol %. The 70-fold increase in content is due to combination of oxygen with hemoglobin.

Respiratory pigments are complexes of proteins and metallic ions, and each one has a characteristic color. Vertebrates use *hemoglobin* as a circulating respiratory pigment and *myoglobin* as a storage respira-tory pigment in muscle. The antarctic ice fish is an exception among vertebrates; the blood of this fish lacks a respiratory pigment and therefore has a low oxygen content. It compensates for the absence of hemoglobin with an increased blood volume and cardiac output, but its rate of oxygen uptake is re-duced compared with other species from the same habitat that possess hemoglobin. Ice fish live in antarctic waters and low temperatures are probably a factor in the evolution of fish lacking hemoglobin. Low temperatures are associated with low metabolic rates in poikilotherms, and oxygen, like all gases, has a higher solubility at low temperatures.

Different groups of invertebrates have different respiratory pigments, including hemerythrin (Priapulida, Branchiopoda, Annelida), chlorocruorin (Annelida), hemocyanin (many invertebrate groups), and hemoglobin (many invertebrate groups). Many invertebrates do not have a respiratory pigment. Hemocyanin is a large copper-containing molecule; 1 mole of O_2 combines with approximately 50,000 to 75,000 g of this respiratory pigment.

Vertebrate hemoglobin, except that of cyclostomes, has a molecular weight of 68,000 and contains four iron porphyrin prosthetic groups—heme—associated with the protein *globin* (Fig. 14-2), which in turn is made up of two equal parts, each consisting of two polypeptide chains (an α-chain and a β, γ, or ε-chain). Hemoglobin will dissociate into four subunits of approximately equal weight, each containing one polypeptide chain and one heme group. Iron in the ferrous state is bound into the porphyrin ring of the heme, forming coordinate links with the four pyrrole nitrogens. The two remaining coordinate linkages are used to bind the heme group to an imidazole ring of the globin and to bind oxygen. If oxygen is bound, the molecule is referred to as *oxyhemoglobin;* if O_2 is absent, the term *deoxyhemoglobin* is used. The oxygen-binding characteristics of hemoglobins vary. These differences are related to variations in the structure of the globin molecule.

Methemoglobin, which does not bind oxygen and is therefore nonfunctional, is formed if ferrous iron of heme is oxidized to the ferric state. This occurs normally, but red blood cells contain the enzyme methemoglobin reductase, which reduces methemoglobin to the functional ferrous form. Certain compounds (nitrates or chlorates) act either to oxidize hemoglobin or to inactivate methemoglobin reductase, thereby increasing the level of methemoglobin and impairing oxygen transport.

The affinity of hemoglobin is about 200 times as great for carbon monoxide as for oxygen. As a result, carbon monoxide will displace oxygen and saturate hemoglobin, even at very low partial pressures of carbon monoxide, causing a marked reduction in oxygen transport to the tissues. Hemoglobin saturated with carbon monoxide is called *carboxyhemoglobin.* The effect of such saturation on oxidative metabolism is similar to that of oxygen deprivation, which is why the carbon monoxide produced by cars or improperly stoked coal or wood stoves is so extremely toxic. Even the levels found in city traffic can impair brain function due to partial anoxia.

OXYGEN TRANSPORT IN BLOOD

Each hemoglobin molecule can combine with four oxygen molecules, each heme combining with one molecule of oxygen. The extent to which oxygen is bound to hemoglobin varies with the partial pressure of the gas. If all sites on the hemoglobin molecule are occupied by oxygen, the blood is 100% saturated and the *oxygen content* of the blood is equal to its oxygen *capacity.* A millimole of heme can bind a millimole of oxygen, which represents a volume of 22.4 ml of oxygen. Human blood contains about 0.9 mmole of heme per 100 ml of blood. The oxygen capacity is therefore $0.9 \times 22.4 = 20.2$ vol %. The oxygen content of a unit volume of blood includes the oxygen in physical solution as well as the oxygen combined with hemoglobin, but in most cases the O_2 in physical solution is only a small fraction of the total O_2 content.

The oxygen capacity increases in proportion to the hemoglobin concentration; consequently, in order to compare blood of different hemoglobin content, we use the term percent saturation, expressing O_2 content as a percentage of O_2 capacity. *Oxygen dissociation curves* (Figs. 14-3 to 14-5) describe the relationship between percent saturation and the partial pressure of oxygen.

The curves of myoglobin (a storage respiratory pigment in muscles) and lamprey hemoglobin are hyperbolic, whereas other vertebrate hemoglobin oxygen dissociation curves are sigmoid (Fig. 14-3).

14-3. Oxygen dissociation curves for hemoglobin and myoglobin. Note the hyperbolic shape of the myoglobin curve and the sigmoid shape of the hemoglobin curve. Lamprey hemoglobin, with a single heme group, has a dissociation curve similar to myoglobin.

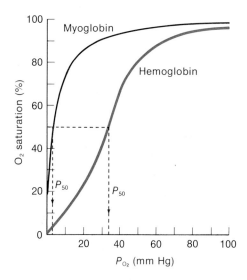

This is correlated with the fact that myoglobin and lamprey hemoglobin have a single heme group, whereas other hemoglobins have several (usually four) heme groups. The sigmoid shape of these curves is explained in terms of *subunit interactions*. Oxygenation of the first heme groups somehow facilitates oxygenation of subsequent heme groups, probably as a result of conformational changes in the protein globin.

Hill described the oxygen-hemoglobin equilibrium mathematically in 1910:

$$y/100 = \frac{KP^n}{1 - KP^n},$$

where y = percent saturation with oxygen, P = partial pressure of oxygen, K = equilibrium constant, and n = measure of subunit interaction. Rearranging and taking logarithms on both sides gives

$$\log \frac{y}{100 - y} = \log K + n \log P.$$

A plot of $\log (y/100 - y)$ against $\log P$ gives a straight line. The slope, n, indicates the extent of subunit interaction. Myoglobin gives an n value of 1, indicating no subunit interaction. If $n > 1$, there is positive subunit interaction; if $n < 1$, the reverse is true. For human hemoglobin between 20 and 98% saturation, $n = 2.7$; outside of this range n approaches 1. The intercept on the $\log (y/100 - y)$ axis yields K, the oxygen-hemoglobin equilibrium constant.

An important functional property of respiratory pigments is that they combine reversibly with O_2 over the range of partial pressures normally encountered in the animal. At low P_{O_2}, only a small amount of oxygen binds to the respiratory pigment; at high P_{O_2}, however, a large amount of oxygen is bound. Because of this property, the respiratory pigment can act as an oxygen carrier, loading at the respiratory surface (a region of high P_{O_2}) and unloading at tissues (a region of low P_{O_2}). In some animals, the predominant role of a respiratory pigment may be to serve as an oxygen store, releasing O_2 to the tissues only when O_2 is relatively unavailable. For instance, seals and other diving mammals have high levels of the respiratory pigment myoglobin in their muscles. Myoglobin acts as an oxygen store, releasing O_2 only during periods when oxygen levels in the muscle decrease, as they do during a dive. It has also been demonstrated that the diffusion of respiratory pigments in a solution facilitates the diffusion of gas molecules attached to the pigments. This process could be important in facilitating the mixing of gases in blood; in the majority of species, however, pigments are intracellular, and diffusion of the pigment is probably an insignificant factor in oxygen transfer.

Hemoglobins with high oxygen affinities are saturated at low partial pressures of oxygen, whereas hemoglobins with low oxygen affinities are completely saturated only at relatively high partial pressures of oxygen. This difference in oxygen affinity is related to differences in the properties of the protein moiety globin, and can be expressed in terms of the P_{50}, the partial pressure of oxygen at which the hemoglobin is 50% saturated with oxygen.

The rate of oxygen uptake increases in proportion to the difference in partial pressure across an epithelium. A hemoglobin with a high oxygen affinity facilitates the movement of oxygen into the blood from the environment because oxygen is bound to hemoglobin at low P_{O_2}. Thus a large difference in P_{O_2} across the respiratory epithelium—and therefore a high rate of oxygen transfer into the blood—is maintained until hemoglobin is fully saturated. Only then does blood P_{O_2} rise. Hemoglobin with a high oxygen affinity, however, will not release oxygen to the tissues until the P_{O_2} of the tissues is very low. In contrast, a hemoglobin with a low oxygen affinity will facilitate the release of oxygen to the tissues, maintaining large differences in P_{O_2} between blood and tissues and a high rate of oxygen transfer to the tissues. Thus a hemoglobin of high oxygen affinity favors the uptake of oxygen by the blood, whereas a hemoglobin of low oxygen affinity facilitates the release of oxygen to the tissues. From a functional viewpoint, therefore, hemoglobin should have a low O_2 affinity in the tissues and a high O_2 affinity at the respiratory surface. Interestingly, hemoglobin O_2 affinity is affected by changes in chemical and physical factors in the blood that favor oxygen binding at the respiratory epithelium and oxygen release in the tissues.

Hemoglobin oxygen affinity is labile and is reduced either by increases in P_{CO_2}, temperature, and *2,3-diphosphoglycerate* (DPG), or by a decrease in pH (Fig. 14-4). The term *Bohr effect*, or *Bohr shift*, is used to describe the interaction between H^+ ions and hemoglobin oxygen affinity. Increases in $[H^+]$ (decrease in pH) cause a reduction in hemoglobin oxygen affinity (Fig. 14-5). Conversely, oxygenation of hemoglobin results in the release of protons from hemoglobin, and therefore a decrease in pH. Carbon dioxide reacts with water to form carbonic acid and with $-NH_2$ groups on plasma proteins and hemoglobin to form carbamino compounds (Fig. 14-9). An increase in P_{CO_2} results in a decrease in blood pH and an increase in carbamino compounds in the blood. Increases in CO_2 cause a reduction in the oxygen affinity of hemoglobin, both by reducing pH (Bohr effect) and by the direct combination of CO_2 with hemoglobin to form carbamino compounds. Carbon dioxide enters the blood at the tissues and facilitates the unloading of oxygen from hemoglobin, whereas CO_2 leaves the blood at the lung or gill and facilitates the uptake of oxygen by the blood.

The oxygen dissociation curve for myoglobin, unlike that for hemoglobin, is relatively insensitive to changes in pH.

In some fish, cephalopods, and crustaceans, an increase in CO_2 or a decrease in pH not only causes a reduction in the oxygen affinity of hemoglobin but also a reduction in oxygen capacity, which is termed the *Root effect*, or *shift* (Fig. 14-6).

A decrease in pH results in an increase in oxygen affinity in hemocyanins from several gastropods and from the horseshoe crab *Limulus*. This is referred to as a *reverse Bohr effect* and may serve to facilitate oxygen uptake during periods of low oxygen availability when there are maintained reductions in blood pH in these animals.

Mammalian red blood cells contain high levels of 2,3-diphosphoglycerate. Hemoglobin and DPG are nearly equimolar in human red blood cells. DPG binds to the α-chains of deoxyhemoglobin and reduces oxygen affinity. Increases in DPG levels accompany reductions in blood oxygen levels, increases in pH, and reductions in hemoglobin concentrations in blood. Low blood oxygen levels may result from a climb to a higher altitude. Barometric pressure and the partial pressure of oxygen in air both decrease with altitude. The resultant DPG rise in response to high altitude is completed in 24 hours with a half-time of about 6 hours. At elevations of 3000 m, there is a 10% increase in DPG over the concentration at sea level. The resultant reduced oxygen affinity enhances oxygen transfer to the tissues, but adversely affects oxygen uptake at the lungs. In some vertebrates, other phosphorylated compounds, such as adenosine triphosphate in fish or inositol phosphate in birds, are in higher concentration in the red cell and have a greater effect on the oxygen affinity of hemoglobin than DPG. Phosporylated compounds in the red cell not only affect the oxygen affinity of hemoglobin but also increase the magnitude of the Bohr effect, and may affect subunit interaction. It appears that the functional significance of increased DPG levels is that they favor the release of oxygen to the tissues under conditions of low oxygen, such as at high altitude.

It is generally assumed that a particular hemoglobin has evolved to meet the special gas-transfer and H^+-buffering requirements of the animal. The properties of hemoglobin (and red cells) vary among species and may change during development (Fig. 14-7). For instance, fetal hemoglobins often have a higher oxygen affinity than the postnatal and adult hemoglobin (Fig. 14-8). The higher O_2 affinity of fetal hemoglobin enhances oxygen transfer from mother to fetus.

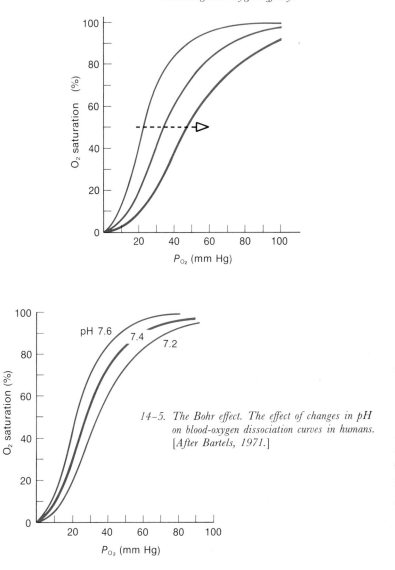

14-4. A rise in temperature, P_{CO_2}, or level of 2,3-diphosphoglycerate or a drop in pH will reduce the hemoglobin oxygen affinity.

14-5. The Bohr effect. The effect of changes in pH on blood-oxygen dissociation curves in humans. [After Bartels, 1971.]

14-6. Oxygen equilibrium curves of eel blood at 14°C and pH from 6.99 to 8.20. Notice the effect of pH on the O_2 capacity (Root effect). Bottom line describes the O_2 content of plasma. Hematocrit of whole blood, 40 vol%. [After Steen, 1963.]

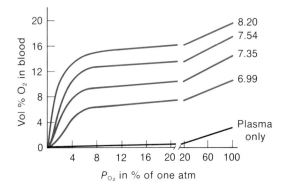

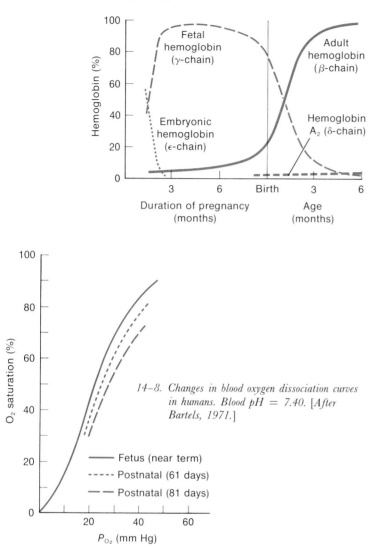

14-7. *Changes in hemoglobins during development in humans.* [*After Young, 1971.*]

14-8. *Changes in blood oxygen dissociation curves in humans. Blood pH = 7.40.* [*After Bartels, 1971.*]

It is important to remember that in most animals hemoglobin is contained within red blood cells. Values of blood parameters usually refer to conditions in the plasma, not the red blood cell. There are differences between the inside and outside of cells, and the red blood cell is no exception. For example, mammalian arterial blood pH at 37°C is usually 7.4. This is the pH of arterial blood *plasma;* the pH inside the red blood cell is less, about 7.2 at 37°C.

CARBON DIOXIDE TRANSPORT IN BLOOD

Carbon dioxide diffuses into the blood from the tissues, is transported in the blood, and diffuses across the respiratory surface into the environment. Figure 14-9 outlines the sequence of reactions involved in the exchange of CO_2 and O_2 and the relative distribution of CO_2 entering the blood from the tissues of a typical mammal.

Carbon dioxide reacts with water to form carbonic acid, a weak acid, which dissociates into bicarbonate and carbonate ions:

$$CO_2 + H_2O \rightleftharpoons H_2CO_3 \rightleftharpoons$$
$$H^+ + HCO_3^- \rightleftharpoons H^+ + CO_3^{2-}$$

The proportion of CO_2, HCO_3^-, and CO_3^{2-} in solution is dependent upon pH, temperature, and the ionic strength of the solution. In blood, the ratio of CO_2 to H_2CO_3 is approximately 1000:1, and the ratio of CO_2 to bicarbonate ions is about 1:20. Bicarbonate is therefore the predominant form of CO_2 in the blood

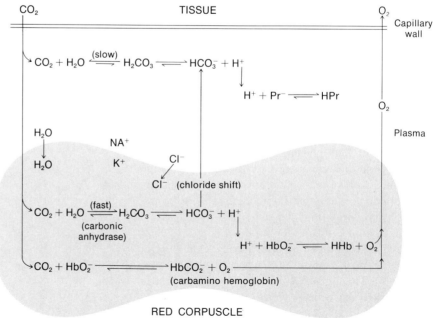

14-9. *Transfer of carbon dioxide between blood and tissues. The reverse process occurs in the lungs. Pr = protein; Hb = hemoglobin.*

at normal blood pH. The carbonate content is usually negligible in birds and mammals; in poikilotherms, however, with their low temperature and high blood pH, the carbonate content may approach 5% of the total CO_2 content of the blood, but bicarbonate is still the predominant form of CO_2.

Carbon dioxide also reacts with $-NH_2$ groups on proteins and, in particular, hemoglobin to form carbamino compounds.

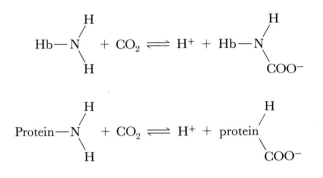

The extent of carbamino formation will depend upon the number of available $-NH_2$ groups, as well as on blood pH and P_{CO_2}.

The total CO_2 content of blood varies with P_{CO_2}. The relationship is described graphically in the form of a CO_2 dissociation curve (Fig. 14-10). The total CO_2 concentration (the sum of all forms of CO_2—i.e., HCO_3^-, CO_2, carbamino compounds) is higher in plasma than in red blood cells. The P_{CO_2} is essentially the same, but bicarbonate levels are considerably higher in plasma than in red blood cells. More carbamino compounds are formed within the red blood cell than in plasma because of the large number of $-NH_2$ groups on hemoglobin compared with plasma proteins. The difference, however, is not sufficient to offset the higher plasma bicarbonate concentration.

Carbon dioxide is added to the blood in the tissues and removed at the respiratory surface, and levels of CO_2, HCO_3^-, and carbamino compounds all change during this transfer. Carbon dioxide both enters and leaves the blood as molecular CO_2 rather than as bicarbonate ion because CO_2 molecules are nonpolar and diffuse through membranes much more rapidly than HCO_3^- ions. In the tissues, CO_2 enters the blood and is either hydrated to form bicarbonate ions or reacts with $-NH_2$ groups of hemoglobin and other proteins to form carbamino compounds. The reverse process occurs when CO_2 is unloaded from the blood.

The CO_2 hydration/dehydration reaction is slow and has an uncatalysed time course of several seconds. In the presence of the enzyme *carbonic anhydrase*, found in red blood cells, the reaction approaches equilibrium in much less than a second. Although plasma has a

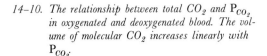

14-10. *The relationship between total CO_2 and P_{CO_2} in oxygenated and deoxygenated blood. The volume of molecular CO_2 increases linearly with P_{CO_2}.*

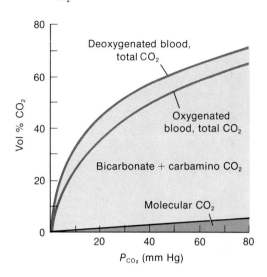

higher total CO_2 content than red blood cells, most of the CO_2 entering and leaving the plasma does so via the red blood cell. The reason for this is that carbonic anhydrase is present in the red blood cell and not in the plasma. Therefore, bicarbonate or CO_2 formation occurs much more rapidly in the red blood cell, and bicarbonate ions subsequently diffuse either from or into the plasma (Fig. 14-9). A second reason why most of the CO_2 entering or leaving the blood passes through the red blood cell is that deoxygenated hemoglobin (Hb) acts as a proton acceptor, facilitating the formation of bicarbonate:

$$CO_2 + H_2O \rightleftharpoons H_2CO_3 \rightleftharpoons$$
$$HCO_3^- + H^+ + HbO_2 \rightleftharpoons HHb + O_2$$

Thus changes in pH caused by the hydration of CO_2 are minimized because of the binding of protons with the formation of deoxyhemoglobin as oxygen is released to the tissues. For every HCO_3^- or carbamino compound formed, a proton is liberated; as deoxygenation proceeds, however, more proton acceptors become available on the hemoglobin molecule. In fact, complete deoxygenation of saturated hemoglobin, releasing 1 mole O_2, results in the binding of 0.7 mole of hydrogen ions. At a respiratory quotient of 0.7 (pure fat diet), the transport of CO_2 can proceed without any change in blood pH. If the respiratory quotient is 1, then the additional 0.3 mole H^+ is buffered by blood proteins, including hemoglobin, and blood undergoes only a small change in pH.

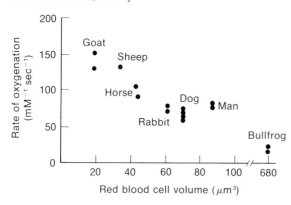

37°C of 0.12 s in human red blood cells. A reduction in temperature always decreases reaction velocities in any one species. Nevertheless, eel red blood cells at 15°C have the same half-time for the Bohr shift as human red blood cells at 37°C. These two species have evolved similar reaction velocities for the Bohr shift at very different temperatures. In most instances, reaction velocities of O_2 and CO_2 in blood are too fast to be important rate-limiting steps in gas transfer, and animals do not adjust reaction velocities in order to regulate rates of gas transfer. Variations in gas transfer rates in mammals are achieved either by adjusting breathing rate and volume or by adjusting the flow rate and distribution of blood in both tissues and the respiratory surface.

CO_2 and Acid–Base Regulation. The relationship between pH and the extent of dissociation of a weak acid, such as carbonic acid, is described by the Henderson Hasselbach equation (see p. 20, Chapter 2). The equation can be rewritten for the CO_2/bicarbonate system in the form

$$pH = pK' + \log \frac{[HCO_3^-]}{\alpha P_{CO_2}} \qquad (14\text{-}1)$$

where P_{CO_2} = the partial pressure of CO_2 in blood, α = the Bunsen solubility coefficient for CO_2, and $[HCO_3^-]$ = the concentration of bicarbonate. Changes in pH will affect the HCO_3^-/P_{CO_2} ratio and vice versa.

Weak acids have their greatest buffering action when pH = pK'. The pK' of plasma proteins and hemoglobin is close to the pH of blood. These compounds are therefore important buffers in the blood. The pK' of the reaction $H_2CO_3 \rightleftharpoons HCO_3^- + H^+$ is about 6.2, and pK' of the reaction $HCO_3^- \rightleftharpoons CO_3^{2-} + H^+$ is around 9.4; thus the CO_2 hydration/dehydration reaction is of less importance than either hemoglobins or proteins in providing a physical buffer system. The importance of the CO_2/HCO_3^- system is that an increase in breathing can rapidly increase pH by lowering CO_2 levels in the blood, and that HCO_3^- can be excreted via the kidney to decrease blood pH. That is, the CO_2/bicarbonate ratio can be adjusted by excretion in order to regulate pH.

It can be seen from the Henderson-Hasselbach equation that changes in pK' will cause changes in pH or in the dissociation of weak acids. Temperature has a marked effect on pK' of plasma proteins, the pK' increasing as temperature decreases. Poikilotherms adjust arterial pH with changes in temperature. As temperature drops, the pH of arterial blood plasma increases (Fig. 14-12) and offsets changes in pK' of plasma proteins (as a result of the temperature change), so that the extent to which the plasma proteins dissociate remains constant. Because the pK' of the CO_2 hydration/dehydration reaction changes

At a given P_{CO_2}, deoxyhemoglobin binds more protons and carbamino CO_2 than oxyhemoglobin; the total CO_2 content of deoxygenated blood at a given P_{CO_2} is therefore higher than that of oxygenated blood (Fig. 14-10). Thus deoxygenation of hemoglobin in the tissues reduces the change in P_{CO_2} and pH as CO_2 enters the blood; this is termed the *Haldane effect.*

Upon entering the blood, carbon dioxide diffuses into red blood cells and bicarbonate is formed rapidly in the presence of carbonic anhydrase. This results in a rise in bicarbonate levels, and as a result, HCO_3^- leaves the red blood cells. Electrical balance within the cells is maintained by anion exchange; as HCO_3^- moves from the red blood cells into the plasma, there is a net influx of Cl^- ions into the erythrocyte. This process is called the *chloride shift.*

The rate of movement of CO_2, HCO_3^-, Cl^-, and O_2 into or out of the red blood cell will be determined by the surface to volume ratio of the cell and the diffusion coefficient of these substances through the red cell, as well as the transport capacity of the HCO_3^-/Cl^- exchange mechanism. The size of erythrocytes varies considerably among species, hence it is not surprising that small erythrocytes, with their larger surface/volume ratio, are oxygenated faster than larger cells (Fig. 14-11). The size of erythrocytes may also be important in determining the rates of HCO_3^- and Cl^- movement between the red blood cell and the plasma. Nevertheless, it is not clear why different species have evolved red blood cells of different sizes.

Since gas transfer is a dynamic process that takes place as blood moves rapidly through capillaries, rates of diffusion, reaction velocities, and steady-state conditions for gases in blood must all be taken into account. For instance, a Bohr shift that occurred after the blood had left the capillaries that supply an active tissue would have little importance. The Bohr shift, in fact, occurs very rapidly, having a half-time at less rapidly with temperature than blood pH, the animal must adjust the CO_2/bicarbonate ratio in the blood (Eq. 14-1). In general, it appears that as temperature falls, air-breathing poikilothermic vertebrates keep bicarbonate levels constant but decrease molecular CO_2 levels. In aquatic animals, CO_2 levels remain the same and bicarbonate levels increase as temperature drops. This results in an adjustment of the CO_2/HCO_3^- ratio (Eq. 14-1), and hence regulation of pH.

Oxygen and Carbon Dioxide Movement Between Compartments

The previous section considered the properties of oxygen and carbon dioxide and, in particular, described how these gases are carried in the blood. This section examines the ways in which oxygen and carbon dioxide move from one compartment to another —for example, between air and blood across the lungs or between tissues and blood across capillary walls. The transfer of oxygen and carbon dioxide between gaseous and liquid compartments is considered first, followed by a discussion of gas transfer between two liquid compartments. This presentation was chosen because the structure of a system for gas exchange is influenced by the properties of the media, as well as the requirements of the animal. For example, the lungs of mammals have a very different structure from the gills of fish and are ventilated in a different manner. This is because the density and viscosity of water are both approximately 1000 times greater than that of air, but water contains only 1/30th as much molecular oxygen. Moreover, gas molecules diffuse 10,000 times more rapidly in air than water. Thus, in general, air-breathing consists of the reciprocal movement of air into and out of the lung (Fig. 14-13,A), whereas water-breathing consists of a unidirectional flow of water over the gills (Fig. 14-13,B). These variations in the environment, in the structure of the respiratory apparatus, and in the nature of ventilation result in differences in the partial pressures of gases in the blood and tissues of air-breathing and water-breathing animals, particularly in P_{CO_2}. On the other hand, in both air-breathing and water-breathing animals, there have evolved similar systems for the transfer of gases between liquid compartments. For example, the mammalian placenta, which evolved for the exchange of substances between maternal and fetal blood, functions in many respects much like the gills of fishes.

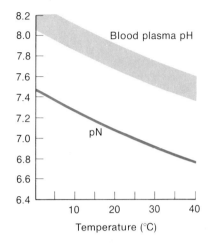

14-12. Blood pH in turtles, frogs, and fish at various temperatures, together with the change in neutrality of water, pN. [After Rahn, 1967.]

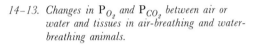

14-13. Changes in P_{O_2} and P_{CO_2} between air or water and tissues in air-breathing and water-breathing animals.

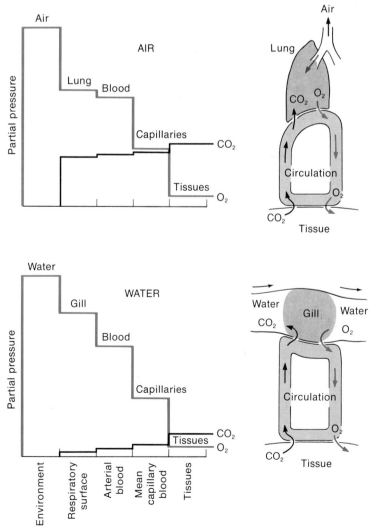

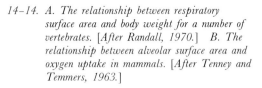

14-14. A. The relationship between respiratory surface area and body weight for a number of vertebrates. [After Randall, 1970.] B. The relationship between alveolar surface area and oxygen uptake in mammals. [After Tenney and Tremmers, 1963.]

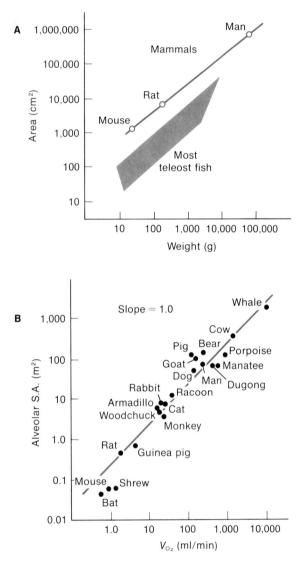

MOVEMENT BETWEEN GASEOUS AND LIQUID COMPARTMENTS

The most-studied and best-known system of transfer between a gaseous and liquid compartment is the movement of oxygen and carbon dioxide across the mammalian lung. Nevertheless, there are numerous other interesting examples that illustrate evolutionary solutions to particular problems. For instance, insects have developed a tracheal system that bypasses the need for the transport of oxygen and carbon dioxide in blood. Oxygen and carbon dioxide are exchanged across the shell of bird's eggs. How are the developing bird embryo's increasing requirements for oxygen satisfied when the surface area of the egg shell remains fixed? Finally, fish can secrete oxygen into the swim bladder from blood even though the partial pressure of oxygen in the swim bladder is much higher than in arterial blood. How is this possible?

LUNGS: ORGANS FOR AIR BREATHING

The *vertebrate lung* develops as a diverticulum of the gut, and consists of a complex network of tubes and sacs, the actual structure varying considerably among species. If one compares the lungs of amphibia, reptiles, and mammals in that order, the sizes of terminal air spaces are seen to become smaller, but the total number per unit volume of lung are seen to become greater. The structure of the amphibian lung is variable, ranging from a smooth-walled pouch in some urodeles to a lung subdivided by septa and folds into numerous interconnected air sacs in frogs and toads. The degree of subdivision is increased in reptiles, and increases even more in mammals, the total effect being an increase in respiratory surface area per unit volume of lung. There is considerable variation in area of the respiratory surface in mammals; in general, the area increases with body weight (Fig. 14-14,A) and oxygen uptake (Fig. 14-14,B).

The mammalian lung consists of millions of blind-ending, interconnected sacs. The *trachea* subdivides to form *bronchi*, which branch repeatedly, leading eventually to *terminal* and then *respiratory bronchioles*, each of which is connected to a terminal spray of alveolar ducts and sacs (Fig. 14-15). The total cross-sectional area of the airways increases rapidly as a result of extensive branching, although the diameter of individual air ducts decreases from trachea to terminal bronchioles. Gases are transferred across the thin-walled alveoli (Fig. 14-16,A,B) found throughout the portion of the lung distal to the terminal bronchiole, termed the *acinus*. The acinus, made up of the respiratory bronchioles, the alveolar ducts, and the alveolar sacs, constitutes the respiratory portion of the lung. The airways leading to the acinus constitute the nonrespiratory portion of the lung. Alveoli in adjoining acini are interconnected by a series of holes, the pores of Kohn, allowing the collateral movement of air, which may be a significant factor in gas distribution during lung ventilation.

Air ducts leading to the respiratory portion of the lung contain cartilage and a little smooth muscle and are lined with cilia, which move particles toward the mouth. Cartilage is absent, and is replaced by smooth muscle in the respiratory portions of the lung. Activity

14-15. *The structure of the mammalian lung.*

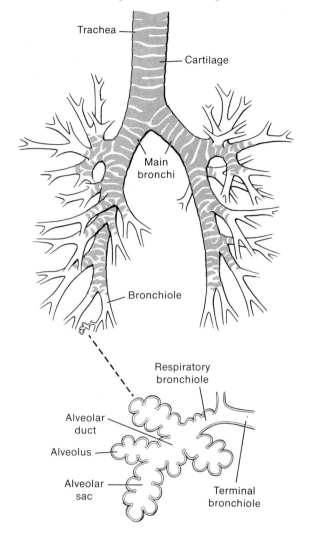

14-16. *A. The anatomy of the respiratory portion of the mammalian lung. B. The dimensions and structure of the alveolar capillary membrane. [After Hildebrandt and Young, 1965.]*

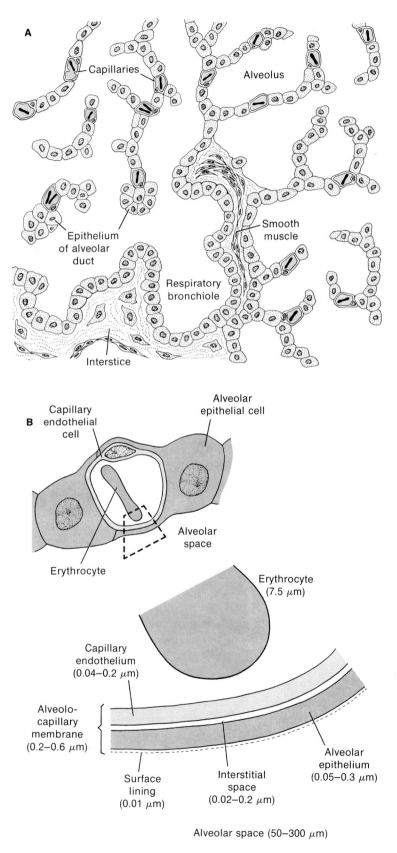

in this smooth muscle can have a marked effect on the dimensions of the airways in the lungs.

Small mammals have a higher resting oxygen uptake per unit body weight than large mammals; this is associated with their greater alveolar surface area per unit body weight. The increase in area is achieved by a reduction in the size but an increase in the number of alveoli per unit volume of lung. In the human lung, most alveoli develop after birth. There is a rapid increase in number of alveloi, the adult complement of about three-hundred million being attained by the age of 8 years; subsequent increases in respiratory area are achieved by increases in the volume of each alveolus. The resting oxygen uptake per unit weight is higher in children than in adults, and once again there is a correlation between oxygen uptake per unit weight and alveolar surface area per unit body weight.

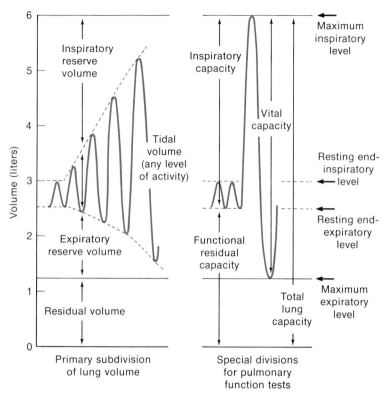

Primary subdivision of lung volume

Special divisions for pulmonary function tests

ables being lung area and diffusion distance between air and blood.

Lung Ventilation. Various terms are used to describe different types of breathing. *Eupnea* refers to the normal, quiet breathing typical of an animal at rest. *Hyperventilation* (= *hyperpnea*) and *hypoventilation* refer, respectively, to an increase or decrease in the amount of air moved in or out of the lung by changes in either or both the rate and depth of breathing. *Apnea* refers to the absence of breathing. *Dyspnea* denotes labored breathing associated with the unpleasant sensation of breathlessness, whereas *polypnea* indicates an increase in breathing rate without an increase in the depth of breathing.

Air exchanged between the alveoli and the environment must pass through a series of tubes (trachea, bronchi, nonrespiratory bronchioles) not directly involved in gas transfer. The volume of air contained in these nonrespiratory tubes is referred to as the *anatomical dead space.* Some air may be supplied to nonfunctional alveoli, or certain alveoli may be ventilated at too high a rate, increasing the volume of air not directly involved in gas exchange. This "volume of air" is termed the *physiological dead space,* and is equal to or greater than but includes the anatomical dead space. The amount of air moved in or out of the lung with each breath is referred to as the *tidal volume.* The amount of air moving in and out of the alveolar air sacs is the tidal volume minus the anatomical dead-space volume, and is referred to as the *alveolar ventilation volume.* Only this "gas volume" is directly involved in gas transfer. The lungs are not completely emptied even at maximal expiration, leaving a *residual volume* of air in the lungs. The maximum amount of air that can be moved in or out of the lungs is referred to as the *vital capacity* of the lungs (Fig. 14-17).

Oxygen content is lower and CO_2 content higher in gas in alveoli than in ambient air because only a portion of the lung's gas volume is changed with each breath. There are differences in the movement of oxygen and carbon dioxide along the air ducts, oxygen diffusing toward the alveoli and carbon dioxide away from them. Alveolar ventilation in humans is about 350 ml/breath, whereas functional residual volume of the lungs exceeds 2000 ml. The volume of alveoli increases during inspiration by elongation and widening of the ducts leading to the alveoli. During breathing, air moves in and out of the acinus, and may also move between adjacent alveoli through the pores of Kohn. Mixing of gases in the ducts and alveoli occurs by diffusion and by convection currents caused by breathing (Fig. 14-18). Partial pressures of oxygen and carbon dioxide are probably fairly uniform across the alveoli, because diffusion is rapid in air and the distances involved are small. The partial pressures of gases within the alveoli oscillate in phase with the breathing

There is a tendency for alveoli to collapse (see p. 488), and this increases with decrease in size of alveoli. This tendency, although reduced by the presence of surfactants, may determine the minimum size of alveoli. The smallest alveoli are about 35 μm in diameter, whereas the air capillaries (the functional equivalent of the alveolus) of bird lungs are much smaller, approximately 10 μm in diameter. The air capillaries are less susceptible to collapse, because the bird lung is a more rigid structure with a different means of ventilation than the mammalian lung (see p. 486). When expressed as a percentage of body weight, lung weights are similar in mammals and birds; the smaller air capillaries of bird lungs increase the area per unit lung volume.

There is a reduction in the magnitude of the diffusion barrier between air and blood across the respiratory surface if one compares fish, amphibia, reptiles and mammals, decreasing from about 5 μm to 1 μm. The diffusion barrier in mammals is made up of an aqueous surface film, the epithelial cells of the alveolus, the interstitial layer, endothelial cells of the blood capillaries, plasma, and the wall of the red blood cell (Fig. 14-16). It is generally assumed, but not demonstrated, that the coefficient of diffusion for gases does not vary in tissues obtained from the lungs of different animals, the only structural vari-

EXPIRATION   INSPIRATION

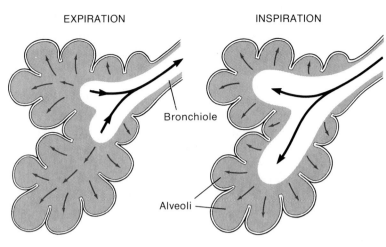

Bronchiole

Alveoli

14–18. *Changes in air flow (large arrows) and the pattern of diffusion (small arrows) in the respiratory portions of the lung during breathing.*

14–19. *The extremely long trachea of the trumpeter swan results in a large anatomical dead-space volume. [After Banko, 1960.]*

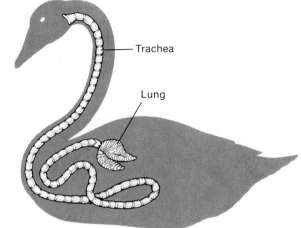

Trachea

Lung

movements, the magnitude depending on the extent of tidal ventilation.

The oxygen and carbon dioxide levels in alveolar gas will be determined by the rate of gas transfer across the respiratory epithelium and the rate of alveolar ventilation. Alveolar ventilation will depend on breathing rate, tidal volume, and anatomical dead-space volume. Variations in the magnitude of the anatomical dead space will alter gas tensions in the alveolus in the absence of changes in tidal volume. Thus artificial increases in anatomical dead space, produced in human subjects breathing through a length of hose, result in a rise in CO_2 and a fall in O_2 in the lung and a subsequent increase in tidal volume. Many animals, such as the giraffe and the swan, have long necks, but not for reasons directly related to breathing. Nevertheless, there is an increase in tracheal length and therefore anatomical dead space. The trumpeter swan is an extreme example of tracheal elongation (Fig. 14-19). Without concomitant increases in tidal volume, gas tensions in the lungs and blood would be adversely affected.

Breathing rate and tidal volume vary considerably in animals. Humans breathe about twelve times per minute and have a tidal volume at rest of about one-tenth of total lung volume. The exclusively aquatic but air-breathing amphibian *Amphiuma* rises to the surface of the swamp water in which it lives about once each hour to breathe; its tidal volume, however, is more than 50% of its lung volume. This produces large, slow oscillations in P_{O_2} in the lung and blood; compared with the rather small oscillations in the more rapidly breathing human, these oscillations are more or less in phase with the breathing movements (Fig. 14-20). *Amphiuma* is preyed upon by snakes and is most vulnerable when it rises to breathe. As it lives in water of low oxygen content, aquatic respiration is not a suitable alternative. The hazard of being eaten

14–20. *Changes in oxygen and carbon dioxide tensions in the lung, dorsal aorta, and inferior vena cava of a 515-g* Amphiuma *during two breathing-diving cycles. Heart rate and systolic and diastolic blood pressures in the dorsal aorta are also plotted. Vertical arrows indicate times when the animal surfaced and ventilated its lungs. [After Toews et al., 1971.]*

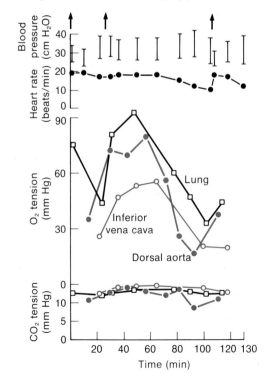

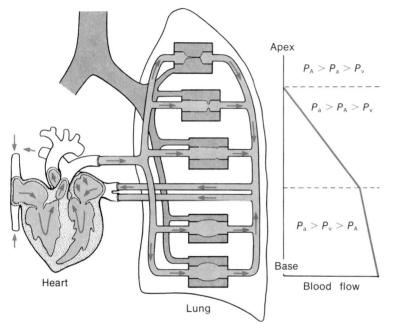

14-21. *The pattern of blood flow in the vertical human lung. The boxes within the lung represent the condition of vessels in the interalveolar septum in different portions of the lung.* P_A = *alveolar pressure;* P_a = *arterial pressure;* P_v = *venous pressure.* [*After West, 1970.*]

while surfacing to breathe may have influenced the evolution of its very low breathing rate, its large tidal and lung volume, and the cardiovascular adjustments it is capable of for maintaining O_2 delivery to the tissues in the face of widely oscillating blood gas levels.

In summary, oxygen and carbon dioxide levels in alveolar gas are determined by ventilation and the rate of gas transfer. Ventilation of the respiratory epithelium is determined by breathing rate, tidal volume, and anatomical dead-space volume. The nature and extent of ventilation also influences the magnitude of oscillations in oxygen and carbon dioxide in blood during a breathing cycle.

Blood Circulation to the Lung. The lung, like the heart, receives blood from two sources. Deoxygenated blood from the pulmonary artery perfuses the lung and is involved in O_2 uptake and CO_2 excretion. A second supply, the bronchial circulation, comes from the systemic (body) circulation, and supplies the lung tissues with O_2 and other substrates for growth and maintenance. Our discussion here is confined to the pulmonary circulation.

In mammals, the lung is perfused at low pressures compared with that of the systemic (body) circulation. Although blood pressure tends to drive water across the capillary walls, the retention of plasma proteins within the capillaries creates an osmotic gradient

across the capillary wall that exceeds the relatively low pulmonary blood pressure. Thus there is minimal accumulation of interstitial fluid in the lung tissue. Nevertheless, there is a lymphatic drainage of the lungs.

The mean arterial pressure in the human lung is about 17 cm H_2O oscillating between 10 and 30 cm H_2O with each contraction of the heart. In the vertical (upright) human lung, arterial pressure is just sufficient to raise blood to the apex of the lung, hence flow is minimal at the top and increases toward the base of the lung (Fig. 14-21). Blood is distributed more evenly to different parts of the horizontal lung.

The pulmonary vessels are very distensible and are subject to distortion by breathing movements. Small vessels within the interalveolar septa are particularly sensitive to changes in alveolar pressure. The diameter of these thin-walled collapsible capillaries is determined by the transmural pressure (blood pressure within capillaries minus alveolar pressure), and if alveolar pressure exceeds blood pressure within the capillaries, they collapse and blood flow ceases. This may occur at the apex of the vertical human lung, where blood pressures are low (Fig. 14-21). If pulmonary arterial pressure is greater than alveolar pressure, which in turn is greater than pulmonary venous pressure, then the difference between arterial and alveolar pressure will determine the diameter of capillaries in the interalveolar septa and, in the manner of a sluice gate, control blood flow through the capillaries. Venous pressure will not affect flow into the venous reservoir as long as alveolar pressure exceeds venous pressure. Flow in the upper portion of the vertical lung is probably determined in this way by the difference between arterial blood pressure and alveolar pressure. Arterial blood pressure, and therefore blood flow, increases with distance from the apex of the lung. In the bottom half of the vertical lung, where venous pressure exceeds alveolar pressure, blood flow is determined by the difference between arterial and venous blood pressures. This pressure difference does not vary, but both the arterial and venous pressures increase toward the base of the lung. This increase in absolute pressure results in an expansion of vessels and, therefore, a decrease in resistance to flow. Thus flow increases toward the base of the lung, even though the arterial-venous pressure difference does not change (Fig. 14-21).

There is an absence of well-defined arterioles in the mammalian lung circulation, but there are sympathetic adrenergic and parasympathetic cholinergic innervations of the smooth muscle around blood vessels and bronchioles. Compared with the systemic (body) circulation, the extent of innervation is much less, and the pulmonary circulation is relatively unresponsive to nerve stimulation or injected drugs.

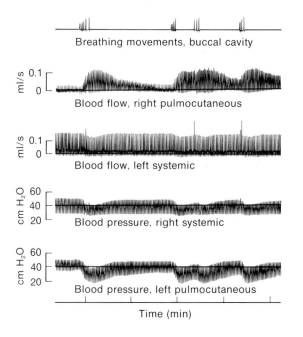

Breathing movements, buccal cavity

Blood flow, right pulmocutaneous

Blood flow, left systemic

Blood pressure, right systemic

Blood pressure, left pulmocutaneous

Time (min)

14–22. *Pressures and flows in the arterial arches of Xenopus, 85 g. Pressure changes in the buccal cavity produced by movements of the buccal floor are recorded on the upper trace. Each of the bursts of movement recorded was of the lung ventilating type. The effect of breathing movements on individual flow and pressure pulses can be seen. [After Shelton, 1970.]*

14–23. *Changes in pressure and volume in the buccal cavity and lung of a frog during buccal movements alone and during buccal and lung movements. [After West and Jones, 1975.]*

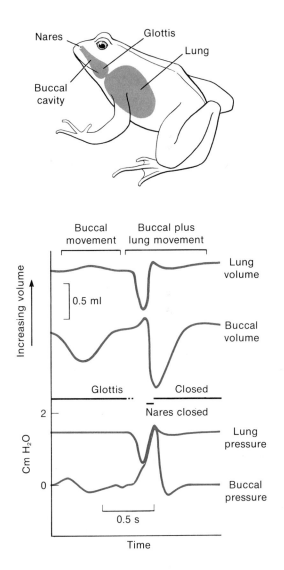

Sympathetic nerve stimulation or the injection of noradrenaline causes a slight increase in resistance to blood flow, whereas parasympathetic nerve stimulation or acetylcholine has the opposite effect.

Reductions in either oxygen levels or in pH have a marked direct effect on pulmonary blood vessels: both cause a local vasoconstriction. The response to low oxygen is considered to be important in distributing blood to well-ventilated portions of the lung. Those regions of the lung that are poorly ventilated will have low alveolar oxygen levels, and this will cause a local vasoconstriction and therefore a reduction in blood flow to that area of the lung. Alternatively, a well-ventilated area of the lung will have high alveolar oxygen levels, local blood vessels will be dilated, and blood flow will be high. This vasoconstrictor response to low oxygen, which is the opposite to that observed in systemic capillary networks, ensures that blood flows to where the air is distributed within the lung.

Cardiac output to the pulmonary circuit is identical to cardiac output in the systemic (body) circuit in mammals. In amphibians and reptiles, with a single or partially divided ventricle that ejects blood into both the lung and body circulations, the ratio of lung to body blood flow can be altered. In turtles and frogs, there is a marked increase in blood flow to the lung following a breath (Fig. 14-22). During periods between breaths in the frog *Xenopus*, lung blood flow decreases, but systemic blood flow is hardly changed (Fig. 14-22).

Mechanisms of Ventilation. The mechanism of lung ventilation varies considerably in vertebrates. In frogs, the nose opens into a buccal cavity, which is connected via the glottis to paired lungs. The frog can open and close its nares and glottis. Air is drawn into the buccal

cavity and then forced into the lungs by raising the buccal floor with the nares closed and the glottis open. This lung-filling process may be repeated several times in sequence. Reducing lung volume may also be a step process, the lungs releasing air in portions to the buccal cavity (Fig. 14-23). There may be alternate lung-

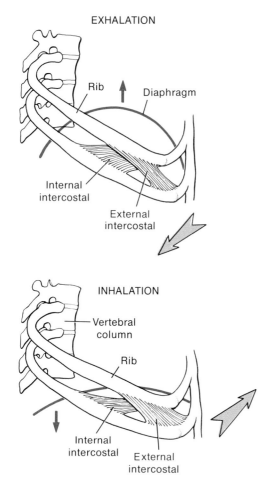

14-24. *Changes in the position of the ribs and diaphragm during inspiration and expiration in mammals.*

EXHALATION

Rib

Diaphragm

Internal intercostal

External intercostal

INHALATION

Vertebral column

Rib

Internal intercostal

External intercostal

filling and emptying movements in which some air is exhaled but the remainder, mixed with air in the buccal cavity, is pumped back into the lung. That is, a mixture of lung air, presumably low in O_2 and high in CO_2, is mixed with fresh air in the buccal cavity and returned to the lung. The reason for this complex method of lung ventilation is not clear. Ventilation may be directed toward reducing oscillations in CO_2 levels in the lungs in order to stabilize and regulate blood P_{CO_2} and control blood pH.

The ribs of reptiles form a thoracic cage around the lungs. During inhalation, the ribs are moved cranially and ventrally, enlarging the thoracic cage. This reduces the pressure within the cage below atmospheric pressure, the nares and glottis are open and air flows into the lungs. Relaxation of muscles that enlarge the thoracic cage releases energy stored in stretching the elastic component of the lung and body wall, allowing passive exhalation. Reptiles do not possess a diaphragm, but pressure differences between these two cavities have been recorded, indicating at least a partial functional separation of thoracic and abdominal cavities. In tortoises and turtles, the ribs are fused to

a rigid shell. Expansion of the thoracic cavity is not possible. The lungs are filled, however, by outward movements of the limb flanks and forward movement of the shoulders. The reverse process results in lung deflation. As a result, limb movements are coupled to changes in lung volume, and the retraction of limbs and head into the shell occurs at the expense of lung volume.

Mammals possess a muscular diaphragm that separates the thoracic and abdominal cavities. The elasticity of the lungs creates a pressure a few mm Hg below atmospheric in the fluid-filled pleural space between the lungs and the wall of the thoracic cage. The relaxed diaphragm is forced upward, forming a concave surface at the caudal end of the thoracic cavity. During inspiration, the external intercostal muscle situated between the ribs contracts and moves the ribs in a cranial and ventral direction, enlarging the thoracic cavity (Fig. 14-24). Moreover, contractions of the diaphragm move its center in a caudal direction, further enlarging the thoracic cage. The resultant reduction in pressure within the lung as it expands causes air to flow into it. During eupneic breathing, expiration may be passive. Increased expiration can be achieved, however, by contraction of internal intercostal muscles, forcing the ribs in a caudal and dorsal direction and actively reducing the volume of the thoracic cage.

In birds, gas transfer takes place in small air capillaries (10 μm in diameter) that branch from tubes—the parabronchi (Fig. 14-25), the functional equivalent of the mammalian alveolar sac. The parabronchi are a series of small tubes extending between large dorsobronchi and ventrobronchi, both of which are connected to an even larger tube, the mesobronchus, which joins the trachea anteriorly (Fig. 14-26,B). The parabronchi and connecting tubes form the lung, which is contained within a thoracic cavity. A tight horizontal septum closes the caudal end of the thoracic cage. The ribs are curved to prevent lateral compression, and move forward only slightly during respiration; the volume of the thoracic cage and lung change little during breathing. The large flight muscles of birds are attached to the sternum, and have little influence on breathing. Although there is no mechanical relation between flight and respiratory movements in birds, "in phase" flight and breathing movements may result from synchronous neural activation of the two groups of muscles involved.

How, then, is the avian lung ventilated? The answer lies in the associated air-sac system connected to the lungs (Fig. 14-26,A,B). As these air sacs are squeezed, air is forced through the parabronchi. The system of air sacs extends as diverticula and penetrates into adjacent bones and between organs, reducing the density of the bird. Of the many air sacs, only the tho-

14–25. *Semischematic drawing of the parabronchi characteristic of song birds. Oxygen and carbon dioxide are exchanged between air and blood in the air capillaries branching from the parabronchi. [After Duncker, 1972.]*

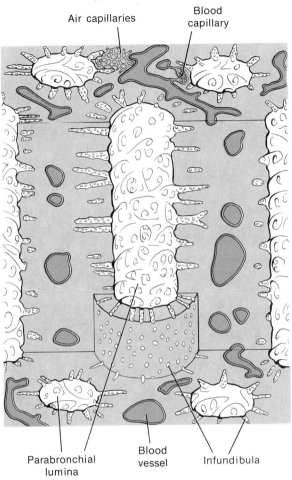

Air capillaries

Blood capillary

Parabronchial lumina

Blood vessel

Infundibula

14–26. *A. Position of air sacs and lungs in a bird. [After Salt, 1964.] B. Diagram of a bird lung The arrows indicate the qualitative flow direction, but not the flow rates. C. Schematic diagram of the bronchial tree, with the connections to the air sacs. The air sacs of the cranial group (cervical, interclavicular, and prethoracic sacs) depart from the three cranial ventrobronchi, whereas the air sacs of the caudal group (postthoracic and abdominal sacs) are connected directly to the mesobronchus. [Parts B and C after Scheid et al., 1972.]*

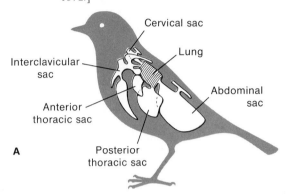

Cervical sac

Lung

Interclavicular sac

Abdominal sac

Anterior thoracic sac

Posterior thoracic sac

A

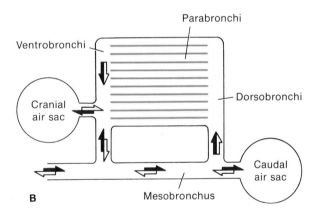

Parabronchi

Ventrobronchi

Dorsobronchi

Cranial air sac

Caudal air sac

Mesobronchus

B

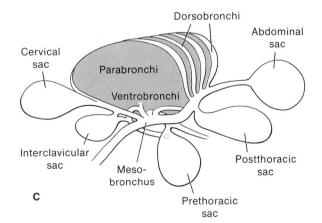

Dorsobronchi

Abdominal sac

Cervical sac

Parabronchi

Ventrobronchi

Interclavicular sac

Meso-bronchus

Prethoracic sac

Postthoracic sac

C

racic (cranial) and abdominal (caudal) sacs show marked changes in volume during breathing. Volume changes in the air sacs are achieved by a rocking motion of the sternum against the vertebral column and by lateral movements of the posterior ribs. Air flow is two-directional in the mesobronchus, but unidirectional through the parabronchi (Fig. 14-26,B). During inspiration, air flows into the caudal air sacs through the mesobronchus; air also moves into the cranial air sacs via the ventrobronchus, the dorsobronchus, and the parabronchi. During expiration, air leaving the caudal air sacs passes through the parabronchi and, to a lesser extent, through the mesobronchus to the trachea. The cranial air sacs, whose volume changes less than that of the caudal air sacs, are reduced somewhat in volume by air moving from the cranial sac via the ventrobronchi and the mesobronchus to the trachea. Thus there is a unidirectional flow of air through the parabronchi during both phases of breathing. This is achieved not by mechan-

Oxygen and Carbon Dioxide Movement Between Compartments   487

14-27. *A. Laplace's Law states that the pressure (P) in a bubble decreases with increased radius (R) if the wall tension (Y) remains constant. The pressure in the small bubble is 4 times that of the large bubble, which is double the radius but has the same wall tension as the small bubble. The equation is written 4Y/R rather than 2Y/R because the bubble in air has an inner and an outer surface. B. If the bubbles are joined, the small bubble (higher pressure) collapses into the large bubble (lower pressure). C. The problem of alveolar collapse is ameliorated by a surfactant lining. As the surfactant film expands with the alveolus, the thickness of the film decreases and the surface tension increases, tending to stabilize the alveoli.*

A Two bubbles in air

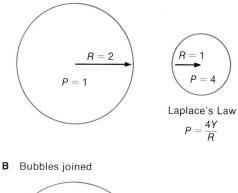

Laplace's Law
$$P = \frac{4Y}{R}$$

B Bubbles joined

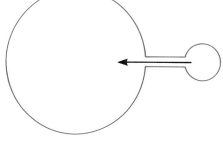

C Properties of surfactant

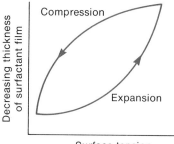

ical valves but instead by aerodynamical valving. The openings of the ventro and dorsobronchi into the mesobronchus show a variable, direction-dependent resistance to air flow. The structure of the openings is such that eddy formation, and therefore resistance to flow, varies with the direction of air flow.

There is variety among the lungs of invertebrates; some are ventilated, and others are not, relying only on diffusion of gases between the lung and the environment. Spiders have paired, nonventilated lungs on the abdomen. The respiratory surface consists of a series of thin, blood-filled plates that extend like the leaves of a book into a cavity guarded by an opening, or *spiracle.* The spiracle can be opened or closed to regulate the rate of water loss from these *book lungs.* Snails and slugs have ventilated lungs that are well-vascularized invaginations of the body surface, the mantle cavity. The volume change that the snail lung is capable of undergoing enables the animal to emerge from and withdraw into its rigid shell. When the snail retracts into its shell, the lung empties, a situation similar to that seen in tortoises. In aquatic snails, the lung serves to reduce the animal's density.

Problems of Alveolar Collapse. The small dimensions of the fragile alveolar sacs create mechanical problems; they tend to collapse. This problem can be discussed by considering each alveolus as a tiny balloon or bubble that is alternately inflated and then deflated. According to the Law of LaPlace, the pressure differential between the inside and outside of a bubble is proportional to $2Y/R$, where Y is the wall tension per unit length and R the radius of the bubble. If one considers two bubbles of similar wall tension but different radius, the pressure in the small bubble will be higher than that in the large bubble. As a result, if the bubbles are joined, the small bubble will empty into the large bubble (Fig. 14-27).

A similar situation exists in the lung. We can consider the alveoli as a number of interconnected bubbles. If the wall tension is similar in alveoli of different size, the small alveoli will tend to collapse, emptying into the larger alveoli. There is evidence, however, that wall tension varies with expansion, thereby stabilizing the alveoli and reducing the probability of alveolar collapse. The wall tension depends on the properties of the alveolar wall and the surface tension at the liquid-air interface. The lungs are lined with a "surfactant," a lipoprotein complex with a preponderance of dipalmitoyl lecithin. This lipoprotein complex bestows a very low surface tension on the liquid-air interface, which increases if the surface film is expanded and decreases if it is compressed. Because the film is expanded as the alveolar volume increases, the surface tension of the alveolus will also increase, compensating for the effects of increased radius. The effect will be to minimize pressure differences between large and small alveoli and reduce the chance of collapse and permit easy inflation of any collapsed alveoli.

Surfactants are found in the lungs of amphibians, reptiles, birds, and mammals, and may exist in some fish that build bubble nests. Surfactants appear prior to birth in mammals. Their presence reduces the forces required to inflate the lung at birth. The lipoprotein film is stable, the lipid probably forming an outer monolayer firmly associated with a protein layer underneath. Surfactants are produced rapidly by specialized cells within the alveolar lining, and have a half-life of about half a day.

Heat and water loss with Respiration. Increases in lung ventilation not only increase gas transfer but also result in increased heat and water loss. Thus the evolution of lungs has involved some compromises. Air in contact with the respiratory surface is saturated with water vapor and is in thermal equilibrium with the blood. Cool dry air entering the lung of mammals is humidified and heated. Exhalation of this hot humid air results in considerable loss of heat and water, which will be proportional to the rate of ventilation of the lung surface. Many air-breathing animals live in very dry environments, where water conservation is of paramount importance. It is therefore not surprising that these animals in particular have evolved means of minimizing the loss of water.

The rates of heat and water loss from the lung are intimately related. As air is inhaled, it is warmed and humidified. Because the evaporation of water cools the nasal mucosa, a temperature gradient exists along the nasal passages. As the moist air leaves the lung, it is cooled, so that water condenses on the nasal mucosa, since the water-vapor pressure for 100% saturation decreases with temperature. Thus the cooling of exhalent air in the nasal passages results in the conservation of both heat and water (Fig. 14-28). The extent of water conservation will depend on the ability of the animal to cool exhalent air, which in turn will be related to the thermal gradient established in the nasal passages. Evaporation can, in some animals, reduce surface temperatures in distal portions of the nasal passages to less than the ambient temperature. The thermal gradient established will be determined by the velocity of air flow, the dimensions of the nasal passages, and the extent and pattern of blood flow to the nose, as well as the temperature and humidity of inhalent air. The blood circulation to the nasal mucosa is capable of supplying water to saturate the inhalent air, but the temperature gradients established by water evaporation and air movement are not destroyed by the circulation.

The structure of the nasal passages in vertebrates is variable, and to some extent can be correlated with the ability of animals to regulate heat and water loss

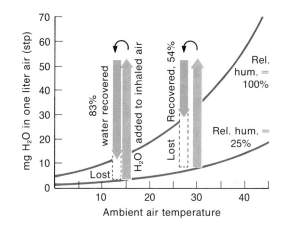

14-28. Diagram showing recovery of water from exhaled air in the kangaroo rat. When air is inhaled at 15°C and 25% relative humidity, the amount of water needed to bring this air to saturation at body temperature (38°C) is indicated by the gray bar placed at 15°C on the abscissa. Under these atmospheric conditions, the kangaroo rat exhales air at 13°C, and the amount of recondensed water is represented by the colored column. The columns to the right give evaporation and recovery at ambient air of 30°C and 25% relative humidity. [After Schmidt-Nielsen, et al., 1970.]

from the lung. Humans have only a limited ability to cool exhaled air, which is saturated with water vapor and at a temperature only a few degrees below core body temperature. The kangaroo rat, which dwells in the desert and breathes dry air, is able to reduce the temperature of distal portions of the nasal mucosa to less than the ambient temperature due to the evaporation of water. The exhaled air is also cooled to less than the ambient temperature, but is no longer dry. Reduced water loss is associated with reduced heat loss via the lungs. In animals that live in hot, arid environments, heat loss must occur via other pathways if water loss via the lungs is to be reduced.

Reptiles and amphibia, whose body temperatures adjust to the ambient temperature, exhale air saturated with water at temperatures about 0.5 to 1.0°C below body temperature. Lung air temperatures and body surface temperatures are often slightly below ambient because of the continual evaporation of water. In some reptiles, however, body temperature is maintained above ambient. In the iguana heat and water loss is conserved in a manner similar to that observed in mammals. In addition, this lizard conserves water by humidifying air with water evaporated from an excretory fluid. The iguana excretes NaCl via nasal salt glands (p. 421). The saline solution produced by these glands collects in the nasal passages, where it evaporates, humidifying the inhalent air,

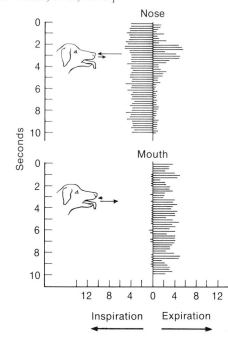

14-29. *Top. Air flow through the nose of a panting dog. Horizontal lines extending to the left of the vertical mid-line indicate inspiration; to the right, expiration. Mean inhaled and exhaled volumes are indicated by vectors placed adjacent to the dog's nose.   Bottom. Air flow through the mouth of a panting dog. Inspiration through the mouth is virtually zero; expiration through the mouth carries most of the air taken in through the nose. [After Schmidt-Nielsen, et al., 1970.]*

14-30. *As the total respiratory ventilation (abscissa) increases in the panting ox, the dead-space ventilation increases steadily. The alveolar ventilation, however, does not increase until the total ventilation exceeds about 200 liter/min. In extreme panting, the respiratory frequency (f) is decreased as tidal volume (V$_T$) is increased (figures at top of graph). [After Hales, 1966.]*

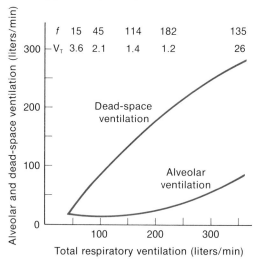

leaving salt crystals, which presumably are then blown out of the nose.

Mammals and birds control heat loss via the respiratory system so as to regulate body temperature. To increase heat loss, mammals breathe through the mouth. Heat is carried away in exhalent air because the dimensions of the mouth are such that exhalent air is not cooled below body temperature. Mammals also hyperventilate to increase heat loss. A change in alveolar ventilation, however, will result in a change in blood P_{CO_2} and blood pH. This is avoided by increasing lung ventilation, but not alveolar ventilation, in order to increase heat loss. Breathing rate is increased but tidal volume reduced, so that dead-space ventilation (i.e. flow through the mouth and trachea) but *not* alveolar ventilation is increased (Figs. 14-29, 14-30); this, of course, is called "panting." Overheated dogs pant, inhaling through the nose and breathing out through the mouth, exposing the tongue to encourage further water evaporation and therefore heat loss.

THE INSECT TRACHEAL SYSTEM: ANOTHER APPROACH TO AIR-BREATHING

The system that insects have evolved for transferring gases between the tissues and the environment differs fundamentally from that found in air-breathing vertebrates. The insect tracheal system takes advantage of the fact that oxygen and carbon dioxide diffuse 10,000 times more rapidly in air than in water, blood, or tissues. Consisting of a series of air-filled tubes that penetrate from the body surface to the cells (Fig.

14-31. *Some types of respiratory system in insects (schematic).   A. Simple anastomosing tracheae, with sphincters in the spiracles. B. Mechanically ventilated air sacs developed. C. Tracheal system entirely closed with abdominal gills, formed as evaginations of the tracheoles. [After Wigglesworth, 1965.]*

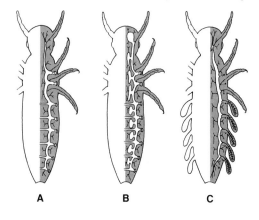

A   B   C

14-31), this system acts as a pathway for the rapid movement of oxygen and carbon dioxide, thereby avoiding the need for a circulatory system to transport gases between the respiratory surface and the tissues. The tracheae (Fig. 14-32), having a wall structure similar to that of the cuticle, are invaginations of the body surface that branch everywhere in the tissues. The smallest branches, or tracheoles, are blind-ending and poke between and into individual cells (without disrupting the cell membrane). At various intervals, the system of branching tubes may have a number of air sacs (Fig. 14-31,B) which enlarge tracheal volume and therefore oxygen stores. In some cases, these air sacs reduce the specific gravity of organs, either for buoyancy or balance.

Except in a few primitive forms, the tracheal entrances are guarded by spiracles, which control air flow into the tracheae, regulate water loss, and keep out dust. The bug *Rhodnius*, for example, dies in three days if its spiracles are kept open in a dry environment.

The air sacs and tracheae are often compressible, allowing changes in tracheal volume. Some insects ventilate the larger tubes and air sacs of the tracheal system by alternate compression and expansion of the body wall, particularly the abdomen. Different spiracles may open and close during different phases of the breathing cycle so as to control the direction of air flow. In the locust, air enters through the thoracic spiracles but leaves through more posterior openings. Tracheal volume in insects is highly variable; it is 40% of body volume in the beetle *Melolontha* but only 6–10% of body volume in the larva of the diving beetle *Dytiscus*. Each ventilation results in a maximum of 30% of tracheal volume being exchanged in *Melolontha* and 60% in *Dytiscus*. Not all insects ventilate their tracheal system; in fact, many calculations have shown that diffusion of gases in air is rapid enough to supply tissue demands in many species. Ventilation occurs in larger insects, and during high levels of activity in some smaller insects in order to augment gas transfer.

Gases are transferred between air and tissues across the walls of the tracheoles. The walls are very thin, with an approximate thickness of only 40 to 70 nm. The tracheolar area is very large, and only rarely are insect cells more than three cells away from a tracheole. The tips of the tracheoles, except in a few species, are filled with fluid so that gases diffusing from the tracheoles to the tissues move through the fluid in the tracheoles, the tracheolar wall, the extracellular space (often negligible), and the cell membrane to the mitochondria. This diffusion distance can be altered in active tissues either by an increase in tissue osmolarity, which causes water to move out of the tracheoles and into tissues (Fig. 14-33) or by changes in the activity of an ion pump, which results in the

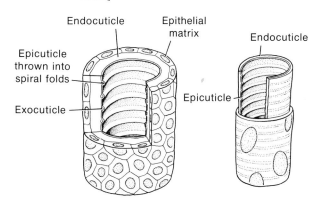

14–32. *Structure of tracheae. A. Tracheal branch close to spiracle. B. Small tracheal branch, more highly magnified.* [After Wigglesworth, 1965.]

Endocuticle   Epithelial matrix   Endocuticle
Epicuticle thrown into spiral folds   Epicuticle
Exocuticle

14–33. *Tracheoles running to a muscle fibre (semischematic). A. Muscle at rest; terminal parts of tracheoles (shown in gray) contain fluid. B. Muscle fatigued; air extends far into tracheoles.* [After Wigglesworth, 1965.]

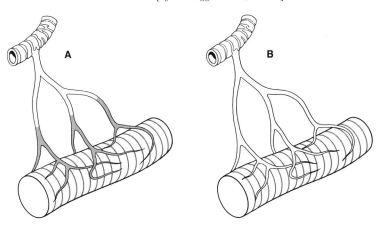

net flow of ions and water out of the tracheoles. The fluid is replaced by air, so that oxygen can more rapidly diffuse into the tissues. Insect flight muscle has the highest recorded O_2 uptake rate of any tissue, with O_2 uptake increasing 10- to 100-fold above the resting value during flight. In general, more active tissues have more tracheoles, and in larger insects the tracheal system is more adequately ventilated.

There are many modifications of the generalized tracheal system that has been described above. Some larval insects rely on cutaneous respiration, the tracheal system being closed off and filled with fluid. Other aquatic insects have a closed, air-filled tracheal system in which gases are transferred between water and air across tracheal gills. The gills are evaginations

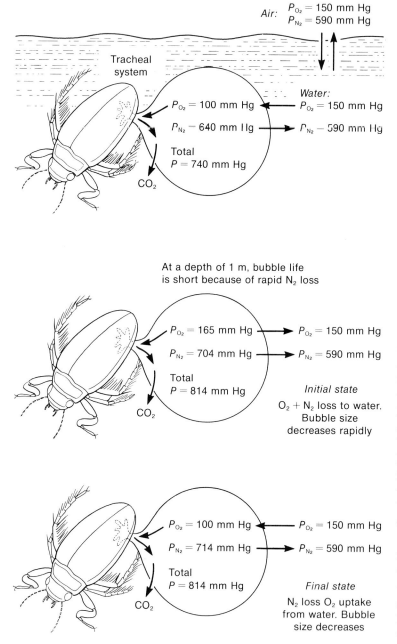

14-34. *Partial pressures of O_2, CO_2, and N_2 and total pressure (P) in bubbles under water. Arrows indicate diffusion of gas molecules.*

Air:
$P_{O_2} = 150$ mm Hg
$P_{N_2} = 590$ mm Hg

Tracheal system

$P_{O_2} = 100$ mm Hg

$P_{N_2} = 640$ mm Hg

Total
P = 740 mm Hg

CO_2

Water:
$P_{O_2} = 150$ mm Hg

$P_{N_2} = 590$ mm Hg

At a depth of 1 m, bubble life is short because of rapid N_2 loss

$P_{O_2} = 165$ mm Hg

$P_{N_2} = 704$ mm Hg

Total
P = 814 mm Hg

CO_2

$P_{O_2} = 150$ mm Hg

$P_{N_2} = 590$ mm Hg

Initial state

$O_2 + N_2$ loss to water. Bubble size decreases rapidly

$P_{O_2} = 100$ mm Hg

$P_{N_2} = 714$ mm Hg

Total
P = 814 mm Hg

CO_2

$P_{O_2} = 150$ mm Hg

$P_{N_2} = 590$ mm Hg

Final state

N_2 loss O_2 uptake from water. Bubble size decreases

of the body that are filled with trachea, the air of which is separated from the water by a membrane 1 μm thick. This tracheal system is not readily compressible, allowing the insect to change depth under water without impairment of gas transfer.

Many aquatic insects, such as mosquito larvae, breathe through a hydrofuge (water-repellent) syphon that protrudes above the surface of the water; others take bubbles of air beneath the surface with them. The water bug *Notonecta* carries air bubbles that cling to hydrofuge velvet-like hairs on its ventral surface when under water, and the larva of the beetle *Dytiscus* dives with air bubbles beneath its wings or attached to its rear end. When such insects dive, gases are transferred between the bubble and the tissues via the tracheal system; gases can also diffuse however, between the bubble and the water. The rates of O_2 transfer from water to bubble will depend on the gradients established and the area of the air-water interface.

The oxygen content of the bubble will decrease due to uptake by the animal; this will establish an O_2 gradient between the bubble and the water (assuming the water is in gaseous equilibrium with air), and oxygen will diffuse into the bubble from the water. As P_{O_2} in the bubble is reduced, P_{N_2} will increase; if the bubble is just below the surface, the pressure will be maintained at approximately atmospheric pressure. Nitrogen will therefore diffuse slowly from the bubble into the water (Fig. 14-34). (Because of the high solubility of CO_2 in water, CO_2 levels in the bubble are always negligible.) If the bubble is taken to depth, however, the pressure will increase by 0.1 atm for every meter of depth, increasing both P_{O_2} and P_{N_2} and speeding the diffusion of both N_2 and O_2 from the bubble into the water. The bubble will gradually get smaller and eventually disappear as nitrogen leaves the bubble. Thus the life of the bubble depends on the insect's metabolic rate, the initial size of the bubble, and the depth to which it is taken. It collapses because nitrogen is lost from the bubble as the insect uses the oxygen. It has been calculated that up to seven times the initial O_2 content diffuses into the bubble from the water and is therefore available to the insect before the bubble disappears.

If the bubble were noncollapsible, the animal would not need to surface; oxygen would diffuse from the water via the bubble into the tracheal system and thence to the tissues. The insect *Aphelocheirus* has such a structure (Fig. 14-35); it consists of a plastron of hydrofuge hairs (10^6/mm^2) that contain a small volume of air. The plastron can withstand pressures of several atmospheres before collapsing. In the small air space, N_2 is presumably in equilibrium with the water, P_{O_2} is low and oxygen therefore diffuses from water into the plastron, which is continuous with the tracheal system.

14–35. *Hydrofuge hairs on the surface of some insects and insect eggs have an incompressible air space that acts as a gill under water. Oxygen diffuses from water into the air space contained within the plastron and then into the animal via the tracheal system. The lower diagram indicates partial pressures of oxygen and nitrogen in the air and water phases. Most of the hairs have been removed for simplicity.*

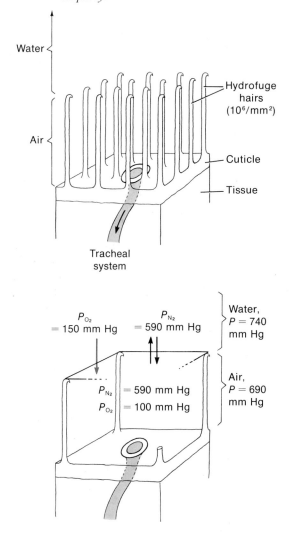

14–36. *A. Diagram of the diffusion pathway between air and chick embryo blood across the egg shell in the region of the air cell. B. Plot of oxygen tension versus incubation age, comparing measurements of air cell and allantoic venous blood P_{O_2}. C. Plot of carbon dioxide tension of air cell and allantoic venous blood versus incubation age. In contrast to data for oxygen, there is no P_{CO_2} difference between air-cell gas and allantoic venous blood during a chick embryo's development. [After Wagenstein, 1972.]*

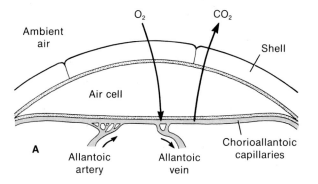

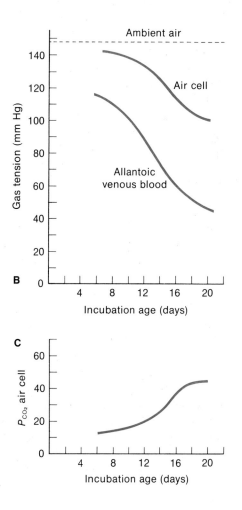

BIRD EGGS: A PROBLEM OF FIXED DIMENSIONS AND CHANGING GAS-TRANSFER REQUIREMENTS

The egg shells of birds have fixed dimensions but contain an embryo whose gas-transfer requirements increase by a factor of 10^3 between laying and hatching. Thus the transfer of oxygen and CO_2 must take place across the shell at ever-increasing rates during development while the dimensions of the transfer surface (egg shell) do not change. Gases diffuse through small air-filled pores in the egg shell and then through underlying membranes, including the allantoic membrane (Fig. 14-36,A). The allantoic circulation is in close apposition to the egg shell, and increases with the development of the embryo. If the egg is kept in a hypoxic environment, more capillaries develop in the allantoic membrane. The key to increasing rates of gas transfer during development in the bird's egg is the development of an underlying circulation in the allantoic membrane and an increase in the P_{CO_2} and P_{O_2} difference across the egg shell, both of which increase transfer rates of O_2 and CO_2 between the environment and the embryo (Fig. 14-36,B,C).

Water is lost from the egg during development, and this loss results in the gradual enlargement of an air space within the egg, which is as much as 12 ml at hatching in the chicken egg. Just before they hatch, birds ventilate their lungs by poking their beak into the air space. Blood P_{CO_2} is initially low, but rises to 40 mm Hg just before hatching (Fig. 14-36,C). This pressure is maintained after hatching, thus avoiding any marked acid-base changes when the bird switches from the shell to its lungs for gas exchange.

THE SWIM BLADDER OF THE FISH: THE ACCUMULATION OF O_2 AGAINST AN APPARENT GRADIENT

Many aquatic animals maintain a neutral buoyancy; that is, they compensate for a dense skeletal structure by the incorporation of lighter materials in specialized organs. These "buoyancy tanks" may be NH_4Cl solutions (squids), lipid layers (many animals, including sharks), and air-filled swim bladders (many fish). NH_4Cl and lipid floats have the advantage of being incompressible, not changing volume with changes in hydrostatic pressure that accompany vertical movement in water. Swim bladders are less dense, and can be much smaller than NH_4Cl and lipid floats, but they are compressible and change in volume, thus changing the buoyancy of the animal with changes in depth. Hydrostatic pressure increases by approximately 1 atm for every 10 m of depth. If a fish is swimming just below the surface and suddenly dives to a depth of 10 m, the total pressure in its swim bladder doubles from 1 to 2 atm and the bladder volume is reduced by one half, thus increasing the density of the fish. The fish will now continue to sink because it is more dense than water. Similarly, if the fish rises to a shallower depth, its swim bladder will expand, decreasing the fish's density, so that it continues to rise. One advantage of swim bladders is that they are of low density, but they are essentially unstable because of the volume changes they undergo with changes in depth. One means of preventing volume changes is for gas to be added or removed as the fish ascends or descends. Many fish do have mechanisms for increasing or decreasing the amount of gas in the swim bladder in order to maintain a constant volume over a wide range of pressures.

Fish with swim bladders spend most of their time in the upper 200 m of lakes, seas, and oceans. The pressure in the bladder will range from 1 atm at the surface to about 20 atm at 200 m. Water is in equilibrium with air, and the gas content in water will not vary much with depth (Fig. 14-37). The swim bladder gas in most fish consists of oxygen, but those of some species are filled with CO_2 or N_2. If the fish dives from a depth of 100 m, oxygen is added to the swim bladder. The environment is the source, and O_2 is moved from the environment to the swim bladder against a pressure difference—in this example, of nearly 10 atm (water $P_{O_2} = 0.0228$ atm, bladder $P_{O_2} = 10$ atm). In order to understand how this occurs, let us review the structure of the swim bladder.

The teleost swim bladder is a pouch of the foregut (Fig. 14-38). In some fish, there is a duct between gut and bladder; in others, the duct is absent in the adult. The bladder wall is tough and impermeable to gases, with very little leakage even at very high pressures, but the wall is *not* highly resistant to stretch. Those animals capable of moving oxygen into the bladder at high pressure have a rete mirabile. The rete consists of several bundles of capillaries (both arterial and venous) in close apposition, the blood flow being

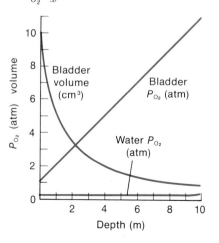

14-37. *Changes in volume and P_{O_2} in water and gas bubble with depth in water. Hydrostatic pressure increases by approximately 1 atm every 10 m. In this example, oxygen is assumed to be the only gas present, and is neither added nor removed from the bubble. Fish can maintain constant density only by maintaining constant bladder volume. This can be achieved by adding O_2 to the bladder with increasing depth. Note the increasing P_{O_2} difference between water and bladder with depth. Oxygen must be moved from water into the swim bladder in the presence of this P_{O_2} difference.*

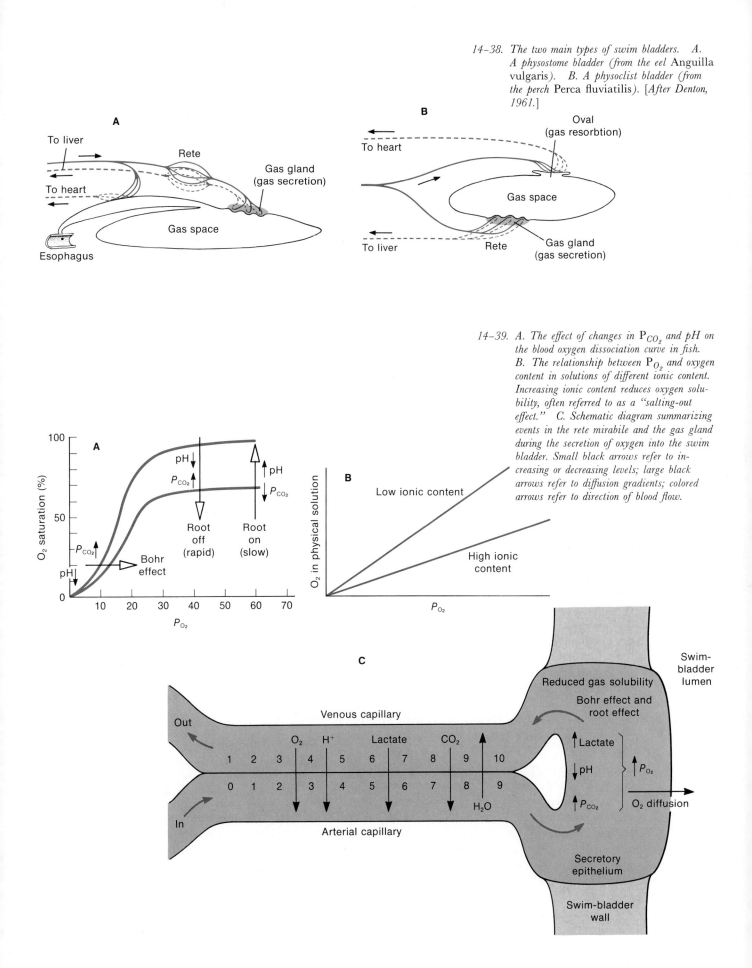

14-38. *The two main types of swim bladders. A. A physostome bladder (from the eel* Anguilla vulgaris*). B. A physoclist bladder (from the perch* Perca fluviatilis*). [After Denton, 1961.]*

A

To liver

To heart

Rete

Gas gland (gas secretion)

Gas space

Esophagus

B

To heart

Oval (gas resorbtion)

Gas space

To liver

Rete

Gas gland (gas secretion)

14-39. *A. The effect of changes in* P_{CO_2} *and pH on the blood oxygen dissociation curve in fish. B. The relationship between* P_{O_2} *and oxygen content in solutions of different ionic content. Increasing ionic content reduces oxygen solubility, often referred to as a "salting-out effect." C. Schematic diagram summarizing events in the rete mirabile and the gas gland during the secretion of oxygen into the swim bladder. Small black arrows refer to increasing or decreasing levels; large black arrows refer to diffusion gradients; colored arrows refer to direction of blood flow.*

A

O_2 saturation (%)

pH↓
P_{CO_2}↑

Root off (rapid)

pH↑
P_{CO_2}↓

Root on (slow)

P_{CO_2}↑

Bohr effect

pH↓

P_{O_2}

B

O_2 in physical solution

Low ionic content

High ionic content

P_{O_2}

C

Swim-bladder lumen

Venous capillary

Out

Reduced gas solubility

Bohr effect and root effect

↑Lactate

↓pH

↑P_{CO_2}

O_2 H⁺   Lactate CO_2

1 2 3 4 5 6 7 8 9 10

0 1 2 3 4 5 6 7 8 9

H_2O

}P_{O_2}

In

O_2 diffusion

Arterial capillary

Secretory epithelium

Swim-bladder wall

countercurrent between arterial and venous blood. It has been calculated that eel retia have 88,000 venous capillaries and 116,000 arterial capillaries containing about 0.4 ml of blood. The surface area of contact between the venous and arterial capillaries is about 100 cm². Blood passes first through the arterial capillaries of the rete, then through a secretory epithelium in the bladder wall, and finally back through the venous capillaries in the rete. The arterial and venous blood in the rete are separated by a distance of about 1.5 μm.

The rete structure allows blood to flow into the bladder wall without a concomitant large loss of gas from the swim bladder. Blood leaving the secretory epithelium at high P_{O_2} passes into the venous capillaries, and oxygen diffuses into the arterial capillaries within the rete. P_{O_2} decreases in both arterial and venous capillaries with distance from the secretory epithelium. The P_{O_2} difference between arterial and venous blood at the end of the rete distal to the swim bladder is small compared with the P_{O_2} difference between the environment and swim bladder. The rete therefore acts as a countercurrent exchanger (Box 12-2), reducing the loss of oxygen from the swim bladder.

The rete structure acts as a countercurrent exchanger, reducing gas loss from the swim bladder, but *how is oxygen secreted into the swim bladder?* First, consider the relationship between P_{O_2}, oxygen solubility, and oxygen content. Oxygen is carried in blood bound to hemoglobin and in physical solution. If oxygen is released from hemoglobin into physical solution, P_{O_2} will increase. The release of oxygen from hemoglobin can be caused by a reduction in pH via the Bohr, or Root, effect (Fig. 14-39). An increase in ionic concentration reduces oxygen solubility and also results in an increase in P_{O_2}, as long as oxygen content in physical solution remains unchanged (Fig. 14-39). Thus an increase in blood P_{O_2} can be achieved by releasing oxygen from hemoglobin or increasing the ionic concentration of the blood.

Glycolysis occurs in the secretory epithelium of the swim bladder, even in an oxygen atmosphere, resulting in the production of two lactate molecules for each glucose molecule. This results in (1) a decrease in pH, which causes the release of oxygen from hemoglobin (Root "off" shift), and (2) an increase in ionic concentration, and therefore a reduction in oxygen solubility (sometimes termed the "salting-out effect"); both changes cause the P_{O_2} in the secretory epithelium to increase more than that in the swim bladder, so that oxygen diffuses from blood into the gas space of the swim bladder. The "salting out effect" will also reduce the solubility of other gases, such as nitrogen and carbon dioxide, and may explain the high levels of these gases sometimes observed in swim bladders.

Gas Exchange Across Capillary Walls

Gases diffuse slowly in blood, water, and tissues compared with rates in air. In order to keep diffusion distances to a minimum and maintain adequate rates of gas exchange between two compartments, the separating epithelial layer must be thin. Large diffusion distances can be further reduced by mixing the fluid compartments on either side of the epithelium. In the exchange of gases between maternal and fetal blood across the placenta or between water and blood across the fish gill, the exchange takes place between two flowing liquids separated by a thin epithelium. These gas-exchange surfaces are ventilated to avoid dead spaces and to reduce diffusion distances to not much more than the thickness of the epithelium separating the two compartments.

The gas-exchange surfaces, with a few exceptions, are ventilated with a steady, unidirectional flow of blood or water rather than a tidal flow, which would be inefficient because of the high density and viscosity of blood and water. The direction of flow of the two liquids can be concurrent, countercurrent, or intermediate (Fig. 14-40). The advantage of a countercurrent system is that a larger difference in partial pressure of gases can be maintained across the whole gas-exchange surface, allowing more gas transfer per unit area of surface (Fig. 14-41). A countercurrent arrangement of flows is most advantageous if the flow rate and gas solubility are similar in the two liquids. For instance, if flow or gas solubility is very high in one liquid compared with the other, there will be little change in P_{O_2} in the first liquid, and the gradient established will be similar in both a concurrent and countercurrent arrangement of flows (Fig. 14-41). Thus there is no advantage of countercurrent flow over concurrent. Having reviewed the above features, we offer the following discussion of gas transfer between liquid compartments—namely, blood and tissues and water and blood.

OXYGEN AND CARBON DIOXIDE EXCHANGE ACROSS CAPILLARIES

The reason why cells are seldom far from a capillary is that P_{O_2} drops rapidly with distance from the blood supply (Fig. 14-42). The rate of oxygen uptake by tissues depends, as it does in the lungs, on the oxygen concentration difference, the diffusion coefficient, the area available for diffusion, and the diffusion distance. The rate of oxygen transfer in an organ is regulated by changes in the number of open capillaries and by the rate of blood flow within the tissue, which in turn change the area available for diffusion, the diffusion

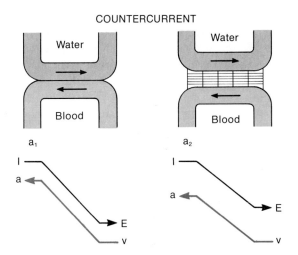

COUNTERCURRENT

Water

Blood

a_1

I
a
E
v

Water

Blood

a_2

I
a
E
v

CONCURRENT

Water

Blood

I
E
v
a

MULTICAPILLARY

Water

Blood

I
a
E
v

14-40. *Various arrangements for the flows of water and blood at the respiratory surface in aquatic animals. Relative changes in* P_{O_2} *in water and blood are indicated below each diagram. I, inhalant; E, exhalant; a, arterial blood; v, venous blood.*

14-41. *Changes in* P_{O_2} *in two fluids on either side of a respiratory surface are nearly independent of the arrangement of flows (countercurrent or concurrent), because fluid a has a much higher flow rate and/or oxygen solubility coefficient compared with fluid b. A countercurrent arrangement of flows is most advantageous if the flows and oxygen solubility coefficients of the two fluids are equal.*

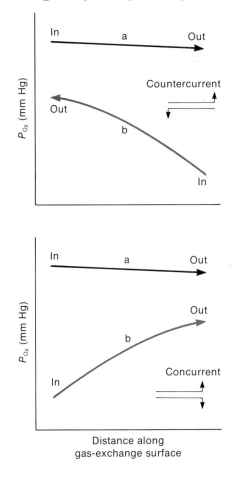

In   a   Out

Out

P_{O_2} (mm Hg)

b

Countercurrent

In

In   a   Out

Out

P_{O_2} (mm Hg)

b

In

Concurrent

Distance along
gas-exchange surface

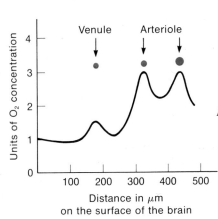

Venule   Arteriole

Units of O_2 concentration

Distance in μm
on the surface of the brain

14-42. *Relative* P_{O_2} *of cerebral cortex of cat measured at various distances from two arterioles and a venule. [After Comroe, 1962.]*

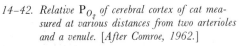
Gas Exchange Across Capillary Walls 497

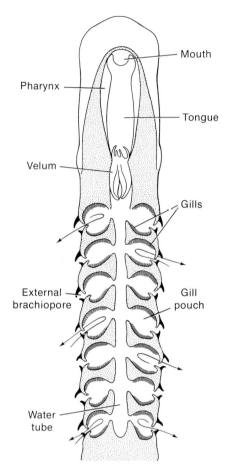

14-43. *Longitudinal transverse section through the head of an adult lamprey. Water is moved in and out of each gill pouch via the external branchiopore. Arrows mark the direction of water flow. The valves of the external branchiopore move in and out with the oscillating water flow.*

Mouth

Pharynx

Tongue

Velum

Gills

External branchiopore

Gill pouch

Water tube

distance, and the magnitude of the difference between oxygen levels in blood and tissues.

The quantitative aspects of the response to increased oxygen demands vary from tissue to tissue. The most dramatic changes are observed by comparing oxygen uptake in resting and active skeletal muscle. The number of open capillaries can increase by a factor of 10 with the onset of activity in skeletal muscles, resulting in a marked increase in blood flow as well as oxygen uptake. The regulation of this increase in oxygen uptake is complex. In vertebrates, most arterioles are innervated by sympathetic adrenergic fibers which constrict the vessels, but skeletal muscle vessels are innervated by sympathetic cholinergic fibers which dilate them. Increases in sympathetic discharge alters the distribution of blood flow to various organs, resulting in a preferential flow to skeletal muscle at the onset and during exercise. Contractions squeeze blood vessels within the muscle and,

with the help of venous valves, augment flow through the muscle. The production of metabolites (increased P_{CO_2} and $[H^+]$) and the reduction of O_2 in active muscles cause local vasodilation, which also increases blood flow. The drop in cell P_{O_2} increases the oxygen difference between blood and the muscle fibers, thereby enhancing oxygen uptake. Finally, the rise in CO_2 favors the release of O_2 from hemoglobin because of the Bohr shift. The net effect of all these processes is to increase oxygen uptake and CO_2 removal from the active tissue.

THE VERTEBRATE GILL

The arrangement of flow of both water and blood on either side of the respiratory surface in aquatic animals is usually unidirectional and countercurrent. The lamprey is an exception. The mouth of this parasitic animal is often blocked by attachment to a host. The gill pouches, although connected internally to the pharyngeal and mouth cavities, are ventilated by tidal movements of water through a single external opening to each pouch (Fig. 14-43). This unusual method of gill ventilation is clearly associated with a parasitic mode of life. The ammocoete larvae of lampreys are not parasitic and maintain a unidirectional flow of water over their gills, typical of aquatic animals in general.

Flow of water over the gills of teleost fish is maintained by the action of skeletal muscle pumps in the buccal and opercular cavities. Water is drawn into the mouth, passes over the gills, and exits through the opercular clefts (Fig. 14-44). Valves guard the entrance to the buccal cavity and opercular cleft, maintaining a unidirectional flow of water over the gills. The buccal cavity changes volume by raising and lowering the floor of the mouth. The operculum swings in and out, enlarging and reducing the size of the opercular cavities. Changes in volume in the two cavities are nearly in phase, but a pressure differential is maintained across the gills throughout most of each breathing cycle. The pressure in the opercular cavity is a few mm Hg below that in the buccal cavity, resulting in a unidirectional flow of water across the gills throughout most, if not all, of the breathing cycle (Fig. 14-44).

Many active fish "ram-ventilate" their gills, opening their mouths so as to ventilate the gills by the forward motion of the body. The Remora, a fish that attaches itself to the body of a shark, ventilates its own gills only when the shark stops swimming; normally, it relies upon the motion of its host to ventilate its gills.

The details of gill structure vary among species, but the general plan is similar. The gills of teleost fish, described here in detail, are taken to be representative of an aquatic respiratory surface. The four gill arches

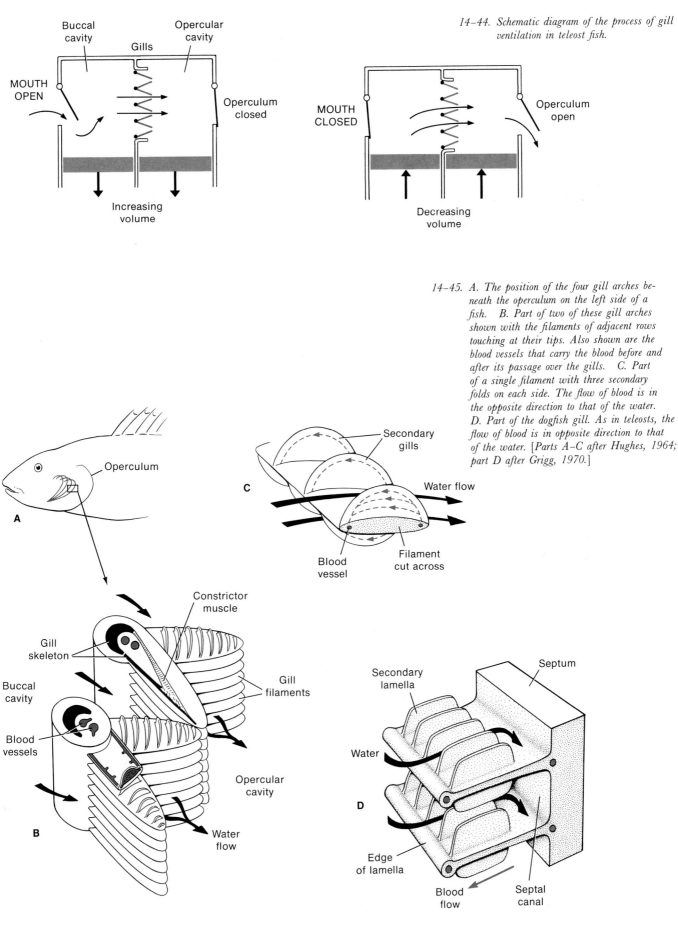

14-44. *Schematic diagram of the process of gill ventilation in teleost fish.*

Buccal cavity
Opercular cavity
Gills

MOUTH OPEN

Operculum closed

Increasing volume

MOUTH CLOSED

Operculum open

Decreasing volume

14-45. *A. The position of the four gill arches beneath the operculum on the left side of a fish. B. Part of two of these gill arches shown with the filaments of adjacent rows touching at their tips. Also shown are the blood vessels that carry the blood before and after its passage over the gills. C. Part of a single filament with three secondary folds on each side. The flow of blood is in the opposite direction to that of the water. D. Part of the dogfish gill. As in teleosts, the flow of blood is in opposite direction to that of the water. [Parts A–C after Hughes, 1964; part D after Grigg, 1970.]*

Operculum

A

Secondary gills

C

Water flow

Blood vessel

Filament cut across

Constrictor muscle

Gill skeleton

Buccal cavity

Blood vessels

Gill filaments

Opercular cavity

Water flow

B

Secondary lamella

Septum

Water

D

Edge of lamella

Blood flow

Septal canal

14-46. *Transverse section through gill lamella of trout, showing the water-blood barrier. Magnification 40,000×. B. Scanning electron micrograph of a plastic cast of the vasculature of a trout gill filament, showing several lamellae. Magnification 160×. [Courtesy of B. J. Gannon.]*

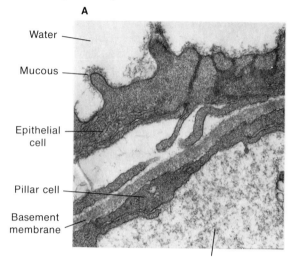

Water
Mucous
Epithelial cell
Pillar cell
Basement membrane
Blood plasma

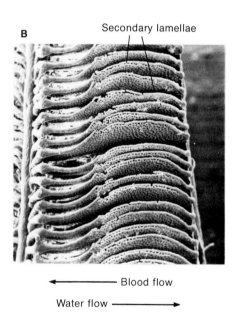

Secondary lamellae

Blood flow ⟵

Water flow ⟶

14-47. *Details of the vascular system of the gill arch and filaments of a teleost fish. [Courtesy of B. J. Gannon.]*

on either side of the head separate the opercular and buccal cavities (Fig. 14-45,A). Each arch has two rows of filaments, and each filament, flattened dorsoventrally, has an upper and a lower row of secondary lamellae (Fig. 14-45,B,C). The lamellae of successive filaments in a row are in close contact. The tips of filaments of adjacent arches are juxtapositioned so that the whole gill forms a sieve-like structure in the path of water flow. Water flows in slit-like channels between neighboring lamellae. These channels are about 0.02 to 0.05 mm wide and about 0.2 to 1.6 mm long, the lamellae are about 0.1 to 0.5 mm high (Fig. 14-46). As a result, the water flows in thin sheets between the lamellae, which represent the respiratory portion of the gill, and diffusion distances in water are reduced to a maximum of 0.01 to 0.025 mm (half the distance between adjacent lamellae on the same filament).

The lamellae are covered by thin sheets of epithelial cells (Fig. 14-46), the internal walls of which are held together by pillar cells, which occupy about 20–40% of the internal volume of the lamella. Blood flows in the spaces between the pillar cells. The diffusion distance between the center of the red blood cell and the water is between 3 and 8 μm. The total area of the lamellae is large, varying from 1.5 to 15 cm^2/g of body weight, depending on the size of the fish and whether it is generally active or sluggish. Blood and water flow in a countercurrent arrangement (Fig. 14-47).

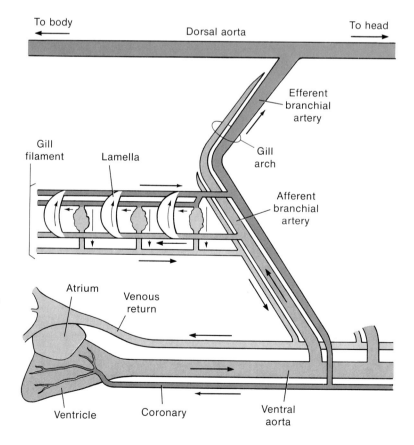

To body
To head
Dorsal aorta
Efferent branchial artery
Gill arch
Gill filament
Lamella
Afferent branchial artery
Atrium
Venous return
Ventricle
Coronary
Ventral aorta

Fish can adjust the flow to each arch and to lamellae in each filament. The gill vessels are innervated by sympathetic adrenergic nerves, which liberate norepinephrine, and probably also by parasympathetic cholinergic nerves, which secrete acetylcholine. Norepinephrine increases blood flow to secondary lamellae, whereas acetylcholine decreases it. These nerves, therefore, may function to regulate the extent of perfusion of the secondary lamellae in order to adjust gas-transfer rates to meet changing demands of the animal. This is of adaptive significance, since increases in area result in an increase in the transfer of ions and water as well as O_2 and CO_2 across the gills. By regulating the blood perfusion of the gill, the fish can adjust the functional area of the gills to the minimum required for O_2 and CO_2 exchange, and thereby eliminate unnecessary flux of ions and water across the gill.

Regulation of Gas Transfer and Respiration

The regulation of the rate of oxygen and carbon dioxide transfer has been studied extensively only in mammals. Thus this section is confined mainly to a discussion of the regulation of gas transfer in mammals. The movement of oxygen and carbon dioxide between the environment and mitochondria in mammals is regulated by altering lung ventilation and blood flow and distribution within the body. Here the emphasis is placed on the control of breathing; the reader is referred to Chapter 13 for details of the control of the cardiovascular system.

VENTILATION/PERFUSION RATIOS

Energy is expended in ventilating the respiratory surface with air or water and in perfusing the respiratory epithelium with blood. The total cost of these two processes is difficult to assess, but probably amounts to 4–30% of the total aerobic energy output of the animal, depending on the species in question and the physiological state of the animal. Thus gas transfer between environment and cell accounts for a considerable proportion of the total energy output of the animal, and represents a significant selective pressure in favor of the evolution of mechanisms for the close regulation of ventilation and perfusion in order to conserve energy.

The rate of blood perfusion of the respiratory surface is related to the requirements of the tissues for gas transfer and to the gas transport capacities of the blood. To ensure that sufficient oxygen is delivered to the respiratory surface to saturate the blood with oxygen, the rate of ventilation must be adjusted in accord with the perfusion rate.

The ventilation/perfusion ratio at the respiratory surface depends on the difference in gas content between arterial and venous blood and between inhalent and exhalent air or water. This in turn will depend on the partial pressure of oxygen and the gas content per unit volume per mm Hg of P_{O_2} in the blood and in the medium. The oxygen content of arterial blood in humans is similar to the oxygen content of air, the $\dot{V}_A/\dot{Q}$ ratio, therefore, is about 1 (Fig. 14-48). Water, however, contains only about one thirtieth as much dissolved oxygen as an equivalent volume of air at the same P_{O_2} and temperature. Thus the ratio between water flow over and blood flow through the gills in fish is between 10:1 and 20:1, much higher than the $\dot{V}_A/\dot{Q}$ ratio in air-breathing mammals. The ratio of ventilation to perfusion in fish is not 30:1 (as might be expected comparing dissolved oxygen content in water and air) because the oxygen capacity of the blood of many lower vertebrates is only half that of mammalian blood.

Changes in P_{O_2} also affect the $\dot{V}_A/\dot{Q}$ ratio. A reduction in P_{O_2} in inhalent air or water must be compensated by an increase in ventilation, and hence an increase in the ventilation/perfusion ratio, if the rate of oxygen uptake is to be maintained.

The ventilation/perfusion ratio must be maintained over each portion of the respiratory surface as well as the whole system. The pattern of capillary blood flow changes in both gills and lungs, changing the distribution of blood over the respiratory surface. The distribution of air or water must reflect the blood distribution. Perfusion of an alveolus without ventilation is as pointless as ventilating an alveolus without blood perfusion. This is an extreme example; the maintenance of too high or too low a blood flow or ventilation rate will also result in a reduction in gas transfer per unit of energy expended. For efficient gas transfer, the optimal ventilation/perfusion ratio should be maintained over the whole respiratory surface. This does not preclude differential rates of blood perfusion over the respiratory surface, but states only that the flows of blood and medium be matched.

The efficiency of gas exchange is diminished if some of the blood entering the lungs either bypasses the respiratory surface of perfuses a portion of the respiratory surface that is inadequately ventilated (Fig. 14-49). The magnitude of this *venous shunt* can be expressed as a percentage of total flow to the respiratory epithelium and calculated from arterial and venous blood oxygen content, assuming an ideal arterial oxygen content. In the lung, for instance, blood is almost in equilibrium with alveolar gas tensions. If these and the blood-oxygen dissociation curves are

BOX 14-2 VENTILATION/PERFUSION RATIOS

The actual ratio of ventilation to perfusion is affected by a number of factors. The oxygen uptake by the blood as it passes through the respiratory surface is given by

$$\dot{V}_{O_2} = \dot{Q}(C_{aO_2} - C_{vO_2}),\tag{1}$$

where $\dot{V}_{O_2}$ is oxygen uptake per unit time, $\dot{Q}$ is blood flow per unit time, and C_{aO_2} and C_{vO_2} are, respectively, the oxygen content of blood leaving (oxygenated) and entering (deoxygenated) the respiratory epithelium.

Similarly, the amount of oxygen leaving the medium is given by

$$\dot{V}_{O_2} = \dot{V}_A(C_{IO_2} - C_{EO_2}),\tag{2}$$

where $\dot{V}_A$ is alveolar ventilar volume and C_{IO_2} and C_{EO_2} are, respectively, the O_2 content in inhalent and exhalent medium. Equation 2 is true only if inspired and expired volumes are equal, which they generally are not in air-breathing animals. Therefore, mean values from replicates of samples taken during several breathing movements should be used. From Equations 1 and 2, we obtain

$$\dot{Q}(C_{aO_2} - C_{vO_2}) = \dot{V}_A(C_{IO_2} - C_{EO_2})$$

and

$$\dot{V}_A/\dot{Q} = (C_{aO_2} - C_{vO_2})/(C_{IO_2} - C_{EO_2}).$$

14–48. An approximation of volumes and flows in lung (human) and gills (trout). Actual values vary considerably. Note that the ventilation/perfusion ratio is about 1 in the lung and about 10 in the gill.

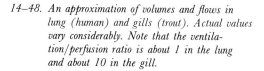

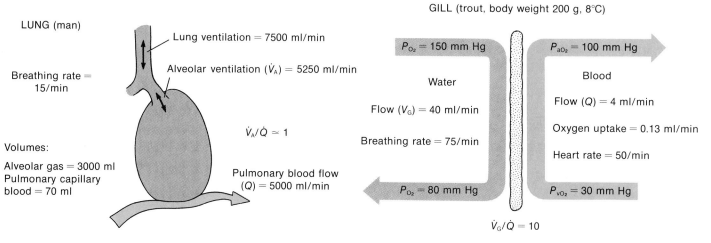

GILL (trout, body weight 200 g, 8°C)

LUNG (man)

Lung ventilation = 7500 ml/min

Alveolar ventilation ($\dot{V}_A$) = 5250 ml/min

Breathing rate = 15/min

$\dot{V}_A/\dot{Q} \simeq 1$

Volumes:
Alveolar gas = 3000 ml
Pulmonary capillary blood = 70 ml

Pulmonary blood flow (Q) = 5000 ml/min

P_{O_2} = 150 mm Hg

Water

Flow (V_G) = 40 ml/min

Breathing rate = 75/min

P_{O_2} = 80 mm Hg

P_{aO_2} = 100 mm Hg

Blood

Flow (Q) = 4 ml/min

Oxygen uptake = 0.13 ml/min

Heart rate = 50/min

P_{vO_2} = 30 mm Hg

$\dot{V}_G/\dot{Q}$ = 10

---

known, the expected ideal oxygen content of arterial blood can be determined. Let us assume that this is 20 ml of O_2 per 100 ml of blood (20 vol %) and the measured values for arterial and venous blood are respectively, 17 and 5 vol %. This reduction in measured arterial oxygen content from the ideal situation can be explained in terms of a venous shunt, oxygenated arterial blood (20 vol %) being mixed with venous blood (5 vol %) in the ratio of 4:1 to give a final O_2 content of 17 vol %; that is, 20% of the blood perfusing the lung is passing through a venous shunt.

Flows of blood and air or water are regulated to maintain the optimal ventilation/perfusion ratio over the surface of the respiratory epithelium under a variety of conditions. In general terms, $\dot{Q}$ is regulated to meet the requirements of the tissues, $\dot{V}_A$ to maintain adequate rates of O_2 and CO_2 transfer. Such mechanisms as hypoxic vasoconstriction of blood vessels help to maintain optimal $\dot{V}_A/\dot{Q}$ ratios in different parts of the respiratory surface. Low oxygen levels cause a vasoconstriction in lung vessels, tending to reduce blood flow to poorly ventilated, and therefore hypoxic, regions and to increase blood flow to well-ventilated regions of the respiratory surface.

Neural Regulation of Breathing

The lung is ventilated by the action of the diaphram and muscles between the ribs. These muscles are activated by spinal motoneurons that receive inputs from groups of neurons that constitute the medullary respiratory centers (Fig. 14-50). The control of respiratory muscles can be very precise, allowing extremely fine control of air flow, as is required for such complex actions in humans as singing, whistling, or talking, as well as simply breathing.

The medullary respiratory center in mammals consists of at least two groups of neurons. Those whose activity coincides with inspiration make up the inspiratory neurons, and those whose activity is associated with expiration make up the expiratory neurons.

It is clear that rhythmic breathing in mammals is maintained by a central generator that is situated within the medulla and which maintains alternate activity in inspiratory and expiratory motoneurons. Brain sections indicate that rhythmic activity is maintained by neurons in the pons (pneumotaxic center) and in the medulla, and that some neurons just anterior to the medulla (apneustic center) cause prolonged inspiration in the absence of rhythmic drive from the pneumotaxic center and reflex vagal inhibition from lung stretch receptors (Fig. 14-50). More recent studies, in which neuronal activity has been recorded from individual cells, have indicated that the rhythm generator probably consists of a group of neurons in the nucleus tractus solitarius in the medulla. This rhythm generator activates other inspiratory neurons in the rostral regions of the nucleus retroambigualis, also within the medulla. These inspiratory neurons, when active, inhibit expiratory neurons in the caudal region of the nucleus retroambigualis. In the absence of any inhibition, these expiratory neurons are tonically active. The neurons in both the nucleus tractus solitarius and the nucleus retroambigualis send activity into nerves innervating the respiratory muscles.

REFLEX CONTROL OF BREATHING

The rate and depth of breathing are influenced by changes in O_2, CO_2, and pH; by the emotions; by sleep; by lung inflation and deflation and lung irri-

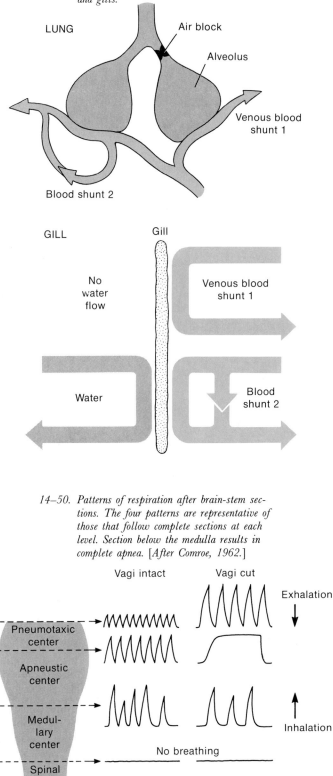

14–49. Problems of inefficient gas transfer can arise because blood flows to a portion of the respiratory surface without adequate ventilation (shunt 1) or because blood does not flow in proximity to the respiratory epithelium (shunt 2). Blood flow is regulated to avoid the development of blood shunts in the lung and gills.

14–50. Patterns of respiration after brain-stem sections. The four patterns are representative of those that follow complete sections at each level. Section below the medulla results in complete apnea. [After Comroe, 1962.]

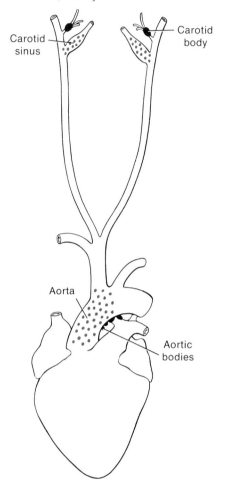

14–51. *The carotid and aortic bodies (dog). Approximate location of the carotid and aortic chemoreceptors and stretch receptors. [After Comroe, 1962.]*

Carotid sinus

Carotid body

Aorta

Aortic bodies

14–52. *The effect of alterations in arterial* P_{O_2} *upon lung ventilation in the duck. This relationship is affected by changes in arterial* P_{CO_2} *[After Jones and Purves, 1970.]*

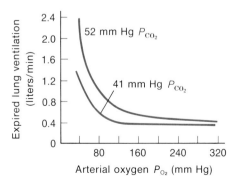

52 mm Hg P_{CO_2}

41 mm Hg P_{CO_2}

Expired lung ventilation (liters/min)

Arterial oxygen P_{O_2} (mm Hg)

tation; by variations in light and temperature; and by the requirements for speech. These influences are integrated by neurons in the medullary respiratory centers.

Most, if not all, animals respond to changes in O_2 and CO_2 with changes in ventilation. The receptors involved have only been localized in a few groups of animals. Chemoreceptors monitor changes in O_2 and CO_2 in arterial blood in the *carotid and aortic bodies* of mammals, in the carotid body of birds, and in the carotid labyrinth of amphibia. In all cases, the chemoreceptors are innervated by branches of the IXth (Glossopharyngeal) or Xth (vagus) cranial nerve.

The carotid body of mammals (Fig. 14-51) receives a generous blood supply and has a high oxygen uptake per unit weight. Sensory fibers innervating the carotid body show an increase in activity when P_{O_2} is decreased or P_{CO_2} increased in the carotid body perfusate. It has been reported that changes in arterial CO_2 and O_2 levels in the intact animal cause reflex changes in ventilation via the carotid body. The response to a change in P_{O_2} depends on the CO_2 level and vice versa (Fig. 14-52). Electrical stimulation of efferent sympathetic nerve fibers innervating the carotid body reduces blood flow, oxygen uptake of the carotid body, and the activity in its afferent sensory fibers.

Increases in blood CO_2 affect CO_2 levels and pH in the cerebral spinal fluid (CSF) of mammals and, via H+ *receptors in the brain,* cause an increase in breathing. The cerebral spinal fluid of mammals, and possibly of other vertebrates, is produced by the choroid plexus of the brain, modified by exchange with the brain and glial cells, and finally absorbed by the arachnoid plexus of the brain. The production rate is extremely variable, ranging from 2 to 164 $\mu l/min$ in a variety of mammalian species. The CSF is very low in protein and is essentially a solution of NaCl and $NaHCO_3$ with low but closely regulated levels of K+, Mg^{2+}, and Ca^{2+}. Changes in blood P_{CO_2} cause corresponding changes in the P_{CO_2} of the CSF, and these in turn result in changes in the pH of the CSF. A decrease in pH stimulates receptors that are possibly located in the region of medullary respiratory center, causing the reflex increases in breathing (Fig. 14-53). Prolonged changes in P_{CO_2} result in the adjustment of the pH of the CSF by changes in HCO_3^- levels.

Many reflexes participate in regulating inflation of the lung and preventing mechanical or chemical irritation of the respiratory surface. In 1868, Hering and Breuer observed that inflation of the lungs decreases the frequency of breathing. This Hering-Breuer reflex is abolished by cutting the vagus nerve. Inflation stimulates stretch receptors in the bronchi and/or bronchioles, which have a reflex inhibitory effect, via the vagus, on the medullary inspiratory center (nucleus tractus solitarius) and, therefore on inspiration.

CO$_2$-sensitive mechanoreceptors have been localized in the lungs of rabbits. Increased CO$_2$ levels reduce the inhibitory effects of these lung stretch receptors on the respiratory center, thereby increasing depth of breathing and lung ventilation. It is not clear if the CO$_2$-sensitive receptors investigated in the lungs of birds are pure CO$_2$ receptors or CO$_2$-sensitive mechanoreceptors, as observed in mammals. Increased CO$_2$ in the lungs of birds, however, has a greater effect on sensory discharge from the lung than that observed in mammals.

In addition to pulmonary stretch receptors, there are a variety of irritant receptors in the lung that are stimulated by mucus and dust or other irritant particles and cause reflex bronchioconstriction and coughing. A third group of receptors is positioned close to the pulmonary capillaries in interstitial spaces; these are called *juxtapulmonary capillary receptors* or, more simply, *type J receptors*. The type J receptors were previously termed "deflation receptors," but their natural stimulus appears not to be lung deflation but an increase in interstitial volume. Stimulation of the type J receptors elicits a sensation of breathlessness. Violent exercise probably results in a rise in pulmonary capillary pressure and an increase in interstitial volume, which could cause stimulation of J receptors and therefore breathlessness.

INTEGRATED RESPONSES TO CHANGES IN OXYGEN AND CARBON DIOXIDE LEVELS

Reduced availability of oxygen. Aquatic animals are subjected to more frequent and rapid changes in oxygen levels than air-breathing animals. The changes in oxygen levels in water may or may not be accompanied by changes in carbon dioxide. In air, the oxygen and carbon dioxide levels are relatively stable, and local environments of low O$_2$ or high CO$_2$ are rare and more easily avoided. There is, of course, a gradual reduction in P_{O_2} with altitude, and animals vary in their capacity to climb to altitude and withstand the reduction in oxygen levels in the air. The highest permanent human habitation is at about 18,000 feet, where the P_{O_2} is 79 mm Hg. Many birds migrate over long distances at altitudes above 6000 m, where atmospheric pressures would cause severe respiratory distress in many mammals. High altitudes are associated with low temperatures as well as low pressures, and this also has a marked effect on animal distribution. Many aquatic animals can withstand very long periods of hypoxia. Some fish—for example, carp—overwinter in the bottom mud of lakes, where the P_{O_2} is very low. Many invertebrates also bury themselves in mud of low P_{O_2} but high nutritive content. Some parasites live in hypoxic regions during one or more phases of their life cycle. Limpets and bivalve mollusks close

14–53. Central H$^+$ receptors are influenced by the [H$^+$] of cerebrospinal fluid (CSF) and by arterial P$_{CO_2}$. Carbon dioxide molecules diffuse readily across the walls of the brain capillaries and alter CSF pH, but there is a barrier to other molecules. Across some capillary walls, exchange of HCO$_3^-$ and Cl$^-$ helps to maintain a constant [H$^+$] of the CSF in the face of a maintained change in P$_{CO_2}$. [After Comroe, 1962.]

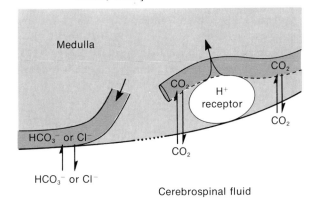

their shells during exposure at low tide to avoid dessication, but as a consequence are subjected to a period of hypoxia. Many of these animals utilize a variety of anaerobic metabolic pathways in order to survive the period of reduced oxygen availability. Others also adjust the respiratory and cardiovascular systems in order to maintain oxygen delivery in the face of reduced oxygen availability.

A reduction in oxygen in air results in a decrease in blood P_{O_2} and causes an increase in lung ventilation in mammals as a result of hypoxic stimulation of the carotid and aortic body chemoreceptors. The rise in lung ventilation results in an increase in CO$_2$ elimination and a decrease in blood P_{CO_2}. The decrease in blood P_{CO_2} results in a reduction in P_{CO_2}, and therefore an increase in pH of the CSF. Decreases in blood P_{CO_2} and increases in cerebral spinal fluid pH tend to reduce ventilation, and, in the example given above, result in attenuation of the increase in lung ventilation because of hypoxia. If, however, the hypoxic conditions are maintained, as occurs when animals move to high altitude, then both blood and cerebral spinal fluid pH are returned to normal levels by the elimination of bicarbonate. This process takes about one week in man. Thus, as cerebral spinal fluid pH returns to normal, the reflex effects of hypoxia on ventilation predominate, and the result is a gradual increase in ventilation as the animal acclimatizes to altitude. This response to prolonged hypoxia may also involve modulation of the effects of CO$_2$ on the carotid and aortic bodies in order to reset these chemoreceptors to the new lower CO$_2$ level at altitude.

Low oxygen levels cause a local vasoconstriction in the pulmonary capillaries in mammals, producing a rise in pulmonary arterial blood pressure. This response normally has some importance in redistributing blood away from portions of the lung that are not adequately ventilated and are therefore hypoxic. When hypoxia is general, however, the increase in the resistance to flow through the whole lung can have detrimental effects. In some mammals that live at high altitudes, there is a reduced local pulmonary vasoconstrictor response to hypoxia which is probably genetically determined.

Long-term adaptations also occur during prolonged exposure to hypoxia. Most vertebrates respond by increasing the number of red blood cells and the blood hemoglobin content, and therefore the oxygen capacity of the blood. The level of phosphorylated compounds, such as 2,3-diphosphoglycerate, adjusts to alter the oxygen affinity of hemoglobin. In humans, a climb to altitude is accompanied by an increase in 2,3-diphosphoglycerate levels and by an adaptive reduction in the hemoglobin oxygen affinity (see p. 475). The gills of fish and amphibia are larger in species exposed to prolonged periods of hypoxia. Similar enlargement of the respiratory surface appears not to occur in mammals. These processes augment the transfer of oxygen, its transport in the blood, and its delivery to the tissues, but they take from several hours to days or weeks to reach completion.

Problems of Diving. Diving mammals and birds are subjected to periods of anoxia during submergence. The vertebrate central nervous system cannot withstand anoxia, and must be supplied with oxygen throughout the dive. Diving animals solve this problem by utilizing oxygen stores in the body. To maximize the use of available stores, oxygen is utilized only by the brain and the heart during a dive, blood flow to other organs is reduced, and these tissues adopt anaerobic metabolic pathways. There is a marked slowing of heart rate and a reduction of cardiac output (see Chapter 13). The blood volume is stored in the veins and is recirculated through the brain and the heart. Many diving animals exhale before diving. During a deep dive, the increase in hydrostatic pressure results in lung compression. By reducing lung volume before a dive, air is forced out of the alveoli as the lungs collapse and is contained within the more rigid but less-gas-permeable trachea and bronchi. If gases remained in the alveoli, they would diffuse into the blood as pressure increased. At the end of the dive, the partial pressure of nitrogen in the blood would be high, and a rapid ascent would result in the formation of bubbles in the blood—the equivalent of decompression sickness or the "bends" in humans.

Situated near the glottis and near the mouth and nose (depending on the species) are receptors that detect the presence of water and which inhibit inspiration during a dive; blood oxygen levels fall and carbon dioxide levels rise, but this does not stimulate ventilation via the carotid and aortic body chemoreceptors. The information from these receptors is ignored by the respiratory neurons during the dive.

During birth, a mammal emerges from an aqueous environment into air and survives a short period of anoxia between the time the placental circulation stops and the first inhalation of air. The respiratory and circulatory responses of the fetus during this period are similar in several respects to those of a diving mammal.

Increased P_{CO_2} levels. In many animals, an increase in P_{CO_2} results in an increase in ventilation. In mammals, the increase is proportional to the rise in CO_2 level in the blood. The effect is mediated by modulation of the activity of several receptors that send messages to the medullary respiratory center. These receptors include the aortic and carotid body chemoreceptors, the H^+ receptors within the medulla, and mechanoreceptors in the lungs (see p. 465). A marked increase in ventilation occurs almost immediately in response to an increase in CO_2. The increase is maintained in the presence of increased CO_2 for long periods of time, but eventually returns to a level slightly above the ventilation volume that prevailed before to hypercapnia. This return to a value only slightly greater than the initial level is related to increases in levels of plasma bicarbonate and CSF bicarbonate, with the result that pH returns to normal even though the raised CO_2 levels are maintained.

Effects of exercise. Exercise increases O_2 utilization, CO_2 production, and metabolic acid production. Cardiac output increases to meet the higher demands of the tissues. Transit time for blood through the lung capillaries is reduced, but there is still adequate time for gas transfer (Fig. 14-54). Ventilation volume increases in order to maintain gas tensions in arterial blood in the face of increased blood flow. The increase in ventilation in mammals is rapid, coinciding with the onset of exercise. This sudden increase in ventilation volume is followed by a more gradual rise until a steady state is obtained both for ventilation volume and oxygen uptake (Fig. 14-55). When exercise is terminated, there is a sudden decrease in breathing, followed by a gradual decline in ventilation volume. During exercise, O_2 levels are reduced and CO_2 and H^+ levels raised in venous blood, but the mean partial pressures of O_2 and CO_2 in arterial blood do not vary markedly, except during severe exercise. The oscillations in arterial blood P_{O_2} and P_{CO_2} associated with each breath increase in magnitude, although the mean level is unaltered.

There appear to be a number of receptor systems involved in the responses to exercise, not all of which may have been identified. Large changes in CO_2 and O_2 are required to produce equivalent changes in ventilation in the absence of exercise. It would seem that the chemoreceptors in both the aortic and the carotid body and in the medulla are probably not directly involved in the ventilatory responses to exercise, because mean P_{O_2} and P_{CO_2} levels in arterial blood do not change very much during exercise. It is possible, however, that the sensitivity of the receptors is increased during exercise, so that only small changes cause the increase in ventilation. In this regard, it is significant that catecholmines, which are released in increased quantities during exercise, increase the sensitivity of medullary receptors to changes in CO_2.

Contractions of muscles stimulate stretch, acceleration, and position mechanoreceptors in muscles, joints, and tendons. Activity in these receptors reflexly stimulates ventilation, and this system probably causes the sudden changes in ventilation that occur at the beginning and end of a period of exercise. It has also been suggested that changes in activity in the brain and spinal chord that cause muscle contraction, and therefore exercise, may also affect the medullary respiratory center, causing an increase in ventilation.

Muscle contraction generates heat, and raises body temperature, which increases ventilation via action on temperature receptors in the hypothalamus. The exact response elicited by stimulation of the hypothalamus depends on the ambient temperature. The increase in ventilation is more pronounced in a hot environment. Since the rise and fall of temperature that follow exercise and subsequent rest are gradual, only the slow changes in ventilation can be caused by changes in body temperature during exercise.

Summary

At the level of the mitochondria, the number of oxygen molecules that an animal extracts from the environment and utilizes is approximately the same as the number of carbon dioxide molecules it produces and releases into the environment. In very small animals, gases are transferred between the surface and the mitochondria by diffusion alone, but in larger animals a circulatory system has evolved for the bulk transfer of gases between the respiratory surface and the tissues.

Large surface-to-volume ratios are maintained in animals by the elaboration of a respiratory surface characterized by large surface areas and small distances for diffusion between the medium and the blood in order to facilitate gas transfer. Breathing movements assure a continual supply of oxygen and prevent stagnation of the medium close to the respiratory epithelium. The design of the respiratory surface and the mechanism of breathing are related to the nature of the medium (i.e., gills in water, lungs in air).

Bulk transport of oxygen and carbon dioxide in the blood is augmented by the presence of a respiratory pigment (e.g., hemoglobin); the pigment not only increases the oxygen-carrying capacity of the blood, but also aids the uptake and release of oxygen and carbon dioxide at the lungs and tissues.

Insects have evolved a tracheal system that takes advantage of the rapid diffusion of gases in air and avoids the necessity of transporting gases in the blood. The tracheal system consists of a series of air-filled,

14–54. Diagram of the way in which P_{O_2} rises as blood flows along the pulmonary capillaries. Note that blood P_{O_2} rapidly reaches near equilibrium with alveolar P_{O_2}. During exercise, blood flow increases; blood spends less time in the lung capillaries, but equilibration is still almost complete. [After West, 1970.]

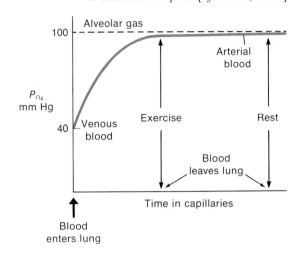

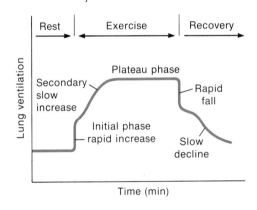

14–55. Changes in lung ventilation during exercise and recovery in mammals. [After Dejours, 1966.]

thin-walled tubes that extend throughout the body and serve as diffusion pathways for oxygen and carbon dioxide between the environment and the cells. In some large active insects, the tracheal system is ventilated.

The rate of gas transfer across a respiratory surface depends upon the ratio of ventilation of the respiratory surface to blood flow, as well as upon absolute ventilation volume and cardiac output. These factors are closely regulated in order to maintain adequate rates of gas transfer to meet the requirements of the tissues. The control system has been studied extensively only in mammals. It consists of a number of mechano- and chemoreceptors that feed information into a central integrating region, the medullary respiratory center.

This center, through a variety of effectors, causes appropriate changes in breathing and blood flow to maintain rates of oxygen and carbon dioxide transfer at a level sufficient to meet the requirements of metabolism.

The bird's egg and the swim bladder of fish present interesting problems in gas transfer. A bird's egg contains an embryo whose oxygen requirements, which must be transferred across a shell of fixed dimensions, increase by 10^3 between laying and hatching. Gas tensions in the fish swim bladder often exceed that in the blood by several orders of magnitude, but the design of the blood supply and gas gland are such that gases move from the blood into the swim bladder.

EXERCISES

1. Calculate the percent change in volume when dry air at $20°C$ is inhaled into the human lung ($T = 37°C$).

2. Define the following terms: (a) oxygen capacity, (b) oxygen content, (c) percent saturation, (d) methemoglobin, (e) Bohr effect, (f) Haldane effect.

3. Describe the role of hemoglobin in the transfer of oxygen *and* carbon dioxide.

4. Describe the effects of gravity on the distribution of blood in the human lung. What effect does alveolar pressure have on lung blood flow?

5. Compare and contrast ventilation of the mammalian and bird lung.

6. What mechanisms have evolved to reduce heat and water loss via the lung?

7. What is the functional significance of the presence of surfactants in the lung?

8. How have insects avoided the necessity of transporting gases in the blood?

9. The number and dimensions of air pores in egg shells is constant for a given species. What effect would doubling the number of pores have on the transfer of oxygen, carbon dioxide, and water across the egg shell?

10. Discuss the role of the rete mirabile in the maintenance of high gas pressures in the fish swim bladder.

11. How is oxygen moved into the swim bladder of teleost fish?

12. Describe the structural and functional differences between gills and lungs.

13. Why is the ventilation/perfusion ratio much higher in water-breathing than air-breathing animals?

14. Describe the role of central chemoreceptors in the control of carbon dioxide excretion.

15. What is the importance of the Hering-Breuer reflex in the control of breathing?

16. Describe the processes involved in the acclimation of mammals to high altitude.

SUGGESTED READING

Bolis, L., K. Schmidt-Nielsen, and S. H. P. Maddrell. 1973. *Comparative Physiology.* American Elsevier, New York.

Comroe, J. H. 1965. *Physiology of Respiration.* Year Book Medical Publishers, Inc. Chicago.

Davenport, H. W. 1969. *The A.B.C. of Acid Base Chemistry* (5th ed.). Univ. of Chicago Press, Chicago.

Dejours, P. (ed.). 1972. Comparative physiology of respiration in vertebrates. *Resp. Physiol.* 14.

Dejours, P. 1975. *Principles of Comparative Respiratory Physiology.* American Elsevier, New York.

de Reuck, A. V. S., and R. Porter (eds.). 1962. *Development of the Lung.* A Ciba Foundation Symposium. J. & A. Churchill Ltd., London.

Farner, D. S., and J. R. King (eds.). 1972. *Avian Biology* (Vol. II). Academic Press, New York.

Hoar, W. S., and D. J. Randall (eds.) *Fish Physiology* (Vol. IV). Academic Press, New York.

Hochachka, P. W., and G. N. Somero. 1973. *Strategies of Biochemical Adaptation.* Saunders, Philadelphia.

Johansen, K. 1971. Comparative physiology: Gas exchange and circulation in fishes. *Ann. Rev. Physiol.* 33:569–612.

Jones, J. D. 1972. *Comparative Physiology of Respiration.* Edward Arnold Ltd., London.

Krogh, A. 1968. *The Comparative Physiology of Respiratory Mechanisms.* Dover, New York.

Leusen, I. 1972. Regulation of cerebral spinal fluid composition with reference to breathing. *Physiol. Revs.* 52:1–56.

Rahn, H. 1966. Aquatic gas exchange theory. *Resp. Physiol.* 1:1–12.

Ruch, T. C., and H. D. Patton. (eds.) 1974. *Physiology and Biophysics* (20th ed.). Vol. II. Philadelphia.

Schmidt-Nielsen, K. 1972. *How Animals Work.* Cambridge Univ. Press, New York.

Steen, J. B. 1971. *Comparative Physiology of Respiratory Mechanisms.* Academic Press, New York.

West, J. B. 1974. *Respiratory Physiology: The Essentials.* Williams & Wilkins, Baltimore.

REFERENCES CITED

Banko, W. E. 1960. *The Trumpeter Swan.* North American Fauna, No. 63. U.S. Dept. Interior, Fish & Wildlife Service. Washington, D.C.

Bartels, H. 1971. *In* P. L. Altman and D. W. Dittmer (eds.), *Respiration and Circulation.* Federation of American Societies for Experimental Biology. Bethesda, Maryland.

Comroe, J. H. 1962. *Physiology of Respiration.* Year Book Medical Publ., Inc., Chicago.

Dejours, P. 1966. *Respiration.* Oxford Univ. Press, New York.

Denton, E. J. 1961. The buoyancy of fish and cephalopods. *Progr. Biophys.* 11:178–234.

Duncker, H. R. 1972. The lung air sac system of birds. A contribution to the functional anatomy of the respiratory apparatus. *Ergebn. Anat. Entwickl. Gesch.* 45(6):1–171.

Federation Proceedings. 1950. Standardization of definitions and symbols in respiratory physiology. *Fed. Proc.* 9:602–605.

Grigg, G. C. 1970. Water flow through the gills of Port Jackson sharks. *J. Expt. Biol.* 52:565–568.

Hales, J. R. S. 1966. The partition of respiratory ventilation of the panting ox. *J. Physiol.* (Lond.) 188:45–68.

Hildebrandt, J., and A. C. Young. 1965. Anatomy and physics of respiration. *In* T. C. Ruch and H. D. Patton (eds.), *Physiology and Biophysics* (19th ed.). Saunders, Philadelphia.

Holland, R. A. B., and R. E. Forster. 1966. The effect of size of red cells on the kinetics of their oxygen uptake. *J. Gen. Physiol.* 49:727–742.

Hughes, C. M. 1964. How a fish extracts oxygen from water. *New Scientist* 11:346–348.

Jones, D. R., and M. J. Purves. 1970. The carotid body in the duck and the consequences of its denervation upon the cardiac responses to immersion. *J. Physiol.* 211:279–294.

McGilvery, R. W. 1970. *Biochemistry: A Functional Approach.* Saunders, Philadelphia.

Rahn, H. 1967. Gas transport from the external environment to the cell. *In* A. V. S. de Reuck and R. Porter (eds.), *Development of the Lung. A Ciba Foundation Symposium.* J. & A. Churchill Ltd., London.

Randall, D. J. 1970. Gas exchange in fish. *In* W. S. Hoar and D. J. Randall (eds.), *Fish Physiology* (Vol. IV). Academic Press, New York.

Roughton, F. J. W. 1962. Transport of oxygen and carbon dioxide. *In* W. O. Fenn and H. Rahn (eds.), *Handbook of Physiology.* American Physiological Society, Washington, D.C.

Salt, G. W. 1964. Respiratory evaporation in birds. *Biol. Revs.* 39:113–136.

Scheid, P., H. Slama, and J. Piiper. 1972. Mechanisms of unidirectional flow in parabronchi of avian lungs: Measurements in duck lung preparations. *Resp. Physiol.* 14:83–95.

Schmidt-Nielsen, K., W. L. Bretz, and C. R. Taylor. 1970. Panting in dogs: Unidirectional air flow over evaporative surfaces. *Science* 169:1102–1104.

Schmidt-Nielsen, K., F. R. Hainsworth, and D. E. Murrish. 1970. Countercurrent heat exchange in the respiratory passages: Effect on water and heat balance. *Respir. Physiol.* 9:263–276.

Shelton, G. 1970. The effect of lung ventilation on blood flow to the lungs and body of the amphibian *Xenopus laevis. Respir. Physiol.* 9:183–196.

Steen, J. B. 1963. The physiology of the swimbladder of the eel *Anguilla vulgaris.* I. The solubility of gases and the buffer capacity of the blood. *Acta. Physiol. Scand.* 58:124–137.

Tenney, S. M., and J. E. Temmers. 1963. Comparative quantitative morphology of the mammalian lung: Diffusing area. *Nature* (Lond.) 197:54–57.

Toews, D. P., G. Shelton, and D. J. Randall. 1971. Gas tensions in the lungs and major blood vessels of the urodele amphibian, *Amphiuma tridactylum. J. Exp. Biol.* 55:47–61.

Wagenstein, O. D. 1972. Gas exchange by a bird's embryo. *Resp. Physiol.* 14:64–74.

West, J. B. 1970. *Ventilation/blood flow and gas exchange.* (2nd. Ed.) Blackwell Scientific Publications, Oxford.

West, N. H., and D. R. Jones. 1975. Breathing movements in the frog *Rana pipiens.* I. The mechanical events associated with lung and buccal ventilation. *Canad. J. Zool..* 53:332–344.

Wigglesworth, V. B. 1965. *The Principles of Insect Physiology* (6th ed.). Methuen and Co. Ltd., London.

Young, M. 1971. *In* P. L. Altman and D. W. Dittmer (eds.), *Respiration and Circulation.* Federation of American Societies for Experimental Biology, Bethesda, Maryland.

Appendixes

Appendix 1: SI Units

Basic SI Units.

Physical Quantity	Name of Unit	Symbol for Unit
Length	meter	m
Mass	kilogram	kg
Time	second	s
Electric current	ampere	A
Temperature	kelvin	K
Luminous intensity	candela	cd

SI Multipliers.

Multiplier	Prefix	Symbol
10^9	giga	G
10^6	mega	M
10^3	kilo	k
10^2	hecto	h
10	deka	da
10^{-1}	deci	d
10^{-2}	centi	c
10^{-3}	milli	m
10^{-6}	micro	μ
10^{-9}	nano	n
10^{-12}	pico	p

Derived SI Units.

Physical Quantity	Name of Unit	Symbol for Unit	Definition of Unit
Acceleration	meter per second squared	m/s^2	
Activity	1 per second	s^{-1}	
Electric capacitance	farad	F	A-s/V
Electric charge	coulomb	C	A-s
Electric field strength	volt per meter	V/m	
Electrical resistance	ohm	Ω	V/A
Entropy	joule per kelvin	J/K	
Force	newton	N	$kg\text{-}m/s^2$
Frequency	hertz	Hz	s^{-1}
Illumination	lux	lx	lm/m^2
Luminance	candela per square meter	cd/m^2	
Luminous flux	lumen	lm	cd-sr
Power	watt	W	J/s
Pressure	newton per square meter	N/m^2	
Voltage, potential difference,	volt	V	W/A
Work, energy, heat	joule	J	N-m

Appendix 2: Selected Atomic Weights

Atomic Weights

Element	Symbol	Atomic Number	Atomic Weight	Valence
Aluminum	Al	13	26.9815	3
Barium	Ba	56	137.34	2
Boron	B	5	10.811	3
Cadmium	Cd	48	112.40	2
Calcium	Ca	20	40.08	2
Carbon	C	6	12.01115	2, 4
Cesium	Cs	55	132.905	1
Chlorine	Cl	17	35.453	1, 3, 5, 7
Chromium	Cr	24	51.996	2, 3, 6
Cobalt	Co	27	58.9332	2, 3
Copper	Cu	29	63.54	1, 2
Fluorine	F	9	18.9984	1
Gold	Au	79	196.967	1, 3
Helium	He	2	4.0026	0
Hydrogen	H	1	1.00797	1
Iodine	I	53	126.9044	1, 3, 5, 7
Iron	Fe	26	55.847	2, 3
Lanthanum	La	57	138.91	3
Lead	Pb	82	207.19	2, 4
Lithium	Li	3	6.939	1
Magnesium	Mg	12	24.312	2
Manganese	Mn	25	54.9380	2, 3, 4, 6, 7
Mercury	Hg	80	200.59	1, 2
Nickel	Ni	28	58.71	2, 3
Nitrogen	N	7	14.0067	3, 5
Osmium	Os	76	190.2	2, 3, 4, 8
Oxygen	O	8	15.9994	2
Palladium	Pd	46	106.4	2, 4, 6
Phosphorus	P	15	30.9738	3, 5
Platinum	Pt	78	195.09	2, 4
Plutonium	Pu	94	244	3, 4, 5, 6
Potassium	K	19	39.102	1
Radium	Ra	88	226	2
Rubidium	Rb	37	85.47	1
Selenium	Se	34	78.96	2, 4, 6
Silicon	Si	14	28.086	4
Silver	Ag	47	107.870	1
Sodium	Na	11	22.9898	1
Strontium	Sr	38	87.62	2
Sulfur	S	16	32.064	2, 4, 6
Thallium	Tl	81	204.37	1, 3
Zinc	Zn	30	67.37	2

Appendix 3:

Conversions, Formulas, Physical and Chemical Constants, Definitions

Temperature Conversion

$$°C = 5/9(°F - 32)$$
$$°F = 9/5(°C) + 32$$
$$0°K = -273.15°C = -459.67°F$$
$$0°C = 273.15°K = 32°F$$

Units and Conversion Factors

To Convert from	to	Multiply by
angstroms	inches	3.937×10^{-9}
	meters	1×10^{-10}
	micrometers (μm)	1×10^{-4}
atmospheres	bars	1.01325
	dynes per square centimeter	1.01325×10^6
	grams per square centimeter	1033.23
	torr (=mm Hg; 0°C)	760
	pounds per square inch	14.696
bars	atmospheres	0.9869
	dynes per square centimeter	1×10^6
	grams per square centimeter	1019.716
	pounds per square inch	14.5038
	millimeters of mercury (0°C)	750.062
calories	British thermal units	3.968×10^{-3}
	ergs	4.184×10^7
	foot-pounds	3.08596
	kilocalories	10^{-3}
	horsepower-hours	1.55857×10^{-6}
	joules	4.184
	watt-hours	1.1622×10^{-3}
	watt-seconds	4.184
ergs	British thermal units	9.48451×10^{-11}
	calories	2.39×10^{-8}
	dynes per centimeter	1
	foot-pounds	7.37562×10^{-8}
	gram-centimeters	1.0197×10^{-3}
	joules	1×10^{-7}
	watt-seconds	1×10^{-7}
grams	daltons	6.024×10^{23}
	grains	15.432358
	ounces (avdp)	3.52739×10^{-2}
	pounds (avdp)	2.2046×10^{-3}

To Convert from	to	Multiply by
inches	angstroms	2.54×10^8
	centimeters	2.54
	feet	8.333×10^{-2}
	meters	2.54×10^{-2}
joules	calories	0.239
	ergs	1×10^7
	foot-pounds	0.73756
	watt-hours	2.777×10^{-4}
	watt-seconds	1
liters	cubic centimeters	10^3
	gallons (US,liq)	0.2641794
	pints (US,liq)	2.113436
	quarts (US,liq)	1.056718
lumens	candle power	7.9577×10^{-2}
lux	lumens per square meter	1
meters	angstroms	1×10^{10}
	micrometers (μm)	1×10^6
	centimeters	100
	feet	3.2808
	inches	39.37
	kilometers	1×10^{-3}
	miles (statute)	6.2137×10^{-4}
	millimeters	1000
	yards	1.0936
newtons	dynes	10^5
pints (US,liq)	cubic centimeters	473.17647
	gallons	0.125
	liters	0.47316
	ounces	16
	quarts	0.5
watts	British thermal units per second	9.4845×10^{-4}
	calories per minute	14.3197
	ergs per second	1×10^7
	foot-pounds per minute	44.2537
	horsepower	1.341×10^{-3}
	joules per second	1

Electric potential	$E = IR = q/C$
	E = electric potential (voltage)
	I = current
	R = resistance
	q = charge
	C = capacitance
Power	$p = w/t$
	w = work
	t = time
Electric power	$p = RI^2 = EI$
	E = electric potential
Work	$W = RI^2t = EIt = Pt$
Pressure	P = force (f)/unit area
Weight	$W = mg$
	m = mass
	g = acceleration of gravity
Force	$f = ma$
	m = mass
	a = acceleration
Dalton's Law of Partial Pressures	$PV = V(p_1 + p_2 + p_3 + \cdots + p_n)$
	P = pressure of gas mixture
	V = volume
	p = pressure of each gas alone
Electrostatic force of attraction	$F = \dfrac{q_1 q_2}{\epsilon r^2}$
	r = distance separating q_1 and q_2
	ϵ = dielectric constant
Potential energy	$E = mgh$
	h = height of mass above the surface of the earth
Kinetic energy	$E = 1/2mv^2$
	v = velocity of mass
Energy of a charge	$E = 1/2qV$
	q = charge
	V = electric potential
Perfect Gas Law	$PV = nRT$
	P = pressure
	V = volume
	n = number of moles
	R = gas constant
	T = absolute temp.

Hooke's Law of Elasticity	$F = kT$
	k = spring constant
	F = force
	T = tension

Energy of a photon	$E = h\nu$
	h Planck's constant
	ν = frequency

Physical and Chemical Constants

Avogadro's number	$N_A = 6.022 \times 10^{23}$
Faraday constant	$F = 96,487$ coulombs/mole
Gas constant	$R = 8.314$ joule/°K-mole
	$= 1.98$ cal/°K-mole
	$= 0.082$ liter-atm/°K-mole
Planck's constant	$h = 6.62 \times 10^{-27}$ ergs/s
	$= 1.58 \times 10^{-34}$ cal/s
Speed of light in a vacuum	$c = 2.997 \times 10^{10}$ cm/s
	$= 186,000$ mi/s

Chemical Definitions

1 mole = the mass in grams of a substance equal to its molecular or atomic weight. This mass contains Avogadro's number (N_A) of molecules or atoms.

Molar volume = the volume occupied by a mole of gas at standard temperature and pressure (25°C, 1 atm) = 22.414 liters.

1 molal solution = 1 mole per 1000 g of solvent.

1 molar solution = 1 mole of solute in 1 liter of solution.

1 equivalent = 1 mole of 1 unit charge.

1 einstein = 1 mole of photons.

Dimensions of Plane and Solid Figures

Area of a square = l^2

Surface area of a cube = $6l^2$

Volume of a cube = l^3

Circumference of a circle = $2\pi r$

Area of a circle = πr^2

Surface area of a sphere = $4\pi r^2$

Volume of a sphere = $4/3\pi r^3$

Surface area of a cylinder = $2\pi rh$

Volume of a cylinder = $\pi r^2 h$

Glossary

A-band. A region of a muscle sarcomere that corresponds to the myosin thick filaments.

Absolute temperature. (Kelvin scale, °K) Temperature measured from absolute zero, the state of no atomic or molecular thermal agitation. 0°K is equal to -273.15°C or -459.67°F.

Accommodation. The temporary increase in threshold that develops during the course of a subthreshold stimulus.

Acetylcholine (ACh). An acetic acid ester of choline ($CH_3—CO—O—CH_2—CH_2—N(CH_3)_3—OH$), important as a synaptic transmitter.

Acetylcholinesterase. An enzyme that hydrolyzes ACh and resides on postsynaptic membrane surface.

Acid. Proton donor.

Acromegaly. Hypersecretion of growth hormone in adulthood, causing enlargement of the skeletal extremities and facial structures.

Actin. A muscle protein. G-actin is the globular monomer that polymerizes to form F-actin, the backbone of the thin filaments of the sarcomere.

Action potential (nerve impulse, spike). Transient all-or-none reversal of a membrane potential produced by regenerative inward current in excitable membranes.

Action spectrum. The degree of response to incident light of a given energy as a function of wavelength.

Activating reaction. A reaction that changes an inactive enzyme into an active catalyst.

Activation energy. The energy required to bring reactant molecules to velocities sufficiently high to break or make chemical bonds.

Activation heat. Heat produced during excitation and activation of muscle tissue, but independent of shortening.

Active site. Catalytic region of an enzyme molecule.

Active state. Condition of relative inextensibility of muscle, before and during contraction, due to attachment of myosin cross bridges to actin filaments.

Active transport. Energy-requiring translocation of a substance across a membrane, usually against its concentration or electrochemical gradient.

Activity. Capacity of a substance to react with another. The effective concentration of an ionic species in the free state.

Activity coefficient. A proportionality factor obtained by dividing the effective reactive concentration of an ion (as indicated by its properties in a solution) by its molar concentration.

Actomyosin. A complex of the muscle proteins actin and myosin.

Acuity. Resolving power.

Adductor muscle. One that brings a limb toward the median plane of the body.

Adenine. A white, crystalline base 6-amino-purine, $C_5H_5N_5$. Purine base constituent of DNA and RNA.

Adenohypophysis (anterior pituitary gland, anterior lobe). The glandular anterior lobe of the hypophysis, consisting of the pars infundibularis and pars distalis.

Adenosine triphosphate (ATP). A nucleotide used as a common energy currency by all cells.

Adenylate cyclase (= adenyl cyclase). A membrane-bound enzyme that catalyzes the conversion of ATP to cAMP.

Adipose. Fatty.

Adrenalin. Trade name for epinephrine.

Adrenergic. Relating to neurons or synapses that release epinephrine, norepinephrine, and other catecholamines when stimulated.

α-Adrenergic receptors. Receptors on cell surfaces that bind norepinephrine and, less effectively, epinephrine. The binding leads to enzymatically-mediated responses by the cells.

β-Adrenergic receptors. Epinephrine binding sites.

Adrenocorticotrophic hormone (ACTH; adrenocorticotropin; corticotropin). A hormone released by cells in the adenohypophysis that acts mainly on the adrenal cortex, stimulating growth and corticosteroid production and secretion in that organ.

Aequorin. A protein extracted from the jellyfish *Aequorea*. Upon combining with Ca^{2+}, it emits a photon of blue-green light.

Aerobic. Utilizing molecular oxygen.

Afferent. Transporting or conducting toward a central region; centripetal.

Ia Afferent fiber. An axon with a peripheral sensory ending innervating a muscle spindle organ and responding to stretch of the organ. Its central terminals synapse directly onto alpha motoneurons of the homonymous muscle.

Ib Afferent fiber. An axon whose sensory terminals innervate the tendons of skeletal muscle and respond to tension.

Afferent fiber. An axon that relays impulses from a sensory receptor to the central nervous system.

Affinity sequence (or selectivity sequence). The order of preference with which an electrostatic site will bind different species of counterions.

Aldehydes. A large class of substances derived from the primary alcohols by oxidation and containing the —CHO group.

Aldosterone. A mineralocorticoid secreted by the adrenal cortex. The most important electrolyte-controlling steroid, acting on the renal tubules to increase the resorption of sodium.

Alkali earth metals. A group of grayish-white, malleable metals easily oxidized in air, comprising Be, Mg, Ca, Sr, Ba, Ra.

All-or-none. Pertaining to the independence of response magnitude from the strength of the stimulus. Response is "all" if the stimulus achieves threshold and "none" if the stimulus fails to achieve threshold.

Allantoic membrane. One of the membranes within a bird egg shell. Important in the respiration of the unhatched chick.

Allantoin. Waste product of purine metabolism.

Allosteric site. Area of an enzyme that binds a substance other than the substrate, changing the conformation of the protein so as to alter the catalytic effectiveness of the active site.

Alpha helix. Helical secondary structure of many proteins in which each NH group is hydrogen-bonded to a CO group at a distance equivalent to three amino acid residues. The helix makes a complete turn for each 3.6 residues.

Alpha motoneurons. Large spinal neurons that innervate extrafusal skeletal muscle fibers of vertebrates.

Alveolar ventilation volume. The volume of fresh atmospheric air entering the alveoli during each inspiration.

Alveoli. Small cavities, especially those microscopic cavities that are the functional units of the lung.

Amacrine cells. Neurons without axons, found in the inner plexiform layer of the vertebrate retina.

Ambient. Surrounding, prevailing.

Amide. An organic derivative of ammonia in which a hydrogen atom is replaced by an acyl group.

Amine. Derivative of ammonia in which at least one hydrogen atom is replaced by an organic group.

Amino acids. Class of organic compounds containing at least one carboxyl group and one amino group. The alpha-amino acids, $RCH(NH_2)COOH$, make up proteins.

Amino group. $—NH_2$.

Ammonia. NH_3, toxic, water-soluble, alkaline waste product of deamination of amino acids and uric acid.

Ampere (amp). MKS unit of electric current; equal to the current produced through a one-ohm resistance by a potential difference of one volt. The movement of 1 coulomb of charge per second.

Amphipathic. Pertaining to molecules bearing groups with different properties, such as hydrophilic or hydrophobic groups.

Amphoteric. Having opposite characteristics; behaving as either an acid or a base.

Anabolism. Synthesis by living cells of complex substances from simple substances.

Anastomose. To interconnect.

Anatomical dead space. The nonrespiratory conducting pathways in the lung.

Androgens. Hormones having masculinizing activity.

Aneurism. Localized dilation of an artery wall.

Angiotensin. A protein in the blood, converted from angiotensinogen by the action of renin. It first exists as a decapeptide (angiotensin I) that is acted upon by a peptidase, which cleaves it into an octapeptide (angiotensin II), a potent vasopressor and stimulator of aldosterone secretion.

Anion. Negatively charged ion; attracted to the anode or positive pole.

Anode. Positive electrode or pole to which negatively charged ions are attracted.

Anoxia. A lack of oxygen.

Anoxemia. A lack of oxygen in the blood.

Antagonist muscle. A muscle acting in opposition to the movement of another muscle.

Antennal gland. Crustacean osmoregulatory organ.

Antibody. An immunoglobulin, a 4-chain protein molecule of a specific amino acid sequence. An antibody will only interact with the antigen that brought about its production or one very similar to it.

Antidiuretic hormone (ADH). A hormone made in the

hypothalamus and liberated from storage in the neurohypophysis; acts on the epithelium of the renal collecting duct by stimulating osmotic resorption of water, thereby producing a more concentrated urine; also acts as a vasopressor.

Antigen. A substance capable of bringing about the production of antibodies and then to react with them specifically.

Antimycin. An antibiotic that is isolated from a *Streptomyces* strain; acts to block electron transport from cytochrome *b* to cytochrome *c* in the electron-transport chain.

Aorta. The main artery leaving the heart.

Aortic body. A nodule on the aortic arch containing chemoreceptors that sense the chemical composition of the blood.

Apnea. The suspension or absence of breathing.

Apoenzyme. The protein portion of an enzyme. The apoenzyme and coenzyme form the functioning holoenzyme.

Aporepressor. A repressor gene product that, in combination with a corepressor, reduces the activity of particular structural genes.

Arteriole. A tiny branch of an artery; in particular, one nearest a capillary.

Arteriosclerosis. A class of diseases marked by an increase in thickness and a reduction in elasticity of the arterial walls.

Asynchronous muscle. A type of flight muscle found in the thorax of some insects. Contracts without any one-to-one relation to motor impulses. *See also* Fibrillar muscle.

ATPase (adenosine triphosphatase). A class of enzymes that catalyze the hydrolysis of ATP.

ATPS. Ambient temperature and pressure, saturated with water vapor; referring to gas volume measurements.

Atrio-ventricular node. Specialized conduction tissue in the heart, which, along with Purkinje tissue, forms a bridge for electrical conduction of the impulse from atria to ventricles.

Autonomic nervous system. The efferent nerves that control involuntary visceral functions. It is classically subdivided into the sympathetic and parasympathetic sections.

Autoradiography. The process of making a photographic record of the internal structures of a tissue by utilizing the radiation emitted from incorporated radioactive material.

Autorhythmicity. The generation of rhythmic activity without extrinsic control.

Avogadro's law. Equal volumes of different gases at the same temperature and pressure contain equal numbers of molecules. 1 mole of an ideal gas at 0°C and 1 atm occupies 22.414 liters. Avogadro's number equals 6.02252×10^{23} molecules/mole.

Axon. The elongated cylindrical process of a nerve cell along which action potentials are conducted. A nerve fiber.

Axon hillock. The transitional region between an axon and the nerve cell body.

Axoneme. Complex of microtubules and associated structures within the flagellar or ciliary shaft.

Axoplasm. The cytoplasm within an axon.

Azide. Any compound bearing the N_3^- group.

Basal body (kinetosome). Microtubular structure from which a cilium or flagellum arises. Homologous with centriole.

Base. Proton acceptor.

Basilar membrane. The delicate ribbon of tissue bearing the auditory hair cells in the cochlea of the vertebrate ear.

Bell-Magendie Law. The dorsal root of the spinal cord contains only sensory axons, whereas the ventral root contains only motor axons.

Beta keratin. Insoluble, sulfur-rich scleroprotein; constituent of epidermis, horns, hair, feathers, nails, and tooth enamel. *Beta* refers to the protein's secondary structure, which is in pleated sheets.

Bipolar cell. A neuron with two axons emerging from opposite sides of the soma. One class of such neurons is found in the vertebrate retina, where they transmit signals from the visual receptor cells to the ganglion cells of the optic nerve.

Birefringence. Double refraction; the ability to pass preferentially light that is polarized in one plane.

Bleaching. Fading of photopigment color upon absorption of light.

Bohr effect (Bohr shift). A change in hemoglobin-oxygen affinity due to a change in pH.

Bombykol. Sex attractant pheromone of the female of the silkworm moth. *Bombyx.*

Book lungs. The respiratory surface in spiders.

Bowman's capsule (glomerular capsule). A globular expansion at the beginning of a renal tubule and surrounding the glomerulus.

Bradycardia. A reduction in heart rate from the normal level.

Bradykinin. A hormone formed from a precursor normally circulating in the blood. It is a very potent cutaneous vasodilator.

Brain hormone (prothoracotropin; activating hormone). A hormone synthesized by the neurosecretory cells of the pars intercerebralis and released by the corpora cardiaca of insects. It activates the prothoracic glands to secrete ecdysone.

Bronchi. Conducting airways in the lung; branches of the trachea.

Bronchioles. Small conducting airways in the lung; branches of bronchi.

Brood spot. A prolactin-induced bald area on the ventral surface of some brooding birds that receives a rich supply of blood for the incubation of eggs.

Brush border. A free epithelial cell surface bearing numerous microvilli.

BTPS. Body temperature, atmospheric pressure, saturated with water vapor.

Buffer. A chemical system that stabilizes the concentration of a substance; acid-base systems serve as pH buffers, preventing large changes in hydrogen ion concentration.

Bundle of His. Conducting tissue within the interventricular septum of the mammalian heart.

Bungarotoxin. A group of neurotoxins isolated from the venom of members of the snake genus *Bungarus* (the krait) of the cobra family. Binds selectively and irreversibly to acetylcholine receptors.

Bunsen solubility coefficient. The quantity of gas at STPD that will dissolve in a given volume of liquid per unit partial pressure of the gas in the gas phase. This coefficient is used only for gases that do not react chemically with the solvent.

Bursicon. A hormone secreted by neurosecretory cells of the insect central nervous system. It tans and hardens the cuticle of freshly molted insects.

Cable properties. Passive resistive and capacitive electrical properties of a cell, akin to those exhibited by a submarine cable.

Calcitonin (thyrocalcitonin). A protein hormone secreted by the mammalian parafollicular cells of the thyroid in response to elevated plasma calcium levels.

Calcium response. A graded depolarization due to a weakly regenerative inward calcium current.

Capacitance. The property of storing electric charge by electrostatic means.

Capacitive current. Current entering and leaving a capacitor.

Capacity. The ability of a capacitor or other body to store electric charge. The unit of measure is the farad, F, which describes the proportionality between charge stored and potential for a given voltage, $C = q/V =$ coulombs/volts.

Carbohydrate. Aldehyde or ketone derivative of alcohol. Utilized by animal cells primarily for the storage and supply of chemical energy. Most important are the sugars and starches.

Carbonic anhydrase. An enzyme reversibly catalyzing the degradation of carbonic acid to carbon dioxide and water.

Carbonyl. The organic radical $-C=O$, which occurs in such compounds as aldehydes, ketones, carboxylic acids, and esters.

Carboxyhemoglobin. The compound formed when carbon monoxide combines with hemoglobin. Carbon monoxide competes successfully with oxygen for combination with hemoglobin, producing tissue anoxia.

Carboxyl group. The radical $-COOH$, which occurs in the carboxylic acids.

Carboxylates. $R-COO-$, salts or esters of carboxylic acids.

Cardiac output (CO). The total volume of blood pumped by the heart per unit of time. Cardiac output equals heart rate times stroke volume.

Carotid body. A nodule on the occipital artery just above the carotid sinus, containing chemoreceptors that sense the chemical composition of arterial blood.

Carotid sinus baroreceptors. Receptors that sense arterial blood pressure; located in the carotid sinus, a dilatation of the internal carotid artery at its origin.

Carrier molecules. Lipid-soluble molecules that act within biological membranes as carriers for certain molecules that have lower mobility in the membrane.

Catabolism. Disassembly of complex molecules into simpler ones.

Catalysis. An increase in the rate of a chemical reaction promoted by a substance—the catalyst—not consumed by the reaction.

Catalyst. A substance that increases the rate of a reaction without being used up in the reaction.

Catecholamines. A group of related compounds exerting a sympathomimetic action on nervous tissue. Examples are epinephrine, norepinephrine, and dopamine.

Cathode. The negative electrode, so called because it is the electrode to which cations are attracted.

Cation. A positively charged ion; attracted to a negatively charged electrode.

Caudal. Pertaining to the tail end.

Central sulcus. A deep, almost vertical furrow on the cerebrum, dividing the frontal and parietal lobes.

Cerebellum. The part of the hind brain that is involved in coordination of motor output.

Cerebral hemispheres. The large paired structures of the cerebrum, connected by the corpus callosum.

Cerebrospinal fluid. A clear fluid that fills the cavities (ventricles) within the brain. It is a complex filtrate of blood plasma and is modified by brain cells before returning to the venous system.

Chemoreceptor. A sensory receptor specifically sensitive to certain molecules.

Chief cells. Epithelial cells of the gastric epithelium that release pepsin.

Chitin. A structural polymer of D-glucosamine that serves as the primary constituent of arthropod exoskeletons.

Chloride cells. Epithelial cells of fish gills that engage in active transport of salts.

Chloride shift. The movement of chloride ions across the red blood cell membrane to compensate for the movement of bicarbonate ions.

Chlorocruorin. A green respiratory pigment found in some marine polychaetes. Similar to hemoglobin.

Cholecystokinin (CCK; pancreozymin). A hormone liberated by the upper intestinal mucosa that induces gall bladder contraction and release of pancreatic enzymes.

Cholesterol. A natural sterol; precursor to the steroid hormones.

Cholinergic. Relating to acetylcholine or substances with actions similar to ACh.

Choroid plexus. Highly vascularized, furrowed projections into the brain ventricles that secrete cerebrospinal fluid.

Choroid rete. A countercurrent arrangement of arterioles and venules behind the retina in the eyes of teleost fish.

Chromaffin cells. Epinephrine-secreting cells of the adrenal medulla; named for their high affinity for chromium salt stains.

Chromophore. A chemical group that lends a distinct color to a compound containing it.

Ciliary body. A thick region of the anterior vascular tunic of the eye; joins the choroid and the iris.

Ciliary muscle. A muscle of the ciliary body of the vertebrate eye; influences the shape of the lens in visual accommodation.

Ciliary reversal. A change in the direction of the power stroke of a cilium causing it to beat in reverse.

Cis. A configuration with similar atoms or groups on the same side of the molecular backbone.

Cis-trans isomerization. Conversion of a *cis* isomer into a *trans* isomer.

Cochlear microphonics. Electrical signals recorded from the cochlea, having a frequency identical to that of the sound stimulus.

Coelom. The body cavity of higher metazoans, situated between the gut and the body wall and lined with mesodermal epithelium.

Coenzyme. An organic molecule that combines with an apoenzyme to form the functioning holoenzyme.

Coenzyme A. A derivative of pantothenic acid to which acetate becomes attached to form acetyl CoA.

Cofactor. An atom, ion, or molecule that combines with an enzyme to activate it.

Coitus. Sexual intercourse.

Colchicine. An agent that disrupts microtubules by interfering with the polymerization of tubulin monomers.

Collar cells. Flagellated cells lining the internal chambers of sponges (porifera).

Collaterals. Minor side branches of a nerve or blood vessel.

Collecting duct. The portion of the renal tubules in which the final concentration of urine occurs.

Colligative properties. Characteristics of a solution that depend on the number of molecules in a given volume.

Colloid. A system in which fine solid particles are suspended in a liquid.

Competitive inhibition. Reversible inhibition of enzyme activity due to competition between a substrate and an inhibitor for the active site of the enzyme.

Compliance. The change in dimension per unit change in the applied force.

Compound eye. The multifaceted arthropod eye; the functional unit is the ommatidium.

Condensation. A reaction between two or more organic molecules leading to the formation of a larger molecule and the elimination of a simple molecule, such as water or alcohol.

Conductance. A measure of the ease with which a conductor carries an electric current; the unit is the mho, reciprocal of the ohm.

Conductivity. The intrinsic property of a substance to conduct electric current; reciprocal of resistivity.

Conductor. A material that carries electrical current.

Cone. A vertebrate visual receptor cell having a tapered outer segment in which the lamellar membranes remain continuous with the surface membrane.

Conjugate acid-base pair. Two substances related by gain or loss of an H$^+$ ion (proton).

Contracture. A more-or-less sustained contraction in response to an abnormal stimulus.

Contralateral. Pertaining to the opposite side.

Conus. A chamber invested with cardiac muscle, and found in series with and downstream from the ventricle in elasmobranchs.

Corepressor. A low-molecular-weight molecule that unites with an aporepressor to form a substance that inhibits the synthesis of an enzyme.

Corpora allata. Nonneural insect glands existing as paired organs or groups of cells dorsal and posterior to the corpus cardiaca. The corpora allata secrete juvenile hormone.

Corpora cardiaca. Major insect neurohemal organs existing as paired structures immediately posterior to the brain. They liberate brain hormone.

Corpus luteum. The yellow ovarian glandular body that arises from a mature follicle that has released its ovum; it secretes progesterone. If the ovum released has been fertilized, the corpus luteum grows and secretes during gestation; if not, it atrophies and disappears.

Cortex. External or surface layer of an organ.

Coulomb. MKS unit of electric charge; equal to the amount of charge transferred in one second by one ampere of current.

Coupled transport. Uptake of one substance into a cell that depends upon the downhill diffusion exit of another substance into the cell.

Countercurrent multiplier. A pair of opposed channels containing fluids flowing in opposed directions and having an energetic gradient directed transversely from one of the channels into the other. Since exchange due to the gradient is cumulative with distance, the exchange per unit distance will be multiplied, so to speak, as a function of the total distance over which exchange takes place.

Counterion. An ion associated with, and of opposite charge to, an ion or an ionized group of a molecule.

Covalent bond. A bond formed by electron-pair sharing between two atoms.

Creatine phosphate. A phosphorylated nitrogenous compound found primarily in muscle. Acts as a storage form of high-energy phosphate for the rapid phosphorylation of ADP to ATP.

Creatinine. Nitrogenous waste product of muscle creatine.

Cretinism. A chronic condition caused by hypothyroidism in childhood. Characterized by arrested physical and mental development.

Critical fusion frequency. The number of light flashes per second at which the light is perceived to be continuous.

Crop milk. A nutrient-rich substance fed by regurgitation to pigeon chicks by both parents.

Cross-bridge link. The thin connection between the globular head of the myosin cross bridge and the myosin thick filament.

Cross bridges. Spirally arranged projections from the myosin thick filaments that interact with the actin thin filaments during muscle contraction.

Crustecdysone. Steroid hormone which promotes molting in crabs.

Cupula. A small upside-down cup or domelike cap housing another structure; in lateral-line and equilibrium organs, the cupula covers hair cells in a gelatinous matrix.

Curare (*d*-tubocurarine). South American arrow poison; blocks synaptic transmission at motor endplate by competitive inhibition of acetycholine receptors.

Cyanide. A compound containing cyanogen and one other element. Blocks transfer of electrons from the terminal cytochrome a and a_3 to oxygen in the respiratory chain.

Cybernetics. The science of information communication and control in animals and machines.

Cyclic AMP (cAMP; 3′,5′-cyclic adenosine monophosphate). A ubiquitous cyclic nucleotide produced from ATP by the enzymatic action of adenylate cyclase; important cellular regulatory agent that acts as the "second messenger" for many hormones and transmitters.

Cyclic GMP (cGMP; guanosine 3′,5′-monophosphate). A cyclic nucleotide analogous to cAMP but present in cells at a far lower concentration and producing target cell responses that are usually opposite to those of cAMP.

Cyclostomes. A group of jawless vertebrates, including lampreys and hagfishes.

Cytochalasin. A drug that disrupts cytoplasmic microfilaments.

Cytochromes. A group of iron-containing proteins that function in the electron-transport chain in aerobic cells. They accept and pass on electrons.

Cytoplasm. The semifluid substance within a cell, exclusive of the nucleus but including other organelles.

Cytosine. Oxyamino-pyrimidine, $C_4H_5N_3O$. Base component of nucleic acid.

Cytosol. The unstructured aqueous phase of the cytoplasm between the structured organelles.

D600. α-Isopropyl-α-[(N-methyl-N-homoveratryl)-α-aminopropyl]-3,4,5-trimethoxyphenylacetonitrile; an organic drug that blocks calcium influx through cell membranes.

Dark current. Steady sodium current leaking into a visual receptor cell at the outer segment. The sodium is actively pumped out at the inner segment, completing the circuit. The dark current is reduced by photoexcitation.

Decerebration. Experimental elimination of cerebral activity by section of the brain stem or by interruption of the blood supply to the brain.

Decussation. Crossing over from one side to the other.

Dehydrogenase. An enzyme that "loosens" the hydrogen of a substrate in preparation for passage to a hydrogen receptor.

Dehydroretinal. An aldehyde of dehydroretinol.

Dalton's Law. The partial pressure of a gas in a mixture is independent of other gases present. The total pressure is the sum of the partial pressures of all gases present.

Dehydroretinol (retinol 2; vitamin A_2). The form of vitamin A occurring in the liver and retina of freshwater fish, some invertebrates, and amphibians.

Delayed (or late) outward current. Current carried by K^+ through channels that open with a time lag after onset of a depolarization. Responsible for repolarization of the action potential.

Denaturation. Alteration or destruction of the normal nature of a substance by chemical or physical means.

Dendrites. Fine processes of a neuron, often providing the main receptive area of the cell for synaptic contacts.

Deoxyhemoglobin. Hemoglobin in which oxygen is not combined to the Fe^{3+} of the heme moiety.

Depolarization. The reduction or reversal of the potential difference that exists across the cell membrane at rest.

Diabetes mellitus. A metabolic malady in which there is a partial or complete loss of activity in the pancreatic islets. The concomitant insulin insufficiency leads to inadequate uptake of glucose into cells and loss of blood glucose in the urine.

Dialysis. The process by which crystalloids and macromolecules are separated by utilizing the differences in their diffusion rates through a semipermeable membrane.

Dielectric constant. A measure of the degree to which a substance is able to store electric charge under an applied voltage. Depends on charge distribution within molecules.

Diffusion. Dispersion of atoms, molecules, or ions as a result of random thermal motion.

1,25-Dihydroxycholecalciferol. A substance that is converted from vitamin D in the liver and increases Ca^{2+} absorption by the kidney.

Dimer. A molecule made by the joining of two molecules (i.e., monomers) of the same kind.

Dinitrophenol (DNP). Any of a group of six isomers, $C_6H_3(OH)(NO_2)_2$, that act as aerobic metabolic inhibitors by virtue of their ability to uncouple oxidation from phosphorylation in mitochondrial electron transport.

Dipole. A molecule with separate regions of net negative and net positive charge, so that one end acts as a positive pole and the other as a negative pole.

Dipole moment. The electrostatic force required to align a dipolar molecule parallel to the electrostatic field. The force required increases as the separation of the molecular charges decreases.

Dissociation. Separation; resolution by thermal agitation or solvation of a substance into simpler constituents.

Dissociation constant. $K' = [H^+][A^-]/[HA]$ Empirical measure of the degree of dissociation of a conjugate acid-base pair in solution.

Distal. More distant from a point of reference in the centrifugal direction—i.e., away from the center.

Distal convoluted tubule. The renal tubules located in the rental cortex leading from (and continuous with) the ascending limb of the loop of Henle to the collecting duct.

Distance of closest approach. Shortest possible span between centers of two atoms.

Diuretic. An agent that increases urine secretion.

Divalent. Carrying an electric charge of two units; a valence of two.

DNA (deoxyribonucleic acid). Class of nucleic acids responsible for hereditary transmission and for the coding of amino acid sequences of proteins.

Donnan equilibrium. Electrochemical equilibrium that develops when two solutions are separated by a membrane permeable to only some of the ions of the solutions.

Dopamine (hydroxytyramine). A product of the decarboxylation of dopa, an intermediate in norepinephrine synthesis; possibly a central nervous system transmitter.

Dorsal root. A nerve trunk that enters the spinal cord near the dorsal surface. Contains sensory axons only.

Duodenum. The initial section of the small intestine, situated between the pylorus of the stomach and the jejunum.

Dwarfism. An abnormally small size in humans; a result of insufficient growth hormone secretion during childhood and adolescence.

Dynein. A ciliary protein with Mg-activated ATPase activity.

Dynein arms. Projections from tubule A of one microtubule doublet toward tubule B of the next, composed of a protein exhibiting ATPase activity.

Dyspnea. Labored, difficult breathing.

Early inward current. Depolarizing current of excitable tissues, carried by Na^+ or Ca^{2+}. Responsible for the upstroke of the action potential.

Early receptor potential (ERP). An almost instantaneous potential change recorded from the retina in response to a short flash of light that probably corresponds to a movement of charge that occurs as the photopigment undergoes conformational change.

Eccentric cell. In the ommatidium of *Limulus*, the afferent neuron that is surrounded by retinular cells.

Ecdysone. A steroid hormone secreted by the thoracic gland of arthropods that induces molting.

Ectopic pacemaker. A pacemaker situated outside the area where it is normally found.

Edema. Retention of interstitial fluid in organs or tissues.

EDTA. Ethylenedinitrilo tetraacetic acid; a calcium- and magnesium-chelating agent.

Effector. A tissue or organ that produces a response (i.e., contraction, secretion, etc.) to nerve signals or to a hormone.

Efferent. Centrifugal; carrying away from a center.

EGTA. Ethyleneglycol-*bis* (в-aminoethylether)-*N*, *N*'-tetraacetic acid, a calcium-chelating agent.

Elastic. Capable of being distorted, stretched, or compressed with subsequent spontaneous return to original shape; resilience.

Electric potential. Electrostatic pressure, analogous to water pressure. A potential difference (i.e., voltage) across a resistance is required for the flow of current.

Electrocardiogram. The record of electrical events associated with contractions of the heart; obtained with electrodes placed on other portions of the body.

Electrochemical equilibrium. The state at which the concentration gradient of an ion across a membrane is precisely balanced by the electric potential.

Electrode. An electrical circuit element used to make contact with a solution, a tissue, or a cell interior. Used either to measure potential or to carry current.

Electrogenic. Giving rise to an electric current or voltage.

Electrolyte. A compound that dissociates into ions when dissolved in water.

Electromotive force (emf). The potential difference across the terminals of a battery or other source of electric energy.

Electron shells. Energy levels of electrons surrounding the nucleus.

Electron-transport chain (respiratory chain). A series of enzymes that transfer electrons from substrate molecules to molecular oxygen.

Electronegativity. Affinity for electrons.

Electroneutrality rule. For a net potential of zero, the positive and negative charges must add up to zero. A solution must contain essentially as many anionic as cationic charges.

Electro-osmosis. Movement of water through a membrane of fixed charge in response to a potential gradient.

Electroretinogram (ERG). An electrical signal recorded from the cornea of the eye; it represents the total activity of the visual receptors and neurons.

Electrotonic potential. Potential generated locally by currents flowing across the membrane; not actively propagated and not all-or-none.

Endergonic. Characterized by a concomitant absorption of energy.

Endocardium. The internal lining of the heart chamber.

Endocrine glands. Ductless organs or tissues that secrete a hormone into the circulation.

Endolymph. Aqueous liquid with a high K^+ concentration found in the scala media of the cochlea.

Endometrium. An epithelium that lines the uterus.

Endplate. The traditional name of the vertebrate neuromuscular synapse, where the motor axon ramifies into fine terminal branches over a specialized system of folds in the postsynaptic membrane of the muscle cell.

End-product (feedback) inhibition. Inhibition of a biosynthetic pathway by the end product of the pathway.

Energy. Capacity to perform work.

Enterogastrone. A hormone that is secreted from the duodenal mucosa in response to fat ingestion and which suppresses a gastric motility and secretion.

Entropy. Measure of that portion of energy not available for work in a closed system; measure of molecular randomness. Entropy increases with time in all irreversible processes.

Enzyme. Protein with catalytic properties.

Enzyme activity. A measure of the catalytic potency of an enzyme: the number of substrate molecules that react per minute per enzyme molecule.

Enzyme induction. Enzyme production stimulated by the specific substrate (inducer) of that enzyme or by a molecule structurally similar to the substrate.

Epicardium. The external covering of the heart wall.

Epididymis. A long, string-like duct along the dorsal edge of the testis, its function is to store sperm.

Epinephrine. Generic name for the catecholamine released from the adrenal cortex; also known by the trade name Adrenalin.

Equilibrium. The state in which a system is in balance due to equal action by opposing forces arising from within the system.

Equilibrium potential. That voltage difference across a membrane at which the ionic species in question is in electrochemical equilibrium; it is dependent on the concentration gradient of the ions, as described by the Nernst equation.

Equimolar. Having the same molarity.

Eserine (physostigmine). An alkaloid ($C_{15}H_{21}N_3O_2$) of plant origin that blocks the enzyme cholinesterase.

Estradiol-17β. The most active natural estrogen.

Estrogens. A family of female sex steroids responsible for producing estrus and the female secondary sex characteristics. It also prepares the reproductive system for fertilization and implantation of the ovum. Synthesized primarily in the ovary, although some is made in the adrenal cortex and male testis.

Estrus cycle. Periodic episodes of "heat," or estrus, marked by sexual receptivity in mature females of most mammalian species.

Ethers. A class of compounds in which two organic groups are joined by an oxygen atom, R_1—O—R_2.

Eupnea. Normal breathing.

Euryhaline. Able to tolerate wide variations in salinity.

Exchange diffusion. A process by which the movement of one molecule across a membrane enhances the movement of another molecule in the opposite direction. Most likely involves a common-carrier molecule.

Excitability. The property of altered membrane conductance (and often membrane potential) in response to stimulation.

Excitation-contraction coupling. The process by which electrical excitation of the surface membrane leads to activation of the contractile process in muscle.

Excitation-secretion coupling. The concept that depolarization brings about secretion of transmitter at nerve endings by one or more intermediate steps known to include the influx of extracellular Ca^{+2}.

Excitatory. In neurophysiology, pertaining to the enhanced probability of producing an action potential.

Exergonic. Characterized by a concomitant release of heat energy.

Exocrine gland. A gland that secretes a fluid via a duct.

Exocytosis. Fusion of the vesicle membrane to the surface membrane and subsequent expulsion of the vesicle contents to the cell exterior.

Extensor. A muscle that extends or straightens a limb or other extremity.

Exteroceptors. Sense organs that detect stimuli arriving at the surface of the body from a distance.

Facilitation. An increase in the efficacy of a synapse as the result of a preceding activation of that synapse.

Facilitated, or carrier-mediated, diffusion. Downhill transmembrane diffusion aided by a carrier molecule that enhances the mobility of the diffusing substance in the membrane.

Farad. The unit of electrical capacitance (F).

Faraday. *See* Faraday's constant.

Faraday's constant (*F*). The equivalent charge of a mole of electrons, equal to 9.649×10^{-4} coulombs per mole of electrons.

Feedback. The return of output to the input part of a system. In *negative feedback,* the sign of the output is inverted before being fed back to the input so as to stabilize the output. In *positive feedback,* the output is unstable because it is returned to the input without a sign inversion, and thus becomes self-reinforcing, or regenerative.

Fermentation. Enzymatic decomposition; anaerobic transformation of nutrients without net oxidation or electron transfer.

Ferritin. A large protein molecule opaque to electrons, used as a marker in electron microscopy; normally present in the spleen as a storage protein for iron.

Fibrillar muscle. Oscillatory insect flight muscle; also termed asynchronous muscle because contractions are not individually controlled by motor impulses.

Fibroblast. A connective tissue cell that can differentiate into chrondroblasts, collagenoblasts, and osteoblasts.

Final common pathway. The concept that the sum total of neural integrative activity expressed in motor output is channeled through the motoneurons to the muscles.

Firing level. Potential threshold for the generation of an action potential.

First Law of Thermodynamics. Net energy is conserved in any process.

First-order enzyme kinetics. Describes enzymatic reactions, the rates of which are directly proportional to one reactant's concentration (either substrate or product).

Flagellum. A motile, whip-like organelle similar in organization to a cilium, but longer and generally present on a cell only in small numbers.

Flame cells. Flagellated cells at the ending of the excretory collecting tubules of flatworms and nemerteans.

Flavin adenine dinucleotide (FAD). A coenzyme formed by the condensation of riboflavin phosphate and adenylic acid; it performs an important function in electron transport and is a prosthetic group for some enzymes.

Flavoproteins. Proteins combined with flavin prosthetic groups important as intermediate carriers of electrons between the dehydrogenases and cytochromes in the respiratory chain.

Flexor. A muscle that flexes or bends an extremity.

Fluorescence. The property of emitting light upon molecular excitation by an incident light. The emitted light is always less energetic (has a longer wavelength) than the light producing the excitation.

Flux. Rate of flow of matter or energy across a unit area.

Follicle. A sac, cavity, or depression.

Follicle-stimulating hormone (FSH). An anterior pituitary gonadotropin that stimulates the development of ovarian follicles in the female and testicular spermatogenesis in the male.

Follicular phase. That part of the estrus and menstrual cycles that is characterized by formation of and secretion by the Graafian follicles.

Foramen. An orifice or opening.

Fovea. A depression in the center of the retina containing closely packed cone cells.

Free energy. The energy available to do work at a given temperature and pressure.

Fructose. A ketohexose, $C_6H_{12}O_6$, found in honey and many fruits.

Fusimotor system. The gamma motoneurons and the intrafusal fibers that they innervate.

Gain. The increase in signal produced by amplification.

Gamma aminobutyric acid (GABA). Inhibitory transmitter identified in crustacean motor-synapses and in the vertebrate central nervous system.

Gamma efferents. The motor axons innervating the intrafusal muscle fibers of spindle organs.

Gamma motoneurons. Nerve cells of the ventral spinal cord that innervate the intrafusal muscle fibers.

Gamma rays. Electromagnetic radiation of very short wavelength (10^{-12} cm) and very high energy.

Ganglion. An anatomically distinct concentration of neuron cell bodies.

Ganglion cells. A nonspecific term applied to some nerve cell bodies, especially those located in ganglia of invertebrates or outside the vertebrate central nervous system proper.

Gap junctions. Specializations for electrical coupling between cells, where intercellular spacing is only about 20 Å and tubular assemblies of particles connect the apposed membranes.

Gastric juice. Fluid secreted by the cells of the gastric epithelium.

Gastrin. A protein hormone that is liberated by the gastrin cells of the pyloric gland and induces gastric secretion and motility.

Geiger counter. An instrument that detects the presence of ionizing radiation.

Generator potential. A receptor potential that depolarizes the spike-initiating zone of an axon.

Geniculate body. A projection of the geniculate nucleus that relays incoming sensory information to the cortex. Named for its knee-like shape in cross section.

Gestation. Pertaining to pregnancy.

Gigantism. Excessive growth due to pituitary GH hypersecretion from birth.

Glomerular filtration rate (GFR; inulin clearance). The amount of total glomerular filtrate produced per minute by all nephrons of both kidneys. Equal to the clearance of a freely filtered and nonresorbed substance such as inulin.

Glomerulus. A coiled mass of capillaries.

Glucagon. A protein hormone released by the alpha cells of the pancreatic islets. Its secretion is induced by low blood sugar or by growth hormone. Stimulates glycogenolysis in the liver.

Glucocorticoids. Steroids synthesized in the adrenal cortex with wide-ranging metabolic activity. Included are cortisone, cortisol, corticosterone, and 11-deoxycorticosterone.

Gluconeogenesis. Synthesis of carbohydrates from noncarbohydrate sources, such as fatty acids or amino acids.

Glutamate. A putative excitatory synaptic transmitter in the vertebrate central nervous system and in arthropod neuromuscular junctions.

Glycogen synthetase. An enzyme that catalyzes the polymerization of glucose to glycogen.

Glycogenesis. The synthesis of glycogen.

Glycogenolysis. The breakdown of glycogen to glucose-6-phosphate.

Glycolipid. A lipid containing carbohydrate groups, in most cases galactose.

Glycolysis (Embden-Meyerhof pathway). The metabolic pathway by which hexose and triose sugars are broken down to simpler substances, especially pyruvate or lactate.

Glycosuria (glucosuria). The excretion of excessive amounts of glucose in the urine.

Goiter. An abnormal increase in size of the thyroid gland, usually due to a dietary lack of iodine.

Golgi tendon organs. Tension-sensing nerve endings of the lb afferent fibers found in muscle tendons.

Gonadotropic (-phic) hormones. (gonadotropins). Hormones that influence the activity of the gonads; in particular, those secreted by the anterior pituitary.

Graafian follicle. A mature ovarian follicle in which fluid is accumulating.

Graded response. One that increases as a function of the energy applied. A membrane response that is not all-or-none.

Graham's Law. The rate of diffusion of a gas is proportional to the square root of the density of that gas.

Gray matter. Tissue of the central nervous system consisting of cell bodies, unmyelinated fibers, and glial cells.

Growth hormone (GH; somatotropin). A protein hormone that is secreted by the anterior pituitary and stimulates growth. It directly influences protein, fat, and carbohydrate metabolism and regulates growth rate.

Guanine. 2-amino-6-oxypurine, $C_5H_5N_5O$, a white, crystalline base; a breakdown product of nucleic acids.

Guano. White, pasty waste product of birds and reptiles; high in uric acid content.

Guanosine triphosphate (GTP). A high-energy molecule similar to ATP that participates in several energy-requiring processes, such as peptide bond formation.

Guanylate cyclase. An enzyme that converts GTP to cyclic GMP.

Gustation. The sense of taste; chemoreception of ions and molecules in solution by specialized epithelial sensory receptors.

H-zone. The light zone in the center of the muscle sarcomere, where the myosin filaments are not overlapped by actin filaments; the region between actin filaments.

Habituation. The progressive loss of behavioral response probability with repetition of a stimulus.

Hair cell. Mechanosensory epithelial cell bearing stereocilia and in some cases a kinocilium.

Halide. A binary compound of a halogen and another element.

Halogens. A family of related elements that form similar salt-like compounds with most metals. They are fluorine, chlorine, bromine, and iodine.

Heat. Energy in the form of molecular or atomic vibration that is transferred by conduction, convection, and radiation down a thermal gradient.

Heat of shortening. Thermal energy associated with muscle contraction. It is proportional to the distance the muscle has shortened.

Heat of vaporization. Heat necessary per mass unit of a given liquid to convert all of the liquid to gas at its boiling point.

Heavy meromyosin (HMM; H-meromyosin). The "head" and "neck" of the myosin molecule, the portion containing ATPase activity.

Helicotrema. The opening that connects the scala tympani and the scala vestibuli at the cochlear apex.

Hematocrit. The percentage of total blood volume occupied by red blood cells. In humans, the hematocrit is normally 40–50%.

Heme. $C_{34}H_{33}O_4N_4FeOH$, an iron protoporphyrin portion of many respiratory pigments.

Hemerythrin. An invertebrate respiratory pigment that is a protein but does not contain heme.

Hemocyanin. An invertebrate respiratory pigment that is a protein, contains copper, and is found in mollusks and crustaceans.

Hemolymph. The blood of invertebrates with open circulatory systems.

Henderson-Hasselbach equation. pH = pK + log ([H^+ acceptor]/[H^+ donor]). Formula for calculation of the pH of a buffer solution.

Henry's Law. The quantity of gas that dissolves in a liquid is nearly proportional to the partial pressure of that gas in the gas phase.

Hering-Breuer reflex. A reflex in which lung inflation activates lung stretch receptors that inhibit further inspiration during that cycle. Activity from stretch receptors is carried in the vagus nerve.

Hertz. Cycle(s) per second (Hz).

Hexose. A 6-carbon monosaccharide.

Histaminergic. Refers to nerves that release histamine.

Histone. A simple, repeating, basic protein that combines with DNA.

Hodgkin cycle. The regenerative or positive-feedback loop responsible for the up stroke of the action potential: depolarization causes an increase in the Na permeability, permitting an increased influx of Na^+, which further depolarizes the membrane.

Homeotherms. Animals that regulate their own internal temperature within a narrow range, regardless of the ambient temperature; mammals and birds.

Homonymous. Pertaining to the same origin.

Horizontal cell. A nerve cell whose fibers extend horizontally in the outer plexiform layer of the retina.

Hormone. A chemical compound synthesized and secreted by an endocrine tissue into the blood stream. Influences the activity of a target tissue.

Horseradish peroxidase. A large protein molecule that is opaque in the electron microscope.

Hydration. Combination with water.

Hydride. Any compound consisting of an element or radical combined with hydrogen.

Hydrofuge. Pertains to structures with nonwetting surfaces.

Hydrogen bond. A weak electrostatic attraction between a hydrogen atom bound to a highly electronegative element in a molecule to another highly electronegative atom in the same or a different molecule.

Hydrolysis. Fragmentation or splitting of a compound by the addition of water, whereupon the hydroxyl group joins one fragment and the hydrogen atom the other.

Hydronium ion. A hydrogen ion (H^+) combined with a water molecule; H_3O^+.

Hydrophilic. Having an affinity for water.

Hydrophobic. Lacking an affinity for water.

Hydrostatic pressure. Force exerted over an area due to pressure in a fluid.

Hydroxyl group (or radical). The $-OH^-$ group.

Hypercalcemia. Excessive plasma calcium levels.

Hypercapnia. Increased levels of carbon dioxide.

Hyperemia. Increased blood flow to a tissue or organ.

Hyperglycemia. Excessive blood glucose levels.

Hyperpnea. Increased lung ventilation; hyperventilation.

Hyperpolarization. An increase in potential difference across a membrane, making the cell interior more negative than it is at rest.

Hyperosmotic. Containing a greater concentration of osmotically active constituents than the solution of reference.

Hypertrophy. Excessive growth or development of an organ or tissue.

Hyperventilation. *See* Hyperpnea.

Hypoglycemia. Low blood glucose levels.

Hypophysis. The pituitary gland.

Hypopnea. Hypoventilation; decreased lung ventilation.

Hypoosmotic. Containing a lower concentration of osmotically active constituents than the solution of reference.

Hypothalamicohypophysial relay system. Portal veins linking the capillaries of the hypothalamic median eminence with those of the adenohypophysis. These transport hypothalamic neurosecretions directly to the adenohypophysis.

Hypothalamus. The part of the diencephalon that forms the floor of the median ventricle of the brain. It includes the optic chiasm, mamillary bodies, tuber cinereum, and infundibulum.

Hypothyroidism. Reduced thyroid activity.

Hypoxia. Reduced oxygen levels.

I-band. The region between the A-band and Z-disc of a muscle sarcomere that appears light when viewed microscopically. It contains the actin thin filaments without overlap from the myosin filaments.

Impedance. The dynamic resistance to flow met by fluids moving in a pulsatile manner.

Impulse-initiating region (spike-initiating zone). The proximal portion of the axon, which has a lower threshold for action potential generation than either the soma or the dendrites.

Infrared. Thermal radiation. Electromagnetic radiation of wavelengths greater than 7.7×10^{-5} cm and less than 12×10^{-4} cm; the region between red light and radio waves.

Inhibitory. In neurophysiology, pertaining to a reduction in probability of generating an action potential.

Initial segment. The portion of axon and axon hillock proximal to the first myelinated segment; generally the site of impulse initiation.

Inner segment. The portion of a vertebrate photoreceptor cell that contains the cell organelles and synaptic contacts.

Instinct. A species-specific set of unlearned behaviors and responses.

Insulin. A protein hormone synthesized and secreted by the beta cells of the pancreatic islets. It controls cellular uptake of carbohydrate and influences lipid and amino acid metabolism.

Integration, neural. Synthesis of an output based on the sum of inputs to a neuron or neural network.

Interneuron. A nerve cell connecting two or more other neurons.

Interstitial. Between cells or tissues.

Interstitial cell-stimulating hormone (ICSH). Identical to luteinizing hormone, but in the male.

Intrafusal fibers. The muscle fibers located within a muscle spindle organ.

Inulin. An indigestible vegetable starch. Used in studies of kidney function because it is freely filtered and not actively transported.

In vitro. "In a glass"; in an artificial environment outside the body.

In vivo. Within the living organism or tissue.

Iodoacetic acid. An agent that poisons glycolysis by inhibiting glyceraldehyde phosphate dehydrogenase.

Ion. An atom bearing a net charge due to loss or gain of electrons.

Ion battery. The emf capable of driving an ionic current across a membrane; results from unequal concentrations of an ion species in the two compartments separated by the membrane.

Ion exchanger site (or ion-binding site). An electrostatically charged site that attracts ions of the opposite charge.

Ionic bond. Electrostatic bond.

Ionization. The dissociation into ions of a compound in solution.

Ionophores. Molecules that carry certain ions or molecules across membranes, sometimes having a donut-like configuration.

Ipsilateral. Relating to the same side.

Iris. The pigmented circular diaphragm located behind the cornea of the vertebrate eye.

Ischemia. The absence of blood flow (to an organ or tissue).

Islets of Langerhans. Microscopic endocrine structures dispersed throughout the pancreas. They consist of three cell types: the alpha cells, which secrete glucagon; the beta cells, which secrete insulin; and the delta cells.

Isoelectric point. The pH of a solution at which an amphoteric molecule has a net charge of zero.

Isomer. A compound having the same chemical formula as another, but with a different arrangement of its atoms.

Isometric contraction. Contraction during which the muscle does not shorten significantly.

Isosmotic. Having the same osmotic pressure.

Isoteric interaction. Chemical interaction involving molecules with the same number of valence electrons in the same configuration but made up of different types and numbers of atoms.

Isotonic contraction. Contraction in which force remains constant while the muscle shortens.

Isotope. Any of two or more forms of an element with the same number of protons (atomic number) but a different number of neutrons (atomic weight).

Isovolumetric. Having the same volume.

Juvenile hormone (JH). A class of insect hormones that are secreted by the corpora allata and which promote retention of juvenile characteristics.

Juxtaglomerular cells. Specialized secretory cells situated in the afferent glomerular arterioles. They act as receptors that respond to low blood pressure by secreting renin, which converts angiotensinogen to angiotensin, resulting in the stimulation of aldosterone secretion.

Kelvin. *See* Absolute temperature.

Ketones. Compounds having a carboxyl group (CO) attached (by the carbon) to hydrocarbon groups.

Ketone bodies. Acetone, acetoacetic acid, and β-hydroxybutyric acid. Products of fat and pyruvate metabolism formed from acetyl-CoA in the liver. They are oxidized in muscle and by the central nervous system during starvation.

Kinematic viscosity. Viscosity divided by density. Gases of equal kinematic viscosity will become turbulent at equal flow rates in identical airways.

Kinetic energy. Energy inherent in the motion of a mass.

Kininogen. Precursor of bradykinin.

Kinocilium. A true "9 + 2" cilium present in sensory hair cells.

Kirchhoff's Laws. *First law:* The sum of the currents entering a junction in a circuit equals the sum of the currents leaving the junction. *Second law:* The sum of the potential changes encountered in any closed loop in a circuit is equal to zero.

Labeled lines concept. Sensory modalities are determined by the stimulus sensitivity of peripheral sense organs and the anatomical specificities of their central connections.

Lamella. A thin sheet or leaf.

Laminar flow. Fluid flow in which the direction of motion in neighboring regions is the same.

Larva. The immature, active feeding stage characteristic of many invertebrates.

Lateral inhibition. Reciprocal suppression of excitation by neighboring neurons in a sensory network. The effect is enhanced lateral contrast and an increase in dynamic range.

Lateral-line system. Series of hair cells (see *neuromast*) on the medial wall of canals running the length of the head and body of fish and many amphibians. These channels have openings to the outside; the system is sensitive to water movement.

Law of Laplace. The transmural pressure in a thin-walled tube is proportional to the wall tension divided by the inner radius of the tube.

Lecithin. A group of phospholipids found in animal and plant tissues; composed of choline, phosphoric acid, fatty acids, and glycerol.

Length constant (λ). Distance along a cell over which a potential change decays in amplitude by $1 - 1/e$ or 63%.

Leucocytes. White blood cells.

Leydig cells (interstitial cells). Cells of the testes that are stimulated by LH to secrete testosterone.

Light meromyosin (LMM). The rod-like fragment of the myosin molecule that constitutes most of the molecule's backbone.

Lipid. Fatty acids, neutral fats, waxes, steroids, and phosphatides. Lipids are hydrophobic and feel greasy.

Lipogenesis. The formation of fat from nonlipid sources.

Lipophilic. Having an affinity for lipids.

Local circuit current. The current that spreads electrotonically from the excited portion of an axon during conduction of the nerve impulse, flowing longitudinally along the axon, across the membrane, and back to the excited portion.

Loop of Henle. A U-shaped bend in the portion of a renal tubule that lies in the renal medulla.

Lumen. The interior of a cavity or duct.

Luteal phase. The part of the estrus or menstrual cycle characterized by formation of and secretion by the corpus luteum.

Luteinizing hormone (LH). A gonadotropin that is secreted by the adenohypophysis and which acts with FSH to induce ovulation of the ripe ovum and liberation of estrogen from the ovary. It also influences formation of the corpus luteum and stimulates growth in and secretion from the male testicular Leydig cells.

Lysolecithin. A lecithin without the terminal acid group.

Lysosome. Minute electron-opaque organelles in many cell types that contain hydrolytic enzymes and are normally involved in localized intracellular digestion.

Malpighian tubules. Insect excretory-osmoregulatory organs responsible for the active secretion of waste products and formation of urine.

Mass Action Law. The velocity of a chemical reaction is proportional to the active masses of the reactants.

Mastoid bone. Posterior process of the temporal bone, situated behind the ear and in front of the occipital bone.

Mechanism. A theory that proposes that life is based purely on the action of physical and chemical laws.

Mechanoreceptors. A sensory receptor sensitive to mechanical distortion or pressure.

Median eminence. A structure at the base of the hypothalamus that is continuous with the hypophyseal stalk. It contains the primary capillary plexus of the hypothalamico-hypophyseal portal system.

Medulla oblongata. A cone-shaped neural mass connecting the pons and spinal cord.

Medullary cardiovascular center. A group of neurons in the medulla involved in the integration of information used in the control and regulation of the circulation.

Melanocyte- or **melanophore-stimulating hormone.** A peptide hormone released by the adenohypophysis that effects melanin distribution in mammals and creates skin-color changes in fish, amphibians, and reptiles.

Melting point. The lowest temperature at which a solid will begin to liquify.

Membrane potential. The electrical potential measured from within the cell relative to the potential of the extracellular fluid, which is by convention at zero potential. The potential difference between opposite sides of the membrane.

Menarche. The onset of the menstruation during puberty.

Menopause. The cessation of the menstrual cycle in the mature female human.

Menstrual cycle. Recurring physiological changes that include menstruation.

Menstruation. The shedding of the endometrium, an event that usually occurs in the absence of conception throughout the fertile period of the female of certain primate species, including humans.

Messenger RNA (mRNA). A fraction of RNA that is responsible for transmission of the informational base sequence of the DNA to the ribosomes.

Metabolism. The totality of physical and chemical processes involved in anabolism, catabolism, and cell energetics.

Metabolic pathway. A sequence of enzymatic reactions involved in the alteration of one substance into another.

Metabolic water. Water evolved from cellular oxidation.

Metachronism. The progression of in-phase activity in a wave-like manner over a population of organelles, such as cilia.

Metamorphic climax. The last stage of amphibian metamorphosis, in which the adult form is attained.

Metamorphosis. A change in morphology—in particular, from one stage of development to another, such as juvenile to adult.

Metarhodopsin. Product of the absorption of light by rhodopsin. It decomposes to opsin and *trans*-retinal.

Methemoglobin. Hemoglobin in which the Fe^{3+} of heme has been oxidized to Fe^{2+}.

Mho. The unit of electrical conductance. Reciprocal of the ohm.

Micelle. A microscopic particle made from an aggregation of amphipathic molecules in solution.

Michaelis-Menten constant (K_M). The concentration (moles/liter) of the substrate at half the maximal velocity of an enzymatic reaction.

Microfilaments. Filaments within the cytoplasmic substance with a diameter of less than 100 Å.

Microtubules. Cylindrical cytoplasmic structures made of polymerized tubulin and found in many cells, especially motile cells, as constituents of the mitotic spindle, cilia, and flagella.

Microvilli. Tiny cylindrical projections on a cell surface that function to increase surface area. They are frequently found on absorptive epithelia.

Micturition. Urination.

Mineralocorticoids. Steroid hormones that are synthesized and secreted by the adrenal cortex and which influence plasma electrolyte balance—in particular, by sodium and chloride resorption in the kidney tubules. *See also* Aldosterone.

Miniature endplate potentials (m.e.p.p.'s). Tiny depolarizations (generally 1 mv or less) of the postsynaptic membrane of a motor endplate; produced by presynaptic release of single packets of transmitter.

Miniature postsynaptic potentials (m.p.p.'s). Potentials produced in a postsynaptic neuron by presynaptic release of single vesicles of transmitter substance.

Mobility. A quantity proportional to the migration rate of an ion in an electric field.

Molality. The number of moles of solute in a kilogram of a pure solvent.

Molarity. The number of moles of solute in a liter of solution.

Mole. Avogadro's number (6.023×10^{23}) of molecules of an element or compound; equal to the molecular weight in grams.

Monomer. A compound capable of combining in repeating units to form a dimer, trimer, or polymer.

Monopole. An object or particle bearing a single unneutralized electric change, as, for example, an ion.

Monosaccharide sugar. An unhydrolyzable carbohydrate; a simple sugar. They are sweet-tasting, colorless crystalline compounds with the formula $C_n(H_2O)_n$. *See also* saccharide.

Monosynaptic. Relating to or transmitted through one synapse only.

Monovalent. Having a valence of one.

Monozygotic. Arising from one ovum or zygote.

Motoneuron (motor neuron). A nerve cell that innervates muscle cells.

Motor cortex. The part of the cerebral cortex that controls motor function; situated anterior to the central sulcus, which separates the frontal and parietal lobes.

Motor program. An endogenous coordinated motor output of central neural origin and independent of sensory feedback.

Motor unit. The unit of motor activity consisting of a motoneuron and the muscle fibers it innervates.

Mucosa. Mucous membrane facing a cavity or the exterior of the body.

Müllerian ducts. Paired embryonic ducts originating from the peritoneum that connect with the urogenital sinus to develop into the uterus and Fallopian tubes.

Multineuronal innervation. Innervation of a muscle fiber by several motoneurons, as in many invertebrates, especially arthropods.

Multiterminal innervation. Numerous synapses made by a single motoneuron along the length of a muscle fiber.

Muscle fiber. A skeletal muscle cell.

Muscle spindle (stretch receptor). A length-sensitive receptor organ located between and in parallel with extrafusal muscle fibers. Gives rise to the myotatic or stretch reflex of vertebrates.

Mutation. A transmissible alteration in genetic material.

Myelin sheath. Layers of Schwann cell membrane wrapped tightly around segments of axon in vertebrate nerve. Serves as electrical insulation in saltatory conduction.

Myoblasts. Embryonic cell precursor for muscle.

Myocardium. Heart muscle.

Myofibril. Longitudinal unit of muscle function made up of sarcomeres and surrounded by sarcoplasmic reticulum.

Myogenic pacemaker. A pacemaker that is a specialized muscle cell.

Myoglobin. Iron-containing protoporphyrin-globin complex found in muscle. Serves as a reservoir for oxygen. Gives muscle its pink color.

Myosin. The protein that makes up the thick filaments and cross bridges of the A-band.

Myotatic (or stretch) reflex. Reflex contraction of a muscle in response to stretch.

Myotube: A developing muscle fiber.

Nares. Nostrils.

Nephron. The morphological and functional unit of the vertebrate kidney. It is composed of the glomerulus and Bowman's capsule, the proximal and distal tubules, the loop of Henle (birds, mammals), and the collecting duct.

Nernst equation. Equation for calculating the potential difference across a membrane that will balance the osmotic gradient of an ion.

Nerve. As a noun, it means a bundle of axons held together as a unit by connective tissue; as an adjective, it means "neural."

Neural network. A system of interacting nerve cells.

Neurilemma. Connective tissue sheath covering a bundle of axons.

Neurin. A filamentous protein found attached to the inner surface of the plasmalemma of nerve endings in the brain. It is similar to muscle actin and may play a role in exocytosis. *See also* Neurostennin.

Neurogenic pacemaker. A pacemaker that is a specialized nerve cell.

Neuroglia. Inexcitable supporting tissue of the nervous system; also termed *glia*.

Neurohemal organ. Organs for storage and discharge into the blood of the products of neurosecretion.

Neurohumor. Synaptic transmitters and neurosecretory hormones.

Neurohypophysis (pars nervosa). A neurally derived reservoir for hormones with antidiuretic and oxytocic action. Consists of the neural stalk, which is connected to and passes neurosecretions from the hypothalamus, and the neural lobe, which makes up the bulk of the neurohypophysis.

Neuromast. Collections of hair cells embedded in a cupula in lateral-line mechanoreceptors of the lower vertebrates.

Neuron. Nerve cell.

Neurophysins. Proteins associated with neurohypophysial hormones stored in granules in the neurosecretory terminals. Cleaved from the hormones before secretion.

Neuropil. A dense mass of closely interwoven and synapsing nerve cell processes (axon collaterals and dendrites) and glial cells.

Neurosecretory cells. Nerve cells that liberate neurohormones.

Neurostennin. (*see* Neurin and Stennin). A complex of two proteins found in brain nerve cell endings, possibly associated with exocytosis.

Neurotransmitter. A chemical mediator released by a presynaptic nerve ending that interacts with receptor molecules in the postsynaptic membrane. This generally induces a permeability increase to an ion or ions and thereby influences the electrical activity of the postsynaptic cell.

Nicotinamide adenine dinucleotide (NAD). A coenzyme widely distributed in living organisms, participating in many enzymatic reactions. Made up of adenine, nicotinamide, and two molecules each of *d*-ribose and phosphoric acid.

Node of Ranvier. Regularly spaced interruptions (about every millimeter) of the myelin sheath along an axon.

Noncompetitive inhibition. Enzyme inhibition due to alteration or destruction of the active site.

Norepinephrine (noradrenalin). A neurohumor secreted by the peripheral sympathetic nerve terminals, some cells of the central nervous system, and the adrenal medulla.

Nucleic acid. Nucleotide polymers of high molecular weight. *See* DNA and RNA.

Nucleotide. A product of enzymatic (nuclease) splitting of nucleic acids. Nucleotides are made up of a purine or pyrimidine base, a ribose or deoxyribose sugar, and a phosphate group.

Nucleus. *Of an atom:* The central, positively charged mass surrounded by a cloud of electrons. *Of a cell:* The membrane-bound body within eucaryotic cells that houses the genetic material of the cell. *Of nerve cells:* A related group of neurons in the central nervous system.

Nymph. A juvenile developmental stage in some arthropods; morphology resembles the adult.

Nystatin. A rod-shaped, antibiotic molecule that creates channels through membranes that allow the passage of molecules of a diameter less than 4 Å.

Obligatory osmotic exchange. An exchange between an animal and its environment that is determined by physical factors beyond the animal's control.

Occipital lobe. The most posterior region of the cerebral hemisphere.

Ohm. The MKS unit of electrical resistance, equivalent to the resistance of a column of mercury one millimeter square in cross section and 106 centimeters long.

Ohm's Law. $I = V/R$; the strength of an electric current, I, varies directly as the voltage, V, and inversely as the resistance, R.

Olfaction. The sense of smell; chemoreception of molecules suspended in air.

Ommatidium. The functional unit of the invertebrate compound eye, consisting of an elongated structure with a lens, focusing cone, and photoreceptor cells.

Oocyte. A developing ovum.

Operator gene. A gene that regulates the synthetic activity of closely linked structural genes via its association with a regulator gene.

Operon. A segment of DNA consisting of an operator gene and its associated structural genes.

Opsin. Protein moiety of visual pigments; it combines with 11-*cis* retinal to become a visual pigment.

Optic axis. An imaginary straight line passing through the center of curvature of a simple lens.

Optic chiasma. A swelling under the hypothalamus, where the two optic nerves meet and the optic fibers from the nasal portions of the retinae cross to the contralateral sides of the brain.

Organ of Corti. The tissue in the cochlear channel of the inner ear that contains the hair cells.

Ornithine cycle (urea cycle). A cyclic succession of reactions that eliminate ammonia and produce urea in the liver of ureotelic organisms.

Osmoconformer. An organism that exhibits little or no osmoregulation, so that the osmolarity of its body fluids follows changes in the osmolarity of the environment.

Osmole. The standard unit of osmotic pressure.

Osmometer. An instrument for the measurement of the osmotic pressure of a solution.

Osmoregulation. Maintenance of internal osmolarity with respect to the environment.

Osmoregulator. An organism that controls its internal osmolarity in the face of changes in environmental osmolarity.

Osmosis. The movement of pure solvent from a solution of a low solute concentration to one of higher concentration through a semipermeable membrane separating the two solutions.

Osmotic flow. The solvent flux due to osmotic pressure.

Osmotic pressure. Pressure that can potentially be created by osmosis between two solutions separated by a semipermeable membrane; the amount of pressure necessary to prevent osmotic flow between the two solutions.

Ossicles. Little bones. Auditory ossicles are the tiny bones (malleus, incus, stapes) of the middle ear, which transmit sound vibrations from the tympanic membrane to the oval window.

Ouabain. Cardiac glycoside, a drug capable of blocking some sodium pumps.

Outer segment. That portion of a vertebrate visual receptor that contains the pigmented receptor membranes. Attached to the inner segment by a thin cilium-like connection.

Oval window. An opening in the inside wall of the middle ear, closed by the base of the stapes.

Overshoot. The reversal of membrane potential during an action potential. The voltage above zero to the peak of the action potential.

Ovulation. The release of an ovum from the ovarian follicle.

Ovum. An egg cell; the reproductive cell (gamete) of the female.

Oxidant. An electron acceptor in a reaction involving oxidation and reduction.

Oxidation. Loss of electrons or the increase in net positivity of an atom or molecule. Biological oxidations are usually achieved by removal of a pair of hydrogen atoms from a molecule.

Oxidative phosphorylation (respiratory chain phosphorylation). The formation of high-energy phosphate bonds via phosphorylation of ADP to ATP, accompanied by the transport of electrons to oxygen from the substrate.

Oxygen debt. The extra oxygen necessary to oxidize the products of anaerobic metabolism that accumulate in the muscle tissues during intense physical activity.

Oxygen dissociation curves. Curves that describe the relationship between the extent of combination of oxygen with the respiratory pigment and the partial pressure of oxygen in the gas phase.

Oxyhemoglobin. Hemoglobin with oxygen combined to the Fe atom of the heme group.

Oxytocin. An octapeptide hormone secreted by the neurohypophysis. Stimulates contractions of the uterus in childbirth and the release of milk from mammary glands.

P-wave. That portion of the electrocardiogram associated with depolarization of the atria.

Pacemaker. An excitable cell or tissue that fires spontaneously and rhythmically.

Pacemaker potentials. Spontaneous and rhythmical depolarizations produced by pacemaker tissue.

Pacinian corpuscle. Pressure receptors found in skin, muscle, joints, connective tissue of vertebrates; they consist of a nerve ending enclosed in a laminated capsule of connective tissue.

Pancreozymin. *See* cholecystokinin.

Parabiosis. The experimental connection of two individuals to allow mixing of their body fluids.

Parabronchi. Air-conduction pathways in the bird lung.

Parafollicular cells (C cells). Cells in the mammalian thyroid that secrete calcitonin.

Parasympathetic nervous system. The craniosacral part of the autonomic nervous system.

Parathyroid glands. Small tissue masses (usually two pairs) close to the thyroid gland that secrete parathormone (or parathyroid hormone).

Parathyroid hormone (PH; parathormone). A polypeptide hormone of the parathyroid glands secreted in response to a low plasma calcium level. It stimulates calcium release from bone and calcium absorption by the intestines while reducing calcium excretion by the kidneys.

Paraventricular nucleus. A group of neurosecretory neurons in the supraoptic hypothalamus that send their axons into the neurohypophysis.

Pars intercerebralis. The dorsal part of the insect brain, which contains the cell bodies of neurosecretory cells that secrete brain hormones from axon terminals in the corpora cardiaca.

Partition coefficient. Ratio of the distribution of a substance between two different liquid phases (e.g., oil and water).

Parturition. The process of giving birth.

Pentose. A 5-carbon monosaccharide sugar.

Peptide bond. The center bond of the $-CO-NH-$ group, created by the condensation of amino acids into peptides.

Perfusion. The passage of fluid over or through an organ, tissue, or cell.

Pericardium. The connective-tissue sac that encloses the heart.

Perilymph. Aqueous liquid contained within the scala tympani and scala vestibuli of the cochlea.

Peripheral resistance units (PRU). The drop in pressure (in mm Hg) along a vascular bed divided by mean flow in milliliters per second.

Peritoneum. The membrane that lines the abdominal and pelvic cavities.

Permeability. The ease with which substances can pass through a membrane.

pH scale. Negative log scale (base 10) of hydrogen ion concentration of a solution. $pH = -\log [H^+]$.

Phagocyte. A cell that engulfs other cells, microorganisms, or foreign particulate matter.

Phagocytosis. The ingestion of particles, cells, or microorganisms by a cell into its cytoplasmic vacuoles.

Phasic. Transient.

Pheromone. A species-specific substance released into the environment for the purpose of signalling between individuals of the same species.

Phlorizin. A glycoside that inhibits active transport of glucose.

Phosphagen. High-energy phosphate compounds (e.g., phosphoarginine and phosphocreatine) that serve as phosphate-group donors for rapid rephosphorylation of ADP to ATP.

Phosphoarginine. A compound that has phosphagen properties similar to those of phosphocreatine and which occurs in the muscles of some invertebrates.

Phosphocreatine. A compound that is broken down in muscle metabolism into inorganic phosphorus and creatine in the rephosphorylation of ADP to ATP.

Phosphodiesterase. A hydrolytic cytoplasmic enzyme that degrades cAMP to AMP.

Phosphodiester group. —O—P—O—.

Phospholipid. A phosphorus-containing lipid that hydrolyzes to fatty acids, glycerin, and a nitrogenous compound.

Phosphorylase *a*. Activated (phosphorylated) form of phosphorylase that catalyzes the cleavage of glycogen to glucose-1-phosphate.

Phosphorylase kinase. Enzyme that, when phosphorylated by a protein kinase, converts phosphorylase *b* to the more active phosphorylase *a*.

Phosphorylation. The incorporation of a PO^{3-} group into an organic molecule.

Photopigments. Pigment molecules that can become excited by light.

Photoreceptors. A sensory cell specifically sensitive to light energy.

Physiological dead space. That portion of inhaled air not involved in gas transfer in the lung.

Pinocytosis. Fluid intake by cells via surface invaginations that seal off to become vacuoles filled with liquid.

Pituitary gland (hypophysis). A complex endocrine organ situated at the base of the brain and connected to the hypothalamus by a stalk. It is of dual origin: the anterior lobe (adenohypophysis) is derived from embryonic buccal epithelium, whereas the posterior lobe is derived from the diencephalon.

pK'. The negative log (base 10) of an ionization constant K'. $pK' = -\log K'$.

Plane-polarized light. Light vibrating in only one plane.

Plasma kinins. Hormones carried in blood—for example, bradykinin.

Plasma skimming. The separation of plasma from blood within the circulation.

Plasmalemma. Cell membrane; surface membrane.

Plasticity. Compliance to external influence.

Plastron. The ventral shell of a tortoise or turtle. Also a gas film held in place under water by hydrofuge hairs, creating a large air-water interface.

Pleura. The membranes that line the pleural cavity.

Pleural cavity. The cavity between the lungs and the wall of the thorax.

Pneumotaxic center. A group of neurons in the pons, thought to be involved in the maintenance of rhythmic breathing in mammals.

Poikilotherm. An animal whose body temperature more or less follows the ambient temperature.

Poiseuille's Law. In laminar flow, the flow is directly proportional to the driving pressure, and resistance is independent of flow.

Polymer. A compound composed of a linear sequence of simple molecules or residues.

Polypeptide chain. A linear arrangement of more than two amino acid residues.

Polypnea. Increased breathing rate.

Polysynaptic. Refers to transmission through a sequence of more than one synapse.

Polytene. Having many duplicate chromatin strands.

Pores of Kohn. Small holes between adjacent regions of the lung, permitting collateral air flow.

Porphyrins. A group of cyclic tetrapyrrole derivatives.

Porphyropsin. A purple photopigment present in the retinal rods of some freshwater fish.

Portal vessels. Blood vessels that carry blood directly from one capillary bed to another.

Postsynaptic. Located distal to the synaptic cleft.

Post-tetanic depression. Reduced postsynaptic response following prolonged presynaptic stimulation at a high frequency; believed due to presynaptic depletion of transmitter.

Post-tetanic potentiation (PTP). Increased efficacy of synaptic transmission following presynaptic stimulation at a high frequency. Often occurs after post-tetanic depression.

Potassium activation. An increase in the conductance of a membrane to potassium in response to depolarization.

Potential energy. Stored energy that can be released to do work.

Premetamorphosis. The developmental stage just preceding amphibian metamorphosis, during which iodine binding and hormone synthesis occur in the thyroid gland.

Presynaptic. Located proximal to the synaptic cleft.

Primary follicle. An immature ovarian follicle.

Primary structure. The sequence of amino acid residues of a polypeptide chain.

Proboscis. An elongated, protruding mouth part.

Procaine. 2-diethylaminoethyl-*p*-aminobenzoate. A local anesthetic that interferes with some of the ion conductances of excitable membranes.

Progesterone. A hormone of the corpus luteum, adrenal cortex, and the placenta that promotes growth of a suitable uterine lining for implantation and development of the fertilized ovum.

Prolactin. An adenohypophyseal hormone that stimulates milk production and lactation after parturition in mammals.

Prometamorphosis. The first stage of amphibian metamorphosis, during which there is increased development and activity in the thyroid gland and median eminence.

Proprioceptors. Sensory receptors situated primarily in muscles, tendons, and the labyrinth that relay information about the position and motion of the body.

Prostaglandins. A family of recently discovered natural fatty acids that arise in a variety of tissues and are able to induce contraction in uterine and other smooth muscle, lower blood pressure, and modify the actions of some hormones.

Prostate gland. A gland located around the neck of the bladder and urethra in males that contributes to the seminal fluid.

Prosthetic group. An organic compound essential to the function of an enzyme. Prosthetic groups differ from coenzymes in that they are more firmly attached to the enzyme protein.

Protagonistic muscles. Muscles whose contractions co-operate to produce a movement.

Protein kinase. Any enzyme that catalyzes the transfer of a phosphate group from ATP to a protein, creating a phosphoprotein.

Proteins. Large molecules composed of one or more chains of alpha amino acid residues (i.e., polypeptide chains).

Proteolysis. The splitting of proteins by hydrolysis of peptide bonds.

Prothoracic glands. Ecdysone-secreting tissues situated in the anterior thorax of insects.

Proximal convoluted tubule. Coiled portions of the renal tubules located in the renal cortex, beginning at the glomerulus and leading to (and continuous with) the descending limb of the loop of Henle.

Pseudopodium. Literally, false foot; a temporary projection of an ameboid cell for engulfment of food or for locomotion.

Psychophysics. The branch of psychology concerned with relationships between physical stimuli and perception.

Pulmonary. Pertaining to or affecting the lungs.

Pupa. A developmental stage of some insect groups; between the larva and the adult.

Pupil. The opening at the center of the iris through which light passes.

Purinergic. Referring to nerve endings that release purines or their derivatives as transmitter substances.

Purines. A class of nitrogenous heterocyclic compounds, $C_5H_4N_4$, derivatives of which (purine bases) are found in nucleotides. They are colorless and crystalline.

Pylorus. The distal stomach opening, ringed by a sphincter, that releases the stomach contents into the duodenum.

Pyramidal tract. A bundle of nerve fibers orginating in the motor cortex and descending down the brain stem to the medulla oblongata and to the spinal cord. Responsible for mediating control of voluntary muscle movements.

Pyrimidine. A class of nitrogenous heterocyclic compounds, $C_4H_4N_2$, derivatives of which (pyrimidine bases) are found in nucleotides.

QRS-wave. That portion of the electrocardiogram related to depolarization of the ventricle.

Quantal transmission. The concept that neurotransmitter is released in multiples of discrete "packets." It is now apparent that the quantal packets represent individual presynaptic vesicles, or groups of simultaneously released vesicles.

Quaternary structure. The characteristic ways in which the subunits of a protein containing more than one polypeptide chain are combined.

Radial links. Extensions from peripheral doublets to the central sheath in cilia and flagella.

Radioisotope. A radioactive isotope.

Rate constant (specific reaction rate). The proportionality factor by which the concentration of a reactant in an enzymatic reaction is related to the reaction rate.

Rbc. Red blood cell, or erythrocyte.

Receptive field. That area of a sensory field (e.g., the retina) that when stimulated influences the activity of a given neuron is the receptive field of that neuron.

Receptor current. A stimulus-induced change in the movement of ions across a receptor cell membrane.

Receptor molecules. Molecules that are situated on the outer surface of the cell membrane and which interact specifically with messenger molecules, such as hormones or transmitters.

Receptor potential. A membrane potential change elicited in receptor cells by the flow of receptor current.

Reciprocal inhibition. Inhibition of the motoneurons innervating one set of muscles during the reflex excitation of their antagonists.

Redox pair. Two compounds, molecules, or atoms involved in mutual reduction and oxidation.

Reductant. Donor of electrons in a redox reaction.

Reduction. The addition of electrons to a substance.

Reduction potential. A measurement of the tendency of a reducer to yield electrons in a redox reaction, expressed in volts.

Reflex. An action that is reflected; an involuntary motor response mediated by a neural arc in response to sensory input.

Reflex arc. A neural pathway used in reflex action. Consists of afferent nerve input to a nerve center that produces activity in efferent nerves to an effector organ.

Refraction. The bending of light rays as they pass from a medium of one density into a medium of another density.

Refractive index. The refractive power of a medium compared with that of air, designated 1.

Refractory period. The period of increased membrane threshold immediately following an action potential.

Regenerative. Self-reinforcing; utilizing positive feedback; autocatalytic.

Release-inhibiting hormone (or factor; RIH or RIF). A hypothalamic neurosecretion carried by portal vessels to the adenohypophysis, where it restrains the release of a specific hormone.

Releasing hormones (or factors; RH's). Hypothalamic neurosecretions that stimulate the liberation of a specific hormone from the adenohypophysis.

Renal clearance. That volume of plasma containing the quantity of a freely filtered substance that appears in the glomerular filtrate per unit time. Total renal clearance is the amount of ultrafiltrate produced by the kidney per unit time.

Renshaw cells. Short inhibitory interneurons in the ventral horn excited by branches of the motoneuron axons that feed back on the motoneuron pool:

Repolarization. The return to resting polarity of a cell membrane that has been depolarized.

Repressor gene (regulator gene). A gene that produces a substance (repressor) that shuts off the structural gene activity of an operon by an interaction with its operator gene.

Residual volume. The volume of air left in the lungs after maximal expiratory effort.

Respiratory quotient (RQ). The ratio of carbon dioxide produced divided by the oxygen utilized by a body, organ, or tissue.

Rete mirabile. An extensive countercurrent arrangement of arterial and venous capillaries.

Reticulum. A small network.

Retinal. The aldehyde of retinol obtained from the enzymatic oxidative cleavage of carotene. It unites with opsin in the retina to form the visual pigment.

Retinol. Vitamin A ($C_{20}H_{30}O$), an alcohol of 20 carbons.

It is converted reversibly to retinal by enzymatic dehydrogenation.

Retinular cell. A photoreceptor cell of the arthropod compound eye.

Reserpine. A botanically derived tranquilizing agent that interferes with the uptake of catecholamine from the cytosol by secretory vesicles. Its effect is to deplete the catecholamine content of adrenergic cells.

Resistance. Opposition to electric current presented by a conductor.

Resistivity. The resistance inherent in a given material; measured as the resistance (in ohms) between opposing sides of a one-centimeter cube of the material.

Resting potential. The normal, unstimulated cell membrane potential of a cell at rest.

Reversal potential. The membrane potential at which current through an activated synapse or receptor membrane is null.

Reynolds number. A unitless number. The tendency of a flowing gas or liquid to become turbulent is proportional to its velocity and density and inversely proportional to its viscosity. Calculated from these parameters, the Reynolds number indicates whether flow will be turbulent or laminar under a particular set of conditions.

Rhabdome. The aggregate structure consisting of a longitudinal rosette of rhabdomeres located axially in the ommatidium.

Rhabdomere. That portion of a retinular cell in which the photopigment-bearing surface membrane is thrown into closely packed microvilli. This region faces the central axis of the ommatidium.

Rhodopsin (visual purple). A purplish-red, light-sensitive chromoprotein with 11-*cis* retinal as its prosthetic group. Found in the rods of the retina. It is bleached to visual yellow (all-*trans* retinal) by incident light.

Ribose. A pentose monosaccharide with the chemical formula $HOCH_2(CHOH)_3CHO$; a constituent of RNA.

Ribosome. Riconucleoprotein particles found within the cytoplasm; the sites of intersection of mRNA, tRNA, and the amino acids during the synthesis of polypeptide chains.

Rigor mortis. The rigidity that develops in dying muscle as ATP becomes depleted and cross bridges remain attached.

Ringer solution. Physiological saline solution.

RNA (ribonucleic acid). A nucleic acid made up of adenine, guanine, cytosine, uracil, ribose, and phosphoric acid. Responsible for the transcription of DNA and the translation into protein.

Rods. One class of vertebrate visual receptor cells, the cones being the other. Highly sensitive, but colorblind in most species.

Root effect (Root shift). A change in blood oxygen capacity as a result of a pH change.

Round window. A membrane-covered opening that is located in the inside wall of the middle ear and through which pressure waves leave the cochlea after entering via the oval window.

Saccharide. A family of carbohydrates that includes the sugars. They are grouped as to the number of saccharide ($C_nH_{2n}O_{n-1}$) groups comprising them; the mono-, di-, tri-, and polysaccharides.

Salt glands. Osmoregulatory organs of many birds and reptiles that live in desert or marine environments. A hypertonic aqueous exudate is formed by active salt secretion into the small tubules situated above the eyes and is excreted via the nostrils.

Saltatory. Jumping; discontinuous.

"Salting out." A decrease in Bunsen solubility coefficient as a result of increased ionic strength of the solvent.

Sarcolemma. The surface membrane of muscle fibers.

Sarcomere. The contractile unit of a myofibril, being the span between two Z-lines.

Sarcoplasmic reticulum (SR). A smooth, membrane-limited network surrounding each myofibril. Calcium is stored in the SR and released in ionic form during muscle excitation.

Sarcotubular system. The sarcoplasmic reticulum plus the transverse tubules.

Scala media (membranous labyrinth). The cochlear duct containing the organ of Corti and the tectorial membrane; it is filled with endolymph.

Scala tympani. A cochlear chamber connected with the scala vestibuli through the helicotrema; it is filled with perilymph.

Scala vestibuli. A cochlear chamber beginning in the vestibule, connecting with the scala tympani through the helicotrema; it is filled with perilymph.

Schwann cell. A neuroglial cell that wraps its membrane around axons during development to produce a myelinated insulating sheath between nodes of Ranvier.

Second Law of Thermodynamics. All natural or spontaneous processes are accompanied by an increase in entropy.

Second messenger. A term applied to cAMP, cGMP, Ca^{2+}, or any other intracellular regulatory agent that is itself under the control of an extracellular "first messenger," such as a hormone.

Second-order enzyme kinetics. Describes enzymatic reactions whose rates are determined by the concentrations of two reactants multiplied together or of one reactant squared.

Secondary structure. Refers to the straight or helical configuration of polypeptide chains.

Secretagogue. A substance that stimulates or promotes secretion.

Secretin. A polypeptide hormone secreted by the duodenal and jejunal mucosa in response to the presence of acid chyme in the intestine. It induces pancreatic secretion into the intestine. Chemically identical to enterogastrone.

Secretory granules (secretory vesicles). Membrane-bound cytoplasmic granules containing secretory products of a cell.

Seminal vesicles. Paired sacs attached to the posterior urinary bladder that have tubes joining the vas deferens.

Semipermeable membrane. A membrane that allows certain molecules but not others to pass through it.

Sensillum. Chitinous, hollow, hair-like projections of the arthropod exoskeleton that serve as auxiliary structures for sensory neurons.

Sensory filter network. Neural circuits that selectively transmit some features of a sensory input and ignore other features.

Series elastic components (SEC). Elasticity in series with contractile elements in muscle.

Serosal. Pertaining to the side of an epithelial tissue facing the blood, as opposed to the mucosal side, which faces the exterior or luminal space.

Serotonin (5-hydroxytryptamine; 5-HT; 3-(2-aminoethyl-5-indolol). A neurotransmitter, $C_{10}H_{12}N_2O$.

Servomechanism. A control system that utilizes negative feedback to correct deviations from a selected level, the set point.

Set point. In a negative feedback system, the state to which feedback tends to bring the system.

Sign stimulus. The most basic essential pattern of sensory input required to release an instinctual pattern of behavior.

Sinus. A cavity or sac; a dilated part of a blood vessel.

Sinus node. The junction between the right atrium and the vena cava, the location of the pacemaker. Also called the sino-atrial node, or SA node.

Sliding-filament theory. Shortening of muscle sarcomeres occurs by active sliding of the actin thin filaments toward the midregion of the myosin thick filaments.

Sliding-tubule hypothesis. Bending movements of cilia and flagella are produced by active longitudinal sliding of the axonemal microtubules past one another.

Smooth muscle. Muscle without sarcomeres and hence without striations. Myofilaments are nonuniformly distributed within small, uninucleated spindle-shaped cells.

Sodium activation. An increased conductance of excitable membranes to sodium ions in response to membrane depolarization. Believed to result from an opening of Na "gates" associated with membrane channels.

Sodium hypothesis. The upstroke of an action potential is due to an inward movement of Na^+ down its electro-chemical gradient as a result of a transient increase in sodium permeability.

Sodium inactivation. Loss of responsiveness of Na gates to depolarization. Develops with time during a depolarization and persists for a short period after repolarization of the membrane.

Sodium pump. Membrane mechanism responsible for active extrusion of Na from the cell at the expense of metabolic energy. In some Na pumps, there is a $3:2$ exchange of intracellular Na^+ for extracellular K^+.

Solvation. The process of dissolving a solute in a solvent; hydration, or clustering, of water molecules around individual ions and polar molecules.

Soma. The nerve cell body, or perikaryon; in general, the body.

Somatic. Referring to the body tissues as distinct from the germ cells.

Somatosensory cortex. That region of the cerebral cortex devoted to sensory input from the body surface.

Spatial summation. Integration of simultaneous synaptic current by a neuron.

Specific resistance (R_m). Resistance per unit area of a membrane in ohm-cm².

Spectrum. Specific, charted bands of electromagnetic radiation wavelengths produced by refraction or diffraction.

Sphincter. A ring-shaped band of muscle fibers capable of constricting an opening or passageway.

Spinal cord. The portion of the vertebrate central nervous system that is encased in the vertebral column, extending from the medulla oblongata to the upper lumbar region. It is constructed of a core of gray matter and an outer layer of white matter.

Spindle organ. A stretch receptor of vertebrate skeletal muscle.

Sphingolipid. A lipid formed by a fatty acid attached to the nitrogen atom of sphingosine, a long-chain, oily amino alcohol ($C_{18}H_{37}O_2N$). The sphingolipids occur primarily in the membranes of brain and nerve cells.

Spiracle. Surface openings of the tracheal system in insects.

Standard temperature and pressure. 25°C, 1 atmosphere.

Standing wave. A resonating wave with fixed nodes.

Stapes (stirrup). The innermost auditory ossicle, which articulates at its apex with the incus and whose base is connected to the oval window.

Starch. A polysaccharide of plant origin, formula $(C_6H_{10}O_5)_n$.

Starling curves. Curves that describe the relationship between heart work and filling pressure.

Statocysts. Gravity-sensing sensory organs made up of mechanoreceptor cells and associated statoliths.

Statolith. A small, dense solid granule found in statocysts.

Steady state. Dynamic equilibrium.

Stennin. A protein found in brain nerve endings; exhibits ATPase activity and some similarities with muscle myosin. *See also* Neurin.

Stenohaline. Able to tolerate only a narrow range of salinities.

Stereocilia. Nonmotile filament-filled projections of the surface of 8th-nerve hair cells. Not to be confused with true $9 + 2$ cilia.

Steric. Pertaining to the spatial arrangement of atoms.

Sterols. A group of solid, primarily unsaturated polycyclic alcohols.

Stimulus. A substance, action, or other influence that when applied with sufficient intensity to a tissue causes a response.

STPD. Standard temperature and pressure, dry.

Stria vascularis. Vascular tissue layer over the external wall of the scala media. It secretes the endolymph.

Striated muscle. Characterized by sarcomeres aligned in register. Skeletal and cardiac muscle are striated.

Stroke volume. The volume of blood pumped by one ventricle during a single heart beat.

Structural gene. A gene coding for the sequence of amino acids that make up a polypeptide chain.

Strychnine. A poisonous alkaloid ($C_{21}H_{22}N_2O_2$) that blocks inhibitory synaptic transmission in the vertebrate CNS.

Substrate. A substance that is acted upon by an enzyme.

Sulfhydryl group. The radical —SH.

Supraoptic nucleus. A distinct group of neurons in the hypothalamus, just above the optic chiasm. Their neurosecretory endings terminate in the neurohypophysis.

Surface tension. The elasticity of the surface of a substance (particularly a fluid), which tends to reduce the surface area at each interface.

Surfactant. A surface-active substance that tends to reduce surface tension.

Swim bladder. A gas filled bladder used for flotation; found in many teleost fishes.

Sympathetic nervous system. Thoracicolumbar part of the autonomic nervous system.

Synapse. A conjunction between two directly interacting nerve cells, where impulses in the presynaptic cell influence the activity of the postsynaptic cell.

Synaptic cleft. The space separating the nerve cells at a synapse.

Synaptic delay. The characteristic time lag encountered from the time on impulse reaches a presynaptic nerve terminal to the time a postsynaptic potential change occurs.

Synaptic efficacy. Effectiveness of a presynaptic impulse in producing a postsynaptic potential change.

Synaptic inhibition. A change in a postsynaptic cell that reduces the probability of its generating an action potential. It is produced by a transmitter substance that elicits a postsynaptic current having a reversal potential more negative than the threshold for the action potential.

Synaptic noise. Irregular changes in postsynaptic membrane potential produced by irregular subthreshold synaptic input.

Syneresis. Contraction of a jell-like mixture so that a liquid is squeezed out from molecular interstices.

Systemic. Pertaining to or affecting the body; for example, systemic circulation.

T-wave. That portion of the electrocardiogram associated with repolarization (and usually relaxation) of the ventricle.

Tachycardia. Refers to an increase in heart rate above the normal level.

Target cells. Cells that preferentially bind and respond to specific hormones.

Taxis. Locomotion oriented with respect to a stimulus direction or gradient.

Tectorial membrane. A fine gelatinous sheet lying on the organ of Corti of the ear in contact with the cilia of the hair cells.

Temporal. Referring to the lateral areas of the head above the zygomatic arch. Also, relating to time; time limited.

Temporal lobe. A lobe of the cerebral hemisphere, situated in the lower lateral area, at the temples.

Temporal summation. Summation of membrane potentials over time.

Terminal cisternae. Part of the sarcoplasmic reticulum on both sides of the Z-line, making close contact with the T-tubules.

Tertiary structure. Refers to the way a polypeptide chain is folded or bent to produce the overall conformation of the molecule.

Testosterone. A steroid androgen synthesized by the testicular interstitial cells of the male. Responsible for the production and maintenance of secondary male sex characteristics.

Tetanus. An uninterrupted muscular contraction due to a high frequency of motor impulses. Also the name of a neurotoxin that exhibits retrograde (toward the cell body) transport in axons.

Tetraethylammonium (TEA). A quaternary ammonium agent $(C_2H_5)_4N$, that can be used to block some potassium channels in membrane.

Tetrodotoxin (TTX). The pufferfish poison, which selectively blocks sodium ion channels in the membranes of excitable cells.

Theca interna. Ovarian follicle cell layer responsible for estrogen biosynthesis and secretion.

Theophylline. A crystalline alkaloid $(C_7H_8N_4\ H_2O)$ found in tea. Inhibits the enzyme phosphodiesterase, thereby increasing the level of cAMP. Also releases Ca^{2+} from Ca-sequestering organelles.

Thermoreceptors. Sensory nerve endings responsive to temperature changes.

Thick filament. A myofilament made of myosin.

Thin filament. A myofilament made of actin.

Threshold potential. The potential just large enough to produce the response (e.g., action potential, muscle twitch).

Threshold stimulus. The minimum strength of stimulation necessary to produce a detectible response or an all-or-none response.

Thymine. A pyrimidine base, 5-methyluracil $(C_5H_6N_2O)$, a constituent of DNA.

Thyroid-stimulating hormone (TSH). An adenohypophyseal hormone that stimulates the secretory activity of the thyroid gland.

Thyroxine. An iodine-bearing tyrosine derivative hormone that is synthesized and secreted by the thyroid gland. It raises cellular metabolic rate.

Tidal volume. The volume of air moved in or out of the lungs with each breath.

Tight junctions. An area of membrane fusion between adjoining cells; prevents passage of extracellular material between the cells.

Time constant (T). A measure of the rate of accumulation or decay of an exponential process. The time required for an exponential process to reach 63% completion. In electricity, it is proportional to the product of resistance and capacitance.

Tonic. Steady, slowly adapting.

Tonicity (hyper-, hypo-, or iso-). The relative osmotic pressure of a solution under given conditions (e.g., its osmotic effect on a cell relative to the osmotic effect of plasma on the cell).

Tonus. Sustained resting contraction of muscle, produced by basal neuromotor activity.

Trachea. The large respiratory passageway that connects the pharynx and bronchioles in the vertebrates.

Tracheal system. Air-filled tubules that carry respiratory gases between the tissues and the exterior in insects.

Tracheoles. Minute subdivisions of the tracheal system of insects.

Train of impulses. A rapid succession of action potentials propagated down a nerve fiber.

Trans. A configuration with particular atoms or groups on opposite sides.

Transcription. The formation of an RNA chain of a complementary base sequence from the informational base sequence of DNA.

Transducer. A mechanism that translates energy or signals of one form into a different kind of energy or signals.

Transducer molecule. Hypothesized intermediate molecule within the cell membrane that transmits a hormone-initiated signal from the externally facing hormone receptor to the internally facing adenylate cyclase.

Transduction. General term for the modulation of one kind of energy by another kind of energy. Thus sense organs transduce sensory stimuli into nerve impulses.

Transfer RNA (tRNA). A small RNA molecule that is responsible for the transfer of amino acids from their activating enzymes to the ribosomes. There are twenty tRNAs, one for each amino acid.

Translation. Utilization of the DNA base sequence for linear organization of amino acid residues on a polypeptide; carried out by mRNA.

Transmitter substance. A chemical mediator liberated from a presynaptic ending, producing a conductance change or other response in the membrane of the postsynaptic cell.

Transmural blood pressure. The difference in pressure across the walls of a blood vessel.

Transphosphorylation. The transfer of phosphate groups between organic molecules, bypassing the inorganic phosphate stage.

Transverse tubules (T-tubules). Branching membrane-limited intercommunicating tubules that come into close apposition with the lateral cisternae of the sarcoplasmic reticulum and are continuous with the surface membrane.

Traveling wave. A wave that traverses the propagating medium, as opposed to a standing wave.

Tricarboxylic acid cycle (TCA cycle; Krebs cycle; citric acid cycle). The metabolic cycle responsible for the complete oxidation of the acetyl portion of the acetyl coenzyme A molecule.

Trichromacy theory. The postulate that three kinds of photoreceptor cells exist in the retina, each exhibiting maximal sensitivity to a different part of the color spectrum.

Triglyceride. A neutral molecule composed of three fatty acid residues esterified to glycerol. It is formed in animals from carbohydrates.

Triiodothyronine. An iodine-bearing tyrosine derivative synthesized in and secreted by the thyroid gland; raises cellular metabolic rate, as does thyroxine.

Trimer. A compound made up of three simpler identical molecules.

Trimethylamine oxide. A nitrogenous waste product, probably from choline decomposition.

Tritium. A radioactive isotope of hydrogen with an atomic mass of three (H^3).

Triton X-100. A nonionic detergent used in cell biology to solubilize lipids and certain cell proteins.

Trophic substances. Hypothetical chemical substances believed to be released from neuron terminals, and believed to influence the chemical and functional properties of the postsynaptic cell.

Tropomyosin. A long protein molecule located in the grooves of the actin filament of muscle. Inhibits contraction by blocking the interaction of myosin cross bridges with actin filaments.

Troponin. A complex of globular Ca-binding proteins associated with the actin and tropomyosin of the thin filaments of muscle. On combining with Ca^{2+}, a conformational change in the troponin complex allows the tropomyosin to move out of its myosin-blocking position on the actin filament.

Tubulin. An actin-like, 40 Å globular protein molecule that is the building block of microtubules.

Turbulent flow. Flow in which the fluid moves in all directions.

Turgor. Distension; swollenness.

Twitch muscle (fast muscle). The most common, striated vertebrate skeletal muscle type, usually pale in color because of its low myoglobin content. Has few mitochondria, and its fibers are constructed of many clearly defined fibrils. These contract rapidly and derive most of their energy from anaerobic metabolism.

Tympanic membrane. Ear drum.

Tympanum. The middle ear cavity just inside the tympanic membrane, which houses the auditory ossicles.

Ultraviolet light. Light of wavelengths between 1.8×10^{-5} and 3.9×10^{-5} cm.

Unit membrane. The sandwich-like profile of biological membrane seen in electron micrographs and believed to represent the bimolecular leaflet with hydrophobic center region between hydrophilic surfaces.

Uracil. A pyrimidine ($C_4H_4O_2N_2$) constituent of RNA.

Urea. The primary nitrogenous waste product in the urine of mammals.

Ureter. A muscular tube passing urine to the bladder from the kidney.

Urethra. The channel passing urine from the bladder out of the body.

Uric acid. A crystalline waste product of nitrogen metabolism found in the feces and urine of birds and reptiles. Poorly soluble in water.

Vacuole. A membrane-limited cavity in the cytoplasm of a cell.

Vagus nerve (10th nerve). A major cranial nerve that sends sensory fibers to the tongue, pharynx, larynx, and ear; motor fibers to the esophagus, larynx, and pharynx; and parasympathetic and afferent fibers to the viscera of the thoracic and abdominal regions.

Valence. The number of missing or extra electrons of an atom or molecule.

Van der Waals forces. The close-ranging, relatively weak attraction exhibited between atoms and molecules with hydrophobic properties.

Vas deferens. A testicular duct that joins the excretory duct of the seminal vesicle to form the ejaculatory duct.

Vasopressin. *See* Antidiuretic hormone (ADH).

Vasopressor. A substance that induces arterial and capillary smooth muscle contraction.

Vector. A carrier; an animal transferring an infection from host to host. Mathematical term for a quantity with direction, magnitude, and sign.

Venous shunt. A direct connection between arterioles and venules, bypassing the capillary network.

Ventral. Toward the belly surface.

Ventral horn. The ventral portion of gray matter in the vertebrate spinal cord in which motor nerve cell bodies are situated.

Ventral root. A nerve trunk leaving the spinal cord near its ventral surface. Contains only motor axons.

Ventricle. A small cavity. A chamber of the vertebrate heart.

Venule. A small vessel that connects a capillary bed with a vein.

Viscosity. A physical property of fluids that determines the ease with which layers of a fluid move past each other.

Visible light. Light of wavelengths between 3.9×10^{-5} to 7.4×10^{-5} cm.

Visual cortex. The outermost thin layer of gray matter in the occipital region of the cerebrum; devoted to the processing of visual information.

Vital capacity. The maximum volume of air that can be inhaled into or exhaled from the lungs.

Vitalism. The theory that postulates that biological processes cannot adequately be explained by physical and chemical processes and laws.

Volt. MKS unit of electromotive force; the force required to induce a one-ampere current to flow through a one-ohm resistance.

Voltage. Electromotive force.

Voltage-clamping. An electronic method of imposing a selected membrane potential across a membrane by means of feedback control.

Watt. A unit of electrical power; the work performed at 1 joule per second.

Weber-Fechner Law. Sensation increases arithmetically as stimulus increases geometrically; the least perceptible change in stimulus intensity above any background is proportional to the intensity of the background.

White matter. Tissue of the central nervous system, consisting mainly of myelinated nerve fibers.

Wolffian ducts. The embryonic ducts that are associated with the primordial kidney and which become the excretory and reproductive ducts in the male.

Work. Force exerted upon an object over a distance; force $\times$ distance.

X-ray diffraction. The method of examining crystalline structure using the pattern of scattered X-rays.

Xylocaine. The trade name for lidocaine, a local anesthetic related to procaine.

Z-disc (Z-line, Z-band). A narrow zone at either end of a muscle sarcomere, consisting of a latticework from which the actin thin filaments originate.

Zero-order kinetics. Kinetics in which the rate of the reaction is independent of the concentration of any of its reactants. This would occur if the enzyme concentration were the limiting factor.

Zonula occludens. Tight junctions between epithelial cells, usually having a ring-shaped configuration and serving to occlude transepithelial extracellular passages.

Zwitterion. A molecule carrying both negatively and positively ionized or ionizable sites.

Zygote. A fertilized ovum before first cleavage.

Index

Page numbers printed in *italics* indicate references to figures.

osmotic regulation by, 98–101
permeability of, 22–24, 88–101
(*See also* Membrane
permeability)
channels in, 89, 98
pumps (*See* Active transport)
selectivity of, 97–98
transport in, 88–98
structure of, 83–87
unit (lipid bilayer), 83–*84*, 86
Menstrual cycle, 341, 367–370
m.e.p.p. *See* Miniature endplate
potentials
Meromyosins, 283
Mescaline, 180
Messenger molecules
extracellular, 336–337 (*See also*
Hormones)
intracellular
cyclic nucleotides, 376–386
ions, 336–337
Metabolism
and ATP production, 64–76
of cells, 46
effect of hormones on, 349–360
efficiency of, 75
intermediary, 64–65
membrane regulation of, 103–105
and osmotic exchange, 396
regulation of, 62–64
Metachronism, 329, 331–332
Metamorphosis
amphibian, *357*
insect, 373–*376*
Methyl xanthines
and cAMP levels, 377, 384
and muscle contracture,
296–297, 384
and release of intracellular
calcium, 296–297
Micelle, 17
Michaelis-Menten kinetics, 60
and carrier-mediated
transport, 93
Microelectrode, 112–*113*, 170
Microtubules
and ciliary bending, 324–327
and ciliary structure, 302–322
and exocytosis, 102
in hair cell cilia, *208*, 209
Microvilli, in renal tubule, *406*, 413
Migration
by birds, 269, 273–274
by teleosts, 421
Mineralocorticoids, 360, 362, 367
(*See also* Aldosterone)
Miniature endplate potentials
(m.e.p.p.), 181–183
Miniature postsynaptic potentials,
242–243

Mitochondria, *66*
Ca^{2+} sequestration by, 100,
104, 186
and energy metabolism, 65, 70, 74
membranes of, 65, 70, 74, 81–82,
84, *87*
Molality, 21
Molarity, 21
Monactin, *93*
Monamines, 180
Mosaic bilayer model, 84–*85*
Motoneurons, *149*
alpha, 241, 258–262
integration by, 241–245
and motor units, 155, 241, 305
of stretch reflex, 258–262
trophic action of, 177, 306
Motor cortex, *157*
Motor endplate (neuromuscular
junction), 168–*170*
of arthropods, 305, 307
potentials of, 169–176
miniature, 181–182
transmitter release at, 181–186
acetylcholine, 169, 176–*178*, 182
of vertebrates, 305
Motor units, 155, 305–307
arthropod, 305–307
vertebrate, 305
MSH. *See* Melanocyte-stimulating
hormone
Multineuronal innervation, 307
Multiterminal innervation, 307
Muscle (*See also* Cardiac muscle;
Smooth muscle; Striated
muscle)
excitable membrane of, 125
innervation of, 168–169,
305–309
Muscle spindles. *See* Stretch
receptors
Musculo-skeletal systems, 312–313
Mutation, 3
Myelin sheath, *87*, 164–*165*
Myoblasts, 280
Myocardial potentials, 141–143,
437–440
electrical transmission of, 167,
310, 437–440
refractoriness of, 310, 438
Myofibrils, *280*
Myofilaments
sliding of, in contraction, 284–289
substructure of, 282–283
Myoglobin, 472
in muscle fibers, 306
oxygen affinity of, 473–474
oxygen dissociation curves of,
473–474
subunit interactions in, 474

Myosin,
ATPase activity of, 286, 306
filaments, 283
in nonmuscle cells, 292
in skeletal muscle, 280–283
role in contraction, 284–289
Myotatic reflex (stretch reflex),
258–261
Myotubes, 280
Mytilus, gill cilia of, 328–329

NAD. *See* Nicotinamide adenine
dinucleotide
Nasal epithelium, and olfaction, 207
Navigation, 269
celestial, by birds, 273–274
geoelectric, by American eel, 269
Necturus, lateral-line hair cells of, 209
Nephron
adaptations of, 418–419
anatomy of, *406*
formation of urine by, 407–417
water retention by, 417–418
Nernst relation, 121–122
Nerve cells. *See* Neurons
Nerve nets, 152
Nervous system, 150 (*See also* Central
nervous system)
autonomic, 158–159, 344–345
(*See also* Sympathetic nervous
system; Parasympathetic
nervous system)
evolution of, 152–154
invertebrate, 152–154
specificity of connections in,
240–241
vertebrate, 154–159
Nets, nerve, 152
Neural networks, 150, 241, 245–267
evolution of, 152–154
neuromotor, 258–265
as pattern generators, 241,
263–265
and programmed behavior,
266–267
as sensory filters, 241, 247
Neural signals, 241
Neurin, 102
Neuroendocrine relationships,
344–349
Neurohormones, 337
Neurohumor, 345
Neurohypophysis, *347*–349
Neuroid hypothesis, 332
Neuromuscular junction (motor
endplate)
arthropod, 305, 307
potentials at, 169–176
miniature, 181–182

Water (*continued*)
metabolic, 396
and osmoregulation, 392–395
possible active transport of, 403, 423, 426
properties of, 15
resorption of, by insect hindgut, 423–426
retention of, by vertebrate kidney, 417–418
sea, composition of, 11, 392
as solvent, 15–16
structure of, 14
transport of, across epithelia, 403–405
Water of hydration, 16
"Water" receptors, 464–466
Weber–Fechner law, 199
White matter, 155
Work, definition of, 47

X-ray diffraction, analysis of muscle by, 287
Xylocaine, 137

Z-lines, *280–281*
and T-tubules, 294
Zwitterions, 19